# DATE DUE

| | | |
|---|---|---|
| | | |
| | | |
| | | |
| | | |
| | | |
| | | |
| | | |
| | | |
| | | |
| | | |
| | | |
| | | |
| | | |
| | | |
| | | |
| | | |
| | | |

DEMCO 38-296

# ANTARCTICA

# ANTARCTICA
## *An Encyclopedia*

### JOHN STEWART

*Foreword by*
*Sir Edmund Hillary*

### VOLUME I
*Foreword, Prefaces, A–L*

McFarland & Company, Inc., Publishers
*Jefferson, North Carolina, and London*

British Library Cataloguing-in-Publication data are available

Library of Congress Cataloguing-in-Publication Data

Stewart, John, 1952–
Antarctica : an encyclopedia / by John Stewart.
p. cm.
Includes bibliographical references.
(lib. bdg. : 50# alk. paper)∞
1. Antarctic regions—Dictionaries. I. Title.
G855.S74 1990
919.8′9–dc20 89-43631
CIP

ISBN 0-89950-470-1 (2 vol. set)
ISBN 0-89950-597-X (Vol. I)
ISBN 0-89950-598-8 (Vol. II)

Printed in the United States of America

*McFarland & Company, Inc., Publishers*
*Box 611, Jefferson, North Carolina 28640*

*For Susan*

# FOREWORD
## (Sir Edmund Hillary)

Thirty-three years ago, when I first arrived at the South Pole, much of the Antarctic Continent was still largely unknown. Since those days it has been opened up beyond all expectations but there are still many areas that remain unexplored.

Hundreds of books have been written about different aspects of Antarctica—its history, its geography, the sciences, the expedition reports, and explorers' own narratives (including my own). In my younger days I revelled in these heroic stories and they gave me the inspiration to go south myself.

But many of these books, although still fascinating, are now out of date, or out of print, and certainly unsuitable for any lay individual who wishes to start out on his or her own "Antarctic Journey." This book you are holding is, I believe, the first encyclopaedia ever written about the Antarctic. I feel sure it will be welcomed by libraries and Antarcticans, as well as by the general reader, now that there is such an explosion of serious interest in the Southern Continent and especially in its preservation.

An encyclopaedic guide to Antarctic matters is a useful book on anyone's shelf, particularly when one considers that so much information can be found crammed together in a single work.

Speaking for myself, I'm not quite sure how I feel about being catalogued so neatly, but if I must be in the book, then I bow to the inevitable, and wish this undertaking well.

Sir Edmund Hillary.
*March 16, 1990*

# TABLE OF CONTENTS

## VOLUME I

## VOLUME II

# PREFACE

Somewhat like Sir Edmund Hillary, a model for millions of former school children, who writes in his foreword to this book that he was inspired to go south by tales of the pioneer explorers, I have long been inspired by Antarctica. I was also curious as to why this great southern continent was never given what might be called its own name. "Antarctica" means anti–Arctic, i.e. "Not the Arctic," as for instance Australia might have been called "Antasia." Perhaps it is that a national pride of sorts has been missing in the humanless frozen wasteland of Antarctica. That excuse may not be so valid now. Because Antarctica is still, today, far away, obscure, and ill-defined, many people are not sure if it is the North or the South Pole, or whether it is the place with penguins or polar bears.

I have here written an A-to-Z of Antarctica, incorporating geographical features, expeditions, people, scientific subjects, and entries of general interest—anything that would be useful and informative to the average reader as well as to the specialist.

A study of the literature on Antarctica revealed a mountain of book and periodical material, but very few works of a general nature, and fewer still that would appeal to the beginner, and none of encyclopedic intent. What started out as a volume of moderate size became, after thousands of hours of research, the largest, most comprehensive book ever written on Antarctica, defined herein as from 60° south latitude all the way to the Pole, at 90° south.

It was felt necessary to drop all thoughts of photos, graphics, maps and the like, for this would have added enormously to the size and cost of the book. The biographical entries are, for the most part, limited to the person's involvement with Antarctica. The Bibliography beginning on page 1173 guides the reader to 420 or so books that contain useful information. All the better atlases have good color maps of Antarctica.

This book has a bias toward the geographical and the historical. The other sciences have not been ignored, by any means, but as this writer is not a scientist, it seemed prudent to treat those subjects in a reportorial manner, and to present in the Bibliography more authoritative sources to lead the reader to in-depth study.

I felt it necessary to include all the geographic features of Antarctica. They are generally entered under the names formally approved by the United States. Alternative and old names are cross-referenced in the *"see"* entries. A typical geographic feature entry will list name, coordinates, other names (if applicable), height in meters (very occasionally in feet) if appropriate, a description if necessary, its location in relation to other features, perhaps other information of a historical or scientific nature, when and by whom it was discovered, charted, mapped, or surveyed, and by whom and for whom it was named, and when. The tedious repetition of the phrase "Named by the U.S.A.," has been avoided; it should be understood that the feature was named by the United States, unless otherwise stated, or unless obviously otherwise.

Sometimes I have referred to a glacier as, for example, "the Beardmore Glacier" and other times simply as "Beardmore Glacier." This is to show that both ways are acceptable, even within the same sentence. A more meaningful case is that of Oates Land. Sometimes I have written Oates Land, sometimes northern Victoria Land. Both are correct, and in the instances where a feature falls within Oates Land, the two terms are interchangeable in locating or describing it. This is simply to bring awareness of this fact. The reader should be aware of this when reading other books on Antarctica in which one or the other term might otherwise seem wrong.

I have endeavored to provide entries, through 1989, for all major expeditions that have been south of 60°S, as well as for the most important persons who went south of that line before World War II, when the continent started to open up, and thousands poured in. (There are, no doubt, individuals whom I failed to find.) There are three appendices at the back of the book, a Chronology, a summary of Expeditions, and a Bibliography. The books I found to be helpful to me in my research are annotated; some others are annotated too, and the ones that are not annotated I found to be unreliable, out of date, unavailable for research, or simply duplicated by others more comprehensive or authoritative.

When I realized the amount and breadth of study and research that would be necessary to write this book, I was afraid that living in North Carolina might limit me, possibly even handicap me. I need not have worried. This was the late 1980s, in an information society. All you need is a phone, and good competent people to help you. I had both. For example, I could always, and did always, call that terrific institution, the United States Navy, in Washington, Port Hueneme, Atlanta, and elsewhere. To those excellent gentlemen who so willingly helped—Lt. Kevin Wensing of NAVINFO Washington, PO Newberry at Port Hueneme, John Riley of the Naval Historical Center in Washington, my liaison Chief Brown somewhere on an 800 number, and most of all Cdr. J.D. Van Sickel, director, Navy Office of Information, South East, Atlanta (J.D. would say he's only doing his job)—I offer my deepest thanks.

Thanks to the National Science Foundation, if only for being there and doing it, and to the head man, Jack Talmadge, without whose decision I would not have finished this book so expeditiously.

If I had questions I couldn't answer, or arcane material I wanted, I'd probably call Lyn Lay in the library of the Byrd Polar Research Center, at Ohio State University. She'd see to it.

I had the advantage of writing this book in a time when inter-library loans are possible. I'd often go along to Forsyth County Library, in downtown Winston-Salem, and say to any of three excellent people, Bill Sugg, Bob Shar and Ann Hendrix, "What do I do now?" They'd simply do it for me. You can get anything on an inter-library loan. Barbara Anderson and her staff in the science department made a lot of the more tedious parts almost enjoyable. Also in the library is Cindy Jones, head of periodicals, who spent hours making sure I knew how to handle the government documents and computers. Great encouragement and help to a writer, these people.

Wake Forest University has a magnificent library, and again, people who are so cooperative and friendly. Peter Shipman and Renata Evans could have, if they had been staff first, thwarted progress on my book. But they are people first, and wanted to see this book done. They remove barriers and cut Gordian knots. I like that. Ellen Knott is always there when I need her, no matter how eccentric some of my data requests are. John Dombrowski, government documents specialist, is another who uses the Alexandrian method of cutting through red tape. There is so much Antarctic material to be gotten from government documents, and without John Dombrowski's going out on a long limb for me on several occasions, I would not have been able to compile the book with the thoroughness it has now.

I would like to thank Ed Hillary for his lifelong inspiration and his gracious foreword to the present work. I would also like to thank my publisher, Robert Franklin, for the guidance, humor, and above all, the wings on his feet. Thanks too to leading Antarctic authority Jack Child of American University in Washington, who volunteered to proofread the manuscript. I couldn't inflict that on you, Jack, it's a tad too big, but I appreciate it. Every writer needs a major supporter; I had two, Mary Lyons Rearden and Gayle Winston. If I ever have momentary doubts that I was born under a lucky star, these two friends remove those doubts. Thanks to Morris Bernstein who, with his firsthand knowledge of Antarctica, was the direct inspiration for this book. Everything is black and white with young Morris, and that helped me through the gray areas. The unnerving task of hitting about 10 million typewriter keys was made easier listening to that great drummer, Big Sid Catlett. I would like to doff my hat to Eduardo Orso the filmmaker, for his sage and sometimes eccentric advice on Antarctica-related movies.

I had other friends who helped me by their constant encouragement: Don and Kathy Burns, Senator Anne Bagnal, Senator Harry Bagnal, Julian Crockett, Joe Gleason, Dick Page, J.W. Tatum, Carlos Wight, King Triplett,

Luigi Bozzo, Charlie Williams, David Boden, Jim Finney, Dewey Wilkerson, Tom Anderson, Gwynn Hooks, Keith Monroe, King Alexander I of Edelweiss, Gary Sluder, Judith Sutherin, J.A.C. Dunn, Clarke Worthington, Essie Q and Mr. K.P., Eric the Owl, T.B., Joey and Benji, Russ Womble, Jerry Beauchamp, Marc Lehmann, Linda Weaver, Sharon Chunn, and too many others to thank individually.

And Susan. For a third of my life Susan has shared my adventures, real life and literary, on six continents. And I have shared hers, real life and theatrical. Susan makes it all fun.

The gathering of the material for this book was the work of the author alone.

# A CAPSULE HISTORY

About 450 million years ago Antarctica was probably part of a supercontinent, Pangaea, the Earth's only landmass. Subsequently this landmass broke into two parts, Laurasia and Gondwanaland. At this stage Antarctica may well have been where the Sahara is now. It has been suggested that Gondwanaland itself split up about 120 million years ago, propelling Antarctica southward to its present location. The continent was considerably smaller then, the vast ice sheets that cover it today and that add so much territory having not yet been formed. There were plants and animals there 100 million years ago, probably forests, all flourishing in a large, ice-free southern land.

In time, the extreme southern latitudes, in relation to the tilt of the Earth, forced an accumulation of ice on top of the highest peaks, and these formed glaciers which ran down valleys to form ice sheets and ice shelves. This period of glaciation began about 40 or 50 million years ago, and by and by the entire continent became a land of ice. The more ice, the whiter the surface of the terrain, and the less the sun's rays could be absorbed. Consequently it became a very cold, inhospitable place, and it is still that way today. The fact remains, however, that for most of its history Antarctica has been ice-free, and may become so again.

The first human contact with Antarctica was theoretical. The Greeks argued that because there was an Arctic (Arktos, "the Bear," referring to the Great Bear in the northern skies), there had to be an Antarctica (anti–Arktos) to balance the world. Some European philosophers' ideas about this great southern continent were quite fantastic, and over the centuries Terra Australis Incognita (as it became known in the Middle Ages) was pictured on maps in a variety of imaginative ways, even though no one had ever been there.

The first to visit "The Ice" was, perhaps, Ui-Te-Rangiora, the 7th-century Cook Islander. To the degree that legend is based on truth, it would seem that this gentleman led a war-canoe crew to an icy land in the South Seas. It is not clear what drove this band southward, or how far south they actually got on their trip, but the myth indicates that other civilizations, apart from the Europeans, were aware of a great frozen continent in the high austral latitudes.

The discovery by Columbus of the New World in 1492 led to his successors' pushing ever further south along the coast of South America, eager to find the lands and riches awaiting them. Navigators like Vespucci, Magellan, and Drake opened up the way to the Horn, and in 1599 Dirck Gerritsz claimed to have been blown off course in a storm, sighting land at 64° in southern latitudes. In 1603 a similar thing may have happened to the ship *Blyde Bootschap*. There are several other accounts of "prehistoric" Antarctica adventures, most of them as related by buccaneers, and all of which fall into the realm of the doubtful.

It is generally accepted that 60° south marks the northern boundary of the Antarctic proper, and the first navigator certain to have crossed this barrier was Captain James Cook, in 1773, during his second great voyage. On January 17, 1773, he crossed the Antarctic Circle (66°30'S), and went on to reach 71°10'S without sighting land. He concluded that if there were an Antarctic continental landmass, it would have to be very cold indeed, and of no use to humans.

On his way south Cook discovered South Georgia (54°S), and in his later written account of the voyage he described the great numbers of seals he had seen in these southern lands. This led to the era of the sealers. In 1819 William Smith found the South Shetlands, the first undisputed land south of 60°S (even though, for a short time, his find was questioned, even by his superiors). This opened the gates for the fast and furious seal rush of the next couple of years, in which an enormous number of vessels from all over the world descended on the South Shetlands, wiping out the fur seal population there. In this period some of the sealers searched for fresh beaches, and in this way the South Orkneys were discovered by Palmer and Powell in 1821, and the northern extremities of the Antarctic Peninsula were first sighted and landed on.

The Antarctic island waters became filled with ships from the United States, Argentina, Britain and Australia, and well-organized sealing expeditions were sent from New England ports to bring back as many seals as possible. Adventures abounded, as did wrecks, and tales of death, hardship and triumphs, and bit by bit the northern extremities of Antarctica were charted and mapped.

By 1822 the fur seals were gone and the ships all but stopped coming. Those few that carried on in the area mostly combined navigation and charting with the search for fresh sealing pastures, and in this way discoveries continued. In 1828–31 the *Chanticleer* arrived in the South Shetlands on a purely scientific expedition, and this foreshadowed the great Antarctic voyages of the next two decades, the expeditions of Biscoe, Dumont d'Urville, Balleny, Wilkes, and Ross. These commanders were motivated by a combination of interest in whaling possibilities, national honor, a zeal for exploration, scientific curiosity, mapping needs and the quest for the elusive South Magnetic Pole. Ships' crews made isolated sightings of various parts of the continental coastline. When Ross's expedition ended in 1843, the era of the great Antarctic sea voyages came to an end too.

A long lull in Antarctic activities followed, only the occasional sealer or whaler venturing into the dangerous southern waters. A brief resurgence of the seal population prompted a rash of vessels in the 1870s, but it was not until the 1890s that the next wave of exploration began.

In 1892 the Dundee Whaling Expedition arrived in Antarctica, as did Carl Anton Larsen in the *Jason*. The era of the Antarctic whaler was beginning. In 1895 the Sixth International Geographical Congress decided to devote major attention to Antarctica. The first International Polar Year (1882–83) had not taken much notice of Antarctica, concentrating almost exclusively on the Arctic (as the second such gathering was to do in 1932–33), but from 1895 to 1917 it became a matter of national pride among the British, Norwegians, Germans, Belgians, Swedes, French, Argentinians, Japanese, and Australians to see who could discover the most, and who could bring the greatest glory to their country. Almost subconsciously at first, and then more and more openly, the main aim now became not the South Magnetic Pole, as it had been for the navigators of the 19th century, but the actual South Pole, 90° S, the bottom of the world. The race was on for the ultimate prize, and this Heroic Era, as it has become known, produced the great explorers of the frozen waste, men such as Scott and Amundsen, Shackleton and Mawson, Nordenskjöld and von Drygalski, Borchgrevink and Bruce, Shirase and Filchner, Charcot and de Gerlache, men who pioneered the land traverse with their sledges, dogs and ponies, out there alone in the face of almost unimaginable hardship and cold, dicing with death on a daily basis, and stimulating the imagination of generations of schoolboys. The high point was reached in 1911 when Amundsen beat Scott to the Pole, bringing the four corners of the world together in his mad, glorious dash.

Over the next few decades, in fact up to World War II, whaling activity increased in leaps and bounds, extinction being the inevitable end for several species of whale; science assumed an ever-greater role in Antarctica, especially with the Discovery Investigations conducted by the British. The late 1920s signaled the arrival of the mechanical era and the end to the days of the great land traverses. The airplane and the motorized land vehicle were ushered in by Admiral Byrd, who was to dominate Antarctic exploration for decades. World War II brought the conflict to the Antarctic, not in a big way, but enough to leave a stain on the otherwise pristine continent, and around this time the claiming of Antarctic territory became a major item for certain countries.

After the war Britain launched its FIDS (Falkland Islands Dependencies Surveys) which explored much of the Antarctic Peninsula. Scientific stations were set up, and methodical scientific and charting expeditions took place. The United States conducted a massive assault on Antarctica, Operation Highjump, and the Argentinians and Chileans began sending down yearly expeditions. During the postwar years Antarctica became more and more embedded in the international consciousness. The exploration, the scientific discoveries, the fact that it was the last frontier, contributed to making Antarctica a hot topic.

The mid–1950s brought the IGY (International Geophysical Year), the epitome of international cooperation, where several countries banded together to "discover" Antarctica. This opened up the continent even more and a natural outcome of the IGY was the Antarctic Treaty, signed in 1959 by twelve nations, and over the course of the next three decades by dozens of other nations. This treaty guarantees peace and neutrality for Antarctica. The treaty works.

Now there are scores of scientific stations scattered over the ice, manned by personnel from several countries. Women are now a major factor (having been excluded from Antarctica for such a long time) in scientific work. Although tourism is on the increase, it is the sentiment of many that Antarctica should remain as pure as possible. In 1985 the unhappy discovery of something called the Ozone Hole was announced. Scientists don't really know what has caused this periodic thinning of the ozone layer over Antarctica, but they suspect it has something to do with humans polluting their own atmosphere. This problem is occupying more and more of the scientific community's time.

# A NOTE ON
# ALPHABETIZATION

In this book entries are arranged alphabetically word by word (rather than letter by letter), under the primary word (frequently, the proper name), avoiding inversions except of persons' names. Inversion, particularly of names in a range of languages, can often be confusing or misleading.

Often there are several entries with the same primary word, but with it appearing in various positions. Using a fictitious entry name, *Surman,* this is the order of precedence for the Surman entries:

1. The *Surman* (a ship); or The Surman (a geographic feature).

2. Cape Surman, Isla Surman, Mount Surman, etc., geographic features where the primary (proper) word comes second or even third, and thus the entry is subalphabetized by the first word(s).

3. Surman (person's name; first name unknown).

4. Surman, Capt. (person's name; only a rank or title known).

5. Surman, Aaron; Surman, Frank, etc. — personal name entries where both first and last names are known. These entries, and the ones in 4. above, are the only ones to be inverted, partly to make it clear at a glance that they are entries for persons and partly because the reader expects this convention.

6. Surman Bluff, Surman Cliffs, Surman Mountains, The *Surman of Boston* (a ship), Surman Strait, Surman Valley, etc. — all entries where the primary word comes first (thus they are subalphabetized by the second word).

Entries coming after the Surman entries might be Surmane Glacier, Surmano Terrace, Surmanov Sea, Surman's Straits.

Hyphens are to be ignored, both those that join complete words (example: "All-Blacks," which would be found under All, its primary word) and those that are orthographic conventions within words ("Lake O-ike," for instance, which would be listed, not at the very beginning of the O's as if O were the primary word, but under Oike as if the hyphen did not exist).

A decision was made, because the alternative proved unacceptable, that names like "Mount A. Beck," "Mount S. Hassel," etc., would come at the beginning of the A's and S's respectively, as if "A." and "S." were the primary words. Even so, such entries are frequently merely *"see"* references (as is **"Mount A. Beck** *see* **Beck Peak"**).

Proper last names consisting of two or more parts (La Grange or Van der Essen) are alphabetized as if all one word (Lagrange or Vanderessen).

Mc, Mac and M' entries have been listed together, as if there were no difference.

All entries are alphabetized without reference to English-language definite and indefinite articles. For convenience, non–English language articles are, however, incorporated into the alphabetization (*Las Palmas,* the ship, is word-by-word under L). All accents are ignored in alphabetization.

Abbreviations are kept to a minimum in this book. The most frequently occurring ones are listed separately on pages xxi–xxii, and or in their alphabetical place within the main section of the book.

# ABBREVIATIONS

**AAE**    Australasian Antarctic Expedition 1911–14

**ANARE**    Australian National Antarctic Research Expeditions

**AWS**    Automatic Weather Station

**BANZARE**    British, Australian and New Zealand Antarctic Research Expedition 1929–31

**BAS**    British Antarctic Survey

**BCTAE**    British Commonwealth Transantarctic Expedition 1955–57

**BGLE**    British Graham Land Expedition 1934–37

**FIBEX**    First International BIOMASS Experiment

**FIDASE**    Falkland Islands Dependencies Aerial Survey Expedition 1955–57

**FIDS**    Falkland Islands Dependencies Survey

**IGY**    International Geophysical Year 1957–58

**IWSOE**    International Weddell Sea Oceanographic Expedition

**JARE**    Japanese Antarctic Research Expedition

**LCE 1936–37**    Lars Christensen Expedition 1936–37

**m.**    meters

**NBSAE 1949–52**    Norwegian-British-Swedish Antarctic Expedition 1949–52

**NOZE**    National Ozone Expedition

**NZ**    New Zealand

**NZGSAE**    New Zealand Geological Survey Antarctic Expedition

**NSF**    National Science Foundation

**RAAF**    Royal Australian Air Force

**RAF**    Royal Air Force

**RARE**    Ronne Antarctic Research Expedition 1947–48

**RN**    Royal Navy

**RNR**    Royal Naval Reserve

**RNZAF**    Royal New Zealand Air Force

**Run**    deserted from ship
**SANAE**    South African National Antarctic Expedition
**SPA**    Specially Protected Area
**SSSI**    Site of Special Scientific Interest
**UK**    United Kingdom
**US, USA**    United States
**USAAF**    United States Army Air Force
**USAF**    United States Air Force
**USAP**    United States Antarctic Program
**USARP**    United States Antarctic Research Program
**USAS**    United States Antarctic Service [Expedition]
**USCG**    United States Coast Guard
**USGS**    United States Geological Survey
**USN**    United States Navy
**USNR**    United States Naval Reserve
**USSR**    Soviet Union
**VUWAE**    Victoria University of Wellington Antarctic Expedition
**VX-6, VXE-6**    [see that entry in the encyclopedia]

# THE ENCYCLOPEDIA

**Mount A. Beck** *see* **Beck Peak**

**Mount A. Ditte** *see* **Mount Ditte**

**Sommet A. Gaudry** *see* **Mount Gaudry**

**Mount A. Lindström** *see* **Lindström Peak**

**Aagard Glacier.** 66°46′S, 64°31′W. 8 miles long. Just east of Gould Glacier, it flows into Mills Inlet, on the east coast of Graham Land. Named by the FIDS for Bjarne Aagard, Norwegian authority on whaling.

**Aagard Islands.** 65°51′S, 53°40′E. Also called Bjarne Aagard Islands. Group of small islands just west of Proclamation Island and Cape Batterbee. Discovered Jan. 1930 by the BANZARE, and named for Bjarne Aagard (*see* **Aagard Glacier**).

**Mount Aaron.** 74°31′S, 64°53′W. In the NW sector of the Latady Mountains in Palmer Land. Named for W.T. Aaron, electrician at Amundsen-Scott South Pole Station in 1963.

**Aaron Glacier.** 85°08′S, 90°40′W. 4 miles long. Flows from the Ford Massif between Janulis Spur and Gray Spur in the Thiel Mountains. Bermel & Ford, co-leaders of the US Geological Survey Thiel Mountains Party of 1960–61, named it for John M. Aaron, member of the party and of a similar one the following year.

**Abbey Nunatak.** 85°37′S, 134°43′W. 2 miles SE of Penrod Nunatak, on the west side of Reedy Glacier, just north of the mouth of Kansas Glacier. Named for

Gordon Abbey, radioman at Byrd Station, 1957.

**Mount Abbott.** 74°42′S, 163°51′E. 1,020 m. Highest point in the Northern Foothills of Terra Nova Bay in Victoria Land. 3 miles NE of Cape Canwe. Mapped by Campbell's Northern Party during Scott's last expedition, and named for George P. Abbott.

**Abbott, George P.** Petty Officer, RN. One of Campbell's Northern Party during Scott's last expedition, he went mad on his return to Hut Point.

**Abbott Ice Shelf.** 72°45′S, 96°W. 250 miles long. 40 miles wide. It fronts the Eights Coast from Cape Waite to Phrogner Point. Discovered 1940 by the USAS. Named later for Rear Adm. J. Lloyd Abbott, Jr., commander, US Naval Support Force, Antarctica, 1967–69.

**Abbott Island.** 64°06′S, 62°08′W. 1 mile west of Davis Island in the south part of Bouquet Bay off the NE side of Brabant Island. Charted by Charcot 1903–5. Named by the UK for Maude Abbott (1869–1940), US authority on congenital heart disease.

**Abbott Peak.** 77°26′S, 167°E. Also called Abbott's Peak. Pyramidal. Between Mounts Erebus and Bird on Ross Island. Charted during Scott's last expedition, and named for George P. Abbott.

**Abbott's Peak** *see* **Abbott Peak**

**Mount Abbs.** 70°36′S, 66°38′E. 2,135 m. The most prominent peak in the cen-

1

tral part of the Aramis Range, just west of Thomson Massif. Discovered Dec. 1956 by W.G. Bewsher's ANARE party, and named by the Australians for Gordon Abbs, radio operator at Mawson Station, 1956.

**Abel Nunatak.** 63°33′S, 57°41′W. The more easterly of two isolated nunataks on the south side of Broad Valley, Trinity Peninsula. Named by the FIDS in 1961 in association with nearby Cain Nunatak.

**Abele, C.A., Jr.** One of the shore party on Byrd's 1933-35 expedition.

**Abele Nunatak.** 76°18′S, 143°15′W. 2 miles east of Hutcheson Nunataks at the head of Balchen Glacier in Marie Byrd Land. Named for C.A. Abele, Jr.

**Abele Spur.** 83°13′S, 51°05′W. In the Pensacola Mountains.

**Abendroth Peak.** 71°05′S, 62°W. 4 miles NE of Stockton Peak, between the Murrish and Gain Glaciers in Palmer Land. Named for Ernst K. Abendroth, US biologist at Palmer Station in 1968.

**Ablation.** The wearing away of a rock or glacier, or any snow or ice surface, by any means. Ablation is offset by accumulation.

**Ablation Bay** *see* **Ablation Valley**

**Ablation Lake.** 70°49′S, 68°26′W. On the east coast of Alexander Island. Named in association with Ablation Valley.

**Ablation Point.** 70°48′S, 68°30′W. On the north side of the entrance to Ablation Valley (in association with which it was named by the FIDS), on the east coast of Alexander Island. Photographed aerially by Ellsworth on Nov. 23, 1935.

**Ablation Valley.** 70°48′S, 68°30′W. Also called Ablation Bay. 2 miles long. Ice-free. On the east coast of Alexander Island, it opens on George VI Sound. Named by its first visitors, the BGLE, in 1936, because of the small amounts of ice and snow here.

**Abolin Rock.** 71°50′S, 11°16′E. 1 mile west of the north end of Vindegga Spur in the Liebknecht Range of the Humboldt Mountains in Queen Maud Land. Discovered aerially by Ritscher's expedition 1938-39, and named by the USSR in 1966 for botanist R.I. Abolin.

**Mount Abrams.** 75°22′S, 72°27′W. 2½ miles east of Mount Brice in the Behrendt Mountains of Ellsworth Land. Discovered by the RARE 1947-48 and named by Ronne for Talbert Abrams, instrument manufacturer and supporter of the expedition.

**Abrupt Island.** 67°S, 57°46′E. ½ mile in width. 1½ miles east of Lang Island, just east of the Øygarden Group and Edward VIII Bay. Photographed by the LCE 1936-37, and named Brattøy (Abrupt Island) by the Norwegians.

**Abrupt Point.** 66°54′S, 56°42′E. 3 miles SW of the Patricia Islands, on the west side of Edward VIII Bay. Photographed by the LCE 1936-37, and named Brattodden (Abrupt Point) by the Norwegians.

**Mount Absalom.** 80°24′S, 25°24′W. 1,640 m. The highest and most southerly of the Herbert Mountains. Named by the BCTAE in 1957 for Henry W.L. Absalom, member of the scientific committee for that expedition.

**Abyssal plains.** Extremely flat areas of the ocean and sea floors, at abyssal depths of between 2 and 4 miles, under the oceans surrounding continents. The surface (up to ½ mile thick) is sediment deposited over the centuries.

**Academy Glacier.** 84°15′S, 61°W. Flows between the Patuxent and Neptune Ranges in the Pensacola Mountains, and enters the Foundation Ice Stream. Named for the US National Academy of Sciences.

**Acarospora Peak.** 86°21′S, 148°28′W. 1 mile east of Mount Czegka at the SW end of the Watson Escarpment. Named by the New Zealanders in 1969-70 for the lichen *Acarospora emergens* found on the peak.

**Access Point.** 64°50'S, 63°47'W. Just SE of Biscoe Point. 2 miles NW of Cape Lancaster, on the south side of Anvers Island. Charted by Charcot 1903–5. Surveyed in 1955 by the FIDS who named it because it had a landing place for boats, and thus leads to the interior of the island.

**Accidents** *see* **Disasters**

**Achaean Range.** 64°30'S, 63°38'W. In the central part of Anvers Island. Surveyed by the FIDS in 1955 and named by the UK for the Achaeans of Homer's time.

**Mount Achala.** 62°55'S, 60°42'W. On the north part of Telefon Ridge on Deception Island. Named by the Argentines in 1956.

**Mount Achernar.** 84°11'S, 160°56'E. Forms the NE end of the MacAlpine Hills, on the south side of Law Glacier, at the top of the Bowden Névé, in the Queen Maud Mountains. Named by the New Zealanders in 1962 for the star Achernar, which one of their expeditions used in fixing the survey baseline.

**Achernar Island.** 66°58'S, 57°12'E. 1½ miles long. 1 mile west of Shaula Island in the Øygarden Group. Photographed by the LCE 1936–37 and named Utøy (Outer Island) by the Norwegians. First visited by the ANARE in 1954 and renamed by the Australians for the star.

**¹Mount Achilles.** 64°29'S, 63°35'W. 1,280 m. Snow-covered and steep-sided. 4 miles SW of Mount Nestor in the Achaean Range of central Anvers Island. Surveyed by the FIDS in 1955 and named by the UK for the Greek hero.

**²Mount Achilles.** 71°53'S, 168°08'E. 2,880 m. Pyramidal. Between Fitch Glacier and Man-o-War Glacier in the Admiralty Mountains. Named by the New Zealanders in 1957–58 for the former NZ cruiser, the *Achilles* (which never got to the Antarctic).

**Achilles Heel.** 64°30'S, 63°38'W. 915 m. Snow-covered hill. Between Mounts Helen and Achilles in the Achaean Range of central Anvers Island. Surveyed

by the FIDS in 1955 and named by the UK in association with Mount Achilles.

**Mount Aciar.** 64°25'S, 62°34'W. Also called Monte E, Monte Primer Teniente Aciar, Monte Ferrer, Mount Ehrlich. Between the heads of the Rush and Jenner Glaciers in the Solvay Mountains of SW Brabant Island. Originally (before 1957) called Monte Primer Teniente Aciar, by the Argentines, for a 1st Lt. Aciar.

**Ackerman, Peter.** Seaman on the Wilkes Expedition of 1838–42. Joined in the USA and served the cruise.

**Ackerman Nunatak.** 82°41'S, 47°45'W. 655 m. Isolated. 6½ miles SSE of Butler Rocks in the northern Forrestal Range. Named for Thomas A. Ackerman, aerographer at Ellsworth Station in 1957.

**Ackerman Ridge.** 86°34'S, 147°30'W. Forms the NW extremity of the La Gorce Mountains in the Queen Maud Mountains. Discovered by Quin Blackburn in Dec. 1934, and later named for Lt. Rennie J. Ackerman, VX-6 navigator, 1965 and 1966.

**Ackroyd Point.** 70°46'S, 166°47'E. Just east of the O'Hara Glacier, on the south side of the inner portion of Yule Bay, on the north coast of Victoria Land. Named for Lt. Frederick W. Ackroyd, USN, Medical Officer at McMurdo Base in 1958.

**The *Active*.** 340-ton whaler, part of the Dundee Whaling Expedition 1892–93. Under the command of Thomas Robertson. C.W. Donald was the naturalist aboard. On Jan. 10, 1893, it ran areef on Active Reef for six hours during a gale.

**Active Reef.** 63°23'S, 55°52'W. Isolated. In the Firth of Tay, just off the north coast of Dundee Island. Discovered by Thomas Robertson of the *Active* in 1892–93, who named it because his ship ran areef here for 6 hours on Jan. 10, 1893.

**Active Sound.** 63°25'S, 56°10'W. Average of 2 miles wide. With the Firth of Tay it separates Joinville Island from Dundee Island. Discovered by Thomas

Robertson in 1892–93. He named it for his vessel, the *Active*.

**Mount Acton.** 70°58'S, 63°42'W. On the west ridge of the Welch Mountains of Palmer Land. Named for Cdr. William Acton, USN, operations officer on the staff of the commander, US Naval Support Force, Antarctica, 1967–68, and executive officer, 1968–69.

**Islote Acuña** *see* **Acuña Rocks**

**Acuña, Hugo.** 1885–1953. Hugo Alberto Acuña. Pioneer Argentine meteorologist at Omond House in the South Orkneys with Bruce's expedition in 1904, just before the station became Argentine.

**Acuña Island.** 60°46'S, 44°37'W. Also called Delta Island. Just south of Point Rae, off the south coast of Laurie Island in the South Orkneys. Charted in 1903 and named in 1904–5 by Bruce for Hugo Acuña.

**Acuña Rocks.** 63°18'S, 57°56'W. Two rocks almost ½ mile west of Largo Island in the Duroch Islands off Trinity Peninsula. Named Islote Acuña by the Argentines before 1959, almost certainly for Hugo Acuña.

**Mount Adam.** 71°47'S, 168°38'E. 4,010 m. 2½ miles WNW of Mount Minto in the Admiralty Mountains. Discovered and named by Ross in Jan. 1841, for Sir Charles Adam, a lord of the admiralty.

**Adams.** Bosun on the *Aurora* during the AAE 1911–14.

**Cape Adams.** 75°04'S, 62°20'W. Also called Cape Charles J. Adams. An abrupt rock scarp, it forms the north side of the entrance to Gardner Inlet at the south end of the Lassiter Coast on the east side of Palmer Land, and juts out into the northernmost part of the Ronne Ice Shelf. Discovered by the RARE 1947–48 and named by Ronne for Charles J. Adams.

**Mount Adams** *see* **Adams Mountains**

**Adams, Charles J.** Lt. USAAF. Pilot on the RARE 1947–48.

**Adams, Harry.** Retired naval lieutenant with 30 years service when he

went as second mate on the *Eleanor Bolling* and later the *City of New York* during Byrd's 1928–30 expedition.

**Adams, Jameson B.** b. 1880. Lt. Jameson Boyd Adams, later knighted. Meteorologist and second-in-command of the shore party during Shackleton's 1907–9 expedition. One of the first to climb Mount Erebus in 1908, and one of Shackleton's Pole party which almost made it to the South Pole in 1908–9.

**Adams, Joseph.** Captain of the *Stranger* in the South Shetlands 1820–21.

**Adams Bluff.** 82°09'S, 159°55'E. 5 miles north of Peters Peak in the Holyoake Range of the Churchill Mountains. Named for Paul L. Adams, meteorologist at Byrd Station, 1961–62, 1962–63, and at McMurdo Station, 1963–64, 1964–65.

**Adams Fjord.** 66°50'S, 50°30'E. Also called Seven Bay, Bukhta Semerka. 13 miles long. In the NE part of Amundsen Bay, just south of Mount Riiser-Larsen. On Feb. 14, 1958, the *Thala Dan* sent a motor launch into the fjord, and its ANARE crew, led by Phillip Law, landed at the foot of Mount Riiser-Larsen. Named by the Australians for Ian L. Adams, officer-in-charge at Mawson Station, 1958.

**¹Adams Glacier.** 66°45'S, 109°24'E. Over 20 miles long, this broad glacier feeds Vincennes Bay from the Budd Coast. Named John Quincy Adams Glacier for the US president who greatly helped forward the Wilkes Expedition of 1838–42. The name was later shortened.

**²Adams Glacier.** 78°08'S, 163°45'E. Just south of Miers Glacier in Victoria Land. Named by the New Zealanders in 1957–58 for Jameson B. Adams.

**Adams Island.** 66°33'S, 92°35'E. On the west side of McDonald Bay, about 11 miles west of Mabus Point. Discovered and named by the Western Party of the AAE 1911–14 for Adams, the bosun on the *Aurora*.

**Adams Mountains.** 84°30′S, 166°20′E. In the Queen Alexandra Range. Discovered by Shackleton 1907–9 and named the Adams Range by him for Lt. Jameson B. Adams. Scott, on his 1910–13 expedition, trimmed the term to one peak in the range, and called it Mount Adams. The term mountains is now considered appropriate.

**Adams Nunatak.** 71°44′S, 68°34′W. On the south side of Neptune Glacier, 6 miles west of Cannonball Cliffs, in eastern Alexander Island. Named by the UK for John C. Adams (1819–92), astronomer who discovered the planet Neptune.

**Adams Peak.** 81°38′S, 160°04′E. 1,540 m. On the east side of Starshot Glacier, 2 miles SE of Heale Peak in the Surveyors Range. Named by the New Zealanders in 1960–61 for 19th century NZ surveyor C.W. Adams.

**Adams Range** *see* **Adams Mountains**

**Adams Rocks.** 76°14′S, 145°39′W. Two large rock outcrops that overlook the inner part of Block Bay from northward. 7 miles west of Mount June in the Phillips Mountains of the Ford Ranges of Marie Byrd Land. Named for James G. Adams, USN, builder at Byrd Station, 1967.

**Mount Adamson.** 73°55′S, 163°E. 3,400 m. 6½ miles ENE of Mount Hewson, in the Deep Freeze Range of Victoria Land. Named by the Northern Party of the NZGSAE 1965–66 for R. Adamson, geologist with the party.

**Cape Adare.** 71°17′S, 170°14′E. A cape of black basalt in sharp contrast to the rest of the snow-covered coast at the foot of the Admiralty Mountains, at the western edge of the Ross Sea, in Oates Land. Discovered and named by Ross in Jan. 1841 for Viscount Adare, a friend in Wales. First landed on by a party from the *Antarctic* in 1895. Borchgrevink

was the first to winter over here, in 1899.

**Adare Peninsula.** 71°40′S, 170°30′E. Also called Cape Adare Peninsula. High, ice-covered. 40 miles long. Cape Adare is at its northern tip. In Oates Land. Named by the New Zealanders in association with Cape Adare

**Adare Saddle.** 71°44′S, 170°12′E. 900 m. An ice-saddle where the Admiralty Mountains meet Adare Peninsula, and where Newnes Glacier meets Moubray Glacier which falls steeply from this saddle. Named by the New Zealanders in 1957–58 for nearby Cape Adare.

**Adelaide Anchorage.** 67°47′S, 68°57′W. West of Avian Island, off the south end of Adelaide Island. Ships normally anchor here when visiting Base T (now Teniente Carvajal Station).

**Adelaide Island.** 67°15′S, 68°30′W. Also called Isla Belgrano. 20 miles wide. Mainly ice-covered. Off the west coast of the Antarctic Peninsula, at the north end of Marguerite Bay. Discovered and named by Biscoe on Feb. 15, 1832, as Queen Adelaide Island for the British queen. At first thought to be only 8 miles long, but Charcot, in 1909, proved it to be over 70 miles long. The British Base T was here (it is now Teniente Carvajal Station, a Chilean station).

**Adélie Coast** *see* **Adélie Land**

**Adélie Depression** *see* **Mertz-Ninnis Valley**

**Adélie Land.** Centers on 67°S, and lies between Pourquoi Pas Point (136°11′E) and Point Alden (142°02′E), or more generally between George V Land and the Wilkes Coast in Wilkes Land. An ice-covered plateau, it rises from the Indian Ocean and covers 166,800 sq. miles. Discovered Jan. 20, 1840, by Dumont d'Urville and named Terre Adélie or Terre d'Adélie by him for his wife, Adèle. Charcot began urging the French Government to claim it in 1926, and they finally did on April 1, 1938. The French did not establish a base here until the

*Commandant Charcot* pulled in on Jan. 20, 1950.

**Adélie penguin.** This is the best known of all the penguins. Also known as the black-throated penguin, it is about 30 inches high, about 9–14 pounds in weight, and lays one or two eggs. It was discovered by Hombron and Jacquinot, and named *Pygoscelis adeliae* after Adélie Land.

**Adélie Trough**  *see*  **Adélie Valley**

**Adélie Valley.** 66°S, 136°E. Submarine feature off the coast of Adélie Land. Also called Adélie Trough, Dumont d'Urville Trough.

**Mount Ader.** 64°10′S, 60°29′W. On the north side of Breguet Glacier, and just SE of Mount Cornu, in northern Graham Land. Named by the UK in 1960 for Clément Ader (1841–1925), pioneer French aviator.

**Adie, R.J.** South African geologist with the FIDS in 1947–49.

**Adie Inlet.** 66°25′S, 62°20′W. Ice-filled. 25 miles long. East of Churchill Peninsula, on the east side of Graham Land. Named by the FIDS for R.J. Adie.

**Adit Nunatak.** 65°54′S, 62°48′W. 3 miles WNW of Mount Alibi on the north side of Leppard Glacier in Graham Land. Surveyed by the FIDS in 1955. Named by the UK in 1957 for the adit (or opening) to an unsurveyed inland area between Leppard and Flask Glaciers.

**Mount Adkins.** 73°03′S, 62°02′W. On the north side of Mosby Glacier, just west of the mouth of Fenton Glacier, on the Black Coast of the Antarctic Peninsula. Named for Thomas Adkins, cook at Palmer Station, 1965.

**Admiral Byrd Bay**  *see*  **Byrd Bay**

**The *Admiralen*.** The first modern floating factory whaling ship. It first operated in Admiralty Bay in the South Shetlands in Jan. 1906, Alexander Lange, captain.

**Admiralen Peak.** 62°06′S, 58°30′W. Also called Admiration Peak, Pico Puño. 305 m. Almost ¾ mile SSW of Crépin Point at the west side of Admiralty Bay on King George Island in the South Shetlands. Named by the UK in 1960 for the *Admiralen*. This may be the peak Charcot called Le Poing.

**Admiralty Bay.** 62°10′S, 58°25′W. Also called Bahía Lasserre. Indents the southern coast of King George Island for ten miles between Demay Point and Martins Head (5 miles wide), in the South Shetlands. Named in or before 1822 by Powell for the British Admiralty. The British had their Base G here, and the Poles have Arctowski Station. The western side of the bay is SSSI 8 (*see* **Sites of Special Scientific Interest**).

**Admiralty Inlet**  *see*  **Admiralty Sound**

**Admiralty Mountains.** 71°45′S, 168°30′E. Also called the Admiralty Range. A large group of high mountains, ranges, and ridges at the extreme north of Victoria Land. First sighted Jan. 11, 1841, by Ross, and named by him for the British Admiralty who sent him on this expedition.

**Admiralty Range**  *see*  **Admiralty Mountains**

**Admiralty Sound.** 64°20′S, 57°10′W. Separates Snow Hill Island and Seymour Island from James Ross Island. Ross discovered the broad NE part of this sound on Jan. 6, 1843, and named it Admiralty Inlet, for the British Admiralty (*see* **Admiralty Mountains**). Nordenskjöld redefined it in 1902.

**Admiration Peak**  *see*  **Admiralen Peak**

**Adolph Islands.** 66°19′S, 67°11′W. Group of small islands and rocks off the NW part of Watkins Island in the Biscoe Islands. Named by the UK for Edward F. Adolph, US physiologist specializing in the cold.

**Adolph Ochs Glacier** *see* **Ochs Glacier**

**Cape Adriasola.** 67°39′S, 69°11′W. Ice-cliffed. At the SW end of Adelaide Island, 10 miles NW of Avian Island. Discovered by Charcot 1908–10, and named by him for a friend in Chile.

**Advance Base** *see* **Bolling Advance Weather Station**

**Advent Island** *see* **Bauprés Rocks**

**The *Adventure*.** The smaller of Cook's two ships which crossed the Antarctic Circle in 1773. Formerly the *Raleigh*, it was 336 tons, carried cannon and a large ship's launch, and had a crew of 91 commanded by Tobias Furneaux. It was not with the *Resolution* when Cook reached his southing record of 71°10′S, having then been lost twice by the flagship and on its way back to England.

**Adventure Network International, Inc.** Canadian tour company which began in the Antarctic in the 1985–86 season after having formed Antarctic Airways in 1984. One of the more imaginative of the Antarctic tour operators, it flew 20 tourists to the Pole on Jan. 11, 1988. That was a first. Another 15 came on other flights. The following year, 1988–89, the same expedition was offered at $28,500 for 8–12 days. Their Antarctic Ski Expedition was offered at $10,000 for 12 days, and the Mount Vinson climbs at $16,500 for 21 days. In 1988–89 it supplied logistical backup for the Mountain Travel expedition. They claim to be the only land operator in North America for the Antarctic, and most of their programs are sold through Mountain Travel, Special Odysseys, and Lindblad Travel. Incorporated in 1984, it is part owned by Martyn Williams, and the managing director is Hugh Culver. Address: 200-1676 Duranleau St., Vancouver, B.C., Canada V6H 3S5. Tel: (604) 683-8033.

**Mount Aeolus.** 77°29′S, 161°16′E. Over 2,000 m. Between Mounts Boreas and Hercules in the Olympus Range of Victoria Land. Named by the New Zealanders in 1958–59 for the Greek god of the winds.

**Aerial photography.** Photographs taken from the air. In the case of Antarctica, more than any other continent, aerial photography opened up much of the land, and the photos were later checked by ground controls. As far as the US operation is concerned, VXE-6 is responsible for aerial photography. The most notable landmarks in this field are The Lars Christensen Expedition of 1936–37, which photographed a vast amount of East Antarctica; the German New Schwabenland Expedition, led by Ritscher in 1938–39, which photographed about 77,000 sq. miles from an altitude of 10,000 feet in the course of one flight (many of these were in color, and without ground controls were practically useless); and Operation Highjump, which took 40,000 photos. Expeditions subsequent to this one have stressed the importance of aerial photography in the Antarctic.

**Aerodromnaya Hill.** 70°47′S, 11°38′E. Isolated. 1 mile south of the Schirmacher Hills in Queen Maud Land. Discovered by Ritscher in 1938–39. The USSR named it in 1961 (name means "aerodrome") because of the airstrip here which services nearby Novolazarevskaya Station.

**The *Aeronaut*.** US whaler/sealer from Mystic, Conn. In the South Shetlands 1852–53 under Capt. Eldridge. It sailed with the *Lion*. In 1853–54, with the *Lion* and the *Wilmington*, it was back in the South Shetlands, again under Eldridge.

**Aeronaut Glacier.** 73°18′S, 163°24′E. 25 miles long. Flows from Gair Mesa into the upper part of Aviator Glacier, near Navigator Nunatak in Victoria Land. Named by the New Zealanders in 1962–63 for the aeronauts in VX-6 who supported their New Zealand Geological Survey Antarctic Expedition of that year, and also in association with Aviator Glacier.

**Aeroplanes** *see* **Airplanes**

**AFAN McMurdo.** The world's most southerly radio station, at McMurdo.

**Mount Afflick.** 70°46'S, 66°12'E. 3 miles west of Mount Bunt in the Aramis Range. Named by the Australians for G.M. Afflick, weather observer at Mawson Station, 1965.

**Afuera Islands.** 64°20'S, 61°36'W. Also called Dodge Rocks, Penguin Island. Group of three small islands north of Challenger Island, and just outside the south entrance point to Hughes Bay, off the west coast of Graham Land. Charted by Charcot 1908–10. The name means "outside" in Spanish.

**Mount Agamemnon.** 64°38'S, 63°31'W. 2,575 m. Snow-covered. Marks the southern limit of the Achaean Range in central Anvers Island. It is part of the Mount Français massif, but has a separate summit 1½ miles west of the main peak of the massif. Surveyed by the FIDS in 1944 and 1955, and named by the UK for the Homeric hero.

**Cape Agassiz.** 68°29'S, 62°56'W. It is the eastern tip of Hollick-Kenyon Peninsula, and juts out into the Larsen Ice Shelf on the eastern side of the Antarctic Peninsula, just at the dividing line between Palmer Land and Graham Land. Discovered in Dec. 1940 by the USAS from East Base, who named it Cape Joerg for W.L.G. Joerg, the geographer. Joerg insisted it be renamed for Louis Agassiz, the US naturalist.

**Agate Peak.** 72°57'S, 163°48'E. At the SE end of Intention Nunataks, at the SW edge of the Evans Névé, in northern Victoria Land. Named by the New Zealanders for the agate found here in 1966–67.

**Aguda Point.** 65°02'S, 63°41'W. Also called Eclipse Point, Punta Natho, Punta Larga. Forms the east side of the entrance to Hidden Bay on the west coast of Graham Land. De Gerlache charted it in 1897–99. Name means "sharp" in Spanish.

**Cerro Agudo** see **Buddington Peak**

**Pico Agudo** see **Sharp Peak**

**Caleta Águila** see **Eagle Cove**

**Aguirre Cerda** see **Presidente Pedro Aguirre Cerda Station**

**Aguirre Passage.** 64°49'S, 62°51'W. Off the west coast of the Antarctic Peninsula.

**Pico Agujo** see **Needle Peak**

**The Agulhas.** South African ship of the 1980s. It supplied Sanae Station.

**Agurto Rock.** 63°18'S, 57°54'W. Just NW of Silva Rock in the Duroch Islands off Trinity Peninsula.

**Mount Ahab.** 65°26'S, 62°10'W. 925 m. Between the lower ends of Mapple Glacier and Melville Glacier on the east coast of Graham Land. Surveyed by the FIDS in 1947 and 1955. Named by the UK in 1962 for the *Moby Dick* character.

**Ahern Glacier.** 81°47'S, 159°10'E. Flows from the Churchill Mountains between Mounts Lindley and Hoskins, and enters Starshot Glacier. Named by the New Zealanders for B. Ahern, a NZ geologist here in 1964–65.

**Ahlmann Glacier.** 67°52'S, 65°45'W. The more southerly of two glaciers flowing into Seligman Inlet on the east coast of Graham Land. Charted in 1947 by the FIDS who named it for Hans Ahlmann (see **Ahlmann Ridge**).

**Ahlmann Ridge.** 71°50'S, 2°30'W. The Norwegians call it Ahlmannryggen. Broad, ice-covered ridge, 70 miles long, surmounted by scattered, low peaks. It rises between the Schytt and Jutulstraumen Glaciers and extends from the Borg Massif northward to the Fimbul Ice Shelf in Queen Maud Land. Named for the Swedish geologist Hans Ahlmann (1889–1974), who was chairman of the Swedish Committee for the NBSAE 1949–52.

**Ahlstad Hills.** 71°50'S, 5°30'E. Just east of Cumulus Mountain in the Mühlig-Hofmann Mountains of Queen Maud Land. Named Ahlstadhottane (Ahlstad Hills) by the Norwegians.

**Ahmadjian Peak.** 83°41'S, 168°42'E. 2,910 m. Ice-covered. 4½ miles SW of Mount Fox in the Queen Alexandra Range. Named for Vernon Ahmadjian, biologist at McMurdo Station, 1963–64.

**Ahrnsbrak Glacier.** 79°48'S, 82°18'W. In the Enterprise Hills of the Heritage

Range, it flows between Sutton Peak and Shoemaker Peak to the lower end of the Union Glacier. Named for William F. Ahrnsbrak, glaciologist at Palmer Station, 1965.

**Mount Aidwich** *see* **Mount Aldrich**

**Ailsa Craig.** 60°47′S, 44°37′W. Also called Ailsa Craig Islet. 1 mile south of Point Rea, off the south coast of Laurie Island in the South Orkneys. Charted by Bruce in 1903 and named by him for the Scottish island.

**Aim Rocks.** 62°42′S, 61°15′W. East of Cape Timblón in the middle of Morton Strait in the South Shetlands. Named descriptively by the UK in 1961. If you line up the rocks they are a guide through the southern entrance of Morton Strait.

**Ainsworth, G.F.** Member of the AAE 1911–14. During 1911–13 he was leader and meteorologist of the expedition's party on Macquarie Island (not in the Antarctic).

**Ainsworth Bay.** 67°47′S, 146°43′E. Ice-filled indentation into the coast, 5 miles wide, between Capes Bage and Webb. Discovered by the AAE 1911–14, and named by Mawson for G.F. Ainsworth.

**Air-Cushion Vehicles.** In Jan. 1988 the Hake Hover Systems Husky 1500 ACV arrived at McMurdo Station. It was soon reassembled, and it was the first time an ACV had been used in Antarctica by Americans as a cargo transporter. The Japanese have been experimenting at Showa Station with ACVs. The Husky can reach 35 mph and carry 14 people. It can operate in strong headwinds, and can stop very suddenly. It did a trip on the Ross Ice Shelf in 47 minutes. This would have taken an ordinary vehicle 3 hours.

**Aircraft** *see* **Aerial photography, Airplanes, Autogiros, Ballooning, Helicopters**

**Airdevronsix Icefalls.** 77°31′S, 160°25′E. At the head of the Wright Upper Glacier in Victoria Land. Named in 1956–57 for VX-6 (AirDevRon Six).

**Airdrop Peak.** 83°44′S, 172°45′E. 890 m. Twin-peaked mountain at the north end of the Commonwealth Range, on Ebony Ridge. Named by the New Zealanders in 1959–60 because a VX-6 airplane airdropped a spare radio to them on Dec. 11, 1959.

**Airdrops.** Essentially airdrops stock and re-stock bases. They were especially significant during Operation Deep Freeze (which began in 1955 and continues to this day). During IGY they were led by the 61st Troop Carrier Group headed by Col. William Forwood.

**Airfields** *see* **Airstrips**

**Airglow.** Faint luminescence of the entire upper atmosphere (*see also* **Phenomena**). Caused probably by the breakdown of air molecules by solar radiation, and their subsequent recombination.

**Airlifts.** Opposite to airdrops. The first was the rescue of Balchen, June, and Gould on March 22, 1929, by Byrd and Smith during Byrd's 1928–30 expedition. The three men had flown out to the Rockefeller Mountains in the *Virginia*. The plane was destroyed in a gale near the Washington Ridge at 78°48′S, 155°15′W. Parts of it were salvaged by Dane, Moody, and Swan during Byrd's 1933–35 expedition.

**Airplanes.** Airplanes have revolutionized Antarctic exploration, taking only a few hours to do a trip which it took the old explorers months to make by land. It also cut out a great deal of the hardship and heroics. Following are some of the landmarks in Antarctic aviation history. **Dec. 2, 1912:** The first test run of an airplane in Antarctica. Actually it was broken and didn't have any wings. Mawson took a collapsible Vickers REP monoplane (cost: £900) with him on the AAE 1911–14. It got damaged in Adelaide before he even left Australia, and he decided to try it as an "air tractor sledge" without the wings. It was still a failure. **Nov. 16, 1928:** The first plane to fly in Antarctica. A wheel-equipped Lockheed Vega monoplane flown by C.B. Eielson and Hubert Wilkins on Deception Island. **Nov. 26, 1928:** Wilkins' 2 Lockheed Vega monoplanes took off from Deception Island looking for a more suitable base. **Dec. 20, 1928:** Wilkins and Eielson flew 1,300 miles in 11 hours over Graham Land at 6,000 feet at 120 mph to as far south as 71°20′S, 64°15′W before they turned back. **Jan. 10, 1929:** Wilkins and Eielson flew 500 miles over Graham Land. **Jan. 15, 1929:** Byrd made his first Antarctic flight. Byrd pioneered the use of the plane in Antarctica throughout his many expeditions, using ski planes more and more. On his first expedition, 1928–30, his three planes were the *Floyd Bennett,* the *Virginia,* and the *Stars and Stripes.* A fourth plane never got to the Antarctic. **Jan. 27, 1929:** Balchen and Byrd flew across the Ross Ice Shelf. **March 7, 1929:** Balchen, June, and Gould flew to the Rockefeller Mountains in the *Virginia. See* Airlifts (above) to see what happened to them. **Nov. 29, 1929:** The first flight over the South Pole. Balchen, Byrd, June, and McKinley in the *Floyd Bennett.* Byrd had already flown over the North Pole (or so he claimed). **Dec. 5, 1929:** Byrd discovered Marie Byrd Land by plane. **Dec. 7, 1929:** Riiser-Larsen flew over the Enderby Land coast in a seaplane from his ship, the *Norvegia.* **Dec. 22, 1929:** Riiser-Larsen discovered much territory in Queen Maud Land. He had brought two planes to Antarctica, and, during the 1930s, in their exploration of Queen Maud Land, the Norwegians used planes a great deal. **Dec. 27, 1929:** Wilkins and Cheesman flew over Charcot Land. **Dec. 29, 1929:** Wilkins and Cheesman flew over Charcot Land again, proving it to be an island, and claiming it for Britain. **1929–1931:** Mawson used planes on the BANZARE where ice prevented an approach to the mainland by ship. **Jan. 5, 1930:** Wilkins flew from Port Lockroy to Deception Island. **Jan. 30, 1930:** Wilkins managed a local flight over the pack ice. **Feb. 1, 1930:** Wilkins and

Cheesman flew 460 miles round trip over Graham Land. **1933–1935:** Byrd took 3 planes and an autogiro on his expedition (*see* **Byrd's 1933–35 expedition**). **Nov. 23–Dec. 15, 1935:** The first transantarctic crossing, by Ellsworth and Hollick-Kenyon. **1946–1947:** Operation Highjump (q.v.) took a total of 25 aircraft, including 7 helicopters (q.v.). This was the first time planes of the size of Dakotas had landed on the continent. **1947–1948:** The RARE 1947–48 took 3 planes: a twin-engine Beechcraft C-45, the photographic plane; a Noorduyn C-64 Norseman, a single-engine cargo plane developed in Canada for cold-weather operations; and a Stinson L-5, a two-seater reconnaissance plane. All three aircraft had skis. **Oct. 31, 1956:** The *Que Sera Sera,* piloted by Gus Shinn and carrying Adm. Dufek, was the first plane to land at the South Pole. By the 1950s planes were a fundamental part of Antarctic life, being used as support, supply, and exploration vehicles. **Oct. 15, 1957:** The first commercial flight to visit the continent came to McMurdo and brought, among others, two stewardesses (*see* **Women in Antarctica**). **Jan. 1960:** The first Hercules flew into Antarctica. **April 9, 1961:** The first nocturnal flight and landing was the American mission to take Leonid Kuperov out of Byrd Station for medical treatment. **Dec. 2, 1967:** The last flight of the "Gooney Bird," the nickname of the LC-47H Dakotas, from Hallett Station to McMurdo. The Gooney Bird had served with VX-6 from 1963. It was replaced by the Hercules LC-130, "The Workhorse of Antarctica," which revolutionized scientific exploration on the continent. **1982:** An air route was established by the USSR between Maputo (Mozambique) and Molodezhnaya Station. **1989:** The arrival of the Galaxy in Antarctica (*see* the Chronology appendix).

**Airstrips.** Included in this entry are airports, airfields, aerodromes, runways, etc. Most of the scientific stations in Antarctica have an airstrip of one kind or another. The biggest and most used by far is Williams Field ("Willy Field") at McMurdo Station. The original (it has gone through several metamorphoses— see **Williams Field** for details) was built in 2 days, Dec. 18–20, 1955, and a flight came in from an outside base for the first time in Antarctic history. It was also the first time wheeled aircraft had landed on the ice. The strip was 8,000 feet long. But it was not the first airstrip, by any means. The first was on the ice in Port Foster, Deception Island, during the Wilkins-Hearst expedition of 1928–29. It was 880 yards long and very dangerous. Wilkins took off from here on the first Antarctic flight (see **Airplanes**). The first airstrip proper was built at Little America IV in 1946–47 during Operation High-jump. Many airstrips were built during IGY (1957–58). Byrd Station's airstrip was called Byrd Airfield, and Little America V's was called Kiel Field. The Russians seem to favor packed-snow air-strips—one was built at Novolazarev-skaya in 1985, similar to the one already in operation at Molodezhnaya, which has an improvised snow and ice strip. In 1982–83 the French started a permanent, all-weather runway at Dumont d'Urville Station of 3,608 feet in length. Chiloé Station (Chile) has one over 13,000 feet long, and Teniente Rodolfo Marsh Sta-tion has one almost 4,000 feet in length. The Chileans constructed several small ones on the Antarctic Peninsula during 1982–83. Showa Station (Japan) has only a temporary, summer-only runway on the ice.

**Airy Glacier.** 69°12'S, 66°20'W. 20 miles long. 6 miles wide. Flows into the Forster Ice Piedmont, near the west coast of the Antarctic Peninsula. Named by the UK for Sir George Airy, British Astronomer Royal for most of the 19th century.

**Aitcho Islands.** 62°24'S, 59°47'W. Group of small islands between Table and Dee Islands in the South Shetlands. They extend across the central part of the

northern entrance to English Strait. Named before 1948, possibly for the Hydrographic Office. They include Emeline I., Cecilia I., Passage Rock, Mor-ris Rock, Jorge Rock.

**Aitken.** British able seaman on the *Aurora* during the British Imperial Transantarctic Expedition led by Shack-leton. His name is also spelled Atkin.

**Aitken Cove.** 60°45'S, 44°32'W. Just NE of Cape Whitson on the south coast of Laurie Island in the South Orkneys. Named by Bruce in 1903 for A.N.G. Aitken, solicitor for the expedition.

**Aitken Nunatak.** 85°42'S, 173°49'E. 2,785 m. Small rock nunatak to the im-mediate east of the Otway Massif, and 3 miles SW of Mount Bumstead in the Grosvenor Mountains. Named for Wil-liam M. Aitken, aurora scientist at Amundsen-Scott South Pole Station, 1962.

**Aitkenhead Glacier.** 63°57'S, 58°44'W. 10 miles long. Flows from the Detroit Plateau in Graham Land to the Prince Gustav Channel just north of Alectoria Island. Named by the UK for Neil Ait-kenhead, FIDS geologist at Base D, 1959–60.

**The** *Ajax.* British ship sent to help look for a boat crew from the *Discovery II,* missing on King George Island in the South Shetlands, in Jan. 1937. The cap-tain was C.S. Thomsen, and the governor of the Falklands was aboard.

**Mount Ajax.** 71°49'S, 168°27'E. 3,770 m. 1 mile WSW of Mount Royalist in the Admiralty Mountains. Named by the New Zealanders in 1957–58 for the NZ ship, the *Ajax* (not to be confused with the British ship of the same name—see that entry).

**Ajax Icefall.** 62°04'S, 58°23'W. Be-tween Stenhouse Bluff and Ullmann Spur at the head of Visca Anchorage on King George Island in the South Shetlands. Charted by Charcot 1908–10, and named by the UK in 1960 for the *Ajax*.

**Akar Peaks** *see* **Aker Peaks**

**Cape Akarui.** 68°29′S, 41°23′E. Also called Cape Miho. 11 miles NE of Cape Omega on the Queen Maud Land coast. The Japanese named it Akarui-misaki (bright cape).

**Akebono Glacier.** 68°07′S, 42°53′E. Flows to the Queen Maud Land coast between Cape Hinode and Akebono Rock. Named by the Japanese.

**Akebono Rock.** 68°04′S, 42°55′E. Just east of the mouth of Akebono Glacier on the Queen Maud Land coast. Named by the Japanese.

**Aker Peaks.** 66°37′S, 55°13′E. Also called Akar Peaks, Aker Range. A series of mainly snow-covered peaks, the highest being 1,800 m. They extend for 9 miles. 4 miles west of the Nicholas Range and 30 miles WNW of Edward VIII Bay. Discovered Jan. 14, 1931, by Otto Borchgrevink.

**Aker Range** *see* **Aker Peaks**

**Åkerlundh, Gustav.** A member of the Nordenskjöld expedition of 1901–4.

**Åkerlundh Nunatak.** 65°04′S, 60°10′W. 2 miles NW of Donald Nunatak, between Bruce Nunatak and Murdoch Nunatak in the Seal Nunataks, off the east coast of the Antarctic Peninsula. Charted in 1947 by the FIDS who named it for Gustav Åkerlundh.

**Akkuratnaya Cove.** 70°45′S, 11°48′E. 3 miles ESE of Nadezhdy Island, indenting the north side of the Schirmacher Hills in Queen Maud Land. Discovered by Ritscher in 1938–39, mapped by the USSR in 1961, and named by them Bukhta Akkuratnaya (accurate cove).

**The *Alabama Packet*.** US sealing brig in the Fanning-Pendleton Sealing Expedition of 1821–22. It had a crew of 21 led by William A. Fanning. On Nov. 6, 1821, it anchored at Deception Island.

**Aladdin's Cave.** Depot set up on Aug. 9, 1912, by Mawson, Madigan, and Ninnis in an ice-shelter 5½ miles south of Main Base during the AAE 1911–14. In September food was ferried there.

**Alamein Range.** 72°10′S, 163°30′E. West of Canham Glacier, in the Freyberg Mountains of Oates Land. Named for the battle in North Africa taken part in by Lord Freyberg (*see* **Freyberg Mountains**).

**Alamode Island.** 68°43′S, 67°32′W. Largest and most southerly of the Terra Firma Islands in Marguerite Bay. Discovered by the BGLE in 1936, and named in 1948 by its surveyors, the FIDS, for its resemblance in shape to the dessert.

**Alan Peak.** 72°39′S, 0°11′E. On the west side of the mouth of Reece Valley in the southern part of the Sverdrup Mountains of Queen Maud Land. Discovered by Ritscher in 1938–39, and later named for Alan Reece.

**Mount Alan Thompson** *see* **Mount Allan Thomson**

**Alasheyev Bight.** 67°33′S, 45°40′E. Also called Alasheyev's Bay. On the Enderby Land coast. Molodezhnaya Station is here. Named by the USSR in 1957 for hydrographer D.A. Alasheyev.

**Alaska Canyon.** 86°S, 136°33′W. In the north face of Michigan Plateau. Named for the University of Alaska, which has sent researchers to the Antarctic.

**The *Alatna*.** US tanker of the 1950s and 1960s. Participated in Operation Deep Freeze in the seasons 1958–59, 1959–60.

**Alatna Valley.** 76°52′S, 161°10′E. Icefree. 4 miles north of Mount Gran. It extends 10 miles along the SE side of the Convoy Range. Named in 1963 for the *Alatna*.

**Albanus Glacier.** 85°52′S, 151°W. Also called Phillips Glacier. 25 miles long. Feeds into the Robert Scott Glacier between the Tapley Mountains and the Hays Mountains. Discovered Dec. 1934 by Quin Blackburn, and named by Byrd for Albanus Phillips, Jr., a manufacturer, and patron of Byrd's first two expeditions.

**Albanus Phillips Mountains** *see* **Phillips Mountains**

**Albatross.** Also known as mollymawk and gooney. This bird belongs to the order Procellariiformes, and to the family Diomedeidae. Albatrosses are actually a branch of the petrel family and have the largest wing span of any bird in the world. They drink seawater and live normally on squid. They come ashore only to breed, in colonies, and lay a single white egg. They have a long life span. The wandering albatross *(Diomedia exulans)* nests on islands near the Antarctic Circle, but really does not breed south of 54°S (South Georgia). Other albatrosses seen in Antarctic skies are the black-browed albatross *(Diomedia melanophris)*, the light-mantled sooty albatross *(Phoebetria palpebrata)*, and (rarely), the gray-headed albatross *(Diomedia chrysostoma)*.

**Albatross Cordillera.** Centers on 45°S, 115°W, although parts of it extend south of 60°S. Also called the Antarctic Rise, Easter Island Cordillera, Easter Island Swell, Easter Island Rise, South Pacific Cordillera. It is a submarine mountain range beyond the Ross Ice Shelf.

**Alberich Glacier.** 77°36'S, 161°36'E. Flows from Junction Knob toward the east flank of Sykes Glacier in the Asgard Range of Victoria Land. Named by the New Zealanders for the Teutonic mythical figure.

**Albert, J.D.** Crew member on the *Bear of Oakland* 1933–34.

**Cape Albert de Monaco** *see* **Cape Monaco**

**Mount Albert Markham.** 81°23'S, 158°12'E. 3,205 m. Flat-topped. Between Mount Nares and Pyramid Mountain in the Churchill Mountains, overlooking the Ross Ice Shelf. Named by Scott for Sir Albert Markham, cousin of Sir Clements Markham, the patron of the Royal Society Expedition.

**Isla Alberti** *see* **Epsilon Island**

**Isla Alberto** *see* **Sinclair Island**

**Mount Alberts.** 73°02'S, 167°52'E. 2,320 m. Snow-covered. 11 miles east of Mount Phillips on the eastern edge of Malta Plateau in Victoria Land. Just south of the terminus of Line Glacier, and overlooking the western edge of the Ross Sea. Named in 1966 by the New Zealanders for Fred G. Alberts, American compiler of *Geographic Names of the Antarctic* (*see* the Bibliography).

**Alberts Glacier.** 66°52'S, 64°50'W. On the Antarctic Peninsula.

**Mount Albion.** 70°18'S, 65°40'E. 2 miles SSE of Mount O'Shea in the southern part of the Athos Range. Discovered in 1956–57 by W.G. Bewsher's ANARE party, and named by the Australians for Patrick Albion, radio operator at Mawson Station, 1956.

**Albone Glacier.** 64°13'S, 59°42'W. Narrow. Deeply entrenched. On the east side of Wolseley Buttress flowing from the Detroit Plateau of Graham Land. Named by the UK for Dan Albone, British designer of the Ivel tractor, the first successful tractor with an internal combustion engine.

**Al'bov Rocks.** 66°28'S, 126°46'E. Just south of Cape Spieden, on the west side of Porpoise Bay. Charted by the USSR in 1958, and named by them for Nikolay M. Al'bov (1806–1899), botanical geographer and explorer of Tierra del Fuego.

**Albrecht Penck Glacier.** 76°40'S, 162°20'E. Also called Penck Glacier. Between the Fry Glacier and the Evans Piedmont Glacier, flowing toward Tripp Bay on the coast of Victoria Land. Charted by Shackleton's 1907-9 expedition, and named by them for Albrecht Penck, director of the Institute of Oceanography and of the Geographical Institute in Berlin.

**Mount Albright.** 82°49′S, 155°06′E. Surmounts the SE end of the Endurance Cliffs in the Geologists Range. Named for John C. Albright, geologist on the South Pole–Queen Maud Land Traverse 1964-65.

**Alcock Island.** 64°14′S, 61°08′W. Called Islote Arriagada by the Argentines and Isla Barros by the Chileans. West of Charles Point in Hughes Bay off the west coast of Graham Land. Whalers in the area in 1922 called it Penguin Island, but later the name was officially given for Sir John W. Alcock (1892–1919), pioneer aviator.

**Mount Aldaz.** 76°03′S, 124°25′W. 2,520 m. Mostly ice-covered. On the Usas Escarpment, 22 miles ESE of Mount Galla, in Marie Byrd Land. Named for Luis Aldaz, meteorologist and scientific leader at Byrd Station, 1960.

**Islas Aldea** *see* **Büdel Islands**

**Aldea Island.** 69°13′S, 68°30′W. Off the west coast of the Antarctic Peninsula.

**Aldebaran Rock.** 70°50′S, 66°41′W. Nunatak of bright red rock near the head of Bertram Glacier, 5 miles NE of the Pegasus Mountains in western Palmer Land. Named by the UK for the giant red star Aldebaran.

**Point Alden.** 66°48′S, 142°02′E. Ice-covered. Marks the west side of the entrance to Commonwealth Bay, and the division between Adélie Land and George V Land. Discovered Jan. 30, 1840, by Wilkes.

**Alden, James.** American naval lieutenant on the *Vincennes* during the Wilkes Expedition of 1838–42. Transferred to the *Porpoise* at San Francisco in Oct. 1841.

**Alderdice Peak.** 68°12′S, 49°35′E. 6 miles SE of Mount Underwood in the

eastern part of the Nye Mountains. Named by the Australians for W. Alderdice, weather observer at Wilkes Station, 1959.

**Mount Aldez** *see* **Mount Aldaz**

**Mount Aldrich.** 80°07′S, 158°13′E. Also called Mount Aidwich, Mount Aldwich. Flat-topped. On the east side of Ragotzkie Glacier in the Britannia Range. Discovered during Scott's first expedition and named by Scott for Pelham Aldrich.

**Aldrich, Pelham.** British naval lieutenant on the *Challenger* 1872–76. Later an admiral, and a supporter of Scott's first expedition.

**Aldridge Peak.** 72°27′S, 167°24′E. 2,290 m. Between Hearfield and Trafalgar Glaciers in the Victory Mountains of Victoria Land. Named for James A. Aldridge, VX-6 aviation machinists mate at McMurdo Station, 1967.

**Mount Aldwich** *see* **Mount Aldrich**

**Alectoria Island.** 63°59′S, 58°37′W. Nearly ice-free. Less than one mile long. In the Prince Gustav Channel, ½ mile from the terminus of Aitkenhead Glacier on Trinity Peninsula. Surveyed in 1945 by the FIDS, who named it for the lichen Alectoria, which was abundant here then.

**Mount Alekseyev.** 67°28′S, 50°40′E. 6 miles NE of McNaughton Ridges in the Scott Mountains of Enderby Land. Named by the USSR in 1961–62 for A.D. Alekseyev, polar pilot.

**Alençar Peak.** 65°24′S, 63°53′W. 1,555 m. Also called Mount de Alençar. At the head of Lind Glacier, 6 miles east of Cape Pérez on the west side of Graham Land. Discovered and named by Charcot in 1908–10, for Adm. Alexandrino de Alençar, minister of marine in Brazil.

**[1]Cape Alexander.** 66°44′S, 62°37′W. Also called Cape Foyn. Forms the southern end of Churchill Peninsula and the east side of the entrance to Cabinet Inlet, as it juts out into the Larsen Ice Shelf from the east side of the Antarctic Peninsula. Named by the FIDS for Albert V. Alexander, first lord of the admiralty.

**²Cape Alexander** *see* **Mount Alexander**

**Mount Alexander.** 63°18′S, 55°48′W. Has several summits, the highest being 595 m. Forms the peninsula separating Gibson Bay from Haddon Bay on the south side of Joinville Island. Thomas Robertson in the *Active* discovered the cliff marking the extremity of the peninsula on Jan. 8, 1893, and named it Cape Alexander. The FIDS surveyed it in 1953–54 and the British redefined it in 1956.

**¹Alexander, Captain.** Captain of the *George IV* in the South Shetlands 1821–22. This could well be the same Capt. Alexander who was in the South Shetlands 1822–23 in the *King George*.

**²Alexander, Captain.** Captain of the *King George* in the South Shetlands 1822–23. Probably the same Capt. Alexander who commanded the *George IV* in the South Shetlands 1821–22.

**Alexander, C.D.** Member of Byrd's 1933–35 expedition.

**Alexander I Coast, Land, Island** *see* **Alexander Island**

**Alexander Hill.** 77°17′S, 166°25′E. 220 m. South of Harrison Stream and Cinder Hill on the lower western slopes of Mount Bird on Ross Island. Named by the New Zealanders for B.N. Alexander, a surveyor here, 1958–59.

**Alexander Humboldt Mountains** *see* **Humboldt Mountains**

**Alexander Island.** 71°S, 70°W. Large island in the Bellingshausen Sea, separated from the mainland by the George VI Sound. Rugged, with high peaks, it is 270 miles long and up to 115 miles wide. Discovered Jan. 28, 1821, by von Bellingshausen, he named it Alexander I Coast, for the tsar, not knowing it was an island. It later became Alexander I Land. Wilkins, in a flight over it in 1929, suspected that it was an island, and this was proved in 1940 by the USAS. Its name was changed to Alexander I Island, which in time became Alexander Island. Meanwhile Britain had claimed it in 1908, Chile claimed it in 1940, and Argentina did the same in 1942.

**Alexander McKay Cliffs** *see* **McKay Cliffs**

**Alexander Nunatak** *see* **Alexander Nunataks**

**Alexander Nunataks.** 66°30′S, 110°39′E. Formerly Alexander Nunatak. Two coastal nunataks at the southern limit of the Windmill Islands on the shore of Penney Bay, almost ½ mile east of the base of Browning Peninsula. Named for H.N. Alexander, photographer on Operation Windmill 1947–48.

**Alexander Peak.** 77°28′S, 146°48′W. At the northern end of the Haines Mountains in the Ford Ranges of Marie Byrd Land. First seen aerially by Byrd's 1928–30 expedition, and later named for C.D. Alexander.

**Alexander Wetmore Glacier** *see* **Wetmore Glacier**

**Cape Alexandra.** 67°45′S, 68°36′W. Also called Punta Yerbas Buena. Forms the SE extremity of Adelaide Island. Discovered in 1909 by Charcot and named by him for the Queen of England.

**Alexandra Mountains.** 77°30′S, 153°30′W. Also called Alexandria Mountains, and are not to be confused with the Queen Alexandra Range. These are on the Edward VII Peninsula, just SW of Sulzberger Bay in Marie Byrd Land. Discovered in Jan. 1902 by Scott's first expedition before they docked in McMurdo Sound, and named by them for the Queen of England.

**Alexandra Range** *see* **Queen Alexandra Range**

**Alexandria Mountains** *see* **Alexandra Mountains**

**Alexandria Range** *see* **Queen Alexandra Range**

**Île Alexis Carrel** *see* **Carrel Island**

**Mount Alf.** 77°55'S, 86°07'W. Over 3,200 m. Between Mounts Sharp and Dalrymple in the northern Sentinel Range. Named for Edward A. Alf, meteorologist at Byrd Station, 1957.

**Isla Alfa** *see* **Alpha Island**

**Punta Alfaro** *see* **Hospital Point**

**Isla Alférez Maveroff** *see* **Pickwick Island**

**Punta Alfiler** *see* **Renier Point**

**Alfons Island** *see* **Kolven Island**

**Mount Alford.** 71°55'S, 161°37'E. 1,480 m. Flat-topped. Ice-free. On the south end of Boggs Valley in the Helliwell Hills. Named for Montague Alford, geologist at McMurdo Station, 1967–68.

**Mount Alfred.** 70°18'S, 69°14'W. Over 2,000 m. Ice-capped. 5½ miles inland from George VI Sound, 8 miles south of Mount Athelstan in the Douglas Range of Alexander Island. Photographed aerially on Nov. 23, 1935, by Ellsworth. The FIDS named it in 1949 for the English king of old.

**Algae.** Primitive plant-like organisms (*see also* **Flora** and **Diatoms**). There are 25,000 species worldwide, many of them in Antarctica. Most of them are freshwater.

**Algae Inlet** *see* **Algae Lake**

**Algae Lake.** 66°18'S, 100°48'E. Narrow, winding lake, 9 miles long, and between ¼ mile and a mile wide, in the Bunger Hills. First named by the Americans as Algae Inlet because of the algae here, but redefined in 1956–57 by the USSR.

**Algal Lake.** 77°38'S, 166°25'E. Small, roughly circular meltwater lake between Skua Lake and Island Lake on Cape Evans, Ross Island. Named by biologists David T. Mason, Charles R. Goldman and Brian J.B. Wood, Jr., who studied it in 1961–62 and 1962–63. There are blue-green algal remains here.

**Algie Glacier.** 82°13'S, 162°10'E. 25 miles long. Flows into the Nimrod Glacier, just west of the Nash Range.

Named by the New Zealanders for R.M. Algie, minister in charge of scientific and industrial research, who, in 1957–58, strongly supported the NZ part of the BCTAE.

**Mount Alibi.** 65°55'S, 62°40'W. 3 miles ESE of Adit Nunatak on the north side of Leppard Glacier in Graham Land. Discovered aerially by Wilkins on Dec. 20, 1928, and named Mount Napier Birks. Appropriately renamed by the UK in 1955 to avoid confusion with nearby Mount Birks.

**Isla Alice** *see* **Lecointe Island**

**Alice Creek.** 64°50'S, 63°29'W. Cove which forms the most southerly part of Port Lockroy on Wiencke Island. Discovered by Charcot in 1903–5 and named by him for the wife of Édouard Lockroy (*see* **Port Lockroy**).

**Mount Alice Gade.** 85°45'S, 163°40'W. Over 3,000 m. Mainly ice-covered. Marks the NE extremity of the Rawson Plateau, just to the west of the Amundsen Glacier in the Queen Maud Mountains. It stands next to Mount Ruth Gade, and was discovered by Amundsen on his trek to the Pole in 1911. The Gade girls were daughters of the Norwegian Minister to Brazil, a supporter of Amundsen's expedition.

**Alice Glacier.** 83°58'S, 170°E. 13 miles long. Flows from the Queen Alexandra Range and enters the Beardmore Glacier at Sirohi Point. Discovered on Shackleton's expedition of 1907–9 and named for Eric Marshall's mother.

**Mount Alice Wedel-Jarlsberg** *see* **Mount Wedel-Jarlsberg**

**All-Blacks Nunataks.** 81°29'S, 155°45'E. Between Wallabies Nunataks and Wilhoite Nunataks on the SE edge of the Byrd Névé to the west of the Churchill Mountains. Named by the New Zealanders in 1960–61 for the rugby team.

**Allaire Peak.** 84°52'S, 170°54'W. 1,900 m. 3 miles NW of Mount Hall, between the Gough Glacier and the Le Couteur Glacier in the Prince Olav

Mountains. Named for Capt. C.J. Allaire, US Army, in Antarctica, 1963.

**Mount Allan.** 69°59'S, 67°45'W. On the west coast of the Antarctic Peninsula.

**Allan, David.** Petty officer, RN. On the Royal Society Expedition, 1901–4.

**Allan Hills.** 76°45'S, 159°40'E. Mainly ice-free. 12 miles long. Just NW of the Coombs Hills near the heads of the Mawson and Mackay Glaciers. Just to the west of the Convoy Range in southern Victoria Land. Named by the NZ Party of the BCTAE 1957–58 for Prof. R.S. Allan of the University of Canterbury, NZ. Meteorites are abundant here.

**Allan McDonald Glacier** *see* **McDonald Ice Rumples**

**Allan Nunatak.** 76°38'S, 159°54'E. In the Allan Hills of southern Victoria Land. Named in association with the hills.

**Mount Allan Thomson.** 76°57'S, 161°47'E. Over 1,400 m. 3 miles west of the mouth of Cleveland Glacier, overlooking the Mackay Glacier in Victoria Land. Charted and named during Scott's last expedition 1910–13 for J. Allan Thomson, British geologist who helped write the scientific reports of Shackleton's 1907–9 expedition.

**Allegheny Mountains.** 77°15'S, 143°12'W. 10 miles west of the Clark Mountains in the Ford Ranges of Marie Byrd Land. Discovered aerially in 1934 during Byrd's 1933–35 expedition. Named for Paul Siple's alma mater, Allegheny College, Meadville, Pa.

**Allegro Valley.** 71°18'S, 160°15'E. Steep-sided, glacier-filled indentation into the eastern side of the Daniels Range, just north of White Spur, in the Usarp Mountains. Named by the New Zealanders in 1963–64 for Milton's poem, "L'Allegro," for the good weather here.

**Allemand Peak.** 78°24'S, 158°36'E. 1½ miles south of Moody Peak in the northern part of the Boomerang Range. Named in 1964 for Lawrence J. Allemand, construction driver at Little America in 1958.

**Cape Allen.** 83°33'S, 171°E. 3 miles SW of Mount Hope, near the mouth of the Beardmore Glacier. Forms the western side of the approach to The Gateway. Discovered by Shackleton's expedition of 1907–9, and named for Sir Robert Allen of the Franklin Relief Expedition to the Arctic.

**¹Mount Allen.** 77°24'S, 162°32'E. 1,400 m. Between the Clark Glacier and the head of Greenwood Valley in Victoria Land. Charted by the VUWAE 1959–60, and named for A.D. Allen, geologist with the party.

**²Mount Allen.** 78°43'S, 84°56'W. 3,430 m. 5 miles SE of Mount Craddock in the Sentinel Range. Named for Lt. Forrest M. Allen, USNR, co-pilot on reconnaissance flights from Byrd Station, 1957–58.

**Allen Knoll.** 63°40'S, 58°35'W. Steep-sided snow dome. 2 miles NW of the head of Russell West Glacier on the Trinity Peninsula. Named by the UK for Keith Allen, FIDS radio operator at Base D, 1959 and 1960.

**Allen Peak.** 77°34'S, 86°51'W. 1,880 m. 5 miles west of Mount Wyatt Earp, it forms the northern extremity of the main ridge of the Sentinel Range. Discovered aerially by Ellsworth on Nov. 23, 1935. Named for Robert J. Allen, US cartographer.

**Mount Allen Young.** 83°27'S, 166°54'E. 2,755 m. Pyramidal. Just south of Fegley Glacier in the Holland Range, to the west of the Lennox-King Glacier. Discovered by Shackleton's 1907–9 expedition, and named for Sir Allen Young, Arctic explorer.

**Alley Spur.** 82°32'S, 51°47'W. On the north side of the Dufek Massif, just south of the Sapp Rocks in the Pensacola Mountains. Named for Capt. Dalton E. Alley, USAF, navigator, a member of the US Air Force Electronics Test Unit 1957–58.

**The *Alliance*.** US whaler out of Newport, R.I., which on a return trip from the Pacific sighted an island at 59°S, 90°W on May 21, 1824. Probably crept below the 60°S line of latitude.

**Alligator Island.** 66°34′S, 97°38′E. Also called Alligator Nunatak. ½ mile long. In the Bay of Winds. 4 miles west of Jones Rocks. Discovered by the Western Base Party of the AAE 1911–14. Named for its shape by Mawson.

**Alligator Nunatak** *see* **Alligator Island**

**Alligator Peak.** 78°28′S, 158°45′E. Conical. At the head of Alligator Ridge in the Boomerang Range. Named by the NZ Party of the BCTAE 1957–58 because of its proximity to the ridge.

**Alligator Ridge.** 78°28′S, 158°46′E. Spectacular serrated rock ridge. Runs 2 miles from Alligator Peak in the Boomerang Range to the Skelton Névé. Named for its shape by the NZ Party of the BCTAE of 1957–58.

**Punta Allipen** *see* **Shmidt Point**

**Mount Allison.** 72°31′S, 162°22′E. 3 miles NE of Mount Stuart in the Monument Nunataks. Named for Richard G. Allison, biologist at McMurdo Station, 1965–66, and 1967–68.

**Allison Automatic Weather Station.** 89°53′S, 60°W. USA. Near the South Pole, at an elevation of approx. 10,000 feet. Began Jan. 28, 1986.

**Allison Bay.** 67°30′S, 61°17′E. Small bay just west of Utstikkar Glacier, on the coast of Mac. Robertson Land. Photographed by the LCE 1936–37 and named Isvika (Ice Bay) by the Norwegians. Renamed by the Australians for Dr. Robert Allison, medical officer at Mawson Station, 1955.

**Allison Glacier.** 78°16′S, 161°57′E. Its head is just north of Mount Huggins, and it flows from the western slopes of the Royal Society Range to the Skelton Glacier. Named in 1963 for Lt. Cdr. John K. Allison, USN, VX-6 commander at McMurdo Base, 1959.

**Allison Islands.** 66°21′S, 110°29′E. Small chain of islands in the north side of the entrance to Sparkes Bay in the Windmill Islands. Named for William L. Allison, ionosphere physicist at Wilkes Station, 1958.

**Allison Peninsula.** 73°10′S, 85°50′W. Narrow, ice-covered. Juts out into the Bellingshausen Sea from Ellsworth Land, forming the eastern edge of the Venable Ice Shelf. Named for Cdr. Paul Allison, USN, plans officer, US Naval Support Force, Antarctica, 1967 and 1968.

**Allison Ridge.** 70°46′S, 66°19′E. Partly snow-covered. ½ mile west of Mount Bunt in the Aramis Range. Named by the Australians for D. Allison, electrical engineer at Mawson Station, 1965.

**Allman, James.** Private on the Wilkes Expedition of 1838–42. Joined in the USA. Served the cruise.

**Mount Allo.** 63°58′S, 61°48′W. Conical. Snow-covered. 285 m. Rises from Neyt Point at the NE end of Liège Island. Discovered and named by de Gerlache 1897–99.

**Allowitz Peak.** 71°08′S, 167°39′E. 1,240 m. West of Mount Troubridge in Hedgpeth Heights in the Anare Mountains. Named for Ronald D. Allowitz, biologist at Hallett Station, 1962–63.

**Mount Allport.** 68°01′S, 56°27′E. Snow-free. Just west of Leslie Peak. About 5 miles south of Mount Cook in the Leckie Range. Named by the Australians for B. Allport, radio officer at Mawson Station in 1964, who traversed by this mountain in a 1965 ANARE party.

**Allshouse, Joseph.** Private on the Wilkes Expedition of 1838–42. Joined in the USA. Died Oct. 30, 1841, hit by a falling spar while en route to Hawaii from the USA.

**Mount Allsup.** 84°01′S, 159°36′E. 2,580 m. Rock peak. Marks the SW limit of the Canopy Cliffs, at the south end of the Queen Elizabeth Range. Named for Clifford C. Allsup, USN, aviation machinist's mate injured during Operation Deep Freeze II, 1956–57.

**Mount Alma McCoy** *see* **Mount McCoy**

**The *Almirante Brown*.** Cruiser which took part in Argentine Naval maneuvers in the South Shetlands in 1948 under the overall command of Contra-Almirante Cappus.

**Almirante Brown Station.** Argentine base built in 1951 in Paradise Bay on the Antarctic Peninsula. Rebuilt in 1965 and partially destroyed by fire in April 1984. In 1985 it was reactivated as a year-round station.

**Caleta Almirante Fliess** *see* **Fliess Bay**

**The *Almirante Irízar*.** 14,000-ton Argentine naval icebreaker/research ship of the 1980s.

**The Almond.** 78°19′S, 163°27′E. A bare, almond-shaped ridge of granite just west of The Pyramid on the west side of Koettlitz Glacier. Named by the New Zealanders in 1960–61.

**Almond Point.** 63°53′S, 59°28′W. Between Whitecloud Glacier and McNeile Glacier at the head of Charcot Bay. Charted in 1945 by the FIDS who named it for its shape.

**Alpha Bluff.** 78°53′S, 162°30′E. On the west side of Shults Peninsula, on the east side of the Skelton Glacier. Named by the NZ party of the BCTAE in 1957 because it is the most southerly of all the bluffs on the Skelton Glacier.

**The *Alpha Helix*.** Ice-strengthened vessel of 464 tons displacement belonging to the Scripps Institution of Oceanography. 133 feet long, it can carry 10 scientists and a crew of 12. Designed and equipped especially for experimental biologists, it has a large lab on the main deck. It arrived at Palmer Station on Jan. 2, 1971, and continued as a research ship into the 1980s.

**Alpha Island.** 64°19′S, 63°W. Also called Isla Alfa, Isla Huidobro. Between Epsilon Island and Delta Island in the Melchior Islands. The Discovery Committee surveyed it in 1927 and probably named it.

**Alphard Island.** 66°58′S, 57°25′E. Rises to 150 m. 2½ miles long. North of Shaula Island in the Øygarden Group. Photographed by the LCE 1936–37 and later named Meøya (The Middle Island) by the Norwegians. Robert Dovers was the first to visit it in 1954, and the island was later renamed by the Australians for the star.

**Mount Alpheratz.** 70°59′S, 66°58′W. On the SE ridge of Pegasus Mountains, 10 miles ENE of Gurney Point on the west coast of Palmer Land. Named by the UK for the star Alpheratz, which is in the Great Square of Pegasus.

**Alpine Tours.** A Tokyo-based company that sends tours to the Antarctic.

**Alt Glacier.** 71°06′S, 162°31′E. Sometimes given (erroneously) as Art Glacier. 4 miles long. Flows from the Explorers Range into Rennick Glacier, just north of Mount Soza. Named by the USA for Jean Alt, French observer and Weather Central meteorologist at Little America in 1958.

**The Altar.** 71°39′S, 11°22′E. Flat-topped rock summit of 2,200 m. At the head of Grautskåla Cirque, just west of Altarduken Glacier, in the Humboldt Mountains of Queen Maud Land. Discovered and named by Ritscher in 1938–39. The Norwegians call it Altaret (the Altar).

**Altar Mountain.** 77°54′S, 160°54′E. Over 2,000 m. At the head of Arena Valley in southern Victoria Land. Discovered probably no earlier than 1907–9 during Shackleton's expedition, and named descriptively in 1958–59 by the New Zealanders.

**Altarduken Glacier.** 71°39′S, 11°26′E. Small glacier just east of The Altar in Queen Maud Land. Discovered by Ritscher in 1938–39, and later named Altarduken (the altar cloth) by the Norwegians.

**Altitude**  *see*  **Highest points**

**Álvarez Glacier.** 70°53'S, 162°20'E. Flows from the SW side of Stanwix Peak in the Explorers Range into Rennick Glacier, to the north of Sheehan Glacier. Named by the USA for Lt. Cdr. José A. Álvarez, Argentine navy, observer and Weather Central meteorologist at Little America, 1957.

**Alvaro Cove.** 64°51'S, 63°01'W. On the east coast of Graham Land.

**Islas Alzogaray**  *see*  **Theta Islands**

**The *Amana*.** Argentine ship of the 1970s.

**Amanda Bay**  *see*  **Hovde Cove**

**Pico Amarillo**  *see*  **Bolinder Bluff**

**Ambalada Peak.** 75°57'S, 158°23'E. 2,160 m. 2 miles SE of Griffin Nunatak in the Prince Albert Mountains of Victoria Land. Named for Cesar N. Ambalada, electrician at Amundsen-Scott South Pole Station, 1966.

**Ambrose Rocks.** 65°16'S, 64°22'W. Small cluster of rocks. SW of the southern Argentine Islands and NW of Gaunt Rocks, off the west coast of Graham Land. Named by the UK for David A. Ambrose, survey assistant of the Hydrographic Survey Unit from the *Endurance* in 1968–69.

**Ambush Bay.** 63°10'S, 55°26'W. Also called Bahía Carminatti. 3½ miles wide. Indentation into the northern coast of Joinville Island, just east of King Point. Surveyed by the FIDS in 1953, and named for the lurking dangers here.

**American Geographical Society Bay** *see*  **Gardner Inlet**

**American Highland.** 72°30'S, 78°E. Interior plateau region of East Antarctica, extending from Enderby Land in the west to Wilkes Land in the east, and inland from the Ingrid Christensen Coast and the Amery Ice Shelf. Lying east of the Lambert Glacier, it is an ice-capped upland with an average of 7,000 to 10,000 feet above sea level. It was discovered and named on Jan. 11, 1939, by

Ellsworth, and is the central part of a large area of East Antarctica claimed by Australia.

**Cape Amery.** Mapped on Feb. 11, 1931, by the BANZARE under Mawson, who named it for William B. Amery, governor-general of Australia, 1925–28. In 1947 the Americans interpreted this to be the coastal angle of an ice shelf in the area, and called the whole ice shelf the Amery Ice Shelf (q.v.), dropping the name Cape Amery altogether.

**Amery Ice Shelf.** 69°30'S, 72°E. The southernmost part of the Indian Ocean, it lies between the Lars Christensen Coast and the Ingrid Christensen Coast, east of the American Highland in East Antarctica. It extends from Prydz and MacKenzie Bays inland more than 200 miles to the foot of the Lambert Glacier. This glacier is the primary feeding source of ice for the shelf, but other contributors are the Scylla, Charybdis, Nemesis, and Kreitzer Glaciers. Australia claimed it in 1933. Named in 1947 by the Americans in association with Cape Amery.

**Amery Ice Shelf Station.** (i) Australian scientific base in the 1960s, on the Amery Ice Shelf. (ii) A USSR base on the east side of the Amery Ice Shelf, on Sandefjord Bay at 69°42'S, 73°42'E. This was a summer station only during the seasons 1971–72, 1972–73, and 1973–74, and was closed permanently on Feb. 25, 1974.

**Amery Peaks.** 70°36'S, 67°25'E. 18 miles in extent. On the SE side of Nemesis Glacier, in the eastern Aramis Range. Discovered by the ANARE in 1956–57, and named for their proximity to the Amery Ice Shelf.

**Ames Glacier**  *see*  **Boyd Glacier**

**Ames Range.** 75°42'S, 132°20'W. Also called Joseph Ames Range. Snow-covered, flat-topped, steep-sided mountains, 20 miles in extent, which form a right angle with the eastern end of the Flood Range, behind the Getz Ice Shelf, in Marie Byrd Land. Discovered by the USAS 1939–41 and named by Byrd for his father-in-law, Joseph Ames.

**Mount Amherst.** 86°33'S, 153°W. In the Pensacola Mountains.

**Amiot Islands.** 67°36'S, 69°38'W. Comprise the Ward Islands and Cumbers Reef. 9 miles west of Cape Adriasola on Adelaide Island. Discovered by Charcot in 1908–10, and named by him for A. Amiot, engineering director of the French Montevideo Company in Uruguay, which repaired the *Pourquoi Pas?*

**Amos Lake.** 60°42'S, 45°39'W. Small lake near the west coast of Signy Island. 550 yards south of Thulla Point. Named by the UK for Stephen C. Amos, BAS limnologist here in 1972–73.

**Amphibole Peak.** 84°43'S, 173°24'W. 1,660 m. Highest peak in the Gabbro Hills. 4 miles north of Mount Llano in the Queen Maud Mountains. The New Zealanders named it in 1964 for the minerals of the Amphibole group found here.

**Amphibolite Point.** 60°41'S, 45°21'W. Pyramidal. 1½ miles NW of Saunders Point on the south coast of Coronation Island in the South Orkneys. Surveyed in 1948–49 by the FIDS and named by them for the amphibolite found here.

**¹The Amphitheatre.** 68°06'S, 66°34'W. A depression, ¾ mile in diameter, at the south side of the head of Northeast Glacier in Graham Land. Surveyed and named by the FIDS in 1946.

**²The Amphitheatre.** 78°18'S, 163°03'E. A large cirque, now occupied only by névé, on the north side of Mount Dromedary, on the east side of the Royal Society Range. Named by the New Zealanders in 1960–61 for its enormous size and near-perfect amphitheatrical shape.

**Amphitheatre Lake.** 68°06'S, 48°45'E. Smooth-surfaced meltwater lake, 1½ miles long, in the western part of the Amphitheatre Peaks in the Nye Mountains. Almost completely enclosed by rock and ice cliffs, it forms an amphitheater, with an outlet to Rayner Glacier at the western end. Named by the Australians.

**Amphitheatre Peaks.** 68°06'S, 48°52'E. A group of peaks surrounding and extending to the east of Amphitheatre Lake in the NW part of the Nye Mountains. Named by the Australians for their nearness to the lake.

**Amputations.** The first recorded amputation in Antarctica was the removal of Aeneas Mackintosh's eye on Jan. 31, 1908. Brocklehurst had some of his frozen toes removed on April 6, 1908, after his Mount Erebus climb. On Dec. 24, 1908, Charcot saved a Norwegian sailor from gangrene by removing his hand at Deception Island. Blackborrow lost some toes to surgery in 1916, and on July 21, 1951, Alan Reece's eye was removed. Ralph P. LeBlanc, a victim of the Martin Mariner plane crash of 1946, was badly burned and his feet frozen. Gangrene set in and both of his legs had to be removed below the knee on board the *Philippine Sea* on the way home.

**Mount Amundsen.** 67°14'S, 100°45'E. A nunatak, east of Denman Glacier, about 11 miles NE of Mount Sandow, behind the Shackleton Ice Shelf. Discovered by the Western Base Party of the AAE 1911–14, and named by Mawson for Amundsen.

**Amundsen, Roald.** Roald Engebreth Gravning Amundsen. b. July 16, 1872, Borge, near Christiania (now Oslo), Norway. d. ca. June 18, 1928, somewhere in the Arctic in rescue of his enemy Nobile. Norwegian naval captain, explorer, and discoverer, who was the first leader to reach the South Pole, on Dec. 14, 1911, at the head of the Norwegian Antarctic Expedition. He arrived a month ahead of Scott, his rival, but he got back and Scott didn't. As a young man he was second mate on the *Belgica* expedition, and wintered-over in 1898, being the first man to ski in Antarctica, and one of the first to sledge. From 1903–6 he was north, searching for the Northwest Passage. He found it in 1906. He was on his way to discover the North Pole in the *Fram* in 1910 when news arrived that Peary had beaten him to it. So Amundsen carried on, but the other way, with a new Pole in mind. After 1912 he went into the shipping business, and conducted much Arctic activity. He wrote a couple of books (*see* the Bibliography).

**Amundsen Arm.** An ice cape 3½ miles south of Little America I. It is no longer there.

**Amundsen Basin** *see* **Southeast Pacific Basin**

**Amundsen Bay.** 66°55'S, 50°E. Also called Ice Bay, Isfjorden. 24 miles wide. On the coast of Enderby Land, between Casey Bay and Tula Mountains. Seen Jan. 14, 1930, by Mawson as an ice-filled indentation in the coastline. Seen aerially the following day by Riiser-Larsen more for what it really is. Mapped in detail by the Australians in 1956 and 1958. Named by Mawson for Amundsen.

**Amundsen Coast.** 85°30'S, 162°W. To the south of the Ross Ice Shelf, between Morris Peak (on the east side of the Liv Glacier) and the west side of the Robert Scott Glacier. The New Zealanders named it in 1961 for Amundsen, who was here in 1911.

**Amundsen Glacier.** 85°35'S, 159°W. 4–6 miles wide. 80 miles long. Flows from the Polar Plateau, through the Queen Maud Mountains, into the Ross Ice Shelf. Discovered by Byrd on his flight to the Pole in Nov. 1929, and named by Gould for Amundsen.

**Amundsen Icefall.** 85°28'S, 166°42' W. Steep, turbulent. At the point where the Axel Heiberg Glacier comes off the Polar Plateau, between Mount Fridtjof Nansen and Mount Don Pedro Christophersen, in the Queen Maud Mountains. Named by the New Zealanders in 1961–62 for Amundsen.

**Amundsen-Scott South Pole Station.** US base at the South Pole, the only base ever at 90°S. Called simply South Pole Station until 1961, it was renamed for the first two leaders to reach this spot. On Oct. 31, 1956, Adm. Dufek landed here in the *Que Sera Sera* to inspect the ter-

rain and see if it was suitable for an IGY base. It was. On Nov. 20, 1956, Lt. Richard Bowers was dropped off at the Pole and construction began. Strictly a navy base, it was a dark hole underground, buried by the snow, and consisted of 6 tunnels, a radio and meteorology shack, barracks for 12 men, a recreation room and quarters for 6 men, an inflation shelter, an astronomical observatory, a weather balloon, a garage, a power house and water supply unit, a Rawin tower, a snow-filled fire-break, a science building and the scientific leader's office, a galley and mess hall, an Aurora tower, a photo lab, a latrine, a radio antenna, as well as meteorological instruments connected to the base by a snow tunnel. The 18 men who wintered-over in 1957 were the first men ever to do so at the Pole. They were Dr. Paul A. Siple, scientific leader (replaced Nov. 30, 1957, by Palle Mogensen); John Tuck, military leader (replaced Nov. 9, 1957, by V.N. Houk); Willi S. Hough, ionosphere physicist from Colorado; Bob F. Benson, geomagnetist and seismologist from Minnesota; Arlo U. Landolt, aurora physicist from Illinois; Ed W. Remington, geologist from Maryland; Edwin C. Flowers, meteorologist from Maryland; John F. Guerrero, meteorologist from California; Herbert L. Hansen, meteorologist from Nebraska; William F. Johnson, meteorologist from Oklahoma; Howard C. Taylor III, Lt., USN, medical officer from New York; William C. McPherson, Jr., USN, radioman from Rhode Island; Cliff R. Dickey, Jr., USN, electronics man from California; Tom M. Osborne, USN, builder from Pennsylvania; Earl F. Johnson, USN, utilitiesman from Ohio; Melvin C. Havener, USN, mechanic from Iowa; Kenneth L. Waldron, USN, electrician from Iowa; Chester W. "Chet" Segers, USN, cook from Rhode Island. Also on board was Bravo, a Malemute husky born at Dogheim at McMurdo Base on Aug. 14, 1956, the only survivor of a litter of 7. He flew to the Pole with his master, Tuck, and was the spoiled mascot at the station.

Leaders for the 1959 winter were Sidney Tolchin (military) and Julian Posey (scientific). Built at an altitude of 9,370 feet, and 820 miles from McMurdo, it drifted with the ice cap 27–30 feet per year in the direction of 43°W, until it was no longer at the Pole. It was decided to build a new station. It was begun in 1970–71 and finished 1974–75. It was dedicated Jan. 9, 1975, and is really space-age, covered by a huge aluminum geodesic dome, big enough to enclose three 2-story buildings if it needed to. Over the entrance it says, "The United States Welcomes You to the South Pole." It is permanently inhabited, and in the summer houses 80–100 people. It has all the facilities of home. Sometimes only a handful winter-over, sometimes the number is in the 20s, or anywhere in between. Women have been wintering-over since Michele Raney did so as physician in 1979. It is now (1990) about 150 yards west of the South Pole, due to the movement of the ice cap (see above).

**Amundsen Sea.** 72°30′S, 112°W. Also called Roald Amundsen Sea, Franklin D. Roosevelt Sea, Roosevelt Sea. Off the coast of Marie Byrd Land, between Cape Dart on Siple Island in the west, and Cape Flying Fish on Thurston Island in the east, or more generally, between the Ross Sea and the Bellingshausen Sea. Named by Nils Larsen in Feb. 1929, for Amundsen.

**Amy Guest Island** *see* **Guest Peninsula**

**Anagram Islands.** 65°12′S, 64°20′W. Also called Islotes Roca. Group of small islands and rocks including Maranga Island and Nob Island between Roca Islands and Argentine Islands in the Wilhelm Archipelago. Charted by de Gerlache in 1897–99, by Charcot in 1903–5 and 1908–10, and by Rymill in 1934–37. Named by the UK in 1959 for the confusion in naming groups of islands in this area.

**Mount Anakiwa.** 73°S, 165°43′E. 2,640 m. 3 miles north of Mount Supernal, in the Mountaineer Range of Vic-

toria Land. Named by the New Zealanders for the Cobham Outward Bound School at Anakiwa in NZ.

**Mount Analogue.** 85°49′S, 138°08′W. In the Horlick Mountains.

**ANARE** *see* **Australian National Antarctic Research Expeditions**

**Anare Mountains.** 70°55′S, 166°E. Large group of mainly snow-covered peaks and ridges in Oates Land. First sighted by Ross in 1841, they were named by the New Zealanders in 1963–64 for the ANARE of 1962 led by Phillip Law.

**Anare Nunataks.** 69°58′S, 64°37′E. A group of mainly snow-covered ridges with exposed rock summits rising to 2,035 m. 16 miles south of Stinear Nunataks in Mac. Robertson Land. Visited in Nov. 1955 by an ANARE party led by J.M. Béchervaise.

**Anare Pass.** 71°13′S, 166°37′E. Broad and ice-covered, it is 1,200 m above sea level. It is the highest point on the glaciers that delimit the south side of the Anare Mountains. It separates the Anare Mountains from the Admiralty Mountains and Concord Mountains to the south.

**Ancestor Pass** *see* **Celebration Pass**

**Anchor Crag.** 69°12′S, 66°12′W. On the north side of Airy Glacier, 4 miles NNE of Mount Gilbert, in the central part of the Antarctic Peninsula. Photographed aerially by the RARE on Nov. 27, 1947, and surveyed by the FIDS on Nov. 4, 1958. Named by the UK for an anchor-shaped snow patch here in 1958.

**Anchor ice.** Also called ground ice, grounded ice, bottom ice. Ice formed at the bottom of streams while the temperature of the water is above freezing point. It is formed only under a clear night sky, and most readily on dark rocks. The prime cause is probably radiation of heat from the stream bottom.

**Anchor Peak** *see* **Archer Peak**

**Anchorage Island.** 67°36′S, 68°13′W. Almost ¾ mile SE of Lagoon Island in the

Léonie Islands, off the SE coast of Adelaide Island. Discovered by Charcot in 1908–10, and named by Rymill, who visited it in Feb. 1936.

**Anchorage Patch.** 68° 34′ S, 77° 55′ E. Small, isolated shoal within Davis Anchorage, about ½ mile NW of Torckler Rocks. Positioned in 1961 by the ANARE party from the *Thala Dan* led by D'A.T. Gale.

**Anckorn Nunataks.** 70° 14′ S, 63° 12′ W. Group of nunataks and snow-covered hills, 15 miles in extent, between Mounts Bailey and Samsel in the eastern part of Palmer Land. Named by the UK for J.F. Anckorn, BAS geologist who worked here.

**Mount Ancla.** 64° 49′ S, 63° 41′ W. Also called Mount Hindson. 815 m. Mostly snow-covered. 2 miles north of Cape Lancaster in the southern part of Anvers Island. Surveyed by the members of Operation Tabarin in 1944, and named by the Argentines before 1950.

**Andean Chain.** Geologic formation which runs from the tip of South America, through the Drake Passage, the South Shetlands, down the Antarctic Peninsula, to Marie Byrd Land.

**Andean Province** *see* **West Antarctica, Geology**

**Anders Peak.** 71° 45′ S, 9° 01′ E. 2,135 m. A mile south of Gruvletindane Crags in the Holtedahl Peaks in the Orvin Mountains of Queen Maud Land. Named by the Norwegians for Anders Vinten-Johansen, medical officer with the Norwegian Antarctic Expedition of 1957–58.

**Andersen, Capt. Lars.** Commander of the whale catcher *Falk* in 1930–31.

**Andersen, Normann.** Captain of the *Ole Wegger* when it was taken over by the Nazis in 1941.

**Andersen, Søren.** b. Veierland, Norway. First mate on the *Jason* 1892–93.

**Andersen Escarpment.** 85° 08′ S, 91° 37′ W. A steep rock and snow escarpment south of Reed Ridge on the west side of the Ford Massif in the Thiel Mountains.

Named by Bermel and Ford, co-leaders of the US Geological Survey Thiel Mountains Party of 1960–61, for Bjorn G. Andersen, a Norwegian member of the expedition.

**Andersen Harbor.** 64° 19′ S, 62° 56′ W. Small harbor formed by the concave west side of Eta Island, and the north end of Omega Island, in the Melchior Islands. Named before 1927.

**Andersen Island.** 67° 26′ S, 63° 22′ E. Also called Lars Andersen Island. 4 miles west of Thorgaut Island in the Robinson Group. Mapped by the BANZARE in Feb. 1931, and at about the same time by personnel from the *Thorgaut*. Named for Capt. Lars Andersen.

**Cape Anderson.** 60° 46′ S, 44° 35′ W. Also called Cape Nan Anderson. Marks the east side of the entrance to Mill Cove, on the south coast of Laurie Island. Charted in 1903 by Bruce, who named it for his secretary Nan Anderson.

**Mount Anderson.** 78° 09′ S, 86° 13′ W. 4,255 m. 2 miles south of Mount Bentley in the Sentinel Range. Discovered by Charles R. Bentley on the Marie Byrd Land Traverse Party of 1957–58, and named for Vernon H. Anderson, glaciologist at Byrd Station, 1957, and a member of the traverse party.

**Anderson, A.S.** Captain of the *Odd I,* 1926–27.

**Anderson, George H.** Lt. USN. The second man to pilot a plane over the Pole, on Feb. 15, 1947. He carried Byrd and crew (*see* **South Pole**).

**Anderson, James.** Ordinary seaman on the Wilkes Expedition of 1838–42. Joined at Callao and served the cruise.

¹**Anderson, John.** Ordinary seaman on the Wilkes Expedition of 1838–42. Joined in the USA. Served the cruise.

²**Anderson, John.** Seaman on the Wilkes Expedition of 1838–42. Joined at Callao. Killed by the natives at Drummond Island, in 1841.

**Anderson, John D.** Gunner on the *Peacock* during the Wilkes Expedition of 1838–42.

**Anderson, Robert.** Gunner on the *Resolution* during Cook's voyage of 1772–75.

**Anderson, William.** b. 1750. d. Aug. 3, 1778, of tuberculosis, off the coast of Alaska. Surgeon's mate on the *Resolution* during Cook's second voyage. He was surgeon on Cook's third voyage.

**Anderson Dome.** 73°30′S, 93°54′W. 1,475 m. Ice-covered mountain on the east side of Gopher Glacier. 4 miles east of Bonnabeau Dome in the Jones Mountains. Mapped by the University of Minnesota–Jones Mountains Party of 1960–61 and named by them for Joe M. Anderson, topographic engineer with the party.

**Anderson Glacier.** 66°24′S, 63°55′W. Heavily crevassed. 12 miles long. Flows into Cabinet Inlet between Cape Casey and Balder Point on the east coast of Graham Land. Named by the FIDS for Sir John Anderson, member of the British War Cabinet in WWII.

**Anderson Heights.** 84°49′S, 178°15′ W. Rectangular, snow-covered tableland. 7 miles long by 6 miles wide. Over 2,400 m high. Between Mounts Bennett and Butters in the eastern part of the Bush Mountains. Named for George H. Anderson.

**Anderson Hills.** 84°30′S, 64°W. Irregular group of hills, ridges, and peaks between Mackin Table and Thomas Hills in the Patuxent Range of the Pensacola Mountains. Named by Finn Ronne in 1957–58 for Robert Anderson, US deputy secretary of defense, 1954–55, who had responsibility for US operations in Antarctica.

**Anderson Icefalls.** 71°21′S, 169°E. At the lower end of Pitkevich Glacier, just SE of Atkinson Cliffs on the north coast of Victoria Land. Charted in 1911 by Victor Campbell's Northern Party. Named by the UK for John Anderson, NZ businessman and supporter of Scott's last expedition.

**Anderson Massif.** 79°10′S, 84°45′W. Ice-covered. 10 miles across. Rises to 2,190 m. At the junction of Splettstoesser Glacier and Minnesota Glacier in the Heritage Range. Named for John J. Anderson, geologist, field leader of the University of Minnesota Ellsworth Mountains Party, 1961–62.

**Anderson Nunataks.** 75°06′S, 68°18′ W. Also called Shimizu Nunatak. Group forming the NE end of the Sweeney Mountains. Discovered by the RARE 1947–48, and named later for Richard E. Anderson, aviation electronics technician in Antarctica in 1961.

**Anderson Peninsula.** 69°48′S, 160°13′ E. Ice-covered. 7 miles long. Ends in Belousov Point. Between Gillett Ice Shelf and Suvorov Glacier on the coastal edge of the Wilson Hills. Named for Lt. Richard E. Anderson, USN, base public works officer at McMurdo Base, 1955–56, 1956–57, and 1957.

**Anderson Pyramid.** 70°46′S, 159°57′ E. Most southerly of the Bigler Nunataks, in the Usarp Mountains. Named for Staff Sgt. Robert J. Anderson, US Army, here in 1962–63.

**Anderson Ridge.** 85°47′S, 155°24′W. 2 miles long. Rises above the middle of the head of Koerwitz Glacier in the Queen Maud Mountains. Named for Arthur J. Anderson, meteorologist at South Pole Station, 1960.

**Anderson Summit.** 85°03′S, 90°53′ W. 2,810 m. (13,957 ft.). A mountain on top of the Ford Massif, directly south of Walker Ridge, the highest peak in the Thiel Mountains. Named by Bermel and Ford of the US Geological Survey Thiel Mountains Party of 1960–61 for chief geologist of the US Geological Survey, Charles A. Anderson (1902–1990). Ford climbed it in 1961.

**Andersson, J. Gunnar.** Swedish doctor. Second-in-command of Nordenskjöld's 1901–4 expedition.

**Andersson, Karl Andreas.** Zoologist on Nordenskjöld's 1901–4 expedition.

**Andersson Island.** 63°35'S, 56°35'W. 7 miles long by 4 miles wide. ½ mile south of Jonassen Island at the west side of the south entrance to Antarctic Sound. Named Uruguay Island by Nordenskjöld's expedition of 1901–4 for the *Uruguay*. Renamed by the UK for J. Gunnar Andersson.

**Andersson Nunatak.** 63°22'S, 57°W. A mile west of Sheppard Point on the north shore of Hope Bay. Discovered by J. Gunnar Andersson in 1903, and it was named for him by the FIDS in 1945.

**Andersson Peak.** 64°52'S, 61°02'W. Ice-capped. 1,230 m. 9 miles north of Mount Fairweather, on the east coast of Graham Land. Charted in 1947 by the FIDS, and named by them for Karl Andreas Andersson.

**Andersson Ridge.** 74°43'S, 162°37'E. 4 miles long. Forms the north wall of Reeves Glacier, between the mouths of Anderton and Carnein Glaciers, behind Terra Nova Bay, in the southern Eisenhower Range, in northern Victoria Land. Named for Lars E. Andersson, cosmic radiation scientist at Amundsen-Scott South Pole Station, 1966.

**Anderton Glacier.** 74°41'S, 162°22'E. 7 miles long. Flows down the southern slopes of the Eisenhower Range to enter the Reeves Glacier between Mount Matz and Andersson Ridge, in Victoria Land. Named for Peter W. Anderton, glaciologist at McMurdo Station, 1965–66.

**Mount Andes.** 85°53'S, 146°46'W. 2,525 m. In the SE part of the Tapley Mountains. Named for Lt. Cdr. Paul G. Andes, USN, pilot at McMurdo Station, 1962–63, 1963–64.

**Andøya** *see* **Oldham Island**

**Cabo Andrada** *see* **Rip Point**

**Cape Andreas.** 64°S, 60°43'W. Also called Cape Karl Andreas. Marks the east side of the entrance to Curtiss Bay, on the west coast of Graham Land. Discovered on the Nordenskjöld expedition of 1901–4, and named by them for Karl Andreas Andersson.

**Andreassen, F.L.** First mate on the *Antarctic* during Nordenskjöld's expedition of 1901–4.

**Andreassen Point.** 63°54'S, 57°46'W. Ice-free. On northern James Ross Island. It fronts on Herbert Sound, 8 miles south of Cape Lachman. First seen by Nordenskjöld in 1903, it was surveyed by the FIDS in 1945, and named by the UK for F.L. Andreassen.

**Andrée Island.** 64°31'S, 61°31'W. In Recess Cove, Charlotte Bay, off the west coast of Graham Land. Named by the UK in 1960 for Salomon A. Andrée (1854–1897), balloonist who died over the North Pole.

**Andresen, Hans.** Norwegian captain of the *Nilsen-Alonzo* 1928–29, and of the *Kosmos* 1929–31.

**Andresen, Monsieur.** Manager of the Magellan Whaling Co., on Deception Island in 1908–9. He gave coal for Charcot's expedition.

**Andresen Island.** 66°53'S, 66°40'W. Over 610 m. 2 miles long. In the middle of the entrance to Lallemand Fjord, off the west coast of Graham Land. Discovered by Charcot in 1908–10, and named by him for M. Andresen.

**Andrew, Dr. J.D.** Medical officer at Base D, the FIDS station at Hope Bay, from 1946–47.

**Andrew Glacier.** 63°53'S, 59°40'W. 3 miles long. Flows into Charcot Bay, just west of Webster Peaks, in northern Graham Land. Charted in 1948 by the FIDS, who named it for Dr. J.D. Andrew.

**Mount Andrew Jackson** *see* **Mount Jackson**

**Mount Andrews.** 85°57'S, 149°40'W. 2,480 m. Between Mount Danforth and Mount Gerdel on the south side of Albanus Glacier in the Queen Maud Mountains. Named for Ensign Stanley J. Andrews, USN, who flew over here with Lt. George W. Warden during Operation Highjump, 1946–47.

**Andrews, Thomas.** Surgeon on the *Adventure* 1772–76, during Cook's second voyage.

**Andrews Peaks.** 77°08′S, 144°03′W. A line of rock peaks 3 miles long, near the head of the Arthur Glacier, between Mounts Warner and Crow in the Ford Ranges of Marie Byrd Land. Named for Stephen T. Andrews, ionosphere physicist and scientific leader at Byrd Station, 1969.

**Andrews Point.** 64°30′S, 62°55′W. Between Hackapike Bay and Inverleith Harbor on the NE coast of Anvers Island. Charted in 1927 by the *Discovery* personnel and named by them.

**Andrews Ridge.** 77°39′S, 162°50′E. The northern arm of Nussbaum Riegel, south of Suess Glacier and Lake Chad in the Taylor Valley of Victoria Land. Named by Grif Taylor during Scott's expedition of 1910–13.

**Cape Andreyev.** 68°55′S, 155°12′E. Marks the SE limit of the Slava Ice Shelf. Named by the USSR in 1960 for Prof. A.I. Andreyev, historian.

**Mount Andreyev.** 71°46′S, 10°13′E. 2,320 m. SW of Mount Dallmann, where it forms part of the SW wall of Brattebotnen Cirque in the Orvin Mountains of Queen Maud Land. Discovered by Ritscher in 1938–39, and named in 1963 by the USSR for A.I. Andreyev (*see* **Cape Andreyev**).

**Mount Andrus.** 75°48′S, 132°14′W. Volcano 2 miles SE of Mount Boennighausen in the SE extremity of the Ames Range. Lichens are found here. Named for Lt. Carl H. Andrus, USN, medical officer and officer-in-charge of Byrd Station, 1964.

**Andrus Point.** 73°53′S, 165°48′E. Juts out into Lady Newnes Bay from Victoria Land. Named for Cdr. H.R. Andrus, logistics officer with the staff of the commander, US Naval Support Force, Antarctica, 1962–66.

**Andvord Bay.** 64°50′S, 62°39′W. Also called Andword Bay. 9 miles long. 3 miles wide. Between Beneden Head and Duthiers Point on the Danco Coast, on the western coast of the Antarctic Peninsula. Discovered by de Gerlache 1897–99 and named by him for Rolf Andvord, Belgian consultant at Christiania.

**Andword Bay** *see* **Andvord Bay**

**Anemometer Hill.** 68°11′S, 67°W. 25 m high. NE of Fishtrap Cove on Stonington Island. The UK named it for the anemometer placed here in 1961.

**The *Angamos*.** Part of the Chilean Antarctic Expedition 1946–47, it was commanded by Gabriel Rojas Parker. On March 7, 1947, it visited Stonington Island, putting a crew ashore on March 8, 1947. The ship left March 9, 1947. It was back in Antarctic waters as part of the Chilean Antarctic Expedition of 1950–51. During the Chilean Antarctic Expedition of 1951–52 it was commanded by Capt. Carvajal, and in the 1956–57 expedition by Hernán Bravo.

**Mount Angier.** 83°21′S, 161°02′E. In the Moore Mountains in the southern sector of the Queen Elizabeth Range. Named by the New Zealanders in 1961–62 for Lt. Cdr. Donald C. Angier, USN, pilot here that season.

**Angino Buttress.** 78°14′S, 158°42′E. Mountain near the center of the Skelton Icefalls. Named in 1964 for Ernest A. Angino, geologist at McMurdo Station, 1959–60.

**Angle Peak.** 71°45′S, 62°03′W. On the north side of Condor Peninsula, just south of where Cline Glacier enters Odom Inlet, on the east coast of Palmer Land. Named for J. Phillip Angle, ornithologist here in 1966 (*see* the Bibliography, under George E. Watson).

**Angot Point.** 63°48′S, 61°41′W. Marks the southern tip of Hoseason Island. Named by Charcot in 1903–5 for Alfred Angot, assistant director of the French Meteorological Service.

**Mount Angus** *see* **Mount Argus**

**Angus Nunatak.** 85°22′S, 124°14′W. The more northerly of 2 nunataks, just north of Mount Brecher in the Wisconsin Range. Named for Gordon W. Angus, ionosphere physicist at Byrd Station, 1961.

**Animals** *see* **Fauna**

[1]**The *Ann*.** British sealer from Liverpool in the South Shetlands for the 1820–21 season. Captain unknown. Wrecked approximately Dec. 30, 1820.

[2]**The *Ann*.** British sealer from Liverpool in the South Shetlands for the 1821–22 season, under the command of Capt. J. Kitchen. Moored at New Plymouth for the season. In March 1822 it visited South Georgia (54°S).

**Cape Ann.** 66°10'S, 51°22'E. Also spelled (erroneously) Cape Anne. At the foot of the Napier Mountains, on the coast of Enderby Land. Mount Biscoe is located on it. Discovered by Biscoe on March 6, 1831, and named by him for his wife. Photographed aerially on Dec. 22, 1929 by Riiser-Larsen's *Norvegia* expedition, and photographed from the *Discovery* on Jan. 14, 1930, by the BANZARE.

**Ann Island.** 68°08'S, 67°06'W. SE of Barbara Island, in the Debenham Islands, off the west coast of Graham Land. Discovered by the BGLE 1934–37, and named by Rymill for one of the daughters of Frank Debenham (q.v.), a member of the expedition's advisory committee.

**Mount Ann Shirley** *see* **Mount Shirley**

**Cape Anna.** 64°35'S, 62°26'W. Rises to 280 m. Forms the northern tip of Arctowski Peninsula, on the west coast of Graham Land. Charted and named by de Gerlache, who landed here on Jan. 30, 1898.

**Anna Cove.** 64°35'S, 62°26'W. Just east of Cape Anna, at the northern end of Arctowski Peninsula, on the west coast of Graham Land. Charted and named by de Gerlache, who landed here on Jan. 30, 1898.

**Annandags Peaks.** 72°32'S, 6°18'W. Group of small, isolated peaks, 15 miles

SW of Jule Peaks, in Queen Maud Land. The Norwegians called them Annandagstoppane (the next day's peaks).

**The *Annawan*.** Brig on the Palmer-Pendleton Expedition of 1829–31. Owned by Nat Palmer, among others. Palmer was captain, and there were 28 crew and 5 scientists.

**Cape Annawan.** 72°18'S, 95°24'W. Ice-covered. Marks the eastern extremity of Thurston Island and the NW entrance to Seraph Bay. Discovered in Feb. 1960 during helicopter flights from the *Burton Island* and the *Glacier* while part of the USN Bellingshausen Sea Expedition of that season. Named for the *Annawan*.

[1]**Cape Anne** *see* **Cape Ann**

[2]**Cape Anne.** 73°37'S, 169°51'E. Marks the SE extremity of Coulman Island in the Ross Sea. Discovered by Ross in Jan. 1841, and named by him for his wife.

**Mount Anne.** 83°48'S, 168°30'E. 3,870 m. 6 miles north of Mount Elizabeth, just to the west of the Beardmore Glacier, in the Queen Alexandra Range. Discovered on Shackleton's 1907–9 expedition, and named by him for Anne Dawson-Lambton, a supporter.

**Anne Island** *see* **Ann Island**

**Annelids** *see* **Worms**

**Annenkov, Mikhail.** Lt. Officer on the *Mirnyy*, 1819–21.

**Annexstad Peak.** 76°41'S, 125°52'W. 2,610 m. Partially ice-free. On the western side of the crater rim of Mount Cumming in the Executive Committee Range of Marie Byrd Land. Named for John O. Annexstad, seismologist at Byrd Station, 1958.

**Anniversary Nunataks** *see* **Blånabbane Nunataks**

**Annual ice.** Or Sea ice. Ice that breaks up during the summer. It is distinguished from the permanent ice of glaciers, ice shelves, and the ice cap of the Polar Plateau.

**Ansell.** Steward on the *Nimrod*, 1907–9. Not a part of the shore party.

**Ant Hill.** 78°47'S, 161°27'E. 1,310 m. On the west side of the Skelton Glacier, between Ant Hill Glacier and Dilemma Glacier. Surveyed and named in 1957 by the NZ party of the BCTAE for the prominent anticline in the bluff below the hill.

**Ant Hill Glacier.** 78°49'S, 161°30'E. Between Ant Hill and Bareface Bluff, rising in the Worcester Range and flowing into the Skelton Glacier. Surveyed and named in 1957 by the NZ party of the BCTAE in association with nearby Ant Hill.

**¹The *Antarctic*.** Norwegian ship, formerly an old steam whaler called the *Kap Nor*. 226 tons, 8 whaleboats, 11 harpoon guns and an average crew of 31. It took two expeditions to the Antarctic: (i) Svend Foyn (1809–94), the sealing magnate and inventor of the harpoon gun, financed an 1893–95 sealing and exploration expedition led by Henryk J. Bull. Captain of the *Antarctic* was Leonard Kristensen, and the two men were to quarrel over leadership. The ship left Norway on Sept. 30, 1893, and went via Melbourne, and through many adventures, to NZ, where 2 men deserted and 7 others were fired for refusing to go to Antarctica. 4 new men were taken aboard. On Dec. 25, 1894, they crossed the Antarctic Circle, and on Jan. 16, 1895, sighted Cape Adare. On Jan. 18, 1895, a party (including Carsten Borchgrevink) made a landing on Possession Islands. Here Borchgrevink discovered lichens, the first vegetation discovered within the Antarctic Circle. On Jan. 24, 1895, they landed on the coast itself, at Ridley Beach, Cape Adare, the first substantiated landing on the continent proper. Kristensen, Borchgrevink, and von Tunzelman all claim to have been the first to step out of the landing boat onto the shore (Bull was also in the landing boat). After another few weeks they left Antarctica on Feb. 8, 1895. (ii) Nordenskjöld (q.v. for details of the expedition) led a 1901–4 expedition from Göteborg in Sweden on Oct. 16, 1901, in the *Antarctic*, with Carl Anton Larsen as captain. After putting ashore Nordenskjöld's party on Snow Hill Island, the ship wintered in the Falkland Islands, returning to pick up the Swedish party in Feb. 1903. It was crushed in the pack ice on Feb. 12, 1903, and sank at 63° 50'S, 57°W, and the crew took refuge on Paulet Island. Nordenskjöld's party was forced to winter-over again on Snow Hill Island until all the members of the expedition were picked up by the *Uruguay*.

**²The *Antarctic*.** Norwegian whaling ship in Antarctic waters in 1930–31 under the command of Otto Borchgrevink.

**Antarctic airlift** *see* **Airlifts**

**Antarctic Airways.** The world's first real commercial airline for the Antarctic. Founded in 1984 by Adventure Travel International. Chief pilot was Giles Kershaw (*see also* **Mountain Travel**). In 1987–88 they operated a Douglas DC-4 and Twin Otters.

**Antarctic Anticyclone.** Large atmospheric high pressure center in continual existence over Antarctica. It contains the world's coldest air.

**Antarctic Archipelago** *see* **Palmer Archipelago**

**Antarctic Bottom Water.** Or ABW. Produced by shelf water escaping in short periods of time, not necessarily during winter. It is produced in the Ross Sea, Weddell Sea, and off Adélie Land.

**Antarctic Circle.** Latitude 66°30'S, (or 66½°S), and called the circle because it goes all around the continent at that latitude. On Midwinter's Day (June 21) the sun reaches only this far south due to the earth's 23½° axial tilt to its ecliptic (*see also* **Seasons**). Only a few coastal areas of Antarctica lie north of the Antarctic Circle, and the line crosses through places like the Larsen Ice Shelf, Biscoe Islands, Balleny Islands, Wilkes Coast, Norths Highland, Sabrina Coast, Cape Mikhaylov, Budd Coast, Knox Land, the Bunger Hills, Queen Mary

Land, Mirnyy Station, West Ice Shelf, and the Napier Mountains. The first ships to cross it were Cook's *Resolution* and *Adventure* on Jan. 17, 1773. Cook crossed a second time on Dec. 20, 1773, and a third time on Jan. 26, 1774. Von Bellingshausen was the next to cross it, on Jan. 26, 1820, and again on Dec. 24, 1820. The first steamship to cross it was the *Challenger* on Feb. 16, 1874.

**Antarctic Circumpolar Current.** Also called the West Wind Drift Current. A surface oceanic current flowing from west to east and encircling Antarctica. It is the greatest ocean current in the world, and the earth's only circumpolar current. It flows 14,913 miles as it circles the earth, and is between 124 and 621 miles in width. First studied properly in 1978.

**Antarctic cod.** *Notothenia nudifron.* A cod-like fish of the order Gadidae, living at the sea bottom near the coasts. The giant Antarctic cod is *Dissostichus mawsoni.*

**Antarctic Conferences.** The first Antarctic Conference, as such, was held in Paris in July 1955 as a prelude to IGY. Entirely scientific, they coordinated plans for the expeditions. There have also been many conferences relating to Antarctica, the most notable being in July 1895 when the Sixth International Geographical Congress decided that Antarctica must be investigated. It was this decision which sparked off the rash of expeditions in the late 1890s/early 1900s.

**Antarctic Convergence.** Also called the Antarctic Polar Front and the Southern Hemisphere Polar Front, it is the easily identifiable oceanic boundary, 20–30 miles wide, where the warm, subtropical waters of the Indian, Pacific, and Atlantic Oceans meet the cold, polar waters of Antarctica. It lies in a staggered, zig-zagging line between 48°S and 61°S, and is very influential on climate, marine life, and the ice (*see also* **Subantarctic Surface Water** and **Antarctic Intermediate Water**). It was discovered by the Discovery Committee.

**Antarctic Derby.** Held on June 15, 1915, by the crew of the *Endurance* while they were stuck on the ice. It was a 700-yard dog-team race won by Frank Wild who had started 6–4 favorite. All 28 men had a bet of chocolate or cigarettes.

**Antarctic Developments Project 1947** *see* **Operation Highjump**

**Antarctic Dragonfish.** Family of about 15 species of fish belonging to Bathydraconidae, and to the super family of Nototheniodia.

**Antarctic Front.** Semipermanent, semicontinuous front that separates continental Antarctic air from maritime polar air. The first slides underneath the second, causing violent storms moving from east to west. There is not much rain because of the coldness of both air masses.

**Antarctic Ice Sheet.** The vast ice cap that covers almost all of Antarctica, and parts of the sea around it. Average thickness is about 6,900 feet.

**Antarctic Intermediate Water.** Ocean water mass found in all the southern oceans at the Antarctic Convergence, at a depth of between 1,500 and 4,000 feet. Temperatures range from 37–45°F.

**Antarctic Ocean.** A term used principally by the USSR and UK, it is also called the Southern Ocean. The southernmost of all the oceans (*see* **Oceans**), its existence as an individual ocean is not universally accepted. Some say that it is really the southern part of the Atlantic, Pacific, and Indian Oceans, and others put the southern limit of these oceans at the Antarctic Circle (66½°S). But those who accept the Antarctic Ocean generally place its northern limits at the Subtropical Convergence (40°S) and its southern boundary as the land mass of Antarctica itself (*see* **Subantarctic Surface Water** for more details). The waters are less saline than those of other oceans because of the lower temperature and lesser evaporated concentration of dissolved salts.

**Antarctic Pacific Ridge** *see* **Pacific-Antarctic Ridge**

**Antarctic Peninsula.** 69°30'S, 65°W. At surface level it forms the most northerly tip of the Antarctic continental land mass (or rather, ice mass). It reaches out toward South America like an 800-mile-long stubby finger. Tierra del Fuego is only 600 miles away across the Drake Passage, and is connected geologically with the Peninsula. Also speaking geologically, the Peninsula is a string of islands separated from the real continent at bedrock level, the ice-covering of the whole continent joining it all together at the surface. Its main features are Graham Land, Palmer Land, the Larsen Ice Shelf, and the Eternity Range. The highest point is Mount Jackson at over 13,000 feet. Discovered probably by the Russian, von Bellingshausen, in 1820, and reputedly named by him as Palmer's Land (later Palmer Land) for Nat Palmer, the US navigator he met in these waters at that time. The British navigator Biscoe called it Graham Land, as did many countries later on. The Americans were calling it Palmer Land. Later, in the next century, the Chileans called it O'Higgins Land (actually Tierra de O'Higgins), and the Argentines called it San Martín Land (actually Tierra San Martín). By 1958 more and more people were calling it the Antarctic Peninsula, and in 1964 the US, UK, Australia, and NZ made an international agreement to make that its official name. Graham Land now refers to the northern half, and Palmer Land to the southern half. The whole was proved to be a peninsula by Dallmann in 1874.

**Antarctic Perch.** Order: Nototheniiformes. Nearly three quarters of the 90 or so species of fish (q.v.) living at the bottom of the Antarctic waters belong to this order.

**Antarctic Petrels** *see* **Fulmars**

**Antarctic Polar Front** *see* **Antarctic Convergence**

**Antarctic Services, Inc.** *see* **ITT/Antarctic Services, Inc.**

**Antarctic Services Associates.** Took over as the National Science Foundation's Antarctic support contractor on April 1, 1990, from ITT/Antarctic Services, Inc. (q.v.). This was announced on Oct. 3, 1989. ASA is a joint venture comprising EG&G of Wellesley, Mass., and Holmes & Narver (q.v.) of Orange, Calif. EG&G used to operate the *Hero* (q.v.). ASA is out of Denver, Colorado.

**Antarctic Shield** *see* **Geology**

**Antarctic Sound.** 63°20'S, 56°45'W. 30 miles long. 7–12 miles wide. Separates Trinity Peninsula from Joinville Island, Bransfield Island, and Dundee Island. Named by Nordenskjöld's expedition, for the *Antarctic,* which in 1902 became the first vessel to sail in this sound.

**Antarctic Support Activities.** The support staff for the USA's Operation Deep Freeze in Antarctica. They build, operate, repair, doctor, etc., and the commander operates out of McMurdo Station, and is responsible to the Commander, US Naval Support Force, Antarctica (*see* **US Naval Support Force, Antarctica**). It is a mixture of Seabees and general Navy personnel. Synonymous with US Naval Support Force, Antarctica.

**Antarctic Surface Water.** Cold, north-flowing Antarctic water. At the Antarctic Convergence it sinks to about 3,000 feet beneath the warmer, Subantarctic Surface Water (q.v.), to become the Subantarctic Intermediate Water (q.v.).

**Antarctic Terns.** *Sterna vittata.* Similar in looks to the Arctic terns (q.v.). They breed all over the Antarctic and lay 1–3 eggs apiece.

**Antarctic Tetons** *see* **Lyttelton Ridge**

**Antarctic Treaty.** The International Geophysical Year (IGY), 1957–58, had placed a successful moratorium over Antarctica, all the participating nations working together with one common aim—scientific research. On May 2, 1958, Dwight D. Eisenhower, then president of the USA, proposed a treaty which would continue this spirit. After much discussion, it was signed in Washington, D.C., on Dec. 1, 1959, by the 12 governments with active interests in the Antarctic—Great Britain, USA, USSR, Chile, Australia, Argentina, NZ, Norway, South Africa, Japan, Belgium, and France. It entered into full force on June 23, 1961, and is binding for 30 years after that date, and then renewable. Other countries joined later (see list below). Unprecedented in its international cooperation, it has been hugely successful, and was important as a thaw in the cold war, and as a neutralizer of space. A provision of the treaty requires periodic meetings, and such Consultative meetings have established the conservation of Antarctic flora and fauna, the preservation of historic sites, codes of conduct at bases, and other activities while on the continent, the establishment of sites of special scientific interest, and specially protected areas. It won't be long until tourism is looked on with doubtful eyes by these meetings, but at the moment the big subject of discussion is minerals, and what is going to happen to them when and if they are discovered in large quantities. There have been 14 such meetings since 1961:

Canberra 1961, Buenos Aires 1962, Brussels 1964, Santiago 1966, Paris 1968, Tokyo 1970, Wellington 1972, Oslo 1975, London 1977, Washington 1979, Buenos Aires 1981, Canberra 1983, Brussels 1985, Rio de Janeiro 1987.

The 12 original signatories are all Consultative Parties, i.e. those with a decision-making role within the Antarctic Treaty system, those carrying out substantial scientific activities in Antarctica. There has been much discontent in the late 1980s, by certain nonconsultative members, or Acceding Members, as they are called, who say that the Consultative powers are getting ready to divide the wealth of Antarctica among themselves. Would it not be a logical step for these discontented parties to develop a serious activity in Antarctica, and thus become

Consultative powers themselves? Other countries to have become Consultative have been:

Poland, July 29, 1977; West Germany, March 3, 1981; Brazil, Sept. 12, 1983; India, Sept. 12, 1983; Uruguay, Oct. 7, 1985; China, Oct. 7, 1985; East Germany, Oct. 5, 1987; Italy, Oct. 5, 1987; Sweden, Sept. 1988; Spain, Sept. 1988.

Below is the list of members in sequence of Ratification. (* means one of the 12 original signatories in 1959) (C means claimant to territory. See Territorial claims.)

1. Great Britain, May 31, 1960*C; 2. South Africa, June 21, 1960*; 3. Belgium, July 26, 1960*; 4. Japan, Aug. 4, 1960*; 5. USA, Aug. 18, 1960*; 6. Norway, Aug. 24, 1960*C; 7. France, Sept. 16, 1960*C; 8. NZ, Nov. 1, 1960*C; 9. USSR, Nov. 2, 1960*; 10. Poland, June 8, 1961; 11. Argentina, June 23, 1961*C; 12. Australia, June 23, 1961*C; 13. Chile, June 23, 1961*C; 14. Czechoslovakia, June 14, 1962; 15. Denmark, May 20, 1965; 16. Netherlands, March 30, 1967; 17. Rumania, Sept. 15, 1971; 18. East Germany, Nov. 19, 1974; 19. Brazil, May 16, 1975; 20. Bulgaria, Sept. 11, 1978; 21. West Germany, Feb. 5, 1979; 22. Uruguay, Jan. 11, 1980; 23. Papua New Guinea, March 16, 1981; 24. Italy, March 18, 1981; 25. Peru, April 10, 1981; 26. Spain, March 31, 1982; 27. China, June 8, 1983; 28. India, Aug. 19, 1983; 29. Hungary, Jan. 27, 1984; 30. Sweden, April 24, 1984; 31. Finland, May 15, 1984; 32. Cuba, Aug. 16, 1984; 33. South Korea, Nov. 28, 1986; 34. Greece, Jan. 8, 1987; 35. North Korea, Jan. 21, 1987; 36. Austria, Aug. 25, 1987; 37. Ecuador, Sept. 15, 1987; 38. Canada, May 4, 1988; 39. Colombia, Jan. 1989.

The main aim of the Antarctic Treaty is to prohibit military presence and to use the continent for scientific purposes, although there is nothing in the treaty prohibiting commercial enterprise. There are 14 articles, and they are laid out here in an abridged form:

Article I. Concerns the peaceful use of Antarctica; Article II. For international cooperation and freedom of scientific investigation; Article III. For free exchange of plans, scientific results, and personnel; Article IV. Prohibits new claims of territory, but upholds those already made; Article V. Prohibits nuclear explosions or waste disposal (*see* **Nuclear**); Article VI. For application of the Treaty to all areas south of Latitude 60° S, excluding the high seas (which come under International Law); Article VII. For open inspection of any country's Antarctic operations by any other member country (*see* **Inspections**); Article VIII. Observers (in Article VII) and scientists (in Article III) are under the jurisdiction of their own states; Article IX. The Treaty states shall meet periodically to consult; Article X. Treaty states will discourage any improper activity by another country in Antarctica; Article XI. For reference of disputes to the International Court of Justice, if they can not otherwise be peaceably settled; Article XII. For a review of the Treaty in 1991, if such a review is requested by any contracting party; Article XIII. The Treaty is subject to ratification and is open for accession by any UN state or state that all signatories want in; Article XIV. The USA is the repository and the secretary of the Treaty.

Note: the Antarctic Treaty is not a product or agency of the United Nations Organization.

**Antarctic Trough.** Permanent ring of low pressure around Antarctica at about 60° S.

**Antarctic Year.** 1901–3. Brought into being by the Geographical Congress of 1900, in Berlin. Sir Clements Markham, president of the Royal Geographical Society in London, determined to send the British south on an expedition. He picked Scott to lead the Royal Society Expedition. The Germans sent von Drygalski in the *Gauss,* Sweden sent Otto Nordenskjöld in the *Antarctic,* and France sent Jean-Baptiste Charcot in the *Français.*

**Antarctica.** Defined herein as all area, land, and water south of latitude 60° S.

This is the most widely held definition of Antarctica, although some authorities include all area south of the Antarctic Convergence, which would take in Heard Island, Bouvetøya, the South Sandwich Islands, South Georgia, and the other sub–Antarctic islands. Antarctica is a continental mass, lying concentrically around the South Pole, and mostly covered in ice. It is the southernmost continent and would be roughly circular if it were not for the Antarctic Peninsula and the Ross and Weddell Seas. The Antarctic Peninsula juts out northward like a thumb toward South America, and the two seas are deep embayments into the coast. Islands surround the giant land mass, of course, and the continent itself is composed of two unequal sized parts, East Antarctica and West Antarctica, separated by the Transantarctic Mountains. It has a volume of 7.2 million cubic miles. Antarctica has gone by other names in history. Before Cook's time it was called Southern Thule, and in the early days of the sealers, in the 1820s, some called it New South Iceland. But the most common name applied throughout history before "Antarctica" really caught on in the 1820s was Terra Australis Incognita (the unknown southern land). Capt. Robert Johnson called it New South Greenland in the early 1820s, but by that time Antarctica was on its way to becoming the official name.

*Antarctica.* Japanese movie of 1984. A spectacular commercial film, the biggest Japanese hit of the year. Directed by Koreyoshi Kurahara, it told the story of the JARE (Japanese Antarctic Research Expedition) of 1958. Akira Shiizuka was director of photography, and Vangelis provided the music. It was 112 minutes long, and in color. The players were Ken Takakura, Tsunekiko Watase, Eiji Okada, Masako Natsume, Keiko Oginome, Takeshi Kusaka, Shigeru Koyama, and So Yamamura.

**Antarctica Tours.** A Chilean tour company.

**Antarcticite.** A new mineral, calcium chloride hexahydrate, discovered in late 1961 in Don Juan Pond in the Wright Valley, Victoria Land, by George H. Meyer and his party.

**Antenna Island.** 69°S, 39°35'E. Between Nesøya and East Ongul Island. Named Antena-jima (Antenna Island) by the Japanese in 1972.

**Antevs Glacier.** 67°15'S, 66°47'W. Also called North Heim Glacier. On Arrowsmith Peninsula in Graham Land, flowing between Humphreys Hill and Boyle Mountains to Lallemand Fjord. Named by the UK in 1960 for Ernest V. Antevs, US glacial geologist.

**Anthony Bluff.** 79°06'S, 160°05'E. Along the south wall of Mulock Glacier. 9 miles NW of Cape Lankester. Named for Capt. Alexander Anthony, USAF, on the staff of the US Antarctic Projects Officer, 1963–65.

**Anthony Glacier.** 69°47'S, 62°45'W. Terminates opposite the southern tip of Hearst Island, in eastern Graham Land. The upper part was discovered by the BGLE 1934–37, and the seaward side in 1940 by the USAS from East Base. Photographed aerially by the RARE in 1947, and named by Ronne for Alexander Anthony of the J.P. Stevens Co. in New York, which contributed windproof clothing to the RARE.

**Anthracite.** Hard coal. It is the highest ranked coal (i.e. that which has been subjected to the highest pressure for the longest period of time). It is black and brilliant and is found in Antarctica.

**Antimony.** Stibnite, symbol Sb. Metallic element belonging to the nitrogen family. It has been found in Antarctica.

**The *Anton Bruun.*** US research ship in Antarctic waters in the 1960s.

**Anton Island.** 66°02'S, 134°28'E. Ice-capped. ½ mile long. 5 miles NNE of Lewis Island, just outside the eastern side of the entrance to Davis Bay. Discovered

in 1956 by Phillip Law's ANARE party off the *Kista Dan.* A helicopter party led by Law landed on the island on Jan. 18, 1960. Named by the Australians for Anton Moyell, first officer on the *Magga Dan* in 1960.

**The *Antonina Nezhdanova.*** Lindblad Travel's ship, built in 1978, it is the newest passenger vessel visiting Antarctica. Very modern, it has a stabilizing and satellite system, a library, sauna, seawater pool, and 3 decks—upper, main, and second. It takes 6 Zodiac landing craft. All public rooms underwent extensive renovations in Hong Kong in April 1988, and it can accommodate 188 passengers (although Lindblad takes 90 maximum). It has an ice classification, is 3,941 gross tons, 330 feet long, 50 feet wide, has a 23-foot draft, and has two 2,600 hp engines. Its cruising speed is 15 knots. Registered in the USSR, it is owned and operated by the Far Eastern Shipping Company (the largest USSR ship owner in the Pacific).

**Antonio Moro Refugio.** Argentine refuge hut built on Tabarin Peninsula by Esperanza Station personnel in 1955.

**Antwerp Island** *see* **Anvers Island**

**Anuchin Glacier.** 71°17'S, 13°31'E. Flows to Lake Unter-See in the northern part of the Gruber Mountains in Queen Maud Land. Discovered by Ritscher, 1938–39, and named by the USSR in 1966, for geographer D.N. Anuchin.

**Anvers Island.** 64°33'S, 63°35'W. Also called Antwerp Island. 46 miles long and 35 miles wide, it is the largest of the Palmer Archipelago. It is also the most southerly of that chain of islands, off the west coast of Graham Land. Biscoe, in Feb. 1832, made the first landing, and thinking that it was part of the continent called it Graham Land. De Gerlache got the true geographic picture in 1898, and he named it for the Belgian province of Anvers (Antwerp). It was first occupied in 1954–55 by the British Base N, and later the US Palmer Station was built here.

**Anvil Crag.** 62°12'S, 58°29'W. On King George Island in the South Shetlands.

**Anvil Rock.** 65°14'S, 64°16'W. A rock in the water between Grotto Island and the SE end of Forge Islands in the Argentine Islands. Named descriptively by the BGLE in 1935.

**Aogori Bay.** 69°13'S, 39°44'E. Small indentation in the western side of the Langhovde Hills on the Queen Maud Land coast, just south of Mount Futago. Named Aogori-wan (blue-ice bay) by the Japanese in 1972.

**Mount Aorangi.** 72°25'S, 166°22'E. 3,135 m. Highest mountain in the Millen Range. Named by the New Zealanders in 1962–63. The name in Maori means "the cloud-piercer."

**Apatite.** Clear, fragile, soft series of phosphate minerals, the major source of phosphorus. Found in Antarctica.

**Apéndice Island.** 64°11'S, 61°02'W. Also called Sterneck Island, and formerly called Isla Telegrafista Rivera or Isla Rivera for a telegraphist on the Chilean Antarctic Expedition of 1947, which first defined it as an island. NW of Charles Point in Hughes Bay, off the west coast of Graham Land. It looks like an appendix.

**Apfel, Dr. Earl T.** Professor of geology at Syracuse University, NY. He was Task Force 39's geologist during Operation Windmill, 1947–48.

**Apfel Glacier.** 66°25'S, 100°35'E. 5 miles wide and 20 miles long. Flows along the southern flank of the Bunger Hills, and ends in the Edisto Ice Tongue. Named for Earl T. Apfel.

**Aphrodite Glacier.** 68°50'S, 64°32'W. 15 miles long. It flows to the east coast of the Antarctic Peninsula, 3 miles west of Victory Nunatak. Photographed by Wilkins in Dec. 1928, by Ellsworth in Nov. 1935, and by the RARE in Dec. 1947. Surveyed by the FIDS in Dec. 1958 and in Nov. 1960, and named by the UK for the Greek goddess.

**Apocalypse Peaks.** 77°23'S, 160°50'E. A group east of Willett Range, between the Barwick and Balham Valleys of Victoria Land. The highest peak is 2,360 m. Named by the New Zealanders in 1958–59 because the peaks look like the Four Horsemen of the Apocalypse.

**Apollo Glacier.** 68°50'S, 64°45'W. 9 miles long. Flows into Aphrodite Glacier, in the eastern part of the Antarctic Peninsula. Surveyed in Nov. 1960 by the FIDS, who named it for the Greek god.

**Apollo Ice Rise** *see* **Apollo Island**

**Apollo Island.** 70°15'S, 1°55'W. Also called Apollo Ice Rise. Small, ice-covered island 18 miles ENE of Blåskimen Island in the NW part of the Fimbul Ice Shelf. 10 miles ENE of Sanae Station. Named by the South Africans prior to 1969.

**Mount Apolotok.** 72°16'S, 164°29'E. 2,555 m. A red granite peak in the Salamander Range of the Freyberg Mountains. It is an Eskimo word meaning "the big red one," and was named by the New Zealanders in 1963–64.

**Apostrophe Island.** 73°31'S, 167°25'E. Small, ice-covered island just off Spatulate Ridge in Lady Newnes Bay in Victoria Land. Named descriptively by the New Zealanders in 1966.

**Appalachia Nunataks.** 69°44'S, 71°09'W. In the northern part of Alexander Island.

**Point Appleby.** 67°25'S, 59°36'E. Almost a mile south of Warren Island, in the William Scoresby Archipelago, it forms part of the western side of an unnamed island. Discovered, charted, and named by personnel on the *William Scoresby* in Feb. 1936.

**Appleton, James.** Name also seen as Appleman. Captain of the *Charles Shearer* on its last voyage, 1877–78. Appleton disappeared with his vessel.

**The *Aquiles*.** Chilean naval ship under charter to Lindblad Travel.

**Isla Aragay** *see* **Gulch Island**

**Arago Glacier.** 64°51′S, 62°23′W. Flows into Andvord Bay just NW of Moser Glacier on the west coast of Graham Land. Named in 1960 for D.F.J. Arago (1786–1853), French geodesist.

**Arai Terraces.** 83°12′S, 163°26′E. Series of crevassed terraces and icefalls just south of the Fazekas Hills near the head of Lowery Glacier. Named by the New Zealanders in 1959–60, because this is a barrier to sledging. The Maori word for barrier is "arai."

**Aramis Range.** 71°S, 65°15′E. Extends for 30 miles. The most southerly of the Prince Charles Mountains in Mac. Robertson Land. It overlooks the Amery Ice Shelf from the west. 11 miles SE of the Porthos Range. First visited in Jan. 1957 by W.G. Bewsher's ANARE party. Bewsher named it for the character in *The Three Musketeers.*

**Arcas Rocket.** US atmospheric sounding rocket (*see* **Rockets**).

**Archambault Ridge.** 73°42′S, 162°55′E. Descends from the Deep Freeze Range to Campbell Glacier between Rainey and Recoil Glaciers in Victoria Land. Named for Lt. John L. Archambault, USN, medical officer at McMurdo Station in 1967.

**Archangel Nunataks** *see* **Arkhangel'skiy Nunataks**

**Cape Archer.** 76°51′S, 162°52′E. Marks the northern side of the entrance to Granite Harbor on the eastern coast of Victoria Land. Named by Campbell's Northern Party during Scott's 1910–13 expedition, for W.W. Archer.

**Mount Archer.** 69°10′S, 157°38′E. Just south of Archer Point on the west side of Harald Bay. Named in association with the point.

**Archer, W.W.** Chief steward, late of the RN, on Scott's 1910–13 expedition.

**Archer Glacier.** 65°10′S, 63°05′W. Flows into the head of Bolsón Cove in Flandres Bay on the west coast of Graham Land. Charted by de Gerlache in 1897–99. Named by the UK in 1960 for Frederick S. Archer (1813–1857), photographic processing pioneer.

**Archer Peak.** 71°52′S, 171°10′E. Also called Anchor Peak. 110 m. On the SW end of Possession Island. Named by Borchgrevink in 1898–1900 for A. Archer, of Australia, mentioned in Borchgrevink's book, *First on the Antarctic Continent,* or perhaps for Colin Archer, designer of the *Southern Cross.*

**Archer Point.** 69°08′S, 157°38′E. Marks the west side of Harald Bay. Discovered in Feb. 1911, by Lt. Harry Pennell in the *Terra Nova,* and named for W.W. Archer.

**Archibald Point.** 63°13′S, 56°40′W. On the SW side of Bransfield Island in Antarctic Sound. Named by the UK in 1963 for George K. Archibald, first officer on the *Shackleton.*

**Arcondo Nunatak.** 82°08′S, 41°37′W. 780 m. 5 miles south of Mount Spann in the Panzarini Hills of the Argentina Range in the Pensacola Mountains. Named by the US for Mayor Pedro Arcondo, officer-in-charge at General Belgrano Station, 1959–61.

**Arctic Tern.** *Sterna paradisaea.* The world's greatest traveler, it nests each summer in the North Pole area, and then immediately flies to Antarctica for another summer, coming down in large numbers. It has the greatest annual migration of any bird.

**Arctowski, Henryk.** 1871–1958. Polish meteorologist/geologist/oceanographer, born in Warsaw. He was a pioneer in the field of meteorology, and proposed that wind can be as harmful as cold. He was on the *Belgica* in 1897–99, and after 1939 was in the USA.

**Arctowski Nunatak.** 65°06′S, 60°W. 2 miles NW of Hertha Nunatak in the Seal Nunataks, off the east coast of the Antarctic Peninsula. Charted by Nordenskjöld's expedition in 1902 during a sledge journey, and named by the Swedish leader for Henryk Arctowski.

**Arctowski Peak.** 73°44′S, 61°28′W. 1,410 m. Isolated. Ice-covered. 8 miles WSW of the head of Howkins Inlet on the east coast of Palmer Land. Discovered by the USAS in 1940. Named by the FIDS for Henryk Arctowski.

**Arctowski Peninsula.** 64°45′S, 62°25′W. 15 miles long. Between Andvord Bay and Wilhelmina Bay on the west coast of Graham Land. Discovered by de Gerlache, 1897–99, and later named by the Americans for Henryk Arctowski.

**Arctowski Station.** 62°10′S, 58°28′W. Also called Henryk Arctowski Station, for Henryk Arctowski. Polish scientific station belonging to the Polish Academy of Sciences. Located on Admiralty Bay, King George Island, South Shetlands. It was opened Feb. 26, 1977, and studied mainly birds and seals. By 1982 there were only 9 persons there, mostly doing small-scale krill research. The station continues.

**Ardery Island.** 66°22′S, 110°28′E. A steep, rocky island, just over ½ mile long. 7 miles south of Wilkes Station, in Vincennes Bay, or just over a mile west of Odbert Island, in the Windmill Islands. With Odbert Island it forms a Specially Protected Area, because of the abundant petrel life here. Named for Maj. E.R. Ardery, Army Medical Corps observer on Operation Windmill, 1947–48.

**Ardley, R.A.B.** Lt., RNR. Officer on the *Discovery II* in 1929–31 and 1931–33, during the Discovery Investigations.

**Ardley Island.** 62°13′S, 58°56′W. 1 mile long. Off the east coast of Fildes Peninsula, in Maxwell Bay, just off the SW end of King George Island, in the South Shetlands. Charted as a peninsula in 1935 by the personnel on the *Discovery II,* and named Ardley Peninsula. The South Americans called it Península Hardley. It was named for Lt. R.A.B. Ardley. It has since been redefined, aerially, as an island.

**Ardley Peninsula** *see* **Ardley Island**

**Ardley Refugio.** Argentine refuge hut built on Ardley Peninsula (now known to be an island, Ardley Island), off King George Island, in 1954.

**Area.** Antarctica is the fifth largest continent, covering about 5½ million square miles. 10 percent of the area is ice shelf. The continent covers more than 9 percent of the earth's surface. Its coastline is 18,500 miles. The diameter of the continent is 2,800 miles. Antarctica is roughly circular. There are one million square miles of ocean ice in summer, and 7.3 million square miles of it in winter.

**Arena Corner.** 69°51′S, 68°02′W. On the west coast of the Antarctic Peninsula.

**Arena Glacier.** 63°24′S, 57°03′W. 3 miles long. Flows from Mount Taylor into Hope Bay, 2 miles SW of Sheppard Point, at the end of Trinity Peninsula. Mapped in 1948 and 1955 by the FIDS, and named by them for the flat ice floor of the glacier's upper half which, surrounded by the steep slopes of Twin Peaks, Mount Taylor, and Blade Ridge, looks like an arena.

**Arena Saddle.** 77°53′S, 160°46′E. At the head of the Arena Valley in southern Victoria Land.

**Arena Valley.** 77°50′S, 160°58′E. A dry valley between East Beacon and New Mountain in the Quartermain Range of southern Victoria Land. Named descriptively by the New Zealanders in 1958–59.

**Arenite Ridge.** 69°41′S, 69°30′W. On the west coast of the Antarctic Peninsula.

**Ares Cliff.** 71°49′S, 68°15′W. Rises to 500 m. Formed of pale-colored sandstone. East of Mars Glacier, and 1 mile north of Two Step Cliffs, on the east side of Alexander Island. Named by the UK for the Greek god.

**Areta Rock.** 82°06′S, 41°05′W. 3 miles SE of Mount Spann in the Panzarini Hills of the Argentina Range in the Pensacola Mountains. Named by the US for Lt.

Eduardo Ferrin Areta, Argentine officer-in-charge at Ellsworth Station in 1961.

**Arêtes.** Sharp-crested, steep-sided, serrate ridges separating the heads of opposing valleys (or cirques) that were once occupied by glaciers.

**Argentina.** In 1904 the Argentines took over Bruce's Laurie Island station at Omond House, at his invitation. This was the first scientific station in Antarctica, and Argentina has maintained it ever since, calling it Orcadas Station (Orcadas is the Spanish word for Orkneys). They claimed the South Orkneys as early as 1925 (*see* **Territorial Claims**), and in 1942 and 1943 they sent expeditions to Antarctica (*see* the Expeditions appendix), claiming the sector between 74°W and 25°W, in 1942. This area includes the Antarctic Peninsula, and they have since disputed this area with Great Britain and Chile, both of whom claim roughly the same area. Argentina was pro–Nazi during World War II, and Britain established a permanent base on Deception Island as a counter-thrust. Expeditions followed from 1947, and bases were built at several sites in the area as a counter-counter move to the British. In 1951 the Instituto Antártico Argentino was established and placed under the army. This instituto is at the head of all Argentine scientific programs here. In 1952 some Argentinians fired on a British party at Hope Bay (*see* **Wars**), but in 1959 both countries were among the 12 original signatories of the Antarctic Treaty. The Argentines call the Antarctic Peninsula Tierra San Martín. They first flew to the Pole in 1963, and trekked there in 1965. In 1986 Argentina tripled its Antarctic scientific staff, and discovered dinosaur fossils (*see* **Fossils**). Other stations (*see* **Scientific stations**) have included General Belgrano, Melchior, Primero de Mayo, San Martín, Almirante Brown, Esperanza, Teniente Camara, Petrel, Vicecomodoro Marambio, Sobral, Jubany, Teniente Matienzo, Primavera, General Belgrano II, General Belgrano III. After IGY (1957–58) Argentina operated Ellsworth Station.

**Argentina Range.** 82°20′S, 42°W. 42 miles long. 35 miles east of the northern part of the Forrestal Range in the NE portion of the Pensacola Mountains. The Panzarini Hills are here. Discovered aerially on Jan. 13, 1956 (*see* the Chronology). Named by the US for the country of Argentina.

**Argentine Antarctic Expedition 1947.** Led by Luís Miguel García. It was for political purposes, although surveys and lighthouse construction were done, and Orcadas Station was relieved. Melchior Station was built. The ships were *King, Murature, Ministro Ezcurra, Don Samuel, Patagonia, Chaco, Fournier.*

**Argentine Antarctic Expedition 1947–48.** Led by Ricardo Hermelo until March 1948, when Luís Miguel García took over. It was conducted primarily to build Primero de Mayo Station, do naval maneuvers, and an aerial survey. The ships involved were *Bouchard, Granville, King, Pampa, Ministro Ezcurra, Murature, Chiriguano, Seaver, Parker, Robinson, Esiv Brunt, Charua, Sanavirón.*

**Argentine Islands.** 65°14′S, 64°15′W. 5 miles SW of Petermann Island, and 4 miles west of Cape Tuxen. Discovered and named Îles Argentine by Charcot in 1903–5. The BGLE operated out of here, and the British Base F was here. Islands in the group include The Barchans, Black Island, Anvil Rock, the Buttons, Channel Rock, Corner Island, Fanfare Island, Forge Islands, Galíndez Island, Grotto Island, Skua Island, Irízar Island, Winter Island, Uruguay Island, Corner Rock, Leopard Island, Shelter Islands.

**Canal Argentino** *see* **Lientur Channel**

**Argentino Channel.** 64°54′S, 63°01′W. Also called Brazo Sur, Ferguson Channel, Canal Lautaro. This is not to be confused with Canal Argentino (*see* **Lientur Channel**). Between Bryde Island and the west coast of Graham Land, connecting Paradise Harbor with Gerlache

Strait. Charted by de Gerlache in 1897–99. The Argentines named it Canal Argentino before 1950, and, translated, this is Argentino Channel.

**Argles, H.J.** Trimmer who joined the *Quest* expedition at Rio in 1921.

**Argo Glacier.** 83°17'S, 157°35'E. 10 miles long. The southernmost of the glaciers in the Miller Range. Flows into Marsh Glacier just south of McDonald Bluffs. Named by the New Zealanders in 1961–62 for Jason's ship in Greek mythology.

**Argo Point.** 66°15'S, 60°55'W. Rises to 260 m. On the east side of Jason Peninsula, 22 miles NE of Veier Head, on the east coast of Graham Land. First seen by Carl Anton Larsen in 1893 from his ship, the *Jason.* Surveyed by the FIDS in 1953 and named by the UK in 1956 for Jason's ship in Greek mythology.

**Argonaut Glacier.** 73°13'S, 166°42'E. 10 miles long. In the Mountaineer Range of Victoria Land. Flows into Mariner Glacier just north of Engberg Bluff. Named by the New Zealanders in 1962–63 in association with the nearby glaciers—Astronaut, Cosmonaut, and Cosmonette.

**Argosy Glacier.** 83°08'S, 157°40'E. 15 miles long. Enters Marsh Glacier, north of Kreiling Mesa in the Miller Range. Named by the New Zealanders in 1961–62.

**Estrecho Arguindeguy** *see* **Picnic Passage**

**Mount Argus.** 68°54'S, 63°50'W. Also spelled (erroneously) as Mount Angus. Large, isolated mountain mass, surmounted by three separate peaks, the highest being 1,220 m. Between Poseidon Pass and Athene Glacier, 10 miles WNW of Miller Point, in NE Palmer Land. Named by the UK in 1963 for the son of Zeus in Greek mythology.

**Mount Ariel.** 71°22'S, 68°40'W. 1,250 m. Marks the southern limit of Planet Heights, and overlooks the north side of Uranus Glacier, in the eastern part of

Alexander Island. Ellsworth saw and photographed it aerially on Nov. 23, 1935. The UK named it later because Ariel is one of the satellites of the planet Uranus.

**The Ark.** 80°43'S, 24°47'W. 1,790 m. Mountain summit in the central part of the Read Mountains, in the Shackleton Range. Named by the BCTAE because it looks like an ark from the west.

**Arkell Cirque.** 80°41'S, 24°08'W. Just to the east of the Shackleton Range.

**Arkhangel'skiy Nunataks.** 69°28'S, 156°30'E. Formerly called Archangel Nunataks, and White Nunataks. Group of scattered rock outcrops 15 miles west of the central part of the Lazarev Mountains. In 1958 the USSR named the largest of these Arkhangel'skiy Nunatak, for geologist A.D. Arkhangel'skiy, and later the Australians broadened the application of the name.

**Arkticheskiy Institut Rocks.** 71°18'S, 11°27'E. 8 miles north of Nordwestliche Insel Mountains at the NW extremity of the Wohlthat Mountains. Discovered by Ritscher, 1938–39, and named by the USSR for their Arctic Institute.

**Armadillo Hill.** 68°07'S, 66°22'W. 1,760 m. Ice-covered. 4 miles ESE of the head of Northeast Glacier, and 8 miles NE of the head of Neny Fjord, on the Graham Land plateau. The BGLE surveyed it in 1934–37, and the USAS resurveyed it on sledging parties in 1940. They named it Sawtooth for its appearance. The FIDS did another survey in 1946–47 and renamed it, because, when viewed from the NE, it looks like an armadillo.

**Mount Armagost.** 71°38'S, 166°01'E. 2,040 m. Between Mirabito Range and Homerun Range in Victoria Land. 9 miles SW of Mount LeResche. Named for Harry M. Armagost, USN, chief equipment operator at McMurdo Station in 1963 and 1967.

**Årmålsryggen.** 73°12'S, 2°08'W. A ridge at the west end of the Neumayer

Cliffs in Queen Maud Land. Photographed aerially by Ritscher's expedition in 1938–39. Name means "the year's goal ridge" in Norwegian.

**Armbruster Rocks.** 73°57′S, 116°48′W. In the Amundsen Sea, just off the Marie Byrd Land coast.

**Cape Armitage.** 77°52′S, 166°40′E. The southernmost cape on Ross Island, at the tip of Hut Point Peninsula, where lie Scott Base, Hut Point and McMurdo Station. Discovered by Scott and named by him for Albert P. Armitage, during the first expedition, 1901–04.

**Mount Armitage** *see* **Mount Armytage**

**Armitage, Albert P.** 1864–1943. Merchant officer with the P & O Line, he had Arctic experience when asked to lead the Royal Society Expedition of 1901–4. However, Scott was finally picked as the leader, and Armitage was relegated to navigator and second-in-command of the expedition. Nicknamed "The Pilot," he was the first onto the polar ice cap itself, and in 1903 discovered and named Ferrar, Taylor, and Blue Glaciers during his western trip from McMurdo Sound. Wrote a couple of books (*see* the Bibliography).

**Armitage Saddle.** 78°09′S, 163°15′E. At the head of the Blue Glacier, overlooking the Howchin and Walcott Glaciers. It is at the south end of the Snow Valley (the upper part of the Koettlitz Glacier). Mapped by Armitage in 1902. The NZ Blue Glacier party of the BCTAE established a survey station here in Sept. 1957, and they named it for Albert P. Armitage.

**Armlenet** *see* **Mayr Ridge**

**Armlenet Ridge.** 71°59′S, 2°52′E. Runs for 3 miles between Stabben Mountain and Jutulhogget Peak, and forms the eastern arm of Jutulsessen Mountain in the Gjelsvik Mountains of Queen Maud Land. Name means "the arm rest" in Norwegian.

**Armonini Nunatak.** 71°11′S, 65°51′E. Partly snow-covered. 5 miles ESE of Mount Reu in the Prince Charles Mountains. Named by the Australians for G.C. Armonini, weather observer at Davis Station, 1962.

**Armour Inlet.** 73°38′S, 124°39′W. Ice-filled indentation in the north side of Siple Island, just west of Armour Peninsula on the coast of Marie Byrd Land. Named for the Armour Institute of Technology in Chicago, whose funds for the USAS 1939–41 purchased the Snowcruiser (q.v.).

**Armour Peninsula.** 73°42′S, 124°10′W. Ice-covered. Just east of Armour Inlet on Siple Island, on the Marie Byrd Land coast. Named in association with the inlet.

**Mount Armstrong.** 85°50′S, 157°12′W. 2,330 m. 5 miles SSE of Mount Goodale in the Hays Mountains. Named for Thomas B. Armstrong, USARP representative at Palmer Station, 1966–67.

**Armstrong, W.J.** Seaman on the *City of New York,* during Byrd's 1928–30 expedition.

**Armstrong Glacier.** 71°31′S, 67°30′W. Flows from the south side of Mount Bagshawe into George VI Sound. The only known safe route for mechanical vehicles from George VI Sound to the Palmer Land plateau. Named by the UK for Edward B. Armstrong, BAS surveyor at Stonington Island, 1964–65.

**Armstrong Peak.** 66°24′S, 53°23′E. 1,470 m. 15 miles SE of Mount Codrington, Enderby Land. Photographed by the LCE 1936–37, and named later by the Norwegians as Austnuten (the east peak). Renamed by the Australians in 1960 for J.C. Armstrong, ANARE surveyor at Mawson Station, who obtained an astrofix near here in Dec. 1959.

**Armstrong Platform.** 70°32′S, 160°10′E. Mainly ice-covered plateau, or height. It is a NE extension of the Pomerantz Tableland. 5 miles long. Between 1,200 and 1,800 meters in height. Directly north of Helfferich Glacier in the Usarp Mountains. Named for biologist Richard L. Armstrong, at McMurdo Station, 1967–68.

**Armstrong Reef.** 65°54'S, 66°18'W. Also called Arrecife Espinosa. A large number of small islands and rocks lie within this reef, which extends 5 miles from the SW end of Renaud Island in the Biscoe Islands. Named by the UK for Terence E. Armstrong, British sea-ice specialist.

**Army Range** *see* **LeMay Range**

**Mount Armytage.** 76°02'S, 160°45'E. 1,855 m. Dome-shaped. North of the Mawson Glacier, and 14 miles west of Mount Smith, in Victoria Land. Charted by Shackleton's 1907-9 expedition, who named it for Bertram Armytage.

**Armytage, Bertram.** 1869-1943. In charge of the ponies on the shore party of Shackleton's 1907-9 expedition.

**Arne Nunataks.** 71°43'S, 8°20'E. The Norwegians call it Arnesteinen. The largest of the Hemmestad Nunataks in the Drygalski Mountains of Queen Maud Land. Photographed aerially by Ritscher, 1938-39. Named by the Norwegians for Arne Hemmestad, mechanic on the Norwegian Antarctic Expedition of 1956-57.

**The *Arneb.*** US attack cargo ship used during Operations Deep Freeze I and II, in other words during IGY. Helped build Hallett Station in 1957.

**Arneb Glacier.** 72°25'S, 170°02'E. 3 miles long. 2 miles wide. Between Hallett Peninsula and Redcastle Ridge. It flows into Edisto Inlet as a floating ice tongue. Named by the New Zealanders in 1957-58 for the *Arneb.*

**Arnel Bluffs.** 68°07'S, 56°12'E. Series of rock outcrops in a steeply falling ice scarp south of the Leckie Range. Named by the Australians for R.R. Arnel, geophysical assistant at Mawson Station, 1958.

**Arnold Cove.** 77°25'S, 163°46'E. Between Marble Point and Gneiss Point in southern Victoria Land. Named for Charles L. Arnold, an engineer studying here in 1971-72.

**Aronson Corner.** 80°29'S, 20°56'W. Just to the east of the Shackleton Range.

**Islote Arriagada** *see* **Alcock Island**

**Arriens, Dr. Pieter.** Geologist on David Lewis' *Solo* expedition of 1977-78.

**Arrival Bay.** The little bay to the east of Cape Royds on Ross Island. Discovered and named by Scott in Feb. 1902, for the place where the *Discovery* arrived.

**Arrival Heights.** 77°48'S, 166°39'E. Also called Harbour Heights. Cliff-like heights overlooking Arrival Bay, on Hut Point Peninsula, Ross Island, 1½ miles north of Hut Point. Elevation, approximately 620 feet. Discovered by Scott in 1902, and named by him for the arrival of the *Discovery*. It is an SSSI, and there is an AWS here.

**Arrol Icefall.** 64°35'S, 60°40'W. A steep icefall, 3 miles long. Flows from the southern side of Detroit Plateau in Graham Land, about 8 miles NW of Cape Worsley. Mapped from surveys by the FIDS in 1960-61. Named by the UK for the Arrol-Johnston automobile (*see* **Automobiles**).

**Mount Arronax.** 67°40'S, 67°22'W. 1,585 m. Ice-covered. 6 miles WSW of Nautilus Head. It dominates the northern part of Pourquoi Pas Island off the west coast of Graham Land. Surveyed by the BGLE in 1936, and again in 1948 by the FIDS who named it for the Jules Verne character.

**Arrow Island** *see* **Pila Island**

**Arrowhead Nunatak.** 82°34'S, 157°22'E. Long, narrow nunatak. 7 miles SE of Sullivan Nunatak, near the end of the Nimrod Glacier. From the air it looks like an arrowhead, hence the name given by the New Zealanders in 1960-61.

**Arrowhead Range.** 73°24'S, 164°10'E. 20 miles long. Just north of Cosmonaut Glacier and west of Aviator Glacier in the Southern Cross Mountains of Victoria Land. It is shaped like an arrowhead, the eastern end forming the head.

**Mount Arrowsmith.** 76°46'S, 162°18'E. A jagged rock peak near Mount Perseverance, 2 miles along a ridge running NE from that mountain, and 2 miles east of Mount Whitcombe, in Victoria Land. Named by the NZ Northern Survey Party of the BCTAE for the mountain of that name in NZ.

**Arrowsmith Peninsula.** 67°15'S, 67° 15'W. 40 miles long. On the Antarctic Peninsula, across from Adelaide Island. Surveyed by the FIDS in 1955–58, and named by them for Edwin P. Arrowsmith, governor of the Falkland Islands.

**Arruiz Glacier.** 70°39'S, 162°09'E. Flows from Stanwix Peak in the Explorers Range of the Bowers Mountains, to enter Rennick Glacier north of Frolov Ridge. Named for Lt. Alberto J. Arruiz, Argentine observer at Weather Central (q.v.) at Little America in 1958.

**Arsen'yev Rocks.** 71°51'S, 11°12'E. 2½ miles west of Mount Deryugin in the Liebknecht Range of the Humboldt Mountains. Named in 1966 by the USSR for geographer K.I. Arsen'yev.

**Art Glacier** *see* **Alt Glacier**

**Arthropods.** The only native form of terrestrial microfauna in Antarctica. They consist of 130 species, 44 being parasitic on birds and seals. There are 67 species of mites, 19 of springtails, 37 of biting lice, 4 of sucking lice (*see* **Lice**), 2 of midges, and 1 of fleas. Arthropoda is the largest phylum in the animal kingdom (spiders, insects, crustaceans, etc., are members).

**Bahía Arthur** *see* **Wylie Bay**

**Mount Arthur.** 67°39'S, 49°52'E. 1,290 m. Just west of Mount Douglas, at the west end of the Scott Mountains in Enderby Land. Named by the Australians for J. Arthur, electrical fitter at Mawson Station, 1960.

**Arthur Davis Glacier** *see* **Davis Glacier**

**Arthur Glacier.** 77°03'S, 145°15'W. Also called Arthur Davis Glacier, Davis Glacier, Warpasgiljo Glacier. 25 miles long. Flows to the Sulzberger Ice Shelf between the Swanson Mountains on the north and Mounts Rea and Cooper on

the south, in the Ford Ranges of Marie Byrd Land. Discovered aerially in Nov.–Dec. 1940 by the USAS from West Base, and named for Rear Adm. Arthur C. Davis, USN, a leader in aviation.

**Arthur Harbor.** 64°46'S, 64°04'W. Small harbor on the SW coast of Anvers Island, between Bonaparte Point and Norsel Point. Charcot charted it in 1903–5, and the FIDS surveyed it in 1955. Base N was built here by the British in 1955, and later the Americans built Palmer Station here. Named by the UK in 1960 for Oswald R. Arthur, Governor of the Falkland Islands.

**Mount Arthur Owen** *see* **Mount Owen**

**Arthur Sulzberger Bay** *see* **Sulzberger Bay**

**Arthurson Bluff.** 70°45'S, 166°05'E. Mostly ice-covered. Overlooks the confluence of the Ludvig Glacier and the Kirkby Glacier from the west, near the northern coast of Victoria Land. Landed on by helicopter in 1962, when ANARE leader Phillip Law did so. He named it for the pilot of the helicopter, Capt. J. Arthurson.

**Arthurson Ridge.** 69°22'S, 158°30'E. Short promontory extending north from the Wilson Hills, between Cook Ridge and the terminus of the McLeod Glacier, at the head of Davies Bay. First visited by an ANARE airborne field party in March 1961, and named for the pilot of the helicopter, J. Arthurson (*see* **Arthurson Bluff**).

**Artigas Station.** 62°10'S, 58°50'W. Uruguayan scientific station established in Dec. 1984 in Collins Harbor, King George Island, South Shetlands. It is very near to the Great Wall Station of the Chinese. Started as a summer station, it became a year-round station in 1986.

**Ascent Glacier.** 83°13'S, 156°22'E. 2 miles wide. Flows into the Argosy Glacier, just east of Milan Ridge, in the Miller Range. Named by the NZGSAE 1961–62. They used it to get to the central Miller Range.

**Asgard Automatic Weather Station.**
77°36'S, 161°06'E. American AWS in the dry valleys of Victoria Land, at an elevation of approximately 5,300 feet. It operated from Feb. 5, 1980, until Dec. 31, 1982.

**Asgard Range.** 77°37'S, 161°30'E. Between the Wright Valley and the Taylor Valley, in southern Victoria Land. Named by the New Zealanders in 1958–59 for the home of the Norse gods.

**Mount Ash.** 79°57'S, 156°40'E. 2,025 m. Overlooks the north side of Hatherton Glacier in the Darwin Mountains, 11 miles WSW of Junction Spur. Named for mechanic Ralph E. Ash, a member of the US McMurdo-Pole Traverse Party of 1960–61.

**Ash Point.** 62°29'S, 59°39'W. Also called Punta Bascope, Punta Ceniza. At the entrance to Discovery Bay in Greenwich Island. Apparently named in 1935 by personnel on the *Discovery II*.

**Asher Peak.** 75°44'S, 129°11'W. 2,480 m. In the SW portion of Mount Flint in the McCuddin Mountains of Marie Byrd Land. Named for Bill F. Asher, USN, Senior Chief Construction Electrician at Little America in 1958, and nuclear power plant operator at McMurdo Station in 1969.

**Ashley Snow Nunataks** *see* **Snow Nunataks**

**Ashton, L.** FIDS carpenter at Port Lockroy, 1944–45, and at Base D, at Hope Bay, 1945–46.

**Ashton Glacier.** 70°44'S, 61°57'W. 9 miles long. Flows from Mount Thompson to the NW side of Lehrke Inlet on the east coast of Palmer Land. Named by the FIDS for L. Ashton.

**Ashtray Basin.** 77°52'S, 160°58'E. Small basin near the head of Arena Valley in Victoria Land. Named descriptively by the Australians in 1966–67.

**Mount Ashworth.** 70°55'S, 163°06'E. 2,060 m. 4 miles ENE of Mount Ford in

the Bowers Mountains. Named by the ANARE for Squadron Leader N. Ashworth, RAAF, here in 1962.

**Asimutbreen Glacier.** 71°23'S, 13°42'E. Small, steep glacier flowing between Solhøgdene Heights and Skuggekammen Ridge in the eastern Gruber Mountains of the Wohlthat Mountains in Queen Maud Land. Feeds into Vangemgeym Glacier. Discovered by Ritscher, 1938–39. Name means "the azimuth glacier" in Norwegian.

**Asman, Adam.** Driver at West Base during the USAS 1939–41.

**Asman Ridge.** 77°10'S, 144°48'W. 6 miles long. On the south side of Arthur Glacier, just north of Bailey Ridge in the Ford Ranges. Discovered aerially in 1934 by members of Byrd's 1933–35 expedition, and named by the USAS 1939–41 for Adam Asman.

**Aspland Island.** 61°30'S, 55°49'W. Also called Aspland's Island. South of Elephant Island, and 4 miles west of Gibbs Island, it is one of the easterly group of the South Shetlands. Named before 1821.

**Mount Asquith** *see* **Asquith Bluff**

**Asquith Bluff.** 83°30'S, 167°21'E. Also called Mount Asquith. Wedge-shaped rock bluff on the west side of the Lennox-King Glacier, 4 miles SE of Mount Allen Young. Discovered during Shackleton's 1907–9 expedition, and named by them for the British prime minister, Lord Asquith, who helped get Shackleton's expedition debts paid off.

**Assender Glacier.** 67°36'S, 46°25'E. Flows into Spooner Bay in Enderby Land. Named by the Australians for Pilot Officer K. Assender, pilot at Mawson Station, 1959.

**Asses Ears.** 62°20'S, 59°45'W. Also called Islas Orejas de Burro. Formerly thought to be two islands, this is, in fact, a twin-peaked rock in the water, in the northern part of the Potmess Rocks, in the English Strait, in the South Shetlands. Discovered by the early sealers of 1819–21. Named descriptively by the personnel on the *Discovery II* in 1935.

**Astakhov Glacier.** 70°45'S, 163°21'E. Just south of Chugunov Glacier in the Explorers Range of the Bowers Mountains. Flows from Mount Hager and enters Ob' Bay just west of Platypus Ridge. Named by the US for Pyotr Astakhov, USSR exchange scientist at Amundsen-Scott South Pole Station, 1967.

**Astapenko, Pavel D.** USSR observer at Weather Central at Little America, 1958.

**Astapenko Glacier.** 70°40'S, 162°52'E. 11 miles long. Flows from Stanwix Peak in the Bowers Mountains, into Ob' Bay. Named by the US for Pavel D. Astapenko.

**Astarte Horn.** 71°40'S, 68°52'W. Pyramidal peak in eastern Alexander Island. Near Venus Glacier. Named by the UK for the Phoenician goddess.

**Mount Astor.** 86°01'S, 155°30'W. Also called Mount Vincent Astor. 3,710 m. (12,175 feet). 2 miles north of Mount Bowser in the Hays Mountains of the Queen Maud Mountains. Discovered by Byrd on the Nov. 1929 flight to the Pole, and named by him for Vincent Astor, a contributor to Byrd's 1928–30 expedition.

**Astor, B.** Crew member of the *Jane Maria* in 1819–21, who, on the instruction of Donald McKay, brought back rocks and minerals to be studied in New York.

**Astor Island.** 62°39'S, 61°11'W. Between Rugged Island and Livingston Island in the South Shetlands. Named by the UK in 1958 for B. Astor.

**Astor Rocks.** 71°48'S, 12°44'E. Two small rock outcrops 4 miles SE of Mount Ramenskiy at the SE extremity of the Wohlthat Mountains. Named by the Norwegians for Astor Ernstsen, meteorologist with the Norwegian Antarctic Expedition of 1958–59.

**Astraea Nunatak.** 71°59'S, 70°25'W. 6 miles south of Staccato Peaks in southern Alexander Island. Surveyed by the FIDS

in 1948–50, and named by the UK for the asteroid.

**Astro Cliffs.** 66°40'S, 62°26'W. Rock cliffs 60 meters high. At the SE extremity of the Churchill Peninsula, 6 miles NE of Cape Alexander on the east coast of Graham Land. Surveyed by the FIDS in 1955, they were the southernmost point of the survey. Named by the UK for the FIDS astrofix taken here.

**Astro Glacier.** 82°57'S, 157°20'E. The northernmost of the glaciers in the Miller Range, between the Turner Hills and Tricorn Peak. It flows into Marsh Glacier. Named by the New Zealanders who set up an astro station on the bluff at the mouth of the glacier in Dec. 1961.

**Astro Peak.** 83°29'S, 57°W. 835 m. 1 mile off the west end of Berquist Ridge in the Neptune Range of the Pensacola Mountains. Named by the Americans for an astro control station they built on this peak in 1965–66.

**The *Astrolabe*.** Dumont d'Urville's flagship during his 1837–40 expedition to Antarctica. Called, until 1825, the *Coquille,* it had twice sailed around the world in the 1820s, the second time under Dumont d'Urville, but it was not equipped for the ice. A small, old French corvette of 380 tons displacement, it was 94 feet long, 29 feet in the beam, and 13 feet deep in the hold. It carried 10 guns, 17 officers, and 85 men.

**Astrolabe Glacier.** 66°45'S, 139°55'E. Also called Glacier Géologie, Glacier Terra-Nova. 4 miles wide. 10 miles long. Feeds Commonwealth Bay from Adélie Land, and becomes Astrolabe Glacier Tongue. First sighted by Dumont d'Urville in 1840. Named by the French in 1950 for the *Astrolabe.*

**Astrolabe Glacier Tongue.** 66°42'S, 140°05'E. 3 miles wide. 4 miles long. The seaward extension of Astrolabe Glacier, at the east end of Géologie Archipelago. Named in association with the glacier.

**Astrolabe Island.** 63°17'S, 58°40'W. 3 miles long. 14 miles NW of Cape

Ducorps, in the Bransfield Strait, off the northern tip of the Antarctic Peninsula. Discovered by Dumont d'Urville in 1837–40 and named by him for his ship, the *Astrolabe*.

**Astrolabe Islet** *see* **Dobrowolski Island**

**Astrolabe Needle.** 64°08′S, 62°36′W. 105 m. A monolith in the water, 1 mile south of Claude Point on Brabant Island. Discovered and named descriptively by Charcot in 1903–5 for the *Astrolabe*.

**Astronaut Glacier.** 73°S, 164°30′E. Flows into the upper part of the Aviator Glacier, just west of Parasite Cone, in Victoria Land. Named by the New Zealanders in 1962–63 in association with the nearby Aeronaut Glacier.

**Islote Astrónomo Romero** *see* **Romero Rock**

**Cape Astrup.** 64°43′S, 63°11′W. Also called Cap Edvind Astrup. Bold, dark-colored bluff marking the northern end of Wiencke Island in the Palmer Archipelago. Discovered during the *Belgica* expedition of 1897–99, and named at that time by Amundsen for his friend, the Arctic explorer, Edvind Astrup.

**Astudillo Glacier.** 64°53′S, 62°51′W. In Graham Land.

**Asuka Camp.** 71°32′S, 24°08′E. The third Japanese scientific station in Antarctica (*see also* **Showa** and **Mizuho**). This one was built in 1986 as a summer station.

**Mount Athelstan.** 70°10′S, 69°16′W. 1,615 m. Partly ice-covered. On the north side of Trench Glacier, on the east coast of Alexander Island. Surveyed in 1936 by the BGLE, and again in 1948 and 1949 by the FIDS, and named by the FIDS for the 10th century king of Wessex.

**Athene Glacier.** 68°56′S, 64°07′W. 10 miles long. Merges with the terminus of Casey Glacier where it flows into Casey Inlet, on the east coast of the Antarctic Peninsula. Surveyed by the FIDS in Nov. 1960, and named by the UK that year for the Greek goddess.

**Atherton Islands.** 62°06′S, 58°59′W. Group of small islands, 2 miles WNW of Bell Point off the west side of King George Island in the South Shetlands. Charted and named in 1935 by personnel on the *Discovery II*.

**Athos Range.** 70°14′S, 65°15′E. Also called Moonlight Range. The most northerly of the ranges in the Prince Charles Mountains, on the west flange of the Amery Ice Shelf. 40 miles long, it was first seen aerially during Operation Highjump, 1946–47, and first visited by Béchervaise's ANARE party in Nov. 1955, and then again by Bewsher's ANARE party of 1956–57. Bewsher named it for the *Three Musketeers* character.

**The *Atka*.** US icebreaker of 6,000 tons, 296-foot hull, 6 diesel engines giving 10,000 hp. Launched in 1943, it was the principal element of the US Navy Antarctic Expedition 1954–55, and scouted the Antarctic coast for potential US bases for the upcoming IGY. Cdr. Glen Jacobsen was captain. It found that Little America had been calved off into the sea in Feb. 1955. It returned to the USA in April 1955. It also took part in Operation Deep Freeze II, III, 60, 62, 64, 66, 68 and 69. On Oct. 31, 1966, it was transferred from the Navy to the Coast Guard, and on Jan. 18, 1967, its name was changed to the *Southwind*.

**Atka Bay** *see* **Byrd Bay**

**Atka Glacier.** 76°40′S, 161°33′E. Just east of Flagship Mountain, flowing into Fry Glacier in Victoria Land. Discovered in 1957 by the NZ Northern Survey Party of the BCTAE, and named by them for the *Atka*.

**Atka Iceport.** 70°35′S, 7°45′W. 10 miles long and wide. Permanent indentation in the front of the Ekström Ice Shelf, on the coast of Queen Maud Land. Named by Cdr. Glen Jacobsen of the *Atka*, which moored here in Feb. 1955, while investigating possible IGY base sites.

**Atkins, Joseph R.** Ordinary seaman on the Wilkes Expedition 1838–42. Joined in Sydney and served the cruise.

**Atkins, Silas.** Seaman on the Wilkes Expedition 1838–42. Joined in the USA. Returned in the *Relief*, 1839.

**Mount Atkinson.** 78°39'S, 85°30'W. In the Sentinel Range.

**Atkinson, Dr. Edward L.** 1882–1929. Edward Leicester Atkinson. Royal Navy surgeon known as "Atch," he was the parasitologist and bacteriologist on the British Antarctic Expedition 1910–13, led by Scott, and was in command at Cape Evans during the last year of the expedition, after Scott's death.

**Atkinson Cliffs.** 71°18'S, 168°55'E. High coastal cliffs, 4 miles long. Between the lower ends of Fendley Glacier and Pitkevich Glacier, on the north coast of Victoria Land. Named by Campbell's Northern Party in 1911–13, during Scott's last expedition, for Dr. Edward L. Atkinson.

**Atlantic-Antarctic Basin** *see* **Atlantic-Indian Basin**

**Atlantic-Indian Basin.** Latitude about 60°S. Approximate longitude between 5°E and 70°E. Also called the Atlantic-Antarctic Basin, Western Indian Antarctic Basin, Atlantic-Indian Antarctic Basin, Valdivia Basin. A submarine depression off the coast of Antarctica, between the Indian and Atlantic Oceans.

**Atlantic Ocean.** Second largest ocean (*see* **Oceans**) in the world, it extends down to Antarctic waters. If one dismisses the notion of the Antarctic Ocean (q.v.), then the Atlantic's southern boundaries are the Antarctic Peninsula, the Weddell Sea, and New Schwabenland.

**Atmosphere.** The Antarctic atmosphere has a low temperature, and contains about one-tenth the water vapor found in more temperate latitudes. It comes from the ice-free regions of the southern oceans, and is transported to Antarctica in the troposphere. Most of it comes down as snow around the margin of the continent. Rainfall is almost unknown. Because of the lack of a water layer present in most atmospheres (which absorbs and radiates to earth long-wave solar radiation), the Antarctic loses much heat energy into space.

**Atoll Nunataks.** 71°21'S, 68°47'W. Group on the north side of Uranus Glacier, 3 miles west of Mount Ariel, in eastern Alexander Island. Named descriptively by the UK.

**Atom Rock.** 66°28'S, 66°26'W. Insular rock, ½ mile NE of Rambler Island in the Bragg Islands (see that entry for the reason for the name of this rock). Surveyed by the FIDS, 1958–59, and named by the UK.

**Atomic energy** *see* **Nuclear power**

**Atriceps Island.** 60°47'S, 45°09'W. The most southerly of the Robertson Islands, 3 miles south of the SE end of Coronation Island, in the South Orkneys. Surveyed by the FIDS in 1948–49, and named by them for the colony of blue-eyed shags *(Phalacrocorax atriceps)* found on the island.

**Attlee Glacier.** 66°13'S, 63°46'W. 8 miles long. Flows to the head of Cabinet Inlet, on the east side of Graham Land, to the north of Bevin Glacier. Charted by the FIDS in Dec. 1947, and named by them for Clem Attlee, British secretary of state for dominion affairs.

**Atwater Hill.** 66°11'S, 66°38'W. 2½ miles south of Benedict Point, on the east side of Lavoisier Island, in the Biscoe Islands. Named by the UK for Wilbur O. Atwater (1844–1907), US physiologist.

**Mount Atwood.** 77°16'S, 142°17'W. 1,180 m. On the west edge of the Clark Mountains, in the Ford Ranges of Marie Byrd Land. Discovered by personnel from West Base during the USAS 1939–41, and named by Byrd for W.W. Atwood, Sr., and his son, W.W. Atwood, Jr., geologists of Clark University.

**Audrey Island.** 68°08'S, 67°07'W. Most southerly of the Debenham Islands, off the west coast of Graham Land. Discovered by the BGLE 1934–37, and named by Rymill for one of Frank Debenham's daughters.

**Augen Bluffs.** 83°30′S, 157°40′E. Between Orr Peak and Isocline Hill, on the west side of Marsh Glacier, in the Miller Range. Named by the Ohio State University Geological Party of 1967–68 for the augengneiss in the rocks here.

**Aughenbaugh Peak.** 82°37′S, 52°49′ W. Over 1,800 m. Almost ¾ mile NE of Neuberg Peak, in the SW part of the Dufek Massif. Named for Nolan B. Aughenbaugh, glaciologist at Ellsworth Station, a member of the first party to visit the Dufek Massif, in Dec. 1957.

**Mount Augusta.** 84°47′S, 163°06′E. 2½ miles east of Mount Wild, at the south end of the Queen Alexandra Range. Discovered on Shackleton's 1907–9 expedition, and named by him for Augusta Edwards, a relative.

**Auguste Island.** 64°04′S, 61°37′W. Flat-topped. Less than one mile long. 4 miles NE of Two Hummock Island in the Gerlache Strait. Discovered by de Gerlache in 1897–99, and named by him for his father.

**Islote Augusto** *see* **Lobodon Island**

**Aurdalen Valley.** 71°42′S, 12°22′E. Small, moraine-covered valley between Gråkammen Ridge and Aurdalsegga Ridge in the Petermann Ranges. Discovered by Ritscher in 1938–39, and later named Aurdalen (the gravel valley) by the Norwegians.

**Aurdalsegga Ridge.** 71°44′S, 12°23′E. 5 miles long. Surmounted by Mount Nikolayev. In the Südliche Petermann Range of the Wohlthat Mountains, just SE of Aurdalen Valley. Discovered by Ritscher in 1938–39, and later named by the Norwegians as Aurdalsegga (the gravel valley ridge).

**Aureole Hills.** 63°45′S, 58°54′W. Two smooth, conical, ice-covered hills, the higher being 1,080 m. Just west of the north end of the Detroit Plateau, on the Trinity Peninsula. Surveyed by the FIDS in 1947–48, and named descriptively by them.

**Aurhø Peak.** 72°08′S, 3°11′W. 1 mile east of Slettfjell in the Ahlmann Ridge of

Queen Maud Land. Name means "gravel height" in Norwegian. There is gravel moraine on the NW side of it.

**Auriga Nunataks.** 70°42′S, 66°38′W. Small group of nunataks in Palmer Land. 21 miles east of Wade Point at the head of the Bertram Glacier. Named by the UK for the constellation.

**Aurkjosen Cirque.** 71°21′S, 13°33′E. Ice-free. On the east side of Lake Unter-See, in the Gruber Mountains. Discovered by Ritscher, 1938–39. Name means "the gravel cove" in Norwegian. There are several old gravel moraines here.

**Aurkleven Cirque.** 71°58′S, 7°31′E. A large cirque, its bottom is largely covered with moraine. Between Kubus Mountain and Klevekampen Mountain in the Filchner Mountains. Name means "the gravel closet" in Norwegian.

**Aurkvaevane Cirques.** 71°52′S, 14°26′ E. Three cirques with moraine-covered floors, indenting the west side of Kvaevefjellet Mountain in the Payer Mountains. Discovered by Ritscher, 1938–39.

**Aurnupen Peak.** 71°59′S, 3°22′W. 1 mile north of Flårjuven Bluff on the Ahlmann Ridge of Queen Maud Land. Name means "the gravel peak" in Norwegian, because of the gravel moraine on the NW side.

**[1]The *Aurora*.** A US sealing brig built at Saybrook, Conn., in 1815. It was registered on July 1, 1820, at 190 tons, and 82 feet long. Under Captain Robert Macy, it was part of the New York Sealing Expedition of 1820–21, which arrived late in the season at the South Shetlands, in Feb. 1821. It was accidentally beached from March 21 to 24, 1821, and was sold for salvage in the Falklands on Aug. 1, 1821, for $1,100.

**[2]The *Aurora*.** A 600-ton Newfoundland sealer with a 98 hp auxiliary engine, it was built in 1876 in Dundee. In 1911 John King Davis took it from London to Hobart to pick up the AAE 1911–14. It was this expedition's ship throughout this time. Afterwards it was left in NZ for when it was next used, by the Ross Sea Party of Shackleton's disastrous British Imperial Transantarctic Expedition of 1914–17, after which the vessel returned to NZ. Its anchor it still embedded in the ground at Cape Evans. Captains: 1911–14 — John King Davis; 1914–15 — Aeneas Mackintosh; 1915–16 — J.R. Stenhouse; 1916–17 — John King Davis.

**¹Mount Aurora.** 78°14′S, 166°20′E. Not to be confused with Aurora Peak or Aurora Heights. 1,040 m. Volcanic. Round-topped. The highest point on Black Island, in the Ross Archipelago. Named by the New Zealanders in 1958–59 for the 20th century ship, the *Aurora*.

**²Mount Aurora** *see* **¹Aurora Peak**

**Aurora Australis.** Display of light patterns filling the sky during the Antarctic night. Electric particles emitted by the sun speed through space and are caught by the earth's magnetic field. They then race toward the earth's magnetic poles, and as they do, they excite the tenuous, ionized gases that form the high layers of the atmosphere. They can be seen every clear night within 20 degrees of the South Magnetic Pole, and occur most frequently around 70°S. Aurorae range in height from 45 miles to 620 miles above the earth, with an average height of 62 miles. Discovered and named by Cook in 1773, they are the counterpart of those other Polar Lights phenomena, the Aurora Borealis in the Arctic.

**The *Aurora Australis*.** Shackleton's magazine produced during the 1907–9 expedition. At first it was to be called "Antarctic Ice Flowers" (*see* the Bibliography).

**Aurora Glacier.** 77°37′S, 167°38′E. One of the 3 major glaciers on Ross Island (cf. Terror Glacier, Barne Glacier). It flows between Mounts Erebus and Terra Nova into the Windless Bight. Named by A.J. Heine (*see* **Mount Heine**) in 1963 for the 20th century ship, the *Aurora*.

**Aurora Heights.** 83°07′S, 157°06′E. Also called Aurora Peak. Not to be confused with the other Aurora Peak. 5

miles long. They border the north side of the Argosy Glacier in the Miller Range. Named by the New Zealanders in 1961–62 for the 20th century ship, the *Aurora*.

**¹Aurora Peak.** 67°23′S, 144°12′E. Also called Mount Aurora, and not to be confused with the other Mount Aurora, or Aurora Heights. 535 m. On the west side of the Mertz Glacier, 4 miles south of Mount Murchison. Discovered by the AAE 1911–14, and named by Mawson for his ship, the *Aurora*.

**²Aurora Peak** *see* **Aurora Heights**

**Austbanen Moraine.** 71°32′S, 12°21′E. A medial moraine in the glacier between Westliche and Mittlere Petermann Ranges in the Wohlthat Mountains, beginning at Svarttindane and going north for 12 miles. Name means "the east path" in Norwegian (cf. Vestbanen, 7 miles to the west).

**Auster Glacier.** 67°12′S, 50°45′E. 2 miles wide. Flows into the SE extremity of Amundsen Bay. Sighted in Oct. 1956 by an ANARE party led by P.W. Crohn, and named for the Auster aircraft used on the expedition.

**Auster Islands.** 67°25′S, 63°50′E. Group of small islands at the NE end of the Robinson Group. 5½ miles north of Cape Daly in Mac. Robertson Land. The Australians named them for the Auster aircraft used on many of their expeditions.

**Auster Pass.** 78°19′S, 162°38′E. In the Royal Society Range, between Mount Huggins and Mount Kempe. It leads into the Skelton Glacier area from McMurdo Sound. Named by the NZ Northern Survey Party of the BCTAE, for the Auster aircraft.

**Auster Point.** 63°49′S, 59°28′W. On the east shore of Charcot Bay on Trinity Peninsula. Named by the UK for the Auster aircraft.

**Austhamaren Peak.** 71°44′S, 26°42′E. 2,060 m. Just east of Byrdbreen in the Sør Rondane Mountains. Photographed by the LCE 1936–37. Name means "the east hammer" in Norwegian.

**Austhjelmen Peak.** 71°42'S, 26°28'E. 1,740 m. 2 miles east of Vesthjelmen Peak in the Sør Rondane Mountains. Photographed by the LCE 1936-37. Name means "the east helmet" in Norwegian.

**Austhovde Headland.** 69°42'S, 37°46' E. Icy headland. Forms the eastern part of Botnneset Peninsula on the south side of Lützow-Holm Bay. Photographed by the LCE 1936-37. Name means "east knoll" in Norwegian.

**Mount Austin.** 74°53'S, 63°10'W. Also called Mount Stephen Austin. 955 m. At the southern end of the Lassiter Coast, where the eastern side of the Antarctic Peninsula meets the Ronne Ice Shelf. It projects into the head of Gardner Inlet. Discovered by the RARE 1947-48, and named by Ronne for Stephen F. Austin, Texan patriot (Ronne's ship was the *Port of Beaumont, Texas*).

**Austin, H.** Crew member on the *Eleanor Bolling,* 1929-30, during the second half of Byrd's 1928-30 expedition.

**Austin, H.F.** Lt. With Foster on the *Chanticleer,* 1828-31.

**Austin Group** *see* **Austin Rocks**

**Austin Peak.** 71°38'S, 165°29'E. In the eastern central sector of the Mirabito Range. Named by the New Zealanders in 1963-64 for William T. Austin, an American that season at McMurdo Station who organized support for the NZ field parties.

**Austin Rocks.** 63°26'S, 61°04'W. Also called the Austin Group. Rocks extending for 3 miles off the SW of Spert Island in the Bransfield Strait. Charted by Foster in 1828-31, and named by him for Lt. H.F. Austin.

**Austin Valley.** 73°30'S, 93°20'W. Small. Ice-filled. On the east side of Avalanche Ridge in the Jones Mountains. Named for Jerry W. Austin of VX-6, here in 1961.

**Austkampane Hills.** 71°47'S, 25°15'E. 2,210 m. A group 5 miles north of Menipa Peak in the Sør Rondane Mountains. Photographed by the LCE 1936-37. Name means "the east crags" in Norwegian.

**Austnes Peninsula.** 66°42'S, 57°17'E. Also called Austnes Point. Short, broad, ice-covered. Forms the SE end of the Edward VIII Plateau, and the north side of the entrance to Edward VIII Bay. Cape Gotley is on the extreme end of the peninsula. Photographed in Jan.-Feb. 1937 by the LCE 1936-37.

**Austnes Point** *see* **Austnes Peninsula**

**Austnestangen** *see* **Cape Gotley**

**Austnuten** *see* **Armstrong Peak**

**Austpynten.** 69°37'S, 38°23'E. Forms the NE end of Padda Island in Lützow-Holm Bay. Photographed by the LCE 1936-37. Name means "east point" in Norwegian.

**The** *Austral.* Argentine ship which relieved Orcadas Station in 1905-6. Captain Lorenzo Saborido. It was wrecked in Dec. 1907, just after leaving Buenos Aires for Booth Island (off the west coast of Graham Land). All passengers were saved by the *Amazone.*

**Bahía Austral** *see* **Gould Bay**

**Austral Island.** 66°30'S, 110°39'E. Small island in the extreme south of Penney Bay in the Windmill Islands, of which it is the southernmost (hence the name).

**Australasian Antarctic Expedition.** 1911-14. Abbreviated as AAE 1911-14. Led by Douglas Mawson. Other personnel: Frank Wild, Dr. S.E. Jones, Andrew D. Watson, Dr. Leslie Whetter, Adams, A.L. Kennedy, G.F. Ainsworth, R. Bage, Frank H. Bickerton, J.H. Blair, John H. Close, Percy E. Correll, G. Dovers, Frank D. Fletcher, C.A. Hoadley, Alfred J. Hodgeman, F.J. Gillies, Percy Gray, Frank L. Stillwell, Cecil Madigan, Ninnis, Azi Webb, Hurley, Mertz, McLean, John King Davis, Harrisson, John C. Hunter, Murphy, Laseron, Walter Hannam, Morton H. Moyes.

Mawson, at first, wanted it to be part of Scott's 1910-13 expedition, but Scott didn't want this. However, he did want

Mawson on his team, but Mawson decided to go it alone. With a £1000 donation from the Australasian Association for the Advancement of Science, and other privately raised funds, Mawson was able to get an expedition together. The men were mostly from Australian and New Zealand universities. They met up at Hobart in late 1911, where they joined their expedition ship, the *Aurora,* commanded by John King Davis, who had brought the ship down from London. On Dec. 2, 1911, they left Hobart Town and established a 5-man station on Macquarie Island, halfway to the Antarctic. They left Macquarie Island on Dec. 23, 1911, and on Jan. 8, 1912, set up their Main Base, at Cape Denison, in Commonwealth Bay. By Jan. 19, 1912, unloading was finished, and the *Aurora* took the Western Base Party of 8, led by Frank Wild, to the Shackleton Ice Shelf, where they set up their main base, "The Grottoes." The *Aurora* then set out on its own mission—to explore the coast as far as Cape Adare in Victoria Land. Meanwhile, back at Main Base, on Cape Denison, Mawson and his 17 men tried the useless airplane (*see* **Airplanes**), and on April 4, 1912, began construction of the radio masts. This chore lasted until Sept. 1, 1912, because the wind was so strong. This was the first Antarctic expedition to use radio. On Aug. 9, 1912, Mawson, Madigan, and Ninnis headed south, and set up a supply depot at Aladdin's Cave. Several sledging parties went out. On Nov. 10, 1912, Mawson, Mertz, and Ninnis set out as the Far Eastern Party, heading for Aladdin's Cave. The conditions were terrifying, and they knew they had to be back by Jan. 15, 1913, when the *Aurora* would be waiting to take them home. Bage, the leader of the Southern Party, which also consisted of Webb and Hurley, headed toward the South Magnetic Pole, and on Dec. 21, 1912, got to within 50 miles of it before returning. Madigan led the Eastern Coastal Party, and on Dec. 18, 1912, they reached their furthest east, 270 miles from Main Base. The Near Eastern Party supported the Far

Eastern Party and the Eastern Coastal Party, for the first few miles of those parties' trips. Frank Bickerton led the Western Party to the highlands west of Main Base, and discovered the first meteorite in Antarctica. They reached 158 miles west of Main Base on Dec. 25, 1912. By Jan. 15, 1913, everyone was back at Main Base, waiting for Mawson's Far Eastern Party. Mawson, Ninnis, and Mertz left Aladdin's Cave on Nov. 17, 1912, with 18 Greenland dogs and 3 sledges. They crossed an incredible number of crevasses in desperate weather. On Dec. 14, 1912, Ninnis disappeared down a crevasse, taking with him one sledge, the tent, most of the food and spare clothing, and the 6 fittest dogs. At this point, having crossed the Mertz and Ninnis Glaciers into George V Land, they were 315 miles from Main Base, and this was their furthest east. There was 10 days food for the 2 of them, and none at all for the dogs. They turned back. The dogs were fed worn-out finnesko shoes, rawhide straps, and mitts. On Dec. 15, 1912, they killed the weakest of the dogs, in order to feed the remaining dogs, and themselves. Ten days later the last animal collapsed, and they killed that one too, and ate it. By Dec. 25, 1912, they were still 160 miles from home, and conditions were disastrous. By Jan. 1, 1913, Mertz was in a bad way. On Jan. 7, 1913, Mertz died, 100 miles from Main Base. Mawson buried him. Mawson's hair was falling out. The soles of his feet were coming off, and he bandaged them back on. His fingers and toes were festered with frostbite. On Jan. 15, 1913, he covered only 1 mile. On Jan. 17, 1913, he fell into a crevasse. He managed to haul himself out, but then he fell back in. Finally, after a considerable time, he dragged himself out again. On Jan. 29, 1913, he arrived at a cairn built by McLean, Hodgeman, and Hurley. It had food in it, and a note, left only a few hours before. Mawson was now only 23 miles from Aladdin's Cave, itself only 5½ miles south of Main Base. He arrived at the cave on Feb. 1, 1913, at 7 p.m., but was trapped in it for a week due to very bad weather. He finally arrived back at Cape Denison. The *Aurora* had sailed. Meanwhile the Western Base Party, led by Wild, on the Shackleton Ice Shelf, had done 5 exploratory journeys in 1912–13, including a 215-mile trip from the Scott Glacier to Gaussberg and back. They had wintered over in 1912, and were relieved by the *Aurora* on Feb. 23, 1913. Six men had stayed at Main Base when the *Aurora* left to pick up Wild's party, in the hope that Mawson's Far Eastern Party was still alive. After Mawson staggered in to Main Base, the 7 men wintered-over in comparative comfort, and the *Aurora* returned on Dec. 12, 1913. On Feb. 5, 1914, the *Aurora* headed for Australia, arriving on Feb. 26, 1914. The AAE made more geographical and scientific discoveries than any previous expedition. It discovered 1,320 miles of land, including the Mertz Glacier, the Denman Glacier, the Scott Glacier, and the Davis Sea. It mapped 800 miles of coastline between 89°E and 153°E, i.e. between Gaussberg and Cape Adare, all along the Adélie Land coast and beyond. And, as mentioned above, it was the first expedition to take an airplane (although it didn't work) and the first expedition to use radio.

**Australia.** Australia claims 42 percent of Antarctica, all in the east (*see* **Australian Antarctic Territory**), based on the explorations of Douglas Mawson. In 1954 Mawson Station was built as a substantive basis for this outrageous claim. During IGY they built Davis Station. After IGY Australia operated the former American station, Wilkes. Other stations include Casey, Law Dome, and Edgeworth David. In 1947 the ANARE (Australian National Antarctic Research Expeditions—q.v.) were created, and in 1947–48 the first ANARE party went down to Antarctica. In 1969 Kay Lindsay became the first Australian woman to reach the Pole. By the 1980s the Australian Antarctic effort was headquartered in Kingston, Tasmania.

**Australian Antarctic Basin** *see* **South Indian Basin**

**Australian Antarctic Territory.** Created in 1933 by the Australian Antarctic Territory Acceptance Act, by which territory was transferred from Great Britain to Australia. Also called The Australian Dependency, it is formed from 2 sectors of the continent, and covers 2,400,000 square miles (excluding ice shelves), and encompasses all land and islands between 60°S and the Pole, and between the longitudes of 160°E and 45°E, with the exception of Adélie Land, which is claimed by France. Its only human inhabitants are the personnel of the research stations.

**Australian Dependency** *see* **Australian Antarctic Territory**

**Australian National Antarctic Research Expeditions.** More commonly known as ANARE. Australia's Antarctic effort, ongoing from 1947. The first ANARE party, led by Stuart Campbell, went down on the *Wyatt Earp*, captained by K.E. Oom, in 1947–48, to look for a base on George V Land. They failed. In 1949 the Australian government set up the Antarctic Division of the Department of External Affairs. This controlled ANARE from that time. From 1948–54 ANARE stayed in the sub–Antarctic islands, with Phillip Law as the most famous of its leaders. In Feb. 1954, they set up Mawson Station, and Law continued to be the man most associated with leading ANARE. The *Kista Dan* is the vessel best remembered for taking the ANARE parties down to Antarctica every year.

**Austranten Rock.** 71°24′S, 14°02′E. Isolated. 2 miles SE of Todt Ridge, at the east end of the Gruber Mountains. Discovered by Ritscher, 1938–39. Name means "east ridge" in Norwegian.

**Austreskorve Glacier.** 71°50′S, 5°40′E. In the Mühlig-Hofmann Mountains. Named by the Norwegians.

**Austria.** The 36th signatory of the Antarctic Treaty, ratified on Aug. 25, 1987. Austria took part in the Filchner Ice Shelf Program.

**Austskjera.** 67°31'S, 64°E. Rocks in water, 5 miles east of Cape Daly, and 2 miles ESE of Safety Island. Photographed by the LCE 1936–37. Name means "the east skerry" in Norwegian.

**Austskotet** *see* **East Stack**

**Austvollen Bluff.** 72°06'S, 3°48'E. Forms the east side of Festninga Mountain, in the Mühlig-Hofmann Mountains of Queen Maud Land. Name means "the east wall" in Norwegian.

**Austvorren Ridge.** 73°06'S, 1°35'W. The more easterly of two rock ridges that go north from the Neumayer Cliffs in Queen Maud Land. Name means "the east jetty" in Norwegian (cf. Vestvorren).

**Autogiros.** Also spelled autogyros, and also known as gyroplanes. Rotary-winged aircraft, designed by Juan de la Cierva (*see* **Cierva Cove**) in 1923. First used in the Antarctic by Byrd during his 1933–35 expedition. His Kellett Autogiro was called *Pep Boy's Snowman!*, and first flew on Sept. 1, 1934. After 10 flights, it crashed on Sept. 25, 1934. They were superseded after 1945 by helicopters (q.v.).

**Automatic Weather Stations** *see* **Weather Stations**

**Automobiles.** *See also* **Tractors.** Shackleton tried an auto on skis in 1908 at Cape Royds, Ross Island. It was unloaded from the *Nimrod* on Jan. 3, 1908, and was a 12–15 hp new Arrol-Johnston, 4-cylinder engine car, with an air-cooling system. It wouldn't ride the snow, kept getting bogged down, but after its final trial run on Sept. 19, 1908, it proved to be a success. It did serviceable work around the base, but then on Dec. 1, 1908, it fell into a crevasse. It was rescued, but was out of commission. Remains of some of the wheels can still be seen at Cape Royds. In 1928 Wilkins took down an Austin car to haul fuel from the ship to the plane during the Wilkins-Hearst expedition of 1928–30. During IGY the USSR used the GAZ 69, a wheeled car made by Gorki Automobile Works, weighing 3,350 pounds,

with 55 hp. It was used for light haulage. The Z1S 151 was also used by the USSR as a repair truck. It weighed 5½ tons. Currently, in order to simplify the spare parts situation, the US uses Ford pick-ups at McMurdo Station.

**Auvert Bay.** 66°14'S, 65°45'W. Also called Auvert Fjord, Evensen Bay. 8 miles wide, it indents the west coast of Graham Land for 3 miles between Cape Evensen and Cape Bellue. Discovered by Charcot, 1908–10.

**Auvert Fjord** *see* **Auvert Bay**

**Avalanche Bay.** 77°01'S, 162°44'E. Little bay on the southern shore of Granite Harbor. 1 mile wide, just SE of Discovery Bluff. Mapped by members of Scott's 1910–13 expedition, and named by them for the avalanches heard nearby.

**Avalanche Corrie.** 60°40'S, 45°22'W. An ice-filled cirque just north of Amphibolite Point on the south coast of Coronation Island in the South Orkneys. Surveyed in 1948–49 by the FIDS, and named by them for the avalanches here.

**Avalanche Ridge.** 73°30'S, 94°22'W. 1 mile long. Extends north from Pillsbury Tower, and separates Basecamp Valley from Austin Valley in the Jones Mountains. Named by the University of Minnesota–Jones Mountains Party here in 1960–61, for the avalanches here.

**Avalanche Rocks.** 66°30'S, 98°01'E. 185 meters high. Between Delay Point and Jones Rocks on the west side of Melba Peninsula. Discovered in Sept. 1912 by the AAE 1911–14. While the men were camped nearby, a huge avalanche took place.

**Islas Avellaneda** *see* **Pitt Islands**

**Mount Avers.** 76°30'S, 145°18'W. 2 miles north of Mount Ferranto, in the Fosdick Mountains. Discovered in Dec. 1929 during Byrd's 1928–30 expedition, and named by Byrd for Henry G. Avers, a mathematician who helped determine that Byrd had, in fact, reached the Pole by plane.

**Avery, Capt.** Commander of the *Lively* during Biscoe's expedition of 1830–32. He took over from Capt. Smith at the Falklands on the way south, probably in Nov. 1830.

**Avery Plateau.** 66°50′S, 65°30′W. 1,830 m. 40 miles long. Ice-covered. Between the Loubet Coast and the Foyn Coast in Graham Land. Surveyed in 1946–47 by the FIDS, and named by them for Capt. Avery.

**Islote Aviador Tenorio** *see* **Tenorio Rock**

**Avian Island.** 67°46′S, 68°54′W. ¾ mile long. 40 meters high. Just off the southern tip of Adelaide Island. Discovered by Charcot, 1908–10. Visited 1948–49 by the FIDS, who named it for the large number of birds here.

**Aviation** *see* **Airplanes**

**Aviation Islands.** 69°16′S, 158°45′E. Group of small rocky islands, 3 miles north of Cape Kinsey and the Wilson Hills. Mapped by the USSR and named by them as Polar Aviation Islands. The name has subsequently been shortened. There is an Adélie penguin rookery here.

**Aviator Glacier.** 73°55′S, 165°15′E. Also called Lady Newnes Glacier. 60 miles long. 5 miles wide. Flows along the west side of the Mountaineer Range, and enters Lady Newnes Bay between Cape Sibbald and Hayes Head, where it forms Aviator Glacier Tongue. Photographed from the air on Dec. 17, 1955, by Trigger Hawkes. Named by the New Zealanders in 1958–59 for the airmen who have served in Antarctica.

**Aviator Glacier Tongue.** 74°S, 165°50′E. The seaward extension of Aviator Glacier into the Ross Sea between Wood Bay and Lady Newnes Bay on the coast of Victoria Land. Named in association with the glacier.

**Aviator Nunatak.** 85°11′S, 168°58′W. The most northerly of 3 large nunataks in the upper Liv Glacier, 4 miles east of Mount Wells. Named by the New Zealanders in 1961–62 for the aviators on Byrd's 1929 flight to the Pole.

**Avicenna Bay.** 64°26′S, 62°23′W. Also called Avicenza Bay. Small bay 1½ miles SW of D'Ursel Point on the east side of Brabant Island. Charted by de Gerlache in 1897–99, and named later by the UK for Arabian physician Avicenna (980–1037).

**Avicenza Bay** *see* **Avicenna Bay**

**Islotes Avión** *see* **Sigma Islands**

**Avsyuk Glacier.** 67°07′S, 67°15′W. On Arrowsmith Peninsula, Graham Land. Flows into Shumskiy Cove. Named by the UK in 1960 for USSR glaciologist Gregori A. Avsyuk.

**The *Awahnee*.** 54-foot ferro cement-hulled, blue and buff highmasted sailing yacht out of Honolulu, Hawaii, built and operated by Robert Griffith and flying the US flag. Griffith, a retired veterinarian from California, now living in NZ, decided to take the summer of 1970–71 and sail around Antarctica with his wife Nancy and their 16-year-old son Reid, and two NZ crewmen. It was in at Palmer Station from Jan. 22–29, 1971, for radio repairs.

**Awl Point.** 63°49′S, 60°37′W. 4 miles NE of Borge Point on the east side of Trinity Island. Named descriptively by the UK in 1960.

**Axel Heiberg Glacier.** 85°25′S, 163°W. Also called Heiberg Glacier. One of the most famous glaciers in the world, it is a 30-mile-long valley glacier flowing from the Polar Plateau between the Herbert Range and Mount Don Pedro Christophersen, on the east coast of the Ross Ice Shelf, which it feeds. Amundsen pioneered this glacier as a short, steep route to the Polar Plateau in Nov. 1911 (Scott used the longer, gentler Beardmore Glacier). Amundsen first named this glacier on Nov. 17, 1911, as Folgefonni, but shortly thereafter renamed it for Consul Axel Heiberg, Norwegian businessman and polar contributor.

**Mount Axtell.** 81°18′S, 85°06′W. 1½ miles SE of Mount Tidd in the Pirrit Hills. Named for William R. Axtell, Jr., USN, cook at Ellsworth Station in 1958.

**Axthelm Ridge.** 69°35'S, 159°02'E. 4 miles long. 1½ miles SE of Parkinson Peak in the Wilson Hills. Named for Cdr. Charles E. Axthelm, USN, commander of the US Naval Support Force, Antarctica, during Operation Deep Freeze 69 and 70. He had been executive officer on the *Glacier* in 1965 and 1966.

**Mount Axworthy.** 73°06'S, 62°44'W. In the NW part of the Dana Mountains, in Palmer Land. Named for Charles S. Axworthy, at Palmer Station, 1965.

**Mount Ayres.** 79°20'S, 156°28'E. 2,500 m. 10 miles south of the west end of the Finger Ridges in the Cook Mountains. Climbed in Dec. 1957 by the Darwin Glacier Party of the BCTAE. Harry H. Ayres was one of the two men who comprised this party.

**Ayres, Harry H.** Doghandler in the NZ depot-laying party under Hillary during the BCTAE, 1957–58. One of the 2 men in the Darwin Glacier Party that year. New Zealand's leading mountain climber of the 1940s.

**Azarashi Rock.** 70°01'S, 38°54'E. Also spelled Azarasi Rock. 1 mile north of Insteckleppane Hills, near the east side of Shirase Glacier, on the coast of Queen Maud Land. Named Azarashi-iwa (seal rock) by the Japanese.

**Azimuth Hill.** 63°45'S, 58°16'W. 85 m. Just south of the mouth of Russell East Glacier, in the area of the Prince Gustav Channel, on Trinity Peninsula. Surveyed by the FIDS in 1946 and named by them for the sun azimuth obtained from here.

**Azimuth Island.** 67°32'S, 62°44'E. The largest of the Azimuth Islands in Holme Bay. Photographed by the LCE 1936–37, and later named by the Australians because this island was included in a triangular survey done by the ANARE in 1959.

**Azimuth Islands.** 67°32'S, 62°44'E. Group of four small islands, the largest being Azimuth Island. NW of Parallactic Islands in Holme Bay, Mac. Robertson Land. Photographed by the LCE 1936–

37, and later named by the Australians for the triangular survey done here by the ANARE in 1959 (the azimuth is a term used in this survey).

**Estrecho Azopardo** *see* **Herbert Sound**

**Aztec Mountain.** 77°48'S, 160°31'E. Over 2,000 m. Pyramidal. Just SW of Maya Mountain, and west of Beacon Valley, in Victoria Land. Named by the New Zealanders in 1958–59 for the resemblance here to Aztec temple structures.

**Azufre Point.** 65°03'S, 63°39'W. Also called Punta Pedro, Wedgwood Point. 3 miles SE of Cape Renard, on the south side of Flandres Bay, on the west coast of Graham Land. Charted by de Gerlache in 1897–99. Named before 1954 by the Argentines (the name means "brimstone").

**Azuki Island.** 69°53'S, 38°56'E. Small island 1 mile west of Rundvågs Head in the SE part of Lützow-Holm Bay. Named Azuki-shima (Azuki bean island) by the Japanese.

**Azure Bay** *see* **Azure Cove**

**Azure Cove.** 65°04'S, 63°35'W. Also known as Azure Bay. 1 mile long. Just east of Cangrejo Cove, in the SW part of Flandres Bay, on the west coast of Graham Land. Discovered and named by de Gerlache, 1897–99, as Baie d'Azur, because of the blue pervading everything he saw here.

**B-9.** A massive iceberg that broke away from the Ross Ice Shelf in early Oct. 1987. 98 miles long and 25 miles wide, it was, at 2,540 square miles, twice the size of Rhode Island. 750 feet thick. It represents two to three times the annual ice discharge of the entire Antarctic continent. It occurred near the Bay of Whales and eliminated the Bay of Whales as a geographical feature in the process. Terry Cooke of McMurdo Station was the first to observe it. By Nov. 1987 it was 53 miles away, and heading north, as all icebergs do from the Antarctic, and it was shrinking as it went. It does/did not pose a threat.

**Babb, Philip.** Private on the Wilkes Expedition 1838–42. Joined in the USA. Served the cruise.

**Babel Rock.** 63°53'S, 61°24'W. North of Intercurrence Island, in the Palmer Archipelago. James Hoseason, in the *Sprightly* in 1824, named the small group to which this rock belongs the Penguin Islands. The largest was later renamed for the noise from the penguin colony here.

**Babis Spur.** 82°13'S, 163°03'E. In the south part of the Nash Range, 6 miles west of Cape Wilson. Named for William A. Babis, oceanographer on the *Eastwind*, 1962–63, and on the *Burton Island*, 1963–64.

**Babordsranten Ridge.** 72°17'S, 3°26' W. 1 mile south of Stamnen Peak, at the SW end of the Ahlmann Ridge in Queen Maud Land. Name means "the port side ridge" in Norwegian.

**Babushkin Island.** 69°06'S, 157°36'E. Also spelled Babuskin Island. 5½ miles north of Archer Point and 5 miles east of Matusevich Glacier Tongue. Named by the USSR for Mikhail S. Babushkin (1893–1938), polar aviator lost in the Arctic.

**Bach, Lt.** Nazi raider-commando officer who took over the Norwegian factory ship *Ole Wegger* on Jan. 13, 1941, not far out from the coast of Queen Maud Land.

**Bach Ice Shelf.** 72°S, 72°W. Irregular in shape. 45 miles long. On the south side of Alexander Island, between Berlioz and Rossini Points. Named by the UK in 1960 for J.S. Bach, the composer.

**Bacharach Nunatak.** 66°41'S, 65°11' W. Overlooks the northern arm of the Drummond Glacier in Graham Land. Named by the UK in 1958 for Alfred L. Bacharach, nutritionist.

**Bachstrom Point.** 65°29'S, 63°51'W. On the NE side of Beascochea Bay, 8 miles SE of Cape Pérez, on the west coast of Graham Land. Charted by the BGLE 1934–37. Named by the UK in 1959 for J.F. Bachstrom, 18th century expert on scurvy.

**Back Bay.** 68°11'S, 67°W. Also called Back Bay Cove. ½ mile wide. The little bay behind Stonington Island, in Marguerite Bay, on the west coast of Graham Land. Surveyed by the USAS 1939–41, and descriptively named in relation to Stonington Island.

**Back Bay Cove** *see* **Back Bay**

**Back Rock** *see* **Sack Island**

**Backdoor Bay.** 77°34'S, 166°12'E. The bay just south of Cape Royds, on Ross Island. Shackleton's 1907–9 expedition unloaded supplies here, and it was named by them because it is at the back of Cape Royds, opposite Front Door Bay.

**Backer Islands.** 74°25'S, 102°40'W. Chain of small islands on the south side of Cranton Bay, off the Walgreen Coast of Marie Byrd Land. They extend for 12 miles. Named for Walter K. Backer, USN, chief construction mechanic at Byrd Station in 1967.

**Backstairs Passage Glacier.** 75°02'S, 162°36'E. Also called Backstairs Passage. 2 miles long. Flows along the north side of Mount Crummer into the Ross Sea, behind Terra Nova Bay, in Victoria Land. David, Mawson, and Mackay used this long route to get to the Larsen Glacier on their way to the South Magnetic Pole in 1908–9, and thus named it.

**Bacon, Frederick A.** Passed midshipman on the *Sea Gull* when it went to Deception Island in March 1839, during the Wilkes Expedition 1838–42.

**Bacteria.** Microorganisms of the class Scizomycetes. There are 1,500 species throughout the world, many of them in Antarctica (*see also* **Flora**). Many bacteriologists have studied in Antarctica.

**Bader Glacier.** 67°37'S, 66°45'W. Flows into Bourgeois Fjord, just south of Thomson Head, on the west coast of Graham Land. Named by the UK in 1958 for Henri Bader, Swiss glaciologist, specialist in the snowflake.

**Arrecife Baeza** *see* **Herald Reef**

**Baffle Rock.** 68°12'S, 67°05'W. A tiny islet 1½ miles west of Stonington Island in Marguerite Bay. Just over ½ mile NW of the western tip of Neny Island, off the west coast of Graham Land. Surveyed in 1947 by the FIDS, and named by them because it is only just visible at the surface at high-tide.

**Cape Bage.** 67°44'S, 146°33'E. Between the Mertz and Ninnis Glaciers, between Murphy and Ainsworth Bays, on the coast of East Antarctica. Discovered in 1912 by the AAE 1911–14, and named by Mawson for Lt. R. Bage.

**Bage, R.** Lt. Astronomer/assistant magnetician/recorder of tides on the AAE 1911–14. He led the Southern Party to the area of the South Magnetic Pole in 1912, accompanied by Webb and Hurley.

**Baggott Ridge.** 70°19'S, 64°19'E. Snow-covered. 1½ miles west of Baldwin Nunatak. 7 miles SSW of Mount Starlight in the Prince Charles Mountains of Mac. Robertson Land. Named by the Australians for P.J. Baggott, radio officer at Mawson Station in 1965.

**Bagnold Point.** 67°02'S, 67°29'W. Between the Gunnel Channel and Shumskiy Cove on Arrowsmith Peninsula, in Graham Land. Named by the UK in 1960 for Ralph A. Bagnold, British expert on deserts.

**Mount Bagritskogo** *see* **Ormehausen Peak**

**Mount Bagshawe.** 71°27'S, 67°06'W. 2,225 m. The southernmost and highest of the Batterbee Mountains. 8 miles inland from George VI Sound, on the west coast of Palmer Land. Photographed aerially on Nov. 23, 1935, by Ellsworth. Surveyed in 1936 by the BGLE. Named by the UK in 1954 for Sir Arthur W.G. Bagshawe, tropical medicine expert and supporter of the BGLE 1934–37.

**Bagshawe, Thomas W.** b. April 18, 1901. "Geologist" on the infamous British Imperial Expedition of 1920–21. He stayed behind to winter over with his enemy, M.C. Lester! Wrote *Two Men in the Antarctic* in 1939, and also wrote articles on penguins.

**Bagshawe Glacier.** 64°56'S, 62°38'W. Flows from the NE side of Mount Theodore into Lester Cove, at Andvord Bay, on the west coast of Graham Land. Discovered by de Gerlache in Feb. 1898. Surveyed by Ken Blaiklock from the *Norsel* in April 1955. Named by the UK for Thomas Bagshawe.

**Bahamonde Point.** 63°19'S, 57°55'W. Also called Punta Bahamondes. Marks the west end of Schmidt Peninsula on Trinity Peninsula. Charted by the Chileans in 1947–48 and named by them for 1st Lt. Arturo Bahamonde Calderón, engineer of the expedition that year.

**The *Bahía Aguirre*.** Argentine vessel which took part in various Antarctic expeditions sent from Argentina: 1951–52 (captain unknown), 1952–53 (Capt. Eugenio Fuenterrosa), 1953–54 (captain unknown), 1954–55 (Capt. Benigno Ignacio Varela), 1955–56 (Capt. David O. Funcia), 1956–57 (Capt. José C.T. Carbone). An Argentine vessel of this name put in at Palmer Station in the 1970–71 season.

**The *Bahía Buen Suceso*.** Argentine vessel which took part in various Antarctic expeditions from Argentina: 1950–51 (Capt. Sánchez Moreno), 1951–52 (Capt. Luís M. Iriate), 1952–53 (Capt. Juan C. Balcazar), 1953–54 (captain unknown), 1954–55 (Capt. Aurelio C. López de Bertodano).

**The *Bahía Paraíso*.** Mountain Travel's tour vessel to Antarctic waters until 1989. Bought by the Argentines in 1979 as a polar research/supply vessel, it was not a tourist ship as such. Its main purpose was to supply food and fuel to the Argentine scientific stations on the Antarctic Peninsula, but was chartered by the American tour company. Built at a cost of $50 million in 1979, it was owned by the Argentine Antarctic Institute and operated by the Argentine navy. It had a reinforced twin steel hull, was 10,000 tons, 433 feet long, and 63½ feet wide. It had a 23½-foot draft, 2 diesel engines of 8 cylinders—6,000 hp each. Maximum speed 17 knots. It could carry up to 80 passengers and had modern equipment

— 3 landing craft-type launches (EDPVs), 2 Zodiacs, 2 rowboats, 2 rescue power boats, 2 Sikorsky Sea King helicopters, and life rafts. On Jan. 28, 1989, it ran aground and spilled oil (*see* **Pollution**), and then capsized.

**The *Bahía Thetis*.** Argentine vessel used on that country's 1956–57 Antarctic expedition.

**Baia Terra Nova Station.** 72°46′S, 164°07′E. Italian scientific station established at Terra Nova Bay, Victoria Land, as a year-round establishment. Built over the Dec. 1988–Feb. 1989 period, it was Italy's first Antarctic station.

**The *Baikal*.** USSR motor ship carrying passengers to Antarctica.

**Mount Bailey.** 69°58′S, 63°13′W. 1,445 m. South of Anthony Glacier. 6 miles WSW of Lewis Point, in the Eternity Range of the Antarctic Peninsula. Charted in 1936 by the BGLE and again in 1947 by the Weddell Coast Sledge Party (q.v.). Named by Ronne for Clay Bailey.

**Bailey, Claude E.** Cdr., USN. Captain of the *Henderson* during Operation Highjump, 1946–47.

**Bailey, Clay W.** USN. One of the shore party on Byrd's 1933–35 expedition. He was at Little America III (West Base) during the USAS 1939–41. He helped to outline the radio requirements of the RARE 1947–48.

**Bailey, Dana K.** He succeeded Eric T. Clarke as physicist for the second, i.e. 1940–41, season of the USAS 1939–41.

**Bailey Glacier** *see* **Friederichsen Glacier**

**Bailey Island** *see* **Bailey Peninsula**

**Bailey Nunatak.** 75°40′S, 140°02′W. 1,010 m. On the north flank of White Glacier, between Partridge Nunatak and Wilkins Nunatak, in Marie Byrd Land. Named for Andrew M. Bailey, meteorologist at Byrd Station in 1963.

**Bailey Peninsula.** 66°17′S, 110°32′E. Also called Rocky Peninsula. Almost 2 miles long. 1 mile wide. Between Newcomb Bay and O'Brien Bay, at the east side of the Windmill Islands, on the

Budd Coast of Wilkes Land. Cartographers working from Operation Highjump photos assumed it to be an island, and named it Bailey Island, for Claude Bailey. It was redefined by the Wilkes Station party in 1957.

**Bailey Ridge.** 77°12′S, 145°02′W. 4 miles long. Between Mount Blades and the Fleming Peaks, in the Ford Ranges of Marie Byrd Land. Discovered aerially during Byrd's 1933–35 expedition, and named by the USAS 1939–41 for Clay Bailey.

**Bailey Rocks.** 66°17′S, 110°32′E. Small chain of rocks, including Nicholson Island, in the Windmill Islands. Named by Carl Eklund in 1957 for Carl T. Bailey, USN, aerographer's mate 1st class at Wilkes Station in 1957.

**Baillie Peak.** 83°22′S, 161°E. Over 2,800 m. 2 miles SSE of Mount Angier, in the Moore Mountains of the Queen Elizabeth Range. Named by the Ohio State University Geological Party of 1967–68, for Ralph J. Baillie, field assistant with the party.

**Baillieu Peak.** 67°51′S, 60°46′E. 1,380 m. 25 miles south of Cape Bruce, and 10 miles WSW of Pearce Peak. Discovered in Feb. 1931 by the BANZARE, and named by Mawson for Clive Baillieu, a patron of the expedition.

**Baily Head.** 62°58′S, 60°30′W. An indentation in the east side of Deception Island, between South East Point and Rancho Point. This is *not* synonymous with Rancho Point.

**Bailys Island** *see* **Ohlin Island**

**Mount Bain.** 66°33′S, 65°26′W. Also called Monte Villarrica. 2,090 m. Between the Hopkins and Erskine Glaciers on the west coast of Graham Land. Named by the UK in 1958 for James S. Bain, polar food specialist in London.

**Bain Crags.** 70°30′S, 71°45′E. On the south part of the west side of Gillock Island, in the Amery Ice Shelf. Visited in Jan. 1969 by J.H.C. Bain, ANARE geologist, for whom the Australians named this feature.

**Bain Nunatak.** 71°06'S, 71°35'E. One of the Manning Nunataks, on the east side of the Amery Ice Shelf. Named for J.H.C. Bain, weather observer at Mawson Station in 1969.

**Baines Nunatak.** 80°19'S, 23°59'W. In the Shackleton Range.

**Bainmedart Cove.** 70°51'S, 68°03'E. 1 mile long. In eastern Radok Lake, in the Prince Charles Mountains. It leads to Pagodroma Gorge, which joins Radok Lake and Beaver Lake. Three ANARE geologists surveyed here in Jan.–Feb. 1969—J.H.C. Bain, A. Medvecky, and J. Dart; and the name given by the Australians to this feature is a compound of all their names.

**Punta Baja** see **Penfold Point**

**Båken Nunatak.** 71°18'S, 2°57'W. A small, isolated nunatak which surmounts the northern part of Båkeneset Headland in Queen Maud Land. Name means "the beacon" in Norwegian.

**Båkenesdokka Valley.** 71°26'S, 3°03' W. Ice-filled. On the east side of Roberts Knoll. It runs into the Jelbart Ice Shelf, in Queen Maud Land. Name means "the beacon cape depression" in Norwegian.

**Båkeneset Headland.** 71°23'S, 2°48' W. Ice-covered. Båken Nunatak stands on the seaward end. It forms the NW end of the Ahlmann Ridge in Queen Maud Land. Name means "the beacon cape" in Norwegian.

**Mount Baker.** 84°44'S, 172°21'W. 1,480 m. In the SE part of the Gabbro Hills, near the edge of the Ross Ice Shelf. On the west side of Gough Glacier, 6 miles east of Amphibole Peak. Discovered by Albert Crary's Ross Ice Shelf Traverse Party of 1957–58, and named by Crary for Gladys E. Baker, who analyzed the lichens brought back by Byrd's 1933–35 expedition.

**Baker, Francis.** Ordinary seaman on the Wilkes Expedition 1838–42. Joined in the USA. Served the cruise.

**Baker Glacier.** 72°46'S, 169°15'E. Flows into Whitehall Glacier just north of Martin Hill in the Victory Mountains.

Named for John R. Baker, biologist at Hallett Station in 1967–68 and 1968–69.

**Baker Nunatak.** 85°23'S, 124°40'W. 1 mile NW of Mount Brecher in the northern Wisconsin Range. Named for Travis L. Baker, meteorologist at Byrd Station in 1961.

**Baker Ridge.** 83°20'S, 55°40'W. In the north part of the Washington Escarpment, in the Neptune Range. Named for Clifford E. Baker, aviation electronics technician at Ellsworth Station in 1958.

**Baker Rocks.** 74°14'S, 164°45'E. 2 miles west of Wood Bay, and 7 miles north of Mount Melbourne, on the coast of Victoria Land. Named for Billy A. Baker, radioman at McMurdo Station in 1963 and 1967.

**Baker Three Glacier** see **Lambert Glacier**

**Bakewell, William L.** American who posed as a Canadian to go on the British Imperial Transantarctic Expedition of 1914–17. The only American on the expedition, he sailed as an able seaman on the *Endurance*. He later returned to the USA to become a farmer in Michigan.

**Bakewell Island.** 75°40'S, 18°55'W. A small, ice-covered island near the Princess Martha Coast. East of Lyddan Island, in the southern part of the Riiser-Larsen Ice Shelf. Discovered aerially on Nov. 5, 1967, by VX-6. Named for William L. Bakewell.

**Bakhallet Slope.** 72°08'S, 2°56'E. An ice slope between Terningskarvet Mountain and Brugda Ridge in the Gjelsvik Mountains of Queen Maud Land. Name means "the back slope" in Norwegian.

**Mount Bakker.** 70°19'S, 64°36'E. Isolated. 6½ miles SSE of Mount Starlight, in the Prince Charles Mountains. Named by the Australians for F.C.R. Bakker, radio supervisor at Davis Station in 1964.

**Bakkesvodene Crags.** 71°56'S, 6°32'E. They overlook the eastern side of Lunde Glacier in the Mühlig-Hofmann Mountains of Queen Maud Land. Name means "the hill slopes" in Norwegian.

**Bakutis, Fred E.** Rear Admiral, USN. Commander of Operation Deep Freeze from 1965 to 1967.

**Bakutis Coast.** 74°30′S, 120°W. Between the Hobbs Coast and the Kohler Range, on the coast of Marie Byrd Land. It actually extends from 74°42′S, 127°05′W (opposite the eastern part of Dean Island) to Cape Herlacher. Discovered by the USAS 1939–41. Named for Fred Bakutis.

**¹The *Balaena*.** 400-ton Dundee whaler which led the Dundee Whaling Expedition of 1892–93. Capt. Alexander Fairweather. William S. Bruce was the naturalist aboard.

**²The *Balaena*.** British whaling factory ship belonging to United Whalers Ltd. In 1946–47 it was in the waters off East Antarctica, doing not only whaling but also scientific work and aerial spotting, in an expedition led by Rupert Trouton, director of the expedition. Reider Pedersen was captain of the vessel, and H.H. Lamb was meteorologist. Also on board was John Grierson, the filmmaker. The ship operated off the coast from Jan.–Feb. 1947. It was named for the original *Balaena*.

**Balaena Islands.** 66°S, 111°07′E. A small group of rocky islands off the Budd Coast. 10 miles NE of Cape Folger. They include Thompson Island. Named for the 1947 ship, the *Balaena*.

**Balaena Valley.** 63°20′S, 56°23′W. Ice-filled. East of Suspiros Bay in the western part of Joinville Island. Surveyed by the FIDS in 1953–54. Named by the UK in 1956 for the original *Balaena*.

**Punta Balcarce** *see* **Fildes Point**

**Mount Balch.** 65°16′S, 63°59′W. Also called Mount Swift Balch. Between Mount Peary and Mount Mill, on the west coast of Graham Land. Has several sharp peaks, the highest being 1,105 m. Discovered by Charcot in 1908–10, and named by him for Edwin Swift Balch, US authority on Antarctic exploration (*see also* the Bibliography).

**Balch Glacier.** 66°50′S, 64°48′W. 9 miles long. On the east coast of Graham Land. Flows into Mill Inlet. Surveyed by the FIDS in 1946–47, and named by them as East Balch Glacier. Another feature nearby was called West Balch Glacier. A later, 1957, survey showed no connection between the two glaciers as had been thought. East Balch Glacier became Balch Glacier, and the western one became Drummond Glacier. Named for Edwin Swift Balch (*see* **Mount Balch**).

**Mount Balchen.** 85°22′S, 166°12′W. 3,085 m. 6 miles east of the summit of Mount Fridtjof Nansen, in the Herbert Range. Named by the New Zealanders in 1961–62 for Bernt Balchen. Not to be confused with Balchen Mountain.

**Balchen, Bernt.** b. 1900, Norway. d. Oct. 18, 1973, Mount Kisco, NY. A lieutenant in the Royal Norwegian Naval Air Force. He went on two Amundsen-Ellsworth Arctic aerial explorations, and was on the transatlantic flight of the *America*—all before 1928. In that year he became chief pilot on Byrd's 1928–30 Antarctic expedition. On Jan. 27, 1929, he and Byrd crossed the Ross Ice Shelf by plane, Balchen piloting, and between March 7 and 10, 1929, he, June, and Gould were trapped in the Rockefeller Mountains (*see* **Byrd's 1928–30 expedition** and **Airlifts**). He was the pilot of the *Floyd Bennett* during Byrd's historic flight to the South Pole in 1929. They took off from Little America at 3:29 a.m., on Nov. 28, 1929, and at 1:15 p.m. reached the Pole. They were back at Little America at 8:20 p.m. The flight took 15 hours and 51 minutes. (Of the two previous leaders to reach the Pole—by land—Amundsen had taken 99 days for the round trip. Scott had never made it back.) Balchen became a US citizen in 1931, and was Ellsworth's chief pilot on his first two Antarctic expeditions, 1933–34 and 1934–35. One of the leading experts on polar flying, he helped build Scandinavian Airlines after World War II. He retired as a colonel in the USAF.

**Balchen Glacier.** 76°26′S, 145°30′W. Also called Bernt Balchen Glacier, Bernt Balchen Valley. A crevassed glacier between the Phillips Mountains and the Fosdick Mountains of Marie Byrd Land. It flows into Block Bay on the Ruppert Coast, between the Hobbs Coast and Guest Peninsula. Discovered on Dec. 5, 1929, by Byrd's 1928–30 expedition, and named by Byrd for Bernt Balchen.

**Balchen Mountain.** 72°S, 27°12′E. Also called Balchenfjella. 2,820 m. At the east side of Byrdbreen in the Sør Rondane Mountains. Named by the Norwegians for Bernt Balchen. Not to be confused with Mount Balchen.

**Balchenfjella** *see* **Balchen Mountain**

**Balchunas Pass.** 75°46′S, 128°45′W. Between Mount Flint and Mount Petras in the McCuddin Mountains of Marie Byrd Land. Named for Robert C. Balchunas, USN, part of Operation Deep Freeze as executive officer for Antarctic Support Activities, 1971, 1972, 1973.

**Bald Head.** 63°38′S, 57°36′W. Also called Cabo Circular. An ice-free headland, 8 miles SW of View Point on the south side of Trinity Peninsula. First seen in 1902-3 by Dr. J. Gunnar Andersson's party during the Nordenskjöld expedition of 1901–4. Charted by the FIDS in 1945, and named descriptively by them.

**Balder Point.** 66°27′S, 63°45′W. Between Frigga Peak and Cabinet Inlet, on the east coast of Graham Land. Charted in 1947 by the FIDS, and named by them for the Norse god.

**Mount Baldr.** 77°35′S, 160°34′E. Also called Mount Baldur. West of Mount Thor and south of the Wright Upper Glacier in the Asgard Range of Victoria Land. Named by the New Zealanders in 1958–59 for the Norse god.

**Baldred Rock.** 60°44′S, 44°26′W. In Fitchie Bay, Laurie Island, in the South Orkneys. Just off the south side of Ferrier Peninsula, ¾ mile ESE of Graptolite Island. Mapped by Bruce in 1902-4, and later named Bass Rock because of its

similarity to the Scottish rock of that name. Renamed in 1954 by the UK for the saint who lived on the original Bass Rock in the 6th century.

**Mount Baldur** *see* **Mount Baldr**

**Mount Baldwin.** 72°15′S, 163°18′E. 5 miles south of Smiths Bench, in the Freyberg Mountains of Oates Land. Named for T.T. Baldwin, transport specialist here in 1959–60.

**Baldwin, A.S.** Acting master on the *Porpoise* during the Wilkes Expedition 1838–42.

**Baldwin, George E.** Sgt. US Marines. Photographer on Flight 8A which flew over the South Pole (q.v. for further details) on Feb. 16, 1947.

**Baldwin Bluff.** 72°06′S, 169°27′E. On the SW side of Ironside Glacier. 5 miles SW of the summit of Mount Whewell, in the Admiralty Mountains. Named for Howard A. Baldwin, biologist at McMurdo Station, 1966–67.

**Baldwin Glacier.** 85°05′S, 177°W. Flows from the icefalls west of Mount Rosenwald, and enters the Shackleton Glacier south of Mount Heekin. Discovered aerially on Feb. 16, 1947, during Operation Highjump, 1946–47 (*see* **South Pole** for details of that flight). Named for George E. Baldwin.

**Baldwin Nunatak.** 70°19′S, 64°24′E. 6½ miles SSW of Mount Starlight in the Prince Charles Mountains. Named by the Australians for J.W. Baldwin, weather observer at Mawson Station in 1965.

**Baldwin Peak.** 64°24′S, 60°45′W. Between Lilienthal Glacier and Mount Berry in northern Graham Land. Named by the UK in 1960 for Thomas S. Baldwin (1860–1923), American inventor of parachute vents.

**Baldwin Point.** 66°50′S, 120°48′E. On the Sabrina Coast of Wilkes Land.

**Baldwin Rocks.** 66°24′S, 98°45′E. 5 miles NW of Watson Bluff on the north side of David Island. Charted by the AAE 1911-14 and named by Mawson for Joseph M. Baldwin of the Melbourne Observatory.

**Baldwin Valley.** 77°18′S, 162°20′E. Ice-filled. In the Saint Johns Range, NW of Pond Peak, in Victoria Land. Named for Russell R. Baldwin, USN, in charge of the Airfield Maintenance Branch at McMurdo Station in 1962.

**Mount Baleen.** 65°36′S, 62°12′W. 910 m. Pyramidal when viewed from the Larsen Ice Shelf. Between the Rachel and Starbuck Glaciers on the east coast of Graham Land. Named by the UK for the baleen whales.

**Baleen whales.** There are seven species of baleen whales, or whalebone whales, which inhabit Antarctic waters (*see* **Whales** for further details). The baleen is a structure in the mouth of a toothless whale, used for straining plankton and krill.

**Mount Balfour.** 69°19′S, 67°13′W. 1,010 m. At the mouth of Fleming Glacier, close to the junction with the Wordie Ice Shelf on the west side of the Antarctic Peninsula. Surveyed by the BGLE in 1936, and again in 1948 by the FIDS, and named for Henry Balfour, president of the Royal Geographic Society, 1936–38.

**Lake Balham.** 77°26′S, 160°57′E. A small lake near the center of Balham Valley in Victoria Land. Named in 1964 by American geologist here, Parker Calkin, for its location in the valley.

**Balham, Dr. Ron.** NZ marine biologist in the NZ party of the BCTAE 1957–58.

**Balham Valley.** 77°24′S, 161°06′E. A dry valley between the Insel Range and Apocalypse Peaks, in southern Victoria Land. Named by the New Zealanders in 1958–59 for Ron Balham.

**Balin Point.** 60°42′S, 45°36′W. Marks the north side of the entrance to Borge Bay, on the east side of Signy Island, in the South Orkneys. Named before 1933.

**Balin Rocks.** 60°42′S, 45°36′W. A small group just south of Balin Point, on the east side of Signy Island, in the South Orkneys. Named before 1933.

**Balish Glacier.** 79°25′S, 84°30′W. 18 miles long. Flows from the Soholt Peaks and enters Splettstoesser Glacier, just NE of Springer Peak, in the Heritage Range. Named for Cdr. Daniel Balish, VX-6 executive officer, 1965, and commander of VX-6 in 1967.

**Ball, James L.** Lt. (jg) USN. Co-pilot of the plane which found the survivors of the crashed Martin Mariner, *George-I*, in 1947, during Operation Highjump. He operated off the *Pine Island*.

**Ball Stream.** 77°26′S, 163°44′E. A meltwater stream. 2 miles west of Marble Point. It issues from the front of the Wilson Piedmont Glacier, and flows into Surko Stream, just west of where the latter enters Arnold Cove, in southern Victoria Land. Named by visiting scientist Robert L. Nichols in 1957–58 for Donald G. Ball, soil physicist.

**Ballance Peak.** 76°46′S, 159°29′E. The highest peak at the southern end of the Allan Hills, in Victoria Land. Named by the New Zealand Allan Hills Expedition of 1964 for P.F. Ballance, geologist with the expedition.

**Mount Ballard.** 75°12′S, 70°05′W. In the western part of the Sweeney Mountains in Ellsworth Land. Named for G.E. Ballard, equipment operator at Amundsen-Scott South Pole Station in 1963.

**Ballard Spur.** 82°08′S, 163°40′E. 5 miles north of Cape Wilson, on the east side of the Nash Range. Named for Thomas B. Ballard, aurora scientist at Hallett Station in 1961.

**Balleny, John.** British whaling captain who, from 1798–1831 plied the seas in British ships, and from 1831 to 1838 presumably in foreign ships, as captain most of the time. In 1838–39 he was working for Enderby Brothers as leader of the expedition to Antarctica involving the *Eliza Scott* and the *Sabrina*. He discovered the Balleny Islands on Feb. 9, 1839, and the Sabrina Coast on March 2, 1839. He reached 69°02′S, 174°E, the furthest south in these longitudes up to that time, on Feb. 1, 1839.

**Balleny Basin.** 66°30′S, 175°E. A submarine feature in the Pacific Ocean, beyond the Ross Sea. Named for John Balleny.

**Balleny Fracture Zone.** Centers on 62° S, 156°E. A fracture zone under the ocean, out to sea from the Oates Coast. Named for the Balleny Islands.

**Balleny Islands.** 66°55′S, 163°20′E. Group of heavily glaciated islands, volcanic in origin, 150 miles NNE of Cape Kinsey, Oates Land. They extend for 100 miles on and near the Antarctic Circle. They consist of 2 larger islands, Young Island and Sturge Island, and 3 smaller ones, Sabrina Island, Borradaile Island, and Row Island. Also included in the group are the Seal Rocks, Beale Pinnacle, and The Monolith. Discovered by John Balleny on Feb. 9, 1839. Capt. Freeman from the expedition landed on the islands. Named for Balleny by Capt. Beaufort, hydrographer to the Admiralty.

**Balleny Trough.** A submarine trough centering on 66°S, 158°E.

**Islotes Ballesteros** *see* **Psi Islands**

**Balloon Bight.** In the area where the Bay of Whales used to be. Thomas Williamson named it Discovery Nook in 1902 during the early stages of the Royal Society Expedition. It disappeared in the calving process sometime after 1904.

**Balloons.** Scott was the first person to see Antarctica from the air, when he went up in a captive army balloon called *Eva,* to a height of 790 feet on Feb. 4, 1902, at the Bay of Whales. Shackleton went up next, to take photos. On the *Discovery* were six enormous gas tanks from which to fill *Eva,* as well as the other models of the army's captive balloons. *Eva* was inflated with 8,500 cubic feet of gas from 19 cylinders. Scott's balloon section consisted of Skelton, Shackleton, Lashly, Kennar, and Heald, and had been trained at Aldershot in England, under Col. Templar. Von Drygalski used one on his expedition around the same time. Finn Ronne used balloons in the 1940s. The Supernova Observer Project took place in Jan. 1988. On Jan. 8, 1988, just after noon, the Antarctic's largest

ever high-altitude, helium-filled balloon went up from Williams Field, McMurdo, to a height of 115,000 feet, carrying a gamma ray detector to study emissions from Supernova 1987A in outer space. It also tested the detector. The balloon, 11.6 million cubic feet, and made of very thin plastic, rose at 1,000 feet per minute, and after 3 days it came down 200 miles from Vostok Station (it had been due to stay up 21 days). US pilots went out to retrieve the information from its gondola on Jan. 13, 1988.

**Mount Ballou.** 73°14′S, 163°03′E. 2,900 m. Forms the south end of Pain Mesa, and the north side of the entrance to Pinnacle Gap, in the Mesa Range of Victoria Land. Named for Cdr. Justin G. Ballou, USN, at McMurdo Station in 1966.

**The *Bam.*** The *BAM* was a USSR tanker sometimes in the Antarctic.

**Bamse Mountain.** 72°15′S, 22°18′E. 2,500 m. 11 miles west of Mount Nils Larsen in the Sør Rondane Mountains. Named Bamsefjell (bear mountain) by the Norwegians.

**Mount Banck.** 64°54′S, 63°03′W. Also called Monte Guillermo, Monte William, Monte Laprida. 675 m. Conspicuous. Made of red rock. Just west of Mascías Cove, on the west coast of Graham Land. Discovered by de Gerlache in 1898 and considered by him to be an island. He named it Île Banck. It was later redefined as a small peninsula whose main feature is this mountain.

**Bancroft Bay.** 64°34′S, 61°52′W. Between Charlotte Bay and Wilhelmina Bay on the west coast of Graham Land. Named by the UK in 1960 for Anthony D. Bancroft, FIDS surveyor here during the FIDASE 1955–57.

**Banded Bluff.** 85°20′S, 169°30′W. 4 miles long. 3 miles SE of McKinley Nunatak. Named for the alternating bands of snow and rock here.

**Banded Peak.** 85°03′S, 166°05′W. 1,400 m. 3 miles NE of Mount Fairweather in the Duncan Mountains. It

It has a snow band across the south face, and for this reason was named by the New Zealanders in 1963–64.

**Banding birds.** Birds are banded to study their movements. Studies show that some Antarctic birds travel the world. Others cross the Antarctic continent. Some skuas are banded with colored, plastic anklets, while some are dyed scarlet. Giant fulmars and penguins are banded too.

**Bandstone Block.** 71°40′S, 68°12′W. A rock on land, 2 miles north of Triton Point, at the mouth of Venus Glacier, on the east coast of Alexander Island. Surveyed in 1949 by the FIDS, who named this rectangular block of sandstone for its conspicuous sedimentary bands.

**Bandy Island.** 75°04′S, 137°49′W. Small and ice-covered. In Hull Bay, 1½ miles west of Lynch Point on the coast of Marie Byrd Land. Named for Orville L. Bandy (1917–1973), geologist who studied several times in the Antarctic since 1961.

**Mount Banfield** *see* **Mount Gjeita**

**Banks.** Or marine banks. Rocky or sandy submerged elevations of the sea floor with a summit not more than 650 feet below the surface but not so high as to endanger navigation (if they become dangerous they are called shoals).

**BANZARE** *see* **British, Australian and New Zealand Antarctic Research Expedition 1929–31**

**Banzare Coast.** 67°S, 126°E. Also called Banzare Land. Between Cape Southard (122°05′E) and Cape Morse (130°10′E), just south of the Voyeykov Ice Shelf, in Wilkes Land. Discovered aerially by the BANZARE in the 1930–31 season, and named by Mawson for his expedition.

**Banzare Land** *see* **Banzare Coast**

**Baptiste, John.** Seaman on the Wilkes Expedition 1838–42. Joined at Valparaiso. Served the cruise.

**The *Baquedano*.** Chilean vessel which took part in 2 Antarctic expeditions sent by that country: 1955–56 (Capt. Wilfredo Bravo), and 1956–57 (Capt. Jorge Paredes).

**Bar Island.** 68°17′S, 67°12′W. A long, low, rocky islet ¼ mile off the west end of Red Rock Ridge on the Antarctic Peninsula. Surveyed by the BGLE in 1936, and again by the FIDS in 1948–49, and named by the FIDS for its shape.

**The *Barão de Teffe*** *see* **Thala Dan**

**Barbara Island.** 68°08′S, 67°06′W. Largest and most northerly of the Debenham Islands, in the area of Stonington Island, off the west coast of Graham Land. Discovered by the BGLE 1934–37, and named by them for one of Frank Debenham's daughters (*see* **Debenham Islands**).

**Barbaro Point** *see* **Leniz Point**

**Barbedes, Peter.** Crewman on the *Jacob Ruppert*, 1933–34.

**Barber, Noel.** Correspondent for the *London Daily Mail*, he became the first Englishman to reach the South Pole since Scott's party, the first Englishman to reach the Pole and get back alive, and one of the first 50 people ever to stand at the Pole. He was covering the BCTAE 1955–58 at the time. Altogether he made 3 trips to the South Pole, and wrote *White Desert* (*see* the Bibliography), an account of his experiences during the IGY.

**Barber Glacier.** 70°26′S, 162°42′E. Rises just east of Mount Bruce in the Bowers Mountains and flows to the coast between the Stuhlinger Ice Piedmont and Rosenau Head. Named for Capt. Don W. Barber, in Antarctica in 1967 and 1968 as construction and equipment officer.

**Barbière Island.** 65°11′S, 64°10′W. A small island, the most southerly of the islands lying off the south end of Petermann Island in the Wilhelm Archipelago. Discovered and named by Charcot in 1908–10.

**The Barchans.** 65°14′S, 64°20′W. A group of small, snow-capped islands marking the western end of the Argentine Islands. Charted by the BGLE 1934–37 and named by them because the snow caps resemble barchans.

**Barclay Bay.** 62°33′S, 60°58′W. Between Cape Shirreff and Essex Point, on the north side of Livingston Island, in the South Shetlands. Named Barclay's Bay before 1825. The name was later shortened slightly.

**Barclay's Bay** *see* **Barclay Bay**

**Barcroft Islands.** 66°27′S, 67°10′W. A group of small islands and rocks, including Bedford Island and Irving Island. 5 miles in extent. Just south of Watkins Island, in the Biscoe Islands. Named by the UK for Sir Joseph Barcroft (1872–1947), Irish physiologist and specialist in cold.

**Barcus Glacier.** 74°15′S, 62°W. In the Hutton Mountains. Flows to the north of Mount Nash and Mount Light, into Keller Inlet in Palmer Land. Named for James R. Barcus, ionosphere physicist at Byrd Station in 1966–67 and 1967–68.

**Bardell Rock.** 65°20′S, 65°23′W. Almost 1 mile south of Dickens Rocks in the Pitt Islands. Named by the UK in 1971 for Mrs. Bardell, the Dickens character.

**Mount Barden.** 77°51′S, 86°13′W. 2,910 m. 2½ miles NW of Mount Sharp in the northern part of the Sentinel Range. Named for Virgil W. Barden, ionosphere physicist at Byrd Station in 1957.

**Bardsdell Nunatak.** 70°16′S, 63°54′W. Ice-free. Just north of Dalziel Ridge in the Columbia Mountains of Palmer Land. Named for Mark Bardsdell, Columbia University geologist in the area, 1970–71.

**Bare Rock.** 60°43′S, 45°36′W. 175 yards NE of Berntsen Point in the entrance to Borge Bay, off the east side of Signy Island, in the South Orkneys. Named by personnel on the *Discovery* in 1927.

**Bareface Bluff.** 78°50′S, 161°40′E. 940 m. Snow-free. Rises above Skelton Glacier, between Ant Hill Glacier and Mason Glacier. Surveyed and named descriptively by the NZ party of the BCTAE in 1957.

**Barela Rock.** 77°01′S, 148°52′W. In the south part of Przybyszewski Island in the Marshall Archipelago. Named for Ruben A. Barela, USN, aviation structural mechanic at McMurdo Station in 1967.

**Bargh Glacier.** 73°05′S, 168°46′E. 6 miles long. In the SW part of Daniell Peninsula, Victoria Land. 2 miles north of Langevad Glacier, and it flows parallel to it, and into Borchgrevink Glacier. Named for Kenneth A. Bargh, seismologist at Hallett Station in 1958.

**Barilari Bay.** 65°55′S, 64°43′W. Also spelled (erroneously) as Barilar Bay. 12 miles long. 6 miles wide. Between Cape García and Loqui Point, on the west coast of the Antarctic Peninsula, north of the Biscoe Islands. Discovered by Charcot in 1903–5, and named by him for Rear-Admiral Atilio S. Barilari of the Argentine navy.

**Barkell Platform.** 72°40′S, 68°16′E. A narrow, level rock platform, 100 meters wide and 1,285 meters high, on the north end of the Mawson Escarpment. There was a geodetic survey station here during the 1971 ANARE Prince Charles Mountains Survey. Named by the Australians for V.G. Barkell, helicopter pilot with the survey.

**Barkley, Erich.** Biologist on the German New Schwabenland Expedition led by Ritscher in 1938–39.

**Barkley Mountains.** 72°22′S, 1°05′E. A small group which includes Kvitkjølen Ridge and Isingen Mountain. Between Kvitsvodene Valley and Rogstad Glacier in the Sverdrup Mountains of Queen Maud Land. Discovered by Ritscher in 1938–39 and named by him for Erich Barkley.

**Barkov Glacier.** 71°46′S, 10°27′E. Flows between Mount Dallmann and the central part of the Shcherbakov Range in the Orvin Mountains of Queen Maud

Land. Named by the USSR in 1966 for geographer A.S. Barkov.

**Mount Barkow.** 73°22′S, 62°48′W. 1,390 m. 20 miles west of Court Nunatak and New Bedford Inlet, in the SW part of the Dana Mountains on the Lassiter Coast of Palmer Land. Discovered aerially in Dec. 1940 by the USAS. Named by the FIDS in 1947 for Erich Barkow.

**Barkow, Erich.** Meteorologist on the German Antarctic Expedition of 1911–12, led by Filchner.

**Cape Barlas.** 60°43′S, 45°W. Also called Cape Barles. Marks the north end of Fredriksen Island in the South Orkneys. Discovered in Dec. 1821 by Palmer and Powell. Named before 1933 for William Barlas.

**Barlas, William.** British representative at Deception Island and the South Shetland Islands in general, 1914–15, there to protect the British claim to Antarctica. Between 1928–41 he spent several seasons at South Georgia (54°S) (cf. Arthur G. Bennett).

**Barlas Channel.** 67°13′S, 67°45′W. 8 miles long. 2 miles wide. In the northern part of Laubeuf Fjord. It separates Day Island from Adelaide Island. Surveyed in 1936 by the BGLE, and again in 1948 by the FIDS. Named by the FIDS for William Barlas.

**Barlatier-Demas, François-Edmond-Eugène.** Lieutenant in the French navy. 2nd officer on the *Astrolabe* during Dumont d'Urville's 1837–40 expedition.

**Cape Barles** *see* **Cape Barlas**

**Cape Barlow** *see* **Barlow Island**

**Barlow Island.** 62°52′S, 62°21′W. A small island 1 mile WNW of the northern tip of Smith Island in the South Shetlands. Foster, in 1828–31, named a cape on the east side of Smith Island, as Cape Barlow, for Peter Barlow, British physicist. In 1951–52 the FIDS decided that a cape did not exist, and accordingly named this feature thus.

**Barn Rock.** 68°41′S, 67°32′W. 92 m. Near the north end of the Terra Firma

Islands, in Marguerite Bay. Visited and surveyed by the BGLE in 1936, and resurveyed by the FIDS in 1948, and named by them because of its appearance when seen from the west.

**Barnacles.** 85 species of cirripeds have been taken in Antarctic waters. This represents 29 genera, or 9 families. Of these, 20 species, 9 genera, and 1 family were newly discovered in Antarctica.

**Mount Barnard** *see* **Mount Friesland**

**Barnard, Capt.** Captain of the *Courier* in the South Shetlands, 1831–33.

**Barnard, Charles H.** Veteran American sealing captain who bought the *Charity* at Pernambuco, Brazil, on June 2, 1820, and sailed it as captain/sole owner to the Falkland Islands where he teamed up with the New York Sealing Expedition on their South Shetlands cruise of 1820–21. He was back again with the *Charity* for the 1821–22 season. That season he and Weddell (q.v.) took a tour on the *Beaufoy of London* together, under McLeod.

**Barnard Peak** *see* **Mount Friesland**

**Barnard Point.** 62°46′S, 60°21′W. Also called Pointe Bernard. Marks the SE side of the entrance to False Bay, on the south coast of Livingston Island, in the South Shetlands. Formerly called Friesland Point, it was renamed in the early 1920s in association with Mount Barnard (now called Mount Friesland).

**Barnards Peak** *see* **Needle Peak**

**Cape Barne.** 77°35′S, 166°14′E. 120 m. A steep, rocky bluff. South of Cape Royds, it is the westernmost cape on Ross Island. Discovered by Scott in 1902 and named by him for Michael Barne.

**Barne, Michael.** 1877–1961. 2nd lt. RN. The assistant magnetic observer on the Royal Society Expedition of 1901–4. Leader of the supporting party during Scott's push to the Pole in 1902.

**Barne Glacier.** 77°36′S, 166°22′E. Also called Cape Barne Glacier. A steep glacier that flows from Mount Erebus, and forms a steep cliff on the coast of Ross Island, between Cape Evans and Cape Barne, where it calves into McMurdo Sound. Discovered by Scott in 1902, and named by Shackleton in 1908 in association with the cape.

**Barne Inlet.** 80°15'S, 160°15'E. 17 miles wide. A Ross Ice Shelf inlet into the Transantarctic Mountains (a re-entrant), between Cape Kerr and Cape Selborne, at the foot of Mount Albert Markham. It receives the ice of Byrd Glacier. Discovered by Scott in 1902–3. Barne and Mulock mapped the coastline this far south, in 1903. It was named for Michael Barne.

**¹Mount Barnes** *see* **Cheeks Nunatak**

**²Mount Barnes.** 77°38'S, 163°35'E. 985 m. Surmounts the west central side of New Harbor, and marks the east end of the Kukri Hills, in Victoria Land. Discovered during Scott's 1901–4 expedition, and named by them as New Harbour Heights. Scott renamed it in 1910–12 for a Canadian ice physicist, Howard T. Barnes.

**Barnes, Haldor.** Medical officer on the *Eleanor Bolling* during Byrd's 1928–30 expedition. Transferred to the Norwegian whaler *Kosmos* in 1930.

**Barnes, Stephen S.** Took over as scientific leader at Byrd Station from George Toney, on Dec. 8, 1957. He served through the 1958 winter.

**Barnes Bluff.** 74°46'S, 110°19'W. On the Bear Peninsula, on the coast of Marie Byrd Land.

**Barnes Glacier.** 67°32'S, 66°25'W. Flows into Blind Bay on the west coast of Graham Land. Named by the UK in 1958 for Howard T. Barnes (*see* **Mount Barnes**).

**Barnes Icefalls.** 83°49'S, 55°53'W. Along the Washington Escarpment, between Mount Dover and Bennett Spires, in the Neptune Range. Named for James C. Barnes, meteorologist and scientific leader at Ellsworth Station in 1962.

**Barnes Nunatak** *see* **Cheeks Nunatak**

**Barnes Peak.** 84°23'S, 167°34'E. 3,360 m. 4 miles SE of Mount Dickerson in the Queen Alexandra Range. Named for Elwood E. Barnes, cosmic ray scientist at Hallett Station in 1963.

**Barnes Ridge.** 78°08'S, 84°50'W. 7 miles long. Between the Young and Ellen Glaciers on the east side of the Sentinel Range. Named for Stephen S. Barnes.

**Barnett Glacier.** 70°59'S, 167°40'E. In the Anare Mountains. Flows along the south side of Tapsell Foreland into Smith Inlet, in northern Victoria Land. Named for Donald C. Barnett, photographer here in 1961–62, and again in 1962–63.

**Barnum Peak.** 85°23'S, 171°40'W. 2,940 m. Near the head of Liv Glacier. Just south of the mouth of LaVergne Glacier. Discovered by Byrd during his flight to the Pole in Nov. 1929, and named by him for J.D. Barnum, publisher of the Syracuse *Post-Standard,* and a supporter.

**Baronick Glacier.** 78°36'S, 161°50'E. 6 miles SW of Mount Cocks, in the Royal Society Range of southern Victoria Land. It flows into the Skelton Glacier. Named in 1963 for Michael P. Baronick of VX-6. Baronick was based at McMurdo Base in 1956, and that season established Beardmore Glacier Camp. He subsequently returned to Antarctica for several summer seasons.

**Mount Barr Smith.** 67°10'S, 99°12'E. 1,310 m. The most northerly of a line of peaks along the west side of the Denman Glacier. Discovered in Dec. 1912 by the Western Base Party of the AAE 1911–14, and named by Mawson for a patron of the expedition, Robert Barr Smith.

**Barracouta Ridge.** 85°20'S, 166°35'W. A long, jagged ridge that ends at Webster Knob in the north. It is an extension from the base of Mount Fridtjof Nansen into the head of Strom Glacier, in the Queen Maud Mountains. Discovered by Gould's Dec. 1929 party during Byrd's 1928–30 expedition. Climbed, and descriptively named, by the New Zealanders in 1963–64.

**Barracuda.** Order: Perciformes. Family: Sphyraenidae. One type of this deep sea fish is found in Antarctic waters (*see also* **Fish**).

**Barratt Island.** 68°33′S, 77°52′E. A small island off the Vestfold Hills. 1 mile west of Bluff Island. Photographed by the LCE 1936–37. Named later by the Australians for N.R. Barratt, weather observer at Davis Station in 1960.

**Mount Barré.** 67°30′S, 68°33′W. 2,195 m. Has an ice-covered, pyramidal peak. 2 miles NE of Mount Gaudry in the southern part of Adelaide Island. Discovered and surveyed by Charcot in 1909, and resurveyed by the FIDS in 1948. Named by the UK for Michel Barré.

**Barré, Michel.** French explorer who led the 1951 French Polar Expedition winter party of 1951, relieving Liotard at Port-Martin on Jan. 9, 1951. On June 10, 1951, he was the first person to see emperor penguins incubating, and early in 1952 suffered through the Port-Martin fire. He and his party were taken off by the *Tottan* on Feb. 2, 1952.

**Barré Glacier.** 66°35′S, 138°40′E. A channel glacier. 5 miles wide. 5 miles long. Flows from the continental ice to the coast of East Antarctica, just east of Cape Pépin. Named by the USA for Michel Barré.

**Barren Bluff.** 73°04′S, 161°18′E. In the southern part of the Sequence Hills on the west side of the upper Rennick Glacier, in Victoria Land. Named descriptively by the New Zealanders in 1962–63.

**Barrett, Peter J.** NZ geologist with the University of Minnesota Ellsworth Mountains Party of 1962–63, and with the NZGSAE 1963–64. On Dec. 28, 1967, while working at 9,000 feet on Granite Peak at the edge of the Polar Plateau with a party from Ohio State University, he discovered the fossilized jawbone of a primitive lizard. This was a labyrinthodont, about 220 million years old. Other labyrinthodonts have been found in other continents, and this made Gondwanaland (q.v.) into an acceptable

theory. In 1970 Barrett led an expedition into the Darwin Mountains.

**Barrett Buttress.** 72°13′S, 65°36′W. On the west side of Palmer Land.

**Barrett Glacier.** 84°37′S, 174°10′W. Flows from the northern slopes of the Prince Olav Mountains, between the Longhorn Spurs and the Gabbro Hills, to the Ross Ice Shelf. 15 miles long. Named by the New Zealand Geological Survey Antarctic Expedition (NZGSAE) 1963–64 for Peter J. Barrett.

**Barrett Island.** 72°09′S, 95°30′W. 2 miles long. Ice-covered. Just within the northern part of the mouth of Morgan Inlet, Thurston Island. Named for Lt. (jg) Barry B. Barrett, VX-6 pilot in 1964.

**Barrett Nunataks.** 79°19′S, 81°24′W. On the east side of the Dott Ice Rise, overlooking Constellation Inlet in the Heritage Range. Named by the University of Minnesota Ellsworth Mountains Party of 1962–63 for Peter J. Barrett.

**Barrier Bay.** 67°45′S, 81°15′E. At the west end of the Leopold and Astrid Coast, and the Chelyuskintsy Ice Tongue. An open bay, it was photographed by the LCE 1936–37, and named Barriervika (barrier bay) by the Norwegians because of its proximity to the West Ice Shelf (the old name for an ice shelf was "barrier").

**Barrier Island.** 68°26′S, 78°23′E. ½ mile long. At the northern end of the Vestfold Hills, just north of the entrance to Tryne Fjord in Tryne Sound. Photographed by the LCE 1936–37. Visited in 1957 by an ANARE party, and named by them because the island seemed to form a barrier to the passage of icebergs up Tryne Fjord.

**Barrier Wind Phenomenon.** The barrier wind develops when a stable air stream blows against a mountain barrier, which causes strong mountain-parallel winds. Werner Schwerdtfeger identified it in 1970 in Vol. 14, "Climates of Polar Regions" of the *World Survey of Climatology* (Ed. H.E. Landsberg — Elsevier Science Publishers, Amsterdam).

Schwerdtfeger was an authority on Antarctic meteorology and died in Jan. 1985.

**Barrios Rocks.** 63°19'S, 57°58'W. A group of 3 small rocks, 1 mile west of Toro Point, Trinity Peninsula. Named Islotes Barrios by the Chilean Antarctic Expedition of 1947–48 for Gen. Guillermo Barrios Tirado (*see* **Distinguished Visitors**).

**Barron, Alexander.** Ordinary seaman on the Wilkes Expedition 1838–42. Joined in the USA. Discharged at Oahu, Nov. 2, 1840.

**Isla Barros** *see* **Alcock Island**

**Barros Rocks.** 65°17'S, 64°12'W. Group between the Berthelot Islands and the Argentine Islands, 2 miles SW of Cape Tuxen, off the west coast of Graham Land. Discovered and named by Charcot in 1908–10.

**¹Cape Barrow.** 63°42'S, 61°43'W. A cape in the form of a steep cliff. It forms the north end of Hoseason Island. Named by Foster in 1828–31 for Sir John Barrow, secretary of the admiralty and founder of the Royal Geographical Society in 1830.

**²Cape Barrow.** 71°22'S, 169°20'E. The northern point of Flat Island, Victoria Land. It marks the west side of the entrance to Robertson Bay. In Jan. 1840 Ross applied the name, for Sir John Barrow (*see* the other **Cape Barrow**) to a mainland cape. Scott's 1910–13 expedition mapped it where it is now.

**Barrows Isle** *see* **Elephant Island**

**Barry Hill.** 85°10'S, 174°44'W. Ice-free. Just west of the mouth of the LaPrade Valley. 1 mile NNE of Mount Kenyon, in the Cumulus Hills. Named for Lt. Richard P. Barry, USN, communications officer at McMurdo Base in 1957, and for the summer seasons of 1955–56, 1956–57, and 1957–58.

**Barry Island.** 68°08'S, 67°07'W. The central of the Debenham Islands, off the Fallières Coast, on the west coast of Graham Land. Charted by the BGLE, who used this island as a base in 1936 and 1937. Named by Rymill for the oldest son of Frank Debenham.

**Mount Barsoum.** 82°04'S, 88°07'W. Partly snow-free. On the west end of the Martin Hills. Positioned on Dec. 10, 1958, by the US Ellsworth-Byrd Traverse Party and named for Lt. Adib H. Barsoum, USN, medical officer at Ellsworth Station in 1958.

**Barter, Leland L.** American seaman who took part, as ship's crew only, on the first two Byrd expeditions to Antarctica. On Byrd's 1928–30 expedition he was an ordinary seaman on the *Eleanor Bolling* for the first half of the expedition, and then in 1929 he stepped up to 2nd assistant engineer, replacing Elbert Thawley. On Byrd's 1933–35 expedition he was chief engineer on the *Bear of Oakland* from 1933–34, and 1st assistant engineer on the *Jacob Ruppert* from 1934–35.

**Barter Bluff.** 75°10'S, 114°W. 1½ miles west of Leister Peak in the Kohler Range of Marie Byrd Land, on the east side of Kohler Glacier. Named for Leland L. Barter.

**Barth Seamount.** 63°S, 44°W. Subsurface feature, just south of the South Orkneys.

**Bartholin Peak.** 67°17'S, 66°42'W. Near the north end of the Boyle Mountains, in Graham Land. Named by the UK in 1958 for Erasmus Bartholin, the first man to write about snow crystals, in 1661.

**¹Mount Bartlett.** 66°57'S, 51°06'E. 3 miles SE of Mount Storer in the Tula Mountains of Enderby Land. Named by the Australians for A.J. Bartlett.

**²Mount Bartlett.** 84°56'S, 163°56'E. 2,560 m. Ice-free. 2 miles north of Mount Buckley at the head of the Beardmore Glacier. Discovered by Shackleton in 1908, and named by him for A.H. Bartlett of London, a supporter.

**Bartlett, A.J.** Member of the *Discovery* crew during the BANZARE 1929–31.

**Bartlett, David.** Seaman on the Wilkes Expedition 1838–42. Joined at Rio. Served the cruise.

**Bartlett Bench.** 86°24′S, 152°18′W. Bare, flat, benchlike elevation overlooking the Bartlett Glacier from the east. 6 miles SSW of Mount Ruth in the Queen Maud Mountains. Named by the New Zealanders in 1969–70, in association with the glacier.

**Bartlett Glacier.** 86°15′S, 152°W. 30 miles long. 5 miles wide at its terminus. Feeds the Robert Scott Glacier in the Queen Maud Mountains, just north of Mount Gardiner. Discovered in Dec. 1934 by Quin Blackburn's party during Byrd's 1933–35 expedition, and named Bob Bartlett Glacier by Byrd for Robert A. Bartlett of Newfoundland, Arctic explorer who recommended the purchase of the *Bear of Okland*. The name was later shortened.

**Bartlett Inlet.** 77°12′S, 156°40′W. 16 miles wide. A frozen inlet at the northern tip of the Edward VII Peninsula, with Cape Colbeck forming its western fringe. Named for Lt. Eugene F. Bartlett, USN, officer-in-charge of Byrd Station in 1960.

**Bartley Glacier.** 77°32′S, 162°10′E. A hanging glacier on the south wall of the Wright Valley, in Victoria Land, just west of the Meserve Glacier. Named for Ollie B. Bartley (*see* **Deaths, 1957**).

**Bartok Glacier.** 69°38′S, 71°W. 7 miles long. 3 miles wide. Flows from the south end of the Elgar Uplands in the northern part of Alexander Island. Named by the UK for the Hungarian composer.

**Barton Peninsula.** 62°14′S, 58°46′W. Between Marian Cove and Potter Cove on King George Island, in the South Shetlands. Named by the UK in 1963 for Colin M. Barton, FIDS geologist here in 1959–61.

**Bartrum Glacier.** 79°44′S, 158°44′E. A small, steep, highly-crevassed glacier in the Brown Hills. Flows between Bowling Green Plateau and the Blank Peaks. Named for the NZ geology professor, John A. Bartrum.

**Bartrum Plateau.** 83°10′S, 159°55′E. 11 miles long. 6 miles wide. Ice-covered. West of Mount Bonaparte in the Queen Elizabeth Range. Named by the New Zealanders in 1961–62 for Prof. John A. Bartrum (*see* **Bartrum Glacier**).

**Barwick Valley.** 77°21′S, 161°10′E. A dry valley north of Apocalypse Peaks, in Victoria Land. It is SSSI #3. Named by the New Zealanders in 1958–59 for R.E. Barwick, summer biologist on the NZ party of the BCTAE, who worked here in 1957–58 and 1958–59.

**Basaltspitze** *see* **Haslum Crag**

**Båsbolken Spur.** 71°54′S, 5°17′E. Near the head of Tvibåsen Valley, in the Mühlig-Hofmann Mountains. It divides the upper valley into two equal parts.

**Punta Bascope** *see* **Ash Point**

**Base A.** *see* **Port Lockroy Station**

**Base B.** 62°59′S, 60°34′W. British military station built on Whaler's Bay, Deception Island, by the personnel of Operation Tabarin, in 1944, to guard British interests in the South Shetlands. This was the first ever permanent station built in Antarctica. W.R. Flett led the first, 1944, wintering party. In 1945 Alan Reece was leader, and it became a FIDS scientific station that year. In 1946 H.P. Featherstone was leader, and in Sept. of that year the station was destroyed by fire. It was rebuilt in 1947 when J.R.S. Huckle was leader. Subsequent leaders were 1948—A.J. Scadding, 1949—G. Stock, 1950—J.R. Green, 1951—Ralph A. Lenton, 1952—E.D. Stroud, 1953—I.W.N. Clarke, 1954—G.E. Hemmen, 1955—C.H. Palmer, 1956—P. Guyver, 1957—J. Paisley. The station conducted meteorological studies during the IGY. It was destroyed by a volcano in 1969. There was an old whaling station next to it, and this is now partially buried under mud and volcanic ash, as is the Whaler's Graveyard.

**Base C.** British scientific station established by the FIDS at Cape Geddes, Laurie Island, in the South Orkneys, in 1946. M.A. Choyce was leader for the 1946 winter. In 1947 all personnel were transferred to the new station, Base H, on Signy Island (*see* **Signy Island Station**).

**Base D.** 63°24′S, 56°59′W. British military station built at Hope Bay, Trinity Peninsula, by personnel of Operation Tabarin, in 1945. It was the third ever permanent station in Antarctica (*see* **Base B** and **Port Lockroy Station**). The *Eagle* landed the first crew, in Feb. 1945, and A. Taylor led the first wintering party, in 1945. Later that year it became a FIDS scientific station, studying geography and geology. V.I. Russell led the 1946 party, and F.K. Elliott was station leader in 1947 and 1948. In Nov. 1948 the original building burned down, killing two scientists, and the base was vacant from 1949–52. In Feb. 1952, when the FIDS attempted to land at Hope Bay, they were repulsed by the Argentinians (*see* **Wars**). After that dispute was settled, the FIDS re-established the base, with G.W. Marsh as leader in 1952 and again in 1953. Subsequent leaders were 1954— W. Turner, 1955—W.E. Anderson, 1956—R.F. Worswick, 1957—L. Rice. The station conducted meteorological studies during the IGY. It closed in 1964. There is a large Adélie penguin rookery here.

**Base E.** British scientific base built by E.W. Bingham and his FIDS crew on Stonington Island, 250 yards south of the old USAS East Base, between Feb. 24 and March 13, 1946. Bingham led the 1946 wintering party, and K.S. Pierce-Butler led the 1947 wintering party. Vivian Fuchs was leader in 1947 and, because of the ice, relief for Fuchs and his crew was impossible at the end of their stint. Consequently they were forced to winter-over again in 1949, until Feb. 1950. It was then that the British discontinued it as a year-round base. For a few years it carried on as a summer-only station, was abandoned, then re-opened in 1957–58, with new buildings, for the IGY. In March 1975 the base was finally closed, and is now used for emergency and summer work only.

**Base F** *see* **Faraday Station**

**Base G.** 62°05′S, 58°25′W. British scientific station on Admiralty Bay, King George Island, in the South Shetlands. In 1947 it was reconnoitered, and a small hut built. It was established as a permanent meteorological station in 1948. Leaders of the wintering parties have been 1948—E. Platt, 1949—G. Hattersley-Smith, 1950—J.A. Kendall, 1951— K.R. Gooden, 1952—W.J. Meehan, 1953—R.F. Worswick, 1954—D.J. George, 1955—J.R. Noble, 1956—C.C. Clement, 1957—A. Precious. During the IGY meteorology and glaciology were studied. The station was not occupied after 1960.

**Base H** *see* **Signy Island Station**

**Base J.** 66°S, 65°24′W. Also called Prospect Point Station. British scientific station built at Ferin Head, Prospect Point, on the west coast of Graham Land, in 1957. R. Miller was the first leader, in 1957. Meteorology was studied during the IGY.

**Base K** *see* **Fossil Bluff Station**

**Base N.** 64°46′S, 64°05′W. Also called Arthur Harbour Station, Anvers Island Station. British scientific station built by the personnel of the *Norsel* in 1955, at the NW corner of Arthur Harbor, Anvers Island. P.R. Hooper was FIDS leader in 1955 and 1956, and J.W. Thompson in 1957. It was not an IGY station, and closed in 1958. It was used as a lab by the Americans' Palmer Station in 1965, the station that had replaced it at Arthur Harbor. The original building later burned down.

**Base O.** 64°44′S, 62°32′W. British scientific station built by the FIDS personnel off the *Shackleton* in 1956, on Danco Island, off the Danco Coast of the Antarctic Peninsula. It conducted survey and geological programs. R.A. Foster was leader in 1956 and 1957. It was not an IGY station.

**Base T.** 67°46'S, 68°54'W. British scientific base on Adelaide Island, unused since 1977. In 1985 it was transferred to Chile, and renamed Teniente Carvajal Station.

**Base V.** 63°32'S, 57°23'W. At View Point, Duse Bay. A British base built as a hut in Dec. 1953 by personnel from the FIDS Base D at Hope Bay, nearby on the Trinity Peninsula. It was occupied semipermanently March–Nov. 1953, Jan.–Nov. 1955, and then intermittently until 1961.

**Base W.** 66°52'S, 66°48'W. British scientific station built on Détaille Island, off the Loubet Coast of the Antarctic Peninsula, by the FIDS personnel off the *John Biscoe* in 1956. T.L. Murphy was leader in 1956, and A.B. Erskine was leader in 1957. It conducted meteorological studies for the first part of the IGY until it closed later in 1957.

**Base Y.** 67°49'S, 67°17'W. British scientific station established in 1955 on Horseshoe Island, off the coast of the Antarctic Peninsula, by FIDS personnel off the *Norsel*. Kenneth M. Gaul was the first leader, in 1955. D.J.H. Searle was leader in 1956, and P. Guyver in 1957. During the IGY, meteorological studies were conducted. The station operated until 1960.

**Basecamp Valley.** 73°30'S, 94°22'W. A small, ice-filled valley on the west side of Avalanche Ridge in the Jones Mountains. Mapped and named by the University of Minnesota–Jones Mountains Party of 1961–62, who established a base camp, Camp Minnesota (q.v.) here.

**Baseline Nunataks.** 70°46'S, 66°55'E. A small group. 5 miles south of Mount McKenzie, on the south side of the Aramis Range, in the Prince Charles Mountains. Bewsher's ANARE southern party visited them in Jan. 1957. They formed the eastern end of a photo baseline, hence the name.

**Baseline Rock.** 67°36'S, 62°44'E. Isolated. Between Nøst Island and the Flat Islands in Holme Bay. Photographed by the LCE 1936–37, and later named by the Australians because the rock was used as one end of the baseline of a 1959 ANARE triangulation of the area.

**Bases.** *See also* **Scientific stations.** Some of the older bases are now covered over by drifting snows, or the ones built on ice shelves have left the continent and disappeared on icebergs. Certainly in the case of the Antarctic Peninsula where so many Chilean, British, and Argentinian bases exist, it seems that today the prime raison d'être is one of military intelligence rather than science.

**The *Bashkiria*.** USSR passenger motor steamship, sometimes seen in the Antarctic in the 1970s.

**Basil Halls Island** *see* **Snow Island**

**Basilica Peak.** 70°02'S, 159°21'E. 1,810 m. A granite peak. 2 ½ miles SE of Mount Gorton in the south part of the Wilson Hills. Named by the New Zealanders because of its shape.

**Basissletta.** 72°17'S, 3°36'W. A small, gently-sloping, ice-covered plain between Pyramiden Nunatak and Stamnen Peak near the SW end of the Ahlmann Ridge, in Queen Maud Land. Name means "the base plain" in Norwegian.

**Bass, Joseph.** Ordinary seaman on the Wilkes Expedition 1838–42. Joined in the USA. Served the cruise.

**Bass Rock** *see* **Eden Rocks, Baldred Rock**

**Basso, Juan.** Chief storekeeper on the *Iquique*, 1946–47.

**Basso Island.** 62°30'S, 59°44'W. A small island linked by a mostly submerged spit to the southern shore of Discovery Bay, Greenwich Island, in the South Shetlands. Charted by the Chilean Antarctic Expedition of 1946–47, and named for Juan Basso.

**Mount Bastei.** 71°22'S, 13°32'E. Also called Bastionen. 2,460 m. 2 miles west of Mount Mentzel, in the Gruber Mountains of Queen Maud Land. The Ritscher expedition of 1938–39 discovered it and named it. Bastei means "bastion" in German. It is a buttress, bastion-type mountain.

**Bastien Glacier** *see* **Union Glacier**

**Bastien Range.** 78°50′S, 86°W. Extends for 40 miles in the Ellsworth Mountains. Named for Thomas W. Bastien, geologist, leader of the University of Minnesota Geological Party here in 1963–64. He had been to the Ellsworth Mountains in 1961–62 with the Camp Minnesota team.

**Mount Bastin.** 72°32′S, 31°15′E. 2,000 m. 1 mile north of Mount Perov in the Belgica Mountains. Discovered by the Belgian Antarctic Expedition of 1957–58 led by Gaston de Gerlache, and named by him for Capt. Frank Bastin, who helped the scientific preparation of the expedition. Bastin went on to lead the next Belgian Antarctic Expedition, of 1958–59.

**Mount Bastion.** 77°19′S, 160°29′E. 2,530 m. West of Webb Glacier and Gibson Spur, in the Barwick Valley of Victoria Land. Named descriptively by the New Zealanders in 1959–60.

**Bastion Hill.** 79°50′S, 158°19′E. Ice-free. In the Brown Hills. 1,490 m. It projects southward into the Darwin Glacier, just east of the Touchdown Glacier. Descriptively named by the Darwin Glacier Party of the BCTAE 1956–58.

**Bastion Peak.** 66°10′S, 63°35′W. 1,610 m. Ice-capped. On the east coast of Graham Land. Named by the FIDS in 1948 because it forms a buttress or bastion to the plateau escarpment west of Morrison Glacier.

**Bastlen, Erich.** Fishing biology student on the German New Schwabenland Expedition of 1938–39, led by Ritscher. On Jan. 31, 1939, he was flown in the *Boreas* to a point on the coast, and took 5 emperor penguins and returned them to the *Schwabenland.*

**Batchelor, Henry.** Seaman on the Wilkes Expedition 1838–42. Joined in the USA. Served the cruise.

**Bateman, David.** Private in the marines on the Wilkes Expedition 1838–42. Joined in the USA. Died of a lung ailment at Fiji on June 30, 1840.

**Bates, J.G. "Jim."** NZ engineer who went to the South Pole with Hillary during the BCTAE 1956–58.

**Bates Glacier.** 74°13′S, 163°51′E. A small glacier flowing from the west side of Mount Queensland, into the west side of the Campbell Glacier just north of Mills Peak, in Victoria Land. Named by the New Zealanders in 1965–66 for D.R. Bates, geologist here that year.

**Bates Island.** 65°49′S, 65°38′W. Also called Isla Videla. A narrow island, 3 miles long. 3 miles east of Jurva Point on Renaud Island in the Biscoe Islands. Named by the UK in 1959 for Charles C. Bates, US oceanographer.

**Bates Nunataks.** 80°15′S, 153°30′E. Three isolated nunataks, 18 miles west of Vantage Hill in the Britannia Range, in the area of the Byrd Glacier, in the Queen Maud Mountains. Discovered by the Darwin Glacier Party of the BCTAE 1956–58. Named by NZ for J.G. Bates.

**Bates Peak.** 69°35′S, 72°55′W. On the NW coast of Alexander Island.

**Bates Point.** 70°43′S, 166°47′E. Ice-covered. Forms the north side of the entrance to Yule Bay, on the north coast of Victoria Land. Named for Lt. Thomas R. Bates, USN, flight surgeon and medical officer at McMurdo Station in 1964.

**Bathurst Island** *see* **Ford Island**

**Cape Batterbee.** 65°51′S, 53°48′E. Ice-covered. The most northerly projection of Enderby Land, just east of Proclamation Island. Discovered on Jan. 13, 1930, by the BANZARE, and named by Mawson for Sir Harry Fagg Batterbee, assistant secretary of the dominions office.

**Batterbee Mountains.** 71°23′S, 66°55′W. 2,225 m. Part of the Dyer Plateau of Palmer Land, it overlooks the George VI

Sound. Discovered aerially by Ellsworth on Nov. 23, 1935. Named by Rymill during the BGLE 1934–37 for Sir Harry Batterbee (*see* **Cape Batterbee**).

**Battle Point.** 67°10'S, 64°45'W. SE of Mount Dater, on the east coast of Graham Land. Named by the UK for Walter R.B. Battle, British glaciologist.

**Battlements Nunatak.** 76°32'S, 159°21'E. Large and ice-free. Several small peaks run in a line west from the main peak. 6 miles NW of the Allan Hills in Victoria Land. Near the head of Mawson Glacier. Discovered and descriptively named by the NZ party of the BCTAE 1956–58.

**Battleship Promontory.** 76°55'S, 160°55'E. A sandstone promontory rising from the floor of the Alatna Valley near its head, in Victoria Land. Named by US geologist Parker Calkin, here in 1960–61, for its resemblance in shape to a battleship.

**Battye Glacier.** 70°53'S, 67°54'E. Flows into Radok Lake in the Aramis Range of the Prince Charles Mountains. Named by the Australians for A.C. Battye, glaciologist at Wilkes Station in 1962.

**Baudin Peaks.** 68°49'S, 67°03'W. Group rising to higher than 750 m. At the SE corner of Mikkelsen Bay, just SW of the mouth of Clarke Glacier. 9 miles ENE of Cape Berteaux, on the west coast of Graham Land. Surveyed by the BGLE in 1936, but unnamed. In 1948–49 the FIDS determined that they were what Charcot had called Cap Pierre Baudin in 1909, when he discovered them, thinking that the feature was a cape, and naming them for Pierre Baudin, the port engineer at Pernambuco, Brazil.

**Bauhs Nunatak.** 84°12'S, 163°24'E. 2,225 m. On the north side of the Walcott Névé. 3½ miles SSE of Mount Sirius, in the Queen Maud Mountains. Named for Luvern R. Bauhs, ionosphere physicist at South Pole Station in 1959.

**Baulch Peak.** 83°20'S, 163°04'E. 8 miles NE of Claydon Peak, in the Queen Elizabeth Range. Named for DeeWitt M. Baulch, meteorologist at South Pole Station in 1958.

**Bauprés Rocks.** 64°54'S, 63°37'W. Also called Advent Island. Two rocks in the middle of the southern entrance to Peltier Channel in the Palmer Archipelago. First charted by Charcot in 1903–5. Named before 1952 by the Argentines as Rocas Bauprés (bowsprit rocks) because from afar the rocks look like a bowsprit.

**Bautaen Peak.** 71°58'S, 25°57'E. 2,240 m. On the NE side of Mount Bergersen in the Sør Rondane Mountains. Name means "the monolith" in Norwegian.

**Mount Baxter.** 74°22'S, 162°32'E. 2,430 m. Just south of O'Kane Canyon, at the very east of the Eisenhower Range in Victoria Land. Discovered by Scott in 1902, and named by him for Sir George and Lady Baxter of Dundee, supporters of the Royal Society Expedition.

**Bay of Sails** *see* **Sails, Bay of**

**Bay of Whales** *see* **Whales, Bay of**

**Bay of Winds** *see* **Winds, Bay of**

**Bay Point.** 64°46'S, 63°26'W. Marks the east side of the entrance to Börgen Bay on the SE coast of Anvers Island. Discovered by de Gerlache in 1897–99 and named before 1927.

**Bayard Islands.** 64°56'S, 63°14'W. A small group 1 mile NE of Cape Willems, off the west coast of Graham Land. Charted by de Gerlache in 1897–99. Named by the UK in 1960 for Hippolyte Bayard, 19th century photography pioneer.

**Bayer, John J.** 1st assistant engineer on the *City of New York* during Byrd's 1928–30 expedition.

**Bayet Peak.** 65°02'S, 63°01'W. 1,400 m. Overlooks the southern shore of Briand Fjord in Flandres Bay, on the west coast of Graham Land. Charcot named the SE entrance to Briand Fjord as Pointe Bayet, for Charles Bayet, director of instruction and member of the Commission of Scientific Work of the expedition.

Air photos have shown no point here, so the name has been relocated (*see* **Pelletan Point**).

**Bayet Point**    *see*    **Pelletan Point**

**Cape Bayle.** 64°17'S, 63°10'W. Forms the NE end of Anvers Island. Charted by Charcot in 1903–5, and named by him as Pointe Bayle for Vice-Adm. Bayle. The name has since been anglicized.

**Mount Bayliss.** 73°32'S, 62°44'E. Extends for 9 miles. 6 miles east of Mount Menzies in the Prince Charles Mountains. Named by the Australians for E.P. Bayliss, Australian cartographer who drew the map of Antarctica in 1939.

**Isla Bayley**    *see*    **Bob Island**

**Bayly, William.** Astronomer on the *Adventure* during Cook's voyage of 1772–75.

**Bayly Glacier.** 64°37'S, 61°50'W. Flows into the head of Bancroft Bay, on the west coast of Graham Land. Named by the UK in 1960 for Maurice B. Bayly, FIDS geologist at Base O in 1956.

**Bayne, H.** First officer on the *Jacob Ruppert*, 1933–34.

**Mount Bayonne.** 68°56'S, 70°59'W. 1,500 m. Forms the northern extremity of the Rouen Mountains on Alexander Island. Charcot named it in 1908–10 for the French city.

**Bazett Island.** 66°18'S, 67°06'W. A small island just south of the west end of Krogh Island in the Biscoe Islands. Named by the UK for Henry C. Bazett, US physiologist (1885–1950).

**Bazzano Island.** 65°11'S, 64°10'W. A small island off the south end of Petermann Island, between Lisboa and Boudet Islands, in the Wilhelm Archipelago. Discovered and named by Charcot in 1908–10.

**Beaches.** There are several beaches in Antarctica, but not enough to make them commonplace. There are two in the vicinity of Cape Evans on Ross Island— Home Beach and West Beach, and more in the area of Cape Bird on the same

island—Romanes, McDonald, Waipuke, and Caughley Beaches. Ridley Beach is an example of a beach in another part of Antarctica—Cape Adare, in Oates Land.

**Beacon Dome.** 86°08'S, 146°25'W. 3,010 m. A large, domelike mountain at the head of the Griffith Glacier along the Watson Escarpment. Named by the New Zealanders in 1969–70 because it is composed partly of the Beacon series.

**Beacon Group.** Flat-lying Devonian to Jurassic strata laid down about 200 or 300 million years ago on top of Precambrian rock, in the Pensacola Mountains.

**Beacon Head.** 67°49'S, 67°21'W. A small headland at the north side of the entrance to Lystad Bay on Horseshoe Island, off Graham Land. Named by the UK for a timber beacon built here by the Argentines, and used by the FIDS from 1955–57 during a survey on Horseshoe Island.

**Beacon Heights.** 77°50'S, 160°50'E. A ridge of peaks, including East Beacon, West Beacon, and South Beacon. South of Taylor Glacier, between Beacon Valley and Arena Valley in Victoria Land. Named by Hartley Ferrar in 1903 for the beacon sandstone found here.

**Beacon Hill.** 68°04'S, 66°23'W. 1,810 m. Ice-covered. Dome-shaped. 2½ miles NE of McLeod Hill, in the center of the Antarctic Peninsula, between Northeast Glacier and Bills Gulch. Named by the USAS 1939–41. There was probably a beacon placed here during the expedition.

**Beacon Sandstone formation.** In ancient days the mountain ranges were worn away by erosion, and replaced by a series of mainly quartzose sediments. This formation of platform sediments contains a rich record of extinct Antarctic life (*see* **Fossils**). This is the Beacon Sandstone formation.

**Beacon Valley.** 77°49'S, 160°39'E. One of the dry valleys in Victoria Land. Between Pyramid Mountain and the

Beacon Heights, in the Quartermain Range. Named by the New Zealanders in 1958–59 in association with the heights.

**Beagle Island.** 63°25'S, 54°40'W. One of the Danger Islands, off the SE coast of Joinville Island. Named by the UK in 1963 for the *Beagle* (Darwin's ship, not in Antarctic waters) due to the island's proximity to Darwin Island in the same group.

**Beagle Peak.** 69°36'S, 71°45'W. In the NW part of Alexander Island.

**Beaglehole Glacier.** 66°33'S, 64°07' W. Between Spur Point and Friederichsen Glacier on the east coast of Graham Land. Named by the UK for John C. Beaglehole (1901–1971), NZ historian of the Antarctic (*see* the Bibliography).

**Beak Island.** 63°37'S, 57°18'W. 360 m. Arc-shaped. 4 miles long. ½ mile NE of Eagle Island in the NE part of the Prince Gustav Channel. First seen by the Swedes in 1902–3 during Nordenskjöld's expedition. Surveyed by the FIDS in 1945, and named because of its shape, and also because of its relation to Tail and Eagle Islands.

**Beaked whales.** *Hyperoodontidae.* An uncommon species of whale, but found frequently in Antarctic waters. Actually the southern bottlenose whale is *Hyperoodon planifrons.* (See also **Whales.**)

**Beakers.** Local slang term for scientists in Antarctica.

**Beakley Glacier.** 73°51'S, 119°50'W. On the west side of Duncan Peninsula on Carney Island, flowing into the Amundsen Sea. Named for Vice Adm. W.M. Beakley, USN, administrator during the IGY.

**Cape Beale.** 66°35'S, 162°45'E. Steep bluff along the SE side of Borradaile Island in the Balleny Islands. Named for W. Beale, a merchant who joined with Charles Enderby in sending out the Balleny expedition of 1838–40.

**Beale Pinnacle.** 66°36'S, 162°45'E. 60 m. A boot-shaped rock pinnacle in wa-

ter, lying close off Cape Beale in the Balleny Islands. Named for W. Beale (*see* **Cape Beale**).

**Beall Island.** 66°18'S, 110°29'E. A rocky island, just over a mile long. It has small coves indenting it on the east and west sides. 350 yards NW of Mitchell Peninsula in the Windmill Islands. Named for James M. Beall, US Weather Bureau observer on Operation Windmill, 1947–48.

**Beall Reefs.** 66°18'S, 110°27'E. Submarine ridges with depths of less than one fathom. ½ mile west of Beall Island, in the Windmill Islands. Discovered from the launch at Wilkes Station in 1961. Named for Beall Island.

**Beals, Artimeus W.** Captain of the hold on the Wilkes Expedition 1838–42. Joined at Upolu. Served the cruise.

**Beaman Glacier.** 70°58'S, 164°38'E. In the SW part of the Anare Mountains. Flows into Ebbe Glacier. Named for 1st Lt. Charles W. Beaman, US Army helicopter pilot here in 1962–63.

**Bean Peaks.** 75°58'S, 70°W. Group including Carlson Peak and Novocin Peak. They form the SW part of the Hauberg Mountains. Discovered aerially by the RARE 1947–48. Named for Lawrence D. Bean, electrician at Amundsen-Scott South Pole Station in 1967.

**The *Bear*** *see* **The *Bear of Oakland***

**[1]Bear Island.** 68°11'S, 67°04'W. About ¼ mile long, and a couple of hundred yards wide. Just under a mile west of Stonington Island in Marguerite Bay, off the west coast of Graham Land.

**[2]Bear Island** *see* **Bear Peninsula**

**The *Bear of Oakland*.** A square-sailed wooden barquentine built in 1858, and refitted by Stephen and Sons of Dundee in 1874. Originally named the *Bear*, it was called "the strongest wooden ship ever built." It was renamed the *Bear of Oakland* and used by Byrd as one of his two ships on his 1933–35 expedition. Later, with its name changed back to the *Bear*, it was chartered to Byrd for his USAS Expedition of 1939–41. The cost to Byrd was a dollar a year. It was his flagship for that expedition, and Cruzen commanded.

**Bear Peninsula.** 74°36'S, 110°48'W. 50 miles long. 25 miles wide. Ice-covered. 30 miles east of Martin Peninsula, on the coast of Marie Byrd Land, in the Dotson Ice Shelf. It juts out into the Amundsen Sea. At first thought to be an island, and called Bear Island, for the *Bear*. It was later redefined.

**Beard Peak.** 86°40'S, 145°25'W. 2,360 m. On the north edge of the La Gorce Mountains, 4 miles south of the east tip of Mount Mooney. Named for Philip H. Beard, VX-6 photographer in 1966 and 1967.

**Bearded penguin** *see* **Chinstrap penguin**

**Beardmore Glacier.** 83°45'S, 171°E. One of the world's largest valley glaciers, it is over 100 miles long and averages 12 miles wide. It divides the Queen Alexandra Range from the Commonwealth Range, and its head is 9,820 feet above sea level. It descends about 8,200 feet from the Polar Plateau to the Ross Ice Shelf. It contains petrified wood and fossils of fern and coral, evidence of a temperate climate once enjoyed by Antarctica. Shackleton discovered the Beardmore and pioneered it as a route to the South Pole, naming it for his employer and principal backer, Sir William Beardmore. Scott used the same basic route in 1911–12.

**Beardmore Glacier Camp.** 84°56'S, 166°W. Established at the foot of the Beardmore Glacier, on the Ross Ice Shelf. It was an Operation Deep Freeze II camp 400 miles from the South Pole. Construction of Beardmore Air Operating Facility (as it was designated, strictly speaking) was led by Michael Baronick, and finished by Oct. 28, 1956. It was used to help in support of operations to the Pole during the IGY, and as a refueling station for South Pole flights by the Americans. It was relocated 122 miles to the east, to the foot of the Liv Glacier, and its name was changed to Liv Glacier Auxiliary Naval Air Facility. Later still, the name reverted to Beardmore.

**Beardmore South Camp.** 84°03'S, 164°15'E. A large, temporary US field camp built by ITT/Antarctic Services Inc., on the Bowden Névé near the Beardmore Glacier. Built in 1984–85 to support about 60 scientists for more than 70 days in the following, 1985–86, season, it consisted of Jamesway huts. In one 40-foot-long Jamesway hut were 4 showers, 7 toilets, 8 sinks, and 3 urinals. Three 80-foot-long Jamesways provided the sleeping areas, and an 84-foot hut the galley/dining area. There was a 64-foot hut for helicopter maintenance, and other buildings. Geology was the main study. David H. Elliott was chief scientist and David B. Waldrip was station manager.

**Beards.** For most men in Antarctica they are almost necessary. There is a lot of variety, and a lot of vanity. Some men dislike them because they attract too much ice.

**Bearing Island.** 64°33'S, 62°02'W. A small island between Nansen Island and Enterprise Island, in Wilhelmina Bay, off the west coast of Graham Land. An old whalers' name, it was also called Direction Island, because of its use in the area.

**Mount Bearskin.** 78°20'S, 85°37'W. 2,850 m. 5 miles NE of Mount Tyree, between the Patton and Cornwall Glaciers, in the Sentinel Range. Named for Leland Bearskin.

**Bearskin, Leland S.** Capt., USAF. Participated in the setting up of the South Pole Station in the 1956–57 season, and therefore was one of the first men ever to stand at the Pole (*see* the Bibliography under Paul Siple, his book *90° South,* for list of those with Bearskin).

**Beascochea Bay.** 65°30'S, 64°W. 10 miles long. 5 miles wide. An indentation into the west coast of Graham Land, south of Cape Pérez. Discovered by de Gerlache in 1897–99. Named by Charcot in 1903–5 for Cdr. Beascochea of the Argentine Navy.

**Beaudoin Peak.** 79°48'S, 81°W. 980 m. Snow-free. Surmounts the SE part of the Meyer Hills, in the Heritage Range.

Named for Douglas W. Beaudoin, meteorologist at Ellsworth Station in 1961.

**Mount Beaufort** *see* **Mount Foster**

**Beaufort Island.** 76°55′S, 166°56′E. 2,530 feet high. 12 miles to the north of Cape Bird, Ross Island, in the Ross Sea. It is an SPA because of its breeding grounds. Discovered by Ross in 1841, and named by him for Capt. Francis Beaufort, RN, hydrographer to the admiralty (*see also* **Balleny Islands**).

**The *Beaufoy of London*.** British 65-ton sloop with a crew of 13. It was tender to the *Jane* during Weddell's 1819–22 expeditions in Antarctic waters, and during that time was commanded by Capt. Michael McLeod. From 1822–24 it was again the *Jane's* consort vessel, but this time commanded by Capt. Matthew Brisbane. In 1824–26 it was on its own in the South Shetlands, again under Brisbane.

**Beaufoy Ridge.** 60°38′S, 45°33′W. A black ridge. 1,650 meters at its NW end. At the west side of the Sunshine Glacier. Just north of Iceberg Bay, on the south side of Coronation Island, in the South Orkneys. Surveyed by the FIDS in 1948–49, and named by them for the *Beaufoy of London*.

**Mount Beaufurt** *see* **Mount Foster**

**Beaumont Bay.** 81°31′S, 161°22′E. A Ross Ice Shelf indentation into the Transantarctic Mountains (this type of bay is called a re-entrant), on the Shackleton Coast, between Young Head and Harris Point. Dickey Glacier flows into it. Discovered by members of Scott's 1901–4 expedition, and named for Adm. Sir Lewis Beaumont, RN, Arctic explorer and a supporter of Scott's expedition.

**Beaumont Glacier.** 72°02′S, 62°W. Also called Tejas Glacier. Flows into Hilton Inlet on the east coast of Palmer Land. Discovered aerially in 1940 by the USAS 1939–41. Ronne named it for the Texas city and also for the Tejas chapter of the Daughters of the Republic of Texas, both of whom supported the RARE 1947–48.

**Beaumont Hill.** 64°01′S, 61°59′W. 4½ miles NE of Chauveau Point on the west side of Liège Island. Named by the UK for William Beaumont, US surgeon (1785–1853).

**Beaumont Island.** 68°12′S, 66°57′W. A tiny island, no more than a rock, in Neny Bay, almost ½ mile from the mouth of Centurion Glacier, off the west coast of Graham Land. The BGLE discovered and charted it in 1936. The FIDS surveyed it in 1947 and named it for the *Port of Beaumont, Texas*, which wintered near here in 1947.

**Beaumont Skerries.** 64°46′S, 64°19′W. Two small islands and several rocks. 1 mile east of the Joubin Islands, off the SW coast of Anvers Island. Named for Malcolm J. Beaumont, electronics technician on the *Hero*, on that vessel's first Antarctic voyage in 1968.

**Beaupré Cove.** 64°42′S, 62°22′W. 1 mile wide. Just NW of Piccard Cove in Wilhelmina Bay, on the west coast of Graham Land. Charted by de Gerlache in 1897–99. Named by the UK in 1960 for Charles-François Beautemps-Beaupré (1766–1854), French hydrographer who briefed the Dumont d'Urville expedition of 1837–40.

[1]**Beaver Glacier.** 67°02′S, 50°40′E. 15 miles long, and 4 miles wide. Flows into Amundsen Bay between Auster Glacier and Mount Gleadell, from the Napier Mountains of Enderby Land. Visited by an ANARE party on Oct. 28, 1956. Named by the ANARE for the Beaver aircraft used in coastal exploration.

[2]**Beaver Glacier.** 83°24′S, 169°30′E. 15 miles long. Flows from the Queen Alexandra Range, between the Lennox-King and Beardmore Glaciers, into the Ross Ice Shelf at McCann Point. Named by the New Zealanders in 1959–60 for the *City of Auckland* (q.v.), which was a Beaver airplane.

**Beaver Island.** 67°07′S, 50°47′E. 2 miles long. 1 mile wide. On the south flank of Beaver Glacier in Amundsen Bay. P.W. Crohn led an ANARE party here in 1956, and named it because of its proximity to the glacier.

**Beaver Lake.** 70°48'S, 68°20'E. A lake of smooth ice, 7 miles long and 5 miles wide. Enclosed on the south and east by Flagstone Bench and Jetty Peninsula. 17 miles ESE of the Aramis Range in the Prince Charles Mountains. Discovered in 1956 by the ANARE. Used as a landing area by Beaver aircraft.

**Beaver Rocks.** 63°40'S, 59°21'W. A group 2 miles off the Trinity Peninsula between Notter Point and Cape Kjellman. Named by the UK for the type of aircraft.

**Mount Beazley.** 85°51'S, 142°51'W. 2,410 m. Surmounts the northern extremity of the California Plateau. Named for Lt. Robert M. Beazley, USN, officer-in-charge of Amundsen-Scott South Pole Station in 1965.

**Beche Blade.** 80°43'S, 24°19'W. A ridge in the Shackleton Range.

**Mount Béchervaise.** 70°11'S, 64°48'E. 2,360 m. A massif in Mac. Robertson Land. 1 mile east of Mount Lacey in the Athos Range. It is bare, except for an ice cap on the flat summit. Visited in Nov. 1955 by John M. Béchervaise and his ANARE party. Béchervaise was officer-in-charge of Mawson Station in 1955 and 1959 (*see also* the Bibliography).

**Béchervaise Island.** 67°35'S, 62°49'E. Largest of the Flat Islands in Holme Bay. Found to be a separate island in 1954 by the ANARE, and later named for John Béchervaise (*see* **Mount Béchervaise**).

**Cape Beck.** 78°18'S, 166°16'E. Forms the southern end of Black Island in the Ross Archipelago. Named by the New Zealanders in 1958–59 for A.C. Beck, here at the time.

[1]**Mount Beck.** 71°02'S, 67°01'E. Also called Mount Bent. Partly snow-covered. 2 miles SW of Taylor Platform in the Prince Charles Mountains. Named by the Australians for J.W. Beck, assistant cook at Mawson Station in 1964, and storeman at Wilkes Station in 1966.

[2]**Mount Beck** *see* **Beck Peak**

**Beck, Andreas.** Norwegian Arctic sealing skipper who was ice-pilot on the *Fram* with Amundsen during the Norwegian Antarctic Expedition of 1910–12.

**Beck Peak.** 86°05'S, 158°58'W. Also called Mount Beck, Mount A. Beck. 2,650 m. On the east flank of Amundsen Glacier, 2 miles NW of Mount Stubberud, in the Queen Maud Mountains. In Nov. 1911, when Amundsen was speeding toward the Pole, and without much time to bother too much about accuracy of his plotting of features, he saw a mountain in this general area and called it Mt. A. Beck, naming it for Andreas Beck. Modern geographers can not be sure where this peak is, or was, but they know it was definitely in this general area, so they arbitrarily named this particular peak as Beck Peak.

**Mount Becker.** 75°06'S, 72°02'W. 1 mile NE of Mount Boyer in the Merrick Mountains. Discovered aerially by the RARE 1947–48, and named by Ronne for Ralph A. Becker, legal counsel who helped get the expedition together.

**Beckett Nunatak.** 76°02'S, 160°11'E. 9 miles west of Mount Armytage, and south of Harbord Glacier, in Victoria Land. Named in 1964 for W.T. Beckett, utilitiesman at McMurdo Station in 1963.

**Bedford Island.** 66°28'S, 67°09'W. 1 mile long. At the south end of the Barcroft Islands, in the Biscoe Islands. Named by the UK for Thomas Bedford, British physicist.

**Bednarz Cove.** 66°21'S, 110°32'E. Indentation into the south side of the Mitchell Peninsula in the Windmill Islands. Named for Chief Electronics Technician Donald F. Bednarz, USN, at Wilkes Station in 1958.

**Bedrock.** If there were no ice cap in Antarctica, it would be a small continent of 2.7 million square miles, consisting of bedrock. In other words, it would be like any other continent in that respect. This continent would comprise East Antarctica (the actual continental land mass) and a nearby island archipelago (West

Antarctica). There would be vast lowland plains and reasonably high mountains, and the terrain would be generally hilly to mountainous. All this has been borne out by echo soundings, which give a lay of the land below the ice. The continental bedrock has been depressed by about 2,000 feet on average by the sheer weight of the ice on top of it. At the South Pole, for example, there are 336 feet of bedrock beneath 9,186 feet of ice.

**The Beehive** *see* **Mount Ruth Gade**

**Beehive Hill.** 68°16′S, 66°10′W. 2,030 m. Ice-covered. On the Graham Land plateau. 10 miles east of the head of Neny Fjord, and just north of the head of Wyatt Glacier. Surveyed in 1940 by the USAS, who called it Sphinx. Resurveyed in 1946 by the FIDS, who renamed it descriptively.

**Beehive Mountain.** 77°40′S, 160°33′E. 5 miles north of Finger Mountain, at the northern edge of the Taylor Glacier, in Victoria Land. Discovered by Armitage in 1902 during Scott's 1901–4 expedition, and named descriptively by him (Armitage).

**Beehive Nunatak** *see* **Teall Nunatak**

**Beer Island.** 66°S, 65°41′W. Also called Mutton Cove Island. 1 mile long. Just south of Jagged Island. 8 miles west of Prospect Point, off the west coast of Graham Land. Named by the BGLE 1934–37.

**Beethoven Peninsula.** 71°40′S, 73°45′W. 60 miles long. 60 miles wide at its broadest. Deeply indented and ice-covered. Forms the SW part of Alexander Island. Discovered aerially in 1940 by the USAS. Named by the UK for the composer.

**Beetle Spur.** 84°10′S, 172°E. 2 miles north of Mount Patrick in the Commonwealth Range. First seen by Shackleton in 1908. From the west it looks like a beetle, and was so named by John Gunner of the Ohio State University Geological Expedition of 1969–70.

**Beetles.** There are two species of beetles living in Antarctica. They are probably alien to the continent. They inhabit islands near the Antarctic Peninsula.

**Behaim Peak.** 68°47′S, 66°43′W. 1,150 m. Pyramid-shaped. A rock peak between Meridian Glacier and Doggo Defile, at the southern end of a chain of mountains, on the west side of the Antarctic Peninsula. Named by the UK for Martin Behaim (1459–1506), navigator.

**Mount Behling.** 85°40′S, 161°04′W. 2,190 m. Ice-covered. Flat-topped. Between Steagall Glacier and Whitney Glacier. 5 miles north of Mount Ellsworth in the Queen Maud Mountains. Named for Robert E. Behling, glaciologist on the South Pole–Queen Maud Land Traverse II, 1965–66.

**Behr Glacier.** 72°55′S, 168°05′E. 7 miles long. Flows along the north side of Clapp Ridge, to enter Borchgrevink Glacier, in Victoria Land. It first appeared on a 1960 NZ map of Antarctica. Named by the USA for Col. Robert Behr, USAF, an Antarctic administrator of policy, 1970–71.

**Behrendt Mountains.** 75°20′S, 72°30′W. 20 miles long. Shaped like a horseshoe. In eastern Ellsworth Land, just to the north of the Orville Coast. 7 miles SW of the Merrick Mountains. Named for John C. Behrendt, traverse seismologist at Ellsworth Station in 1957. He was in these mountains in the 1961–62 season, in Marie Byrd Land in 1963–64, and in the Pensacola Mountains in 1965–66.

**Beiszer Nunatak.** 83°29′S, 51°57′W. 1,630 m. 1 mile south of Ray Nunatak, at the SW end of the Forrestal Range. Named for John E. Beiszer, aviation structural mechanic at Ellsworth Station in 1957.

**Beitzel Peak.** 80°17′S, 82°18′W. 1½ miles SE of Minaret Peak in the Marble Hills of the Heritage Range. Named for John E. Beitzel, geophysicist on the South Pole–Queen Maud Land Traverses I and II, 1964–65 and 1965–66.

**Bekker Nunataks.** 64°42′S, 60°50′W. Three nunataks below Ruth Ridge on the north side of the Drygalski Glacier, in Graham Land. Named by the UK for Lt. Col. Mieczyslaw G. Bekker, Canadian engineer specializing in the ice.

**Belding Island.** 66°24′S, 67°13′W. 3 miles long. West of the south end of Watkins Island in the Biscoe Islands. Named by the UK for Harwood S. Belding, US physiologist specializing in the cold.

**Mount Belecz.** 85°34′S, 163°27′W. 2,120 m. Ice-covered. Flat-topped. 6 miles NE of Mount Ruth Gade in the Quarles Range. Named for Dan M. Belecz, meteorologist at Amundsen-Scott South Pole Station in 1962.

**Belemnite Point.** 70°40′S, 68°32′W. Between Lamina Peak and Ablation Point, on the east coast of Alexander Island. It is 2 miles inland from George VI Sound, and forms the eastern end of an ice-free ridge. Photographed aerially by Ellsworth on Nov. 23, 1935. Surveyed by the BGLE in 1936, and again by the FIDS in 1949. Named by the FIDS for the belmnite fossils found here.

**Belgen Valley.** 73°35′S, 4°W. Broad and ice-filled. Between Enden Point and the Heksegryta Peaks in the Kirwan Escarpment of Queen Maud Land. Name means "the shell" in Norwegian.

**The *Belgica*.** Belgian 3-masted steam/sailing ship sent by Belgium to the Antarctic on an expedition led by Adrien de Gerlache in 1897–99. Originally a whaler called the *Patria,* it was bought for 60,000 francs, overhauled and renamed for the ancient Roman province of Belgica. A gray ship, with natural wood and cream trimmings, it was bark-rigged with patent single topsails. 110 feet long, 26 feet wide, and had a draft of 15 feet. It had auxiliary steam power aft, and could reach 7 knots maximum speed. A modern steam sealer, it had a new boiler and a 150 hp engine. Equipped as a scientific laboratory, its lab measured 15 feet by 12 feet in a special deck house. The Belgian Antarctic Expedition left Antwerp on Aug. 16, 1897, and Ostend on Aug. 24, 1897. Aside from the leader, de Gerlache, others on board included Lecointe (ship's captain and second-in-command of the expedition), Danco, Wiencke, Amundsen, Dobrowolski, Racovitza, Arctowski, Malaerts, Tollefsen, Knudsen, Somers, Van Rysselbergh, Van Mirlo, Hjalmar Johansen, Koren, Michotte, and Dufour (there was one other, but he deserted in Chile). The ship arrived at Madeira on Sept. 13, 1897, and left there on Sept. 16, 1897, bound for Rio. It reached the Brazilian port on Oct. 22, 1897. On Oct. 30, 1897, Frederick Cook, the surgeon, boarded, and the same day the ship sailed for Buenos Aires, Montevideo and Punta Arenas (this last port being where the 20th member deserted). They arrived in Antarctic waters on Jan. 19, 1898. Truly an international crew, 19 men from 5 nations, the expedition arrived at the South Shetlands on Jan. 20, 1898. On Jan. 23, 1898, Carl Wiencke drowned. Between Jan. 23 and Feb. 12, 1898, the expedition ship made 20 separate landings on the islands off the Antarctic Peninsula, the first scientific vessel to visit the continent itself. On Jan. 26, 1898, Amundsen became the first man to ski in Antarctica, when he did so on Two Hummock Island. On Jan. 31, 1898, de Gerlache, Cook, Amundsen, Danco, and Arctowski sledged across Brabant Island. On Feb. 15, 1898, the *Belgica* crossed the Antarctic Circle. On March 3, 1898, it got trapped in the pack ice at 70°20′S, 85°W, in the Bellingshausen Sea, and drifted for a year due to the failure of the weak, inefficient engines to pull it out. Danco died in June, and by Nov. 19, 1898, Amundsen had resigned due to prejudice by the Belgian majority against the non–Belgians on board. Two men, Tollefsen and Knudsen, went insane. The crew cut its way out of the ice beginning Jan. 11, 1899, finally escaping on Feb. 15, 1899. Scurvy was rampant. Amundsen refused to travel back to Belgium on the *Belgica,* taking Tollefsen home to Norway on a mail boat. When the *Belgica* got home it did so to celebration. It had coasted Graham Land, and discovered the Belgica Strait (now the Gerlache Strait) and the Danco Coast.

**Belgica Glacier.** 65°23'S, 63°50'W. 8 miles long. Flows into Trooz Glacier to the east of Lancaster Hill, on the west coast of Graham Land. Charted by the BGLE 1934–37, and named by the UK in 1959 for the *Belgica.*

**Belgica Mountains.** 72°35'S, 31°10'E. An isolated chain, 10 miles long, at the fringe of Queen Maud Land, between the Sør Rondane Mountains and the Queen Fabiola Mountains. They include Mounts Bastin, Boë, Brouwer, Collard, Gillet, Hoge, Hulshagen, Imbert, Kerckhove de Denterghem, Lahaye, Launoit, Perov, Van der Essen, and Victor. Discovered by the Belgian Antarctic Expedition of 1957–58, led by Gaston de Gerlache, and named by him for his father's ship, the *Belgica.*

**Belgica Sea**  *see*  **Bellingshausen Sea**

**Belgica Strait**  *see*  **Gerlache Strait**

**Belgium.** In 1897 Belgium sent to Antarctica the ill-fated *Belgica* expedition, led by Adrien de Gerlache. The next was the Belgian Antarctic Expedition of 1957–58 led by Gaston de Gerlache, son of the pioneer. This expedition established Belgium's only scientific station in Antarctica, Roi Baudouin Station (which was to close in 1967). Frank Bastin led the Belgian Antarctic Expedition of 1958–59, and Guido Derom led the one of 1959–61. One of the original 12 signatories of the Antarctic Treaty in 1959, Belgium still sends research parties to Antarctica, though in cooperation with other countries. It took part in the Filchner Ice Shelf Program.

**Isla Belgrano**  *see*  **Adelaide Island**

**Belknap Nunatak.** 72°26'S, 97°45'W. 6 miles WNW of Shelton Head on the south coast of Thurston Island. Named for William Belknap, field assistant at Byrd Station in 1964–65.

**Mount Bell.** 84°04'S, 167°30'E. 4,305 m. Forms part of the NE edge of the Grindley Plateau. 6 miles SE of Mount Mackellar, in the Queen Alexandra Range. Named by Shackleton in 1907–9 for William Bell, one of his relatives, and a supporter.

**Bell, Dennis R.** b. 1934. FIDS meteorological assistant at Base G on King George Island from 1958 to July 26, 1959, when he died in a crevasse.

**Bell, Thomas G.** Bosun on the Wilkes Expedition 1838–42.

**Bell Bay.** 67°11'S, 58°25'E. Between Mount Saint Michel and the Kring Islands, on the coast of Enderby Land. Photographed by the LCE 1936–37, and named Indrefjord (inner fjord) by the Norwegians. Renamed by the Australians for Sgt. S. Bell, RAAF, wireless fitter at Mawson Station in 1959.

**Bell Bluff.** 84°04'S, 170°E. On the west side of the Beardmore Glacier, just north of the mouth of Garrard Glacier. Named for Charles A. Bell, utilitiesman at Hallett Station in 1964.

**¹Bell Glacier.** 66°40'S, 125°05'E. Flows into Maury Bay, just east of Blair Glacier, on the coast of East Antarctica. Mapped by G.D. Blodgett in 1955. Named for Thomas G. Bell.

**²Bell Glacier**  *see*  **Mackellar Glacier**

**Bell Island**  *se*  **Guesalaga Island**

**Bell Peak.** 85°22'S, 164°14'W. 1,620 m. In the Herbert Range, just SW of Sargent Glacier. Seen by Amundsen in 1911, and mapped by Byrd's 1928–30 expedition. Named for G. Grant Bell, cosmic ray scientist at McMurdo Station in 1962.

**Bell Point.** 62°07'S, 58°53'W. 6 miles SW of Stigant Point, near the west end of King George Island, in the South Shetlands. Named Rocky Point by the personnel on the *Discovery II* in 1935. In 1960 the UK renamed it for Dennis R. Bell.

**Bell Rock.** 71°35'S, 66°26'W. Isolated. On Goodenough Glacier, 12 miles east of Mount Ward, in Palmer Land. Named by the UK for Charles M. Bell, BAS geologist at Fossil Bluff Station in 1968–71.

**Bell Valley.** 79°51'S, 82°W. A small, ice-free valley south of Urban Point, in the Enterprise Hills of the Heritage Range. Named by the University of Minnesota Geological Party of 1963–64 for the Bell helicopters used here.

**Mount Bellingshausen.** 75°07'S, 162°06'E. 1,380 m. Cone-shaped. 5 miles NE of Mount Priestley, between the Larsen and David Glaciers, in the Prince Albert Mountains of Victoria Land. Discovered by Scott's 1901–4 expedition, and named by Scott for von Bellingshausen.

**Bellingshausen, Fabian von** see **Von Bellingshausen, Fabian**

**Bellingshausen Abyssal Plain** see **Bellingshausen Plain**

**Bellingshausen Basin** see **Southeast Pacific Basin**

**Bellingshausen Plain.** Also called Bellingshausen Abyssal Plain. An enormous subsurface feature beneath the Amundsen and Bellingshausen Seas. It wends a snakelike course between 60°S and 72°S, and between 77°W and 172°W. Named for von Bellingshausen.

**Bellingshausen Sea.** 71°S, 85°W. Also called Belgica Sea. A vast sea, constantly ice-floed, between Thurston Island in the west and the Antarctic Peninsula in the east. It is part of the southern Pacific Ocean and reaches depths of from 500 feet to 13,000 feet and more. Named for von Bellingshausen.

**Bellingshausen Station.** 62°12'S, 58°56'W. USSR year-round scientific station built over the 1967–68 summer on Potter Cove, Fildes Peninsula, King George Island, in the South Shetlands. It was opened on Feb. 22, 1968. Its studies were atmosphere, meteorology, geomagnetism, and coastal hydrology. The original buildings were wooden, but now they are metal. It has a winter population of about 15. Named for von Bellingshausen.

**Mount Bellows.** 84°50'S, 178°58'E. 2,390 m. 3 miles west of Layman Peak, at the east side of the Ramsey Glacier. Named for Frederick A. Bellows, USN, radioman at McMurdo Station in 1964.

**Cabo Bellue** see **Phantom Point**

**Cape Bellue.** 66°18'S, 65°53'W. Forms the north side of the entrance to Darbel Bay, on the west coast of Graham Land. Discovered by Charcot in 1908–10, and named by him for Admiral Bellue, superintendent of the dockyard at Cherbourg. Not to be confused with Cabo Bellue (see **Phantom Point**).

**Mount Belolikov.** 70°29'S, 162°07'E. 1,120 m. Along the west wall of Gannutz Glacier, about 8 miles WNW of Mount Bruce, in the Bowers Mountains. Named by the USSR in 1961 for A.M. Belolikov (see **Deaths, 1960**).

**Belousov Point.** 69°50'S, 160°21'E. Ice-covered. Forms the southern tip of Anderson Peninsula just north of the terminus of Suvorov Glacier. Named for Russian polar captain Mikhail P. Belousov (1904–1946).

**Cape Belsham.** 61°06'S, 54°52'W. ½ mile west of Point Wild, on the north coast of Elephant Island. Named before 1822.

**Bender Mountains.** 85°31'S, 140°12'W. A small group in the vicinity of the Leverett Glacier, just to the east of the Harold Byrd Mountains, in Marie Byrd Land. Mount Mahan is the chief peak. 4 miles SW of the Berry Peaks. Named for Lt. Cdr. Leslie C. Bender, USN, aircraft commander at McMurdo Station in 1962–63 and 1963–64.

**Beneden Head.** 64°46'S, 62°42'W. Also called Cape Van Beneden. 700 m. A headland forming the north side of the entrance to Andvord Bay, on the west coast of Graham Land. Discovered by de Gerlache in 1897–99, and named by him for Prof. E. Van Beneden, president of the *Belgica* Commission, and author of several of the zoological reports of the expedition.

**Benedict Peak.** 75°17'S, 110°30'W. Ice-covered. 6 miles NE of the summit of Mount Murphy, in Marie Byrd Land. Named for Philip C. Benedict, aurora scientist at Byrd Station in 1966.

**Benedict Point.** 66°09'S, 66°36'W. 5 miles south of Cape Leblond, on the east side of Lavoisier Island, in the Biscoe Islands. Named by the UK for Francis G. Benedict, US physiologist specializing in metabolism.

**Benes Peak.** 76°02'S, 124°07'W. 2,450 m. Snow-covered. 4 miles east of Mount Aldaz, on the Usas Escarpment in Marie Byrd Land. Named for Norman S. Benes, meteorologist at Byrd Station in 1961.

**Mount Beney.** 80°16'S, 27°45'W. In the Shackleton Range.

**Beney Nunataks** see **La Grange Nunataks**

**Bengaard Peak.** 83°19'S, 163°29'E. 2,110 m. 6 miles south of the Fazekas Hills, on the east side of the Queen Elizabeth Range. Named for Hans J. Bengaard, US ionosphere physicist at Little America V in 1957.

**Mount Benjamin.** 85°48'S, 160°06'W. 1,750 m. On the west side of Amundsen Glacier. 5 miles SE of Mount Ellsworth in the Queen Maud Mountains. Discovered during Byrd's 1928–30 expedition. Named for Benjamin F. Smith, meteorologist at McMurdo Station in 1963.

**The *Benjamin Bowring*.** NZ ship conducting seismic surveys in the Ross Sea during the 1980–81 season.

**Mount Benkert.** 73°38'S, 76°40'W. The most easterly of the Snow Nunataks. 8 miles ESE of Mount Thornton, on the coast of Ellsworth Land. Discovered by the USAS 1939–41. Named for Capt. W.M. Benkert, US Coast Guard, commander of the *Eastwind* in 1966 and 1967.

**Benlein Point.** 66°29'S, 110°29'E. The southern point of Peterson Island in the Windmill Islands. Named for Franklin J. Benlein, USN, construction man at Wilkes Station in 1958.

**Cape Bennett.** 60°37'S, 45°13'W. Also spelled Cape Bennet. On the NE coast of Coronation Island in the South Orkneys. Discovered in Dec. 1821 by Powell and Palmer. Bennett was the name of Powell's employer.

**¹Mount Bennett** see **Stor Hånakken Mountain**

**²Mount Bennett.** 84°49'S, 178°54'W. 3,090 m. 3 miles east of Mount Boyd. Surmounts the western part of the Anderson Heights in the Queen Maud Mountains. Discovered by the USAS 1939–41. Surveyed by Crary's Ross Ice Shelf Traverse Party of 1957–58, and named by Crary for Hugh Bennett, seismologist with the party.

**Bennett, Arthur G.** British whaling representative in the South Shetlands and South Orkneys for many years between 1913 and 1927. From 1924–38 he was acting government naturalist on the Falkland Islands (cf. William Barlas).

**Bennett Bluff.** 75°08'S, 134°35'W. 810 m. Behind the Hobbs Coast in Marie Byrd Land. Between the upper reaches of the Venzke Glacier and the Berry Glacier. 7 miles SSW of the Perry Range. Discovered on Dec. 18, 1940, by the USAS. Named for Clarence E. Bennett, USN, VX-6 technician at McMurdo Station in 1963.

**Bennett Escarpment.** 70°36'S, 64°19'E. Curves SW for 20 miles from Mount Pollard in the Prince Charles Mountains. Named by the Australians for J.M. Bennett, physicist at Mawson Station in 1965.

**Bennett Islands.** 66°56'S, 67°40'W. At the SW side of Liard Island, in Hanusse Bay, off the west coast of Graham Land. They extend for 6 miles, and include Jona Island, Gränichen Island, Mügge Island, Pfaff Island, and Weertman Island. Discovered aerially by the BGLE in Feb. 1937. Named by the UK in 1954 for Arthur G. Bennett.

**Bennett Nunataks.** 84°47'S, 116°25'W. Two rock nunataks, ½ mile apart. ½ mile north of Lackey Ridge in the Ohio

Range. Named for John B. Bennett, geo-magnetist/seismologist at Byrd Station in 1960.

**Bennett Platform.** 85°13′S, 177°50′W. A high, nearly flat, snow-free, dark mesa. 5 miles long. 2½ miles wide. Just east of Mount Black, on the west side of the Shackleton Glacier, in the Transant-arctic Mountains. Discovered during the Feb. 16, 1947, flights to the Pole during Operation Highjump. Named for Floyd Bennett, Byrd's North Pole companion (see The *Floyd Bennett* for details).

**Bennett Saddle.** 77°05′S, 126°26′W. A deep snow saddle between Mounts Waesche and Sidley in the Executive Committee Range of Marie Byrd Land. Named for Gerard A. Bennett, traverse specialist at Byrd Station, who took part in the Executive Committee Range Tra-verse in Feb. 1959, and who was on the Marie Byrd Land Traverse of 1959–60.

**Bennett Spires.** 83°51′S, 56°10′W. Two sharp peaks overlooking the head of Jones Valley in the Neptune Range. Named for Staff Sgt. Robert E. Bennett, USAF, with the US Air Force Electronics Test Unit (q.v.), 1957–58.

**Bennett Spur.** 82°26′S, 50°38′W. In the northern part of the Pensacola Mountains.

**Benoit Peak.** 72°06′S, 163°40′E. 5 miles NNE of Mount Camelot in the Ala-mein Range of the Freyberg Mountains. Named for Robert E. Benoit, biologist at McMurdo Station, 1966–67 and 1967–68.

**Mount Bensley.** 70°19′S, 64°15′E. 1,920 m. 8½ miles SSW of Mount Starlight in the Prince Charles Moun-tains. Named by the Australians for P.A. Bensley, carpenter at Mawson Station in 1965.

**Mount Benson.** 78°37′S, 84°27′W. 2,270 m. On the NE side of the Thomas Glacier, 4 miles east of Mount Osborne, in the SE part of the Sentinel Range. Named for Robert F. Benson, seismolo-gist at the South Pole Station in 1957.

**Benson, Elof.** Originally Elof Berndt-son. Born in Göteborg, Sweden, he came to the USA as a young man, and lived in Stonington, Conn. He was mate on the *Hersilia*, 1819–20, and kept the log-book, which turned up in 1956 after hav-ing been presumed lost (his descendants had it). In 1820–21 he was first mate on the *Catharina*, on a voyage to the South Shetlands. He later became captain of an American sealer called the *Adventure*. He was lost at sea in the 1820s.

**Benson Glacier.** 76°50′S, 162°12′E. 20 miles long. Flows between the Fry and Mackay Glaciers into the northern part of Granite Harbor, where it forms a floating tongue. Named by the NZ party of the BCTAE in 1957 for W.N. Benson, petrologist from the University of Otago, NZ.

**Benson Hills.** 70°28′S, 62°17′W. A cluster of coastal hills near the head of Smith Inlet, 3 miles east of the Berry Massif, on the east side of Palmer Land. Named for Lt. Arthur K. Benson, USN, medical officer at Palmer Station in 1969.

**Benson Knob.** 75°45′S, 159°17′E. 1,540 m. A hill at the southern extremity of the Ricker Hills in the Prince Albert Mountains of Victoria Land. Named for Anthony J. Benson, hospital corpsman at Amundsen-Scott South Pole Station in 1966.

**Benson Point.** 62°39′S, 61°18′W. Forms the SW end of Rugged Island, in the South Shetlands. Named by the UK in 1958 for Elof Benson.

**Benson Ridge.** 82°46′S, 164°48′E. Be-tween Robb Glacier and Bondeson Gla-cier. 5 miles west of the north end of the Holland Range. Named for Carl S. Ben-son, US glaciologist at Roosevelt Island, 1961–62.

**Mount Bent**   *see*   **Mount Beck**

**Benten Island.** 69°01′S, 39°13′E. A small island 5 miles west of Ongulkalven Island in the east part of Lützow-Holm Bay. Named Benten-shima (goddess of fortune island) by the Japanese.

**Mount Bentley.** 78°07'S, 86°14'W. 4,245 m. 2 miles north of Mount Anderson in the main western ridge of the Sentinel Range. Discovered by the Marie Byrd Land Traverse Party of 1957–58, led by Charles R. Bentley, for whom this feature is named.

**Bentley, Charles R.** b. Dec. 23, 1929, Rochester, NY. Charles Raymond Bentley. Glaciologist, and one of the leading figures in Antarctic history. A professor at Columbia University when he went to Antarctica during the IGY. He was the chief traverse seismologist at Byrd Station from 1957–59. He led the Marie Byrd Land Traverse Party of 1957–58, and the Ellsworth Highland Traverse from Byrd Station between Nov. 14, 1960, and Feb. 11, 1961. He studied seismics of the polar caps and the sea floors, and used geophysical methods when dealing with glaciological problems. He wrote *Land Beneath the Ice* (*see also* the Bibliography).

**Bentley Crag.** 67°17'S, 66°53'W. Between Humphreys Hill and Seue Peaks on Arrowsmith Peninsula, in Graham Land. Named by the UK for Wilson A. Bentley, US photographer.

**Bentley Subglacial Trench.** 78°S, 110°W. The deepest depression in the world, it is 8,326 feet below sea level. It is part of the Byrd Subglacial Basin, in Marie Byrd Land, and lies partly under the West Antarctic land mass, and partly under the Amundsen Sea. Named for Charles R. Bentley, who discovered it in 1957–58.

**Benton Island.** 77°04'S, 147°53'W. 4 miles long. Ice-covered. 5 miles NW of Nolan Island in the Marshall Archipelago. Named for William T. Benton, USN, bosun's mate on the *Glacier,* 1961–62.

**Benz Pass.** 63°41'S, 58°22'W. Between the southern cliffs of Louis Philippe Plateau and a rock nunatak 2 miles NE of the head of Russell East Glacier, on Trinity Peninsula. Named by

the UK for Karl Benz, the automobile manufacturer.

**Beresino Island** *see* **Greenwich Island**

**Berg, Dr. Reals.** Medical officer from Oslo. He was on Ellsworth's 1933–34 expedition.

**Berg Bay.** 71°27'S, 169°27'E. A small bay between Birthday Point and Islands Point on the west side of Robertson Bay, in northern Victoria Land. Charted and named in 1911 by Campbell's Northern Party during Scott's 1910–13 expedition. There are icebergs here.

**Berg Ice Stream.** 73°42'S, 78°20'W. 30 miles long. Flows into Carroll Inlet between Rydberg Peninsula and Espenschied Nunatak, on the coast of Ellsworth Land. Named for Capt. Harold Berg, commander of the *Eltanin,* 1964–65.

**Berg Mountains.** 69°13'S, 156°04'E. Also called Mount Dwyer. A mountain and 2 ridges. 14 miles south of Cape Buromskiy, on the Krylov Peninsula. Named by the USSR for geographer Lev Berg.

**Berg Peak.** 71°32'S, 161°47'E. 1,870 m. 3 miles south of El Pulgar, in the northern part of the Morozumi Range. Named for Thomas E. Berg, geologist at McMurdo Station in 1961. He was in Victoria Land for three successive summers in the 1960s, and died in 1969 (*see* **Deaths, 1969**).

**Bergan Castle.** 80°36'S, 21°21'W. A mountain in the Shackleton Range.

**Bergel Rock.** 65°10'S, 64°58'W. Almost 1 mile south of Quintana Island, in the SW part of the Wilhelm Archipelago. Named by the UK for Alexandra Bergel, granddaughter of Shackleton, who sponsored the *Endurance* which made surveys here in Feb. 1969.

**Mount Bergen.** 76°59'S, 160°48'E. 2,110 m. 2 miles west of Mount Gran, on the north side of the Mackay Glacier, in Victoria Land. Surveyed in 1957 by the NZ party of the BCTAE 1956–58, and named by them for Tryggve Gran's birthplace.

**Bergen Nunataks.** 72°25'S, 64°53'W. In Palmer Land.

**Mount Berger.** 75°04'S, 71°57'W. 2 miles NE of Mount Becker, in the Merrick Mountains. Named for Lt. Cdr. Raymond E. Berger, USN, pilot who flew the University of Wisconsin Traverse Party to this area in 1965–66.

**Mount Bergersen.** 72°04'S, 25°48'E. Also called Mount Birger Bergersen. 3,170 m. At the west side of Byrdbreen in the Sør Rondane Mountains. Photographed by the LCE 1936–37. Named by the Norwegians for Ambassador Birger Bergersen, chairman of the Norwegian Whaling Board.

**Mount Bergin.** 67°42'S, 48°55'E. 700 m. 4 miles west of Mount Maslen, in the Raggatt Mountains of Enderby Land. Named by the Australians for R.D. Bergin, radio officer at Mawson Station in 1956.

**Bergnes** *see* **Byrd Head**

**Bergschrund.** The crevasse, at the head of a valley glacier, that separates the ice from the rock behind it.

**Bergy bit.** A small bit of floating ice, usually under the water.

**Berkley Island.** 66°13'S, 110°39'E. ½ mile long. Marks the NE end of the Swain Islands. Named by Carl Eklund in 1957 for Richard J. Berkley, geomagnetician at Wilkes Station in 1957.

**Berkner, Lloyd V.** b. Feb. 1, 1905, Milwaukee, Wisc. d. June 4, 1967, Washington, DC. Lloyd Viel Berkner. Ionosphere physicist who was assigned by the Department of Commerce to Byrd's 1928–30 expedition as radio technician. A naval officer since 1926, he helped develop radar during the 1940s. In 1949 he proposed a third International Polar Year, which became the IGY in 1957–58 while he was President of ICSU (the International Council of Scientific Unions).

**Berkner Bank.** 75°S, 48°W. A submarine feature in the Weddell Sea.

**Berkner Island.** 79°30'S, 47°30'W. Also called Hubley Island. 30,000 square miles in area. 200 miles long. 85 miles wide. An ice-drowned island in the Weddell Sea, between the Ronne and Filchner Ice Shelves. It rises to a height of 975 m. Discovered by the Americans from Ellsworth Station in 1957–58. Named for Lloyd Berkner.

**Mount Berlin.** 76°03'S, 135°52'W. 3,500 m. A conical volcano, 10 miles west of Mount Moulton at the west end of the Flood Range, overlooking the Hobbs Coast, in Marie Byrd Land. Lichens are to be found here. Discovered aerially in Nov.–Dec. 1934 during Byrd's 1933–35 expedition, and named by Byrd as Mount Hal Flood, but renamed later by the USA for Leonard R. Berlin.

**Berlin, Arthur.** Seaman on the *City of New York* during Byrd's 1928–30 expedition.

**Berlin, Leonard R.** Cadastral engineer at West Base during the USAS 1939–41. Leader of a party that sledged to Mount Berlin in Dec. 1940.

**Berlin Crater.** 76°03'S, 135°52'W. High, circular, ice-filled. Near the summit of Mount Berlin, in the Flood Range of Marie Byrd Land. Named in association with the mountain.

**Berlin Crevasse Field.** 76°S, 136°30'W. 10 miles in extent. Just west of Mount Berlin. Named in association with the mountain.

**Berlioz Point.** 72°10'S, 73°36'W. Snow-covered. On the south side of Beethoven Peninsula, on Alexander Island. Named by the UK for the composer.

**Bermel Escarpment.** 85°17'S, 89°30'W. 15 miles long. Extends from the base of the Ford Massif to King Peak, in the Thiel Mountains. Named for Peter Bermel of the US Geological Survey, co-leader with Arthur B. Ford of the Thiel Mountains Party in 1960–61, and leader of the US Geological Survey Topo West Party which surveyed between Cape Adare and the Wilson Hills, 1962–63.

**[1]Cape Bernacchi.** 77°29'S, 163°51'E. Forms the northern fringe of New Harbor, in southern Victoria Land. Discovered by Scott in 1902, and named by him for Louis Bernacchi.

²Cape Bernacchi *see* Bernacchi Head

**Bernacchi, Louis C.** 1876–1940. Australian physicist who was the magnetic and meteorological observer during Borchgrevink's 1898–1900 expedition, and wintered over in 1899. He was physicist on the Royal Society Expedition of 1901–4, joining in NZ.

**Bernacchi Bay.** 77°27'S, 163°28'E. 3 miles wide. Just to the south of Marble Point in southern Victoria Land. Discovered during Scott's 1910–13 expedition, and named in association with nearby Cape Bernacchi.

**Bernacchi Head.** 76°08'S, 168°20'E. Forms the southern extremity of Franklin Island, in the Ross Sea. Named Cape Bernacchi by Borchgrevink in 1900, for Louis Bernacchi. The name was later changed because of the other feature with the same name.

**Bernal Islands.** 66°22'S, 66°28'W. 4 mainly snow-covered islands and several rocks, in Crystal Sound, 10 miles east of the south end of Lavoisier Island, in the Biscoe Islands. Named by the UK for John D. Bernal, British physicist specializing in ice.

**Pointe Bernard** *see* **Barnard Point**

**Bernard, Robert C.** Quartermaster on the Wilkes Expedition 1838–42. Joined at Valparaiso. Served the cruise.

**Mount Bernard Horne** *see* **Mount Horne**

**Bernard Island.** 66°40'S, 140°02'E. Also called Île Claude Bernard. ¼ mile long. 80 yards east of Buffon Island in the Géologie Archipelago. Charted by the French in 1951, and named by them for Claude Bernard (1813–1878), French physiologist.

**Bernard Rocks.** 64°08'S, 62°01'W. A small group between Davis Island and Spallanzani Point, off the NE side of Brabant Island. Mapped by Charcot in 1903–5. Named by the UK for Claude Bernard (*see* **Bernard Island**).

**Bernardo O'Higgins Station** *see* General Bernardo O'Higgins Station

**Bernasconi, Irene.** Argentine hydrographic professor who worked on the Antarctic Peninsula in 1968–69, one of the first women ever to work in Antarctica (*see* **Women in Antarctica**).

**Bernhardi Heights.** 80°20'S, 25°W. In the Shackleton Range.

**Mount Bernstein.** 71°37'S, 163°07'E. 2,420 m. Forms part of the northern wall of Linder Glacier in the Lanterman Range. Named for Capt. Fred J. Bernstein, assistant chief of staff for operations and plans, US Naval Support Force, Antarctica, 1967 and 1968.

**Bernt Balchen Glacier** *see* **Balchen Glacier**

**Bernt Balchen Valley** *see* **Balchen Glacier**

**Berntsen, Søren.** Norwegian skipper of the *Orwell* during the last half of the 1920s.

**Berntsen Point.** 60°43'S, 45°36'W. Forms the south side of the entrance to Borge Bay, on the east side of Signy Island. Charted by the Discovery Investigations personnel on the *Discovery* in 1927, and named for Søren Berntsen.

**Berquist Ridge.** 83°31'S, 56°30'W. 8 miles long. In the Neptune Range. Named for Robert M. Berquist, photographer at Ellsworth Station in 1958.

**Berr Point.** 69°46'S, 39°04'E. A bare rock point. On the SE shore of Lützow-Holm Bay. 4 miles north of the Rundvågs Hills. Photographed by the LCE 1936–37. Named Berrodden (the bare point) by the Norwegians.

**Mount Berrigan.** 66°40'S, 52°43'E. 1 mile east of Budd Peak, in Enderby Land. Named by the Australians for M.G. Berrigan, assistant diesel mechanic at Wilkes Station in 1961.

**Berrnabbane Crags.** 69°44'S, 38°58'E. Along the SE shore of Djupvika, on the SW side of Lützow-Holm Bay. Photographed by the LCE 1936–37. Name means "the bare crags" in Norwegian.

**Berrodden** *see* **Berr Point**

**Mount Berry.** 64°26′S, 60°43′W. 3 miles SE of Baldwin Peak, near the head of Cayley Glacier in northern Graham Land. Named by the UK in 1960 for Albert Berry, US parachuting pioneer.

**Berry, Charles.** Master at arms during the Wilkes Expedition 1838–42. Joined in the USA. Returned in the *Relief* in 1839.

**Berry, James.** Seaman on the Wilkes Expedition 1838–42. Joined at Rio. Served the cruise.

**Berry Glacier.** 75°S, 134°W. 25 miles long. 5 miles wide. Flows between the Perry Range and the Demas Range into the Getz Ice Shelf, on the coast of Marie Byrd Land. Named for Cdr. William H. Berry, USN, air operations officer for Task Force 43, 1969–72. He was operations officer, 1973.

**Berry Head.** 60°42′S, 45°37′W. A point which divides Tern Cove from Stygian Cove on the NE side of Signy Island, in the South Orkneys. Surveyed by the personnel on the *Discovery II* in 1933, and named before that.

**Berry Massif.** 70°27′S, 62°30′W. Circular. Snow-covered. At the south side of the terminus of the Clifford Glacier, where that glacier enters Smith Inlet, on the east coast of Palmer Land. Named for Dale L. Berry, biologist and station scientific leader at Palmer Station in 1971.

**Berry Peaks.** 85°26′S, 138°32′W. To the immediate east of the Bender Mountains. It is a small group, 10 miles south of the terminus of the Reedy Glacier. Named for William Berry, radioman at Byrd Station in 1961.

**Bertalan Peak.** 72°04′S, 167°08′E. 2,320 m. At the NW side of the head of Montecchi Glacier in the Victory Mountains of Victoria Land. Named for Robert E. Bertalan, USN, chief machinery repairman at McMurdo Station in 1967.

**Cape Berteaux.** 68°51′S, 67°27′W. Also called Cape Pierre Baudin. Juts out into Marguerite Bay, forming the north-ern fringe of the Wordie Ice Shelf. Charcot named it Île Berteaux, thinking it was an island, and the name came to be known in English as Berteaux Island. The BGLE 1934–37 redefined it. Berteaux was a supporter of Charcot's expedition.

**Berteaux Island** *see* **Cape Berteaux**

**Bertha Island.** 67°23′S, 59°39′E. Also called Hamreneset. 2½ miles long. 1 mile south of Islay, at the east side of William Scoresby Bay. Discovered in Feb. 1936 by the personnel on the *William Scoresby,* and named by them.

**Berthelot Islands.** 65°20′S, 64°09′W. A group of rocky islands 1½ miles SW of Deliverance Point, off the west coast of Graham Land, near to Petermann Island. Green Island is the largest of the group. Discovered by Charcot in 1903–5, and named by him for Marcellin Berthelot, French chemist.

**Bertoglio Glacier.** 79°18′S, 160°20′E. 7 miles long. Flows from the Conway Range between Cape Lankester and Hoffman Point, to the Ross Ice Shelf. Named for Cdr. Lloyd W. Bertoglio, USN, leader at McMurdo Station in 1960.

**Bertrab Nunatak.** 77°55′S, 34°32′W. On the south side of the Lerchenfeld Glacier, about 5 miles WSW of the Littlewood Nunataks. Discovered by Filchner in 1911–12, and named by him for General von Bertrab, chief quartermaster on the German General Staff and chief of the Land Survey, who was chairman of Filchner's expedition (*see* **German Antarctic Expedition**).

**Bertram, George C.L.** Replaced Brian Roberts as biologist halfway through the BGLE 1934–37. In 1949 he became director of the Scott Polar Research Institute in Cambridge.

**Bertram Glacier.** 70°50′S, 67°28′W. 15 miles long. 18 miles wide at its mouth. Flows from the Dyer Plateau of Palmer Land into George VI Sound between Wade and Gurney Points. Discovered and surveyed in 1936 by Stephenson, Fleming, and Bertram of the BGLE. Named by the UK in 1954 for Bertram.

**Bertrand Ice Piedmont.** 68°31'S, 67°05'W. 11 miles long. 3–5 miles wide. Between Rymill Bay and Mikkelsen Bay on the Fallières Coast of Graham Land. Named by the UK for Kenneth J. Bertrand (see the Bibliography).

**Bertrand Island** see **Stanley Island**

¹**Berwick Glacier** see **Swinford Glacier**

²**Berwick Glacier.** 84°36'S, 165°45'E. 14 miles long. Flows between the Marshall Mountains and the Adams Mountains, to enter the Beardmore Glacier at Willey Point. Named by Shackleton in 1907–9 for the *Berwick*, on which Lt. Jameson B. Adams had served (though this ship was never in Antarctica). Swinford Glacier (sometimes confused with it) lies 12 miles to the SW.

**Mount Besch.** 78°11'S, 84°43'W. 1,210 m. Forms the south end of Barnes Ridge, and overlooks the terminus of the Ellen Glacier, on the east side of the Sentinel Range. Named for Capt. Marvin E. Besch, USAF, who helped build the South Pole Station.

**Besnard, A.** Seaman on the *Français,* during Charcot's 1903–5 expedition.

**Besnard Point.** 64°50'S, 63°29'W. At the SE side of Port Lockroy on Wiencke Island. It marks the east side of the entrance to Alice Creek. Discovered by Charcot in 1903–5, and named by him for A. Besnard.

**Bessinger Nunatak.** 85°05'S, 64°41'W. 1,640 m. Mound-shaped. At the SW end of Mackin Table, 3 miles east of Mount Tolchin, in the southern part of the Patuxent Range. Named for Lt. C.D. Bessinger, Jr., USN, officer-in-charge of Amundsen-Scott South Pole Station in 1963.

**Mount Best.** 66°49'S, 51°23'E. 1½ miles SW of Mount Morrison in the Tula Mountains of Enderby Land. Named by the Australians for F. Best.

**Best, F.** Crew member on the *Discovery* during the BANZARE 1929–31.

**Besvikelsens Kap** see **Cape Disappointment**

**Beta Island.** 64°19'S, 63°W. Also called Isla Rodeada. Just north of Kappa Island, and just SW of Alpha Island, in the Melchior Islands. Named by the personnel on the *Discovery* in 1927 for the Greek letter.

**Beta Peak.** 75°51'S, 160°06'E. 1,620 m. 2 miles NE of Pudding Butte, in the Prince Albert Mountains of Victoria Land. Named by the New Zealanders in 1962–63. They had called it Station B when they were here.

**Cape Betbeder.** 63°37'S, 56°41'W. Marks the SW end of Andersson Island in the Antarctic Sound. Charted by Nordenskjöld's expedition of 1901–4, and named by him for Rear-Adm. Onofre Betbeder, Argentine minister of marine, who sent the *Uruguay* to rescue Nordenskjöld.

**Betbeder Islands.** 65°15'S, 65°03'W. A group of small islands and rocks in the SW part of the Wilhelm Archipelago, 22 miles west of Cape Tuxen. Discovered by Charcot in 1903–5, and named by him for Onofre Betbeder (see **Cape Betbeder**).

**Betbeder Refugio.** Argentine refuge hut built on Snow Hill Island in 1954. Named for Onofre Betbeder (see **Cape Betbeder**).

**Betekhtin Range.** 71°54'S, 11°32'E. 14 miles long. Forms the southern arm of the Humboldt Mountains in Queen Maud Land. Discovered by Ritscher in 1938–39. Named by the USSR in 1963 for academician A.G. Betekhtin.

**Beton, Theodore.** Ordinary seaman on the Wilkes Expedition 1838–42. Joined at Rio. Served the cruise.

**Bettle Peak.** 77°47'S, 163°30'E. 1,490 m. West of the Bowers Piedmont Glacier, and 6 miles north of the Granite Knolls, in Victoria Land. Named for James F. Bettle, meteorologist and scientific leader at McMurdo Station in 1962.

**Mount Betty.** 85°11'S, 163°45'W. 1,250 feet high. A small ridge on the north side of Bigend Saddle, in the NE extremity of the Herbert Range, overlooking the Ross Ice Shelf, between the Storm Glacier and the Axel Heiberg Glacier, in the Transantarctic Mountains. This is almost certainly the same feature that Amundsen discovered on Nov. 17, 1911, and named Betty's Knoll, for Betty Andersson, the Amundsen family housekeeper.

**Betty's Knoll** *see* **Mount Betty**

**Bevin Glacier.** 66°17'S, 63°47'W. 5 miles long. Flows into the NW end of Cabinet Inlet from the plateau escarpment of Graham Land, between the Attlee and Anderson Glaciers. Named by the FIDS for Ernest Bevin, British minister of labour.

**Mount Bewsher.** 70°54'S, 65°28'E. Flat-topped. 6 miles east of Mount McMahon, in the Aramis Range of the Prince Charles Mountains. First visited by the ANARE southern party of 1956–57 led by W.G. Bewsher, officer-in-charge of Mawson Station in 1956. Named for him by the Australians.

**Beyl Head.** 74°05'S, 116°31'W. On the coast of Marie Byrd Land.

**Bibby Point.** 63°48'S, 57°57'W. A steep rocky point at the NE corner of Brandy Bay, on James Ross Island. Named by the UK for John S. Bibby, FIDS geologist at Base D, 1958–59.

**Cape Bickerton.** 66°20'S, 136°56'E. Also called Cape Richardson. Ice-covered. 5 miles ENE of Gravenoire Rock, on the Clarie Coast of Wilkes Land. Charted by the AAE 1911–14, and named by Mawson for Frank Bickerton.

**Bickerton, Frank H.** Motor engineer in charge of the airplane/sledge during the AAE 1911–14. He led the Western Party during that expedition. He was due to go south again on the *Endurance* with Shackleton, in 1914, but World War I took him into the navy.

**Bidlingmaier, Friedrich.** Doctor, magnetician, and meteorologist on the von Drygalski expedition of 1901–3.

**Bielecki Island.** 64°46'S, 64°29'W. ½ mile north of Trundy Island in the west

part of the Joubin Islands. Named for Johannes N. Bielecki, assistant engineer on the *Hero* during that ship's first voyage to Antarctica, in 1968.

**Cape Bienvenue.** 66°43'S, 140°31'E. 44 m. A small, rocky cape, partly ice-covered. Forms the east side of the entrance to Piner Bay, on the Adélie Land coast. Charted and named by Barré in 1951–52. He established an astronomical station here. It was a welcome discovery.

**Bier Point.** 74°10'S, 164°09'E. On the east side of Campbell Glacier, 7 miles NE of Mount Queensland, in Victoria Land. Named for Jeffrey W. Bier, biologist at McMurdo Station, 1966.

**Mount Bierle.** 71°30'S, 167°19'E. 2,360 m. 4½ miles north of Mount Granholm in the Admiralty Mountains. Named for Donald A. Bierle, biologist at McMurdo Station, 1966–67 and 1967–68.

**Big Brother Bluff.** 71°28'S, 159°48'E. 2,840 m. A high, angular, granite bluff. Along the west wall of the Daniels Range, 6 miles north of Mount Burnham, in the Usarp Mountains. Named by the New Zealanders in 1963–64 because it is always visible, even from 50 miles away.

**Big Diamonen Island** *see* **Diamonen Island**

**Big Razorback Island.** 77°41'S, 166°30' E. Also called Large Razorback Island, Razorback Island. The most southeasterly, and the third largest, of the Dellbridge Islands, in Erebus Bay, off the west coast of Ross Island, in McMurdo Sound. Discovered and named descriptively by Scott in 1902.

**The *Bigbury Bay*.** British frigate at Deception Island in the 1949–50 season, with the governor of the Falkland Islands aboard. Captain that year was G.R.P. Goodden. In March, 1953, it joined the *Snipe* at Deception Island during the expulsion of South Americans from the island (*see* **Wars**). Captain that season was A.W.F. Sutton.

**Bigelow, George H.** Technical Sgt., US Marines. Tractor driver/mechanic on

Operation Highjump, 1946–47, and Operation Windmill, 1947–48.

**Bigelow Rock.** 66°10′S, 95°25′E. Also called Burton Island Rock. Low, ice-covered. 150 feet long. Just west of the Shackleton Ice Shelf. 25 miles NE of Junction Corner. Operation Windmill set up an astronomical station here in 1947–48. Named for George H. Bigelow.

**Bigend Saddle.** 85°12′S, 163°50′W. Snow-covered. On the SW side of Mount Betty, in the northern part of the Herbert Range. Traversed in Dec. 1929 by Gould's party during Byrd's 1928–30 expedition. Named by the New Zealanders in 1963–64 because one of the NZGSAE's motor toboggans was abandoned here with a smashed big end bearing.

**Biggs Island.** 67°48′S, 68°53′W. A small island, the easternmost of the Henkes Islands, off the south end of Adelaide Island. Named by the UK in 1963 for Thomas Biggs, a Falkland Islander with the *John Biscoe* here in 1963.

**Bigler Nunataks.** 70°45′S, 159°55′E. A cluster of nunataks SE of the Pomerantz Table, between Keim Peak and Lovejoy Glacier. Named for John C. Bigler, biologist at McMurdo Station in 1966–67.

**Mount Bigo.** 65°46′S, 64°17′W. 1,980 m. Just SW of Mount Perchot, at the head of Bigo Bay, on the west coast of Graham Land. Discovered by Charcot in 1908–10, and named by him for Robert Bigo of Calais, a member of the Ligue Maritime Française.

**Bigo Bay.** 65°43′S, 64°30′W. 8 miles long. 6 miles wide. An indentation into the west coast of Graham Land, between Cape García and Magnier Peaks. Charted by Charcot in 1908–10 as the southern part of Leroux Bay, but redefined and named by the BGLE in association with Mount Bigo.

**Bigourdan Fjord.** 67°33′S, 67°23′W. A sound. 12 miles long. An average of 2 miles wide. Between Pourquoi Pas Island and the SW part of Arrowsmith Peninsula, on the west coast of Graham Land.

Discovered by Charcot in 1908–10, and named by him for Guillaume Bigourdan, astronomer.

**Bildad Peak.** 65°49′S, 62°36′W. Also misspelled as Bilbad Peak. Snow-capped. 5 miles west of Spouter Peak on the south side of the Flask Glacier in Graham Land. Named by the UK for the *Moby Dick* character.

**Bilgeri Glacier.** 66°01′S, 64°47′W. Flows into Barilari Bay south of Huitfeldt Point, on the west coast of Graham Land. Named by the UK in 1959 for Georg Bilgeri (1873–1934), Austrian skiing pioneer.

**The Billboard.** 77°04′S, 145°38′W. A granitic, monolithic upland between Arthur Glacier and Boyd Glacier in the Ford Ranges. Its two principal peaks are Mount Rea and Mount Cooper. Discovered in Nov. 1934 by Paul Siple's sledge party, during Byrd's 1933–35 expedition. It is descriptively named.

**Billey Bluff.** 75°32′S, 140°02′W. Formerly called Landry Peak. 4 miles SW of Mount Langway, in the western part of the Ickes Mountains, on the Ruppert Coast of Marie Byrd Land. Named for John P. Billey, ionosphere physicist and scientific leader at Byrd Station in 1971.

**Billie Peak.** 64°45′S, 63°23′W. 725 m. 1½ miles ENE of Bay Point, on the SE coast of Anvers Island. Discovered by de Gerlache in 1897–99, and charted by the Discovery Investigations team on the *Discovery* in 1927. Named before that.

**Billie Rock** *see* **Billie Rocks**

**Billie Rocks.** 60°43′S, 45°37′W. A group, 150 yards NE of Drying Point in Borge Bay, along the east side of Signy Island. The most easterly of the group is called Billie Rock, and was named before 1927, when the Discovery Investigations personnel were in the waters of the South Orkneys on the *Discovery*, and charted these rocks as a group.

**Mount Billing.** 75°43′S, 160°54′E. 1,420 m. Wedge-shaped. Between Mount Mallis and Mount Bowen, in the Prince

Albert Mountains of Victoria Land. Named by NZ for Graham Billing, PR officer at Scott Base, 1962–63 and 1963–64.

**Billingane Peaks.** 68°21′S, 59°18′E. Also called Maruff Peaks. A cluster of 4 peaks 5 miles ESE of See Nunatak at the east end of the Hansen Mountains. Photographed by the LCE 1936–37, and later named by the Norwegians.

**Billis Islet**  *see*  **Bills Island**

**Bills Gulch.** 68°05′S, 65°50′W. The northern of two glaciers flowing east from the plateau upland into the head of Trail Inlet, on the east coast of Graham Land. Named by the USAS for Bill, the lead dog on Paul Knowles' transpeninsular traverse in 1940. Bill died here.

**Bills Island.** 64°49′S, 63°30′W. Also called Billis Islet. NE of Goudier Island, in the harbor of Port Lockroy, Wiencke Island. Charted by its discoverer, Charcot, in 1903–5. In 1927 the Discovery Investigations personnel on the *Discovery* re-charted it. It had already been named by that time.

**Bills Point.** 64°19′S, 62°59′W. Marks the southern end of Delta Island, in the Melchior Islands. Named in 1927 by the personnel on the *Discovery*, who charted it.

**Billycock Hill.** 68°10′S, 66°33′W. 1,630 m. Rounded. Ice-covered. Just north of the head of Neny Glacier on the west coast of Graham Land. Named by the FIDS because it looks like a billycock hat.

**Binder Rocks.** 74°14′S, 114°51′W. Isolated. 4 miles south of Siglin Rocks, on the west side of Martin Peninsula, in Marie Byrd Land. Lichens and petrels are to be found here. Named for Lt. R.A. Binder, USN, maintenance coordinator at Williams Field in 1967.

**Binders Nunataks.** 72°36′S, 62°58′E. Two nunataks, 37 miles north of Mount Scherger, in the southern Prince Charles Mountains. Named by the Australians for the fictional character in W.E. Bowman's novel, *The Ascent of Rumdoodle* (cf. Rumdoodle Point).

**Bingen Cirque.** 72°41′S, 3°18′W. In the Jøkulskarvet Ridge, in the Borg Massif of Queen Maud Land. Name means "the bin" in Norwegian.

**Bingham, E.W.** Surgeon Lt. Cdr., RN. Had been with Rymill in Greenland before both of them went on the BGLE 1934–37. He was the first FIDS leader, arriving at Stonington Island on Feb. 23, 1946, in the *Trepassey* in order to set up Base E there. On Feb. 24, 1946, he and his FIDS crew occupied the old East Base created by the USAS a few years before, and by March 13, 1946, Bingham had created Base E, 250 yards away. He was relieved on Feb. 5, 1947, by K.S. Pierce-Butler.

**Bingham Col.**  *see*  **Safety Col**

**Bingham Glacier.** 69°23′S, 63°10′W. 15 miles long. Feeds the Larsen Ice Shelf from the Eternity Range. Named by the USA in 1947 for E.W. Bingham.

**Bingham Peak.** 79°26′S, 84°48′W. 1,540 m. 2½ miles SE of Springer Peak in the Heritage Range. Named for Joseph P. Bingham, aurora scientist at Eights Station in 1965.

**Bingley Glacier.** 84°29′S, 167°10′E. Just to the west of the Beardmore Glacier, in the Queen Alexandra Range. 8 miles long, it flows from Mount Kirkpatrick, Mount Dickerson, and Barnes Peak, and enters the Beardmore Glacier just north of the Adams Mountains. Named by Shackleton in 1907–9 for his ancestral home in England. In 1910–13 Scott's expedition inadvertently named it Garrard Glacier. This confusion was sorted out by the New Zealanders in 1961–62.

**Binn, Captain.** Captain of the *Minerva*, in the South Shetlands, 1820–21.

**Binon Hill**  *see*  **Bynon Hill**

**Isla Bio Bio**  *see*  **Rambler Island**

**BIOMASS.** Biological Investigation of Marine Antarctic Systems and Stocks. Project BIOMASS, headed by SCAR (q.v.), came about as the result of concern over the exploitation of krill in the 1970s. In 1981 researchers in the program discovered 10 million tons of krill. Phase 1 of BIOMASS was known as FIBEX (q.v.).

**Birchall Peaks.** 76°29'S, 146°20'W. A group 3 miles west of Mount Iphigene, on the south side of Block Bay, in Marie Byrd Land. Discovered in 1929 by Byrd's 1928–30 expedition, and named by Byrd for Frederick T. Birchall, member of the staff of the *New York Times,* which published the expedition's press dispatches.

**Cape Bird.** 77°09'S, 166°43'E. The northernmost point of Ross Island, jutting out into the Ross Sea below Mount Bird. Discovered in 1841 by Ross, and named by him for Lt. Edward J. Bird.

**Mount Bird.** 77°17'S, 166°43'E. 1,765 m. The smallest mountain on Ross Island, it overlooks Wohlschlag Bay and Lewis Bay. 7 miles south of Cape Bird. Named by Scott in association with the cape, and mapped by his crew.

**Bird, Edward Joseph.** Lt. Officer on the *Erebus,* during the Ross expedition of 1839–43.

**Bird, John R.** Seaman on the *City of New York* during Byrd's 1928–30 expedition.

**Bird Bluff.** 76°30'S, 144°36'W. On the north side of the Fosdick Mountains, 2½ miles east of Mount Colombo, in the Ford Ranges of Marie Byrd Land. Named for Cdr. Charles F. Bird, meteorological officer on the staff of the Commander, US Naval Support Force, Antarctica, 1968.

**Bird Ridge.** 66°47'S, 55°04'E. 7 miles long. Partly ice-covered. 6 miles west of Mount Storegutt, west of Edward VIII Bay. Named by the Australians for G. Bird, senior electronics technician at Mawson Station in 1961.

**Birds.** About 45 species of birds live in Antarctica, but only 3 breed exclusively on the continent—the emperor penguin, the Antarctic petrel, and the south polar skua. Antarctic birds have strong homing instincts and navigational abilities (*see also* **Banding birds**). The sea-birds feed mostly on crustacea, fish, and squid. Shorebirds forage for mollusks, echinoderms, and crustaceans. Birds can live well, as there are few mammalian predators. *See* **Fauna, Penguins, Penguin rookeries, Adélie penguins, Emperor penguins, Chinstrap penguins, Robert Island penguins, Gentoo penguins, Macaroni penguins, Shearwaters, Shags, Cormorants, Fulmars, Petrels, Skuas, Sheathbills, Prions, Arctic terns, Antarctic terns, Albatrosses, Pintails, Phalaropes.** For the "Terror Bird" *see* **Fossils.**

**Birdsend Bluff.** 64°45'S, 62°33'W. Also called Mesa Negra. On the south side of the mouth of Wheatstone Glacier, on the west coast of Graham Land. Surveyed by de Gerlache in 1897–99. In May, 1956, two FIDS men were camping below the bluff when a rock fell and crushed a bird outside their tent.

**Birdwell Point.** 74°18'S, 128°10'W. The NW point of Dean Island, within the Getz Ice Shelf, off the coast of Marie Byrd Land. Named for Keith W. Birdwell, USN, electronics technician at Byrd Station in 1969.

**Biretta Peak.** 73°05'S, 163°13'E. 2,530 m. On the east side of Pain Mesa, in the Mesa Range of Victoria Land. Named by the New Zealanders in 1962–63 for its resemblance to a biretta cap.

**Mount Birger Bergersen** *see* **Mount Bergersen**

**Birkenhauer Island.** 66°29'S, 110°37'E. Ice-free. South of Boffa Island in the Windmill Islands. Named for the Rev. Henry F. Birkenhauer, seismologist at Wilkes Station in 1958.

**Mount Birks.** 65°18'S, 62°10'W. 1,035 m. Pyramid-shaped. At the north side of the mouth of Crane Glacier, on the east coast of Graham Land. For its discovery and naming *see* **Mount Napier Birks.**

**Birley Glacier.** 65°58'S, 64°21'W. 10 miles long. Flows into Barilari Bay on the west coast of Graham Land. Charcot discovered and surveyed it in 1909. The UK later named it for Kenneth P. Birley, supporter of the BGLE 1934–37.

**Birthday Point.** 71°26'S, 169°24'E. Between Pressure Bay and Berg Bay on the northern coast of Victoria Land. Charted and named by Campbell's Northern Party during Scott's 1910–13 expedition.

**Births in Antarctica.** It was not until Jan. 7, 1978, at Esperanza Station, that the first human birth took place — Emilio Marcos de Palma, son of Chief Officer de Palma of that station. Thirty years before, Jennie Darlington was taken off Antarctica in Oct. 1948, at the natural end of the RARE, just before giving birth. One could say, with all propriety, that she was the first woman to conceive of an Antarctic birth. On March 14, 1961, Pandora the hamster, there with Operation Deep Freeze, gave birth to twins at the South Pole Station, the first recorded birth (of any species) at the Pole.

**Bisco Bay**  *see*  **²Biscoe Bay**

**Mount Biscoe.** 66°13'S, 51°22'E. 700 m. Surmounts Cape Ann. 3 miles north of Mount Hurley, on the coast of East Antarctica. Biscoe discovered Cape Ann on March 16, 1831, and named it thus. On Dec. 22, 1929, Riiser-Larsen aerially photographed it, and the mountain, and on Jan. 14, 1930, Mawson did the same thing during the BANZARE. Mawson named the mountain for Biscoe.

**Biscoe, John.** 1794–1843. b. Middlesex, England. British navigator. Joined the RN in 1812, fought in the war of 1812 against the USA, joined the Merchant Navy and progressed through the ranks. While working for the London whaling company of Enderby Brothers he was sent to Antarctica on a sealing-exploring expedition. He left London on July 14, 1830, with two ships, the *Tula* and the *Lively.* He crossed the Antarctic Circle on Jan. 22, 1831, and on Jan. 29, 1831, he reached 69°03'S, then sailed east through the pack-ice. He sighted land on Feb. 24, 1831, and on Feb. 28, 1831, discovered the coast of Enderby Land, naming it for his employers. Earlier that month he had already named and annexed for Britain, Graham Land, discovered Adelaide Island and the Biscoe Islands. He was forced to New Zealand by crew sickness (two died in the Pacific), and in Hobart, Tasmania, the *Tula* met up with the *Lively,* the latter vessel having lost 7 men out of 10 due to sickness. He was back with the two ships in early 1832. By Feb. 3, 1832, he had reached 65°32'S. He circumnavigated Antarctica, and discovered more land than had any other previous expedition. In 1837 Biscoe moved to Sydney, and died in poverty as a passenger on a ship returning to England.

**¹Biscoe Bay**  *see*  **Sulzberger Bay**

**²Biscoe Bay.** 64°48'S, 63°50'W. Also seen spelled as Bisco Bay. An indentation into the SW coast of Anvers Island, just north of Biscoe Point, off Cape Errera, near Palmer Station. Discovered by de Gerlache in 1897–99, and named by him for John Biscoe, who may have landed here in Feb. 1832.

**Biscoe Islands.** 66°S, 66°30'W. A group of islands, lying parallel to the west coast of the Antarctic Peninsula, and extending for 80 miles north of Adelaide Island. Discovered by Biscoe, who explored here on Feb. 17 and 18, 1832. The principal features within the group are the Pitt Islands, Watkins Island, Renaud Island, Lavoisier Island, the Symington Islands, the Adolph Islands, the Barcroft Islands, the Bernal Islands, Rabot Island, Bazett Island, the Büdel Islands, the Hennessey Islands, Decazes Island, Bates Island, the Garde Islands, the Hardy Rocks, the Huddle Rocks, the Karelin Islands, the Vize Islands, the Palosuo Islands, Lacuna Island, Horvath Island, Hook Island, Belding Island, Clements Island, Schule Island, Holmes Island, Wittmann Island, the Trivial Islands, Woolpack Island, Milnes Island, Laktionov Island, Guile Island, Extension Reef, Du Bois Island, Cornet Island, Krogh Island, and Vieugué Island.

**Biscoe Point.** 64°49'S, 63°49'W. Forms the SE side of Biscoe Bay, just north of Access Point, on the south side of Anvers Island. The area was surveyed by Charcot in 1904. He named a small peninsula on the SE side of Biscoe Bay as Presqu'Île de Biscoe, for John Biscoe, who may have landed here in 1832. The FIDS resurveyed it in 1955, and found two rocky points here. They gave the name Biscoe Point to the more prominent.

**Biscuit Step.** 72°22'S, 168°30'E. A steplike rise in the level of the Tucker Glacier above its junction with the Trafalgar Glacier, in Victoria Land. Named by the NZGSAE 1957–58 for biscuits they left here while exploring the Tucker Glacier.

**Mount Bishop.** 83°43'S, 168°42'E. 3,020 m. 2 miles south of Ahmadjian Peak, in the Queen Alexandra Range. Named for Lt. Barry Bishop, USAF, an observer with the Argentine Antarctic Expedition of 1956–57. He served on the staff of the US Antarctic Projects Officer in 1958 and 1959, and in 1962 climbed Mount Everest.

**Bishop Peak.** 78°10'S, 162°09'E. 3,460 m. Surmounts the east end of Rampart Ridge, in the Royal Society Range. Named in 1963 for Bernice P. Bishop Museum, Honolulu, which has sent many researchers to Antarctica.

**Bismarck Strait.** 64°53'S, 63°55'W. Between the south end of Anvers and Wiencke Islands, and the Wilhelm Archipelago, off the west coast of the Antarctic Peninsula. Discovered in 1874 by Dallmann, and named by him for the Prussian statesman, Otto von Bismarck.

**Mount Bistre.** 65°03'S, 62°02'W. On the north side of Evans Glacier on the east side of Graham Land. Named by the UK for its bistre color.

**Mount Bitgood.** 76°29'S, 144°55'W. 1,150 m. Between Mount Lockhart and Mount Colombo, on the north side of the Fosdick Mountains, in the Ford Ranges of Marie Byrd Land. Named for Charles D. Bitgood, geologist in the Fosdick Mountains in 1967–68.

**Bizeux Rock.** 66°49'S, 141°24'E. An island, 175 yards long. 175 yards east of Manchot Island, just NE of Cape Margerie. Charted by the French in 1950 and named by them for the island in the center of the Rance Estuary in France.

**Mount Bjaaland.** 86°33'S, 164°14'W. Also called Mount Olav Bjaaland. 2,675 m. At the head of the Amundsen Glacier, in the Queen Maud Mountains. It may or may not be the actual mountain discovered and named by Amundsen in 1911, but it is the one thus selected by modern geographers. Named for Olav Bjaaland.

**Bjaaland, Olav.** b. 1872, Morgedal, Telemark, Norway. d. June, 1961. Olav Olavson Bjaaland (or Bjåland). A champion skier, he was one of the first men ever to reach the South Pole, as part of Amundsen's team of 1911–12. In fact, he was the first to stand at the actual Pole point. It was he who led the way up the Axel Heiberg Glacier in 1911, en route to the Pole, and the man who led the final run to the Pole area. He lived on his farm until his death, the last of the five polarfarers to die. (*See also* the Bibliography.)

**Bjarne Aagard Islands** *see* **Aagard Islands**

**The *Bjerk*.** Norwegian factory ship which, on Feb. 26, 1921, took Wilkins and Cope to Montevideo during the ill-fated British Imperial Expedition.

**Mount Bjerke.** 71°58'S, 9°43'E. 2,840 m. Forms the southern end of the Conrad Mountains, in the Orvin Mountains of Queen Maud Land. Discovered by Ritscher in 1938–39. Named Bjerkenuten by the Norwegians, for Henry Bjerke, mechanic with the Norwegian Antarctic Expedition of 1957–59.

**Bjerkø, Reidar.** Norwegian gunner on the whale catcher *Bouvet II,* in Antarctic waters in 1930–31. It was from his deck that the MacKenzie Bay coast, including what became known as the Bjerkø Peninsula, was sketched, on Jan. 19, 1931.

**Bjerkø Head** *see* **Cape Darnley**

**Bjerkø Peninsula.** 67°50'S, 69°30'E. A broad, ice-covered peninsula, it forms the west shore of MacKenzie Bay, in East Antarctica. Cape Darnley is at the end of the peninsula. Named by Norwegian whalers in the area in 1931 for Reidar Bjerkø.

**Bjørn Spur.** 71°55'S, 4°39'E. Extends NE from Skigarden Ridge, in the Mühlig-Hofmann Mountains of Queen Maud Land. Named Bjørnsaksa by the Norwegians for Bjørn Grytøyr, scientific assistant with the Norwegian Antarctic Expedition of 1956–57.

**Björnert Cliffs.** 74°58'S, 135°09'W. Series of ice-covered cliffs which face the sea along the north side of McDonald Heights, in Marie Byrd Land. Between Hanessian Foreland and Hagey Ridge. Named by the USA in 1974 for Rolf P. Björnert of the Office of Polar Programs, who was a station projects manager for Antarctica.

**Cape Black** *see* **Black Crag**

**¹Mount Black.** 85°13'S, 178°24'W. 3,005 m. Snow-covered on the SW. Has a steep rock face on the NW. Near the Shackleton Glacier in the Queen Maud Mountains. Discovered by Byrd on his flight to the Pole in Nov. 1929, and named by him for Van Lear Black, supporter of both of Byrd's first two expeditions.

**²Mount Black** *see* **Mount Ruth**

**Black, George H.** The mechanic and supply officer on Byrd's 1928–30 expedition.

**Black, J.** Bosun on the Wilkes Expedition 1838–42.

**Black, John.** Bosun's mate on the Wilkes Expedition 1838–42. Joined in the USA. Discharged at Oahu, Oct. 31, 1840.

**Black, Richard B.** One of the shore party on Byrd's 1933–35 expedition. As a commander, USNR, he was planning his own expedition to Antarctica in the late 1930s when President Roosevelt persuaded him to join the USAS 1939–41. During that expedition he was commander at East Base, and led the building of that base on Stonington Island. He led a flight on Dec. 30, 1940, which discovered the Black Coast. He was acting chief of staff on Operation Deep Freeze from 1955 to Aug. 15, 1957.

**Black Beach** *see* **Blacksand Beach**

**Black Cap.** 79°S, 161°51'E. A black rock peak which surmounts the NW end of Teall Island, just south of the mouth of the Skelton Glacier. Discovered and named by the NZ party of the BCTAE in Feb. 1957.

**Black Coast.** 71°45'S, 62°W. Also called Richard Black Coast. Between Cape Boggs and Cape Mackintosh, on the east coast of Palmer Land. Driscoll Island occupies a third of its area. Discovered aerially by the USAS from East Base on Dec. 30, 1940. Named for Cdr. Richard B. Black.

**Black Crag.** 71°46'S, 98°06'W. Also called Cape Black. A small, steep, cliff rock exposure at the NE end of Noville Peninsula on Thurston Island. Just south of Mulroy Island. Named for George H. Black.

**¹Black Glacier.** 62°58'S. On Deception Island, in the South Shetlands. It seems not to be there any longer.

**²Black Glacier.** 71°38'S, 164°50'E. Marks the SE extent of the Bowers Mountains, and flows into the Lillie Glacier. Named for Robert F. Black, geologist for several summers at McMurdo Station in the 1960s.

**Black Head.** 66°06'S, 65°37'W. Marks the south side of the entrance to Holtedahl Bay, on the west coast of Graham Land. This headland was named descriptively by the BGLE 1934–37.

**Black Hill** *see* **Clark Nunatak**

**¹Black Island.** 65°15'S, 64°17'W. 350 yards long. Just SW of Skua Island in the Argentine Islands. Charted and named by the BGLE in 1935.

**²Black Island.** 78°15'S, 166°29'E. 1,040 m. 12 miles long. A grounded island, of volcanic origin, directly north of Minna Bluff, in the Ross Archipelago, in the western Ross Ice Shelf. Because of the protective bluff, it does not get as much snow as its neighbor, White Island. Discovered by Scott in 1902, and named by him for its black volcanic rocks.

**Black Island Channel.** 65°15'S, 64°17' W. 175 yards wide. Between Black Island and Skua Island, in the Argentine Islands. Charted and named in 1935 by the BGLE.

**Black Nunataks.** 72°59'S, 74°28'E. 9 nunataks, 10 miles WSW of Mount Harding in the Grove Mountains. Named by the Australians for I. Black, geophysicist at Mawson Station in 1963.

**Black Pass.** 67°40'S, 67°34'W. In Graham Land.

**Black Peak** *see* **Greaves Peak**

**Black Point.** 62°29'S, 60°43'W. 2½ miles SE of Cape Shirreff on the north coast of Livingston Island. Discovered by the sealers in the early 1820s. Named by personnel on the *Discovery II* in 1935 when they charted it.

**Mount Black Prince.** 71°47'S, 168°15' E. 3,405 m. An imposing, dark-colored rock mountain. 4 miles west of Mount Ajax, in the Admiralty Mountains of Victoria Land. Named by the New Zealanders in 1957–58 for its appearance and for the NZ cruiser, the *Black Prince* (not in Antarctic waters).

**Black Pudding Peak.** 76°50'S, 161°45' E. An isolated, squat, black mountain in the valley of the Benson Glacier, 2 miles NW of Mount Brøgger. Named by the NZ party of the BCTAE in 1957.

**Black Reef** *see* **Sooty Rock**

**¹Black Ridge** *see* **Hanson Ridge**

**²Black Ridge.** 74°24'S, 163°36'E. 1,500 m. 7 miles long. Forms a divide between Priestley Glacier and Corner Glacier, in the Deep Freeze Range of Victoria Land. First explored by Campbell's Northern Party during Scott's 1910–13 expedition, and named descriptively by them.

**Black Thumb.** 68°25'S, 66°53'W. Also called Black Thumb Mountain. A peak. 1,190 m. Between the Romulus Glacier and the Bertrand Ice Piedmont, it forms the southern edge of Neny Fjord, just north of Marguerite Bay, on the west coast of Graham Land. Named descriptively by the BGLE 1934–37.

**Blackborrow, P. d.** 1949. Got onto the *Endurance* at Buenos Aires as a stowaway, and from then served as a steward on the ship during the ill-fated British Imperial Transantarctic Expedition led by Shackleton in 1914–17. Doctors McIlroy and Macklin amputated the toes on one of his feet while the party was on Elephant Island in 1916.

**Mount Blackburn.** 86°17'S, 147°16'W. Formerly also called Mount Jessie O'Keefe. 3,275 m. Flat-topped. Just east of the Robert Scott Glacier. Discovered by Quin Blackburn in Dec. 1934, during Byrd's 1933–35 expedition, and named for him by Byrd.

**Blackburn, Quin.** The surveyor on Byrd's 1928–30 expedition. He was also one of the shore party of Byrd's 1933–35 expedition, and in Dec. 1934 took a sledging party the length of the Robert Scott Glacier, doing a vast amount of discovering in the process.

**Blackburn Nunatak.** 83°49'S, 66°13' W. 965 m. Marks the northern extremity of the Rambo Nunataks in the Pensacola Mountains. Named for Lt. Archie B. Blackburn, USN, officer-in-charge of Plateau Station in 1967.

**Blackface Point.** 67°57'S, 65°24'W. 3 miles NW of Cape Freeman on the east coast of Graham Land. Named by the UK to describe the extremely black rock exposed at the end of the point.

**Blackfish** *see* **Pilot whale**

**Blackhead Rock** *see* **Blackrock Head**

**Blackrock Head.** 67°15'S, 58°59'E. Also called Blackhead Rock. On the east part of Law Promontory, 3 miles NW of Tryne Point. Discovered in Feb. 1936 by the personnel on the *William Scoresby*, and named descriptively by them.

**Blacksand Beach.** 77°33'S, 166°08'E. Also called Black Beach, Sandy Beach. A beach formed of black volcanic sand. ½ mile north of Flagstaff Point on Cape Royds, on the west coast of Ross Island. Named by Shackleton's 1907–9 expedition, who discovered it near their base.

**Blackstone, Henry.** Seaman on the Wilkes Expedition 1838–42. Joined in the USA. Discharged at Oahu, Oct. 31, 1840.

**Black-throated penguin** *see* **Adélie penguin**

**Blackwall Glacier.** 86°10'S, 159°40'W. 8 miles long. Flows from the Nilsen Plateau along the NE side of Hanson Spur to join the Amundsen Glacier. All the rock walls surrounding this glacier are black, and the feature was descriptively named by the Ohio State University field parties here in 1963–64 and 1970–71.

**Blackwall Mountains.** 68°22'S, 66°48' W. Also called Climbing Range. 1,370 m. They extend for 5 miles south of Neny Fjord, on the west coast of Graham Land. Surveyed by the BGLE in 1936, and again by the FIDS in 1948–49, and named by the FIDS because the black cliffs of the mountains facing Rymill Bay remain snow-free all year.

**Blackwelder Glacier.** 77°56'S, 164°12' E. Also called Ricky Glacier. 1 mile wide. 2 miles long. Between Salmon Hill and Hobbs Glacier in Victoria Land. Studied in 1957–58 by Troy L. Péwé, and named by him for Dr. Eliot Blackwelder, formerly head of geology at Stanford.

**Blade Ridge.** 63°25'S, 57°05'W. Has three peaks on it, the highest being 575 m. Forms the NW wall of Depot Glacier, near the head of Hope Bay, in the NE part of Trinity Peninsula. Discovered by Nordenskjöld's 1901–4 expedition. Surveyed and descriptively named by the FIDS in 1945.

**Mount Blades.** 77°10'S, 145°15'W. 3 miles WNW of Bailey Ridge, on the north side of the Boyd Glacier, in the Ford Ranges of Marie Byrd Land. Discovered and mapped by the USAS 1939–41. Named for Cdr. J.L. Blades, USN, in charge of support activities at McMurdo Station in 1965.

**Blades, William Robert.** Navigator on Operation Highjump, 1946–47, and on the first 4 Operation Deep Freeze expeditions, i.e. I, II, III, and IV (1955–59).

**Blades Glacier.** 77°38'S, 153°W. Flows from the snow-covered saddle just north of La Gorce Peak, in the Alexandra Mountains. Merges with Dalton Glacier on the north side of the Edward VII Peninsula. Named for William Robert Blades.

**Blaiklock, Ken.** Kenneth V. Blaiklock. He was with the FIDS in 1949 and 1955. During the BCTAE 1955–58 he was surveyor, and leader of the Advance Party of that expedition, and accompanied Fuchs across the continent. In 1968 he surveyed the Shackleton Mountains.

**Blaiklock Glacier.** 80°30'S, 29°50'W. 16 miles long. Flows from Turnpike Bluff to Mounts Provender and Lowe, in the western part of the Shackleton Range. Mapped in 1957 by the BCTAE, and named for Ken Blaiklock.

**Blaiklock Island.** 67°33'S, 67°04'W. High, rugged, and irregularly shaped. 9 miles long. Between Bigourdan Fjord and Bourgeois Fjord. It is separated from Pourquoi Pas Island by The Narrows, and from the west coast of Graham Land by the Jones Channel. Charted by the BGLE 1934–37 as a promontory, but redefined in 1949 by Ken Blaiklock, for whom it is named.

**Mount Blair.** 72°32'S, 160°49'E. 2,120 m. 6 miles NW of Mount Weihaupt in the Outback Nunataks. Named for Terence T. Blair, biologist at McMurdo Station in 1966–67.

**Blair, D.** Seaman on the *Eleanor Bolling*, 1929–30, i.e. during the second half of Byrd's 1928–30 expedition.

**Blair, J.H.** Chief officer on the *Aurora*, during the AAE 1911–14.

**Blair, James L.** Midshipman on the Wilkes Expedition 1838–42. He served on the *Peacock*.

**Blair Glacier.** 66°45'S, 124°32'E. Flows into the west corner of Maury Bay, East Antarctica. Named for James L. Blair.

**Blair Islands.** 66°50'S, 143°10'E. A group of small islands, 4 miles west of Cape Gray, at the east side of the entrance to Commonwealth Bay. Discovered by the AAE 1911–14, and named by Mawson for J.H. Blair.

**Blair Peak.** 67°48'S, 62°53'E. 960 m. 2 miles SE of Rumdoodle Peak in the Masson Range of the Framnes Mountains. Photographed by the LCE 1936–37. Named by the Australians for James Blair, senior diesel mechanic at Mawson Station in 1958.

**Blåisen Valley.** 72°32'S, 3°42'W. A small, cirquelike valley on the west side of Borg Mountain. Just north of Borggarden Valley, in the Borg Massif of Queen Maud Land. Name means "blue ice" in Norwegian.

**Cape Blake.** 68°26'S, 148°55'E. A rocky cape on the Organ Pipe Cliffs, 4 miles west of Cape Wild. Discovered by the AAE 1911–14, and named by Mawson for L.R. Blake, geologist and cartographer with the Macquarie Island (not in Antarctica) party of the expedition.

**Blake, John L.** Ordinary seaman on the Wilkes Expedition 1838–42. Joined at Rio. Discharged on June 30, 1840.

**Blake, Patrick J.** Midshipman on the *Williams*, 1820.

¹**Blake Island.** 63°38'S, 59°01'W. Narrow, ice-free, 1½ miles long. In Bone Bay, along the NW coast of Trinity Peninsula. Charted in 1948 by the FIDS. Named by the UK for Patrick J. Blake.

²**Blake Island** *see* **Koll Rock**

**Blake Nunataks.** 74°10'S, 66°40'E. Also called Blake Peaks. Three low, flat-topped nunataks between Wilson Bluff and Mount Maguire, near the head of the Lambert Glacier. Discovered aerially by Flying Officer J. Seaton, RAAF, during a photographic flight in Nov. 1956. Named by the Australians for J.R. Blake, aurora physicist at Mawson Station in 1958.

**Blake Peak.** 76°01'S, 143°44'W. Isolated. On the SW side of Siemiatkowski Glacier in Marie Byrd Land. Named for Dale G. Blake, ionosphere physicist at Byrd Station in 1964.

**Blake Peaks** *see* **Blake Nunataks**

**Blake Rock.** 85°11'S, 64°50'W. Isolated. 5 miles south of the south end of Mackin Table, in the Patuxent Range of the Pensacola Mountains. Named for Joseph A. Blake, Jr., construction electrician at South Pole Station in 1960.

**Blakeney Point.** 66°14'S, 110°35'E. The north point of Clark Peninsula in the Windmill Islands. Named for A.A. Blakeney, photographer's mate on Operation Highjump flights in this area in 1946–47.

**Blåklettane Hills.** 72°26'S, 21°30'E. 18 miles SW of Bamse Mountain, at the SW end of the Sør Rondane Mountains. Name means "the blue hills" in Norwegian.

**Blånabbane Nunataks.** 68°03'S, 63°E. Also called Anniversary Nunataks. A small group 15 miles east of Mount Twin-top in Mac. Robertson Land. Photographed by the LCE 1936–37, and later named by the Norwegians.

**Sommet Blanchard** *see* **Blanchard Ridge**

**Blanchard Glacier.** 64°44'S, 62°05'W. Flows into Wilhelmina Bay between Garnerin and Sadler Points, on the west coast of Graham Land. Charted by de Gerlache in 1897–99. Named by the UK in 1960 for Jean P. Blanchard (1753–1809), the first professional balloon pilot.

**Blanchard Hill.** 80°26'S, 21°56'W. In the Shackleton Range.

**Blanchard Nunataks.** 72°S, 64°50'W. A group, 16 miles long, which marks the south end of the Gutenko Mountains in central Palmer Land. Named for Lloyd G. Blanchard of the Division of Polar Programs and assistant editor of the *Antarctic Journal.*

**Blanchard Peak** *see* **Blanchard Ridge**

**Blanchard Ridge.** 65°12'S, 64°04'W. Also called Sommet Blanchard, Blanchard Peak. 520 m. At the north side of the mouth of Wiggins Glacier, on the west coast of Graham Land. Mapped by Charcot, and named by him for the French Consul at Punta Arenas, Chile.

**Blancmange Hill.** 64°S, 57°40'W. Ice-free. 3 miles south of Stark Point, on the east side of Croft Bay, James Ross Island. Surveyed by the FIDS in 1958–61, and named descriptively by the UK.

**The *Bland*.** US cargo ship of the 1970s, sometimes in Antarctic waters.

**Blank Peaks.** 79°45'S, 158°45'E. Also called Blank Peninsula. A cluster of ice-free peaks, between the Bartrum and Foggydog Glaciers. They are situated on a ridge in the Brown Hills. Named by the New Zealanders for H. Richard Blank, a geologist here in 1960–61.

**Blank Peninsula** *see* **Blank Peaks**

**Blåskimen Island.** 70°25'S, 3°W. The USSR calls it Kupol Kruglyy. High, ice-covered. 8 miles north of Novyy Island, at the juncture of the Fimbul and Jelbart Ice Shelves. Originally thought to be a part of Novyy Island. The USSR proved otherwise in 1961.

**Blauvelt, Abraham.** American sealing captain, commander of the *Jane Maria,* 1821–22.

**Bleclic Peaks.** 74°59'S, 134°16'W. Two peaks, near the south end of the Perry Range in Marie Byrd Land. Named for John P. Bleclic, senior aerographer's mate on the *Glacier,* 1961–62.

**Bleikskoltane Rocks.** 72°16'S, 27°22'E. 7 miles south of Balchen Mountain, in the SE part of the Sør Rondane Mountains. Name means "the pale knolls" in Norwegian.

**Blériot Glacier.** 64°25'S, 61°10'W. Short and wide. East of Salvesen Cove, on the west coast of Graham Land. Named by the UK in 1960 for Louis Blériot (1872–1936), French aviation pioneer.

**Bleset Rock.** 73°39'S, 3°57'W. 5 miles ESE of Enden Point, between Utråkket Valley and Belgen Valley. It surmounts the ice divide between the two valleys, in the Kirwan Escarpment. Named by the Norwegians.

**Blessing Bluff.** 77°19'S, 163°03'E. Marks the east end of Staeffler Ridge. Overlooks the Wilson Ice Piedmont, 6½ miles west of Spike Cape, Victoria Land. Named for Cdr. George R. Blessing, USN, officer-in-charge of McMurdo Station in 1963.

**Bleue Cove.** 66°49'S, 141°24'E. Just east of Cape Margerie. Charted by the French in 1950, and named by them as Anse Bleue (blue bay) because the waters are blue.

**Blind Bay.** 67°31'S, 66°32'W. A small bay which forms the NE extremity and the head of Bourgeois Fjord. It marks the junction of the Fallières Coast and the Loubet Coast, along the west coast of Graham Land. Surveyed in 1936 by the BGLE, and again by the FIDS in 1949. Named by the FIDS because the bay was a blind alley to sledging parties.

**Blissett, A.H.** Private in the R.M.L.I. Took part in the Royal Society Expedition of 1901–4.

**Bliznetsov Point.** 67°40'S, 45°54'E. On Alasheyev Bight, about 1½ miles east of Molodezhnaya Station.

**The *Blizzard*.** A ten-page magazine produced by Shackleton at Hut Point in the winter of 1902 as an "alternative" to the *South Polar Times*. The title page showed a figure wreathed in snowflakes, holding a bottle, with the caption, "Never Mind the Blizzard, I'm All Right." It contained things like poems, and ribald caricatures by Michael Barne. Only one edition appeared, on May 1, 1902. Everyone on the expedition got a copy.

**Blizzard Heights.** 84°37'S, 164°08'E. A high, flat area in the Marshall Mountains, in the Queen Alexandra Range. 2 miles long. 550 m. above the surrounding snow surface. 2 miles NW of Blizzard Peak, from which it is separated by a broad snow col, and in association with which it was named by the Ohio State University party here in 1966–67.

**Blizzard Peak.** 84°38'S, 164°08'E. 3,375 m. The highest peak in the Marshall Mountains, in the Queen Alexandra Range. 4 miles NW of Mount Marshall. Named by the Northern Party of the NZGSAE 1961–62 because a blizzard prevented them from reaching it for several days.

**Blizzards.** Brief, localized snowstorms where no snow falls but the snow on the ground is caught up in the greatly turbulent katabatic winds and swept up. They appear suddenly, and the sky above is generally clear, although visibility on the ground can be zero. The temperature is low, and the winds can be 100 mph or more.

**The Blob.** 73°24'S, 124°56'W. A snow-covered, mound-shaped, knoll-like nunatak. Between Thurston Glacier and Armour Inlet on the north coast of Siple Island. Named descriptively by the USA.

**Mount Block.** 85°46'S, 176°13'E. Formerly called Mount Paul Block. A nunatak of 10,000 feet, in the Grosvenor Mountains of the Queen Maud Mountains, 5 miles south of Block Peak. Discovered by Byrd on his flight to the Pole in Nov. 1929, and named by him for Paul Block, Jr., son of Paul Block, a patron.

**Block Bay.** 76°15'S, 146°22'W. Also called Paul Block Bay. A frozen bay between the Guest Peninsula and the Ruppert Coast, Marie Byrd Land. Discovered in 1929 by Byrd's 1928–30 expedition, and named by Byrd for Paul Block, newspaper publisher and patron.

**Block Mountain.** 70°28'S, 68°52'W. 1,460 m. A block-shaped mountain. Just south of Transition Glacier, in the Douglas Range of Alexander Island. Photographed aerially by Ellsworth on Nov. 23, 1935. Surveyed by the BGLE in 1936, and again by the FIDS in 1949, and named descriptively by the FIDS.

**Block Peak.** 85°41'S, 176°13'E. 2,770 m. 4 miles NW of Mauger Nunatak in the Grosvenor Mountains. Discovered by Byrd on his flight to the Pole in Nov. 1929 and named by him as Mount William Block, for the son of Paul Block (*see* **Block Bay**). The name was later shortened.

**Blodget, David.** Officer's cook on the Wilkes Expedition 1838–42. Joined in the USA. Died at Navigator's Islands, Nov. 6, 1839.

**Blodgett Basin.** 65°30'S, 130°E. Submarine feature off the Wilkes Coast.

**Blodgett Iceberg Tongue.** 66°10'S, 130°12'E. Extends seaward from the Cape Morse and Cape Carr area, on the east side of Porpoise Bay, off the Wilkes Coast. Named for Gardner D. Blodgett, cartographer with the Office of Geography, Department of the Interior.

**Mount Blood.** 85°01'S, 167°30'W. At the south side of the mouth of Somero Glacier, 2½ miles NE of Mount Johnstone in the Queen Maud Mountains. Named for Richard H. Blood, ionosphere physicist at Amundsen-Scott South Pole Station.

**Mount Bloomfield.** 72°59'S, 65°37'E. Low, domed, boulder-covered. 5 miles west of Mount Rymill in the southern Prince Charles Mountains. Named by the Australians for Flying Officer E. Bloomfield, RAAF, navigator at Mawson Station in 1960.

**Bloor Passage.** 65°14′S, 64°15′W. Leads north from the Meek Channel, between Corner Island and Uruguay Island, in the Argentine Islands. Named by the UK in 1959 for Able Seaman Vincent T. Bloor, RN, a member of the British Naval Hydrographic Survey Unit here in 1957–58.

**Blount Nunatak.** 83°16′S, 51°19′W. 1,630 m. 3 miles SW of Mount Lechner, on the west side of the Forrestal Range in the Pensacola Mountains. Discovered aerially on Jan. 13, 1956, on an American transcontinental nonstop flight from McMurdo Station to the Weddell Sea and back. Named for Hartford E. Blount, VX-6 operative in Antarctica in 1956.

**Blow-Me-Down Bluff.** 68°03′S, 66°40′W. 1,820 m. At the north flank of Northeast Glacier, on the west side of Graham Land. Named by the FIDS because it stands in the windiest part of the glacier, and many explorers have been blown down here.

**Mount Blowaway.** 69°40′S, 158°10′E. 1,320 m. A gneissic mountain. Has extensive areas of exposed rock. 12 miles WNW of Governor Mountain, in the Wilson Hills. Named by the Northern Party of the NZGSAE 1963–64 because 3 members of that party were forced by a blizzard to abandon their proposed survey and gravity station there.

**Blubaugh Nunatak.** 85°45′S, 134°06′W. Ridgelike. Just south of the mouth of Kansas Glacier where it enters Reedy Glacier. Named for Donald D. Blubaugh, construction mechanic at Byrd Station in 1957.

**The *Blue Blade*.** NC331N. The single-engine Fokker F-14 monoplane taken by Byrd on his 1933–35 expedition. It crashed at Little America on March 13, 1934.

**Blue Glacier.** 77°47′S, 164°E. A large glacier that flows into the Bowers Piedmont Glacier about 10 miles south of New Harbor, in Victoria Land, at McMurdo Sound. Discovered in 1903 by Armitage and named by him for its clear blue ice.

**Blue Lake.** 77°32′S, 166°10′E. About 400 yards long and 150 yards wide. The largest of the several small frozen lakes near Cape Royds, on the west coast of Ross Island. ½ mile NNE of Flagstaff Point, Cape Royds. Named by Shackleton's 1907–9 expedition for the striking blue color of the ice here.

**Blue whale.** *Balaenoptera musculus.* Also called sulfur-bottom whale, Sibbald's rorqual. The largest animal in the world, it can grow up to 110 feet long, and weigh almost 200 tons. A newly-born calf can be over 20 feet long and weigh about 3 tons. The blue makes the loudest noise of any creature and can be heard over 500 miles away. When frightened, a blue whale can maintain a speed of 23 mph for 10 minutes. In winter they migrate to warmer climates for breeding, but in summer they are often seen in Antarctic waters. Hunted mercilessly from 1910 to 1966, more than 330,000 blues were slaughtered during that period. 29,400 were captured in 1931 alone. Almost wiped out by whaling (q.v.), the blue whale has been a protected species since 1966, but despite this fact there are only about 1,500 left, and they may well become extinct.

**Bluff Depot.** 79°S. Used by the Ross Sea Party during the British Imperial Transantarctic Expedition of 1914–17. Named for its location, at Minna Bluff.

**¹Bluff Island.** 68°33′S, 77°54′E. ½ mile south of Magnetic Island. 2 miles west of Breidnes Peninsula in the Vestfold Hills, in Prydz Bay. Photographed by the LCE 1936–37. Named by the Australians because the south end of the island is marked by a steep cliff face.

**²Bluff Island** *see* **Murray Island**

**Bluff Point.** A high bluff on the SW side of Trinity Island, rising to over 2,000 feet. This is a name no longer used.

**Blümcke Knoll.** 66°50'S, 68°W. 11 miles SW of Mount Vélain, in the northern part of Adelaide Island. Named by the UK for Adolf Blümcke (1854–1914), German glaciologist.

**Blundell Peak.** 69°24'S, 76°06'E. On the Stornes Peninsula in Prydz Bay. Photographed by the LCE 1936–37, and later named by the Australians for A.A. Blundell, radio operator at Mawson Station in 1968.

**Mount Blunt.** 68°48'S, 65°48'W. 1,500 m. Ice-covered. Rises from the west flank of the Weyerhaeuser Glacier on the east side of the Antarctic Peninsula. Photographed aerially by the USAS on Sept. 28, 1940. Named by the UK for Edmund Blunt (1770–1862), American chart publisher.

**Blunt, Simon F.** Passed midshipman on the *Vincennes* during the Wilkes Expedition 1838–42. Joined at Orange Harbor, and left sick at Honolulu in April 1841.

**Blunt Bay** *see* **Blunt Cove**

**Blunt Cove.** 66°54'S, 108°50'E. Also called Blunt Bay. In the SW extremity of Vincennes Bay. Named for Simon F. Blunt.

**Blustery Cliffs.** 71°25'S, 67°53'E. 3½ miles long. In the north part of the Fisher Massif in Mac. Robertson Land. J. Manning, surveyor with the ANARE Prince Charles Mountains survey party in Jan. 1969, occupied a survey station on one of the cliffs at 1,135 m. There is a lot of turbulence here, hence the name.

**The *Blyde Bootschap*.** Correctly the *Blijde Bootschap* (the "Good News"). In 1603 this Dutch ship was captured by Spanish pirates and blown off course. Laurens Claess, one of the captives, tells of getting to 64°S, and seeing a large and miserably bleak island. This could have been the South Shetlands.

**¹Blythe Bay.** 62°28'S, 60°20'W. Also called Desolation Harbor. An anchorage at the SE side of Desolation Island, in the South Shetlands. Named before 1821, probably for William Smith's home in England.

**²Blythe Bay** *see* **Hero Bay**

**Mount Bo** *see* **Mount Boë**

**Bob Bartlett Glacier** *see* **Bartlett Glacier**

**Bob Island.** 64°56'S, 63°26'W. Also called Isla Bayley, Isla Poisson. 145 m. 1 mile long. 4 miles SE of Cape Errera, Wiencke Island. Surveyed and photographed by de Gerlache in 1898, and named by him as Île Famine. In his reports however, it was featured as Île Bob. The FIDS anglicized the name in 1955.

**Bobby Rocks.** 75°49'S, 159°11'E. Ice-free. 4 miles south of the Ricker Hills, in the Prince Albert Mountains of Victoria Land. Named for Bobby J. Davis, commissaryman at Amundsen-Scott South Pole Station in 1966.

**Bobo Ridge.** 85°51'S, 150°48'W. Isolated. 2 miles long. On the north side of Albanus Glacier. Marks the SW extremity of the Tapley Mountains. Named for Robert Bobo, meteorologist at McMurdo Station in 1963.

**Boccherini Inlet.** 71°42'S, 72°W. Ice-filled. 18 miles long. 16 miles wide. Indentation into the south side of Beethoven Peninsula. Forms the northern extremity of the Bach Ice Shelf, on Alexander Island. Named by the UK for the composer.

**Mount Boda.** 68°05'S, 48°52'E. Just north of Amphitheatre Peaks, at the west end of the Nye Mountains. Named by the Australians for Dr. J. Boda, medical officer at Wilkes Station in 1959.

**Bode Nunataks.** 72°30'S, 75°07'E. Two nunataks. Partly snow-covered. 23 miles north of Mount Harding in the Grove Mountains. Named by the Australians for O. Bode, weather observer at Mawson Station in 1962.

**Cape Bodman** *see* **Bodman Point**

**Bodman, Dr. Gösta.** Hydrographer/meteorologist on Nordenskjöld's Swedish Antarctic Expedition of 1901–4.

**Bodman Point.** 64°14′S, 56°48′W. On the west side of Seymour Island. Surveyed by Nordenskjöld's expedition of 1901–4, and named by them as Cape Bodman, for Dr. Gösta Bodman. Resurveyed and redefined by the FIDS in 1952.

**Mount Bodys.** 67°09′S, 67°48′W. Over 1,220 m. Mostly ice-covered. The most easterly mountain on Adelaide Island. Surveyed by Charcot in 1909. Resurveyed by the FIDS in 1949, and named by them for Sgt. William S. Bodys, mechanic for the expedition's Norseman airplane in 1950.

**Mount Bodziony.** 74°34′S, 111°54′W. On the coast of Marie Byrd Land.

**Mount Boë.** 72°35′S, 31°19′E. Also called Mount Bo, Mont Bo. 2,520 m. 1 mile NE of Mount Victor, in the Belgica Mountains. Discovered by the Belgian Antarctic Expedition of 1957–58, led by Gaston de Gerlache, who named it for Capt. Sigmund Boë, captain of the *Polarhav*, which transported the expedition.

**Lake Boeckella.** 63°24′S, 57°W. 600 yards south of Hope Bay. It is a small lake which drains by a small stream into Eagle Cove at the NE end of Graham Land. Discovered and named by Nordenskjöld's expedition of 1901–4. Boeckella is a species of crustaceans found here.

**Boeger Peak.** 75°49′S, 116°06′W. 3,070 m. Snow-covered. 2 miles west of Richmond Peak on the Toney Mountain massif in Marie Byrd Land. Named for Alvin C. Boeger, USN, chief aerographer's mate in the Antarctic in 1972.

**Boehning, Max E.** Seaman on the *City of New York* during Byrd's 1928–30 expedition.

**Mount Boennighausen.** 75°47′S, 132°18′W. 2,970 m. Snow-covered. 4 miles SSW of Mount Kosciusko, in the Ames Range of Marie Byrd Land. Named for Lt. Cdr. Thomas L. Boennighausen, USN, officer-in-charge of the nuclear power plant at McMurdo Station in 1966.

**Boffa Island.** 66°28′S, 110°37′E. Almost a mile long. ½ mile east of the Browning Peninsula, between the Bosner and Birkenhauer Islands, in the south part of the Windmill Islands. Named for W.C. Boffa, SAC observer on Operation Windmill, 1947–48.

**Cape Boggs.** 70°33′S, 61°23′W. Also called Cape Eielson. An ice-covered headland forming the tip of Eielson Peninsula, on the east coast of Palmer Land. Discovered by members from East Base during the USAS 1939–41. Named for S.W. Boggs, geographer with the US Department of State, who studied Antarctica.

**Boggs Strait** *see* **Stefansson Strait**

**Boggs Valley.** 71°55′S, 161°30′E. Heavily strewn with morainal debris. Between Mount Van der Hoeven and Mount Alford in the Helliwell Hills of Oates Land. Named for William J. Boggs, biologist at McMurdo Station in 1967–68.

**Böhnecke Glacier.** 72°23′S, 61°25′W. 3 miles wide. Flows into the NW side of Violante Inlet, on the east coast of Palmer Land. Discovered aerially by the USAS in Dec. 1940. Named by the FIDS in 1948 for Gunther Böhnecke, German oceanographer and member of the German expedition to Bouvetøya (not in this book) in the *Meteor*, 1925–26.

**Bohyo Heights.** 68°08′S, 42°44′E. A small, rocky elevation which overlooks the coast of Queen Maud Land. 2 miles ESE of Cape Hinode. Named Bohyo-dai (ice view heights) by the Japanese in 1973.

**The Boil.** 74°09'S, 161°34'E. A nunatak on the NE side of the Reeves Névé, Victoria Land. Over 2,300 m. 4 miles east of Shepard Cliff. Named descriptively by the New Zealanders in 1962–63.

**Boker Rocks.** 72°25'S, 98°40'W. 5 miles NE of Von der Wall Point, in the Walker Mountains, on the south coast of Thurston Island. Named for Helmut C. Boker, meteorologist at Byrd Station in 1964–65.

**Bol, Peter.** Lt. Cdr., USN. Chaplain with the 1956 winter party at McMurdo Base.

**Bol Glacier.** 77°52'S, 162°34'E. Between Darkowski Glacier and Condit Glacier. Flows from the Cathedral Rocks into the Ferrar Glacier in Victoria Land. Named in 1964 for Lt. Cdr. Peter Bol.

**Boland.** Seaman, and later lieutenant, on the *Pourquoi Pas?* during Charcot's 1908–10 expedition.

**Mount Boland.** 65°18'S, 63°50'W. Over 1,065 m. 6 miles east of Lumière Peak, on the ridge between Bussey Glacier and Trooz Glacier, on the west side of Graham Land. Discovered by Charcot in 1908–10, and named Sommet Boland by him for Boland (q.v.). The name was later anglicized.

**Bold Cliff** *see* **Williams Cliff**

**Bolin, Jacob.** Captain of the fo'c's'le during the Wilkes Expedition 1838–42. Joined in the USA. Served the cruise.

**Bolinder Beach** *see* **Bolinder Bluff**

**Bolinder Bluff.** 61°56'S, 57°58'W. Also called Bolinder Beach, Pico Amarillo. A bluff crowned by three buttresses. Overlooks Venus Bay, 3 miles SE of False Round Point, on the north coast of King George Island, in the South Shetlands. Named by personnel on the *Discovery II* in 1937, when the Bolinder engine broke down on one of their boats, causing 6 men to be marooned for 9 days on the beach at the foot of the bluff.

**Bølingen Islands.** 69°30'S, 75°45'E. A group of small islands, 8 miles in extent, off the north side of the Publications Ice Shelf, in the SE part of Prydz Bay. Discovered by Klarius Mikkelsen in Feb. 1935. Name means "the herd" in Norwegian.

**Mount Bolle.** 71°54'S, 6°50'E. 2,685 m. Above the Larsen Cliffs, 3 miles south of Kyrkjeskipet Peak, in the eastern Mühlig-Hofmann Mountains of Queen Maud Land. Named Bolle-Berg (or rather, some peak in this vicinity was called that) by Ritscher in 1938–39, for Herbert Bolle.

**Bolle, Herbert.** Aviation supervisor on the German New Schwabenland Expedition of 1938–39, led by Alfred Ritscher.

**Bollene Rocks.** 72°15'S, 27°14'E. A group just west of Bleikskoltane Rocks at the head of Byrdbreen, in the Sør Rondane Mountains. Name means "the buns" in Norwegian.

**The** *Bolling* *see* **The** *Eleanor Bolling*

**Bolling Advance Weather Station.** 80°08'S, 163°57'W. This was the place where Byrd holed up alone from March 28 to Aug. 11, 1934, during his 1933–35 expedition. 123 miles from Little America II, it was named by Byrd for his mother, Eleanor Bolling Byrd. A structure prefabricated in Boston by Tinglof, it was 800 cubic feet, and weighed 1,500 pounds. It had 4-inch-thick walls. It was shipped to Antarctica and assembled at Little America for a trial run of 6 weeks, and on Feb. 15, 1934, it was dismantled. It was taken to 80°08'S, by a 9-man party led by June and Demas, and assembled on March 21, 1934, in a hole 15 feet long by 11 feet wide by 8 feet deep, dug in the ice. Outside the structure was a windspeed gauge on a 12-foot pole, and 200 feet of radio antenna strung on bamboo sticks by Bud Waite. On March 22, 1934, Byrd, Bailey, and Bowlin flew in the Pilgrim from Little America, and almost a week later Byrd began his lonely vigil, to test man's ability to live alone in the heart of Antarctica, during the winter. His supplies included 360 pounds of meat, 792 pounds of vegetables, 73 pounds of soup, 176 pounds of canned fruit, 90 pounds of dried fruit, 56 pounds of desserts, ½ ton of various staples including cereals, a 5-gallon can stuffed with toilet paper, 350 candles, 3 flashlights, a 300-candlepower gasoline pressure lantern, 2 sleeping bags (one fur, one eiderdown), 2 primus stoves, 2 kerosene lanterns, 2 decks of playing cards, and a Victrola. He almost died from the slow leakage of fumes from the faulty generator, and on Aug. 11, 1934, Demas, Poulter, and Waite arrived overland, being greeted by Byrd's "Hello, fellows, come on below. I've got a bowl of hot soup waiting for you." They spent until Oct. 14 there with Byrd, helping him to recuperate. On Oct. 14 Bowlin and Schlossbach arrived in the Pilgrim, and flew Byrd back to Little America. See Byrd's book, *Alone.*

**Bolsón Cove.** 65°09'S, 63°05'W. Also called Bahía Cruz, Schulze Cove. At the head of Flandres Bay, just east of Étienne Fjord, on the west coast of Graham Land. Charted by de Gerlache in 1897–99. Named descriptively by the Argentines before 1954. A bolsón is a large salt valley.

**Mount Bolt.** 71°06'S, 165°42'E. 2,010 m. On the north side of the Ebbe Glacier. 5 miles NW of Peterson Bluff in the Anare Mountains. Named for Lt. Ronald L. Bolt, USN, pilot here in 1961–62 and 1962–63.

**Bolten Peak.** 71°49'S, 1°44'W. Isolated, 3 miles north of Litvillingane Rocks, on the east side of the Ahlmann Ridge, in Queen Maud Land. Name means "the bolt" in Norwegian.

**Mount Bolton.** 85°56'S, 129°43'W. 2,840 m. In the west part of the Wisconsin Range. 6 miles SE of Mount Soyat, along the east side of the Reedy Glacier. Named for Lt. James L. Bolton, USN, helicopter pilot here in 1965, 1966, and 1967.

**Bolton Glacier.** 65°01'S, 62°58'W. Flows into the head of Briand Fjord, Flandres Bay, on the west coast of Graham Land. Named by the UK for William B. Bolton (1848–1889), British photography pioneer.

**Mount Boman.** 82°33'S, 162°E. 1,630 m. Between the Tranter and Doss Glaciers, in the northern part of the Queen Elizabeth Range. Named for William M. Boman, American traverse engineer at Roosevelt Island in 1962–63, and at McMurdo Station in 1965.

**Bomb Peak.** 77°32'S, 169°15'E. 805 m. 2 miles west of Cape Crozier, on Ross Island. Charted by the New Zealanders in 1958–59, and named by them for the bomblike geological formations here.

**Bombardier Glacier.** 64°19'S, 59°59'W. Flows from the Detroit Plateau in Graham Land, into the Edgeworth Glacier. Named by the UK for J.A. Bombardier, Canadian engineer and developer of the snowmobile.

**Bombay Island** *see* **D'Hainaut Island**

**Bommen Spur.** 72°37'S, 3°08'W. Runs between Jøkulskarvet Ridge and Flogstallen in the Borg Massif of Queen Maud Land. Name means "the bar" in Norwegian.

**Bon Docteur Nunatak.** 65°40'S, 140°01'E. 28 m. On the west side of the Astrolabe Glacier Tongue. 350 yards south of Rostand Island in the Géologie Archipelago. Charted by the French in 1952–53, and named by them for Dr. Jean Cendron.

**Mount Bonaparte.** 83°05'S, 160°50'E. 3,430 m. 4 miles NW of Mount Lecointe in the Queen Elizabeth Range. Discovered by Shackleton in 1908 and named for Prince Roland Bonaparte, president of the Geographical Society of Paris.

**Bonaparte Channel.** Off Anvers Island, in the area of Palmer Station. A term no longer used.

**Bonaparte Point.** 64°47'S, 64°05'W. Also called Roland Bonaparte Point. A narrow point at the south side of Arthur Harbor, Anvers Island, in the immediate area of Palmer Station (q.v.). Charted by Charcot in 1903–5, and named by him for Prince Roland Bonaparte (see **Mount Bonaparte**).

**Mount Bond.** 66°49'S, 51°07'E. Just south of Mount Rhodes, in the Tula Mountains of Enderby Land. Named by the Australians for E. Bond.

**¹Bond, Capt.** British commander of the *Enchantress* in 1821–22. This is not Ralph Bond.

**²Bond, Capt.** Commander of the *Martha*, in the South Shetlands, 1821–23. Almost certainly this is Ralph Bond (q.v.).

**Bond, Charles A.** Lt. Cdr., USN. Led the Western Group of Operation Highjump, 1946–47.

**Bond, E.** Crew member on the *Discovery* during the BANZARE 1929–31.

**Bond, Ralph.** British sealing captain, commander of the *Hetty* in 1820–21. This is almost certainly the same Captain Bond who brought down the *Martha* for the 1821–23 period.

**Bond Glacier.** 66°58'S, 109°E. Heavily crevassed. To the west of Ivanoff Head, it flows from the continental ice to Blunt Cove, at the head of Vincennes Bay. Named for Capt. Charles A. Bond.

**Bond Nunatak.** 67°09'S, 68°10'W. Snow-capped. North of Mount Bouvier on Adelaide Island. Named by the UK in 1963 for Flight Lt. Peter R. Bond, RAF, BAS pilot at Base T in 1962–63.

**Bond Peaks.** 72°11'S, 25°24'E. Called Bondtoppane by the Norwegians. 3,180 m. A group on the SW side of Mount Bergersen, in the Sør Rondane Mountains. Named by the USA for Capt. Charles A. Bond.

**Bond Point.** 62°41'S, 60°48'W. NE of Elephant Point on the south side of Livingston Island, in the South Shetlands. Named by the UK in 1958 for Ralph Bond.

**Bond Ridge.** 70°16'S, 65°13'E. 1 mile NE of Moore Pyramid on the north side of

Scylla Glacier, in the Prince Charles Mountains. Named by the Australians for D.W.G. Bond, senior diesel mechanic at Mawson Station.

**Bondeson Glacier.** 82°44'S, 165°E. 7 miles long. Flows along the east side of Benson Ridge into the lower portion of the Robb Glacier. Named for W. Bondeson, captain of the *Towle* in 1964 and 1965.

**Bondtoppane** *see* **Bond Peaks**

**Bone, Thomas M.** Midshipman on the *Williams* under Bransfield, in the early part of 1820.

**Bone Bay.** 63°38'S, 59°04'W. Also called Bone Cove. 10 miles wide at the entrance. Between Notter Point and Cape Roquemaurel, along the NW coast of Trinity Peninsula. Named by the UK for Thomas M. Bone.

**Bone Cove** *see* **Bone Bay**

**Bone Point.** 66°25'S, 110°40'E. Forms the SE extremity of Herring Island in the Windmill Islands. Named for Steven D. Bone, meteorologist at Wilkes Station in 1962.

**Bonert, Capt.** Federico Bonert Holzappel. Chilean naval officer. As a lt. 1st class, he accompanied the USAS 1939–41, as an observer. Later, as a capitán de corbeta, he was commander of the *Angamos,* and second-in-command of the Chilean Antarctic Expedition of 1946–47.

**Bonert Rock.** 62°27'S, 59°43'W. ½ mile SE of Canto Point, Greenwich Island, in the South Shetlands. Surveyed by the Chilean Antarctic Expedition of 1946–47, and named by them as Islote Bonert, or Islote Capitán Bonert, for Capt. Bonert (q.v.).

**Cape Bongrain** *see* **Bongrain Point**

**Bongrain, Maurice.** French naval officer who was first officer and second-in-command of Charcot's 1908–10 expedition to Antarctica on the *Pourquoi Pas?* A surveyor, his other specialties were hydrography, astronomy, seismology, and terrestrial gravitation. He made the first map of the NW coast of Alexander Island. He later became an admiral.

**Bongrain Ice Piedmont.** 69°S, 71°30′W. 27 miles long. 12 miles wide at its broadest. Occupies the NW coastal area of Alexander Island. First seen by Charcot in 1908–10. Photographed aerially on Aug. 15, 1936, by the BGLE. Named by the UK in 1954 for Maurice Bongrain.

**Bongrain Point.** 67°43′S, 67°48′W. Also called Cape Bongrain, Punta Yungay. Forms the south side of the entrance to Dalgliesh Bay, on the west side of Pourquoi Pas Island, off the west coast of Graham Land. Named by the FIDS for Maurice Bongrain.

**Bonnabeau Dome.** 73°31′S, 94°09′W. Ice-covered, dome mountain on the west side of Gopher Glacier, 4 miles west of Anderson Dome, in the Jones Mountains. Mapped by the University of Minnesota–Jones Mountains Party of 1960–61, and named by them for Dr. Raymond C. Bonnabeau, Jr., medical officer with the party.

**Lake Bonney.** 77°43′S, 162°23′E. A meromictic, permanently ice-covered lake to the south of the Asgard Range, and at the head of the Taylor Valley, in southern Victoria Land. About 330 feet above sea level. Visited by Scott's expedition of 1910–13, and named by them for T. Bonney, Cambridge professor of geology.

**Bonney Bowl.** 80°21′S, 25°35′W. In the Shackleton Range.

**Bonney Riegel.** 77°43′S, 162°22′E. A ridge running from the Kukri Hills across the Taylor Valley to Lake Bonney in southern Victoria Land. Named by Grif Taylor's Western Journey Party during Scott's 1910–13 expedition, in association with the lake.

**Bonnier Point.** 64°28′S, 63°57′W. Marks the north side of the entrance to Hamburg Bay, on the NW coast of Anvers Island. Charted by Charcot in 1903–5, and named by him for J. Bonnier, who installed a laboratory on the *Français.*

**Boobyalla Islands.** 67°15′S, 46°34′E. Two small islands. 2 miles NE of Kirkby Head, in Enderby Land. Named by the Australians for their native tree.

**Books.** The first book published in Antarctica was *Aurora Australis,* a 120-page book written in 1908 by Shackleton and his 14-man crew of winterers to ward off boredom. They wrote it, printed it, and bound it. Joyce and Wild typeset it, Marston illustrated, and Day created the covers. Shackleton's printing press had been presented to him by Messrs. Joseph Causton and Sons, and they had trained Joyce and Wild in printing and typesetting. During Charcot's *Pourquoi Pas?* expedition of 1908–10, Jules Rouch wrote a novel for a bet. It was called *L'Amant de la Dactylographe (The Typist's Lover).* Charcot brought 1,500 books with him on that trip. The Ross Sea party of 1914–17, under Mackintosh, had an *Encyclopaedia Britannica* available. On the other side of Antarctica Hurley salvaged some volumes of *Britannica* when the *Endurance* went down in 1915.

**Mount Bool.** 70°11′S, 64°57′E. Between Mount Peter and Mount Dwyer in the Athos Range of the Prince Charles Mountains. Named by the Australians for G.A. Bool, weather observer at Mawson Station in 1969.

**Boomerang Glacier.** 74°33′S, 163°54′E. 10 miles long. Flows from Mount Dickason in the Deep Freeze Range, and enters Browning Pass at the north side of the Nansen Ice Sheet, in Victoria Land. Discovered by Campbell's Northern Party during Scott's 1910–13 expedition, and named by them for its gentle curve.

**Boomerang Range.** 78°30′S, 158°45′E. Just to the east of the Warren Range, in southern Victoria Land. A narrow range, it curves like a boomerang. It extends for 16 miles, and forms a part of the western limits of the Skelton Névé. Mapped and descriptively named by the NZ party of the BCTAE in 1957.

**Booth Island.** 65°05′S, 64°W. 4 miles long, by 4 miles wide at its broadest. In the Palmer Archipelago. Dallmann discovered it in 1873–74, and named it for Oskar and Stanley Booth, members of the Hamburg Geographical Society which had sent out the expedition. In 1898 de Gerlache charted it, and renamed it as Wandel Island, for Carl F. Wandel, Danish hydrographer who helped de Gerlache's expedition. Charcot wintered over here, at Port Charcot, in 1904. The name Booth Island was later reapplied officially.

**Booth Peninsula.** 66°06′S, 101°13′E. Also called Booth Ridge. 4 miles long. 1 mile wide. 3 miles SW of Remenchus Glacier. Named for George H. Booth, who flew with Bunger during Operation Highjump, 1946–47.

**Booth Ridge** *see* **Booth Peninsula**

**Booth Spur.** 75°37′S, 142°01′W. On the north side of El-Sayed Glacier. 1½ miles SW of Mount Shirley, on the coast of Marie Byrd Land. Named for Lt. Cdr. Robert M. Booth, USN, public works officer in Antarctica, 1968 and 1969.

**Cape Boothby.** 66°34′S, 57°16′E. 4 miles north of Kloa Point, at the western end of the Edward VIII Gulf, at the foot of the Napier Mountains of Enderby Land. Discovered on Feb. 28, 1936, by personnel on the *William Scoresby,* and named for the captain, Lt. Cdr. C.R.U. Boothby.

**Boothby, C.R.U.** Lt. Cdr., RNR. British captain of the *William Scoresby* during the Discovery Investigations tours of 1934–35, 1935–36, and 1936–37.

**Boots.** The standard, especially for tourists, is the pull-on, rubber, unlined, waterproof, knee-high (14″–16″ high) boot with a strong, rubber-ridged, non-skid sole. Leather boots are inappropriate. *See also* **Finneskoes.**

**Borceguí Island.** 61°03′S, 55°09′W. Also called Buskin Rocks. Ice-free. Between Cape Yelcho and Gibbous Rocks, 1 mile off the north coast of Elephant Island, in the South Shetlands. Named by the *Chiriguano* personnel in 1954–55. The name signifies a half-boot in Spanish, and denotes the shape of the island.

**Mount Borchgrevink.** 72°07′S, 23°08′E. Also called Otto Borchgrevinkfjella. 2,390 m. 3 miles south of Tanngarden Peaks, in the Sør Rondane Mountains. Named by the Norwegians for Otto Borchgrevink.

**Borchgrevink, Carsten E.** b. 1864, Oslo. d. 1934, Norway. Norwegian explorer, with an English mother named Ridley (cf. Ridley Beach). Went to Australia in 1888. Was a deckhand and part-time scientist on the *Antarctic* during Bull's expedition of 1894–95. He collected the first vegetation ever found within the Antarctic Circle, and on Jan. 24, 1895, was one of the first to set foot on the continent, at Cape Adare. He claimed to be the very first, and wrote a book, *First on the Antarctic Continent.* In 1898 he led his own expedition, the British Antarctic Expedition of 1898–1900, out of England, on the *Southern Cross.* Sponsored by publisher Sir George Newnes, the expedition's purpose was to winter over and to do scientific work. The *Southern Cross* left London on Aug. 22, 1898, under the command of Capt. Jensen. It sighted the Balleny Islands on Jan. 12, 1899, and crossed the Antarctic Circle on Jan. 23, 1899, arriving at Cape Adare, Oates Land, on Feb. 18, 1899. On March 2, 1899, the *Southern Cross* left, and the first deliberate wintering-over in Antarctica took place. 75 dogs, and 10 men, including Borchgrevink, Fougner, Hugh Evans, Hanson, Ellifsen, Bernacchi, Johansen, Colbeck, and 2 Finns (one of whom was Klövstad) brought along as dog handlers (this was the first time that dogs were ever used on the continent). On July 24, 1899, a fire in the hut almost burned it down (one of Borchgrevink's huts is still standing, another is partially ruined), and on Oct. 16, 1899, Hanson, the naturalist, died, probably of scurvy. The *Southern Cross* returned on Jan. 28, 1900, and picked the men up on Feb. 2, 1900, for Part II of the expedition, which was to sail around the coast into the Ross Sea, and along the Ross Ice Shelf. They landed on the Possession Islands and on Coulman Island, as well as making several other landings on the eastern shore of Victoria Land. On Feb. 16, 1900, Borchgrevink, Colbeck, and one of the Finns sledged 10 miles south over the Ross Ice Shelf, setting a new southing record of 78°50′S. On Feb. 19, 1900, Bernacchi, Evans, Fougner, and Johansen got there as well. Borchgrevink discovered the northward movement of the Ross Ice Shelf, made meteorological observations, made geological collections, discovered the emperor penguin rookery at Cape Crozier, and made the first sledge journey on the Ross Ice Shelf. They left due to the advanced season, and by Feb. 28, 1900, were over the Antarctic Circle and headed for home. Unpopular in England, Carsten Egeberg Borchgrevink lived the rest of his life in Norway.

**Borchgrevink, Otto.** Norwegian whaling captain who worked for the Antarctic Whaling Company out of Tønsberg, Norway. As skipper of the *Antarctic* (the second ship of that name), he was leader of the Norwegian Whaling Expedition of 1930–31 which mapped the coast of Antarctica between 51°30′E and 59°E. On Jan. 14, 1931, they discovered the Aker Peaks.

**Borchgrevink Coast.** 73°S, 171°E. Between Cape Adare and Cape Washington, on the Ross Sea coast of northern Victoria Land. Named by NZ in 1961 for Carsten Borchgrevink.

**Borchgrevink Glacier.** 73°04′S, 168°30′E. In the Victory Mountains of Victoria Land. Flows between the Malta Plateau and the Daniell Peninsula, and ends in the Borchgrevink Glacier Tongue. Named by the New Zealanders in 1957–58 for Carsten Borchgrevink.

**Borchgrevink Glacier Tongue.** 73°21′S, 168°50′E. Seaward extension of the Borchgrevink Glacier in Victoria Land. It

discharges into Glacier Strait in the Ross Sea, just south of Cape Jones. Named in association with the glacier.

**Borchgrevink Nunatak.** 66°03′S, 62°30′W. 650 m. 1½ miles long. On the south side of the entrance to Richthofen Pass, on the east coast of Graham Land. Discovered in 1902 by Nordenskjöld's expedition of 1901–4, and named by him for Carsten Borchgrevink.

**Borchgrevinkisen.** 72°10′S, 21°30′E. Also called Carsten Borchgrevinkisen. A glacier flowing to the west of Taggen Nunatak, at the west end of the Sør Rondane Mountains. Named by the Norwegians for Carsten Borchgrevink.

**Mount Borcik.** 86°12′S, 153°38′W. 2,780 m. 4½ miles NNW of Mount Dietz, in the southern sector of the Hays Mountains, in the Queen Maud Mountains. Named for Lt. Cdr. Andrew J. Borcik, photographic pilot in Antarctica, 1965–67.

**Boreal Point.** 63°07′S, 55°48′W. Forms the west side of Rockpepper Bay, on the north coast of Joinville Island. Surveyed by the FIDS in 1953–54. Named by the UK for its northerly (boreal) position.

**The *Boreas*.** 10-ton, pusher-propellor Dornier Super Wal hydroplane owned by Lufthansa, and loaned to the German New Schwabenland Expedition of 1938–39 led by Ritscher. It carried pilot, navigator, mechanic, and photographer. *See also* **The *Passat*.**

**Mount Boreas.** 77°29′S, 161°06′E. 2,180 m. Between Mounts Aeolus and Dido, in the Olympus Range of Victoria Land. Named by the New Zealanders in 1958–59 for the Greek mythological figure.

**Boreas Nunatak.** 71°19′S, 3°57′W. 220 m. 1 mile SW of Passat Nunatak, at the mouth of the Schytt Glacier in Queen Maud Land. Discovered by Ritscher in 1938–39, and named for the *Boreas*.

**Boreas Peak.** 69°38′S, 68°20′W. On the west coast of the Antarctic Peninsula.

**Boree Islands.** 67°41′S, 45°19′E. Two small islands. 2 miles west of Point Widdows in Enderby Land. Named by the Australians for their native tree.

**Borg Island.** 66°58′S, 57°35′E. 1 mile long. In the eastern part of the Øygarden Group. Photographed by the LCE 1936–37. Named Borgøy (castle island) by the Norwegians.

**Borg Massif.** 72°45′S, 3°30′W. A spectacular mountain massif. 30 miles long. Has summits over 2,700 m. Along the NW side of the Penck Trough in Queen Maud Land. Divided into three rough groups by the ice-filled Raudberg Valley and Frostlendet Valley. Discovered aerially during the Ritscher expedition of 1938–39. The Norwegians later named it Borgmassivet (the castle massif) in association with Borg Mountain, its most prominent feature.

**Borg Mountain.** 72°32′S, 3°30′W. Also called Borga, Borgen. Large, flat, and ice-topped. At the north end of the Borg Massif, in Queen Maud Land, it is part of the Ritscher Upland in New Schwabenland. The Norwegian name Borga means "the castle."

**Borga Massif** see **Borg Massif**

**Borga Station.** A South African camp in Queen Maud Land.

**Borge, Hans.** Captain of the *Polynesia* in the South Shetlands in 1913–14. In 1914–15 he was surveying Mikkelsen Harbor in Trinity Island.

**Borge Bay.** 60°43′S, 45°37′W. Also called Borge Harbor, Queens Bay. Between Balin Point and Berntsen Point, on the east side of Signy Island, in the South Orkneys. Charted in 1912 by Petter Sørlle. Named for Capt. Hans Borge.

**Borge Harbor** see **Borge Bay**

**Borge Point.** 63°54′S, 60°45′W. Also called Punta Fuenzalida. Forms the east side of Mikkelsen Harbor, Trinity Island. Charted and named by Hans Borge, 1914–15, during his survey of Mikkelsen Harbor.

**Borgen** see **Borg Mountain**

**Börgen Bay.** 64°45′S, 63°30′W. Also called William Bay. 4 miles wide. An indentation into the SE coast of Anvers Island, just west of Bay Point. Discovered by de Gerlache in 1897–99, and named by him for Karl Börgen, German astronomer.

**Borgen Mountains** see **Borg Massif**

**Mount Borgesen** see **Mount Borgeson**

**Mount Borgeson.** 72°07′S, 99°10′W. Also seen spelled (erroneously) as Mount Borgesen. 5 miles ESE of Smith Peak in the Walker Mountains of Thurston Island. Named for Warren T. Borgeson, topographic engineer here in 1960.

**Borggarden Valley.** 72°34′S, 3°48′W. Broad, ice-filled, and 10 miles long. Between Borg Mountain and Veten Mountain in the NW part of the Borg Massif in Queen Maud Land. Name means "the castle courtyard" in Norwegian.

**Borghallet.** 72°25′S, 3°30′W. A gently sloping plain with an area of 100 square miles. North of Borg Mountain in Queen Maud Land. Name means "the castle slope" in Norwegian.

**Mount Borgstrom.** 74°16′S, 162°53′E. 2,610 m. 2 miles SE of Mount Meister on Nash Ridge in the Eisenhower Range of Victoria Land. Named for Charles O. Borgstrom, VX-6 commander in 1966.

**Mount Borland.** 74°25′S, 67°45′E. 5 miles south of Mount Twigg, near the head of the Lambert Glacier. Discovered aerially by Flying Officer J. Seaton, RAAF, on a Nov. 1956 flight for the ANARE. Named by the Australians for R.A. Borland, meteorologist at Mawson Station in 1958.

**Cape Borley.** 65°56′S, 55°10′E. Ice-covered. Between Capes Close and Boothby, or between Cape Batterbee and Magnet Bay, on the coast of Enderby Land, overlooked by the Napier Mountains. Discovered in Jan. 1930 by the BANZARE, and named by Mawson for John Oliver Borley, a member of the Discovery Committee (q.v.), who helped the BANZARE acquire the *Discovery* as their ship.

**Bornmann, Robert C.** Lt., USN. Took over as military leader of Hallett Station from Juan Tur on Jan. 16, 1958. In turn, Albert Bridgeman took over from Bornmann.

**Bornmann Glacier.** 72°20′S, 170°13′E. Flows from the west side of Hallett Peninsula, 1 mile south of Seabee Hook, and forms a short floating ice tongue on the shore of Edisto Inlet. Named by the New Zealanders in 1957–58 for Robert C. Bornmann.

**Borns Glacier.** 77°47′S, 162°01′E. Just west of Mount Coates, in the Taylor Valley, it flows from the Kukri Hills of Victoria Land. Charted by members of Scott's 1910–13 expedition. Named by the USA for Harold W. Borns, Jr., geologist here in 1960–61.

**Mount Borodin.** 71°32′S, 72°41′W. 250 m. Mostly ice-covered. 7 miles NNW of Gluck Peak, in the SW part of Alexander Island. Discovered by the RARE 1947–48. Named by the UK for the composer.

**Borodino Island** *see* **Smith Island**

**Borradaile Island.** 66°35′S, 162°45′E. One of the Balleny Islands. 2 miles long. 1 mile wide. 4 miles SE of Young Island, in the same group. Discovered in Feb. 1839 by Balleny, who named it for W. Borradaile, merchant who teamed with Charles Enderby in sending out the expedition.

**Borrello Island.** 66°19′S, 110°22′E. A small island off the west side of Hollin Island, in the Windmill Islands. Named for Sebastian R. Borrello, geomagnetician at Wilkes Station in 1958.

**Boschert Glacier.** 74°43′S, 111°30′W. On the coast of Marie Byrd Land.

**Bosner Island.** 66°27′S, 110°36′E. Also called Bosner Rock. 600 yards long. 200 yards NW of Boffa Island, and ½ mile east of Browning Peninsula, in the southern part of the Windmill Islands. Named for Paul Bosner, photographer on Operation Windmill, 1947–48.

**Bosner Rock** *see* **Bosner Island**

**Boss Peak.** 71°52′S, 166°15′E. 2,170 m. An isolated black peak on the east side of the terminus of Jutland Glacier. 8 miles NNE of Thomson Peak, in the NW part of the Victory Mountains of Victoria Land. Named by the New Zealanders in 1963–64 for Shackleton's nickname.

**Bosse Nunatak.** 72°08′S, 65°22′E. A small nunatak, 20 miles west of Mount Izabelle, in the Prince Charles Mountains. Discovered by J. Manning, surveyor with the ANARE Prince Charles Mountains Survey Party of 1971. Named by the Australians for H.E. Bosse, helicopter pilot with the survey party.

**The Boston Expedition.** Not an expedition as such, but rather 3 Boston vessels in the South Shetlands together during the summer of 1820–21. The *O'Cain* sailed from Boston on Aug. 19, 1820, captained by Jonathan Winship. The other two did belong together, the *Esther*, commanded by F.G. Low, and the *Emerald*, commanded by John G. Scott, both leaving Boston on Sept. 23, 1820. On Dec. 25, 1820, the *O'Cain* lost a man and a little later the other two ships saved the crew of the *Venus* when it was wrecked on March 7, 1821. The *Esther* and the *Emerald* collected 9,000 sealskins between them and sailed for Chile, where the *Emerald* was sold. The *O'Cain* left Antarctica on March 18, 1821, with 12,000 sealskins, in company with a British ship, the *King George*. It arrived in Boston on June 8, 1821, also with minerals, stones, and shells.

**Bostwick, William.** Member of the Wilkes Expedition 1838–42. Joined in the USA. Served the cruise.

**Botany Bay.** 77°S, 162°35′E. A little bay on the southern coast of Granite Harbor, between Cape Geology and Discovery Bluff, Victoria Land. Mapped by Scott's expedition of 1910–13. Named in 1911–12 by Grif Taylor and Frank Debenham, both Australians on that expedition, for Botany Bay, New South Wales.

**Botany Peak** *see* **Lichen Peak**

**Bothy Bay.** 62°09′S, 58°57′W. On the south coast of King George Island, in the South Shetlands.

**Bothy Lake.** 60°44′S, 45°40′W. On the south side of Signy Island, in the South Orkneys.

**Botnfjellet Mountain.** 71°45′S, 11°25′ E. 2,750 m. Forms the NE and eastern walls of Livdebotnen Cirque in the Humboldt Mountains of Queen Maud Land. Discovered by Ritscher in 1938–39. Name means "the cirque mountain" in Norwegian.

**Botnfjorden** *see* **Cirque Fjord**

**Botnneset Peninsula.** 69°44′S, 37°35′ E. Mainly ice-covered. Between Fletta Bay and Djupvika on the south, or "bottom," side of Lützow-Holm Bay. Photographed by the LCE 1936–37, and later named by the Norwegians. The name means "the bottom ness."

**Botnnuten.** 70°24′S, 38°01′E. An isolated rock peak. 1,460 m. South of Havsbotn. 22 miles SW of Shirase Glacier in Queen Maud Land. Photographed by the LCE 1936–37. Name means "the bottom peak" in Norwegian.

**Bottle-nosed whales** *see* **Beaked Whales**

**Bottom ice** *see* **Anchor ice**

**Bottrill Head.** 67°42′S, 66°57′W. On the east side of Bourgeois Fjord. Forms the northern side of the entrance to Dogs Leg Fjord, on the west coast of Graham Land. The FIDS named it for Harold Bottrill, shipping agent of assistance to the BGLE (who surveyed this feature in 1936) and to the FIDS (who resurveyed it in 1948).

**The** *Bouchard.* Ship used on the Argentine Antarctic Expedition of 1947–48. Captain Morroni.

**Boucot Plateau.** 82°25′S, 155°40′E. Small and ice-covered. West of the Wellman Cliffs and south of the McKay Cliffs in the Geologists Range. Named for Arthur J. Boucot, geologist at Byrd Station in 1964–65.

**Boudet Island.** 65°11′S, 64°10′W. The largest of the several small islands off the southern end of Petermann Island, in the Wilhelm Archipelago. Discovered by Charcot in 1908–10, and named by him for the French consul in Brazil.

**Boudette Peaks.** 76°50′S, 126°02′W. Two peaks, of 2,810 m. and 2,815 m. 1 mile WSW of Lavris Peak, in the northern portion of Mount Hartigan, in the Executive Committee Range of Marie Byrd Land. Lichens are to be found here. Named for Eugene L. Boudette, geologist, a member of the Marie Byrd Land Traverse Party of 1959–60.

**Boulder Point.** 68°11′S, 67°W. The southern extremity of Stonington Island, just off the west coast of Graham Land. Surveyed in 1940 by the USAS, and again in 1948 by the FIDS, and named by the FIDS for a large granite boulder here.

**Boulder Rock.** 71°19′S, 170°14′E. On the west side of Adare Peninsula, just south of Ridley Beach, in Victoria Land. Charted and named in 1911 by Campbell's Northern Party during Scott's last expedition.

**Boulding Ridge.** 68°02′S, 66°55′W. Separates Todd Glacier from McClary Glacier, on the west side of Graham Land. Named by the UK for Richard A. Boulding, BAS surveyor at Base E, 1965–68.

**Islotes Boulier** *see* **Rho Islands**

**Boulton Peak.** 64°06′S, 60°42′W. On the SE side of Curtiss Bay, 5 miles south of Cape Andreas, in Graham Land. Named by the UK for Matthew P.W. Boulton, aircraft pioneer in the 19th century.

**Bounty Nunatak.** 71°37′S, 160°E. 2,350 m. Mostly ice-free. 4 miles SE of Mount Burnham, in the south part of the Daniels Range in the Usarp Mountains. Named by the NZGSAE 1963–64 because the party was out of food when it arrived at a cache near here.

**Bouquet Bay.** 64°03′S, 62°10′W. 7 miles wide. Between Liège Island and the northern part of Brabant Island. Discovered by Charcot in 1903–5, and named by him for Jean Bouquet de la Grye, French hydrographic engineer who helped publish the scientific results of the expedition.

**Bouquet de la Grye Bay** *see* **Bouquet Bay**

**Bourgeois Fjord.** 67°40′S, 67°05′W. An inlet, 30 miles long, and between 3 and 5 miles wide. Between the eastern sides of Pourquoi Pas Island and Blaiklock Island, and the west coast of Graham Land. Discovered by Charcot in 1908–10, and named by him for Col. Joseph E. Bourgeois, director of the Geographic Service of the French Army.

**Bourgeois Nunataks.** 69°54′S, 158°22′E. A group 12 miles SW of Governor Mountain, in the Wilson Hills. Named for William L. Bourgeois, USN, chief aviation machinist's mate in the Antarctic, 1967 and 1968.

**Bousquet Island.** 66°25′S, 110°41′E. 600 yards long. Just east of Herring Island in the Windmill Islands. Carl Eklund named it for Edward A. Bousquet, USN, utilitiesman 2nd class at Wilkes Station in 1957.

**Boutan Rocks.** 64°54′S, 63°10′W. A small group 1½ miles SW of Bruce Island, off the west coast of Graham Land. Named by the UK in 1960 for L.M.A. Boutan (1859–1934), French photography pioneer.

**The *Bouvet III*.** A Norwegian whale catcher off the East Antarctica coast in Jan. 1931, under the command of Carl Sjövold.

**The *Bouvet II*.** A Norwegian whale catcher off the coast of Mac. Robertson Land in Jan. 1931. Gunner was Reidar Bjerkø.

**Mount Bouvier.** 67°14′S, 68°09′W. 2,070 m. Mostly ice-covered. Just north of the head of Stonehaide Bay in the eastern part of Adelaide Island. Discovered and named by Charcot in 1903–5. He named it Pic Bouvier, for Louis Bouvier,

the French naturalist. The name was later anglicized.

**Bøving Island.** 66°17′S, 110°31′E. A small island in the southern part of Newcomb Bay. 175 yards east of McMullin Island, in the Windmill Islands. Named by the Australians for F. Bøving, 3rd officer on the *Thala Dan* in 1965, who assisted in a hydrographic survey in the area.

**Bowden Névé.** 83°35′S, 165°E. 20 miles wide. South of Mount Miller, between the Queen Elizabeth and Queen Alexandra Ranges, near Beardmore Glacier, in the Queen Maud Mountains. Discovered by the NZ Southern Party of the BCTAE in 1958, and named for Charles M. Bowden, chairman of the Ross Sea Committee, which organized the NZ party of the BCTAE.

**Bowditch Crests.** 68°30′S, 65°22′W. A line of steep cliffs surmounted by four summits overlooking the NW corner of Mobiloil Inlet, in eastern Graham Land. Named by the UK for Nathaniel Bowditch (1773–1838), US astronomer and author in 1801 of *The New American Practical Navigator*.

**Mount Bowen.** 75°45′S, 161°02′E. 1,875 m. 6 miles SW of Mount Howard, in the Prince Albert Mountains of Victoria Land. Discovered during Scott's 1901–4 expedition, and named by them for C.C. Bowen, a supporter in NZ.

**Bowen, Peter.** Seaman on the Wilkes Expedition 1838–42. Joined at Rio. Run at Valparaiso.

**Bowen Cirque.** 80°42′S, 23°27′W. In the Shackleton Range.

**Mount Bower.** 72°37′S, 160°30′E. 2,610 m. In the Outback Nunataks of northern Victoria Land. 6 miles ENE of Roberts Butte. Named for John R. Bower, ionosphere physicist at Amundsen-Scott South Pole Station in 1968.

**Bower Canyon** *see* **Bowers Canyon**

**Bower Hills** *see* **Bowers Mountains**

**Mount Bowers.** 85°02′S, 164°05′E. 2,430 m. 2 miles SSE of Mount Buckley, at the head of the Beardmore Glacier, just to the south of the Queen Alexandra Range. Named by the members of Scott's 1910–13 expedition for Henry Bowers.

**Bowers, Henry R.** b. 1883, Scotland. d. about March 29, 1912, Antarctica. Henry Robertson Bowers. Known as "Birdie" because of his beaky nose. Son of a sailor, he was in the merchant navy at 16, and from 1905 in the R.I.M. (Royal Indian Marine). In 1909 he became a lieutenant, and joined Scott's 1910–13 expedition as ship's officer in charge of stores on the *Terra Nova.* Scott chose him for the shore party because of his organizational and navigation abilities. He took part in the "worst journey in the world," along with Wilson and Cherry-Garrard, to Cape Crozier, to collect emperor penguins' eggs, and Scott chose him for the Pole party of 1911. Short (5'4") for an explorer, he was, however, the toughest of the polar party, and was one of the first 10 men ever to reach the South Pole. He didn't make it back.

**Bowers, Richard A.** Lt. (jg), USNR. Led the party that built the South Pole Station over the 1956–57 summer season. He was delivered to the Pole area on Nov. 20, 1956, in one of the R4D airplanes. He had sledges, and other equipment, such as a Weasel and 11 dogs. The Weasel broke down, and he had to make the 9-mile trip to the Pole by dog sledge. Paul Siple joined him later and headed up the establishment when it was ready for occupation. Bowers headed back to McMurdo when his job was done. He was the second Lt. Bowers to stand at the South Pole in 44 years (for the list of his advance party *see* **South Pole**), and the fourth leader to stand at the Pole (*see* **Amundsen, Scott,** and **Dufek**).

**Bowers Automatic Weather Station.** 85°12′S, 163°24′E. An American AWS at an elevation of approximately 6,400 feet. Began operating on Jan. 11, 1986.

**Bowers Canyon.** 71°S, 173°E. Also known (erroneously) as Bower Canyon. Submarine feature of the Ross Sea, off northern Victoria Land.

**Bowers Corner.** 79°01′S, 84°21′W. A peak, 9 miles SE of Lishness Peak at the extreme south end of the Sentinel Range. At the east side of the terminus of the Nimitz Glacier. Named for Lt. Richard A. Bowers.

**Bowers Glacier.** 72°37′S, 169°05′E. On the west side of Mount Northampton in the Victory Mountains of Victoria Land. It flows into the Tucker Glacier. Named for Chester H. Bowers, meteorologist and senior US representative at Hallett Station in 1962.

**Bowers Hills** *see* **Bowers Mountains**

**Bowers Mountains.** 71°10′S, 163°15′E. Also called Bower Hills, Bowers Hills. 90 miles long. 35 miles wide. In Oates Land, northern Victoria Land. When Pennell sighted the seaward end in Feb. 1911, from the *Terra Nova,* he called them the Bowers Hills for Lt. Henry Bowers. The name was later amended by the USA.

**Bowers Peak.** 71°45′S, 163°20′E. 2,140 m. Between the Hunter Glacier and the Hoshko Glacier, in the Lanterman Range of the Bowers Mountains. Named by the NZGSAE 1963–64 for Lt. John M. Bowers, Jr., VX-6, who flew support flights for this party.

**Bowers Piedmont Glacier.** 77°41′S, 164°24′E. 40 square miles in area. Just south of New Harbor, on the SW coast of McMurdo Sound. It merges at its south side with Blue Glacier, in Victoria Land. Discovered by Scott's 1901–4 expedition, and called Butter Point Piedmont by them. Renamed by Scott's 1910–13 expedition for Henry R. Bowers.

**Bowie Crevasse Field.** 79°03′S, 84°45′W. On the Minnesota Glacier, between the SE end of the Bastien Range and the Anderson Massif, in the Ellsworth Mountains. Named by the University of Minnesota Ellsworth Mountains Party of 1962–63, for Glenn E. Bowie, geophysicist with the party.

**Bowin Glacier.** 84°53′S, 177°20′E. 5 miles long. Flows between Sullivan

Ridge and Fulgham Ridge, to enter the Ramsey Glacier. Named for C.F. Bowin, USN, commissaryman in Antarctica in 1965 and 1966.

**Bowl Island.** 67°09′S, 50°50′E. Has a bowl-like depression in the center. Just south of Crohn Island, at the head of Amundsen Bay, in Enderby Land. Discovered by the ANARE in 1956, and named descriptively by them.

**Bowler Rocks.** 62°21′S, 59°50′W. A group, ½ mile SW of Table Island, in the South Shetlands. Named by the UK for David M. Bowler, surveying recorder for the RN Hydrographic Survey Unit on the *Nimrod* here in 1967.

**Cape Bowles.** 61°19′S, 54°06′W. The southern tip of Clarence Island, in the South Shetlands. Named in 1820 by Bransfield.

**¹Mount Bowles** *see* **Mount Irving**

**²Mount Bowles.** 62°38′S, 60°12′W. Over 800 m. Ice-covered. 3 miles north of Mount Friesland in the eastern part of Livingston Island, in the South Shetlands. Perhaps this was the peak charted by Foster in 1828–31.

**Mount Bowlin.** 86°28′S, 147°18′W. 2,230 m. Between the mouths of the Van Reeth Glacier and the Robison Glacier in the Queen Maud Mountains. Discovered in Dec. 1934 by Quin Blackburn, and named by Byrd for William H. Bowlin.

**Bowlin, William H.** A long-time navy man, he was 2nd pilot on the shore party of Byrd's 1933–35 expedition.

**Bowling Green Plateau.** 79°42′S, 158°36′E. Ice-covered. At the north side of the Brown Hills in the Cook Mountains. Named by the VUWAE 1962–63. Prof. Charles C. Rich, geologist and deputy leader of the expedition, was affiliated with Bowling Green State University of Ohio.

**Bowman Coast.** 68°S, 65°W. Between Cape Northrop and Cape Agassiz, on the east side of the Antarctic Peninsula. It is on the other side of the Peninsula across from Marguerite Bay. Discovered aerially by Wilkins on Dec. 20, 1928, and named by him for Isaiah Bowman, director of the American Geographical Society, 1915–35, and president of Johns Hopkins University, 1935–49.

**Bowman Glacier.** 85°34′S, 162°W. Also called Isaiah Bowman Glacier. Deeply entrenched. 40 miles long. Flows from the Polar Plateau, between the Quarles Range and the Rawson Plateau, into the Amundsen Glacier, where that glacier enters the Ross Ice Shelf. Discovered in Dec. 1929 by Gould's party during Byrd's 1928–30 expedition. Named by Byrd for Isaiah Bowman (*see* **Bowman Coast**).

**Bowman Inlet.** 68°42′S, 64°23′W. A Larsen Ice Shelf indentation into the east coast of the Antarctic Peninsula.

**Bowman Island.** 65°20′S, 103°08′E. A high, ice-covered island. 24 miles long. Shaped like a figure 8. It rises above the NE part of the Shackleton Ice Shelf, 25 miles NE of Cape Elliott, off the Knox Coast. Discovered on Jan. 28, 1931, by the BANZARE, and named by Mawson for Isaiah Bowman (*see* **Bowman Coast**).

**Bowman Peak.** 77°29′S, 153°13′W. Formerly called John Bowman Peak. On the south side of Butler Glacier in the Alexandra Mountains of Marie Byrd Land. Discovered during Byrd's 1928–30 expedition, and named by Byrd for John McEntee Bowman, president of Bowman Biltmore Hotels, and a patron of the expedition.

**Bowman Peninsula.** 74°47′S, 62°22′W. 25 miles long. 15 miles wide in its northern and central portions. Ice-covered. Between Nantucket Inlet and Gardner Inlet, south of Smith Peninsula, in Trinity Land. It terminates in Cape Adams, on the Antarctic Peninsula. Discovered by the RARE 1947–48. Named by Ronne for Isaiah Bowman (*see* **Bowman Coast**).

**Mount Bowser.** 86°03′S, 155°36′W. 3,655 m. 2 miles south of Mount Astor at the north end of Fram Mesa, in the Queen Maud Mountains. Named for

Carl J. Bowser, geologist at McMurdo Station in 1965–66 and 1966–67.

**Bowyer Butte.** 74°57'S, 134°45'W. 1,085 m. 3 miles wide. An isolated nunatak on the Hobbs Coast, between the lower end of the Johnson Glacier and the lower end of the Venzke Glacier, in Marie Byrd Land. Lichens and mosses are to be found here. Discovered aerially by the USAS 1939–41. Named for Donald W. Bowyer, meteorologist at Byrd Station in 1962.

**Box Reef.** 67°45'S, 69°03'W. A line of drying rocks between the Esplin Islands and League Rock, off the south end of Adelaide Island. Named by the UK in 1963 in association with nearby Cox Reef (the old story of Box and Cox).

**Boxing Island.** 64°35'S, 61°41'W. A small island in Charlotte Bay. East of Harris Peak, off the west coast of Graham Land. De Gerlache charted it in 1897–99. Named by the FIDS who saw it on Dec. 26, 1955 (Boxing Day).

**Mount Boyd.** 84°48'S, 179°25'W. 2,960 m. Pyramidal. 3 miles west of Mount Bennett in the Bush Mountains. Discovered by the USAS 1939–41. Surveyed by Crary, leader of the Ross Ice Shelf Traverse Party of 1957–58, and named by him for Walter Boyd, Jr., glaciologist with the party.

**Boyd, Vernon D.** US Marine many times in Antarctica. He was one of the shore party on Byrd's 1933–35 expedition, and was a member of West Base during the USAS 1939–41. During Operation Highjump, 1946–47, he was head of the motorized section at Little America IV, and was transportation officer on Operation Windmill, 1947–48.

**Boyd Escarpment.** 82°26'S, 50°30'W. At the extreme north of the Pensacola Mountains.

**Boyd Glacier.** 77°14'S, 145°25'W. Also called Ames Glacier. Heavily crevassed. 45 miles long. Flows from the Ford Ranges of Marie Byrd Land, between Bailey Ridge and Mount Douglass, into the Sulzberger Ice Shelf. Discovered aerially in 1934 during Byrd's 1933–35 expedition, and named by Byrd for Vernon D. Boyd.

**Boyd Head.** 75°17'S, 110°01'W. Just east of the mouth of Vane Glacier, on the coast of Marie Byrd Land. Over 1,000 m. Named for Capt. Hugh F. Boyd III, US Army, construction projects officer, 1972 and 1973.

**Boyd Nunatak.** 69°50'S, 74°44'E. 8 miles SE of Mount Caroline Mikkelsen on the south side of the Publications Ice Shelf. Photographed by the LCE 1936–37. Later named by the Australians for J.S. Boyd, physicist at Wilkes Station in 1965.

**Boyd Ridge.** 76°57'S, 116°57'W. Ice-covered. 22 miles long. Forms the south end of the Crary Mountains, in Marie Byrd Land. It is separated from the main peaks of the group by Campbell Valley. Named for John C. Boyd, biologist at McMurdo Station in 1965–66 and 1966–67.

**Boyd Strait.** 62°50'S, 61°50'W. Also called Estrecho Larrea. Over 20 miles wide. Separates Smith Island from Snow Island and the rest of the group, in the South Shetlands. Named Boyd's Straits in 1823 by Weddell for Capt. David Boyd (who had nothing to do with Antarctica). The name was later simplified.

**Boydell Glacier.** 64°11'S, 59°04'W. 9 miles long. Flows from the Detroit Plateau of Graham Land, and merges with the Sjögren Glacier. Named by the UK for James Boydell, 19th century British inventor.

**Boyds Straits** *see* **Boyd Strait**

**Mount Boyer.** 75°07'S, 72°04'W. 1 mile SW of Mount Becker in the Merrick Mountains. Named for Francis C. Boyer, USN, hospital corpsman and officer-in-charge of Eights Station in 1964.

**Boyer, Joseph.** Joseph Emmanuel Prosper Boyer. French naval élève on the *Astrolabe* during Dumont d'Urville's 1837–40 expedition. He was promoted to ensign on Aug. 10, 1839, but was put ashore sick in NZ on April 29, 1840.

**Boyer Butte** *see* **Bowyer Butte**

**Boyer Glacier.** 73°19′S, 167°18′E. 10 miles west of Index Point, in the eastern part of the Mountaineer Range. It flows into the lower part of the Mariner Glacier in Victoria Land. Named for Jack W. Boyer, USN, radioman at Hallett Station in 1962.

**Boyer Rocks.** 63°35′S, 59°W. A small group in the NE corner of Bone Bay, 3 miles SW of Cape Roquemaurel, Trinity Peninsula. Named by the UK for Joseph Boyer.

**Boyer Spur.** 71°51′S, 62°48′W. Between the Kellogg and Gruening Glaciers on the east side of Palmer Land. About 5 miles WNW of Malva Bluff and the NW head of Hilton Inlet. Named for Stephen J. Boyer, geologist here in 1972–73.

**Boyle, Robert.** Seaman on the Wilkes Expedition 1838–42. Joined in the USA. Run at Sydney.

**Boyle Mountains.** 67°21′S, 66°38′W. A wall of mountains between the heads of Lallemand and Bourgeois Fjords in Graham Land. Named by the UK for Robert Boyle (1627–1691), natural philosopher specializing in cold.

**Boyson, John W.** 1st class boy on the Wilkes Expedition 1838–42. Joined in Fiji. Run at Oahu.

**Bozu Peak.** 69°25′S, 39°48′E. 235 m. The central and highest of the Byvågåsane Peaks, on the east shore of Lützow-Holm Bay. Photographed by the LCE 1936–37. Later named by the Japanese as Bozu-san (treeless peak).

**Cape Braathen.** 71°48′S, 96°05′W. Ice-covered. At the NW termination of Evans Peninsula, on Thurston Island. Named for Christoffer Braathen.

**Braathen, Christoffer.** Ski expert and dog driver on Byrd's 1928–30 expedition. He was the mechanic on Ellsworth's 1933–34 and 1934–35 expeditions.

**Brabant Island.** 64°15′S, 62°20′W. 34 miles long. An average of 12 miles wide. Mount Parry, its highest peak, rises to 2,520 m. Between Anvers Island and Liège Island, it is the second largest island in the Palmer Archipelago, off the west coast of Graham Land. Discovered in 1898 by de Gerlache, and named by him for the Belgian province.

**Brabazon Point.** 64°24′S, 61°16′W. Forms the east side of the entrance to Salvesen Cove, on the west coast of Graham Land. De Gerlache charted it in 1897–99. In 1960 the UK named it for Lord Brabazon, pioneer aviator and aerial photographer.

**Mount Brabec.** 73°34′S, 165°24′E. 2,460 m. Surmounts the east wall of Aviator Glacier, 10 miles north of Mount Monteagle, in the Mountaineer Range of Victoria Land. Named for Lt. Cdr. Richard C. Brabec, USN, Hercules aircraft commander on Operation Deep Freeze 66.

**Bracken Peak.** 77°51′S, 85°24′W. 1,240 m. South of the terminus of Newcomer Glacier, 3 miles NE of Mount Malone, on the east side of the Sentinel Range. Named for H.C. Bracken, pilot over the area in Dec. 1959.

**Braddock Nunataks.** 70°48′S, 65°55′W. A group inland from the Bertram Glacier, 9 miles SE of the Perseus Crags, on the western edge of the Dyer Plateau, in Palmer Land. Named for Lt. Robert L. Braddock, Jr., USN, officer-in-charge of Amundsen-Scott South Pole Station in 1974.

**Bradford Glacier.** 65°51′S, 64°18′W. Flows from Mount Dewey into Comrie Glacier, on the west coast of Graham Land. Named by the UK for Samuel C. Bradford (1878–1948), pioneer of scientific information services.

**Bradford Rock.** 66°13′S, 110°34′E. An ice-covered rock, in water, marks the NW end of the Swain Islands. Named by Carl Eklund in 1957 for Don L. Bradford, USN, radioman at Wilkes Station in 1957.

**Mount Brading.** 64°17′S, 59°17′W. Topped by a snow peak. 4 miles east of the NE corner of Larsen Inlet, in Graham

Land. Named by the UK for Christopher G. Brading, FIDS surveyor at Base D, 1959–60. First climbed by Brading, Ian Hampton, R. Harbour, and J. Winham, in early 1960.

**Mount Bradley.** 63°53'S, 58°37'W. 835 m. Pyramidal. At the SE end of a ridge descending from the Detroit Plateau, 4 miles SW of Mount Reece, in the southern part of the Trinity Peninsula of Graham Land. Climbed in 1945 by the FIDS, who named it for K.G. Bradley, colonial secretary in the Falkland Islands.

**Bradley, B.O.J.** Crewman on the *Jacob Ruppert*, 1933–34.

**Bradley Nunatak.** 81°24'S, 85°58'W. 10 miles SW of Mount Tidd, in the Pirrit Hills. Positioned on Dec. 7, 1958, by the US Ellsworth-Byrd Traverse Party, and named for the Rev. A. Bradley, seismologist with the party.

**Bradley Ridge.** 70°14'S, 65°15'E. 7 miles SE of Mount Peter, in the Athos Range of the Prince Charles Mountains. Named by the Australians for R.G. Bradley, weather observer at Mawson Station in 1964.

**Bradley Rock.** 65°S, 64°42'W. An island 9 miles NW of the entrance to French Passage in the Wilhelm Archipelago. Named by the UK in 1973 for Lt. Cdr. Edgar M. Bradley, RN, who directed a hydrographic survey in the area in 1965.

**Mount Bragg.** 84°06'S, 56°43'W. 1,480 m. 6 miles SW of Gambacorta Peak, in the southern part of the Neptune Range. Named for Ralph L. Bragg, VX-6 photographer at McMurdo Station in 1964.

**Bragg Islands.** 66°28'S, 66°26'W. A small group in Crystal Sound, 7 miles north of Cape Rey, Graham Land. Included are Rambler Island, Alan Rock, Molecule Island, Sunday Island, Vagrant Island. Named by the UK for Sir William H. Bragg (1862–1942), British physicist.

**Brahms Inlet.** 71°25'S, 73°55'W. Ice-filled. 25 miles long. 6 miles wide. Indentation into the north side of Beetho-

ven Peninsula on Alexander Island, between Mendelssohn and Verdi Inlets. Named by the UK for the composer.

**Braillard, A.T.** Able seaman, RN, on the *Discovery II*, 1931–33 and 1933–35.

**Braillard Point.** 62°13'S, 58°55'W. Forms the NE end of Ardley Island, off the SW end of King George Island, in the South Shetlands. Charted by personnel on the *Discovery II* in 1935, and named by them for A.T. Braillard.

**Bramble Peak.** 72°22'S, 166°59'E. 2,560 m. Surmounts the NE side of the head of Croll Glacier in the Victory Mountains of Victoria Land. Named for Edward J. Bramble, USN, VX-6 machinist's mate at McMurdo Station in 1967.

**Mount Bramhall.** 72°10'S, 98°24'W. 5 miles east of Mount Hawthorne, in the Walker Mountains of Thurston Island. Named for Dr. E.H. Bramhall.

**Bramhall, Dr. E.H.** Physicist on the shore party of Byrd's 1933–35 expedition.

**Mount Branco** *see* **Mount Rio Branco**

**Brand Peak.** 70°01'S, 63°55'W. Snow-covered. 10 miles ESE of the Eternity Range, 4 miles NW of Mount Duemler, in Palmer Land. Named for Timothy Brand, biologist at Palmer Station in 1974.

**Brandau Glacier.** 84°54'S, 173°45'E. 15 miles long. Flows from an ice divide between Haynes Table and Husky Heights, into the Keltie Glacier just west of Ford Spur. Named for Lt. Cdr. James F. Brandau, USN, VX-6 pilot, 1964 and 1965.

**Brandau Rocks.** 76°53'S, 159°20'E. ½ mile west of Carapace Nunatak in Victoria Land. Named by the New Zealanders in 1964 for Lt. Cdr. James F. Brandau (*see* **Brandau Glacier**), who helped an expedition out here that year.

**Brandau Vent.** A volcanic vent in southern Victoria Land. Named for Lt. Cdr. James F. Brandau (*see* **Brandau Glacier**).

**Brandenburger Bluff.** 75°58'S, 136°05'
W. 1,650 m. A steep rock bluff at the extreme north side of Mount Berlin in the
Flood Range of Marie Byrd Land. Algae
and lichens are to be found here. Named
for Arthur J. Brandenburger, US glaciologist with the Byrd Station Traverse of
1962–63.

**Mount Brandt.** 72°10'S, 1°07'E. 1,540
m. The most northerly nunatak of the
Rømlingane Peaks, in the Sverdrup
Mountains of Queen Maud Land. Discovered by Ritscher in 1938–39, and
named by him as Brandt-Berg for Emil
Brandt. This may or may not be precisely
the mountain that Ritscher named, but
modern geographers have decided that it
is close enough.

**Brandt, Emil.** Sailor on the German
New Schwabenland Expedition led by
Ritscher in 1938–39.

**Brandy Bay.** 63°50'S, 57°59'W. 2
miles wide. On the NW coast of James
Ross Island. Nordenskjöld was probably
the first to see it, in 1903. The FIDS
surveyed it in 1945, and again in 1952.
While they were here in 1952 they were
discussing the efficacy of brandy for
dogbites.

**The *Bransfield*.** British Royal research /
supply ship commissioned at Leith, Scotland, on Dec. 31, 1970. It then sailed for
the Weddell Sea.

**Mount Bransfield.** 63°17'S, 57°05'W.
760 m. Ice-covered. 2 miles SW of Cape
Dubouzet, on the northern tip of the
Antarctic Peninsula. This is probably the
peak sighted by Bransfield on Jan. 20,
1820, and named by him as Mount
Wakefield. That name was later changed
to Mount Hope, and in turn to Mount
Bransfield.

**Point Bransfield** *see* **Bransfield
Island**

**Bransfield, Edward.** b. ca 1795. d.
1852. British naval lieutenant. He was in
Chile as captain of the *Andromache*
when William Smith arrived reporting
his discovery of the South Shetlands in
1819. Bransfield was placed in command

of Smith's ship, the *Williams,* and with
Smith as pilot, they sailed from
Valparaiso on Dec. 20, 1819, in order to
chart the South Shetlands. They arrived
at the islands on Jan. 16, 1820. They
landed on King George Island to take
possession, explored for a week, then, on
Jan. 27, 1820, sailed SW. They went to
Deception Island, and went further
south still. On Jan. 30, 1820, they saw
"high mountains covered with snow."
These were the peaks of Trinity Land, on
the mainland, and they charted part of it
(crudely). They also discovered the
Bransfield Strait. On Feb. 4, 1820, they
landed at Clarence Island. Bransfield left
the navy later that year.

**Bransfield Island.** 63°11'S, 56°36'W. 5
miles long. 3 miles SW of D'Urville
Island, off the northern tip of the Antarctic Peninsula. Ross named it Point Bransfield, for Edward Bransfield. The FIDS
redefined it in 1947.

**Bransfield Rocks.** 61°46'S, 56°51'W.
Between O'Brien Island and Ridley Island in the South Shetlands. Apparently
these rocks have disappeared, for the
term is no longer used.

**Bransfield Strait.** 63°S, 59°W. Also
called Mar de Flota. 60 miles wide. It extends for 200 miles in a NE–SW direction,
and separates the northern tip of the Antarctic Peninsula from the South Shetlands. Discovered by Bransfield in 1820,
and named for him by Weddell in 1825.

**Bransfield Trough.** A submarine
trough centering on 61°30'S, 54°W.

**Branson Nunatak.** 67°55'S, 62°46'E.
Between Mount Burnett and Price Nunatak, in the Framnes Mountains of Mac-
Robertson Land. Photographed by the
LCE 1936–37, and named Horntind
(horn peak) by the Norwegians. Renamed by the Australians for J. Branson,
geophysicist at Mawson Station in 1962.

**Branstetter Rocks.** 70°08'S, 72°37'E.
A small group 1 mile ENE of Thil Island,
in the eastern part of the Amery Ice
Shelf. Named by US cartographer John
H. Roscoe in 1952, for J.C. Branstetter,

air crewman on Operation Highjump flights over this area in 1946–47.

**Bråpiggen Peak.** 72°54'S, 3°18'W. One of the ice-free peaks at the south side of Frostlendet Valley, 1 mile south of Friis-Baastad Peak, in the Borg Massif of Queen Maud Land. Name means "the abrupt peak" in Norwegian.

**Brash ice.** Or brash. Small (must be under 6 feet across) fragments and nodules of ice, resulting from a floe breaking up.

**Brash Island.** 63°24'S, 54°55'W. About 7 miles SE of Joinville Island. Isolated, it is 5 miles NW of Darwin Island. Surveyed in 1953 by the FIDS, and named by the UK for the brash ice in the area.

**The Bråtegg.** Norwegian ship in Antarctic waters in 1947–48 on an expedition organized by the Federation of Norwegian Whaling Companies. Holger Holgersen led the expedition, which conducted research in oceanography, zoology, and geography. Nils Larsen captained the ship.

**Bråtegg Bank.** 65°16'S, 68°35'W. Also called Bråteggen. A submarine feature.

**Bråteggen** see **Bråtegg Bank**

**Bratholm** see **Steepholm**

**Bratina Island.** 78°S, 165°32'E. A small island at the northern tip of Brown Peninsula, in the Ross Ice Shelf. Named in 1963 for Chief Aviation Machinist's Mate Joseph Bratina, of VX-6, at McMurdo Station, 1958–59, 1960–61, and 1961–62.

**Brattebotnen Cirque.** 71°45'S, 10°15'E. On the west wall of Mount Dallmann, in the Orvin Mountains of Queen Maud Land. Name means "the steep cirque" in Norwegian.

**Brattnipane Peaks.** 71°54'S, 24°33'E. 2,660 m. A group 9 miles NW of Mefjell Mountain in the Sør Rondane Mountains. Photographed by the LCE 1936–37. Named Brattnipane (the steep peaks) by the Norwegians.

**Brattodden** see **Abrupt Point**

**Brattøy** see **Abrupt Island**

**Brattskarvbrekka Pass.** 72°10'S, 1°25'E. Between Brattskarvet Mountain and Vendeholten Mountain in the Sverdrup Mountains of Queen Maud Land. Name means "the steep mountain slope" in Norwegian.

**Brattskarvet Mountain.** 72°06'S, 1°27'E. 2,100 m. Just north of Vendeholten Mountain in the Sverdrup Mountains of Queen Maud Land. Name means "the steep mountain" in Norwegian.

**Brattstabben** see **Jennings Bluff**

**Brattstrand Bluffs.** 69°13'S, 77°E. 3 miles ENE of Hovde Island, on Prydz Bay and part of the Ingrid Christensen Coast, about 20 miles north of the Larsemann Hills. The Norwegian name Brattstranda means "the abrupt shore." Photographed by the LCE 1936–37.

**Mount Braun.** 69°26'S, 71°31'W. In the NW part of Alexander Island.

**Braunsteffer Lake.** 68°32'S, 78°22'E. ½ mile long. 1 mile west of the central part of Lake Zvezda in the Vestfold Hills. Named by the Australians for C. Braunsteffer, weather observer at Davis Station in 1959.

**Brautnuten Peak.** 71°46'S, 1°21'W. 5 miles SE of Snøkallen Hill, on the east side of the Ahlmann Ridge in Queen Maud Land.

**Rocas Bravo** see **Snag Rocks**

**Bravo Hills.** 84°41'S, 171°W. A group of low peaks rising to 780 m. They border the Ross Ice Shelf between the Gough and Le Couteur Glaciers. Named by the Southern Party of the NZGSAE 1963–64 for their supply depot B (Bravo) near here.

**Bråvold, Capt.** Commander of the *Thorshammer*, 1936–37.

**Brawhm Pass.** 77°53'S, 160°41'E. A small pass which provides easy passage between Beacon Valley and Arena Valley, on the east side of Farnell Valley, in southern Victoria Land, between Beacon Valley and the Ferrar Glacier.

Named by NZ in 1968 for the 6 members of the University of New South Wales (Australia) expeditions of 1964–65 and 1966–67, who used this pass (Bryan, Rose, Anderson, Williams, Hobbs, and McElroy).

**Brawn Rocks.** 73°12′S, 160°45′E. Isolated. They extend over 3 miles. 12 miles SW of the Sequence Hills in Victoria Land. Named for James E. Brawn, VX-6 machinist's mate at McMurdo Station in 1966.

**Mount Bray.** 74°50′S, 113°52′W. Ice-capped. On the SE side of Martin Peninsula, in the Kohler Range of Marie Byrd Land. 1 mile NW of Klimov Bluff. Named for Thomas K. Bray, topographic engineer with the Marie Byrd Land Survey Party of 1966–67.

**Bray Nunatak** *see* **Office Girls**

**Brazil.** Ratified as the 18th signatory of the Antarctic Treaty on May 16, 1975, Brazil became the 15th nation to achieve Consultative status on Sept. 12, 1983. After years of planning, a two-ship expedition was sent to the Antarctic Peninsula in the summer of 1982–83, in a major reconnaissance effort. In 1984 two ships made three scientific cruises in Antarctic waters, and that year Comandante Ferraz Summer Research Station was established.

**Mount Brazil.** 72°03′S, 167°59′E. 2,090 m. At the south end of the McGregor Range in the Admiralty Mountains. Named for CWO John D. Brazil, US Army, helicopter pilot in the area, 1961–62.

**Brazitis Nunatak.** 84°58′S, 67°23′W. 1,625 m. 5 miles south of DesRoches Nunataks in the SW part of the Patuxent Range of the Pensacola Mountains. Named for Peter F. Brazitis, cosmic ray scientist at Amundsen-Scott South Pole Station in 1967.

**Mount Breaker.** 67°53′S, 67°16′W. Has double summits. The eastern one is 880 m., and is the highest summit on Horseshoe Island, off the coast of Graham Land. Descriptively named by

the UK in 1958. When seen from the west it resembles a breaking wave.

**Breaker Island.** 64°46′S, 64°07′W. A small, rocky island SW of Norsel Point, Anvers Island. 1½ miles NW of Palmer Station. Surveyed by the FIDS in 1955. Named by the UK because the island causes breakers when the sea is rough.

**Breakwater Island.** 64°47′S, 63°13′W. A small island ⅓ mile off the east side of Wiencke Island in the Palmer Archipelago. Descriptively named by personnel on Operation Tabarin in 1944.

**Mount Brearley.** 77°48′S, 161°45′E. 2,010 m. The most westerly of the Kukri Hills in Victoria Land. Named by Grif Taylor's Western Journey Party during Scott's 1910–13 expedition.

**Breccia Crags.** 60°42′S, 45°13′W. 305 m. 1 mile west of Petter Bay, in the SE end of Coronation Island in the South Orkneys. Named by the UK for the brecciated schist here.

**Breccia Island.** 68°22′S, 67°01′W. A small, low island 1 mile NW of the Tiber Rocks in the northern part of Rymill Bay, off the west coast of the Antarctic Peninsula. Named by Robert L. Nichols of the RARE 1947–48 because of the breccia here.

**Mount Brecher.** 85°24′S, 124°22′W. 2,100 m. Just west of Mount LeSchack in the northern Wisconsin Range. Named for Henry H. Brecher, glaciologist at Byrd Station in 1960, and who spent several subsequent summers in Antarctica.

**Mount Breckenridge** *see* **Breckinridge Peak**

**Breckenridge Peak** *see* **Breckinridge Peak**

**¹Mount Breckinridge.** 66°37′S, 53°41′E. 2,050 m. 4 miles south of Stor Hånakken Mountain, in the Napier Mountains of Enderby Land. Photographed by the LCE 1936–37. Named Langnuten (the long peak) by the Norwegians. Renamed by the Australians for J.E. Breckinridge, meteorologist at Wilkes Station in 1961. Not to be confused with Breckinridge Peak.

²**Mount Breckinridge** *see* **Breckinridge Peak**

**Breckinridge Peak.** 78°04'S, 155°07' W. Also called Mount Breckenridge, Mount Breckinridge, Breckenridge Peak. 1 mile SW of Mount Nilsen, in the southern group of the Rockefeller Mountains, on the Edward VII Peninsula. Discovered during Byrd's 1928–30 expedition and named by Byrd for Colonel and Mrs. Henry Breckinridge of New York.

**Breeding Nunatak.** 77°04'S, 142°28' W. Isolated. 10 miles NE of the Allegheny Mountains, in the Ford Ranges of Marie Byrd Land. Named for George H. Breeding, USN, storekeeper at Byrd Station in 1967.

**Breguet Glacier.** 64°10'S, 60°48'W. Flows into Cierva Cove south of Gregory Glacier, on the west coast of Graham Land. Named by the UK in 1960 for Louis and Jacques Breguet, French helicopter pioneers.

**Breid Bay.** 70°15'S, 24°15'E. Also called Broad Bay. 20 miles wide. An indentation into the ice shelf of the Princess Ragnhild Coast of Queen Maud Land. Photographed by the LCE 1936–37 on Feb. 6, 1937. Named Breidvika (broad bay) by Norwegian cartographer H.E. Hansen. The Belgian IGY station, Roi Baudouin, was here.

**Breidhovde** *see* **Law Promontory**

**Breidnes Peninsula.** 68°34'S, 78°10'E. Also called Broad Peninsula. 13 miles long. 5 miles wide. Between Ellis Fjord and Langnes Fjord in the Vestfold Hills. Photographed by the LCE 1936–37, and named by the Norwegians as Breidneset (the broad ness). Davis Station is here.

**Breidneset** *see* **Breidnes Peninsula**

**Breidneskollen** *see* **Gardner Island**

**Breidnesmulen** *see* **Mule Peninsula**

**Breidskaret Pass.** 72°44'S, 3°24'W. A mountain pass between Høgfonna Mountain and Jøkulskarvet Ridge in the Borg Massif of Queen Maud Land. Name means "the wide gap" in Norwegian.

**Breidsvellet.** 72°39'S, 3°10'W. A steep ice slope on the east side of Jøkulskarvet Ridge, in the Borg Massif of Queen Maud Land. Name means "the broad ice sheet" in Norwegian.

**Breidvåg Bight.** 69°20'S, 39°44'E. A small bight on the east shore of Lützow-Holm Bay, just west of Breidvågnipa Peak. Photographed by the LCE 1936–37, and later named Breidvåg (the broad bay) by the Norwegians.

**Breidvågnipa Peak.** 69°21'S, 39°48'E. 325 m. ½ mile SE of Mount Hiroe on the Queen Maud Land coast. Photographed by the LCE 1936–37, and named by the Norwegians as Breidvågnipa (the broad bay peak) in association with nearby Breidvåg Bight.

**Breidvika** *see* **Breid Bay, Gwynn Bay**

**Breitfuss Glacier.** 66°58'S, 64°52'W. Also called Wilson Glacier. 10 miles long. Flows from Avery Plateau into Mill Inlet, to the west of Cape Chavanne, on the east coast of Graham Land. Named by the FIDS for Leonid Breitfuss, German Arctic explorer.

**Brekilen Bay.** 70°08'S, 25°48'E. An indentation into the ice shelf 10 miles SW of Tangekilen Bay, on the coast of Queen Maud Land. Photographed by the LCE 1936–37. Name means "the glacier bay" in Norwegian.

**Brekkerista Ridge.** 72°14'S, 0°18'W. 2 miles NE of the summit of Jutulrøra Mountain in the Sverdrup Mountains of Queen Maud Land. Name means "the slope ridge" in Norwegian.

**Bremot, John.** Ordinary seaman on the Wilkes Expedition 1838–42. Joined at Rio. Run at Callao on July 13, 1839.

**Bremotet Moraine.** 71°41'S, 12°05'E. On the NW side of Zwiesel Mountain, at the point where the Humboldt Graben meets the Parizhskaya Kommuna Glacier, in the Wohlthat Mountains of

Queen Maud Land. Name means "the glacier meeting" in Norwegian.

**Mount Brennan.** 84°15'S, 175°54'E. 2,540 m. Dome-shaped. 7 miles NE of Mount Cartwright in the northernmost portion of the Hughes Range. Discovered aerially by the USAS on Feb. 29–March 1, 1940. Surveyed by Albert P. Crary in 1957–58, and named by him for Matthew J. Brennan.

**Brennan, Dr. Matthew J.** Took over from Finn Ronne as scientific leader of Ellsworth Station on Jan. 16, 1958.

**Brennan Inlet.** 74°28'S, 116°35'W. On the coast of Marie Byrd Land.

**Brennan Point.** 76°05'S, 146°31'W. Ice-covered. Forms the east side of the entrance to Block Bay on the coast of Marie Byrd Land. Discovered on Dec. 5, 1929, on a flight by Byrd during his 1928–30 expedition. Named by Byrd for Michael J. Brennan, who helped select personnel for that expedition.

**Brennecke Nunataks.** 72°14'S, 63°35' W. In Palmer Land.

**Breoddane** *see* **Scoble Glacier**

**Breplogen Mountain.** 71°55'S, 5°27'E. 2,725 m. Mostly ice-covered. West of Austreskorve Glacier in the Mühlig-Hofmann Mountains. Name means "the glacier plow" in Norwegian.

**Mount Bresnahan.** 71°48'S, 161°28'E. 1,630 m. Flat-topped and ice-free. On the east side of the Helliwell Hills, 6 miles NNE of Mount Van der Hoeven. Named for David M. Bresnahan, biologist at McMurdo Station in 1967–68 and 1968–69.

**Breton Island.** 66°48'S, 141°23'E. A small, rocky island, 350 yards SW of Empereur Island. Charted in 1950 by the French, and named by them for the mostly Breton crew of the *Commandant Charcot.*

**Brett.** Cook on the *Discovery* during Scott's Royal Society Expedition of 1901–4. A civilian from New Zealand, he was put in irons in Feb. 1902 by Scott for in-

subordination, and sent home on the *Morning,* in March 1903.

**Brewer Peak.** 71°34'S, 168°28'E. 2,110 m. On the west wall of Pitkevich Glacier, near the head of that glacier, in the Admiralty Mountains of Victoria Land. Named for Thomas J. Brewer, USN, commissaryman at McMurdo Station in 1967.

**Cape Brewster** *see* **Byewater Point**

**Mount Brewster.** 72°57'S, 169°22'E. 2,025 m. In the central part of the Daniell Peninsula, it is the highest point on that feature, in Victoria Land. Named in 1841 by Ross for Sir David Brewster, Scottish physicist.

**Brewster Island.** 64°43'S, 62°34'W. Also called Islote Sorpresa. A small island NE of Danco Island, in Errera Channel, off the west coast of Graham Land. Named by the UK in 1960 for Sir David Brewster (*see* **Mount Brewster**).

**Mount Breyer** *see* **Breyer Mesa**

**Breyer Mesa.** 86°01'S, 161°12'W. Formerly called Mount Breyer. Ice-covered. 5 miles long. 3,000 m. Between the Christy and Tate Glaciers, on the west side of the Amundsen Glacier, in the Queen Maud Mountains. Discovered by Byrd on his South Pole flight of Nov. 1929, and named by him for Robert S. Breyer, a patron.

**Brialmont Bay** *see* **Brialmont Cove**

**Brialmont Cove.** 64°16'S, 61°W. Also called Primavera Bay, Bahía Maldita. In Hughes Bay, between Charles and Spring Points, on the west coast of Graham Land. Charted by de Gerlache in 1898, and named by him for Lt. Gen. Brialmont, a member of the *Belgica* Commission.

**Brian Island.** 68°08'S, 67°07'W. The most westerly of the Debenham Islands, off the west coast of Graham Land. Charted by the BGLE 1934–37, and named by Rymill for Frank Debenham's son (*see* **Debenham Islands**).

**Briand Fjord.** 65°01'S, 63°01'W. Also called Bahía Dedo. Almost 3 miles long.

In the NE part of Flandres Bay, on the west coast of Graham Land. Charted by Charcot in 1903-5, and named by him for Aristide Briand, French politician.

**Mount Brice.** 75°22'S, 72°37'W. 2½ miles west of Mount Abrams, in the Behrendt Mountains. Named for Neil M. Brice, radioscience researcher at Camp Sky-Hi near here, in 1961-62.

**Mount Bride** *see* **Skorefjell**

**Bridge Pass.** 81°46'S, 160°42'E. Between the Surveyors Range and the Nash Range, at the upper reaches of the Dickie and Algie Glaciers. It is a passage from the Nimrod Glacier to Beaumont Bay. Named by the New Zealanders in 1960-61 for Capt. Lawrence D. Bridge, leader at Scott Base from Nov. 1960 to Feb. 1961.

**Bridgeman Island.** 62°04'S, 56°44'W. Also called Helena Island. A volcanic island, ½ mile long, circular, and 240 m. high. 23 miles east of King George Island in the South Shetlands. Named Bridgeman's Island about 1820. The name was later amended slightly.

**Mount Bridger.** 72°17'S, 167°35'E. 2,295 m. On the south side of Pearl Harbor Glacier. 5 miles NNE of Conard Peak, in the Cartographers Range, in the Victory Mountains of Victoria Land. Named for William D. Bridger, USN, aviation machinist's mate and flight engineer at Ross Island in 1968.

**Bridger Bay.** 60°33'S, 45°51'W. Semicircular. 2½ miles wide. West of Tickell Head, on the north side of Coronation Island, in the South Orkneys. Discovered in Dec. 1821 by Palmer and Powell. Named by the UK for John F.D. Bridger, who surveyed Coronation and Signy Islands with the FIDS in the 1956-58 period.

**Mount Bridgman.** 66°50'S, 67°23'W. Dominates the center of Liard Island, off the west coast of Graham Land. Named by the UK for Percy W. Bridgman, US physicist specializing in ice.

**Bridgman, Albert H.** Lt., USN. Surgeon and military leader at Hallett Station during the winter of 1959.

**Bridgman Glacier.** 72°23'S, 170°05'E. Flows from the west side of the Hallett Peninsula, and forms a floating ice tongue on the east shore of Edisto Inlet, between Salmon and Roberts Cliffs, in Victoria Land. Named by the New Zealanders in 1957-58 for Lt. Albert H. Bridgman.

**Bridgman Island** *see* **Bridgeman Island**

**Bridwell Peak.** 71°56'S, 166°28'E. 2,220 m. 6 miles SE of Boss Peak, in the Victory Mountains of Victoria Land. Named for Ray E. Bridwell, meteorologist at Hallett Station, 1964-65.

**Brien Rocks.** 73°13'S, 161°23'E. 6 miles west of the Caudal Hills in Victoria Land. Named for Robert J. Brien, VX-6 technician at McMurdo Station in 1966.

**Mount Briesemeister** *see* **Briesemeister Peak, Mount Martin**

**Briesemeister Peak.** 69°28'S, 62°45'W. Also known as Mount Briesemeister. 690 m. 7 miles WNW of Cape Rymill on the east coast of Palmer Land. Photographed aerially by Wilkins on Dec. 20, 1928. Named by the RARE 1947-48 for William A. Briesemeister, US cartographer.

**Briggs, Alfred Charles.** b. 1905. d. March 11, 1988. British able seaman on the *Discovery*, 1925-27, and on the *Discovery II*, 1931-35, during the Discovery Investigations.

**Briggs Hill.** 77°49'S, 163°E. 1,210 m. Ice-free. On the south side of the Ferrar Glacier, between the Descent and Overflow Glaciers, in Victoria Land. Charted during Scott's 1910-13 expedition. Named for Raymond S. Briggs, meteorologist at McMurdo Station in 1962, and scientific leader there in 1963.

**Briggs Peak.** 68°58'S, 66°41'W. 1,120 m. Isolated. On the NE side of the Wordie Ice Shelf. Named by the UK for Henry Briggs (1556-1630), coinventor of logarithms.

**Briggs Peninsula.** 64°30′S, 63°01′W. Forms the west side of Inverleith Harbor, on the NE coast of Anvers Island. The NE point of the peninsula was charted in 1927 by personnel on the *Discovery,* who named it Briggs Point, for Alfred Charles Briggs. The UK in 1959 dropped the term "point" and extended the name to the whole (small) peninsula.

**Briggs Point** *see* **Briggs Peninsula**

**Bright, Washington.** Gunner on the Wilkes Expedition 1838–42. He joined the *Relief* at Callao, and later transferred to the *Vincennes.*

**Brimblecomb, Joseph.** Seaman on the Wilkes Expedition 1838–42. Joined in the USA. Returned in the *Relief* in 1839.

**Brimstone Bluff** *see* **Brimstone Peak**

**¹Brimstone Peak.** 61°55′S, 57°48′W. Also called Brimstone Bluff, Brimstone Point. Between Venus Bay and Emerald Bay, on the north coast of King George Island, in the South Shetlands. Called North Foreland in 1822, but that name is now applied to a different feature. Renamed in 1937 by personnel on the *Discovery II* because of its yellow color.

**²Brimstone Peak.** 75°50′S, 158°33′E. 2,340 m. Between the Ricker Hills and Griffin Nunatak at the top of the Mawson Glacier in the Prince Albert Mountains of northern Victoria Land. Named by the New Zealanders in 1962–63 for its coloring.

**Brimstone Point** *see* **Brimstone Peak**

**Brindle Cliffs.** 69°23′S, 68°33′W. 610 m. Ice-free. 6 miles east of Cape Jeremy, on the west coast of the Antarctic Peninsula. Discovered by the BGLE on Aug. 16, 1936, and photographed aerially by them. Surveyed in 1948 by the FIDS who named them for their color.

**Brinton Nunatak.** 85°35′S, 132°24′W. A small nunatak, marking the western extremity of the Ford Nunataks in the Wisconsin Range. Named for Curtis C. Brinton, utilitiesman at Byrd Station in 1957.

**Mount Bris.** 63°59′S, 59°50′W. 1 mile west of the head of Sabine Glacier and 11 miles south of Cape Kater, in Graham Land. Named by the UK for Jean Marie Le Bris (1808–1872), the first glider pilot, 1857.

**Brisbane, Matthew.** Captain of the *Beaufoy of London,* 1822–26.

**Brisbane Heights.** 60°36′S, 45°38′W. A series of heights rising to 960 m. They extend in an arc from Worswick Hill to High Stile in the central part of Coronation Island, in the South Orkneys. Surveyed in 1948–49 by the FIDS, and called Brisbane Plateau by them, for Matthew Brisbane. Redefined following a 1956 survey.

**Brisbane Plateau** *see* **Brisbane Heights**

**Brisco, William.** Name sometimes seen as Briscoe. Armorer on the Wilkes Expedition 1838–42. He started off on the *Relief,* and transferred to the *Vincennes* on June 20, 1839.

**The *Brisk.*** Enderby Brothers ship, commanded by Capt. Tapsell, in 1849–50. In Feb. 1850, it sighted the Balleny Islands, then went as far as 143°E, sailing in higher latitudes than Wilkes had done, but without seeing land.

**Bristly Peaks.** 69°23′S, 66°15′W. A series of sharp rock peaks on a ridge separating the Seller and Fleming Glaciers in the central part of the Antarctic Peninsula. Named by the UK for its likeness to the bristles of a brush.

**Britain** *see* **Great Britain**

**The *Britannia.*** The British Royal yacht. In Jan. 1957 Prince Philip and the governor of the Falkland Islands visited FIDS stations in South Georgia and Graham Land. Peter Mitchell was navigator of the yacht. The dignitaries transferred to the *John Biscoe* for part of the cruise, escorted by the *Protector.*

**Mount Britannia.** 64°43′S, 62°41′W. 1160 m. In the center of Rongé Island, off the west coast of Graham Land. Charted by de Gerlache in 1897–99. Named by the UK in 1960 for the *Britannia*, the Royal yacht.

**Britannia Range.** 80°S, 158°E. Just to the north of the Byrd Glacier, in the Transantarctic Mountains, overlooking the western end of the Ross Ice Shelf. Mounts Henderson and McClintock are in it.

**British Antarctic Expedition 1898–1900** *see* **Borchgrevink, Carsten**

**British Antarctic Expedition 1907-9.** Led by Shackleton. It took Shackleton a few years to get the backing for his first expedition, and principal supporters were Sir William Beardmore and the Misses Dawson-Lambton. The *Nimrod* left Torquay on Aug. 7, 1907, arriving in NZ on Nov. 23, 1907. Shackleton traveled on the *India* to Australia, and boarded the *Nimrod* in Lyttelton, NZ. The expedition set out on Jan. 1, 1908, the *Nimrod* being towed by the *Koonya* in order to save it fuel. On Jan. 14, 1908, the two ships were in Antarctic waters, and on Jan. 15, 1908, the *Koonya* left for home. The *Nimrod* arrived at the Ross Sea on Jan. 16, 1908, and on Jan. 23, 1908, they sighted the Ross Ice Shelf. On Jan. 24, 1908, they were at the Bay of Whales, which Shackleton named. On Jan. 29, 1908, the *Nimrod* entered McMurdo Sound. On Jan. 31, 1908, Dr. Marshall was forced to remove Mackintosh's eye. On Feb. 1, 1908, the first automobile in Antarctica was lowered onto the ice, and that same day Adams, Joyce, and Wild sledged to Hut Point from the *Nimrod,* returning to ship on Feb. 3, 1908. Shackleton selected Cape Royds, Ross Island as his base, and the *Nimrod* finally docked there. Cape Royds (indeed, McMurdo Sound), was Shackleton's fourth choice for a base site, at least it was publicly. Scott had asked him in no uncertain terms to leave his old area alone and go another way. However, the hut was built (*see* **Shackleton's Hut**), and on Feb. 22, 1908, the *Nimrod* left for NZ, with Shackleton's mailed instructions aboard to replace Capt. England

with Capt. Evans the next time the ship came to Cape Royds. On March 2, 1908, the crew decided to climb Mount Erebus (it had never been done). On March 5, 1908, Mawson, David, and Mackay set off for the peak, with Adams leading the support party which included himself, Brocklehurst and Marshall. They conquered Erebus at 10 a.m. on March 10, 1908, returning to Cape Royds on March 11, 1908. The climb cost Brocklehurst some of his toes, and on April 6, 1908, Dr. Marshall was busy with his scalpel again. Spring outings started on Aug. 18, 1908, and then the push to the Pole began. That was the primary aim of the expedition. (For further dates *see* the Chronology appendix in this book.) Shackleton led the Polar trek, and he, Adams, Marshall, and Wild got to within 97 miles of the Pole on Jan. 9, 1909, before turning back. Shackleton decided that they couldn't get to the Pole and get back to base alive. At this point they were 360 miles further south than any human being had ever been before. They had pioneered the Beardmore Glacier route (which Scott would follow in 1911–12), they had discovered that glacier and so many other features of consequence on this trip, and now the time had come for Shackleton to make the decision that it was better to live than to be a dead hero. As it was, the party barely made it back to Cape Royds. The other major highlight of the expedition was the first reaching of the elusive South Magnetic Pole. David, Mackay, and Mawson sledged 1,260 miles round trip. Shackleton's expedition, as an overall expedition, collected coal specimens and fossilized plants, was the first Antarctic expedition to take movies, and the first to try out an automobile on the continent. Others on the expedition included Day, Marston, Roberts, James Murray (in charge of the base when Shackleton was away), Priestley, Armytage, Joyce (in charge of provisions and dogs), Ansell, Buckley, Cheetham, Cotton, John King Davis, Dunlop, Ellis, Handcock, Harbord, McGillan, Michell, Montague, Paton, Riches, and J.D. Morrison. The expedition got back to London in triumph in June 1909.

**British Antarctic Expedition 1910–13.** This was Scott's famous last expedition, also referred to as the *Terra Nova* expedition. Scott's mission was to get to the Pole. The *Terra Nova* left England on June 15, 1910, and arrived in Melbourne on Oct. 12, 1910. It was there that Scott received Amundsen's telegram informing him that the *Fram* was proceeding to Antarctica, and that the Norseman would be trying for the Pole also. Now the race was on—Scott and Amundsen the two players, Britain's and Norway's the honors at stake. There were 65 men on the *Terra Nova* when it hit the pack-ice on Dec. 9, 1910. On Dec. 30, 1910, after a miserable 3 weeks in the pack-ice, they got through into the calm of the Ross Sea, and on Jan. 2, 1911, they landed at Cape Evans, Ross Island (Amundsen used the Bay of Whales as his base). On Jan. 5, 1911, they unloaded and on Jan. 28, 1911, the *Terra Nova* sailed east on the Edward VII Land party led by Victor Campbell, his mission being to explore what is now Edward VII Peninsula. On Feb. 3, 1911, the *Terra Nova* met the *Fram,* Amundsen's ship, in the Bay of Whales. Campbell's crew was invited by Amundsen to lunch at Framheim, the Norwegian base nearby, and then Amundsen went aboard the *Terra Nova.* There was no place to land, so Campbell aborted the Edward VII Land effort, and the *Terra Nova* went back to Cape Evans. There they told Scott of the *Fram.* On Feb. 9, 1911, Campbell took the ship north instead, becoming the Northern Party of the expedition. He and his party were dropped at Cape Adare for the 1911 winter. Other members of this party were Levick, Browning, Priestley, Dickason, and Abbott. From a scientific standpoint the Northern Party was generally unsatisfactory, some exploration being done of the Victoria Land coast (more on this party later). The *Terra Nova* continued around the coast of Victoria Land under the command of the

ship's captain, Lt. Harry Pennell. He discovered all the land of the Oates Land coast, and arrived in New Zealand on March 31, 1911. Meanwhile Scott and the main party at Cape Evans had begun laying depots in preparation for their push to the Pole in the 1911–12 austral summer. On Jan. 24, 1911, with 13 men, 8 ponies, and 24 dogs, they set out going south. On Feb. 17, 1911, they laid One-Ton Depot at 79°28'30"S, and arrived back at Cape Evans on March 2, 1911. 7 out of the 8 ponies had died on this trip. On June 27, 1911 began "the worst journey in the world," as described by Apsley Cherry-Garrard, one of the three participants, in his later book of that title. With Wilson and Bowers he went east to Cape Crozier in the dark of winter, to collect emperor penguins' eggs for naturalist Wilson to study. They barely survived the return from this horrific journey. The big push to the Pole began on Nov. 1, 1911. The 5 polar trekkers were Scott, Bowers, Wilson, Edgar Evans, and Oates. Accompanying and preceding them was a support party, from which men would drop off at regular intervals and return to base (for dates en route to the Pole and back, *see* the Chronology appendix in this book). By Dec. 11, 1911, they had all turned back except 12 men: the 5 polar trekkers, Wright, Crean, Teddy Evans, Keohane, Lashly, Atkinson, and Cherry-Garrard. They then went up the Beardmore Glacier. On Dec. 21, 1911, Keohane, Cherry-Garrard, Wright, and Atkinson turned back, and the main party reached the Polar Plateau on Jan. 1, 1912 (at this point, Scott's party and Amundsen's party were both at about the same degree of latitude, in other words they were both about the same distance from the South Pole. The main difference was that Scott was going there, and Amundsen was on his way back after having conquered the Pole. It may be interesting to speculate that if Scott had met Amundsen coming back, which was quite possible, and learned that the Norwegian had already won the prize, might Scott not have pressed on anyway?). On Jan. 4, 1912, Crean, Teddy Evans, and Lashly dropped back to base. At this stage they were only 171 miles from the Pole (it is one of the unsung stories, but for Crean, Evans, and Lashly to make such a trip back by themselves deserves the great recognition it never got). At 6:30 p.m. on Jan. 17, 1912, Scott and his 4 companions reached the Pole — too late. The Norwegian flag which waited for them, and the black tent, and the message from Amundsen, and all the other things left by the polar farers over a month before, devastated Scott and his men. "Great God, this is an awful place," said Scott about the Pole. On Jan. 18, 1912, Scott figured that they were 3 miles out, and they walked the remaining distance. It would seem, from the microscopic examination of Scott's records, that his party never set foot at the actual mathematical Pole point, but then Amundsen probably didn't either. It is not important. It had taken Scott 81 days to get there, and the return journey was beset by hunger, sickness, tiredness, and blizzards. They had started off the trek with 10 Manchurian ponies and 2 dog teams, but none of the animals even got to the Beardmore Glacier. The men really manhauled their sledges most of the way there and back (a round-trip distance of 1,700 miles from Ross Island to the Pole), across the ice, snow, crevasses, and glaciers. On Feb. 7, 1912, they began their descent of the Beardmore. This would get them down off the Polar Plateau, and onto the vastness of the Ross Ice Shelf. That would then give them a clear run back to base. It was at the Beardmore that Evans died, on Feb. 17, 1912. At 79°05′S, Oates walked out of the tent, on his 32nd birthday, March 17, 1912. He was riddled with scurvy and frostbite, and according to Scott's diary, he left the tent voluntarily, and he did so with the noblest motives. He was never seen again. The 3 remaining men, now in shocking condition, mentally and physically, got to within 11 miles of One-Ton Depot (they knew this), when they

got caught in a blizzard. On, or around, March 29, 1912, they all died in their tent, 176 miles from their base at Cape Evans — and a legend was born, and an enormous amount of Amundsen's (and Norway's) thunder was stolen. Questions remain. Why didn't they make it? Despite the astonishing hardship, and despite the condition they were in, these were 3 men with strong powers of endurance. They knew that they had failed themselves and their country by failing to get to the Pole first. Did they feel that they couldn't face Britain when they returned? Did they realize that the only way to salvage their dignity, and Britain's dignity, was to become legends by dying out there in the frozen waste? They were all romantics, for whom life would have been dreadfully dull after what they had just been through. It seems unlikely that the 3 would die together, run out of steam together, unless they chose to. After all, with the survival instinct they had, it seems surprising that at least one would not have tried to press on, come what may, unless it was a deliberate choice not to. Meanwhile, Campbell's Northern Party was picked up by the Terra Nova on Jan. 3, 1912. It took them to Evans Coves on Jan. 8, 1912. The ship would return around Feb. 18, 1912, to pick them up again, so with 6 weeks rations they were left there. That was the plan, but the ship couldn't get through the ice, and the 6 men were forced to winter over again in Victoria Land, this time in desperately horrific circumstances, in an ice cave at Terra Nova Bay. The cave measured 12 feet by 9 feet, and was 5½ feet high. On Sept. 30, 1912, they set out on foot for Cape Evans, and after 40 days reached base to tell their remarkable story of survival and endurance, and to find that Scott hadn't made it back from the Pole. The Terra Nova, after dropping Campbell's Northern Party at Evans Coves, had returned to Cape Evans on Feb. 5, 1912. Later that year a search party went out to look for Scott, and found the 3 men in their tent on Nov. 12, 1912, the bodies lying as they had died, with diaries, records, and 35 pounds of geological specimens from the Beardmore Glacier. The expedition arrived back in England in 1913. Other members of the expedition included Simpson, Taylor, Nelson, Debenham, Ponting (the cameraman and filmmaker), Meares, Day, Gran, Archer, Clissold, Forde, Williamson, Hooper, Omel'-chenko, Gerof, Davies, Lillie, Cheetham, McGillan, McLeod, Paton, Burton, Drake, Mortimer, McCarthy, William McDonald, William Williams, and Rennick.

**British Antarctic Survey.** The official name for the total ongoing British scientific effort in Antarctica (*see also* **British Antarctic Territory**). Until 1962 it was called the FIDS (Falkland Islands Dependencies Survey).

**British Antarctic Territory.** A British colony since 1962. It is a section of Antarctica, between 80°W and 20°W, and south of 60°S, i.e. the Antarctic territory claimed by Great Britain. It includes the South Orkneys, South Shetlands, and the Antarctic Peninsula. Population about 82, mostly scientists who maintain the British Antarctic Survey (BAS) stations. Until 1962 this was part of the larger colony of the Falkland Islands Dependencies, but that year Britain split that colony into two, with 60°S as the dividing line of latitude. All south of that was British Antarctic Territory, while all north was the Falkland Islands Dependencies.

**British, Australian and New Zealand Antarctic Research Expedition.** 1929–31. More commonly known by its initials, the BANZARE. A cooperative venture supported by the British, Australian, and New Zealand governments, and led by Mawson. It was really two summer expeditions in successive years, 1929–30 and 1930–31. It was Mawson's second major Antarctic expedition, and the third time he had been to the Antarctic. Sir Macpherson Robertson of Australia was the chief sponsor, and the aim of the BANZARE was to explore the 2,500 miles

of coastline between the Wilhelm II Coast and Coats Land, including the Kemp Coast and Enderby Land. The *Discovery* (Scott's old ship), sailed from Cape Town on Oct. 19, 1929, commanded by Capt. John King Davis. Leaving for Antarctica about the same time was Riiser-Larsen's Norwegian expedition to the same area of the continent, and the press instigated a rivalry, thinking back to the days of Scott and Amundsen. Also on the BANZARE were J.T. Kyle, A.J. Bartlett, F. Best, E. Bond, Stuart Campbell, J.B. Child, W.R. Colbeck, W.E. Crosby, R.C. Tomlinson, C. Degerfeldt, E. Douglas, F.G. Dungey, H.O. Fletcher, R.A. Falla, H.V. Gage, Lt. K.E. Oom, C.H.V. Selwood, R.G. Simmers, F. Sones, A.M. Stanton, R.V. Hampson, H. Henksen, A. Howard, W.E. Howard, W.H. Letten, K. McLennan, F.L. Marsland, James H. Martin, N.C. Mateer, J. Matheson, J.J. Miller, H.C. Morrison, Morton H. Moyes, J.A. Park, L. Parviainen, O. Peacock, F.W. Porteus, J.E. Reed, and G.J. Rhodes. Airplanes were taken, and on Dec. 29, 1929, Mac. Robertson Land was discovered aerially. On Jan. 13, 1930, they landed on Proclamation Island, and Mawson claimed for Britain all land south of 60°S, and between 47°E and 73°E, i.e. Enderby Land. On Jan. 14, 1930, the *Discovery* met the *Norvegia,* and the British and Norwegians came to a compromise on exploration—the British to the east of 40°E, the Norwegians to the west of that point (this was changed later to 45°E). The *Discovery* then sailed for Australia. The second half of the expedition began on Nov. 22, 1930, when Mawson left Hobart, this time with the *Discovery* under the command of Capt. K.N. MacKenzie. They arrived at Cape Denison on Jan. 4, 1931, and the ship then sailed the coast. More flights were made in the expedition's Gipsy Moth by the pilots, Douglas and Campbell. That season they claimed the George V Coast, and discovered the Banzare Coast, Princess Elizabeth Coast, and MacKenzie Bay. They also rediscovered the Sabrina Coast, and charted 1,000 miles of coastline. The coasts they discovered covered 29° of longitude. They arrived back in Australia on March 19, 1931.

**British Commonwealth Transantarctic Expedition. 1955–58.** More commonly seen by its initials, the BCTAE, or sometimes as the CTAE (i.e. the Commonwealth Transantarctic Expedition). Led by Vivian Fuchs, this was the first successful land traverse of the Antarctic continent, and the last great polar journey. It was a two-pronged operation. Fuchs was to lead the main party from the Weddell Sea, in heated vehicles, with air reconnaissance and radio contact, across a vast stretch of unknown land, to the Pole, and then on to McMurdo Sound, on the other side of the continent, in the summer of 1957–58. On the other side, Sir Edmund Hillary was to lay depots that same season from Ross Island toward the Pole, and to guide Fuchs back to McMurdo Sound. The idea for this expedition had come to Fuchs on Alexander Island, while he had been FIDS leader at Base E in 1949. With the help of Sir James Wordie and others, Fuchs got started. The British government donated £10,000 toward the expedition, and this started the ball rolling. The NZ government took responsibility for the Ross Sea party led by Hillary. On Nov. 14, 1955, Fuchs' part of the expedition left London on the *Theron*, with 2 aircraft, a Sno-cat, some tractors, and 24 dogs. They reached Vahsel Bay, on the Filchner Ice Shelf of the Weddell Sea coast, on Jan. 28, 1956. Hillary was on board as observer. Fuchs oversaw the landing of the supplies and equipment, and then returned to London on the *Theron*, in order to continue his organization of the expedition. Eight men stayed at Vahsel Bay in the winter of 1956, setting up Shackleton Base. Ken Blaiklock was leader of this advance party, and the others were Lenton, La Grange, Homard, R.H.A. Stewart, Jeffries, Taffy Williams, and Goldsmith. Fuchs left London again, this time on the

*Magga Dan*, returning to Vahsel Bay on Jan. 13, 1957. A site was selected for South Ice, a depot en route to the Pole. By Feb. 22, 1957, it was ready, and in March 1957 occupied by a 3-man wintering team. Meanwhile the *Endeavour* (formerly the *John Biscoe*) left New Zealand on Dec. 21, 1956, carrying Hillary's Ross Sea party to McMurdo Sound, on the other side of the continent. It arrived there on Jan. 3, 1957. Hillary built Scott Base on Pram Point, Ross Island, then explored the Ross Sea Basin. He then flew out to the foot of the Skelton Glacier to build a depot there. Later he built Plateau Depot at the top of the glacier. On Sept. 10, 1957, Hillary left to investigate the Ferrar Glacier. He split his crew into 3 teams. His Northern Sledge Party set out from Scott Base on Oct. 4, 1957, to go up the Mackay Glacier to the Polar Plateau. A party of 3 was flown to the Skelton Depot, and Hillary led 3 others to cover the route Fuchs would take on the final leg from the Pole to Scott Base. On Nov. 25, 1957, Hillary created Depot 480. On Dec. 15, 1957, he began work on Depot 700. The NZ depot-laying party, which discovered much on their travels, consisted of Hillary, J.H. Miller, Ayres, Gunn, Mulgrew, Ellis, Bates, Gawn, G. Marsh, R. Brooke, Bucknell, Warren, Carlyon, E. Wright, and Balham. The RNZAF aerial contingent that supported them, were Claydon, Cranfield, and Tarr. On the other side of the continent, Fuchs led the main transantarctic party out of Shackleton Base on Nov. 24, 1957, after thoroughly scouting the trail to South Ice, which he reached on Dec. 21, 1957. He was traveling with 4 Sno-cats, 3 Weasels, a muskeg tractor, and 10 men—Blaiklock, Stratton, La Grange, Homard, Geoffrey and David Pratt, Allan F. Rogers, Lister, Jon Stephenson, and Lowe. Their RAF aerial back-up comprised John Lewis, Haslop, Weston, and Taffy Williams. As Fuchs was crossing the continent toward the Pole, Hillary was at Depot 700, having stocked it with supplies. With a month to wait

for Fuchs, and fearing that the late-
ness in the season might force Fuchs
to abandon the expedition, Hillary
decided to go "hellbent for the Pole."
His mission had been to wait for Fuchs at
Depot 700, and not go to the Pole, that
honor go to the leader, Fuchs. But he
made the decision, which he regarded as
the correct one, and set out with Ellis,
Bates, Mulgrew, and Wright, and arrived
at the Pole on Jan. 4, 1958. Some say he
stole his leader's thunder by this move.
He then flew back to Scott Base, later
returning by plane to the Pole to meet
Fuchs there on Jan. 20, 1958, when the
transantarctic party arrived. "How happy
I am to see you again," said Fuchs to
Hillary, although he may well not have
meant it. Hillary flew off again, and
Fuchs set out on his last leg, on Jan. 24,
1958, from the Pole to Scott Base. He
reached Depot 700 on Feb. 7, 1958, and
Hillary joined the party there, guiding
Fuchs back to the Ross Sea. For Fuchs it
had been a 2,158 mile journey in 99 days,
a huge success for him. A knighthood
was waiting for him when he arrived at
Scott Base at 1:47 p.m., on March 2,
1958.

**British Graham Land Expedition.**
1934–37. More commonly known by its
initials, the BGLE 1934–37, or simply the
BGLE. Led by Australian John Rymill.
Sponsored by the British Colonial Office,
the Royal Geographical Society and
others, its mission was to explore Graham
Land. Rymill planned it, and at a cost of
only £20,000 the expedition left England
on the *Penola,* on Sept. 10, 1934. Of the
16 men on board, the only professionals
were the *Penola's* captain and chief
engineer—all the rest were amateur explorers, although some had had previous
experience in Greenland. They took
a plane, a small single-engine de Havilland Fox Moth. At the Falkland Islands the *Penola* was refitted for the ice,
and the *Discovery II* transported the aircraft, dogs, and heavy stores to Port
Lockroy, Wiencke Island, in the Palmer
Archipelago. The *Penola* arrived at Port

Lockroy on Jan. 22, 1935. After an
airplane flight Rymill chose the Argentine Islands as a base, picking Winter
Island specifically as the location. On
Feb. 28, 1935, another flight convinced
Rymill to move his base further south the
next summer. Sledging began in earnest.
Their hut was finished after 3 weeks
building. They wintered-over in 1935,
then on Feb. 17, 1936, the *Penola* set out
on a southern exploration cruise with
everyone on board except Wilfred E.
Hampton and Alfred Stephenson. They
came down later. On Feb. 29, 1936, the
*Penola* eased into the Debenham
Islands, and Rymill set up the base on
Barry Island. On March 12, 1936, the
*Penola* left to winter in the Falklands.
The new hut was completed and occupied on March 24, 1936. In June 1936,
their one tractor had to be abandoned
when an ice floe broke. On Aug. 15,
1936, they aerially discovered the George
VI Sound, their most important single
find. On Sept. 5, 1936, sledging parties
went out looking for the Stefansson
Strait, and the Casey and Lurabee Channels, all of which Wilkins had claimed
earlier connected the eastern and western
parts of the Antarctic Peninsula (as it
later became known). The BGLE failed to
find these features, concluded that they
might not exist, and that therefore the
entire peninsula might well be a part of
the Antarctic continent, as was originally
thought before Wilkins had made his
flight in 1928. On Sept. 24, 1936, they
found a suitable landing place for the
Moth, and Rymill and E.W. Bingham
turned back to fetch it. At this point they
were 90 miles from base, in the interior
of Graham Land. By Oct. 10, 1936, 6
flights had been made here, and they set
up a depot. From the Barry Island base
Rymill and Bingham returned to the
depot, and then made the first ever land
crossing of the Antarctic Peninsula, exploring the Graham Land coast as far as
Cape Evensen. They arrived on the east
coast on Nov. 22, 1936. They got back to
base on Jan. 25, 1937. The *Penola* arrived
on Feb. 13, 1937, and on March 12, 1937,

the expedition left for home. The BGLE mapped much of Graham Land, and found that it is really an 8,000-foot-high, plateau. They explored Alexander Island, and conducted aerial photography. Other members of the expedition included Lisle Ryder, Robert Ryder, Brian B. Roberts, Ian F. Meiklejohn, James H. Martin, Hugh M. Millett, James I. Moore, George Bertram, W.L.S. Fleming, Verner D. Carse, and Norman Gurney.

**British Imperial Expedition.** 1920–22. Grand name for a minor effort, by 4 youths, one of whom should have known better (and did—Sir Hubert Wilkins). A poorly planned expedition led by John Cope, it intended to take some aircraft to Graham Land, and make the first ever flight from there to the Pole. However, Cope couldn't get a plane. The 4, Cope, M.C. Lester, Thomas Bagshawe, and Wilkins, met up at Deception Island on Dec. 24, 1920. Wilkins claimed later to have been inveigled into going. From Deception Island they planned to go by whaler to Hope Bay. Hope Bay was iced in so they went to Paradise Bay instead, with the revised intention of crossing Graham Land by foot. They got to Paradise Bay on Jan. 12, 1921, and slept under an old boat beached there by whalers 8 years before. They built a tiny hut, but realized they would never be able to continue with the expedition. On Feb. 26, 1921, Cope, Lester, and Wilkins left Bagshawe alone while they went in search of a whaler to take them to Montevideo, in order to look there for a boat to take them to Hope Bay, their original destination. A week later they returned, in the *Bjerk,* and Cope and Wilkins left Lester and Bagshawe alone together for the winter. These 2 were not good friends, and the picture of them living and quarreling together in the most desolate place on earth has amused Antarctic historians for decades. Actually the 2 did substantial work there, and on Dec.

18, 1921, refused a lift in the *Graham,* a whale catcher from the Norwegian factory ship *Svend Foyn.* On Jan. 13, 1922, however, they accepted a second offer, and headed home. Cope had already gone home, and Wilkins had departed in disgust to take a position with Shackleton.

**British Imperial Transantarctic Expedition.** 1914–17. Led by Shackleton. Its aim was to cross the Antarctic by land. The whole scheme ended in disaster and glorious failure. Scott's failure to be the first to reach the South Pole in 1911–12 led Shackleton to try to recapture some glory for the British Empire in 1914, a bad year, as it turned out, due to World War I. So, even if he had succeeded, his achievement would have gone largely unnoticed. The principal backer was Sir James Caird. The expedition was to be two-pronged. Shackleton was to go down to the Weddell Sea in the *Endurance,* establish a base on the coast, and then cross the continent with 5 other men, via the Pole, to McMurdo Sound, 1,800 miles away. Aeneas Mackintosh, on the *Aurora,* was to go to Ross Island, McMurdo Sound, and lay depots en route to the Pole from the other end, for the last stages of Shackleton's trip. 5,000 people applied to join the expedition, including a few women, and the *Endurance* sailed from Plymouth on Aug. 8, 1914, with 28 men aboard, including Shackleton, Frank Wild (second-in-command), Crean, Cheetham, Marston, Hurley, Worsley, Hudson, Greenstreet, Rickinson, Kerr, McIlroy, Macklin, R.S. Clark, How, Hussey, Wordie, R.W. James, McNeish, Orde-Lees, MacArty, Vincent, C.J. Green, Blackborrow, Bakewell, McLeod, H. Stephenson, and Holness. They went via Buenos Aires to South Georgia, leaving there on Dec. 5, 1914. On Dec. 7, 1914, they were in Antarctic waters, and on Jan. 5, 1915, they moored to an ice floe, got out, and played soccer. On Jan. 12, 1915, they discovered the Caird Coast, and on Jan. 19, 1915, ran into trouble in the pack-ice.

On Feb. 22, 1915, the *Endurance* got truly caught in the ice, and drifted 573 miles to the north for 9 months. On Oct. 27, 1915, the men got out in anticipation of the *Endurance* going down. They began living on an ice floe. On Nov. 1, 1915, they set up Ocean Camp, 1½ miles from the stricken ship. On Nov. 21, 1915, what they were waiting for happened. "She's gone, boys," Shackleton said as the *Endurance* was crushed by the ice and disappeared. For 5 months the 28 men lived on the northbound floe as it took them away from Antarctica. On Dec. 31, 1915, they floated over the Antarctic Circle. Finally, on April 10, 1916, they escaped from their icy home, and using their 3 whaleboats, the *Stancomb-Wills*, the *James Caird*, and the *Dudley Docker*, they reached Cape Valentine on deserted Elephant Island, on April 14, 1916. On April 17, 1916, they shifted to Cape Wild, and on April 24, 1916, Shackleton decided that he must strike out for help. He took 5 companions, Crean, Worsley, MacArty, Vincent, and McNeish, in the *James Caird* (an open boat) and left Elephant Island to look for help. After crossing 800 miles of Antarctic waters in the most bizarre and nightmarish conditions, they reached South Georgia (54°S) on May 10, 1916. Further around the island was the Norwegian whaling station of Grytviken, but separating that station from Shackleton's crew were the high, dangerous mountains that no one had ever crossed. On May 15, 1916, Shackleton took Crean and Worsley and set out again, this time to cross the mountains that it was thought by others could not be crossed. The other 3 men stayed behind. After a mad crossing, Shackleton and his men arrived at an astonished Grytviken, and sought help. Three efforts were made to get to Elephant Island, on the *Southern Sky*, the *Instituto de Pesca I*, and the *Emma*, before they finally succeeded in the *Yelcho* in picking up the 22 men led by Frank Wild, on Elephant Island, on Aug. 30, 1916. "Are you all well?," demanded Shackleton on seeing his men again. No

lives were lost. The same could not be said for the other half of the expedition, on the other side of the continent. The *Aurora* left Sydney on Dec. 15, 1914, the Ross Sea party having got there from England in Sept. 1914. Ship's party included John King Davis, Aitken, D'Anglade, Donnelly, Downing, Glidden, Grady, Kavenagh, Larkman, Mugridge, Paton, Shaw, L.J.F. Thomson, Warren, and Wise. The ship arrived at Hut Point on Jan. 7, 1915. On Jan. 21, 1915, three parties went ashore to establish two depots, one at 79°S and one at 80°S. Ninnis, Hooke, and Stenhouse got back after 3 weeks and were picked up by the *Aurora*, and the ship anchored at Cape Evans for the winter. Stevens, Richards, Gaze, and Spencer-Smith occupied Scott's hut at Cape Evans. On May 6, 1915, the *Aurora* drifted away in a blizzard, leaving the men on shore stranded. On June 2, 1915, the remaining 6 men, Mackintosh, Ernest Wild, Hayward, Joyce, Cope, and Jack, arrived from their depot-laying in the far south. Meanwhile the *Aurora* was beginning a 10-month entrapment in the ice which would take the vessel 1,100 miles to the north. On Sept. 1, 1915, a series of relaying expeditions set out from Ross Island, to set up a depot at every degree south, as far south as Mount Hope (83°34'S), at the southern edge of the Ross Ice Shelf. Six finally went the last stretch, Mackintosh, Hayward, Spencer-Smith, Wild, Joyce, and Richards. Spencer-Smith was left alone, sick, at 83°S, while the other 5 pressed on, getting to Mount Hope on Jan. 26, 1916. On Jan. 29, 1916, they were back with Spencer-Smith, who was now incapable of walking. They were now headed back to base, their job having been completed under terrible conditions. Mackintosh was becoming progressively worse and incapable. The (mostly) inexperienced dogs had all died on the bad return trip, and from Feb. 17 to 23, 1916, the men were trapped immobile in a blizzard 10 miles south of Bluff Depot (79°S). On March 1, 1916, they all reached the depot. On March 8,

1916, the Rev. Spencer-Smith died of scurvy and exhaustion, and on March 11, 1916, the remaining 5 reached the Discovery Hut on Ross Island. They were in terrible condition. Their aim was to get to Scott's other hut, at Cape Evans, not too far away, but because the sea ice was still soft, they didn't dare venture across it. Mackintosh and Hayward finally became impatient and died trying to get across. On July 15, 1916, Wild, Joyce, and Richards made it to Cape Evans, and were picked up by the *Aurora* on Jan. 10, 1917. The irony of the Ross Sea party was that they need not have gone through all that. But they could not know that Shackleton was never going to use the depots, that his side of the expedition had been aborted. The first successful land traverse of the entire continent did not take place until March 2, 1958, when Fuchs arrived at Ross Island during the IGY.

**British Royal Society IGY Expedition** *see* **Dalgliesh, David**

**Britt Peak.** 76°03'S, 135°07'W. 3,070 m. Just SW of Mount Moulton, in the Flood Range of Marie Byrd Land. Named for Dale R. Britt, USN, builder at Amundsen-Scott South Pole Station in 1969.

**Britten Inlet.** 72°36'S, 72°30'W. An indentation into the SW part of Alexander Island. Named by the UK for the composer.

**Broad Bay** *see* **Breid Bay**

**Broad Peninsula** *see* **Breidnes Peninsula**

**Broad Valley.** 63°32'S, 57°55'W. Broad and glacier-filled. On the south side of Laclavère Plateau, Trinity Peninsula. Named descriptively by V.I. Russell of the FIDS following his 1946 survey.

**Brock Gulley.** 76°44'S, 159°44'E. 1 mile south of Windwhistle Peak in the Allan Hills of Victoria Land. Named by the New Zealanders in 1964 for its resemblance to English badger country.

**Mount Brockelsby.** 67°34'S, 50°11'E. 1,290 m. 7 miles north of Simpson Peak, in the Scott Mountains of Enderby Land. Named by the Australians for W.K. Brockelsby, ionosphere physicist at Mawson Station in 1961.

**Brockhamp Islands.** 67°17'S, 67°56'W. Two small islands in Laubeuf Fjord, 3 miles SW of Mothes Point, Adelaide Island. Named by the UK for Bernhard Brockhamp, German glaciologist in the 1920s.

**Mount Brocklehurst.** 76°08'S, 161°27'E. 1,310 m. Dome-shaped. North of the Mawson Glacier. 6 miles west of Mount Murray, in Victoria Land. Charted by Shackleton's 1907–9 expedition, and named by them for Sir Philip Lee Brocklehurst.

**Brocklehurst, Sir Philip Lee.** A British baronet who met Shackleton in 1906 and paid to go on that explorer's British Antarctic Expedition 1907–9, as junior geologist. He climbed Mount Erebus in 1908, but suffered severe frostbite as a result, and had to have some of his toes amputated. He was one of the supporting party during Shackleton's push to the Pole in 1908. He was later a lieutenant-colonel.

**Brocklehurst Ridge.** 71°02'S, 67°06'E. Partly snow-covered. 1 mile south of Taylor Platform in the Prince Charles Mountains. Named by the Australians for F.J. Brocklehurst, electrical fitter at Mawson Station in 1964.

**Brockton Station.** 80°10'S, 178°25'W. American camp on the Ross Ice Shelf.

**Mount Brocoum.** 70°12'S, 63°45'W. The dominant peak on the eastern ridge of the Columbia Mountains, in Palmer Land. Named for Stephan J. Brocoum and his wife Alice V. Brocoum, Columbia University geologists who studied the structure of the Scotia Ridge area in 1970–71. Mr. Brocoum had been there before, in 1968–69.

**Brodie Peak.** 69°25'S, 66°05'W. In the Eternity Range of the Antarctic Peninsula.

**Brødrene Rocks.** 66°17′S, 56°06′E. Also called Wheeler Rocks. A group in the entrance to Wheeler Bay just NW of Magnet Bay. Photographed by the LCE 1936–37, and named Brødrene (the brothers) by the Norwegians.

**Mount Brøgger.** 76°52′S, 161°48′E. Over 1,400 m. Part of the north wall of the Cleveland Glacier, about 4 miles north of Referring Peak, in Victoria Land, just north of the Mackay Glacier. Charted by Scott's 1910–13 expedition, and named by them for Waldemar C. Brøgger, Norwegian geologist, mineralogist, and parliamentarian.

**Broka Island.** 67°07′S, 58°36′E. 140 m. 4 miles long. 2 miles north of Law Promontory. 1 mile west of Havstein Island. Photographed by the LCE 1936–37 and named Broka (the trousers) by the Norwegians for the outline of the island.

**Broken Island.** 67°49′S, 66°57′W. 2½ miles long. 1½ miles north of Centre Island, in the northern part of Square Bay, off the west coast of Graham Land. Discovered and named by the BGLE 1934–37.

**Cape Broms.** 64°20′S, 58°18′W. Marks the south side of the entrance to Röhss Bay, on the west side of James Ross Island. Discovered in 1901–4 by the Nordenskjöld expedition, who named it for G.E. Broms, a patron.

**Mount Bronk.** 84°24′S, 175°48′E. 3,530 m. Snow-covered. 4 miles NE of Mount Waterman, in the Hughes Range. Discovered aerially by Byrd on Nov. 18, 1929, and surveyed by Crary in 1957–58. Crary named it for Detlev W. Bronk, president of the US National Academy of Sciences.

**Mount Brooke.** 76°50′S, 159°56′E. 2,675 m. 17 miles NW of Mount Gran. Named for F. Richard Brooke.

**Brooke, F. Richard.** NZ Lt. in the RN. Surveyor in Hillary's party during the BCTAE 1957–58, and leader of the Northern Survey Party during that expedition.

**Brookins, John.** Ordinary seaman on the Wilkes Expedition 1838–42. Joined at Upolu. Served the cruise.

**Brooklyn Island.** 64°39′S, 62°05′W. 2½ miles long. 1 mile south of Nansen Island, in the eastern part of Wilhelmina Bay, off the west coast of Graham Land. Discovered by de Gerlache in 1897–99, and named by him for the home of Dr. Frederick Cook.

**Brookman Point.** 74°19′S, 131°51′W. Snow-covered. The NW point of Grant Island, off the Marie Byrd Land coast. Discovered and charted by the *Glacier* in Feb. 1962. Named for Lt. Peter J. Brookman, USN, officer-in-charge at Byrd Station in 1970.

**Cape Brooks.** 73°36′S, 60°46′W. Forms the south side of the entrance to New Bedford Inlet, on the east coast of Palmer Land. Discovered aerially in Dec. 1940 by the USAS. Named by the FIDS for Charles E.P. Brooks, British meteorologist on the staff of the Met Office from 1907–49.

**Brooks, John.** Seaman on the *Vincennes* during the Wilkes Expedition 1838–42. Joined in the USA. Served the cruise.

**Brooks Island** *see* **Ivanoff Head**

**Brooks Nunatak.** 84°59′S, 66°18′W. 1,615 m. Isolated. 6 miles SW of the Shurley Ridge on the south side of the Mackin Table, in the Patuxent Range of the Pensacola Mountains. Named for Robert E. Brooks, biologist at Amundsen-Scott South Pole Station in 1966–67.

**Brooks Point.** 66°45′W, 108°25′E. On the west shore of Vincennes Bay, 5 miles WNW of Mallory Point. Named in 1972 for John Brooks.

**Mount Broome.** 73°35′S, 61°45′W. Between the mouths of the Douglas Glacier and the Bryan Glacier, in the Werner Mountains of Palmer Land. Named for Howard W. Broome, Jr., electrician at Amundsen-Scott South Pole Station in 1967.

**Brörvika** *see* **Wheeler Bay**

**Brosnahan Island.** 79°28′S, 160°59′E. 1 mile long. On the western part of the Ross Ice Shelf. 11 miles NE of Cape Murray. Named for Cdr. James J. Brosnahan, USN, commander of McMurdo Base, 1961.

**Brothers Hill** *see* **Three Brothers Hill**

**Brouardel Point.** 65°03′S, 63°59′W. North of Port Charcot, on the west side of the Mount Lacroix peninsula, on Booth Island, in the Wilhelm Archipelago. Charted and named by Charcot in 1903–5 for Dr. Brouardel of the Institut de France.

**The *Brough.*** US ship DE-148, in Antarctica between 1956–59.

**Broune Insel** *see* **Brown Peninsula**

**Mount Brounov.** 71°58′S, 14°20′E. 2,370 m. 1½ miles south of Mount Kibal'chich, in the Payer Mountains of Queen Maud Land. Named by the USSR in 1966 for P.I. Brounov, geographer.

**Mount Brouwer.** 72°35′S, 31°26′E. 2,460 m. Between Mount Hoge and Mount Launoit, in the Belgica Mountains. Discovered by the Belgian Antarctic Expedition of 1957–58 led by Gaston de Gerlache, and named by him for Carl de Brouwer, a patron of the expedition.

**Cape Brown.** 69°16′S, 69°42′W. Ice-covered. 5½ miles NNE of the summit of Mount Nicholas, marking the eastern side of the entrance to Schokalsky Bay. It juts out from the northern part of Alexander Island into the southern part of Marguerite Bay, opposite Cape Jeremy. First seen by Charcot in 1909, and charted by him as part of a small island. Later redefined. Surveyed by Colin C. Brown of the FIDS in 1948–49, and named for him by the UK. He was stationed at Base E, Stonington Island, that season.

**Mount Brown.** 68°18′S, 86°25′E. 160 miles east of the Vestfold Hills, and 100 miles SSW of Cape Penck. Named for Lt. (jg) Eduardo P. Brown, USN, photographic officer for the Western

Group on Operation Highjump, 1946–47.

[1]**Brown, Capt.** Commander of the *Sprightly* in the South Shetlands, 1821–22, during that vessel's second tour of the islands. May be the same Capt. Brown who commanded the *Susanna Ann* in 1823–25.

[2]**Brown, Capt.** Commander of the *Susanna Ann* in the South Shetlands, 1823–25. May be the same captain who commanded the *Sprightly* in 1821–22.

**Brown, Franklin.** Ordinary seaman on the Wilkes Expedition 1838–42. Joined in the USA. Served the cruise.

**Brown, Gustav L.** Captain of the *Eleanor Bolling* during Byrd's 1928–30 expedition.

[1]**Brown, James.** Leader of the *Pacific* expedition of 1829–31.

[2]**Brown, James.** Carpenter's mate on the Wilkes Expedition 1838–42. Joined in the USA. Served the cruise.

[1]**Brown, John.** 1st class boy on the Wilkes Expedition 1838–42. Joined at Rio. Run at Sydney on Dec. 31, 1839.

[2]**Brown, John.** Seaman on the Wilkes Expedition 1838–42. Joined in the USA. Served the cruise.

**Brown, John B.** Seaman on the Wilkes Expedition 1838–42. Joined in the USA. Returned in the *Relief* in 1839.

**Brown, Peter.** Ordinary seaman on the Wilkes Expedition 1838–42. Joined at Rio. Run at Upolu on Nov. 10, 1839.

**Brown, Dr. R.N. Rudmose.** Naturalist on the Scottish National Antarctic Expedition of 1902–4 led by Bruce. He was a member of the Scott Polar Research Committee from 1939–41 (*see also* the Bibliography).

**Brown, Robert.** Bosun's mate on the Wilkes Expedition 1838–42. Joined in the USA. Discharged at Oahu on Oct. 31, 1840.

**Brown, Samuel.** Captain of the fo'c's'le on the Wilkes Expedition 1838–42. Joined in the USA. Discharged at Oahu on Nov. 2, 1840.

**Brown, William.** Ordinary seaman on the Wilkes Expedition 1838–42. Run at Rio.

**Brown Bay.** 66°17′S, 110°33′E. Just SE of Casey Station, on Bailey Peninsula, in the Windmill Islands. Named by the Australians for A.M. Brown, senior engineer with the Antarctic Division, Melbourne, who helped supervise the construction of Casey Station.

**Brown Bluff.** 63°32′S, 56°55′W. 745 m. An ice-capped, flat-topped mountain that has a prominent cliff of red-brown volcanic rock on the north face (hence the name). 9 miles south of Hope Bay on the east side of Tabarin Peninsula. Named by the FIDS after their 1946 survey.

**Brown Hills.** 79°46′S, 158°33′E. To the immediate north of the Darwin Glacier, they are a group of mainly snow-free hills in the Cook Mountains, in the Queen Alexandra Range. Named for their color by the Darwin Glacier Party of the BCTAE 1956–58.

**¹Brown Island.** 64°58′S, 63°47′W. Small, brown, and snow-free. In the SE part of the Wauwermans Islands, 2 miles SW of Wednesday Island. Charted by the BGLE 1934–37, and named by Rymill because its color stands out among all the other snow-capped islands.

**²Brown Island** *see* **Brown Peninsula**

**Brown Nunataks.** 82°37′S, 53°30′W. Three nunataks 1 mile NW of Walker Peak, at the SW extremity of the Dufek Massif. Named for John B. Brown, ionosphere physicist at Ellsworth Station in 1957.

**Brown Peak.** 67°25′S, 164°35′E. 1,705 m. In the north part of Sturge Island, in the Balleny Islands. Discovered in Feb. 1839 by Balleny, who named it for W. Brown, one of his sponsors. In 1841 Ross accidentally renamed it Russell Peak, but the earlier name prevails.

**Brown Peaks.** 85°35′S, 158°05′W. A series of low peaks, 7 miles east of Robinson Bluff, at the east side of the Amundsen Glacier, in the Queen Maud Mountains. Named for Kenneth R. Brown, biologist at McMurdo Station in 1964.

**Brown Peninsula.** 78°07′S, 165°30′E. Also called Broune Insel. Nearly ice-free. 10 miles long. 4 miles wide. The highest point on it is 2,654 feet. At the bottom of the northern slopes of Mount Discovery leading to McMurdo Sound, in the southern part of Victoria Land. Discovered on Scott's 1901–4 expedition, and named by them as Brown Island because of its color and islandlike quality. Later redefined.

**Brown Range** *see* **Sørtindane Peaks**

**Brown Ridge.** 83°38′S, 55°06′W. 3 miles long. Extends NNW from Nelson Peak in the Neptune Range. Named for Robert D. Brown, geologist with the Patuxent Range field party of 1962–63.

**Brown Valley.** 75°38′S, 132°12′W. Ice-covered. Between Mount Kauffman and Mount Kosciusko, in the NE end of the Ames Range of Marie Byrd Land. Named for Thomas I. Brown, meteorologist at Byrd Station in 1963.

**Mount Brown-Cooper.** 70°42′S, 64°12′E. Partly ice-covered. 1 mile SW of Mount Forecast, on the SE end of the Bennett Escarpment, in the Prince Charles Mountains. Named by the Australians for P.J. Brown-Cooper, geophysicist at Wilkes Station in 1965.

**Mount Browning.** 74°37′S, 164°04′E. 760 m. 2 miles to the north of the Gerlache Inlet at the north of Terra Nova Bay, in northern Victoria Land. Opposite the terminus of Boomerang Glacier, in the Northern Foothills. Mapped by Shackleton's 1907–9 expedition, and explored and mapped in greater detail by Campbell's Northern Party of 1911–12. They named it for Frank Browning.

**Browning, Frank V.** Petty officer, 2nd class, RN. Was part of Campbell's Northern Party during Scott's 1910–13 expedition. He came close to dying on this trip.

**Browning Island** *see* **Browning Peninsula**

**Browning Pass.** 74°36'S, 164°E. 10 miles long. Ice-covered. Just to the north of the Gerlache Inlet, at the north end of Terra Nova Bay, in northern Victoria Land. Between the Deep Freeze Range and the Northern Foothills. One passes from the lower ends of the Priestley and Campbell Glaciers using this pass, which was first mapped by Campbell's Northern Party of 1911–12 as part of Campbell Glacier. Remapped by the New Zealanders in 1962–63, and named by them for Frank Browning.

**Browning Peninsula.** 66°28'S, 110°33' E. Also called Browning Island. 4 miles long. Separates Penney and Eyres Bays at the south end of the Windmill Islands. Named for Cdr. Charles L. Browning, USN, chief staff officer with Operation Windmill, 1947–48, and later staff officer with Task Force 43, 1955–56.

**Browns Bay.** 60°43'S, 44°36'W. 1½ miles wide. Between Thomson Point and Cape Geddes, on the NW side of Laurie Island, in the South Orkneys. Charted in 1903 by Bruce, who named it for Dr. R.N. Rudmose Brown.

**Browns Butte.** 85°16'S, 167°30'E. At the north side of the mouth of the Koski Glacier, in the Dominion Range. Named for Craig W. Brown, meteorologist at Amundsen-Scott South Pole Station in 1963.

**Browns Glacier.** 68°57'S, 77°58'E. 4 miles north of Chaos Glacier, it flows into the northern extremity of Ranvik Bay. Photographed by the LCE 1936–37 and again by Operation Highjump, 1946–47. Named by US cartographer John H. Roscoe, in 1952, for Lt. (jg) Eduardo P. Brown (*see* **Mount Brown**).

**The *Brownson*.** American destroyer which took part in Operation Highjump, 1946–47, as part of the Eastern Task Group. Commanded by Cdr. H.M.S. Gimber.

**Brownson Islands.** 74°10'S, 103°36'W. 20 or so small islands just outside the entrance to Cranton Bay, about 14 miles SW

of the SW tip of Canisteo Peninsula. Named for the *Brownson*.

**Lake Brownworth.** 77°26'S, 162°45'E. Also called Wright Lake. A meltwater lake west of Wright Lower Glacier at the east end of the Wright Valley, in Victoria Land. Named for Frederick S. Brownworth, topographic engineer in Antarctica for several seasons. In 1970–71 he supervised aerial photography of the dry valleys of Victoria Land, including this lake.

**¹Cape Bruce** *see* **Bruce Point**

**²Cape Bruce.** 67°25'S, 60°47'E. The northern tip of a small, unnamed, island, at the east side of Oom Bay, just west of the Taylor Glacier. The BANZARE landed here on Feb. 18, 1931, and Mawson named it for the prime minister of Australia.

**Mount Bruce.** 70°32'S, 162°30'E. 1,640 m. The northernmost of the Bowers Mountains in Oates Land. Just south of the Stuhlinger Ice Piedmont, and between the Gannutz and Barber Glaciers. Discovered by the personnel on the *Terra Nova* in 1911, and named for Wilfred M. Bruce.

**Bruce, Wilfred M.** Lt., RNR. Robert Falcon Scott's brother-in-law. He was a lieutenant on the P&O Line, and joined Scott's 1910–13 expedition in New Zealand, as the man in charge of zoological work aboard the *Terra Nova*. He was not a member of the shore party.

**Bruce, William S.** b. 1867, London. d. 1921. William Spiers Bruce. Scottish explorer. Son of a surgeon, he was raised in Edinburgh. In 1892–93 he was naturalist/doctor on the *Balaena* during the Dundee Whaling Expedition, and planned also to go on the *Antarctic* expedition, led by Bull in 1894–95, but couldn't get to Melbourne in time to meet the ship. Around this time he conceived the idea of a transantarctic traverse, in order to test the theoretic Ross-Weddell Graben. He refused the post of naturalist on Scott's 1901–4 expedition because he was planning his own—the

Scottish National Antarctic Expedition of 1902–4. The British government, however, refused to back his expedition and so, being intensely patriotic toward Scotland, Bruce approached the Coats family, who became his main backers. Purely Scottish-financed, the *Scotia* left Scotland on Nov. 2, 1902. The main themes of the expedition were to conduct hydrography in the Weddell Sea and to survey the South Orkneys. On Feb. 3, 1903, they sighted the South Orkneys, and got to 70°25′S, 17°12′W before being squeezed by ice on Feb. 22, 1903. They wintered over on Laurie Island in the South Orkneys, and while there worked at botany and meteorology at their base, Omond House. Much hydrography was done, and the expedition made a major contribution to science, collecting more unknown specimens than any expedition before it. The *Scotia* was icebound during the winter of 1903 (from March to November). On Aug. 6, 1903, Allan Ramsey, the chief engineer of the *Scotia,* was buried on Laurie Island. On Nov. 22, 1903, the *Scotia* was freed, and on Nov. 27, 1903, it sailed to Buenos Aires to be refitted, leaving behind 6 men to continue the summer study. The men made the first thorough study of penguins, and skied for relaxation. While in Buenos Aires, Bruce arranged for the Argentinians to take over Omond House (seeing that the British expressed no interest), and the *Scotia* set sail again with 3 Argentinians aboard. Four of the 6 shore party reembarked and in Feb. 1904 went sailing south with Bruce, while the 3 Argentinians remained to winter over with 2 of the original shore party—R.C. Mossman and the cook. On March 3, 1904, the *Scotia* reached 72°18′S, discovered Coats Land (guessing it to be a continuation of Enderby Land), and on March 12, 1904, reached 74°01′S. The *Scotia* got back to Northern Ireland on July 15, 1904, to a tremendous reception. Meanwhile, Mossman, the cook, and the 3 Argentinians left behind on Laurie Island carried on working. The *Uruguay* arrived on Dec. 30, 1904, with

relief Argentinians, and from then on Omond House became Orcadas Station (q.v.). Bruce himself continued in science, and in Arctic research. In 1915–16 he managed a whaling station in the Seychelles. His ashes were scattered over the Indian Ocean. Others on the Scottish National Antarctic Expedition included Harvey Pirie, Alastair Ross, David Wilton, R.N. Rudmose Brown, J. Davidson, John Fitchie, J. McDougal, J. Martin, and Kerr the bagpipe player. There was also a meteorologist, a botanist, and a zoologist.

**Mount Bruce Harkness** *see* **Mount Harkness**

**Bruce Island.** 64°54′S, 63°08′W. ½ mile off the SW corner of Bryde Island, in the Gerlache Strait. Discovered and mapped by de Gerlache in 1897–99. Named by David Ferguson in 1913 for William S. Bruce.

**Bruce Islands.** 60°41′S, 44°54′W. A group 1½ miles NW of Eillium Island and 3 miles NW of Route Point, the NW tip of Laurie Island, in the South Orkneys. Discovered in Dec. 1821 by Powell and Palmer. Named by the personnel on the *Discovery II* in 1933 for William S. Bruce.

**Bruce Nunatak.** 65°05′S, 60°15′W. 2 miles west of Donald Nunatak in the Seal Nunataks, off the east coast of the Antarctic Peninsula. Charted in 1902 by Nordenskjöld's expedition, who named it for William S. Bruce.

**Bruce Plateau.** 65°50′S, 63°35′W. Ice-covered. 90 miles long. 1,830 m. Extends from the heads of the Gould and Erskine Glaciers to the area of Flandres Bay, in Graham Land. Named by the UK for William S. Bruce.

**Bruce Point.** 75°38′S, 162°26′E. Also called Cape Bruce, Cape William Bruce. A point, on the south side of Charcot Cove, on the coast of Victoria Land. Discovered by Scott's first expedition (i.e. the Royal Society Expedition of 1901–4), and named by Scott for William S. Bruce.

**Bruce Ridge.** 60°S, 35°W. A submarine feature to the east of the South Orkneys.

**Bruce Rise** *see* **Bruce Spur**

**Bruce Spur.** 63°S, 101°15′E. Also called Bruce Rise. A submarine feature.

**Bruces Peak** *see* **Summers Peak**

**Brückner Glacier.** 67°14′S, 66°56′W. Flows through Arrowsmith Peninsula and enters the southern part of Lallemand Fjord, just west of Humphreys Hill. Named by the UK for Eduard Brückner, German glaciology pioneer.

**Brugda Ridge.** 72°05′S, 2°50′E. Extends ESE from the south side of Jutulsessen Mountain in the Gjelsvik Mountains of Queen Maud Land. Name means "the basking shark" in Norwegian.

**Brugmann Mountains.** 64°02′S, 61°55′W. 850 m. On the east side of Liège Island. Discovered by de Gerlache in 1897–99, and named by him for Georges Brugmann, a patron of the expedition.

**The** *Brulson* *see* **The** *Brusso*

**Mount Brundage.** 75°16′S, 65°28′W. Also called Mount Burr Brundage. 12 miles WSW of Mount Terwileger in the southern part of the Scaife Mountains. Discovered by the RARE 1947–48, and named by Finn Ronne for Burr Brundage, Department of State, who helped the expedition.

**Bruner Hill.** 75°39′S, 142°25′W. 770 m. Mostly snow-covered. On the north side of the El-Sayed Glacier, 8 miles west of Mount Shirley, in Marie Byrd Land. Named for Lt. Michael J. Bruner, USN, LC-130 Hercules aircraft commander, 1970 and 1971.

**Brunhilde Peak.** 77°38′S, 161°27′E. Between Donner Valley and Sykes Glacier in the Asgard Range of Victoria Land. Named by NZ for the mythical Teutonic figure.

**Brunner Glacier.** 85°14′S, 175°38′W. 2 miles long. Flows from the west slope of the Cumulus Hills between Landry Bluff and Halfmoon Bluff, into the Shackleton Glacier. Named by the Texas Tech Shackleton Glacier Expedition of 1964–65 for Staff Sgt. Donald R. Brunner, member of the US Army Aviation Detachment that supported the expedition.

**Brunow, Benjamin J.** American captain of the *Henry*, 1820–21, and probably second-in-command of the New York Sealing Expedition of that year. He was back in the *Henry* for the second part of the expedition, 1821–22.

**Brunow Bay.** 62°43′S, 60°09′W. A small indentation into the SE side of Livingston Island in the South Shetlands. Named by the UK in 1958 for Ben Brunow.

**Mount Bruns.** 84°29′S, 64°23′W. In the Patuxent Range of the Pensacola Mountains.

**Bruns, Herbert.** Electrical engineer on the German New Schwabenland Expedition of 1938–39, led by Ritscher.

**Bruns Nunataks.** 72°05′S, 1°10′E. A small group, including Tua Hill, 2½ miles WNW of Brattskarvet Mountain in the Sverdrup Mountains of Queen Maud Land. Ritscher discovered them in 1938–39, and named them Bruns-Berge, for Herbert Bruns. Later geographers, unsure of Ritscher's aerial photography, selected these nunataks as the ones he intended, and named them in English.

**Brunt Ice Shelf.** 75°30′S, 25°W. Borders the coast of Coats Land between Dawson-Lambton Glacier and Stancomb Wills Glacier Tongue. The new Halley Station opened on this ice shelf in Feb. 1984. Named by the UK for David Brunt, British meteorologist.

**Brunt Icefalls.** 75°55′S, 25°W. A line of icefalls extending along the Caird Coast for almost 50 miles where the steep, ice-covered coast descends to the Brunt Ice Shelf. Discovered on Nov. 5, 1967, on a VX-6 flight, and named in association with the ice shelf.

**Brunvoll, Arnold.** Brother of Saebjørn Brunvoll. They were both Norwegian whaling captains who explored the coast of East Antarctica in the *Seksern* in Jan. 1931.

**Brunvoll, Saebjørn.** Brother of Arnold Brunvoll (see above).

**Brunvoll Glacier.** 67°48′S, 66°48′E. Flows between Murray Monolith and Torlyn Mountain on the east, and Scullin Monolith and Mikkelsen Peak on the west, as far as the coast. Named by Bjarne Aagard (*see* **Aagard Glacier**) for the Brunvoll Brothers, Arnold and Saebjørn.

**Brusen Nunatak.** 68°12′S, 58°13′E. Also called Foley Nunatak. Isolated. 3 miles west of Mount Gjeita in the Hansen Mountains. Photographed by the LCE 1936–37, and later named by Norwegian cartographers.

**Brush Glacier.** 74°29′S, 111°38′W. In the NW part of the Bear Peninsula, flowing into the Dotson Ice Shelf to the north of Jeffrey Head, in Marie Byrd Land. Named for Bernard E. Brush, station engineer at Byrd VLF Station in 1966.

**Brusilov Nunataks.** 66°42′S, 51°24′E. A group 6 miles north of Mount Morrison in the Tula Mountains of Enderby Land. Named by the USSR in 1962 for Polar explorer, G.L. Brusilov.

**The *Brusso*.** Also called the *Brulson*. A British sealer in the South Shetlands for the 1821–22 season, under the command of Capt. Greaves. Anchored in Clothier Harbor for the summer.

**Brustad, A.C.** Seaman on the *City of New York* during Byrd's 1928–30 expedition.

**Bryan Coast.** 73°35′S, 84°W. Between Pfrogner Point (at the very edge of the Eights Coast) and the north tip of the Rydberg Peninsula (at the edge of the English Coast), on the Bellingshausen Sea. Originally called the George Bryan Coast, for Rear Adm. George S. Bryan, hydrographer of the US Navy, 1938–46.

**Bryan Glacier.** 73°30′S, 61°33′W. Flows from the Werner Mountains into Douglas Glacier at New Beford Inlet, in Palmer Land. Named for Terry E. Bryan, glaciologist at Byrd Station in 1967.

**Cape Bryant.** 71°12′S, 60°55′W. High and snow-covered, it forms the north side of the entrance to Palmer Inlet. Juts out from the east coast of the Antarctic Peninsula into the southern end of the Larsen Ice Shelf, below Steele Island. Discovered in 1940 by the members of East Base during the USAS 1939–41, and named by them for Herwil M. Bryant.

**Bryant, Herwil M.** Biologist at East Base during the USAS 1939–41.

**Bryde Channel** *see* **Lientur Channel**

**Bryde Island.** 64°52′S, 63°02′W. 6 miles long. 3 miles wide. Just SW of Lemaire Island, at the entrance to Paradise Bay, in Graham Land. Discovered by de Gerlache in 1897–99, and named by him for the expedition's representative in Norway.

**Bryde Refugio.** Argentine refuge hut built on Orne Harbor–Paradise Harbor.

**Bryde's Whale.** Like the Sei Whale, but it has a smaller dorsal fin and longer, stiffer baleen plates.

**Bryggeholmen** *see* **Gibbney Island**

**Bryozoans.** Aquatic invertebrates which lie on the sea bed, near the shore (*see also* **Fauna**).

**Bryse Peaks.** 72°43′S, 74°50′E. A small nunatak with two peaks. 4 miles NNE of Mason Peaks, in the Grove Mountains. Named by the Australians for R.A. Bryse, major Australian cartographer of Antarctica.

**Mount Bubier.** 71°51′S, 97°48′W. Also called Bubier Head. About 4 miles south of Edwards Peninsula, on Thurston Island. Named for Kennard F. Bubier.

**Bubier, Kennard F.** Aviation mechanic on Byrd's 1928–30 expedition.

**Bubier Head** *see* **Mount Bubier**

**Buchan Bay.** 60°47′S, 44°42′W. Between Cape Hartree and Cape Murdoch near the SW end of Laurie Island, in the South Orkneys. Charted in 1903 by Bruce, and named by him for Scottish meteorologist, Alexander Buchan.

Cape Buchanan *see* Cape Vala-vielle

**Buchanan, J.Y.** Chemist on the *Challenger* expedition of 1872–76. Much later he was a patron of the AAE 1911–14.

**Buchanan Bay.** 67°05′S, 144°42′E. Formed by the junction of the west side of the Mertz Glacier Tongue and the mainland. Cape de la Motte marks the western entrance point. Discovered by the AAE 1911–14, and named by Mawson for J.Y. Buchanan.

**Buchanan Channel** *see* **Southwind Passage**

**Buchanan Hills.** 79°39′S, 82°55′W. North of the Union Glacier, and between the Collier Hills and the Nimbus Hills, in the Heritage Range. Named for Roger Buchanan, biologist in Antarctica in 1964–65.

**Buchanan Passage.** 66°48′S, 67°42′W. A marine channel separating Liard Island from Adelaide Island, at the north end of Hanusse Bay. Discovered and charted by Charcot in 1908–10, and much later named by the UK for Capt. Peter W. Buchanan, RN, commander of the *Endurance,* 1968–70.

**Buchanan Point.** 60°43′S, 44°28′W. 2½ miles NW of Cape Dundas. 1 mile SE of Mackintosh Cove, at the NE end of Laurie Island, in the South Orkneys. This name was originally given by Bruce in 1903 to a point 3 miles to the NW which Dumont d'Urville had already named Cape Valavielle in 1838. In 1954 the UK created the present situation.

**Bucher Glacier.** 67°39′S, 66°50′W. Flows into Bourgeois Fjord just north of Bottrill Head on the west coast of Graham Land. Named by the UK in 1958 for Edwin Bucher, Swiss glaciologist.

**Bucher Peak.** 75°20′S, 110°52′W. 2,445 m. In the west central summit area of the Mount Murphy massif, in Marie Byrd Land. Named for Walter H. Bucher, professor of geology at Columbia University, 1940–56.

**Bucher Rim.** 76°19′S, 112°09′W. On the southern portion of the rim of the

extinct volcano Mount Takahe, in eastern Marie Byrd Land. Named for Peter Bucher from the University of Bern, Switzerland. He was a geologist at Byrd Station in 1969–70.

**Buckett, Henry.** Quartermaster on the Wilkes Expedition 1838–42. Joined in the USA. Discharged at Sydney.

**Buckeye Table.** 84°49′S, 114°45′W. A plateau. 12 miles long. Between 2 and 5 miles wide. Occupies the central part of the Ohio Range. William H. Chapman, a surveyor here in 1958–59, named it for Ohio State University (Ohio being nicknamed the Buckeye State), which has sent many researchers here.

**Buckle Island.** 66°47′S, 163°14′E. 13 miles long. 3 miles wide. Between Sturge Island and Young Island in the Balleny Islands. Discovered in Feb. 1839 by Balleny, who named it for J.W. Buckle, one of his sponsors.

**Buckle Island Automatic Weather Station.** 66°49′S, 163°14′E. American AWS on Buckle Island, in the Balleny Islands. Elevation approximately 1,100 feet. Began operating Feb. 20, 1987.

**Mount Buckley.** 84°58′S, 163°56′E. 2,645 m. Ice-free. The central and highest summit of Buckley Island at the head of the Beardmore Glacier. It is on the Polar Plateau, in the most southerly sector of the Queen Alexandra Range. Discovered by Shackleton in 1907–9, and named by him for George Buckley.

**Buckley, George.** d. 1935. George A. McLean Buckley. A wealthy sheepfarmer from Ashburton, NZ, who, on the spur of the moment, went along on the *Nimrod* in 1907–8 during Shackleton's expedition. He was a backer of the expedition, and went only as far as the Ross Sea before returning on the *Koonya,* the ship which had towed the *Nimrod* that far. He later backed the AAE 1911–14, and later still became a lieutenant-colonel.

**Buckley Bay.** 68°16′S, 148°12′E. Between the east side of the Ninnis Glacier Tongue and the mainland, on the western side of the Cook Ice Shelf, at the base of the George V Coast, in Wilkes Land. Discovered by the AAE 1911–14, and named by Mawson for George Buckley.

**Buckley Island.** 84°58′S, 163°56′E. An islandlike mountain massif, surmounted by Mount Bartlett, Mount Buckley and Mount Bowers. It rises above the ice at the head of the Beardmore Glacier. Discovered by Shackleton in 1907–9, and named in association with Mount Buckley.

**Buckmaster, G.H.** Captain of the *Lion* on its second and last trip to the South Shetlands, in 1853–54. The ship was wrecked on English Bank (not in Antarctic waters) on March 22, 1854.

**Bucknell, E.S.** The cook on the NZ party of the BCTAE 1957–58. He was a member of the Darwin Glacier party of that expedition.

**Bucknell Ridge.** 79°58′S, 158°38′E. Just above the Cranfield Icefalls, on the south side of the Darwin Glacier. Mapped by the Darwin Glacier party of the BCTAE 1957–58, and named for E.S. Bucknell.

**Budd, Thomas A.** US naval lieutenant on the Wilkes Expedition 1838–42. Joined the *Vincennes* at Fiji. Was acting captain of the *Peacock* for a while.

**Budd Coast.** 66°30′S, 112°E. Also called Budd Land. Between Hatch Islands (109°16′E) and Cape Waldron (115°33′E), or between Totten Glacier and Vincennes Bay, in Wilkes Land. Discovered on Feb. 12, 1840, by Wilkes, and named by him as Budd's High Land, for Thomas Budd. The name was later amended.

**Budd Land** *see* **Budd Coast**

**Budd Peak.** 66°40′S, 52°40′E. 1 mile west of Mount Berrigan, 23 miles WSW of Stor Hånakken Mountain in Enderby Land. Named by the Australians for W. Budd, glaciologist at Wilkes Station in 1961.

**Buddenbrock Range.** 71°52′S, 5°24′E. A group of scattered mountains and nunataks between Austreskorve Glacier and Vestreskorve Glacier, in the Mühlig-Hofmann Mountains of Queen Maud Land. Ritscher discovered and named the general area in 1938–39 as Buddenbrock-Kette, for the director of Lufthansa. The name was later translated into English.

**Lake Buddha.** 78°03′S, 163°45′E. Large proglacial lake on the south margin of the Joyce Glacier in Shangri-la. Named by the New Zealanders in 1960–61 in association with the valley of Shangri-la.

**Buddington, James W.** A Yankee sealing captain from New London, Conn., who was a major force in the reopening of the Antarctic sealing idea in 1871. The first time a Captain Buddington appeared in southern waters was in 1858–60, when an expedition led by a man of this name visited Heard Island (53°S) on the *Cornelia* (Eldridge's vessel the season before). As far as can be ascertained, this expedition did not venture into Antarctic waters proper, but in 1874–75 a Captain Buddington commanded the *Franklin* on an expedition in the South Shetlands. James W. Buddington was in the South Shetlands looking for fur seals, as captain of the *Florence* in 1876–77, and he seems not to have returned until 1888–89, when he commanded the *Sarah W. Hunt* there. As he took only 39 sealskins that season, he probably returned for the 1889–90 summer to try again. He would have had no luck. All the seals were gone. It is likely that all of these Captains Buddington were the same man. If so, it was a career that spanned at least 32 years as a captain. Nat Palmer (q.v.) was a captain at 20. Buddington may have been too.

**Buddington Peak.** 62°12′S, 58°49′W. Also called Cerro Agudo. Between Collins Harbor and Marian Cove, in the SW part of King George Island, in the South Shetlands. Named by the UK in 1960 for James W. Buddington.

**Budd's High Land** see **Budd Coast**

**Büdel Islands.** 65°47'S, 65°38'W. Also called Islas Aldea. A group between Laktionov Island and Schule Island, off the east side of Renaud Island, in the Biscoe Islands. Named by the UK in 1959 for Julius Büdel, German sea ice specialist.

**Budnick Hill.** 66°17'S, 110°32'E. On the south side of Newcomb Bay in the Windmill Islands, between Crane Cove and Geoffrey Bay. It is joined by a narrow strip of land to the northern part of Bailey Peninsula. Named by the Australians for K. Budnick, ANARE surveyor here from Wilkes Station in 1964.

**Buell Peninsula.** 70°36'S, 164°24'E. Ice-covered. Ends in Cape Williams. Between the lower ends of the Lillie, George, and Zykov Glaciers at the NW end of the Anare Mountains. 15 miles long and 8 miles wide at its broadest. Named for Lt. Kenneth R. Buell, USN, VX-6 navigator, 1965–66 and 1966–67.

**Cabo Buen Tiempo** see **Cape Fairweather**

**Islotes Buen Tiempo** see **Symington Islands**

**Buennagel Peak.** 77°30'S, 146°46'W. 1 mile east of Alexander Peak, in the north part of the Haines Mountains, in the Ford Ranges of Marie Byrd Land. Named for Lawrence A. Buennagel, geomagnetist at Byrd Station in 1968.

**Glaciar Buenos Aires** see **Dawson-Lambton Glacier**

**Buettner Peak.** 75°17'S, 110°55'W. On the north wall of Roos Glacier in the NW part of the Mount Murphy massif in Marie Byrd Land. Named for Robert J. Buettner (1914–1975), manager of contract logistics support for Holmes and Narver. He was in Antarctica at least 5 times between 1969 and 1974.

**Buff Island.** 64°51'S, 64°35'W. 3 miles SW of the Joubin Islands. 10½ miles SW of Cape Monaco, Anvers Island. First shown on a 1936 BGLE chart.

**Buffer Ice Rise.** 69°09'S, 67°18'W. On the Wordie Ice Shelf. 9 miles north of

Mount Balfour, in southern Graham Land. Named by the UK because it obstructs the westward flow of ice.

**Buffon Islands.** 66°40'S, 140°01'E. 3 adjoining, rocky islands. Altogether about ¼ mile in extent. 175 yards east of Pétrel Island in the Géologie Archipelago. Charted by the French in 1951, and named by them for Buffon the naturalist (1707–1788).

**Bugge Islands.** 69°12'S, 68°25'W. A small, ice-covered group in the southern part of Marguerite Bay, just off the front of the Wordie Ice Shelf. Between 4 and 11 miles NW of Mount Guernsey, off the west coast of the Antarctic Peninsula. Discovered aerially by the BGLE in 1936. Named Ruth Bugge Islands by Finn Ronne in 1947 for his niece, Ruth Bugge. The name was later shortened.

**Monte Bulcke** see **Bulcke Finger**

**Mount Bulcke.** 64°29'S, 62°37'W. 1,030 m. Just south of the Solvay Mountains, in the south of Brabant Island. Discovered by de Gerlache and named by him in 1897–99 for a patron of the expedition.

**Bulcke Finger.** 64°29'S, 62°37'W. Also called Monte Bulcke. A fingerlike pinnacle on top of Mount Bulcke, in the southern part of Brabant Island. Discovered by de Gerlache in 1897–99, and named later by the FIDS in association with the mountain.

**Bulgaria.** Ratified as the 20th signatory of the Antarctic Treaty on Sept. 11, 1978.

**Bulken Hill.** 71°51'S, 26°58'E. 2,220 m. 3 miles north of Balchen Mountain in the Sør Rondane Mountains. Name means "the lump" in Norwegian.

**Bulkington Pass.** 65°49'S, 62°43'W. On the south side of Flask Glacier, and west of Bildad Peak, on the east side of Graham Land. 4 miles long. Named by the UK for the *Moby Dick* character.

**Bulkisen.** 71°48'S, 26°47'E. A blue icefield between Austhamaren Peak and Bulken Hill, in the Sør Rondane Mountains. Named in association with the hill.

**Lake Bull.** 77°32'S, 161°42'E. Also called Bull Pond. ½ mile east of Lake Vanda, in the Wright Valley of Victoria Land. Named in the 1960s for Colin Bull (*see* **Bull Pass**). From here the Onyx River feeds Lake Vanda.

**Mount Bull** *see* **Gustav Bull Mountains**

**Bull, Gustav B.** Manager/Commander of the *Thorshammer,* 1930–31 and 1932–33.

**Bull, Henryk J.** 1844–1930. Henryk Johan Bull. Norwegian businessman who emigrated to Australia in 1885. He led the *Antarctic* expedition of 1894–95, and in 1896 wrote *The Cruise of the* Antarctic *to the South Polar Regions.* He continued sealing and whaling after this.

**Bull Island.** 71°58'S, 171°06'E. Between Kemp Rock and Heftye Island in the Possession Islands. Named for Henryk J. Bull.

**Bull Nunatak.** 65°05'S, 60°23'W. 3 miles west of Bruce Nunatak in the Seal Nunataks, off the east coast of the Antarctic Peninsula. Charted in 1902 by Nordenskjöld, and named by him for Henryk J. Bull.

**Bull Pass.** 77°28'S, 161°43'E. A dry valley in the Olympus Range of Victoria Land. Between Mount Jason and Mount Orestes, it joins the McKelvey and Wright Valleys. Named by the VUWAE 1958–59, for Colin Bull, the leader of the expedition.

**Bull Pond** *see* **Lake Bull**

**Bull Ridge.** 64°41'S, 63°28'W. South of Mount Français, in the south of Anvers Island. Named by the UK for George J. Bull, diesel mechanic at Signy Island Station in 1955, and general assistant and mountain climber at Base N in 1956.

**Bullseye Lake.** 77°25'S, 161°15'E. A very small pond in the Insel Range, 4½ miles NE of Mount Boreas, in Victoria Land. Named in 1964 by US geologist Parker Calkin, for its size.

**Bullseye Mountain.** 83°55'S, 160°05' E. Ice-covered. On Peletier Plateau. 4

miles NW of Mount Ropar in the Queen Elizabeth Range. Named for the semi-circular bands of snow on the south side of the mountain.

**Bulnes Island.** 63°18'S, 57°58'W. A small island 2 miles NW of Cape Legoupil on Trinity Peninsula. Charted by the Chilean Antarctic Expedition of 1947–48, and named by the expedition leader Capt. González (q.v.) for Manuel Bulnes Sanfuentes, Chilean politician.

**Buls Bay.** 64°23'S, 62°19'W. 2 miles wide. Indents the east side of Brabant Island, just north of D'Ursel Point. Discovered by de Gerlache in 1897–99, and named by him for Charles Buls, a supporter of the expedition.

**Buls Island** *see* **Maipo Island**

**The Bulwark.** 78°18'S, 163°34'E. A steep-walled, granite bastion-type mountain on the west side of the Koettlitz Glacier, around which the glacier flows on its descent to Walcott Bay. First mapped by Scott's 1910–13 expedition, and named in 1960–61 by the New Zealanders because of its shape.

**Mount Bumstead.** 85°39'S, 174°16'E. Also called Windy Nunatak. 2,990 m. Isolated. 10 miles SE of the Otway Massif, in the Grosvenor Mountains of the Queen Maud Mountains. Discovered by Byrd on his flight to the Pole in Nov. 1929, and named by him for Albert H. Bumstead, inventor of the sun compass.

**Bundermann, Max.** Aerial photographer on the flying boat *Passat* during the German New Schwabenland Expedition of 1938–39, led by Ritscher.

**Bundermann Range.** 72°01'S, 2°42'E. A small range just north of Nupskammen Ridge and Terningskarvet Mountain, in the Gjelsvik Mountains of Queen Maud Land. A range in this area (it may not have been this one exactly) was discovered by Ritscher in 1938–39, and named by him as Bundermann-Ketten, for Max Bundermann. Later geographers arbitrarily selected this range as the one discovered by Ritscher.

**Bunger, David E.** Pilot. Lt. Cdr., US Navy. Discovered the Bunger Hills when he landed on a frozen lake here on Feb. 11, 1947, during Operation Highjump.

**Bunger Hills.** 66°17′S, 100°47′E. Also called Bunger Lakes, Bunger Oasis. A group of low, rounded coastal hills overlain by morainal drift, and ice-free in the summer. Many meltwater ponds are here, and Algae Lake cuts the hills in two. Just south of the Highjump Archipelago, on the coast of Queen Mary Land, just behind the Shackleton Ice Shelf. Discovered on Feb. 11, 1947, by David Bunger, they became the best-known of all the Operation Highjump discoveries, especially after the press started calling the area "Shangri-la." Named for Bunger.

**Bunger Lakes** *see* **Bunger Hills**

**Bunger Oasis** *see* **Bunger Hills**

**Bunker, Calvin.** American whaler from Nantucket who was owner/manager/captain of the *Diana* in 1820–21.

**Bunker Bluff.** 73°04′S, 166°40′E. Just south of the mouth of Gair Glacier in Victoria Land. Named for William H. Bunker, meteorologist at Hallett Station in 1962.

**Bunner Glacier.** 74°26′S, 110°18′W. In the NE part of the Bear Peninsula. Flows to the sea along the SE side of Gurnon Peninsula, in Marie Byrd Land. Named for Sgt. Donald R. Bunner, US Army, here in 1965 and 1966.

**Mount Bunt.** 70°46′S, 66°20′E. 2,315 m. 7 miles east of Mount Hollingshead in the Aramis Range of the Prince Charles Mountains. Discovered in Jan. 1957 by W.G. Bewsher's ANARE Southern Party, and named by the Australians for J.S. Bunt, biologist at Mawson Station in 1956.

**Bunt Island.** 67°09′S, 50°57′E. Just east of Bowl Island, at the head of Amundsen Bay, in Enderby Land. Discovered in 1956 by an ANARE airborne field party. Named by the Australians for J.S. Bunt (*see* **Mount Bunt**).

**Buntley Bluff.** 79°12′S, 160°22′E. A rock cliff 2 miles long. Just north of Cape Lankester at the mouth of the Mulock Glacier. Named for Ensign Ronald E. Buntley, USN, personnel manager at Williams Field in 1964.

**Mount Burch.** 70°50′S, 164°25′E. 1,400 m. 3 miles SE of Mount Kelly on the south side of the George Glacier, in the Anare Mountains. Named by the ANARE for W.M. Burch, geophysicist with the ANARE on the *Thala Dan* in 1962, and geophysicist at Wilkes Station in 1961.

**Burch Peaks.** 66°52′S, 53°02′E. A group, 6 miles east of Mount Torckler in Enderby Land. Named by the Australians for W.M. Burch (*see* **Mount Burch**).

**Cape Burd.** 63°39′S, 57°09′W. A low rock cliff forming the SW extremity of Tabarin Peninsula, at the NE end of the Antarctic Peninsula. Charted by the FIDS in 1946, and named for Oliver Burd.

**Burd, Oliver.** FIDS meteorologist. Leader of the wintering party at Base F in 1947. He died in the Base D fire at Hope Bay in Nov. 1948.

**Burden, Eugene.** Captain of the *Trepassey*, 1946–47.

**Burden Passage.** 63°08′S, 56°32′W. Separates D'Urville Island from Bransfield Island, off the NE end of the Antarctic Peninsula. Charted in 1947 by the FIDS, who named it for Eugene Burden.

**Burdick, Christopher.** Captain (and one of the 4 owners) of the *Huntress*, a vessel in the South Shetlands for the 1820–21 season, and which teamed up with the *Huron* during that period in order to maximize the take of seals. On Feb. 15, 1821, Burdick sighted the continent of Antarctica while in command of the *Cecilia* during a Feb. 12–19, 1821, exploration of Low Island.

**Burdick Channel** *see* **Pendleton Strait**

**Burdick Peak.** 62°38′S, 60°15′W. SW of Mount Bowles on Livingston Island, in the South Shetlands. Named by the UK in 1958 for Christopher Burdick.

**Burgess Glacier.** 85°26'S, 171°55'E. 7 miles long. Flows through the Otway Massif and enters Mill Stream Glacier. Named for Robert W. Burgess, ionosphere physicist at Amundsen-Scott South Pole Station in 1963.

**Burgess Ice Rise.** 70°23'S, 73°21'W. On Wilkins Sound, off the NW coast of Alexander Island.

**The** *Burghead Bay.* British frigate in Antarctic waters in 1952 when it went to Hope Bay with the governor of the Falkland Islands aboard in order to investigate the fracas with the Argentinians there (*see* **Wars**). Captain that year was J.A. Ievers. It did some charting and visited all the FIDS stations except Port Lockroy. In 1954–55, under Capt. P.D. Hoare, it visited the South Orkneys and South Shetlands.

**Burke, Arleigh A.** Adm., USN. Chief of Naval Operations for Operation Deep Freeze, 1956–61.

**Burke, Thomas.** Private on the Wilkes Expedition 1838–42. Joined in the USA. Served the cruise.

**Burke Island.** 73°08'S, 105°06'W. Ice-covered. 16 miles long. 37 miles SW of Cape Waite (at the end of King Peninsula), at the entrance to Pine Island Bay, in the Amundsen Sea. Named for Adm. Arleigh A. Burke.

**Burkett Islands.** 66°56'S, 50°20'E. A group of small islands just west of Mount Gleadell, in the eastern part of Amundsen Bay, in Enderby Land. Named by the Australians for G.E.L. Burkett, radio officer at Wilkes Station in 1960.

**Burkett Nunatak.** 72°42'S, 162°14'E. 2,180 m. 1 mile east of Minaret Nunatak, in the Monument Nunataks. Named for Willis A. Burkett, VX-6 technician, an Antarctic veteran of many years.

**Burkitt Nunatak.** 69°42'S, 66°53'W. On the west side of the Antarctic Peninsula.

**Cape Burks.** 74°45'S, 136°50'W. Marks the east side of the entrance to Hull Bay, on the coast of Marie Byrd Land. It forms the NW seaward extension of the McDonald Heights. Discovered and mapped by personnel on the *Glacier* on Jan. 31, 1962. Named for Lt. Cdr. Ernest Burks, USN, senior helicopter pilot with the *Glacier,* and the first person to set foot on the cape.

**Burlock Peak.** 86°03'S, 132°20'W. 2,070 m. In the area of Mount Simsarian, on the east face of the Watson Escarpment. Named for James U. Burlock, builder at Byrd Station in 1962.

**Burmeister Dome.** 83°22'S, 50°56'W. In the Pensacola Mountains.

**Burn Cliffs.** 70°06'S, 69°52'W. In the western part of Alexander Island.

**Cape Burn Murdoch** *see* **Cape Murdoch**

**Burn Murdoch Nunatak** *see* **Murdoch Nunatak**

**Mount Burnett.** 67°53'S, 62°45'E. 1,050 m. 1½ miles SW of Trost Peak in the Masson Range of the Framnes Mountains. Photographed by the LCE 1936–37. Later named by the Australians for Eric Burnett, radiophysicist at Mawson Station in 1958.

**Burnett, Donald R.** Lt. (jg), USN. Military leader of Wilkes Station throughout 1957, until Jan. 30, 1958, when he handed over to Lt. R.S. Sparkes.

**Burnett Island.** 66°13'S, 110°36'E. 1 mile long. North of Honkala Island. It is the central feature in the Swain Islands. Named by Carl Eklund for Donald R. Burnett.

**Burnette Glacier.** 72°01'S, 170°04'E. In the Admiralty Mountains. Flows between Honeycomb Ridge and Quartermain Point, into Moubray Bay. Named for Airman 2nd Class Robert L. Burnette, USAF (*see* **Deaths, 1958**).

**Burnette Rock.** 75°23'S, 143°13'W. 45 m. About .7 mile NW of Groves Island, off the coast of Marie Byrd Land. Named for CWO Desmond Burnette, US Army, helicopter pilot on the Marie Byrd Land Traverse of 1966–67. He landed on this rock, on Dec. 4, 1966, and the feature was named by Charles E. Morrison, Jr., who was also on this traverse.

**Burney, Captain.** Commander of the *Nelson,* a British sealer in the South Shetlands, 1820–21 and 1821–23.

**Burney, James.** b. 1750, London. d. 1821. Joined the navy as a cabin boy at the age of 10, and died a rear-admiral. He was the brother of the novelist Fanny Burney, and son of the musician Charles Burney. He was a second lieutenant on the *Adventure* during Cook's second voyage.

**Burney Peak.** 62° 19′ S, 58° 52′ W. West of Duthoit Point, in the eastern part of Nelson Island, in the South Shetlands. Named by the UK in 1960 for Captain Burney.

**¹Mount Burnham.** 71° 34′ S, 159° 50′ E. 2,810 m. On the west wall of the Daniels Range. 6 miles south of Big Brother Bluff, in the Usarp Mountains. Named for James B. Burnham, ionosphere physicist at the South Pole Station in 1958 and 1961.

**²Mount Burnham.** 77° 16′ S, 142° 05′ W. 1,170 m. 2 miles north of Mount Van Valkenburg, in the Clark Mountains, of the Ford Ranges in Marie Byrd Land. Discovered aerially in 1940 by members from West Base during the USAS, and named for Guy Burnham, Clark University cartographer.

**Burns, David.** Officer's cook on the Wilkes Expedition 1838–42. Joined in the USA. Returned on the *Relief* in 1839.

**Burns Bluff.** 70° 22′ S, 67° 56′ W. On the west coast of Palmer Land, just to the south of Naess Glacier. Named by the UK for Frederick M. Burns, BAS geophysicist at Base E in 1967–68.

**Burns Glacier.** 73° 57′ S, 164° 15′ E. 12 miles long. Flows along the east side of Pinckard Table and enters the SW side of Tinker Glacier, in Victoria Land. Named for John P. Burns, radioman at McMurdo Station in 1963 and 1967.

**Burnside Ridges.** 69° 14′ S, 157° 10′ E. Three roughly parallel ridges running ap-

proximately NE–SW with their NE end at Matusevich Glacier. Named by the Australians for Lt. Cdr. I.M. Burnside, RAN, hydrographic surveyor on the *Magga Dan,* 1958–59.

**Cape Buromskiy.** 69° S, 156° 05′ E. The north point of Krylov Peninsula. Named by the Soviet Antarctic Expedition in 1958 for N.I. Buromskiy (*see* **Deaths, 1957**), the expedition's hydrographer.

**Buromskiy Island.** 66° 32′ S, 93° E. In the Haswell Islands. Named for N.I. Buromskiy (*see* **Cape Buromskiy**) by the USSR.

**Mount Burr Brundage** *see* **Mount Brundage**

**Burrage Dome.** 75° 33′ S, 161° 05′ E. 840 m. An ice-covered hill. 4 miles NE of the summit of Mount Joyce in the Prince Albert Mountains of Victoria Land. Named for Roy E. Burrage, Jr., construction mechanic at Amundsen-Scott South Pole Station, 1966.

**Mount Burrill.** 72° 50′ S, 167° 30′ E. 2310 m. On the east edge of the Malta Plateau, 4 miles south of Mount Hussey, at the head of Hand Glacier, in the Victory Mountains of Victoria Land. Named by NZ for Dr. Meredith F. Burrill, executive secretary of the US Board on Geographic Names, 1943–73.

**Burris Nunatak.** 71° 47′ S, 160° 27′ E. Near the north end of Emlen Peaks, 2 miles NW of Mount Cox, in the Usarp Mountains. Named for James M. Burris, assistant to the USARP representative at McMurdo Station, 1967–68.

**Burro Peaks.** 62° 26′ S, 59° 47′ W. On Dee Island, in the South Shetlands.

**Mount Burrows.** 74° 17′ S, 163° 39′ E. 2,260 m. 5 miles WSW of Mount Queensland in the Deep Freeze Range of Victoria Land. Dominates the lower side of the Priestley Glacier. Named by NZ for A.L. Burrows, scientific leader at Scott Base, 1964–65.

**Mount Bursey.** 76° S, 132° 40′ W. 2,780 m. Ice-covered. A volcano that forms the east end of the Flood Range, overlooking the Hobbs Coast, in Marie Byrd Land. Discovered aerially in 1940 by the USAS. Named for Jack Bursey.

**Bursey, Jack.** Jacob Bursey. Radio operator and later lieutenant commander in the US Coast Guard. He was radio operator on Byrd's 1928–30 expedition, and was back in Antarctica as a member of West Base during the USAS 1939–41. During that expedition he led a 1,250-mile dog-sledge traverse out of Little America III (also known as West Base) to the Hal Flood Range in Marie Byrd Land. During Operation Deep Freeze I he led 6 volunteers out of Little America V on Jan. 14, 1956, into Marie Byrd Land, to pioneer the 600-mile trail to what was to become Byrd Station.

**Bursey Icefalls.** 75°59′S, 132°48′W. They drain the northern slope of Mount Bursey, in the Flood Range of Marie Byrd Land. Named in association with Mount Bursey.

**Mount Bursik.** 79°43′S, 84°23′W. 2,500 m. The central peak of the Soholt Peaks, in the Heritage Range. Named for Capt. Vlada D. Bursik, USN, deputy commander, US Naval Support Force, Antarctica, 1966.

**Burt, H.R.** Crewman on the *Jacob Ruppert*, 1933–34.

**Burt Rocks.** 69°35′S, 159°09′E. At the west edge of Noll Glacier, 1½ miles south of Axthelm Ridge, in the Wilson Hills. Named for DeVere E. Burt, biologist at Hallett Station in 1968–69.

**Burtis Island.** 73°04′S, 125°29′W. A small island, 10 miles east of Cape Dart, Siple Island, off the coast of Marie Byrd Land. Named for William J. Burtis, ionosphere physicist at Byrd Station in 1965.

**Mount Burton.** 72°33′S, 166°44′E. 2,740 m. At the west side of the mouth of Osuga Glacier, where that glacier enters Trafalgar Glacier, in the Victory Mountains of Victoria Land. Named by the New Zealanders in 1962–63 for William Burton.

**Burton, Charles.** A member of the Trans-Globe Expedition of 1980–82,

which crossed Antarctica, via the Pole, in 66 days.

**Burton, William.** Crew member on the *Terra Nova* during Scott's 1910–13 expedition. He was still alive into the 1980s in New Zealand, and in 1962–63 was a guest of the US Navy in Antarctica.

**The *Burton Island*.** 6,515-ton, 10,000 hp, US Navy wind-class icebreaker launched in 1946. It was part of Task Force 68 during Operation Highjump, and was commanded by Gerald L. Ketchum. It carried a helicopter on board. During 1947–48 it took part in Operation Windmill, and this time was under the command of Edwin A. McDonald. It circumnavigated Antarctica, and rescued the *Port of Beaumont, Texas* (the RARE [q.v.] ship) from the ice on Feb. 20, 1948. It also took part in Operation Deep Freeze III (1957–58), and Operation Deep Freeze 60 (its commander during this expedition, from Dec. 7, 1959, to Nov. 14, 1960) was Cdr. Griffith C. Evans, Jr. The ship was back in Antarctica during Operation Deep Freeze 62, 64, 66, 68, and 69. It transferred from the Navy to the Coast Guard on Dec. 15, 1966.

**Burton Island Glacier.** 66°50′S, 90°20′E. A channel glacier. 9 miles wide. 7 miles long. Flows from the continental ice to Posadowsky Bay, just west of Cape Torson. Named for the *Burton Island*.

**Burton Island Rock** *see* **Bigelow Rock**

**Burton Lake.** 68°35′S, 78°06′E. A small hypersaline lake with its surface at sea level. It is in Marine Plain in the Vestfold Hills, and opens into Crooked Fjord, therefore it is affected by the tides. Detailed, year-round limnological research is conducted here.

**Burton Point.** 66°16′S, 66°56′W. The NE point of Krogh Island in the Biscoe Islands. Named by the UK for Alan C. Burton, Canadian physiologist specializing in the cold.

**Burton Rocks.** 68°14′S, 67°02′W. 3 rocks in Marguerite Bay, a mile south of

Neny Island, off the west coast of Graham Land. Surveyed in 1947 by the FIDS, and named by them for the *Burton Island*.

**Mount Bush**  *see*  **Mount Wade**

**Bush Mountains.** 84°57'S, 179°35'E. Also called Prince Olav Mountains (but see also that entry for the other feature of that name). They extend from Mount Weir in the west to Anderson Heights in the east. They overlook the Ross Ice Shelf from between the Shackleton Glacier and the Beardmore Glacier. Named by Byrd for James Bush, a patron of the 1928–30 expedition led by Byrd.

**Bushell Bluff.** 71°28'S, 67°36'W. On the west coast of Palmer Land, just south of Norman Glacier. Named by the UK for Anthony N. Bushell, BAS general assistant at Fossil Bluff Station in 1969–70.

**Mount Bushnell.** 85°36'S, 150°48'W. 840 m. Between Mount Durham and Pincer Point in the NW part of the Tapley Mountains. Named for Vivian C. Bushnell, editor of the American Geographical Society's *Antarctic Map Folio* series.

**Buskin Rocks**  *see*  **Borceguí Island**

**Buskirk Bluffs.** 70°49'S, 165°38'E. On the west side of McMahon Glacier in the Anare Mountains of Victoria Land. Named by the ANARE for Major H. Buskirk, official US observer with ANARE on the *Thala Dan* in 1962.

**Bussey Glacier.** 65°16'S, 64°01'W. Flows from Mount Peary to the head of Waddington Bay, on the west coast of Graham Land. Charted by Charcot in 1908–10, and named by the UK in 1959 for Group Capt. J. Bussey of the Directorate of Overseas Surveys.

**Butcher Nunatak.** 76°32'S, 146°30'W. At the south end of the Birchall Peaks, 4 miles SW of Swarm Peak, in the Ford Ranges of Marie Byrd Land. Named for Robert S. Butcher, USN, builder at Byrd Station in 1967.

**Butcher Ridge.** 79°12'S, 155°48'E. Just to the north of the Darwin Mountains in southern Victoria Land. Mostly ice-free, it is in the west part of the Cook Mountains. Extends NW from Mount Ayres in the form of an arc. Named for Cdr. H.K. Butcher, USN, air operations officer on the staff of the commander, US Naval Support Force, Antarctica, 1963 and 1964.

**Butchers Shoulder**  *see*  **Butchers Spur**

**Butchers Spur.** 85°34'S, 166°30'W. Ice-covered. Runs from Mount Don Pedro Christophersen to the Polar Plateau, on the southern edge of the Queen Maud Mountains. Amundsen's "Butcher Shop" was here, where, in Nov. 1911 they slaughtered the excess dogs during their push to the South Pole.

**Mount Butler.** 78°10'S, 155°17'W. Also called Mount Navy. The most southerly of the Rockefeller Mountains, on the Edward VII Peninsula, in Marie Byrd Land. Discovered aerially on Jan. 27, 1929, during Byrd's 1928–30 expedition, and named by Byrd for Raymond Butler.

**Butler, Raymond A.** Member of West Base during the USAS 1939–41. He was one of the party which occupied the Rockefeller Mountains seismic station in Nov. and Dec. of 1940.

**Butler Glacier.** 77°25'S, 152°40'W. Flows from the north side of the Edward VII Peninsula near Clark Peak, through the Alexandra Mountains, to its terminus at Sulzberger Bay. Named for Lt. F.M. Butler, USN, navigator on the *Glacier*, 1961–62.

**Butler Island.** 72°13'S, 60°08'W. 185 m. Circular. Ice-covered. 6 miles wide. 7 miles east of Merz Peninsula, below Hilton Inlet, off the east side of Palmer Land. Discovered by the USAS in Dec. 1940. Named by the FIDS for K.S. Pierce-Butler.

**Butler Island Automatic Weather Station.** 72°12'S, 60°21'W. An American AWS on Butler Island, off the east coast of Palmer Land. Elevation approximately

300 feet. Began operating on March 1, 1986.

**Butler Nunataks.** 68°03′S, 62°24′E. A small group just north of Mount Twintop in the Framnes Mountains. Named by the Australians for W.J. Butler, senior diesel mechanic at Mawson Station in 1967.

**Butler Passage.** 64°58′S, 63°44′W. A marine channel between the Wauwermans Islands and the Puzzle Islands, connecting Peltier Channel and Lemaire Channel, off the west coast of Graham Land. Named by the UK in 1959 for Capt. Adrian R.L. Butler, RN, commander of the *Protector* here in 1957–58 and 1958–59.

**Butler Peaks.** 71°31′S, 67°10′W. A group at the south end of the Batterbee Mountains, 4 miles south of Mount Bagshawe, between the Armstrong and Conchie Glaciers. Named by the UK for Peter F. Butler, BAS geophysicist at Base E in 1969–70 and 1973.

**Butler Rocks.** 82°35′S, 47°57′W. 910 m. Two rock nunataks. 2½ miles SW of Vanguard Nunatak, in the northern part of the Forrestal Range of the Pensacola Mountains. Named for William A. Butler, aerographer at Ellsworth Station in 1957.

**Butson, Dr. Richard C.** Arthur Richard C. Butson. British physician with the FIDS at Base E on Stonington Island, in 1947. In July of that year he rescued a member of the RARE 1947–48 from a crevasse in Northeast Glacier.

**Butson Ridge.** 68°05′S, 66°53′W. Has several ice-covered summits on it, the highest being 1,305 m. Forms the north wall of Northeast Glacier on the west coast of Graham Land. Surveyed by the BGLE in 1936, and again by the FIDS in 1946–48. Named by the FIDS for Dr. Richard C. Butson.

**Butter, George.** Officer's cook on the Wilkes Expedition 1838–42. Joined in the USA. Served the cruise.

**Butter Point.** 77°39′S, 164°13′E. On the south side of New Harbor, Victoria Land. Discovered by Scott's 1901–4 expedition, and named by them for the can of butter left here by the Ferrar Glacier party of that expedition.

**Butter Point Piedmont** *see* **Bowers Piedmont Glacier**

**Butterfly Knoll.** 80°21′S, 28°09′W. In the Shackleton Range.

**Mount Butters.** 84°53′S, 177°26′W. 2,440 m. Snow-capped. At the SE end of the Anderson Heights, between Mincey Glacier and Shackleton Glacier. Discovered aerially on Feb. 16, 1947, during Operation Highjump. Named for Capt. Raymond J. Butters.

**Butters, Raymond J.** Capt. US Marines. Navigator of Flight A, which flew over the South Pole (q.v. for further details of this flight) on Feb. 15–16, 1947, during Operation Highjump.

**Mount Butterworth.** 70°42′S, 66°45′E. Has 4 peaks. 5 miles south of Thomson Massif, in the Aramis Range of the Prince Charles Mountains. Named by the Australians for G. Butterworth, radio officer at Wilkes Station in 1963 and at Mawson Station in 1966.

**The Buttons.** 65°14′S, 64°16′W. Two small islands, 350 yards NW of Galíndez Island, in the Argentine Islands. Charted and descriptively named by the BGLE in 1935.

**Buttress Hill.** 63°34′S, 57°03′W. 690 m. Flat-topped. 2 miles east of the most northern of the Seven Buttresses, on Tabarin Peninsula, in the NE end of the Antarctic Peninsula. Charted by the FIDS in 1946 and named by them because of its proximity to the Seven Buttresses.

**Buttress Nunataks.** 72°22′S, 66°47′W. A group of nunataks, the highest being 635 m. Inland from George VI Sound, and 10 miles WNW of the Seward Mountains, on the west coast of Palmer Land. Discovered by the BGLE in 1936. Named descriptively by the FIDS in 1949.

**Buttress Peak.** 84°27′S, 164°15′E. 2,950 m. The eastern part projects as a rock buttress into the head of Berwick Glacier, 3 miles south of Mount Stonehouse, in the Queen Alexandra Range. Named descriptively by the New Zealanders in 1961–62.

**Buys, John.** Seaman on the *Eleanor Bolling* during Byrd's 1928–30 expedition.

**Buzfuz Rock.** 65°28'S, 65°53'W. 1½ miles west of Snubbin Island in the Pitt Islands, in the northern part of the Biscoe Islands. Named by the UK in 1971 for the Dickens character.

**Mount Byerly.** 81°53'S, 89°23'W. In the eastern part of the Nash Hills. Named for Perry Byerly, an IGY official.

**Cabo Byers** *see* **Cape Page**

**Byers Peninsula.** 62°38'S, 61°05'W. Ice-free. On the extreme west of Livingston Island, in the South Shetlands. It is SSSI #6. Named by the UK in 1958 for James Byers, a New York shipowner who, in Aug. 1820, tried unsuccessfully to get the US government to found a settlement in, and take possession of, the South Shetlands. It was he who sent out the New York Sealing Expedition (q.v.).

**Cape Byewater** *see* **Byewater Point**

**Byewater Point.** 62°45'S, 61°30'W. Also called Cape Brewster. On the west side of Snow Island, in the South Shetlands. Charted and named Cape Byewater by Foster in 1829. It has since been redefined.

**Bynon Hill.** 62°55'S, 60°36'W. Also called Goddard Hill. Also seen spelled as Binon Hill. 340 m. Ice-covered. Dome-shaped. Has two rounded summits, and is the most northerly elevation on Deception Island, in the South Shetlands. 1½ miles north of Pendulum Cove. Named before 1953.

**Bynum Peak.** 85°03'S, 173°41'W. 3 miles SE of Mount Finley, overlooking the north side of McGregor Glacier, in the Queen Maud Mountains. Named for Gaither D. Bynum, satellite geodesist at McMurdo Station in 1965.

**Byobu Rock.** 68°22'S, 42°E. 1 mile east of Gobamme Rock, on the coast of Queen Maud Land. Named Byobu-iwa (folding screen rock) by the Japanese.

**Bypass Hill.** 72°28'S, 168°28'E. 660 m. Where Tucker Glacier meets Trafalgar Glacier, in Victoria Land. Named by the NZGSAE 1957–58, who established a survey station at this point.

**Bypass Nunatak.** 68°01'S, 62°30'E. 2 miles south of Mount Tritoppen in the David Range of the Framnes Mountains. Photographed by the LCE 1936–37, and later called Steinen (the stone) by the Norwegians. Renamed by the ANARE because the 1958 ANARE party bypassed dangerous terrain here.

**Cape Byrd.** 69°38'S, 76°07'W. Ice-covered. Forms the NW extremity of Charcot Island, at the easternmost end of the Ruppert Coast of Marie Byrd Land. Discovered aerially by Wilkins on Dec. 29, 1929, during a flight from the *William Scoresby,* and named by him for Richard Byrd.

**Mount Byrd.** 77°10'S, 144°38'W. 810 m. 1 mile north of the east end of Asman Ridge in the Sarnoff Mountains of the Ford Ranges of Marie Byrd Land. Named for Richard E. Byrd, Jr., son of the admiral.

**Byrd, Richard Evelyn.** b. Oct. 25, 1888, Winchester, Virginia. d. March 11, 1957, Boston. Arguably the most famous of all the Antarctic heroes. He was born into an old Virginia family, and followed a naval career. He claimed to have flown over the North Pole on May 9, 1926, and in June 1927 he flew across the Atlantic Ocean. He led 5 major expeditions to Antarctica. Byrd's 1928–30 expedition was his first, during which he established Little America, and made his first Antarctic flight on Jan. 15, 1929. Also during that expedition he flew to the South Pole and back, in Nov. 1929, the first leader to do so. During Byrd's 1933–35 expedition he became the first man to winter over alone in the heart of the continent, from March 28 to Aug. 10, 1934 (see his book, *Alone,* and *see also* the entry **Bolling Advance Weather Station**

in this book). He headed the USAS 1939–41 (the United States Antarctic Service Expedition), but did not winter-over. In 1946–47 he led Operation Highjump. During this stay he flew over the Pole again, on Feb. 15–16, 1947. From 1955 until his death in 1957 he was technical director and overall titular head of Operation Deep Freeze. He had married Marie Ames (Marie Byrd as she became), who died in 1974. Byrd himself died quietly at his home in Boston. Richard Byrd opened up the Antarctic continent more than any other man, propelled Antarctic exploration into the modern, mechanized age, proved that Antarctica really is a continent and that the Ross-Weddell Graben does not exist, developed the use of 2-way radio, and wrote 5 books (see the Bibliography). There is a memorial to Admiral Byrd at McMurdo Station (see **Richard E. Byrd Memorial**). In 1988 some of his belongings were sold. It was the 100th anniversary of his birth. That year also, his son Richard E. Byrd, Jr. (q.v.), died.

**Byrd, Richard Evelyn, Jr.** d. 1988 in mysterious circumstances. The son of Admiral Byrd. He took part in Operation Highjump, 1946–47, and later assisted in naming several Antarctic features.

**Byrd Automatic Weather Station.** 80° S, 120°W. An American climate-monitoring site at an elevation of approximately 4,800 feet, at Byrd Station. Began operating on Feb. 5, 1980.

**Byrd Bay**  see  **Atka Iceport**

**¹Byrd Glacier.** 80°15′S, 160°20′E. 85 miles long, and 15 miles wide. Flows between the Britannia Range and the Churchill Mountains into the Ross Ice Shelf at Barne Inlet. The fastest (it flows at a rate of 7½ feet per day) and one of the largest of the Antarctic glaciers, it was named by the New Zealanders for Richard Byrd.

**²Byrd Glacier**  see  **Byrdbreen**

**Byrd Head.** 67°27′S, 61°01′E. Also called Bergnes. A headland 1 mile SE of the Colbeck Archipelago, just west of Howard Bay. Discovered in Feb. 1931 by the BANZARE, and named by Mawson for Richard Byrd.

**Byrd Land**  see  **Marie Byrd Land**

**Byrd Mountains**  see  **Harold Byrd Mountains**

**Byrd Névé.** 81°S, 154°E. A gigantic névé at the head of Byrd Glacier. Named in association with the glacier.

**Byrd–South Pole Overland Trek.** Also called the Byrd-Pole Tractor Train. 1960–61. The first American land party to traverse to the South Pole. An 11-man party, Task Group 43.4, led by Major Antero Havola, US Army, left Byrd Station on Dec. 8, 1960, taking two 38-ton D-8 tractors (the heaviest pieces of equipment to arrive by land at the Pole to that date), two sledge-mounted wanigans, three 20-ton sledges, one 10-ton sledge, and two tracked Weasels. The other men were Forrest Dowling, Meredith Radford, Walter Davis, Edward Martens, Marvin Madling, James Douglas, S.F. Mahan, Willard Cunningham, and Henry Rosenthal. CWO George W. Fowler was land navigator and scout, and went up ahead in a Weasel, while a VX-6 (q.v.) Dakota aircraft scouted the terrain ahead. Using an untraveled route across Marie Byrd Land, and via the eastern end of the Horlick Mountains, they arrived at South Pole Station 34 days later, on Jan. 11, 1961.

**Byrd Station.** Lonely US scientific base set up in 1957 at 79°59′S, 120°01′W, in Marie Byrd Land, at an elevation of 5,012 feet above sea level, and 885 miles from McMurdo Sound. Named for Admiral Byrd, it was established for the US involvement in the IGY by Operation Deep Freeze II, as an all-year station. Little America V was its home base, 600 miles away. It had 11 buildings, and was designed to hold 25 people. Its first program (1957) was the same as that of South Pole Station (see **Amundsen-Scott South Pole Station**), and its first wintering-over party, that year, consisted of 23 personnel — 10 military under Dr. Brian C. Dalton, lt. USN, and 13 IGY scientists under Dr. George R. Toney. The "Byrd Knights," aside from the two leaders, were meteorologists Wesley R. Morris, R.S. Johns, N.F. Helfert, and Ed A. Alf; seismologists Charles Bentley and N.A. Ostenso; gravity physicist Anthony J. Morency; aurora and airglow specialist Dan P. Hale; ionosphere physicist Virgil W. Barden; the Argentine glaciologist observer Mario B. Giovinetto; and the other two IGY scientists, Anderson and Reynolds. The USN personnel were radioman Gordon Abbey; electronics man W.D. Welch; and D.D. Blubaugh, R.D. Marsh, C.C. Brinton, W.L. Nichols, Jack R. Penrod, W.E. Lowe, and Davis. On Dec. 8, 1957, Peter Ruseski took over from Dalton, and S.S. Barnes took over from Toney, both for the 1958 winter. Edward Galla was military leader for the 1959 winter, and scientific leader was John Pirrit. By 1960 the ice and snow were crushing the station, and the site for a new one was selected on Nov. 10, 1960. It was built by Lt. Dave de Vicq and his 65 Seabees, beginning on Dec. 12, 1960. This was New Byrd Station (the old one is now known as Old Byrd Station) or New Byrd for short. It is 6.1 miles away from the old station, and has 15 buildings. Its new exact location is 80°00′37.224″S, 119°30′07.443″W, at the site of the Byrd Airfield. On Jan. 19, 1972, it became a summer-only station, after having been continuously occupied since Feb. 13, 1962. It is now known as Byrd Surface Camp, and is a fuel stop and weather station for planes flying between McMurdo Station and other destinations, such as the Siple Station area. It consists of sledge-mounted modules.

**Byrd Subglacial Basin.** A subsurface feature centering on 85°S, 125°W. The major subglacial basin of West Antarctica, it is beneath Marie Byrd Land. Named by the USA in 1961 for Admiral Byrd.

**Byrd VLF Station.** A small outpost of Byrd Station, about 15 miles from it, set up in 1965, and nicknamed "Longwire

Station" because its principal piece of equipment was a 21-mile-long radio antenna. It was built on the surface, but was covered by snow until it lay beneath the ice. It was composed of 3 trailer vans covered by a big Jamesway hut. It tested very low frequency radio waves (hence its name). It was closed permanently on Dec. 1, 1970, the last complement of staff including 2 women, Irene Peden (the scientific leader) and Julia Vickers.

**Byrdbreen.** 72°25′S, 26°30′E. Also called Byrd Glacier (the English translation of the Norwegian original). 40 miles long. 11 miles wide. A glacier flowing between Mount Bergersen and Balchen Mountain, in the Sør Rondane Mountains of Queen Maud Land. Named by the Norwegians for Richard Byrd.

**Byrd's 1928–30 Expedition.** This was Richard Byrd's first expedition to Antarctica. He was already an American hero, having flown over the North Pole and across the Atlantic Ocean. The expedition was backed by the likes of John D. Rockefeller, Jr., Edsel Ford, Charles Evans Hughes, Vincent Astor, Paul Block, Harold S. Vanderbilt, and the American Geographical Society. There were two ships that took the men down. The *City of New York* left Hoboken, N.J., on Aug. 25, 1928, bound for Panama. The *Eleanor Bolling* left Norfolk, Va., on Sept. 25, 1928, with Laurence Gould, Haines, and McKinley aboard. A third party of Byrd's men went on the Norwegian whaler *Sir James Clark Ross,* a fast vessel, which transported the dogs as well as Walden, Vaughan, Goodale, and Crockett. The fourth party of Byrd's men went on the *C.A. Larsen.* Both of these Norwegian ships left Norfolk, Va., the *C.A. Larsen* taking the airplanes aboard. These ships had volunteered to assist Byrd in transporting men and supplies to Antarctica. Byrd, Brophy, Owen, Shropshire, Roth, Van der Veen, and Lofgren crossed the USA by land and boarded the *C.A. Larsen* at San Pedro. On Oct. 10, 1933, they put out to sea, and by that date all four ships were in the Pacific, en route to New Zealand. On Nov. 5, 1928, the *C.A. Larsen* docked at Wellington, NZ, and on Nov. 18, 1928, the *Eleanor Bolling* arrived. On Nov. 26, 1928, the *City of New York* arrived at Dunedin, NZ. The *C.A. Larsen* then went whaling in Antarctic waters. On Dec. 2, 1928, the *City of New York*, with Byrd aboard, sailed with the *Eleanor Bolling* in tow, and on Dec. 28, 1928, they reached 62°10'S, 174°27'E. The following day they saw their first Antarctic iceberg, and on Dec. 10, 1928, Byrd saw and confirmed the existence of Scott Island, unseen since Colbeck sighted it in 1903. On Dec. 11, 1928, the *Eleanor Bolling,* as planned, broke away from its tow to the lead ship and returned to New Zealand. The *C.A. Larsen* then took the *City of New York* in tow, in order to get it through the pack-ice, on Dec. 12, 1928. On Dec. 13, 1928, the *Sir James Clark Ross* got stuck in the pack ice. On Dec. 17, 1928, the *C.A. Larsen* and the *City of New York* were at 69°07' S, and in the pack-ice. On Dec. 23, 1928, the two ships got through the pack-ice to emerge in the Ross Sea, and at that point the *C.A. Larsen* left to go whaling. On Dec. 25, 1928, Byrd sighted the Ross Ice Barrier (as the Ross Ice Shelf was then called), and reached it at 177°25'W. On Dec. 26, 1928, they moored in Discovery Inlet. Alton Parker was the first ashore. Meantime the *Eleanor Bolling* had reached NZ on Dec. 20, 1928. (For dates of the expedition while in the Antarctic, *see also* the Chronology appendix). Byrd unloaded the ship at the Bay of Whales, and created his base, Little America. He had brought 95 sledge dogs, 3 airplanes (the *Floyd Bennett,* the *Stars and Stripes,* and the *Virginia*), a tractor, radio, and 650 tons of equipment. This expedition was a mixture of the old and the new, but it really heralded the new age of mechanized Antarctic exploration, as well as the USA's re-entry into the field of Antarctica. By early Jan. 1929 Little America was completed. The 1929 wintering-over shore party comprised Byrd, Laurence Gould (second-in-

command), Balchen, C.D. Alexander, George H. Black, Blackburn, Braathen, Bubier, Bursey, Arnold H. Clark, Coman, Crockett, Czegka, Frank T. Davies, de Ganahl, Demas, Feury, Goodale, Chips Gould, Haines, Malcolm Hanson, Henry Harrison, June, Lofgren, Mason, McKinley, Mulroy, O'Brien, Owen, Parker, Carl Petersen, Martin Rønne, Roth, Rucker, Siple, Dean Smith, Strom, Tennant, Thorne, Van der Veen, Vaughan, and Walden. On Jan. 15, 1929, Byrd made his first Antarctic flight, and on Jan. 27, 1929, Byrd and Balchen flew across the Ross Ice Shelf, discovering the Rockefeller Mountains. On March 7, 1929, the first airborne expedition ended in disaster (*see* **Airlifts**). On Nov. 4, 1929, Larry Gould led his 6-man Southern Geological Party (himself, Barter, Foster, Kessler, Goodale, and Clark) to survey the Queen Maud Mountains. They returned to Little America on Jan. 19, 1930. The highlight of the entire expedition, however, was Byrd's flight to the Pole and back in the *Floyd Bennett.* At 3:29 p.m. (GMT), on Nov. 28, 1929, Thanksgiving Day, the plane took off from Little America, with Balchen (pilot), Byrd (navigator and commander), June, and McKinley. At 8:45 p.m. they sighted Gould's party below on the Ross Ice Shelf, and parachuted some supplies, messages, and aerial photos taken by McKinley on Nov. 18. The plane reached the Transantarctic Mountains and Byrd chose to fly up the Liv Glacier. They had to jettison perhaps 300 pounds of food to be able to clear the plateau ridge at the top of the glacier. At 1:14 a.m., on Nov. 29, 1929, Byrd radioed Little America that the Pole had been reached. Byrd dropped a US flag weighted by a stone from Floyd Bennett's grave (the late Floyd Bennett had been Byrd's pilot over the North Pole, and a close friend). They failed to find Amundsen's Carmen Land, and at 4:47 a.m., on Nov. 29, 1929, they made their first landing, at their fuel cache at the foot of the Queen Maud Mountains. This cache had been laid on Nov. 18. About 6 a.m. they took off again, arriving back at Little America at 10:08 a.m., on Nov. 29, 1929, after 18 hours 39 minutes, of which 17 hours 26 minutes had been in the air. 1,600 miles had been covered. On Dec. 5, 1929, the Edsel Ford Range and Marie Byrd Land were discovered. Little America was closed on Feb. 19, 1930, and the expedition returned home. The crew of the *Eleanor Bolling* consisted of Gustav Brown, McGuinness, Harry R. King, McPherson, Cody, Thawley, Haldor Barnes, Grenlie, Shrimpton, Barter, Buys, Denson, Carroll B. Foster, Fritzson, Kessler, Olsen, Perkins, Perks, Sjogren, Womack, Harry Adams, Samson, H. Austin, Blair, Dobson, Gavronski, Harvey, J. Jones, Newbold, Paape, and Reichart. The crew of the *City of New York* consisted of Melville, Bendik Johansen, Harry Adams, S.D.I. Erickson, Shropshire, Esmonde O'Brien, Bayer, Sutton, Berkner, Arthur Berlin, Boehning, Creagh, Strom, Gavronski, Greason, John Jacobson, Konter, Reichart, Roos, Vojtech, Wallis, A.B. Robinson, Willcox, Orbell, W.J. Armstrong, John Bird, Brustad, Eva, Gribben, Leuthner, Lockwood, J. Robinson, Innes-Taylor, Woolhouse, R. Young. Some of these names appear more than once. That is because they changed ships for the second half of the expedition. Also, some of these ship's crewmen took part in land parties, even though they were not members of the 1929 winteringover shore party. This is a complete list of all the direct participants in the expedition, and all have their own entries.

**Byrd's 1933-35 Expedition.** This was Byrd's second expedition to Antarctica. The expedition left Boston in Oct. 1933, in two ships, the *Bear of Oakland* and the *Jacob Ruppert*. On Jan. 17, 1934, they arrived at the Bay of Whales. For dates during this expedition see the Chronology Appendix. Little America II was set up on top of their old base, and the shore party of 56 men were Byrd, Poulter (second-in-command), Haines (third-in-command), Abele, Clay Bailey, Richard

Black, Blackburn, Bramhall, Boyd, Bowlin, Carbone, Leroy Clark, Corey, Cox, Dane, Demas, Dustin, Dyer, Eilefsen, Fleming, Grimminger, Herrmann, Jo Hill, Jr., Hutcheson, Innes-Taylor, June, Lewisohn, Lindsey, McCormick, Miller, Moody, Morgan, Murphy, Noville, Paige, Pelter, Perkins, Carl Peterson, Paine, Potaka, Finn Ronne, Rawson, Russell, Siple, Skinner, Stancliffe, Sterrett, Schlossbach, Ralph W. Smith, Swan, Tinglof, Von der Wall, Wade, Waite, H.R. Young, and Zuhn. There were 3 airplanes, the *William Horlick,* the *Miss American Airways,* and the *Blue Blade.* There was also an autogiro, the first in Antarctica, the *Pep Boy's Snowman!* There were 153 dogs, 4 head of cattle, and 4 tractors. This was the largest motorized squadron to date in Antarctica, and in one year the tractors covered 12,500 miles of snow and ice. Between Sept. 27 and Oct. 18, 1934, a 4-man party went in one of the Citroën tractors to lay dumps of food every 35 miles and a depot at Mount Grace McKinley 230 miles from Little America, for the benefit of a sledge party which would later travel into Marie Byrd Land. They arrived back with only 25 gallons of fuel left, and proved the worth and practicality of automotive land transport in Antarctica. The airplanes explored 450,000 square miles of territory. A purely scientific expedition, no attempt was made to reach the Pole, although Byrd winteredover alone at Bolling Advance Weather Station, 123 miles from Little America, from March 28 to Aug. 10, 1934 (*see* **Byrd, Richard E.**), almost dying in the process. The expedition gathered masses of scientific information, and almost certainly disproved the existence of the Ross-Weddell Graben. Harold E. Saunders was cartographer to the expedition, although he didn't personally go down. (*See also* **C.D. Alexander, Victor Czegka, Jack La Gorce.**) The following were the ships' officers and crew: J.D. Albert, H. Bayne, Peter Barbedes, B.O.J. Bradley, H.R. Burt, Leland L. Barter, Louis P. Colombo, L.W. Cox,

A.B. Creagh, E.W. Christian, W.H. Clement, J.A. Callahan, A. Christensen, P. Dempster, Gordon B. Desmond, P.O. Dornan, Percy Dymond, O.E. Davis, N.B. Davis, T.J. D'Amico, W.H. Dornin, H. Dickey, Robert A.J. English, J.A. Ellis, H.L. Fleming, George J. Frizzell, Jr., Robert Fowler, Gordon Fountain, Hjalmar Gjertsen, Philip Gargan, W.P. Gaynor, F.W. Giroux, James McGillies, E.H. Griffiths, G.J. Garner, Edward A. Griswold, J. Hawley, Joseph D. Healy, H.A. Hambleton, W.B. Highet, T. Johnson, Bendik Johansen, T.W. Joss, L.H. Kennedy, G. Kerr, Paul Kallenberg, T.E. Litchfield, G.P. Lindley, W.H. Lowd, Howard Lawson, J.J. Muir, John H. Morrison, Peter MacCurrach, Jr., T.M. McLennon, John McNamara, M.P. MacKintosh, D.R. Mackintosh, G.M. Mitchell, Cecil Melrose, Walfred Miller, John Murphy, William McCristel, J.V. Mathias, Neville Newbold, Victor Niewoehner, B.P. O'Brien, Irving Spencer Ortiz, S.A. Pinkham, B.W. Paul, W.K. Queen, Stephen D. Rose, A.G.B. Robinson, J. Robinson, C.P. Royster, P.E. Round, W.A. Robertson, R.S. Robinson, S. Edward Roos, J.W. Sorensen, F.H.P. Schonyan, F.W. Smoothy, S.J. Sullivan, J.G. Sisson, W.C. Stewart, T. Sanderson, E.L. Tigert, F.C. Voight, Rudolph Van Reen, Thomas Van Reen, W.F. Verlager, R.D. Watson, G.B. Wray, and Max Winkle.

**Bystander Nunatak.** 71°21'S, 159°38' E. 2,435 m. 5 miles SW of Forsythe Bluff, on the west side of the Daniels Range, in the Usarp Mountains. Named descriptively by the New Zealanders in 1963–64.

**Bystrov Rock.** 71°47'S, 12°35'E. 1 mile SSE of Isdalsegga Ridge in the Südliche Petermann Range of the Wohlthat Mountains of Queen Maud Land. Named by the USSR in 1966 for paleontologist A.P. Bystrov.

**Byvågåsane Peaks.** 69°25'S, 39°48'E. Three aligned peaks surmounting the eastern shore of Byvågen Bay on the east side of Lützow-Holm Bay. Photographed

by the LCE 1936–37, and later named Byvågåsane (the town bay peaks) by the Norwegians, in association with Byvågen Bay.

**Byvågen Bay.** 69°23'S, 39°44'E. A small indentation into the eastern shore of Lützow-Holm Bay, between Skarvsnes Foreland and Byvågåsane Peaks. Photographed by the LCE 1936–37, and later named Byvågen (the town bay) by the Norwegians.

**Byway Glacier.** 66°30'S, 65°12'W. A tributary of the Erskine Glacier, flowing from Slessor Peak in Graham Land. Named by the UK in 1958 because it is a sledging route inferior to the one up the Erskine Glacier.

**The *C.A. Larsen*.** Enormous Norwegian factory whaling ship, of 8,000 hp, and 17,000 tons displacement, Many times in Antarctic waters in the 1920s, it volunteered to play a part in Byrd's 1928–30 expedition. Under the command of Capt. Nilsen, it took a quarter of Byrd's crew, and the airplanes for the expedition, out of Norfolk, Va., in 1928, went around to San Pedro, Calif., and thence to New Zealand, docking at Wellington on Nov. 5, 1928. It then went whaling in Antarctic waters. It later met up with Byrd's ship, the *City of New York*, and towed that ship through the pack-ice. On Dec. 17, 1928, they were at 69°07'S, and on Dec. 23, 1928, they broke through the ice into the Ross Sea. At that point the *C.A. Larsen* went off whaling again.

**Isla Caballete** *see* **Ridge Island**

**Mount Cabeza.** 64°09'S, 62°11'W. Also called Mount Morgagni. On the SE side of Paré Glacier, 1 mile SW of Hales Peak, in the NE portion of Brabant Island. It was first named, as Monte Cabeza (head mountain), on a 1957 Argentine hydrographic chart. This was a descriptive name.

**Cabinet Inlet.** 66°30'S, 63°W. 36 miles long. 27 miles wide at its entrance. It is a Larsen Ice Shelf indentation into the east coast of the Antarctic Peninsula, between Cape Alexander and Cole Peninsula. Named by the FIDS for the British war cabinet, which authorized Operation Tabarin (the precursor of the FIDS) in 1943.

**Islas Cabrales** *see* **Hennessy Islands**

**Cabrera Nunatak.** 75°46'S, 128°12'W. 6½ miles NE of Putzke Peak, in the McCuddin Mountains of Marie Byrd Land. Named for Quirino Cabrera, USN, construction mechanic at Byrd Station in 1966 and 1969.

**The** *Cacapon.* American tanker in the Western Task Group of Operation Highjump, 1946–47. Captain Ray A. Mitchell commanding.

**Cacapon Inlet.** 66°10'S, 101°E. 2 miles wide. 9 miles long. Between Thomas Island and Fuller Island, in the Highjump Archipelago. Bounded on the west by the Edisto Ice Tongue and on the east by the coast. Named for the *Cacapon.*

**Cachalot Peak.** 65°38'S, 62°16'W. 1,040 m. Between the Stubb and Starbuck Glaciers, 3½ miles west of Mount Queequeg, near the east coast of Graham Land. Named by the UK for a type of whale.

**Cachalot Rock.** 60°48'S, 45°47'W. A term no longer used. Seems to have been a rock to the SW of Buchan Bay, Laurie Island, in the South Orkneys. Named for a type of whale.

**Cache Heights.** 73°28'S, 94°05'W. 3 miles long. 2 miles wide. Snow-covered. Just NE of Bonnabeau Dome in the Jones Mountains. Mapped and named by the University of Minnesota–Jones Mountains Party of 1960–61. A food cache placed here by the party during a blizzard was never recovered.

**Mount Cadbury.** 71°21'S, 66°38'W. 1,800 m. The most easterly of the Batterbee Mountains. ESE of Mount Ness, and 18 miles inland from the George VI Sound, on the west coast of Palmer Land. Surveyed by the BGLE in 1936, and named by the UK in 1954 for Mrs. Henry Tyler Cadbury, who helped get the *Penola* refitted in 1936.

**Cadenazzi Rock.** 76°18'S, 112°39'W. 1½ miles east of Roper Point, on the west slope of Mount Takahe, in Marie Byrd Land. Named for Lt. Michael P. Cadenazzi, USN, helicopter commander in Antarctica, 1969–70 and 1970–71.

**Cadete Guillochón Refugio.** Argentine refuge hut built in Bills Gulch in 1956.

**Cadle Monolith.** 71°40'S, 60°58'W. An isolated bare rock, or headland. At the east end of Condor Peninsula, 9 miles SE of Cape MacDonald, on the east coast of Palmer Land. Named for Gary L. Cadle, USN, electrician at Palmer Station, 1973.

**Cadman Glacier.** 65°37'S, 63°49'W. 1½ miles wide at its mouth. 7 miles long. Flows into the head of the southern arm of Beascochea Bay, on the west side of the Antarctic Peninsula. Discovered and charted by Charcot in 1909. Surveyed in 1935 by the BGLE. Later named by the UK for Lord Cadman, patron of the BGLE 1934–37.

**Cadwalader Beach.** 76°59'S, 166°54'E. Nearly a mile long. At the south end of Beaufort Island, in the Ross Archipelago. There is a large Adélie penguin rookery here. Named by the NZGSAE 1958–59 for Capt. John Cadwalader, USN, who assisted the expedition.

**Cadwalader Inlet.** 72°04'S, 96°18'W. 22 miles long. Ice-filled. Indentation into the NE coast of Thurston Island, between the Evans and Lofgren Peninsulas. Discovered in Feb. 1960 on helicopter flights from the *Burton Island* and the *Glacier.* Named for Capt. John Cadwalader (*see* **Cadwalader Beach**).

**Cady Nunatak.** 77°13'S, 142°51'W. 3 miles east of Mount Zeigler, in the NE part of the Allegheny Mountains, in the Ford Ranges of Marie Byrd Land. Named for Frederick M. Cady, ionosphere physicist at Byrd Station in 1968.

**Café Point.** 64°39'S, 61°59'W. Also called Lana Point. 2 miles south of Zapato Point. 2 miles east of Nansen Island, on the west coast of Graham

Land. Charted by de Gerlache in 1897–99.

**Cagle Peaks.** 79°33′S, 85°28′W. A group that surmounts the southern end of the White Escarpment, in the Heritage Range. Named by the University of Minnesota Geological Party in 1963–64 for Major Paul M. Cagle, helicopter commander who assisted the party.

**Cahoon, Sister Mary Odile.** A biologist. A teaching nun from Saint Scholastica College in Duluth, Minn., she lived at McMurdo Station in 1974 under the direction of Dr. Mary Alice McWhinnie.

**Cain Nunatak.** 63°34′S, 57°42′W. The more westerly of two isolated nunataks on the south side of Broad Valley, in Trinity Peninsula. Named by the FIDS in 1960–61 for nearby Abel Nunatak.

**Caird Coast.** 76°S, 24°30′W. Also called Caird Land. Between the terminus of the Stancomb Wills Glacier (20°W) and the Hayes Glacier (27°54′W), it is one of the coasts of Coats Land. Discovered by Shackleton on Jan. 12, 1915, and named by him for Scottish jute magnate, Sir James Caird, principal backer of the British Imperial Transantarctic Expedition of 1914–17.

**Cairn Hill.** 63°30′S, 57°04′W. Has two summits, the higher being 475 m. 2 miles east of Duse Bay and 1 mile SW of Mineral Hill, on Tabarin Peninsula. Charted by the FIDS in 1946, and named by them for a cairn they built on the eastern of the two summits.

**Cairn Ridge.** 82°35′S, 52°50′W. On the north side of the Dufek Massif, 2 miles NE of Hannah Peak, in the Pensacola Mountains. A cairn was built here during a visit in Dec. 1957 by the US-IGY traverse party from Ellsworth Station.

**Mount Calais.** 69°11′S, 70°15′W. Also called Calais Massif. 2,345 m. At the NW side of Schokalsky Bay, in the extreme NE part of Alexander Island. Surveyed in 1909 by Charcot, who named it for the French city.

**The _Calcaterra_.** US ship DER-390. In Antarctica in 1965–66, 1967–68.

**Mount Caldwell.** 72°04′S, 101°46′W. In the Walker Mountains, 3 miles SE of Mount Lopez, near the west end of Thurston Island. Named for Capt. Henry Howard Caldwell.

**Caldwell, Henry H.** USN. Henry Howard Caldwell. Captain of the _Pine Island_ during Operation Highjump, 1946–47. On Dec. 30, 1946, he narrowly escaped death when the plane in which he was an observer crashed during a white-out, killing Hendersin, Lopez, and Williams.

**Calf Point.** 71°30′S, 169°45′E. Between the terminus of the Nielsen Glacier and Penelope Point, on the west shore of Robertson Bay, in northern Victoria Land. Charted by Campbell's Northern Party during the British Antarctic Expedition of 1910–13, and named by them in 1911 for the calf seals here.

**Calf Rock.** 70°31′S, 68°38′W. 500 m. On the east coast of Alexander Island. 2 miles NE of Lamina Peak, and 2 miles inland from the George VI Sound. Surveyed in 1949 by the FIDS, and named by them for its calved position from Lamina Peak.

**Calfee Nunatak.** 74°19′S, 161°40′E. Isolated. On the east side of the Reeves Névé, 4 miles west of Mount Fenton, in Victoria Land. Named for David W. Calfee, field assistant at McMurdo Station in 1965–66.

**California Plateau.** 86°04′S, 145°10′W. 30 miles long. Between 2 and 12 miles wide. Ice-covered. Undulating. Rises to 3,000 meters at the eastern side of the Robert Scott Glacier. Its maximum height is Mount Blackburn (3,275 m.) at the southern end. The Watson Escarpment is on the north side. Named for the California universities which have sent researchers here.

**Caliper Cove.** 73°33′S, 166°56′E. Rounded. Ice-filled. In Lady Newnes Bay, between the mouths of Wylde and Suter Glaciers, on the coast of Victoria Land. Named by NZ in 1966 for its likeness to calipers.

**Calkin Glacier.** 77°46'S, 162°17'E. Flows from the Kukri Hills to the terminus of the Taylor Glacier, near the Wright Valley of Victoria Land. Just west of Sentinel Peak. Charted by Scott's 1910–13 expedition. Named for Parker Calkin, geologist here in 1960–61 and 1961–62.

**Callahan, J.A.** Crewman on the *Bear of Oakland,* 1933–35.

**Callender Peak.** 75°18'S, 110°19'W. Mainly ice-covered. On the Mount Murphy massif. 9 miles ENE of the summit of Mount Murphy itself, in Marie Byrd Land. Named for Lt. Gordon W. Callender, USN, officer-in-charge of Byrd Station in 1966.

**Callisto Cliffs.** 71°03'S, 68°20'W. 550 m. Two cliffs. One forms the southern edge of Jupiter Glacier, the other the eastern edge of Alexander Island. Named by the UK for Callisto, one of the moons of the planet Jupiter.

**Cape Calmette.** 68°04'S, 67°13'W. On the western extremity of a peninsula, it forms the southern shore of Calmette Bay, on the west coast of Graham Land. Discovered in 1909 by Charcot, who thought it was an island, and named it Île Calmette for Gaston Calmette, editor of *Figaro,* a supporter. Redefined by the BGLE 1934–37.

**Calmette Bay.** 68°03'S, 67°10'W. Between Camp Point and Cape Calmette on the west coast of Graham Land, in the north of Marguerite Bay, just north of Stonington Island. Charted by the BGLE 1934–37, who named it in association with the cape.

**Caloplaca Cove.** 60°43'S, 45°35'W. Between Rethval Point and Pantomime Point, on the east coast of Signy Island. Named by the UK for the type of lichens found here.

**Caloplaca Hills.** 86°07'S, 131°W. East of the Watson Escarpment, on the west side of the Reedy Glacier. They include Mount Carmer and Heathcock Peak. Named by John H. Mercer for the caloplaca here.

**Mount Calvin.** 71°17'S, 165°06'E. Over 1,600 m. 4 miles SE of Pilon Peak, in the southern part of the Everett Range. Named for Lt. Calvin Luther Larsen, USN, navigator and VX-6 photographer in Antarctica in 1969. He had been chief photographer's mate at Little America V in 1957.

**Calving.** The discharging of icebergs into the sea from ice-shelves, ice-sheets, or glaciers around the coast, as they break off. Icebergs also calve into smaller ones. Warning: if you set up base on an ice-shelf, it might calve into the sea, leaving you stranded.

**The *Calypso.*** Jacques Cousteau's vessel. Anchored at Palmer Station in the 1972–73 summer season.

**Calypso Cliffs.** 68°48'S, 64°13'W. Two cliffs rising to 850 m. On the south side of Mobiloil Inlet, just west of the mouth of Cronus Glacier, on the east coast of the Antarctic Peninsula. Named by the UK for the Greek mythological figure.

**Cam Rock.** 60°43'S, 45°37'W. 200 yards east of Waterpipe Beach, and 200 yards NNW of Billie Rocks, in Borge Bay, Signy Island, in the South Orkneys. Surveyed and descriptively named by the personnel on the *Discovery* in 1927.

**Mount Camber.** 64°41'S, 63°16'W. 1,400 m. Snow-covered. 1 mile NE of Molar Peak, in the Osterrieth Range of Anvers Island. First seen by de Gerlache in 1897–99. Named High Peak by J.M. Chaplin (q.v.), here in 1927 with the Discovery Committee, on the *Discovery.* Surveyed in 1955 by the FIDS. Renamed by the UK for its camberlike summit.

**Cambrian Bluff.** 82°25'S, 160°33'E. Forms the south end of the Holyoake Range, just to the north of the Queen Elizabeth Range, on the other side of the Nimrod Glacier. Named by the New Zealanders in 1960–61 because of its Cambrian rock of pink and white marble.

**Cambridge Glacier.** 76°58'S, 160°30'E. Between the Convoy Range and the Coombs Hills, flowing into the Mackay

Glacier, between Mount Bergen and Gateway Nunatak. Surveyed in 1957 by the NZ Northern Survey Party of the BCTAE, and named by them for Cambridge University, where many Antarctic scientific reports were written.

**Camel Nunataks.** 63°25'S, 57°26'W. Two similar rock nunataks rising to 450 m. 1 mile apart. 8 miles north of View Point, Trinity Peninsula. Named descriptively by the FIDS about 1959.

**Camelback Ridge.** 73°31'S, 94°24'W. Just west of Pemmican Bluff, in the Jones Mountains. Mapped by the University of Minnesota–Jones Mountains Party of 1960–61, and named by them for its humped appearance.

**Camell, William.** On Oct. 1, 1719, this sailor fell from the mainsail and drowned, reputedly at about 60°37'S, 5° W, during Shelvocke's voyage.

**Mount Camelot.** 72°11'S, 163°37'E. 2,590 m. The highest peak in the Alamein Range. Named by NZ in 1968.

**Camels Hump.** 77°56'S, 162°34'E. 2,320 m. A dark, bare, rock knob (small mountain). 3 miles south of Cathedral Rocks, in the northern part of the Royal Society Range, in Victoria Land. Discovered and named descriptively by members of Scott's 1901–4 expedition.

**Cameras** *see* **Photography, Aerial photography**

**Mount Cameron.** 71°20'S, 66°30'E. 5 miles south of Mount Woinarski, in the Prince Charles Mountains. Named by the Australians for Dr. A.S. Cameron, medical officer at Mawson Station in 1965.

**Cameron, Richard L.** Chief American glaciologist on the IGY (1957–58), based at Wilkes Station in 1957.

**Cameron Island.** 66°13'S, 110°36'E. A small island, just north of Hailstorm Island, in the Swain Islands. Named by Carl Eklund in 1957 for Richard L. Cameron.

**Cameron Nunataks.** 72°38'S, 163°43' E. A small cluster of nunataks on the west margin of the Evans Névé, at the south end of the Freyberg Mountains. Named for Roy E. Cameron, biologist at McMurdo Station in 1966–67 and 1967–68.

**Camp Hill.** 63°41'S, 57°52'W. 120 m. Ice-free. 2 miles east of Church Point, on the south side of Trinity Peninsula. Charted by the FIDS in 1946, and named by them for the geological camp established at its foot.

**Camp Hills.** 78°56'S, 85°50'W. Between the south portion of the Bastien Range and the Minnesota Glacier, in the Ellsworth Mountains. Named by the University of Minnesota Geological Party of 1963–64, for their base camp (Camp Gould) here.

**Camp Lake.** 68°33'S, 78°05'E. ½ mile west of the head of Weddell Arm on Breidnes Peninsula, in the Vestfold Hills. A camp was established near the NE end of the lake in Jan. 1955, by the first visitors, an ANARE party.

**Camp Norway** *see* **Norway, Camp**

**Camp Point.** 67°58'S, 67°19'W. Between Square Bay and Calmette Bay, on the west coast of Graham Land. Discovered by Charcot in 1908–10. The BGLE 1934–37 camped here, hence the name.

**Camp Ridley** *see* **Ridley, Camp**

**Camp Spur.** 83°16'S, 50°50'W. On the north wall of May Valley, in the Forrestal Range of the Pensacola Mountains. Named for Gary C. Camp, aerographer at Ellsworth Station in 1957.

**Cape Campbell** *see* **Cape Tennyson**

**Monte Campbell** *see* **Mount Pond**

**Mount Campbell.** 84°55'S, 174°W. 3,790 m. 3½ miles SE of Mount Wade, in the Prince Olav Mountains. Discovered by the USAS 1939–41. Surveyed by Albert Crary in 1957–58, and named by him for Joel Campbell of the US Coast and Geodetic Survey, Antarctic Project

Leader for geomagnetic operations, 1957–60.

**Campbell, Clifford M.** Cdr., USN. Commander of Base Group at Little America IV during Operation Highjump, 1946–47. He was senior officer on Flight A during Byrd's flight to the Pole on Feb. 16, 1947.

**Campbell, Dr.** Doctor/naturalist on the *Diana* during the Dundee Whaling Expedition of 1892–93.

**Campbell, Lord George.** Sub-lieutenant on the *Challenger,* 1872–76.

**Campbell, Robert.** Private on the Wilkes Expedition 1838–42. Joined in the USA. Served the cruise.

**Campbell, Stuart A.C.** Flight lt. RAAF pilot on the BANZARE 1929–31. Later a group captain. In 1947–48 he established an ANARE station on Heard Island (53°S). In 1948 he led the first ANARE party to Antarctica, scouting George V Land for a base.

**Campbell, Victor.** Victor L.A. Campbell, RN. On the emergency list to go on Scott's 1910–13 expedition, he led the Northern Party that wintered-over twice in Victoria Land, in 1911 and 1912. He served in the Royal Navy during World War I, retired to Newfoundland in 1922, and died in 1956.

**Campbell Cliffs.** 84°46'S, 174°55'E. Mostly snow-covered. Form the east wall of Haynes Table, in the Hughes Range. Discovered aerially on Flight A of Feb. 16, 1947, during Byrd's flight to the Pole, on Operation Highjump, 1946–47. Named for Cdr. Clifford M. Campbell.

**Campbell Glacier.** 74°25'S, 164°22'E. Also called Melbourne Glacier. 60 miles long. Starts near the end of the Mesa Range, and flows between the Deep Freeze Range and Mount Melbourne, in Victoria Land, and terminates at Terra Nova Bay in the form of the Campbell Glacier Tongue. Named for Victor Campbell.

**Campbell Glacier Tongue.** 74°36'S, 164°24'E. The seaward extension of the Campbell Glacier, in Victoria Land. It juts out into the Ross Sea at Terra Nova Bay. Named in association with the glacier.

**Campbell Head.** 67°25'S, 60°40'E. On the west side of Oom Bay. Discovered in Feb. 1931 by the BANZARE, and named by Mawson for Stuart Campbell.

**Campbell Hills.** 82°26'S, 163°47'E. 5 miles WSW of Cape Lyttelton, on the south side of the Nimrod Glacier, in the central Transantarctic Mountains. Named for William J. Campbell, glaciologist on the Ross Ice Shelf in 1962–63.

**Campbell Nunatak.** 66°29'S, 110°45'E. Also seen as Nunatak Kempbell. At the SE limit of the Windmill Islands, on the coast, overlooking the SE extremity of Penney Bay, 3 miles ENE of the Alexander Nunataks. Named for H. Campbell, Jr., Operation Windmill photographer, 1947–48.

**Campbell Ridges.** 70°23'S, 67°35'W. An irregular complex of ridges between Creswick Gap and Mount Courtauld, in Palmer Land. Named for Lt. Cdr. Bruce H. Campbell, USN, LC-130 Hercules commander on the Lassiter Coast and elsewhere in 1969–70 and 1970–71.

**Campbell Valley.** 76°55'S, 117°40'W. Ice-filled. Between the Crary Mountains and Boyd Ridge, in Marie Byrd Land. Named for Wallace H. Campbell, ionosphere physicist at McMurdo Station in 1964–65.

**Mount Campleman.** 84°51'S, 64°20'W. 1,970 m. Flat-topped. On the north edge of Mackin Table. 3 miles west of Stout Spur, in the Patuxent Range of the Pensacola Mountains. Named for Richard Campleman, USN, petty officer in charge of Palmer Station in 1967.

**Canada.** On May 4, 1988, Canada was ratified as the 38th signatory of the Antarctic Treaty.

**Canada Glacier.** 77°36′S, 163°E. Flows into the north side of Taylor Glacier, just west of Lake Fryxell, in the Taylor Valley of southern Victoria Land. It is SSSI #12. Charted by Scott's 1910–13 expedition, and named by them for Charles S. Wright's home.

**Punta Candado**  *see*  **Stone Point**

**Punta Canelo**  *see*  **Duthiers Point**

**Cangrejo Cove.** 65°04′S, 63°39′W. Also called Bahía Chávez. 1½ miles long. Just west of Azure Cove in Flandres Bay, on the west coast of Graham Land. Charted by de Gerlache in 1897–99. Named Bahía Cangrejo (crawfish bay) by the Argentine Antarctic Expedition of 1951–52. Seen from the air, the cove resembles a crawfish.

**Mount Canham.** 70°29′S, 64°35′E. At the north end of the Bennett Escarpment. 2 miles south of the Corry Massif, in the Porthos Range of the Prince Charles Mountains. Named by the Australians for J.R. Canham, officer-in-charge at Wilkes Station in 1967.

**Canham, David W., Jr.** Lt. cdr., USN. First base commander at AirOpFac (the base that later became McMurdo Base), for the winter of 1956.

**Canham Glacier.** 71°49′S, 163°E. 30 miles long. Flows from the NW part of the Evans Névé, between the Alamein and Salamander Ranges of the Freyberg Mountains, and enters Rennick Glacier to the west of Bowers Peak, in Oates Land. Named for Lt. Cdr. David Canham.

**Mount Canicula.** 63°43′S, 58°28′W. Formed of two rock peaks, one at 890 meters, and the other at 825 meters. 3 miles east of Sirius Knoll, between Russell East Glacier and Russell West Glacier, in the central part of Trinity Peninsula. Charted in 1946 by the FIDS,

and named by them. Canicula = Sirius, the star.

**Caninus Nunataks.** 71°06′S, 70°10′W. On Alexander Island.

**Canis Heights.** 70°26′S, 66°19′W. Snow-covered ridge between the two upper tributaries of the Millett Glacier. On the west edge of the Dyer Plateau of Palmer Land. Named by the UK for the constellations Canis Major and Canis Minor.

**The *Canisteo*.** US tanker with the Eastern Task Group during Operation Highjump, 1946–47. Captain Edward K. Walker commanding.

**Canisteo Peninsula.** 73°48′S, 102°20′W. 30 miles long. 20 miles wide. Ice-covered. Between Ferrero and Cranton Bays, in the eastern extremity of the Amundsen Sea. Named for the *Canisteo*.

**Cann, Roswell.** 1st class boy on the Wilkes Expedition 1838–42. Joined in the USA. Lost on the *Sea Gull* in late April 1839.

**Cannonball Cliffs.** 71°47′S, 68°15′W. At the south side of the terminus of the Neptune Glacier, on the east side of Alexander Island. Named by the UK for the "cannonball" concretions in the sandstone here.

**Cañon Point.** 64°34′S, 61°55′W. Also called Icarus Point. Marks the SW side of the entrance to Bancroft Bay, on the west coast of Graham Land. Charted by de Gerlache in 1897–99, and named by the Argentinians before 1954.

**Lake Canopus.** 77°33′S, 161°31′E. Just above the southern shore of Lake Vanda, in Victoria Land. Named by the 8th VUWAE, in 1963–64, for Canopus, pilot of Menelaus, King of Sparta.

**Mount Canopus.** 81°50′S, 161°E. 1,710 m. Ice-free. On the west edge of the Nash Range, 4½ miles east of Centaur Bluff. Named by the New Zealanders in 1960–61 for the star.

**Canopus Crags.** 71°10′S, 66°38′W. A cluster of peaks extends for 3 miles between Vela Bluff and Carina Heights, on the south side of Ryder Glacier, in Palmer Land. Named by the UK for the star Canopus (in the constellation Carina).

**Canopus Island.** 67°32′S, 62°59′E. The southern of the two largest of the Canopus Islands, in Holme Bay, which were photographed by the LCE 1936–37, mapped by the Norwegians as one island, and named Spjotøy by them. Renamed and redefined by the ANARE in 1959, for the star Canopus.

**Canopus Islands.** 67°32′S, 62°59′E. A group of small islands just north of the Klung Islands, in the eastern part of Holme Bay. Photographed by the LCE 1936–37. Named in 1959 by the ANARE for the star Canopus. This group comprises Canopus Island and Canopus Rocks.

**Canopus Pond.** Unofficial name given to a small, undrained pond, 200 feet by 200 feet, ½ mile SW of Lake Vanda, in Victoria Land. During winter it is frozen completely to the bottom.

**Canopus Rocks.** 67°31′S, 62°57′E. Two small rocks, 1 mile NW of Canopus Island, in the eastern part of Holme Bay. Named by the Australians for Canopus Island, which, with these rocks, forms a major part of the overall group called the Canopus Islands.

**Canopy Cliffs.** 84°S, 160°E. Extend from Mount Allsup to Mount Ropar on the SE side of the Peletier Plateau, in the Queen Elizabeth Range. They are precipitous cliffs, and were descriptively named by the New Zealanders in 1961–62.

**Canso Rocks.** 63°39′S, 59°18′W. Two rocks, west of Bone Bay. 2 miles NW of Notter Point, Trinity Peninsula. Named by the UK for the Canso aircraft used by the FIDASE in 1955–57.

**Mount Cantello.** 70°52′S, 163°07′E. 1,820 m. On the north side of Crawford Glacier, 4 miles NW of Mount Keith, in the Bowers Mountains. Named for Dominic Cantello, Jr., USN, electrician at Amundsen-Scott South Pole Station in 1965.

**Canto Point.** 62°27′S, 59°44′W. Also called Spark Point. Forms the NW side of the entrance to Discovery Bay, Greenwich Island. For a few years after 1935 this was wrongly called Fort William (q.v. for details), and in 1947 it was surveyed by the Chilean Antarctic Expedition of that year, who named it for Capitán del Canto (see **Del Canto**).

**Cantrell Peak.** 71°12′S, 165°13′E. 1,895 m. 6 miles NNE of Mount Calvin. Overlooks Ebbe Glacier, in the northern part of the Everett Range. Named for Major Robert L. Cantrell, US Marines, pilot in Antarctica in 1968 and 1969.

**Canty Point.** 64°45′S, 63°32′W. Forms the west side of the entrance to Börgen Bay, on the SE coast of Anvers Island. Charted by de Gerlache in 1897–99. Surveyed by the FIDS in 1955. Named by the UK for John Canty, FIDS radio operator/mechanic at Base N in 1955, and a member of the sledging party that visited this point.

**Canvas tanks** *see* **Tanks**

**Cape Canwe.** 74°43′S, 163°41′E. Also called Cape Mossyface. A bluff 3 miles north of Vegetation Island. It forms the western extremity of the Northern Foothills, in Victoria Land. Explored and named by Campbell's Northern Party during Scott's 1910–13 expedition. "*Can we* reach it?" asked they, from afar.

**Canyon Glacier.** 83°57′S, 175°20′E. 35 miles long. Flows from the NW slopes of Mount Wexler, between steep canyon walls (hence the name), between the Hughes Range and the Commonwealth Range in the Queen Maud Mountains, into the Ross Ice Shelf just west of the Giovinco Ice Piedmont. Named by the New Zealanders in 1959–60.

**Canyons.** Submarine features, notably off the East Antarctica coast: Nash, Porpoise, Carroll, Ketchum, Kuznetsov, d'Urville, Mawson, Somov, Leonard, Mertz; and those off the Ross Ice Shelf: Bowers, Scott, Hillary, Shackleton.

Cape Adare Peninsula *see* Adare Peninsula

Cape Armitage Promontory *see* Hut Point Peninsula

Cape Barne Glacier *see* Barne Glacier

Cape Bird Station. NZ summer station at Cape Bird, Ross Island.

Cape Keeler Advance Base. An advance base built on Cape Keeler, in the Antarctic Peninsula, by the RARE 1947–48, 125 miles from their main base on Stonington Island. It was built on Sept. 29, 1947, and dismantled on Dec. 22, 1947. It was used as a field base for exploring parties.

Cape petrels *see* Petrels

Cape pigeon. Or pintado. *Procellario capensis,* or *Daption capense.* A bird sometimes seen in Antarctica.

Cape-Pigeon Rocks. 66°58′S, 143°50′E. Twin rocky promontories forming a headland on the west side of Watt Bay, 3 miles south of Garnet Point. Discovered by the AAE 1911–14, and named by Mawson for the large Cape Pigeon rookery here.

Capella Rocks. 70°39′S, 66°32′W. A low, rocky ridge comprising several nunataks, near the head of Bertram Glacier, 2 miles NE of Auriga Nunataks, in Palmer Land. Named by the UK for the star Capella.

Monte Capitán *see* Doumer Hill

Capitán Arturo Prat Station. 62°29′S, 59°38′W. Year-round Chilean scientific station on the coast of Discovery Bay, Greenwich Island, in the South Shetlands. Named for naval hero Arturo Prat Chacón, it was established by the Chilean Antarctic Expedition of 1946–47 under Guesalaga, in Feb. 1947, the first Chilean Antarctic station. Leaders of the first wintering parties were 1947 Boris Kopaitic O'Neil, 1948 Francisco Araya Prorromont, 1949 Augusto Varas Orrego, 1950 Fernando Dorión, 1951 Gaston Kulczewski, 1952 Julio Navarrete, 1953 Ramón Capetillo, 1954 Hernán Sepúlveda, 1955 Galvarino Sazo, 1956 Julio Tagle, 1957 Edgardo T. Apel.

Capitán Estivariz Refugio. Argentine refuge hut built on Watkins Island in the Biscoe Islands, in 1956.

Monte Capitán Mendioroz *see* Mount William

Mount Capley. 79°33′S, 83°12′W. 1,810 m. In the Nimbus Hills. Named for Lt. Cdr. Joe H. Capley, USN, pilot in Antarctica in 1965 and 1966.

Capling Peak. 72°26′S, 167°08′E. 2,730 m. On the north side of the Croll Glacier, 5 miles SE of Bramble Peak, in the Victory Mountains of Victoria Land. Named for Robert W. Capling, USN, flight engineer at McMurdo Station in 1967 and 1968.

Cappellari Glacier. 85°52′S, 158°40′W. 11 miles long. In the Hays Mountains. Flows from the NW shoulder of Mount Vaughan, to enter the Amundsen Glacier, just north of Mount Dort, in the Queen Maud Mountains. Named for Lewis K. Cappellari, ionosphere physicist at McMurdo Station in 1965.

Cappus, Contra Almirante Harald. Leader of Argentine Naval maneuvers in the South Shetlands and the Palmer Archipelago, in 1948. His ships were the *Veinticinco de Mayo,* the *Almirante Brown,* the *Entre Ríos,* the *San Luís,* the *Misiones,* the *Santa Cruz,* the *Mendoza,* the *Cervantes,* the *Patagonia,* the *Ushuaia,* and other auxiliary vessels.

Capsize Glacier. 74°02′S, 163°20′E. In the Deep Freeze Range. It flows between Mount Cavaney and Mount Levick, to enter Campbell Glacier, in Victoria Land. Named by the New Zealanders in 1965–66 because of the alarming capsize that the Northern Party of the NZGSAE had there that season.

Capstan Rocks. 64°57′S, 63°26′W. A small group, 1 mile south of Bob Island, in the southern entrance to Gerlache Strait, off the west coast of Graham Land. Named descriptively by the UK.

Mount Cara. 82°45′S, 161°06′E. 3,145 m. 4 miles NNW of Mount Lysaght, in the Queen Elizabeth Range. Named by Shackleton in 1907–9.

**Carapace Nunatak.** 76°54′S, 159°24′E. An isolated nunatak just to the north of the Mackay Glacier, near the head of that glacier, just west of the Convoy Range, in Victoria Land. 8 miles SW of Mount Brooke. Named in 1957 by the NZ party of the BCTAE for the carapaces of small crustaceans found in the rocks here.

**The *Caraquet*.** Liverpool sealing ship in the South Shetlands, 1821–22. Captain J. Usher.

**Caraquet Rock.** 62°07′S, 59°02′W. 4 miles WSW of Bell Point, off the west part of King George Island, in the South Shetlands. Named by the UK in 1960 for the *Caraquet*.

**Mount Carbone.** 76°22′S, 144°30′W. 3 miles east of Mount Paige, in the Phillips Mountains of Marie Byrd Land. Discovered aerially during Byrd's 1928–30 expedition. Named by Byrd later, for Al Carbone.

**Carbone, Al.** Cook on the shore party of Byrd's 1933–35 expedition.

**Carbutt Glacier.** 65°09′S, 62°49′W. Enters the Goodwin Glacier to the east of Maddox Peak, just east of Flandres Bay, on the west coast of Graham Land. Named by the UK in 1960 for John Carbutt (1832–1895), photography pioneer.

**Mount Cardell.** 70°13′S, 65°10′E. 2 miles NW of Bradley Ridge, in the Athos Range of the Prince Charles Mountains. Named by the Australians for N. Cardell, senior electronics technician at Mawson Station in 1964.

**Cardell Glacier.** 66°25′S, 65°32′W. Flows into Darbell Bay between Shanty Point and Panther Cliff, on the west coast of Graham Land. Named by the UK in 1959 for John D.M. Cardell, snow goggles designer.

**Mount Cardinall.** 63°27′S, 57°10′W. 675 m. SW of Mount Taylor, it overlooks the NE head of Duse Bay, at the NE end of the Antarctic Peninsula. Discovered by Dr. J. Gunnar Andersson's party in 1903, during Nordenskjöld's expedition. Charted in 1945 by the FIDS, and named

by them for Sir Allan Cardinall, governor of the Falkland Islands.

**Cardozo Cove.** 62°10′S, 58°37′W. The northern of two coves at the head of Ezcurra Inlet, Admiralty Bay, King George Island, in the South Shetlands.

**Care Heights.** 69°25′S, 70°50′W. In the NW part of Alexander Island.

**Carey, W.M.** Cdr., RN. First captain of the *Discovery II*, in 1929–31. He was its captain again in 1931–32.

**Carey Glacier.** 78°53′S, 83°55′W. On the east side of Miller Peak, in the south end of the Sentinel Range, flowing into Minnesota Glacier. Named for Lt. David W. Carey (*see* **Deaths, 1956**).

**Carey Range.** 72°53′S, 62°37′W. On the east side of Palmer Land.

**Cargo ships.** Some are ordinary ships, others are designed specifically for Antarctica. Usually they have reinforced hulls, sloping bows, and very powerful engines. The controls are normally at the top of the ship so the captain can plot his course far ahead of time.

**Caria, Maria Adela.** Prof. Argentine hydrographer who, in 1968–69, became one of the first women scientists to work on the continent (*see* **Women in Antarctica**).

**Carina Heights.** 71°09′S, 66°08′W. Near the head of Ryder Glacier, at the west edge of the Dyer Plateau of Palmer Land. Named by the UK for the constellation Carina.

**Carleton Glacier.** 78°01′S, 162°29′E. Flows from the NW slopes of Mount Lister, in the Royal Society Range, into Emmanuel Glacier. Named for Carleton College, Northfield, Minn., which has sent researchers here.

**Carlota Cove.** 62°22′S, 59°42′W. Between Coppermine Peninsula and Misnomer Point, on the west coast of Robert Island, in the South Shetlands. Named Bahía Carlota by the Chileans before 1961.

**Carlson Buttress.** 82°35′S, 52°27′W. In the Pensacola Mountains.

**Carlson Glacier.** 69°25'S, 68°03'W. On the west side of Palmer Land.

**Carlson Inlet.** 78°S, 78°30'W. 100 miles long. 25 miles wide. Ice-filled. Between the Fletcher Ice Rise and the Fowler Ice Rise, in the SW part of the Ronne Ice Shelf. Named for Lt. Ronald F. Carlson, USN, pilot often in Antarctica in the 1950s and 1960s. On Dec. 14, 1961, his flight photographed this feature.

**Carlson Island.** 63°53'S, 58°16'W. Also called Wilhelm Carlson Island. 1 mile long. 300 meters high. In the Prince Gustav Channel, 3 miles SE of Pitt Point. Discovered in 1903 by Nordenskjöld's expedition, and named by Nordenskjöld for Wilhelm Carlson, a major patron.

**Carlson Peak.** 75°57'S, 70°33'W. In the Bean Peaks of the Hauberg Mountains. Named for Paul R. Carlson, meteorologist at Byrd Station in 1965–66.

**Carlsson Bay.** 64°24'S, 58°04'W. Also called J. Carlson Bay, John Carlson Bucht (both erroneous spellings). 2½ miles in extent. 3 miles NW of Cape Foster, on the SW side of James Ross Island. Discovered by Nordenskjöld's expedition in 1903, and named by them for J. Carlsson of Sweden, a supporter.

**Carlyon, Roy A.** Surveyor in the NZ party during the BCTAE 1957–58. He and Ayres made up the Darwin Glacier Party of that season.

**Carlyon Glacier.** 79°37'S, 160°E. Flows from the névé east of Mill Mountain, in the northern portion of the Cook Mountains, and feeds the Ross Ice Shelf through the Hillary Coast. Mapped in 1958 by the Darwin Glacier Party of the BCTAE, and named by NZ for Roy Carlyon.

**Carmen Land.** South of the Queen Maud Mountains, en route to the Pole. Discovered by Amundsen in 1911, but Byrd failed to confirm its existence when he flew over this area in Nov. 1929. Subsequent explorations have failed to turn up the elusive Carmen Land. Perhaps it was a mirage.

**Mount Carmer.** 86°06'S, 131°11'W. On the east side of Wotkyns Glacier, 2 miles WNW of Heathcock Peak, in the Caloplaca Hills. Named for John L. Carmer, electronics technician at Byrd Station in 1962.

**Carmey, Isaac.** 1st class boy on the Wilkes Expedition 1838–42. Joined in the USA. Served the cruise.

**Bahía Carminatti** *see* **Ambush Bay**

**The** *Carnarvon Castle.* In 1943 this British ship, under the command of Capt. E.W. Kitson, recovered a bronze cylinder deposited by the pro–Nazi Argentinians on Deception Island the year before. This cylinder claimed possession of all land between 25°W and 68°34'W. It was replaced by a British flag and record of visit. The cylinder was returned to Argentina.

**Carnations.** *Colobanthus crassifolius.* These flowers are found on Jenny Island, Graham Land, and nowhere else in Antarctica, it seems.

**Carnein Glacier.** 74°41'S, 162°54'E. Flows from the SE corner of the Eisenhower Range, then along the west side of the McCarthy Ridge, to merge with the lower Reeves Glacier at the Nansen Ice Sheet, in Victoria Land. Named for Carl R. Carnein, glaciologist at McMurdo Station in 1965–66.

**Carnell Peak.** 79°28'S, 85°18'W. 1,730 m. In the Watlack Hills, 2½ miles from the SE end of that group, in the Heritage Range. Named for Lt. D.L. Carnell, USN, maintenance officer at Williams Field, 1965–66.

**Mount Carnes.** 77°39'S, 161°21'E. 2 miles east of Saint Pauls Mountain, in the Asgard Range of Victoria Land. Named for Philip A. Carnes, engineering and construction manager for ITT/ Antarctic Services (q.v.), who supervised construction and maintenance performed at Amundsen-Scott South Pole Station, Siple Station, and McMurdo Station in 1973–74, 1974–75 and 1975–76.

**Carnes Crag.** 71°28'S, 162°41'E. 1310 m. In the NW extremity of the Lanterman Range of the Bowers Mountains. Overlooks the junction of Sledgers Glacier and Rennick Glacier. Named for James J. Carnes, USN, chief electrician's mate at McMurdo Station in 1967.

**Carney Island.** 73°57′S, 121°W. 70 miles long. Ice-covered. Between Siple Island and Wright Island, it lies mostly within the Getz Ice Shelf, on the coast of Marie Byrd Land. Named for Adm. R.B. Carney, USN, chief of naval operations during the organization of Operation Deep Freeze, in the pre–IGY period.

**The *Caroline*.** Australian sealer out of Hobart, Tasmania, under the command of Capt. D. Taylor. It was in the South Shetlands in the 1821–22 season. On March 17, 1825, it was wrecked on Macquarie Island (not in Antarctica), and the crew was rescued by the *Wellington* in Aug. of that year.

**Caroline Bluff.** 61°55′S, 57°42′W. 1 mile SE of North Foreland on King George Island, in the South Shetlands. Charted and named North Foreland Head by David Ferguson in 1921. The UK later changed the name, for the *Caroline*.

**Mount Caroline Mikkelsen.** 69°45′S, 74°24′E. 235 m. 4 miles NNW of Svarthausen Nunatak. Between Hargreaves Glacier and Polar Times Glacier, on the Ingrid Christensen Coast of the American Highland, in the area of Prydz Bay. Discovered on Feb. 20, 1935, by Klarius Mikkelsen, and named for his wife, Caroline.

**Carpenter Island.** 72°39′S, 98°03′W. 7 miles long. Oval-shaped. In the Abbott Ice Shelf of Peacock Sound. 17 miles east of Sherman Island. Named for Donald L. Carpenter, radio scientist at Byrd Station in 1966–67.

**Carpenter Nunatak.** 73°37′S, 61°15′E. Isolated. Between Mount Mather and the Mount Menzies massif in the southern Prince Charles Mountains. Named by the Australians for G.D.P. Smith, carpenter at Mawson Station in 1961.

**Cape Carr.** 66°07′S, 130°51′E. Ice-covered. 15 miles NE of Cape Morse, on the Wilkes Coast. Discovered by Wilkes on Feb. 7, 1840, and named by him for Overton Carr.

**Carr, Charles.** b. 1891. Charles Roderick Carr. Aviator on the *Quest*, 1921–22. Later became an air marshal in the RAF.

**Carr, Overton.** USN. First lieutenant on the *Vincennes* during the Wilkes Expedition of 1838–42.

**Carrefour.** 66°50′S, 139°18′E. A small French station 25 miles SW of Dumont d'Urville Station.

**Mount Carrel.** 63°26′S, 57°03′W. 650 m. Horseshoe-shaped. At the east side of Depot Glacier. 1½ miles south of Hope Bay, at the NE end of the Antarctic Peninsula. Discovered by Dr. J. Gunnar Andersson's party in 1903, during Nordenskjöld's expedition of 1901–4. Named by the FIDS in 1945 for Tom Carrel.

**Carrel, Tom.** Bosun on the *Eagle*, 1944–45, during the second phase of Operation Tabarin.

**Carrel Island.** 66°40′S, 140°01′E. Also known as Île Alexis Carrel. ¼ mile long. 175 yards south of Pétrel Island, in the Géologie Archipelago. Charted in 1950 by the French, and named by them for the French surgeon, Alexis Carrel (1873–1944).

**Isla Carrera** *see* **Piñero Island**

**Punta Carrera Pinto** *see* **Rock Pile Point**

**Carro Pass.** 63°57′S, 58°09′W. Links Holluschickie Bay and the bay between Rink Point and Stoneley Point, on the NW coast of James Ross Island. Named for Capitán Ignacio Carro, who first traversed the pass in 1959.

**Mount Carrol Kettering** *see* **Mount Giles**

**Carroll, Arthur J.** Chief aerial photographer on the flights from East Base during the USAS 1939–41.

**Carroll Canyon.** 64°30′S, 130°E. Submarine feature off the Wilkes Coast.

**Carroll Inlet.** 73°18'S, 78°30'W. 40 miles long. 6 miles wide. Between Rydberg Peninsula and Smyley Island, on the English Coast. Case Island is in the middle of it. Discovered aerially on Dec. 22, 1940, by the USAS and named for Arthur J. Carroll.

**Carryer Glacier.** 71°17'S, 162°38'E. 12 miles long. Heavily crevassed. Flows from the central part of the Bowers Mountains into Rennick Glacier, between Mount Soza and Mount Gow. Named by the Northern Party of the NZGSAE 1963–64, for S.J. Carryer, geologist with the party.

**Carse, Verner D.** Verner Duncan Carse. Member of the BGLE 1934–37. Father of V. Duncan Carse, leader of 4 expeditions to South Georgia (54°S) in the 1950s.

**Carse Point.** 70°13'S, 68°13'W. On the south side of the mouth of Riley Glacier, Palmer Land. It fronts on the George VI Sound. Surveyed in 1936 by the BGLE, and named by the UK in 1954 for Verner D. Carse.

**Mount Carson.** 73°27'S, 163°10'E. 2 miles west of the Chisholm Hills, in the Southern Cross Mountains of Victoria Land. Named for Gene A. Carson, USN, construction electrician at McMurdo Station in 1963 and 1967.

**Carsten Borchgrevinkisen** see **Borchgrevinkisen**

**Carstens Shoal.** 67°34'S, 62°51'E. Just north of East Budd Island, in Holme Bay, Mac. Robertson Land. Charted in Feb. 1961 by d'A.T. Gale, hydrographic surveyor on the *Thala Dan* during the ANARE of that year. Named by the Australians for D.R. Carstens, surveyor at Mawson Station in 1962, who assisted the hydrographic survey of 1961.

**Carter, William.** Captain of the maintop during the Wilkes Expedition 1838–42. Joined in the USA. Served the cruise.

**Carter Island.** 73°58'S, 114°43'W. A small, ice-covered island just off the west side of Martin Peninsula, in the Amundsen Sea. Named for Lt. G.W. Carter, USN, maintenance coordinator at Williams Field, 1966.

**Carter Peak.** 70°19'S, 64°12'E. 1 mile west of Mount Bensley and 9 miles SW of Mount Starlight, in the Prince Charles Mountains. Named by the Australians for D.B. Carter, electronics technician at Mawson Station in 1965.

**Carter Ridge.** 72°37'S, 168°37'E. 11 miles long. Between Coral Sea Glacier and Elder Glacier, in the Victory Mountains of Victoria Land. Named for Herbert E. Carter, chemist, member of the National Science Board, National Science Foundation, 1964–72, and chairman of that organization from 1970–72.

**Mount Cartledge.** 70°17'S, 65°43'E. Just east of Mount Albion, in the Athos Range of the Prince Charles Mountains. Named by the Australians for W.J. Cartledge, plumber at Wilkes Station in 1962, and carpenter at Mawson Station in 1966.

**Cartographers Range.** 72°21'S, 167°50'E. 25 miles long. In the Victory Mountains of Victoria Land. Named for the cartographers of the US Geological Survey.

**Cartography** see **Map making**

**Mount Cartwright.** 84°21'S, 175°08'E. 3,325 m. 7 miles NNW of Mount Waterman in the Hughes Range. Discovered by the USAS 1939–41 on Flight C of Feb. 29–March 1, 1940. Surveyed by Crary in 1957–58, and named by him for Gordon Cartwright, the first US exchange scientist to a USSR station, at Mirnyy Station in 1957.

**Casabianca Island.** 64°49'S, 63°31'W. In the Neumayer Channel. ½ mile NE of Damoy Point, on Wiencke Island. Discovered by Charcot in 1903–5, and named by him for M. Casabianca, French administrator of Naval Enlistment.

**Cascade Bluff.** 84°57'S, 178°10'W. Ice-covered. Forms the SW wall of Mincey Glacier, in the Queen Maud Mountains. Named by the Texas Tech Shackleton Glacier Party of 1962–63 because of the water cascading over this bluff in the summertime.

**Cascade Glacier**  *see*  **Delta Glacier**

**Point Case.** A term no longer used. On Jan. 23, 1840, Wilkes was in a body of water that he called Disappointment Bay and he saw a feature on the coast of what is now George V Land. He named it for A.L. Case. It may well be what we call Mount Hunt today (*see* **Cape de la Motte** for further details).

**Case, A.L.** Lt., USN. Joined the *Vincennes* at Callao for the Wilkes Expedition 1838–42.

**Case Island.** 73°19′S, 77°48′W. 12 miles wide. Circular. Ice-covered. Off the coast of Ellsworth Land. It is in the middle of Carroll Inlet, between the mainland and Smyley Island. Named by Finn Ronne for Senator Francis H. Case, supporter of the RARE 1947–48.

**Cape Casey.** 66°22′S, 63°35′W. Surmounted by a peak of 755 m. Marks the east end of the peninsula projecting into Cabinet Inlet, just south of Bevin Glacier, on the east coast of Graham Land. Named by the FIDS for Richard G. Casey, Australian statesman.

**Mount Casey.** 73°43′S, 165°47′E. 2,100 m. On the north side of the head of Oakley Glacier, 5 miles ENE of Mount Monteagle, in the Mountaineer Range of Victoria Land. Named for Lt. Dennis Casey, USNR, chaplain at McMurdo Station in 1967.

**Casey Bay.** 67°20′S, 48°E. Also called Lena Bay. Between Tange Promontory and Dingle Dome, or between the Prince Olav Coast and the Mawson Coast, in Enderby Land. Named by the Australians for Richard G. Casey (*see* **Cape Casey**).

**Casey Channel**  *see*  **Casey Glacier**

**Casey Glacier.** 69°S, 63°50′W. 6 miles wide. Flows from the Scripps Heights into the Larsen Ice Shelf at Casey Inlet, on the east coast of the Antarctic Peninsula. Discovered aerially by Wilkins on Dec. 20, 1928. He thought it was a chan-

nel cutting right across the Antarctic Peninsula, and named it Casey Channel for Richard G. Casey (*see* **Cape Casey**). It also became known as Casey Strait, and was later redefined.

**Casey Inlet.** 69°S, 63°35′W. Ice-filled. At the terminus of the Casey Glacier, between Miller Point and Cape Walcott, on the east coast of Palmer Land. Named in association with the glacier.

**Casey Islands.** 64°44′S, 64°16′W. Off the west coast of Graham Land.

**Casey Range.** 67°47′S, 62°12′E. A razor-backed ridge and a few nunataks in a line. 8 miles west of the David Range, in the Framnes Mountains. Discovered by the BANZARE 1929–31, and named by Mawson for Richard G. Casey (*see* **Cape Casey**).

**Casey Station.** 66°16′S, 110°32′E. Year-round Australian scientific station on the Budd Coast of Wilkes Land. Construction was begun in Jan. 1965, and it was finally ready in Jan. 1969. It was opened on Feb. 19, 1969. It replaced Wilkes Station, which had been used by the Australians since the summer of 1958–59 when the Americans left. There are 12 buildings set on elevated frames in a line across the prevailing wind, with a half-round passageway, facing the wind, connecting them.

**Casey Strait**  *see*  **Casey Glacier**

**Cassandra Nunatak.** 64°27′S, 63°24′ W. 425 m. Marks the east side of the mouth of Iliad Glacier, in the northern part of Anvers Island. Named by the UK for the character in the Iliad.

**Cassedy, Alfred.** Ordinary seaman on the Wilkes Expedition 1838–42. Joined in the USA. Run at Callao.

**Monte Cassino**  *see under* **M**

**Castillo Point.** 75°30′S, 141°18′W. Ice-covered. Marks the east side of the terminus of Land Glacier, on the coast of Marie Byrd Land. Named for Rudy Castillo, USN, aerographer with the Marie Byrd Land Survey Party of 1968, and at Hallett Station in 1969.

**The Castle** *see* **Mount Macey**

**Castle Crags.** 82°01'S, 159°12'E. 4 miles north of Hunt Mountain, on the ridge extending north from the Holyoake Range. Named descriptively by the New Zealanders in 1964–65.

**Castle Peak.** 67°S, 65°53'W. 2,380 m. Ice-covered. Just south of Murphy Glacier and just to the west of the Avery Plateau, in Graham Land. Surveyed by the FIDS in 1946, and named by them for its appearance.

**¹Castle Rock** *see* **Fort Point**

**²Castle Rock.** 62°48'S, 61°34'W. 175 m. A rugged island in the South Shetlands, 2 miles off the west side of Snow Island. Named descriptively before 1822.

**³Castle Rock.** 77°48'S, 166°46'E. 415 m. (1,350 feet). A high, precipitous-sided rock with a flat top. 3 miles NE of Hut Point, it is the most conspicuous landmark on Hut Point Peninsula, Ross Island. Discovered and named descriptively by Scott in Feb. 1902.

**The** *Castor.* Norwegian sealer, under the command of Capt. Morten Pedersen, in the South Shetlands in the 1893–94 season, in company with the *Hertha.*

**Castor Insel** *see* **Castor Nunatak**

**Castor Nunatak.** 65°10'S, 59°55'W. Also spelled Kastor Nunatak. 3 miles SW of Oceana Nunatak, in the Seal Nunataks, off the east coast of the Antarctic Peninsula. First seen by Larsen in 1893, and he mapped it as an island which he called Castor Insel, for the *Castor.* Redefined by Nordenskjöld's expedition in 1902.

**Mount Castro.** 69°20'S, 66°06'W. 1,630 m. On the north side of Seller Glacier, 5 miles SE of Mount Gilbert, in the central part of the Antarctic Peninsula. Named by the UK for João de Castro (1500–1548), Portuguese navigator.

**Casy Island.** 63°14'S, 57°30'W. Also called Casy Rock. The largest island in a group of small islands 2 miles SE of Lafarge Rocks, and 3 miles NE of Coup-vent Point, off the north side of the Trinity Peninsula. Discovered and named by Dumont d'Urville in 1837–40.

**Casy Rock** *see* **Casy Island**

**Cat Island.** 65°47'S, 65°13'W. ½ mile long. Between Duchaylard and Larrouy Islands, at the south end of the Grandidier Channel. Discovered and named by the BGLE 1934–37.

**Cat Ridge.** 71°10'S, 61°50'W. In the middle of Gain Glacier, in eastern Palmer Land. It is descriptive when viewed from the NE.

**Catacomb Hill.** 78°04'S, 163°25'E. 1,430 m. On the east side of Blue Glacier in Victoria Land. The granite of the peak has been weathered into spectacular caverns, hence the name given by the NZ Blue Glacier Party of the BCTAE, who established a survey station on its summit in Dec. 1957.

**Caterpillar Tractors.** Have been used in Antarctica since Scott took 3 with him on his 1910–13 expedition. He and Charcot had tested these sledges equipped with a motor and caterpillar tracks in the Alps before Scott took them south on the *Terra Nova.* D-6s were used on Operation Highjump, 1946–47, and there has been a wide range of tracked vehicles used in Antarctica.

**The** *Catharina.* US sealing brig of 160 tons and 71 feet long. Registered in New London on July 17, 1820, it took part in Alexander Clark's expedition to the South Shetlands in the summer of 1820–21. Captain Joseph Henfield commanded, and Elof Benson was the first mate. Mr. Perry (one of the mates), and another sailor, were drowned at the Falkland Islands on the way south on Oct. 27, 1820.

**Cathedral Crags.** 62°59'30"S, 60°34'W. 140 m. An ice-free hill that is actually a volcanic vent composed of massive, yellow lapilli breccia showing indistinct, nearly horizontal stratification. Between Neptunes Window and Fildes Point, on Deception Island, in the South Shetlands. Pre–1930 whalers called it the

Convent, or Weathercock Hill, and it was renamed before 1953.

**Cathedral Peaks.** 84°45'S, 175°40'W. North of Lubbock Ridge, they extend for 8 miles on the east edge of the Shackleton Glacier. From the glacier they look like a cathedral. Named by Alton Wade in 1962–63.

**¹Cathedral Rocks** *see* **Granite Pillars**

**²Cathedral Rocks.** 77°51'S, 162°30'E. A series of 4 abrupt cliffs interspersed by short glaciers, and surmounted by sharp peaks. They extend for 8 miles along the south side of the Ferrar Glacier. They form part of the north shoulder of the Royal Society Range, in Victoria Land. Discovered on Dec. 7, 1902, by A.B. Armitage, and named descriptively by him.

**The *Catherine*.** American schooner which, under Smyley, sailed from Newport, R.I., on Sept. 10, 1845, going to the South Shetlands. It was wrecked against a glacier in 1846.

**Mount Catherine** *see* **Mount Kathleen**

**Catherine Sweeney Mountains** *see* **Sweeney Mountains**

**Catodon Rocks.** 63°28'S, 60°W. A small group just NE of Ohlin Island, in the Palmer Archipelago. Named by the UK in 1960 for the sperm whale *(Physeter catodon)*.

**Cats.** Not many have gone down to Antarctica. Lumus was the only one of the BGLE's cats to survive the 1935 winter.

**Catspaw Glacier.** 77°43'S, 161°42'E. Just west of Stocking Glacier, it flows from the slopes north of Taylor Glacier in Victoria Land. Named by Grif Taylor during Scott's 1910–13 expedition because of its resemblance to a cat's paw.

**The Catwalk.** 64°31'S, 60°56'W. A col between the Herbert and Detroit Plateaus, in northern Graham Land. Named descriptively by the UK in 1960.

**Caudal Hills.** 73°10'S, 161°50'E. Between the Sequence Hills and the Lichen Hills on the west edge of the upper Rennick Glacier, in Victoria Land. A series of spurs "tail" out to the north, hence the name "caudal" given by the New Zealanders in 1962–63.

**Caughley Beach.** 77°14'S, 166°25'E. Just south of Cape Bird in Ross Island. It is SSSI #10. Named by the New Zealanders for Graeme Caughley, biologist here in 1958–59.

**Caulfeild Glacier.** 66°11'S, 65°W. The northern of two glaciers flowing into Hugi Glacier, near the mouth of that glacier, on the west coast of Graham Land. Named for Vivian Caulfeild (1874–1958), British pioneer ski instructor.

**Punta Caupolicán** *see* **Entrance Point**

**Caution Point.** 65°16'S, 62°01'W. 4 miles NE of Mount Birks. Marks the east end of the north wall of Crane Glacier, on the east coast of Graham Land. Photographed aerially by Wilkins on Dec. 20, 1928. The FIDS charted and named it in 1947.

**Cavalier Rock.** 67°50'S, 69°28'W. Isolated. 13 miles SW of Cape Adriasola, off the south part of Adelaide Island. Named by the UK in 1963 for Sub.-lt. Geoffrey A. Cavalier, RN, helicopter pilot on the *Protector* that year.

**Mount Cavaney.** 74°03'S, 163°03'E. 2,820 m. Just north of the head of Capsize Glacier, in the Deep Freeze Range of Victoria Land. Named by the Northern Party of the NZGSAE 1965–66 for R.J. Cavaney, geologist with the party.

**Cave Island.** 62°27'S, 60°04'W. The second largest of the Meade Islands, it is a tiny island between Greenwich Island and Livingston Island, in the South Shetlands. Marked by a large cave on its south side. Charted by the personnel on the *Discovery II* in 1935, and named by them as Cave Rock. This name was also seen as Cove Rock. It was later redefined as an island.

**Cave Landing.** 66°22'S, 110°27'E. An ice foot near Cave Ravine, Ardery Island, in the Windmill Islands. Discovered in 1961 by Dr. M.N. Orton, medical officer at Wilkes Station that year. Named by the Australians in association with Cave Ravine.

**Cave Ravine.** 66° 22′ S, 110° 27′ E. A ravine 300 yards from the west end of Ardery Island, in the Windmill Islands. Named by the Australians because of the cave in the western wall of the ravine.

**Cave Rock**    *see*    **Cave Island**

**Cavenaugh, Lawrence.** Private on the Wilkes Expedition 1838–42. Joined in the USA. Served the cruise.

**Cavendish Icefalls.** 77° 49′ S, 161° 20′ E. Also called Cavendish Falls. In the Taylor Glacier, between Solitary Rocks and Cavendish Rocks, in Victoria Land. Named by Charles S. Wright during Scott's 1910–13 expedition, for the Cavendish Laboratory in Cambridge, where Wright researched.

**Cavendish Rocks.** 77° 50′ S, 161° 24′ E. Just south of the Cavendish Icefalls in the middle of Taylor Glacier, in southern Victoria Land. Named in 1964 in association with the icefalls.

**Caverns**    *see*    **Ice caverns**

**Cayley Glacier.** 64° 20′ S, 60° 58′ W. Flows into the south side of Brialmont Cove, on the west coast of Graham Land. Named by the UK in 1960 for Sir George Cayley (1773–1857), aeronautics pioneer and designer of the first caterpillar tractor, in 1826.

**Mount Caywood.** 75° 18′ S, 72° 25′ W. Between Mounts Chandler and Huffman in the Behrendt Mountains. Named for Lindsay P. Caywood, Jr., geomagnetist at Sky-Hi Station in 1961–62.

**CCAMLR.** Convention on the Conservation of Antarctic Marine Living Resources. The convention was negotiated at Canberra between May 7 and 20, 1980, and ratified in 1981. Sixteen countries signed it — the 2 Germanys, Argentina, Australia, Belgium, Chile, France, Japan, NZ, Norway, Poland, South Africa, USSR, USA, UK, and India. It went

into effect on April 7, 1982. It established a protection zone for marine organisms south of a line that zigzags between 45° S and 60° S (effectively the Antarctic Convergence), around the continent and all the way to the South Pole. A permanent secretariat is in Hobart, Tasmania, where they held the third convention to discuss limits to fin-fishing, and the recovery of fish stocks.

**Cecil Cave.** 68° 46′ S, 90° 42′ W. A sea cave, indenting the southern part of Cape Ingrid, on the west coast of Peter I Island. Discovered and named by personnel on the *Odd I* in Jan. 1927. Capt. Eyvind Tofte and the second mate rowed into the cave in an unsuccessful attempt to land on the island.

**The** *Cecilia*. A seminal figure in Antarctic history, this was the vessel from which John Davis made the first reputed landing on the continent, on Feb. 7, 1821. A small sealing schooner, it was taken along in kit form aboard the *Huron* from the USA, and assembled by Davis' men in the Falkland Islands. Also known as the *Young Huron* (probably a nickname), it served as tender (or shallop) to not only the *Huron,* but also the *Huntress.* A much-used little vessel, it was from Low Island that Davis made his first landing (*see* **Landings**), and later, on Feb. 15, 1821, Capt. Burdick sighted the continent from it. From Feb. 22 to 24, 1821, Capt. Donald McKay took it out on a cruise. It accompanied the *Huron* (q.v. for details of that vessel's cruise) from March 1821 to Feb. 1822, and made it back to the USA on June 29, 1822.

**Cecilia Island.** 62° 25′ S, 59° 43′ W. Also called Isla Torre. The most southerly of the Aitcho Islands, in the South Shetlands. Named by the UK in 1961 for the *Cecilia*.

**Cecilias Straits**    *see*    **English Strait**

**Mount Cecily.** 85° 52′ S, 174° 18′ E. 2,870 m. 2½ miles NW of Mount Raymond, in the Grosvenor Mountains. To the east of the Otway Massif, in the Queen Maud Mountains. Discovered by

Shackleton in 1907–9, and named by him for his daughter. Shackleton incorrectly thought it was in the Dominion Range.

**Celebration Pass.** 83°59'S, 172°31'E. Also called Ancestor Pass. Just north of Mount Cyril in the Commonwealth Range, it allows passage between the Beardmore and Hood Glaciers. Crossed on Christmas Day, 1959, by the NZ Alpine Club Antarctic Expedition of 1959–60, and named appropriately by them.

**Celestial Peak.** 69°33'S, 158°03'E. 1,280 m. A granite peak 8 miles north of Mount Blowaway, in the Wilson Hills. Named by the New Zealanders because of star observations made here by the NZGSAE 1963–64.

**Celsus Peak.** 64°25'S, 62°26'W. 2 miles west of D'Ursel Point, in the southern part of Brabant Island. Named by the UK for the Latin medical writer Celsus.

**Cemetery Bay.** 60°42'S, 45°37'W. A SW arm of Borge Bay, just below Orwell Glacier, on the east coast of Signy Island, in the South Orkneys. Named by the UK for the whalers' graves on the east side of the bay.

**Cemetery Lake.** In the Mule Peninsula of the Vestfold Hills.

**Cendron, Jean.** French medical doctor and biologist on the French Polar Expedition of 1951. In July 1951 he twice operated on a crewman for an intestinal obstruction.

**Punta Ceniza** *see* **Ash Point**

**Cenobite Rocks.** 67°35'S, 69°18'W. A small, isolated group 5 miles NW of Cape Adriasola, off the SW coast of Adelaide Island. Named by the UK in 1963 because the religious order of Cenobites are isolated too.

**Cenotaph Hill.** 85°13'S, 167°12'W. 2,070 m. Between the Strom and Liv Glaciers in the Queen Maud Mountains. 8 miles NNE of Mount Fridtjof Nansen. Visited by the Southern Party of the NZGSAE 1963–64, who named it for the cenotaph-type hill forming the summit.

**Centaur Bluff.** 81°50'S, 160°30'E. On the east side of the Surveyors Range, 4½ miles west of Mount Canopus. Named by the New Zealanders for the star Centauri, used here to fix survey stations.

**Centennial Peak.** 84°57'S, 174°W. 4,070 m. 6½ miles SSE of Mount Wade, in the Prince Olav Mountains. Named for the centennial of Ohio State University in 1970. Ohio State has sent many researchers here.

**Center Island** *see* **Centre Island**

**Central Masson Range.** 67°50'S, 62°52'E. Central part of the Masson Range. It extends 4 miles and rises to 1,120 m. Photographed by the LCE 1936–37, and later named Mekammen (the middle crest) by the Norwegians. Later still, in 1960, it was renamed by the Australians.

**Centre Island.** 67°52'S, 66°57'W. Also called Isla del Centro, and also spelled Center Island. 4 miles long. 2 miles wide. 1 mile south of Broken Island, in the southern part of Square Bay, off the west coast of Graham Land. Discovered and named by the BGLE 1934–37.

**Isla del Centro** *see* **Centre Island**

**Monte Centro** *see* **Pavlov Peak**

**Centurion Glacier.** 68°12'S, 66°56'W. Flows to Neny Bay between Mount Nemesis and Roman Four Promontory, on the west coast of Graham Land. Surveyed by the BGLE in 1936, and again in 1947 by the FIDS, who named it in association with Roman Four Promontory.

**Mount Cerberus.** 77°26'S, 161°53'E. Over 1,600 m. Between Lake Vida and Mount Orestes, in the Olympus Range of Victoria Land. Named by the New Zealanders for the three-headed dog of Greek mythology because of its many side peaks.

**Cerberus Peak.** 82°01'S, 158°46'E. 2,765 m. At the head of the Prince Philip Glacier, 6 miles NW of Hunt Mountain, in the Churchill Mountains. Named by the New Zealanders for the three-headed dog of Greek mythology.

**Ceres Nunataks.** 72°03'S, 70°25'W. 3 nunataks just east of the base of Shostakovich Peninsula, in southern Alexander Island. Named by the UK for the asteroid.

**The *Cervantes*.** Argentine destroyer which took part in the Argentine Naval maneuvers in the South Shetlands in 1948 under the general command of Contra Almirante Harald Cappus.

**Mount Cervin.** 66°40'S, 140°01'E. 30 m. A hill on the east side of Pétrel Island, in the Géologie Archipelago. Charted in 1951 by the French, and named by them because it resembles the European mountain of that name (also known as the Matterhorn).

**Cape Cesney.** 66°06'S, 133°54'E. Ice-covered. Marks the west side of the entrance to Davis Bay. Named for A.M. Cesney.

**Cesney, A.M.** Master's mate on the *Flying Fish* during the Wilkes Expedition 1838–42. Detached at Honolulu.

**Cetacea Rocks.** 63°43'S, 61°38'W. A small group off the NE side of Hoseason Island. Charted by Charcot in 1908–10. Named by the UK in 1960 for the cetacea (whales and porpoises).

**Cetus Hill.** 70°56'S, 66°10'W. Ice-covered. At the head of Ryder Glacier, in the western part of Palmer Land. 27 miles ENE of Gurney Point. Named by the UK for the constellation of Cetus.

**Cézembre Point.** 66°48'S, 141°26'E. ½ mile NE of Cape Margerie. Charted in 1950 by the French and named by them for an island in the Golfe de Saint-Malo, in France.

**Chabrier Rock.** 62°11'S, 58°18'W. ½ mile SW of Vauréal Peak, in the eastern side of the entrance to Admiralty Bay, King George Island, in the South Shetlands. Charted and named in Dec. 1909 by Charcot.

**Chacabuco Refugio.** Argentine refuge hut built in Bills Gulch in 1956.

**The *Chaco*.** Argentine ship which took part in various Antarctic expeditions sent

by that country: 1946–47 (Capt. Brashariot), 1948–49 (captain unknown), 1949–50 (Capt. Ezequiel N. Vega).

**Islote Chaco** *see* **Låvebrua Island**

**Lake Chad.** 77°38'S, 162°46'E. A small lake east of the mouth of Suess Glacier, immediately to the west of Lake Leon, in the Taylor Valley of southern Victoria Land. Charted by Scott's 1910–13 expedition, and named by them for the African lake.

**Mount Chadwick.** 72°30'S, 160°26'E. 2,440 m. A bare rock mountain. 2½ miles ESE of Mount Walton in the Outback Nunataks. Named for Dan M. Chadwick, meteorologist at Amundsen-Scott South Pole Station in 1968.

**Chaigneau Peak.** 65°13'S, 64°01'W. 760 m. Just SE of Blanchard Ridge, on the west coast of Graham Land. Named by Charcot in 1908–10 for the governor of Provincia de Magallanes, Chile.

**Chair Peak.** 64°43'S, 62°43'W. West of Mount Britannia, on Rongé Island, off the west coast of Graham Land. Named descriptively by Lester and Bagshawe of the British Imperial Expedition of 1920–22.

**The *Challenger*.** A 200-foot-long British corvette of 2,306 tons, built for war use for the Royal Navy in 1858, and converted in 1872 into a survey ship. A square-rigged 3-master with steam power, its auxiliary engine produced 1,234 hp. The ship was used for one of the greatest scientific explorations up to that time, the *Challenger* Expedition of 1872–76. Sponsored in part by the Royal Society, it left England on Dec. 21, 1872. The ship was commanded by Capt. George Nares, and the expedition was led by Wyville Thomson, whose brainchild this expedition was. Among the 240 or so men aboard the *Challenger* were John Murray, J.J. Wild, Rudolf von Willemoës-Suhm, Pelham Aldrich, William Spry, Lord George Campbell, Herbert Swire, N. Moseley, and J.Y. Buchanan. Devoted to oceanography, the voyage really founded that science. It went around the world, and during that time it left Kerguélen Island in Feb. 1874 and crossed the Antarctic Circle (66°30'S) at 78°22'E, on Feb. 16, 1874, the first steam-powered vessel to do so. It reached 66°40'S, 78°22'E. On Feb. 27, 1874, the *Challenger* headed out of Antarctic waters, bound for Melbourne. It covered 68,890 miles in 719 days, and arrived back in England on May 24, 1876. The reports of the expedition filled 50 volumes. The *Challenger* itself later became a coal hulk, and was decommissioned in 1921.

**Passe du Challenger** *see* **Neptune's Bellows**

**Challenger Island.** 64°21'S, 61°35'W. Also called Isla Chica, Isla Kahn. Just north of Murray Island, off the west coast of Graham Land. Named probably by Nordenskjöld's 1901-4 expedition, for the *Challenger*.

**Mount Chalmers.** 79°20'S, 159°29'E. On the east escarpment of the Conway Range, 5 miles south of the summit of Mount Keltie. Discovered by the first Scott expedition in 1901-4, and named by them for Robert Chalmers, assistant secretary to the treasury, 1903-7.

**Chamberlain Harbor.** On the west coast of the Bay of Whales, 5 miles NW of Little America I. It is gone now, because the Bay of Whales is gone.

**Chamberlin Glacier.** 67°34'S, 65°33'W. Flows into Whirlwind Inlet, 4 miles SE of Matthes Glacier, on the east coast of Graham Land. Discovered aerially by Wilkins on Dec. 20, 1928. Charted in 1947 by the FIDS, who named it for Thomas C. Chamberlin, glaciologist/geologist/professor at the University of Wisconsin and the University of Chicago.

**Chambers Glacier.** 83°17'S, 49°25'W. Flows from Mount Lechner and Kent Gap, at the junction of the Saratoga and Lexington Tables, in the Forrestal Range of the Pensacola Mountains. It then flows into Support Force Glacier. Discovered

aerially on Jan. 13, 1956. Named for Capt. Washington I. Chambers, USN, airplane catapult pioneer for ships.

**Chameau Island.** 66°46'S, 141°36'E. 175 yards long. Almost a mile east of Cape Découverte, in the Curzon Islands. Charted and named in 1951 by the French. The island looks like a chameau (camel).

**Champness Glacier.** 71°27'S, 164°15'E. 15 miles long. Flows from near Ian Peak, in the Bowers Mountains, and enters Lillie Glacier at Griffith Ridge. Named by the NZGSAE 1967-68 for G.R. Champness, field assistant with the party.

**Chan Rocks.** 72°45'S, 160°30'E. 5 miles SE of Miller Butte, in the Outback Nunataks. Named for Lian Chan, lab management technician at McMurdo Station in 1968.

**Chance Rock.** 63°59'S, 61°13'W. Isolated. In the center of Gerlache Strait, near its junction with Orléans Strait, in the Palmer Archipelago. Named by the UK in 1960 for its danger to shipping.

**Chancellor Lakes.** 78°13'S, 163°18'E. Small twin lakes near the crest of the ridge north of the Walcott Glacier. Named by the VUWAE 1960-61 for the chancellor of that university (i.e. Victoria University of Wellington, NZ).

**Rocas Chanchito** *see* **Pig Rock**

**Mount Chandler.** 75°17'S, 72°33'W. 2½ miles NW of Mount Caywood, in the Behrendt Mountains. Named for Lt. Cdr. J.L. Chandler, USN, pilot here in 1961-62.

**Chandler Island.** 77°21'S, 153°10'W. 4 miles long. The most southerly of the White Islands, at the head of Sulzberger Bay. Named for Alan Chandler, electrical engineer at Byrd Station in 1969.

**Chang Peak.** 77°04'S, 126°38'W. 2,920 m. Snow-covered. On the NW slope of Mount Waesche in the Executive Committee Range of Marie Byrd Land. Named by the USA for Feng-Keng Chang, traverse seismologist at Byrd

Station in 1959, and a member of the Marie Byrd Land Traverse Party here in 1959–60.

**Changing Lake.** 60°42'S, 45°37'W. The central of 3 lakes in Paternoster Valley, in the NE part of Signy Island, in the South Orkneys. Named by the UK because this proglacial lake slowly changes shape and size as the retaining land ice gradually retreats.

**Channel Glacier.** 64°47'S, 63°19'W. 1½ miles long. Flows across Wiencke Island, between Nipple Peak and the Wall Range, in the Palmer Archipelago. Discovered by de Gerlache in 1897–99. Probably named by the Discovery Committee personnel on the *Discovery* in 1927.

**¹Channel Rock.** 62°28'S, 60°05'W. Also called Roca Escarceo. The larger of two rocks in McFarlane Strait, ½ mile south of the Meade Islands, in the South Shetlands. Charted and named by the Discovery Committee on the *Discovery II* in 1935.

**²Channel Rock.** 65°14'S, 64°16'W. In the NW entrance to Meek Channel, in the Argentine Islands. Charted and named in 1935 by the BGLE.

**Mount Channon** *see* **Nevlingen Peak**

**The** *Chanticleer.* British ship commanded by Henry Foster, which conducted an 1828–31 expedition that included the South Shetlands and charted part of the Antarctic Peninsula. In 1829 they landed in Deception Island, and conducted research there. Other personnel on the expedition included Lt. Edward N. Kendall, Lt. H.F. Austin.

**Chanticleer Island.** 63°43'S, 61°48'W. Also called Islote Vallenar. 1 mile long. Almost snow-free. Off the NW end of Hoseason Island. Named by the UK in 1960 for the *Chanticleer.*

**Chanute Peak.** 63°56'S, 59°58'W. On the east side of Lanchester Bay, 4 miles south of Wennersgaard Point, Graham Land. Named by the UK for Octave

Chanute (1832–1910), US glider designer.

**Chaos Glacier.** 69°S, 77°58'E. 4 miles south of Browns Glacier. Flows from the Ingrid Christensen Coast into the central part of Ranvik Bay. Photographed by the LCE 1936–37. Named in 1952 by US cartographer John H. Roscoe as he worked off photos taken by Operation Highjump in 1946–47. The terminal glacial flowage appears chaotic.

**Chaos Reef.** 62°22'S, 59°46'W. Almost ¾ mile NE of Morris Rock, at the north end of the Aitcho Islands, in the South Shetlands. Named descriptively by the UK in 1971 because this is a confused area of breakers and shoal water.

**Chapel Hill.** 63°41'S, 57°58'W. 140 m. Forms the summit of a headland 1½ miles WSW of Church Point, on the south coast of Trinity Peninsula. Charted by the FIDS in 1946, and named by them because of its nearness to Church Point.

**Chapel of the Snows** *see* **Churches**

**Chapin Peak.** 85°58'S, 131°40'W. 2,170 m. On the west side of Reedy Glacier. 2 miles SE of Stick Peak, in the Quartz Hills. Named for Capt. Howard Chapin, US Marine pilot with VX-6, at McMurdo Station in 1962–63.

**Chaplains Tableland.** 78°S, 162°38'E. A plateau just north of Mount Lister, in the Royal Society Range. Named in 1963 for the chaplains who have served at McMurdo Station and elsewhere in Antarctica. One can see the tableland from McMurdo Station.

**Chaplin, J.H.** Lt. cdr., RN. Second-in-command of the *Discovery* in 1926–27, under Stenhouse. In 1950 he led the wintering party at Port Lockroy.

**Mount Chapman.** 82°35'S, 105°55'W. 2,715 m. Triple-peaked. At the west end of the Whitmore Mountains. Named for William H. Chapman, cartographer here in 1958–59. He was also here in 1957–58 and several other times.

**Chapman, Charles.** Captain of the maintop on the Wilkes Expedition 1838–42. Joined in the USA. Served the cruise.

¹**Chapman Glacier.** 70°17'S, 67°55'W. 11 miles long. 10 miles wide at the center. 3 miles wide at the mouth. Flows from the Dyer Plateau of Palmer Land to the George VI Sound, just south of Carse Point. Surveyed by the BGLE in 1936, and named by the UK in 1954 for Frederick S. Chapman, Arctic explorer and supporter of the BGLE 1934–37.

²**Chapman Glacier.** 70°43'S, 166°22'E. At the head of Yule Bay in northern Victoria Land. Named by the ANARE for A. Chapman, a member of the helicopter team here in 1962 on the *Thala Dan.*

**Chapman Hump.** 70°13'S, 67°30'W. A nunatak in the center of Chapman Glacier, in Palmer Land. 10 miles inland from the George VI Sound. Named by the UK in association with the glacier.

**Chapman Nunatak.** 71°08'S, 64°45'E. 2 miles east of Mount Hicks in the Prince Charles Mountains. Named by the Australians for P.R. Chapman, weather observer at Wilkes Station in 1963.

**Chapman Peak.** 78°11'S, 85°13'W. 2,230 m. On the east side of Ellen Glacier. 5 miles NE of Mount Jumper, in the central part of the Sentinel Range. Named for Capt. John H. Chapman, USAF, one of the men who built the South Pole Station in the 1956–57 season, led by Richard A. Bowers.

**Chapman Point.** 65°56'S, 61°19'W. Marks the eastern limit of Scar Inlet, on the north side of Jason Peninsula, Graham Land. Surveyed by the FIDS in 1955. Named by the UK for Sydney Chapman, British geophysicist, president of the Commission for the IGY, 1957–58.

**Chapman Ridge.** 67°28'S, 60°58'E. 300 m. Extends SW from Byrd Head for 3 miles. Discovered by the BANZARE 1929–31. Photographed by the LCE 1936–37, and later named by the Australians for P. Chapman, aurora physicist at Mawson Station in 1958.

**Chapman Rocks.** 62°30'S, 60°29'W. A group in Hero Bay, Livingston Island, in the South Shetlands. 3½ miles SW of

Desolation Island. Named by the UK in 1961 for Thomas Chapman who, by discovering a method of processing fur seal skins for use in the hat trade, helped propel the seal rushes from London in the early part of the 19th century.

**Chappel Island.** 66°11'S, 110°25'E. The largest of the Donovan Islands. 5 miles NW of Clark Peninsula, in the eastern part of Vincennes Bay. There are several large Adélie penguin rookeries here. Named for CWO R.L. Chappel, US Marine motion picture officer during Operation Highjump, 1946–47.

**Chappel Islets** *see* **Donovan Islands**

**Chappell Nunataks.** 82°18'S, 158°12'E. A group 3 miles west of the central part of the Cobham Range. Named by the NZGSAE 1964–65, for J. Chappell, geologist on the expedition.

**Chappell Peak.** 79°57'S, 82°54'W. 1,860 m. 3 miles south of Schoeck Peak on the south side of the Enterprise Hills, overlooking the head of Horseshoe Valley, in the Heritage Range. Named for Richard L. Chappell, scientific aide at Little America V in 1957.

**Cape Charbonneau** *see* **Sharbonneau, Cape**

**Cape Charcot.** 66°27'S, 98°33'E. At the NE end of Melba Peninsula. 3 miles west of David Island. Discovered by the AAE 1911–14, and named by Mawson for Dr. Jean-Baptiste Charcot.

**Port Charcot.** 65°04'S, 64°W. A bay, 1½ miles wide. On the north side of Booth Island. Charcot charted it in 1903–5 and wintered-over here in 1904. He named it for his father, Jean-Martin Charcot, the French neurologist.

**Charcot, Dr. Jean-Baptiste.** b. July 15, 1867, Neuilly-sur-Seine, France. d. about Sept. 16, 1937, at sea, somewhere off Iceland. Jean-Baptiste Étienne Auguste Charcot. Son of the world famous neurologist, Jean-Martin Charcot. His first Antarctic expedition, of 1903–5, was a national one, carried out with government assistance. Its primary intention was to rescue the missing Swedish explorer Nordenskjöld, but the Argentinians beat him to that. Instead, Charcot charted much of the Antarctic Peninsula, and the Gerlache Strait, and sailed as far south as the north end of Adelaide Island. Twenty-one men left Le Havre, France, on Aug. 15, 1903, on the *Français* (q.v. for names of crew). Two minutes out of port, a sailor by the name of F. Maignan, was struck on board by the hawser and killed. The ship returned to port. On Aug. 27, 1903, it left again, with Adrien de Gerlache on board as adviser. The *Français* arrived at Buenos Aires on Nov. 16, 1903, and de Gerlache left and returned to Belgium. Turquet and Gourdon joined the expedition at this point, and the ship left Buenos Aires on Dec. 23, 1903. By Feb. 1, 1904, they were past the South Shetlands, and on Feb. 5, 1904, the engine started to give trouble. They sheltered in Biscoe Bay, off Cape Errera, and on Feb. 7, 1904, arrived at Flandres Bay, where they stayed until Feb. 18, 1904. On Feb. 19, 1904, they discovered Port Lockroy, and got as far south as 65°05'S, 64°W, and wintered-over at Port Charcot, Booth Island (then known as Wandel Island). On May 30, 1904, Charcot took a party for a picnic to neighboring Hovgaard Island. They broke out of the ice in late Dec. 1904, and on Jan. 13, 1905, sighted Alexander Island. On Jan. 15, 1905, the *Français* struck a rock. On Jan. 29, 1905, they just made it back to Port Lockroy where, for 10 days, repairs were carried out. On Feb. 15, 1905, the ship was struggling past Smith Island, in the South Shetlands, and via Tierra del Fuego, got to Buenos Aires, where the Argentinians bought the ship. On May 5, 1905, Charcot and his companions boarded the *Algérie* for home. It had been a successful expedition. Charcot, an oceanographer, had made studies in that field on this Antarctic trip. On his return to France his wife, the granddaughter of Victor Hugo, divorced him for desertion. He signed a prenuptial agreement with his second wife,

Meg, in 1907, and on Aug. 15, 1908, his second expedition to Antarctica, 1908–10, left Le Havre on the *Pourquoi Pas?* Nine of the men aboard had sailed with him on the *Français* in 1903–5 (for the rest of the crew of the *Pourquoi Pas?* see that entry). Bongrain was second in command of the expedition, and Charcot's wife was on board too. She got off at Punta Arenas, Chile. On Dec. 16, 1908, the ship left Punta Arenas, and on Dec. 22, 1908, was at Smith Island, in the South Shetlands, and soon after that Charcot and his men were socializing with Norwegian whalers on Deception Island. Charcot charted that island in detail, and left there on Dec. 25, 1908, reaching Booth Island, his old wintering base, on Dec. 29, 1908. "I feel as though I've never been away" he said. On Jan. 1, 1909, the *Pourquoi Pas?* anchored in Port Circumcision, Petermann Island. On Jan. 4, 1909, Charcot, Gourdon, and Godfroy left the ship in a launch to scout the coast near Cape Tuxen. It was meant to be only a short trip, of a few hours, but it was 3 days before they got back to the ship—barely alive. On Jan. 8, 1909, the ship hit a rock. At the end of Jan. 1909 it went across the Antarctic Circle, and cruised along Adelaide Island, charting it in detail, and proving it to be much longer than was previously thought. They discovered Marguerite Bay, and Charcot continued his charting of the Antarctic Peninsula, as well as discovering the Fallières Coast. He froze the *Pourquoi Pas?* in at Port Circumcision, on Petermann Island, and wintered-over, building 4 huts on the island. On Dec. 27, 1909, they were back at Deception Island. They left for the south again on Jan. 7, 1910. On Jan. 10, 1910, they discovered Charcot Land (later proved to be an island), and on Jan. 22, 1910, they headed north, arriving in Punta Arenas, Chile, on Feb. 11, 1910. On June 4, 1910, they got back to France. In 1912 Charcot wrote *Autour du Pôle Sud,* and during World War I commanded a Q boat in the British Royal Navy, being awarded the D.S.C. In 1925–26 he pushed the French government to claim Adélie Land (q.v.).

¹**Charcot Bay.** 63°50′S, 59°37′W. 10–15 miles wide. An indentation into the west coast of Graham Land, between Cape Kater and Cape Kjellman. Discovered by Nordenskjöld's expedition of 1901–4 and named by them for Dr. Jean-Baptiste Charcot. Not to be confused with Charcot Cove.

²**Charcot Bay** *see* **Charcot Cove**

**Charcot Cove.** 76°07′S, 162°24′E. Between Cape Hickey and Bruce Point, it is the northernmost indentation into the Scott Coast, on the coast of southern Victoria Land. Immediately to the south of the Nordenskjöld Ice Tongue. Discovered by Scott's 1901–4 expedition, and named Charcot Bay by them, for Dr. Jean-Baptiste Charcot. It was later redefined.

**Charcot Island.** 69°45′S, 75°15′W. 30 miles long. 25 miles wide. Ice-covered except for some mountain tops. 55 miles west of Alexander Island, in the Bellingshausen Sea. Charcot discovered it on Jan. 10, 1910, and named it Charcot Land, for his father, the surgeon Jean-Martin Charcot. The explorer thought it to be part of the mainland. Wilkins flew around it on Dec. 29, 1929, thus proving its insularity. The first people to set foot on it were members of the RARE, on Dec. 23, 1947, when a plane landed there.

**Charcot Land** *see* **Charcot Island**

**Charcot Station.** 69°22′S, 139°02′E. French scientific base built for the IGY. Robert Guillard set out from the coast on Oct. 1, 1956, to build it in the region of the South Magnetic Pole. Jacques Dubois was the first leader of the station, arriving in Jan. 1957, and 4 men wintered-over that year, including Dr. Goy, the surgeon. René Garcia relieved Dubois in 1958. It had one small building that first winter.

**Charcot Strait** *see* **The Gullet**

**The *Charity*.** New York sealing brig of 122 tons and 72 feet long, built at St.

Michaels, Md., in 1817. Its captain was Charles H. Barnard, who bought it outright on June 2, 1820. It was in the South Shetlands for the 1820–21 season, allied with the New York Sealing Expedition. It left Antarctica on March 30, 1821, and was back in the South Shetlands for the 1821–22 season, again allied with the New York Sealing Expedition. It left Antarctica finally on Jan. 26, 1822, and on his return to New York, Barnard registered the vessel on May 27, 1822.

**Mount Charity.** 69°54′S, 64°34′W. 2,680 m. 9 miles south of Mount Hope, in the Eternity Range, on the Antarctic Peninsula. Discovered aerially by Lincoln Ellsworth on Nov. 21 and Nov. 23, 1935, and named by him in association with nearby Mount Hope and Mount Faith. Surveyed by the BGLE in Nov. 1936.

**Charity Glacier.** 62°44′S, 60°20′W. North of Barnard Point, on the south coast of Livingston Island, in the South Shetlands. Named by the UK in 1959 for the *Charity*.

**Charlat Island.** 65°11′S, 64°10′W. A small island just west of the south end of Petermann Island, in the Wilhelm Archipelago. Discovered by Charcot in 1908–10, and named by him for the French vice-consul at Rio, M. Charlat.

**Cap Charles** *see* **Sherlac Point**

**Cape Charles** *see* **Cape Sterneck, Charles Point**

**Mount Charles.** 67°23′S, 50°E. 1,110 m. 3 miles south of Mount Cronus, in Enderby Land. In 1830–31 Biscoe charted and named 4 mountains in what are now the Scott Mountains—Charles, Henry, Gordon, and George, for the Enderby Brothers, owners of Biscoe's vessels. This may or may not be the exact mountain Biscoe had in mind, but in 1962 the UK arbitrarily decided it was.

**The *Charles Adams*.** US sealer from Stonington, in the South Shetlands in the 1831–33 period, under the command of Capt. Alexander S. Palmer, and in company with the *Courier*.

**Charles Glacier.** 72°34'S, 3°26'W. Flows from the south side of Borg Mountain, in the Borg Massif of Queen Maud Land. Named Charlesbreen (Charles Glacier) by the Norwegians, for Charles Swithinbank.

**Charles Gould Peak** *see* **Gould Peak**

**Cape Charles J. Adams** *see* **Cape Adams**

**Charles Nunataks.** 73°19'S, 2°10'W. An isolated group 8 miles south of the west end of the Neumayer Cliffs, in Queen Maud Land. Named Charlesrabbane by the Norwegians, for Charles Swithinbank.

**Charles Peak.** 79°44'S, 83°11'W. 990 m. Surmounts the SE end of the Collier Hills, in the Heritage Range. Named for Charles E. Williams, meteorologist at Little America V in 1958.

**Charles Point.** 64°14'S, 61°W. Forms the north side of the entrance to Brialmont Cove, on the west coast of Graham Land. In 1831 it wa: .alled Cape Charles, and was later re .uned.

**Charles Koux Island** *see* **Roux Island**

**The** *Charles Shearer.* US sealer out of Stonington, in the South Shetlands during the 1874–75 season. It left for these islands again in late 1877, under the command of James Appleton. It left a gang of sealers at Islas de Diego Ramírez (not in Antarctica), and then set sail for the South Shetlands, and disappeared without a trace. Other ships looked for it in the 1879–80 season, including the *Thomas Hunt,* but the *Shearer* (as it was more commonly known) was never found.

**Charles V. Bob Range.** A term no longer used. East of the Queen Maud Mountains, it was discovered by Byrd during his flight of Nov. 18, 1929.

**Charlesbreen** *see* **Charles Glacier**

**Charlesrabbane** *see* **Charles Nunataks**

**Charlesworth Cliffs.** 80°14'S, 25°18' W. In the Shackleton Range.

**Charlotte Bay.** 64°30'S, 61°35'W. Between Reclus Peninsula and Cape Murray, it indents the west coast of Graham Land between Brabant Island and the Danco Coast. Discovered by de Gerlache in 1897–99, and named by him for the fiancée of Georges Lecointe.

**Charlton Island.** 66°13'S, 110°09'E. The most westerly of the Frazier Islands, in Vincennes Bay. Named by Carl Eklund for Frederick E. Charlton, USN, chief electronics technician at Wilkes Station in 1957.

**Charpentier Pyramid.** 80°16'S, 25°37' W. In the Shackleton Range.

**The** *Charua.* Argentine ship which took part in the 1947–48 Antarctic expedition sent by that country. Capt. Raul Kolbe commanded. It was back again for the 1948–49 expedition, in company with the *Pampa* and the *Sanavirón.*

**Charybdis Glacier.** 70°25'S, 67°30'E. Flows between the Porthos and Aramis Ranges in the Prince Charles Mountains, and feeds the Amery Ice Shelf. Discovered by W.G. Bewsher's ANARE southern party in Dec. 1956, and named by the Australians for the Greek mythological whirlpool.

**Charybdis Icefalls.** 70°42'S, 161°12'E. In the lower Harlin Glacier. They join the Rennick Glacier. Named by the New Zealanders in 1963–64 for the whirlpool in Greek mythology.

**Chastain Peak.** 85°10'S, 94°35'W. 2,225 m. Near the center of the Moulton Escarpment, at the west end of the Thiel Mountains. Named for William W. Chastain (*see* **Deaths, 1961**), USN, aviation structural mechanic.

**Chata Rock.** 64°52'S, 63°44'W. Also called Exposure Rock, Roca Expuesta. Isolated. ½ mile south of Cape Lancaster, the southern end of Anvers Island. Chata means "flat" in Spanish. Named by the Argentines before 1950.

**Chatos Islands.** 67°39'S, 69°10'W. A group of small islands and rocks. South of Cape Adriasola on Adelaide Island. Named Islotes Chatos by the Argentine Antarctic Expedition of 1952–53 (name means "flat islands").

The *Chattahoochee*. USNS tanker in at McMurdo Sound in 1961–62 and 1962–63. In the latter season it made 4 fuel-carrying trips between New Zealand and McMurdo.

Chattahoochee Glacier. 76°34'S, 160°42'E. Flows between Wyandot Ridge and Eastwind Ridge, in the Convoy Range. Named in 1964 for the *Chattahoochee*.

Chaucer Island   *see*   Sinclair Island

Chaucheprat Point. 63°32'S, 56°42'W. At the NW corner of Jonassen Island in Antarctic Sound. In 1838 Dumont d'Urville named a cape somewhere in this area as Cap Chaucheprat, and if it was indeed this one, it was determined later and redefined as a point.

Mount Chauve. 66°49'S, 141°23'E. 33 m. A hill at the NW extremity of Cape Margerie. Charted and named by the French in 1950. Chauve means bald.

Cap Chauveau   *see*   Chauveau Point

Chauveau Point. 64°05'S, 62°02'W. Marks the SW end of Liège Island. Charcot charted and named it Cap Chauveau, for an associate in the Central Meteorological Office in Paris. Later this point was unidentifiable. This particular point was therefore chosen to preserve Charcot's naming in the area.

Cape Chavanne. 66°59'S, 64°45'W. A partly ice-free bluff, east of the mouth of Breitfuss Glacier, at the head of Mill Inlet, on the east coast of Graham Land. Named by the FIDS for Josef Chavanne, Austrian polar bibliographer.

Bahía Chávez   *see*   Cangrejo Cove

Chavez Island. 65°38'S, 64°32'W. 550 m. 3 miles long. Just west of the peninsula between Leroux and Bigo Bays, off the west coast of Graham Land. Discovered by Charcot and named by him for Commandant Alfonso Chaves (sic), of Ponta Delgada, Azores.

Île du Chaylard   *see*   Duchaylard Island

The *Che Sera Sera*   *see*   The *Que Sera Sera*

Cheal Point. 60°38'S, 45°59'W. 1 mile ESE of Return Point, the SW extremity of Coronation Island, in the South Orkneys. Surveyed in 1933 by the personnel on the *Discovery II*. Named by the UK for Joseph J. Cheal of the FIDS, general assistant in 1950 and leader in 1951 of the Signy Island Station.

Cheeks Nunatak. 74°58'S, 72°49'W. Also called Mount Barnes, Barnes Nunatak. The largest and most southerly of 3 nunataks, 12 miles NW of the Merrick Mountains. Named for Noble L. Cheeks, aviation electronics technician who helped set up Eights Station in 1961.

Cheesman, S.A. Pilot on Wilkins' flight of 1929.

Cheesman Island. 69°31'S, 74°58'W. A small island off the north coast of Charcot Island, 1 mile north of Mount Martine. Discovered aerially by Wilkins in 1929. Named by the USA in 1950 for S.A. Cheesman.

Cape Cheetham. 70°17'S, 162°42'E. Ice-covered. Forms the NE extremity of the Stuhlinger Ice Piedmont, Oates Land. First charted by the crew on the *Terra Nova*, under Harry Pennell, in Feb. 1911, and named by him for Alfred B. Cheetham.

Cheetham, Alfred B. He was on the *Morning* in 1902–4. He took part in Shackleton's first expedition of 1907–9, as 3rd officer and bosun. He was bosun on the *Terra Nova*, 1910–13, and 3rd officer on the *Endurance* during Shackleton's disastrous British Imperial Transantarctic Expedition of 1914–17. Shackleton called him "the veteran of the Antarctic." He was torpedoed and drowned in 1918 during World War I.

Cheetham Glacier Tongue   *see* Cheetham Ice Tongue

Cheetham Ice Barrier Tongue   *see* Cheetham Ice Tongue

**Cheetham Ice Tongue.** 75°45′S, 162°55′E. Also called Cheetham Ice Barrier Tongue, Cheetham Glacier Tongue. A small glacier tongue (sic) on the east coast of Victoria Land, between Lamplugh Island and Whitmer Peninsula. It juts out into the Ross Sea, and is fed partly by the Davis Glacier and partly by ice draining from Lamplugh Island and Whitmer Peninsula. Charted by Shackleton's 1907–9 expedition, and named by Shackleton for Alfred B. Cheetham.

**Chelyuskintsy Ice Tongue.** 66°20′S, 82°E. Forms the western fringe of the West Ice Shelf, off the Leopold and Astrid Coast. Named by the USSR.

**Cheney Bluff.** 79°39′S, 159°46′E. On the south side of the mouth of Carlyon Glacier, 5 miles SW of Cape Murray. Named for Lt. Cdr. D.J. Cheney, RNZN, commander of the *Rotoiti.*

**Mount Cheops.** 65°52′S, 64°38′W. Over 610 m. 8 miles SSE of Cape García on the west coast of Graham Land. Named by the UK for its pyramidal shape.

**Cherevichny, Ivan E.** Hero of the Soviet Union, who commanded the air fleet during the USSR IGY effort in the late 1950s.

**Chernushka Nunatak.** 71°35′S, 12°01′E. 1,640 m. 2 miles SW of Sandseten Mountain, on the west side of the Westliche Petermann Range, in the Wohlthat Mountains of Queen Maud Land. Discovered by Ritscher in 1938–39. Named by the USSR in 1966.

**Chernyy Island.** 66°08′S, 101°04′E. A small island, ½ mile south of the eastern tip of Thomas Island, in the Highjump Archipelago. The USSR named it Ostrov Chernyy (black island) in 1966.

**Mount Cherry-Garrard.** 71°18′S, 168°40′E. Between Simpson Glacier and Fendley Glacier, on the north coast of Victoria Land. Charted by Campbell's Northern Party during Scott's 1910–13 expedition, and named by them for Apsley Cherry-Garrard.

**Cherry-Garrard, Apsley.** 1886–1959. Apsley George Benet Cherry-Garrard. Son of a British general, he bought his way into the British Antarctic Expedition of 1910–13 with a donation of £1,000. This versatile Englishman who was introduced to Scott by Wilson, went south on the *Terra Nova* as assistant zoologist, even though he had no scientific qualifications. Known as "Cherry," he edited the *South Polar Times* (the expedition's magazine), and took part in all the major sledge traverses, including the "worst journey in the world" (he later wrote a book with this title; in it he was the first to say "all the world loves a penguin") to Cape Crozier and back with Bowers and Wilson. He tried, and failed, to relieve Scott's polar party on their return trip, and suffered great remorse afterwards.

**Cherry Glacier**  *see*  **Cherry Icefall**

**Cherry Icefall.** 84°27′S, 167°40′E. A small, steep icefall on the south side of Barnes Peak. It descends toward the Beardmore Glacier, in the Queen Alexandra Range. Scott's 1910–13 expedition named it Cherry Glacier for Apsley Cherry-Garrard, but in 1961–62 the New Zealanders redefined it.

**Cherry Island.** 73°45′S, 123°32′W. 3 miles long. Ice-covered. Between Siple Island and Carney Island, and just within the Getz Ice Shelf, on the coast of Marie Byrd Land. Named for CWO J.M. Cherry, US Army, in Antarctica in 1966.

**Chervov Peak.** 71°50′S, 10°33′E. 2,550 m. 1 mile north of Mørkenatten Peak, in the Shcherbakov Range, in the Orvin Mountains of Queen Maud Land. Named by the USSR in 1966 for geologist Yevgeniy I. Chervov.

**Cheshire Rock.** 62°22′S, 59°45′W. 175 yards SE of Passage Rock, in English Strait, in the South Shetlands. Named by the UK for Lt. Cdr. Peter J.E. Cheshire, leader of the RN Hydrographic Survey Unit here in 1967.

**Chester, Capt.** Captain of the *Essex,* in the South Shetlands for the 1820–21 and 1821–22 seasons.

**Chester, H.C. Capt.** Commander of the *Franklin,* in the South Shetlands for the 1873–74 season.

**Chester Cone.** 62°38′S, 61°05′W. A peak on Byers Peninsula, Livingston Island, in the South Shetlands. Named by the UK in 1958 for Capt. Chester.

**Chester Mountains.** 76°41′S, 145°W. Just north of the mouth of Crevasse Valley Glacier, and 10 miles north of Saunders Mountain, in the Ford Ranges of Marie Byrd Land. Mapped by Byrd's 1933–35 expedition, and named by Byrd for Colby M. Chester, president of General Foods, and a supporter.

**Mount Chetwynd.** 76°19′S, 162°02′E. Over 1,400 m. Just south of Mount Gauss, in the Kirkwood Range of Victoria Land. Discovered by Scott's 1901–4 expedition, and named by Scott for his friend, Sir Peter Chetwynd.

**Cheu Valley.** 85°11′S, 173°54′W. 3 miles long. In the Cumulus Hills. Just west of Gatlin Glacier. Named by the Texas Tech Shackleton Glacier Expedition of 1964–65, for Specialist 5th Class Daniel T.L. Cheu, a member of the US Army Aviation Detachment which supported the expedition.

**Chevreul Cliffs.** 80°32′S, 20°36′W. In the Shackleton Range.

**Mount Chevreux.** 65°46′S, 64°W. 5 miles SE of Leroux Bay, on the west coast of Graham Land. Discovered by Charcot in 1908–10, and named by him for French zoologist Édouard Chevreux.

**Chevron Rocks.** 84°07′S, 173°05′E. At the north end of Retrospect Spur, near the head of Hood Glacier, in the Queen Maud Mountains. Named by the New Zealanders in 1959–60 because of their chevron-type appearance.

**Isla Chica** *see* **Challenger Island**

**Chick, Amos.** Carpenter on the Wilkes Expedition 1838–42. Joined the *Vincennes* at Callao.

**Chick Island.** 66°47′S, 121°E. Isolated. 10 miles NE of the Henry Islands, off the Sabrina Coast. Named for Amos Chick.

**Isla Chico** *see* **Guyou Islands**

**Mount Chider.** 72°06′S, 169°10′E. 3,110 m. 2 miles SE of Mount Hart, in the Admiralty Mountains of Victoria Land. Named for Lt. Cdr. Thomas J. Chider, VX-6 helicopter pilot at McMurdo Station, 1968.

**Chijire Glacier.** 68°03′S, 43°23′E. Also called Tizire Glacier. Flows to the coast, just east of the Chijire Rocks, in Queen Maud Land. Named by the Japanese.

**Chijire Rocks.** 68°02′S, 43°18′E. Also called Tizire Rocks. On the coast of Queen Maud Land, just west of the mouth of Chijire Glacier. Named by the Japanese.

**Child, J.B.** 3rd officer on the *Discovery* during the BANZARE 1929–31.

**Child Rocks.** 67°26′S, 63°16′E. At the west end of the Robinson Group, off the coast of Mac. Robertson Land. Photographed by the LCE 1936–37, and named Vestskjera (the west skerries) by the Norwegians. Renamed by the Australians for J.B. Child.

**Childs Glacier.** 83°24′S, 58°40′W. Flows from Roderick Valley into the Foundation Ice Stream, in the Neptune Range. Named for John H. Childs, builder at Ellsworth Station in 1958.

**Chile.** On Nov. 6, 1940, Chile claimed the sector of Antarctica from 90°W to 53°W, most of which Great Britain had claimed since 1908 (*see* **Falkland Islands Dependencies**). From 1947 on Chile established several bases on and around the Antarctic Peninsula. Their first expedition was in 1946–47 (*see* **Chilean Antarctic Expedition 1946–47**). The Presidential Expedition came next, in 1947–48, and there has been a Chilean Antarctic Expedition every year since. In 1959 Chile was one of the 12 original signatories of the Antarctic Treaty. In 1985 they acquired Base T from the British, and renamed it Teniente Carvajal Station. Currently the Chilean staff in Antarctica are mostly uniformed. Other scientific stations in Antarctica are Capitán Arturo Prat (the first to go up), General Bernardo O'Higgins, Presidente Gabriel González Videla, Presidente Pedro Aguirre Cerda, Yankee Bay, Coppermine Cove, Diego Ramírez, Presidente Frei, Chiloé, Teniente Rodolfo Marsh, Yelcho.

**Chile Bay**    *see*    **Discovery Bay**

**Chilean Antarctic Expedition 1946–47.** This was Chile's first Antarctic expedition, and was led by Capitán Federico Guesalaga Toro (*see* Guesalaga). There were 2 ships, the *Angamos* and the *Iquique*. Captain of the *Angamos* was Gabriel Rojas Parker, and captain of the *Iquique* was Ernesto González Navarrete (*see* **González**). Other personnel included Capitán Bonert (second-in-command of the *Angamos*), Raul del Canto (chief engineer on the *Iquique*), Juan Basso (storekeeper on the *Iquique*), Osvaldo Vidal, Humberto Tenorio (helicopter pilot), and Carlos Toro. The expedition established Capitán Arturo Prat Station, the first Chilean scientific base in Antarctica, and visited the British at Base E on Stonington Island.

**Ventana Del Chileno**    *see*    **Neptune's Window**

**Chiloé Station.** Chilean scientific station built in 1981 in the mountains of Graham Land. A 4,000 meter-long airstrip was built here.

**China.** China sent scientists to work in Antarctica with Australian and New Zealand expeditions in 1982 and 1983, and on June 8, 1983, the country became ratified as the 27th signatory of the Antarctic Treaty. The China Institute on Polar Regions was formed in 1984, located in Shanghai, and Chinese scientists continued to work with other nations. In 1985 the first Chinese scientific station in Antarctica, the Great Wall Station, was built. China achieved Consultative status within the Antarctic Treaty system on Oct. 7, 1985.

**Chinese Wall**    *see*    **Great Wall Station**

**Chinook Pass.** 69° 29′ S, 68° 33′ W. On the west coast of the Antarctic Peninsula.

**Chinstrap Cove.** 61° 14′ S, 54° 11′ W. 3 miles NE of Escarpada Point, on the NW coast of Clarence Island. Named by the UK for the chinstrap penguins here.

**Chinstrap penguins.** *Pygoscelis antarctica.* One of the handful of penguin species available in Antarctica, they occur only in the northern Antarctic Peninsula coasts, notably on Nelson Island, in the South Shetlands. They are also seen in the South Orkneys, and on Peter I Island. Also known as the ringed penguin, bearded penguin, and stonecracker, they were discovered by John R. Forster. They look like the Adélie penguin, but have a black "chinstrap." They grow to around 30 inches, and weigh about 8 pounds. They are pugnacious and have a very loud voice. They prefer rocky slopes and higher elevations, and lay 2 eggs.

**Chionis Island.** 63° 50′ S, 60° 38′ W. South of Awl Point, Trinity Island. In the 1920s whalers called it Snow Island, but because a Snow Island already existed in the South Shetlands, the UK renamed it in 1960 for the sheathbill (*Chionis alba*).

**The *Chiriguano*.** Argentine ocean-going tug in the South Shetlands and Antarctic Peninsula areas during the following expeditions sent down by Argentina: 1947–48 (Capt. Pedro B. Cabello Moya), 1948–49 (Capt. Enrique G.M. Grünwaldt), 1949–50 (Capt. Benigno Ignacio Varela), 1950–51 (Capt. Ricardo O. Saiz), 1951–52 (Capt. O.E. Eguia), 1952–53 (Capt. Carlos A. Brañas), 1953–54 (Capt. Beláustegui), 1954–55 (Capt. Adolfo V.R. Bluthgen), 1955–56 (Capt. Juan C. Kelly), 1956–57 (Capt. Angel L. Bernasconi).

**Chisel Peak.** 67° 40′ S, 67° 42′ W. On the west coast of Graham Land.

**Chisholm Hills.** 73°26'S, 163°21'E. 6 miles east of Gair Mesa, in the Southern Cross Mountains of Victoria Land. Named by the Southern Party of the NZGSAE 1966–67, for Ross Chisholm, leader of the party.

**Mount Chivers.** 82°32'S, 161°26'E. 1,755 m. Between the mouths of the Otago and Tranter Glaciers, in the northern part of the Queen Elizabeth Range. Named for Hugh J.H. Chivers, upper atmosphere physicist at Byrd Station, Amundsen-Scott South Pole Station and Hallett Station in 1962–63.

**Cape Chocolate.** 77°56'S, 164°34'E. Small and dark, it forms the south side of Salmon Bay, on the coast of southern Victoria Land. It is made up of dark, morainic material from the western edge of the Koettlitz Glacier. Discovered by Scott's 1901–4 expedition, and named descriptively by them.

**Cholet, Ernest.** Captain of the *Français*, 1903–5, and of the *Pourquoi Pas?*, 1908–10, both times under Charcot in the Antarctic.

**Cholet Island.** 65°04'S, 64°02'W. A small island just north of Booth Island, in the Wilhelm Archipelago. Discovered by Charcot in 1903–5, and named by him for Ernest Cholet.

**Chopin Hill.** 71°36'S, 73°46'W. 250 m. Snow-covered. 2 miles SW of Mount Schumann, on Beethoven Peninsula, in the SW part of Alexander Island. Named by the UK for the composer.

**Mount Choto.** 69°12'S, 39°40'E. Also spelled Mount Tyoto. 350 m. Surmounts the north end of the Langhovde Hills, on the coast of Queen Maud Land. Photographed by the LCE 1936–37. Later named Choto-san (Mount Long-head) by the Japanese as a translation of the Norwegian Langhovde.

**Cape Choyce** *see* **Choyce Point**

**Choyce Point.** 67°42'S, 65°23'W. 3 miles SW of Tent Nunatak, it juts out into the Larsen Ice Shelf from the east coast of the Antarctic Peninsula, op-

posite Francis Island. Named Cape Choyce in 1947 by the FIDS. Redefined in 1975. M.A. Choyce was FIDS meteorologist at Base D in 1947.

**Caleta Choza** *see* **Hut Cove**

**Mount Christchurch.** 82°28'S, 164°10'E. 1,355 m. 7 miles SW of Cape Lyttelton, south of the Shackleton Inlet, it is the most northerly of the peaks in the Queen Elizabeth Range. Discovered during Scott's 1901–4 expedition, and named by Scott for the NZ city that supported the expedition (and which was to prove a loyal supporter of so many Antarctic expeditions from many countries).

**Mount Christen Christensen** *see* **Christensen Nunatak**

**Cape Christensen** *see* **Christensen Nunatak**

**¹Mount Christensen** *see* **Mount Mervyn, Christensen Nunatak**

**²Mount Christensen.** 67°57'S, 48°E. Also spelled Mount Kristensen. 1,475 m. Ice-covered. On the SW side of Rayner Glacier, it overlooks Casey Bay, in Enderby Land. Discovered on Jan. 13, 1930, by the BANZARE, and named by Mawson for Lars Christensen.

**Christensen, A.** Crewman on the *Bear of Oakland*, 1933–35.

**Christensen, Christen.** Christen Fredrik Christensen. Norwegian naval architect from Sandefjord who introduced the first factory whaling ship in the South Shetlands, in 1906.

**Christensen, Ingrid.** Wife of Lars (see below), she was on the LCE 1936–37.

**Christensen, Lars.** b. 1884, Sandefjord, Norway. d. 1965, NYC. Norwegian whaling industrialist, born into a whaling family. He operated out of Sandefjord. Between 1927 and 1931 he sent the *Odd I* once and the *Norvegia* four times to Antarctica. He himself went down on the *Thorshavn* in 1931–32, 1932–33, 1933–34, and 1936–37. The latter expedition is referred to in this book as the LCE 1936–37 (Lars Christensen Expedition 1936–37), and the *Firern* also took part in this expedition. Ingrid Christensen, Lars's wife, also came on this 1936–37 expedition. Lars came down on these occasions to direct personally the exploration by his whaling ships and seaplanes. He also financed the 1935–36 expedition of the *Thorshavn,* under Capt. Klarius Mikkelsen. Lars, who was also a consul, wrote *Such Is the Antarctic.*

**Christensen Nunatak.** 65°06'S, 59°31' W. Also known as Mount Christensen, Mount Christen Christensen, Cape Christensen, Christensen Peak, Christensen Volcano. 1 mile north of Robertson Island, in the Seal Nunataks, off the east coast of the Antarctic Peninsula. Named for Christen Christensen, it has been defined and redefined several times, as is evident by the number of names it has gone by.

**Christensen Peak** *see* **Christensen Nunatak, Lars Christensen Peak**

**Christensen Volcano** *see* **Christensen Nunatak**

**Mount Christi.** 62°55'S, 62°24'W. 1,280 m. 3 miles NE of Mount Pisgah, in the NE part of Smith Island, in the South Shetlands. In 1828–31 Foster called the north cape of the island Cape Christi, but that cape had already been called Cape Smith. In 1953 this mountain was so named by the UK in order to preserve Foster's naming in the area.

**Christiaensen Glacier.** 71°32'S, 35°37'E. Flows between Mount Eyskens and Mount Derom in the Queen Fabiola Mountains. Discovered on Oct. 7, 1960, by the Belgian Antarctic Expedition of 1959–61, led by Guido Derom. He named it for Leo Christiaensen, captain of the *Erika Dan.*

**Christian, E.W.** Crewman on the *Jacob Ruppert,* 1933–34.

**Christiania Islands.** 63°57'S, 61°28'W. Also spelled Kristiania Island (sic). Four islands in the Palmer Archipelago, between Liège Island and Trinity Island, off the west coast of Graham Land. The largest is Intercurrence Island, and the others include Small Island and Gulch Island.

Charted by de Gerlache in 1897–99, and named by him for the Norwegian capital, Christiania (now called Oslo).

**Cape Christie.** 72°18'S, 170°02'E. 5 miles WNW of Cape Hallett. Marks the west side of the entrance to Edisto Inlet, on the coast of Victoria Land. Discovered on Jan. 15, 1841, by Ross, and named by him for Prof. Samuel Hunter Christie of the Royal Military Academy, Woolwich.

**Christie Peaks.** 71°15'S, 67°25'W. Just south of the terminus of Ryder Glacier, on the west coast of Palmer Land. Named by the UK for Timothy J.C. Christie, BAS surveyor at Base E, 1970–71.

**Christine Island.** 64°48'S, 64°02'W. ½ mile long. 1 mile off the south coast of Anvers Island, near Palmer Station, and 1½ miles SE of Bonaparte Point. There is a penguin colony here. The name was recommended by Dietland Müller-Schwarze, for his wife Christine. The USA officially adopted the name.

**Cape Christmas.** 72°20'S, 60°41'W. 320 m. Marks the north side of the entrance to Wüst Inlet, on the east coast of Palmer Land. Discovered aerially by the USAS in Dec. 1940. The FIDS spent Christmas of 1947 here, and named it accordingly.

**Mount Christmas.** 81°54'S, 161°56'E. 1,745 m. 9 miles WSW of Cape May, in the Nash Range, between Mount Markham and Mount Albert Markham. Discovered by Scott's 1901–4 expedition, and named by them on Dec. 25, 1902.

**Christmas Cliffs.** 73°33'S, 94°17'W. 2 miles SSE of Pillsbury Tower, in the Jones Mountains. Named by the University of Minnesota–Jones Mountains Party of 1960–61, who were here on Dec. 25, 1960.

**Christmas Island** *see* **Rosamel Island**

**Christoffersen Heights.** 73°36'S, 94°06'W. Snow-covered. They form the south central portion of the Jones Mountains. South of Bonnabeau and Anderson Domes. Named for Lt. Ernest H.

Christoffersen, USNR, pilot here in 1961–62.

**Christoffersen Island.** 60°44'S, 45°03'W. A small island west of the south end of Powell Island, in the South Orkneys. It is part of SPA #15. Named before 1912.

**Mount Christophersen** *see* **Mount Wilhelm Christophersen**

**Christophersen Island** *see* **Christoffersen Island**

**Christy Glacier.** 86°06'S, 161°30'W. Flows along the SW side of Breyer Mesa into the Amundsen Glacier, in the Queen Maud Mountains. Named for Clarence C. Christy, maintenance shop supervisor at Williams Field, 1967.

**Chromium.** Or chromite. Has been found in the Antarctic.

**Chugunov Glacier.** 70°40'S, 163°12'E. 15 miles long. Just north of Astakhov Glacier in the Bowers Mountains. Flows from the eastern slopes of the Explorers Range into Ob' Bay. Named by the USSR for N.A. Chugunov (*see* **Deaths, 1958**).

**Chugunov Island.** 65°54'S, 99°29'E. A small, ice-covered island at the seaward extremity of the Shackleton Ice Shelf, between the projections of the Denman and Scott Glaciers. Named by the USSR for aerographer N.A. Chugunov (*see* **Deaths, 1958** and also **Chugunov Glacier**).

**Chun, Karl.** Leader of the *Valdivia* expedition in 1898–99.

**Cape Church.** 67°51'S, 65°35'W. Projects into the head of Seligman Inlet, just north of the Ahlmann Glacier, on the east coast of Graham Land. Charted by the FIDS in 1947. They named it for Prof. James E. Church, snow surveying pioneer.

**Church, Capt.** This name figures prominently in US sealing/whaling history between 1846 and 1882. There were probably several men by this name, possibly belonging to the same family, for they all issued forth from New London. The first was Capt. Church of the *Exile*, at the Kerguélen Islands (not in Antarctica) in 1846–48. The next record of a Capt. Church is Simeon Church, on the *Marcia*, at the Kerguélens, 1851–53 and 1853–56. Also in the Kerguélens, 1853–56 was another Capt. Church, in the *Alert*, and this latter captain was back, on the same ship, in 1856–58. In 1859–62 a Capt. Church was at the Kerguélens in the *Franklin*, and a Capt. Church commanded the *Arab* at Heard Island in 1864–65 and 1865–66. Yet another record of a Captain Church at the Kerguélens is 1864–67, on the *Roswell King*. Simeon Church was at the Kerguélens 1865–68 on the *Golden West*, and a Capt. Church was commander of the *Roman* at the Kerguélens in 1866–67 and at Heard Island in 1867–68, and back again at the Kerguélens in 1868–69. More confusing, a Capt. Church led the *Golden West* back to the Kerguélens in 1868–71, but this was apparently not Simeon. The first South Shetland visit by a Church was 1872–73 by Capt. Church of the *Flying Fish*. He was back again, in the same ship, in 1873–74. In 1882 the last of the Churches, Rastus Church, came in the *Delia Church,* around Bouvetøya (not in Antarctica).

**Church Glacier.** 71°51'S, 167°34'E. 10 miles long. Flows along the west side of Church Ridge, and enters Leander Glacier to the NW of Shadow Bluff, in the Admiralty Mountains. Named for Brooks D. Church, lab management technician at McMurdo Station in 1966–67 and 1967–68.

**Church Mountain** *see* **Mount Kjerka**

**Church Nunataks.** 66°48'S, 52°39'E. A line of small nunataks, 1 mile NE of Mount Smethurst. 28 miles SW of Stor Hånakken Mountain, in Enderby Land. Named by the Australians for S.W. Church, radio officer at Wilkes Station in 1961.

**Church Point.** 63°41'S, 57°55'W. 2 miles west of Camp Hill, on the south coast of Trinity Peninsula. Charted by the FIDS in 1945, and named by them because of its steeplelike appearance (a dark, distinctive rock peak of 340 meters surmounts this point).

**Church Ridge.** 71°49'S, 167°45'E. 10 miles long. Has several peaks over 200 m. high. It separates the flow of the Church and Leander Glaciers, in the Admiralty Mountains. Named for Cdr. A.E. Church, USN, assistant chief of staff for civil engineering with the US Naval Support Force, Antarctica, in 1967 and 1968.

**Churches.** Until the time of the IGY there were no churches in Antarctica. In early 1956 a Quonset chapel was erected at McMurdo Sound, and called Chapel of the Snows. It was a Catholic church, of which Father John C. Condit was priest. Condit was the first priest of Operation Deep Freeze, and was at McMurdo during Operation Deep Freeze I (summer season of 1955–56). His parish was the world's most southerly. It had been planned to hold religious services in the mess hall at AirOpFac McMurdo (the forerunner of McMurdo Station) because there were no plans or materials for a church, as such. Soon though, the chaplain scrounged materials and the men went to work after hours. Lt. Cdr. Peter Bol was chaplain during the winter over of 1956 at McMurdo, and he was succeeded by Chaplain Leon S. Darkowski for Operation Deep Freeze II (summer of 1956–57). Later in 1956 Our Lady of the Snows Shrine was erected about 330 yards NE of the Discovery Hut. It was a small rock cairn with the statue of the Virgin Mary, and honors the memory of Richard T. Williams. During Deep Freeze II Robert H. Wakeman was the lay leader of the Protestant service, while Darkowski led the Catholic mass. Lt. Donald C. Hauck played organ at Wakeman's services. Pope Pius blessed Operation Deep Freeze, and religious medallions were designed in sterling silver by the men of Deep Freeze III. The Catholic one said "Our Lady of the Snows Protect Us" and had a picture of the Virgin in the middle. The Protestant one had a map of Antarctica, and the words, "In God We Trust, Psalm 39:9,10." On the back of both were the words, "Operation Deep Freeze" and in the middle "USN IGY," and space for the owner's name (*see also* **Medals**). The Chapel of the Snows burned down on Aug. 22, 1978. A temporary one was dedicated on Easter Sunday 1979, and on Jan. 29, 1989, a new one was dedicated, built by the National Science Foundation. It is 2,016 square feet, with an organ, and seats 63 people.

**Churchill Mountains.** 81°30'S, 158°30' E. Between the Nimrod Glacier and the Byrd Glacier, behind the Shackleton Coast, in the Transantarctic Mountains. Includes Mount Egerton, Mount Field, Mount Wharton, Mount Nares, Mount Albert Markham. Discovered by Scott's 1901–4 expedition, and named by them for Winston Churchill.

**Churchill Peninsula.** 66°30'S, 62°45' W. Also called Flint Peninsula. Ice-covered. Between Cabinet and Adie Inlets. Extends 30 miles from the east coast of Graham Land. Named by the FIDS for Winston Churchill, leader of the war cabinet which in 1943 authorized Operation Tabarin, the forerunner of the FIDS.

**Churchill Point.** 66°24'S, 110°23'E. The NW point of Holl Island, in the Windmill Islands. Named for Robert W. Churchill, USN, radioman at Wilkes Station in 1958.

**Cierva Cove.** 64°09'S, 60°53'W. 6 miles SE of Mount Sterneck, in Hughes Bay, on the west coast of Graham Land. Named by the UK in 1960 for Juan de la Cierva (1895–1936), Spanish designer of the autogiro, in 1923.

**Cierva Point.** A term no longer used. On the Danco Coast. This, and nearby islands, form SSSI #15.

**Ciliate Protozoans.** Microfauna of Antarctica (*see* **Fauna**). There are 29 species, and they dominate soil and freshwater communities.

**Cinder Hill.** 77°17'S, 166°26'E. 305 m. A dissected volcano, between the

Harrison and Wilson Streams, on the ice-free lower west slopes of Mount Bird, about 6 miles south of Cape Bird, Ross Island. Descriptively named by the New Zealanders in 1958–59.

**Cinder Spur.** 62°09′S, 58°11′W. Juts out into Legru Bay, 1½ miles west of Low Head, on the south coast of King George Island, in the South Shetlands. Named by the UK in 1963 for the volcanic cinders that comprise it.

**Mount Circe.** 77°29′S, 160°58′E. Over 2,000 m. Just north of Mount Dido, in the Olympus Range, near Wright Valley, in Victoria Land. Named by the New Zealanders in 1958–59 for the Greek mythological figure.

**Circle Icefall.** 79°38′S, 156°30′E. 45 m. 15 miles long. Near Tentacle Ridge, across the Darwin Glacier. Named by the Darwin Glacier Party of the BCTAE 1957–58 for its resemblance to the circle of an opera house.

**Cabo Circular**   *see*   **Bald Head**

**Port Circumcision.** 65°10′S, 64°08′W. A cove indenting the SE side of Peter-mann Island, in the Wilhelm Archipel-ago. Discovered by Charcot on Jan. 1, 1909, and named by him for Bouvet de Lozier's discovery of Cape Circumcision on Bouvetøya (not in Antarctica) in 1739. The *Pourquoi Pas?* wintered-over here in 1909.

**Circumnavigations of Antarctica.** The first 8 circumnavigations of Antarctica at high latitudes were (1) Cook 1773–75, (2) von Bellingshausen Dec. 1819–Feb. 1821, eastward, (3) Biscoe 1831–32, (4) the *Norvegia* 1930–31, (5) the *Discovery II.* The first in winter—1932, (6) The *Thors-havn* 1933–34, (7) the *Discovery II* 1937–38, (8) the *Burton Island* and the *Edisto* 1947–48. Between Dec. 28, 1982, and March 7, 1983, the *Polar Star* circum-navigated Antarctica. Although this seems unlikely, this voyage may well have been only the ninth circumnaviga-tion of Antarctica.

**CIROS.** Cenozoic Investigations in the Ross Sea. A 3-year offshore drilling project by New Zealand, off Butter Point in McMurdo Sound, begun in 1985. A major storm destroyed the camp early on, but it was repaired.

**Cirque Fjord.** 67°18′S, 58°39′E. An ice-filled inlet on the south side of Law Promontory, opening into Stefansson Bay, in Enderby Land. Photographed by the LCE 1936–37, and named Botnf-jorden (the cirque fjord) by the Norwegians.

**Cirque Peak.** 72°11′S, 165°58′E. 1 mile south of Le Couteur Peak, in the Millen Range. Named by the New Zealanders because it is at the head of a large cirque.

**Cirques.** Amphitheater-, or bowl-shaped basins, with precipitous walls cut into the sides of mountains, at the heads of glacier valleys. A cirque usually develops due to erosion beneath the bergschrund of a glacier.

**Citadel Bastion.** 72°S, 68°32′W. A flat-topped, rocky elevation at the south side of the terminus of Saturn Glacier, on the east side of Alexander Island. Named descriptively by the UK.

**Citadel Peak.** 85°57′S, 154°27′W. On the south side of the Vaughan Glacier, 6 miles east of Mount Vaughan, in the Queen Maud Mountains. Named de-scriptively by the New Zealanders in 1969–70.

**Citroën.** French auto company which financed several expeditions throughout the world. The company furnished 3 light trucks with caterpillar tracks for Byrd's 1933–35 expedition. One of these, in the party led by Poulter, rescued Ad-miral Byrd from Bolling Advance Weather Station during his "alone" stay there in the winter of 1934.

**The *City of Auckland.*** Beaver aircraft that crashed in the Queen Alexandra Range, in Jan. 1960.

**The *City of New York.*** Byrd's flagship on his 1928–30 expedition. Formerly called the *Samson,* it was a Norwegian whaler built in 1882. It had a 512-ton dis-placement, was 170 feet long, and had a

31-foot beam. The thick hull was made of spruce and oak, and it had oak ribs. Its sides were 34 inches thick. It carried auxiliary steam power. Byrd bought this barkentine on Amundsen's advice, and converted it into a bark by putting yards on the mainmast. It cost $165,000 to buy and outfit. Captain in 1928–30 was Frederick C. Melville.

**Claess, Laurens.** Bosun on the *Blyde Bootschap*, in 1603. He reported the adventure in writing.

**Clague Ridge.** 71°14′S, 65°40′E. Partially snow-covered. 5 miles SW of Armonini Nunatak, in the Prince Charles Mountains. Named by the Australians for E.L. Clague, weather observer at Wilkes Station in 1962.

**Claiborne, M.G.** Lieutenant on the *Porpoise* during the Wilkes Expedition 1838–42, which he joined at Callao.

**Clapp Ridge.** 72°54′S, 167°54′E. 9 miles long. Forms the north wall of Hand Glacier, in the Victory Mountains of Victoria Land. Named for James L. Clapp, glaciologist at Roosevelt Island, in 1967–68.

**Claquebue Island.** 66°46′S, 14°35′E. ¼ mile long. Almost 100 yards east of Dru Rock, in the Curzon Islands. Charted in 1951 by the French and named by them for the village in the novel *La Jument Verte*, a book much read in the Antarctic.

**Clare Range.** 77°10′S, 161°05′E. Extends WSW from Sperm Bluff to the Willett Range, on the south side of the Mackay Glacier, in Victoria Land. Explored in 1957 by the NZ Northern Survey Party of the BCTAE, and named by them for Clare College, Cambridge.

**Clarence Island.** 61°12′S, 54°05′W. Also called Shishkoff's Island. The most easterly of the South Shetlands, it is 12 miles long. Was named before 1821.

**Mount Clarence MacKay** *see* **MacKay Mountains**

**Clarie Coast** *see* **Wilkes Coast**

**¹Clark, Capt.** British sealing captain who commanded the *Lord Melville* in 1819–20. He and his 10 seal hunters were the first known men to winter-over—albeit involuntarily—in Antarctica, when they spent 1820 on King George Island, in the South Shetlands.

**²Clark, Capt.** Commander of the *Lion* on its first trip to the South Shetlands, in 1852–53.

**Clark, Alexander B.** A Nantucket sealing captain who led the second sealing expedition (sometimes called the Clark Fleet) out of Stonington, Conn., to the South Shetlands (the first had been the *Hersilia*, the year before) in 1820–21. Clark himself commanded the *Clothier* which, with its tender, the *Spark*, left Stonington on Aug. 9, 1820. The brigs *Catharina* and *Emmeline* had sailed on July 30, 1820, and July 31, 1820, respectively. They all arrived in the South Shetlands from the Falkland Islands, on Dec. 1, 1820, and on Dec. 7, 1820, the *Clothier*, the flagship of the fleet, was wrecked. The seal catch was successful, and the two remaining brigs left the South Shetlands on March 9, 1821. Crew members of the *Clothier* sailed back to the USA on the *O'Cain*. The sailing date of the *Spark* is unknown.

**Clark, Arnold H.** Assistant physicist on the shore party of Byrd's 1928–30 expedition.

**Clark, Daniel W.** First mate on the *Hersilia*, 1820–21. He was in charge of a sealing gang on the South Beaches of Livingston Island, in the South Shetlands. He described the activities in writing.

**Clark, George W.** Midshipman on the Wilkes Expedition 1838–42. He started on the *Vincennes*, then joined the *Peacock* at Tahiti, and later rejoined the *Vincennes* at San Francisco.

**¹Clark, Joseph.** Corporal of Marines on the Wilkes Expedition 1838–42. Joined in the USA. Served the cruise.

**²Clark, Joseph.** Seaman on the Wilkes Expedition 1838–42. Joined in the USA. Served the cruise.

**Clark, Leroy.** One of the shore party on Byrd's 1933–35 expedition.

**Clark, Levin.** Captain of the maintop on the Wilkes Expedition 1838–42. Joined in the USA. Served the cruise.

**Clark, Robert S.** 1882–1950. Robert Selbie Clark. Scottish biologist on the *Endurance* during the British Imperial Transantarctic Expedition of 1914–17.

**Clark Glacier.** 77°25′S, 162°25′E. Between Mount Theseus and Mount Allen, in the east part of the Olympus Range, in the vicinity of the Wright Valley, in Victoria Land. Named by the VUWAE 1958–59 for Prof. R.H. Clark, head of the Geology Dept. at the Victoria University of Wellington, NZ, who was immediately responsible for the sponsoring of the expedition.

**Clark Hills.** 70°43′S, 63°25′W. Mainly snow-covered. 4 miles in extent. 5 miles SW of the Eland Mountains, in Palmer Land. Named for Kerry B. Clark, US biologist on the International Weddell Sea Oceanographic Expedition in 1968 and 1969.

**¹Clark Island** *see* **Clark Peninsula**

**²Clark Island.** 74°05′S, 105°17′W. 2 miles long. The largest island of a small group 38 miles WSW of Canisteo Peninsula, in the eastern Amundsen Sea. Named for F. Jerry Clark, glaciologist/geologist at Roosevelt Island in 1961–62, and who was on traverses from Byrd Station in 1963–64.

**Clark Knoll.** 76°53′S, 146°59′W. Ice-covered. 4 miles SW of Mount Dane, in the west part of Radford Island, in the Marshall Archipelago. Named for Elton G. Clark, USN, utilitiesman at Byrd Station in 1967.

**Clark Mountains.** 77°16′S, 142°W. 10 miles east of the Allegheny Mountains, in the Ford Ranges of Marie Byrd Land. Discovered aerially by the USAS in 1940. Named by them for Clark University, Worcester, Mass.

**Clark Nunatak.** 62°40′S, 60°55′W. Also called Black Hill. On the south side of Rotch Dome, in the west part of Livingston Island, in the South Shetlands. Named by the UK in 1958 for Daniel W. Clark.

**Clark Peak.** 77°31′S, 154°12′W. 645 m. On the west side of Larson Glacier, in the northern part of the Edward VII Peninsula. Named for Leroy Clark.

**Clark Peninsula.** 66°15′S, 110°33′E. 2 miles long. 2 miles wide. On the north side of Newcomb Bay, in the Windmill Islands, it is frozen to the side of Vincennes Bay. Named Clark Island in 1947 for John E. Clark, USN, captain of the *Currituck* during Operation Highjump, 1946–47. In 1957 it was redefined. It is SSSI #17.

**Clark Point.** 66°33′S, 123°55′E. Ice-covered. At the east side of the entrance to Paulding Bay. Named for George W. Clark.

**Clark Ridge.** 84°32′S, 64°50′W. 4 miles long. 4 miles west of Mount Lowry, in the Anderson Hills, in the northern part of the Patuxent Range of the Pensacola Mountains. Named for Larry Clark, cook at Plateau Station in 1967.

**Clark Spur.** 84°47′S, 169°12′W. 3 miles long. Extends from the foothills of the Prince Olav Mountains to the edge of the Ross Ice Shelf. Forms the east side of the mouth of Morris Glacier, 6 miles NW of Mount Henson. Discovered by Byrd's 1928–30 expedition, and named by Byrd for Arnold H. Clark.

**Mount Clarke.** 85°05′S, 172°15′E. 3,210 m. 13 miles east of Mount Iveagh, it rises along the east margin of the Snakeskin Glacier, just to the south of the Keltie Glacier, in the Queen Maud Mountains. Discovered and named by Shackleton in 1907–9.

**Clarke, Charles.** Assistant cook, 1901–3, and cook, 1903–4, on the *Discovery* during Scott's Royal Society Expedition.

**Clarke, Eric T.** Physicist from the Bartol Foundation in Pennsylvania. He conducted observations on the *North Star,* and set up the cosmic ray recording equipment at West Base during the first half of the USAS 1939–41, i.e. from 1939–40. He was succeeded on the second half of the expedition by Dana K. Bailey.

**Clarke Barrier** *see* **Clarke Glacier**

**Clarke Bluff.** 69°38′S, 159°13′E. 840 m. At the east end of Feeney Ridge, in the Wilson Hills. Named for Lt. (jg) Jon B. Clarke, USN, navigator in Antarctica in 1967 and 1968.

**¹Clarke Glacier.** 68°48′S, 66°56′W. 2 miles wide. 20 miles long. Flows into Mikkelsen Bay, along the north side of Sickle Mountain and the Baudin Peaks, on the west coast of Graham Land. Named by the FIDS for Louis C.G. Clarke, director of the Fitzwilliam Museum, Cambridge, 1937–46, who helped the BGLE in 1934–37. The BGLE surveyed the glacier in 1936.

**²Clarke Glacier.** 75°34′S, 162°05′E. Also called Clarke Barrier. 5 miles long. Flows to the Victoria Land coast, just north of Lewandowski Point. Discovered and named by Shackleton's 1907–9 expedition.

**Clarkson Cliffs.** 80°28′S, 27°04′W. In the Shackleton Range.

**Clarkson Peak.** 83°19′S, 164°32′E. 2,825 m. At the head of Robb Glacier between the Holland Range and the Queen Elizabeth Range. Named by the NZ Southern Party of the BCTAE for T.R. Clarkson, a member of the Ross Sea Committee for that expedition of 1955–58.

**Clarkson Point** *see* **Pylon Point**

**Clarsach Glacier.** 69°57′S, 70°17′W. In the northern part of Alexander Island.

**Cape Claude** *see* **Claude Point**

**Claude Point.** 64°07′S, 62°36′W. Also called Cape Claude. Forms the south side of the entrance to Guyou Bay, on the west side of Brabant Island. Discovered by Charcot in 1903–5, and named by him for M. Claude, an associate member of the Bureau des Longitudes.

**Claude Swanson Mountains** *see* **Swanson Mountains**

**Clausen Glacier.** 76°10′S, 112°03′W. Flows from the summit of Mount Takahe, to just west of Knezevich Rock, in Marie Byrd Land. Named for Henrik B. Clausen, American glaciologist at McMurdo Station in 1966.

**Clausnitzer Glacier.** 74°02′S, 164°41′E. Flows from the Random Hills into Tinker Glacier, just north of Harrow Peaks, in Victoria Land. Named for Frazer W. Clausnitzer, ionosphere physicist at McMurdo Station in 1966.

**Islote Clavo** *see* **Huemul Island**

**Claydon, John R.** RNZAF squadron leader who led the aircraft support team on Hillary's trip to the Pole during the BCTAE 1957–58.

**Claydon Peak.** 83°25′S, 162°04′E. 3,040 m. In the SE sector of the Queen Elizabeth Range. Named by the NZ Southern Survey Party of the BCTAE in early 1958, for John R. Claydon.

**Claymore Peak** *see* **Mount Ulla**

**Clayton Hill.** 65°11′S, 64°10′W. 125 m. In the north central part of Petermann Island. Charted and named by Charcot in 1908–10.

**Clayton Ramparts.** 80°44′S, 27°25′W. In the Shackleton Range.

**Clean Air Automatic Weather Station.** 90°S. An American AWS at the South Pole. It began operating on Jan. 29, 1986.

**Clear Island.** 64°55′S, 63°44′W. Also called Isla Coy. A small, snow-capped island, just north of Wednesday Island. It is the most northeasterly of the Wauwermans Islands. Named by the UK in 1958 because one can see it from almost everywhere.

**¹Clear Lake.** In the Mule Peninsula of the Vestfold Hills.

**²Clear Lake.** 77°32′S, 166°09′E. A small lake just WNW of Blue Lake at Cape

Royds, Ross Island. It is the deepest lake in the area. Named descriptively by Shackleton in 1907–9.

**Cleaves Glacier.** 82°57'S, 165°E. In the Holland Range, it flows from Mount Reid into the east side of Robb Glacier. Named for Harold H. Cleaves, captain of the *Private Joseph F. Merrell,* 1964–65.

**Cleft Island.** 69°21'S, 75°38'E. A small island north of the Bølingen Islands. 2½ miles SE of Lichen Island, in the southern part of Prydz Bay. Photographed by the LCE 1936–37, and named Lorten by the Norwegian cartographers. Visited by personnel from the *Nella Dan* in Feb. 1966, and renamed by this ANARE party because of the deep channel.

**Cleft Peak.** 83°55'S, 173°34'E. 1,245 m. Its eastern side is cleft from summit to base by a huge fissure. In the west part of the Separation Range, overlooking the terminus of Hood Glacier. Named by the NZ Alpine Club Antarctic Expedition of 1959–60, whose four members were landed here by VX-6 aircraft.

**Cleft Point.** 60°37'S, 45°46'W. On the east side of Norway Bight, on the south coast of Coronation Island, in the South Orkneys. When the Discovery Investigations personnel on the *Discovery II* mapped it in 1933, they thought it was on Coronation Island. In 1950 the FIDS found that it was the western extremity of an island separated (or cleft) from the big island by a narrow channel.

**Clegg, William.** Ordinary seaman on the Wilkes Expedition 1838–42. Joined in the USA. Returned on the *Relief* in 1839.

**Clem Nunatak.** 78°31'S, 160°40'E. 1,260 m. Isolated. On the west side of the Skelton Glacier. 7 miles SW of Halfway Nunatak. Named in 1964 for Willis R. Clem, construction mechanic at McMurdo Station in 1959.

**Clemence Massif.** 72°10'S, 68°43'E. 1,400 m. 15 miles long. Mostly ice-free. 30 miles SE of the Shaw Massif, on the east side of the Lambert Glacier, at the northern end of the Mawson Escarpment, in the Prince Charles Mountains. Discovered aerially by D.M. Johnston, RAAF, an ANARE flying officer, in 1957. Named by the Australians for Squadron Leader P.H. Clemence, commander of the RAAF Antarctic Flight at Mawson Station that year.

**Clement, W.H.** Crewman on the *Jacob Ruppert,* 1934–35.

**Clement Hill.** 62°13'S, 58°58'W. Just to the SW of Suffield Point, on Fildes Peninsula, on King George Island, in the South Shetlands.

**Clements building.** An easily assembled kit building with 4-by-8-foot panels for top and sides. Invented by the Clements Company, and developed by the US Navy for the Antarctic.

**Clements Island.** 65°56'S, 66°W. Also called Clements Markham Island, Markham Island. 1 mile long. Just south of Rabot Island, in the Biscoe Islands. In 1903–5 Charcot named an island in this area as Île Clements Markham. The UK later redefined the island and the name. (*See* the **Royal Society Expedition** for information on Clements Markham.)

**Clements Markham Bay** *see* **Markham Bay**

**Clements Markham Island** *see* **Clements Island**

**Clemons Spur.** 82°31'S, 51°13'W. In the Pensacola Mountains.

**Clemson, H.A.** Midshipman on the Wilkes Expedition 1838–42. Joined the *Vincennes* at Rio. Detached at Callao.

**Clerke, Charles.** b. 1743, Weatherfield, Essex, d. July 22, 1779, of tuberculosis, off Kamchatka. Entered the Royal Navy at 12. He was 2nd lt. on the *Resolution* during Cook's second voyage, of 1772–75.

**Cléry Peak.** 65°03'S, 63°58'W. 640 m. On the north side of Mount Lacroix, at the north end of Booth Island. Charted by Charcot in 1903–5, and named by him for his father-in-law, L. Cléry, a

French lawyer of note, and himself son-in-law of Victor Hugo.

**Cletrac Peak.** 64°20'S, 59°38'W. At the NW corner of Larsen Inlet, just north of Muskeg Gap, in Graham Land. Named by the UK for the cletracs.

**Cletracs.** Heavy tractors built by King White's Cleveland Tractor Company in Ohio. They weighed 6 tons and could tow a 10-ton load. Byrd had one on his 1933–35 expedition (he was the first to use it); it was used only around Little America II because it was too heavy for the crevasses. They were also used on Operation Highjump, 1946–47.

**Cleveland Glacier.** 76°55'S, 162°14'E. 2 miles wide. Flows from Mounts Morrison and Brøgger into the Mackay Glacier. It is just north of that glacier, in Victoria Land. Discovered during Scott's 1910–13 expedition and named by Frank Debenham. Cleveland was his mother's original name.

**Cleveland Mesa.** 86°19'S, 130°W. 5 miles long. 3 miles wide. Ice-covered. At the SE end of the Michigan Plateau. Named for Harlan Cleveland, chairman of the Antarctic Policy Group, 1965.

**Cliff Island.** 66°S, 65°39'W. A narrow, cliffed island, at the south side of Mutton Cove. Just south of Upper Island, and 8 miles west of Prospect Point, off the west coast of Graham Land. Charted and named descriptively by the BGLE 1934–37.

**Clifford, Charles.** Captain of the maintop on the Wilkes Expedition 1838–42. Joined in the USA. Discharged at Oahu, Nov. 2, 1840.

**Clifford Glacier.** 70°25'S, 62°30'W. 40 miles long. Flows into Smith Inlet, on the east coast of Palmer Land. Named by the FIDS in 1952 for Sir G. Miles Clifford, governor of the Falkland Islands.

**Clifford Peak.** 64°34'S, 62°53'W. 1,160 m. At the NE end of the Osterrieth Range, on Anvers Island. Discovered by de Gerlache in 1897–99. Named in 1948

for Sir G. Miles Clifford (*see* **Clifford Glacier**) by personnel on the *Snipe*, following a cruise there in Jan. 1948.

**Climate.** The Antarctic is cold (*see* **Temperatures**). Its great elevation and perpetually reflective snow-cover intensify the Polar climate.

**Climbing Range** *see* **Blackwall Mountains**

**Cline Glacier.** 71°40'S, 62°W. To the east of Mount Jackson, it flows between the Schirmacher Massif and the Rowley Massif, into the head of Odom Inlet, on the east side of Palmer Land. Named for David R. Cline, biologist on the International Weddell Sea Oceanographic Expedition in 1968 and 1969.

**Clingman Peak.** 73°50'S, 161°12'E. 2,150 m. The last peak along the south wall at the head of Priestley Glacier, in Victoria Land. Named for Otis Clingman, Jr., biologist at McMurdo Station in 1965–66.

**Clinker Bluff.** 78°31'S, 161°35'E. Within the Skelton Glacier, west of Mount Tricouni. Surveyed in 1957 by the NZ party of the BCTAE, and named descriptively by them. A clinker is a rectangular nail used in alpine boots, and a tricouni is a saw-toothed nail used on the soles.

**Clinton Spur.** 82°39'S, 52°45'W. On the south side of the Dufek Massif, 1½ miles SE of Neuburg Peak, in the Pensacola Mountains. Named for Lt. Clinton R. Smith, USN, at Ellsworth Station in 1957.

**Clissold, Thomas.** Late of the RN, cook on Scott's 1910–13 expedition.

**Cape Cloos.** 65°07'S, 64°W. Fronts on the Lemaire Channel, and marks the north side of the entrance to Girard Bay, on the west coast of Graham Land. Discovered and named by de Gerlache in 1897–99.

**Massif Cloos** *see* **Mount Cloos**

**Mount Cloos.** 65°07'S, 63°57'W. Also called Massif Cloos. Over 915 m. Dome-shaped. On the north side of Girard Bay.

2 miles NE of Cape Cloos, on the west coast of Graham Land. Discovered by de Gerlache in 1897–99. Named by Charcot in 1908–10 in association with the cape.

**Cape Close.** 65°55'S, 52°30'E. Between Cape Ann and Cape Borley in Enderby Land, at the foot of the Napier Mountains. 30 miles west of Cape Batterbee. Discovered by the BANZARE 1929–31, and named by Mawson for Sir Charles Close, president of the Royal Geographical Society, 1927–30.

**Close, John H.** Member of the AAE 1911–14.

**Close Islands.** 67°02'S, 144°27'E. 3 small islands in the western part of the entrance to Buchanan Bay. Discovered by the AAE 1911–14, and named by Mawson for John H. Close.

**The *Clothier*.** A 94-foot-long, 285-ton Stonington, Conn., sealer, built in Philadelphia in 1810, and registered in New London on Aug. 2, 1820. It was commanded by Capt. Alexander B. Clark as the flagship of his fleet going down to the South Shetlands in 1820–21. On Dec. 7, 1820, it was wrecked on the NW coast of Robert Island, in the South Shetlands, and on Feb. 1 of that year was salvage auctioned in Clothier Harbor where it had gone down.

**Clothier Harbor.** 62°22'S, 59°40'W. Also called Clothier's Harbor. An indentation in the NW coast of Robert Island, in the South Shetlands. Named by Alexander B. Clark, captain of the *Clothier*, which was wrecked here on Dec. 7, 1820.

**Clothing.** The best way to keep warm (in the Antarctic) is to layer the clothing, and to avoid tight clothing. Wool is better than cotton. *See also* **Boots, Finneskoes, Mukluks, Socks, Trousers, Underwear, Sweaters, Sunglasses.**

**The *Cloudmaker*.** 84°17'S, 169°25'E. 2,681 m. A mountain with a high, ice-free slope. A cloud is usually at its summit. Just south of Hewson Glacier, in the Queen Alexandra Range, overlooking the Beardmore Glacier, halfway to the South Pole. Discovered by Shackleton in 1907–9. Named descriptively.

**Clouds.** There is hardly any rain in the Antarctic, so clouds, as such, are not seen. Practically all of the "clouds" in Antarctica are composed of ice crystals, and this can lead to phenomena (q.v.).

**Mount Clough.** 85°54'S, 158°26'W. 2,230 m. Ice-free. 2 miles east of Mount Dort, at the south side of Cappellari Glacier, in the Queen Maud Mountains. Discovered by Byrd's 1928–30 expedition. Named for John W. Clough, geophysicist on the South Pole–Queen Maud Land Traverse II in 1965–66.

**Clowes Bay.** 60°44'S, 45°38'W. 1 mile wide. Between Confusion Point and the Oliphant Islands, on the south side of Signy Island, in the South Orkneys. Charted in 1933 by the personnel on the *Discovery II,* and named by them for Archibald J. Clowes, British oceanographer on the staff of the Discovery Committee, 1924–26.

**Clowes Glacier.** 72°56'S, 60°41'W. 2 miles wide. Flows into Mason Inlet, on the east coast of Palmer Land. Discovered aerially in Dec. 1940 by the USAS. Named by the FIDS for Archibald J. Clowes (*see* **Clowes Bay**).

**Cloyd Island.** 66°25'S, 110°33'E. Also spelled Kloyd Island. Just over ½ mile long. Between Ford Island and Herring Island, in the Windmill Islands. Named for J.R. Cloyd, observer on Operation Windmill, 1947–48.

**Mount Club** *see* **Mount Touring Club**

**Club Lake.** 68°33'S, 78°14'E. A saltwater lake in the central part of the Breidnes Peninsula, in the Vestfold Hills. 1½ miles long, and club-shaped, it was named by the ANARE in 1957–58.

**Clute, Daniel.** Quartermaster on the Wilkes Expedition 1838–42. Joined in the USA. Lost in the *Sea Gull* in late April 1839.

**Coal.** Shackleton discovered coal in Antarctica in 1907–9, and it has been found ever since. Semi-anthracite, an-thracite, and coke. The coal in Antarctica is generally high in ash, fixed carbon, and oxygen, and low in hydrogen and sulfur. The coals are not as good as for-eign coals (*see also* **Fuel**).

**Coal Nunatak.** 72°07′S, 68°32′W. Flat-topped. 2 miles SW of Corner Cliffs on the SE coast of Alexander Island. Dis-covered aerially by Ellsworth on Nov. 23, 1935. It was not clear whether this was a nunatak or an island in the George VI Sound, and it was finally determined by the FIDS to be the former, and was named by them for the thin lenses of coal here.

**Coal Point Island.** A term no longer used. It was off the Danco Coast, just north of Paradise Bay.

**Coal Rock.** 83°29′S, 50°38′W. 4 miles SE of Fierle Peak, at the south end of the Forrestal Range, in the Pensacola Moun-tains. Named by Dwight L. Schmidt (*see* **Schmidt Hills**) for the Permian coal well-exposed on this nunatak.

**Coalsack Bluff.** 84°15′S, 162°25′E. A small rock bluff at the northern limits of the Walcott Névé, at the southern end of the Queen Alexandra Range. 6 miles WSW of Bauhs Nunatak. A great fossil source. Named by the New Zealanders in 1961–62 for the coal seams here.

**Coalseam Cliffs.** 79°10′S, 28°50′W. They form the NW part of Mount Faraway, in the Theron Mountains. Named by the BCTAE in 1956–57 for the coal seam found here.

**Coast Lake.** 77°32′S, 166°08′E. A small lake ¾ mile north of Flagstaff Point, almost a mile north of Cape Royds, Ross Island. Named by members of Shackleton's 1907–09 expedition because of its position close to the coast.

**Coasts.** The major ones, working east from 0° longitude, are Princess Astrid, Princess Ragnhild, Prince Olav, Kemp, Ingrid Christensen, Leopold and Astrid, Queen Mary, Knox, Budd, Sabrina, Ban-zare, Wilkes, Adélie, George V, Oates, Siple, Hobbs, Walgreen, Eights, Bryan, English, Luitpold, Caird, and Princess Martha.

**¹Mount Coates.** 67°52′S, 62°31′E. 1,280 m. Just south of Mount Lawrence, in the David Range of the Framnes Mountains. Discovered and named in Feb. 1931 by the BANZARE.

**²Mount Coates.** 77°48′S, 162°04′E. 2,060 m. Just east of the Borns Glacier, in the Kukri Hills of Victoria Land. Named by Grif Taylor and his Western Journey Party during Scott's 1910–13 expedition.

**Coates Rocks.** 72°32′S, 164°20′E. A small group in the NW part of the Evans Névé, at the south side of the Freyberg Mountains. Named for Donald A. Coates, geologist at Hallett Station in 1964–65, and at McMurdo Station in 1966–67.

**Coats Land.** 77°S, 28°W. Extends be-tween 20°W and 36°W, and forms the eastern shore of the Weddell Sea. It is to the east of the Filchner Ice Shelf, and ex-tends 300 miles to Queen Maud Land, and includes the Luitpold Coast and the Caird Coast. Discovered on March 3, 1904 by Bruce, and named by him for the principal backers of his expedition, the Coats family of Scotland. The eastern sector is claimed by Norway, the central sector by Great Britain, and the western sector by Argentina.

**Cobalescou Island.** 64°11′S, 61°39′W. Small and snow-free, it has two rounded summits. 1 mile SE of Two Hummock Island, in the Palmer Archipelago. Dis-covered by de Gerlache in 1897–99, and named by him on the suggestion of Emile Racovitza (q.v.) for Grigore Cobalescu (sic), a Rumanian geologist of note.

**Cobham Range.** 82°23′S, 159°E. Ex-tends for 20 miles west of the Prince Philip Glacier, in the southern part of the Churchill Mountains, just to the north of the Nimrod Glacier. Named by the New Zealanders for Lord Cobham, a former governor-general of New Zea-land.

**Coblentz Peak.** 66°07′S, 65°08′W. On the north side of the head of Holtedahl Bay, on the west coast of Graham Land. Named by the UK in 1959 for William W. Coblentz of the US National Bureau of Standards, a snow goggles pioneer.

**Cochran Peak.** 79°39′S, 84°39′W. In the south part of the Gifford Peaks, in the Heritage Range. Named for Henry B. Cochran, Weather Central (q.v.) meteorologist at Little America V in 1958.

**Isla Cocinero Honores** *see* **Honores Rock**

**Cape Cockburn.** 64°01′S, 62°18′W. Marks the NE extremity of Pasteur Peninsula, on Brabant Island. Probably named by Foster in 1828–31 for George Cockburn, admiral of the fleet in 1851, and in Foster's time an RN officer. In the 1830s he was senior naval lord of the admiralty.

**Cockburn Island.** 64°12′S, 56°51′W. A tiny island, about 3 square miles in area. It is nearly circular, extremely steep-sided, has a flat, broad surface, and a cone-shaped profile. North of Seymour Island. It was discovered by Ross, who named it for George Cockburn (*see* **Cape Cockburn**).

**Cockerell Peninsula.** 63°24′S, 58°08′W. A narrow isthmus, 7 miles SW of Cape Legoupil, on the northern coast of the Trinity Peninsula. Cape Ducorps forms its extremity.

**Mount Cocks.** 78°31′S, 162°30′E. 2,440 m. In the south part of the Royal Society Range, at the head of the Koettlitz Glacier. Discovered by Scott's 1901–4 expedition, and named by them for E.L. Somers Cocks, treasurer of the Royal Geographical Society.

**Cocks Glacier.** 78°41′S, 162°E. Flows from the SW face of Mount Cocks into the Skelton Glacier, opposite the Delta Glacier, in southern Victoria Land. Surveyed in 1957 by the NZ party of the BCTAE, and named by them in association with the mountain.

**Cockscomb Buttress.** 60°37′S, 45°42′W. 465 m. An isolated spur, 1 mile NW of Echo Mountain, overlooking the east side of Norway Bight, on the south coast of Coronation Island, in the South Orkneys. Named descriptively by the FIDS following their 1950 survey.

**Cockscomb Hill.** 62°05′S, 58°30′W. Also called Cerro Cono. 140 m. Rises through the glacier at the head of Mackellar Inlet, in Admiralty Bay, King George Island, in the South Shetlands. Surveyed by Charcot in 1908–10, and again in 1951–52 by Lt. Cdr. F.W. Hunt, RN, who named it descriptively.

**Mount Codrington.** 66°18′S, 52°52′E. 1,520 m. 24 miles SSE of Cape Close. 17 miles east of Johnston Peak. Charted in 1930 by the BANZARE as being the peak thus named by Biscoe in March 1831.

**Cody, John.** 1st assistant engineer on the *Eleanor Bolling* during the first half of Byrd's 1928–30 expedition. He was replaced by Elbert Thawley.

**Coffer Island.** 60°45′S, 45°08′W. Also seen as Koffer, Kotter. A small island in the entrance to the bay on the east side of Matthews Island, in the Robertson Islands, of the South Orkneys. The personnel on the *Discovery II* who charted it in 1933 were the first to name it Coffer Island.

**Mount Cohen.** 85°16′S, 164°27′W. 1,765 m. 6 miles SW of Mount Betty, in the Herbert Range of the Queen Maud Mountains. Discovered aerially by Byrd in Nov. 1929, and named by him for Manny Cohen of Paramount Pictures, who helped assemble Byrd's movie footage.

**Cohen Glacier.** 85°12′S, 164°15′W. A small glacier that flows from Mount Cohen into Strom Glacier, near the head of the Ross Ice Shelf. Named by the New Zealanders in 1963–64 in association with the mountain.

**Cohen Islands.** 63°18′S, 57°53′W. A cluster of small islands between Ponce Island and Pebbly Mudstone Island, in the SE part of the Duroch Islands. Named for Theodore J. Cohen, geologist here in 1961–62.

**Cohen Nunatak.** 85°24'S, 136°12'W. 1 mile west of the lower part of Reedy Glacier. 7 miles east of the Berry Peaks. Named for Lt. (jg) Harvey A. Cohen, public affairs officer on the staff of the commander, US Naval Support Force, Antarctica, 1966 and 1967.

**Coker Ice Rise.** 69°04'S, 67°08'W. On the west coast of the Antarctic Peninsula.

**Isla Cola** *see* **Tail Island**

**Cape Colbeck.** 77°06'S, 157°54'W. Ice-covered. At the head of the Edward VII Peninsula. Discovered in Jan. 1902 by Scott's 1901–4 expedition, and named for William Colbeck.

**Colbeck, W.R.** 2nd officer on the *Discovery* during the BANZARE 1929–31.

**Colbeck, William.** From Yorkshire. Merchant Navy officer who went on Borchgrevink's expedition of 1898–1900. He wintered over on Victoria Land in 1899, and took part in the southing record set by Borchgrevink on Feb. 16, 1900. He became a lieutenant in the RNR, and was commander of the *Morning*, the ship sent to relieve Scott in 1903 and 1904.

**Colbeck Archipelago.** 67°26'S, 60°58' E. Several small, rocky islands, 1 mile NW of Byrd Head, just east of Taylor Glacier. Sometimes confused with the Thorfinn Islands. Discovered in Jan. 1930, and charted in Feb. 1931 by the BANZARE, and named by Mawson for W.R. Colbeck.

**Colbeck Bay.** 71°38'S, 170°07'E. Between Duke of York Island and Cape Klövstad, in the southern part of Robertson Bay, Victoria Land. Charted by Borchgrevink in 1898–1900, and named by him for William Colbeck.

**Mount Colbert.** 86°12'S, 153°05'W. In the Queen Maud Mountains.

**Colbert Hills.** 84°12'S, 162°35'E. A line of hills and bluffs, including Coalsack Bluff. East of the Lewis Cliffs, between Law Glacier and the Walcott Névé. They trend SW for 16 miles from Mount Sirius. Named for Edwin H.

Colbert, paleontologist here in 1969–70 as leader of the Ohio State University Geological Expedition, which discovered the Lystrosaurus fossil here.

**Colbert Mountains.** 70°35'S, 70°35' W. Also called Colbert Range, United States Navy Range, Navy Range. An isolated mountain mass with several rounded, snow-covered summits, the highest being 1,500 m. They overlook the Handel Ice Piedmont, between Haydn and Schubert Inlets, in the west central part of Alexander Island. Finn Ronne named them for Rear-Adm. Leo O. Colbert, head of the US Coast and Geodetic Survey, which furnished equipment for the RARE 1947–48.

**Colbert Range** *see* **Colbert Mountains**

**Mount Colburn.** 74°25'S, 132°33'W. 520 m. On Shepard Island, in Marie Byrd Land. Named for Lt. (jg) Richard E. Colburn, USN, communications officer on the *Glacier*, which mapped this mountain on Feb. 4, 1962.

**Coldblow Col.** 60°37'S, 45°41'W. 300 m. Snow-covered. A col between Echo Mountain and Cragsman Peaks, on Coronation Island, in the South Orkneys. In Sept. 1948 a FIDS party had their tent blown down in a gale when camped here.

**Mount Cole.** 84°40'S, 177°08'W. Over 1,400 m. On the west side of Shackleton Glacier, between the mouths of the Forman and Gerasimou Glaciers, in the Queen Maud Mountains. Discovered during Operation Highjump, 1946–47. Named for Nelson D. Cole.

**Cole, Garret.** Ordinary seaman on the Wilkes Expedition 1838–42. Joined in the USA. Served the cruise.

**Cole, John H.** Captain of the maintop on the Wilkes Expedition 1838–42. Joined in the USA. Discharged at Oahu, Nov. 2, 1840.

**Cole, Nelson D.** Aviation machinist's mate with VX-6 at McMurdo Base in 1957. The ninth victim of Operation Deep Freeze, he died in a helicopter crash on McMurdo Sound on July 12, 1957.

**Cole Glacier.** 68°42′S, 66°06′W. On the east side of the Godfrey Upland. 11 miles long, it flows into the Traffic Circle, in southern Graham Land. Discovered by the USAS in 1940. Surveyed by the FIDS in 1958, and named by the UK for Humphrey Cole, 16th century instrument maker.

**Cole Peak.** 85°45′S, 136°38′W. 2,140 m. 6 miles NE of Mount Doumani, on the north side of the Watson Escarpment. Named for Jerry D. Cole, VX-6 airman at McMurdo Base in 1957 and 1960.

**Cole Peninsula.** 66°50′S, 64°W. 15 miles long. 8 miles wide. Mostly ice-covered. Juts out from the east side of the Antarctic Peninsula into the Larsen Ice Shelf, just south of Cape Alexander, between Cabinet Inlet and Mill Inlet. Discovered aerially in Dec. 1940 by East Base members during the USAS. Named by Finn Ronne for W. Sterling Cole, congressman from New York, who helped get Ronne a ship for his RARE 1947–48.

**Cole Point.** 74°39′S, 127°30′W. At the south end of Dean Island, inside the Getz Ice Shelf, just off the coast of Marie Byrd Land. Named for Lawrence M. Cole, USN, builder at Byrd Station in 1969.

**Mount Coleman.** 77°32′S, 163°23′E. 1,110 m. Just east of the Commonwealth Glacier, at the head of New Harbor, in Victoria Land. Mapped by Scott's 1910–13 expedition, and named by Charles S. Wright for Prof. Coleman, geologist at Toronto University.

**Coleman, William.** First mate on the *Huntress*, 1820–21.

**Coleman Bluffs.** 72°28′S, 160°37′E. Near the center of the Outback Nunataks. 10 miles NW of Mount Weihaupt. Named for Harold L. Coleman, meteorologist at Amundsen-Scott South Pole Station.

**Coleman Glacier.** 75°47′S, 132°33′W. Flows from Mount Andrus in the south part of the Ames Range, in Marie Byrd Land. Named for Master Sgt. Clarence N. Coleman, US Army, member of the Army-Navy Trail Party that traversed Marie Byrd Land to establish Byrd Station in 1956–57.

**Coleman Nunatak.** 75°19′S, 133°39′W. Near the head of Berry Glacier, in the area of Patton Bluff, Marie Byrd Land. Lichens are found here. Named for Richard I. Coleman, meteorologist at Byrd Station in 1962.

**Mount Coley.** 81°15′S, 158°13′E. 2,570 m. 3 miles south of Mount Frost, in the Churchill Mountains. Named for Cdr. Vernon J. Coley, commander of VX-6, 1957–58.

**Coley Glacier.** 64°09′S, 57°14′W. 5 miles long. On the east side of James Ross Island. Flows into Erebus and Terror Gulf, just north of Cape Gage. Surveyed by the FIDS in 1945 and 1953. Named by the UK for John A. Coley, FIDS meteorological assistant at Base D in 1952 and 1953.

**Isla de la Colina** *see* **Heywood Island**

**Mount Collard.** 72°38′S, 31°07′E. 2,350 m. 3½ miles south of Mount Perov, at the south end of the Belgica Mountains. Discovered by the Belgian Antarctic Expedition of 1957–58, under Gaston de Gerlache, and named by him for Léo Collard, Belgian minister of public instruction.

**Lake Colleen.** 78°02′S, 163°52′E. A small meltwater lake between the lower parts of the Joyce and Garwood Glaciers, in Victoria Land. Discovered by geologist Troy L. Péwé on Jan. 14, 1958. Named by him in association with the clear, reflecting lakes in Ireland.

**Collerson Lake.** 68°35′S, 78°11′E. A small, kidney-shaped lake, 1½ miles SW of Club Lake, in the Vestfold Hills. K. Collerson, a geologist at Davis Station in 1969–70, established a camp here, and the Australians named the lake for him.

**Cape Collier.** 70°10′S, 61°54′W. Ice-covered. Juts out from the east coast of the Antarctic Peninsula into the Larsen Ice Shelf, between Cape Boggs and the south end of Hearst Island. Discovered in 1940 by the USAS, and named for Zadick Collier.

**Collier, Zadick.** Machinist at East Base during the USAS 1939–41.

**Collier Hills.** 79°42′S, 83°24′W. Ice-free. Between the mouths of the Schanz and Driscoll Glaciers, where the two meet Union Glacier, in the Heritage Range. Named by the University of Minnesota Ellsworth Mountains Party of 1962–63 for Robert M. Collier, topographic engineer with the party.

**Mount Collins.** 71°30′S, 66°41′E. A flat, dark-colored ridge, 13 miles west of the Fisher Massif, in the Prince Charles Mountains. Discovered in Nov. 1956 by Flying Officer John Seaton, RAAF. Named by the Australians for P.J. Collins, senior diesel mechanic at Mawson Station in 1957.

**Collins Bay.** 65°21′S, 64°04′W. Between Deliverance Point and Cape Pérez on the west coast of Graham Land. Charted by de Gerlache in 1897–99. Named by the UK in 1959 for Rear-Adm. Kenneth St. B. Collins, RN, hydrographer of the navy in the 1950s.

**Collins Glacier.** 73°41′S, 65°55′E. 11 miles wide at its confluence with the Mellor Glacier, which it feeds. North of Mount Newton in the Prince Charles Mountains. Named by the Australians for N.J. Collins, senior diesel mechanic at Mawson Station in 1960.

**Collins Harbor.** 62°11′S, 58°51′W. A bay that indents the south coast of King George Island, in the South Shetlands, just east of Fildes Peninsula. Named before 1913.

**Collins Peak.** 72°58′S, 167°49′E. 1,810 m. On the east side of the Malta Plateau, in the Victory Mountains of Victoria Land. Named for Eric J. Collins, biologist at Hallett Station in 1965–66.

**Collins Point.** 63°S, 60°35′W. Also called Punta Fontana. As you pass through Neptune's Bellows into Port Foster, Deception Island, in the South Shetlands, it is the first point on your left.

**Collins Ridge.** 85°35′S, 160°48′W. Ice-covered. Extends from Mount Behling to the Bowman Glacier, then between the Bowman and Amundsen Glaciers. Named for Henry C. Collins, US cartographer.

**Collins Rock.** 66°17′S, 110°33′E. At the south side of the entrance to McGrady Cove, Newcomb Bay, in the Windmill Islands. Named by Lt. Robert C. Newcomb, USN, navigator of the *Glacier* in 1956–57, for Engineman 3rd Class Frederick A. Collins, USN, a member of the *Glacier* party that surveyed this feature in Feb. 1957.

**Collinson Ridge.** 85°13′S, 175°21′W. Just to the east of the Shackleton Glacier. Just north of Halfmoon Bluff, in the NW part of the Cumulus Hills, in the Queen Maud Mountains. Named for Prof. James W. Collinson, of Ohio State University, a member of the Institute of Polar Studies geological expedition here in 1970–71.

**Colnett, James.** Midshipman on the *Resolution* during Cook's second voyage, of 1772–75.

**Colombia.** Ratified in Jan. 1989 as the 39th signatory of the Antarctic Treaty.

**Mount Colombo.** 76°31′S, 144°44′W. 3 miles north of Mount Richardson, in the Fosdick Mountains. Discovered on the eastern flight of Dec. 5, 1929, during Byrd's 1928–30 expedition. Named later by Byrd for Louis P. Colombo.

**Colombo, Louis P.** Crewman on the *Jacob Ruppert*, 1933–34, who became assistant mechanic on the shore party of Byrd's 1933–35 expedition. He was a dog driver and biologist at West Base during the USAS 1939–41.

**Colorado Glacier.** 85°53'S, 133°05'W. 10 miles long. Flows from the Michigan Plateau into Reedy Glacier, between the Quartz Hills and the Eblen Hills. Named for the University of Colorado, which has sent many researchers here.

**Colosseum Cliff.** 77°36'S, 161°27'E. A banded cliff between Sykes Glacier and Plane Table, in the Asgard Range of Victoria Land. Named descriptively by the New Zealanders.

**Colosseum Ridge.** 79°47'S, 156°20'E. Between Haskell Ridge and Richardson Hill, in the Darwin Mountains. Contains pyramidal peaks and 5 large cirques; the cirques resemble the Roman Colosseum. Named by the New Zealanders in 1962–63.

**Coloured Peak.** 85°30'S, 156°20'W. 660 m. Near the head of the Ross Ice Shelf, in the coastal foothills of the Queen Maud Mountains. 2 miles SE of O'Brien Peak. Named by the New Zealanders in 1969–70 for its colored strata of yellow, pink, and brown.

**Colson, Charles J.** Hospital steward on the Wilkes Expedition 1838–42. Joined in the USA. Discharged at Oahu, Oct. 31, 1840.

**Columbia Mountains.** 70°14'S, 63°51' W. A group of peaks, ridges, and nunataks. Mostly ice-free. Near the east edge of the Dyer Plateau, 20 miles SE of the Eternity Range, in Palmer Land. Named for Columbia University, New York City, which, in the 1960s and 1970s, sent many geological researchers here.

**Column Rock.** 63°11'S, 57°19'W. Also called Roca Faro. A rock pinnacle, 1 mile north of Gourdin Island, off the coast of Trinity Peninsula. Named descriptively by the UK.

**Colvocoresses, George M.** Passed midshipman on the Wilkes Expedition 1838–42. He joined the *Peacock* at Rio, and the *Vincennes* at Fiji, and also served on the *Porpoise*. He wrote the book *Four Years in a Government Exploring Expedition* in 1852–55, and was later promoted to captain, USN.

**Colvocoresses Bay.** 66°20'S, 114°38'E. Formed by the right angle of the Budd Coast at Williamson Glacier. It is 30 miles wide at the entrance. Named for George M. Colvocoresses.

**Mount Coman.** 73°49'S, 64°18'W. Also called Mount Dana Coman. 12,000 feet. Isolated. Just west of the Playfair Mountains, between the English Coast and the Lassiter Coast. Discovered by the RARE 1947–48, and named by Ronne for F. Dana Coman.

**Coman, Dr. F. Dana.** Francis Dana Coman. Dietician, bacteriologist, biologist. Staff surgeon at Johns Hopkins University. He was physician on Byrd's 1928–30 expedition, and medical officer on Ellsworth's 1934–35 expedition. He had served with the French Army during World War I.

**Cabo Comandante Byers** *see* **Cape Page**

**Paso Comandante Cordovez** *see* **Croker Passage**

**Comandante Ferraz Summer Research Station.** 62°05'S, 58°23'W. Brazilian base built in 1984 on Keller Peninsula, King George Island, in the South Shetlands. It was Brazil's first and, as of 1990, only scientific station in Antarctica. It specializes in marine biology, geology, and geophysics.

**Comb Ridge.** 63°55'S, 57°28'W. 105 m. Forms the east part of the hill at the end of The Naze, on James Ross Island. Named descriptively by the FIDS in 1946.

**Mount Combs.** 73°29'S, 79°09'W. Isolated. At the base of the Rydberg Peninsula, between the Bryan Coast and the English Coast of Ellsworth Land. Discovered by Ronne during the RARE 1947–48, and named by him for J.M. Combs, congressman from Beaumont, Texas, a supporter of the expedition.

**The *Commandant Charcot*.** 1,200-ton French polar dispatch boat, formerly the USS *Lancewood*, bought in San Francisco, and renamed by the French Polar Expeditions for Jean-Baptiste Charcot. It was fitted by the French Navy. Commanded by Max Douguet, it landed the first French party on Adélie Land on Jan. 20, 1950, during the 1949–50 expedition led by Liotard.

**Commandant Charcot Glacier.** 66°25′ S, 136°50′E. Also called Commandant Drovcot Glacier. 3 miles wide. 12 miles long. Flows from the continental ice into Victor Bay, terminating in the Commandant Charcot Glacier Tongue, on the coast of East Antarctica. Charted by the French in 1950–52, and named by them for the *Commandant Charcot.*

**Commandant Charcot Glacier Tongue.** 66°22′S, 136°35′E. 2 miles long. The seaward extension of the Commandant Charcot Glacier, on the coast of Adélie Land. Charted by the French in 1950–52, and named by them in association with the glacier.

**Commandant Drovcot Glacier** *see* Commandant Charcot Glacier

**Committee on Polar Research.** Committee created by the American National Academy of Sciences to study Antarctica after the IGY (1957–58).

**Committee Range** *see* **Executive Committee Range**

**Commonwealth Bay.** 66°54′S, 142°40′ E. 30 miles wide at its entrance, between Point Alden and Cape Gray, on the Adélie Land coast. It is the windiest place on earth, with gusts up to 200 mph. Discovered in 1912 by the AAE 1911–14, and named by Mawson for the Commonwealth of Australia. Mawson established his Main Base at Cape Denison, at the head of this bay.

**Commonwealth Creek** *see* **Commonwealth Stream**

**Commonwealth Glacier.** 77°35′S, 163°25′E. Flows into the north side of Taylor Glacier, just west of Mount Coleman, in Victoria Land, in the area of McMurdo Sound. Charted by Scott's 1910–13 expedition, and named by them for the Commonwealth of Australia, which sent money and men on the expedition.

**Commonwealth Range.** 84°15′S, 172° 20′E. 60 miles long. Between the Hughes Range and the Beardmore Glacier, or between the Ross Ice Shelf and the South Pole. It contains, among others, Mounts Kathleen, Robert Scott, Kyffin, and Patrick. Discovered by Shackleton in 1907–9 and named by him for the Commonwealth of Australia, which helped the expedition greatly.

**Commonwealth Stream.** 77°35′S, 163° 30′E. Runs into New Harbor from the Commonwealth Glacier, in Victoria Land. Named by geologist Troy L. Péwé in association with the glacier.

**Isla Comodor de Quito** *see* **Nupkins Island**

**Compass Island.** 68°38′S, 67°48′W. 15 m. A small island in Marguerite Bay, 7 miles NW of the Terra Firma Islands. Discovered aerially on Feb. 1, 1937, by the BGLE 1934–37. First visited by the FIDS in 1948, and surveyed by them in 1949. Named by them because iron wiring in an anorak hood caused havoc with the compass.

**Compton Valley.** 85°01′S, 91°20′W. Ice-filled. Indents the north side of Ford Massif, between Reed Ridge and Walker Spur, in the Thiel Mountains. Named for Lt. (jg) Romuald P. Compton, USN (*see* **Deaths, 1961**).

**Comrie Glacier.** 65°48′S, 64°20′W. 13 miles long. Flows into Bigo Bay, on the west coast of Graham Land. Discovered by Charcot in 1909. Named by the UK for Leslie J. Comrie, superintendent of the Nautical Almanac Office in 1934. He provided advance copies of the *Nautical Almanac* to the BGLE 1934–37.

**Conard Point.** 72°22′S, 167°26′E. 2,230 m. On the north side of the Hearfield Glacier, 5 miles north of Aldridge Peak, in the Cartographers Range of the Victory Mountains, Victoria Land. Named for Ralph W. Conard, VX-6 ground handler at Williams Field in 1968.

**Conception Point.** 60°31′S, 45°41′W. On the north central side of Coronation

Island, in the South Orkneys. It is the northernmost point on the island. Discovered on Dec. 8, 1821, by Powell and Palmer, and named by Powell.

**Conchie Glacier.** 71°36'S, 67°15'W. On the west coast of Palmer Land. Flows into George VI Sound, between the Batterbee Mountains and the Steeple Peaks. Named by the UK for Flight Lt. Bertie J. Conchie, RAF, pilot with the BAS, 1969–75.

**Concord Mountains.** 71°35'S, 165°10' E. In the NW part of Victoria Land. It comprises the Everett Range, the Mirabito Range, the King Range, the Leitch Massif, the East Quartzite Range, and the West Quartzite Range. Named by the New Zealanders in 1963–64 for the international harmony in Antarctica.

**Islotes Condell**  *see*  **Pauling Islands**

**Condit, John C.** Lt. (jg), USN. The first Catholic priest at AirOpFac McMurdo (which became McMurdo Base). His tour of duty was 1955–56, during the summer season of Operation Deep Freeze I. He built Chapel of the Snows, the first church in Antarctica. He was succeeded at the end of Deep Freeze I by Chaplain Peter Bol, who took over for the 1956 winter. Bol, in turn, was succeeded by Chaplain Leon S. Darkowski (McMurdo's priest for the 1956–57 summer, Operation Deep Freeze II).

**Condit Glacier.** 77°52'S, 162°48'E. On the east side of Cathedral Rocks, it flows into the Ferrar Glacier, in Victoria Land. Charted by Scott's 1910–13 expedition. Named by the USA in 1964 for John C. Condit.

**Condon Hills.** 67°53'S, 48°38'E. 840 meters high at the highest point. On the east side of Rayner Glacier, in Enderby Land. Named by the Australians for M.A. Condon, assistant director of the Bureau of Mineral Resources in Australia.

**Punta Condor**  *see*  **Cape Wollaston**

**Condor Peninsula.** 71°46'S, 61°30'W. 30 miles long. 10–15 miles wide. Moun-

tainous. Ice-covered. Between Odom Inlet and Hilton Inlet, on the east coast of Palmer Land. Discovered aerially on Dec. 30, 1940, on the Condor flight from USAS East Base, with Black, Snow, Perse, Carroll, and Dyer aboard. Named for the Condor biplane.

**Condyle Point.** 63°35'S, 59°48'W. The SE point on Tower Island. Named descriptively by the UK. A condyle is the rounded prominence at the end of a bone.

**Cone Hill.** 77°47'S, 166°51'E. 2 miles NE of Castle Rock, on Hut Point Peninsula, Ross Island. Named Cone Hill I by Scott's 1910–13 expedition, but the name was gradually shortened (*see also* **Cone Hill II**).

**Cone Hill I**  *see*  **Cone Hill**

**Cone Hill II**  *see*  **Ford Rock**

**Cone Island**  *see*  **Cono Island**

**Cone Nunatak.** 63°36'S, 57°02'W. 350 m. Appears conical on its northern side. 3 miles SSE of Buttress Hill, in Tabarin Peninsula, at the NE end of the Antarctic Peninsula. Named by the FIDS following their survey of the area in 1946.

**Cone Rock.** 62°27'S, 60°07'W. Also called Conical Rock. A small rock, 1½ miles NE of Williams Point, and almost a mile south of Pyramid Island, in the South Shetlands. Charted and named by the personnel on the *Discovery II* in 1935.

**Confluence Cone.** 68°56'S, 66°39'W. A small nunatak 4 miles SE of Sickle Mountain, near the west coast of the Antarctic Peninsula. Named by the UK for its position at the confluence of several glaciers.

**Cape Confusion.** 74°50'S, 163°50'E. A rocky point that projects from the SW part of the Northern Foothills, 4 miles NW of Cape Russell, on the coast of Victoria Land. Named by the New Zealanders in 1962–63 for the geological confusion here.

**Confusion Island.** 60°44'S, 45°38'W. 350 yards long. At the west side of the entrance to Clowes Bay, off the south side of Signy Island, in the South Orkneys. The southern point on this island was named Confusion Point by personnel on the *Discovery II* in 1933, but in 1974 the UK extended the name to the whole island.

**Confusion Point** *see* **Confusion Island**

**Conger, Richard R.** USN. Chief photographer's mate on Operation Windmill, 1947–48.

**Conger Glacier.** 66°02′S, 103°33′E. 5 miles east of the Glenzer Glacier, it flows into the eastern part of the Shackleton Ice Shelf. Named for Richard R. Conger.

**Conical Hill.** 77°39′S, 168°34′E. 655 m. On the south side of Mount Terror, in the southern part of Ross Island. Just north of Cape MacKay. Named descriptively by Scott's 1910–13 expedition.

**¹Conical Rock** *see* **Cone Rock**

**²Conical Rock.** 62°43′S, 61°11′W. Also called Rocas Conicas, Rocher Conique. In the east part of Morton Strait, 2 miles south of the SW tip of Livingston Island. Named by the personnel on the *Discovery II* in 1930–31.

**Connell Canyon.** 79°51′S, 83°01′W. Ice-filled. Scenic. In the NW part of the Enterprise Hills, extending from Linder Peak to Union Glacier, in the Heritage Range. Named for Lt. Davis B. Connell, USN, supply officer at McMurdo Station in 1965 and 1966.

**Connors Point.** 66°18′S, 110°29′E. The NW point of Beall Island, in the Windmill Islands. Named for William J. Connors, USN, aerographer's mate at Wilkes Station in 1958.

**Cerro Cono** *see* **Cockscomb Hill**

**Cono Island.** 67°41′S, 69°10′W. Also called Cone Island. A conical island south of the Chatos Islands, off Adelaide Island. Named Islote Cono (Cone Islet) by the Argentine Antarctic Expedition of 1952–53.

**The *Conrad*.** US research ship of the 1970s, sometimes in Antarctic waters.

**Mount Conrad.** 69°26′S, 158°46′E. 600 m. 6 miles south of Cape Kinsey, in the central part of the Goodman Hills, in the Wilson Hills. Named for Max Conrad.

**Conrad, Max.** "The Flying Grandfather," as he was called. An around-the-world flyer (from the USA) in his Piper Aztec. On Dec. 21, 1968, he landed at Palmer Station, spent two days there, and headed off for Adelaide Island, where he got stuck for 3 weeks. He was back in Antarctica on Jan. 13, 1970, landing at McMurdo Station. On Jan. 19, 1970, he flew to the South Pole, the first solo flight to reach 90°S. On Jan. 23, 1970, his plane crashed on take-off, but Max was not injured.

**Conrad Mountains.** 71°50′S, 9°40′E. A narrow chain, 19 miles long, between the Gagarin Mountains and Mount Dallmann, in the Orvin Mountains of Queen Maud Land. Discovered by Ritscher in 1938–39, and named for Adm. Conrad, director of the Meteorological Division of the German Admiralty.

**Conradi Peak.** 66°08′S, 54°34′E. 1,040 m. Isolated. North of the Napier Mountains. 19 miles SW of Cape Borley. Discovered in Jan. 1930 by the BANZARE 1929–31, and named by Mawson for the South African government minister who helped the expedition in Cape Town.

**Conrow Glacier.** 77°34′S, 162°07′E. In the Wright Valley area, between Heimdall Glacier and Bartley Glacier. Named by Roy E. Cameron (*see* **Cameron Nunataks**) for Howard P. Conrow, here in 1966–67.

**Conrow Valley.** A dry valley in the Asgard Range of Victoria Land. The term is not yet official.

**Conroy Point.** 60°44′S, 45°41′W. On the NW side of Moe Island, in the South Orkneys. Named by the UK for James W.H. Conroy, ornithologist on Signy Island in 1967–68.

**Conseil Hill.** 67°36′S, 67°28′W. On the north side of Pourquoi Pas Island. Named by the UK for the Jules Verne character.

**Conservation.** The Antarctic Conservation Act was signed into effect by the president of the USA on Oct. 28, 1978. Aside from these measures, the Antarctic Treaty itself designates the Antarctic continent as a Special Conservation Area, and whaling and sealing, etc., are all but prohibited (*see also* CCAMLR).

**Consort Islands.** 67°52′S, 68°42′W. Two small islands in Marguerite Bay, ½ mile NE of Emperor Island, in the Dion Islands. Surveyed in 1948 by the FIDS, and named by the UK in association with Emperor Island, in a continuation of the courtly theme predominant among features in this area.

**Constable, Love.** Midshipman on the *Adventure* under Cook in 1772–75.

**Cape Constance** *see* **Cape Jones**

**Constellation Dome.** 81°06′S, 160°11′E. 1,330 m. An ice-covered summit, the highest feature in the Darley Hills. 5 miles west of Gentile Point, between the Ross Ice Shelf and the Nursery Glacier. Named by the Northern Party of the NZGSAE 1960–61 for the first astro fix of the journey that was made here.

**Constellation Inlet.** 78°30′S, 80°30′W. 30 miles long. 10 miles wide. Between the Dott and Skytrain Ice Rises, at the SW edge of the Ronne Ice Shelf. Named for the Constellation aircraft (popularly known as the "Connie").

**Construction Point.** 72°19′S, 170°13′E. Marks the west side of the entrance to Willett Cove, and the south end of Seabee Hook, in the area of Cape Hallett, Victoria Land. Surveyed in Jan. 1956 by the *Edisto*. Named because of its association with Seabee Hook (q.v.).

**Consul Reef.** 67°54′S, 68°42′W. A line of drying and submerged rocks forming the south end of the Dion Islands, off the south end of Adelaide Island. Named by the UK in 1963 in association

with nearby Emperor Island and the Consort Islands.

**Contact Peak.** 67°46′S, 67°29′W. 1,005 m. The SE peak of Pourquoi Pas Island, off the west coast of Graham Land. Discovered by Charcot in 1909. Named by the FIDS in 1948 because the peak marks the granite-volcanic contact in the cliffs.

**Contact Point.** 63°23′S, 56°59′W. Just west of Sheppard Point, on the north side of Hope Bay, Trinity Peninsula. Nordenskjöld's expedition of 1901–4 charted it as an island, but the FIDS redefined it in 1955. Geological contacts of greywacke, tuff, and diorite were discovered here.

**Continental Polar Air Mass.** A shallow dome of very cold air, which usually forms in winter around the South Pole and surrounding areas. It causes cold weather throughout the world.

**Isla Contramaestre Rivera** *see* **Sawyer Island**

**The Convent** *see* **Cathedral Crags**

**Convoy Range.** 76°45′S, 160°40′E. A series of small mountains and valleys made up of dense, igneous rock, which is red on the exposed surfaces and gray underneath. Extends south from the Fry Saddle to the Mackay Glacier, about 100 miles north of Taylor Valley, and about 30 miles inland from the Ross Sea, in Victoria Land. Named by the NZ Northern Survey Party of the BCTAE in 1957 for the main convoy into McMurdo Sound in the 1956–57 season. The names of the vessels are used for the features in the range.

**Cape Conway.** 62°51′S, 61°24′W. The southernmost part of Snow Island, in the South Shetlands. Named by Foster in 1828–31 for the *Conway*, one of his old ships (not in the Antarctic).

**Conway Island.** 66°08′S, 65°28′W. In Holtedahl Bay, to the west of Lens Peak, off the west coast of Graham Land. Named by the UK in 1959 for William M. Conway (1856–1937), Arctic pioneer skier.

**Conway Range.** 79°18′S, 159°30′E. In the Cook Mountains, between Carlyon and Mulock Glaciers. Discovered during Scott's 1901-4 expedition, and apparently named by Shackleton's 1907-9 expedition.

**Mount Cook.** 67°55'S, 56°28'E. 1,900 m. The highest point of the Main Massif of the Leckie Range. Named by the Australians for B.G. Cook, geophysicist at Mawson Station in 1958.

**Cook, Frederick.** b. 1865, Hortonville, NY. d. Aug. 5, 1940. Frederick Albert Cook. American medical officer on the *Belgica* expedition of 1897-99, which he joined at Rio on Oct. 22, 1897. While wintering-over in Antarctica, he invented a new type of tent which weighed 12 pounds and held 3 men. Later, he claimed to have reached the North Pole on March 21, 1908, the first man to do so. Since then, however, he has been discredited (more so even than Peary, his rival). He later spent 5 years in jail for fraud.

**Cook, Isaac.** Ordinary seaman on the Wilkes expedition 1838-42. Joined in the USA. Served the cruise.

**Cook, James.** b. Oct. 27, 1728, Marton, Yorkshire, England. Son of a Scotsman. d. Feb. 14, 1779, at the age of 50, killed by Hawaiians. The greatest navigator of all time, he discovered more than any other human being in history. He circumnavigated the world 3 times, and it is the second voyage with which Antarctica is concerned. He left Plymouth with the *Resolution* and the *Adventure,* captained by John Gilbert and Tobias Furneaux respectively. In search of Terra Australis Incognita (the Unknown Southern Land), he became the first to cross the Antarctic Circle, on Jan. 17, 1773, repeating this feat on Dec. 20, 1773, and on Jan. 26, 1774. He circumnavigated Antarctica at high latitudes (again, the first to do so), and concluded that if Antarctica existed at all it must be very cold indeed (Cook reached a new southing record of 71°10'S) and completely barren. He did discover the South Sandwich Islands, however, as well as

South Georgia, and it was his publication of this fact that led to the seal rush of the late 18th-early 19th centuries, and thus to real exploration of Antarctica. Cook returned to England on July 30, 1775, finally being promoted to captain. Also on the second voyage were Robert Anderson, John Marra, John Forster and his son George Forster, William Anderson, James Burney, Charles Clerke, Lt. Robert F. Cooper, Richard Pickersgill, Charles Plymouth, Thomas Willis, George Vancouver, James Patton, William Wales, William Hodges, Oddidy the man from Bora Bora, Arthur Kempe, Thomas Woodhouse, Love Constable, Richard Hergert, George Moorey, Henry Lightfoot, John Lambrecht, Peter Fannin, John Rowe, John Edgecumbe, Thomas Andrews, William Bayly.

**¹Cook, John.** Bosun's mate on the Wilkes Expedition 1838-42. Joined in the USA. Served the cruise.

**²Cook, John.** Seaman on the Wilkes Expedition 1838-42. Joined in the USA. Returned in the *Relief* in 1839.

**Cook Bay** *see* **Cook Ice Shelf**

**Cook Ice Shelf.** 68°40'S, 152°30'E. Also called Cook Bay, Joseph Cook Bay. 55 miles wide. Between Capes Freshfield and Hudson, or between George V Land and Oates Land, in East Antarctica. Defined as a bay by Mawson during the AAE 1911-14, and named by him for Joseph Cook, prime minister of Australia in 1914. Later redefined.

**Cook Mountains.** 79°25'S, 158°E. At the south of the Hillary Coast in the Transantarctic Mountains. First seen by Scott's 1901-4 expedition. Named by New Zealand for Capt. Cook.

**Cook Nunataks.** 67°05'S, 55°50'E. A group of 4 nunataks at the NE end of the Schwartz Range in Enderby Land. Named by the Australians for P.J. Cook, geologist here on the *Nella Dan* in 1965, with the ANARE.

**Cook Peak.** 85°36'S, 156°50'W. 4½ miles west of Feeney Peak, surmounting the west wall of Goodale Glacier, in the foothills of the Queen Maud Mountains. Named for David L. Cook, logistics assistant at McMurdo Station in 1965.

**Cook Peninsula** *see* **Riiser-Larsen Peninsula**

**Cook Ridge.** 69°23'S, 158°35'E. Mostly ice-covered. Parallels the west side of Paternostro Glacier, and extends into the SE corner of Davies Bay. Named by the Australians for surveyor David Cook of the ANARE here in March 1961, led by Phillip Law.

**Cooke Crags.** 83°10'S, 50°43'W. In the Pensacola Mountains.

**Cooke Peak.** 72°27'S, 74°46'E. 6 miles NW of Bode Nunataks, in the Grove Mountains. Named by the Australians for D.J. Cooke, cosmic ray physicist at Mawson Station in 1963.

**Coombes Ridge.** 69°09'S, 157°03'E. 2 miles west of Magga Peak. Forms the eastern extremity of Lauritzen Bay. Named by the Australians for Bruce Coombes, airport engineer who was here in Feb. 1959 on the *Magga Dan* with Phillip Law's ANARE party, to investigate potential airfield sites at Wilkes Station and elsewhere.

**Coombs Hills.** 76°52'S, 160°04'E. Largely snow-free hills and valleys between the Odell and Cambridge Glaciers, just to the north of the Mackay Glacier, in Victoria Land. Discovered in 1957 by the NZ Northern Survey Party of the BCTAE, and named by them for D.S. Coombs, professor of geology at the University of Otago, NZ, who helped the expedition.

**Mount Cooper.** 77°08'S, 145°22'W. On The Billboard, 4 miles west of Asman Ridge, on the south side of Arthur Glacier, in the Ford Ranges of Marie Byrd Land. Discovered aerially in 1934 by Byrd's 1933–35 expedition, and named by Byrd for Merian C. Cooper (1893–1973), producer of the movie *King Kong*.

**Cooper, John.** Armorer on the Wilkes Expedition 1838–42. Joined in the USA. Served the cruise.

**Cooper, Robert P.** Lt. Robert Palliser Cooper. Officer on the *Resolution* during Cook's voyage of 1772–75.

**Cooper Bluffs.** 70°39'S, 165°E. Also called Cooper Ridge. Ice-covered. On the east side of Zykov Glacier, in the Anare Mountains. Named by the ANARE for Flying Officer G. Cooper, RAAF, who explored the area from the *Thala Dan* in 1962.

**Cooper Glacier.** 85°30'S, 164°30'W. Also called Kent Cooper Glacier. 15 miles long. Flows between Butchers Spur and the Quarles Range into the Axel Heiberg Glacier. Discovered aerially by Byrd in Nov. 1929, and named by him for Kent Cooper, an official of the Associated Press.

**Cooper Icefalls.** 82°32'S, 160°E. The main icefalls of the Nimrod Glacier, in the vicinity of Kon-Tiki Nunatak. Named by the Southern Party of the NZGSAE 1960–61 for Christopher Neville Cooper, a member of the expedition, and a member of the NZ Alpine Club Antarctic Expedition of 1959–60.

**Cooper Nunatak.** 79°45'S, 159°11'E. 5 miles north of Diamond Hill, east of the Brown Hills. Named for R.A. Cooper, geologist with the VUWAE 1960–61.

**Cooper Ridge** *see* **Cooper Bluffs**

**Cooper Spur.** 70°38'S, 165°03'E. Extends north from the east end of Cooper Bluffs, on the north coast of Victoria Land. Named for Ronald R. Cooper, USN, chief builder at McMurdo Station in 1967.

**Coor Crags.** 74°29'S, 136°36'W. 3½ miles SE of Cox Point, in the northern part of Erickson Bluffs, near the Marie Byrd Land coast. Named for Lt. Cdr. Lawrence W. Coor, USN, pilot in the Antarctic in 1970 and 1971.

**Mount Cope.** 84°01'S, 174°33'E. On the east side of the Separation Range, in the Queen Maud Mountains. Overlooks the west side of Canyon Glacier, 4 miles NW of Nadeau Bluff. Named for Lt. Ronald P. Cope, USN, officer-in-charge of the nuclear power plant at McMurdo Station in 1963.

**Cope, John L.** British biologist/surgeon of the Ross Sea party of the British Imperial Transantarctic Expedition of 1914–17. He was a very young man at this time. In 1920–22 he led the British Imperial Expedition, in which he and three others tried, but failed, to cross the Antarctic Peninsula by land.

**Cope Hill.** 75°07'S, 114°47'W. 1 mile west of Manfull Ridge, on the north side of the Kohler Range, in Marie Byrd Land. Named for Lt. Winston Cope, USNR, medical officer at Amundsen-Scott South Pole Station in 1974.

**Co-pilot Glacier.** 73°11'S, 164°22'E. Flows from the west and south slopes of Mount Overlord into the upper part of the Aviator Glacier in Victoria Land. Named by the New Zealanders in 1962–63 in recognition of pilots and co-pilots of VX-6, and in association with nearby Pilot Glacier.

**Copper.** Scott and Mawson both found copper in the Antarctic. Both chalcocite and chalcopyrite have been found. The largest deposits are in the Copper Nunataks, in Palmer Land (*see also* **Coppermine Cove**).

**Copper Col.** 64°44'S, 63°23'W. 305 m. A col between Copper Peak and Billie Peak in the Osterrieth Range of Anvers Island. Discovered by de Gerlache in 1897–99. Named Copper Glacier by the personnel on the *Discovery* in 1927. They saw it from afar and misjudged its characteristics. Redefined in 1955 by the FIDS.

**Copper Cove.** 72°09'S, 170°E. 2 miles north of Helm Point, indenting the east side of Honeycomb Ridge, at the west edge of Moubray Bay. Named by the New Zealanders in 1957–58 because its cliffs are stained green in places by the action of weather on the copper ores.

**Copper Glacier** *see* **Copper Col**

**Copper Nunataks.** 74°22'S, 64°55'W. A cluster of nunataks, 4 miles in diameter. At the head of Wetmore Glacier. 11 miles WSW of Mount Crowell, in southern Palmer Land. Named by Peter D. Rowley (*see* **Rowley Massif**) who discovered the largest Antarctican deposits of copper here.

**Copper Peak.** 64°43'S, 63°21'W. Also called Pico Verde. 1,125 m. Vivid green in color. 2 miles NNE of Billie Peak, on the SE side of Anvers Island. Discovered by de Gerlache in 1897–99. Named probably by the personnel on the *Discovery* in 1927.

**Coppermine Cove.** 62°22'S, 59°45'W. Just SE of Fort William, the western tip of Robert Island, in the South Shetlands. The early sealers, in 1820–21, found a lot of copper ore in a larger cove further SE along the westside of Robert Island, and named that as Coppermine Cove. Recently however, the smaller cove has assumed the name, and it is now official. A Chilean refuge hut was built here in 1950, and it is now a scientific station.

**Coppermine Peninsula.** 62°22'S, 59°43'W. 1 mile long. Between Carlota Cove and Coppermine Cove, at the west end of Robert Island, in the South Shetlands. It is an SPA (q.v.). Named by the UK in 1971 in association with the cove.

**Copperstain Ridge.** 71°27'S, 164°22'E. 3 miles long. Descends from Mount Freed in the Bowers Mountains. Named by the New Zealanders in 1967–68 because of the extensive copper staining here.

**The *Cora*.** Liverpool sealing brig in the South Shetlands in the 1820–21 season, under the command of Capt. Robert Fildes. It struck a rock and was wrecked in Blythe Bay off Desolation Island, on Jan. 6, 1821. Fildes island-hopped and made charts for a few weeks, and then he and some of his crew were taken to Liverpool by the *Indian*.

**Cora Cove.** 62°28'S, 60°21'W. In the NW part of Blythe Bay, indenting the SE side of Desolation Island, in the South Shetlands. The *Cora* was lost near here in 1821.

**Coral.** Common name for a variety of invertebrate marine organisms of the class Anthozoa (*see also* **Fauna**). They live on the sea bed, near shore.

**Coral Sea Glacier.** 72°33′S, 168°27′E. Feeds Trafalgar Glacier in Victoria Land. Named by the New Zealanders in 1957–58 for the Battle of the Coral Sea (1943).

**Cora's Cove** *see* **Cora Cove**

**Cora's Island.** A tiny island in the South Shetlands. Named by Fildes in 1820–21. It does not seem to be there anymore, but it could be Cornwall Island, or one of several others.

**Mount Corbató.** 85°04′S, 165°42′W. 1,730 m. 4½ miles east of Mount Fairweather, in the Duncan Mountains. Mapped geologically on Jan. 13, 1975, by the Ohio State University field party, and named by the USA for Charles E. Corbató, geologist with the party.

**Cordell Hull Bay** *see* **Hull Bay**

**Cordell Hull Glacier** *see* **Hull Glacier**

**Cordiner, Douglas L.** USN captain who was an observer on the nonstop transcontinental flight in the P2V-2N Neptune aircraft from McMurdo Sound to the Weddell Sea and back on Jan. 13, 1956. He was one of the crew on the *Que Sera Sera* on Oct. 31, 1956, which landed at the Pole, the first plane to do so.

**Cordiner Peaks.** 82°48′S, 53°30′W. Cover a 6 mile area. 8 miles SW of the Dufek Massif. Include: Rosser Ridge, Jackson Peak, Jaburg Glacier, Sumrall Peak. Discovered aerially on the nonstop flight from McMurdo Sound to the Weddell Sea and back on Jan. 13, 1956. Named for the observer on this flight, Douglas L. Cordiner (see above).

**Cordini Glacier.** 70°01′S, 62°30′W. Flows from Mount Bailey, between Lewis Point and James Nunatak, to the east coast of Palmer Land. Named for I. Rafael Cordini, Argentine scientist, and author of several reports on the geology and ice of the Antarctic Peninsula and the Weddell Sea area.

**Islote Cordovez** *see* **Lobodon Island**

**Mount Cordwell.** 66°52′S, 53°09′E. 2 miles east of the Burch Peaks. 21 miles SSW of Stor Hånakken Mountain, in Enderby Land. Named by the Australians for T.S. Cordwell, radio officer at Wilkes Station in 1961.

**Core samples.** Core sampling is a technique used in underground or undersea exploration and prospecting. A special drill goes beneath the surface, and brings up a cylindrical piece of material for examination. This way the strata of history can be seen at a glance. In Antarctica the age and rate of ice accumulation can be determined from core samples.

**Corelli Horn.** 70°42′S, 69°49′W. 100 m. A rocky pinnacle with a pointed summit. 4 miles west of the north end of the LeMay Range, in central Alexander Island. Named by the UK for the composer.

**Mount Corey.** 76°40′S, 145°08′W. Also called Corey Mountains. Between the Fosdick Mountains and the Chester Mountains, in the Ford Ranges of Marie Byrd Land. Discovered in Nov. 1934 on a sledging expedition during Byrd's 1933–35 expedition. Named by Byrd for Stevenson Corey.

**Corey, Stevenson.** One of the shore party of Byrd's 1933–35 expedition.

**Corey Mountains** *see* **Mount Corey**

**Cormorant Island.** 64°48′S, 63°58′W. Off Anvers Island, about 2 miles SE of Palmer Station. Named by the UK in 1958 for the many cormorants here.

**Cormorants.** The most common shore birds in Antarctica. They nest close to the sea. The blue-eyed cormorant *(Phalacrocorax atriceps)* breeds on the Antarctic Peninsula, in the South Shetlands and the South Orkneys.

**Cape Cornely.** 76°14′S, 162°45′E. 3 miles north of Cape Day, on the coast of Victoria Land, at the south side of the terminus of the Mawson Glacier. Named for Joseph R. Cornely, USN, radioman at Little America V in 1958, at South Pole Station in 1961, and at McMurdo Station in 1963.

**Corner Camp.** Just to the east of White Island, on the Ross Ice Shelf. It was here that Scott's route to the Pole in 1911 turned the "corner" from east to south.

**Corner Cliffs.** 72°04′S, 68°25′W. Just south of Saturn Glacier, on the southern end of Alexander Island. Named by the FIDS in 1949. This is where the exposed rock of eastern Alexander Island turns a corner from a north-south direction toward the SE.

**Corner Glacier.** 74°27′S, 163°40′E. Flows down the Deep Freeze Range, between Black Ridge and Mount Dickason, to merge with the Nansen Ice Sheet, in Victoria Land. Explored by Campbell's Northern Party during Scott's 1910–13 expedition, and named by them for its location with respect to the Nansen Ice Sheet.

**Corner Island.** 65°15′S, 64°14′W. Part of the Corner Islands. A small island, 180 yards NE of Galíndez Island, in the Argentine Islands. Charted and named in 1935 by the BGLE.

**Corner Islands.** 65°15′S, 64°14′W. Collective term for a group of features 180 yards NE of Galíndez Island, in the Argentine Islands. Corner Island is the main feature, and the others are rocks in the immediate area, such as Corner Rock. This term is not accepted universally, the more common mapping of this feature being Corner Island, its "cornerstone."

**Corner Nunatak.** 82°52′S, 157°39′E. Also called Corner Peak. Between Nimrod Glacier and Marsh Glacier, it is the most northerly point in the Miller Range. Named by the New Zealanders in 1961–62.

¹**Corner Peak** *see* **Corner Nunatak**

²**Corner Peak.** 63°35′S, 58°39′W. 930 m. 8 miles ESE of Cape Roquemaurel. It marks a corner in the glacial valley in the

area. Named by the FIDS following a 1946 survey.

**Corner Rock.** 65°15′S, 64°14′W. In the Corner Islands. Between Galíndez Island and Corner Island, at the SE entrance to Meek Channel, in the Argentine Islands. Charted and named by the BGLE in 1935.

**Cornerpost Peak.** 71°57′S, 164°39′E. 2,160 m. At the SE end of the Leitch Massif, in the Concord Mountains. Named by the New Zealand Federated Mountain Clubs Antarctic Expedition 1962–63, because it was here, at the turning point of their traverse, that they established their most northerly survey station.

**The Cornet.** 61°07′S, 54°47′W. A cone-shaped peak on the south side of Pardo Ridge, between Muckle Bluff and The Stadium, on Elephant Island, in the South Shetlands. Named descriptively (ice cream cornet means ice cream cone) by the UK Joint Services Expedition of 1970–71.

**Cornet Island.** 65°34′S, 64°58′W. 1½ miles NE of Milnes Island, on the west side of Grandidier Channel, in the Biscoe Islands. Charted by the BGLE 1934–37. Named by the UK in 1959 for its shape as seen from the air.

**Cornice Channel.** 65°15′S, 64°15′W. A marine channel in the Corner Islands, it separates Galíndez Island from the east part of Skua Island, in the Argentine Islands. Surveyed by the BGLE 1934–37, and named by the UK in 1954 for the cornice that overhangs the ice cliff on Galíndez Island.

**Cape Cornish.** 66°42′S, 163°08′E. Forms the north tip of Buckle Island, in the Balleny Islands. Named in 1938 by personnel on the *Discovery II* for A.W. Cornish.

**Cornish, A.W.** Meteorologist with the Australian Central Bureau. An observer on the *Discovery II* in 1937–38.

**Cornish Islands.** 66°59′S, 67°28′W. Two small snow-capped islands with a rock between them. 4 miles south of

Liard Island, in Hanusse Bay, Graham Land. Named by the UK for Vaughan Cornish (1863-1948), British geographer and pioneer student of snowdrift forms.

**Mount Cornu.** 64°09'S, 60°35'W. At the head of Gregory Glacier, and north of Breguet Glacier, in northern Graham Land. Named by the UK in 1960 for Paul Cornu, French helicopter pioneer.

**¹Cornwall Glacier.** 80°48'S, 26°15'W. 9 miles long. Flows from Crossover Pass to Recovery Glacier, east of Ram Bow Bluff, in the Shackleton Range. Mapped in 1957 by the BCTAE, and named for Gen. Sir James H. Marshall-Cornwall, member of the Committee of Management for the BCTAE 1955-58.

**²Cornwall Glacier.** 83°04'S, 162°20'E. Flows to the south of Crowell Buttresses into Lowery Glacier, in the Queen Elizabeth Range. Named by the New Zealanders in 1961-62 for the English county.

**Cornwall Island.** 62°21'S, 59°42'W. Nearly ½ mile long. Between Heywood Island and Robert Island in the South Shetlands. Fildes discovered it in 1821, but did not name it. In 1934-35 the Discovery Investigations personnel saw it from a distance in the *Discovery II,* and named it Cornwall Point. It was later redefined.

**¹Cornwall Point** *see* **Cornwall Island**

**²Cornwall Point** *see* **Misnomer Point**

**Cornwallis Island.** 61°04'S, 54°28'W. Also called Cornwallis Islands, Michailoff's Island. A tiny island between Elephant Island and Clarence Island in the South Shetlands. 1 mile long. 5 miles NE of the east end of Elephant Island. Named before 1821.

**Mount Cornwell.** 77°40'S, 86°09'W. 2,460 m. 2 miles south of Mount Washburn, on the NE side of Newcomer Glacier, in the northern part of the Sentinel Range. Named for Lt. James W. Cornwell, in Antarctica with VX-6 in 1959-60.

**Coronas** *see* **Phenomena**

**Coronation Island.** 60°37'S, 45°35'W. 25 miles long. Between 3 and 8 miles wide. Has a permanent ice cap. The highest point on the island is 1,265 m. The northern part of the island is SPA #18. The largest of the South Orkney Islands, it was discovered by Powell on Dec. 6, 1820, and named by him in honor of George IV's recent coronation. It was here that Powell took possession of the island group for Britain. In 1822 Weddell re-discovered the island, and named it Pomona, for the island in the Scottish Orkneys. He also called it Mainland, not knowing that Powell had already named it. Weddell's names were published in 1825, but did not survive.

**Coronet Peak.** 71°39'S, 164°21'E. 2,175 m. On the east side of the terminus of Leap Year Glacier, in the SE extremity of the Bowers Mountains. Descriptively named by the New Zealanders in 1967-68.

**The Corral.** Steam whaler owned by the Corral Whaling Company of Bergen, Norway. In the South Orkneys in 1912-13 with its sister whaler, the *Fyr,* and their factory ship, the *Tioga.*

**Corral Point.** 60°45'S, 45°43'W. Forms the SW extremity of Moe Island, in the South Orkneys. Surveyed by the FIDS in 1947, and named by them for the Corral Whaling Company.

**Corral Whaling Company.** Out of Bergen, Norway, a subsidiary of Messrs. Christensen and Co., of Corral, Chile. They operated the *Tioga* in South Orkneys waters in 1912-13.

**Pasaje Correa** *see* **Graham Passage**

**Correll, Percy E.** Mechanic on the AAE 1911-14.

**Correll Nunatak.** 67°37'S, 144°12'E. Within the western part of the Mertz Glacier. 13 miles south of Aurora Peak. Discovered by the AAE 1911-14, and named by Mawson for Percy E. Correll.

**Cape Corry** *see* **Corry Island**

**Mount Corry** *see* **Purka Mountain**

**Corry Island.** 63°43'S, 57°31'W. 510 m. 2 miles long. Between Vega Island and Eagle Island, off the south coast of Trinity Peninsula. Ross sighted what may have been this feature, and named it Cape Corry, for Thomas L. Corry, lord commissioner of the admiralty. Redefined by the FIDS in 1945.

**Corry Massif.** 70°27'S, 64°36'E. 3 miles WNW of the Crohn Massif, in the Porthos Range of the Prince Charles Mountains. Named by the Australians for M.J. Corry, surveyor at Mawson Station in 1965, and leader and glaciologist of the Amery Ice Shelf party in 1968.

**Corry Rocks.** 70°20'S, 71°41'E. A cluster of rocks at the north end of Gillock Island, in the Amery Ice Shelf. One of them was occupied by the ANARE in 1968 as a survey station. Named by the Australians for M.J. Corry (*see* **Corry Massif**).

**Corse, James.** Seaman on the Wilkes Expedition 1838–42. Joined in Rio. Sent home on the *Relief* in 1839.

**Mount Cortés.** 68°29'S, 66°06'W. 1,490 m. Mainly ice-covered. On the SW side of Gibbs Glacier, in southern Graham Land. Named by the UK for Martín Cortés, Spanish author of *Arte de Navigar* (1551), an important navigation manual.

**Cosgrove Glacier.** 67°29'S, 59°10'E. Flows into Stefansson Bay, just west of Mulebreen. Named by the Australians for M. Cosgrove, radio supervisor at Mawson Station in 1959.

**Cosgrove Ice Shelf.** 73°25'S, 101°W. 35 miles long. 25 miles wide. Between the King and Canisteo Peninsulas, in the area of the Walgreen Coast. Named for Lt. Jerome R. Cosgrove, USNR, assistant communications officer on the staff of the commander, US Naval Support Force, Antarctica, 1967 and 1968.

**Cosmonaut Glacier.** 73°25'S, 164°30'E. About a mile from Aviator Glacier, in northern Victoria Land. 15 miles long, it enters Aviator Glacier after flowing along the south side of the Arrowhead Range, in the Southern Cross Mountains. Named by the New Zealanders in 1962–63 in association with the Aviator, Aeronaut, and Astronaut Glaciers.

**Cosmonette Glacier.** 73°37'S, 164°51'E. In the Southern Cross Mountains, it flows along the north side of the Daley Hills to Aviator Glacier, in Victoria Land. Named by the New Zealanders in 1962–63 in association with the other glaciers in the area, such as Aviator, Cosmonaut, and Astronaut Glaciers, and also to honor the first woman astronaut.

**Cape Cotter** *see* **Cotter Cliffs**

**Cotter, Pownall P.** Master of the *Terror*, 1839–43, during Ross' expedition.

**Cotter Cliffs.** 72°29'S, 170°19'E. A line of spectacular bare rock cliffs. They form the seaward face of Hallett Peninsula, in Victoria Land. In 1841 Ross named a cape somewhere in this area as Cape Cotter, for Pownall P. Cotter. Modern-day explorers failed to find it, but named these cliffs thus, in order to preserve Ross' naming.

**Cotton, Leo A.** b. 1883. Leo Arthur Cotton. Sailed to McMurdo Sound and back on the *Nimrod* in 1907–8. In 1925 he became professor of geology at the University of Sydney.

**Cotton Glacier.** 77°15'S, 161°45'E. 10 miles long. Flows between Sperm Bluff and Queer Mountain, on the south side of the Clare Range, between the Mackay and Debenham Glaciers, in Victoria Land. Discovered by Grif Taylor's Western Journey Party during Scott's 1910–13 expedition, and named by Taylor for Leo Cotton.

**Cotton Plateau.** 82°52'S, 159°30'E. Snow-covered. Just to the south of the Nimrod Glacier, and just east of the mouth of the Marsh Glacier, in the Queen Elizabeth Range. Named by the

New Zealanders in 1961–62 for Sir Charles Cotton, noted NZ authority on glacial landforms.

**Coughtrey Island** *see* **Coughtrey Peninsula**

**Coughtrey Peninsula.** 64°54'S, 62°53' W. Also called Península Sanavirón. A small, hook-shaped peninsula at the north side of the entrance to Skontorp Cove, Paradise Harbor, on the west coast of Graham Land. In 1913–14 David Ferguson mapped it as an island, Coughtrey Island. It was later redefined. Almirante Brown Station is here.

**Couling Island.** 67°19'S, 59°39'E. Also called Froa. 1 mile long. 1 mile north of Islay, in the William Scoresby Archipelago. Discovered and named by the personnel on the *William Scoresby* in Feb. 1936.

**Couling Islands** *see* **Couling Island**

**Coulman Island.** 73°28'S, 169°45'E. 18 miles long. 8 miles wide. 9 miles east of Cape Jones, off the extreme southern end of the Borchgrevink Coast, at the western end of the Ross Sea, off the coast of northern Victoria Land. Discovered in 1841 by Ross, and named by him for his father-in-law, Thomas Coulman.

**Couloir Cliffs.** 77°01'S, 162°50'E. 30 to 60 meters high. 3 miles long. On the east side of Avalanche Bay, in Granite Harbor, Victoria Land. Named by the Granite Harbor Geological Party, led by Grif Taylor during Scott's 1910–13 expedition, because these cliffs have several chimneys and couloirs.

**Coulston Glacier.** 72°25'S, 167°58'E. Flows from the Cartographers Range into Trafalgar Glacier, 10 miles west of Bypass Hill, in the Victory Mountains of Victoria Land. Named for Peter W. Coulston, VX-6 aviation electronics technician at McMurdo Station in 1967.

**Mount Coulter.** 83°17'S, 58°02'W. 3 miles NW of Mount Gorecki, in the Schmidt Hills of the Neptune Range. Named for Le Roy G. Coulter, cook at Ellsworth Station in 1958.

**Coulter Glacier.** 69°20'S, 71°53'W. In the NW extremity of Alexander Island.

**Coulter Heights.** 75°21'S, 138°15'W. Snow-covered. Between the Strauss and Frostman Glaciers, near the coast of Marie Byrd Land. Included in this group are Kuberry Rocks, Matikonis Peak, and Lambert Nunatak. Named for Neil M. Coulter, meteorologist at Byrd Station in 1963.

**Coulter Point.** 75°15'S, 138°38'W. On the coast of Marie Byrd Land. A term no longer used.

**Countess Peninsula.** 66°09'S, 101°14' E. Also called Countess Ridge. 1½ miles long. 1½ miles wide. Juts out from the coast between Booth Peninsula and the base of the Bunger Hills. Named for Julian Countess, air crewman who worked on Bunger's plane during Operation Highjump, 1946–47.

**Countess Ridge** *see* **Countess Peninsula**

**Mount Counts.** 83°11'S, 160°26'E. On the east side of Marsh Glacier, it marks the end of the spur running west from Mount Rabot, in the southern sector of the Queen Elizabeth Range. Named by the New Zealanders in 1961–62 for William D. Counts (*see* **Deaths, 1961**).

**Counts Icefall.** 85°13'S, 90°48'W. Heavily crevassed. At the juncture of the Ford Massif and the west end of the Bermel Escarpment, in the Thiel Mountains. Named for Lt. Cdr. William D. Counts (*see* **Deaths, 1961**).

**Couperin Bay.** 72°08'S, 74°22'W. On the SW side of Alexander Island.

**Coupvent Point.** 63°16'S, 57°36'W. Has several offlying rocks. Juts out from Trinity Peninsula, 5 miles SW of the Lafarge Rocks. Dumont d'Urville named a feature near here as Roche Coupvent, for Auguste Coupvent-Desbois. Modern-day cartographers can not find this rock, so they named this point thus, in order to preserve Dumont d'Urville's naming.

**Coupvent-Desbois, Auguste Élie Aimé.** An ensign on the *Zélée* during

Dumont d'Urville's expedition of 1837–40. He was transferred to the *Astrolabe,* and on Dec. 12, 1840, was promoted to lieutenant commander.

**The *Courier*.** US sealer from Stonington, in the South Shetlands for the 1831–33 period, under the command of Capt. Barnard, and in company with the *Charles Adams.*

**Court, Arnold.** US Weather Bureau observer at West Base during the USAS 1939–41. Studied meteorology.

**Court Nunatak.** 73°22′S, 61°36′W. 685 m. 3 miles long. Just east of the mouth of Meinardus Glacier, on the west side of New Bedford Inlet, on the east coast of Palmer Land. Discovered aerially in Dec. 1940 by personnel from East Base during the USAS 1939–41. Named by the FIDS for Arnold Court.

**Court Ridge.** 77°20′S, 146°52′W. Runs from the NW extremity of the Haines Mountains to the Sulzberger Ice Shelf, in the Ford Ranges of Marie Byrd Land. Discovered aerially on Dec. 15–16, 1934, on the northeast flight during Byrd's 1933–35 expedition. Named later for Arnold Court.

**Mount Courtauld.** 70°21′S, 67°28′W. 2,105 m. Mainly ice-covered. 9 miles east of the George VI Sound, at the northern end of that sound, on the west coast of the Antarctic Peninsula. Named by the UK in 1954 for Augustine Courtauld, British Arctic explorer who helped the BGLE 1934–37. The BGLE surveyed here in 1936.

**Courtier Islands.** 67°52′S, 68°44′W. 24 small islands and rocks in Marguerite Bay, just SW of Emperor Island, in the Dion Islands, off the west coast of the Antarctic Peninsula. The highest is 30 meters. Visited and surveyed in 1949 by the FIDS, and named by the UK in association with Emperor Island.

**Courtney Peak.** 79°14′S, 83°35′W. 1,060 m. In the northern part of the Gross Hills, in the Heritage Range. Named for Kenneth N. Courtney, USN, electronics

technician who was in the Antarctic six summers between 1960 and 1966.

**Cousins Rock.** 75°16′S, 133°31′W. Isolated. East of the upper part of Berry Glacier and Patton Bluff. 3½ miles NE of Coleman Nunatak, in Marie Byrd Land. Named for Michael D. Cousins, ionosphere physicist at Siple Station in 1969–70.

**Cousteau, Jacques-Yves.** b. June 11, 1910, Saint-André-de-Cubzac, France. French naval officer and undersea explorer. He spent the summer of 1972–73 in the Antarctic Peninsula area, in his vessel, the *Calypso.*

**Couzens Bay.** 80°35′S, 160°30′E. 10 miles long. Ice-filled. Between Senia Point and Cape Goldschmidt, on the west coast of the Ross Ice Shelf. Named by the New Zealanders in 1960–61 for Lt. Thomas Couzens, RNZAF (*see* **Deaths, 1961**).

**The *Covadonga*.** Chilean ship which took part in various Antarctic expeditions undertaken by Chile: 1946–47 (captain unknown), 1953–54 (Capt. Raul del Solar Grove), 1954–55 (captain unknown).

**Paso Covadonga** *see* **Roman Passage**

**Covadonga Harbor.** 63°19′S, 57°55′W. Also called Puerto Covadonga. A small extension of the NE corner of Huon Bay, just south of Cape Legoupil, in Trinity Peninsula. Named by the Chileans for their ship, the *Covadonga,* which first anchored here in 1946–47.

**¹Cove Rock** *see* **Cave Island**

**²Cove Rock.** 61°54′S, 57°51′W. 3 miles west of North Foreland, the NE tip of King George Island, in the South Shetlands. Charted and named in 1937 by personnel on the *Discovery II.*

**Covey Rocks.** 67°33′S, 67°43′W. A small group in Laubeuf Fjord, between Piñero Island and Cape Sáenz, off the west coast of Graham Land. Surveyed by the BGLE in 1936, and again in 1948 by the FIDS, and named by the FIDS for its resemblance to a covey of partridges sitting in a field.

**Lake Cowan.** 68°32′S, 78°25′E. ½ mile south of Lake Vereteno, in the eastern part of the Vestfold Hills. In plan it resembles a seal. Named by the Australians for D. Cowan, weather observer at Davis Station in 1969. He was at this lake in March 1969 with an ANARE party.

**Mount Cowart.** 83°42′S, 56°09′W. 1,245 m. On Gale Ridge, in the Neptune Range. Named for Master Sgt. Ray J. Cowart, USAF, flight engineer and member of the USAF Electronics Test Unit 1957–58.

**Cowell Island.** 69°16′S, 76°43′E. A small island partly contained in a glacier tongue. 3 miles WSW of Hovde Island. Photographed by the LCE 1936–37. M.J. Corry and his ANARE party visited it in Feb. 1969. Named by the Australians for W.D. Cowell, cook at Mawson Station in 1969, and a member of the ANARE Prince Charles Mountains survey party that year.

**Cowie Dome.** 86°25′S, 152°W. A dome-shaped summit at the east side of the Bartlett Glacier, 2 miles west of Lee Peak, in the Queen Maud Mountains. Named by NZ for George Donald (Don) Cowie, leader of the NZGSAE 1969–70, which was here.

**Cowley, Ambrose.** A pirate who reported that he had gone south of 60°S at the beginning of the 17th century.

**Cows.** Not many cows have been imported to Antarctica. Byrd brought 4 with him to Little America II during his 1933–35 expedition.

**Cape Cox.** 75°20′S, 63°08′W. Forms the NE extremity of Dodson Peninsula, on the west side of the Ronne Ice Shelf. Discovered aerially by the RARE 1947–48. Named for Larry E. Cox, radioman at Amundsen-Scott South Pole Station in 1964.

**Mount Cox.** 71°49′S, 160°32′E. 1,960 m. In the north central part of the Emlen Peaks, 5 miles north of Killer Nunatak.

Named for Allen N. Cox, USN, aircraft crew chief in Antarctica in 1962–63, 1963–64, and 1964–65.

**Cox, E.F.** Carpenter on the shore party on Byrd's 1933–35 expedition.

**Cox, L.W.** Crewman on the *Jacob Ruppert*, 1933–34.

**Cox Bluff.** 75°49′S, 115°11′W. Composed of rock and ice. Just west of Spitz Ridge, on the north side of Toney Mountain, in Marie Byrd Land. Named for Tony L. Cox, geomagnetist/seismologist at Byrd Station in 1966.

**Cox Glacier.** 72°11′S, 101°15′W. Just east of Rochray Glacier, on Thurston Island. It flows into the Abbott Ice Shelf, in Peacock Sound. Named for Lt. (jg) Jerry G. Cox, USN, helicopter pilot on the *Burton Island* in 1959–60.

**Cox Nunatak.** 82°26′S, 50°34′W. 795 m. 1 mile south of Rankine Rock, in the NE part of the Dufek Massif. Named for Walter M. Cox, photographer at Ellsworth Station in 1957.

**Cox Peaks.** 86°03′S, 153°30′W. 5 miles SE of Mount Crockett, just east of the Hays Mountains, in the Queen Maud Mountains. They actually extend from the Hays Mountains to the Robert Scott Glacier on a ridge. Named for Allan V. Cox, geologist at McMurdo Station in 1965–66.

**Cox Point.** 74°56′S, 136°43′W. At the SW side of the terminus of Garfield Glacier, where that glacier discharges into Hull Bay, on the coast of Marie Byrd Land. Named for E.F. Cox.

**Cox Reef.** 67°45′S, 69°06′W. A group of drying rocks NW of Box Reef, off the south end of Adelaide Island. Named by the UK in 1963 for Able Seaman Edward F. Cox, member of the RN Hydrographic Survey Unit, which charted the reef that year.

**Coxcomb Peak.** 76°40′S, 159°50′E. Overlooks the south end of Plumstead Valley, in the Allan Hills of Victoria Land. Named by the New Zealanders in 1964 for its coxcomblike appearance in profile.

**Isla Coy** *see* **Clear Island**

**Coyer Point.** 74°24'S, 113°13'W. On Martin Peninsula, on the coast of Marie Byrd Land.

**Coykendall, Capt.** At Little America V in 1958 he discovered Byrd's old "Snow-cruiser," buried near the camp under 16 feet of snow.

**Crab Stack** *see* **Fortín Rock**

**Crabeater Point.** 68°45'S, 64°08'W. At the SE end of Mobiloil Inlet, 4 miles east of Victory Nunatak, on the east coast of the Antarctic Peninsula. Surveyed in Dec. 1958 by the FIDS, and named descriptively by them. From the air it looks like a crabeater seal.

**Crabeater seal.** *Lobodon carcinophagus.* The most common seal in the world; there are between 6 and 15 million. Native to Antarctica, the crabeater is the fastest pinniped on land, able to travel at 15 or 16 mph. Average length is 8 feet, average weight is 450 pounds. The female is the larger. It feeds on krill rather than on crabs, and is itself the prey of killer whales.

**Mount Crabtree.** 77°S, 144°58'W. 4 miles ESE of Mount Fonda, in the north-central part of the Swanson Mountains, in the Ford Ranges of Marie Byrd Land. Named by Byrd for Dr. E. Granville Crabtree, consultant to Byrd for Operation Deep Freeze.

**Crack Bluff.** 86°33'S, 158°38'W. 2,810 m. 8 miles SE of Kutschin Peak, on the west side of the Nilsen Plateau, in the Queen Maud Mountains. Named by Edmund Stump of the Ohio State University field party 1969–70, which geologically mapped the bluff on Dec. 27, 1969. It has a peculiar subhorizontal crack containing breccia fragment exposed on the SW face.

**Mount Craddock.** 78°38'S, 85°12'W. 4,650 m. Marks the highest point on the southern end of the Vinson Massif, in the Sentinel Range. Named for J. Campbell Craddock, leader of the University of Minnesota Expedition of 1962–63 to this area. In 1960–61 he had led a Minnesota geological expedition to the Jones Mountains.

**Craddock Nunatak** *see* **Cape Menzel**

**Craft Glacier.** 72°11'S, 101°33'W. A valley glacier, 5 miles long. Just west of Hendersin Knob, on Thurston Island. Flows south to the Abbott Ice Shelf, in Peacock Sound. Named for Ensign Charles Craft, USN, helicopter pilot on the *Glacier*, 1959–60. He made exploratory flights over here in Feb. 1960.

**Craggy Island.** 62°28'S, 60°19'W. A narrow, craggy island just off the east side of Desolation Island, in the South Shetlands. It forms the NE side of Blythe Bay. Charted and named descriptively by the personnel on the *Discovery II* in 1935.

**Craggy Point** *see* **Escarpada Point**

**Cragsman Peaks.** 60°38'S, 45°40'W. On the west side of Marshall Bay, extending from Cape Vik to Coldblow Col, on the south coast of Coronation Island, in the South Orkneys. Surveyed by the FIDS in 1956–58, and named by the UK because the feature is excellent for mountain climbers.

**Craig Ridge.** 77°32'S, 86°04'W. Just NE of Polarstar Peak, in the Sentinel Range. Named by the University of Minnesota Geological Party 1963–64 for James A. Craig, helicopter pilot who assisted the party here that year.

**Crain Ridge.** 74°45'S, 63°50'W. On the north flank of Strange Glacier, in the Latady Mountains of Palmer Land. Named for Harold D.K. Crain, utilitiesman at Amundsen-Scott South Pole Station in 1967.

**Isla Cramer** *see* **Lautaro Island**

**Crandall Peak.** 71°27'S, 168°41'E. 1,840 m. Mostly snow-covered. On the west wall of Pitkevich Glacier, in the Admiralty Mountains. Named for Lt. Eugene D. Crandall, USNR, aircraft commander with VX-6 in 1968.

**Crane Channel** *see* **Crane Glacier**

**Crane Cove.** 66°17'S, 110°31'E. 175 yards in extent. In the Windmill Islands, in the area of Bailey Peninsula. Named in 1957 by Lt. Robert C. Newcomb (*see* Newcomb Bay) for Electronics Technician 3rd Class Robert I. Crane, USN, member of the *Glacier* survey party here in Feb. 1957.

**Crane Glacier.** 65°20'S, 62°15'W. Off the Foyn Coast of Graham Land, flowing into the Larsen Ice Shelf. Discovered on Dec. 29, 1929, by Wilkins as he flew over this area. He thought it was a major channel cutting the Antarctic Peninsula in half from east to west, and called it Crane Channel, for C.K. Crane of Los Angeles. It was redefined as an inlet, Crane Inlet, by the BGLE in 1936, and more correctly redefined by the FIDS in 1947.

**Crane Inlet** *see* **Crane Glacier**

**Cranfield, William J.** RNZAF flying officer who flew with Claydon in support of Hillary's depot-laying party during the BCTAE 1957–58. He was also a member of the Darwin Glacier Party of that year, and of that expedition.

**Cranfield Icefalls.** 79°56'S, 158°40'E. 8 spectacular icefalls in a series, running east-west. They fall steeply from Bucknell Ridge into the Darwin Glacier. Named by the Darwin Glacier Party of the BCTAE 1957–58, for William J. Cranfield.

**Cranfield Peak.** 83°38'S, 160°55'E. 2,850 m. 6 miles south of Mount Weeks, in the most southerly sector of the Queen Elizabeth Range. Named Sentinel Peak by the New Zealanders in 1958, and later renamed for William J. (Bill) Cranfield.

**Cranton Bay.** 74°10'S, 102°10'W. 20 miles long and 20 miles wide. South of Canisteo Peninsula, at the east end of the Amundsen Sea. Named for Lt. Elmer M. Cranton, USN, medical officer and officer-in-charge at Byrd Station in 1967.

**Crary, Albert P.** b. July 25, 1911, Pierrepont, NY. d. Oct. 29, 1987, Washington, DC. Albert Paddock Crary. Geophysicist, a pioneer in polar glaciogeo-

physics, Crary was the first person to stand at both Poles (he had flown to the North Pole in 1952), and is one of the leading figures in Antarctic history. During IGY (1957–58) he was the scientific leader at Little America V. That season he made a seismic traverse of the Ross Ice Shelf. He was deputy leader of the US scientific program in Antarctica in 1957–59, and from 1959 chief scientist with USARP, being coordinator of all scientific developments on the continent. He was back in Antarctica for the 1960–61 season. On Dec. 10, 1960, he led a scientific traverse party out of McMurdo Sound in a Sno-cat, and 63 days later arrived at the South Pole, on Feb. 12, 1961. His last trip to Antarctica was in 1966, aboard the *Eltanin*.

**Crary Bank.** 75°S, 169°E. A submarine feature of the Ross Sea.

**Crary Ice Rise.** 82°56'S, 172°30'W. On the Ross Ice Shelf, at the Siple Coast, between the Transantarctic Mountains and Roosevelt Island. Named for Albert P. Crary.

**Crary Mountains.** 76°48'S, 117°40'W. 35 miles long. Ice-covered. 50 miles SW of Toney Mountain, just to the east of the Executive Committee Range, in Marie Byrd Land. Named for Albert P. Crary.

**Crash Nunatak.** 75°47'S, 160°38'E. Isolated. Between Beta Peak and Mount Bowen, in the Prince Albert Mountains of Victoria Land. Named in 1963 by the New Zealanders for the helicopter crash here on Nov. 25, 1962.

**Crater Cirque.** 72°38'S, 169°22'E. On the south wall of Tucker Glacier, just west of its junction with Whitehall Glacier. There is a lake here with red and green algae in it, nests of several types of birds, running streams, moss, and lichens. Named descriptively by the New Zealanders in 1957–58.

**Crater Heights.** Just to the north of Crater Hill, on Hut Point Peninsula, Ross Island. Discovered and named by Scott in Feb. 1902.

**Crater Hill.** 77°50'S, 166°43'E. 300 m. (1,050 feet.) A volcanic hill just over 1 mile NE of McMurdo Station, on Hut Point Peninsula, Ross Island. The view from here is outstanding. Scott discovered and named it in Feb. 1902, and climbed it many times during the Royal Society Expedition of 1901–4.

**Crater Lake.** 62°59'S, 60°40'W. A volcanic crater now filled with water. NW of Mount Kirkwood, on the south side of Deception Island, in the South Shetlands. Named descriptively by the UK in 1959.

**Mount Craven.** 71°08'S, 165°15'E. 1,500 m. In the north part of the Everett Range, 4 miles north of Cantrell Peak. It overlooks Ebbe Glacier from the south. Named for Lt. Cdr. Alexander T. Craven, USN, pilot here in 1962–63 and 1963–64.

**Craven, Thomas T.** Lieutenant on the *Vincennes* during the Wilkes Expedition 1838–42. Left at Valparaiso on June 6, 1839.

**Mount Crawford.** 77°43'S, 86°28'W. Has two summits, 2,360 m. and 2,255 m. 3½ miles NW of Mount Dawson, in the north part of the main ridge of the Sentinel Range. Discovered aerially by Ellsworth on Nov. 23, 1935. Named for William B. Crawford, Jr., cartographer who drew up the map of the Sentinel Range in 1962.

**Crawford Glacier.** 70°53'S, 163°13'E. Flows from the east slopes of the Explorers Range, between Mount Hagar and Mount Ford, into Lillie Glacier south of Platypus Ridge. Named for Douglas I. Crawford, biologist at McMurdo Station, 1965–66.

**Creagh, Arthur B.** Seaman on the *City of New York*, 1928–30, and a crewman on the *Jacob Ruppert*, 1933–34.

**Mount Creak.** 76°34'S, 162°09'E. 1,240 m. Just north of Shoulder Mountain, in the south end of the Kirkwood Range. Discovered by Scott's 1901–4 expedition, and named by them for Capt.

E.W. Creak, director of compasses at the British admiralty.

**Mount Crean.** 77°54'S, 159°28'E. 3,550 m. Forms the central and highest summit in the Lashly Mountains of Victoria Land. Named by NZ for Tom Crean.

**Crean, Thomas.** d. 1938. Royal Navy man from Co. Kerry, Ireland. He first went to the Antarctic in 1901 as an able seaman on the Royal Society Expedition under Scott. Ten years later he was a petty officer, and back in the Antarctic on Scott's last expedition. He was a major figure in the supporting party to the Pole during that expedition. By 1914–17 he was second officer on the *Endurance* during Shackleton's British Imperial Transantarctic Expedition (which failed to get on the ground). During this expedition Crean went with Shackleton in the *James Caird,* and was still with him as the "Boss" crossed South Georgia in search of help for his other men.

**Creaney Nunataks.** 83°14'S, 51°43'W. SW of the Herring Nunataks. 5½ miles west of Mount Lechner, in the western portion of the Forrestal Range, in the Pensacola Mountains. Named for David B. Creaney, aviation electrician at Ellsworth Station in 1957.

**Creehan Cliff.** 75°47'S, 115°26'W. 6 miles ENE of Richmond Peak, on the north side of Toney Mountain, in Marie Byrd Land. Named for Lt. Patrick E. Creehan, USNR, VX-6 flight surgeon, 1971 and 1972.

**Mount Creighton.** 70°25'S, 65°39'E. 3 miles ENE of Mount Gavaghan in the Porthos Range of the Prince Charles Mountains. Named by the Australians for D.F. Creighton, electronics engineer at Mawson Station in 1963.

**Cape Crépin** *see* **Crépin Point**

**Crépin Point.** 62°06'S, 58°29'W. A point, also called Cape Crépin, which marks the west side of the entrance to Mackellar Inlet in Admiralty Bay, King George Island, in the South Shetlands.

Charcot charted it in 1909 and named it Cap Crépin. It was later redefined.

**Crescent Bay.** 71°37'S, 170°05'E. A cove in the NE side of Duke of York Island, in Robertson Bay, Victoria Land. Charted and named descriptively by Borchgrevink in 1898–1900. There is an Adélie penguin rookery here.

**Crescent Glacier.** 77°40'S, 163°14'E. Just east of Howard Glacier, it is a small alpine glacier in the Kukri Hills, and flows into Taylor Valley, in Victoria Land. Troy L. Péwé (*see* **Lake Péwé**) studied it and named it in Dec. 1957, for its shape when seen from the floor of Taylor Valley.

**Crescent Scarp.** 69°39'S, 66°20'W. 1,400 m. 8 miles long. An escarpment of rock and ice cliffs. On the south side of Fleming Glacier, in northern Palmer Land. Named by the UK for its shape.

**Cressey Peak.** 85°29'S, 143°10'W. 870 m. Between the Bender Mountains and the Harold Byrd Mountains. Between the SE edge of the Ross Ice Shelf and the Watson Escarpment. Named for Richard N. Cressey, storekeeper at Byrd Station in 1958.

**Mount Cresswell.** 72°47'S, 64°20'E. Also spelled Mount Creswell. A domed mountain with a small conical peak at the west end. 25 miles NNE of Mount Dummett, in the Prince Charles Mountains. Named by the Australians for G. Cresswell, aurora physicist at Mawson Station in 1960.

**The Crest.** 63°25'S, 56°59'W. 125 m. The summit of a moraine just east of Lake Boeckella, and ½ mile south of Hut Cove, at Hope Bay, on Trinity Peninsula. Named about 1945 by the FIDS. It is the top of the first steep slope up from the FIDS base here (Base D).

**Mount Creswell** *see* **Mount Cresswell**

**Creswick Gap.** 70°23'S, 67°44'W. Between the Creswick Peaks and the Campbell Ridges, on the west side of Palmer Land. Extends from Chapman

Glacier to Meiklejohn Glacier. One uses this gap to get from George VI Sound to the Dyer Plateau. Named by the UK for the peaks nearby.

**Creswick Peaks.** 70°28'S, 67°43'W. A massif with several peaks, the highest being 1,465 m. On the NE side of Moore Point, between the Naess and Meiklejohn Glaciers. 3 miles inland from the northern end of George VI Sound, on the west coast of Palmer Land. Named by the UK in 1954 for Frances E. Creswick, assistant to the director of the Scott Polar Research Institute, 1931–38. She helped organize the BGLE 1934–37, which surveyed these peaks. She married James I. Moore.

**Crevasse Detectors.** Composed of 5 semi-spherical electrodes mounted on the front of a vehicle, which rub over the surface of the ice like feelers. If a crevasse is forthcoming, electric currents cause a red light to flash in the driver's area. Crevasse detectors were developed in Greenland, and first used in Antarctica during the IGY. One of the Weasels that left Little America V on Nov. 5, 1956, to build Byrd Station, had one.

**Crevasse Valley Glacier.** 76°46'S, 145°W. Also called Crevassed Valley. 30 miles long. Flows between the Chester Mountains and Saunders Mountain into the Sulzberger Ice Shelf of Marie Byrd Land. Discovered in Dec. 1934 on a sledging party led by Quin Blackburn during Byrd's 1933–35 expedition, and descriptively named.

**Crevassed Valley** *see* **Crevasse Valley Glacier**

**Crevasses.** Fissures, or cracks, in glaciers or ice shelves. They can be of all sizes and depths, and are not always visible. They can be a danger, especially when a snow bridge has formed over one, rendering it invisible. (*see* **Crevasse Detectors**). There are gruesome stories of men, dogs, ponies, and vehicles plunging to their doom, others hanging by a rope upside down until rescued, etc. If a party gets to a wide, uncrossable crevasse, it normally dynamites the edges so that snow falls in the crevasse to the height of the ground. Previously, explorers had to go around such a crevasse. Crevasses are caused by stress produced by movement. There are longitudinal crevasses, transverse crevasses, marginal crevasses, and bergschrund crevasses.

**Crilly Hill.** 85° 06′ S, 174° 29′ W. The central of 3 ice-free hills on the north side of McGregor Glacier, 6 miles SSW of Mount Finley, in the Queen Maud Mountains. Named by the Texas Tech Shackleton Glacier Expedition of 1964–65, for Specialist 6th Class Clifford L. Crilly, US Army medic with the US Army Aviation Detachment, which supported the expedition.

**Crimson Hill.** 62° 57′ S, 60° 36′ W. Also called Morro Varela. 95 m. Ice-free. On the south side of Pendulum Cove, on Deception Island, in the South Shetlands. Named by Foster in 1829, because of the prominent strata of brickstone in the hill.

**Crisp Glacier.** 77° 12′ S, 162° 12′ E. Between Killer Ridge and Second Facet, it flows into the Debenham Glacier in Victoria Land. Named for Kelton W. Crisp, USN, in charge of the electric shop at McMurdo Station in 1962.

**Cristo Redentor Refugio.** Argentine refuge hut built on Duse Bay by personnel from Esperanza Station in 1955.

**Mount Crockett.** 86° 01′ S, 155° 04′ W. 3,470 m. Between Robert Scott Glacier and Amundsen Glacier, in the Queen Maud Mountains. 2 miles NE of Mount Astor, in the Hays Mountains, of the Queen Maud Mountains. Discovered by Gould's Southern Geological Party during Byrd's 1928–30 expedition, and named by Byrd for Freddy Crockett. Modern geographers think this is the mountain thus named by Gould, and regardless of whether it is, this is now the mountain with Crockett's name.

**Crockett, Freddy.** Frederick E. Crockett. One of the 6-man Southern Geo-

logical Party led by Gould during Byrd's 1928–30 expedition.

**Croft Bay.** 64° S, 57° 45′ W. An indentation into the north-central side of James Ross Island. It forms the south part of the Herbert Sound. Discovered in 1903 by Nordenskjöld's expedition. Charted in 1945 by the FIDS, and named by them for W.N. Croft, FIDS geologist at Base D in 1946.

**Crohn Island.** 67° 07′ S, 50° 51′ E. ½ mile east of Beaver Island, at the head of Amundsen Bay, in Enderby Land. Discovered in 1956 by an ANARE airborne field party led by P.W. Crohn, geologist at Mawson Station in 1955 and 1956.

**Crohn Massif.** 70° 29′ S, 64° 59′ E. Domed. 3 miles west of Mount Kirkby, in the Porthos Range of the Prince Charles Mountains. Discovered by the ANARE southern party led by W.G. Bewsher in 1956–57, and named by the Australians for P.W. Crohn (*see* **Crohn Island**).

**Croker Inlet**  *see*  **Croker Passage**

**Croker Passage.** 64° S, 61° 42′ W. Also called Paso Comandante Cordovez, Paso Federico Puga Borne. Between the Christiania Islands and Two Hummock Island to the east and Hoseason Island and Liège Island to the west. Foster named it Croker Inlet in 1829 for John W. Croker (1780–1857), secretary to the admiralty. Later redefined.

**Croll Glacier.** 72° 29′ S, 167° 18′ E. Flows along the north side of Handler Ridge into Trafalgar Glacier, in the Victory Mountains of Victoria Land. Named by the New Zealanders in 1962–63 for W.G. Croll, a surveyor here that year.

**Mount Cromie.** 84° 50′ S, 179° 14′ W. 2,950 m. Snow-covered. 1½ miles SE of Mount Boyd, in the Bush Mountains. Discovered by the USAS 1939–41. Surveyed by Albert Crary in 1957–58, and named by him for William Cromie, assistant glaciologist with Crary on his US Ross Ice Shelf Traverse Party of 1957–58.

**Cronenwett Island.** 77° S, 149° 59′ W. Ice-covered. 20 miles long. The second largest of the grounded islands in the Marshall Archipelago, in the Sulzberger Ice Shelf of Marie Byrd Land. Named for Cdr. Wilson R. Cronenwett, photo officer during Operation Deep Freeze II (1956–57) and on Operation Deep Freeze 61.

**Cronk Islands.** 66°19′S, 110°25′E. A group NE of Hollin Island, in the Windmill Islands. Named for Caspar Cronk, glaciologist at Wilkes Station in 1958.

**Crontu, James.** Ordinary seaman on the Wilkes Expedition 1838–42. Joined in the USA. Run at Sydney.

**Mount Cronus.** 67°18′S, 50°03′E. 900 m. Conical. Partly snow-covered. 8 miles south of Amundsen Bay, and 9 miles WSW of Reference Peak. Discovered by an ANARE party in Oct. 1956, and aptly named by the Australians for the Greek god, Cronus.

**Cronus Glacier.** 68°51′S, 64°04′W. 6 miles long. 3 miles wide. Flows into Mobiloil Inlet, between Calypso Cliffs and Crabeater Point, on the east coast of the Antarctic Peninsula. Named by the UK for the Greek god.

**Crooked Fjord** *see* **Krok Fjord**

**Crooked Island** *see* **Krok Island**

**Crooked Lake** *see* **Krok Lake**

**Mount Crooker.** 71°03′S, 67°15′W. Gable-shaped. On the north side of Ryder Glacier, and at the south end of the Pegasus Mountains, in Palmer Land. Named for Allen R. Crooker, biologist at Palmer Station in 1972.

**Crookes Peak.** 66°14′S, 65°18′W. On the east side of Widmark Ice Piedmont, between Stair Hill and Rugg Peak, on the west coast of Graham Land. Named by the UK in 1959 for Sir William Crookes (1832–1919), snow goggles pioneer.

**Croom Glacier.** 70°18′S, 62°25′W. Flows into Smith Inlet between Moe Point and Hughes Ice Piedmont, on the east coast of Palmer Land. Named for John M. Croom, biologist at Palmer Station, 1968–69, and US exchange scientist at Bellingshausen Station in 1970.

**Crosby, Joseph.** Carpenter's mate on the Wilkes Expedition 1838–42. Joined in the USA. Returned in the *Relief* in 1839.

**Crosby, W.E.** Crewman on the *Discovery* during the BANZARE 1929–31.

**Crosby Nunataks.** 66°46′S, 51°33′E. Three nunataks 2 miles NE of Mount Morrison in the northern part of the Tula Mountains of Enderby Land. Named by the Australians for W.E. Crosby.

**Cape Cross** *see* **Cape Hinks**

**Mount Cross.** 84°37′S, 63°38′W. 1,005 m. 2½ miles NE of King Ridge, in the Anderson Hills of the Patuxent Range, in the Pensacola Mountains. Named by Finn Ronne in 1957–58 for Dr. Allan S. Cross, who helped prepare Ronne's own RARE of the previous decade.

**Cross, Jacob.** Petty officer on the Royal Society Expedition of 1901–4. Helped Wilson with the bird-skinning.

**Cross Hill** *see* **Laguna Hill**

**Cross Valley.** 64°16′S, 56°42′W. Also called Querthal. 2 miles long. On the north end of Seymour Island. Discovered by the Nordenskjöld expedition of 1901–4, and named by him for the transverse alignment of the valley.

**Mount Crosscut** *see* **Crosscut Peak**

**Crosscut Peak.** 72°22′S, 166°19′E. Also called Mount Crosscut. 3,120 m. Just north of Joice Icefall, in the Millen Range. Named by the New Zealanders in 1962–63 for its jagged northern ridge and summit.

**Crosse Passage.** 67°47′S, 68°55′W. Between the Henkes Islands and the Skeen Rocks, off the south end of Adelaide Island. Named by the UK in 1963 for Lt. Cdr. Anthony G. Crosse, RN, 1st lt. of the *Protector* in 1961–63.

**Cape Crossfire.** 73°11′S, 168°23′E. At the SE end of the Malta Plateau. Here Mariner Glacier and Borchgrevink Glacier merge in Victoria Land. Named by NZ in 1966 for the crossfire of ice flows here.

**Crosson Ice Shelf.** 75°05'S, 109°25'W. 30 miles long. 20 miles wide. North and NE of Mount Murphy, on the coast of Marie Byrd Land. Named for Cdr. W.E. Crosson, USN, CO of the Antarctic Construction Group, 1973.

**Crossover Pass.** 80°38'S, 26°30'W. Between the Gordon and Cornwall Glaciers in the Shackleton Range. It provides a sledging route across the range, hence the name given by the BCTAE who first mapped it in 1957.

**Crosswell Glacier.** 78°17'S, 85°24'W. 10 miles long. Flows from Mount Shinn into Ellen Glacier, in the central part of the Sentinel Range. Named for Col. Horace A. Crosswell, USAF, pilot who helped set up the South Pole Station in 1956–57.

**Crouch Island.** 67°49'S, 68°58'W. The second largest of the Henkes Islands, off the south end of Adelaide Island. Named by the UK for Alan Crouch, BAS general assistant at Base T in 1961–62, and a member of the first party to winter over on Adelaide Island.

**Croucher, George B.** Able Seaman, RN, on the Royal Society Expedition of 1901–4.

**Crouse Spur.** 82°53'S, 48°35'W. 3 miles south of Kester Peaks, in the Forrestal Range, in the Pensacola Mountains. Named for Carl L. Crouse, construction man at Ellsworth Station in 1957.

**Mount Crow.** 77°11'S, 144°04'W. Just east of Mount McClung, in the Ford Ranges of Marie Byrd Land. Discovered by the USAS 1939–41. Named for Lt. J.L. Crow, USN, officer-in-charge of Byrd Station in 1963.

**Mount Crowder.** 72°03'S, 166°23'E. Overlooks the upper part of the Jutland Glacier, 6 miles NE of Mount Tararua, in the Victory Mountains. Named for Dwight F. Crowder, geologist at Hallett Station in 1964–65.

**Mount Crowell.** 74°20'S, 64°05'W. In the north part of the Rare Range, in Palmer Land. Named for John C.

Crowell, geologist at McMurdo Station in 1966–67.

**Crowell, Mason.** Landsman on the Wilkes Expedition 1838–42. Joined in the USA. Served the cruise.

**Crowell Buttresses.** 83°03'S, 162°30'E. 10 miles long. A series of high snow and rock buttress-type peaks, which form the north wall of Cornwall Glacier for 5 miles, and then trend NE for another 5 miles along the west side of Lowery Glacier, in the Queen Elizabeth Range. Named for John T. Crowell, Antarctic vessel project officer with the National Science Foundation, 1960–63, and special projects officer with the same organization, 1963–68. He was in the Antarctic Peninsula in 1963 looking for a US scientific station location.

**Crown Head.** 60°37'S, 45°19'W. A headland that forms the east side of Palmer Bay, on the north coast of Coronation Island, in the South Orkneys. Discovered by Powell and Palmer in Dec. 1821. Named by the UK in 1959 in association with Coronation Island.

**Crown Mountain.** 86°18'S, 158°45'W. 3,830 m. Surmounts the west side of the Nilsen Plateau. 4 miles ENE of Mount Kristensen, in the Queen Maud Mountains. Named for its resemblance to a crown.

**Crown Peak.** 63°34'S, 58°33'W. 1,185 m. Ice-covered. Has a crown-shaped ice formation on top. Forms the highest summit and the south end of Marescot Ridge. 10 miles east of Cape Roquemaurel, on the NW side of Trinity Peninsula. Named by the FIDS following a 1946 survey.

**Crown Prince Gustav Channel** *see* **Prince Gustav Channel**

**Crown Prince Olav Coast** *see* **Prince Olav Coast**

**Crown Prince Olav Land** *see* **Prince Olav Coast**

**Crown Prince Olav Mountains** *see* **Prince Olav Mountains**

**Crown Princess Martha Land** *see* **Princess Martha Coast**

**Cape Crozier.** 77°31′S, 169°23′E. The easternmost cape of Ross Island. Discovered by Ross in 1841, and named by him for Francis Crozier. It is SSSI #4.

**Crozier, Francis.** b. ca. 1796, Ireland. d. in the spring of 1848 of starvation in the Arctic. Francis Rawdon Moira Crozier. Joined the RN in 1810, and in 1839–43 was commander of the *Terror* during Ross' expedition to Antarctica. Known mostly as an Arctic explorer with Ross and Parry, he took command of the Franklin expedition to the Northwest Passage, and died there.

**Crozier Shoal.** 77°45′S, 171°E. Subterranean feature beneath the Ross Ice Shelf, just to the east of Ross Island.

**Cruchleys Island**  *see*  **Powell Island**

**Cruiser Rocks.** 61°13′S, 55°28′W. Also spelled Cruizer Rocks. A group 7 miles south of Cape Lindsey, Elephant Island, in the South Shetlands. Known to sealers as Cruisers as early as 1822.

**Cruisers**  *see*  **Cruiser Rocks**

**Cruizer Rocks**  *see*  **Cruiser Rocks**

**Crulls Islands**  *see*  **Cruls Islands**

**Cruls Islands.** 65°11′S, 64°32′W. Also spelled Crulls Islands. A group of small islands 1 mile west of the Roca Islands, in the southern part of the Wilhelm Archipelago. Discovered by de Gerlache in 1897–99, and named by him for Luis Cruls, Belgian astronomer.

**Crume Glacier.** 71°33′S, 169°21′E. 5 miles long. Flows into Ommanney Glacier, near the north coast of Victoria Land. Named for William R. Crume, USN, support equipment maintenance supervisor of VX-6, at McMurdo Station in 1968.

**Mount Crummer.** 75°04′S, 162°34′E. 895 m. A massive, brown, granite mountain, just south of Backstairs Passage Glacier, on the coast of northern Victoria Land. Charted and named during Shackleton's 1907–9 expedition.

**Crummey Nunatak.** 76°47′S, 143°36′ W. A linear rock nunatak. 1½ miles

long. At the NE end of the Gutenko Nunataks, in the Ford Ranges of Marie Byrd Land. Named for Glenn T. Crummey, USN, construction electrician at Byrd Station in 1967.

**Crust.** The average thickness of the Earth's crust in Antarctica is about the same as for other continents. The crust thickens along the front of the Transantarctic Mountains, and is about 25 miles thick in East Antarctica and about 20 miles thick in West Antarctica. Because the ancient crust was highly mobile, the bedrock shape of Antarctica is very different today then what it was.

**Crustaceans.** Crustacea are a class of the invertebrate phylum Arthropoda (q.v.). They include crabs, shrimp, lobsters, krill, isopods, copepods, ostracods, amphipods, etc. There is a variety that live on the Antarctic sea bed, near the shore (*see* **Fauna**).

**Crutch Peak**  *see*  **Crutch Peaks**

**Crutch Peaks.** 62°28′S, 59°56′W. Also called Crutch Peak, Pico Muleta. The highest is 275 m. 1½ miles east of Greaves Peak. 2½ miles east of the NW tip of Greenwich Island, in the South Shetlands. Named in the singular by the personnel on the *Discovery II* in 1934–35. Aerial photos later proved the existence of two pairs of high peaks, and several lower ones.

**Cruyt Spur.** 64°37′S, 60°42′W. 4 miles NE of Ruth Ridge. 2 miles SE of the south wall of Detroit Plateau, Graham Land. Named by the UK for William Cruyt, Belgian army engineer who designed the autopolaire in 1907.

**Bahía Cruz**  *see*  **Bolsón Cove**

**The *Cruz de Forward*.** Chilean ship in Antarctic waters in 1988–89.

**Cruzen, Richard H.** b. 1898. d. 1970, Camp Pendleton, Calif. Joined the USN in 1920, and during the USAS 1939–41 he commanded the *Bear* and was second-in-command of the expedition. As an admiral, he was the tactical leader of Operation Highjump, 1946–47 (Byrd was technical leader).

**Cruzen Island.** 74°47'S, 142°42'W. Mostly snow-covered. 50 miles NNE of the mouth of Land Glacier, off the Ruppert Coast of Marie Byrd Land. Discovered aerially in 1940 by the USAS from West Base, and named for Richard Cruzen.

**Cryptogram Ridge.** Unofficial name as yet. On top of Mount Melbourne, in Victoria Land.

**Crystal Hill.** 63°39'S, 57°44'W. 150 m. Ice-free. Between Bald Head and Camp Hill on the south side of Trinity Peninsula. Named by the FIDS for the crystals collected at the foot of the hill in 1945 and 1946.

**Crystal Sound.** 66°23'S, 66°30'W. Between the southern part of the Biscoe Islands, and the west coast of Graham Land. The northern limit is Cape Leblond to Cape Evensen. The southern limit is Holdfast Point, Roux Island, Liard Island, and the Sillard Islands. Named by the UK in 1960 because many of the features in the sound are named for ice crystal researchers.

**Mount Csejtey.** 82°30'S, 155°50'E. 1½ miles south of Mount Macpherson, in the central part of the Geologists Range. Named by the USA for Bela Csejtey, geologist at McMurdo Station in 1962–63.

**Ctenophores.** Ctenophora is a phylum of about 80 species of small marine invertebrates, many of them found in Antarctica.

**Bahía Cuadrada**   *see*   **Square Bay**

**Isla Cuadrada**   *see*   **Square End Island**

**Morro Cuadrado Negro**   *see*   **Elephant Point**

**Cuba.** On Aug. 16, 1984, Cuba was ratified as the 32nd signatory of the Antarctic Treaty. Cuba has sent scientists to work in Antarctica with the Russians.

**The Cube**   *see*   **Kubus Mountain**

**Cube Rock.** 63°37'S, 56°22'W. A small rock in the south entrance to Antarctic Sound. 3 miles SE of Cape Scrymgeour, Andersson Island, off Trinity Peninsula. Named Roca Cubo by the Argentines before 1960. This is a descriptive name, and was translated into English.

**Cucumbers.** Cosmic microwave background radiation, or CMBR.

**Cape Cuff**   *see*   **Cuff Cape**

**Cuff Cape.** 77°S, 162°22'E. Also called Cape Cuff. A dark rock point which juts out into Granite Harbor just to the south of the Mackay Glacier Tongue. Mapped by Scott's 1910–13 expedition, and named because it looks like a hand coming out of a snowy cuff.

**Cugnot Ice Piedmont.** 63°38'S, 58°10'W. 15 miles long. Between 3 and 6 miles wide. Extends from the Russell East Glacier to Eyrie Bay, on Trinity Peninsula. Bounded on the landward side by the Louis Philippe Plateau. Named by the UK for Nicolas J. Cugnot (1725–1804), the automobile pioneer.

**Cumbers Reef.** 67°35'S, 69°40'W. A group of rocks which form the north and west part of Adelaide Island. Named by the UK for Roger N. Cumbers, 3rd officer on the *John Biscoe*, 1961–62.

**Cumbie, William A., Jr.** Radioman on the *Que Sera Sera* during the famous flight to the South Pole on Oct. 31, 1956.

**Cumbie Glacier.** 77°13'S, 154°12'W. Just east of Scott's Nunataks, it flows into the Swinburne Ice Shelf, on the SW side of Sulzberger Bay, in Marie Byrd Land. Named for William A. Cumbie, Jr.

**Mount Cumming.** 76°40'S, 125°48'W. Mostly snow-covered and volcanic in origin. Between Mount Hampton and Mount Hartigan in the Executive Committee Range of Marie Byrd Land. A circular snow-covered crater occupies the summit area. Discovered aerially on Dec. 15, 1940, by the USAS, and named Mount Winifred Cumming, for the wife of Hugh S. Cumming, Jr., State Department member of the USAS Executive Committee. The name was shortened.

**Mount Cummings.** 73°14'S, 61°37'W. At the east end of Galan Ridge, in the Dana Mountains of Palmer Land. Named for Jack W. Cummings, radioman at Palmer Station in 1965.

**Cummings, James.** Seaman on the Wilkes Expedition 1838–42. Joined in the USA. Discharged at Oahu, Oct. 31, 1840.

**Cummings, Thomas W.** Passed midshipman on the Wilkes Expedition 1838–42. Left sick at Rio.

**Cummings, W.H.** Bosun's mate on the Wilkes Expedition 1838–42. Joined in the USA. Served the cruise.

**Cummings Cove.** 60°44'S, 45°41'W. Between Jebsen Point and Porteous Point, on the west side of Signy Island, in the South Orkneys. Named by the UK for E.T. Cummings, FIDS radio operator at Cape Geddes in 1946 and at Deception Island in 1947.

**Cumpston Glacier.** 66°59'S, 65°02'W. Flows between Breitfuss Glacier and Quartermain Glacier into the head of Mill Inlet, on the east coast of Graham Land. Named by the UK for J.S. Cumpston of the Australian Department of External Affairs, historian of the Antarctic, who, with E.P. Bayliss, drew up the 1939 map of Antarctica.

**Cumpston Massif.** 73°33'S, 66°53'E. 2,070 m. Flat-topped. 9 miles long. At the junction of the Lambert and Mellor Glaciers, in the southern part of the Prince Charles Mountains. Discovered aerially by the ANARE in Nov. 1956. Named by the Australians for J.S. Cumpston (see **Cumpston Glacier**).

**Cumulus Hills.** 85°15'S, 175°W. Several groups of largely barren hills, divided by the Logie Glacier, in the Queen Maud Mountains, overlooking the Shackleton Glacier, which bounds the hills on the west. The McGregor Glacier bounds them on the north, and the Zaneveld Glacier on the south. Cumulus clouds form here, hence the name given by the New Zealanders in 1961–62.

**Cumulus Mountain.** 71°51'S, 5°23'E. Also called Mount Cumulus. 2,335 m. Just north of Høgsenga Crags, in the Mühlig-Hofmann Mountains of Queen Maud Land, about 5 miles from Svarthamaren Mountain. The Norwegians named it Cumulusfjellet (Cumulus Mountain).

**Cuneiform Cliffs.** 73°06'S, 167°38'E. At the south end of the Malta Plateau, on the north side of the lower Mariner Glacier, in Victoria Land. Named by NZ in 1966 for the wedgelike (cuneiform) spurs which project from the face of the cliffs.

**Cunningham Glacier.** 84°16'S, 173°45'E. Flows into Canyon Glacier, 5 miles north of Gray Peak, in the Queen Maud Mountains. Named for Willard E. Cunningham, Jr., cook at McMurdo Station in 1960 and at Amundsen-Scott South Pole Station in 1963.

**Cunningham Peak.** 79°16'S, 86°12'W. 2,170 m. Mostly ice-covered. At the head of Gowan Glacier, along the Founders Escarpment, in the Heritage Range. Named for John B. Cunningham, USN, ship's serviceman at McMurdo Station in 1966.

**Mount Cupola.** 69°21'S, 70°27'W. 2,500 m. Dome-shaped. Marks the southern limit of the Rouen Mountains, in the northern part of Alexander Island. Named descriptively by the UK in 1960.

**Isla Curanilahue** see **Andresen Island**

**Curie Island.** 66°39'S, 140°03'E. A small island near the east end of the Géologie Archipelago. 1 mile SW of Derby Island, just north of the Astrolabe Glacier Tongue. Charted by the French in 1949–51, and named by them for the French scientific family.

**Curie Point.** 64°50'S, 63°29'W. Also called Pointe P. Curie. Forms the NE extremity of Doumer Island, in the Palmer Archipelago. Discovered by Charcot in 1903–5, and named by him for Pierre Curie (1859–1906), the scientist.

**Mount Curl.** 70°48'S, 63°07'W. Snow-covered. 4 miles ENE of Mount

Gatlin, just NE of the Welch Mountains, in Palmer Land. Named for James E. Curl, glaciologist in the South Shetlands in 1971–72, 1972–73, and 1973–74.

**Curran Bluff.** 68°13′S, 65°02′W. On the east coast of Graham Land.

**Currents.** The ocean currents go clockwise around Antarctica, pulled by the winds. (*See also* **Antarctic Circumpolar Current, Antarctic Surface Water.**)

**Mount Currie.** 67°42′S, 49°12′E. 1,110 m. Between Mount Maslen and Mount Merrick, in the Raggatt Mountains of Enderby Land. Named by the Australians for G.J. Currie, radio supervisor at Mawson Station in 1960.

**The *Currituck*.** Seaplane tender, and flagship of the Western Task Group of Operation Highjump, 1946–47. Capt. John E. Clark commanding.

**Currituck Island.** 66°05′S, 100°40′E. 7 miles long. On the NW side of the Edisto Channel, in the Highjump Archipelago. The southern part of the island was named by the USA in 1956 for the *Currituck*. It was thought that the northern part was a separate island named Mohaupt Island. The USSR in 1956–57 corrected that impression, and the name was applied to the whole island.

**Curtis Island.** 65°56′S, 65°38′W. Over 1 mile long. 2 miles NE of Jagged Island, off the west coast of Graham Land. Named by the UK in 1959 for Robin Curtis, FIDS geologist at Prospect Point in 1957.

**Curtis Peaks.** 84°55′S, 169°35′W. A small cluster of peaks east of Mount Hall, in the Lillie Range of the Queen Maud Mountains. Discovered by the US Ross Ice Shelf Traverse Party led by Crary in 1957–58, and named by him for Lt. Cdr. Roy E. Curtis, USN, VX-6 pilot during the IGY.

**The *Curtiss*.** US ship used on Operation Deep Freeze II (1956–57).

**Curtiss Bay.** 64°02′S, 60°47′W. Also called Bahía Guesalaga. 4 miles wide. Indentation into the west coast of Graham

Land, between Cape Sterneck and Cape Andreas. It is not useless as the Argentine chart of 1957 suggests (they named it Bahía Inútil). It has been used as an anchorage. Renamed by the UK in 1960 for Glenn Curtiss (1878–1930), US seaplane pioneer.

**Curzon Archipelago** *see* **Curzon Islands**

**Curzon Islands.** 66°46′S, 141°35′E. Also called Curzon Archipelago, Curzon Islets. A small group just off Cape Découverte. They include Chameau Island, Claquebue Island, Dauphin Island, Guano Island, Retour Island, Dru Rock, Nord Island, Piton Island. Discovered in Jan. 1840 by Dumont d'Urville, but not charted. Charted in 1912 by John King Davis in the *Aurora*, during the AAE 1911–14, and named by Mawson for Lord Curzon, president of the Royal Geographical Society, 1911–14. Mapped in detail by the French in 1950–52.

**Curzon Islets** *see* **Curzon Islands**

**Cushing Peak.** 64°06′S, 62°25′W. 1½ miles SE of Guyou Bay, at the head of Lister Glacier, in the north of Brabant Island. Named by the UK for Harvey Cushing (1869–1939), US neurosurgery pioneer.

**Cutcliffe Peak.** 70°32′S, 65°17′E. Just south of Mount Mervyn in the Porthos Range of the Prince Charles Mountains. Named by the Australians for M.A. Cutcliffe, electrical fitter at Mawson Station in 1966.

**Cutler, Ben.** Benjamin S. Cutler. Commander of the *Free Gift* during the 1821–22 sealing expedition to the South Shetlands put together by the Fannings. He was also co-owner of the *Frederick*, Ben Pendleton's flagship during the expedition. In 1827–29, as captain of the *Uxor*, he visited the Prince Edward Islands in 1829, but did not go south of 60°S.

**Cutler Stack.** 62°36′S, 60°59′W. A stack in the water, NE of Lair Point, off the north coast of Livingston Island, in the South Shetlands. Named by the UK in 1958 for Ben Cutler.

**Cuttlefish.** A marine cephalopod of the order *Sepioidea.* Related to the octopus and squid. Found in Antarctica.

**¹Cuverville Island** *see* **Rongé Island**

**²Cuverville Island.** 64°41'S, 62°38'W. In Errera Channel, between Arctowski Peninsula and the northern part of Rongé Island, off the west coast of the Antarctic Peninsula. Discovered by de Gerlache in 1897–99 and named by him for the Chevalier de Cuverville, a vice-admiral of the French Navy. Not to be confused with Rongé Island itself.

**Cuvier Island.** 66°39'S, 140°01'E. 175 yards long. 350 yards north of the west part of Pétrel Island, in the Géologie Archipelago. Charted in 1951 by the French, and named by them for Georges Cuvier (1769–1832), French naturalist.

**Cyclops Peak.** 68°S, 55°40'E. A triangular peak marked by a round patch of light-colored rock which makes the feature look like the one-eyed giant of the *Odyssey.* At the NE end of the Dismal Mountains, in Enderby Land. Named by the ANARE in 1958.

**Mount Cyril.** 84°02'S, 172°36'E. 1,190 m. Ice-covered. 2 miles south of Celebration Pass, in the Commonwealth Range, just to the east of the foot of the Beardmore Glacier. Discovered by Shackleton in 1908, and named by him for Cyril Longhurst, secretary of the Royal Society Expedition of 1901–4. He was best man at Shackleton's wedding.

**Czamanske Ridge.** 82°35'S, 52°42'W. In the Pensacola Mountains.

**Czechoslovakia.** On June 14, 1962, this country was ratified as the fourteenth signatory of the Antarctic Treaty.

**Mount Czegka.** 86°21'S, 148°41'W. 2,270 m. On the east side of the Robert Scott Glacier, just north of the terminus of the Van Reeth Glacier, in the Queen Maud Mountains. Discovered in Dec. 1934 by Quin Blackburn's party during Byrd's 1933–35 expedition. Named by Byrd for Victor H. Czegka.

**Czegka, Victor H.** US Marine warrant officer on Byrd's 1928–30 expedition. He was supply manager for Byrd's 1933–35 expedition, on duty in the USA.

**D-80.** 70°S, 132°42'E. American automatic weather station in Adélie Land, at an elevation of approximately 7,800 feet. Studies katabatic winds. Began operating on Dec. 11, 1985.

**D-57.** 68°12'S, 137°30'E. An American automatic weather station in Adélie Land, at an elevation of approximately 6,400 feet. It monitors katabatic winds. It began operating on Nov. 17, 1985.

**D-47.** 67°24'S, 138°42'E. An American automatic weather station in Adélie Land, at an elevation of approximately 5,000 feet. It monitors katabatic winds. It began operating on Nov. 13, 1985.

**D-17.** 66°42'S, 139°42'E. American automatic weather station in Adélie Land, at an elevation of approximately 1,350 feet. It monitored katabatic winds. Began operating on Jan. 11, 1980, and ceased operating on June 19, 1980.

**D-10.** 66°42'S, 139°48'E. American automatic weather station in Adélie Land, at an elevation of approximately 800 feet. It monitors katabatic winds. Began operating on Jan. 15, 1984.

**D'Abnour Bay.** 64°16'S, 63°14'W. 3 miles ESE of Cape Grönland in the northern part of Anvers Island. Charted by Charcot in 1903–5, and named Baie Richard d'Abnour by him for Contre-Amiral Richard d'Abnour, a French naval officer. The name was later shortened.

**Daedalus Point** *see* **Zapato Point**

**Daehli, Capt.** Norwegian skipper of the *Hilda Knudsen,* 1930–31.

**Dagger Peak.** 63°55'S, 57°29'W. Rises sharply at the west end of Comb Ridge, near the end of The Naze on James Ross Island. 90 meters high. Charted by personnel on Operation Tabarin in 1945. Named descriptively by them.

**Daggoo Peak.** 65°45'S, 62°20'W. 905 m. On the north side of the mouth of Flask Glacier. 5 miles WSW of Tashtego Point on the east side of Graham Land.

Named by the UK in 1956 for the *Moby Dick* character

**Daguerre Glacier.** 65°07'S, 63°25'W. Joins the Niepcé Glacier and flows into Lauzanne Cove, Flandres Bay, on the west coast of Graham Land. Named by the UK in 1960 for Louis J.M. Daguerre (1787-1851), French photography pioneer with Niepcé.

**Dahl.** Norwegian chief steward on the *Wyatt Earp*, 1938-39, during Ellsworth's last expedition to the Antarctic. He had been to the Antarctic at least once before with Ellsworth.

**Dahl Reef.** 66°15'S, 110°29'E. Almost 1½ miles NW of Stonehocker Point on the Clark Peninsula. Charted by the ANARE under d'A.T. Gale in 1962, and named by him for Egil Dahl, third mate on the ANARE ship the *Thala Dan,* that year.

**Daiichi Rock** *see* **Tensoku Rock**

**Dailey, Fred E.** Warrant officer, RN. Carpenter on the Royal Society Expedition 1901-4.

**Dailey Archipelago** *see* **Dailey Islands**

**Dailey Islands.** 77°53'S, 165°06'E. Also called Dailey Archipelago. Volcanic islands 5 miles NE of Cape Chocolate, in McMurdo Sound, just off the Ross Ice Shelf. Discovered by Scott's 1901-4 expedition, who named it for Fred E. Dailey.

**Mount Daimler.** 63°45'S, 58°29'W. Between Russell East Glacier and Victory Glacier. 3 miles south of Mount Canicula, in Trinity Peninsula. Named by the UK for Gottlieb Daimler (1834-1900), German automobile pioneer.

**Dais.** 77°33'S, 161°15'E. An elongated mesa between Labyrinth and Lake Vanda in the western part of the Wright Valley in Victoria Land. Named descriptively by the New Zealanders in 1958-59.

**Dakers Island.** 64°46'S, 64°23'W. Between Hartshorne Island and McGuire Island in the eastern Joubin Islands. Named for Hugh B. Dakers, cook on the *Hero* during its first voyage to Palmer Station in 1968.

**Dakota Pass.** 83°52'S, 160°35'E. In the Queen Elizabeth Range, to the east of Peletier Plateau. Named by the New Zealanders in 1961-62 for the Dakota R4D aircraft.

**Dakshin Gangotri Weather Station.** 70°45'S, 11°38'E. On the Princess Astrid Coast. India's only permanent base in Antarctica. Built in 1982, it has a satellite link with India.

**Dale, John B.** Lieutenant on the Wilkes Expedition 1838-42. Joined the *Relief* at Callao, and later transferred to the *Porpoise.*

**Dale Glacier.** 78°17'S, 162°E. Flows from the SW slopes of Mount Huggins in the Royal Society Range, into the Skelton Glacier. Visited by F. Richard Brooke and Bernie Gunn of the NZ party of the BCTAE in 1957-58. Named by the USA in 1963 for Lt. Cdr. Robert L. Dale, USN, VX-6 commander at McMurdo Station in 1960.

**Dales Island.** 67°11'S, 59°44'E. A small island 1 mile north of the Warnock Islands, to the north of the William Scoresby Archipelago. Discovered and named by the personnel on the *William Scoresby* in Feb. 1936.

**Daley Hills.** 73°42'S, 164°45'E. Ice-covered. On the west side of Aviator Glacier, between the mouths of the Cosmonette and Shoemaker Glaciers in Victoria Land. Named for Robert C. Daley, USN, flight engineer in Antarctica in 1966, 1967, and 1968.

**Dalgliesh, David G.** Surgeon and lt. cdr., RN. FIDS medical officer at Base E in the 1948-49 season. He was the first leader of the British Royal Society IGY Expedition of 1955-58. He came to the Weddell Sea in the 1955-56 season on the *Tottan* and he and 10 men built Halley Station in Jan.-Feb. 1956. The *Tottan,* again commanded by Capt. Leif Jakobsen, returned for the 1956-57 season, carrying Robin Smart, leader of the 1957 wintering party at Halley Bay. The *Magga Dan* accompanied it on this trip. David Dalgliesh was the brother of

A.R.F. "Robin" Dalgliesh (b. 1928, d. Dec. 25, 1987), tractor driver during IGY.

**Dalgliesh Bay.** 67°42′S, 67°45′W. 1 mile wide. It indents for 3 miles between Lainez Point and Bongrain Point on the west side of Pourquoi Pas Island, off the west coast of Graham Land. Named by the FIDS for David G. Dalgliesh.

**Dålk Glacier.** 69°25′S, 76°26′E. 8 miles long. Flows into the SE part of Prydz Bay between the Larsemann Hills and Steinnes. Photographed by the LCE 1936–37. Named by John H. Roscoe, the US cartographer, in 1952, in association with Dålk Island.

**Dålk Island.** 69°23′S, 76°30′E. A small island at the terminus of Dålk Glacier in the SE part of Prydz Bay. Photographed by the LCE 1936–37. Named Dålköy (Dålk Island) by the Norwegians.

**Dålköy** *see* **Dålk Island**

**Mount Dallmann.** 71°48′S, 10°20′E. 2,485 m. 11 miles east of the northern part of the Conrad Mountains in the Orvin Mountains of Queen Maud Land. Discovered by Ritscher in 1938–39, and named for Eduard Dallmann.

**Dallmann, Eduard.** 1830–1896. German whaler, the first German leader of an expedition in Antarctica. Under the sponsorship of the German Society for Polar Navigation he went sealing and exploring in the South Shetlands, the Palmer Archipelago and the northern part of the Antarctic Peninsula in 1873–75, in his ship, the *Grönland*. He discovered the Bismarck Strait and the Kaiser Wilhelm Archipelago. It was Dallmann who proved that the Antarctic Peninsula was indeed a peninsula (a fact later "disproved" by Wilkins, in 1928, then proved again after that by the BGLE in 1934–37).

**¹Dallmann Bay.** 64°20′S, 62°55′W. Also spelled (erroneously) as Dallman Bay. A large indentation into the west side of Brabant Island. Not to be confused with Flandres Bay. Discovered by

Eduard Dallmann in 1874 and named for him by the Society for Polar Navigation in Hamburg.

**²Dallmann Bay** *see* **Flandres Bay**

**Dallmann Nunatak.** 65°01′S, 60°18′W. 1½ miles north of Bruce Nunatak in the Seal Nunataks, off the east coast of the Antarctic Peninsula. Charted in 1902 by Nordenskjöld and named by him for Eduard Dallmann.

**Dallmeyer Peak.** 64°53′S, 62°45′W. 1,105 m. 2 miles SE of Steinheil Point, on the south side of Andvord Bay, on the west coast of Graham Land. Named by the UK in 1960 for John H. Dallmeyer (1830–1883), German-English photography pioneer.

**Mount Dalmeny.** 71°08′S, 166°55′E. 1,610 m. 6 miles ESE of Drabek Peak, and 3 miles west of Redmond Bluff, in the Anare Mountains of Victoria Land. Discovered and named by Ross in 1841 for Lord Dalmeny of the Admiralty.

**Mount Dalrymple.** 77°56′S, 86°03′W. 3,600 m. Between Mount Alf and Mount Goldthwait in the northern part of the Sentinel Range. Named for Paul C. Dalrymple, meteorologist at Little America in 1957 and at South Pole Station in 1958.

**Dalsnatten Crag.** 72°31′S, 0°30′E. On the east side of the Skarsdalen Valley in the Sverdrup Mountains of Queen Maud Land. Name means "the valley crag" in Norwegian.

**Dalsnuten Peak.** 72°36′S, 3°11′W. In the NE part of Raudberg Valley, just north of Jøkulskarvet Ridge in the Borg Massif of Queen Maud Land. Name means "the valley peak" in Norwegian.

**Dalten Nunatak.** 72°23′S, 3°42′W. Isolated. 1½ miles ESE of Dilten Nunatak. 7 miles NW of Borg Mountain in Queen Maud Land. Named by the Norwegians.

**Cape Dalton.** 66°53′S, 56°44′E. Marks the SE end of a snow-covered island 1 mile north of Abrupt Point on the western side of Edward VIII Bay. Photographed by the LCE 1936–37. Named by the Australians for R.F.M. Dalton, officer-in-charge of ANARE at Macquarie Island (not in the Antarctic) in 1953. (*See also* Skutenes.) For more information on Dalton, see **Dalton Iceberg Tongue.**

**Mount Dalton.** 69°28′S, 157°52′E. 1,175 m. On the east side of Matusevich Glacier. 6 miles SE of Thompson Peak in the NW part of the Wilson Hills. Named by the Australians for R.F.M. Dalton (*see* **Cape Dalton, Dalton Iceberg Tongue**).

**Dalton, Dr. Brian C.** From Halifax, Mass. He was the USN leader at Byrd Station during the winter of 1957.

**Dalton, David.** Officer's steward on the Wilkes Expedition 1838–42. Joined in the USA. Served the cruise.

**Dalton Glacier.** 77°33′S, 152°25′W. On the east side of the Alexandra Mountains on Edward VII Peninsula. Flows into Butler Glacier, just south of Sulzberger Bay. Named for Lt. Brian C. Dalton.

**Dalton Iceberg Tongue.** 66°15′S, 121°30′E. Extends seaward from the eastern part of the Moscow University Ice Shelf, off the Sabrina Coast. Named by the Australians for R.F.M. Dalton, who, in the late 1950s was technical officer (aircraft) of the Antarctic Division in Melbourne, and second-in-command under Phillip Law, of the 1958–59 and the 1959–60 ANARE expeditions in the *Magga Dan*. For more information on Dalton, see **Cape Dalton.**

**Cape Daly.** 67°31′S, 63°47′E. Ice-covered promontory on the coast, 3 miles west of Safety Island, and just SE of the Robinson Group. Discovered in Feb. 1931 by the BANZARE under Mawson, and named by Mawson for Senator Daly of the Australian Senate.

**Dalziel Ridge.** 70°15′S, 63°55′W. The western ridge of the Columbia Mountains in Palmer Land. Named for Ian W.D. Dalziel, British geologist working for the USA in the Scotia Ridge area from the late 1960s to 1976.

**D'Amico, T.J.** Crewman on the *Bear of Oakland*, 1933–35.

**Mount Damm.** 82°36′S, 162°37′E. 1,130 m. Snow-covered. Between Heidemann and Nottarp Glaciers in the Queen Elizabeth Range. Named for Robert Damm, biologist at McMurdo Station in 1963–64.

**Dammon, William.** Ordinary seaman on the Wilkes Expedition 1838–42. Joined at Callao. Served the cruise.

**Damocles Point.** 69°39′S, 69°21′W. 3 miles ESE of Mount Tyrrell, on the east coast of Alexander Island. Named by the FIDS in 1948 because a 60-meter-high ice cliff overhanging the area where the FIDS collected rock samples seemed like the Sword of Damocles.

**Damoy Point.** 64°49′S, 63°32′W. ½ mile WNW of Flag Point, the north entrance point to the harbor of Port Lockroy, on the west side of Wiencke Island. There is an airfield here. Discovered and named by Charcot in 1903–5.

**Damschroder Rock.** 85°38′S, 69°14′W. 1,595 m. A rock on land 2½ miles west of the central part of Pecora Escarpment in the Pensacola Mountains. Named for Gerald H. Damschroder, construction mechanic at Plateau Station in 1966.

**Mount Dana Coman** *see* **Mount Coman**

**Dana Glacier.** 70°55′S, 62°23′W. 30 miles long. Flows from the east side of the Welch Mountains into Lehrke Inlet just north of the Parmelee Massif, on the east side of Palmer Land. Named for Cdr. John B. Dana, USN, VXE-6 commander in 1972–73. He had been executive officer of VXE-6 in 1972 and operations officer in 1971.

**Dana Mountains.** 73°12′S, 62°25′W. Just NW of New Bedford Inlet, on the Lassiter Coast of eastern Palmer Land. Discovered aerially by the USAS 1939–41. Named for US geologist James Dwight Dana (1813–95).

**Danco, Émile.** b. 1869. Belgian lieutenant and geophysicist who paid to go on the *Belgica* expedition of 1897–99. He was one of the Jan. 31, 1898, sledging party on Brabant Island, and died of scurvy on June 5, 1898. He was buried in a hole in the ice.

**Danco Coast.** 64°40′S, 62°W. Between Cape Sterneck and Cape Renard, on the NW coast of the Antarctic Peninsula. Discovered and explored during Jan. and Feb. 1898 by de Gerlache in the *Belgica* expedition, and named by him as Danco Land, for Émile Danco. The British had Base O here.

**Danco Island.** 66°44′S, 62°37′W. Also called Isla Dedo. 1 mile long. In the south part of Errera Channel, off the west coast of Graham Land. Charted by de Gerlache in 1897–99. Surveyed by the FIDS from the *Norsel* in 1955, and named by the UK for Émile Danco.

**Danco Land** *see* **Danco Coast**

**Mount Dane.** 76°51′S, 146°40′W. 3 miles WNW of Eilefsen Peak in the northern part of Radford Island, in the Sulzberger Ice Shelf, off the coast of Marie Byrd Land. Named for F.S. Dane.

**Dane, F.S.** Dog driver on the shore party of Byrd's 1933–35 expedition.

**Îles Danebrog** *see* **Dannebrog Islands**

**Mount Danforth.** 85°56′S, 150°01′W. Over 2,000 m. Ice-free. Pyramidal. Just east of Mount Zanuck, on the south side of Albanus Glacier, in the Queen Maud Mountains. Discovered in Dec. 1934 by Quin Blackburn during Byrd's 1933–35 expedition and named by Byrd for William H. Danforth, of Purina Mills in St. Louis, a supporter.

**D'Angelo Bluff.** 87°18′S, 154°W. 6 miles long. Trends west from Mount McIntyre, on the west side of the Robert Scott Glacier, 13 miles south of Mount Early. Discovered by Quin Blackburn in Dec. 1934 during Byrd's 1933–35 expedition. Visited on Dec. 5, 1962, by a geological party of the Ohio State University

Institute of Polar Studies, led by George Doumani. Named by him for CWO John D'Angelo, US Army, who landed the party here.

**Cape Danger.** 62°27′S, 60°23′W. Forms the NW end of Desolation Island in the South Shetlands. Charted in 1935 by personnel on the *Discovery II*. Named because a group of sunken rocks extends about ½ mile north from here.

**Danger Islands.** 63°25′S, 54°40′W. A group of 7 tiny islands, including Darwin Island and Beagle Island, which lie about 15 miles SE of Joinville Island. Discovered on Dec. 28, 1842, by Ross, who named them for their danger to shipping.

**Danger Slopes.** 77°49′S, 166°40′E. An ice slope just south of Knob Point. It is very steep for 400 yards and then ends in a sheer drop to Erebus Bay, on Hut Point, Ross Island. Named by Scott in 1902 because it was here that George Vince fell to his death that year.

**D'Anglade, E.** Steward on the *Aurora*, 1914–16.

**Mount Daniel.** 84°54′S, 170°17′W. 2,440 m. 1 mile north of Mount Hall, in the Lillie Range of the Queen Maud Mountains. Discovered during Byrd's 1928–30 expedition and named by Byrd for Robert W. Daniel, of Lower Brandon, Virginia, a supporter.

**Daniel Island.** 66°14′S, 110°36′E. A small island south of Honkala Island. It marks the south end of the Swain Islands. Named by Carl Eklund in 1957 for Dave Daniel, USN, cook at Wilkes Station in 1957.

**Mount Daniel Rex** *see* **Mount Rex**

**Cape Daniell.** 72°42′S, 169°57′E. At the NE end of Daniell Peninsula, which marks the south side of the entrance to Tucker Inlet in Victoria Land. Discovered and named on Jan. 15, 1841, by Ross for Professor Daniell, former secretary of the Royal Society.

**Daniell Peninsula.** 72°50′S, 169°35′E. 2,000 m. An elongated basalt dome, similar to the Adare and Hallett Peninsulas.

Between Cape Daniell and Cape Jones, on the Borchgrevink Coast of Victoria Land. Named by the New Zealanders in 1957–58 in association with the cape.

**Daniels Hill.** 70°34′S, 64°36′W. A solitary nunatak in the eastern part of the Dyer Plateau in Palmer Land. 15 miles west of the head of Clifford Glacier. Named for Robert Daniels, biologist at Palmer Station in 1975.

**Daniels Range.** 71°15′S, 160°E. 50 miles long. 10 miles wide. To the west of the Rennick Glacier in the Usarp Mountains of northern Victoria Land. Named for Ambassador Paul C. Daniels, who helped formulate the Antarctic Treaty.

**Îles Dannebrog** see **Dannebrog Islands, Wilhelm Archipelago**

**Dannebrog Islands.** 65°03′S, 64°08′W. Also called Îles Danebrog. A group of islands and rocks, including Rollet Island, between the Wauwermans Islands and the Vedel Islands, in the Wilhelm Archipelago. For history see **Wilhelm Archipelago.**

**Darbel Bay.** 66°30′S, 65°55′W. An indentation between Cape Bellue and Cape Rey, in the west coast of the Antarctic Peninsula, just north of Adelaide Island. 25 miles wide. It was discovered and charted by Charcot in 1908–10, and named by him as Baie Marin Darbel. The name was later shortened by the UK.

**Darbel Islands.** 66°23′S, 65°58′W. Also called Islas Quirihue. A group of islands and rocks which extend 5 miles SW from Cape Bellue across the entrance to Darbel Bay, off the west coast of Graham Land. Charted by personnel on the *Discovery II* in 1930, and named by them as Marin Darbel Islands, in association with the bay, which was in those days called Baie Marin Darbel. Both names have since been shortened by the UK.

**Darboux Island.** 65°25′S, 64°15′W. 270 m. 1 mile long. 3 miles west of Cape Pérez, off the west coast of Graham Land. Discovered by Charcot in 1903–5,

and named by him for the French mathematician, Gaston Darboux.

**Mount Darbyshire.** 78°28′S, 158°05′E. 2,100 m. Ice-free. Just west of the Warren Range in Victoria Land. Named for Major Leslie L. Darbyshire, US Marines, VX-6 pilot in 1960–61 and 1961–62.

**Darkowski, Leon S.** Lt., USN. Chaplain at McMurdo Base in 1956–57. He replaced Peter Bol.

**Darkowski Glacier.** 77°52′S, 162°25′E. In the Cathedral Rocks, flowing between the Zoller and Bol Glaciers into the Ferrar Glacier of Victoria Land. Charted by Scott's 1910–13 expedition and named by the USA in 1964 for Chaplain Leon Darkowski.

**Darley Hills.** 81°06′S, 160°10′E. Ice-covered. They overlook the Ross Ice Shelf and extend for 20 miles between Cape Douglas and Cape Parr. Named for James M. Darley, chief cartographer of the National Geographic Society, 1940–63, and a seminal figure in Antarctic map making.

**Mount Darling.** 77°15′S, 143°20′W. Highest peak in the Allegheny Mountains. 1 mile west of Mount Swartley, in the Ford Ranges of Marie Byrd Land. Discovered aerially from West Base in 1940 during the USAS, and named for Prof. Chester A. Darling of Allegheny College, Meadville, Pa.

**Darling Ridge.** 84°46′S, 115°54′W. 2,350 m. Flat-topped. Snow-covered. 2½ miles long. At the NW corner of Buckeye Table in the Ohio Range. Surveyed by the USARP Horlick Mountains Traverse Party in Dec. 1958. Named for Fredric L. Darling, glaciological assistant with the party.

**Cape Darlington.** 72°S, 60°43′W. 305 m. Ice-covered headland. At the southern edge of the Hilton Inlet, on the east side of the Antarctic Peninsula. Discovered by the USAS in 1940. They thought it was an island, and named it Darlington Island, for Harry Darlington III. It was redefined by the RARE in Nov. 1947 when they flew over it.

**Darlington, Harry III.** Virginian machinist at East Base during the USAS 1939–41. He was a pilot on the RARE, 1947–48. He described himself incorrectly as second-in-command of the whole expedition; others have described him as the chief of aviation. Ronne, the leader of the expedition, and with whom Darlington had a severe row on this trip, describes him in his autobiography only as a "reserve pilot." No mention in the index even, of Darlington or his wife, Jennie, who also went on the trip (*see* **Jennie Darlington**).

**Darlington, Jennie.** b. 1924. American woman (*see* **Women in Antarctica**), married to Harry Darlington III, one of the pilots on the RARE 1947–48. She went to Antarctica with her husband and, indeed, honeymooned there. While Finn Ronne, the leader of the expedition, had a hut to himself and his wife, the Darlingtons lived at the end of the main hut, which put a strain on everybody. Jennie co-wrote a book about the experience, *My Antarctic Honeymoon* (*see* the Bibliography). She became pregnant, and if the expedition had not left when it did, her daughter would have been the first human being to be born in Antarctica (*see* **Births in Antarctica**). She and Edith Ronne were probably the first two women to winter in Antarctica.

**Darlington Island** *see* **Cape Darlington**

**Darnell Nunatak.** 80°27′S, 155°53′E. 1,405 m. 4 miles NW of Mount Rummage in the SW part of the Britannia Range. Named for Chief Aviation Machinist's Mate Shepard L. Darnell, with VX-6, 1962–63.

**Cape Darnley.** 67°43′S, 69°30′E. Also called Bjerkø Head, Bjerkø Headland. Ice-covered. Forms the northern extremity of Bjerkø Peninsula, at the west side of MacKenzie Bay, near the Amery Ice Shelf. Seen on Dec. 26, 1929, by Mawson from the masthead of the *Discovery,* during a mirage while on the BANZARE

1929–31. He returned, closer, on Feb. 10, 1931, to see it properly, and named it for E.R. Darnley, chairman of the Discovery Committee of the Colonial Office, London, 1923–33.

**Darryl Zanuck Mountain** *see* **Mount Zanuck**

**The *Dart*.** London sealing vessel in the South Shetlands in the 1822–23 season, under the command of Capt. Duell.

**¹Cape Dart.** 73°06′S, 126°09′W. On Siple Island, at the eastern edge of the Getz Ice Shelf. Mount Siple is on it. Discovered in Dec. 1940 by the USAS on a flight from West Base. Named for Justin W. Dart, of the Walgreen Co., a supporter of the expedition.

**²Cape Dart** *see* **Cape Flying Fish**

**Mount Dart.** 70°12′S, 65°07′E. 1½ miles SE of Mount Dwyer in the Athos Range of the Prince Charles Mountains. Named by the Australians for J.R. Dart, radio operator at Mawson Station in 1969.

**Dart Island.** 62°14′S, 59°01′W. In the west entrance to Fildes Strait, in the South Shetlands. Part of the 70 Islets surveyed and named by the personnel on the *Discovery II* in 1934–35. The name 70 Islets was changed by the UK in 1961, and the largest of these islets was called Dart Island, for the *Dart*.

**Dart Moraine.** 70°54′S, 68°E. Extends for 7 miles south of Radok Lake and Pagodroma Gorge, and west of Flagstone Bench, at the east end of the Aramis Range in the Prince Charles Mountains. Crossed many times in Jan. and Feb. 1969 by J.R. Dart (*see* **Mount Dart**).

**Daruma Rock.** 68°32′S, 41°11′E. A coastal rock (on land) on the west side of the Nishi-naga-iwa Glacier in Queen Maud Land. Named Daruma-iwa (tumbler rock) by the Japanese.

**Mount Darwin.** 85°02′S, 163°08′E. 8,200 feet. Ice-free. 5 miles WSW of Mount Bowers, it is the most southerly peak in the Queen Alexandra Range, at the top of the Beardmore Glacier. Discovered by Shackleton in 1908, and named by him for Major Leonard Darwin, president of the Royal Geographical Society, 1908-11.

**Darwin Glacier.** 79°50'S, 159°15'E. Feeds the Ross Ice Shelf from the Darwin Mountains, in the Transantarctic Horst. Named for the mountains.

**Darwin Island.** 63°26'S, 54°46'W. About ½ mile by ½ mile in area. The largest of the Danger Islands, 11 miles ESE of Joinville Island. Discovered by Ross in 1842 and named by him for Charles Darwin, the naturalist.

**Darwin Mountains.** 79°50'S, 156°15'E. Between the Darwin and Hatherton Glaciers, or between the Cook Mountains and the Britannia Range, in southern Victoria Land. Discovered on Scott's 1901-4 expedition, and named for Major Leonard Darwin (*see* **Mount Darwin**), at that time honorary secretary of the Royal Geographical Society.

**Darwin Névé.** 79°26'S, 155°E. On the west side of the Cook Mountains and Darwin Mountains. Named by the NZ Darwin Glacier party of the BCTAE 1956-58 in association with nearby Darwin Glacier.

**Dash Patrol.** Shirase's small team of 7 men who made a dash for the South Pole from the Bay of Whales during the Japanese South Polar Expedition of 1910-12. Two men stayed behind at the edge of the Ross Ice Shelf while Shirase, Mitsui, Takeda, and four others sledged to the SE across the shelf, each dog pulling 57 pounds. They did 8 miles the first day and were stopped by a blizzard. On Jan. 28, 1912, they reached 80°05'S, having covered 160 miles. That was their limit and they buried a copper case with a record of their visit, and then returned to the *Kainan Maru*. Was this a serious dash for the Pole? Did they suspect that Amundsen and Scott might not make it? (Shirase had no way of knowing, but the Norwegian and British parties had already made it to the Pole.) Some historians have doubted that this was a realistic

attempt to get Japan to the South Pole first.

**Mount Dasinger.** 83°13'S, 55°03'W. 1,360 m. 6 miles NE of Neith Nunatak, in the northern part of the Neptune Range. Named for Lt. (jg) James R. Dasinger, USN, at Ellsworth Station in 1958.

**Daspit Glacier.** 68°10'S, 65°45'W. 6 miles long. Flows along the south side of Mount Shelby to the head of Trail Inlet, on the east coast of Graham Land. Discovered by members of East Base during the USAS 1939-41. Named by Ronne during the RARE 1947-48 for Capt. Lawrence R. Daspit, USN, who helped get US Navy support for the RARE.

**Mount Dater.** 67°08'S, 64°49'W. A flat-topped coastal mountain over 1,000 m. Just SW of Monnier Point on the east side of Graham Land. Named by the UK in 1976 for Henry M. Dater.

**Dater, Henry M.** b. Brooklyn, NY. d. June 26, 1974, Washington, DC. Known as Harry. In 1956 he became Byrd's staff historian, and remained the official historian of the US Antarctic program until he died. He was founding editor of the *Bulletin of the U.S. Antarctic Projects Officer*, and co-founding editor of its successor, the *Antarctic Journal of the United States*. He co-wrote the book *Antarctica* (*see* the Bibliography) and was 6 times in Antarctica.

**Dater Glacier.** 78°14'S, 84°30'W. A valley glacier, 24 miles long and between 1 and 3 miles wide. Flows from the eastern slopes of the Vinson Massif to the east flank of the Sentinel Range, joining with Ellen Glacier. Discovered aerially by VX-6 on Dec. 14-15, 1959. Named for Henry M. Dater.

**Dates** *see* the Chronology appendix

**Daughtery Peaks.** 73°29'S, 164°20'E. 2,680 m. Ice-free. Surmount the south wall of Cosmonaut Glacier in the Southern Cross Mountains of Victoria Land. Named for Franklin J. Daughtery, aviation structural mechanic with VX-6 for 6 seasons.

**Dauphin Island.** 66°46'S, 141°35'E. Also called Île des Dauphins. Just over ⅛ mile long. Has two small summits, one at the north end, one at the south. Between Claquebue Island and Chameau Island in the Curzon Islands. Charted by the French in 1951, and named by them for the ancient French province of Dauphiné.

**Dausay Island** *see* **Hope Island**

**Davern Nunatak.** 70°54'S, 69°20'E. 1½ miles west of Mount Bewsher in the Aramis Range of the Prince Charles Mountains. Named by the Australians for E.V. Davern, radio operator at Wilkes Station in 1963, and senior weather observer (radio) there in 1967.

**Davey Nunataks.** 72°58'S, 74°52'E. In the Grove Mountains of the American Highland.

**Davey Peak.** 75°53'S, 115°45'W. 1,855 m. 8 miles west of Scudder Peak on the south side of Toney Mountain in Marie Byrd Land. Named for Gary R. Davey, meteorologist at Byrd Station in 1966.

**Davey Point.** 61°58'S, 58°34'W. 3 miles SW of Round Point on the north coast of King George Island in the South Shetlands. Charted and named Round Island by the personnel on the *Discovery II* in 1935. It was redefined and renamed in 1962 by the UK for Graham J. Davey, FIDS assistant surveyor at Base G in 1957 and 1958.

**Mount David** *see* **Mount Kirkwood**

**David, Edgeworth.** b. Jan. 28, 1858, St. Fagans, Wales. d. Aug. 28, 1934, Sydney, Australia. Professor Sir Tannatt William Edgeworth David. Professor of geology at Sydney University for many years, under whom many Antarctic explorers studied and sought to study. Famous for his geological studies of Australia, to which country he emigrated in 1882. An authority on ice ages, he was scientific officer on Shackleton's 1907–9 expedition to Antarctica, and led the 3-man party that was the first to reach the South Magnetic Pole in 1909. Also

during the expedition he led the first ascent of Mount Erebus. He wrote *Glaciological Notes on the British Antarctic Expedition* in 1909. He advised on the AAE 1911–14.

**David Cauldron.** 75°18'S, 160°50'E. An icefall of turbulent iceblocks on the David Glacier in Victoria Land. Named by the New Zealanders in 1962–63 in association with the glacier.

**David Glacier.** 75°19'S, 162°E. Over 60 miles long. Flows from the Polar Plateau, through the Prince Albert Mountains, and enters the Ross Sea between Capes Philippi and Reynolds in Victoria Land. Discovered by Edgeworth David in Nov. 1908, and it was named for him.

**David Island.** 66°25'S, 98°46'E. Ice-covered. 10 miles long. 6 miles wide. Off Davis Peninsula in the Shackleton Ice Shelf. Discovered in Nov. 1912 by the Western Base Party of the AAE 1911–14. Named by Mawson for Edgeworth David.

**David Lee Glacier** *see* **Rivard Glacier**

**David Range.** 67°54'S, 62°30'E. Extends for 16 miles with peaks rising to 1,500 m. 5 miles west of the Masson Range, which it parallels in the Framnes Mountains, on the coast of Enderby Land. Discovered on Feb. 14, 1931, by the BANZARE, and named by Mawson for Edgeworth David.

**David Valley.** 77°37'S, 162°08'E. A dry valley in the Asgard Range of southern Victoria Land. Named by Roy E. Cameron (*see* **Cameron Nunataks**) for Charles N. David, a member of the same party as Cameron here in 1967–68.

**Davidson.** Crew member on the *Morning* in 1903.

**Cape Davidson.** 60°46'S, 44°46'W. Marks the most southerly part of Mackenzie Peninsula, and the west side of the entrance to Wilton Bay, in the west part of Laurie Island, in the South Orkneys. Charted by Bruce in 1903, and named by him for J. Davidson (*see* **James David-son**).

**Mount Davidson.** 76°44′S, 161°58′E. 1,560 m. At the head of Albrecht Penck Glacier in Victoria Land. Discovered by Scott's 1901–4 expedition, and named by them for Davidson of the *Morning*.

**Davidson, James.** Captain of the *Polar Star* during the Dundee Whaling Expedition of 1892–93. This may be (although it is unlikely) the J. Davidson who was later first mate on the *Scotia* during Bruce's Scottish National Antarctic Expedition of 1902–4.

**Davidson, Robert.** Captain of the *Diana* during the Dundee Whaling Expedition of 1892–93.

**Davidson Glacier.** 82°49′S, 166°07′E. Flows along the east side of the Longstaff Peaks in the Holland Range, into the Ross Ice Shelf. Named for Cdr. E.A. Davidson, commander of the *Edisto* in 1963.

**Davidson Island.** 66°26′S, 66°37′W. Small, dome-shaped, and ice-covered. Between Wollan Island and Shull Rocks in Crystal Sound. Named by the UK for William A. Davidson, US physicist who determined the position of hydrogen atoms in ice.

**[1]Cape Davies.** 71°46′S, 100°23′W. Ice-covered. At the NE end of Hughes Peninsula on Thurston Island. Named for Frank Davies.

**[2]Cape Davies** *see* **Davis Ice Piedmont**

**Davies, Francis E.C.** Shipwright on the *Terra Nova*, 1910–13.

**Davies, Frank.** Welsh physicist known as "Taffy." Was on Byrd's 1928–30 expedition.

**Davies, William E.** Geologist on the *Atka* during the US Navy Antarctic Expedition of 1954–55.

**Davies Bay.** 69°18′S, 158°34′E. Also seen (erroneously) as Davis Bay. 10 miles wide. Between Drake Head and Cape Kinsey, off Oates Land. Discovered in Feb. 1911 from the *Terra Nova*, commanded by Harry Pennell. Named for Francis E.C. Davies.

**Davies Escarpment.** 85°32′S, 89°48′W. 10 miles long. An ice escarpment facing east. South of the Bermel Escarpment in the southern part of the Thiel Mountains. Named by Peter Bermel and Arthur Ford, the leaders of the Thiel Mountains party here in 1960–61, for William E. Davies.

**Davies Gilbert Strait** *see* **Gilbert Strait**

**Davies Heights.** 62°11′S, 58°56′W. Just to the west of Collins Harbor, on the south side of King George Island, to the east of Fildes Peninsula, in the South Shetlands.

**Davies Top.** 69°24′S, 64°56′W. 2,360 m. An isolated peak. On the east side of Wakefield Highland, near the head of Lurabee Glacier, in northern Palmer Land. Named by the UK for Anthony G. Davies, FIDS medical officer at Horseshoe Island (Base Y) and Stonington Island (Base E) in 1960.

**Cape Davis.** 66°24′S, 56°50′E. Ice-covered. 9 miles east of Magnet Bay, it forms the western fringe of Edward VIII Bay in Enderby Land. Discovered on Jan. 12, 1930, by the BANZARE, and named by Mawson for John King Davis.

**Mount Davis.** 78°06′S, 86°15′W. Over 3,800 m. 1 mile north of Mount Bentley in the Sentinel Range. Discovered in 1957–58 by the Marie Byrd Land Traverse Party and named by leader Charles Bentley for Leo E. Davis, geomagnetician at Byrd Station in 1957.

**Point Davis.** 60°46′S, 44°39′W. Just over a mile WNW of Point Rae on the north side of Scotia Bay, Laurie Island, in the South Orkneys. Charted in 1903 by Bruce who named it for W.G. Davis, director of the Argentine Meteorological Office.

**Davis, Alonzo B.** Passed midshipman on the *Peacock* during the Wilkes Expedition 1838–42.

**Davis, Edward.** A pirate who reported going south of 60°S.

**Davis, Frank T.** American physicist who went with Byrd to the Antarctic on the *City of New York*, as a seaman, during Byrd's 1928–30 expedition. He became a member of the shore party.

**Davis, Jerome.** Ordinary seaman on the Wilkes Expedition 1838–42. Joined in the USA. Served the cruise.

**Davis, John.** American sealing captain from New Haven, Conn. Commander of the *Huron* which, teamed with Christopher Burdick in the *Huntress*, plied the South Shetlands for seals in the 1820–21 season. While there Davis went south on an exploring expedition in the *Cecilia*, and made what is generally thought to be the first landing on the Antarctic continent itself (as opposed to the islands), near Hughes Bay. The party stayed ashore for less than an hour (Davis himself did not land), on Feb. 7, 1821. It was about this time that he said "I think this southern land to be a continent." He returned to Antarctica with the *Huron* and the *Cecilia* for the 1821–22 season.

**Davis, John E.** Second midshipman/ cartographer/artist on the *Terror* during Ross's expedition of 1839–43.

**Davis, John King.** b. 1884, London. d. 1967, in a Melbourne boarding house. He was at sea by 1900 and was chief officer on the *Nimrod* for most of the British Antarctic Expedition 1907–9. He was captain of the ship during the very final stages of the expedition, and brought it home in 1909. A great navigator, he was captain of the *Aurora* during the AAE 1911–14. He was second-in-command of the BANZARE 1929–31, during the first half of the expedition, i.e. from 1929–30, as well as being captain of the expedition vessel, the *Discovery*, during that same period. He was later director of navigation for the Commonwealth of Australia.

**Davis, Malcolm.** Bird curator from Washington, DC. Biologist on the *North Star* during the first half of the USAS

1939–41 (i.e. in 1939–40), and ornithologist on Operation Windmill, 1947–48.

**Davis, N.B.** 2nd officer on the *Bear of Oakland*, 1933–34.

**Davis, O.E.** Crewman on the *Jacob Ruppert*, 1934–35.

**Davis Anchorage.** 68°34'S, 77°55'E. 1 mile in extent. 10–13 fathoms deep. Off Breidnes Peninsula in the Vestfold Hills. Krat Rocks and Hobby Rocks bound it on the west, and rocks and shoal water ½ mile off Davis Station bound it on the east. Used by the ANARE since 1957 as an anchorage. Named by them for the station.

¹**Davis Bay.** 66°08'S, 134°05'E. 12 miles wide at its entrance between Cape Cesney and Lewis Island. Discovered from the *Aurora* by the AAE 1911–14 and named by Mawson for John King Davis.

²**Davis Bay** *see* **Salmon Bay, Davies Bay**

**Davis Coast.** 64°S, 60°W. Also called Palmer Coast. Between Cape Kjellman and Cape Sterneck on the west coast of the Antarctic Peninsula. Named for John Davis.

**Davis Creek** *see* **Salmon Stream**

**Davis Gilbert Strait** *see* **Gilbert Strait**

¹**Davis Glacier** *see* **Arthur Glacier**

²**Davis Glacier.** 75°45'S, 162°10'E. Heavily crevassed. 15 miles long. Flows from the NW slopes of Mount George Murray to the coast of Victoria Land opposite the south end of Lamplugh Island. Charted by Shackleton's 1907–9 expedition, and named by them for John King Davis.

**Davis Hills.** 86°52'S, 150°W. A small group on the south side of Klein Glacier, where that glacier enters the Robert Scott Glacier in the Queen Maud Mountains. Named for Parker Davis, VX-6 photographer in 1966 and 1967.

**Davis Ice Piedmont.** 70°38'S, 166°16' E. 10 miles long. 4 miles wide. On the north side of Missen Ridge on the north coast of Victoria Land. In 1841 Ross named a feature in this area as Cape Davis, for John E. Davis. This name was also seen spelled (erroneously) as Cape Davies. Modern explorers could not find a cape here, so they named this ice piedmont in the area in order to preserve Ross's naming.

**Davis Ice Rise.** 74°56′S, 110°18′W. On the Bear Peninsula, on the coast of Marie Byrd Land.

**Davis Island.** 64°06′S, 62°04′W. Just east of Abbott Island, in the Palmer Archipelago.

**Davis Islands.** 66°40′S, 108°25′E. A small group, including Hudson Island, in the west part of the entrance to Vincennes Bay. Named for Malcolm Davis.

**Davis Knoll.** 82°10′S, 155°01′E. Partly ice-covered. 6 miles north of Mount Ester at the head of the Lucy Glacier. Named for Thomas C. Davis, Jr., geologist at McMurdo Station, 1961–62.

**Davis Nunataks.** 85°37′S, 166°36′E. 3 miles NW of Mount Ward, they mark the southernmost part of the Dominion Range. Named for Ronald N. Davis, geomagnetist at Amundsen-Scott South Pole Station in 1963.

**Davis Peninsula.** 66°36′S, 98°47′E. Ice-covered. 3 miles wide. Between Reid Glacier and Northcliffe Glacier. Discovered in Nov. 1912 by the AAE 1911–14, and named by Mawson for John King Davis.

**Davis Promontory.** 84°41′S, 96°30′W. Snow-covered. Near the NE end of Havola Escarpment. Named for Walter L. Davis, USN, chief construction mechanic at Ellsworth Station in 1957 and at Byrd Station in 1960. He was on the Byrd–South Pole Overland Trek (q.v.).

**Davis Ridge.** 71°24′S, 63°W. 6 miles east of Mount Jackson in the east part of Palmer Land. Named for Brent L. Davis, biologist at Palmer Station in 1971 and elsewhere in the Antarctic Peninsula in 1974–75.

**Davis Saddle.** 76°25′S, 147°09′W. An ice saddle just east of Mitchell Peak on Guest Peninsula, on the coast of Marie Byrd Land. Named for Clinton S. Davis, USN, bosun's mate on the *Glacier* here in 1961–62.

**Davis Sea.** 66°S, 92°E. Between the West Ice Shelf and the Shackleton Ice Shelf, between the Leopold and Astrid Coast and the Queen Mary Coast of East Antarctica. Discovered by the *Aurora* party during the AAE 1911–14, and named by them for John King Davis.

**Davis Station.** 68°35′S, 77°58′E. Year-round, permanently occupied Australian scientific base on Breidnes Peninsula, in the Vestfold Hills of the Ingrid Christensen Coast. It was opened on Jan. 13, 1957, and the leader of the first wintering party (1957 winter) was W.R.J. Dingle.

**Davis Valley.** 82°28′S, 51°10′W. Ice-free valley just east of Forlidas Ridge in the NE part of the Dufek Massif. The floor of this valley is about 1,550 feet above sea level. Named for Edward H. Davis, construction mechanic at Ellsworth Station in 1957.

**Davisville Glacier.** 85°17′S, 128°30′W. 30 miles long. Flows from the northern slopes of the Wisconsin Range, between Lentz and Moran Buttresses, and merges with the lower portion of the Horlick Ice Stream. Named for Davisville, Rhode Island, location of the Seabees center.

**Mount Dawson.** 77°46′S, 86°21′W. 2,695 m. Pyramidal. 2½ miles NW of Mount Reimer in the Sentinel Range. Discovered by the Marie Byrd Land Traverse Party of 1957–58 and named for Merle R. Dawson.

**Dawson, Merle R.** b. 1909. d. Feb. 14, 1986. Known as "Skip." US Army, 1943–64. Highly decorated, he retired from the army as a colonel. He was a major in 1956 during Operation Deep Freeze II, and from Nov. 7 to Dec. 16 of that year he led the Army-Navy Trail party from Little America V to open up the way to Byrd Station. He was project manager for ship operations for the

National Science Foundation's Office of Polar Programs from 1965–70.

**Dawson Head.** 70°43'S, 61°57'W. On the NW side of Lehrke Inlet on the east coast of Palmer Land. Named for Capt. Opie L. Dawson, US Coast Guard, commander of the *Glacier* during the International Weddell Sea Oceanographic Expedition of 1968.

**Mount Dawson-Lambton.** 78°54'S, 160°37'E. Also called Mount Dawson and Lambton. 2,295 m. 3 miles SW of the summit of Mount Speyer in the Worcester Range. Discovered by Scott's 1901–4 expedition and named by them for the Misses Dawson-Lambton, supporters.

**Dawson-Lambton Glacier.** 76°15'S, 27°30'W. Also called Glaciar Buenos Aires. Heavily crevassed. Enters the SW part of the Weddell Sea, just west of the Brunt Ice Shelf, on the Caird Coast of Coats Land. Probably the world's largest glacier. Discovered in Jan. 1915 by Shackleton, and named by him for Elizabeth Dawson-Lambton, principal backer of Shackleton's 1914–17 expedition in the *Endurance*.

**Dawson Nunatak.** 70°13'S, 65°02'E. 3 miles SSE of Mount Peter in the Athos Range of the Prince Charles Mountains. Named by the Australians for P.L. Dawson, senior diesel mechanic at Mawson Station in 1964.

**Dawson Peak.** 83°50'S, 162°32'E. 2,070 m. Ice-free. 5 miles SW of Mount Picciotto in the Queen Elizabeth Range. Named for John A. Dawson, aurora scientist at South Pole Station in 1958.

**Cape Day.** 76°18'S, 162°46'E. 11 miles east of Mount Gauss, on the coast of Victoria Land. Charted by Shackleton's 1907–9 expedition, and named by them for Bernard Day.

**Day, Bernard C.** b. Aug. 18, 1884. British electrician and motor engineer, in charge of the motor car on the British Antarctic Expeditions of 1907–9 and 1910–13.

**Day Island.** 67°15'S, 67°42'W. 7 miles long. 3 miles wide. Just south of The Gullet, and 2 miles north of Wyatt Island, in the northern part of Laubeuf Fjord, off the west coast of Graham Land. Named Middle Island by the BGLE in 1936, but renamed by the FIDS in 1948 for Vice-Adm. Sir Archibald Day, hydrographer of the navy.

**Daykovaya Peak.** 71°28'S, 12°11'E. 1,995 m. Between Mount Hansen and Kåre Bench in the Westliche Petermann Range of the Wohlthat Mountains. Discovered by Ritscher in 1938–39. Named Gora Daykovaya (dyke mountain) by the USSR in 1966.

**Daylight.** There are 6 months of 24 hours-a-day daylight at the South Pole. The number of such daylight days decreases gradually as one goes north.

**Cape Dayman.** 70°46'S, 167°24'E. On the north side of Tapsell Foreland that forms the south side of the entrance to Yule Bay, on the extreme western end of the Pennell Coast in northern Victoria Land. Discovered by Ross in 1841 and named by him for Joseph Dayman.

**Dayman, Joseph.** Midshipman on the *Erebus*, 1839–43, during Ross' expedition.

**Mount Dayné** *see* **Dayné Peak**

**Dayné, Pierre.** French alpine guide, with Charcot on the *Français*, 1903–5.

**Dayné Peak.** 64°54'S, 63°36'W. Also called Mount Dayné. 730 m. Pyramidal. Just NE of Cape Errera, the SW tip of Wiencke Island. Discovered by de Gerlache in 1897–99. Named by Charcot in 1903–5 for Pierre Dayné.

**Days, Stephen W.** Hospital steward on the Wilkes Expedition 1838–42. Joined in the USA. Served the cruise.

**Mount Dayton.** 85°44'S, 158°41'W. 1,420 m. Mainly ice-free. On the east side of Amundsen Glacier. 5 miles west of Mount Goodale in the Hays Mountains of the Queen Maud Mountains. Named for Paul K. Dayton, III, biologist at McMurdo Station in 1964.

**Cape Deacon.** 73°17'S, 59°53'W. Ice-covered. The southernmost point on the

Kemp Peninsula, on the east coast of Palmer Land. Named by the FIDS for Dr. George E.R. Deacon.

**Deacon, Dr. George E.R.** Oceanographer, member of the hydrological staff of the Discovery Investigations, 1927–39. He led the 1935–37 *Discovery II* Expedition, and picked up Ellsworth and Hollick-Kenyon after their successful transantarctic flight. He was later director of the National Institute of Oceanography, and was knighted (*see also* the Bibliography).

**Deacon Hill.** 60° 34′ S, 45° 48′ W. 330 m. An ice-covered peak on the divide between Bridger Bay and Norway Bight in the western part of Coronation Island, in the South Orkneys. Discovered in Dec. 1821 by Powell and Palmer. Named by the personnel on the *Discovery II* for George Deacon.

**Deacon Peak.** 62° 06′ S, 57° 54′ W. 170 m. Marks the summit of Penguin Island at the east side of the entrance to King George Bay in the South Shetlands. Named by the personnel on the *Discovery II* for George Deacon.

**Dead men.** Logs laid in pits dug in the ice. Water is poured over them, and the "dead men" are frozen in. So solidly are these "men" "dead" that ropes are attached to them and used as ships' moorings in the Antarctic seas.

**Deadmond Glacier.** 71° 58′ S, 96° 20′ W. 6 miles long. Flows from the east side of Evans Peninsula on Thurston Island into Cadwalader Inlet. Discovered by the USN Bellingshausen Sea Expedition in Feb. 1960. Named for Lt. Cdr. Robert B. Deadmond, executive officer on the *Burton Island* that season.

**Mount Deakin.** 84° 40′ S, 170° 40′ E. 2,810 m. On the east side of the Beardmore Glacier, just north of the mouth of Osicki Glacier, between the Hughes Range and the Commonwealth Range, in the Transantarctic Mountains. Discovered by Shackleton in 1907–9, and named by him for Sir Alfred Deakin, PM

of Australia, and a supporter of the expedition.

**Deakin Bay.** 68° 23′ S, 150° 10′ E. The bay fronting the Cook Ice Shelf, between Horn Bluff and Cape Freshfield. Mawson named it during the AAE 1911–14 for Sir Alfred Deakin, PM of Australia. This may well be the Peacock's Bay that Wilkes discovered in 1840 (*see* **Peacock Bay**).

**Mount de Alençar** *see* **Alençar Peak**

**Mount Dean.** 85° 32′ S, 163° W. 1,620 m. At the NE of the Quarles Range, 2 miles NE of Mount Belecz. Named for Jesse D. Dean, meteorologist at Amundsen-Scott South Pole Station in 1962.

**Dean, John N.** Ordinary seaman on the Wilkes Expedition 1838–42. Joined at Sydney. Served the cruise.

**Dean Island.** 74° 30′ S, 127° 35′ W. Ice-covered. 20 miles long. 10 miles wide. Within the Getz Ice Shelf. Between Grant Island and Siple Island. Off the coast of Marie Byrd Land. Discovered by the *Glacier* on Feb. 5, 1962, and named for CWO S.L. Dean, USN, electrical officer on the *Glacier* at that time.

**Dean Nunataks.** 74° 31′ S, 98° 48′ W. Two nunataks. 6 miles ENE of Mount Moses, in the Hudson Mountains. Named for William S. Dean, of Pleasanton, Texas, ham radio contact in the US for several USARP field parties in the late 1960s.

**Dean Rocks.** 67° 48′ S, 68° 56′ W. 4 rocks in water between Preston and Biggs Islands in the Henkes Islands, off the south end of Adelaide Island. Named by the UK for engineer mechanic Thomas Dean of the RN Hydrographic Survey Unit, which charted these rocks in 1963.

**DeAngelo Glacier.** 71° 54′ S, 170° 10′ E. Flows from the slopes of Mount Robinson in the Admiralty Mountains into Moubray Glacier south of Mount Rugg. Named for Richard J. DeAngelo, USAF, airman first class (*see* **Deaths, 1958**).

**Mount Dearborn.** 77° 14′ S, 160° 08′ E. 2,300 m. Between Mount Littlepage and the northern part of the Willett Range in Victoria Land. Named in 1964 for John Dearborn, biologist at McMurdo Base in 1959 and 1961.

**Mount Deardorff.** 85°48'S, 162°34'W. 2,380 m. Between the Moffett and Steagall Glaciers in the Queen Maud Mountains. Named for J. Evan Deardorff, cosmic ray scientist at McMurdo Station in 1964.

**Deaths in Antarctica.** There have been many more deaths in Antarctica than those listed below. To say that those listed below are some of the more salient is a polite way of saying that those are the ones that this writer was able to trace. Listed are human deaths only. For a related entry *see* **Disasters.** From 1946 to the end of 1987, 52 Americans died in Antarctica while participating in a US Government program. Thirty of these were in 9 aircraft crashes (between 1946 and 1961 alone, 22 Americans died in 7 air accidents) before 1970. There were 6 vehicle deaths, 4 aboard ship, 3 at stations, 3 during recreational activities, 3 in the field, and 1 under other conditions. **Oct. 1, 1719:** William Camell drowned. **1819–21:** 3 died on von Bellingshausen's voyage. **Dec. 5, 1820:** A crew member on the *O'Cain.* **Early 1821:** 8 men died on the *Diana,* circumstances unknown. **1821–22:** One man on the Weddell expedition. **Jan. 17, 1823:** The crew of the *Jenny,* presumably in Antarctic waters. **April 23, 1831:** The carpenter on the *Tula* during the Biscoe expedition. **April 27, 1831:** Another of Biscoe's crew on the *Tula.* **1831:** 7 men on the *Lively,* of sickness, during Biscoe's expedition. **March 11, 1839:** William Steward on the *Peacock.* **March 24, 1839:** All the crew of the *Sabrina.* **1840s:** The *Fleetwood's* crew of 20, including a woman. **1873–74:** 7 men on the *Thomas Hunt.* **1877:** Several of the crew of the *Florence,* of exposure on King George Island, in the South Shetlands. **Jan. 22, 1898:** Wiencke drowned from the *Belgica.* **June 5, 1898:** Danco died of scurvy on the *Belgica.* **Oct. 14, 1899:** Hanson died of unknown

causes, probably scurvy. **March 11, 1902:** George T. Vince. **June 7, 1903:** Ole Christiaan Wennersgaard. **Aug. 6, 1903:** Allan Ramsay, chief engineer of the *Scotia,* buried on Laurie Island, in the South Orkneys. **Feb. 16, 1912:** Edgar Evans. **March 17, 1912:** L.E.G. Oates. **March 29, 1912:** Scott, Bowers, and Wilson. **Aug. 8, 1912:** Richard Vahsel. **Dec. 14, 1912:** B.E.S. Ninnis. **Jan. 7, 1913:** Xavier Mertz. **March 8, 1916:** Rev. A.P. Spencer-Smith. **May 8, 1916:** Mackintosh and Hayward. **Dec. 8, 1924:** Carl Anton Larsen, at the edge of the pack-ice. **Jan. 23, 1928:** 15 men on the *Scapa* when it capsized. **Dec. 30, 1946:** Maxwell A. Lopez, navigator, and PO Wendell K. Hendersin, radio operator, killed in the crash of US Martin Mariner on Thurston Island. PO Frederick Williams, engineer, died 2 hours after the crash. **1946–47:** Vance Woodall, USN, in an unloading accident. **1947–48:** Lagarrigue (*see* **Lagarrigue Cove**), fell in a crevasse near Orne Harbor, Graham Land. **Nov. 1948:** 2 young British scientists, Oliver Burd and Michael C. Greene, in a fire at Base D at Hope Bay. **Feb. 24, 1951:** John E. Jelbart, Bertil Ekström, and Leslie Quar together in a Weasel during the NBSAE 1949–52. **Jan. 22, 1955:** Lt. (jg) John P. Moore in a helicopter crash at Kainan Bay. **Jan. 6, 1956:** Richard T. Williams. **Jan. 1956:** I.F. Khmary, USSR tractor driver at Mirnyy Station, when his tractor broke through the ice. **March 5, 1956:** Max R. Kiel. **March 24, 1956:** Ronald G. Napier of the FIDS (*see* **Napier Rock**). **Oct. 18, 1956:** Lt. David W. Carey, USNR, pilot of a Neptune coming in to land at McMurdo when it crashed. Also killed: Marion O. Marze, Charles S. Miller, and Capt. Rayburn A. Hudman (US Marine Corps). **1957:** N.I. Buromskiy of the USSR. **Jan. 14, 1957:** Ollie B. Bartley, USN, construction driver at McMurdo. His Weasel dropped through the sea ice at Hut Point. **Feb. 3, 1957:** Yevgeniy Zykov, USSR student navigator. **July 12, 1957:** Nelson Cole, the 9th victim of Operation Deep Freeze. **Nov. 8, 1957:** Richard T. Oppegaard, USN, apprentice seaman, in a shipboard accident. **1958:** 2 USSR scientists, N.A. Chugunov and geologist M.I. Rokhlin. **Oct. 15, 1958:** 6 died in a Globemaster crash at Cape Roget: Technical Sgt. Iman A. Fendley, Technical Sgt. Nathaniel Wallis, Staff Sgt. Leonard M. Pitkevich, Richard J. DeAngelo, Robert L. Burnette, and Kelly Slone. **Jan. 4, 1959:** Lt. Harvey E. Gardner, pilot, and Lt. (jg) Lawrence J. Farrell, co-pilot, of an Otter which crashed on take-off from Marble Point. **Jan. 7, 1959:** André Prudhomme, head meteorologist of the French Antarctic team, disappeared in a storm near Pétrel Island. A cross has been erected nearby to commemorate him. **July 26, 1959:** Dennis R. Ball (q.v.) on King George Island. **Nov. 19, 1959:** Lt. Thomas Couzens, RNZAF, in a crevasse accident near Cape Selborne. **Nov. 28, 1959:** Paul V. O'Leary, USNR, builder, of accidental poisoning. **1960:** Lt. Cdr. González Pacheco while in charge of Capitán Arturo Prat Station. **Aug. 3, 1960:** O. Kostka, A.M. Belolikov and A.P. Dergach in a fire at Mirnyy Station. **Oct. 1960:** Shin Fukushima, Japanese geophysicist, in a blizzard near Showa Station. **Nov. 2, 1960:** Orlan F. John, USN, steelworker 1st class, in a construction accident at McMurdo Sound. **1961:** John Filer, BAS biologist, fell to his death off the Signy Island cliffs. **Nov. 9, 1961:** 5 killed in a Neptune crash at Wilkes Station: Dr. Edward C. Thiel, geophysicist, Lt. Cdr. William D. Counts, co-pilot, Lt. (jg) Romuald P. Compton, navigator, William W. Chastain, metalsmith, and James L. Gray, flight engineer. **Oct. 18, 1963:** R.F. White, senior technician (electronics) at Mawson Station. **May 8, 1965:** Carl R. Disch, at Byrd Station. **Feb. 2, 1966:** 6 men killed on a LC-47J crash on the Ross Ice Shelf: Lt. Harold M. Morris (pilot), Lt. William D. Fordell (co-pilot), Lt. Cdr. Ronald Rosenthal (navigator), Richard S. Simmons (flight radioman), Charles C. Kelley (flight mechanic) and Wayne M. Shattuck (flight mechanic). **Feb. 13, 1966:** Andrew B. Moulder, USN,

storekeeper, fatally injured in a cargo unloading accident at Amundsen-Scott South Pole Station. **July 22, 1968:** R.N. Sullivan, on a field trip (*see* **Sullivan Nunataks**). **Nov. 19, 1969:** University of Wisconsin investigator Thomas E. Berg and NZ filmmaker Jeremy Sykes. Their helicopter failed, landed on Mount McLennan, and slid 700 feet down the slope. 6 people did survive. **Oct. 11, 1971:** William Dean Decker, the leading chief petty officer of VXE-6, in his sleep at McMurdo Station, of a heart attack. **Dec. 11, 1973:** American professor of biology, Dr. Wolf Vishniac, fell to his death in the Asgard Range. **May 15, 1974:** Greg Nickell, 26, biology lab manager at McMurdo Station, went off the road in his Dodge truck, falling 600 feet (*see also* **Nickell Peak**). **May 1, 1975:** A member of the personnel at Molodezhnaya Station. This was only the second death at this station since it opened. **Oct. 12, 1975:** Jeffrey D. Rude, 26, drowned in McMurdo Sound when his tracked vehicle fell through the ice near Turtle Rock. **Jan. 22, 1976:** Gerald E. Reilly, Jr., 19, a Coast Guard seaman, electrocuted in the boiler room of the *Glacier* while in the Amundsen Sea. **Jan. 2, 1979:** Pilot, co-pilot, and one passenger during take-off of an IL-14 plane from Molodezhnaya Station. **Jan. 19, 1979:** Polish documentary filmmaker Wladzimierz Puchalski, on a hill to the south of Arctowski Station. **Feb. 8, 1979:** Raymond C. Porter, US Coast Guard, while unloading the *Bland* at McMurdo Station. He was driving a small forklift. It went out of control, rolled over, and pinned him underneath. **Nov. 28, 1979:** 257 crew and tourists, on a "champagne" flight, in an Air New Zealand DC-10, into the side of Mount Erebus. **Jan. 9, 1980:** Casey A. Jones, the Holmes & Narver cook at Amundsen-Scott South Pole Station, under a falling column of snow. **Feb. 8, 1982:** Petty Officer Raymond T. Smith, USN, while helping to unload the *Southern Cross* at McMurdo. A 1.5 cubic foot marble block with Smith's hardhat bronzed and mounted on top, was erected as a monument at McMurdo during the 1982–83 season. **Oct. 29, 1985:** Stephen Bunning, 34, a member of the ANARE, of burns, at Davis Station. **Dec. 1985:** 2 Chilean pilots and 8 US tourists in a crash landing (*see also* **Tourism**). **Feb. 1986:** 6 in a USSR L-14 aircraft crash on Philippi Glacier (for more details, *see* **Disasters**). **Nov. 23, 1986:** 2 ITT/Antarctic Services Inc. employees, Matthew M. Kaz, 25, and John E. Smith, 44, who fell into a crevasse while hiking, 2 miles east of McMurdo Station. These were the first deaths of Americans on official business in Antarctica since Feb. 1982. **Nov. 14, 1987:** Mark T. MacMillian, 22, in a diving accident near the coast of southern Victoria Land, at New Harbor. He was collecting samples from under the sea ice for a biological research team. He was the 50th American to die in Antarctica since World War II (that is to say, the 50th American on official business). **Dec. 9, 1987:** 2 US Navy crewmen in a ski-equipped LC-130 Hercules in East Antarctica, while attempting to land. There were 11 people on board the aircraft, which was making a routine supply flight to D-59 (the site of another, long-crashed, Herc—*see* **Disasters, 1971**). The plane was completely destroyed. **March 1990:** Giles Kershaw, pilot (*see* **Kershaw Ice Rumples**).

**DeAtley Island.** 73°18′S, 73°54′W. Ice-covered. 10 miles east of Spaatz Island, at the south side of Ronne Entrance. Discovered aerially during the RARE 1947–48. Later named by Ronne for Col. Ellsworth DeAtley, US Army, and his wife, Thelma DeAtley, contributors of food and clothing to the RARE.

**Débarquement Rock.** 66°36′S, 140°04′E. An ice-free rock in water. 175 yards long. Marks the north end of the Dumoulin Islands and the NE end of Géologie Archipelago. Dumont d'Urville's expedition made a landing (débarquement) here in Jan. 1840, and named it Rocher de Débarquement. Later translated.

**Mount Debenham** *see* **Debenham Peak**

**Debenham, Frank.** b. 1883, Bowral, NSW, Australia. d. 1965, Cambridge, England. Studied geology under Edgeworth David in Sydney, and went as geologist on the British Antarctic Expedition of 1910–13, taking part in both of the western geological parties during that expedition. He helped set up the Scott Polar Research Institute in Cambridge in 1926, and was director from 1926–48. He was a member of the Advisory Committee of the BGLE 1934–37.

**Debenham Glacier.** 77°12′S, 162°38′E. Behind the Wilson Piedmont Glacier, in Victoria Land. Mapped by Scott's 1901–4 expedition. Named by Scott's 1910–13 expedition for Frank Debenham.

**Debenham Islands.** 68°08′S, 67°07′W. Group of islands and rocks between Millerand Island and the west coast of Graham Land, just north of Stonington Island, in Marguerite Bay. They include June Island, Barry Island, Audrey Island, Ann Island, Barbara Island. Discovered by the BGLE 1934–37 and named by Rymill for Frank Debenham. That expedition was based here (on Barry Island) for part of its stay in Antarctica, and later General San Martín Station was located here.

**Debenham Peak.** 67°21′S, 50°26′E. Also called Mount Debenham. 1,140 m. South of Amundsen Bay, in the Scott Mountains. 7 miles east of Mount Cronus. Discovered in Jan. 1930 by the BANZARE, and named by Mawson for Frank Debenham.

**Mount DeBreuck.** 71°16′S, 35°40′E. 2,000 m. Mostly ice-free. The most northerly massif in the Queen Fabiola Mountains. Discovered on Oct. 7, 1960, by the Belgian Antarctic Expedition of 1960–61 under Guido Derom, who named it for William DeBreuck, US glaciologist and observer on the expedition. He was later at Amundsen-Scott South Pole Station, in 1962–63.

**DeBreuck Glacier.** 82°53′S, 162°50′E. 8 miles long. Flows into Kent Glacier in the Queen Elizabeth Range. Named for William DeBreuck (*see* **Mount DeBreuck**).

**Mount DeBusk** *see* **DeBusk Scarp**

**DeBusk Scarp.** 69°23′S, 62°57′W. Also called Mount DeBusk. A nearly vertical rock cliff. 2 miles long. 300 meters high. At the south side of the mouth of Bingham Glacier, on the east coast of Palmer Land. Named by Ronne in 1948 for Clarence DeBusk, Beaumont, Texas Chamber of Commerce executive who helped the RARE 1947–48.

**Debussy Heights.** 69°44′S, 71°17′W. 1,250 m. A mountain, 9 miles long. Overlooks the Mozart Ice Piedmont 8 miles SE of Mount Morley in the northern part of Alexander Island. Named by the UK for the composer.

**Debutante Island.** 69°34′S, 75°30′E. Nearly ice-covered. The most southerly of the Søstrene Islands, in the Publications Ice Shelf. Photographed by the LCE 1936–37. Named by John H. Roscoe, the US cartographer, in 1952, because it is "coming out" of its ice cover.

**De Camp Nunatak.** 72°16′S, 160°22′E. Isolated. 3 miles SE of Welcome Mountain, in the Outback Nunataks. Named for Michael A. de Camp, biologist at McMurdo Station in 1966–67.

**Decazes Island.** 66°26′S, 67°21′W. ½ mile long. 1½ miles SW of Belding Island at the SW end of the Biscoe Islands. Charcot, in 1908–10, named a point in this area as Pointe Decazes, which was later translated into English as Decazes Point. It was later redefined.

**Decazes Point** *see* **Decazes Island**

**Decennial Peak.** 84°22′S, 166°02′E. 4,020 m. 3 miles SW of Mount Kirkpatrick in the Queen Alexandra Range. Named to commemorate the 10th year of the Institute of Polar Studies at Ohio State University, in 1970.

**Decepción Station** *see* **Primero de Mayo Station**

**Deception Glacier.** 78°30′S, 158°30′E. Between the Warren and Boomerang Ranges, flowing into the upper part of the Mulock Glacier. Named by the NZ party of the BCTAE 1957–58 because it seems to flow into the Skelton Névé, but instead flows south into Mulock Glacier.

**Deception Harbor** *see* **Port Foster**

**Deception Island.** 62°57′S, 60°38′W. Also called Teil Island. A volcanic, horseshoe-shaped caldera, 10 miles south of Livingston Island, in the South Shetlands. The island consists of a sunken volcano which forms a natural harbor called Port Foster (although in 1821–22 there are 2 mentions of this harbor as Dunbar's Harbor, or Port Dunbar. It was also called Deception Harbor, Deception Bay, or just Deception. It was only called Port Foster subsequent to Foster's visit in 1829). The volcano is 1,890 feet high, and the crater is 8 miles in diameter, and one of the best anchorages in the Antarctic. The waters here get to 100°F, and tourists swim in them in the summertime. William Smith may have mapped it as Edwards Island, in 1819–20, but Palmer was the first to explore it, on Nov. 15, 1820. The sealers named it in the early 1820s. The island erupted in 1842. In 1908 Britain claimed it and in 1912 gave a 21-year lease to the Hektor Whaling Company, which set up a whaling station here. Deception Island became the administrative center for all British whaling activities in the South Shetlands and operated as such until 1938. By that year Deception Island had a post office, a stipendiary magistrate and telegraph communications. Claimed by Chile and Argentina, as well as by Britain, in the 1940s, it was the scene of rivalry between Argentina and Britain (*see* **Wars**), and the British built Base B, a military station, here during Operation Tabarin. The island erupted on Dec. 4, 1967, the first eruption in modern times, and again on Feb. 21, 1969. The third, and most violent eruption, took place on Aug. 12 and 13, 1970.

**Deception Plateau.** 73°15'S, 164°50'E. Ice-covered. 11 miles long. 6 miles wide. In Victoria Land. Named by the New Zealanders in 1966–67 because from a distance it looks small.

**Decker Glacier.** 77°28'S, 162°47'E. Flows from the NE slopes of Mount Newall, in the Asgard Range of Victoria Land. Named for Chief Aviation Machinist's Mate William D. Decker, USN, of VXE-6 (*see* **Deaths, 1971**).

**Cape Découverte.** 66°46'S, 141°34'E. Also called Cape Discovery. Marks the NW extremity of the Curzon Islands, along the Adélie Land coast. Discovered on Jan. 21, 1840, by Dumont d'Urville, who named it Cap de la Découverte (Cape of the Discovery). It was the first rocky point of the coast seen by the expedition.

**Découverte Ledge.** 66°15'S, 140°15'E. Submarine feature off Adélie Land.

**De Dion Islets** *see* **Dion Islands**

**Bahía Dedo** *see* **Briand Fjord**

**Isla Dedo** *see* **Danco Island**

**Mount Dedo.** 64°39'S, 62°33'W. Also called Zeiss Needle. 695 m. A needle-shaped peak. South of Orne Harbor, on the west coast of Graham Land. Charted by de Gerlache in 1897–99. Named by the Argentines before 1954 (the name means "finger").

**Punta Dedo** *see* **The Toe**

**Dee Ice Piedmont.** 68°40'S, 66°58'W. Between Pavie Ridge and the mouth of the Clarke Glacier, on the east side of Mikkelsen Bay, on the west coast of the Antarctic Peninsula. Named by the UK for John Dee (1527–1608), navigation pioneer and Queen Elizabeth I's astrologer. Some say Dee was the most important man in Elizabethan England.

**Dee Island.** 62°26'S, 59°47'W. 2½ miles east of Ongley Island, just off the north side of Greenwich Island in the South Shetlands. Charted and named in 1935 by the personnel on the *Discovery II*.

**Dee Nunatak.** 74°28'S, 136°31'W. Behind Cape Burks, on the Hobbs Coast, in the western part of McDonald Heights, in Marie Byrd Land. 1 mile west of Rhodes Icefall, and seemingly in the flow of the Garfield Glacier. Named for Lt. Thomas H. Dee, USN, medical officer at Byrd Station in 1970.

**Mount Deeley.** 67°01'S, 66°13'W. 2,150 m. 6 miles NE of Salmon Cove in Graham Land. Named by the UK for Richard M. Deeley, British geologist and glaciology specialist.

**Deep Freeze Range.** 74°15'S, 163°45'E. 80 miles long. 10 miles wide. Between the Priestley and Campbell Glaciers in Victoria Land. Extends from the Polar Plateau to Terra Nova Bay. Named for Operation Deep Freeze.

**[1]Deep Lake.** 68°34'S, 78°11'E. Not yet an official name. One of the two most saline lakes in the Vestfold Hills of Princess Elizabeth Land. 36 meters deep, it originated from the sea. It is now 50.4 meters below sea level, and has a surface temperature of −20°C during winter and +10°C in summer. The bottom 15 meters remain constant at about −14°C.

**[2]Deep Lake.** 77°34'S, 166°13'E. ½ mile north of Cape Barne on Ross Island. Named descriptively by Shackleton in 1907–9.

**Defant Glacier.** 72°32'S, 61°35'W. 2 miles wide at its mouth. Flows to the west side of Violante Inlet, on the east coast of Palmer Land. Discovered in Dec. 1940 by the USAS. Named by the FIDS for Prof. Albert Defant, Austrian-born German oceanographer, director of the German Hydrographic Office, 1927–46.

**The Defile.** 77°39'S, 162°43'E. An ice-free passage between the terminus of Suess Glacier and the Nussbaum Riegel in Taylor Valley, Victoria Land. Charted and named descriptively by Scott's 1910–13 expedition.

**De Flotte, Paul.** Paul François René de Flotte. Embarked on the *Zélée* in Tahiti as an élève on Nov. 15, 1838, as part of

Dumont d'Urville's expedition of 1837–40. He was promoted to ensign on Aug. 20, 1839.

**DeGanahl, Joe.** Navigator and dog driver, and member of the supporting party, during Byrd's 1928–30 expedition.

**DeGanahl Glacier.** 85°13'S, 170°35'W. 10 miles long. Flows from Jones Peak into the west side of Liv Glacier opposite June Nunatak. Discovered by Byrd during his flight to the Pole in Nov. 1929. He named it for Joe DeGanahl.

**Mount Degerfeldt.** 66°58'S, 51°01'E. 3½ miles south of Mount Storer in the Tula Mountains of Enderby Land. Named by the Australians for C. Degerfeldt.

**Degerfeldt, C.** Crew member on the *Discovery* during the BANZARE, 1929–31.

**Cape de Gerlache** *see* **Cape Gerlache**

**Mount de Gerlache** *see* **Mount Gerlache**

**De Gerlache, Adrien.** b. Aug. 2, 1866, Hasselt, Belgium. d. Dec. 4, 1934, Brussels. Adrien Victor Joseph de Gerlache, Baron Gerlache de Gomery. Belgian naval lieutenant who led the 1897–99 Belgian Antarctic Expedition (*see* **The** *Belgica* for details of the expedition), the first Antarctic expedition concentrating on science. Amundsen and Frederick Cook were on this expedition. In 1901 de Gerlache was in the Persian Gulf (the Arabian Gulf) and in 1903 he joined Charcot's expedition on the *Français*, but resigned in Buenos Aires. He assisted Shackleton in planning the British Imperial Transantarctic Expedition of 1914–17, and in fact sold his yacht to the British explorer (it was renamed the *Endurance*). Most of de Gerlache's later years were spent in the Arctic regions. He was the father of Gaston de Gerlache.

**De Gerlache, Gaston.** Baron Gaston de Gerlache de Gomery. Son of Adrien de Gerlache. Led the Belgian Antarctic Expedition of 1957–58, which set up Roi Baudouin Station.

**De Gerlache Point** *see* **Gerlache Island**

**De Gerlache Strait** *see* **Gerlache Strait**

**DeGoes Cliff.** 71°44'S, 161°54'E. On the west side of the Morozumi Range. Over 6 miles long, its northern end is 6 miles SW of Mount Van Veen. Named for Louis DeGoes of the US National Academy of Sciences, executive secretary of the Committee on Polar Research.

**De Guébriant Islets** *see* **Guébriant Islands**

**De Haven, Edmund H.** Acting master on the Wilkes Expedition 1838–42. Joined the *Vincennes* at Callao, and later transferred to the *Peacock* at Fiji.

**De Haven Glacier.** 66°59'S, 127°32'E. Flows to the SW corner of Porpoise Bay. Named for Edmund H. De Haven.

**Deildedalen Valley.** 71°24'S, 12°43'E. Partly ice-filled. Between Mount Deildenapen and a similar mountain mass to the west, in the Östliche Petermann Range of the Wohlthat Mountains in Queen Maud Land. Discovered by Ritscher in 1938–39. Name means "the dividing valley" in Norwegian.

**Deildegasten Ridge.** 71°29'S, 12°42'E. 5 miles long. Just south of the Deildedalen Valley in the Östliche Petermann Range of the Wohlthat Mountains of Queen Maud Land. Discovered by Ritscher in 1938–39. Named by the Norwegians.

**Mount Deildenapen.** 71°24'S, 12°46'E. 2,050 m. Forms the east wall of the Deildedalen Valley in the Östliche Petermann Range of the Wohlthat Mountains of Queen Maud Land. Discovered by Ritscher in 1938–39. Name means "the dividing mountain" in Norwegian.

**Deimos Ridge.** 71°56'S, 68°36'W. 3 miles SW of Phobos Ridge and Mars Glacier in the SE corner of Alexander Island. Discovered by Ellsworth on his Nov. 23, 1935 flight. Surveyed in 1949 by the FIDS and named by the UK in association with the planet Mars and its moons.

**Dekefjellet Mountain.** 71°58'S, 13°25' E. 3 miles long. Surmounted by Kamskaya Peak. 1½ miles west of Skavlrimen Ridge in the Weyprecht Mountains of Queen Maud Land. Discovered by Ritscher in 1938–39. Named by the Norwegians.

**Dekefjellrantane Hills.** 72°02'S, 13°23'E. At the south end of the Weyprecht Mountains in Queen Maud Land. Named for nearby Dekefjellet Mountain.

**De Kermadec, Félix Huon.** Member of Dumont d'Urville's 1837–40 expedition.

**DeLaca Island.** 64°47'S, 64°07'W. A tiny U-shaped island a mile west of Palmer Station, off Anvers Island. Named for Ted E. DeLaca, biologist here in the 1971–74 period.

**De la Farge, Antoine de Pavin.** Known as Tony. Ensign on the *Zélée* during Dumont d'Urville's 1837–40 expedition. Died on board, Nov. 20, 1839.

**Delaite Island.** 64°33'S, 62°12'W. 1 mile long. 3 miles NE of Emma Island in the north-central part of Wilhelmina Bay, off the west coast of Graham Land. Discovered by de Gerlache in 1897–99, and named by him for J. Delaite, a supporter of the *Belgica* expedition.

**Cape de la Motte.** 67°S, 144°25'E. Separates Watt and Buchanan Bays on the coast of East Antarctica. Mount Hunt rises to 520 meters behind it. This may be the Point Case that Wilkes discovered in 1840. Charted by the AAE 1911–14, and named by Mawson for C.P. de la Motte.

**De la Motte, C.P.** 3rd officer on the *Aurora* during the AAE 1911–14.

**Delay Point.** 66°28'S, 98°14'E. 185 m. On the west side of Melba Peninsula. 6 miles west of Cape Charcot. Discovered by the AAE 1911–14, and named by the Eastern Sledge Party of the Western Base because bad weather delayed the party near here for several days in Nov. 1912.

**Delbridge Islands** *see* **Dellbridge Islands**

**Del Canto, Raul.** Capitán de corbeta. Engineer on the *Iquique* during the Chilean Antarctic Expedition of 1947.

**Mount Deleon.** 80°51'S, 159°57'E. 780 m. Mainly ice-free. On the south side of Entrikin Glacier, 9 miles WNW of Cape Douglas. Named by the US for Emilio A. Deleon, USN, hauling equipment operator at Byrd Station in 1963.

**Delius Glacier.** 69°32'S, 70°50'W. 8 miles long. 3 miles wide. Flows west from the Elgar Uplands into the Nichols Snowfield, in the northern part of Alexander Island. Named by the UK for the composer.

**Cape Deliverance** *see* **Deliverance Point**

**Deliverance Point.** 65°18'S, 64°07'W. Also called Cape Deliverance. 2½ miles south of Cape Tuxen on the west coast of Graham Land. Discovered and named by Charcot after he and his companions were rescued here in early Jan. 1909 in a long boat while exploring the coast. They called it Cap de la Délivrance.

**Dell, James.** James William Dell. Able seaman, RN. He first went to Antarctica on the Royal Society Expedition of 1901–4, as bosun's yeoman/butcher/sailmaker. He was back again on the *Quest* in 1921–22, as bosun/electrician.

**Dellbridge, James H.** Second engineer on the *Discovery* during the Royal Society Expedition of 1901–4.

**Dellbridge Islands.** 77°41'S, 166°25'E. Also seen spelled (erroneously) as Delbridge Islands. Four little volcanic islands in Erebus Bay, just south of Cape Evans, in McMurdo Sound, off the west coast of Ross Island. Tent Island is the biggest, followed in order by Inaccessible Island, Big Razorback Island, and Little Razorback Island. Scott named them in 1902 for James H. Dellbridge.

**Deloncle Bay.** 65°05'S, 63°56'W. 1½ miles long. It indents the west coast of Graham Land between Loubat and Glandaz Points. It opens on the Lemaire Channel opposite Booth Island. Discovered by de Gerlache in 1897–99. Recharted and named by Charcot in 1903–5 for François Deloncle, French diplomat.

**Cape de Loubat** *see* **Loubat Point**

**Delta Bluff.** 78°42′S, 161°22′E. Just north of the mouth of Delta Glacier, on the west side of the Skelton Glacier. Climbed in 1957 by the NZ party of the BCTAE, and named because of its shape.

**Delta Creek** *see* **Delta Stream**

**Delta Glacier.** 78°43′S, 161°20′E. Flows from the Worcester Range, between Northcliffe Peak and Delta Bluff, to enter the west side of the Skelton Glacier. The NZ party of the BCTAE named it Cascade Glacier in 1957 because of its broken lower icefalls. To avoid confusion with another feature of the same name, it was renamed in association with nearby Delta Bluff.

**¹Delta Island.** 64°19′S, 62°59′W. Also called Isla Hermelo. ½ mile long. Just SE of Lambda Island, and east of Alpha Island, in the Melchior Islands. It was named probably in 1927 by the personnel on the *Discovery*, for the Greek letter.

**²Delta Island** *see* **Acuña Island**

**Delta Peak.** 86°35′S, 147°30′W. 6 miles NE of Mount Gjertsen. It forms a corner point on the Ackerman Ridge in the La Gorce Mountains. Named by the New Zealanders in 1969–70 because, seen from the south, its colorful rock strata suggest a "Delta."

**Delta Stream.** 77°38′S, 163°07′E. Also called Delta Creek. A small, intermittent stream flowing from Howard Glacier into Lake Fryxell, in the Taylor Valley of Victoria Land. First studied on the ground by Troy L. Péwé in 1957–58, and named by him for the delta along it.

**Delusion Point.** 65°23′S, 62°W. On the south wall of Crane Glacier, on the east coast of Graham Land. Charted and named by the FIDS in 1947.

**Cap de Margerie** *see* **Cape Margerie**

**Mount Demaria.** 65°17′S, 64°06′W. Also called Demaria Peak. 635 m. Just SE of Cape Tuxen on the west coast of Graham Land. Charted and named by Charcot in 1903–5, for the Demaria Brothers, French photographic pioneers.

**Demaria Peak** *see* **Mount Demaria**

**Demas, E.J.** b. 1905, Allisos, Greece. d. Nov. 17, 1979, Granada Hills, California. Epaminondas James Demas. Known as Pete. A close associate of Admiral Byrd's, he was with him on his first two expeditions to Antarctica.

**Demas, Lt. François Barlatier** *see* **Barlatier-Demas, Lt. François**

**Demas Bluff.** 76°34′S, 144°50′W. On the south side of the Fosdick Mountains. 2 miles west of Mount Richardson in the Ford Ranges of Marie Byrd Land. Named by Byrd in 1939–41 for Dr. Charles J. Demas, who provided medical assistance and supplies for the USAS 1939–41, and also for Byrd's 1933–35 expedition.

**Demas Ice Tongue.** 72°22′S, 103°20′W. It juts out 20 miles from the Abbott Ice Shelf on the Eights Coast, into the NE part of the Amundsen Sea, and forms the westernmost part of Peacock Sound. Discovered on flights from the *Bear* in Feb. 1940, during the USAS 1939–41. Named for E.J. Demas.

**Demas Mountains** *see* **Walker Mountains**

**Demas Range.** 75°S, 133°45′W. 8 miles long. Forms the lower east edge of the Berry Glacier in Marie Byrd Land. Its southernmost peak is Mount Goorhigian. Discovered by the USAS 1939–41. Named for E.J. Demas.

**Demas Rocks.** 63°21′S, 58°02′W. A group of rocks in water off the NW coast of the Trinity Peninsula, in the approach to Huon Bay, 3 miles NE of Cape Ducorps. Discovered in March 1838 by Dumont d'Urville, who named them for Lt. François Barlatier-Demas.

**Demay Point.** 62°13′S, 58°26′W. On the western shore of Admiralty Bay, King George Island, in the South Shetlands.

Discovered before 1822. Named by Charcot in 1908–10.

**Demidov, Dimitri.** Lt. Member of von Bellingshausen's 1819–21 expedition. On Jan. 17, 1820, he and Simonov landed on an iceberg and captured 30 penguins.

**Demidov Island.** 67°29'S, 48°21'E. A small island 5 miles north of the mouth of Rayner Glacier. 9 miles SW of Hydrographer Islands along the coast of Enderby Land. Named by the USSR in 1957 for Dimitri Demidov.

**Deming Glacier.** 72°S, 168°30'E. Flows along the north side of Novasio Ridge into Man-o-War Glacier in the Admiralty Mountains of Victoria Land. Named for Ralph A. Deming, USN, VX-6 aviation electrician at McMurdo Station in 1967.

**Demock, John.** Captain of the topsail on the Wilkes Expedition 1838–42. Joined in the USA. Served the cruise.

**De Montravel, Louis Tardy.** Ensign on the *Zélée* during Dumont d'Urville's 1837–40 expedition. He was promoted to lt. cdr. on March 20, 1839.

**Demorest Glacier.** 67°22'S, 65°35'W. Flows into Whirlwind Inlet between the Flint and Matthes Glaciers, on the east coast of Graham Land. Discovered aerially by Wilkins on Dec. 20, 1928. Charted by the FIDS in 1947, and named by them for the US glaciologist Max H. Demorest.

**Dempster, P.** 2nd officer on the *Jacob Ruppert*, 1933–34.

**Denais.** One of the seamen on the *Pourquoi Pas?* during Charcot's 1908–10 expedition.

**Denais Stack.** 62°08'S, 58°30'W. 1½ miles north of Point Thomas on the west side of Admiralty Bay, King George Island, in the South Shetlands. In 1908–10 Charcot named a cove near here for Denais (q.v.), as Anse Denais. This cove was on the north side of Ezcurra Inlet. Modern geographers cannot find such a

cove, so they gave the name to this stack nearby.

**Mount Denauro.** 86°27'S, 151°30'W. 2,340 m. 3 miles south of Lee Peak, between the Bartlett and Robert Scott Glaciers. Named for Ralph Denauro, VX-6 aviation mechanic in 1966.

**Dendtler Island.** 72°58'S, 89°57'W. 14 miles long. Ice-covered. In the east part of the Abbott Ice Shelf, between Farwell Island and Fletcher Peninsula. Named for Major Robert Dendtler, US Army, coordinating officer on the staff of the commander, US Naval Support Force, Antarctica, 1967 and 1968.

**Denfeld Mountains.** 76°55'S, 144°45'W. Between Crevasse Valley Glacier and Arthur Glacier in the Ford Ranges of Marie Byrd Land. Explored by Byrd's first 3 expeditions. Named by Byrd for Louis E. Denfeld, chief of naval operations, who helped plan Operation Highjump, 1946–47.

**Mount Denham.** 66°55'S, 52°18'E. 1 mile NW of Mount Keyser in the eastern part of the Tula Mountains of Enderby Land. Named by the Australians for W.M. Denham, weather observer at Mawson Station in 1961.

**Den Hartog Peak.** 84°20'S, 178°52'E. At the west side of the mouth of Ramsey Glacier. 3 miles SE of Woodall Peak, to the NE of the Hughes Range in the Transantarctic Mountains, overlooking the Ross Ice Shelf. Discovered on Flight C of Feb. 29–March 1, 1940, during the USAS. Surveyed by Crary in 1957–58, and named by him for Stephen Den Hartog, glaciologist on the Victoria Land Traverse Party of 1958–59, and at Little America V in 1958.

**Mount Denholm.** 68°12'S, 49°07'E. 1 mile SE of Mount Marriner in the Nye Mountains. Named by the Australians for J. Denholm, physicist at Wilkes Station in 1959.

**Deniau Island.** 65°27'S, 64°19'W. A small island between Darboux Island and the Lippmann Islands, off the west coast of Graham Land. Discovered by Charcot in 1908–10, and named by him for a supporter.

**Cape Denison.** 67°S, 142°40′E. 1,700 meters across. A rocky point which juts out 900 meters into Commonwealth Bay from the head of that bay. Discovered by the AAE 1911–14 and named by Mawson for Sir Hugh Denison of Sydney, a patron. Mawson set up his main base here.

**Denison Island.** 66°18′S, 110°27′E. ¼ mile west of Beall Island in the Windmill Islands. Named for Dean R. Denison, aurora scientist at Wilkes Station in 1958.

**Denman Glacier.** 66°45′S, 99°25′E. 70 miles long. Between 7 and 10 miles wide. Flows from Wilkes Land into the Shackleton Ice Shelf, east of David Island. Discovered by the *Aurora* party of the AAE 1911–14. Named by Mawson for Lord Denman, governor-general of Australia, and a patron.

**Denmark.** On May 20, 1965, this country was ratified as the 15th signatory of the Antarctic Treaty.

**Dennes Point.** 76°41′S, 159°45′E. Juts out from the west side of Shipton Ridge into the Shimmering Icefield, in the Allan Hills of Victoria Land. Named by the New Zealanders in 1964 for a similar dolerite feature on Bruny Island, Tasmania.

**Dennison Reef.** 66°29′S, 66°50′W. Between the Shull Rocks and the Pauling Islands, east of the south end of the Biscoe Islands, in Crystal Sound. Named by the UK for David M. Dennison, British physicist and crystal expert.

**Dennistoun, James R.** NZ alpinist in charge of the mules on the *Terra Nova* on its way to Antarctica during Scott's 1910–13 expedition.

**Dennistoun Glacier.** 71°15′S, 168°E. 50 miles long. Flows from the northern slopes of Mounts Black Prince, Royalist, and Adam in the Admiralty Mountains of Victoria Land, between the Lyttelton Range and the Dunedin Range, into Robertson Bay. Named for James R. Dennistoun.

**Denson, Ben.** Seaman on the *Eleanor Bolling* during the second half of Byrd's 1928–30 expedition (i.e. 1929–30).

**Isla Dentada** *see* **Kellick Island**

**Denton Glacier.** 77°29′S, 162°38′E. A hanging glacier which flows from the NW slopes of Mount Newall in the area of the Wright Valley in Victoria Land. Named by US geologist Robert Nichols for glaciologist George H. Denton.

**Mount Denucé.** 66°43′S, 64°12′W. 1,535 m. Between Mounts Hulth and Haskell on the SW side of Cabinet Inlet, on the east coast of Graham Land. Named by the FIDS for Jean Denucé, French polar bibliographer.

**Denys, Charlene.** American biologist, protegée of Dr. Mary Alice McWhinnie. She first went to Antarctica with Dr. McWhinnie in 1975–76, and spent the next 4 summers at Palmer Station. She took over Dr. McWhinnie's work when the latter died in 1980.

**Departure Rocks.** 67°37′S, 62°50′E. 4 rocks in water 1 mile north of Peake-Jones Rock in Holme Bay, Mac. Robertson Land. Photographed by the LCE 1936–37. Named later by the Australians because ANARE parties leaving Mawson Station for the west always pass these rocks.

**Depeaux Point.** 65°11′S, 64°10′W. Forms the south end of Petermann Island, in the Wilhelm Archipelago. Discovered and named in 1908–10 by Charcot.

**Depot Bay** *see* **Farr Bay**

**Depot 480.** 79°51′S, 148°E. Depot established by Hillary on the Polar Plateau in support of the BCTAE 1956–58. Hillary began building it on Nov. 25, 1957, and it was fully stocked by plane on Dec. 6, 1957.

**Depot Glacier.** 63°25′S, 57°03′W. Also called Glaciar Esperanza. A valley glacier which terminates at Hope Bay at the northern end of Graham Land. Discovered by Nordenskjöld in 1901–4, and named by him because it looks like the site for a depot.

¹**Depot Island.** 66°56'S, 57°19'E. A small island in the Øygarden Group. 1 mile north of the west end of Shaula Island. Photographed by the LCE 1936–37. Named later by the Australians because of the depot established here by the ANARE in 1956.

²**Depot Island.** 76°42'S, 162°58'E. 2 miles NW of Cape Ross, off the coast of Victoria Land. Discovered by David in 1908–9 and named by him for the depot of rock specimens he put on the island.

**Dépôt Island.** 66°37'S, 140°05'E. 175 yards long. Just over ½ mile NW of Pasteur Island near the center of the Dumoulin Islands. Charted in 1950–51 by the French, and named by them for the depot built here by personnel from the *Commandant Charcot*.

**Depot Mountains** *see* **Depot Peak**

**Depot Nunatak.** 77°45'S, 16°02'E. 1,980 m. 8 miles west of Finger Mountain, at the head of the Taylor Glacier in Victoria Land. Named by Scott's 1901–4 expedition during their 1903 western journey, for the food depot they made here.

**Depot Peak.** 69°02'S, 64°36'E. An isolated nunatak that has a single, needle-shaped peak. 37 miles north of the Stinear Nunataks, in Mac. Robertson Land. Discovered by Robert Dovers' ANARE party of Dec. 1954, and named by him for the depot he built here.

**Depot 700.** Hillary set it up on the Polar Plateau, 500 miles from the South Pole. Begun on Dec. 15, 1957, it was completed by Dec. 20, 1957, having been fully stocked from the air. This was where Hillary was to have met Fuchs during the BCTAE 1957–58, but instead Hillary pushed on to the Pole from here.

**Depots.** Marked stations of supplies and fuel for a traversing party. A depot-laying party would go out ahead of the main party and lay them for the outward and return trip of the main party. They figured most prominently in the expeditions of Amundsen, Scott, Shackleton,

and Mawson, and during the BCTAE 1955–58. Amundsen's depots, for example, at various points on his way to the Pole in 1911, consisted of a cube of 2 meters, built of hard snow blocks cut from the solid crust, with a dark pennant on top. Scott's and Shackleton's diaries are filled with stories of desperate rushes to get to the depots, while Amundsen's preparations saved him an enormous amount of anguish. (*See also* **Depot 480, Depot 700, 150-Mile Depot, 300-Mile Depot, One-Ton Depot.**)

**Depth of Ice.** The average depth of ice on the Antarctic continent is 6,500 feet, and in some places it is over 2 miles deep. Of course, in some places there is no ice. The greatest recorded depth of ice in Antarctica, measured by radio echo soundings, is 15,670 feet, at 69°09'38"S, 135°20'25"E. At the South Pole the depth of ice is 9,186 feet. The average depth of ice on the Ross Ice Shelf is between 1,100 and 2,300 feet (*see also* **Core samples**).

**Derby Island.** 66°38'S, 140°05'E. A small island north of Astrolabe Glacier Tongue. ½ mile SW of Pasteur Island, at the south end of the Dumoulin Islands. Charted by the French in 1949–51, and named by them for the "Derby" the French field parties had among themselves to reach it.

**Derbyshire Peak.** 72°31'S, 161°06'E. 5 miles NNE of Mount Weihaupt in the Outback Nunataks. Named for Edward Derbyshire, geologist at McMurdo Station in 1966–67.

**DeRemer Nunataks.** 69°45'S, 158°09'E. 4 miles SE of Mount Blowaway in the Wilson Hills. Named for Yeoman 1st Class Dennis L. DeRemer, USN, who served with the US Naval Support Force, Antarctica, from Feb. 1967 to July 1970.

**Mount Dergach.** 70°36'S, 163°01'E. Flat-topped. Ice-covered. Just west of Ob' Bay and south of Lunik Point in the Bowers Mountains. Named by the USSR in 1960–61 for meteorologist A.P. Dergach, a member of the Soviet Antarctic Expedition of 1959–61.

**Mount Derom.** 71°34'S, 35°38'E. A massif of 2,400 m. 2 miles south of Mount Eyskens in the Queen Fabiola Mountains. Discovered on Oct. 7, 1960, by the Belgian Antarctic Expedition of 1960–61 led by Guido Derom. Named for the leader by the Centre National de Recherches Polaires de Belgique.

**Derom, Guido.** Leader of the Belgian Antarctic Expedition of 1960–61.

**De Rongé Island** see **Rongé Island**

**De Roquemaurel, Louis.** Louis François Marie Auguste de Roquemaurel. Lieutenant on the *Astrolabe*, and second-in-command of that ship, during Dumont d'Urville's 1837–40 expedition.

**De Rothschild Islets** see **Splitwind Island**

**Derrick Peak.** 80°04'S, 156°22'E. 2,070 m. Ice-free. 3 miles west of the north end of Johnstone Ridge, it overlooks the Hatherton Glacier in the vicinity of the Byrd Glacier. Named for Robert O. Derrick of the US Weather Bureau, assistant to the USARP representative at Christchurch, NZ, from 1960 until he died in 1966.

**Derrick Point.** ¼ mile NE of Cape Royds, Ross Island.

**Mount Deryugin.** 71°51'S, 11°20'E. 2,635 m. On Vindegga Spur in the Liebknecht Range of the Humboldt Mountains in Queen Maud Land. Discovered by Ritscher in 1938–39. Named by the USSR in 1966 for zoologist K.M. Deryugin.

**De Sauls, James.** Ship's cook on the Wilkes Expedition 1838–42. Joined at Callao. Run at Astoria.

**Descartes Island.** 66°47'S, 141°29'E. 175 yards long. Between Lagrange Island and La Conchée. Almost a mile NNE of Cape Mousse. Charted by the French in 1951, and named by them for the French philosopher René Descartes (1596–1650).

**Descent Cliff.** 77°43'S, 166°53'E. On the west side of Hut Point Peninsula, between the Hutton Cliffs and Erebus Glacier Tongue, on Ross Island. Charted by Scott's 1910–13 expedition, and named by them because they descended from here to the sea ice.

**Descent Glacier.** 77°51'S, 162°52'E. Between Briggs Hill and Condit Glacier, flowing from Descent Pass into the Ferrar Glacier in Victoria Land. Armitage's party descended this glacier in a wild manner in 1901–4, during the Royal Society Expedition. Named because of that incident by Scott's 1910–13 expedition.

**Descent Pass.** 77°52'S, 163°10'E. Leads from Blue Glacier to Ferrar Glacier in Victoria Land. Named by Armitage in 1902 because of his party's wild descent through here to the Ferrar Glacier during Scott's 1901–4 expedition.

**Deschanel Peak.** 68°55'S, 67°14'W. Just south of Cape Berteaux on the west coast of the Antarctic Peninsula. Charcot named it in Jan. 1909 as Sommet Deschanel.

**Desko Mountains.** 69°37'S, 72°30'W. On the east coast of the Antarctic Peninsula.

**Desmond, Gordon P.** Crewman on the *Jacob Ruppert*, 1933–35.

**Island of Desolation** see **Desolation Island**

**Desolation Harbor** see **Blythe Bay**

**Desolation Island.** 62°28'S, 60°22'W. Also called Island of Desolation. A little V-shaped island in the South Shetlands, 5 miles west of Williams Point, Livingston Island, in Hero Bay. Discovered in Jan. 1820 by Bransfield, and named by him for its appearance.

**Despair Rocks.** 60°33'S, 46°10'W. Also called Rocks of Despair. A group of rocks in water, 2 miles south of Melsom Rocks. 7½ miles WSW of Penguin Point, the NW tip of Coronation Island, in the South Orkneys. Discovered and named by Palmer and Powell in Dec. 1821.

**Desprez, Raoul.** Chef on the French Polar Expedition of 1949–51.

**DesRoches Nunataks.** 84°53'S, 67°08' W. 2 nunataks 3 miles east of Postel

Nunatak in the SW part of the Patuxent Range of the Pensacola Mountains. Named for Joseph DesRoches, meteorologist at Amundsen-Scott South Pole Station in 1967.

**Dessent Ridge.** 73°26′S, 166°37′E. Ice-covered. 5 miles east of Mount Murchison in the Mountaineer Range of Victoria Land. Extends for 10 miles. Named for Joseph E. Dessent, meteorologist at Hallett Station in 1961.

**Destruction Bay.** 61°59′S, 57°39′W. Also called Liverpool Bay. 5½ miles wide. Between Taylor Point and Cape Melville on the east side of King George Island in the South Shetlands. Charted and named Bay of Destruction in 1821 by Richard Sherratt from the *Lady Trowbridge*. His vessel was wrecked here.

**Détaille Island.** 66°52′S, 66°48′W. A small island, 2 miles NW of Andresen Island, in the entrance of Lallemand Fjord, off the Loubet Coast, on the west coast of Graham Land. Discovered by Charcot in 1908–10, and named by him for M. Détaille of Punta Arenas, a shareholder in the Magellan Whaling Company, who helped Charcot obtain supplies at the company's whaling station at Deception Island. The British Base W was here.

**Detling Peak.** 75°14′S, 114°48′W. Ice-covered. Cone-shaped. 12 miles SW of Morrison Bluff in the Kohler Range of Marie Byrd Land. Named for James K. Detling, biologist with the Marie Byrd Land Survey Party of 1966–67.

**Detour Island.** 65°01′S, 63°55′W. 2½ miles west of False Cape Renard, on the west side of the Lemaire Channel in the Wilhelm Archipelago. Charted by Charcot in 1903–5. Named by the UK in 1959 because it marks an alternate passage for ships west of Booth Island, other than the Lemaire Channel.

**Detour Nunatak.** 77°08′S, 160°55′E. Between Frazier Glacier and the upper part of Mackay Glacier in Victoria Land. Named in 1957 by the NZ Northern Survey Party of the BCTAE because they had

to make a detour here while going up Mackay Glacier.

**Detroit Aviation Society Plateau** *see* **Detroit Plateau**

**Detroit Plateau.** 64°10′S, 60°W. Varies in height between 1,500 meters and 1,800 meters. Extends 90 miles from the Russell West Glacier in the north, to the Herbert Plateau in the south, just south of Trinity Peninsula, at the northern tip of Graham Land. Discovered aerially by Wilkins on Dec. 20, 1928, and named by him as Detroit Aviation Society Plateau, for the society which helped get his expedition together. The name was later shortened.

**The *Deutschland*.** Filchner's ship during the German Antarctic Expedition of 1911–12. Originally a 3-masted Norwegian sailing ship called the *Björn*, it had been designed for polar work. It had a 300 hp auxiliary engine. Shackleton supervised the strengthening of its hull for Filchner. On the 1911–12 expedition Richard Vahsel was captain, and Alfred Kling was navigator. Kling took over the captaincy when Vahsel died. The ship was later sold to Austria.

**Île des Deux Hummocks** *see* **Two Hummock Island**

**Deverall Island.** 81°29′S, 161°55′E. A small, ice-covered island just NE of Beaumont Bay on the Ross Ice Shelf. Named by the New Zealanders in 1960–61 for William H. Deverall, radio operator at Scott Base in 1961.

**DeVicq Glacier.** 75°S, 131°W. Flows from the Ames Range and the McCuddin Range in Marie Byrd Land, into the Getz Ice Shelf to the SE of Grant Island. Named for David C. deVicq, USN, engineering officer in charge of building the new Byrd Station in 1960–61.

**Devil Island.** 63°48′S, 57°17′W. 1 mile long. Has a low summit on each end. It is in the center of a small bay 1 mile SE of Cape Well-Met in the northern part of Vega Island. Discovered and named by Nordenskjöld's 1901–4 expedition.

**Deville Glacier.** 64°48'S, 62°35'W. Flows along the south side of Laussedat Heights into Andvord Bay, on the west coast of Graham Land. Named by the UK in 1960 for Édouard G. Deville (1849–1924), surveyor-general of Canada from 1885–1924, who, from 1888, introduced and developed photogrammetric methods of survey in Canada.

**The Devil's Ballroom.** 86°50'S, 168°W. A glacier with a treacherous surface of thin ice and snow covering a series of particularly deadly crevasses. On the edge of the Polar Plateau at the top of the Axel Heiberg Glacier. Discovered by Amundsen on Dec. 4, 1911. He originally called it the Devil's Dance Floor. Not to be confused with the nearby Devil's Glacier.

**Devils Corrie.** 60°39'S, 45°25'W. A large, spectacular corrie (or cirque) between Olivine Point and Amphibolite Point on the south coast of Coronation Island, in the South Orkneys. Surveyed and named by the FIDS in 1948–49.

**The Devil's Dance Floor** see **The Devil's Ballroom**

**The Devil's Glacier.** 86°20'S, 168°W. Also called Fandens Brae. At the top of the Amundsen Glacier in the Queen Maud Mountains. Discovered on Nov. 29, 1911, by Amundsen, who named it after being stuck here for 4 days en route to the South Pole.

**Devils Peak.** 60°39'S, 45°27'W. 735 m. Between Sunshine Glacier and Devils Corrie on the south side of Coronation Island in the South Orkneys. Surveyed by the FIDS in 1948–49, and named by them in association with the corrie.

**Devils Point.** 62°40'S, 61°11'W. The most southwesterly point on Byers Peninsula, Livingston Island, in the South Shetlands. Charted and named by Weddell between 1820 and 1823.

**Devils Punchbowl.** 77°01'S, 162°22'E. Also called Punch Bowl. An empty, bowl-shaped cirque in the SW corner of Granite Harbor, between Devils Ridge and the south side of The Flatiron, in Victoria Land. Charted and named by Scott's 1910–13 expedition.

**Devils Ridge.** 77°02'S, 162°21'E. Sickle-shaped. Extends from the south end of The Flatiron, and forms the northern wall of New Glacier, just west of Granite Harbor, in Victoria Land. Charted and named by Scott's 1910–13 expedition.

**Devils Thumb.** 77°02'S, 162°23'E. Just to the west of Granite Harbor, between The Flatiron and New Glacier. A knob, 245 meters high, it marks the central part of Devils Ridge, in Victoria Land. Charted and named descriptively by Scott's 1910–13 expedition.

**Devold, Hallvard.** In 1933 he, Olav Kjelbotn, and Hjalmar Riiser-Larsen attempted a dog-sledge exploration of the Princess Ragnhild Coast.

**Devold Peak.** 72°15'S, 26°44'E. 3,280 m. Between Kjelbotn Peak and the Pukkelen Rocks near the head of Byrdbreen in the Sør Rondane Mountains. Named by the Norwegians for Hallvard Devold.

**Devries Glacier.** 80°20'S, 157°30'E. Just east of Peckham Glacier. Flows from the southern slopes of the Britannia Range into Byrd Glacier. Named for Arthur L. Devries, biologist at McMurdo Station, 1961–62 and 1963–64, who studied fish and their antifreeze systems.

**DeWald Glacier.** 72°19'S, 167°E. 5 miles long. Flows from the NE slopes of Bramble Peak in the Victory Mountains of Victoria Land. Merges with the terminus of Lensen Glacier where both glaciers join Pearl Harbor Glacier. Named for Lt. (jg) Bruce F. DeWald, USN, aerographer at McMurdo Station in 1963 and 1966. He was later forecast duty officer at McMurdo Station in 1972–73 and 1973–74.

**Mount Dewar.** 80°32'S, 21°11'W. In the Shackleton Range.

**Dewar Nunatak.** 67°20'S, 68°15'W. 520 m. Mainly snow-covered. In the middle of Shambles Glacier, on the east coast of Adelaide Island. Named by the UK in 1963 for Graham J.A. Dewar, BAS geologist at Base T, 1961–63.

**Dewart Island.** 66°14'S, 110°10'E. The central island in the Frazier Islands, in Vincennes Bay. Named by Carl Eklund in 1957 for Gilbert Dewart, seismologist at Wilkes Station in 1957.

**Dewdrop Glacier.** 77°01'S, 162°21'E. A hanging glacier at the head of Devils Punchbowl, between The Flatiron and Devils Ridge, at the SW side of Granite Harbor, Victoria Land. Charted by Scott's 1910–13 expedition, and named by them because it hangs on the edge of Devils Punchbowl like a dewdrop.

**Mount Dewe.** 75°58'S, 68°39'W. In the SE part of the Hauberg Mountains, in Ellsworth Land. Named for Michael B. Dewe, glaciologist at Byrd Station in 1965–66.

**Dewees, Thomas.** Corporal on the Wilkes Expedition 1838–42. Joined in the USA. Served the cruise.

**Mount Dewey.** 65°54'S, 64°19'W. 1,830 m. 8 miles SE of Mount Cheops on the west coast of Graham Land. Named by the UK in 1959 for Melvil Dewey (1851–1932), US creator of the Dewey Decimal System in libraries.

**Mount Dewitt.** 77°12'S, 159°50'E. 2,190 m. Just west of Mount Littlepage and the Willett Range, just to the NW of the Wright Valley, in Victoria Land. Named in 1964 for Hugh H. Dewitt, scientific leader of the *Eltanin* cruise of 1962–63. He had also been on the *Glacier* in 1958–59.

**DeWitt Nunatak.** 84°49'S, 67°40'W. 1,295 m. 7 miles west of Snake Ridge in the Patuxent Range of the Pensacola Mountains. Named for Stephen R. DeWitt, meteorologist at Palmer Station in 1966.

**D'Hainaut Island.** 63°54'S, 60°47'W. Also called Hainaut Island, Bombay Island, Islote Norte. A small island in Mikkelsen Harbor, Trinity Island.

Charted by Charcot in 1908–10. Named by the Chilean Antarctic Expedition of 1952 for Lt. Ladislao D'Hainaut.

**Diamond dust.** Tiny crystals of snow. When ice needles (q.v.) reflect sunlight they are called diamond dust.

**Diamond Glacier.** 79°51'S, 158°59'E. Flows into the Darwin Glacier on the north side of Diamond Hill. Named by the New Zealanders in 1962–63 in association with the hill.

**Diamond Hill.** 79°52'S, 159°09'E. Snow-free. Diamond-shaped. 10 miles east of Bastion Hill at the north side of the lower Darwin Glacier. Named by the Darwin Glacier Party of the BCTAE 1957–58, which surveyed the area.

**Diamonen Island.** 64°02'S, 61°17'W. Also called Islote Madariaga, Islote Moreno. North of Moreno Rock in the Gerlache Strait, off the west coast of Graham Land. Charted by de Gerlache in 1897–99. Named Big Diamonen Island in 1921–22 by Capt. Skidsmo. The name was shortened by the UK in 1960.

[1]**The *Diana*.** American sealing and whaling brig, 86 tons, 60 feet long, built at New Bedford in 1794, and registered on Aug. 23, 1820, in Nantucket. Owned, managed, and commanded by Calvin Bunker. It was in the South Shetlands for the 1820–21 season and lost 2 whaling boats and 8 men. It arrived back at Nantucket on May 10, 1821, with 2,000 seal-skins.

[2]**The *Diana*.** 340-ton Scottish whaler on the Dundee Whaling Expedition of 1892–93. Captain Robert Davidson.

**Diana Reef.** 63°26'S, 56°11'W. Isolated. 3 miles east of d'Urville Monument in Joinville Island. Named by the UK in 1956 for the *Diana* of the Dundee Whaling Expedition of 1892–93.

**Diatoms.** A type of algae. Any of the single-celled or colonial algae of the phylum Bacillariophyta found floating in the water. Because of its symmetry and beautiful design it is termed "The Jewel of the Sea." Plentiful in Antarctica.

**Díaz, Emilio L.** Lt. (jg) in the Argentine navy, an observer on the USAS 1939–41. Later, as a captain, he led the 1951–52 Argentine Antarctic Expedition, and in 1955–56 he led another Argentine Antarctic Expedition. His ships on this last venture were *General San Martín, Bahía Aguirre, Chiriguano,* and *Punta Ninfas.*

**Díaz Rock.** 63°18′S, 58°45′W. A rock in water just north of the west end of Astrolabe Island, off the Trinity Peninsula. Named by the Chilean Antarctic Expedition of 1947 for Sub-lieutenant Joaquin Díaz Martínez.

**Dibble, Jonas.** Ship's carpenter on the *Peacock* during the Wilkes Expedition 1838–42. On Jan. 24–25, 1840, he left his sick bed and worked 24 hours with other carpenters without relief to fix a broken rudder after the ship was badly mauled by icebergs in 151°19′E. He then headed for Sydney in the ship.

**Dibble Basin.** 65°20′S, 133°E. Also called Dibble Depression. A submarine feature off the Clarie Coast. Named in association with the Dibble Glacier, which lies roughly in the same degree of longitude.

**Dibble Depression** *see* **Dibble Basin**

**Dibble Glacier.** 66°17′S, 134°36′E. A channel glacier flowing from the continental ice and ending in the Dibble Glacier Tongue. Named by the USA in 1955 for Jonas Dibble.

**Dibble Glacier Tongue.** 66°08′S, 134°32′E. Seaward extension of the Dibble Glacier in East Antarctica. Named by the USA in 1955 in association with the glacier.

**Dibble Iceberg Tongue.** 65°30′S, 135°E. At the seaward end of the Dibble Glacier Tongue, it forms the eastern end of Davis Bay, off the Wilkes Coast. Named by the Australians in association with the glacier tongue.

**Dibdins Island** *see* **Powell Island**

**Mount Dick.** 80°49′S, 158°32′E. 2,410 m. 6 miles east of Mount Egerton, in the Churchill Mountains. Named by the New Zealanders in 1960–61 for R.G. Dick, surveyor-general of New Zealand.

**Dick Glacier.** 84°54′S, 175°50′W. 7 miles long. Flows from Mount Campbell into the Shackleton Glacier just north of Taylor Nunatak, in the Queen Maud Mountains. Named for Lt. Alan L. Dick, with VX-6 in 1964.

**Dick Peaks.** 67°40′S, 49°35′E. 1 mile east of Mount Humble at the east end of the Raggatt Mountains in Enderby Land. Named by the Australians for W. Dick, weather observer at Mawson Station in 1960.

**The *Dick Smith Explorer.*** Boat used by David Lewis on the *Dick Smith Explorer* expedition of 1981–82 and on the Frozen Sea Expedition of 1982–84. A 3-masted schooner, 65 feet long, it had a ¼ inch-thick steel hull, and a 120 hp Mercedes diesel engine.

**The *Dick Smith Explorer* Expedition.** 1981–82. Led by David Lewis in the *Dick Smith Explorer.* The principal supporter was Dick Smith, the Australian millionaire / explorer / adventurer / personality for whom the vessel was named. The sponsor was Lewis' own Oceanic Research Foundation, which he had established in 1977. The all Australian/NZ crew left Sydney on Dec. 12, 1981, arriving at Hobart on Dec. 19, 1981. They left there Dec. 23, 1981, and on Jan. 4, 1982, they came into Antarctic waters. On Jan. 8, 1982, they sighted their first ice at 65°S, just before hitting the Antarctic Circle on Jan. 9, 1982. They reached the South Magnetic Pole (then at sea) and on Jan. 10, 1982, were off George V Land, anchoring at Cape Denison. They left there on Jan. 29, 1982. It was at Cape Denison that Harry Keys, geochemist, was married to Karen Williams, field assistant, by Dick Heffernan, geophysicist, mountain climber, and justice of the peace. The expedition then arrived at the Mertz Glacier Tongue on Feb. 1, 1982, and left there on Feb. 5, 1982. By Feb. 7, 1982, they were at the Antarctic Circle again, arriving at Dumont d'Urville Station on Feb. 8, 1982. They left there on Feb. 22, 1982, leaving Antarctic waters on Feb. 26, 1982. They were back in Sydney on March 15, 1982. Others on the crew were Jeni Bassett and Paul Ensor, both marine biologists; Dot Smith, from Lewis's previous expedition. All mentioned so far had had prior Antarctic experience. Newcomers to the ice were Don Richards, first mate and radio operator; Garry Satherley, mechanic and handyman, and his wife Barbara Muhvich; Malcolm Hamilton, cameraman; and Margaret Hennerbein. It was a 4,500-mile voyage lasting 3 months. They burned their garbage as they went so they would not pollute the Antarctic.

**Mount Dickason.** 74°24′S, 163°58′E. 2,030 m. At the head of Boomerang Glacier in the Deep Freeze Range of Victoria Land. Mapped by Campbell's Northern Party in 1910–13, and named for Harry Dickason.

**Dickason, Harry.** Able seaman, RN. A member of Campbell's Northern Party, during Scott's 1910–13 expedition.

**Dickens Rocks.** 65°19′S, 65°23′W. Two rocks off the north end of the Pitt Islands, in the Biscoe Islands. Named by the UK in 1959 for Charles Dickens, the British novelist.

**Dickenson, Thomas.** Carpenter's mate on the Wilkes Expedition 1838–42. Joined in the USA. Served the cruise.

**Mount Dickerson.** 84°20′S, 167°09′E. 4,120 m. 4 miles east of Mount Kirkpatrick, in the Queen Alexandra Range. Named for Lt. Cdr. Richard G. Dickerson, USN, VX-6 commander in 1964.

**Dickey, H.** Crewman on the *Bear of Oakland*, 1933–34.

**Dickey, W. Mills.** Also known as Willie M. Dickey. Captain, USN. Commander of the US Naval Support Force, Antarctica, 1957. Replaced by Eugene Maher on Nov. 28, 1957.

**Dickey Glacier.** 81°33′S, 161°07′E. 12 miles long. Flows along the east side of

the Surveyors Range into Beaumont Bay on the Ross Ice Shelf. Named for W. Mills Dickey.

**Dickey Peak.** 78°20′S, 84°26′W. In the NW part of the Flowers Hills, in the Sentinel Range. Named for Clifford R. Dickey, Jr., electronics technician at South Pole Station, 1957.

**Dickinson Rocks.** 77°33′S, 147°55′W. Isolated. Near the north end of Hershey Ridge. 9 miles NW of Linwood Peak, in the Ford Ranges of Marie Byrd Land. Named for David N. Dickinson, USN, construction mechanic at Brockton Station in 1965–66 and 1966–67.

**Dickson Icefalls.** 76°S, 133°25′W. Between Mount Moulton and Mount Bursey in the Flood Range of Marie Byrd Land. Named for Donald T. Dickson, glaciologist with the Byrd Station Traverse of 1962–63.

**Dickson Pillar.** 71°55′S, 171°09′E. A rock in water just south of Possession Island, in the Possession Islands. Named for Paul B. Dickson, USN, VX-6 photographer on the flight of Jan. 18, 1958, when this rock was discovered.

**Mount Dido.** 77°30′S, 160°56′E. 2,070 m. Between Mount Electra and Mount Boreas in the Olympus Range of Victoria Land. Named by the New Zealanders in 1958–59 for the Greek mythological figure.

**Dieglman Island.** 66°S, 100°46′E. 4 miles long. Mostly ice-covered. On the NW side of the Edisto Channel, in the Highjump Archipelago. In 1952 the USA called it Dieglman Islets, for E.D. Dieglman, air crewman on Operation Highjump, 1946–47. Redefined by the USSR in 1956–57 as one island with several rock outcrops, and renamed accordingly by the USA.

**Diego Ramírez Station.** 65°30′S, 68°45′W. Chilean scientific base, off the west coast of Graham Land.

**Mount Dietz.** 86°16′S, 153°10′W. 2,250 m. Just north of the confluence of the Souchez and Bartlett Glaciers. Marks the southern limit of the Hays Mountains in the Queen Maud Mountains. Named for Lt. D.L. Dietz, USN, pilot in Antarctica, 1964 and 1965.

**Dietz Bluff.** 72°02'S, 62°08'W. On the east coast of Palmer Land.

**Dike Cirque.** 83°14'S, 157°57'E. A semi-circular glacial cirque. 1 mile wide. In the Miller Range. Carved into Macdonald Bluffs, at the SE base of Kreiling Mesa. Named by the Ohio State University Geological Party of 1967–68 for the several black dikes cutting the cliffs surrounding the cirque.

**Dilemma Glacier.** 78°46'S, 161°25'E. Flows from the Worcester Range into the west side of the Skelton Glacier, to the north of Ant Hill. Named by the NZ party of the BCTAE in 1957 for the dilemmas faced by them when descending the glacier.

**Dillon, William.** Ordinary seaman on the Wilkes Expedition 1838–42. Joined at Sydney. Run at Oahu.

**Dillon Peak.** 73°17'S, 62°40'W. In the Dana Mountains. Surmounts the north side of the terminus of Haines Glacier in Palmer Land. Named for Raymond D. Dillon, biologist at McMurdo Station in 1966–67 and at Palmer Station in 1967–68.

**Dilten Nunatak.** 72°23'S, 3°47'W. Isolated. 1½ miles WNW of Dalten Nunatak. 8 miles NW of Borg Mountain in Queen Maud Land. Named by the Norwegians.

**Dimaryp Peak.** 63°26'S, 57°02'W. 500 m. The NE peak of Mount Carrel. 1 mile south of the head of Hope Bay, Trinity Peninsula. Named by the FIDS for its similarity to the Pyramid (Pyramid—Dimaryp), almost a mile away.

**Dingle Dome.** 67°03'S, 48°54'E. 400 m. An ice-covered dome. Surmounts the north end of Sakellari Peninsula, in the area of Casey Bay, Enderby Land. Discovered in 1956 during ANARE flights. Named by the Australians for Robert Dingle, officer-in-charge at Davis Station in 1957.

**Dingle Lake.** 68°34'S, 78°04'E. Also called Remnant Lake. A saltwater lake. Just west of Stinear Lake, on the Breidnes Peninsula, of the Vestfold Hills. Photographed by the LCE 1936–37. Named by the Australians for Robert Dingle (*see* **Dingle Dome**).

**Dingo Pond.** Just to the east of Mount Fleming, in southern Victoria Land.

**Dingsør, Capt.** Norwegian whale fishery inspector on the *Kosmos,* 1930–31.

**Dingsør Dome.** 68°S, 67°41'E. Also spelled Dingzor Dome. An ice-covered mountain. 11 miles south of Point Williams in Mac. Robertson Land. Discovered in Feb. 1931 by the BANZARE, and named by Mawson for Capt. Dingsør, whaling inspector on the *Kosmos,* which had supplied coal to Mawson's ship, the *Discovery,* on Dec. 29, 1930.

**¹Dinsman, Samuel.** Seaman on the Wilkes Expedition 1838–42. Joined in the USA. Returned in the *Relief* in 1839.

**²Dinsman, Samuel.** Corporal of the marines during the Wilkes Expedition 1838–42. Joined in the USA. Served the cruise. Related to the above in some way.

**Dinsmoor Glacier.** 64°22'S, 59°59'W. Flows from the south edge of the Detroit Plateau of Graham Land, into Edgeworth Glacier to the NE of Mount Elliott. Named by the UK for Charles Dinsmoor, of Warren, Pa., pioneer of tracked vehicles.

**Dint Island.** 69°17'S, 71°49'W. 1½ miles long. 2 miles off the west side of Alexander Island, in Lazarev Bay. Named by the UK because of the dint made on the south side of the island by a distinctive cirque.

**Dion Islands.** 67°52'S, 68°43'W. Also called De Dion Islets, Dion Islets. Group of small islands and rocks, including Embassy Island, Emperor Island, Consul Reef, Envoy Rock, and the Courtier Islands. In the north part of Marguerite Bay, 6 miles SW of Cape Alexandra, Adelaide Island. The only emperor penguin colony on the west side of the Antarctic Peninsula, is here. Discovered by Charcot in 1908–10, and named by him for the Marquis de Dion, automobile manufacturer who donated three motor sledges and equipment to the expedition.

**Dione Nunataks.** 71°56′S, 69°06′W. At the head of Saturn Glacier. 9 miles west of Deimos Ridge, in the SE part of Alexander Island. Named by the UK for one of the satellites of the planet Saturn.

**Diplock Glacier.** 64°03′S, 58°50′W. 10 miles long. Flows from the Detroit Plateau of Graham Land, into the Prince Gustav Channel, 5 miles south of Alectoria Island. Named by the UK for Bramah J. Diplock, pioneer in tracked vehicles.

**Direction Island** *see* **Bearing Island**

**Directions.** At the South Pole any direction you take is north. To make it simpler for those there, they use a system whereby north = Greenwich, and south is behind you as you look toward Greenwich.

**Director Nunatak.** 66°49′S, 65°06′W. Between the heads of the Balch and Breitfuss Glaciers, in Graham Land. Named by the UK in 1958 because this nunatak was used as a landmark by a FIDS sledging party from Base W on Détaille Island in 1957 when traveling on the Avery Plateau.

**¹Cape Disappointment.** 60°42′S, 45°05′W. On the west side of Powell Island in the South Orkneys. Palmer and Powell in Dec. 1821 applied the name to the south end of the island, disappointed at that stage in having to return to their South Shetland bases. Modern explorers have used the term for the western cape.

**²Cape Disappointment.** 65°33′S, 61°43′W. Also called Besvikelsens Kap. Between Exasperation Inlet and Scar Inlet, on the east coast of Graham Land. Discovered in 1902 by Nordenskjöld's 1901–4 expedition, and named by him for the difficult crevasses he found when approaching the cape.

**Disappointment Bay** *see* **Fisher Bay**

**Disasters.** These are only some of the disasters recorded in Antarctica. (For a related entry, *see* **Deaths.**) Sept. 4, 1819: The *San Telmo* abandoned. Dec. 7, 1820: The wreck of the *Clothier.* End of Dec. 1820: The wreck of the *Lord Melville.* Dec. 25, 1820: The wreck of *Lady Trowbridge.* Dec. 25, 1820: The wreck of the *Hannah.* Dec. 30, 1820: The wreck of the *Ann.* Jan. 6, 1821: The wreck of the *Cora.* March 7, 1821: The wreck of the *Venus.* April 8, 1821: *Sarah* lost at sea. Jan. 17, 1823: Death of the crew of the *Jenny.* 1833: The *Rose* crushed between two icebergs at 60°S. March 24, 1839: The *Sabrina* disappeared in a gale. Jan. 24, 1840: The *Peacock* hit by icebergs and badly damaged. Feb. 1845: The wreck of the *Richard Henry* in the South Shetlands. June 24, 1899: A candle left burning in a bunk almost destroyed Borchgrevink's hut. Feb. 12, 1903: The sinking of the *Antarctic.* 1908–9: *The Ørnen* went aground. 1910–13: The whole Scott expedition was a disaster in a way. Feb. 4, 1913: The wreck of the *Tioga.* 1914–17: Shackleton's British Imperial Transantarctic Expedition was a disaster in every way. 1916: The wreck of the *Gouvernøren I.* Jan. 23, 1928: The *Scapa* capsized off Laurie Island, killing 15 out of 17 crew. March 14, 1929: Byrd's Fokker plane, the *Virginia,* destroyed in the Rockefeller Mountains. March 13, 1934: Crash of the *Blue Blade.* Sept. 28, 1934: Crash of the *Pep Boy's Snowman!* Dec. 30, 1946: A US Martin Mariner crashed at 71°23′S, 98°45′W. 3 killed. Jan. 19, 1947: Helicopter lost in the sea. No deaths. Survivors included George Dufek. Jan. 22, 1947: Helicopter crashed into the sea. No deaths. Nov. 1948: Base D burned by fire. 2 deaths. Jan. 13, 1948: Operation Windmill's Bell helicopter crashed in a whiteout in the Bunger Hills. Jan. 24, 1952: 3:20 a.m. The Port-Martin fire. Jan. 22, 1954: Helicopter crash at Kainan Bay. John P. Moore killed. Dec. 22,

**1955:** A US Navy Otter plane crashed on take-off. Cdr. George R. Olliver sustained a broken leg. **Feb. 3, 1956:** A US Navy Otter crashed into the Edward VII Peninsula. No one hurt. **Feb. 10, 1956:** A third Otter wrecked, in a fall to the ice during unloading, at Little America V. **March, 1956:** Blizzard destroyed much of the stores of the BCTAE. **Oct. 18, 1956:** P2V-2N Neptune crashed on landing at McMurdo. 3 died. 4 injured. **Oct. 20, 1956:** A Globemaster crashed on landing at McMurdo. **Dec. 31, 1956:** A *Staten Island* helicopter crashed on the deck of the ship. **Jan. 19, 1957:** A *Glacier* helicopter crashed into the Ross Sea. **1957:** Charles E. Reed had a leg badly smashed by a falling antenna pole at McMurdo. **July 12, 1957:** A helicopter crash killed Nelson Cole. **Aug. 31, 1957:** 80 mph winds blew an Otter away from Little America V. **Dec. 1, 1957:** An *Atka* helicopter crashed on the flight deck. No deaths. **Dec. 3, 1957:** A second *Atka* helicopter crashed into the Ross Sea. No deaths. **Oct. 16, 1958:** A Globemaster crashed into a hill near Cape Roget. 6 dead. **Oct. 22, 1958:** An Otter literally cracked up while taxiing on the Ross Ice Shelf. **1958:** An Otter crashed while taking off from Marble Point. **Feb. 12, 1959:** A *Glacier* helicopter crashed on a test flight after an engine change. **Sept. 15, 1959:** A Dakota crashed on landing at Hallett Station. **Dec. 24, 1959:** A Dakota crashed during a whiteout at Byrd Station. **Jan. 1960:** The *City of Auckland,* a plane, crashed in the Queen Alexandra Range. **Aug. 3, 1960:** Fire at Mirnyy Station. 3 killed. **Oct. 31, 1960:** A US Navy Constellation crashed near McMurdo runway. No deaths. **Feb. 1, 1961:** 2 buildings at McMurdo went up in fire. Damage: $225,000. **Feb. 15, 1961:** Helicopter exploded over the Eights Coast. No injuries. **Nov. 9, 1961:** A Neptune crashed at Wilkes Station. 5 killed. **Nov. 12, 1961:** A Dakota crashed in the Sentinel Mountains. The plane was a total wreck. **Nov. 22, 1962:** Two helicopters crashed, one in the Sentinel Range and one in the Wright Valley.

**Nov. 25, 1962:** A helicopter crashed at Davis Glacier. **Dec. 23, 1962:** A helicopter crashed on take-off at McMurdo. **Nov. 28, 1963:** A helicopter crashed in whiteout outside McMurdo Station. **March 6, 1964:** Original science building at Hallett Station destroyed along with the aurora tower. **Oct. 22, 1964:** LC-47H aircraft crashed. **Nov. 8, 1964:** A helicopter crashed in the Admiralty Mountains. No one injured. **Dec. 5, 1964:** A helicopter crashed. **Jan. 12, 1965:** A helicopter crashed at Camp Ohio in the Horlick Mountains. **Oct. 6, 1965:** An LC-47H crashed on take-off outside Williams Field. **Dec. 5, 1965:** An LC-47H crashed on landing in the Horlick Mountains. **Feb. 2, 1966:** An LC-47J crashed on landing on the Ross Ice Shelf. All 6 men killed. **Nov. 5, 1966:** A helicopter crashed in a whiteout in Marie Byrd Land. **Jan. 22, 1967:** A helicopter landed on its nose during a near whiteout at 71°21′30″S, 169°03′48″E. **Aug. 24, 1967:** New lavatory complex at Williams Field destroyed. **Dec. 4/5, 1967:** Deception Island erupts (*see* **Volcanoes, Deception Island**), and Presidente Pedro Aguirre Cerda Station destroyed. **Jan. 12, 1968:** An LC-117D aircraft fell during loading at McMurdo and was wrecked. **March 19, 1968:** Fire at Plateau Station destroyed the garage containing 3 generators, a Traxcavator, and other equipment. **Aug. 11, 1968:** Snow-melting building at Amundsen-Scott South Pole Station destroyed by fire. **Dec. 18, 1968:** Flash fire at Palmer Station due to a faulty heater spilling oil. A Jamesway hut was destroyed, and certain equipment. **Nov. 19, 1969:** A helicopter crashed at 77°34′S, 162°54′E. 2 killed. **Oct. 8, 1970:** American C-121 airplane veered off the runway at McMurdo, and was wrecked. **Jan. 9, 1971:** An HH-52 helicopter crashed into Mount Erebus while en route to Cape Bird. No deaths. **Feb. 15, 1971:** The *City of Christchurch,* a Hercules LC-130 aircraft, burned on take-off. The first Herc to be lost in Antarctica. **Dec. 4, 1971:** A ski-equipped LC-130 Hercules aircraft called Juliet Delta 321, owned by the National Science Foundation, damaged during a JATO accident at 68°20'S, 137°20'E (this spot was called D-59) in East Antarctica. No one hurt. 16 years later, it was finally (after 3 years of effort) dug out of 30 feet of snow and ice, and fixed up. It had been perfectly preserved. During the recovery another LC-130 crashed, and burned, killing 2 navy crewmen. On Jan. 10, 1988, at 10:56 p.m., Juliet Delta 321 landed again at Williams Field, piloted by Cdr. Jack Rector. The recovery cost was less than one third of the $35 million it would have cost for a new plane (not taking into account the two deaths, of course). Juliet 321 arrived back in the USA on July 2, 1989. **Jan. 28, 1973:** An LC-130 #917 crashed at the South Pole. Although the plane was wrecked, no one was hurt. **July 1974:** McMurdo Station radio shack destroyed and other buildings damaged during 125 mph winds. **Jan. 15, 1975:** 2 US Hercules aircraft damaged in separate incidents. **1978–79:** At Molodezhnaya Station a USSR transport plane crashed during take-off, when an engine failed. It killed the pilot, co-pilot, and a passenger. 11 others were injured. **Jan. 7, 1979:** A UH-1N helicopter crashed into the Gawn Ice Piedmont. No injuries. **Nov. 28, 1979:** An Air New Zealand DC-10 crashed into the side of Mount Erebus, killing 257, all aboard, mostly tourists on this "champagne flight." **Dec. 18, 1981:** The sinking of the *Gotland II.* **1982:** Fire at McMurdo Station. $2 million worth of damage to the transportation building (which was destroyed) and vehicles. **1982:** A Vostok Station fire destroyed the generator facility; the 20 men were forced to winter-over for 8 months and survived by using diesel fuel candles and an ice-drill generator for power. The severe cold caused much damage to the station. The men carried on with their work, and were rescued in 1983. **1982:** The British lost two Twin Otter aircraft in a storm, eliminating much of the planned BAS summer research program. **1984:** Almirante Brown Station partially

destroyed by fire. **Oct. 28, 1985:** An explosion at Davis Station, inside a water tank, killed sprayer Stephen Bunning the following day. **Jan. 12, 1986:** The sinking of the *Southern Quest.* **Feb. 1986:** A USSR IL-14 aircraft, a small cargo plane, crashed on the Philippi Glacier, killing 6, while attempting an emergency landing in a whiteout. **1986:** Druzhnaya Station destroyed by an ice cave-in. **Jan. 28, 1989:** The *Bahía Paraíso* ran aground in the Bismarck Strait, and 3 days later capsized, spilling oil in huge quantities (*see also* **Pollution**).

**Disbrow, John.** Private on the Wilkes Expedition 1838–42. Joined in the USA. Served the cruise.

**Disch Promontory.** 83°34'S, 162°52'E. Ice-covered. 6 miles long. Extends from the east side of the Prince Andrew Plateau, in the Queen Elizabeth Range. Named for Carl R. Disch, ionosphere physicist (*see* **Deaths, 1965**).

**The *Discovery*.** One of the great ships of Antarctic history. Designed by W.E. Smith and built specifically for the Antarctic, in Dundee, at a cost of £34,050. An oak 3-master of 700 tons, with a 483-ton capacity, 177 feet long, and with a 33-foot beam. It had an elm keel, and 400 hp engines. It was the 6th ship of that name, being named specifically for Sir George Nares' *Discovery* of 1876. It was Scott's vessel for the Royal Society Expedition of 1901–4, and had a crew of 43. Scott deliberately froze it in the ice for two years, in McMurdo Sound, 1902–4. After that expedition it was bought by the Hudson Bay Company and used in the Arctic fur trade. In 1923 the Discovery Committee (q.v.) bought it and refitted it. It was involved in the Discovery Investigations from 1925–27, with J.R. Stenhouse as captain, Chaplin as the lieutenant-commander, and Stanley Kemp as expedition leader. With the commissioning of the *Discovery II* in 1929, the older ship became known in some quarters as the *Discovery I.* Mawson used it as his vessel during the BANZARE 1929–31. It was commanded from 1929 to

1930 by Capt. John King Davis, and from 1930–31 by Capt. K.N. MacKenzie.

**Cape Discovery** *see* **Cape Découverte**

**Mount Discovery.** 78°23'S, 165°E. 2,680 m. An isolated, extinct volcano east of Koettlitz Glacier, it overlooks the NW portion of the Ross Ice Shelf, near McMurdo Sound, in southern Victoria Land. Discovered in Feb. 1902 by Scott, and named by him for his ship.

**Discovery Bay.** 62°29'S, 59°41'W. Also called Chile Bay. 3 miles long. 2 miles wide. Indents the north side of Greenwich Island, in the South Shetlands. It is a control area, with summer studies going on here every year. SSSI #26 is here, occupying 2 small areas of the bay, and is of interest for its benthic research, which has been conducted here since 1967. Capitán Arturo Prat Station is also here. Charted and named by the personnel on the *Discovery II* in 1935.

**Discovery Bluff.** 77°02'S, 162°40'E. Juts out into the southern part of Granite Harbor, between Botany Bay and Avalanche Bay, in Victoria Land. Discovered by Scott's 1901–4 expedition, and named Rendezvous Bay by them. Scott's 1910–13 expedition renamed it for the *Discovery.*

**Discovery Committee.** A committee appointed by the British government in 1923 to conduct oceanographic research in Antarctica, with a view to perpetuating and regulating the whaling industry. E.R. Darnley was chairman, 1923–33. A marine biological lab was finished at Grytviken, South Georgia (54°S), in Jan. 1925, and work began here under Neil Mackintosh, and continued each summer until 1931. The next and most important phase, the Discovery Investigations themselves, run by the Falkland Islands Dependencies Administration, was begun on Scott's old ship, the *Discovery* (hence the name of the Committee and the Investigations), in the 1925–27 period. In 1926 the *William Scoresby* was commissioned as the second

Investigations vessel, and in 1927–38 did 6 Antarctic cruises, calling regularly at Deception Island. The *Discovery II* was commissioned in 1929, also for the Investigations, and worked until 1939. The war halted the Discovery Investigations, and in March 1949 the National Institute of Oceanography took over the project. Many reports were drawn up, which are invaluable today. *See also* **J.W.S. Marr,** who was marine biologist on the Investigations, and one of the most prominent figures on the project.

**Discovery Expedition** *see* **Royal Society Expedition**

**Discovery Hut** *see* **Scott's Huts**

**Discovery Inlet.** 78°30'S, 170°W. Intensely cold inlet near the Bay of Whales. It is gone now, but it was used by early navigators like Scott and Byrd. Larsen moored here over the 1923–24 summer.

**Discovery Investigations** *see* **Discovery Committee**

**Discovery Island** *see* **Guépratte Island**

**Discovery Ridge.** 84°44'S, 114°06'W. Projects NW from Buckeye Table, in the Ohio Range. 2 miles NW of Mount Glossopteris. Named by William E. Long, geologist here in 1960–61 and 1961–62, who discovered the first tillite and the first Devonian branchiopods here.

**Discovery Sound.** 64°31'S, 63°01'W. A marine channel, ½ mile wide, between Guépratte Island and the Briggs Peninsula, on the NE side of Anvers Island. Discovered by Dallmann in 1873–74, and charted by Charcot in 1903–5. Named by the personnel on the *Discovery* in 1927.

**The *Discovery II*.** Built by Messrs. Ferguson of Port Glasgow, Scotland, it was an all-steel motor vessel, a Royal Research ship built specifically for oceanographic work. Commissioned in 1929 to replace the *Discovery* as one of the principal ships used in the Discovery Investigations. Its first captain was Cdr. W.M.

Carey, from 1929–33. During his captaincy, the 1929–31 cruise was led by Stanley Kemp, and the 1931–33 cruise was led by D.D. John. In 1932 the ship circumnavigated Antarctica in the winter, the first vessel ever to do that. The captain in the 1933–35 period was A.L. Nelson, and that cruise was led by Neil Mackintosh. On the 1935–37 cruise led by George Deacon, the captain was Lt. L.C. Hill. Richard Walker was first officer of the ship from 1933–37. On Jan. 19, 1936, the ship picked up Ellsworth and Hollick-Kenyon after their aerial transantarctic crossing in the *Polar Star*. Neil Mackintosh led the first part of the 1937–39 cruise, and was succeeded by Henry Herdman. Lt. L.C. Hill was captain again, for that cruise, and in the summer of 1937–38 the ship circumnavigated Antarctica once again. The War halted the Discovery Investigations in 1939. Henry Herdman led the last expedition of the *Discovery II*, in 1950–51, and Capt. J.F. Blackburn commanded the ship.

**Disease.** The big problem in the old, previtamin days was scurvy (q.v.), but that has been eradicated now. Other forms of disease have been and always will be reasonably prevalent in Antarctica. For example, Amundsen turned gray during the wintering-over of the *Belgica* in 1898. Some scientists and explorers come back from Antarctica with their skin dry, cracked, or bleeding. Dehydration is a danger—the cold makes one forget to drink. The winter-over syndrome is depression, hostility, and lack of concentration, while insomnia (the "big eye") affects most people during the summer months when daylight is perpetual. In early 1979 there was a cholera outbreak among skuas at Palmer Station. For tourists going to Antarctica a gamma globulin inoculation, or its equivalent in natural remedies, is recommended. One does not catch cold easily in Antarctica. One's white corpuscles drop from 5,000 per c.c. to 2,500 in about 9 months; upon return to "civiliza-

tion" one is then more susceptible to diseases, colds, etc.

**Dismal Buttress.** 85°27′S, 178°43′W. An ice-free rock bluff overlooking the west side of the head of Shackleton Glacier. 3 miles NW of Roberts Massif. Named by the Southern Party of the NZGSAE 1961–62 because their dog, Dismal, died here.

**Dismal Island.** 68°06′S, 68°50′W. 1 mile long. 60 m. high. Mostly ice-covered. The largest of the Faure Islands in Marguerite Bay, off the west coast of Graham Land. Named by the FIDS in 1949 for its appearance.

**Dismal Mountains.** 68°05′S, 55°25′E. A group of nunataks, 35 miles SW of Rayner Peak, on the border of Kemp Land and Enderby Land. Named by the Australians because of the frequent cloud cover here.

**Dismal Ridge.** 78°17′S, 162°48′E. A forked ridge, which leads north and east from the Mount Kempe–Mount Huggins saddle. The forks descend to Roaring Valley. Named by the New Zealanders in 1960–61 for the dismal conditions here.

**Dismond, John.** Seaman on the Wilkes Expedition 1838–42. Joined in the USA. Served the cruise.

**Disney, Solomon.** Sailmaker's mate on the Wilkes Expedition 1838–42. Joined in the USA. Served the cruise.

**Distinguished Visitors.** All the visitors to Antarctica are, of course, distinguished, because there have not been many. But in Antarctic circles, a DV, as they are called, is anyone of prominent standing in the "civilized" world, a statesman, politician, etc., anyone to whom extra courtesy would normally be extended. Here is a brief list of some interesting DVs to Antarctica over the years. There have been, of course, many more—ambassadors, congressmen, senators, secretaries, undersecretaries, even Isabel Perón, 3rd wife of the famous Argentinian president. **1928:** Sir Arnold Hodson, governor of the Falkland Islands. On the *Fleurus,* to the South Shetlands, Palmer Archipelago, etc. **1947–48:** President Gabriel González Videla of Chile, and Gen. Guillermo Barrios Tirado, minister of national defense, during the Presidential Antarctic Expedition. **Jan. 1957:** Prince Philip, on his own expedition to Graham Land, in the yacht *Britannia.* **Nov. 16, 1957:** Hon. John P. Saylor, congressman from Pennsylvania. The first congressman (from any country) to fly over the South Pole. **Nov. 27, 1957:** The following US senators: Hon. John J. Flynt (Ga.), Hon. Steven B. Derounian (NY), Hon. Samuel N. Friedel (Md.), Hon. Robert Hale (Me.), Hon. Oren Harris (Ark.), Hon. Torbert H. MacDonald (Mass.). **1961:** Hon. Francis A. Russell, US ambassador to New Zealand. **1966–67:** Wernher von Braun. **1967–68:** Brian Lochore, captain of the All-Blacks NZ rugby team. **Nov. 11–14, 1968:** W.H. Crook, Jr., aged 12, the youngest person in modern times to visit Antarctica. He was there with his father, the Hon. W.H. Crook, US ambassador to Australia. **1968 and 1970:** Max Conrad (q.v.), the round-the-world aviator. **Jan. 5–10, 1969:** Sir Arthur Porritt, governor-general of New Zealand. **Jan. 23–28, 1969:** Peter Snell, NZ Olympic gold medallist. **1969:** T.J. Watson, Jr., head of IBM. **Nov. 24, 1969:** Dr. Laurence M. Gould (q.v.). **Jan. 7–14, 1970:** Donald K. Slayton and Col. David R. Scott, astronauts. **Nov. 1970:** Pierre Charpentier, French ambassador and a signer of the Antarctic Treaty 11 years before. **Dec. 1970–Jan. 1971:** Charles Neider, writer/historian. **Dec. 1971:** Senator Allan J. Ellender of Louisiana, president pro tem of the US Senate. **Jan. 1972:** Sen. Barry Goldwater of Arizona, and Sen. Barry Goldwater, Jr., of California. **Jan. 1972:** William F. Buckley, Jr. **1982:** Sir Edmund Hillary (q.v.) and Robert Muldoon, prime minister of New Zealand.

**Mount Ditte.** 67°43′S, 68°37′W. Also called Mount A. Ditte. 1,400 m. Surmounts Cape Alexandra at the SE end of Adelaide Island. Discovered by Charcot in 1908–10, and named by him for Alfred Ditte, the chemist.

**Diversion Hills.** 73°09′S, 163°30′E. On the east side of Pain Mesa in Victoria Land. Named by the Southern Party of the NZGSAE 1966–67 because the party made a diversion eastward from their route at this point in order to visit Navigator Nunatak.

**The Divide.** 60°44′S, 45°10′W. A narrows between Matthews Island and the SE end of Coronation Island in the South Orkneys. Named by personnel on the *Discovery II* in 1933.

**Divide Peaks.** 60°43′S, 45°12′W. Also called Divide Ridge. A series of ice-topped peaks, the highest 640 m. On the SE end of Coronation Island in the South Orkneys. They extend 2 miles. Surveyed in 1948–49 by the FIDS, and named by them for The Divide, nearby.

**Divide Ridge** *see* **Divide Peaks**

**Divin, John W.** Ordinary seaman on the Wilkes Expedition 1838–42. Joined at Rio. Run at Sydney.

**Mount Dixey.** 70°10′S, 68°04′W. 1,250 m. Next to Mount Flower, at the south side of Riley Glacier. 3 miles NE of Carse Point, at the northern end of the George VI Sound, on the west coast of Palmer Land. Surveyed in 1936 by the BGLE and named in 1954 by members of that expedition, for Neville Dixey, chairman of Lloyd's in 1934, and a supporter of the BGLE 1934–37.

**Dixson Island.** 68°08′S, 146°43′E. Ice-covered. 10 miles long. 5 miles wide. At the west side of the mouth of Ninnis Glacier. Discovered by the AAE 1911–14, and named by Mawson for Sir Hugh Dixson of Sydney, a patron.

**Djupedalen Valley.** 71°58′S, 7°06′E. Glacier-filled. Separates the Mühlig-Hofmann Mountains and the Filchner Mountains in Queen Maud Land. Name means "the deep valley" in Norwegian.

**Djupedalshausane Peaks.** 72°05′S, 6°59′E. Between the head of Lunde Glacier and Djupedalen Valley in the Mühlig-

Hofmann Mountains of Queen Maud Land. Name means "the deep valley peaks" in Norwegian.

**Djupedalsleitet Saddle.** 72°05'S, 7°22' E. An ice saddle between the head of Djupedalen Valley and Snuggerud Glacier, just south of the Filchner Mountains in Queen Maud Land.

**Djupvik Point.** 69°43'S, 38°02'E. Marks the east limit of Djupvika, on the SW shore of Lützow-Holm Bay. Photographed by the LCE 1936–37. Named Djupvikodden (the deep bay point) by the Norwegians, in association with nearby Djupvika.

**Djupvika.** 69°44'S, 37°54'E. A bay between Botnneset and Djupvikneset Peninsula in the SW part of Lützow-Holm Bay. Photographed by the LCE 1936–37. Name means "the deep bay" in Norwegian.

**Djupvikneset Peninsula.** 69°47'S, 38°06'E. Ice-covered. Between Djupvika and Havsbotn on the SW shore of Lützow-Holm Bay. Photographed by the LCE 1936–37, and named Djupvikneset (the deep bay ness) by the Norwegians, in association with nearby Djupvika.

**Djupvikodden** *see* **Djupvik Point**

**Dlinnoye Lake.** 70°44'S, 11°39'E. ½ mile long. Just NW of Tsentral'naya Hill, in the Schirmacher Hills of Queen Maud Land. Named by the USSR in 1961 as Ozero Dlinnoye (long lake).

**Dobbratz Glacier.** 79°24'S, 85°05'W. Flows from the south part of the White Escarpment, between the Watlack Hills and the Weber Peaks, into Splettstoesser Glacier, in the Heritage Range. Named by the University of Minnesota Geological Party 1963–64 for Major Joseph Dobbratz, US Marine pilot who supported the party.

**Mount Doble** *see* **Noire Rock**

**Dobleman, Christian.** Master-at-arms on the Wilkes Expedition 1838–42. Joined in the USA. Served the cruise.

**Dobrowolski, Antoine B.** 1872–1954. Polish assistant meteorologist on the *Belgica* expedition 1897–99.

**Dobrowolski Island.** 64°36'S, 62°55' W. A small island close to the east coast of Anvers Island. 3 miles SW of Ryswyck Point. Named Astrolabe Islet in 1927 by personnel on the *Discovery*. The UK renamed it in 1958 for Antoine B. Dobrowolski.

**Dobrowolski Station.** 66°16'S, 100°45' E. In the Bunger Hills. It was formerly Oazis Station, under which name it was built as an IGY scientific base by the USSR in 1957. Transferred from USSR to Poland in 1958 and renamed for Antoine Dobrowolski. Closed in 1959.

**Mount Dobrynin.** 71°42'S, 11°46'E. 1,970 m. 1 mile ESE of Eidsgavlen Cliff on the east side of the Humboldt Mountains in Queen Maud Land. Discovered by Ritscher in 1938–39. Named by the USSR in 1966 for geographer B.F. Dobrynin.

**Dobson, M.W.** Seaman on the *Eleanor Bolling* during the second half of Byrd's 1928–30 expedition.

**Dobson Dome.** 64°02'S, 57°55'W. A snow-covered, dome-shaped mountain. 950 m. Between Röhss Bay and Croft Bay in the northern part of James Ross Island. Surveyed by the FIDS over the 1958–61 period. Named by the UK for Alban T.A. Dobson (1885–1962), secretary of the International Whaling Commission, 1949–59.

**Mount Dockery.** 71°12'S, 164°34'E. 1,095 m. 3 miles west of Mount Matthias in the west part of the Everett Range in the Concord Mountains. Named for Lt. Olan L. Dockery, VX-6 photographer out of McMurdo Station in 1962–63 and 1963–64.

**Doctor Rusch Glacier** *see* **Reusch Glacier**

**Dodd Island.** 69°42'S, 75°38'E. A small island in the SE part of the Publications Ice Shelf. 10 miles south of the Søstrene Islands. Photographed aerially by the LCE 1936–37. Named by the Australians for D.M. Dodd, weather observer at Davis Station in 1963.

**Dodd Nunatak.** 71°50'S, 160°24'E. 2½ miles west of Mount Cox in the NW part of the Emlen Peaks in the Usarp Mountains. Named for Walter H. Dodd, of the National Science Foundation's Public Information Office, who was at McMurdo Station in 1966–67 and 1967–68.

**Mount Dodge.** 84°52′S, 172°22′W. 1,760 m. Mostly ice-free. Just north of the Prince Olav Mountains, at the confluence of the Holzrichter and Gough Glaciers. Discovered by Albert Crary in 1957–58, and named by him for Prof. Carroll W. Dodge, lichen analyst for Byrd's 1933–35 expedition.

**Dodge Rocks** *see* **Afuera Islands**

**Dodman Island.** 65°58′S, 65°46′W. 3½ miles long. 4 miles SE of Rabot Island. 10 miles west of Ferin Head, off the west coast of Graham Land. Charted and named by the BGLE 1934–37.

**Dodson, Robert H.T.** Known as Harry. Assistant geologist/surveyor/trailman on the RARE 1947–48.

**Dodson Island** *see* **Dodson Peninsula**

**Dodson Peninsula.** 75°32′S, 64°12′W. Ice-covered. 40 miles long. Juts out into the Ronne Ice Shelf, at the west end of that shelf, south of Hansen Inlet, at the east side of the base of Palmer Land, in Ellsworth Land. At first thought to be an island by Ronne in 1947, he named it Harry Dodson Island, for Robert H.T. Dodson. This name later became Dodson Island, and then was redefined.

**Dodson Rocks.** 69°55′S, 68°25′E. Two small, dark, rock exposures on the south side of Single Island, on the west side of the Amery Ice Shelf. Discovered aerially by the ANARE in 1969. Named by the Australians for R. Dodson, senior geologist with the ANARE Prince Charles Mountains Survey of 1971.

**Doe Nunatak.** 72°21′S, 160°47′E. Isolated. 3 miles WNW of Doescher Nunatak. 15 miles NNW of Mount Weihaupt in the Outback Nunataks. Named for Wilfrid I. Doe, USN, hospital corpsman at McMurdo Station in 1967.

**Doescher Nunatak.** 72°23′S, 160°59′E. Isolated. 13 miles north of Mount Weihaupt in the Outback Nunataks. Named for Roger L. Doescher, glaciologist at McMurdo Station in 1967–68.

**Dog Island.** 65°49′S, 65°05′W. The most northerly of the Llanquihue Islands, off the west coast of Graham Land. Named by the UK in 1959 because it is opposite Cat Island.

**Doggers Bay.** 69°07′S, 69°09′E. Ice-filled. 16 miles long. 5 miles wide. On the west side of the Amery Ice Shelf, between Foley Promontory and Landon Promontory. Named by the Australians for the dog-sledge party which first visited it in Nov. 1962 during an ANARE party led by I. Landon-Smith.

**Doggers Nunataks.** 67°46′S, 54°51′E. Peaks 30 miles SW of Rayner Peak, on the SW side of Edward VIII Bay. Named by the Australians for the "doggers," the sledging party which surveyed these peaks in Dec. 1958 during the ANARE party led by G.A. Knuckey.

**Doggo Defile.** 68°44′S, 66°48′W. A narrow, steep-sided defile which cuts through the coastal mountains east of the Dee Ice Piedmont, on the west coast of the Antarctic Peninsula. Named descriptively by the UK, because you have to look for this defile.

**Dogs.** The first dog known to have ventured into Antarctica was Sydney, Wilkes' dog, which he picked up in Sydney, Australia, in Dec. 1839. There are pictures of an amused Sydney sitting on icebergs. Although there may have been others before and after Sydney, 60 years went by before the next recorded dog. Borchgrevink was the first explorer to use dogs in Antarctica, during his winter-over of 1899. Scott was the first major pioneer of dogs as Antarctic workers, even though he did not believe in them, did not know how to handle them, and was too humane to see them suffer. In 1902 he went into the unknown with 19 dogs. In 1903 a dog wintered-over with Bruce's shore party on Laurie Island, and

Charcot's dog, Sögen, died during the French expedition of 1903-5. Von Drygalski, during his 1901-3 expedition, took 40 Kamchatka dogs. During the Heroic Era (q.v.) there were two conflicting theories about the use of dogs in Antarctica. Scott and Shackleton, being British, tended to anthropomorphize the dogs. That is why dogs did not work for these two explorers, even though the men knew that in order to get to the South Pole, one must have dogs. But the dogs they did take on their expeditions were token. It was not unknown for the explorers to pull a sick dog on a sledge! Amundsen's theory, on the other hand, was that dogs are animals, and, as much as he loved many of them, some of them had to die if the South Pole were to be attained. Some would be shot at prearranged stages of the trek, thus providing a meal for the others. Dogs quite happily revert to cannibalism at moments of severe hunger. They do not reflect. During the race for the Pole in 1911-12, Scott took 20 male dogs and 3 bitches, not well-trained at all, and more as tokens than anything else. All the dogs died, and Scott suffered because of that. Scott and his party manhauled their sledges to the Pole, an incredible achievement, but they never made it back alive. Amundsen, on the other hand, took 52 dogs of the highest quality and experience, and 4 sledges. His trek went like a dream. Shackleton's British Imperial Transantarctic Expedition of 1914-17 saw the further use of dogs by the British. Because these dogs were inexperienced, many of them (dogs and men) died during the 1916-17 depot-laying venture from Ross Island, led by Mackintosh. On the other side of the continent, Shackleton set up "dogloos," as he called the dogs' quarters, on the ice after his ship had gone down. Tommy was the little black pup on the *Sir James Clark Ross,* during Carl Anton Larsen's 1923-24 whaling expedition into the Ross Sea. At the end of that decade, Igloo was Byrd's fox terrier. On his 1928-30 expedition, Byrd took 95 sledge dogs,

mostly Greenland huskies. 79 came from Labrador, donated by Frank W. Clark of the Clark Trading Co., and 16 came from the farm of Arthur T. Walden of Wonalancet. These latter were heavy draft dogs. The USAS 1939-41 took 160 dogs—West Base got 70 and East Base 90. 7 of them had been born in Antarctica, and many of them were veterans of Byrd's 1933-35 expedition. On the RARE 1947-48 Finn Ronne took a corgi, a whippet, and a sheepdog, as well as 43 huskies, about half of whom died of distemper en route to Antarctica. Ronne's Weddell Coast sledging party made canvas shoes for the dogs out on the trail when their paws were wearing thin. Dogs are still favored by some explorers. For related canine entries, *see* **Taro and Jiro** (a remarkable story), **Amundsen-Scott South Pole Station** (for the mascot of South Pole Station in 1957). The Antarctic Conservation Act of 1978 says, in Subpart 3, Article 670.43, part (b). Dogs. All dogs imported into Antarctica shall be inoculated against the following diseases: (1) distemper, (2) contagious canine hepatitis, (3) rabies, and (4) leptospirosis. Each dog shall be inoculated at least 2 months before importation, and a certificate of inoculation shall accompany each dog. No dog shall be allowed to run free in Antarctica.

**Dogs Leg Fjord.** 67°43'S, 66°52'W. An inlet, 6 miles long and 1½ miles wide. Just east of Ridge Island on the west coast of Graham Land. Discovered by the BGLE 1934-37, and named by them for its shape.

**Dohle Nunatak.** 71°17'S, 66°06'E. Has 2 small peaks and a connecting ridge. Between Mount Gleeson and Mount Gibson in the Prince Charles Mountains. Named by the Australians for C. Dohle, helicopter pilot with the ANARE Prince Charles Mountains Survey in 1971.

**Dokkene Coves.** 69°14'S, 39°38'E. Two coves just NW of Hamna Bay, on the west side of the Langhovde Hills, on the east shore of Lützow-Holm Bay. Photographed by the LCE 1936-37. Named

Dokkene (the docks) by the Norwegians.

**Dolan Peak.** 85°56'S, 133°15'W. 2,070 m. 2 miles WNW of Hendrickson Peak in the NW part of the Quartz Hills. Named for Theodore G. Dolan, glaciologist at Byrd Station in 1960.

**Mount Dolber.** 77°07'S, 145°31'W. 865 m. Snow-free summit. Between Mount Rea and Mount Cooper, in the Sarnoff Mountains of the Ford Ranges, in Marie Byrd Land. Named for Capt. Sumner R. Dolber, US Coast Guard, captain of the *Southwind*, 1967–68 and 1968–69.

**Mount Dolence.** 79°51'S, 83°13'W. Ice-free. Spired. 1,950 m. In the NW end of the Enterprise Hills, in the Heritage Range. Named by the University of Minnesota Ellsworth Mountains Party of 1962–63, for Jerry D. Dolence, geologist in the party.

**Dolevar, Joseph.** Seaman on the Wilkes Expedition 1838–42. Joined at Valparaiso. Served the cruise.

**Dolleman, Hendrik.** Machinist/tractor driver at East Base during the USAS 1939–41.

**Dolleman Island.** 70°37'S, 60°45'W. 13 miles long. A grounded island in the Larsen Ice Shelf, 8 miles east of Cape Boggs, and just south of Hearst Island. Discovered in 1940 by personnel from East Base during the USAS 1939–41. Named for Hendrik Dolleman.

**Dolleman Island Automatic Weather Station.** 70°36'S, 60°45'W. An American AWS on Dolleman Island in the Larsen Ice Shelf. Elevation approximately 1,200 feet. It began operating on Feb. 18, 1986.

**Dolphin Spur.** 84°12'S, 172°48'E. Ice-covered. Just east of Mount Patrick in the Commonwealth Range, descending north into the upper reaches of the Hood Glacier. Named by the New Zealanders in 1959–60 because from further down on the glacier it looks like a school of dolphins.

**Dolphins.** The mammalian dolphins are small whales. The fish dolphins are *Coryphaena hippuras*. Both are occasionally seen south of 60°S. Fossilized species have been discovered.

**Domashnyaya Bank.** 67°39'S, 45°50' E. A shoal, covered by 2 feet of water, near Molodezhnaya Station in Enderby Land. Just off shore, ½ mile SW of Cape Granat. Named by the USSR in 1961–62 as Banka Domashnyaya (domestic bank) for its closeness to the station.

**Domashnyaya Bay.** 67°40'S, 45°50'E. An indentation of Alasheyev Bight into Enderby Land at Molodezhnaya Station. Named by the USSR. The name means "domestic" and relates to its closeness to the station.

**The Dome** *see* **McLeod Hill**

**Dome C.** 74°39'S, 124°10'E. Not a feature exactly, more a location in East Antarctica, with an elevation of approximately 10,000 feet. A US summer camp was established here between Dec. 27, 1974, and Jan. 15, 1975, in order to collect information in anticipation of planned drilling at the site. There is an automatic weather station here now, an American AWS measuring katabatic winds, which began operating on Jan. 13, 1983.

**Dome Nunatak.** 77°01'S, 161°27'E. 990 m. Dome-shaped. Protrudes above the Mackay Glacier, 4 miles NW of Mount Suess, in Victoria Land. Charted and named by Scott's 1910–13 expedition.

**Domen Butte.** 72°43'S, 3°50'W. Snow-topped. Just SW of Høgskavlen Mountain, in the Borg Massif of Queen Maud Land. Named Domen (the dome) by the Norwegians.

**Dominion Range.** 85°22'S, 166°E. 30 miles long. At the top of the Beardmore Glacier, in the Transantarctic Mountains. Discovered by Shackleton in 1908–9, and named by him for the Dominion of New Zealand, a country helpful to Antarctic expeditions of all nationalities from the very beginning.

**Lake Don Juan** *see* **Don Juan Pond**

**Don Juan Pond.** 77°34'S, 161°10'E. Also called Lake Don Juan. A shallow, saline closed lake in the Wright Valley. Discovered by helicopter on Oct. 11, 1961. Shortly thereafter George H. Meyer and others came here several times to study it, and ingeniously named it for Lts. Donald Roe (the Don part—*see* **Mount Roe**) and John Hickey (the Juan part—*see* **Cape Hickey**) who helped the party. Antarcticite was discovered here.

**Mount Don Pedro Christophersen.** 85°31'S, 165°47'W. 3,765 m. Largely ice-covered. Surmounts the divide between the heads of the Axel Heiberg and Cooper Glaciers in the Queen Maud Mountains. Discovered by Amundsen on Nov. 19, 1911, and first named by him as Haakonshallen, after its resemblance to a Norwegian castle of that name. He later renamed it for one of his major patrons.

**Don Quixote Pond.** 77°32'S, 161°07'E. Unofficial American name for a pond in the Wright Valley. It consists of a layer of fresh water over a body of salt water, with an ice topping. It is 30,000 square meters in area, and is several feet deep.

**The *Don Samuel*.** Argentine whale catcher built in 1925. It took part in the Argentine Antarctic Expedition of 1946–47, being commanded by Capt. J.R. Pisani Reilly. It helped set up Melchior Station on Melchior Island, and cruised around the Antarctic Peninsula area. On Feb. 11, 1947, it visited the British Base E on Stonington Island, getting back to Melchior by Feb. 14, 1947. It was later owned by the Compañía Argentina de Pesca in Grytviken, South Georgia, and sank near South Georgia in 1951.

**Donald, C.W.** Doctor/naturalist on the *Active* during the Dundee Whaling Expedition of 1892–93.

**Donald Nunatak.** 65°05'S, 60°06'W. 1½ miles north of Gray Nunatak in the Seal Nunataks, off the east coast of the Antarctic Peninsula. Charted by Dr.

Nordenskjöld in 1902, and named by him for C.W. Donald.

**Donald Ridge.** 79°37'S, 83°10'W. Extends south from Mount Capley in the Pioneer Heights of the Heritage Range. Named for Donald L. Willson, meteorologist at Little America in 1958.

**Mount Donald Woodward** *see* **Mount Woodward**

**Donald Woodward Mountains** *see* **Mount Woodward**

**Mount Donaldson.** 84°37'S, 172°12'E. 3,930 m. 5 miles NNE of Flat Top, west of the head of Ludeman Glacier, between the Hughes Range and the Commonwealth Range. Discovered and named by Shackleton in 1908–9.

**Donaldson, Dr. Peter.** Botanist on David Lewis's *Solo* expedition of 1977–78.

**Isla Donati** *see* **Kappa Island**

**Donnally Glacier.** 81°37'S, 159°18'E. 12 miles long. Flows along the north side of Swithinbank Range and enters Starshot Glacier, in the Churchill Mountains. Named for Cdr. Edward W. Donnally, USN, officer-in-charge of US Naval Support personnel at McMurdo Station in 1962.

**Donnelly, C.A.** 2nd engineer on the *Aurora*, 1914–16.

**Donner Valley.** 77°37'S, 161°27'E. Mainly ice-free. NNE of Mount Thundergut, in the Asgard Range of Victoria Land. Named by NZ, possibly for the German word meaning "thunder," because of its closeness to Mount Thundergut.

**Donovan Islands.** 66°11'S, 110°24'E. Also called Chappel Islands. 8 islands, including Chappel Island, Glasgal Island, Grinnell Island, and Lilienthal Island. 5 miles NW of Clark Peninsula, in the east part of Vincennes Bay. Named by the Australians for J. Donovan, administrative officer of the Antarctic Division, Melbourne, and leader of a few relief expeditions to Macquarie and Heard Islands (not in the Antarctic).

**Doolette Bay.** 67°55'S, 147°E. At the junction of the western side of the Ninnis Glacier Tongue and the mainland. Discovered by the AAE 1911–14, and named by Mawson for G.P. Doolette of Perth, a patron.

**Mount Doorly.** 77°23'S, 162°54'E. Just behind the Wilson Piedmont Glacier, in Victoria Land. Between the Greenwood Valley and the Wright Lower Glacier. Discovered by Scott's 1901–4 expedition, and named by them for Gerald S. Doorly.

**Doorly, Gerald S.** Lt., RN. Junior officer on the *Morning*, 1903.

**Dorchuck Glacier.** 74°44'S, 113°56'W. On Martin Peninsula, on the coast of Marie Byrd Land.

**Dorian Bay.** 64°49'S, 63°30'W. A cove on the NW side of Wiencke Island. ½ mile ENE of Damoy Point. Discovered by Charcot in 1903–5, and named by him for a member of the French Chamber of Deputies.

**Canal d'Orléans** *see* **Orleans Strait**

**Dornan, P.O.** Crewman on the *Jacob Ruppert*, 1933–34.

**Dornin, W.H.** Crewman on the *Bear of Oakland*, 1933–35.

**Dorrel Rock.** 75°27'S, 111°20'W. A rock on land, 9 miles SW of the summit of Mount Murphy, in Marie Byrd Land. Near the head of Pope Glacier. Named by the USARP in the late 1960s for Leo E. Dorrel, USN, hospital corpsman at Byrd Station in 1966.

**Dorrer Glacier.** 82°41'S, 163°05'E. Just south of Mount Heiser. Flows into Lowery Glacier from the NE slopes of the Queen Elizabeth Range. Named for Egon Dorrer, US glaciologist on the Ross Ice Shelf, 1962–63 and 1965–66.

**Dorsey, Herbert G., Jr.** Worked for the US Weather Bureau, and devised an accurate method for predicting suitable flying weather. He was meteorologist at East Base during the USAS 1939–41.

**Dorsey Island.** 70°S, 71°50'W. 10 miles long. Mainly ice-covered. Averages

1½ miles wide. In Wilkins Sound, off the west side of Alexander Island. Discovered aerially by personnel from East Base during the USAS 1939–41. Named for Herbert G. Dorsey, Jr.

**Dorsey Mountains.** 67°04'S, 67°04'W. Just east of Somigliana Glacier, in the northern part of Arrowsmith Peninsula in Graham Land. Named for Noah E. Dorsey (1873–1959), US physicist specializing in ice.

**Mount Dort.** 85°54'S, 158°53'W. 2,250 m. Ice-free. Juts out into the east side of the Amundsen Glacier, just south of the mouth of Cappellari Glacier, in the Queen Maud Mountains. Discovered during Byrd's 1928–30 expedition. Named for Wakefield Dort, Jr., geologist at McMurdo Station in 1965–66, and US exchange scientist at Showa Station in 1967.

**Doss Glacier.** 82°30'S, 162°21'E. Just east of Mount Boman, flowing into the Nimrod Glacier, from the slopes of the Queen Elizabeth Range. Named for Edgar L. Doss, glaciologist at Roosevelt Island, 1962–63.

**Dostupnyy Point.** 67°38'S, 46°08'E. 8 miles east of Molodezhnaya Station, on Alasheyev Bight, Enderby Land.

**Dot Peak.** 79°45'S, 159°11'E. 1,450 m. Marks the highest point of Cooper Nunatak, on the east side of the Brown Hills. Named by the New Zealanders in 1962–63 for its size.

**Dotson Ice Shelf.** 74°24'S, 112°22'W. 30 miles wide. Between the Martin Peninsula and the Bear Peninsula, between the Bakutis Coast and the Walgreen Coast, in Marie Byrd Land. Named for Lt. William A. Dotson, USN, with the Ice Reconnaissance Unit in Alaska, who died on the job in Nov. 1964.

**Dotson Ridge.** 76°46'S, 161°25'E. 1,640 m. 1 mile long. East of Staten Island Heights and the Convoy Range. Named in 1964 for Morris F. Dotson, electrician at McMurdo Station in 1962.

**Dott Ice Rise.** 79°18'S, 81°48'W. A peninsulalike feature, ice-drowned except for the Barrett Nunataks. 20 miles long, it extends east from the Heritage Range in the Ellsworth Mountains. Terminates at Constellation Inlet at the SW edge of the Ronne Ice Shelf. Named for Robert H. Dott, geologist and senior US representative at General Bernardo O'Higgins Station in 1962.

**Dotten Nunatak.** 71°57'S, 24°05'E. 2 miles north of Smalegga Ridge near the mouth of Gillock Glacier, in the Sør Rondane Mountains. Named Dotten (the lump) by the Norwegians.

**Douanier Rock.** 66°49'S, 142°04'E. An island just east of Point Alden, at the juncture of Adélie Land and George V Land. It lies close to the coast, and was discovered by the French under Liotard in 1949-50, and named Rocher de Douanier by them because of its relation to the coast (douanier means customs man in French).

**Double Curtain Glacier.** 77°39'S, 163°31'E. On the south slope of the Kukri Hills, just SW of Mount Barnes, flowing toward the mouth of Ferrar Glacier, in Victoria Land. Mapped and named by Scott's 1910-13 expedition, for its shape.

**Double Islands.** 66°45'S, 141°11'E. 2 small rocky islands just east of the tip of the Zélée Glacier Tongue. Almost ½ mile NNW of Triple Islands. Charted and named by the French in 1949-51.

**Doublefinger Peak.** 76°53'S, 162°15'E. At the top of Hunt Glacier in Victoria Land. It overlooks Granite Harbor, from which it is 4 miles inland. Just NE of Mount Marston. Named by Scott's 1910-13 expedition, because from the east it has two peaks.

**The Doublets.** 66°25'S, 98°39'E. Rocks on land, at the west side of David Island, East Antarctica. Discovered and named by the Western Base Party of the AAE 1911-14.

**Mount Dougherty.** 82°43'S, 161°05'E. 2,790 m. Between Mount Sandved and Mount Cara in the northern part of the Queen Elizabeth Range. Named for Ells-

worth C. Dougherty, biologist at McMurdo Station in 1959-60 and 1961-62.

**Dougherty Island.** Does not exist.

**Doughty, John.** Captain of the topsail on the Wilkes Expedition 1838-42. Joined in the USA. Served the cruise.

**Cape Douglas.** 80°55'S, 160°52'E. Ice-covered. Marks the south side of the entrance to Matterson Inlet, on the west side of the Ross Ice Shelf. Discovered by Scott's 1901-4 expedition, and named by them for Sir Archibald Douglas, lord of the admiralty, who persuaded the Admiralty to assign naval seamen to the expedition.

**Mount Douglas.** 76°33'S, 161°18'E. 1,750 m. Pyramidal. Near the head of Fry Glacier, between the Fry and Mawson Glaciers. Named by the NZ Northern Survey Party of the BCTAE, which established a survey station on its summit in Dec. 1957, for Murray H. Douglas.

**Douglas, E.** Flight lt., RAAF. Australian pilot on the BANZARE 1929-31.

**Douglas, G. Vibert.** George Vibert Douglas. Geologist on the *Quest,* 1921-22.

**Douglas, Murray H.** Member of the NZ Northern Survey Party of the BCTAE 1956-58.

**Douglas Gap.** 71°05'S, 167°44'E. Glacier-filled. 1½ miles wide. Between Hedgpeth Heights and Quam Heights in the Anare Mountains of Victoria Land. Named for Donald S. Douglas, biologist at Hallett Station in 1959-60 and 1960-61.

**Douglas Glacier.** 73°31'S, 61°45'W. Flows through the central Werner Mountains in Palmer Land, and merges with Bryan Glacier, just north of Mount Broome where it enters New Bedford Inlet. Named for Everett L. Douglas, biologist at Palmer Station in 1967-68.

**Douglas Inlet** *see* **New Bedford Inlet**

**Douglas Islands.** 67°23'S, 63°22'E. Two small islands, 12 miles NW of Cape Daly, off the coast of East Antarctica. Discovered aerially from the *Discovery* on Dec. 31, 1929, during the BANZARE 1929–31, and located at 66°40'S, 64°30' E. Mawson named them for Vice-Adm. Percy Douglas (*see* **Douglas Range**), hydrographer of the Royal Navy. In 1931 they were repositioned at 67°20'S, 63°32' E. In 1956 an ANARE sledge party led by P.W. Crohn could not find them in the new position, but did find 2 uncharted islands at 67°23'S, 63°22'E, and thus named them Douglas Islands.

**Douglas Peak.** 66°24'S, 52°28'E. 1,525 m. 11 miles SW of Mount Codrington. 8 miles east of Mount Marr. Discovered in Jan. 1930 by the BANZARE, and named by Mawson for Flight Lt. E. Douglas.

**Douglas Peaks.** 80°S, 81°25'W. South of Plummer Glacier in the SE end of the Heritage Range. Named by the University of Minnesota Ellsworth Mountains Party of 1962–63 for Lt. Cdr. John Douglas, pilot who flew one of the party out for an appendectomy.

**Douglas Range.** 70°S, 69°35'W. Extends 35 miles from Mount Nicholas to Mount Edred, overlooking the northern part of the George VI Sound, on the NE coast of Alexander Island. Found to be a range by Ellsworth on his flight over on Nov. 23, 1935. Named by the BGLE 1934–37 for Vice-Adm. Sir Percy Douglas (*see also* **Douglas Islands**), chairman of the BGLE Advisory Committee, and a member of the Discovery Committee from 1928 until he died in 1939. Mapped using the RARE aerial photos of 1947–48.

**Mount Douglass.** 77°19'S, 145°20'W. Ice-covered. 8 miles ESE of Mount Woodward on the south side of Boyd Glacier, in the Ford Ranges of Marie Byrd Land. Discovered on aerial trips in 1934 during Byrd's 1933–35 expedition. Named for Malcolm C. Douglass.

**Douglass, Malcolm C.** Dog driver at West Base during the USAS 1939–41.

**Douguet, Max.** French commander of the *Commandant Charcot* during the French Polar Expeditions of 1948–51. He had been in Greenland in 1932–33.

**Mount Doumani.** 85°49'S, 137°38'W. 3,240 m. Between the Johns and Kansas

Glaciers at the north side of the Watson Escarpment. Named for George A. Doumani who was many times in Antarctica. He was geologist/seismologist at Byrd Station in 1958–59. He was on the Executive Committee Range Traverse of Feb. 1959, and wintered at Byrd Station in 1959. He was part of the Marie Byrd Land Traverse Party of 1959–60; and in 1960–61 and again in 1961–62 he was in the Horlick Mountains. In 1962–63 he was at Mount Weaver, and in 1964–65 was back in the Horlick Mountains.

**Doumani Peak.** 77°07'S, 126°03'W. 2,675 m. On the southern slopes of Mount Sidley in the Executive Committee Range of Marie Byrd Land. Named for George A. Doumani (*see* **Mount Doumani**).

**Doumer Hill.** 64°51'S, 63°34'W. Also called Monte Capitán, Monte López. Snow-covered. Pyramidal. 515 m. Forms the summit of Doumer Island, in the Palmer Archipelago. Charted by Charcot in 1903–5. Named by the UK in 1958 in association with the island.

**Doumer Island.** 64°51'S, 63°35'W. 4½ miles long. 2 miles wide. Has a snow-covered peak on it of 515 m. (*see* **Doumer Hill**). At the SW entrance to the Neumayer Channel, between Wiencke Island and Anvers Island. Discovered by de Gerlache in 1897–99, and named by Charcot in 1904–5 for Paul Doumer, president of the French Chamber of Deputies, and later president of France.

**The *Dove*.** George Powell's British sloop of 1821–22 which, with the *James Monroe* under Palmer, discovered the South Orkneys on Dec. 6, 1821.

**Dove Channel.** 60°45'S, 45°36'W. Also called Dove Strait. A marine channel cutting through the Oliphant Islands, ½ mile south of Gourlay Peninsula, the SE tip of Signy Island, in the South Orkneys. Named about 1930 for the *Dove*.

**Dove Strait** *see* **Dove Channel**

**Mount Dover.** 83°46'S, 55°50'W. 1,645 m. Surmounts the SE end of Gale Ridge, where the ridge abuts the Washington Escarpment, in the Neptune Range of the Pensacola Mountains. Named for James H. Dover, geologist with the Patuxent Range field party in 1962–63.

**Cape Dovers.** 66°29′S, 97°08′E. Fronts the Shackleton Ice Shelf, 5 miles south of Henderson Island. Discovered by the Western Base Party of the AAE 1911–14. Named by Mawson for G. Dovers.

**Mount Dovers.** 70°08′S, 64°59′E. A ridge, 2 miles NW of Mount Dwyer in the Athos Range of the Prince Charles Mountains. First seen from Stinear Nunataks in 1954 by Robert G. Dovers' ANARE party, and named by the Australians for him.

**Dovers, G.** Cartographer on the AAE 1911–14.

**Dovers, Robert G.** Geologist, surveyor and officer-in-charge of Mawson Station in 1954. He had been on Heard Island (53°S) in 1948. His wife, Wilma, had a glacier named for her (*see* **Wilma Glacier**).

**Dovers Glacier** *see* **Mulebreen**

**Dovers Nunatak** *see* **Dovers Peak**

**Dovers Peak.** 69°42′S, 64°26′E. Also called Dovers Nunatak. In the west part of the Stinear Nunataks in Mac. Robertson Land. Discovered by Robert G. Dovers' ANARE party in 1954, and named by the Australians for him.

**Dow Nunatak.** 75°01′S, 136°14′W. Isolated. 3½ miles NW of Mount Sinha, in the SW part of the McDonald Heights of Marie Byrd Land. Named for Charles R. Dow, glaciologist at Byrd Station, 1969–70.

**Dow Peak.** 71°03′S, 163°04′E. 2 miles ESE of Mount Sturm, in the Bowers Mountains. Named by the NZGSAE to northern Victoria Land in 1967–68 for its senior geologist, J.A.S. Dow.

**Mount Dowie.** 70°42′S, 65°58′E. 4 miles west of Mount Hollingshead in the Aramis Range of the Prince Charles Mountains. Discovered by W.G. Bewsher's ANARE southern party in Jan. 1957, and named by the Australians for Donald A. Dowie, medical officer at Mawson Station in 1956.

**Mount Dowling.** 72°27′S, 98°08′W. 13 miles east of Von der Wall Point, in the Walker Mountains of Thurston Island. Named for Forrest L. Dowling, geophysicist at Byrd Station in 1960–61.

**Downer Glacier.** 66°58′S, 56°25′E. 15 miles long. Flows into the Edward VIII Ice Shelf, just north of Wilma Glacier. Named by the Australians for Sgt. G.K. Downer, RAAF, electrical and instrument fitter at Mawson Station in 1958.

**The Downfall.** 64°48′S, 62°23′W. A peak between the heads of the Arago and Woodbury Glaciers, on the west coast of Graham Land. Named by the UK in 1960 for the very steep drop on its eastern side.

**Downham Peak.** 64°17′S, 58°54′W. Pyramidal. At the south side of the mouth of Sjögren Glacier, on Trinity Peninsula. Named by the UK for Noel Y. Downham, FIDS meteorological assistant at Base D in 1960–61.

**Downs Cone.** 75°50′S, 116°16′W. On the SW side of Toney Mountain in Marie Byrd Land. 3 miles WSW of Boeger Peak. Named for Bill S. Downs, USN, air controlman at Williams Field in 1969–70 and 1970–71. He had also wintered-over at Little America in 1958.

**Downs Nunatak.** 69°36′S, 66°40′W. In the central part of the Antarctic Peninsula.

**Cape Downshire** *see* **Downshire Cliffs**

**Downshire Cliffs.** 71°37′S, 170°36′E. 2,000 m. above the Ross Sea, they form much of the eastern side of Adare Peninsula in northern Victoria Land. Ross called part of them Cape Downshire, at the request of Crozier, for the latter's friend, the Marquis of Downshire. Modern historians could not find this cape, so they renamed the entire cliffs.

**Doyle Glacier.** 66°S, 65°18′W. Flows to the west coast of Graham Land on both sides of Prospect Point. Named by the UK for Sir Arthur Conan Doyle, the first British person to make a full day's journey on skis, in March 1893 (not in the Antarctic). Conan Doyle also wrote *Sherlock Holmes.*

**Doyle Point.** 65°53'S, 54°52'E. Between Cape Batterbee and Cape Borley on the coast of Enderby Land. Discovered on Jan. 12, 1930, by the BANZARE, and named by Mawson as Stuart Doyle Point, for Stuart Doyle (1887–1945), Australian movie magnate who helped Frank Hurley process the expedition's movies. The name was later shortened.

**Drabanten Nunatak.** 73°54'S, 5°55'W. Isolated. 10 miles west of Tunga Spur, just north of the Kirwan Escarpment in Queen Maud Land. Name means "the satellite" in Norwegian.

**Drabek Peak.** 71°05'S, 166°37'E. 2,090 m. 6 miles north of Anare Pass. 9 miles west of Redmond Bluff, in the Anare Mountains of Victoria Land. Named for Charles M. Drabek, US biologist at McMurdo Station in 1964–65 and 1967–68.

**Mount Draeger.** 71°09'S, 163°54'E. 1,690 m. In the NW part of the Posey Range, in the Bowers Mountains. It overlooks from the east the junction of Smithson Glacier with Graveson Glacier. Named for Ernest J. Draeger, USN, chief radioman at McMurdo Station in 1967.

**The *Dragon.*** Liverpool sealing brig, commanded by Capt. McFarlane. In the South Shetlands during the 1820–21 season. It met the *Cora* off Desolation Island on Dec. 16, 1820. The vessel may have made a landing on the Antarctic continent (*see* **Landings**) in early 1821. The expedition took at least 5,000 fur seals.

**Dragon Cove.** 62°28'S, 60°08'W. SE of Williams Point on the NE side of Livingston Island in the South Shetlands. Named by the UK in 1958 for the *Dragon.*

**Dragon Fish.** *Prionodraco evansii.* Coastal fish of Antarctica.

**The Dragons Back.** 80°23'S, 28°33'W. A ridge in the Shackleton Range. Named descriptively.

**Dragons Teeth.** 63°15'S, 58°40'W. A small group of black, tooth-shaped rocks in water off the NE part of Astrolabe Island, off Trinity Peninsula. Named descriptively by the UK.

**Drake, Francis R.H.** British meteorologist on the *Terra Nova,* 1911–12. Not a member of Scott's shore party, he remained on the ship under the command of Lt. Harry Pennell, as the ship cruised to the north after dropping Scott's party at McMurdo Sound.

**Drake Head.** 69°13'S, 158°14'E. A headland which forms the west side of the entrance to Davies Bay. Discovered by Pennell in the *Terra Nova* in Feb. 1911, and named by him for Francis R.H. Drake (q.v.).

**Drake Icefall.** 79°46'S, 83°50'W. 2 miles wide. Between Soholt Peaks and Edson Hills. Flows from the Polar Plateau into Union Glacier, in the Heritage Range. Named by the University of Minnesota Ellsworth Mountains Party of 1962–63 for Benjamin Drake IV, geologist and member of the party.

**Drake Nunatak.** 85°17'S, 89°20'W. 1,935 m. At the base of the Bermel Escarpment. 1 mile east of Elliott Nunatak in the Thiel Mountains. Named by Bermel and Ford of the US Geological Survey Thiel Mountains Party of 1960–61, for Avery A. Drake, Jr., geologist on the *Glacier* to Thurston Island in 1960–61.

**Drake Passage.** Centers on 58°S, 70°W, but stretches over the 60th degree of southern latitude. It is a 600-mile stretch of water which latitudinally separates South America from the Antarctic Peninsula, and longitudinally connects the Atlantic Ocean with the Pacific Ocean. The average depth of water is 11,000 feet, but the southern boundaries can reach up to 15,600 feet deep. Drake discovered it in Sept. 1578, and it was named for him, even though he did not sail through the passage, that honor first going to a Flemish expedition led by Willen Schouten.

**Dråpane Nunataks.** 73°46'S, 5°03'W. Just north of Urnosa Spur, near the SW end of the Kirwan Escarpment in Queen Maud Land. Name means "the drops" in Norwegian.

**Draves Island** *see* **Draves Point**

**Draves Point.** 66°04'S, 101°04'E. The most westerly point of Booth Peninsula. One third of a mile north of the eastern part of Thomas Island. The western part of Booth Peninsula was named Draves Island by the USA in 1956, for Dale Draves, air crewman on Bunger's flights during Operation Highjump, 1946–47. Later redefined by the USSR in 1956–57.

**Dread Point** *see* **Renier Point**

**Dreadnought Point.** 64°S, 57°48'W. On the west side of Croft Bay, James Ross Island. Surveyed by the FIDS in Aug. 1953. Named descriptively by the UK for the dreadnought ships it somewhat resembles.

**Dream Island.** 64°44'S, 64°14'W. 1 mile SE of Cape Monaco, off the SW coast of Anvers Island, in the area of Palmer Station. Named by the UK for its cave, waterfall (in summer, at least), grass, and moss.

**Dreikanter Head.** 76°53'S, 162°30'E. Between Lion Island and Cape Retreat, on the coast of Granite Harbor, in Victoria Land. A dark headland, it looks triangular from the SE (dreikantig means "three-edged" in German).

**Drew Cove.** 66°20'S, 110°30'E. Indents the west side of Mitchell Peninsula, in the Windmill Islands. Named for Chief Construction Electrician John W. Drew, USN, at Wilkes Station in 1958.

**Cape Dreyfus** *see* **Cape Well-Met**

**Cap Driencourt** *see* **Driencourt Point**

**Driencourt Point.** 64°12'S, 62°31'W. 6 miles SE of Claude Point on the west side of Brabant Island. Charted by Charcot in 1903–5, and named Cap Driencourt by him for a French hydrographic engineer of that name. The feature was later called Driencourt Point in English.

**Driscoll Glacier.** 79°42'S, 83°W. 13 miles long. Flows between the Collier Hills and the Buchanan Hills into the Union Glacier in the Heritage Range. Named for Cdr. Jerome M. Driscoll, VX-6 administration officer in 1965.

**Driscoll Island.** 76°12'S, 146°50'W. 16 miles long. A large, ice-covered island in Block Bay, on the Marie Byrd Land coast. Named for Lawrence J. Driscoll, USN, bosun's mate on the *Glacier* here in 1961–62.

**Driscoll Point.** 82°59'S, 168°E. Forms the east side of the entrance to Wise Bay, and overlooks the Ross Ice Shelf. Named for C.E. Driscoll, captain of the *Private Joseph F. Merrell* in 1963.

**Mount Dromedary.** 78°19'S, 163°02'E. Hump-shaped. Over 2,400 m. 4 miles east of Mount Kempe in the Royal Society Range of southern Victoria Land. Mapped by Scott's 1901–4 expedition, but named descriptively by Scott's 1910–13 expedition.

**Dromedary Glacier.** 78°23'S, 163°06'E. Occupies a high cirque on the east side of Mount Dromedary in the Royal Society Range. Named by the New Zealanders in 1960–61 for the nearby mountain.

**Dronning Fabiolafjella** *see* **Queen Fabiola Mountains**

**Dronning Mary Land** *see* **Queen Mary Land**

**Dronning Maud Land** *see* **Queen Maud Land**

**Dronning Maudsfjell** *see* **Queen Maud Mountains**

**Dru Rock.** 66°46'S, 141°35'E. An island, ½ mile long. Between Retour Island and Claquebue Island in the Curzon Islands. Charted in 1951 by the French, and named Rocher des Drus by them in memory of the scaling of the needle-shaped peaks of Chamonix, France. Dru means "strong."

**Drummond Glacier.** 66°40'S, 65°43'W. 10 miles long. 2 miles wide. Flows WNW into Darbel Bay to the south of

Hopkins Glacier on the west coast of Graham Land. Surveyed in 1946–47 by the FIDS, and named by them as West Balch Glacier. In 1957 the FIDS decided that it had no connection with East Balch Glacier (q.v.) and renamed it for Sir Jack C. Drummond (1891–1952), professor of biochemistry at the University of London, who helped select rations for many expeditions from 1920 to 1940.

**Drummond Peak.** 77°51′S, 153°58′W. Isolated. 19 miles SW of La Gorce Peak on the Edward VII Peninsula. Named for Lt. (jg) Glenn N. Drummond, Jr., USN, assistant aerologist on the staff of the commander, US Naval Support Force, Antarctica, 1959–62.

**Drury Nunatak.** 69°14′S, 156°58′E. Snow-free. Isolated. At the head of Lauritzen Bay. 1½ miles NW of Reynolds Peak. Discovered and charted on Feb. 20, 1959, by Phillip Law's ANARE party from the *Magga Dan*. Named by the Australians for Alan Campbell-Drury, photographic officer of the Antarctic Division, Melbourne. He was on this expedition.

**Drury Ridge.** 83°39′S, 55°45′W. 9 miles long. Mainly snow-covered. Extends from Nelson Peak in the Neptune Range of the Pensacola Mountains. Named for David L. Drury, meteorologist at Ellsworth Station in 1959–60 and 1961.

**Rocher des Drus** *see* **Dru Rock**

**Druzhnaya Station.** 77°34′S, 40°13′W. USSR summer camp/scientific base dedicated to geological research. On the Filchner-Ronne Ice Shelf of Queen Maud Land. In 1986 it was destroyed by a massive cave-in on the ice shelf and calved off with an iceberg into the Weddell Sea.

**Druzhnaya III Station.** USSR summer camp/scientific base built at Norsel Iceport near the Quar Ice Shelf in Queen Maud Land in 1988 as a replacement for Druzhnaya Station (which became known in retrospect as Druzhnaya I Sta-

tion). If there was a Druzhnaya II Station, it didn't last long.

**Dry Valley** *see* **Taylor Valley**

**Dry valleys.** The general lowering of ice sheet levels at certain times in geological history caused some glaciers to recede and vanish from their valleys, producing dry valleys, or ice-free valleys as they are sometimes called. Taylor Valley was the first to be discovered — by Scott's expedition in 1902. They were realized as reasonably frequent occurrences by aerial photography during Operation Windmill in 1947–48. *See* **Taylor Valley, Garwood Valley, Victoria Valley, Wright Valley, David Valley, King-David Junction, Wheeler Valley, McKelvey Valley, Barwick Valley, Arena Valley, Beacon Valley, Turnabout Valley, No Name Valley, Pearse Valley, Conrow Valley, King Valley, Matterhorn Valley, Bull Pass, Olympus Range, Balham Valley.** *See also* **Glaciers.**

**The Dry Valley Drilling Project.** Known also as the DVDP. 1971–76. Geophysical exploration, geological reconnaissance and bedrock drilling in the dry valleys north of McMurdo Station in southern Victoria Land. Carried out by NZ, Japan, and the USA. The first borehole was begun on Jan. 21, 1972. Leon Oliver was chief driller 1973–74, and drilling superintendent 1974–75. The goal of the project was to understand better the Cenozoic geologic history of the McMurdo Sound region.

**Mount Dryfoose.** 84°51′S, 169°55′W. 2 miles long. Has peaks on it over 1,600 m. 3 miles NE of Mount Daniel. NE of the southern part of the Lillie Range. Discovered by the US Ross Ice Shelf Traverse Party of 1957–58 under Crary, who named it for Lt. Earl D. Dryfoose, Jr., USNR, VX-6 pilot during IGY.

**Drygalski.** Engine room crew member on the *Sir James Clark Ross*, 1923–24.

**Drygalski, Erich Von** *see* **Von Drygalski, Erich**

**Drygalski Barrier** *see* **Drygalski Ice Tongue**

**Drygalski Basin.** 74°45′S, 167°E. Submarine feature of the Ross Sea.

**Drygalski Bay** *see* **Drygalski Glacier**

**Drygalski Glacier.** 64°43′S, 60°44′W. 18 miles long. Flows from the Herbert Plateau to just north of Sentinel Nunatak on the east coast of Graham Land. Discovered in 1902 by Nordenskjöld and named by him as Drygalski Bay, for Erich von Drygalski. The name also appeared as V. Drygalski Bay. It was redefined by the FIDS in 1947.

**Drygalski Glacier Tongue** *see* **Drygalski Ice Tongue**

**Drygalski Ice Tongue.** 75°24′S, 163°30′E. Also called Drygalski Barrier, Drygalski Glacier Tongue. It is actually a glacier tongue. Between 9 and 15 miles wide. 30 miles long, or more. It forms the foot of David Glacier, and juts out into the Ross Sea from southern Victoria Land. Discovered by Scott in Jan. 1902, and named by him for Erich von Drygalski.

**Drygalski Island.** 65°45′S, 92°30′E. 325 m. Domed. Ice-capped. 11 miles long. 45 miles NNE of Cape Filchner, in the Davis Sea. Discovered in Nov. 1912 by the Western Base Party of the AAE 1911–14. May well be Drygalski's High Land, charted in 1902 by von Drygalski.

**Drygalski Mountains.** 71°45′S, 8°15′E. Between the Filchner Mountains and the Kurze Mountains in the Orvin Mountains of Queen Maud Land. Discovered by Ritscher in 1938–39, and named by him for Erich von Drygalski.

**Drygalski's High Land** *see* **Drygalski Island**

**Drying Point.** 60°43′S, 45°37′W. On the SW side of Borge Bay. 350 yards NW of Mooring Point on the east side of Signy Island in the South Orkneys. Named in 1927 by the personnel on the *Discovery*.

**Duarte, José.** Captain of the *Lautaro*, 1949–50.

**Du Baty, Raymond Rallier.** A cadet in the French merchant marine, he was a naval apprentice seaman on the *Français* during Charcot's 1903–5 expedition.

**DuBeau Glacier.** 66°23′S, 106°27′E. A channel glacier flowing to the coast, 18 miles west of Merritt Island, East Antarctica. Named for Earl P. DuBeau, photo interpreter on Operation Windmill, 1947–48.

**Dublitskiy Bay.** 70°05′S, 7°45′E. 12 miles wide. Indents the ice shelf around the Queen Maud Land coast. 70 miles north of Sigurd Knolls. Named by the USSR in 1961 for K.A. Dublitskiy, former captain of the icebreaker *Litke*.

**Dubois, Jacques.** Leader of Charcot Station from Jan. 1957 until 1958. Replaced by René Garcia.

**DuBois Island.** 66°16′S, 67°10′W. 1 mile west of Krogh Island, near the south end of the Biscoe Islands. Named by the UK for Eugene F. DuBois, US physiologist.

**Cape Dubouzet.** 63°16′S, 57°01′W. 2 miles east of Mount Bransfield at the NE end of the Antarctic Peninsula. Charted by Dumont d'Urville in 1838, and named by him for Joseph-Fidèle-Eugène du Bouzet.

**Du Bouzet, Joseph-Fidèle-Eugène.** French lieutenant on the *Zélée* during Dumont d'Urville's 1837–40 expedition. On Jan. 21, 1840, he claimed Adélie Land for France by landing on an offshore islet.

**DuBridge Range.** 71°30′S, 168°53′E. 20 miles long. In the Admiralty Mountains of Victoria Land. Between Pitkevich Glacier and Shipley Glacier. Named for Lee DuBridge, science advisor to the president of the USA, 1969–70.

**Duce Bay** *see* **Duse Bay**

**Duchaylard Island.** 65°42′S, 65°07′W. 3 miles long. At the west side of the Grandidier Channel, 1 mile SE of Vieugué Island. 10 miles west of Cape García, off the west coast of Graham Land. Discovered by Charcot in 1903–5, and named by him for M. du Chaylard, French minister plenipotentiary in Montevideo. Bongrain (q.v.) used the Duchaylard spelling in his 1914 report, and that is the spelling now used.

**Duclaux Point.** 64°04′S, 62°15′W. Extends into Bouquet Bay, from the east side of Pasteur Peninsula. 3 miles SE of Cape Cockburn on Brabant Island. Charted by Charcot in 1903–5, and named by him for Pierre E. Duclaux, director of the Pasteur Institute in Paris.

**Cape Ducorps.** 63°24′S, 58°08′W. 3 miles long. Joined to the coast by Cockerell Peninsula. 7 miles SW of Cape Legoupil on the northern coast of the Trinity Peninsula. Discovered by Dumont d'Urville in 1837–40, and named by him for Louis Ducorps.

**Ducorps, Louis.** Member of Dumont d'Urville's expedition of 1837–40.

**¹Mount Dudley** *see* **Dudley Head**

**²Mount Dudley.** 68°16′S, 66°30′W. Over 1,375 m. At the head of Neny Fjord. Neny Glacier is on its north and east sides. On the west coast of Graham Land. Named by Ronne in 1948 for Harold M. Dudley, executive secretary of the American Council of Commercial Laboratories, in Washington, who helped the RARE 1947–48.

**The *Dudley Docker.*** One of the 3 longboats used by Shackleton during the British Imperial Transantarctic Expedition of 1914–17.

**Dudley Head.** 84°20′S, 172°25′E. 2,540 m. Snow-covered. Projects into the eastern side of the Beardmore Glacier. 5 miles south of Mount Patrick. Shackleton discovered it in 1907–9 and named it Mount Dudley, but it was redefined later by the USA as a head. Actually it is a ridge.

**Duegen, Charles.** Seaman on the Wilkes Expedition 1838–42. Joined at Rio. Returned to the USA in the *Relief* in 1839.

**Duell, Capt.** Commander of the *Dart* in the South Shetlands, 1822–23.

**Cape Duemler** *see* **Cape Robinson**

**Mount Duemler.** 70°01′S, 63°45′W. 2,225 m. SW of the head of Anthony Glacier, 11 miles west of Mount Bailey, in the Eternity Range of the Antarctic Peninsula. Named by Ronne for R.F. Duemler, vice-president of the Delaware, Lackawanna and Western Coal Co., of New York, which contributed coal to the RARE 1947–48.

**Dufaure de Lajarte Islands** *see* **Lajarte Islands**

**Dufayel Island.** 62°10′S, 58°34′W. Also called Haakon Island. Near the center of Ezcurra Inlet in Admiralty Bay, King George Island, in the South Shetlands. Charted and named in Dec. 1909 by Charcot.

**Dufek, George.** b. Feb. 10, 1903, Rockford, Ill. d. Feb. 10, 1977. George John Dufek. One of the major figures in Antarctic history. His first tour to Antarctica was with the USAS 1939–41, as navigator of the *Bear*. He discovered the mountains of Thurston Island during a flight over. He was a lieutenant-commander during Operation Highjump, 1946–47, and led the Eastern Group during that expedition. He fell into the Bellingshausen Sea during this cruise. Back again for the IGY, he was an admiral in the US Navy by this time, and tactical leader of Operation Deep Freeze, being the commander of the US Naval Support Force, Antarctica (Task Force 43), the military side of the operation. On Oct. 31, 1956, he became the 11th man, and the first American, to stand at the South Pole, when he was flown here in the *Que Sera Sera*. On Aug. 15, 1957, he took over from Byrd as the US Antarctic projects officer, and on April 14, 1959, was replaced as the head American in Antarctica by Admiral Tyree. He wrote *Operation Deep Freeze*, in 1957 (*see* the Bibliography).

**Dufek Coast.** 84°30′S, 179°W. Between Airdrop Peak and Morris Peak, at the south of the Ross Ice Shelf, at the foot of the Transantarctic Mountains, between the Bush Mountains and the Prince Olav Mountains. Named by NZ in 1961 for George Dufek.

**Dufek Massif.** 82°36′S, 52°30′W. Also called Santa Teresita Range. 27 miles long. Largely snow-covered. West of the Forrestal Range, in the northern Pensacola Mountains. Discovered on Jan. 13, 1956, by air, and named by the USA for George Dufek.

**Dufek Mountain.** 72°10′S, 24°45′E. Also called Dufekfjellet. 3,150 m. 2 miles SW of Mefjell Mountain in the Sør Rondane Mountains. Named by the Norwegians for George Dufek.

**Duff Point.** 62°27′S, 60°02′W. The westernmost point of Greenwich Island, in the South Shetlands. Named in 1961 by the UK in order to preserve the name Duff in the area (*see* **McFarlane Strait**).

**Duff's Straits** *see* **McFarlane Strait**

**Duffy Peak.** 71°45′S, 70°40′W. On the west coast of Alexander Island.

**Sierra DuFief.** 64°52′S, 63°28′W. Also called Fief Mountains. A range, 4 miles in length. Has several peaks, the highest being 1,415 m. In the south part of Wiencke Island. Discovered and named by de Gerlache in 1897–99 for Jean DuFief, general secretary of the Belgian Royal Geographical Society.

**Dufour, Gustave.** Belgian sailor on the *Belgica* expedition of 1897–99.

**Dugdale Glacier.** 71°38′S, 169°50′E. 25 miles long. Flows from the Admiralty Mountains into Robertson Bay on the northern coast of Victoria Land. Charted by Borchgrevink in 1898–1900, and named by him for Frank Dugdale of Stratford-on-Avon.

**Dugurdspiggen Peak.** 72°26′S, 2°46′W. Isolated. 4 miles north of the Borg Massif in Queen Maud Land. Name means "the second breakfast peak" in Norwegian.

**Duke Ernst Bay** *see* **Vahsel Bay**

**Duke of York Island.** 71°37′S, 170°04′E. Ice-free. Mountainous. 2½ miles

long. In the south part of Robertson Bay, on the north coast of Victoria Land. Charted in 1899 by Borchgrevink and named by him for the Duke of York.

**Duken Flat.** 73°48′S, 5°10′W. A small, flat, ice-covered area between Urnosa Spur and Framranten Point, near the SW end of the Kirwan Escarpment in Queen Maud Land. Named by the Norwegians.

**Mount Dumais.** 85°02′S, 64°30′W. 1,830 m. On the SW edge of the Mackin Table. 2 miles north of Lekander Nunatak in the southern part of the Patuxent Range of the Pensacola Mountains. Named for Lt. Clarence C. Dumais, USN, officer-in-charge of the South Pole Station in 1960.

**Dumbbell Island.** 68°43′S, 67°35′W. 1 mile west of Alamode Island in the Terra Firma Islands, off the west coast of Graham Land. Surveyed by the FIDS in 1948, and named by them for its shape.

**Mount Dummett.** 73°12′S, 64°E. 11 miles east of Mount McCauley, in the Prince Charles Mountains. Named by the Australians for R.B. Dummett, formerly managing director of BP Australia, supporter of the ANARE for years.

**Dumont d'Urville, Jules-Sébastien-César.** b. May 23, 1790, Condé-sur-Noireau, Calvados, France. d. in the Versailles train crash of May 8, 1842. French explorer, navigator, and naval captain. He joined the navy at 16, and in 1820 discovered the Venus de Milo. In 1821 he helped found the Paris Geographical Society, and circumnavigated the world in 1822–25. On Sept. 7, 1837, he left Toulon on his expedition to Antarctica, and on Jan. 24, 1838, his two ships, the *Astrolabe* and the *Zélée* (the latter commanded by Charles-Hector Jacquinot) were at 63°23′S. The following day they were at 64°42′S. Unable to get through the pack ice, they laid over in the South Orkneys until Feb. 2, 1838. On Feb. 4, 1838, the 2 ships got caught in the pack ice for 5 days, and then went westward. On Feb. 27, 1838, Dumont d'Urville discovered Louis Philippe Land and Joinville Island, at the north of the Antarctic Peninsula. He charted and mapped the north of Graham Land (he had already done survey work in the South Orkneys and the South Shetlands). Because of scurvy on board they left the area in early March 1838. On April 1, 1838, seaman Lepreux died of scurvy, and hydrographer Dumoulin and the *Astrolabe*'s second officer, Barlatier-Demas, were both sick with it. They made Chile in April 1838, and 9 men deserted. Crossing the Pacific many men died. In Jan. 1840, Dumont d'Urville was back in Antarctic waters, in search of the South Magnetic Pole. On Jan. 19, 1840, he sighted the continent itself (around the same time, and in roughly the same area of East Antarctica, as Wilkes did), and on Jan. 21, 1840, du Bouzet led a party onto an islet off the shore of Adélie Land, and claimed this coast for France. On Jan. 29, 1840, they met the *Porpoise* from Wilkes' expedition, but, due to a misunderstanding of the signals on both sides, made no communication, even though the commanders (Ringgold and Dumont d'Urville) both wanted to. On Jan. 31, 1840, they discovered the Clarie Coast. They returned to France on Nov. 6, 1840. Dumont d'Urville was in Antarctic waters only from mid-Jan. 1838 to March 8, 1838, and again from Jan. to Feb. 1840, a total of about 85 days. Also on the expedition were Honoré Jacquinot, Boyer, Coupvent-Desbois, Thanaron, Ducorps, Dumoutier, Duparc, Duroch, Gervaize, Gourdin, de Kermadec, Hombron, de la Farge, Lafond, Le Guillou, de Flotte, and de Roquemaurel.

**Dumont d'Urville Sea.** 63°S, 137°E. Off the shores of Adélie Land. Named for J-S-C Dumont d'Urville.

**Dumont d'Urville Station.** 66°40′S, 140°01′E. French scientific station on Pétrel Island, in the Géologie Archipelago, off the coast of Adélie Land. Built by Robert Guillard in 1956 to replace Port-Martin Station, which had been destroyed by fire. It was an exten-sion of the substation built earlier by Marret. The first commander was Guillard, who led the 1956 wintering party. Imbert led the 1957 wintering party. It has all modern conveniences now, and a staff of around 67 in the summer and 30 in the winter. It has a year-round skiway landing-strip called D-21, 13 miles away.

**Dumont d'Urville Trough** *see* **Adélie Valley**

**Dumoulin, C.A. Vincendon** *see* **Vincendon-Dumoulin, C.A**

**Dumoulin Islands.** 66°37′S, 140°04′E. A small group at the NE end of the Géologie Archipelago. They include Derby Island, Pasteur Island, Dépôt Island. 2½ miles north of the Astrolabe Glacier Tongue. Dumont d'Urville sent a party, led by du Bouzet, onto one of these islands, in 1840. Charted by the AAE 1911–14, and named by Mawson for C.A. Vincendon-Dumoulin.

**Dumoulin Rock** *see* **Jurien Island**

**Dumoulin Rocks.** 63°26′S, 59°48′W. A group of rocks in water 4 miles NE of Cape Leguillou, the northern tip of Tower Island, in the Palmer Archipelago. Named Îles Dumoulin by Dumont d'Urville in 1837–40 for C.A. Vincendon-Dumoulin, or rather one group of rocks was so named by him. There are, in fact, two groups here. The western group has been named more recently as the Kendall Rocks, and the eastern group has retained the original name.

**Cape Dumoutier.** 63°33′S, 59°46′W. Forms the eastern tip of Tower Island, in the Palmer Archipelago. Named by Dumont d'Urville in 1837–40 for Pierre Dumoutier.

**Dumoutier, Pierre.** Pierre Marie Alexandre Dumoutier. Assistant naturalist on Dumont d'Urville's 1837–40 expedition.

**Dun Glacier.** 77°48′S, 162°09′E. Feeds the Ferrar Glacier in Victoria Land. Flows from the southern side of the Kukri Hills, between Mount Coates and Sentinel Peak. Named by Grif Taylor's Western Journey Party during Scott's 1910–13 expedition.

**Port Dunbar.** Probably someone's idea of trying to rename Deception Island in the 1821–22 season. Also called Dunbar's Harbor, it was almost certainly named for Thomas J. Dunbar, Jr. Definitely it was an early name for what later became Port Foster.

**Dunbar, Addison.** Private on the Wilkes Expedition 1838–42. Joined in the USA. Served the cruise.

**Dunbar, Thomas J., Jr.** American sealing captain from Westerly, Rhode Island. He was commander and part owner of the *Free Gift* during the Fanning-Pendleton Sealing Expedition to the South Shetlands in 1820–21. In 1821–22 he was captain of the *Express.*

**Dunbar Islands.** 62°29′S, 60°12′W. A group SW of Williams Point, off the north coast of Livingston Island, in the South Shetlands. Named in 1958 by the UK for Thomas Dunbar.

**Dunbar Ridge.** 79°33′S, 84°16′W. 10 miles long. Separates the upper reaches of the Balish and Schneider Glaciers in the Heritage Range. Named by the University of Minnesota Geological Party of 1963–64 for Warrant Officer William Dunbar, maintenance officer of the 62nd Transportation Detachment who helped the party.

**Dunbar's Harbor** *see* **Port Dunbar** (under D)

**Duncan Mountains.** 85°02′S, 166°W. 18 miles long. Between the Liv and Strom Glaciers in the Transantarctic Mountains, overlooking the Ross Ice Shelf. Discovered in Nov. 1929 during Byrd's 1928–30 expedition, and named James Duncan Mountains by Byrd for James Duncan, manager of Tapley Ltd., Byrd's shipping agent in Dunedin, NZ. The name was later abbreviated.

**Duncan Peninsula.** 73°56′S, 119°30′W. Ice-covered. 30 miles long. Forms the east part of Carney Island along the coast of Marie Byrd Land. Named for Adm. Donald B. Duncan, USN, vice chief of naval operations under Admiral Carney during the IGY.

**Cape Dundas.** 60°44′S, 44°24′W. The most easterly point on Laurie Island, in the South Orkneys. Discovered by Weddell on Jan. 12, 1823, and named by him for the British noble family.

**Dundee Island.** 63°30′S, 55°55′W. At the north of the Antarctic Peninsula, immediately south of Joinville Island. Discovered on Jan. 8, 1893, by Capt. Thomas Robertson of the *Active* during the Dundee Whaling Expedition that summer, and named by him for the town of Dundee.

**Dundee Whaling Expedition.** 1892–93. Four Dundee whalers equipped for the Antarctic by Dundee shipowner and merchant, Robert Kinnes, which went seeking the right whales in the Weddell Sea reported by Ross 50 years before. The *Balaena* (commanded by Alexander Fairweather), the *Active* (commanded by Thomas Robertson), the *Diana* (commanded by Robert Davidson) and the *Polar Star* (commanded by James Davidson). W.G. Burn Murdoch was the artist, and the three naturalists/doctors were Bruce, Donald, and Campbell.

**Dunedin Range.** 71°24′S, 167°54′E. 23 miles long. Between 2 and 4 miles wide. 5 miles east of the Lyttelton Range in the Admiralty Mountains. Named for Dunedin, NZ, for its long history of support to Antarctic expeditions from all countries.

**Dungane Peaks.** 72°11′S, 24°09′E. 2 peaks. 2,870 m. 9 miles west of Dufek Mountain in the Sør Rondane Mountains. Name means "the heaps" in Norwegian.

**Mount Dungey.** 67°S, 51°15′E. 1 mile west of Pythagoras Peak in the Tula Mountains of Enderby Land. Named by the Australians for F.G. Dungey.

**Dungey, F.G.** Crew member on the *Discovery* during the BANZARE 1929–31.

**Cape Dunlop.** 77°14′S, 163°26′E. Also called Dunlop Point. Just west of Dunlop Island on the coast of Victoria Land. Mapped by Shackleton in 1907–9, and named by him as Rocky Point. Later renamed in association with the nearby island.

**Dunlop, H.T.L.** Irishman. Chief engineer on the *Nimrod*, 1907–9.

**Dunlop Island.** 77°15'S, 163°29'E. Also called Terrace Island. A little island, 1½ miles long by a mile wide, just NE of Cape Dunlop, in McMurdo Sound, off the Wilson Piedmont Glacier. Mapped by Shackleton's 1907–9 expedition, and named by them for H.T.L. Dunlop.

**Dunlop Peak.** 67°57'S, 62°28'E. 1,330 m. One of the Smith Peaks. 1 mile south of Mount Hordern in the David Range of the Framnes Mountains. Photographed by the LCE 1936–37. Named later by the Australians for R. Dunlop, cosmic ray physicist at Mawson Station in 1958.

**Dunlop Point** *see* **Cape Dunlop**

**Dunn, James.** Officer's steward on the Wilkes Expedition 1838–42. Joined in the USA. Served the cruise.

**Dunn Glacier.** 73°37'S, 165°43'E. Flows from the NW slopes of Mount Casey into the Icebreaker Glacier in the Mountaineer Range of Victoria Land. Named for Robert Dunn, USN, commissaryman at McMurdo Station in 1967.

**Dunn Spur.** 86°21'S, 147°22'W. Descends from Mount Blackburn and extends for 5 miles along the north side of Van Reeth Glacier in the Queen Maud Mountains. Named for Thomas H. Dunn, VX-6 air crewman, 1964, 1966, and 1967.

**Duparc, Louis.** French naval officer on the *Astrolabe* during Dumont d'Urville's 1837–40 expedition.

**Duparc Rocks.** 63°31'S, 58°50'W. A group of rocks in water, 3 miles NE of Cape Roquemaurel, Trinity Peninsula. Named by the UK for Louis Duparc.

**Duperré Bay.** 64°27'S, 62°41'W. Also called Shackleton Harbor, Bahía Santa Marta. 3 miles long. Just NE of Hulot Peninsula, at the SW end of Brabant Island. Discovered by Charcot in 1903–

5, and named by him for Vice-Adm. Charles Duperré of the French Navy.

**The *Durant*.** US Ship DER-389, in Antarctica 1962–63.

**Mount Durham.** 85°33'S, 151°12'W. 860 m. Mainly ice-free. Between the Leverett Glacier and the Robert Scott Glacier, it marks the NW limits of the Tapley Mountains, overlooking the Ross Ice Shelf. Discovered by Gould's Dec. 1929 party during Byrd's 1928–30 expedition, and climbed in Dec. 1934 by Quin Blackburn's party during Byrd's 1933–35 expedition. Named by Byrd for Durham, N.H., home of Stuart D.L. Paine.

**Durham Point.** 85°32'S, 151°12'W. A spur which extends north from Mount Durham at the NW end of the Tapley Mountains in the Queen Maud Mountains, just to the east of where the Robert Scott Glacier flows into the Ross Ice Shelf. Visited in Dec. 1934 by Quin Blackburn's party during Byrd's 1933–35 expedition, and named in association with the mountain.

**Mount Durnford.** 80°58'S, 158°15'E. 2,715 m. 5 miles SE of Mount Field, between the Byrd Glacier and the Ross Ice Shelf, in the Churchill Mountains. Discovered by Scott's 1901–4 expedition, and named by them as Durnford Bluff, for Adm. Sir John Durnford, naval lord who helped Scott's expedition. Redefined by the New Zealanders in 1960–61.

**Durnford Bluff** *see* **Mount Durnford**

**Duroch, Joseph.** Joseph Antoine Duroch. Ensign on the *Astrolabe* during Dumont d'Urville's 1837–40 expedition. He was promoted to lt. cdr. on Aug. 20, 1839.

**Duroch Islands.** 63°18'S, 57°54'W. A group of islands and rocks which extend for 3 miles just NW of Cape Legoupil on the north coast of Trinity Peninsula. They include Gándara Island, Kopaitic Island, Pebbly Mudstone Island, Silvia Rock, the Acuña Rocks, the Cohen Islands, etc. Discovered in 1837–40 by Dumont d'Urville, who only named one of the larger islands in the group, as Rocher Duroch, for Joseph Duroch. This name was translated into English as Duroch Rock, and was also seen spelled (erroneously) as Durock Rock. The group was charted and redefined by the FIDS in 1946.

**Durrance Inlet.** 73°50'S, 16°30'W. Ice-filled. 10 miles north of Veststraumen Glacier on the Princess Martha Coast. 5 miles wide. Named for Lt. (jg) Frank M. Durrance, Jr., USNR, navigator on the Nov. 5, 1967, VX-6 flight which plotted this inlet.

**Cape D'Ursel** *see* **D'Ursel Point**

**D'Ursel Point.** 64°25'S, 62°20'W. Marks the south side of the entrance to Buls Bay, on the SE coast of Brabant Island. Discovered by de Gerlache in 1897–99, and named by him for Count Hippolyte d'Ursel, a supporter.

**d'Urville** *see* **Dumont d'Urville**

**Mount d'Urville.** 63°31'S, 58°11'W. Also called D'Urville Berg. 1,085 m. Just north of the east end of Louis Philippe Plateau, on Trinity Peninsula. Discovered by Dumont d'Urville in 1837–40, and named for him by the French.

**D'Urville Berg** *see* **Mount d'Urville**

**d'Urville Canyon.** 64°30'S, 137°E. Submarine feature off Adélie Land.

**d'Urville Island.** 63°05'S, 56°20'W. 17 miles long. Immediately north of Joinville Island, the most northerly island south of the Bransfield Strait. Charted by Nordenskjöld's expedition in 1902, and named by them for Dumont d'Urville.

**d'Urville Monument.** 63°25'S, 56°18'W. 575 m. A conical peak at the SW end of Joinville Island. Discovered and named d'Urville's Monument by Ross in 1839–43, for Dumont d'Urville. Renamed slightly later.

**d'Urville Wall.** 75°16'S, 162°13'E. 720 m. A granitic cliff cut by a glacier. Forms the north wall of David Glacier near its terminus, in the Prince Albert Mountains of Victoria Land. Discovered by

Shackleton in 1907–9, and named by him for Dumont d'Urville.

**Duse, Lt. Samuel A.** Cartographer on Nordenskjöld's 1901–4 expedition. He was one of the 3 forced to winter-over at Hope Bay in 1903.

**Duse Bay.** 63°32'S, 57°15'W. Also called Bay of the Thousand Icebergs, and also seen misspelled as Duce Bay. Indentation into the south side of the Trinity Peninsula, between View Point and the west side of Tabarin Peninsula. Discovered by J. Gunnar Andersson's party, in 1902–3, during Nordenskjöld's expedition of 1901–4, and named by Nordenskjöld for Samuel A. Duse.

**Cape Duseberg** *see* **Duseberg Buttress**

**Duseberg Buttress.** 65°10'S, 64°06'W. 500 m. A cone at the SW side of Mount Scott, on the west coast of Graham Land. Discovered and named Cap Duseberg by de Gerlache in 1897–99. Later redefined, as there is no point (cap) here, only a rocky buttress.

**Dusky Mountains** *see* **Dusky Ridge**

**Dusky Ridge.** 80°05'S, 157°02'E. Icefree. 9 miles long. 2 miles wide. Between the Lieske and Hinton Glaciers in the Britannia Range. The Darwin Glacier Party of the BCTAE 1956–58 named it Dusky Mountains because of its ice-free slopes. Redefined by the USA in 1962.

**Dustin, Frederick G.** American veteran of the Antarctic. He was one of the shore party on Byrd's 1933–35 expedition, and was a mechanic at West Base during the USAS 1939–41. He took part in Operation Highjump, 1946–47, and then, in 1955–56, was a commander on the *Glacier*. On Nov. 22, 1968, he visited McMurdo Station for a few hours.

**Dustin Island.** 72°34'S, 94°50'W. An island consisting of a low, snow-covered dome and abrupt coastal cliffs. 18 miles long. 15 miles SE of Cape Annawan, it forms the SE limit of Seraph Bay, east of

Thurston Island. Discovered by Byrd on a flight from the *Bear* on Feb. 27, 1940, and named by him for Frederick G. Dustin.

**Duthie, Alistair.** New Zealander from Dunedin who took part in Ellsworth's 1934–35 expedition as a crew member on the *Wyatt Earp.*

**Duthiers Head**   *see*   **Duthiers Point**

**Duthiers Point.** 64°48′S, 62°49′W. Also called Duthiers Head, Punta Duthon, Punta Canelo. Forms the south side of the entrance to Andvord Bay, on the west coast of Graham Land. Discovered by de Gerlache in 1897–99, and named by him as Cap Lacaze-Duthiers, for Félix-Henri de Lacaze-Duthiers (1821–1901), French naturalist.

**Duthoit Point.** 62°19′S, 58°50′W. Forms the east tip of Nelson Island, in the South Shetlands. Named by the personnel on the *Discovery II* in 1935.

**Punta Duthon**   *see*   **Duthiers Point, Duthoit Point**

**Du Toit Mountains.** 72°28′S, 62°11′W. On the east coast of Palmer Land.

**Du Toit Nunataks.** 80°44′S, 25°50′W. In the Shackleton Range.

**Duyvis Point.** 65°55′S, 64°35′W. On the east side of Barilari Bay. 11 miles SSE of Cape García, on the west coast of Graham Land. Named by the UK for F. Donker Duyvis, Dutch documentalist, secretary of the International Federation for Documentation.

**Dvergen Hill.** 72°13′S, 0°47′E. Isolated. 4 miles north of Fuglefjellet in the Sverdrup Mountains of Queen Maud Land. Name means "the dwarf" in Norwegian.

**Dvořák Ice Rise.** 71°17′S, 72°57′W. 1½ miles in extent. In Mendelssohn Inlet, in the SW part of Alexander Island. Named by the UK for the composer.

**¹Mount Dwyer.** 70°11′S, 65°04′E. 2 miles SE of Mount Dovers in the Athos Range of the Prince Charles Mountains. Named by the Australians for V.J.

Dwyer, radio operator at Mawson Station in 1964.

**²Mount Dwyer**   *see*   **Berg Mountains**

**Dwyer Escarpment.** 70°40′S, 165°24′E. Ice-covered. Overlooks the north coast of Victoria Land between Cooper Spur and Cape North. Mapped by the ANARE in 1962, and named by them for L.J. Dwyer, director of the Australian Commonwealth Bureau of Meteorology, a member of the ANARE Executive Planning Committee.

**Dwyer Nunataks.** 68°13′S, 58°27′E. 6 miles in extent. 3 miles wide. 2 miles SE of Mount Gjeita in the Hansen Mountains. Named by the Australians for V.J. Dwyer (*see* **Mount Dwyer**).

**Dybvadskog Peak.** 79°19′S, 86°20′W. 2,180 m. Isolated. Just west of the southern part of the Founders Escarpment in the Heritage Range. Named for Olav Dybvadskog, Norwegian glaciologist, a member of the USARP South Pole–Queen Maud Land Traverse of 1964–65.

**Dyer, J. Glenn.** American surveyor with the General Land Office, Department of the Interior. He was the cadastral engineer at East Base during the USAS 1939–41.

**Dyer, John N.** Chief radio engineer on the shore party of Byrd's 1933–35 expedition. In 1934 he fell 45 feet from an antenna pole at Little America II, but only scraped his shin.

**Dyer Island.** 67°36′S, 62°52′E. A small island between Lee Island and Entrance Island in Holme Bay, Mac. Robertson Land. Named by the Australians for R. Dyer, cook at nearby Mawson Station in 1960.

**Dyer Plateau.** 71°S, 65°W. A huge plateau on the Antarctic Peninsula, to the east of Alexander Island. Named for J. Glenn Dyer.

**Dyer Point.** 71°52′S, 100°55′W. Ice-covered. Just west of Hughes Peninsula on the north coast of Thurston Island. Named for John N. Dyer.

**Mount Dyke.** 67°35'S, 49°25'E. 1,100 m. 3 miles north of Mount Humble, in the NE part of the Raggatt Mountains. Named by the Australians for Flying Officer G. Dyke, RAAF, pilot at Mawson Station in 1960.

**Dykes Peak.** 77°13'S, 161°01'E. 2,220 m. At the head of the Victoria Upper Glacier. 4 miles east of Skew Peak, in the Clare Range of Victoria Land. Named in 1974 for Leonard H. Dykes, US Government man involved in Antarctica for many years.

**Dyment Island.** 74°08'S, 102°02'W. A small island 5 miles SW of the McKinzie Islands in the central part of Cranton Bay. Named for Donald I. Dyment, USN, cook at Byrd Station in 1967.

**Dymond, Percy.** Crewman on the *Jacob Ruppert,* 1933-35.

**Dyna Hill.** 72°22'S, 0°40'E. 2 miles west of Kvithovden Peak in the Sverdrup Mountains of Queen Maud Land. Name means "the dune" in Norwegian.

**Dynamite Island.** 68°11'S, 67°W. A small island in Back Bay, 175 yards east of Stonington Island, off the west coast of Graham Land. Surveyed by the USAS 1939-41 and named Petrel Island by them. There was already another Petrel Island in South Georgia (54°S), so Finn Ronne renamed it in 1948 for the dynamite he used to blast the *Port of Beaumont, Texas* out of the ice near here in 1947.

**Dyrdal Peak.** 83°25'S, 51°23'W. 1,820 m. At the SW end of the Saratoga Table. 2 miles WNW of Fierle Peak, in the Forrestal Range of the Pensacola Mountains. Named for Frederick F. Dyrdal, aviation structural mechanic at Ellsworth Station in 1957.

**Dzema Peak.** 85°45'S, 138°W. 2,570 m. 5 miles WSW of Mount Ratliff, on the north side of the Watson Escarpment. Named for Lt. (jg) John Dzema of VX-6, at McMurdo Station in 1962-63 and 1963-64.

**Mount Dzhalil.** 72°01'S, 14°36'E. 2,510 m. In the Linnormen Hills of the Payer Mountains in Queen Maud Land. Named by the USSR in 1966 for Musa Dzhalil, poet.

**Dziura Nunataks.** 71°44'S, 161°15'E. 1,480 m. Ice-free. 2 miles NW of Mount Remington, in the NW extremity of the Helliwell Hills. Named for Charles S. Dziura, US meteorologist at Amundsen-Scott South Pole Station in 1967-68.

**Monte E.** *see* **Mount Aciar**

**E. de Rothschild Island** *see* **Rothschild Island**

**Mount E. Gruening** *see* **Mount Jackson**

**Eadie Island.** 61°28'S, 55°57'W. 1 mile long. Between Aspland and O'Brien Islands in the South Shetlands. Charted by von Bellingshausen in Feb. 1821. He named the three islands Ostrova Tri Brata (Three Brothers Islands). This one was renamed by Lt. L.C. Hill on the *Discovery II* in 1936-37 for the dockyard manager of the Melbourne Harbour Trust in Australia.

**Eady Ice Piedmont.** 78°32'S, 165°18'E. Just south of Mount Discovery, on the edge of the Ross Ice Shelf, in the Transantarctic Mountains. Named in 1963 for Capt. Jack A. Eady, USN, chief of staff to the commander, US Naval Support Force, Antarctica, from July 1959-April 1962.

**The Eagle.** Participated in the second phase of Operation Tabarin, i.e. the 1944-45 part. In Feb. 1945 it helped establish Base D at Hope Bay. Captain was R.C. Sheppard, 1st mate was R. Whitten, and bosun was Tom Carrel.

**Eagle Cove.** 63°24'S, 57°W. Just west of Seal Point on the south side of Hope Bay, at the NE end of the Antarctic Peninsula. Discovered by J. Gunnar Andersson during the Nordenskjöld expedition of 1901-4. Later named by the FIDS for the *Eagle.*

**Eagle Island.** 63°40'S, 57°29'W. 5 miles long. 4 miles wide. 560 meters high on the NE side. It is the largest island in the archipelago between Trinity

Peninsula and Vega Island. Charted by the FIDS in 1945, and named by them for the *Eagle*.

**Mount Early.** 87°04'S, 153°46'W. A solitary volcanic cone. 2,720 m. 13 miles north of D'Angelo Bluff, at the top of the Robert Scott Glacier. Discovered in Dec. 1934 by Quin Blackburn's party during Byrd's 1933–35 expedition, from nearby Mount Weaver. First visited by George Doumani's Ohio State University geological party on Nov. 21, 1962. Named for Capt. Neal E. Early, US Army, here that season.

**Early Bluff.** 75°13'S, 113°57'W. On the east side of the Kohler Glacier on the south side of the Kohler Range of Marie Byrd Land. Named by local scientists in the 1960s for Thomas O. Early, paleomagnetician on the Marie Byrd Land Survey party of 1966–67.

**Early Islands.** 73°40'S, 101°40'W. Just west of the Cosgrove Ice Shelf in the SE corner of Ferrero Bay in the Amundsen Sea. Named for Tommy Joe Early, biologist with the Ellsworth Land Survey of 1968–69.

**Earnshaw Glacier.** 68°45'S, 65°11'W. 10 miles long. Flows to the east of Norwood Scarp and enters Maitland Glacier to the south of Werner Peak in the eastern part of the Antarctic Peninsula. Named by the UK for Thomas Earnshaw (1749–1829), pioneer in the chronometer.

**Mount Earp**   *see*   **Mount Wyatt Earp**

**Earthquakes.** Seismologically, Antarctica is the quietest of the continents. There have not been many major earthquakes in modern times, although Antarctica is quite active tectonically, as was shown in 1981 when earthquake activity was picked up by the three seismic stations on Mount Erebus (*see* **Volcanoes**). During the summer of 1982–83 thousands of small earthquakes were recorded by these devices, sometimes as many as 650 a day. Some other interesting ones recently have been **Aug. 11, 1970:** 6 on the Richter Scale. 60°36'S, 25°24'W. At

sea. **Feb. 8, 1971:** 6.3 on the Richter Scale. On Deception Island. No volcanic activity. **Aug. 11, 1971:** 5.4 on the Richter Scale. In the Balleny Islands. **Feb. 25, 1972:** 6.1 on the Richter Scale. 60°36'S, 25°42'W. **Feb. 25, 1973:** 6.4 on the Richter Scale. 61°S, 37°54'W. At sea. **Oct. 6, 1973:** 7.0 on the Richter Scale. 60°48'S, 21°30'W. At sea. Major earthquakes are over 6.9, and large ones are 6.0 to 6.9.

**Earth's crust**   *see*   **Crust**

**Cape Easson**   *see*   **Cape Little**

**East Antarctic Ice Sheet.** A desert. It is now so high and vast that little atmospheric moisture nourishes its central part. It can reach heights of 11,500 feet and more (*see* **Highest points in Antarctica**). (*See also* **East Antarctica**, and **Atmosphere**.)

**East Antarctica.** Centers on 80°S, 80° E. Also called Greater Antarctica, Gondwana Province (because of its geographical affinity with the Gondwana region of India. It may once have been joined to it. *See* **Gondwanaland**). East Antarctica is really a high, ice-covered plateau, the ice cap being unstable, or mobile, and between 50 and 200 million years old. Geologically, though, the 3–5 billion-year-old Pre-Cambrian shield bedrock beneath is stable, and this mass of land is the actual continent of Antarctica, West Antarctica being geologically an archipelago of islands. It is only the thick ice sheet joining the two halves together that adds to the surface size of the continent. East Antarctica comprises Coats Land, Queen Maud Land, Enderby Land, Mac. Robertson Land, Wilkes Land, and Victoria Land. The name was coined by Edwin Swift Balch (*see* the Bibliography) in 1902, and used by Nordenskjöld a few years later. The name grew in popularity until the IGY (1957–58) when the Transantarctic Mountains proved such a natural divide between the two halves of Antarctica, that the name was made official by the USA in 1962.

**East Arm.** 67°36'S, 62°53'E. A peninsula. Forms the eastern limit of Horseshoe Harbor in Holme Bay, Mac. Robertson Land. Photographed by the LCE 1936–37. Visited by an ANARE party on Feb. 5, 1954, and named descriptively by them.

**East Balch Glacier** *see* **Balch Glacier**

**East Base.** Built by Richard Black at the north end of Stonington Island in Marguerite Bay, off the west coast of the Antarctic Peninsula. It was the eastern base of the USAS 1939–41. Black was in command and Finn Ronne was second in command. For other personnel, *see* **United States Antarctic Service Expedition 1939–41.** The site was selected on March 8, 1940. There were 6 prefabricated buildings. The main building had the galley, the leader's quarters, and the sick bay. The others were a science building with a meteorological tower, a machine shop with 2 generators, a small hut, a taxidermy shop, and a storage hut. When Ronne landed here again in 1947 for the RARE, he found that the base had been ravaged by other expeditions. He renamed it Port of Beaumont, Texas, Base and wintered-over there in 1947. Although East Base was the first year-round base on the Antarctic Peninsula, it has not been used since 1948.

**East Beacon.** 77°50′S, 160°52′E. Peak over 2,200 m. Between Beacon Valley and Arena Valley in southern Victoria Land. It is part of the Beacon Heights on the south edge of Taylor Glacier. Named by the New Zealanders in 1962–63.

**East Budd Island.** 67°35′S, 62°51′E. At the north end of the Flat Islands in Holme Bay, Mac. Robertson Land. Photographed by the LCE 1936–37. The northern islands in the group were named Flatöynålane (the flat island needles) by the Norwegians. This island was named by the Australians for Dr. G.M. Budd, medical officer at Mawson Station in 1959.

**¹East Cape.** 60°37′S, 45°10′W. Almost 1½ miles SE of Cape Bennett, on the extreme NE coast of Coronation Island in the South Orkneys. Discovered by Powell and Palmer in Dec. 1821. Named by personnel on the *Discovery II* in 1933.

**²East Cape.** The eastern side of the entrance to the Bay of Whales. It is gone now, along with the Bay of Whales.

**East Commonwealth Range** *see* **Separation Range**

**East Egerton.** 80°50′S, 158°05′E. 2,815 m. A peak, 2 miles east of Mount Egerton (hence the name). In the Churchill Mountains. Named by the New Zealanders in 1960–61.

**East Fork** *see* **Ferrar Glacier**

**East Germany.** East German scientists have been active in Antarctica since before the Berlin Wall went up, but mostly as members of USSR teams. The country was ratified on Nov. 19, 1974, as the 18th signatory to the Antarctic Treaty, being the 19th to achieve Consultative status, on Oct. 5, 1987. In 1986–87 they set up their own scientific station, Georg Foster Base.

**East Gould Glacier** *see* **Gould Glacier**

**East Groin.** 77°39′S, 160°57′E. Narrow rock spur. Forms the east wall of Flory Cirque on the south side of the Asgard Range in Victoria Land. Named descriptively in association with West Groin by Scott's 1910–13 expedition.

**East Melchior Islands.** 64°19′S, 62°55′W. Ice-covered. East of The Sound in the Melchior Islands. *See also* the **West Melchior Islands** and the **Melchior Islands.** Named by the Discovery Committee in 1927.

**East Ongul Island.** 69°S, 39°35′E. 1 mile long. Just east of the north part of Ongul Island, in the eastern part of Lützow-Holm Bay, off the Prince Olav Coast. Showa Station is here. Originally mapped as part of Ongul Island by the Norwegians from the photos taken by the LCE 1936–37. The Japanese in 1957 discovered a strait separating the two islands, and they redefined this one.

**East Pacific Rise** *see* **Albatross Cordillera**

East Perrier Bay   *see*   Perrier Bay

East Quartzite Range. 72° S, 165° 05′ E. 12 miles long. In the SW part of the King Range in the Concord Mountains. 5 miles east of the West Quartzite Range. Named by the New Zealanders in 1962–63 for the distinctive geological formation here.

East Russell Glacier   *see*   Russell East Glacier

East Stack. 67° 05′ S, 58° 12′ E. Also called Austskotet. A coastal rock on land. 60 m. On the east side of Hoseason Glacier, 16 miles SE of Edward VIII Bay. Discovered in Feb. 1936 by personnel on the *William Scoresby,* and named by them in association with West Stack.

Easter Island Cordillera   *see*   Albatross Cordillera

Easter Island Rise   *see*   Albatross Cordillera

Easter Island Swell   *see*   Albatross Cordillera

Eastern-Indian Antarctic Basin   *see* South Indian Basin

Eastern Plain   *see*   Polar Subglacial Basin

Eastface Nunatak. 78° 42′ S, 163° 38′ E. Ice-covered with a notable rock face on its east side (hence the name given in 1963). 11 miles south of Mount Morning in Victoria Land.

Mount Eastman. 65° 10′ S, 62° 59′ W. Overlooks the head of Flandres Bay. 4 miles south of Pelletan Point on the west coast of Graham Land. Named by the UK in 1960 for George Eastman (1854–1932), photography pioneer.

Eastman, Samuel. Quartermaster on the Wilkes Expedition 1838–42. Joined in the USA. Discharged at Oahu, Oct. 31, 1840.

The *Eastwind.* US Coast Guard icebreaker, launched in 1943. Took part in Operation Deep Freeze I (1955–56), and was back in Antarctic waters for Operation Deep Freeze 60, 61, 62, 63, 64, 65, 66, 67.

Eastwind Ridge. 76° 36′ S, 160° 47′ E. 10 miles long. Partly ice-covered. Between Chattahoochee and Towle Glaciers in the Convoy Range. Named in 1964 for the *Eastwind.*

Eastwood, William. Ordinary seaman on the Wilkes Expedition 1838–42. Joined in the USA. Served the cruise.

Mount Eather. 70° 29′ S, 65° 50′ E. 2 miles south of the Martin Massif in the Porthos Range. Named by the Australians for R.H. Eather, aurora physicist at Mawson Station in 1963.

Eaton Nunatak. 75° 10′ S, 72° W. Marks the SE end of the Merrick Mountains in Ellsworth Land. Named for John W. Eaton, aurora scientist at Eights Station in 1963.

Ebba Glacier   *see*   Liotard Glacier

Ebbe, Gordon K. Cdr. USN. The first head of VX-6, from June 1955–June 1956.

Ebbe Glacier. 71° 05′ S, 165° E. 60 miles long. Flows from the Homerun Range and the Robinson Heights, between the Everett Range and the Anare Mountains, or between the Rennick Glacier and Cape Adare in Oates Land, and enters Lillie Glacier. Named for Gordon K. Ebbe.

Eblen Hills. 85° 51′ S, 133° 28′ W. 1,640 m. Just north of the mouth of Colorado Glacier, where that glacier enters the west side of Reedy Glacier. Named for James C. Eblen, aviation machinist at McMurdo Station in 1969 and for several seasons after that.

Ebon Pond. 78° 11′ S, 165° 13′ E. In the SW end of the Brown Peninsula in Victoria Land. Named by Troy L. Péwé, US geologist, in 1957–58 for the black (ebon) volcanic terrain surrounding the pond.

Ebony Ridge. 83° 45′ S, 172° 45′ E. A coastal ridge, 5 miles long. Between Airdrop Peak and Mount Robert Scott. It consists of dark, metamorphosed greywacke, hence the name given by the New Zealanders in 1959–60.

**Ebony Wall.** 63°53'S, 59°08'W. 400 m. A dark, nearly vertical, rock wall cliff, 2 miles long, at the head of Pettus Glacier. It forms a part of the western escarpment of the Detroit Plateau near the base of Trinity Peninsula. Charted and named descriptively by the FIDS in 1948.

**Puerto Echeverría** *see* **New Plymouth**

**Echinoids.** Marine invertebrates that lie on the sea bed near the shore (*see* **Fauna**).

**Echo Mountain.** 60°37'S, 45°41'W. 790 m. Surmounts the west side of the Laws Glacier, just north of Cragsman Peaks on Coronation Island in the South Orkneys. Surveyed by the FIDS in 1948–49, and named by them for the echo experienced here.

**Eckener Point.** 64°26'S, 61°36'W. Marks the NE side of the entrance to Charlotte Bay, on the west coast of Graham Land. Named by the UK in 1960 for Hugo Eckener (1868–1954), German airship pioneer.

**Eckhörner Peaks.** 71°32'S, 11°27'E. Also called Hjornehorne. Six peaks in a line, which form the north wall of Schüssel Cirque in the north-central part of the Humboldt Mountains of Queen Maud Land. Discovered and named descriptively as Eck-Hörner (corner peaks) by Ritscher in 1938–39.

**Eckins Nunatak.** 85°08'S, 175°51'W. Isolated. 5 miles NE of Matador Mountain in the eastern part of the Shackleton Glacier. Named for Henry J. Eckins, meteorologist at South Pole Station in 1961.

**Eckman Bluff.** 74°47'S, 110°22'W. On the Bear Peninsula on the coast of Marie Byrd Land.

**Eclipse Point** *see* **Aguda Point**

**Economy.** Until recently the two economies in Antarctica were whaling and sealing. Now Antarctica exports mostly scientific findings. Tourism may well prove to be an economy of sorts (but for whom?) in the future, and then there is the growing concern of the minerals. When technology reaches a stage when it can dig the minerals out of the frozen continent, the Antarctic Treaty may well receive its first real test. Ice (and, therefore, non-salt water), is abundant to the point that Antarctica contains 90 percent of the world's ice, but transportation costs to civilization would be too high to make exporting the ice economical—as of 1990. If that can be overcome, Antarctica may shrink in size drastically over the next few millennia, and also become a more hospitable place. Could this be the colony of the future for mankind? Krill fishing is limited because it has proved difficult to market, and also because it is supposedly protected by CCAMLR.

**Ecuador.** Ratified as the 37th signatory to the Antarctic Treaty on Sept. 15, 1987.

**The** *Ed Sweeney.* Twin-engined Beechcraft C-45 airplane, the photographic plane for the RARE 1947–48. It was loaded aboard the *Port of Beaumont, Texas,* at Balboa, Panama, as a substitute for the original Beechcraft which had fallen into the dock at Beaumont, Texas, as it was being loaded onto the ship. Test flown in Antarctica on Sept. 30, 1947. Named by Ronne for Cdr. Edward C. Sweeney, USNR, a contributor to the expedition.

**Eddy Col.** 63°26'S, 57°06'W. Between Mount Taylor and Blade Ridge. 1½ miles SW of the head of Hope Bay, Trinity Peninsula. Surveyed and named in 1955 by the FIDS. The wind direction creates eddies in this col as it changes constantly.

**Eddy Point.** 62°14'S, 58°59'W. On the south side of Fildes Peninsula, ½ mile west of Halfthree Point on King George Island in the South Shetlands. Charted and named by the personnel on the *Discovery II* in 1935. It is used as a reference point for finding the rocks in Fildes Strait.

**Eddystone** *see* **Eddystone Rocks**

**Eddystone Rocks.** 62°36'S, 61°23'W. Rocks in water. 4½ miles SW of Start Point on Livingston Island in the South Shetlands. Named before 1822.

**Eden Glacier.** 66°12'S, 63°15'W. 5 miles long. Flows into the head of Cabinet Inlet, NW of Lyttelton Ridge, on the east coast of Graham Land. Named by the FIDS for the British politician, Anthony Eden, a member of the War Cabinet which created Operation Tabarin.

**Eden Island** *see* **Eden Rocks**

**Eden Rocks.** 63°29'S, 55°40'W. Rocks in water, just off the east end of Dundee Island. Ross reported a small island here on Dec. 30, 1842, and called it Eden Island for Capt. Charles Eden, RN. A 1953 survey by the FIDS proved it to be two islands close together. The larger one is sometimes called Eden Island and the smaller one is sometimes called Bass Rock.

**Islote Edgardo** *see* **Walsham Rocks**

**Edge Glacier.** 82°29'S, 51°07'W. Flows into the Davis Valley, in the NE part of the Dufek Massif in the Pensacola Mountains. Named for Joseph L. Edge, VX-6 photographer, 1963 and 1964.

**Edge Hill** *see* **Mount Tranchant**

**Edge Rocks.** 83°59'S, 52°55'W. Two rocks on land at the SE edge of the Iroquois Plateau. 11 miles east of Hill Nunatak in the Pensacola Mountains. Named for their position on the edge of the plateau.

**Edgecumbe, John.** 2nd lt. and commander of the Marines on the *Adventure*, during Cook's second voyage (1772–75).

**Mount Edgell.** 69°26'S, 68°16'W. 1,675 m. East of Cape Jeremy (which it overlooks), the east side of the northern entrance to the George VI Sound, just south of the Wordie Ice Shelf, on the west coast of the Antarctic Peninsula. Discovered in 1908–10 by Charcot, who named it Île Gordon Bennett, for James Gordon Bennett (1841–1918), of the *New York Herald*, a supporter. In 1936–37 the BGLE couldn't find an island here, but did find a mountain. They renamed it for John Edgell, hydrographer of the British Navy from 1932–45.

**Edgell Bay.** 62°16'S, 58°59'W. 1½ miles long and 1½ miles wide. Indents the NE side of Nelson Island in the South Shetlands. Charted by Powell in 1821–22. Recharted in 1934–35 by personnel on the *Discovery II* who named it for Sir John Edgell (*see* **Mount Edgell**).

**Edgeworth David Station.** Australian summer research station built on the Bunger Hills of Queen Maud Land. Named for Edgeworth David.

**Edgeworth Glacier.** 64°23'S, 59°55'W. 12 miles long. Flows from the edge of Detroit Plateau below Wolseley Buttress to the ice shelf to the west of Sobral Peninsula in Graham Land. Named by the UK for Richard L. Edgeworth (1744–1817), inventor of the "Portable Railway" in 1770, the first track-laying vehicle.

**Edholm Point.** 66°15'S, 67°04'W. The most northwesterly of the Krogh Islands in the Biscoe Islands. Named by the UK for Otto G. Edholm, physiologist specializing in the cold.

**Edinburgh Hill.** 62°33'S, 60°01'W. A volcanic knob. Forms the north side of the entrance to Moon Bay in the east part of Livingston Island, in the South Shetlands. Named by David Ferguson in 1913–14. In 1935 the personnel on the *Discovery II* renamed it High Point, but that name did not catch on and the original naming, for the Scottish capital, is now in force.

**The *Edisto*.** US Navy wind-class icebreaker of 6,150 tons launched in 1946. 10,000 hp. Took part in Operation Windmill, 1947–48, as part of Task Force 39. While on this operation it circumnavigated Antarctica with the *Burton Island*, and on Feb. 20, 1948, helped break from the ice the *Port of Beaumont, Texas*, Ronne's ship at Stonington Island. During and after the IGY it was part of Task Force 43, and took part in Operation Deep Freeze I (1955–56. Cdr.

Roger W. Luther was in command), Operation Deep Freeze IV (1958–59), and Operation Deep Freeze 61 (Cdr. Griffith C. Evans, Jr., took over command on Nov. 14, 1960 for this operation), 63, 65, 69. It was transferred from the US Navy to the Coast Guard on Oct. 20, 1965.

**Edisto Bay** *see* **Edisto Inlet**

**Edisto Channel.** 66°05'S, 100°50'E. Marine channel between Taylor Islands and the NW islands in the Highjump Archipelago on the west and the Bunger Hills, Thomas Island, and the rest of the Highjump Archipelago on the east. The SW end is occupied by the Edisto Ice Tongue. Named for the *Edisto*.

**Edisto Glacier.** 72°27'S, 169°53'E. Flows between Felsite Island and Redcastle Ridge into the Edisto Inlet. Named by the New Zealanders in 1957–58 for the *Edisto*.

**Edisto Ice Tongue.** 66°10'S, 100°37'E. Occupies the SW part of the Edisto Channel, in the NW edge of the Bunger Hills, in the Highjump Archipelago. It is fed by the Apfel and Scott Glaciers. Named in association with the channel.

**Edisto Inlet.** 72°20'S, 170°05'E. At the southern end of Moubray Bay. It is 7 miles long and 3 miles wide. Cape Hallett juts out into it from Victoria Land, and it is between that cape and Cape Christie. Originally named Edisto Bay for the *Edisto*, which came in here in Feb. 1956, looking for a station (Hallett, as it happened). It was later redefined.

**Edisto Rock** *see* **Edisto Rocks**

**Edisto Rocks.** 68°13'S, 67°08'W. Almost 1¼ miles SW of the western tip of Neny Island in Marguerite Bay. Surveyed in 1947 by the FIDS and named by them as Edisto Rock, for the *Edisto*. Later redefined.

**Bahía Edith** *see* **Eyrie Bay**

**Edith Ronne Ice Shelf** *see* **Ronne Ice Shelf**

**Edith Ronne Land.** From Mount Austin at the base of the Antarctic Peninsula to Berkner Island in between what are now called the Ronne Ice Shelf and the Filchner Ice Shelf. Named by Finn Ronne in 1947 for his wife (*see* **Edith Ronne**), and claimed by him for the USA. In 1968 it became part of the Ronne Ice Shelf (*see* **Ronne Ice Shelf** for details).

**Mount Edixon.** 71°48'S, 163°23'E. 2,080 m. 6 miles SE of Bowers Peak in the Lanterman Range of the Bowers Mountains. Named by the Northern Party of the NZGSAE 1963–64 for Lt. James R. Edixon, VX-6 pilot who supported the party.

**Edlin Névé.** 71°10'S, 163°06'E. At the south side of Mount Sturm in the Bowers Mountains. Feeds the Carryer, Irwin, McLin, and Graveson Glaciers, as well as others. Named by the New Zealanders in 1967–68 for G. Edlin, the postmaster at Scott Base that season.

**Edman Island.** 66°18'S, 110°32'E. Near the center of O'Brien Bay in the Windmill Islands. Named for Donald H. Edman, ionosphere physicist at Wilkes Station in 1958.

**Edmonson Point.** 74°20'S, 165°08'E. Largely ice-free. Below Mount Melbourne on the west side of Wood Bay in Victoria Land. Named for Larry D. Edmonson, satellite geodesy scientist at McMurdo Station, 1966.

**Mount Edred.** 70°35'S, 69°W. 2,195 m. Ice-covered. 10 miles inland from George VI Sound. Marks the southern limit of the Douglas Range on Alexander Island. Named by the FIDS in 1949 for the old Saxon king.

**Edsel Ford Mountains** *see* **Ford Ranges**

**Edsel Ford Ranges** *see* **Ford Ranges**

**Edson Hills.** 79°49'S, 83°39'W. Mainly ice-free. South of the Drake Icefall, west of the Union Glacier, in the Heritage Range. Named by the University of Minnesota Ellsworth Mountains Party of 1962–63 for Dean T. Edson, topographic engineer with the party.

**Cape Edvind Astrup** *see* **Cape Astrup**

**Mount Edward.** 75°12′S, 69°33′W. 1,635 m. On the southern edge of the Sweeney Mountains in eastern Ellsworth Land. Discovered by the RARE 1947–48, and named by Ronne for Cdr. Ed Sweeney (*see* the *Ed Sweeney*).

**Edward VIII Bay.** 66°50′S, 57°E. Also called Edward VIII Gulf. Between Law Promontory and Cape Boothby in Kemp Land, or between the Edward VIII Plateau and the Øygarden Group. 20 miles in extent. Discovered in 1936 by personnel on the William Scoresby, and named by them for the king.

**Edward VIII Gulf** *see* **Edward VIII Bay**

**Edward VIII Ice Shelf.** 66°50′S, 56°33′E. Occupies the head of Edward VIII Bay. Photographed by the LCE 1936–37. The northern part was named Innviksletta (the inner bay plain) by the Norwegians working off these photos. The whole ice shelf was later redefined and renamed for the bay.

**Edward VIII Plateau.** 66°35′S, 56°50′E. A dome-shaped, ice-covered peninsula between Magnet Bay and Edward VIII Bay. Photographed by the LCE 1936–37 and named Gulfplatået (the gulf plateau) by the Norwegians. The Australians renamed it King Edward Plateau, and the US even later called it Edward VIII Plateau.

**Edward Ridge.** 67°15′S, 55°34′E. Snow-covered. 13 miles NW of Rayner Peak in Enderby Land. Named by the Australians for Edward Nash, aircraft mechanic with the ANARE *Nella Dan* expedition of 1965 under Phillip Law.

**Edward VII Land.** 77°S, 145°W. The land behind and including the famous Edward VII Peninsula. On Jan. 30, 1902, Scott discovered this land, and called it King Edward VII Land, for the new king. What Scott actually discovered was a peninsula, but he had no way of knowing its true character. However, the peninsula is only the largest part of an even greater area of land called Edward VII Land.

**Edward VII Peninsula.** 77°40′S, 155°W. Also called King Edward VII Peninsula. It forms the tip of Edward VII Land, and juts out into the Ross Sea at the NW extremity of Marie Byrd Land. It forms the NE edge of the Ross Ice Shelf. It has on it the Rockefeller Mountains and the Alexandra Mountains. It lies between the NE corner of the Ross Ice Shelf and Sulzberger Bay. This land was discovered on Jan. 30, 1902, by Scott (*see* **Edward VII Land**), who named it King Edward VII Land, a term that was subsequently shortened to Edward VII Land. This was the first Antarctic discovery of the 20th century. During Byrd's 1933–35 expedition it began to look as if this land were in fact a peninsula, and this suspicion was proved to be a fact by the USAS 1939–41. The name for this enormous peninsula was consequently given as Edward VII Peninsula, and the land to the south of it was called Edward VII Land. The term Edward VII Land now covers the peninsula as well, yet the peninsula has retained its own name as a separate feature within that land.

**Mount Edwards.** 76°51′S, 144°07′W. 5 miles ESE of Morris Peak in the Denfeld Mountains of Marie Byrd Land. Named by Byrd for Leroy P. Edwards, financial adviser to Byrd on his first two expeditions.

**Edwards Gap.** 71°15′S, 70°20′W. On Alexander Island.

**Edwards Glacier.** 71°35′S, 160°30′E. Flows from the eastern slopes of the Daniels Range between Thompson Spur and Schroeder Spur in the Usarp Mountains. Named for Lloyd N. Edwards, US geologist at McMurdo Station in 1967–68.

[1]**Edwards Island.** Somewhere in the South Shetlands, in the area of Deception Island. William Smith discovered it in Feb. 1820, and named it. It has remained a mystery as to what exactly is this island. Was it a berg, was it an island which doesn't exist any more, or was it Deception Island itself, or perhaps another island which now has another name?

²**Edwards Island.** 65°35'S, 64°19'W. Second largest in the group of islands in the entrance to Leroux Bay, off the west coast of Graham Land. Named by the UK for Lt. Cecil J.C. Wynne-Edwards, RN, who led a hydrographic survey unit here in 1956–57, 1957–58.

¹**Edwards Islands.** 66°51'S, 50°29'E. Group in the east side of Amundsen Bay. 2½ miles SW of Mount Oldfield in Enderby Land. Named by the Australians for T. Edwards, assistant diesel mechanic at Wilkes Station in 1960.

²**Edwards Islands.** 73°53'S, 103°08'W. Group of 20 small islands. Mostly ice-free. Off the SW tip of Canisteo Peninsula in the Amundsen Sea. Named for Z.T. Edwards, chief quartermaster on the *Glacier* here in 1959–60.

**Edwards Nunatak.** 70°46'S, 65°42'E. 2 miles SW of Mount Kizaki in the Aramis Range. Named by the Australians for D.R. Edwards, radio technician at Mawson Station, 1969.

**Edwards Peninsula.** 71°55'S, 97°46'W. 20 miles long. Ice-covered. Between Murphy and Koether Inlets on the north side of Thurston Island. Named for Lt. Donald L. Edwards, navigator of the *Burton Island* in 1959–60.

**Edwards Pillar.** 73°05'S, 66°20'E. 2 miles NE of Mount Stinear in the Prince Charles Mountains. Named by the Australians for N.F. Edwards, a surveyor with the ANARE Prince Charles Mountains survey party in 1971, which established a geodetic survey station here.

**Edwards Point.** 62°29'S, 59°30'W. Also called Punta Prat. Marks the southern extremity of Robert Island in the South Shetlands. Charted by personnel on the *Discovery II* in 1935, but not named by the UK until 1948.

**Edwards Spur.** 75°59'S, 135°18'W. On the lower NW slopes of Mount Moulton in Marie Byrd Land. Named for Alvah G. Edwards, USN, construction driver with the Army-Navy Trail Party which established Byrd Station in 1956.

**Eel Pout.** *Lycenchelys antarcticus.* Thick-lipped, elongated, eel-shaped coastal fishes of the order Zoarcidae, living at the sea bottom. They may grow up to 3 feet long. Some lay eggs and some are viviparous.

**Mount Egbert.** 69°57'S, 69°37'W. 2,895 m. Mainly ice-covered. 8 miles SSE of Mount Stephenson in the Douglas Range of Alexander Island. In 1948 the FIDS named it for the old Saxon king.

**Mount Ege.** 83°34'S, 55°53'W. 1,350 m. Between Berquist and Drury Ridges in the Neptune Range. Named for John R. Ege, geologist here in 1963–64.

**Egeberg Glacier.** 71°34'S, 169°51'E. Between Scott Keltie Glacier and Dugdale Glacier, flowing into the west side of Robertson Bay in Victoria Land. Charted by Borchgrevink in 1898–1900, and named by him for Consul Westye Egeberg of Christiania (now Oslo). Egeberg was also Borchgrevink's middle name.

**Mount Egerton.** 80°50'S, 157°55'E. 2,830 m. 3 miles NNW of Mount Field in the Churchill Mountains. It overlooks Barne Inlet on the Ross Ice Shelf. Discovered by Scott's 1901–4 expedition and named by Scott for Adm. Sir George Le Clerc Egerton, Arctic explorer and an adviser to Scott.

**Egg Island.** 63°41'S, 57°42'W. 310 m. Circular. 1½ miles across. 1 mile west of Tail Island in the NE part of the Prince Gustav Channel. Charted by the FIDS in 1945, and named by them in association with Tail, Eagle, and Beak Islands.

**Egil Peak.** 72°24'S, 1°18'E. 2,640 m. At the east side of Isingen Mountain in the Sverdrup Mountains of Queen Maud Land. Named by the Norwegians for Egil Rogstad.

**Ehlers Knob.** 72°34'S, 95°04'W. An ice-covered hill on the western part of the north coast of Dustin Island. Named for Robert C. Ehlers, field assistant at Byrd Station in 1966–67.

**Mount Ehrenspeck.** 84°46'S, 175°35'W. 2,090 m. 2 miles SW of Mount

Kenney, in the Cathedral Peaks, on the east side of Shackleton Glacier in the Queen Maud Mountains. Named for Helmut Ehrenspeck, geologist here in 1970–71.

**Mount Ehrlich** *see* **Mount Aciar**

**Eichorst Island.** 64°47′S, 66°04′W. Tiny island about ½ mile south of Palmer Station, off Anvers Island, between Shortcut Island and Surge Rocks. Named for Marvin H. "Ike" Eichorst, of Glenview, Illinois, ham radio operator connecting Palmer Station to the USA between 1964 and 1972.

**Eidsgavlen Cliff.** 71°41′S, 11°42′E. 1 mile south of Eidshaugane Peaks in the Humboldt Mountains of Queen Maud Land. Discovered by Ritscher in 1938–39. Name means "the isthmus gable" in Norwegian.

**Eidshaugane Peaks.** 71°40′S, 11°46′E. 1 mile north of Eidsgavlen Cliff in the Humboldt Mountains of Queen Maud Land. Discovered by Ritscher in 1938–39. Name means "the isthmus hills" in Norwegian.

**Cape Eielson** *see* **Cape Boggs**

**Eielson, C.B.** Carl Ben Eielson. Alaskan bush pilot who was Wilkins' pilot on the first airplane flight made in Antarctica, on Nov. 16, 1928. He and Wilkins then flew on a 10-hour expedition down the Antarctic Peninsula on Dec. 20, 1928, as far as the Stefansson Strait. Eielson disappeared on Nov. 9, 1929, in high Arctic latitudes.

**Eielson Peninsula.** 70°35′S, 61°45′W. 20 miles long. Mainly snow-covered. 10 miles wide on average. Between Smith Inlet and Lehrke Inlet on the east side of the Antarctic Peninsula. It juts out into the southern part of the Larsen Ice Shelf, between Wilkins Coast and Black Coast, opposite Dolleman Island. Wilkins discovered it aerially on Dec. 20, 1928, and named part of it Cape Eielson (now Cape Boggs), for C.B. Eielson. Since then the entire peninsula has assumed the name Eielson.

**Eigg Rock** *see* **Nigg Rock**

**Eights, James.** Geologist from Albany, NY. The first US scientist to visit Antarctica and thought to be the first scientist ever to do field work there (*see,* however, **W.H.B. Webster**), which he did during the Palmer-Pendleton Expedition of 1829–31. He wrote 7 papers, the first by a scientist in Antarctica, and described the pycnogonids (q.v.) to a disbelieving world. He was refused a place on the Wilkes Expedition 1838–42, and was much neglected until recent times.

**Eights Coast.** 73°30′S, 96°W. Between Cape Waite and Phrogner Point, it overlooks the Bellingshausen Sea and is bisected by the Jones Mountains. It is bordered by Thurston Island, the Abbott Ice Shelf, and some islands in the ice shelf. Discovered on flights from the *Bear* in Feb. 1940 by members of the USAS 1939–41. Named for James Eights. It was first explored in Feb. 1960 by the *Glacier* and the *Burton Island* during the USN Bellingshausen Sea Expedition.

**Eights Peninsula** *see* **Thurston Island**

**Eights Station.** 75°14′S, 77°10′W. US scientific station in the Sentinel Mountains at the base of the Antarctic Peninsula in Ellsworth Land. At first it was a camp serving as a conjugate point station to carry on simultaneous measurements of the earth's magnetic field and of the ionosphere during the USARP Project Sky-Hi, and was called Camp Sky-Hi. The site was selected in Nov. 1961 and the first Dakota aircraft landed here on Nov. 26, 1961, to drop men off to prepare a skiway. Construction on the camp and landing strip began in Dec. 1961, and was completed on Feb. 9, 1962. The camp housed 10–11 men. It became Eights Station in the summer of 1962–63, and housed only 5 men for the following 2 winters. It was closed in Nov. 1965.

**Eijkman Point.** 65°37′S, 64°10′W. Juts out into Leroux Bay at the end of a rocky spur, 4 miles SSE of Nuñez Point, on the west coast of Graham Land. Named by the UK in 1959 for Christiaan Eijkman (1858–1930), Dutch biologist and pioneer in the cure of beriberi.

**Eilefsen, Albert.** Driver on the shore party of Byrd's 1933–35 expedition.

**Eilefsen Peak.** 76°52'S, 146°25'W. In the NE part of Radford Island, in the Sulzberger Ice Shelf off the Marie Byrd Land coast. Named for Albert Eilefsen.

**Eillium Island.** 60°42'S, 44°51'W. Almost 1¼ miles NW of Route Point, the NW tip of Laurie Island in the South Orkneys. Discovered by Powell and Palmer in Dec. 1821, and recharted by Bruce in 1903. In 1904 Bruce named it for his son, Eillium (a variant of the Gaelic Uilleam, meaning "William").

**Einstøding Islands.** 67°29'S, 61°42'E. 3 small islands, 2 miles north of the Stanton Group off the coast of Mac. Robertson Land. Photographed by the LCE 1936–37, and named Einstødingane (the hermits) by the Norwegians for their lonely position.

**Einstødingen Island.** 69°39'S, 38°50'E. 10 miles east of Padda Island in the southern part of Lützow-Holm Bay. Photographed by the LCE 1936–37. Named Einstødingen (the hermit) by the Norwegians for its solitary position.

**Einthoven Hill.** 64°14'S, 62°09'W. 3 miles SW of Mitchell Point on the east side of Brabant Island. Named by the UK for William Einthoven (1860–1927), Dutch inventor of the electrocardiograph.

**Eisberg Head.** 75°12'S, 110°27'W. Just west of the mouth of Vane Glacier on the coast of Marie Byrd Land. It is the northernmost part of a ridge that descends from the central part of Mount Murphy. Named for Cdr. Harry B. Eisberg, USN, staff medical officer on Operation Highjump, 1946–47.

**Eisenhower Range.** 74°15'S, 162°15'E. 3,070 m. Flat-topped. 45 miles long. Between Reeves Névé on the west, Reeves Glacier on the south, and Priestley Glacier on the north and east, in Victoria Land. Easily seen from the Ross Sea. Named for President Dwight D. Eisenhower.

**Eisner Peak.** 68°50'S, 65°45'W. On the east coast of the Antarctic Peninsula.

**Mount Eissinger.** 70°02'S, 67°44'W. On the north side of Riley Glacier, on the west side of Palmer Land. Named by the US for Karlheinz Eissinger, topographic engineer with the Ellsworth Land Survey, 1968–69.

**Ekblad Glacier.** 83°05'S, 167°18'E. 8 miles long. Flows from the eastern slopes of the Holland Range into Wise Bay at the Ross Ice Shelf. Named for A. Ekblad, captain of the *Wyandot*, 1964 and 1965.

**Mount Ekblaw.** 77°18'S, 141°48'W. 1,235 m. 3 miles east of Mount Van Valkenburg in the eastern part of the Clark Mountains in Marie Byrd Land. Discovered aerially from West Base in 1940 during the USAS and named for W.E. Ekblaw, professor of geography at Clark University, and Arctic explorer.

**Cape Ekelöf** *see* **Ekelöf Point**

**Ekelöf, Dr. Eric.** Medical officer on Nordenskjöld's 1901–4 expedition.

**Ekelöf Point.** 64°14'S, 57°12'W. 5 miles SW of Cape Gage. Marks the north side of the entrance to Markham Bay on the east side of James Ross Island. Discovered and named Cape Ekelöf by Nordenskjold's 1901–4 expedition, for Eric Ekelöf. Resurveyed and redefined in 1953 by the FIDS.

**Ekesteinen Rock.** 71°46'S, 10°46'E. Isolated. 3½ miles SE of Smirnov Peak in the Shcherbakov Range, at the eastern end of the Orvin Mountains in Queen Maud Land. Name means "the spoke stone" in Norwegian.

**Ekho Mountain.** 71°28'S, 15°26'E. 1,690 m. 3 miles SW of Vorposten Peak in the Lomonosov Mountains of Queen Maud Land. Discovered by Ritscher in 1938–39. Named Gora Ekho (Echo Mountain) by the USSR in 1963.

**Eklund, Carl R.** d. 1962. Carl Robert Eklund. One of the major figures in 20th century Antarctic exploration. He was the ornithologist at East Base during the USAS, and with Ronne sledged through the George VI Sound. He turned down the second-in-command post on the RARE 1947–48 due to family commitments, but was scientific leader at Wilkes Station during the IGY until he handed over to Dr. Willis Tressler on Jan. 30, 1958. He was the first president of the Antarctican Society, founded in Washington on Oct. 8, 1959. In 1972 the Carl R. Eklund Biological Center was named for him at McMurdo Station.

**Eklund Island.** In 1940–41 Finn Ronne and Carl Eklund sledged 1,097 miles from Stonington Island to the SW part of the George VI Sound and back during the USAS 1939–41. In Dec. 1940, near their furthest point out, they found an island, 5 miles in extent and rising to a height of 410 m. Ronne named the island for Eklund. In 1949 Vivian Fuchs and R.J. Adie of the FIDS sledged here in a recession of the ice and found the island to be the largest of a group of mainly ice-drowned islands. The US has since extended the name of Eklund to all these islands (*see* **Eklund Islands**).

**Eklund Islands.** 73°16′S, 71°50′W. Small group of islands off the English Coast, just beyond the head of the Ronne Entrance, near the SW end of the George VI Sound. Mainly ice-covered, they rise through the ice, more prominently as the ice recedes. The largest is Eklund Island (see above for details of discovery).

**Ekspress Nunatak.** 71°48′S, 2°53′E. Isolated. 10 miles north of Stabben Mountain in Queen Maud Land. Named Gora Ekspress (Express Hill) by the USSR in 1961.

**Ekström, Bertil.** Swedish mechanical engineer on the NBSAE 1949–52. Drowned on Feb. 24, 1951, when the Weasel he was driving plunged over the edge of the Quar Ice Shelf.

**Ekström Ice Shelf.** 71°S, 8°W. Also called Ekströmisen, Östre Shelf-Is. Between Søråsen Ridge and Halvfarryggen Ridge on the coast of Queen Maud Land. Named by the Norwegians for Bertil Ekström.

**Elaine Automatic Weather Station.** 85°09′S, 174°27′E. An American AWS at an elevation of approximately 200 feet. Began operating on Jan. 26, 1986.

**Eland Mountains.** 70°40′S, 63°W. 2,440 m. 20 miles in extent. Along the south side of Clifford Glacier, to the east of the Dyer Plateau, on the Antarctic Peninsula. Discovered in 1936 by the BGLE. Named in 1952 by Sir Miles Clifford, governor of the Falkland Islands, for his wife (it was her maiden name) at the request of the FIDS.

**Elbow Peak.** 83°32′S, 56°37′W. 1,195 m. At the southernmost bend of Berquist Ridge in the Neptune Range. Named descriptively for its position on the ridge.

**Eld, Henry.** Passed midshipman on the *Peacock* from 1838–40, during the Wilkes Expedition 1838–42. He claimed to have seen land on Jan. 16, 1840. He transferred to the *Vincennes* at Fiji for the second half of the expedition.

**Eld Peak.** 69°20′S, 157°15′E. 800 m. 6 miles SE of Reynolds Peak on the west side of Matusevich Glacier in the Wilson Hills of East Antarctica. On Jan. 16, 1840, Midshipmen Reynolds and Eld both spotted land from the *Peacock* during the Wilkes Expedition 1838–42. The two conical peaks they sighted were named by Wilkes as Eld's Peak and Reynolds Peak, the SE one for Henry Eld. Due to a mirage, Wilkes charted it inaccurately at 50 miles out to sea beyond the Mawson Peninsula. In 1959 Phillip Law ascertained this peak to be the one Wilkes had had in mind.

**Mount Elder.** 61°13′S, 55°12′W. Also called Misty Mountain. Between Endurance Glacier and Mount Pendragon on Elephant Island in the South Shetlands. Named by the UK for Capt. John P. Elder, RE, surveyor of the Joint Services Expedition to Elephant Island in 1970–71.

**Elder Bluff.** 70°31'S, 61°44'W. On the north side of Eielson Peninsula. It overlooks Smith Inlet on the east coast of Palmer Land. Named for Robert B. Elder, chief of the USCG oceanographic unit on the first IWSOE on the *Glacier* in 1968.

**Elder Glacier.** 72°35'S, 168°46'E. Feeds the Tucker Glacier just west of Oread Spur in the Victory Mountains of Victoria Land. Named for William C. Elder, topographic engineer here in 1961–62.

**Eldred, Andrew J.** Captain of the *Thomas Hunt* out of Stonington, Conn., who visited the South Shetlands in 1873–74. He was probably the captain on the *Thomas Hunt*'s grossly unsuccessful 1874–75 cruise to the South Shetlands, and was definitely its skipper during the 1875–76 season in the same waters. He and the ship were back again in 1878–79, and again in 1879–80 when he helped look for the lost *Charles Shearer.*

**Eldred Glacier.** 61°58'S, 58°16'W. 2½ miles long. Flows to the north coast of King George Island in the South Shetlands, just east of Potts Peak. Named by the UK in 1960 for Andrew J. Eldred.

**Eldred Point.** 75°30'S, 141°58'W. Ice-covered. Marks the west side of the terminus of Land Glacier on the coast of Marie Byrd Land. Named for David T. Eldred, USN, at McMurdo Station, 1958, 1965, and 1969.

**Eldridge, Capt.** Commander of the *Aeronaut* on its two trips to the South Shetlands, 1852–53 and 1853–54. These expeditions included other ships, and Eldridge was senior commander of the fleets. In 1857–58 he led an expedition to Heard Island (53°S) in the *Cornelia.*

**Eldridge Bluff.** 73°27'S, 164°48'E. 5 miles long. Forms part of the west wall of the Aviator Glacier, just south of Cosmonaut Glacier in Victoria Land. Named for Lt. Cdr. David B. Eldridge, Jr., USN, VX-6 officer-in-charge at McMurdo Station, 1967.

**Eldridge Peak.** 84°51'S, 116°50'W. Actually a nunatak. Mainly ice-free. Marks the western extremity of the Ohio Range. Named for Henry M. Eldridge, US Antarctic cartographer.

**The *Eleanor Bolling.*** Formerly called the *Chelsea,* this was one of the two ships of Byrd's 1928–30 expedition. Named by Byrd for his mother, it had dimensions similar to the other ship, the *City of New York.* It was a freighter of 800 tons cargo capacity, had a 200 hp engine, and a top speed of 9 knots. The cost to buy and outfit it was $125,000. Like the *City of New York* it was outfitted at cost by the Todd Ship Yard. Captain during the expedition was Gustav L. Brown.

**Eleanor Bolling Bight.** 4 miles north of Little America I, on the east coast of the Bay of Whales. Named by Byrd for his mother in 1928. It is no longer there, due to the ever-changing coastline of Antarctica.

**Mount Electra.** 77°31'S, 160°52'E. Over 2,000 m. Just west of Mount Dido in the Olympus Range of Victoria Land. Named by the New Zealanders in 1958–59 for the Greek mythological character.

**Elephant Bay.** Near Yankee Harbor in the South Shetlands. A term no longer used.

**Elephant Flats.** 60°43'S, 45°37'W. A mud flat in the form of an inlet on the shore between Cemetery Bay and Marble Knolls on the east side of Signy Island in the South Orkneys. Named by the UK for the elephant seals here.

**Elephant Island.** 61°10'S, 55°14'W. Also called Barrows Isle, Mordrins Island. 24 miles long, with a greatest width of 12 miles. One of the largest of the South Shetland Islands, it was discovered in 1820 by Bransfield. It was named in 1821 by American sealers who found an abundance of elephant seals here. In 1916 Shackleton's party was trapped here during the abortive British Imperial Transantarctic Expedition of 1914–17.

**Elephant Moraine.** An ice-core moraine west of Reckling Peak at the top of Mawson Glacier in Victoria Land.

**¹Elephant Point.** 62°41'S, 60°52'W. Also called Morro Cuadrado Negro (by the Argentines for the square black rock on it). A mainly ice-free promontory that forms the southernmost point of the western half of Livingston Island in the South Shetlands. Charted and named by Fildes in 1820–22.

**²Elephant Point** *see* **Miers Bluff**

**Elephant Rocks.** 64°46'S, 64°05'W. 3 tiny islets at the entrance to Arthur Harbor in the area of Palmer Station. Named about 1971 for the elephant seals that abound here.

**Elephant seals.** *Mirounga leonina.* Also called southern elephant seals, or sea elephants, they belong to the family Phocidae, and are the largest of the pinnipeds (seals, sea lions, and walruses). An adult bull weighs 2 tons and measures 16 feet in length (one was 4 tons and 22 feet long). They have exceptionally large eyes, and an inflatable, trunklike snout. They feed on fish, squid, and cephalopods. They breed north of the Antarctic Convergence, and are often seen in Antarctica. Once hunted mercilessly for their oil, they became almost extinct, but are now growing in number, and total about 700,000.

**Pico Elevado** *see* **Molar Peak**

**Eley Peak.** 79°39'S, 84°20'W. In the northern part of the Soholt Peaks. It overlooks the head of Balish Glacier in the Heritage Range. Named for Richard G. Eley, USN, aerial photographer in Antarctica in 1965–66 and 1966–67.

**Elgar Uplands.** 69°34'S, 70°30'W. 1,500 m. Extend SW from Tufts Pass 15 miles to Sullivan Glacier, between Hampton Glacier and Nichols Snowfield in the northern part of Alexander Island. Named by the UK for the composer.

**Eliason Glacier.** 64°15'S, 59°25'W. 5 miles long. Just west of Mount Hornsby. Flows from the Detroit Plateau into the ice piedmont north of Larsen Inlet,

Graham Land. Named by the UK for the Eliason motor sledge (*see* **Sledges**).

**The *Eliza*.** A London sealer in the South Shetlands in 1820–21, commanded by Capt. Powell. It was often in company with Weddell's expedition. It was back in 1821–22 (captain unknown) with George Powell's *Dove* expedition.

**Eliza Cone.** 66°53'S, 163°13'E. A rock on land, 1 mile west of Cape McNab on the south side of Buckle Island in the Balleny Islands. It has an archway through it. Next to Scott Cone. Both named for the *Eliza Scott*.

**Eliza Rocks.** 62°26'S, 60°14'W. Group of rocks in water, west of the Zed Islands in the South Shetlands. Named by the UK in 1958 for the *Eliza*.

**The *Eliza Scott*.** Balleny's flagship out of London. He commanded it personally (*see also* the **Sabrina**) in the Antarctic during the 1838–39 season. 134-ton schooner. William Moore was chief mate and John McNab was second mate. It returned to England on Sept. 17, 1839, with 178 seal skins. On July 12, 1840, it left England again for the Enderby Brothers Whaling Company, under Capt. Mapleton, but the voyage was abandoned.

**Mount Elizabeth.** 83°53'S, 168°24'E. 4,480 m. 6 miles south of Mount Anne just to the west of the Beardmore Glacier, in the Queen Alexandra Range. Ice-free. Discovered by Shackleton in 1908–9 and named by him for Elizabeth Dawson-Lambton, one of his principal supporters.

**The *Elkhorn*.** A USNS tanker in McMurdo Sound, 1961–62.

**Elkhorn Ridge.** 76°42'S, 160°59'E. 10 miles long. Between Towle and Northwind Glaciers in the Convoy Range of Victoria Land. Named for the *Elkhorn*.

**Mount Elkins.** 66°39'S, 54°08'E. Has three major peaks, the highest is 2,300 m. Just north of the Young Nunataks in the Napier Mountains. Photographed by the LCE 1936–37. The Norwegians named it

Jökelen (the glacier). Later renamed by the Australians for T.J. Elkins, ionosphere physicist at Mawson Station in 1960.

**Ellefsen Harbor.** 60°44'S, 45°03'W. Also called Ellefsen's Harbor, Ellesen Harbor. At the south end of Powell Island between Christoffersen and Michelsen Islands in the South Orkneys. Discovered by Powell and Palmer in Dec. 1821.

**Ellen Glacier.** 78°13'S, 84°30'W. In the central part of the Sentinel Range, flowing from the eastern slopes of Mount Anderson and Long Gables for 22 miles to Barne Ridge, where it joins the Rutford Ice Stream. Named for Lt. Col. Cicero J. Ellen, USAF, who helped construct the South Pole Station in 1956–57.

**Mount Ellery.** 69°54'S, 159°38'E. 1,110 m. Near the head of Suvorov Glacier. 2 miles NW of Hornblende Bluffs in the Wilson Hills. Named by the Australians for R.L.J. Ellery, a member of the Australian Antarctic Exploration Committee of 1886.

**Ellesen Harbor** *see* **Ellefsen Harbor**

**Ellifsen.** One of the wintering-over party on Borchgrevink's expedition of 1898–1900.

**Mount Elliot.** 70°50'S, 166°35'E. Also seen spelled (erroneously) as Mount Elliott, and it is not to be confused with Mount Elliott. 1,500 m. Between Kirkby Glacier and O'Hara Glacier. 5 miles south of Yule Bay, in the Anare Mountains of Victoria Land. Ross saw a mountain in this area in Feb. 1841, and named it for Rear-Adm. George Elliot, commander-in-chief of the Cape of Good Hope Station in the Cape Colony at the southern tip of Africa.

**Elliot Peak.** 84°31'S, 164°04'E. 1 mile NW of Tempest Peak in the Queen Alexandra Range. Named by the Ohio State University party to that range in 1966–67 for David H. Elliot, geologist with the party.

**Cape Elliott.** 65°52'S, 102°35'E. Ice-covered. 28 miles SW of Bowman Island, it fronts the Shackleton Ice Shelf and forms the western edge of the Knox Coast. Named for J.L. Elliott.

**¹Mount Elliott.** 64°24'S, 60°02'W. Not to be confused with Mount Elliot. 1,265 m. 16 miles NW of Cape Sobral on the east coast of Graham Land. Charted in 1947 by the FIDS and named for F.K. Elliott, leader of the FIDS Base D at Hope Bay in 1947 and 1948.

**²Mount Elliott** *see* **Mount Elliot**

**Elliott, George.** 1st class boy on the Wilkes Expedition 1838–42. Joined at Valparaiso. Served the cruise.

**Elliott, J.L.** Chaplain on the *Vincennes* during the Wilkes Expedition 1838–42. Detached at San Francisco in Oct. 1841.

**Elliott, Samuel.** Midshipman on the *Vincennes* during the Wilkes Expedition 1838–42.

**Elliott Glacier.** 66°33'S, 115°14'E. A channel glacier. Flows to the Budd Coast between Cape Hammersly and Cape Waldron, on the coast of East Antarctica. Named for Samuel Elliott.

**Elliott Hills.** 71°25'S, 65°25'W. 12 miles long. They mark the NW end of the Gutenko Mountains in central Palmer Land. Named for Lt. Cdr. David J. Elliott, USN, pilot of Hercules planes in 1970 and 1971.

**Elliott Nunatak.** 85°16'S, 89°43'W. 2,165 m. Juts out from the center of the Bermel Escarpment in the Thiel Mountains. Named by Bermel and Ford of the US Geological Survey Thiel Mountains party here in 1960–61, for Raymond L. Elliott, geologist with the party.

**Elliott Quay.** The steel wharf docking berth area at McMurdo Station. Destroyed in March 1972 in a storm, but replaced with a floating ice wharf.

**Elliott Ridge.** 83°57'S, 57°W. Hook-shaped. 8 miles long. Extends from Wiens Peak in a westerly direction in the southern Neptune Range of the Pensacola Mountains. Named for Cdr. James Elliott, commander of the *Staten Island.*

**Elliotte, James.** Gunner's mate on the Wilkes Expedition 1838–42. Joined in the USA. Sent home on the *Relief* in 1839.

**Ellis.** Steward on the *Nimrod,* 1908–9.

**Mount Ellis.** 79°52′S, 156°14′E. 2,330 m. The highest point in the Darwin Mountains. Surmounts the northern edge of Midnight Plateau. Named by the Darwin Glacier Party of the BCTAE in 1957–58 for Murray R. Ellis.

**Ellis, J.A.** 2nd assistant engineer on the *Jacob Ruppert,* 1933–34.

**Ellis, Murray R.** NZ engineer who went to the Pole with Hillary during the BCTAE 1957–58. He was back in Antarctica, mountain climbing with Hillary in 1967–68.

**Ellis Bluff.** 85°20′S, 175°35′W. 2,280 m. At the south side of the mouth of Logie Glacier in the Cumulus Hills. Named for W. Ellis, chief air controlman, USN, in Antarctica in 1965 and 1966.

**Ellis Cone.** 75°49′S, 116°23′W. On the SW side of Toney Mountain in Marie Byrd Land. Named for Homer L. Ellis, USN, radar air traffic controller at McMurdo Station in 1968, and chief in charge of the ground-controlled approach unit at the Byrd Station skiway landing strip in 1969–70.

**Ellis Fjord.** 68°33′S, 78°06′E. Between Breidnes Peninsula and Mule Peninsula in the Vestfold Hills of East Antarctica. Photographed by the LCE 1936–37 and using these photos the Norwegian cartographers mapped it as a bay (which they called Mulvik; the name means "snout bay") and a remnant lake (which they called Langevatnet; the name means "the long lake"). In 1952 John H. Roscoe, the US cartographer, working off the more recent photos taken by Operation Highjump in 1946–47, determined the two features to be connected, and he redefined them and renamed the feature for Edwin E. Ellis, Operation Highjump photographer on flights over this area.

**Ellis Glacier.** 71°58′S, 24°17′E. 4 miles long. Flows from Mount Walnum, between the Gillock and Jennings Glaciers in the Sør Rondane Mountains. Named Ellisbreen (Ellis Glacier) by the Norwegians for Edwin E. Ellis (*see* **Ellis Fjord**).

**Ellis Rapids.** At the eastern end of Ellis Fjord, on the Mule Peninsula of the Vestfold Hills. Named for the fjord.

**Ellis Ridge.** 74°45′S, 113°54′W. On Martin Peninsula on the coast of Marie Byrd Land.

**Cape Ellsworth.** 66°17′S, 162°20′E. 290 m. Sheer rock bluff. Forms the north end of Young Island in the Ballenys. Named by personnel on the *Discovery II* in 1936 for Lincoln Ellsworth. The vessel picked him up after his transantarctic flight.

**Mount Ellsworth.** 85°45′S, 161°W. 2,925 m. The highest peak on the massif between the Steagall and Amundsen Glaciers in the Queen Maud Mountains. Discovered on the South Pole Flight of Nov. 28–29, 1929, by Byrd, and named by him as Mount Lincoln Ellsworth, for Lincoln Ellsworth. The name was later shortened.

**Ellsworth, Lincoln.** b. May 12, 1880, Chicago. d. May 26, 1951, NYC. American explorer, engineer, scientist, aviator, and adventurer. Son of a Chicago coal magnate, he began his exploring life after leaving school, and financed his own expeditions. In 1926 he crossed the Arctic. In the early 1930s he turned his attention to the Antarctic. In 1933–34 he was down there, intending to be the first to complete a transantarctic crossing—in a plane. The *Wyatt Earp,* his own ship, sailed from Bergen, Norway, on July 29, 1933, to Dunedin, NZ, where Ellsworth joined it on Nov. 9, 1933. It sailed on Dec. 10, 1933, with 17 men and the airplane *Polar Star* on board. Personnel included Ellsworth, the leader, Sir Hubert Wilkins, the manager of the expedition, Bernt Balchen the pilot, Chris Braathen, Walter J. Lanz, Dr. Reals Berg, and Dr. Jorgen Holmboe. Baard Holth was ship's captain, and he and 7 other officers and crewmen were veterans of Norwegian whaling fleets in the Antarctic. Hartveg Olsen was first mate, Liavaag was second mate, and Magnus Olsen, Hartveg's brother, was a member of the crew. On Dec. 17, 1933, the *Wyatt Earp* entered the pack ice of the Ross Sea. On Jan. 9, 1934, it reached the Bay of Whales. The plan was to fly from the Bay of Whales to the Weddell Sea but the *Polar Star* was damaged in an ice breakup and the expedition was abandoned. They were back in Dunedin on Jan. 28, 1934. The *Polar Star* was shipped by Balchen to the USA on an oil tanker, and Ellsworth himself sailed on the *Mariposa* to San Francisco. He was back again at the end of the year to try again. The 1934–35 expedition sailed from Dunedin, again in the *Wyatt Earp*, on Sept. 19, 1934, arriving at Deception Island on Oct. 14, 1934. The personnel were essentially the same, except that Dr. F. Dana Coman replaced Berg as medical officer, and Alistair Duthie replaced a Norwegian crewman who had returned to Europe. This time the plan was to fly from the Antarctic Peninsula over to the Bay of Whales. But they could not find a suitable airstrip, and the expedition was abandoned. On Jan. 21, 1935, they sailed for Dunedin. Back again for a third try, the 1935–36 expedition sailed from Montevideo on Oct. 18, 1935, again on the *Wyatt Earp*, and again carrying their plane, the *Polar Star*. 18 men this time, including Ellsworth and Wilkins. This expedition saw a few changes in personnel. Balchen had resigned as chief pilot and was replaced by Hollick-Kenyon, J.H. Lymburner became reserve pilot, and Patrick Howard replaced Braathen as mechanic. William J. Klenke, Jr., was another airplane mechanic. Dr. Theodore Schlossbach replaced Coman as medical officer. Hartveg Olsen was promoted to captain of the ship on Holth's resignation, Liavaag became first mate and Magnus Olsen second mate. They arrived at Deception Island on Nov. 2, 1935, and on Nov. 12, 1935, arrived at Dundee Island. Ells-

worth and Hollick-Kenyon took off in the *Polar Star* from Dundee Island on Nov. 21, 1935, intending to fly to the Bay of Whales, but returned after 10 hours with mechanical problems. At 8:05 a.m. on Nov. 23, 1935, the same duo left again, Hollick-Kenyon at the controls. Ellsworth was then 55 years old. They flew south along the Antarctic Peninsula, photographing everything they saw, then crossed the continent itself. The trip was 2,300 miles long, and was done in 6 stages. Four unexpected landings were made in bad weather, and then the plane ran out of gas at 79°15'S, 102°W, 16 miles from Little America, which had been their target. They abandoned the *Polar Star* and sledged to Little America II (which Byrd had abandoned earlier that year), arriving there on Dec. 15, 1935. On Jan. 19, 1936, a small plane from the *Discovery II,* which was looking for them, parachuted fruit and their mail. On Jan. 22, 1936, the *Wyatt Earp* arrived to take them off. No one else crossed the Antarctic again until Jan. 1956, when a P2V-2N from VX-6 flew from McMurdo Sound to the Weddell Sea. Ellsworth was back in Antarctica again in 1938–39 on another expedition. This time 19 men took part, including Ellsworth as leader, Wilkins as technical adviser/expedition manager, J.H. Lymburner as chief pilot, Burton J. Trerice as reserve pilot, Harman F. Rhoades, Jr., as medical officer, Frederick Seid as radio operator. All of the officers and crew were Norwegian. The captain was Londer Johansen. Liavaag was first mate. Dahl was chief steward, and Sperre was second engineer. The *Wyatt Earp* sailed from Cape Town on Oct. 29, 1938, this time carrying two planes. One was an all-metal Northrop Delta monoplane (NC14267) with a 750 hp Wright Cyclone engine, and the other was an Aeronca 2-seater scouting plane. Both had skis, wheels and pontoons, and 2-way radios. After several flights, including the major one by Ellsworth and Lymburner over the American Highland (which Ellsworth discovered and named), Liavaag had an accident and Ellsworth canceled the trip immediately. They sailed for Hobart, arriving there on Feb. 4, 1939. Liavaag was operated on there. This was Ellsworth's last expedition, and on it he claimed 430,000 square miles of territory for the USA.

**Ellsworth Highland** *see* **Ellsworth Land**

**Ellsworth Land.** It centers on 75°30′S, and its longitudes are between 80°W and 120°W. Large tract of land between the old Hearst Land and Marie Byrd Land, and between the Ronne Ice Shelf and the Bellingshausen Sea, just south of the Antarctic Peninsula. It includes the Ellsworth Mountains. Discovered by Lincoln Ellsworth and called by him the James W. Ellsworth Highland, for his father. This name got shortened to James W. Ellsworth Land and Ellsworth Highland. In 1962 the US officially named it Ellsworth Land, more for the son than for the father.

**Ellsworth Mountains.** 79°S, 85°W. 200 miles long. 30 miles wide. Just to the east of the Hollick-Kenyon Plateau in Ellsworth Land. They are bisected by the Minnesota Glacier to form two ranges, the Sentinel Range to the north, and the Heritage Range to the south. The highest and least known area of West Antarctica. The Vinson Massif is here. Ellsworth discovered them aerially on Nov. 23, 1935, and named them the Sentinel Range for their imposing, sentrylike position. The mountains were later found to contain the two ranges mentioned above, and the name was changed to honor Ellsworth.

**Ellsworth Station.** 77°43′S, 41°08′W. Elevation 138 feet. US Navy station established for the IGY on the Filchner Ice Shelf in the Weddell Sea, and named for Lincoln Ellsworth. Unloading from the *Wyandot* began on Jan. 27, 1957. The first leader (military and scientific) was Finn Ronne, who led the station through the 1957 winter. He handed over command on Jan. 16, 1958, to Paul Tidd (military) and Dr. Matthew J. Brennan (scientific). Other personnel during that

first, 1957, winter, were Lt. Cdr. Charles J. McCarthy, USNR, officer-in-charge; Lts. (USN) Clinton R. Smith and Conrad J. Jaburg; Lt. (jg) William J. Sumrall, USNR; and enlisted men Thomas A. Ackerman, Ronald D. Brown, John E. Beiszer, Gary C. Camp, William A. Butler, Walter M. Cox, Carl L. Crouse, Frederick F. Dyrdal, Edward H. Davis, Charlie W. Forlidas, Walter L. Davis, David B. Greaney, Jr., Richard W. Grob, Earl F. Herring, James L. Hannah, Allen M. Jackson, Robert E. Haskill, Kenneth K. Kent, Larry R. Larson, Walter H. May, Atles F. Lewis, Clyde J.M. McCauley, Melvin Mathis, Albert Spear, and James A. Ray. The chief seismologist was Edward C. Thiel, and his assistants were Nolan P. Aughenbaugh and John C. Behrendt. The chief glaciologist was Hugo A.C. Neuburg, and his assistant was Paul T. Walker. John B. Brown was the ionosphere physicist and his assistant was Donald D. Skidmore. The chief meteorologist was Gerrard R. Fierle and chief of the Aurora Program was J. McKim "Kim" Malville. After the IGY the station was loaned to Argentina.

**Ellyard Nunatak.** 70°19′S, 64°54′E. On the north side of Scylla Glacier. 7 miles SSE of Mount Béchervaise in the Prince Charles Mountains. Named by the Australians for D.G. Ellyard, physicist at Mawson Station, 1966.

**Elmers Nunatak.** 83°58′S, 55°25′W. 5 miles SE of Mount Hawkes in the Neptune Range of the Pensacola Mountains. Named for Elmer H. Smith, aerographer at Ellsworth Station in 1958 and at McMurdo Station in 1961.

**El-Sayed Glacier.** 75°40′S, 141°52′W. 15 miles long. Flows from the NE slopes of Zunich Hill in Marie Byrd Land and enters Land Glacier at the south side of Mount Shirley. Named for Sayed Z. El-Sayed, US oceanographer on the IWSOE 1967–68 and 1969–70, and one of the leading scientific authorities on Antarctica.

**Else Nunataks.** 67°21′S, 55°40′E. Partly snow-covered. 3 miles north of

Mount Øydeholmen on the south side of the Wilma Glacier in Enderby Land. Named by the Australians for H. Else, ANARE pilot off the *Nella Dan* in 1965. He also supported the 1969 Prince Charles Mountains ANARE party.

**Else Platform.** 70°22′S, 68°48′E. Flat-topped. At the northern end of Jetty Peninsula in Mac. Robertson Land. Named by the Australians for H. Else (*see* **Else Nunataks**).

**Elsner Ridge.** 71°47′S, 167°21′E. 6 miles long. 4 miles NE of the south end of the Homerun Range in the Admiralty Mountains. Named for Robert W. Elsner, biologist at McMurdo Station in 1967–68, 1968–69, and 1969–70.

**The *Eltanin*.** US ice-strengthened floating laboratory research ship. 266 feet, 2 inches long. 51 feet, 6 inches max. beam. 19 feet, 9 inches draft hull. 3,886 tons displacement. Gross tonnage of 2,703 tons. Diesel electric 2,700 hp. Cruising speed of 12.5 knots. Maximum speed of 13.5 knots. Could accommodate 48 crew, 38 scientists. Built in 1957 at Avondale Marineways, Avondale, La., and converted to a research ship in 1962. Between July 5, 1962, and Dec. 29, 1972, it made 52 southern cruises, covering 400,000 miles over 80 percent of the southern oceans between 35°S and the Antarctic continent, in oceanic research sponsored by the National Science Foundation. There were 3 additional, more northerly, cruises, which brought the distance traveled over that 10-year period to 410,000 miles and 3,014 days at sea. These voyages were of immense scientific importance. Scientific leaders included such luminaries as Albert Crary, George Toney, George A. Llano, Kendall Moulton, Merle Dawson, Lawrence Frakes, and Sayed Z. El-Sayed. In 1973 it was leased to Argentina as a research vessel for that nation, changed its name to the *Islas Orcadas,* and in 1974 carried on researching in what really amounted to joint Argentine/US cruises. It made 14 cruises between 1974 and 1979, 8 sponsored by the USA and 6 by Argentina.

It covered 116,736 miles over the 5-year period, and on Aug. 1, 1979, at the end of the lease, it was returned to the USA. It is now out of service.

**Eltanin Bay.** 73°40′S, 82°W. 35 miles wide. In the southern part of the Bellingshausen Sea. Indents the coast of Ellsworth Land west of the Wirth Peninsula. Named for the *Eltanin*.

**Elton Hill.** 68°50′S, 66°36′W. 1,000 m. Marks the SE limit of Meridian Glacier at its junction with Clarke Glacier in southern Graham Land. Discovered aerially by the RARE in Nov. 1947. Surveyed by the FIDS in Dec. 1958. Named by the UK for John Elton, British inventor of the artificial horizon in 1732.

**Elvers Peak.** 79°52′S, 83°33′W. 1,615 m. At the SE end of the Edson Hills in the Heritage Range. Named for Douglas J. Elvers, seismologist on the USARP South Pole–Queen Maud Traverse, 1965–66.

**Ely Nunatak.** 72°08′S, 66°30′E. 4 miles north of Mount Izabelle in the Prince Charles Mountains. Named by the Australians for J. Ely, technical officer (survey) with the ANARE Prince Charles Mountains Survey in 1971.

**Embassy Islands.** 67°53′S, 68°45′W. Two small islands, the most westerly of the Dion Islands. 7 miles south of Adelaide Island. Surveyed by the FIDS in 1949. Only one of the islands was named, by the UK, as Embassy Rock, for its detached position in relation to Emperor Island. In 1963 the Royal Navy Hydrographic Survey Unit redefined it as two islands, and called them Embassy Islands.

**Embassy Rock** *see* **Embassy Islands**

**Embree Glacier.** 77°59′S, 85°10′W. 20 miles long. In the north-central part of the Sentinel Range. Flows from the slopes of Mount Anderson and Mount Bentley, and then east to its terminus opposite Mount Tegge on the east side of the range. Named for Major Henry Embree, USAF, who helped build the South Pole Station in 1956–57.

**Rocas Eme** *see* **Emm Rock**

**The *Emeline*.** US sealing brig. 108 tons. 67 feet long. Built in Lyme, Conn., in 1818. Registered in New London on July 17, 1820. It was part of Alexander Clark's expedition to the South Shetlands in the season of 1820–21. Captain was Jeremiah Holmes.

**Emeline Island.** 62°24′S, 59°48′W. In the Aitcho Islands. 2 miles NW of Cecilia Island, in the South Shetlands. Named by the UK in 1961 for the *Emeline*.

**The *Emerald*.** US sealing brig of 81 tons. Built at Providence, R.I., in 1817, and owned by John and Sullivan Dorr and David W. Child. Registered in Boston on Sept. 16, 1820. It was captained by John C. Scott during the Boston Expedition to the South Shetlands in 1820–21. Sold in Chile on July 12, 1821.

**Emerald Cove.** 61°55′S, 57°46′W. 2 miles wide. Between North Foreland and Brimstone Peak on the north coast of King George Island in the South Shetlands. William Smith called it Shireff's Cove for William Shirreff, RN, Smith's boss in Chile that year (1819–20). A mix-up resulted in that name being applied elsewhere (*see* **Shirreff Cove**). The UK renamed this cove in 1960 for the *Emerald*.

**Emerald Lake.** 60°43′S, 45°39′W. Just over ½ mile SE of Jebsen Point in western Signy Island, in the South Orkneys. Named by the UK for the color of the water here.

**Emerald Nunatak.** 69°39′S, 70°02′W. In the northern part of Alexander Island.

**Emerging Island.** 73°23′S, 168°02′E. 2 miles long. Ice-covered. 1½ miles east of Index Point, Victoria Land, in the northern part of Lady Newnes Bay. Named by NZ in 1966 because the island seems to be emerging from the ice at the terminus of Mariner Glacier.

**Mount Emerson.** 71°35′S, 168°44′E. 2,190 m. 5 miles ESE of Brewer Peak in the southern part of the DuBridge Range in the Admiralty Mountains. Named for

George L. Emerson, USN, steelworker at McMurdo Station in 1967.

**Mount Emily.** 85°50′S, 174°20′E. 2 miles NE of Mount Cecily in the Grosvenor Mountains, to the east of the Otway Massif, in the Queen Maud Mountains. Over 10,000 feet in height, it is separated from the Dominion Range by the Mill Glacier. Named by Shackleton in 1907–9 for his wife.

**Mount Emison.** 74°12′S, 163°44′E. 2,050 m. On the west side of Campbell Glacier, just north of the mouth of Bates Glacier in the Deep Freeze Range of Victoria Land. Named for William B. Emison, biologist at McMurdo Station, 1964–65 and 1965–66.

**Emlen Peaks.** 71°54′S, 160°35′E. 16 miles in extent, and 7 miles wide. 6 miles south of the Daniels Range, in the south end of the Usarp Mountains. Named for John T. Emlen, biologist in Antarctica, 1962–63.

**Emm Rock.** 62°16′S, 58°42′W. Also called Rocas Eme, Roca Ewens. 30 m. high. A rock in water, ½ mile off the south coast of King George Island in the South Shetlands. Named for the letter which it resembles.

**The *Emma*.** British schooner used by Shackleton in July 1916 to make his third unsuccessful attempt to rescue his 22 men trapped on Elephant Island. British and Chilean residents in Punta Arenas, Chile, had subscribed £1500 for this purpose. 100 miles north of Elephant Island the auxiliary engine broke down and the mission had to be aborted.

**Emma Cove** *see* **Rodman Cove**

**Emma Island.** 64°36′S, 62°20′W. 1½ miles long. 4 miles west of Nansen Island in the SW half of the entrance to Wilhelmina Bay, off the west coast of Graham Land. Discovered by de Gerlache in 1897–99, and named by him for his mother.

**Emmanuel Glacier.** 77°54′S, 162°06′E. In the Royal Society Range of Victoria Land. Flows from Mount Lister between

Table Mountain and Cathedral Rocks, into Ferrar Glacier. Named by Scott's 1910–13 expedition for Emmanuel College, Cambridge.

**Point Emmons** *see* **Cape Wild**

**Emmons, George F. Lt.** Officer on the *Vincennes* during the Wilkes Expedition 1838–42.

**Emory Land Bay** *see* **Land Bay**

**Emory Land Glacier** *see* **Land Glacier**

**Empereur Island.** 66°48′S, 141°23′E. 1 mile north of Cape Margerie, just north of Breton Island, in the entrance to Port Martin. Charted by the French under Liotard in 1949–51, and named by them because they captured their first emperor penguin here.

**Emperor Bay.** 75°31′S, 26°52′W. Indents the Brunt Ice Shelf west of Halley Station. Named by the UK for the penguin colony nearby to the west.

**Emperor Island.** 67°52′S, 68°43′W. Just NE of the Courtier Islands in the Dion Islands in Marguerite Bay, off the west coast of the Antarctic Peninsula. Surveyed by the FIDS in 1948. Named by the UK for the penguins who breed here.

**Emperor penguins.** *Aptenodytes forsteri.* The largest of the penguins living in Antarctica (*see* **Penguins**). Thought at one time to be rare, there are over a million, living in 25 colonies. They weigh 55 to 100 pounds, and can stand almost 4 feet high. They congregate in close packed hordes. Females lay a single egg each fall. The male incubates the egg by carrying it on his broad feet beneath a warm fold of abdominal skin. They do not build nests like other penguins do. They are the deepest diving birds in the world, able to reach 870 feet underwater and remain submerged for 18 minutes. They do not migrate north during the winter months. Found exclusively south of 60°S, except in 6 sightings only (once in New Zealand!) by reporters who knew the difference between them and king penguins. In Oct. 1902 Wilson discov-

ered and studied the first colony during Scott's 1901–4 expedition. They were first seen incubating in winter by members of the French Polar Expedition on June 10, 1951. The first emperor chick to have been bred and hatched outside the Antarctic was born Sept. 16, 1980, at Hubbs-Sea World Research Institute in San Diego, California. Sea World has several emperors in an Antarctic-like environment.

**Enceladus Nunataks.** 71°43′S, 69°27′W. 8 nunataks at the head of the drainage basin of the Saturn Glacier, in southern Alexander Island. Named by the UK for one of Saturn's moons.

**Enchanted Valley.** 82°37′S, 53°10′W. Snow-filled and beautifully scenic. Between Walker Peak and Hannah Peak in the SW end of the Dufek Massif in the Pensacola Mountains. Named appropriately by the Americans from Ellsworth Station, who visited it in Dec. 1957.

**The *Enchantress*.** British sealer from Plymouth, in the South Shetlands in the 1821–22 season under the command of Captain Bond.

**Enchantress Rocks.** 62°42′S, 60°49′W. A group of rocks in water, 1½ miles SE of Elephant Point, Livingston Island, in the South Shetlands. Named by the UK in 1961 for the *Enchantress*.

**The *Endeavour*.** Hillary's polar ship, formerly called the *John Biscoe*, which transported the NZ party to McMurdo Sound in 1957 for their part in the BCTAE. Its first commander was Capt. Henry Kirkwood (1955–58).

**Mount Endeavour.** 76°35′S, 161°59′E. 1,810 m. Flat-topped. North of Fry Glacier, NW of Mount Creak and Shoulder Mountain. Forms the southern block of the Kirkwood Range in Victoria Land. Named by the NZ Northern Survey Party of the BCTAE in 1957 for their ship, the *Endeavour*.

**The *Endeavour II*.** NZ supply tanker A184, in Antarctic waters in the 1963–64 season, commanded by Cdr. P.R.H. Silk.

**Enden Point.** 73°37'S, 4°14'W. Also called Mount Kleynshmidt. At the SW side of Belgen Valley, in the Kirwan Escarpment of Queen Maud Land. Name means "the end" in Norwegian.

**Enderby Land.** Centers on 67°30'S, and extends longitudinally from Shinnar Glacier (44°38'E) to William Scoresby Bay (59°34'E). A large stretch of barren, ice-capped plateau in the interior of East Antarctica, between Queen Maud Land and the Amery Ice Shelf. It has high peaks toward the coast, including the Napier Mountains. Discovered by John Biscoe on Feb. 28, 1831, while he was sailing for Enderby Brothers, the largest British whaling company of the day. Britain claimed it on Jan. 13, 1930, and in 1933 they handed it over to Australia.

**Endresen Islands.** 67°17'S, 60°E. A group of small islands. The highest is 60 meters. Just north of the Hobbs Islands, off the coast of East Antarctica. Discovered in Feb. 1936 by personnel on the *William Scoresby.*

**¹The *Endurance.*** 3-masted barquentine of 144 feet long, built by Lars Christensen (q.v.) and launched in 1912. It was called the *Polaris,* and was owned by Adrien de Gerlache (q.v.). Its 350 hp steam engine gave a top speed of 10.5 knots. De Gerlache sold it to Shackleton, who renamed it the *Endurance* and used it as his vessel on the disastrous British Imperial Transantarctic Expedition of 1914–17. The ship was crushed in the ice on Nov. 21, 1915.

**²The *Endurance.*** A British ice patrol/research ship of the 1960s, 1970s, and 1980s. 3,600 tons. It was in the Antarctic several times over those three decades, notably in 1968–70 (Capt. Peter W. Buchanan), again in 1970–71 when it was used to carry the Joint Services Expedition to Elephant Island, and yet again in 1972–74 (Capt. Christopher J. Isacke, RN).

**Glacier Endurance** *see* **Français Glacier**

**Endurance Cliffs.** 82°46'S, 155°05'E. Also called Endurance Nunatak. Between Mount Summerson and Mount Albright in the southern part of the Geologists Range. Named by the New Zealanders in 1961–62 for Shackleton's old ship.

**¹Endurance Glacier** *see* **Veststraumen Glacier**

**²Endurance Glacier.** 61°10'S, 55°08'W. Also called Flog Glaicer. North of Mount Elder, flowing to the south coast of Elephant Island in the South Shetlands. Named by the UK for the *Endurance,* the modern vessel which took the Joint Services Expedition to the island in 1970.

**Endurance Nunatak** *see* **Endurance Cliffs**

**Endurance Reef.** 68°18'S, 67°32'W. 8 miles west of Red Rock Ridge in Marguerite Bay, off the west coast of the Antarctic Peninsula. Named by the UK for the *Endurance,* the modern vessel which in Feb. 1972 hit a rock here.

**Engberg Cliff.** 73°13'S, 166°48'E. Ice-covered. Between the mouths of the Argonaut and Meander Glaciers where these two glaciers enter the southern part of Mariner Glacier in Victoria Land. Named for Larry W. Engberg, meteorologist at Hallett Station in 1961.

**Cape Engel** *see* **Cape Freeman**

**Engel Peaks.** 69°32'S, 63°08'W. Three peaks, the highest being 1,460 m. They extend for 4 miles, 15 miles west of Cape Rymill, in the Eternity Range, on the east side of Palmer Land. Named by Finn Ronne in 1948 for Bud Engel of the Osterman Co., in Milwaukee, who was a sponsor of Ronne's expedition, the RARE 1947–48.

**Mount Engelstad.** 85°29'S, 167°24'W. Also called Mount Ole Engelstad, and also seen spelled (erroneously) as Mount Englestat. Snow-covered. At the head of the Axel Heiberg Glacier, between Helland-Hansen Shoulder and Mount Wilhelm Christophersen. Discovered in Nov. 1911 by Amundsen, and named by him for Norwegian naval captain Ole Engelstad, who was to have been second-in-command of the *Fram,* but had died before it sailed.

**Mount England.** 77°03'S, 162°27'E. 1,205 m. Conical-topped. Just to the south of New Glacier, in the NE part of Gonville and Caius Range of Victoria Land. It overlooks Granite Harbor. Discovered by Scott in 1901–4 and named by him for Rupert England.

**England, Rupert G.** d. 1942. First officer on the *Morning,* 1902–4, and captain of the *Nimrod,* 1907–8. He left the sea in 1909 and founded his own business. However, he served in the navy in World War I, and later was president of the Antarctic Club, 1933–34.

**England Peak.** 82°37'S, 52°49'W. In the northern part of the Pensacola Mountains.

**England Ridge.** 77°01'S, 162°29'E. Juts out NE from Mount England in Victoria Land, above New Glacier. Named in association with the mountain.

**Mount English** *see* **Mount Mooney**

**English, Robert A.J.** Lt. (jg) USN. Commander of the *Bear of Oakland* during Byrd's 1933–35 expedition. Later, as a lieutenant commander, he was executive secretary of the USAS 1939–41.

**English Coast.** 73°45'S, 73°W. Between the northern tip of Rydberg Peninsula and the Buttress Nunataks, on the coast at the neck of Palmer Land, on the west side of the Antarctic Peninsula. Discovered and explored in 1940 by Ronne and Eklund during the USAS 1939–41. Named Robert English Coast for Robert English. The name was later shortened.

**English Rock.** 76°49'S, 118°W. Near the foot of the western slopes of Mount Frakes, in the Crary Mountains of Marie Byrd Land. Named for Claude L. English, Jr., USN, VX-6 helicopter crewman in 1961, 1962, 1965, and 1970.

**English Strait.** 62°27'S, 59°40'W. Also called Estrecho Espora, Spencers Straits. Separates Greenwich Island and Robert Island in the South Shetlands. Named Cecilia Straits by John Davis in 1822 for the *Cecilia,* but it was later renamed.

**Enigma Peak.** 69°24'S, 72°42'W. 1,000 m. North of the Wagner Ice Piedmont.

It surmounts the NW end of the central ridge of Rothschild Island. Named by the UK for the difficulty in finding it off photos during the mapping process.

**Isla Enrique** *see* **Harry Island**

**Enterprise Hills.** 79°50'S, 82°W. Mostly ice-free. Hills and peaks in the form of an arc extending for 30 miles. Form the north and NE boundary of Horseshoe Valley in the Heritage Range. Named in association with the heritage theme.

**Enterprise Island.** 64°32'S, 62°W. Also called Isla Nansen Norte, Isla Lientur. 1½ miles long. At the NE end of Nansen Island in Wilhelmina Bay, off the west coast of Graham Land. This and Nansen Island were charted together as Île Nansen by de Gerlache in 1898. By the early 1900s whalers had spotted that there were in fact two islands here, and were calling them North Nansen Island and South Nansen Island. North Nansen Island became Enterprise Island, named by the UK for the enterprise of the whalers in the area.

**Entrance Island.** 67°36'S, 62°52'E. Just north of the entrance to Horseshoe Harbor in Holme Bay, Mac. Robertson Land. Photographed by the LCE 1936–37. Named later by the Australians for its position at the entrance to the harbor at Mawson Station.

**Entrance Point.** 63°S, 60°34'W. Also called Punta Caupolicán. Southeasterly point on Deception Island, where one passes through Neptune's Bellows to get inside the island. Surveyed by Lt. Cdr. D.N. Penfold, RN, in 1948–49, and named by the British Admiralty following that survey.

**Entrance Shoal.** 67°36'S, 62°52'E. Just west of Entrance Island at the NW entrance to Horseshoe Harbor in Holme Bay, Mac. Robertson Land. Named by the ANARE under d'A.T. Gale in Feb. 1961.

**The *Entre Ríos.*** Destroyer which took part in the Argentine naval maneuvers of 1948 in the South Shetlands under the overall command of Contra-Almirante Harald Cappus.

**Entrikin Glacier.** 80°49′S, 160°E. Flows from the Churchill Mountains into Matterson Inlet. Named for Lt. Cdr. Joseph W. Entrikin, USN, VX-6 pilot in Antarctica in 1955–56.

**Entuziasty Glacier.** 70°30′S, 14°30′E. Flows from the Wohlthat Mountains into the Lazarev Ice Shelf in Queen Maud Land. Named Lednik Entuziastov (enthusiasts' glacier) by the USSR in 1961.

**Envoy Rock.** 67°51′S, 68°42′W. Submerged rock marking the northern limit of the Dion Islands, off the south end of Adelaide Island. Named by the UK following the courtly names given to other islands in the area (Emperor, etc.).

**Mount Ephraim**  *see*  **Ephraim Bluff**

**Ephraim Bluff.** 62°34′S, 59°43′W. Called Mount Ephraim as early as 1820. Modern air photos show it is a high bluff at the south end of Greenwich Island in the South Shetlands. It overlooks the southern entrance to McFarlane Strait, almost 1¾ miles west of Sartorius Point.

**Epidote Peak.** 84°46′S, 176°56′W. Just north of the mouth of Held Glacier, overlooking the west side of Shackleton Glacier in the Queen Maud Mountains. Named by the Texas Tech Shackleton Glacier Expedition of 1964–65 for the epidote found here in abundance.

**Epler Glacier.** 86°15′S, 161°W. 10 miles long. Flows from the Nilsen Plateau in the Queen Maud Mountains into the Amundsen Glacier, just south of Olsen Crags. Named for Charles F. Epler, VX-6 storekeeper, 1966 and 1967.

**Mount Epperly.** 78°26′S, 85°53′W. Over 4,600 m. 2 miles south of Mount Tyree in the main ridge of the Sentinel Range. Named for Lt. Robert M. Epperly, USNR, pilot here, 1957–58.

**Epsilon Island.** 64°19′S, 63°W. Also called Isla Alberti. Small island between Alpha Island and the southern tip of Lambda Island in the Melchior Islands. Named by the Argentines in 1945 for the Greek letter.

**The *Erebus.*** Small signal boat, or bomb (small warship used for carrying mortars) of 378 tons displacement. 106 feet long, with a 29-foot beam, it was launched in 1826. The larger of Ross' two ships which went into Antarctic waters during his 1839–43 expedition. Made entirely of wood, but reinforced for the ice, it was commanded by Ross. There were 3 lieutenants, a purser, 3 executive officers, a surgeon, and an assistant surgeon in charge of zoological and geological observations. Charles T. Tucker was master, and Henry Yule was second master. For other crew *see* **Ross.**

**Mount Erebus.** 77°32′S, 167°09′E. 3,795 m. The most southerly volcano on Ross Island, near the edge of the Ross Ice Shelf. Indeed, it is Antarctica's major volcano, at one time thought to be the only active one on the continent (*see* **Volcanoes**). It is one of only 3 convecting magma lake volcanoes in the world (the other 2 are in Africa). The crater is 900 feet deep and 2,640 feet across. It was first seen on Jan. 25, 1841, by Ross, and thought to be an island (Ross called it High Island, and the next day he renamed it more accurately, for his ship). It was in a state of eruption at the time. Ross estimated its height at 12,367 feet. Scott was the next to see it, in 1902, and he estimated its height at 13,120 feet and then at 12,922 feet. At 10 a.m., on March 10, 1908, during Shackleton's 1907–9 expedition, Edgeworth David and Jameson Adams reached the top at the head of a party which included Douglas Mawson and the Baronet Brocklehurst. Their climb, which took 5 days, made the height 13,370 feet. Raymond Priestley led the second ascent of Erebus in 1911, during Scott's 1910–13 expedition. Estimates of the height varied greatly, but the generally accepted one for a long time was 12,448 feet, until 1957 when a height of 13,200 feet was adopted as the standard. Erebus erupted for 6 hours on Sept. 4, 1974, and last erupted in 1979. The International Mount Erebus Seismic Study (IMESS) was begun in Dec. 1980 (*see* **Earthquakes**).

**Erebus and Terror Gulf.** 63°55′S, 56°40′W. Off the SE part of the northern tip of the Antarctic Peninsula, between Dundee Island and James Ross Island. Named for Ross' two ships of 1839–43.

**Erebus Basin.** 77°15′S, 166°E. Submarine feature off the NW coast of Ross Island in McMurdo Sound.

**Erebus Bay.** 77°44′S, 166°30′E. 13 miles wide. Between Cape Evans and Hut Point Peninsula on the SW coast of Ross Island in McMurdo Sound. Discovered and explored by Scott's 1901–4 expedition and named by his 1910–13 expedition for Ross' ship of 1839–43, and also for Mount Erebus.

**Erebus Glacier.** 77°42′S, 167°E. Flows from Mount Erebus on Ross Island to the coast, forming the Erebus Glacier Tongue on the west side of the island. Named by Scott in 1902 for the mountain.

**Erebus Glacier Tongue.** 77°42′S, 166°40′E. Juts out into McMurdo Sound from the west side of Ross Island. It is caused by the Erebus Glacier. Charted and named by Scott in 1902 for the glacier.

**Ereby Point.** 62°38′S, 60°27′W. 4½ miles ENE of Hannah Point on the north side of South Bay, Livingston Island. Named by the UK in 1961 in order to preserve the name Ereby, which had otherwise become extinct with Erebys Bay (*see* **South Bay**).

**Erebys Bay** *see* **South Bay**

**Eremitten Nunatak.** 72°11′S, 27°13′E. 3 miles south of Balchen Mountain in the Sør Rondane Mountains. Name means "the hermit" in Norwegian.

**Erewhon Basin.** 79°48′S, 158°34′E. Ice-free. In the Brown Hills. Separates the snouts of the Foggydog and Bartrum Glaciers from the northern edge of the Darwin Glacier. Named by the New Zealanders in 1962–63 for Samuel Butler's novel, *Erewhon.*

**Erickson, S.D.I.** Third mate on the *City of New York* during the first half of Byrd's 1928–30 expedition. In 1929–30

he was second mate, replacing Bendik Johansen.

**Erickson Bluffs.** 75°02′S, 136°30′W. They extend from Gilbert Bluff to Mount Sinha, and form the SW edge of the McDonald Heights, near the coast of Marie Byrd Land. Named for Albert W. Erickson, biologist in the Bellingshausen and Amundsen Seas in the *Southwind* in 1971–72.

**Erickson Glacier.** 84°23′S, 179°50′W. 12 miles long. Flows from the Queen Maud Mountains, between Mount Young and O'Leary Peak, and joins Ramsey Glacier at the edge of the Ross Ice Shelf. Named for Cdr. J.L. Erickson, USN, commander of the *Staten Island* in 1965.

**The *Erika Dan.*** Ship which brought the Belgian Antarctic Expedition of 1960 to the Antarctic, under the leadership of Guido Derom. Captain of the vessel was Leo Christiaensen.

**Roca Erizo** *see* **Urchin Rock**

**Erlanger Spur.** 83°16′S, 51°06′W. At the north of the Pensacola Mountains.

**Mount Ernest Gruening** *see* **Mount Jackson**

**Ernst Bay** *see* **Vahsel Bay**

**Eroica Peninsula.** 71°12′S, 72°25′W. Ice-covered. Just north of Beethoven Peninsula and Mendelssohn Inlet in western Alexander Island. Named by the UK for Beethoven's famous symphony.

**Eros Glacier.** 71°18′S, 68°20′W. 7 miles long. 2 miles wide at its mouth. Flows from Planet Heights into the George VI Sound, on the east coast of Alexander Island, just north of Fossil Bluff. Named by the UK for the minor planet Eros.

**Erosion.** Wearing down of the earth's surface features by the elements. Erosion is important in the geologic history of Antarctica. Whole mountain ranges have been eroded (*see* **Beacon Sandstone formation,** for example). Glacial erosion dominates the landscape. Running water erosion has produced little effect (*see also* **Rocks**).

**Errant Glacier.** 82°21'S, 160°58'E. 15 miles long. On the east side of the Holyoake Range, it flows into the Nimrod Glacier. Named by the NZGSAE 1960–61 to describe their zigzag route on the glacier as they looked for a route north from the Nimrod Glacier in Dec. 1960.

**Erratic Valley.** 70°47'S, 68°25'W. On the east side of Alexander Island.

**Erratics.** Ice-worn rocks carried by a glacier to a new position.

**Cape Errera.** 64°55'S, 63°37'W. The southernmost point on Wiencke Island. Discovered by de Gerlache in 1897–99, and named by him for a family who helped sponsor his expedition.

**Errera Channel.** 64°42'S, 62°36'W. A marine channel between Rongé Island and the west coast of Graham Land. Discovered by de Gerlache in 1897–99 and named by him for Leo Errera, professor at the University of Brussels, and a member of the *Belgica* Commission.

**Erskin, Charles.** Ordinary seaman on the Wilkes Expedition 1838–42. Joined in the USA. Served the cruise.

**Erskine Bay** *see* **Erskine Iceport**

**Erskine Glacier.** 66°29'S, 65°40'W. 16 miles long. On the west coast of Graham Land. It flows into Darbel Bay to the north of Hopkins Glacier. Surveyed and named West Gould Glacier in 1947 by the FIDS. In 1957 another survey showed no relation between this glacier and East Gould Glacier. The eastern glacier became Gould Glacier and the western one was renamed for Angus B. Erskine, leader of the first FIDS party to travel down the glacier.

**Erskine Iceport.** 69°54'S, 19°11'E. 3½ miles wide. 2½ miles deep. Indentation into the Princess Astrid Coast. Discovered by the *Glacier* on March 26, 1956, and named for retired Marine Lt. Gen. Graves B. Erskine, assistant secretary of defense for special operations. Originally called General Erskine Bay, then Erskine Bay, it was redefined as an iceport later in 1956.

**Erven Nunataks.** 75°45'S, 128°12'W. 7½ miles NE of Putzke Peak in the McCuddin Mountains of Marie Byrd Land. Named for Raymond D. Erven, meteorologist at Byrd Station in 1964.

**Escalade Peak.** 78°38'S, 159°23'E. 2,035 m. 8 miles east of the south end of the Boomerang Range in Victoria Land. Named by the NZ party of the BCTAE in 1957 because it forms a ladder to the summit with its vertical pitches and platforms.

**Roca Escarce** *see* **Channel Rock**

**Escarpada Point.** 61°17'S, 54°14'W. Also called Craggy Point. The SW point of Clarence Island in the South Shetlands. The Argentines named it in 1953–54. The name Escarpada means "craggy" in Spanish.

**Rocas Escarpadas** *see* **Rugged Rocks**

**The *Esiv Brunt*.** Argentine ship which took part in the 1947–48 expedition fielded by that country to the Antarctic.

**Eskers** *see* **Strand Moraines**

**Eskimo Point.** 74°17'S, 162°33'E. A flat-topped promontory which juts out from the east side of the Eisenhower Range, and forms the north wall of O'Kane Canyon in Victoria Land. Named by the Southern Party of the NZGSAE 1962–63, which built an igloo while waiting for a whiteout to lift here.

**Eskimo Ysbult** *see* **Novyy Island**

**Eskola Cirque.** 80°43'S, 23°49'W. In the Shackleton Range.

**Espenschied Nunatak.** 73°35'S, 77°52'W. The most westerly of the Snow Nunataks on the coast of Ellsworth Land. Named for Peter C. Espenschied, US aurora scientist at the Byrd Auroral Sub-Station in 1960–61.

**Glaciar Esperanza** *see* **Depot Glacier**

**Isla Esperanza** *see* **Hope Island**

**Esperanza Bay** *see* **Hope Bay**

**Esperanza Station.** 63°24'S, 57°01'W. Argentine year-round scientific station built in 1952 on Hope Bay (Esperanza is

Spanish for "hope") on the Trinity Peninsula, next to Britain's Base D. It is now an extensive military base, occupied by whole families. Nordenskjöld's hut is here (see **Historic sites**). Leaders of various wintering parties: 1952—Luís Manuel Casanova; 1953—Juan Carlos Kelly; 1954—Rodrigo. In 1954 a second station was built here, and led by Castro. It closed after that year.

**Espíndola. I.** Surveyor on the *Uruguay* in 1915 in the South Shetlands.

**Arrecife Espinosa** *see* **Armstrong Reef**

The *Espírito Santo*. Argentine sealing brig which was in the South Shetlands in 1819–20 with a British crew.

**Esplin Islands.** 67°45′S, 69°W. Group of 2 small islands and off-lying rocks, NE of Box Reef, off the south end of Adelaide Island. Named by the UK for Sub-Lt. Christopher J. Esplin Jones, RN, a member of the RN Hydrographic Survey Unit here in 1962–63.

**Estrecho Espora** *see* **English Strait**

The *Essex*. Stonington, Conn., sealer in the South Shetlands in 1820–21, and again in 1821–22, both seasons under the command of Capt. Chester.

**Essex Point.** 62°35′S, 61°12′W. Also called Punta Start. 1 mile NE of Start Point at the west end of Livingston Island in the South Shetlands. Named by the UK in 1958 for the *Essex*.

**Estay Rock.** 63°20′S, 57°59′W. A rock in water almost 2 miles WSW of Toro Point, Trinity Peninsula. Named by the Argentines in 1947 for Fidel Estay Cortez of the Chilean government.

**Glaciar Este** *see* **Shoesmith Glacier**

**Mount Ester.** 82°18′S, 155°04′E. Over 2,200 m. Surmounts the western part of McKay Cliffs in the Geologists Range. Named for Donald W. Ester, geologist at McMurdo Station in 1962–63.

The *Esther*. American sealing ship owned by the same people who owned the *Emerald*. It was in the South Shet-

lands as part of the Boston Expedition of 1820–21. Commander was F.G. Low.

**Esther Bay** *see* **Venus Bay**

**Esther Harbor.** 61°55′S, 57°59′W. Also called Esther's Harbor. On the west side of Venus Bay, just west of Pyrites Island, and south of Gam Point, on the north side of King George Island in the South Shetlands. Named by the early American sealers for the *Esther*.

**Esther Islands** *see* **Pyrites Island**

**Esther Nunatak.** 61°57′S, 57°50′W. 2 miles SW of Brimstone Peak in the NE part of King George Island in the South Shetlands. Charted by the personnel on the *Discovery II* in 1937, and named by them in association with nearby Esther Harbor.

**Eta Island.** 64°19′S, 62°55′W. Also called North Star Island, Isla Piedrabuena. 1½ miles long. Just north of Omega Island in the Melchior Islands. Named by the Argentines in 1945 for the Greek letter.

**Mount Etchells.** 80°18′S, 28°21′W. In the Shackleton Range.

¹**Eternity Mountains** *see* **Welch Mountains**

²**Eternity Mountains** *see* **Eternity Range**

**Eternity Range.** 69°46′S, 64°34′W. Also called the Eternity Mountains. 2,860 m. 28 miles long. It is in the middle of what used to be called Hearst Land, in the middle of the Antarctic Peninsula. It bisects the Antarctic Peninsula into Graham Land and Palmer Land. It contains Mounts Faith, Hope, and Charity. Discovered and named by Ellsworth on Nov. 23, 1935.

**Mount Ethelred.** 70°04′S, 69°29′W. 2,470 m. Ice-covered. Three miles south of Mount Ethelwulf. 8 miles inland from George VI Sound in the Douglas Range of Alexander Island. Surveyed in 1936 by the BGLE, and by the FIDS in 1948, and named by them for the Saxon king.

**Mount Ethelwulf.** 70°02′S, 69°34′W. 2,590 m. Ice-covered. Between Mounts

Egbert and Ethelred at the head of Tumble Glacier, in the Douglas Range of Alexander Island. Surveyed by the BGLE in 1936 and again by the FIDS in 1948, and named by them for the Saxon king.

**Étienne Fjord.** 65°09'S, 63°13'W. A bay, 5 miles long, between Bolsón and Thomson Coves on the south side of Flandres Bay, on the west coast of Graham Land. Charted by Charcot in 1903–5, and named Baie Étienne by him for Eugène Étienne (1844–1921), vice president of the Chamber of Deputies in France.

**Etna Island.** 63°05'S, 55°09'W. 6 miles north of the eastern end of Joinville Island, just north of Fliess Bay. Discovered by Ross and named by him because its high summit reminded him of the Sicilian volcano.

**Mount Eubanks.** 70°02'S, 67°15'W. Isolated. Rises 600 m. above the ice-surface, near the head of Riley Glacier in Palmer Land. Named for Lt. Cdr. Paul D. Eubanks, USN, pilot on long-range flights in Antarctica, 1969–70.

**Eubanks Point.** 73°27'S, 93°38'W. 2 miles WSW of Mount Loweth in the Jones Mountains. Named for Staff Sgt. Leroy E. Eubanks, US Marine navigator with VX-6 here in 1961–62.

**Eureka Glacier.** 69°44'S, 68°15'W. 18 miles long. 17 miles wide at its mouth. Flows from the west side of Palmer Land into the George VI Sound. The BGLE found their way to George VI Sound via this glacier in 1936, and named it appropriately.

**Europa Cliffs.** 70°52'S, 68°45'W. On the west side of Jupiter Glacier in eastern Alexander Island. Named by the UK for one of the satellites of the planet Jupiter.

**Cape Eustnes** *see* **Cape Gotley**

**Cape Eva.** 68°42'S, 90°37'W. Also called Evas Cape. Forms the northern end of Peter I Island. Discovered in 1927 by Eyvind Tofte in the *Odd I* and named by him.

**Eva, R.** Seaman on the *City of New York*, 1928–30.

**Cape Evans.** 77°38'S, 166°24'E. 6 miles south of Cape Royds, on the west coast of Ross Island. Discovered in 1902 by Scott, who named it The Skuary. Coming back in 1911, Scott renamed it on Jan. 2 that year for E.R.G.R. Evans, and used it as his base.

**Mount Evans.** 77°16'S, 162°28'E. 1,420 m. Has a double summit. Between the Debenham Glacier and the Wilson Piedmont Glacier in Victoria Land, it dominates the Saint Johns Range. Discovered by Scott in 1901–4, and named by him for E.R.G.R. Evans. Evans later took his title from this mountain.

**Evans, E.R.G.R.** 1881–1957. Edward Ratcliffe Garth Russell Evans. Created Lord Mountevans in 1945. Known as "Teddie." In 1902–3 he was sub-lieutenant on the *Morning* which relieved Scott's expedition and took Shackleton home. In 1910, by now a lieutenant, he went on the *Terra Nova* with Scott's 1910–13 expedition, as navigator and second-in-command of the expedition. Leader of the support party on the way to the Pole, he came down with scurvy on the way back, and barely made it back to Cape Evans (named for him) alive. He was invalided home in 1912, but returned in the *Terra Nova* in 1913 to take charge of the rest of the expedition (Scott had died). He wrote several books, including *South with Scott* in 1921. In 1934 he was at Bouvet Island (not in the Antarctic) in command of the *Milford*, but was unable to land.

**Evans, Edgar.** b. 1876, Rhossili, Wales. d. Feb. 17, 1912, on the Beardmore Glacier, Antarctica, and was buried the following day at the foot of the glacier, during his return trip from the South Pole during Scott's 1910–13 expedition. Known as "Taff" he joined the RN in 1891, and as a petty officer volunteered for the Royal Society Expedition, 1901–4, during which he, Scott and Lashly sledged 680 miles across Victoria Land. He became a gunnery instructor when he got home and then, utterly bored with life, volunteered again to go with Scott on the *Terra Nova* in 1910. Made it to the Pole on Jan. 17, 1912, but was the first to die on the way home.

**Evans, F.P.** Captain of the *Koonya*, 1907–8, and of the *Nimrod*, 1908–9.

**Evans, Griffith C., Jr.** Commander, USN. From Dec. 1959 to Nov. 14, 1960, he was captain of the *Burton Island*. He then became captain of the *Edisto*.

**Evans, Henry.** Officer's cook on the Wilkes Expedition 1838–42. Joined in the USA. Run at Fort George, Columbia River.

**Evans, Hugh Blackwell.** British assistant zoologist on Borchgrevink's 1898–1900 expedition.

**Evans Butte.** 85°55'S, 145°16'W. 2,570 m. Snow-topped. At the head of Albanus Glacier. Marks the SE limit of the Tapley Mountains. Named for Lt. Eldon L. Evans, USN, medical officer at Byrd Station in 1962.

**Evans Cove.** 74°53'S, 163°49'E. An indentation of Terra Nova Bay into the coast of Victoria Land between Inexpressible Island and Cape Russell. Charted by Shackleton's 1907–9 expedition and named by them as Evans Coves for Capt. F.P. Evans. Campbell's Northern Party wintered-over here in 1911–13. The name was later singularized.

**Evans Coves** *see* **Evans Cove**

**¹Evans Glacier.** 65°05'S, 61°40'W. 15 miles long. 4 miles wide. Gently sloping. Flows from the plateau escarpment to join Hektoria Glacier between Shiver Point and Whiteside Hill, on the east coast of Graham Land. Discovered aerially by Wilkins on Dec. 20, 1928, and named Evans Inlet by him for E.S. Evans of Detroit. Redefined by the FIDS in 1955.

**²Evans Glacier.** 83°47'S, 169°55'E. Just south of the Owen Hills, flowing from the Queen Alexandra Range into the Beardmore Glacier. Named by the New Zealanders in 1961–62 for Edgar Evans.

**Evans Heights.** 75°06'S, 161°33'E. Small rock heights on the west side of the mouth of Woodberry Glacier in the Prince Albert Mountains of Victoria Land. Named for John P. Evans, field assistant at McMurdo Station in 1964–65.

**Evans Ice Stream.** 76°S, 78°W. Flows from Ellsworth Land, between Cape Zumberge and the Fowler Ice Rise into the western part of the Ronne Ice Shelf. Named by the British for Stanley Evans, physicist at Halley Bay Station in 1956–57.

**Evans Inlet** *see* **Evans Glacier**

**Evans Island.** 67°36'S, 62°48'E. The most southerly of the Flat Islands in the eastern part of Holme Bay. Photographed by the LCE 1936–37. Later named by the Australians for D. Evans, diesel mechanic at Mawson Station in 1958.

**Evans Knoll.** 74°51'S, 100°25'W. Mainly snow-covered. At the north side of the terminus of Pine Island Glacier. SW of Webber Nunatak, it marks the SW end of the Hudson Mountains on the coast of Marie Byrd Land. Named for Donald J. Evans, VLF scientist at Byrd Station in 1960–61.

**Evans Névé.** 72°30'S, 164°45'E. Feeds the Tucker, Mariner, Aviator, Rennick, and Lillie Glaciers in Oates Land. Named by the New Zealanders in 1963–64 for Edgar Evans.

**Evans Peak.** 78°17'S, 85°58'W. 3,950 m. 3 miles ENE of Mount Ostenso in the Sentinel Range. Named by the University of Minnesota Geological Party here in 1963–64 for John Evans, geologist with the party.

**Evans Peninsula.** 71°58'S, 96°42'W. 30 miles long. Ice-covered. Between Koether and Cadwalader Inlets, it juts out from the north side of Thurston Island. Discovered during the USN Bellingshausen Sea Expedition of Feb. 1960, and named for Griffith C. Evans, Jr.

**Evans Piedmont Glacier.** 76°45'S, 162°40'E. A broad ice sheet occupying the low-lying coastal platform between Tripp Island and Cape Archer, between the Oates Piedmont Glacier and the

Wilson Piedmont Glacier on the coast of Victoria Land. Named by the NZ Northern Survey Party of the BCTAE when they circumnavigated it in 1957, for Edgar Evans.

**Evans Point.** 72°26′S, 99°39′W. Ice-covered. Fronts on Peacock Sound. 15 miles WNW of Von der Wall Point at the south side of Thurston Island. Named for Richard Evans, oceanographer on the *Burton Island* here during the USN Bellingshausen Sea Expedition of Feb. 1960.

**Evans Ridge.** 72°07′S, 166°54′E. Extends for 12 miles between Midway and McKellar Glaciers in the Victory Mountains of Victoria Land. Named in 1966 for Arthur Evans, secretary of the NZ Antarctic Place Names Committee.

**Evas Cape** *see* **Cape Eva**

**Cape Evensen.** 66°09′S, 65°44′W. Also called Cape Waldeck Rousseau. Forms the north side of the entrance to Auvert Bay, on the west coast of Graham Land. Discovered by Charcot in 1903-5 and named by him for C.J. Evensen.

**Evensen, Capt. C.J.** Led the 1893-94 expedition in the *Hertha* to the South Shetlands. Sailed with the *Castor.*

**Evensen Bay** *see* **Auvert Bay**

**Evensen Nunatak.** 64°59′S, 60°22′W. 1½ miles NW of Dallmann Nunatak in the Seal Nunataks off the east coast of the Antarctic Peninsula. Charted by the FIDS in Aug. 1947, and named by them for Capt. C.J. Evensen.

**Everett Nunatak.** 85°28′S, 176°40′W. Just NE of Roberts Massif, at the SW side of the Zaneveld Galcier. Named by the Texas Tech Shackleton Glacier Expedition of 1964-65 for James R. Everett, graduate student of that institution and a member of the expedition.

**Everett Range.** 71°20′S, 165°40′E. 60 miles long. Mainly ice-covered. Forms the east side of the Lillie Glacier, between the Greenwell and Ebbe Glaciers in Oates Land. Named for Cdr. William H. Everett, USN, VX-6 commander in 1962-63.

**Everett Spur.** 71°05′S, 164°30′E. Marks the NW end of the Everett Range and the junction of Ebbe Glacier with Lillie Glacier. Named for Kaye R. Everett, geologist at McMurdo Station, 1967-68 and at Livingston Island, 1968-69.

**Everson Ridge.** 60°43′S, 45°39′W. Extends from Jebsen Point to Tioga Hill on the west coast of Signy Island in the South Orkneys. Named by the UK for Inigo Everson, BAS biologist on Signy Island, 1965-66.

**Cape Evgenov** *see* **Cape Yevgenov**

**Evison Glacier.** 71°42′S, 164°E. Flows from the south end of the Molar Massif in the Bowers Mountains. Named by the New Zealanders in 1967-68 for F.F. Evison, New Zealand's first professor of geophysics.

**Evteev Glacier.** 78°57′S, 161°12′E. Flows from the SE slopes of the Worcester Range to the Ross Ice Shelf, west of Cape Timberlake. Named by the USA in 1964 for Sveneld A. Evteev, glaciologist and USSR exchange scientist at McMurdo Station in 1960.

**Roca Ewens** *see* **Emm Rock**

**Ewing Island.** 69°52′S, 61°12′W. Ice-covered. Dome-shaped. 8 miles across. 15 miles NE of Cape Collier, just south of Hearst Island, off the east coast of the Antarctic Peninsula. Discovered aerially on Nov. 7, 1947, by the RARE, and named by Ronne for Dr. Maurice Ewing of Columbia University, who helped plan the RARE seismological program.

**Exasperation Inlet.** 65°20′S, 62°W. Ice-filled. 16 miles wide at its entrance between Foyn Point and Cape Disappointment on the east coast of Graham Land. Charted by the FIDS in 1947, and named by them for the exasperation experienced here by sledging parties due to the disturbed nature of the ice.

**Executive Committee Range.** 76°50′S, 126°W. Also called Committee Range. 50 miles in extent along the 126th Meridian in Marie Byrd Land. It has 5 major extinct volcanoes: Mounts Sidley,

Waesche, Hampton, and Cumming, and Whitney Peak. Byrd discovered Mount Sidley in 1934 as an individual mountain, but the range itself was discovered aerially on Dec. 15, 1940, by members of the USAS, and named for the Executive Committee of the expedition.

**Exile Nunatak.** 70°19′S, 71°16′W. Isolated (hence the name given by the UK). In the NW part of the Handel Ice Piedmont in the west-central part of Alexander Island.

**Exiles Nunataks.** 69°57′S, 158°E. 8 miles SSW of DeRemer Nunataks in the Wilson Hills. Named by the New Zealanders in 1963–64 for their isolated position.

**Exodus Glacier.** 79°49′S, 156°22′E. 1 mile NE of Mount Ellis. Flows from the northern edge of Midnight Plateau to the SW side of Island Arena in the Darwin Mountains. Named by the New Zealanders in 1962–63 for nearby Exodus Valley.

**Exodus Valley.** 79°50′S, 156°18′E. Moraine-filled. Descends from Midnight Plateau between Colosseum Ridge and Exodus Glacier in the Darwin Mountains. Named by the New Zealanders in 1962–63 because it provides the only easy descent route from Midnight Plateau.

**Expedition Rock.** 60°43′S, 44°45′W. A submerged rock in water. 1½ miles ENE of Cape Robertson in the entrance to Jessie Bay on the north side of Laurie Island in the South Orkneys. Charted and named by personnel on the *Discovery II* in 1933.

**Expeditions** *see* **the Appendixes**

**Explorers.** For a complete list of leaders *see* the Expeditions Appendix. Moreover, each explorer, leader or not, has his own entry in the Encyclopedia. For a guide to who might be the most famous in history, one might (but see end of this section) use the *Encyclopaedia Britannica*. Thus, in order of importance, depending on the size of the entry in that book (and excluding such incidental Antarctic visitors as Hooker and

Murray on the *Challenger*): Cook, Byrd, Dumont d'Urville, Scott, Shackleton, von Drygalski, Wilkes, Ellsworth, Wilkins, Ross, Hillary, von Bellingshausen, Amundsen, Nordenskjöld, Charcot, Filchner, Weddell, David, de Gerlache, Bransfield, Bentley, Smith, Borchgrevink, F. Cook, Fuchs, Mawson, Bruce. This system shows the unreliability of bringing the general to bear on the specific. For example, Scott is much more famous than Dumont d'Urville, and so is Amundsen, and Finn Ronne should have an entry in *Britannica*.

**Explorers Cove.** 77°34′S, 163°35′E. At the NW head of New Harbor in Victoria Land. Named in 1976 for the explorers who have worked near here.

**Explorers Range.** 70°50′S, 162°45′E. Extends from Mount Bruce in the north to the Carryer and McLin Glaciers in the south, in the Bowers Mountains. Named by NZ for the northern party of the NZGSAE 1963–64.

**Explosives.** Sometimes used to clear a path in the ice, or to fill in a crevasse in order to make it passable.

**Exposure Hill.** 73°32′S, 162°43′E. Also called Exposure Hills. At the SW end of Gair Mesa, in the Mesa Range of Victoria Land. Named by the New Zealanders in 1962–63 because of the light-colored sandstone exposed on the west side.

**Exposure Hills** *see* **Exposure Hill**

**Exposure Rock** *see* **Chata Rock**

[1]**The** *Express*. 2-masted, 138-ton American schooner. 76 feet, 9 inches long. Built at Hudson, NY, in 1816, and registered on July 25, 1820. Nat Palmer was part owner during 1820–22 when the *Express* went to the South Shetlands on the two Fanning-Pendleton Sealing Expeditions of 1820–21 and 1821–22. With a crew of 17, Ephraim Williams was first commander, and Thomas Dunbar was his successor.

[2]**The** *Express*. American sealing schooner commanded by Capt. Thomas

B. Lynch, in the South Shetlands, South Orkneys, and around the Trinity Peninsula in 1879–80, looking for the lost *Charles Shearer*. In 1885–86 it was at South Georgia (54° S) under an unknown captain.

**Express Cove.** 60° 42′ S, 45° 39′ W. North of Foca Point on the west coast of Signy Island in the South Orkneys. Charted in 1933 by the Discovery Committee, and surveyed in 1947 by the FIDS. Named by the UK for the *Express* (Capt. Lynch).

**Express Island.** 62° 27′ S, 59° 59′ W. Between Greenwich Island and Livingston Island in the South Shetlands.

**Roca Expuesta** *see* **Chata Rock**

**Extension Reef.** 65° 58′ S, 66° 08′ W. Has a large number of small islands and rocks. Extends 10 miles SW from the south end of Rabot Island in the Biscoe Islands. Charted and named descriptively by the BGLE in 1934–37.

**Exum Glacier.** 73° 30′ S, 94° 13′ W. Flows between Hughes Point and Bonnabeau Dome, in the Jones Mountains. Named by the University of Minnesota–Jones Mountains Party of 1960–61 for Glenn Exum who trained the party in mountain climbing.

**Eyres Bay.** 66° 29′ S, 110° 28′ E. Between the west side of Browning Peninsula and the front of Vanderford Glacier, at the south end of the Windmill Islands. Named for Ensign David L. Eyres, USN, at Wilkes Station, 1958.

**Eyrie Bay.** 63° 35′ S, 57° 38′ W. Also called Bahía Edith. 2 ½ miles wide at its mouth. Extends 3 miles inland. Just north of Jade Point, Trinity Peninsula. Named by the UK in association with nearby Eagle Island.

**Mount Eyskens.** 71° 30′ S, 35° 36′ E. 2,300 m. Just north of Mount Derom in the Queen Fabiola Mountains. Discovered by the Belgian Antarctic Expedition of 1960–61, and named by leader Guido Derom for Albert Eyskens, pilot of one of the two aircraft used on the expedition.

**Eyssen, Robert.** Captain of the *Komet,* 1940–41.

**Ezcurra Inlet.** 62° 10′ S, 58° 34′ W. Also called Fjord Ezcurra. The western branch of Admiralty Bay on King George Island in the South Shetlands. Charcot named it in Dec. 1909.

**Mount F. Gjertsen** *see* **Mount Gjertsen**

**Mount F.L. Smith.** 83° 38′ S, 169° 30′ E. 2,635 m. 1 mile NE of Mount Fox, in the Queen Alexandra Range. Discovered by Shackleton's 1907–9 expedition, and named by them for F.L. Smith, London tobacconist and supporter.

**Factory Bluffs.** 60° 43′ S, 45° 36′ W. 120 m. To the south of Signy Island Station and Factory Cove, on the east side of Signy Island, in the South Orkneys. Named by the UK for the small shore-based whaling station that operated between 1920 and 1930 below the bluffs on the shore of Factory Cove.

**Factory Cove.** 60° 43′ S, 45° 37′ W. Between Knife Point and Berntsen Point, in the southern part of Borge Bay, Signy Island, in the South Orkneys. Discovered by Hans Borge in 1913–14, and named around that time by Petter Sørlle, as Borge Havna. Renamed in 1927 by personnel on the Discovery Investigations, for the ruins of the whaling factory built in 1920–21 by the Tønsberg Hvalfangeri.

**Factory ships.** *See* **Whaling.** The first modern floating factory ship was the *Admiralen,* operating in the South Shetlands in Jan. 1906.

**Fadden Peak.** 85° 29′ S, 142° 43′ W. 920 m. 2 miles east of Cressey Peak, between the SE edge of the Ross Ice Shelf and the Watson Escarpment, between the Bender Mountains and the Harold Byrd Mountains. Named for Dean E. Fadden, utilitiesman at Byrd Station in 1958.

**Mount Faget.** 71° 44′ S, 168° 26′ E. 3,360 m. 4 miles NW of Mount Adam in the Admiralty Mountains. Named for Maxime A. Faget, a NASA official who visited McMurdo Sound in 1966–67.

**Fairchild Peak.** 83°52'S, 165°41'E. 2,180 m. Just over 1½ miles SSE of Portal Rock, at the south side of the mouth of Tillite Glacier. Named for William W. Fairchild, cosmic ray scientist at Mc-Murdo Station in 1961.

**Cape Fairweather.** 65°S, 61°01'W. Also called Cabo Buen Tiempo. 705 m. Mostly ice-covered. Between Drygalski Glacier and Evans Glacier, it forms the southern tip of the Nordenskjöld Coast, on the NE tip of the Antarctic Peninsula. Charted in 1947 by the FIDS. Named for Capt. Alexander Fairweather.

**Mount Fairweather.** 85°04'S, 166°32'W. 1,865 m. At the head of Somero Glacier, 4 miles NE of Mount Schevill, in the Duncan Mountains, of the Queen Maud Mountains. Named by the Southern Party of the NZGSAE 1963–64, who experienced a spell of unusually fine weather here.

**Fairweather, Capt. Alexander.** Commander of the *Balaena* during the Dundee Whaling Expedition of 1892–93.

**Mount Faith.** 69°37'S, 64°29'W. 2,650 m. 9 miles north of Mount Hope, in the Eternity Range, between Graham Land and Palmer Land. Discovered aerially by, and named by, Ellsworth on Nov. 21, 1935. Surveyed by the BGLE in Nov. 1936.

**Mount Falconer.** 77°34'S, 163°08'E. 810 m. Surmounts Lake Fryxell, on the north wall of the Taylor Valley, between Mount McLennan and the Commonwealth Glacier. Named by Grif Taylor's Western Journey Party during Scott's 1910–13 expedition.

**The *Falk*.** Norwegian whale catcher in Antarctic waters in 1930–31, commanded by Capt. Lars Andersen. It helped the *Discovery* with coal during that ship's BANZARE (British, Australian and New Zealand Antarctic Research Expedition).

**Falkenhof Glacier.** 85°02'S, 172°05'E. 7 miles long. Flows from the area of Tricorn Mountain into Snakeskin Glacier, NW of Mount Clarke. Named for Jack J. Falkenhof, meteorologist at

Amundsen-Scott South Pole Station in 1965.

**The *Falkland*.** Norwegian factory whaling ship in the South Orkneys in the 1912–13 season. It was badly damaged while entering what is now Falkland Harbor on Powell Island.

**Falkland Dependency** *see* **British Antarctic Territory**

**Falkland Harbor.** 60°44'S, 45°03'W. On the SW side of Powell Island, in the South Orkneys. Charted by Petter Sørlle in 1912–13. Named for the *Falkland*.

**Falkland Islands Dependencies Aerial Survey Expedition.** 1955–57. Better known as the FIDASE. Led by Peter G. Mott. Hunting Aerosurveys Ltd., under contract to the British Colonial Office, began a program of vertical air photography of the South Shetlands and northern Graham Land, with Canso flying boats based at Deception Island. Helicopters were also used to assist ground control parties. The *Oluf Sven*, a Danish freighter commanded by Capt. J.C. Ryge, was chartered by the expedition to take them to Deception Island in 1955 and 1956, and was used as a mobile base for ground surveys by FIDASE parties. They photographed about 34,000 square miles of territory as far south as 68°S. J.H. Saffery was flying manager, and deputy leader of the expedition. Other personnel included Anthony D. Bancroft (senior surveyor), J.D.L. Symington (senior air photographer), M.R. Milburn (air traffic officer), Frederick W. Sherrell (surveyor/geologist), Christopher B. Gavin-Robinson, J. Greenshields, Robert N. Pettus (airplane pilots), and Jan Patcha (helicopter pilot).

**Falkland Islands Dependencies Surveys.** Better known as the FIDS. A series of British government surveys conducted in the South Shetlands, South Orkneys, and the Antarctic Peninsula area between 1945 and 1962. In reality it was the ongoing British scientific effort in the area of Antarctica claimed by Great Britain. In 1943 the British War Cabinet created Operation Tabarin (q.v.), a military-scientific investigation of the area of the Antarctic in question. This operation was the responsibility of the Admiralty. In 1945, at the end of World War II, responsibility for the stations (or bases) created by Operation Tabarin was transferred from the Admiralty to the Colonial Office, and the FIDS were created. At that time the area of British Antarctica was part of what were called the Falkland Islands Dependencies. A. Taylor was still leading the second phase of Operation Tabarin, and was wintering-over in Antarctica, as leader of Base D, at Hope Bay. Strictly speaking, therefore, he became the first FIDS leader. On Feb. 23, 1946, E.W. Bingham arrived with his men at Stonington Island in the *Trepassey*. He relieved Taylor as leader of the British Antarctic effort, and is generally regarded as the first FIDS leader assigned in that role. Bingham moved to the old East Base (q.v.) on Feb. 24, 1946, and that same day began construction of Base E, 250 yards to the south. It was finished by March 13, 1946, and Bingham led the 1946 wintering party there. On Feb. 5, 1947, the *Trepassey* returned with a replacement FIDS crew headed by Maj. K.S. Pierce-Butler. The ship left on Feb. 7, 1947, and Pierce-Butler led the 1947 wintering party at Base E, and continued the FIDS mission, to explore, chart, plot, map, report, name features, and generally open up the area. Over the 1947–48 season the FIDS teamed up with the RARE led by Finn Ronne, for the Weddell Coast Sledge Party (q.v.). In early 1948 Vivian Fuchs replaced Pierce-Butler as FIDS leader, and in Oct. 1948 responsibility for the FIDS was transferred to the governor of the Falkland Islands, with headquarters at Stanley. Fuchs went on to lead the FIDS again from 1949 to 1953. In 1955–57 the Falkland Islands Dependencies Aerial Survey Expedition (q.v.), better known as the FIDASE, took place, and in 1962 the FIDS became the BAS (British Antarctic Survey—q.v.).

**Mount Falla.** 84°22′S, 164°55′E. 3,825 m. Conical. 3½ miles NE of Mount Stonehouse, between the Prebble and Berwick Glaciers, in the southern sector of the Queen Alexandra Range. Discovered by the NZ party of the BCTAE 1957–58, and named by them for R.A. Falla.

**Falla, R.A.** Ornithologist on the BANZARE 1929–31, he was one of the two New Zealanders (*see also* **Simmers**) on the expedition. Years later he was a member of the Ross Sea Committee for the BCTAE 1955–57 (he did not go to Antarctica this time).

**Falla Bluff.** 67°34′S, 61°29′E. Also called Svarthovden. A coastal bluff at the head of Utstikkar Bay. Discovered in Feb. 1931 by the BANZARE, and named by Mawson for R.A. Falla.

**Fallières Coast.** 68°30′S, 66°30′W. Also called Fallières Land. Between the head of Bourgeois Fjord and Cape Jeremy, on the west coast of Graham Land, behind Marguerite Bay. Discovered by Charcot in 1908–10, and named by him for the president of France, Armand Fallières.

**Fallières Land** *see* **Fallières Coast**

**Fallone Nunataks.** 85°21′S, 142°54′W. A chain, 10 miles long. 10 miles NE of Harold Byrd Mountains, between the edge of the Ross Ice Shelf and the Watson Escarpment. Named for Lt. (jg) Paul R. Fallone, Jr., USN, aide to the commander, US Naval Support Force, Antarctica, 1962.

**Pico Falsa Agujo** *see* **Helmet Peak**

**False Bay.** 62°42′S, 60°22′W. Also called Palmer Bay. 4 miles long. Between Barnard Point and Miers Bluff, on the south coast of Livingston Island, in the South Shetlands. Discovered by Palmer in Nov. 1820, and named by him. Weddell renamed it as Palmer's Bay, for the discoverer of this feature, but it was later renamed False Bay.

**False Cape Renard.** 65°02′S, 63°50′W. 1½ miles SW of Cape Renard, on the west coast of Graham Land. Charted by de

Gerlache in 1897–99, and during his expedition Henryk Arctowski named this point and Cape Renard collectively as The Needles. In 1908–10 Charcot gave them these separate names (*see* **Cape Renard**).

**False Cerro Negro** *see* **False Negro Hill**

**False Island.** 64°31'S, 62°53'W. The largest of 3 islands at the east side of Hackapike Bay, off the NE coast of Anvers Island. Charcot charted two islands here in 1903–5, and the personnel on the *Discovery* in 1927 named this one.

**False Island Point.** 63°55'S, 57°20'W. A headland. 1 mile long and ½ mile wide. Connected to the south side of Vega Island by a low, narrow, almost invisible isthmus. Charted as an island in Feb. 1902 by Nordenskjöld's expedition, and redefined and named by the FIDS in 1945.

**False Negro Hill.** 62°39'S, 61°04'W. Also called False Cerro Negro. On the south side of Byers Peninsula, just to the west of Negro Hill, on Livingston Island, in the South Shetlands.

**False Round Point.** 61°54'S, 58°02'W. 8½ miles west of North Foreland, and 2 miles south of Ridley Island, on the north coast of King George Island, in the South Shetlands. First charted before 1822. In 1937, the personnel on the *Discovery II* recharted it and named it for its similarity to Round Point, 12 miles to the west.

**Île Famine** *see* **Bob Island**

**Fandens Brae** *see* **Devils Glacier**

**Fanfare Island.** 65°13'S, 64°11'W. The most northerly of the Argentine Islands, 1½ miles south of Herald Reef in the Wilhelm Archipelago. Named by the UK in 1961 in association with Herald Reef.

**The Fang** *see* **Fang Ridge**

**Fang Buttress.** 64°41'S, 63°21'W. A crag, just west of Molar Peak, near the south end of the Osterrieth Range, on Anvers Island. It has a small, but notable, fanglike rock in front of it (hence the name given by the UK in 1959). It is a landmark for parties crossing William Glacier. Surveyed by the FIDS in 1955–57.

**Fang Glacier.** 77°29'S, 167°06'E. On the west side of Fang Ridge, halfway up Mount Erebus, Ross Island. Charted by Debenham during Scott's 1910–13 expedition, and named by him in association with Fang Ridge.

**Fang Peak.** 67°48'S, 62°35'E. Conical. 1 mile south of Mount Parsons, in the David Range of the Framnes Mountains, in Mac. Robertson Land. Photographed by the LCE 1936–37, and later named descriptively by the Australians.

**Fang Ridge.** 77°29'S, 167°12'E. Also called The Fang. Halfway up Mount Erebus, on Ross Island, it is part of the original caldera rim of that volcano. Named for its curved shape by Frank Debenham in 1912, during Scott's last expedition.

**Fannin, Peter.** Master of the *Adventure* during Cook's 1772–75 voyage.

**Cape Fanning.** 72°24'S, 60°39'W. Forms the north side of the entrance to Violante Inlet, on the east coast of Palmer Land. Discovered during a flight from East Base during the USAS, on Dec. 30, 1940. Named for Edmund Fanning.

**Fanning, Edmund.** 1770–1841. US sealer out of Stonington, Conn., and NYC. Fanning is a seminal figure in early Antarctic history, even though he never got there. A veteran of many sealing voyages further north, he was long interested in the mysteries of the southern oceans. He was in South Georgia (54°S) in 1800–1. In 1812 he was about to set out on a government expedition to look for the Antarctic (one suspects he would have found it) in the *Volunteer* and the *Hope,* but was prevented by the war with the British. In 1815–17 he sailed around the world in the *Volunteer,* and in 1818 organized his own sealing outfit. He organized the Fanning-Pendleton Sealing Expeditions of 1820–21 and

1821–22, as well as the Palmer-Pendleton Expedition of 1829–31. He was the father of William A. Fanning.

**Fanning, William A.** Son of Edmund Fanning, and owner-manager of the *Hersilia*. He went to the South Shetlands with that vessel in 1819–20, as supercargo. In 1820–21 he was aboard the *Express* during the Fanning-Pendleton Sealing Expedition, of which he was managing agent. He was captain of the *Alabama Packet,* and second-in-command of the Fanning-Pendleton Sealing Expedition of 1821–22.

**Fanning-Pendleton Sealing Expedition 1820–21.** 5 ships commanded by Ben Pendleton (with William Fanning a partner in the scheme), which left Stonington, Conn., for the South Shetlands seal rush of 1820–21, under the aegis of Edmund Fanning. Pendleton left first, in the flagship *Frederick,* on May 14, 1820, a week before the *Hersilia* returned from its pioneering 1819–20 expedition. Thomas Dunbar, skipper of the *Free Gift* left next, and at this stage the *Hero* (under Nat Palmer) and the *Express* (under Ephraim Williams) were added to the fleet. These two and the *Hersilia* (still under the command of Sheffield), left on July 21, 1820, with William Fanning aboard the *Express* as managing agent of the expedition, which had 70 men on it in toto. The expedition spent almost 4 months in the South Shetlands, gathering seals; and Palmer, in the *Hero,* went to Deception Island on Nov. 15, 1820, and was the first man to explore inside this island. The following day he sighted Trinity Island, and on Nov. 17 he discovered Orléans Strait, and must have sighted the Antarctic Peninsula. He discovered Yankee Harbor back in the South Shetlands, where the fleet relocated on Nov. 24, 1820. Another vessel, or maybe the *Hero,* with maybe Palmer and Pendleton, may have explored the western coast of the Antarctic Peninsula to as far south as 68°S, but there is no proof of this. The fleet took a total of 50,895 sealskins between Nov. 27, 1820,

and Jan. 12, 1821. The *Free Gift* left for home on Feb. 4, 1821, in company with the *Frederick.* The others left on Feb. 22, 1821. All except the *Hersilia* arrived back in Stonington between April 29 and May 8, 1821. For the fate of the *Hersilia,* see that entry in this book. The sequel to this expedition was the Fanning-Pendleton Sealing Expedition 1821–22.

**Fanning-Pendleton Sealing Expedition 1821–22.** Sequel to the Fanning-Pendleton Sealing Expedition 1820–21. This time the fleet had 85 men, and a few changes in vessels and leading players. They knew going in that there were not many seals left in the South Shetlands, and, as it turned out, the expedition was just profitable. Pendleton again commanded the expedition, and William Fanning was his second-in-command. The *Frederick* (once again the flagship under Pendleton), the *Alabama Packet* (under Fanning), the *Express* (under Dunbar), the *James Monroe* (under Nat Palmer), and the *Hero* (under Harris Pendleton) left Stonington on July 25, 1821. They based at Deception Island during the summer of 1821–22, and did much exploration for new seal beaches. Also in the area that season was British sealer George Powell, in the *Dove,* who was looking for the Seal Islands. Powell and Palmer ran across each other at Elephant Island, and the two teamed up on Nov. 30, 1821, for an exploration eastward, discovering the South Orkneys on Dec. 6, 1821. The fleet left Deception Island on Jan. 30, 1822, three of them going straight home and arriving in April 1822. Three others sailed to the Pacific, looking for hair sealskins (not as good as fur sealskins, but still profitable). Of these 3 ships, the *Frederick* arrived home on Nov. 1, 1822, while the *Hero* was sold in Chile on Oct. 11, 1822, and the crew returned on the *Alabama Packet,* which got back to Stonington on June 18, 1823.

**Fannings Harbor** *see* **Yankee Harbor**

**Fanning's Islands.** Collective name for Rugged Island, Snow Island, and Livingston Island. These three islands were discovered by the crew of the *Hersilia* on Jan. 22, 1820, and named for William A. Fanning. The name Fanning's Islands became obsolete soon afterward when it was found that the three islands were part of the South Shetlands.

**Cape Faraday.** 60°38′S, 45°04′W. Forms the northern tip of Powell Island, in the South Orkneys. Discovered by Powell and Palmer in Dec. 1821, and named by Powell.

**Faraday Station.** 65°15′S, 64°16′W. British scientific station on Galíndez Island, in the Argentine Islands, off the west coast of Graham Land. It is a geophysical observatory, and atmospheric research is done here. Originally this station was on Winter Island, built there in 1947 by the FIDS as Base F, on the site of the old BGLE hut. Oliver Burd was first leader there, in the winter of 1947. Subsequent leaders were T.M. Nicholl (1948 and 1949), H.G. Heywood (1950), J.R. Green (1951), N.S.W. Petts (1952), D.A. Barrett (1953). In 1953 the site for the new Faraday Station was prepared on Galíndez Island, and occupied in 1954. First leader was Ralph A. Lenton (winter of 1954). Subsequent early leaders were R.V. Hesketh (1955), N.A. Hedderley (1956), D. Emerson (1957). During the IGY, meteorology, geomagnetism, oceanography, and seismology were studied.

**Mount Faraway.** 79°12′S, 28°49′W. 1,175 m. Snow-covered. Marks the southern extremity of the Theron Mountains. Discovered by the BCTAE in 1956, and named by them because, while sledging toward it, they never seemed to get any closer to it for days.

**Farbo Glacier.** 75°50′S, 141°45′W. Flows into Land Glacier, 8 miles west of Mount McCoy, on the coast of Marie Byrd Land. Named for Richard R. Farbo, USN, equipment operator at McMurdo Station in 1959 and 1965, and at Amundsen-Scott South Pole Station in 1969.

**Farewell Rock.** 63°52′S, 61°01′W. A rock in water, ½ mile long, off the SW end of Spert Island. 6 miles NW of Skottsberg Point on Trinity Island. Named in the 19th century.

**Punta Farias** *see* **Skottsberg Point**

**Mount Farley.** 86°35′S, 152°30′W. 2,670 m. 3 miles east of McNally Peak, between the Bartlett and Robert Scott Glaciers, in the Queen Maud Mountains. Discovered by Quin Blackburn's party in Dec. 1934, during Byrd's 1933–35 expedition. Named in 1935 by Byrd for James M. Farley, US Postmaster-General.

**Farley Massif.** 70°13′S, 65°48′E. 1 mile north of Mount Jacklyn, in the Athos Range of the Prince Charles Mountains. Named by the Australians for J.A. Farley, surveyor at Mawson Station in 1964.

**Farman Nunatak.** 64°25′S, 61°07′W. 655 m. West of Mount Morton, in the Blériot Glacier, on the west coast of Graham Land. Named by the UK in 1960 for Henry Farman (1874–1958), aeronautics pioneer.

**Farmer Island.** 76°37′S, 147°04′W. 14 miles long. Ice-covered. 6 miles north of Radford Island, in the Sulzberger Ice Shelf, on the coast of Marie Byrd Land. Named for Floyd L. Farmer, USN, senior ship fitter on the *Glacier* here in 1961–62.

**Farnell Valley.** 77°53′S, 160°39′E. 1 mile long. Ice-free. A southerly spur of Beacon Valley, leading toward the Ferrar Glacier, in southern Victoria Land. Named in 1964 for James B.H. Farnell who assisted in supplying field parties at McMurdo Station in 1960.

**Roca Faro** *see* **Column Rock**

**Farr Bay.** 66°35′S, 94°23′E. 7 miles wide. Just east of Helen Glacier, on the coast of East Antarctica. Discovered in Nov. 1912 by the Western Base Party of the AAE 1911–14, and named Depot Bay by Mawson. He later renamed it for Dr. C.C. Farr of NZ, a member of the expedition's advisory committee.

**Mount Farrell.** 78°21′S, 85°03′W. Over 2,600 m. Just NW of Dater Glacier.

13 miles east of Mount Shear, in the Sentinel Range. Named for Lt. (jg) Lawrence J. Farrell, USN (*see* **Deaths, 1959**).

**Farrington Island.** 67°15'S, 59°42'E. A small island, 4 miles NNE of Couling Island. 1½ miles west of the Klakkane Islands, in the William Scoresby Archipelago. Discovered and named by the personnel on the *William Scoresby* in Feb. 1936.

**Farrington Ridge.** 73°35'S, 94°20'W. Isolated. 1½ miles long. 2 miles WNW of Forbidden Rocks, in the Jones Mountains. Named by the University of Minnesota–Jones Mountains Party of 1960–61 for Lt. Robert L. Farrington, USN, copilot of the Dakota which made the first landing in the Jones Mountains on Dec. 9, 1960.

**Farwell Island.** 72°49'S, 91°10'W. Ice-covered. 38 miles long. 10 miles wide. Between McNamara Island and Dendtler Island, in the eastern section of the Abbott Ice Shelf. Named for Capt. A.F. Farwell, chief of staff to the commander, US Naval Support Force, Antarctica, 1968 and 1969.

**Fasettfjellet.** 72°33'S, 2°59'W. 2,425 m. A mountain north of Flogstallen, in the NE part of the Borg Massif, in Queen Maud Land. Name means "the facet mountain" in Norwegian.

**Fashion Lane.** A particularly treacherous area full of crevasses, 125 miles out of Little America V, on the way to Byrd Station. Named in early Dec. 1956 by the pioneers who went out to establish Byrd Station for the IGY. It took them 2 weeks to get through a 30-foot-wide, 7½-mile-long area (apparently they would not go around it).

**Fast ice.** Sea ice that is attached to land.

**Faulkender Ridge.** 75°03'S, 115°W. Ice-covered. 12 miles long. West of Horrall Glacier, in the NW part of the Kohler Range of Marie Byrd Land. Named for DeWayne J. Faulkender, topographic engineer here in 1966–67 with the Marie Byrd Land Survey party.

**Faulkner Escarpment.** 86°12'S, 156° W. 3,000 m. 30 miles long. Ice-covered. Forms the east edge of the Nilsen Plateau and Fram Mesa, in the Queen Maud Mountains. Discovered in Dec. 1934 by Quin Blackburn's party during Byrd's 1933–35 expedition, and named by Byrd for Charles J. Faulkner, Jr., chief counsel of Armour and Co., patrons of the expedition.

**Faulkner Nunatak.** 69°36'S, 71°48'W. In the NW part of Alexander Island.

**Fault Bluff.** 79°18'S, 157°38'E. 2,320 m. 9 miles NE of Mount Longhurst, in the Cook Mountains. Named in 1957–58 by the Darwin Glacier Party of the BCTAE, for a geological fault here.

**Fauna.** Animal life, of which there is not much on land in Antarctica, but plenty in the sea. All Antarctic life is cold-adapted. In prehistoric days, however, there was abundant land life, as temperatures were tropical. In the Beacon Sandstone formation, for example, there are many fossils, including large reptiles such as Lystrosaurus, and amphibians in Triassic Age rocks. Nowadays, though, native land fauna is wholly invertebrate (there are about 150 species of invertebrates in Antarctica), and very small. The macrofauna consists entirely of arthropods. There are also 2 species of beetles, which may well be alien imports. The microfauna of Antarctica consists of heliozoans, rotifers, tardigrades, nematodes, ciliate protozoans, foraminifera, radialaria, etc. The Antarctic is a haven for birds (q.v.). The mammals are all marine, and include dolphins, seals, whales, and the occasional porpoise (see all these entries). Also in the sea are plankton, krill, fish, squid, cuttlefish, sessile hydrozoans, coral, sponges, bryozoans, pycnogonids, isopods, worms, echinoids, crustaceans, and mollusks (qq.v.). Imported animals have included dogs, goats (Ross took one named Billy on the *Erebus*), cats, and pigs.

**Faure, Alfred.** Leader of the French Polar Expedition of 1959–61.

**Faure Inlet.** 72°37′S, 70°48′W. In the SW part of Alexander Island.

**Faure Islands.** 68°06′S, 68°52′W. Also called Maurice Faure Islands. A group of rocky islands and reefs, 3 miles in extent. 21 miles SW of Cape Alexandra, the SE end of Adelaide Island. Discovered in 1908–10 by Charcot, and named by him for Maurice Faure, French statesman.

**Faure Passage.** 68°14′S, 68°55′W. A marine channel between the Faure Islands and the Kirkwood Islands, in Marguerite Bay, off the west coast of Graham Land. Named Pasaje Faure by the Argentines in association with the islands.

**Faure Peak.** 85°42′S, 128°35′W. 3,940 m. 3½ miles east of Mount Minshew, on the north side of the Wisconsin Plateau, in the Wisconsin Range, of the Horlick Mountains. Named for Gunter Faure, leader of the Ohio State University geological party here in 1964–65.

**Favé Island.** Somewhere in the western part of the Wilhelm Archipelago. Cannot yet be mapped among the many small, ice-capped islands on the aerial photos of the area.

**Favela Rocks.** 76°12′S, 145°21′W. A group at the NW end of the Phillips Mountains, 4 miles NW of Mount June, in the Ford Ranges of Marie Byrd Land. Named for Rafael Favela, Jr., USN, equipment operator at Byrd Station in 1967.

**Favreau Pillar.** 71°57′S, 171°07′E. A pillar rock in water, just east of Foyn Island, in the Possession Islands. Named for Robert D. Favreau, US Marines, VX-6 navigator on the flight which photographed this feature on Jan. 18, 1958.

**Fazekas Hills.** 83°08′S, 163°10′E. Ice-free. They extend for 9 miles. Just east of Mount Oona, on the east side of Lowery Glacier, in the Queen Elizabeth Range. Named for Stephen P. Fazekas, Sr., US meteorologist at South Pole Station in 1958.

**Mount Fazio.** 73°23′S, 162°48′E. 2,670 m. Ice-free. Marks the SW end of the Tobin Mesa, in the Mesa Range of Victoria Land. Named for William Z. Fazio, USN, helicopter crew member in Antarctica in 1966, 1967, and 1968.

**Mount Fearon.** 75°05′S, 161°42′E. 1,140 m. At the east side of Woodberry Glacier, 6 miles NW of Mount Priestley, in the Prince Albert Mountains of Victoria Land. Named for Colin E. Fearon, biologist at McMurdo Station in 1962–63.

**Mount Feather.** 77°58′S, 160°20′E. 2,985 m. On the north side of the Skelton Névé, between Lashly Glacier and the head of Ferrar Glacier, in southern Victoria Land. Just north of Mount Lister. Named for Thomas A. Feather.

**Feather, Thomas A.** Warrant officer, RN. Bosun on the *Discovery*, during the Royal Society Expedition of 1901–4. Went with Scott on the Western Journey of 1903.

**Paso Federico Puga Borne** *see* **Croker Passage**

**Feeley Peak.** 85°26′S, 126°26′W. 1,730 m. 3 miles NW of Sheets Peak, between the Davisville and Quonset Glaciers, on the north side of the Wisconsin Range. Named for Keith E. Feeley, construction mechanic at Byrd Station in 1959.

**Feeney Col.** 85°37′S, 155°45′W. On the NE side of Feeney Peak, near the center of Medina Peaks, in the Queen Maud Mountains. At a height of 970 meters, it provides a good route through these peaks. Named by the New Zealanders in 1969–70 in association with Feeney Peak.

**Feeney Peak.** 85°37′S, 155°50′W. 1,210 m. Near the center of the Medina Peaks. 7 miles north of Patterson Peak, on the east side of Goodale Glacier. Named for Robert E. Feeney, biologist at McMurdo Station for several summer seasons between 1964–65 and 1968–69.

**Feeney Ridge.** 69°40′S, 159°06′E. 6 miles long. Mainly ice-free along the crest. Parallels the SE side of Fergusson Glacier, in the Wilson Hills. Named for Lt. Cdr. Edward J. Feeney, USN, aircraft commander on Hercules planes in 1968.

**Fegley Glacier.** 83°24'S, 167°25'E. Flows into Lennox-King Glacier, in the Holland Range. 5 miles NE of Mount Allen Young. Named for Lt. Charles E. Fegley, III, USN, officer-in-charge of the nuclear power unit at McMurdo Station in 1964.

**Feistmantel Valley.** 76°43'S, 159°35'E. South of Shimmering Icefield, and west of Mount Watters, in the Allan Hills of Victoria Land. There are fossils here. Named by the Allan Hills expedition of 1964 for Professor O. Feistmantel, who made pioneering studies of Gondwanaland flora.

**Mount Feldkotter.** 84°06'S, 56°06'W. 1,510 m. 4 miles south of Gambacorta Peak, in the southern part of the Neptune Range of the Pensacola Mountains. Named for Henry H.J. Feldkotter, aviation electrician at Ellsworth Station in 1958.

**Cape Félicie** *see* **Félicie Point**

**Félicie Point.** 64°42'S, 63°09'W. Also called Cape Félicie. Forms the southern end of Lion Island, just east of Anvers Island. Charted and named by de Gerlache in 1897–99, as Cap Félicie.

**Mount Fell.** 73°26'S, 62°16'W. 8 miles west of Mount Hemmingsen, in the north part of the Werner Mountains of Palmer Land. Named for Jack W. Fell, biologist on the *Eastwind*, 1965–66.

**Felsite Island.** 72°26'S, 169°49'E. 300 m. 1 mile long. At the head of Edisto Inlet, within the northward stream of Edisto Glacier. Named by the New Zealanders in 1957–58 for the felsite found here.

**Felson, Henry A.** Ordinary seaman on the Wilkes Expedition 1838–42. Joined in the USA. Served the cruise.

**Cape Felt.** 73°50'S, 116°10'W. Ice-covered. Marks the north end of Wright Island, on the coast of Marie Byrd Land.

Named for Adm. Harry D. Felt, USN, vice chief of naval operations in the late 1950s.

**Felton Head.** 67°17'S, 46°59'E. A flat-topped, dark brown headland. 3½ miles east of Harrop Island, on the coast of Enderby Land. Named by the Australians for Sgt. K. Felton, RAAF, engine fitter at Mawson Station in 1960.

**Fender Buttress.** 64°34'S, 61°04'W. 1,600 m. A bluff which projects from the south side of Herbert Plateau into the head of Drygalski Glacier, in Graham Land. Named by the UK for Guillaume Fender of Buenos Aires, inventor of an early type of tracked vehicle.

**Fendley Glacier.** 71°20'S, 168°45'E. 17 miles long. Flows from the Admiralty Mountains to the sea, between Mount Cherry-Garrard and the Atkinson Cliffs, on the north coast of Victoria Land. Named for Technical Sgt. Iman A. Fendley, USAF (*see* **Deaths, 1958**).

**Fendorf Glacier.** 79°30'S, 84°50'W. Flows from the Gifford Peaks, and merges with the Dobbratz Glacier, in the Heritage Range. Named for Lt. Cdr. James E. Fendorf, USN, VX-6 pilot in 1966.

**Fenno, John.** Seaman on the Wilkes Expedition 1838–42. Joined in the USA. Served the cruise.

**Fenrir Valley.** 77°37'S, 161°56'E. Mainly ice-free. Between the upper reaches of the Heimdall and Rhone Glaciers, in the Asgard Range of Victoria Land. Named by NZ and the USA for the mythological Norse wolf.

**Fenriskjeften Mountain.** 71°53'S, 8°18'E. Ice-free. Looks like a hairpin from the air. Forms the southern portion of the Drygalski Mountains of Queen Maud Land. Name means "Fenrir's paw" in Norwegian. Named for its shape (*see* **Fenrir Valley**).

**Fenristunga.** 71°52'S, 8°17'E. A glacier within the rock walls of Fenriskjeften Mountain, in the Drygalski Mountains of Queen Maud Land. Name means "Fenrir's tongue" in Norwegian. Named in association with the mountain (*see also* **Fenrir Valley**).

**Mount Fenton.** 74°20'S, 161°55'E. 2,480 m. On the northern part of Skinner Ridge, 2 miles NE of Mount Mackintosh, in Victoria Land. Named for Michael D. Fenton, geologist at McMurdo Station in 1965–66.

**Fenton Glacier.** 73°03'S, 61°48'W. Flows into Mosby Glacier, just east of Mount Adkins, in Palmer Land. Named for Lt. (jg) Ernest R. Fenton, USN, officer-in-charge of Palmer Station in 1971.

**Feoktistov Point.** 67°39'S, 45°58'E. On Alasheyev Bight, in Enderby Land, about 3½ miles east of Molodezhnaya Station.

**Ferguslie Peninsula.** 60°43'S, 44°34'W. 1½ miles long. Between Browns Bay and Macdougal Bay, on the northern coast of Laurie Island, in the South Orkneys. Charted by Bruce in 1903, and named by him for the Scottish residence of James Coats, chief patron of the expedition.

**Mount Ferguson.** 84°56'S, 169°34'W. 1,190 m. Surmounts the southern part of the Mayer Crags, on the west side of Liv Glacier, in the Queen Maud Mountains. Discovered by Byrd's 1928–30 expedition, and named by Byrd for Homer L. Ferguson, president of the Newport News Shipbuilding and Dry Dock Co., of Virginia. This company repaired Byrd's ships.

**Ferguson, David.** Scottish geologist who, in 1913–14, was in the *Hanka* doing geological reconnaissance around the Antarctic Peninsula and in the South Shetlands. In 1911–12 he had been in South Georgia (54°S) doing geological surveys for the firm of Salvesen and Co., out of Leith, Scotland.

**Ferguson Channel** *see* **Argentino Channel**

**Ferguson Nunataks.** 73°33'S, 63°48'W. Between the heads of the

Meinardus and Swann Glaciers in Palmer Land. Named for Charles L. Ferguson, electrician at Palmer Station in 1965.

**Fergusson Glacier.** 69°38'S, 159°10'E. Flows between Serba Peak and Feeney Ridge into Noll Glacier, in the Wilson Hills. Named by the New Zealanders in 1963–64 for Sir Bernard Fergusson, governor-general of New Zealand from 1962–67. Fergusson, or more formally Lord Ballantrae, had been with Orde Wingate in Burma during World War II, and in the 1960s visited Antarctica. He died in 1980.

**Ferin Head.** 65°59'S, 65°20'W. A headland 4 miles north of the entrance to Holtedahl Bay, on the west coast of Graham Land. Charcot discovered it from a distance in 1908–10, and charted it as an island, Île Férin, named for A. Férin, French vice-consul in the Azores. This name became Ferin Island in English, until the BGLE redefined it in 1934–37.

**Ferin Island** *see* **Ferin Head**

**Isla Fernando** *see* **Prevot Island**

**Fernette Peak.** 85°35'S, 176°58'W. 2,700 m. In the south central part of Roberts Massif, in the Queen Maud Mountains. Named for Gregory L. Fernette, USARP field assistant in Antarctica in 1968–69.

**Mount Ferranto.** 76°33'S, 145°25'W. Forms the extreme SW projection of the main massif of the Fosdick Mountains in the Ford Ranges of Marie Byrd Land. Discovered by a sledging party during Byrd's 1933–35 expedition, and named later for Felix Ferranto.

**Ferranto, Felix.** Radio and tractor operator at West Base during the USAS 1939–41. Originally he had been one of the 4 men designated to look after the Snowcruiser (q.v.).

**Ferrar, Hartley T.** Geologist on the Royal Society Expedition of 1901–4.

**Ferrar Glacier.** 77°45'S, 163°30'E. Also called New Harbor Glacier. 35 miles long. Flows from near the Royal Society Range into New Harbor, in southern Victoria Land. Armitage discovered it in 1903 during the Royal Society Expedition, and he climbed it. Scott did likewise the following year. This expedition thought that the Taylor Glacier and this glacier were one and the same, because Taylor Glacier actually joins it for a while in apposition. The term East Fork was applied to what is today Ferrar Glacier, until Grif Taylor redefined the area during Scott's 1910–13 expedition. Scott renamed the two glaciers at that stage. Hartley T. Ferrar was the person honored.

**Mount Ferrara.** 82°15′S, 41°25′W. Also called San Rafael Nunatak. 875 m. 2½ miles NE of Vaca Nunatak, in the Panzarini Hills of the Argentina Range of the Pensacola Mountains. Discovered aerially on Jan. 13, 1956. Named for Chief Aviation Machinist's Mate Frederick J. Ferrara, USN, crew chief of the Neptune which made the flight.

**Ferrell Automatic Weather Station.** 78°S, 170°48′E. An American AWS on the Ross Ice Shelf, just south of Ross Island, at an elevation of approximately 144 feet. It began operating on Dec. 10, 1980.

**Ferrell Nunatak.** 83°54′S, 54°53′W. On Iroquois Plateau, 5 miles NE of Elmers Nunatak, in the Pensacola Mountains. Named for James T. Ferrell, construction mechanic at Ellsworth Station in 1958.

**Monte Ferrer** *see* **Mount Aciar**

**Ferrer Point.** 62°30′S, 59°42′W. Also called Punta Teniente Ferrer. Ice-free. In the south part of Discovery Bay, Greenwich Island, in the South Shetlands. Just over 1 mile SW of Iquique Cove. Charted by the Chilean Antarctic Expedition of 1950–51, and named for Lt. Fernando Ferrer Fougá, hydrographic officer on the *Angamos* during that expedition.

**Ferrer Rocks.** 64°42′S, 62°48′W. Off the west coast of Graham Land.

**Ferrero Bay.** 73°28′S, 102°30′W. 15 miles wide. Just west of the Cosgrove Ice Shelf, between the King and Canisteo Peninsulas. Named for Lt. Cdr. H.H. Ferrero, communications officer on the staff of the Commander, US Naval Support Force, Antarctica, 1966–68.

**Ferri Ridge.** 75°01′S, 113°41′W. Forms the west wall of Simmons Glacier. Terminates in Mount Isherwood, at the north side of the Kohler Range, in Marie Byrd Land. Named for Guy Ferri, US Department of State, chairman of the Interagency Committee on Antarctica, 1969–70.

**Ferrier Peninsula.** 60°44′S, 44°26′W. 1½ miles long. Forms the east end of Laurie Island, in the South Orkneys. Charted by Weddell in 1823. Surveyed by Bruce in 1903, and named by him for J.G. Ferrier, his secretary, and manager in Scotland of the expedition.

**Ferromanganese.** Nodules of this are indicated below the Antarctic Convergence (*see* **Mineral exploitation**).

**Festive Plateau.** 79°24′S, 157°30′E. Over 2,200 m. Ice-covered. 10 miles long. 3 miles wide. Just north of Mount Longhurst, in the Churchill Mountains. Named by the Darwin Glacier Party of the BCTAE, who spent Christmas Day of 1957 here.

**Festninga Mountain.** 72°07′S, 3°43′E. 2535 m. Ice-topped. West of Mount Hochlin, at the west end of the Mühlig-Hofmann Mountains of Queen Maud Land. Name means "the fortress" in Norwegian.

**Festningsporten Pass.** 72°05′S, 3°43′E. An ice-covered gap in the middle of the north face of Festninga Mountain, leading to the mountain's flat summit, in the Mühlig-Hofmann Mountains of Queen Maud Land. Name means "the fortress gate" in Norwegian.

**Mount Feury.** 71°44′S, 98°26′W. Between the Sikorsky and Frankenfeld Glaciers, on the NE side of the Noville Peninsula, on Thurston Island. First thought to be a headland, and named Feury Head, for James A. Feury. Later redefined.

**Feury, James A.** Mechanic and snowmobile driver on Byrd's 1928–30 expedition.

**Feury Head** *see* **Mount Feury**

**Feyerharm Knoll.** 77°S, 125°46'W. Ice-covered. On the lower NE slope of Mount Sidley, in the Executive Committee Range of Marie Byrd Land. Named for William R. Feyerharm, meteorologist at Byrd Station in 1960.

**FIBEX.** The First International BIOMASS Experiment. Held Jan.–Feb. 1981. The largest multiship experiment in biological oceanography ever undertaken in the southern ocean, this was Phase I of BIOMASS (q.v.), and consisted of 18 ships from 11 countries (Japan—4 ships, USSR—3, West Germany—3, and one each from Argentina, Australia, Chile, France, Poland, South Africa, USA, UK). Its main purpose was an acoustic survey of krill in Antarctic waters. The Second International BIOMASS experiment was completed in 1984–85.

**The Fid.** 68°39'S, 65°57'W. 1,640 m. A sharp peak at the east side of the mouth of Cole Glacier, in southern Graham Land. Named by the UK for its shape. A fid is a wooden pin used in splicing.

**FIDASE** *see* **Falkland Islands Dependencies Aerial Survey Expedition**

**Fidase Peak.** 63°23'S, 57°33'W. 915 m. 9 miles east of Mount Jacquinot. At the west end of the Mott Snowfield, on Trinity Peninsula. Named for the Falkland Islands Dependencies Aerial Survey Expedition.

**Fidjeland.** Mechanic on the LCE 1936–37.

**Mount Fidjeland.** 71°42'S, 25°36'E. Also called Fidjelandfjellet. 1,630 m. Just NE of Mehaugen Hill, on the west side of the mouth of Byrdbreen, in the Sør Rondane Mountains. Named by the Norwegians for Fidjeland (q.v.).

**FIDS** *see* **Falkland Islands Dependencies Surveys**

**Mount Fiedler.** 85°33'S, 140°41'W. 1,140 m. In the Bender Mountains. Between the edge of the Ross Ice Shelf and the Watson Escarpment. Named for Leonard G. Fiedler, electrician at Byrd Station in 1960 and 1964.

**Fief Mountains** *see* **Sierra DuFief**

**Mount Field.** 80°53'S, 158°E. 3,010 m. 3 miles SSE of Mount Egerton, just to the south of Byrd Glacier, in the Churchill Mountains. Discovered and named by Scott's 1901–4 expedition.

**Field Glacier.** 67°08'S, 66°24'W. Flows into Lallemand Fjord, 3 miles south of Salmon Cove. Named by the UK for William B.O. Field, glaciologist with the American Geographical Society.

**Field ice** *see* **Pack-ice**

**Field Islands** *see* **Hydrographer Islands**

**Field Rock.** 67°36'S, 62°54'E. ½ mile south of Teyssier Island, on the coast of Mac. Robertson Land. Named by the Australians for E.D. Field, cook at nearby Mawson Station in 1957.

**Fielding Col.** 68°52'S, 67°02'W. Between Baudin Peaks and Hag Pike, in southern Graham Land. It is the best route to get to Morgan Upland from the coast, between Neny Fjord and the Wordie Ice Shelf. Named by the UK for Harold M. Fielding, BAS surveyor at Base E in 1967–69.

**Fields Peak.** 75°59'S, 135°56'W. 2½ miles SE of Brandenburger Bluff, on the lower north slopes of Mount Berlin, in Marie Byrd Land. Named for Master Sgt. Samuel J. Fields, US Army, member of Merle Dawson's Army-Navy Trail Party which opened the way to Byrd Station in 1956–57.

**Fields Strait** *see* **Fildes Strait**

**Fiennes, Sir Ranulph.** b. 1944. British baronet, leader of the Antarctic leg of the Trans-Globe Expedition, 1980–82, which crossed the continent through the South Pole (and the world through both Poles, thus effecting an unusual trans-world crossing).

**Fierle Bay**  *see*  **McCarthy Inlet**

**Fierle Peak.** 83°25′S, 50°58′W. 1,960 m. 3 miles ESE of Dyrdal Peak, at the southern extremity of the Saratoga Table, in the Forrestal Range of the Pensacola Mountains. Named for Gerald R. Fierle, meteorologist at Ellsworth Station in 1957.

**Figaro Nunatak.** 69°56′S, 70°57′W. Isolated. On Mozart Ice Piedmont, in the northern part of Alexander Island. 1 mile south of Puccini Spur. Named by the UK for the Mozart opera.

**Fikkan Peak.** 71°31′S, 159°50′E. Between Big Brother Bluff and Mount Burnham, on the west wall of the Daniels Range, in the Usarp Mountains. Named for Philip R. Fikkan, geologist at McMurdo Station in 1967–68.

**Cape Filchner.** 66°27′S, 91°53′E. Ice-covered. Fronts on the Davis Sea. 17 miles WNW of Adams Island. It divides Wilhelm II Land from Queen Mary Land. Discovered by the AAE 1911–14, and named by Mawson for Wilhelm Filchner.

**Filchner, Wilhelm.** b. Sept. 13, 1877, Munich. d. May 7, 1957, Zurich. German scientist/explorer who led the German Antarctic Expedition of 1911–12, on the *Deutschland,* which discovered the Filchner Ice Shelf and the Luitpold Coast. Independent of William S. Bruce (q.v.), he had conceived the idea of a transantarctic traverse in order to test the legend of the Ross-Weddell Graben, but neither his nor Bruce's traverses ever came off. He wrote some books (*see* the Bibliography). An anti–Nazi, he explored mostly in Asia.

**Filchner Group**  *see*  **Filchner Mountains**

**Filchner Ice Shelf.** 79°S, 40°W. Between the Ronne Ice Shelf and Coats Land, it fills the head of the Weddell Sea. It extends inland for 250 miles to the escarpment of the Pensacola Mountains. Fed by the Slessor, Recovery, and Support Force Glaciers, among others. Discovered in 1911–12 by Wilhelm Filchner,

who named it the Weddell Barrier, for the sea (all ice shelves in those days were called barriers, or ice barriers). Not long afterward he renamed it the Wilhelm Barrier (for the Kaiser). The Kaiser, however, renamed it yet again, for Filchner, calling it the Filchner Barrier, or Filchner Ice Barrier. Over the years this ice shelf has been otherwise seen variously as Wilhelm Ice Barrier, Wilhelm Shelf Ice, Wilhelm Ice Shelf, Filchner Shelf Ice, and Filchner Ice Shelf (its current name). The original Filchner Ice Shelf was much larger than the Filchner Ice Shelf of today. Nowadays there are two large ice shelves in this area, the Filchner Ice Shelf and the Ronne Ice Shelf, the two being separated by Berkner Island. Formerly that whole stretch, from the Bowman Peninsula of Palmer Land to the Luitpold Coast of Coats Land, was called the Filchner Ice Shelf. In 1947–48 Finn Ronne staked his claim to the western half (i.e. the shelf west of Berkner Island) and called it Edith Ronne Land, for his wife. This Land included the interior, behind the present day Ronne Ice Shelf. In 1968 international agreement created the situation we know today.

**Filchner Ice Shelf Program.** Perhaps better known by its initials—FISP. An international program comprising scientists from West Germany, Austria, Belgium, Norway, and the USA.

**Filchner Mountains.** 72°S, 7°40′E. Also called the Filchner Group. 7 miles SW of the Drygalski Mountains, at the west end of the Orvin Mountains of Queen Maud Land. Discovered by Ritscher in 1938–39, and named by him for Wilhelm Filchner.

**Filchner Shelf Ice**  *see*  **Filchner Ice Shelf**

**Filchner Station.** West German scientific station on the Filchner Ice Shelf, it was aborted before being properly built, and was replaced by the Georg von Neumayer Station on the Ekström Ice Shelf.

**Bahía Fildes**  *see*  **Maxwell Bay**

**Fildes, Robert.** Name pronounced like Fields. British sealing captain of the brig *Cora,* in the South Shetlands in 1820–21. On Jan. 6, 1821, his vessel was wrecked in Blythe Bay, on the north coast of Livingston Island, and Fildes sailed about the South Shetlands for the remainder of the season, as a passenger on the ships of other sealing captains, and made charts as he went, preparing the first sailing directions for the South Shetlands. He and part of his crew were taken back to Liverpool in the early part of 1821 on the *Indian.* Fildes was back in the South Shetlands in 1821–22, as captain of the *Robert.*

**Fildes Peninsula.** 62°12′S, 58°58′W. 4½ miles long. Forms the SW end of King George Island, in the South Shetlands. Named by the UK in 1960 for Robert Fildes.

**Fildes Point.** 63°S, 60°34′W. Also called Punta Balcarce. Forms the south side of Whaler's Bay, in Deception Island, in the South Shetlands. Named for Robert Fildes.

**Fildes Strait.** 62°14′S, 59°W. Originally, and erroneously, called Field's Strait. Barely ¼ mile wide at its narrowest, it separates King George Island from Nelson Island, in the South Shetlands. Named for Robert Fildes.

**Filer Haven.** 60°44′S, 45°35′W. Between Pantomime Point and Pageant Point, on the east side of Gourlay Peninsula, Signy Island, in the South Orkneys. Named by the UK for John Filer, BAS biologist (*see* **Deaths, 1961**).

**Filla Island.** 68°50′S, 77°50′E. Over 3 miles long. In the north part of the Rauer Islands, it is the largest of that group. Photographed by the LCE 1936–37. Norwegian cartographers working off these photographs applied the name Filla (the tatters) to this island and several smaller ones nearby, thinking the whole group to be one ragged island. In 1952, John H. Roscoe, the US cartographer, working off Operation Highjump photos taken in 1946–47, redefined the area and gave the name Filla Island to the largest one.

**Film** *see* **Movies, Photography**

**Filson Nunatak.** 67°52′S, 63°03′E. 6 miles east of Trost Peak, in the eastern part of the Framnes Mountains of Mac. Robertson Land. Named by the Australians for R. Filson, carpenter at Mawson Station in 1962.

**Filsponen Nunatak.** 72°12′S, 14°25′E. NE of Steinfila Nunatak, in the southern part of the Payer Mountains of Queen Maud Land. Name means "the filings" in Norwegian.

**Fimbul Ice Shelf.** 70°30′S, 0°. 120 miles long and 60 miles wide, it borders the coast of Queen Maud Land from 3°W to 3°E, and is fed by the Jutulstraumen Glacier. Named Fimbulisen (the giant ice) by the Norwegians. Sanae III, the South African scientific station, is here.

**Fimbulisen** *see* **Fimbul Ice Shelf**

**Fin Nunatak.** 69°03′S, 64°03′W. 805 m. In the middle of Casey Glacier, near the east coast of Palmer Land. Named by the UK for its shape.

**Fin whale.** Also called finner whale, finback whale, razorback whale, common rorqual. The second largest of the rorquals, it is a slender baleen whale, *Balaenoptera physalus.* 60–80 feet long, it has a ridge on its back. It lives in Antarctic waters in the summers, but moves north to breed. It is an endangered species.

**Final Island.** 65°05′S, 64°29′W. The most westerly of the Myriad Islands. 3½ miles NW of Snag Rocks, in the Wilhelm Archipelago. Named by the UK for its position, and also because it is the most westerly of all the islands bordering French Passage.

**Final Rock.** 84°09′S, 56°10′W. An isolated rock on land, 3 miles south of Mount Feldkotter, at the southern end of the Neptune Range. Named for its position at the south of the Neptune Range.

**Finback Massif.** 65°41′S, 62°25′W. Over 1,000 m. Between the Stubb and

Flask Glaciers. 6 miles WNW of Tashtego Point, on the east side of Graham Land. Named by the UK for the type of whale.

**Finback whale** *see* **Fin whale**

**Mount Finch.** 72°34'S, 167°23'E. 2,100 m. On the west side of the mouth of Trainer Glacier, where that glacier enters Trafalgar Glacier, in the Victory Mountains of Victoria Land. Named for Lt. Jerry L. Finch, USN, VX-6 project officer for infrared ice sounding equipment, in 1968.

**Findlay Point.** 60°35'S, 45°23'W. 2 miles NW of Palmer Bay, on the north coast of Coronation Island, in the South Orkneys. Discovered in Dec. 1821 by Palmer and Powell, and charted by Powell. Named by the UK for Alexander G. Findlay (1812–1875), British geographer who compiled charts of the South Orkneys from sailors' reports.

**Finger Mountain.** 77°45'S, 160°38'E. 1,920 m. Just to the north of Turnabout Valley, it is 5 miles south of Beehive Mountain, on the south side of Taylor Glacier, in southern Victoria Land. Named by Scott's 1901–4 expedition for the long tongue of dolerite between the sandstone strata, which looks like a finger.

**¹Finger Point.** 65°15'S, 64°17'W. Forms the SW end of Skua Island, in the Argentine Islands. Charted and named by the BGLE 1934–37.

**²Finger Point.** 77°01'S, 162°25'E. Juts out into Granite Harbor, between Cuff Cape and Cape Geology. Forms the eastern end of The Flatiron, in southern Victoria Land. Mapped and named descriptively by Scott's 1910–13 expedition.

**Finger Ridges.** 79°11'S, 156°58'E. Several mainly ice-free ridges which extend for 12 miles in an east-west direction in the NNW part of the Cook Mountains, between Butcher Ridge and the Ross Ice Shelf, in the extreme south of Victoria Land. The individual ridges are one to two miles long, and project northward from the higher main ridge. Named descriptively by the USA.

**Fingeren Peak.** 72°38'S, 3°47'W. Just NW of Høgskavlipiggen Peak, in the Borg Massif of Queen Maud Land. Name means "the finger" in Norwegian.

**Finland.** Ratified on May 5, 1984, as the 31st signatory of the Antarctic Treaty.

**Finlandia Foothills.** 69°56'S, 70°09' W. In the northern part of Alexander Island.

**Mount Finley.** 85°01'S, 173°58'W. 3,470 m. On the ridge which extends south from Mount Wade. 5 miles SSW of Mount Oliver, in the Queen Maud Mountains. Named by Byrd for John H. Finley, president of the American Geographical Society at the time of Byrd's 1928–30 expedition.

**Finley Glacier.** 73°36'S, 165°35'E. Flows from Mount Monteagle into the upper part of Icebreaker Glacier, in the Mountaineer Range of Victoria Land. Named for Russell H. Finley, VX-6 aviation bosun's mate in 1966, 1967, and 1968.

**Finley Heights.** 69°13'S, 63°13'W. 1,070 m. Between the mouths of the Bingham and Lurabee Glaciers, at the north end of Wilkins Coast, across Stefansson Strait from Hearst Island, on the east coast of the Antarctic Peninsula. Discovered aerially on Dec. 20, 1928, by Wilkins, who named them Finley Islands (thinking that they were islands), for John H. Finley, president of the American Geographical Society. This feature was later redefined as Finley Peninsula, and Finley Ridge, before its true character was determined.

**Finley Islands** *see* **Finley Heights**

**Finley Peninsula** *see* **Finley Heights**

**Finley Ridge** *see* **Finley Heights**

**Finner whale** *see* **Fin whale**

**Finneskoes.** Or finnesko (singular and plural). Boots made completely of fur, including the soles. They are packed with the moisture-absorbing Norwegian hay called sennegrass. They are very warm, but do not have much traction.

**Finney, William.** Landsman on the Wilkes Expedition 1838–42. Joined in Callao. Run at Oahu.

**Finsterwalder Glacier.** 67°19′S, 66°20′ W. 10 miles long. 2 miles wide. Flows from the central plateau of Graham Land to the head of Lallemand Fjord. Its mouth lies between the mouths of the Haefeli and Klebelsberg Glaciers. Discovered by the FIDS in 1947, and named by them for the German father and son glaciologists, Sebastian and Richard Finsterwalder.

**Fire.** A major hazard in Antarctica, because the dryness and the wind spread a fire quickly. Water cannot be used to douse a fire, because it freezes. All buildings are made of fireproof materials (but even so, they do catch alight). There are Canadian CN-110 fire trucks at McMurdo Station (*see also* **Disasters**).

**The *Firern*.** A Norwegian whaler which took part in the LCE 1936–37, with the *Thorshavn,* both under the command of Lars Christensen, owner of both ships.

**Firlingane Nunataks.** 71°52′S, 27°07′ E. 4 nunataks between Bulken Hill and Hesteskoen Nunatak, in the Sør Rondane Mountains. Name means "the quadruplets" in Norwegian.

**Firn snow.** Also called névé. Old, partially compacted granular snow, transformed into dense snow with air spaces containing minute ice crystals. It is the intermediate stage between snow and glacial ice, and is found under the snow that accumulates at the head of a glacier.

**Firnication.** The rounding of large snowflakes through age and compression.

**First Crater.** 77°50′S, 166°39′E. On Arrival Heights, just over a mile north of McMurdo Station, on Hut Point Peninsula, Ross Island. Named by Debenham in 1912.

**First Facet.** 77°09′S, 162°30′E. A steep, ice-free escarpment-type bluff, just east of Second Facet, forming part of the north wall of the Debenham Glacier in southern Victoria Land. Charted and descriptively named by Scott's 1910–13 expedition.

**First View Point.** 77°01′S, 163°03′E. Just to the west of Cape Roberts, on the south coast of Granite Harbor, in southern Victoria Land. Named by the Granite Harbour Geological Party, led by Grif Taylor, during Scott's 1910–13 expedition.

**Firth of Tay** *see* **Tay**

**Fischer Nunatak.** 67°44′S, 63°03′E. Also spelled Fisher Nunatak. 750 m. 2 miles south of Mount Henderson, in the NE part of the Framnes Mountains of Mac. Robertson Land. Photographed by the LCE 1936–37, and named Sörnuten (the south peak) by the Norwegians. Renamed by the ANARE for H.J.L. Fischer, cook at Mawson Station in 1958.

**Fischer Ridge.** 71°58′S, 169°E. Ice-covered. Between the Kirk and Ironside Glaciers, in the Admiralty Mountains of Victoria Land. Named for William H. Fischer, atmospheric chemist at McMurdo Station in 1966–67.

**Fish.** 120 species of fish live in Antarctic waters. 90 percent of these live at the bottom of the sea, and 70 percent of these are Antarctic perches. 90 percent of the fish at the bottom are to be found nowhere else in the world. 65 percent of all Antarctic fish belong to the Nototheniodei. Also at the bottom are eel pouts, sea snails, rat-tailed fishes, and Antarctic cod. (*See also* **Dragon fishes, Plunder fishes, Rays, Ice fish.**) Non-bony types are hagfish and skate. Many deep sea species are known here, but only 3 stay—a barracuda and 2 lantern fishes. There are no sharks in Antarctica, which is strange. Antarctic fish are well adapted to the cold, those living at temperatures below the freezing level of their blood creating a glycoprotein that acts as an antifreeze (Dr. Arthur DeVries discovered this fact in the 1960s).

**Fish Islands.** 66°02'S, 65°25'W. A group of small islands in the north part of the entrance to Holtedahl Bay, off the west coast of Graham Land. Discovered and named by the BGLE in 1934–37. All the features within this group have fish names, like Flounder Island, Mackerel Island, Perch Island, Plaice Island, Salmon Island, Trout Island, The Minnows.

**Mount Fisher.** 85°06'S, 171°03'W. Also called Fisher Mountains. 4,080 m. Domed. Snow-capped. A mountain 2 miles NW of Mount Ray, next to Mount Wade, in the Prince Olav Mountains, between the Shackleton and Liv Glaciers. Discovered aerially by Byrd in Nov. 1929, and named by him for the Fisher Brothers of Detroit, sponsors of Byrd's 1928–30 expedition.

**Fisher Bay.** 67°30'S, 145°45'E. 14 miles wide. East of the Mertz Glacier Tongue, off George V Land. Discovered by the AAE 1911–14, and named Disappointment Bay by Mawson. He later renamed it for Andrew Fisher, prime minister of Australia.

**Fisher Glacier.** 73°15'S, 66°E. 100 miles long. Comes off Mac. Robertson Land, to feed the Lambert Glacier just east of Mount Stinear. Discovered aerially by K.B. Mather of the ANARE in 1957. Named by the Australians for N.H. Fisher, chief geologist at the Bureau of Mineral Resources in Australia.

**Fisher Island.** 77°08'S, 154°W. 7 miles long. Ice-covered. Just north of Edward VII Peninsula, where it marks the west side of the entrance to Sulzberger Bay. Named for Wayne Fisher, of the US Department of State.

**Fisher Massif.** 71°27'S, 67°40'E. 16 miles long. 5 miles wide. At the west side of the Lambert Glacier, 42 miles south of the Aramis Range of the Prince Charles Mountains. Discovered by Bruce Stinear's ANARE party in Oct. 1957. Named by the Australians for Morris M. Fisher, surveyor at Mawson Station in 1957.

**Fisher Mountains** see **Mount Fisher**

**¹Fisher Nunatak.** 77°43'S, 87°27'W. 13 miles west of Mount Crawford, in the Sentinel Range of the Ellsworth Mountains. Discovered by the Marie Byrd Land Traverse Party of 1957–58 led by Charles Bentley. Named for Diana D. Fisher, director, Glaciological Headquarters, US-IGY Program, 1956–59.

**²Fisher Nunatak** see **Fischer Nunatak**

**Fisher Spur.** 71°09'S, 159°50'E. Just north from the west flank of the Daniels Range, just north of Mount Nero, in the Usarp Mountains. Named for Dean F. Fisher, geophysicist at McMurdo Station in 1967–68.

**Fishing.** Fishing in the Antarctic is not commercially viable (neither is krill fishing), and because of its lack of potential (see also **Economy**), has never been fully developed. However, the USSR is over-fishing and some stocks are drying up. As for fishing as a sport, it probably would not be too much fun in the cold.

**Fishtail Point.** 78°58'S, 162°36'E. The most southerly point on Shults Peninsula, at the east side of the mouth of Skelton Glacier. Surveyed and named descriptively by the NZ party of the BCTAE in 1957.

**Fishtrap Cove.** 68°11'S, 67°W. 175 yards NW of Boulder Point, on the SW side of Stonington Island, just off the west coast of Graham Land. Surveyed by members of East Base during the USAS 1939–41, and again in 1946–47 by the FIDS, who named it for the fishtraps which they set here.

**Fisk, John.** Ordinary seaman on the Wilkes Expedition 1838–42. Joined at Rio. Served the cruise.

**Cape Fiske.** 74°21'S, 60°27'W. Forms the eastern tip of Smith Peninsula, and juts out from the Lassiter Coast into the Weddell Sea, on the east coast of Palmer Land. Named by Finn Ronne in 1947–48, first as Cape Light (for Richard U. Light — see **Mount Light**), and then for C.O. Fiske.

**Fiske, C.O.** Climatologist on the RARE 1947-48.

**The Fist** *see* **Wegger Peak**

**Fitch Glacier.** 72°01'S, 168°07'E. Flows along the east side of the McGregor Range, to enter Man-o-War Glacier, in the Admiralty Mountains. Named for Lt. E.E. Fitch, USN, medical officer at Hallett Station in 1963.

**Fitchie, John.** 2nd mate on the *Scotia* during the Scottish National Antarctic Expedition of 1902-4, led by Bruce.

**Fitchie Bay.** 60°45'S, 44°29'W. Between Cape Dundas and Cape Whitson, on the south side of Laurie Island, in the South Orkneys. Charted by Bruce in 1903, and named by him for John Fitchie.

**Fitton Rock.** 67°46'S, 68°34'W. A flat-topped rock in water. SE of Cape Alexandra, off the south end of Adelaide Island. Charted by Charcot in 1908-10. Named by the UK in 1963 for Gordon F. Fitton, FIDS general assistant at Base T in 1961-62, and a member of the first party to winter-over on Adelaide Island.

**FitzGerald Bluffs.** 74°03'S, 77°20'W. 9 miles long. 30 miles south of the Snow Nunataks, in Ellsworth Land. Discovered by the RARE 1947-48, and named by Ronne for Gerald FitzGerald, chief topographic engineer with the US Geological Survey, 1947-57.

**Fitzgerald Glacier.** 77°33'S, 166°15'E. A valley glacier which flows from Mount Murchison in Victoria Land to Lady Newnes Bay, just after coalescing with Icebreaker Glacier. Explored by the NZGSAE 1958-59, and named by NZ for E.B. Fitzgerald (*see* **Fitzgerald Hill**).

**Fitzgerald Hill.** 77°16'S, 166°25'E. 230 m. West of Mount Bird, between Fitzgerald Stream and Shell Glacier, on Ross Island. Named by NZ for E.B. Fitzgerald, deputy leader of the NZGSAE 1958-59, who mapped it.

**Fitzgerald Nunataks.** 66°15'S, 52°49'E. 3 isolated nunataks, 2 miles NE of Mount Codrington, at the NW end of the

Napier Mountains, in Enderby Land. Photographed by the LCE 1936-37, and named Veslenutane (the little peaks) by the Norwegians. Renamed by the Australians for Brigadier L. Fitzgerald, director of survey in the Australian army, 1942-60.

**Fitzgerald Stream.** 77°16'S, 166°21'E. Between Fitzgerald Hill and Inclusion Hill, on the lower, ice-free, western slopes of Mount Bird, Ross Island. It flows across McDonald Beach to McMurdo Sound. Explored by the NZGSAE 1958-59, and named by NZ for E.B. Fitzgerald (*see* **Fitzgerald Hill**).

**Fitzpatrick Rock.** 66°16'S, 110°30'E. An ice-capped rock in water, ½ mile NW of Kilby Island, at the mouth of Newcomb Bay, in the Windmill Islands. Charted in Feb. 1957 by a party from the *Glacier*. Named by Lt. Robert C. Newcomb (*see* **Newcomb Bay**), for Bosun's Mate 2nd Class John A. Fitzpatrick, USN, member of the survey party.

**The *Fitzroy*.** British vessel which took part in Operation Tabarin and various postwar FIDS maneuvers. K.A.J. Pitt was captain in 1943-44 and 1944-45 during both phases of Tabarin, and again in 1945-46 during the first FIDS season. Capt. White was captain in 1946-47 and 1947-48. The *Fitzroy* was not in Antarctic waters after that date.

**Cape Fitzroy** *see* **Fitzroy Point**

**Fitzroy Island.** 68°11'S, 66°58'W. ½ mile east of the southern tip of Stonington Island. In Neny Bay, at the foot of Northeast Glacier, by which it is partially covered, off the west coast of Graham Land. Surveyed in 1947 by the FIDS, who named it for the *Fitzroy*.

**Fitzroy Point.** 63°11'S, 55°07'W. Forms the eastern flange of Fliess Bay, and the NE point on James Ross Island. Discovered on Dec. 30, 1842, by Ross, who named it Cape Fitzroy, for Capt. Robert Fitzroy, RN (1805-65), hydrographer and meteorologist. Later redefined as a point.

**Mount Fitzsimmons.** 77°54'S, 154°55' W. Also called Mount Margaret Wade. Between Mount Jackling and Mount Shideler, in the northern group of the Rockefeller Mountains. Discovered on Jan. 27, 1929, during a fly-over by Byrd during his 1928–30 expedition. Named for Roy G. Fitzsimmons.

**Fitzsimmons, Roy G.** Physicist at West Base during the USAS 1939–41. He was in charge of the Rockefeller Mountains Seismic Station during Nov. and Dec. 1940.

**Fitzsimmons Nunataks.** 72°08'S, 161° 42'E. A group of small nunataks. 27 miles ENE of Welcome Mountain, in the Outback Nunataks and 8 miles SE of the Helliwell Hills. Named for John M. Fitzsimmons, biologist at McMurdo Station in 1966.

**Fivemile Rock.** 63°29'S, 57°03'W. 375 m. A nunatak just NW of Mineral Hill, on Tabarin Peninsula. Named by the FIDS in 1956 because it is 5 miles from their station (Base D) at Hope Bay, on the way to Duse Bay.

**Fizkin Island.** 65°31'S, 65°31'W. 2½ miles SE of Pickwick Island, in the Pitt Islands of the Biscoe Islands. Named by the UK in 1959 for the Dickens character.

**Fjellimellom Valley.** 72°05'S, 2°29'E. Ice-filled. Between Jutulsessen Mountain and Nupskammen Ridge, in the Gjelsvik Mountains of Queen Maud Land. Name means "between the mountains" in Norwegian.

**Fjomet Nunatak.** 73°25'S, 2°55'W. Isolated. 8 miles ESE of Mount Hallgren, on the Kirwan Escarpment of Queen Maud Land. Named by the Norwegians.

**Fladerer Bay.** 73°15'S, 80°20'W. 15 miles long. 6 miles wide. Between the Wirth and Rydberg Peninsulas, in Ellsworth Land. Named for Capt. George Fladerer, commander of the *Eltanin*.

**Flag Point.** 64°49'S, 63°31'W. Just over ¼ mile ESE of Damoy Point. Forms the north side of the entrance to Port Lockroy on Wiencke Island. Discovered by Charcot in 1903–5. Named by personnel on Operation Tabarin in 1944 for the metal Union Jack erected at Port Lockroy Station when it was built here that year.

**Flagon Point.** 72°14'S, 60°41'W. Has 2 peaks on it, 295 m. and 395 m. Marks the south side of the entrance to Schott Inlet, on the east coast of Palmer Land. Discovered aerially in Dec. 1940 by the USAS. Named by the FIDS in 1947 because the two peaks, when seen from north or south, look like a flagon tilted on its side.

**Flagpole Point.** 68°11'S, 67°01'W. 350 yards NW of Fishtrap Cove. Forms the southern part of the western extremity of Stonington Island, just off the west coast of Graham Land. Named by the FIDS in 1947 for the flagpole erected by the USAS East Base personnel here in 1939–41.

**Flagship Mountain.** 76°45'S, 161°28' E. 1,720 m. Conical. Between the Northwind and Atka Glaciers, in Victoria Land. Named by the NZ Northern Survey Party of the BCTAE in 1957 for the *Glacier*, flagship of the convoy into McMurdo Sound in 1956–57.

**Flagstaff Glacier.** 62°05'S, 58°26'W. Just north of Flagstaff Hill, on Keller Peninsula, King George Island, in the South Shetlands. Named about 1958 by the British personnel on the island, in association with the hill.

**Flagstaff Hill.** 62°05'S, 58°25'W. 265 m. ½ mile north of Plaza Point, on Keller Peninsula, King George Island, in the South Shetlands. Named by the FIDS in 1952. There was an iron flagstaff on the summit.

**Flagstaff Point.** 77°33'S, 166°10'E. The tip of Cape Royds, Ross Island. Charted and named by Shackleton's 1907–9 expedition, who erected a flagstaff here at their winter headquarters.

**Flagstone Bench.** 70°50'S, 68°12'E. A large rock bench littered with slabs of sandstone which look like flagstones (hence the name given by the Australians). Borders the SE sides of

Radok Lake and Beaver Lake, in the Prince Charles Mountains.

**Flanagan Glacier.** 79°29'S, 82°42'W. In the Pioneer Heights of the Heritage Range, flowing from the Thompson Escarpment between the Gross Hills and the Nimbus Hills to the lower end of Union Glacier. Named for Lt. Walter B. Flanagan, VX-6 assistant maintenance officer at McMurdo Station in 1963 and 1964.

**Flanders Bay**  *see*  **Flandres Bay**

**Flandres Bay.** 65°S, 63°20'W. Also spelled Flanders Bay, and also called Dallmann Bay. Between Capes Renard and Willems, on the west coast of Graham Land. De Gerlache explored it in 1898, and named it for the area of Flanders, in Europe.

**Flank Island.** 65°07'S, 64°21'W. The most southerly of the Myriad Islands. 2 miles ENE of Snag Rocks, in the Wilhelm Archipelago. Named by the UK for its position.

**Mount Flånuten.** 71°47'S, 11°17'E. 2,725 m. Between Livdebotnen Cirque and Vindegghallet Glacier, in the Humboldt Mountains of Queen Maud Land. Discovered by Ritscher in 1938–39. Name means "the flat summit" in Norwegian.

**Flårjuven Bluff.** 72°02'S, 3°24'W. Flat-topped. Mostly ice-free. 1 mile north of Storkletten Peak, on the Ahlmann Ridge of Queen Maud Land. Named by the Norwegians.

**Flårjuvnutane Peaks.** 72°01'S, 3°32'W. 1 mile west of Flårjuven Bluff, on the Ahlmann Ridge of Queen Maud Land. Named by the Norwegians.

**Flask Glacier.** 65°47'S, 62°25'W. 25 miles long. Flows from Bruce Plateau into Scar Inlet between Daggoo Peak and Spouter Peak, in Graham Land. Named by the UK for the *Moby Dick* character.

**Flat Island.** 71°24'S, 169°18'E. 480 m. Flat-topped. 3 miles long. At the terminus of the Shipley Glacier, off the Pennell Coast. Its NE tip, Cape Barrow,

marks the west side of the entrance to Robertson Bay. Charted and named by Scott's 1910–13 expedition.

**Flat Islands.** 67°36'S, 62°49'E. A small chain of islands, including Fletcher Island, Stinear Island, and Béchervaise Island, which extends for 2½ miles. 2½ miles SW of Welch Island, in the east part of Holme Bay. Photographed by the LCE 1936–37. Norwegian cartographers, working off these photos, named the group at the south end of the chain as Flatøyholmane (the flat island islets). In 1958 the Australians extended the name to the entire chain, as the Flat Islands.

**Flat Isle**  *see*  **The Watchkeeper**

**Flat Spur.** 77°36'S, 161°30'E. Descends NE from Brunhilde Peak, between the north and south branches of the Sykes Glacier, in the Asgard Range of Victoria Land. Named descriptively by NZ.

**¹Flat Top.** A peak on Fildes Peninsula, in King George Island, in the South Shetlands. This is not an official name.

**²Flat Top.** 80°27'S, 28°16'W. 1,330 m. A table mountain (hence the name given by the BCTAE 1955–58 from aerial flights), 4 miles NE of the Lister Heights, in the Shackleton Range. Visited by the BCTAE in 1957.

**³Flat Top.** 84°42'S, 171°50'E. Over 4,000 m. An ice-covered mountain with a flat summit (hence the name given by Scott's 1910–13 expedition), just east of the head of the Osicki Glacier. It is the highest point in the Commonwealth Range.

**Flat Top Peninsula.** 62°13'S, 59°02'W. Also called Península Morro Chato. Flat-topped (hence the name given by the personnel on the *Discovery II* in 1935), 1 mile north of the SW end of King George Island, in the South Shetlands.

**Flatcap Point.** 64°07'S, 58°07'W. On the east side of the northern arm of Röhss Bay, on James Ross Island. There are two flat-topped rock cliffs in this location.

This one is the more northerly. Named descriptively by the UK.

**The Flatiron.** 77°02'S, 162°23'E. A triangular headland just to the south of the Mackay Glacier Tongue, overlooking Granite Harbor, in southern Victoria Land. Charted by Scott's 1910–13 expedition, and named by them for its shape.

**Flatiron Valley.** 70°54'S, 68°29'W. On the west coast of Palmer Land.

**Flatnes Ice Tongue.** 69°16'S, 76°44'E. Forms the western limit of Hovde Cove, in the SE part of Prydz Bay. Fed by drainage from the Ingrid Christensen Coast. It extends for 3 miles into the bay. Named Flatnes (flat point) by Norwegian cartographers working off the photos taken by the LCE 1936–37. John Roscoe, the US cartographer working off Operation Highjump photos taken in 1946–47, redefined this feature in 1952.

**Flattunga.** 68°51'S, 40°E. An ice tongue which juts out into the sea between Tottsuki Point and Tensoku Point, at the western end of the Prince Olav Coast of Queen Maud Land. Photographed by the LCE 1936–37. Name means "the flat tongue" in Norwegian.

**Flatvaer Islands.** 69°01'S, 39°33'E. Also called the Ongul Islands. A group of small islands, of which Ongul Island is the largest, at the east side of the entrance to Lützow-Holm Bay. Photographed by the LCE 1936–37. Name means "flat islands" in Norwegian.

**Fleas.** There is one species of flea in Antarctica—*Siphonateptera*.

**Fleece Glacier.** 65°54'S, 63°10'W. Enters Leppard Glacier on its north side, about 1½ miles east of Moider Peak, on the east side of Graham Land. Named by the UK for the *Moby Dick* character.

**Fleet Point.** 67°37'S, 65°24'W. 4 miles NW of Tent Nunatak, on the east coast of Graham Land. It has a rocky spine ranging from 260 meters to 870 meters in height. Named by the UK for Michael Fleet, general assistant with the BAS Larsen Ice Shelf Party of 1963–64.

**The *Fleetwood*.** A little clipper lost in the ice at 60°S, 70°W, in the 1840s. On May 4 (unknown year) a boat with the mate and four seamen was picked up (by an unknown vessel). The captain's boat, with 16 men and one passenger, as well as the captain's wife and child, were lost.

**Flein Island.** 69°45'S, 39°05'E. Almost ½ mile north of Berr Point, in the SE part of Lützow-Holm Bay. Photographed by the LCE 1936–37, and mapped by subsequent Norwegian cartographers as two islands. They called the larger one Fleinøya (the bare island). Later the Japanese redefined this feature, and continued the use of the Norwegian name.

**Fleiss Bay** *see* **Fliess Bay**

**Mount Fleming.** 77°33'S, 160°08'E. Over 2,200 m. On the SW side of Airdevronsix Icefalls, in the Quartermain Range of southern Victoria Land, in the area of the Wright Upper Glacier. Named by the NZ Northern Survey Party of the BCTAE in 1957 for Dr. C.A. Fleming, senior paleontologist of the NZ Geological Survey, and chairman of the Royal Society's Antarctic Research Committee.

**Fleming, Bernard.** Assistant to the scientific staff on the shore party of Byrd's 1933–35 expedition.

**Fleming, H.L.** Crewman on the *Jacob Ruppert*, 1933–34.

**Fleming, The Rev. W.L.S.** The dean of Trinity Hall, Cambridge. He was chaplain, geologist, and chief scientist on the BGLE 1934–37.

**Fleming Glacier.** 69°25'S, 66°40'W. 25 miles long. On the west side of the Antarctic Peninsula, it terminates in the Forster Ice Piedmont, to the east of the Wordie Ice Shelf. Named by the USA in 1947 for W.L.S. Fleming.

**Fleming Head.** 75°10'S, 162°38'E. A headland which marks the south side of the terminus of Larsen Glacier, where it enters the Ross Sea on the coast of Victoria Land. Named for John P. Fleming, senior chief construction electrician, USN, at McMurdo Station in 1962 and 1966.

**Fleming Peaks.** 77°15′S, 144°30′W. A small group, 6 miles ESE of Bailey Ridge, on the north side of the Boyd Glacier, in the Ford Ranges of Marie Byrd Land. Discovered by the USAS 1939–41. Named for Bernard Fleming.

**Fleming Point.** 64°20′S, 62°35′W. 4½ miles NE of Humann Point, on the west side of Brabant Island. Charted by Charcot in 1903–5. Named by the UK for Sir Alexander Fleming (1881–1955), Scottish discoverer of penicillin in 1928.

**Flenserne** *see* **Flensing Islands**

**Flensing Icefall.** 70°52′S, 163°45′E. At the east side of the Bowers Mountains, at the junction of the Graveson and Rastorguev Glaciers with the Lillie Glacier. Named by the New Zealanders in 1963–64 because the icefall's longitudinal system of parallel crevassing looks like the carcass of a whale being flensed (*see* **Flensing Islands**).

**Flensing Islands.** 60°42′S, 45°41′W. A group of small islands 1 mile west of Foca Point, on the west side of Signy Island, in the South Orkneys. Petter Sørlle named them Flenserne in 1912–13. The personnel on the *Discovery II* renamed them in 1933. Flensing is the process of stripping skin and blubber from whales.

**Flesa Rock.** 72°29′S, 2°25′W. An isolated rock on land, 7 miles east of the NE end of the Borg Massif, in Queen Maud Land. Name means "the low-lying islet" in Norwegian.

**Cape Fletcher.** 67°41′S, 65°35′E. South of Martin Reef, between Strahan Glacier and Scullin Monolith, in East Antarctica. Discovered by the BANZARE 1929–31, and named by Mawson for H.O. Fletcher.

**Fletcher, Frank D.** First officer on the *Aurora* during the AAE 1911–14.

**Fletcher, H.O.** Assistant biologist on the BANZARE 1929–31.

**Fletcher, Robert.** Ordinary seaman on the Wilkes Expedition 1838–42. Joined in the USA. Discharged at Oahu, Oct. 31, 1840.

**Fletcher Ice Rise.** 78°20′S, 81°W. 100 miles long. 40 miles wide. At the SW side of the Ronne Ice Shelf. Ice-covered, it is between the Rutford Ice Stream and Carlson Inlet. Discovered aerially on Dec. 14–15, 1961, by Lt. Ronald F. Carlson, USN. Named for Joseph O. Fletcher, National Science Foundation director of polar programs, 1971–74.

**Fletcher Island.** 66°53′S, 143°05′E. ¼ mile across. Largest of the Fletcher Islands, in the east part of Commonwealth Bay, 6 miles WSW of Cape Gray. Discovered by the AAE 1911–14, and named by Mawson for Frank D. Fletcher.

**¹Fletcher Islands.** 66°53′S, 143°05′E. A small group, 6 miles WSW of Cape Gray, in the east part of Commonwealth Bay. Discovered by the AAE 1911–14. Mawson named the largest island Fletcher Island (see above). The US gave the name collectively to the group as well.

**²Fletcher Islands.** 72°40′S, 94°10′W. Just to the east of Thurston Island, in the Bellingshausen Sea. A term no longer used.

**Fletcher Peninsula.** 72°45′S, 88°50′W. Ice-covered. Extends into the Bellingshausen Sea, between the Abbott and Venable Ice Shelves. Named for Fred C. Fletcher of Boston, a contributor to the USAS 1939–41.

**Mount Flett.** 68°09′S, 49°12′E. Between Mount Marriner and Mount Underwood, in the central Nye Mountains. Named by the Australians for A. Flett, radio officer at Wilkes Station in 1959.

**Flett, W.R.** Leader of the first wintering-over party at Base B on Deception Island, during Operation Tabarin, in 1944.

**Flett Crags.** 80°39′S, 23°35′W. In the Shackleton Range.

**Fletta Bay.** 69°45′S, 37°12′E. Indents the SW shore of Lützow-Holm Bay just west of Botnneset Peninsula. Photographed by the LCE 1936–37, and named Fletta (the braid) by the Norwegians.

**The *Fleurus*.** British ship at Deception Island in 1927, and off the west coast of Graham Land, notably in Wilhelmina Bay, in 1928.

**Fleurus Island.** 64°34'S, 62°13'W. ½ mile south of Delaite Island, in Wilhelmina Bay, off the west coast of Graham Land. Named by the UK in 1956 for the *Fleurus*.

**Flies.** *Belgica antarctica* is a wingless chironomid fly living in the northern parts of the Antarctic Peninsula.

**Fliess, Felipe.** 1878–1952. Argentine naval lieutenant, head of the group detached by the Argentine navy to lead the search for Nordenskjöld's party, in 1903, on the *Uruguay*. Later an admiral.

**Fliess Bay.** 63°12'S, 55°10'W. Also called Caleta Almirante Fliess, and also seen spelled (erroneously) as Fleiss Bay. Just west of Fitzroy Point, on the north coast of Joinville Island. Named by the Argentines in 1957 for Felipe Fliess.

**Flinders Peak.** 69°20'S, 66°40'W. 960 m. Triangular. On the west end of the Bristly Peaks, it overlooks the Forster Ice Piedmont, near the west coast of the Antarctic Peninsula. Named by the UK for Matthew Flinders (1774–1814), British navigator.

**Mount Flint.** 75°45'S, 129°05'W. 2,695 m. Mainly snow-covered. 10 miles NW of Mount Petras, in the McCuddin Mountains of Marie Byrd Land. Lichens are to be found here. Discovered on Dec. 15, 1940, on USAS Flight G from West Base, and was called Mount Gray. Later renamed by the USA for Robert B. Flint, Jr., geomagnetist at Byrd Station in 1964, scientific leader at Plateau Station in 1966, and exchange scientist at Vostok Station in 1974.

**Flint Glacier.** 67°20'S, 65°25'W. Flows into Whirlwind Inlet between Demorest Glacier and Cape Northrop, on the east coast of Graham Land. Discovered aerially by Wilkins on Dec. 20, 1928. Charted in 1947 by the FIDS who named it for Richard F. Flint, professor of geology at Yale.

**Flint Peninsula** *see* **Churchill Peninsula**

**Flint Ridge.** 77°31'S, 163°02'E. 995 m. at its highest point. Just north of Commonwealth Glacier, in Victoria Land. Named for Lawrence A. Flint, manager of the USARP Berg Field Center at McMurdo Station in 1972. There is a US Geological Survey tablet fixed in a rock slab at the top of this ridge, marked "Flint ET 1971–72" by the USGS Electronic Traverse of that season.

**Flog Glacier** *see* **Endurance Glacier**

**Flogeken Glacier.** 72°04'S, 4°25'E. Flows between Mount Grytøyr and Langfloget Cliff, in the Mühlig-Hofmann Mountains of Queen Maud Land. Name means "the rock wall spoke" in Norwegian.

**Flogstallen.** 72°36'S, 2°59'W. A flat, ice-capped mountain just NE of Jøkulskarvet Ridge, in the Borg Massif of Queen Maud Land. Name means "the rock wall stable" in Norwegian.

**Flood Range.** 76°03'S, 134°30'W. 60 miles long. Snow-covered. Extends east-west, and forms a right angle with the southern end of the Ames Range, in Marie Byrd Land. Contains Mount Berlin and Mount Moulton. Discovered in 1934 during Byrd's 1933–35 expedition, and Byrd named the main mountain in the group as Mount Hal Flood, for his uncle, Henry D. Flood. Later the USA applied the name Hal Flood to the range, and it became known as the Hal Flood Range, and the mountain which Byrd had named became Mount Berlin (q.v.). The name of the range was later shortened.

**Flora.** Not much vegetation on land, but there is in the sea (like fauna; and like fauna it is all cold-adapted.) Long ago it was much warmer in Antarctica, and there was much more flora, jungle even, but with the onset of glaciation, about 50 million years ago, most plant life was forced north. Growth now occurs in the remaining plant life in short summer bursts. There are about 850 species of plants in Antarctica. 350

are lichens (q.v.), 100 or so bryophytes (q.v.) (mosses, liverworts—qq.v.), and there are numerous species of molds, yeasts, and other fungi (qq.v.), as well as fresh water algae and bacteria (qq.v.). There are only two species of vascular plants in Antarctica—both on Lagotellerie Island, and also in the South Shetlands and South Orkneys—*Deschampsia antarctica* and *Colobanthus quitensis*. This completes the list of indigenous Antarctic continental flora. Humans have introduced a number of species to the continent. Native flora goes as far south as 87° S, but contributes little to soil formation. Spore reproduction characterizes the plants here. In the seas, however, there is plankton, particularly productive near the coasts, and there is an abundance of diatoms, a form of algae. Leonard Kristensen discovered the first flora ever south of the Antarctic Circle—a lichen—on Possession Island, in 1895. Borchgrevink collected it.

**Mount Flora.** 63° 25′ S, 57° 01′ W. Also called Flora-Berg and Florasberg. 520 m. On the northern tip of the Antarctic Peninsula, at Hope Bay. Discovered by Nordenskjöld's expedition of 1901–4, and named by Dr. J. Gunnar Andersson of that expedition for the flora fossils found here.

**The *Florence*.** A New London, Conn., sealer in the South Shetlands in the 1876–77 season, under the command of Capt. James W. Buddington, during the era of revival of sealing in Antarctica. Some of the crew, led by Mr. King, the mate, were put ashore on Rugged Island, in the South Shetlands, for winter sealing, while the ship went north. In their little boat, King and his crew managed to get to Potter Cove, King George Island, where they all died, except King, who was picked up by the *Francis Allyn* in 1877–78.

**Florence Island.** 66° 38′ S, 140° 05′ E. A small island, almost ½ mile south of Derby Island, near the northern end of the Astrolabe Glacier Tongue. Charted

by the French in 1951, and named by them for the Italian city.

**Florence Nunatak.** 62° 13′ S, 58° 37′ W. 280 m. Also called Yamana Nunatak. Almost 2 miles east of the head of Potter Cove, in King George Island, in the South Shetlands. Named by the UK in 1960 for the *Florence*.

**Florence Rock.** 60° 47′ S, 44° 36′ W. A rock in water, 175 yards long. It has a smaller rock off its NE end. Almost a mile SW of Cape Anderson, off the south coast of Laurie Island, in the South Orkneys. Surveyed by Bruce in 1903, and named by the personnel on the *Discovery II* in 1933.

**Flory Cirque.** 77° 39′ S, 160° 52′ E. Between West Groin and East Groin on the north side of the Taylor Glacier, in Victoria Land. Named for Robert F. Flory, geologist at McMurdo Station in 1968–69, 1969–70, and 1970–71.

**Mar de Flota**  *see*  **Bransfield Strait**

**Flounder Island.** 66° 01′ S, 65° 24′ W. The largest of the Fish Islands (hence the name given by the UK in 1959), at the north side of Holtedahl Bay, off the west coast of Graham Land. Charted by the BGLE 1934–37.

**Mount Flower.** 70° 12′ S, 67° 53′ W. Has two summits, the highest is 1,465 m. 6½ miles inland from Carse Point and the northern end of the George VI Sound. It is next to Mount Dixey, on the Antarctic Peninsula. Named by the UK in 1954 for Geoffrey C. Flower, who helped work out the surveys of the BGLE 1934–37. He was instructor in survey at the Royal Geographical Society from 1933–40.

**Flowers Hills.** 78° 24′ S, 84° 10′ W. 20 miles in extent. These hills have peaks of 1,240 m. and 1,390 m. South of the terminus of Dater Glacier, in the east part of the Sentinel Range. Named for Edwin C. Flowers, meteorologist at South Pole Station in 1957.

**The *Floyd Bennett*.** NX4542. Byrd's famous Ford Tri-motor airplane which flew to the South Pole and back on Nov.

28–29, 1929. The standard 220 hp engine in the nose had been replaced with a 550 hp Wright Cyclone engine, and the plane could carry a 6-ton load at 125 mph. It was named by Byrd for Floyd Bennett, his friend and companion on their 1926 North Pole flight. Bennett had died in 1927. Balchen flew the plane on that November day in Antarctica, and his passengers were Byrd, McKinley, and June. The plane was recovered during Byrd's 1933–35 expedition, and brought back to the USA.

**Floyd Bennett Bay.** On the west coast of the Bay of Whales, 6 miles NW of Little America I. Named by Byrd for his old friend, Floyd Bennett (*see* the *Floyd Bennett*). Along with the Bay of Whales, it is gone now.

**Fløymannen Nunatak.** 73°09′S, 2°14′W. Just north of the west end of the Neumayer Cliffs in Queen Maud Land. Name means "the wing man" in Norwegian.

**Fluted Peak.** 85°37′S, 176°40′W. A fluted snow peak (hence the name given by the New Zealanders in 1961–62) at the SE end of the Roberts Massif. It is the only snow peak on the massif, and is visible as a landmark for many miles to the south.

**Fluted Rock.** 67°34′S, 46°21′E. A columnlike rock on land, on the NE side of Spooner Bay, in Enderby Land. Named by the ANARE in Feb. 1961 for its fluted appearance when seen from the sea.

**Flutter Island.** 68°33′S, 77°58′E. In Prydz Bay, between Trigwell Island and Breidnes Peninsula of the Vestfold Hills. Photographed by the LCE 1936–37, and mapped as two islands by the Norwegian cartographers working from these photos. This is understandable as the island is almost divided in two. The ANARE redefined it in 1957–58, and named it for Maxwell J. Flutter, officer-in-charge of Davis Station in 1958.

**The *Flying Cloud.*** Stonington, Conn., sealer in the South Shetlands for the 1853–54 season, under the command of Capt. Hidden.

**[1]The *Flying Fish.*** American pilot boat of 96-ton displacement, 70 feet, 3 inches long, 19 feet, 9 inches in the beam, 8 foot depth in hold, with 2 guns and a crew of 15. It was sister ship to the *Sea Gull,* both vessels taking part in the Wilkes Expedition 1838–42. Lt. Walker was commander on the first Antarctic cruise, and was succeeded by Lt. Pinckney by late 1839. On all non–Antarctic cruises the vessel was commanded by Lt. Samuel R. Knox. In early 1840, due to unseaworthiness, the *Flying Fish* was taken back to New Zealand by Pinckney. It continued to be part of the expedition, and was sold in Singapore in late Feb. 1842.

**[2]The *Flying Fish.*** New London, Conn., sealer in the South Shetlands in 1872–73 and 1873–74, under the command of Capt. Church. In 1875–76 it visited Heard Island (53°S) under Capt. Neal, and in 1877–78 was at South Georgia (54°S) under an unknown captain. It had been at South Georgia before, in 1870–71, under Capt. Alfred Turner.

**Cape Flying Fish.** 72°06′S, 102°29′W. Also called Cape Dart. Ice-covered. The most westerly point of Thurston Island. Discovered aerially by Byrd in Feb. 1940 during the USAS, and named for the *Flying Fish,* Wilkes' vessel of 1838–42.

**Flynn Glacier.** 81°31′S, 159°21′E. 10 miles long. Flows from Mount Nares in the Churchill Mountains, into Starshot Glacier south of Kelly Plateau. Named for Cdr. William F. Flynn, USN, Seabee commander at McMurdo Base in 1957.

**Flyspot Rocks.** 68°35′S, 68°06′W. 30 m. A group of rocks in water, 14 miles west of the Terra Firma Islands in Marguerite Bay. Ice-covered on their south sides, but ice-free on their north sides. In 1909 Charcot, from a distance, charted a "doubtful" island here. Named about 1940 because of their indistinct appearance as shown on the rough sketch map made by the BGLE on Feb. 1, 1937. Surveyed in 1949 by the FIDS.

**Foale Nunatak.** 70°16′S, 65°20′E. 4 miles ENE of Moore Pyramid, on the north side of Scylla Glacier, in the Prince Charles Mountains. Named by the Australians for K.A. Foale, radio operator at Davis Station in 1963.

The *Foca*. Whale catcher belonging to the Compañía Argentina de Pesca, in the South Orkneys in Dec. 1926.

**Pointe Foca** *see* **Penguin Point**

**Foca Cove.** 60°42′S, 45°39′W. Just south of Foca Point, on the west side of Signy Island, in the South Orkneys. Named by the UK in association with the point.

**Foca Point.** 60°42′S, 45°40′W. Forms the south side of the entrance to Express Cove, on the west side of Signy Island, in the South Orkneys. Surveyed in 1947 by the FIDS. Named by the UK for the *Foca*.

**Fog Bay.** 77°40′S, 168°10′E. A Ross Ice Shelf indentation into the south side of Ross Island, just to the east of Windless Bight. Named by Wilson and his Winter Journey party of July 1911, for the thick white fog here.

**Fog bows.** Phenomena often seen near coasts and on ice shelves, wherein small, supercooled cloud droplets cause diffraction of light in the fog, and produce a wide, white band that may be tinged with red or orange along its outer edge.

**Fogg Highland.** 72°45′S, 60°50′W. On the east coast of Palmer Land.

**Foggydog Glacier.** 79°47′S, 158°45′E. Between Blank Peaks and Mount Rich, in the Brown Hills. Named by the New Zealanders in 1962–63 for its shape when seen from the air. A moraine suggests the collar, and a glacial lake suggests the ears, and thus the outline is like the head and neck of a dog. There is fog here regularly.

**Fogle Automatic Weather Station.** 77°54′S, 166°43′E. An American AWS at an elevation of approximately 640 feet. Named for Benson T. Fogle, a program manager for the National Science Foundation. It operated from Jan. 25, 1984, to Jan. 10, 1985.

**Föhn Bastion.** 69°31′S, 68°36′W. On the west coast of the Antarctic Peninsula.

**Fokker Rocks.** 78°04′S, 155°10′W. Just south of Mount Schlossbach, in the Rockefeller Mountains, on the Edward VII Peninsula. Named for the Fokker airplane damaged and left here during Byrd's 1928–30 expedition.

**Fokknuten Nunatak.** 71°56′S, 23°15′E. 4 miles east of the Perlebandet Nunataks, in the Sør Rondane Mountains. Name means "the spray peak" in Norwegian.

**Fold Island.** 67°17′S, 59°23′E. Also called Folda Island. 6 miles long. 3 miles wide. Between Stefansson Bay and William Scoresby Bay, off the coast of Enderby Land. Discovered by the personnel on the *William Scoresby* in Feb. 1936, and mapped as part of the mainland. The LCE 1936–37 photographed it aerially, and the Norwegian cartographers who worked off these photos determined it to be an island, and named it Foldöya (Fold Island).

**Folda Island** *see* **Fold Island**

**Foley Nunatak** *see* **Brusen Nunatak**

**Foley Promontory.** 68°57′S, 69°24′E. Ice-covered. 5 miles north of Landon Promontory, on the west side of the Amery Ice Shelf. Named by the Australians for N.E. Foley, weather observer at Mawson Station in 1962, and a member of the D.R. Carstens ANARE party which first visited this feature in that year.

**Cape Folger.** 66°08′S, 110°44′E. Ice-covered. Forms the east side of the entrance to Vincennes Bay. This could be the Budd's High Land (q.v.) discovered and named by Wilkes in 1840, or rather the west end of it. Named for Edward C. Folger, Jr.

**Folger, Edward C., Jr.** Cdr. USN. Commander of the *Edisto* during Operation Windmill, 1947–48.

**Folger, Tristan.** Captain of the *William and Nancy* from May 2, 1820–April 21, 1821.

**Folger Rock.** 62°16′S, 59°15′W. A rock in water, 2½ miles north of Harmony Point on Nelson Island, in the South Shetlands. Named by the UK in 1961 for Tristan Folger.

**Folk Ridge.** 73°09′S, 161°49′E. Just SE of Moore Ridge, and parallel to it, in the Caudal Hills of Victoria Land. Named for John E. Folk, biolab technician at McMurdo Station in 1965–66.

**Fomalhaut Nunatak.** 70°58′S, 66°40′W. Isolated. Flat-topped. Near the head of Ryder Glacier, 6½ miles east of Mount Alpheratz, in the Pegasus Range of Palmer Land. Named by the UK for the star.

**Mount Fonda.** 76°59′S, 145°15′W. 695 m. In the NW part of the Swanson Mountains, 6 miles south of Greegor Peak, in the Ford Ranges of Marie Byrd Land. Named by Byrd during the USAS 1939–41 for Howard B. Fonda, who contributed medical supplies to Byrd's first two expeditions to Antarctica.

**Fontaine, Leopoldo.** Leader of the Chilean Antarctic Expedition of 1948–49. This was a station relief expedition, and involved the *Covadonga*, the *Maipo*, and the *Lautaro*.

**Fontaine Bluff.** 79°34′S, 159°40′E. 4 miles west of Cape Murray, on the south side of Carlyon Glacier. Named for Lt. Cdr. R.K. Fontaine, USN, commander of the *Hissem* which plied between Christchurch, NZ and McMurdo Sound in 1963–64, in support of aircraft flight.

**Fontaine Heights.** 65°48′S, 64°28′W. Extends from Mount Dewey to Cape García, on the south side of Bigo Bay, on the west coast of Graham Land. Named by the UK for Henri La Fontaine (1854–1943), Belgian documentalist who created the Universal Decimal Classification.

**Punta Fontana** *see* **Collins Point**

**Fontes, Professor Elena Martínez.** Argentine hydrographer who, in 1968–69, became one of the first women scientists to work in Antarctica (*see* **Women in Antarctica**).

**Food.** Cook was the first navigator into Antarctic regions, during his voyage of 1772–75. He had already discovered a cure for the dreaded scurvy — fresh meat and vegetables. On this trip he took 27 tons of biscuits and over 14,000 pieces of salt pork, 9 tons of sauerkraut, and 3 tons of salted cabbage. Over the next century and a half though, with civilization becoming more and more streamlined, processed food looking like fresh meat and vegetables became the mainstay of all European ships, and scurvy ran rampant among crews as late as the 1920s. The discovery of vitamins ended the scourge, and today the food that is taken down to Antarctica is plentiful and good. In the old days of the pioneers, though, things were not good. There are many stories of explorers, half-crazed through lack of food, scurvy-ridden, and desperate to get their men back to base, killing and eating dogs, ponies, seals, the food for these animals, and even worse — possibly themselves. Although there have been no reports of cannibalism in the Antarctic, not even whispers, it is not improbable given the isolation and need for food. Dogs have reverted easily to cannibalism in the Antarctic on many occasions. Ross, in 1839–43, took concentrated soup, preserved meat, and masses of vegetables (including 5 tons of carrots and 4 tons of pickles). The big foods of the land traverse parties of the early 20th century were pemmican (q.v.), hoosh (pemmican boiled into thick stew), and above all, oatmeal (porridge). Scott used Oxo on his second expedition, and so did Shackleton on his later expeditions. This was Scott's daily ration for his men on the Royal Society Expedition of 1901–4: 12.7 oz. of biscuit (*see* **Sledging biscuit**); 1.6 oz. of oatmeal; 8.8 oz. of pemmican; 2.7 oz. of bacon and pea flour; 2.0 oz. of plasmon (q.v.); 2.1 oz. of cheese; 1.0 oz. of chocolate; 0.7 oz. of cocoa; 3.5 oz. of sugar. Each 3-man crew received a further weekly allowance of 12.3 oz. of tea, 8.8 oz. of onion powder, 4.4

oz. of pepper, 7.0 oz. of salt. Bruce's party, in 1902–4, had for breakfast hot porridge (they were Scottish), bacon, biscuits, and cocoa. Lunch was biscuits, butter, cheese, and chocolate. Dinner was biscuits, meat, and tea. Shackleton, on his 1907–9 expedition, took pemmican made by Beauvais in Copenhagen. These lists illustrate how underfed these men were in the Antarctic, the most inhospitable place on Earth. Those who manhauled sledges hundreds of miles across ice, surviving on food inadequate even for the sedentary, are remembered in this book.

**Foolsmate Glacier.** 74°01'S, 161°55'E. Heavily crevassed. Flows into the Priestley Glacier 11 miles west of Shafer Peak, in Victoria Land. Named by New Zealanders in 1962–63.

**The Football.** 72°30'S, 169°42'E. An ice-free scar shaped like a football (a NZ football, that is). On the north side of Football Mountain. Always visible in the flat snow, it is a landmark for personnel at Hallett Station. Named by the New Zealanders in 1957–58.

**Football Mountain.** 72°31'S, 169°42'E. 830 m. On the ridge between Edisto Inlet and Tucker Glacier, in Victoria Land. The Football (see above) is on its northern side. Named in association with The Football.

**Football Saddle.** 72°31'S, 169°46'E. 700 m. A pass, 2 miles ESE of Football Mountain. Can be crossed by sledge, as it is entirely snow-covered. Named by the New Zealanders in 1957–58 in association with The Football (see above).

**Foote Islands.** 66°12'S, 66°12'W. A small group of snow-capped islands and several rocks, 12 miles SE of Cape Leblond on Lavoisier Island, in Crystal Sound. Named by the UK for Brian L.H. Foote, FIDS radio mechanic at Base N in 1957, and surveyor at Base W in 1958. He made surveys of Crystal Sound.

**Footsteps of Scott Expedition** *see* **In the Footsteps of Scott Expedition**

**Fopay Peak.** 83°03'S, 161°47'E. 5 miles NW of Mount Macbain, on the south side of Cornwall Glacier, in the Queen Elizabeth Range. Named for Charles F. Fopay, Weather Central (q.v.) meteorologist at Little America V in 1958.

**Foraminifera.** Microfauna of Antarctica (*see also* **Fauna**).

**Forbes Glacier.** 67°48'S, 66°44'W. Flows into the NE corner of Square Bay, on the west coast of Graham Land. 10 miles long, and 4 miles wide in its central part, it is 2 miles wide at its mouth. Named by the FIDS in 1948 for James D. Forbes (1809–1868), Scottish physicist and glaciology pioneer.

**Forbes Hill** *see* **Forbes Point**

**Forbes Point.** 64°53'S, 62°33'W. Forms the east side of the entrance to Lester Cove at Andvord Bay, on the west coast of Graham Land. A feature near here (no longer existing) was named Forbes Hill by David Ferguson in 1913–14. The UK later applied the name to this point.

**Forbes Ridge.** 80°09'S, 157°30'E. 7 miles long. In the Britannia Range. It extends north from Mount McClintock along the east side of the Hinton Glacier. Named for Robert B. Forbes of the University of Alaska, geologist in the McMurdo Sound area in 1955–56 and 1962–63.

**Forbidden Plateau.** 64°47'S, 62°05' W. Extends SW from Charlotte Bay to Flandres Bay, in Graham Land. Named by the UK because of the extraordinary difficulty experienced in getting to it (the FIDS were the first to do so, in 1957).

**Forbidden Rocks.** 73°36'S, 94°12'W. A line of rocks, 1 mile long, on the west edge of the Christoffersen Heights, between the Haskell and Walk Glaciers, in the Jones Mountains. Mapped by the University of Minnesota–Jones Mountains Party of 1960–61, and named by them because crevasse fields made their approach to the rocks impossible from the NW.

**Mount Ford.** 70°57'S, 162°52'E. 2,580 m. 2 miles north of Miller Peak. 4 miles WSW of Mount Ashworth, in the Explorers Range of the Bowers Mountains. Named by the northern party of the NZGSAE 1963–64, for M.R.J. Ford, who was surveyor and deputy leader of this northern party (see also **Ford Peak, Ford Rock**).

**Ford, Charles R.** Also known as C. Reginald Ford. Ship's steward and ship's clerk on the *Discovery* during the Royal Society Expedition of 1901–4. He broke his leg while skiing, the first man in the Antarctic to do that.

**Ford, Thomas.** Ordinary seaman on the Wilkes Expedition 1838–42. Joined in the USA. Run at Oahu, Oct. 31, 1840.

**Ford Ice Piedmont.** 82°10'S, 50°W. In the Pensacola Mountains.

**Ford Island.** 66°24'S, 110°31'E. Also called Bathurst Island. Just over 1¼ miles long. Between O'Connor Island and Cloyd Island, in the southern part of the Windmill Islands. Named for Homer D. Ford, photographic officer with the Eastern Task Group of Operation Highjump, 1946–47, and assistant photographic officer on Operation Windmill, 1947–48.

**Ford Massif.** 85°05'S, 91°W. 2,810 m. 15 miles long. 5 miles wide. Snow-topped. Flat. The major feature in the northern part of the Thiel Mountains. Named for Arthur B. Ford, co-leader with Peter Bermel of the US Geological Survey Thiel Mountains survey party of 1960–61, and leader of the 1961–62 geological survey party here. He was leader of several more parties here between 1962–63 and 1978–79.

**Ford Nunataks.** 85°36'S, 131°30'W. 9 miles in extent. 7 miles NW of Murtaugh Peak, in the Wisconsin Range. Named for Franklin E. Ford, construction mechanic at Byrd Station in 1961, and at Amundsen-Scott South Pole Station in 1965.

**Ford Peak.** 75°43'S, 160°27'E. 1,830 m. 6½ miles west of Mount Billing, in the Prince Albert Mountains of Victoria Land. Named by the southern party of the NZGSAE 1962–63 for M.R.J. Ford, assistant surveyor with that party. He had wintered-over at Scott Base in 1962 (see also **Mount Ford, Ford Rock**).

**Ford Ranges.** 77°S, 145°W. Also called Ford Range. Between the Flood Range and the Edward VII Peninsula. They comprise the Fosdick Mountains, the Clark Mountains, the Haines Mountains, the Chester Mountains, the Swanson Mountains, the Mackay Mountains, as well as Mount Woodward, Mount Cooper, Mount Rea, Mount Corey, and Saunders Mountain. They are made up mostly of cretaceous granite-granodiorite platons, and are an older, thick sequence of quartzites, slates, and phyllites. Discovered aerially by Byrd on Dec. 5, 1929, and named by him as Edsel Ford Ranges, for Edsel Ford, a supporter of the expedition. The name was later shortened.

**Ford Rock.** 77°46'S, 166°53'E. A rock halfway up Hut Point Peninsula, on Ross Island, 1 mile NE of Cone Hill. In 1910–13 Scott named it Cone Hill II. The Americans established a survey beacon on this rock in 1955–56. Later it was renamed by A.J. Heine for M.R.J. Ford, NZ surveyor who established a survey beacon network for the McMurdo Ice Shelf Project 1962–63 (see also **Mount Ford, Ford Peak**).

**Ford Spur.** 84°51'S, 173°50'E. Marks the SW end of the Haynes Table, and the confluence of the Keltie and Brandau Glaciers, in the Queen Maud Mountains. Named by the New Zealanders in 1961–62 for Charles R. Ford.

**Mount Forde.** 76°53'S, 162°05'E. Over 1,200 m. At the head of Hurst Glacier, 2 miles NW of Mount Marston, just to the north of the Mackay Glacier, in Victoria Land. Mapped by Scott's 1910–13 expedition, and named by them for Robert Forde.

**Forde, Robert.** Petty officer, RN. On Scott's 1910–13 expedition. A member of the Western Geological Party during that expedition.

**Mount Fordell.** 80°19'S, 82°09'W. 1,670 m. Marks the south end of the Marble Hills, in the Heritage Range. Named for Lt. William D. Fordell, USN, pilot (*see* **Deaths, 1966**).

**Mount Forecast.** 70°40'S, 64°18'E. Has several peaks. Just NE of Mount Brown-Cooper, 12½ miles SW of Mount Pollard, in the Prince Charles Mountains. Named by the Australians for M.J. Forecast, weather observer at Wilkes Station in 1965.

**Forefinger Point.** 67°37'S, 48°04'E. Between McKinnon Island and Rayner Glacier, at the head of Casey Bay, in Enderby Land. Named by the Australians because it looks like a pointing left hand from the air.

**Forel Glacier.** 67°29'S, 66°30'W. 1½ miles wide. 4 miles long. Flows into Blind Bay, on the west coast of Graham Land. Named by the FIDS in 1949 for François A. Forel, Swiss glacier physicist of the 19th century.

**Foreland Island.** 61°57'S, 57°39'W. Also called Islote Promontorio. 1 mile ESE of Taylor Point, off the east side of King George Island, in the South Shetlands. Named for North Foreland, 3½ miles to the NW.

**Foreman, Kinnard.** Sailmaker's mate on the Wilkes Expedition 1838–42. Joined at Callao, and returned to the USA on the *Relief* in 1839.

**Foreman Peak.** 85°45'S, 138°24'W. 2,050 m. 2 miles west of Dzema Peak, on the north side of the Watson Escarpment. Named for Donald L. Foreman, VX-6 mechanic at Little America, 1958, and at McMurdo Station, 1960.

**Forests.** In ancient days there were forests of trees in Antarctica known as Glossopteris (q.v.). (*See also* **Flora.**)

**Forge Islands.** 65°14'S, 64°17'W. A group of small islands, including Smooth Island, NE of the Barchans, and ½ mile NW of Grotto Island, in the Argentine

Islands. Charted by the BGLE in 1934–37, and named by them as the Horseshoe Islands. In 1959 the UK changed the name in order to avoid confusion with the other feature of a similar name, Horseshoe Island, not too far away. The new name keeps the same theme.

**Forgotten Hills.** 72°59'S, 164°E. A small group, 6 miles SE of Intention Nunataks, at the west side of the head of Astronaut Glacier. Named by the New Zealanders in 1966–67 because all of the parties who had come here up to that time had not had time to examine these hills.

**Forlidas Pond.** 82°27'S, 51°21'W. In the Pensacola Mountains.

**Forlidas Ridge.** 82°29'S, 51°16'W. Forms the west side of Davis Valley, in the Dufek Massif of the Pensacola Mountains. Named for Charles W. Forlidas, radioman at Ellsworth Station in 1957.

**Forman Glacier.** 84°39'S, 177°10'W. 4 miles long. Enters Shackleton Glacier between Mount Franke and Mount Cole, in the Queen Maud Mountains. Named for John H. Forman, USN, construction mechanic at McMurdo Station in 1959.

**Forposten** *see* **Vorposten Peak**

**Forrest Pass.** 75°54'S, 132°34'W. Ice-filled. Between Mount Bursey and the southern elevations of the Ames Range, in Marie Byrd Land. Named for Robert B. Forrest, glaciologist with the Byrd Station Traverse of 1962–63.

**Forrestal Range.** 83°15'S, 50°W. 65 miles long. Largely snow-covered. East of the Dufek Massif and the Neptune Range, in the Pensacola Mountains. Discovered aerially on Jan. 13, 1956. Named for the *Forrestal,* first supercarrier of the US Navy (not in Antarctica).

**Forrester Island.** 74°08'S, 132°13'W. 3½ miles long. 13 miles NNE of Shepard Island, in the Getz Ice Shelf, or rather just north of it, off the coast of Marie Byrd Land. Discovered and charted from the *Glacier* on Feb. 5, 1962. Named for Lt. Cdr. John J. Forrester, USN, executive officer on the *Glacier* that season.

**Forsdick, William.** Ordinary seaman on the Wilkes Expedition 1838–42. Joined in the USA. Run at Oahu, Oct. 31, 1840.

**Førstefjell.** 71°50'S, 5°43'W. An isolated nunatak, 5 miles north of Førstefjellsrabben in the NW part of Giaever Ridge, in Queen Maud Land. Name means "the first mountain" in Norwegian.

**Førstefjellsrabben.** 71°55'S, 5°49'W. An isolated nunatak, 5 miles south of Førstefjell, in the NW part of Giaever Ridge, in Queen Maud Land. Name means "the first mountain hill" in Norwegian. Named in association with Førstefjell.

**Førstefjellsryggen** *see* **Giaever Ridge**

**Forster, George.** b. Nov. 27, 1754, Nassenhuben, Prussia. d. in poverty, in Paris, on Jan. 12, 1794, after an eventful international career in science, academia, sailing, and politics. Originally he was Johann Georg Adam Forster. He was on the *Resolution* during Cook's voyage of 1772–75, along with his father John Forster (see below). He published his father's account of the trip 6 weeks before Cook published the official narrative of the voyage, in 1777 (cf. John Marra).

**Forster, John R.** b. Oct. 22, 1729, Dirschau, Prussia. d. Dec. 9, 1798, Halle, Germany. Johann Reinhold Forster. German preacher, sailor, writer, translator, scientist who settled in London in 1766. Naturalist on the *Resolution* during Cook's voyage of 1772–75. His son, George (see above), was also on the trip. The Admiralty forbade him to publish his account of the expedition before Cook published the official version, so his son published it in 1777 (cf. John Marra).

**Forster Ice Piedmont.** 69°22'S, 67°W. On the landward side of the Wordie Ice Shelf, on the west coast of the Antarctic Peninsula. Formed by the confluence of the Airy, Seller, Fleming, and Prospect Glaciers. It is 25 miles long from north-

south, and 12 miles wide. Surveyed by the BGLE in 1936–37, and again by Peter D. Forster and P. Gibbs of the FIDS in 1958. Forster was surveyor at Base E in 1958, and at Base Y in 1960.

**Forsythe Bluff.** 71°16'S, 159°50'E. Over 2,500 m. at its highest. On the west edge of the Daniels Range, in the Usarp Mountains. 11 miles north of Big Brother Bluff. Named for Warren L. Forsythe, geologist at McMurdo Station in 1967–68.

**Fort Point.** 62°34'S, 59°34'W. Also called Castle Rock, Fort Rock, Roca Peñón, Punta Hardy. 85 m. A point which forms the SE end of Greenwich Island, in the South Shetlands. Surveyed by the Discovery Investigations personnel in 1935, and named Castle Rock by them. In 1954 the UK renamed it in order to avoid confusion with the other Castle Rock, just off Snow Island. The name Fort Point is descriptive.

**Fort Rock** *see* **Fort Point**

**¹Fort William** *see* **Canto Point**

**²Fort William.** 62°23'S, 59°43'W. Also called Cape Morris. A flat-topped headland in the form of a cape, which forms the west end of Robert Island, in the South Shetlands. In 1822 Robert Fildes placed it where it is now, i.e. on the eastern side of what is now English Strait. In 1829 he put it on the other side of the strait, i.e. on Greenwich Island. Following a Discovery Investigations survey in 1934–35 this Greenwich Island location assumed the name. It has, however, since then, been officially placed back to the original side of the strait, i.e. Fort William is now on Nelson Island again. The UK renamed the Greenwich Island point as Canto Point.

**Fortenberry Glacier.** 70°48'S, 166°57'E. On the north side of Tapsell Foreland, in Victoria Land. It flows into Yule Bay, 3 miles east of Ackroyd Point. Named for Lt. Ralph M. Fortenberry, USN, medical officer at McMurdo Station in 1960.

**Fortín Rock.** 62°29'S, 60°44'W. Also called Crab Stack, Roca Scarborough

Castle. A sea stack 2 miles SE of Cape Shirreff, off the north coast of Livingston Island, in the South Shetlands. Named descriptively by the Argentines in 1953. Fortín is Spanish for a small fort.

¹The Fortress  see  Mount Pendragon

²The Fortress. 77°18'S, 160°55'E. A platform of Beacon Sandstone dissected to form four promontories bordered by cliffs over 300 m. high. NE of the Webb Glacier. Named by the New Zealanders in 1959–60 for its appearance.

Fortress Hill. 63°56'S, 57°31'W. 120 m. 2 miles north of Terrapin Hill, in the northern part of James Ross Island. Charted and named descriptively by the FIDS in 1946.

Fortress Rocks. 77°51'S, 166°41'E. ½ mile NE of McMurdo Station, on Ross Island. Named by Scott in 1911. They now form McMurdo Station's quarry.

Forwood, William G. Colonel, USAF. Commander of the 61st Troop Carrier Group which handled the enormous airlift/airdrop operation during Operation Deep Freeze, during the IGY.

Fosdick, Stephen. Gunner's mate on the Wilkes Expedition 1838–42. Joined in the USA. Served the cruise.

Fosdick Mountains. 76°S, 145°W. Also called Raymond Fosdick Mountains. They are made up of metamorphic rocks containing mineral assemblages of the medium- to high-amphibolite facies. Individual features include Mount Iphigene, Mount Ferranto, Mount Avers, Mount Lockhart, Mount Colombo, Mount Richardson, Mount Perkins, Marujupu Peak, Ochs Glacier. At the neck of the Guest Peninsula, in the Ford Ranges of Marie Byrd Land. Discovered by Byrd in 1929, and named by him for Raymond B. Fosdick, president of the Rockefeller Foundation.

Cabo Fossati  see  Cape Lookout

Fossil Bluff. 71°20'S, 68°17'W. Prominent rock bluff on the east coast of Alexander Island. Marks the north side of the mouth of Uranus Glacier, where that glacier enters the George VI Sound. Surveyed by the BGLE in 1936, and named by them for the fossils found in the rock here. Resurveyed by the FIDS in 1948.

Fossil Bluff Station. 71°20'S, 68°17'W. British scientific base at Fossil Bluff, near the Uranus Glacier, in Alexander Island. Previously known as Base K. Operative from 1961.

Fossil Wood Point. 70°50'S, 68°02'E. Between Bainmedart Cove and Radok Lake, in the east part of the Aramis Range of the Prince Charles Mountains. Named by the Australians for the deposits of fossil wood here.

Fossils. Jonathan Winship may have been the first to discover fossils in Antarctica, during the 1820–21 season in the South Shetlands. In 1830 James Eights was the first scientist to find Antarctic fossils. In 1892 Larsen found fossils, as Nordenskjöld did in 1901–4, and several other expeditions did over the years, but it was not until 1967 that the fossil explosion began. That year Peter Barrett (q.v.) found a lizard jawbone at Graphite Peak (q.v. for further details of the find). This was a labyrinthodont, about 220 million years old. As other labyrinthodonts have been found in other parts of the world, this suddenly made Gondwanaland (q.v.) a more acceptable theory. In 1982, on Seymour Island, the first fossil remains of an Antarctic land mammal were found by a team of US scientists. The bones were those of a small marsupial, about the size of a rat. Unless it is a hoax, this supports the theory of marsupial migration from the Americas to Australia, via Antarctica, which can only imply the continental shift theory is correct. In 1986 Argentine scientists discovered 70 million-year-old dinosaur fossils on James Ross Island, and the same year US teams near the Beardmore Glacier discovered more than 350 vertebrate bones from 190–225 million years ago, including 4 new amphibians and reptiles. In 1987, on Seymour Island, were discovered fossils of crocodiles, a 6½-foot-tall flightless bird (probably a primordial penguin), and a 32 foot-long whale (discovered by Ewan Fordyce, a NZ paleontologist, on Jan. 3, 1987, and the largest fossil ever recovered in Antarctica). Fossils teem in the Beacon Sandstone formation, for example, including freshwater fish fossils in Devonian Age rocks. Seymour Island and James Ross Island are rich in fossils, and geologically young fossils have been found in the Transantarctic Mountains. In 1987 the beak of an enormous bird was discovered on Seymour Island. Larry G. Marshall called it the "Terror Bird." An alligator fossil has also been found on Seymour Island, as have 50 lobster fossils.

**Cape Foster.** 64°27′S, 57°58′W. 2 miles SE of Carlsson Bay, on the south side of James Ross Island. Discovered by Ross in 1839–43, and named by him for Henry Foster.

**¹Mount Foster** *see* **Mount Pisgah**

**²Mount Foster.** 63°S, 62°33′W. 2,105 m. A triple peak. 4 miles SW of Mount Pisgah, on Smith Island, in the South Shetlands. Foster visited it in 1829 and called it Mount Beaufurt (a name also seen as Mount Beaufort). Mount Foster soon became more popular as its name, however.

**Port Foster.** 62°57′S, 60°39′W. The central part of Deception Island, in the South Shetlands. A basinlike harbor, it is actually a drowned breached crater within the volcano which is Deception Island. 5 miles long and 3 miles wide, its bays include Whaler's Bay, Pendulum Cove, Primero de Mayo Bay, and Telefon Bay. First called Port Williams, for the *Williams,* and Yankee Harbor, for the number of American sealers here (not to be confused with the other Yankee Harbor, the "real" feature of that name). Also before 1821 it was called Deception Harbor, and, sometime around 1821–22 was also called Dunbar's Harbor or Port Dunbar. Renamed in 1829 for Henry Foster. The shores of Port Foster are SSSI #21, and two small areas of benthic habitat in its waters form SSSI #27. Of

interest because of the volcanics, it became a study area on Dec. 31, 1967.

**Foster, Carroll B., Jr.** Seaman on the *Eleanor Bolling* during Byrd's 1928–30 expedition.

**Foster, Henry.** Royal Navy. Fellow of the Royal Society. He was with Smith on the *Williams* in 1819–20, and was therefore one of the first to sight the South Shetlands. He made a drawing of them. He was back in 1828–31, as leader of the *Chanticleer* expedition, entering Deception Island and anchoring in Pendulum Cove, where he conducted gravity studies for the British government, as part of Britain's effort to determine the true shape of the earth. With him was scientist W.H.B. Webster (q.v.). He left two self-recording thermometers (one for high and one for low temperatures) on the island, which were sought unsuccessfully by Johnson in the *Sea Gull* from Dec. 10 to 17, 1838, during the Wilkes Expedition of 1838–42, and found by Smyley in Feb. 1842. Foster also took possession of Hoseason Island on Jan. 7, 1829, and roughly charted part of the Antarctic Peninsula.

**Foster Bluff.** 66°25′S, 110°37′E. In the SW part of Herring Island, in the Windmill Islands. Named for Danny L. Foster, meteorologist at Wilkes Station in 1962.

**Foster Glacier.** 78°25′S, 162°55′E. 4 miles south of Mount Kempe, in the Royal Society Range of Victoria Land. It flows into the Koettlitz Glacier. Named in 1963 for Maj. James Foster, US Marines, assistant air operations officer for Task Force 43 in Antarctica in 1960.

**Foster Island.** 66°03′S, 100°16′E. Just over ¼ mile long. 7 miles WNW of Currituck Island, at the NW end of the Highjump Archipelago. Named for H.C. Foster, motion picture photographer on Operation Highjump, 1946–47.

**Foster Nunatak.** 71°06′S, 71°40′E. Horseshoe-shaped. In the south part of the Manning Nunataks, on the east side of the Amery Ice Shelf. Named by the

Australians for A.L. Foster, electronics engineer at Mawson Station in 1970.

**Foster Peninsula.** 71°18′S, 61°10′W. Ice-covered. Between the Palmer and Lamplugh Inlets, on the east coast of Palmer Land. Named for Theodore D. Foster, US oceanographer on the International Weddell Sea Oceanographic Expedition of 1969. He was also party leader on the Weddell Sea Investigations of 1972–73 and 1974–75.

**Foster Plateau.** 64°43′S, 61°25′W. 80 square miles in area. Between the Drygalski and Hektoria Glaciers, in northern Graham Land. Named by the UK in 1960 for Richard A. Foster, FIDS leader of Base O in 1956 and 1957.

**Fothergill Point.** 64°35′S, 60°12′W. 5 miles NE of Cape Worsley, on the east side of Graham Land. Named by the UK for Ian L. Fothergill, leader and meteorological assistant at Base D from 1959–63.

**Fougner, Anton.** Scientific assistant in Borchgrevink's wintering-over party at Cape Adare in 1899.

**Foul Point.** 60°32′S, 45°29′W. Also called Punta Peligroso. On the central north side of Coronation Island, in the South Orkneys. It is the northern point of the island, and has off-lying rocks. It is at the east side of the entrance to Ommanney Bay. Discovered in Dec. 1821 by Powell and Palmer. Named before 1822.

**Foundation Ice Stream.** 83°15′S, 60°W. In the Pensacola Mountains. Flows northward for 150 miles along the west side of the Patuxent and Neptune Ranges, to enter the Ronne Ice Shelf west of the Dufek Massif. Named for the National Science Foundation (q.v.).

**Founders Escarpment.** 79°12′S, 86°21′W. West of Founders Peaks, in the Heritage Range. Extends from Minnesota Glacier to Splettstoesser Glacier. Named by the University of Minnesota Geological Party of 1963–64 for the nearby peaks.

**Founders Peaks.** 79°10′S, 86°15′W. A cluster of peaks and ridges just east of

Founders Escarpment, and between the Minnesota and Gowan Glaciers, in the Heritage Range. Named in continuation of the heritage theme.

**Fountain, Gordon.** Crewman on the *Bear of Oakland*, 1934–35.

**Four Ladies Bank.** 67°30′S, 77°30′E. A submarine feature, just off the Ingrid Christensen Coast. Named for the four ladies on the LCE 1936–37 (*see* **Women in Antarctica**).

**Four Ramps.** 84°42′S, 177°35′E. 4 small rock spurs, roughly parallel, which project through the snow surface, and which form the NE part of Sullivan Ridge, on the west side of Ramsey Glacier. Discovered during Operation Highjump, 1946–47, and named descriptively by the USA.

**Mount Fourcade.** 64°36′S, 62°30′W. 2 miles SW of Cape Anna, on the west coast of Graham Land. Charted by de Gerlache in 1897–99. Named by the UK in 1960 for H.G. Fourcade, South African photogrammetry pioneer.

**Fourier Island.** 66°48′S, 141°30′E. A small island less than 100 yards off the coast of East Antarctica, and ¾ mile ENE of Cape Mousse. Charted in 1951 by the French, and named by them for Jean-Baptiste Fourier (1768–1830), French geometrician.

**The *Fournier*.** Argentine ship which took part in the Argentine Antarctic Expeditions of 1946–47 (Capt. Díaz) and 1947–48 (Capt. Domingo G. Luís). It was wrecked in the Strait of Magellan in 1948.

**Fournier Bay.** 64°31′S, 63°06′W. 8 miles long. 3 miles wide. Indents the NE coast of Anvers Island, just west of Briggs Peninsula. Charted by Charcot in 1903–5, and named by him for Vice-Adm. Ernest Fournier of the French navy.

**Fournier Island.** 64°33′S, 62°49′W. Also called Ryswick Island. A small island in the southern part of the Schollaert Channel, ½ mile off the eastern end of Anvers Island. Charted by

Charcot in 1903-5. Named in 1950 by the Argentines for the *Fournier*.

**Fournier Ridge.** 69°34'S, 72°42'W. On the NW coast of Alexander Island.

**Fowler, Alexander C.** Seaman on the Wilkes Expedition 1838-42. Joined in the USA. Served the cruise.

**Fowler, Robert.** Crewman on the *Bear of Oakland*, 1933-35.

**Fowler Ice Rise.** 77°30'S, 78°W. Between the Evans Ice Stream and Carlson Inlet, in the SW part of the Ronne Ice Shelf. It is ice-covered except for the Haag Nunataks in the NW portion. Named for Capt. Alfred N. Fowler, USN, Commander US Naval Support Force, Antarctica, 1972-74.

**Fowler Islands.** 66°25'S, 66°26'W. A group of small islands between the Bernal Islands and the Bragg Islands, in Crystal Sound. Named by the UK for Sir Ralph H. Fowler (1889-1944), British mathematician.

**Fowler Knoll.** 84°47'S, 99°14'W. 2,465 m. Snow-covered. In the west central part of the Havola Escarpment. Named for CWO George W. Fowler, US Army, navigator on the Byrd-South Pole Traverse (q.v.), which passed near here on Dec. 25, 1960.

**Mount Fox.** 83°38'S, 169°14'E. 2,820 m. 1 mile SW of Mount F.L. Smith, just to the west of the Beardmore Glacier, in the Queen Alexandra Range. Discovered and named by Shackleton's 1907-9 expedition.

**Fox, Edward.** Officer's steward on the Wilkes Expedition 1838-42. Joined at Sydney. Discharged at Oahu.

**Fox, Dr. J.L.** Assistant surgeon on the *Vincennes* during the Wilkes Expedition 1838-42. Joined the *Porpoise* at San Francisco in Oct. 1841.

**Fox Glacier.** 66°14'S, 114°25'E. Flows from the area NE of Law Dome, to the coast, 12 miles north of Williamson Glacier. It forms a small glacier tongue at its terminus. Named for Dr. J.L. Fox.

**Fox Ridge.** 70°47'S, 67°53'E. On the McLeod Massif, 5 miles west of Beaver

Lake, in the east part of the Aramis Range of the Prince Charles Mountains. Named by the Australians for J. Fox, technical officer (survey), the leader of one of the survey parties in the Prince Charles Mountains.

**Cape Foyn** *see* **Cape Alexander**

**Foyn Coast.** 66°40'S, 64°20'W. Now known to be an island, on the east side of Graham Land, between Capes Alexander and Northrop. About 20 miles long, it runs from NE to SW. Discovered by Larsen in 1893, and named by him as Foyn Land, or Svend Foyn Land, for the inventor of the harpoon gun. The name became Svend Foyn Coast, and then Foyn Coast, and finally, even though it was determined to be an island and not a coast or a land as Larsen and others had thought, it remained Foyn Coast.

**Foyn Harbor.** 64°33'S, 62°01'W. Also called Svend Foyn Harbor. An anchorage between Nansen Island and Enterprise Island, in Wilhelmina Bay, off the west coast of Graham Land. Surveyed by Lester and Bagshawe of the British Imperial Expedition of 1920-22, and named by whalers here for the *Svend Foyn*, moored here that summer.

¹**Foyn Island** *see* **Foyn Point**

²**Foyn Island.** 71°56'S, 171°04'E. Also called Svend Foyn Island. The second largest island in the Possession Islands. 4 miles SW of Possesion Island. Named by Henryk Bull in 1895 as James Ross Island, for Sir James Clark Ross. He later changed the name (to avoid confusion with the more prominent island of that name) to honor Svend Foyn, primary backer of Bull's expedition.

**Foyn Land** *see* **Foyn Coast**

**Foyn Point.** 65°15'S, 61°38'W. Surmounted by a peak of 525 m. Marks the north side of the entrance to Exasperation Inlet, on the Oscar II Coast, on the east coast of Graham Land. Wilkins named it Foyn Island, from photos he took aerially on Dec. 20, 1928, but it was later redefined. Svend Foyn was the inventor of the harpoon gun.

**Mount Frakes.** 76°48′S, 117°43′W. 3,675 m. Highest point in the Crary Mountains of Marie Byrd Land. Lichens are found here. Named for Lawrence A. Frakes, geologist in Antarctica in the mid- to late-1960s.

**The *Fram*.** Norwegian ship designed by Norwegian engineer Colin Archer, following the directions of Arctic explorer Fridtjof Nansen. It was built specifically for Nansen and the Arctic, and was launched on Oct. 26, 1892. The name Fram means "forward" in Norwegian. The ship was 402 tons gross, 307 tons net, it had a 102 foot-long keel, was 113 feet long at the waterline and 128 feet long on deck. It was 36 feet wide, 17 feet deep, and had a draft of between 12½ and 15 feet. It had a reinforced bow and stern, and 220 hp engines, which gave a speed of between 6 and 7 knots. Nansen give it to Amundsen in 1910, and it took the Norwegian to the Bay of Whales, reaching 78°41′S, the furthest south ever reached by a ship. The *Fram* was commanded by Capt. Thorvald Nilsen on this Norwegian Antarctic Expedition of 1910–12. After the expedition it sailed home, and in 1936 was installed in an Oslo museum. Wisting (q.v.) died aboard it while it was in the museum.

**Fram Bank.** 67°18′S, 70°E. A submarine feature which juts out from the Lars Christensen Coast of Mac. Robertson Land. Named for the *Fram*.

**Fram Islands.** 66°38′S, 139°50′E. A small group of rocky islands and rocks in the west portion of the Géologie Archipelago. 2 miles NNW of Cape Géodésie. Charted by the French in 1949–51, and named by them for the *Fram*.

**Fram Mesa.** 86°08′S, 156°28′W. 10 miles long. Between 1 and 3 miles wide. Ice-capped. Forms the NE portion of the Nilsen Plateau, in the Queen Maud Mountains. Named for the *Fram*.

**Fram Peak.** 68°04′S, 58°27′E. The most northerly peak in the Hansen Mountains. Photographed by the LCE 1936–37, and named Framfjellet (the forward peak) by the Norwegians. Translated later by the Australians.

**Frame Ridge.** 78°05′S, 165°26′E. In the central part of Brown Peninsula, in Victoria Land. Named by NZ for A.O. Frame, paleontology technician here in 1964–65.

**Framheim Station.** Amundsen's base on the Bay of Whales during the Norwegian Antarctic Expedition of 1910–12. A hut, with fourteen 16-man military bell-tents around it constituted the camp, whose name meant "the home of *Fram*," the *Fram* being the expedition's ship. Prestrud came up with the name on Feb. 4, 1911. In 1928, when Byrd got to the Bay of Whales and set up Little America only 3 miles away, Framheim had been wiped out by 16 years of snow.

**Cape Framnaes** *see* **Cape Framnes**
**Framnaesodden** *see* **Framnes Head**
**Framnäs** *see* **Cape Framnes**

**Cape Framnes.** 65°57′S, 60°33′W. Also spelled Cape Framnaes, Framnäs. The northeasternmost point of Jason Peninsula, on the east coast of Graham Land. Named descriptively by Larsen in 1893. The name means "forward point" in Norwegian. It was the most advanced point of land which he saw there.

**Framnes Head.** 68°47′S, 90°42′W. Also called Framnaesodden. In Sandefjord Cove, on the west side of Peter I Island. Charted and named by Nils Larsen in the *Norvegia*, who made the first landing on the island at this point, in Feb. 1929.

**Framnes Mountains.** 67°50′S, 62°35′E. In Mac. Robertson Land, behind Mawson Station. They comprise the Casey, Masson, and David Ranges. Discovered by the BANZARE, and by Norwegian sealers, separately, in Feb. 1931. Photographed by the LCE 1936–37 in Jan. 1937, and named by Lars Christensen for Framnesfjellet, a hill near his home in Norway.

**Framrabben Nunatak.** 72°29′S, 3°52′W. 3 miles WNW of Borg Mountain, in Queen Maud Land. Name means "the forward nunatak" in Norwegian.

**Framranten Point.** 73°49'S, 5°13'W. Extends NW from Kuvungen Hill, near the SW end of the Kirwan Escarpment of Queen Maud Land. Named by the Norwegians.

**Framryggen Ridge.** 72°30'S, 3°54'W. 3 miles west of Borg Mountain, in Queen Maud Land. Name means "the forward ridge" in Norwegian.

**Framskotet Spur.** 72°30'S, 3°41'W. Forms the west extremity of Borg Mountain, in Queen Maud Land. Name means "the forward bulkhead" in Norwegian.

**Fran Inlet** see **Nantucket Inlet**

**Franca Glacier.** 68°23'S, 65°34'W. On the east coast of Graham Land, it flows into the Larsen Ice Shelf.

**The *Français*.** Charcot's ship during his 1903–5 expedition. A 3-masted schooner built entirely of oak, and built specifically for the Antarctic by Gauthier, Senior, at the Saint-Malo shipyards in France, at a cost of 450,000 gold francs. It had a reinforced bow and a 125 hp second-hand engine (Charcot had almost run out of money). It was 150 feet long, with a 25 foot beam. It weighed 245 tons. On board were 6 unpaid officers, 14 men (paid) including 5 sailors, 3 stokers, a cook, and a steward. They were Charcot, Cholet (the captain), Pléneau, Rallier du Baty, Turquet, Rey, Gourdon, Matha, Deyné, Libois, Jabet, Besnard, the two Guégnans, Goudier, Hervéou, Paumelle, Poste, Roland, Rozo, and Toby the pig. Charcot froze the ship in at Booth Island for the winter of 1904, and on March 5, 1905, the *Français* called at Patagonia in South America, with 75 cases of collected materials from the Antarctic, as well as scientific notes. The Argentine government bought the ship, which was finally lost on the Rio de la Plata in 1907.

**Mount Français.** 64°38'S, 63°27'W. Also called Monte Teniente Ibáñez. 2,760 m. Snow-covered. Highest point on Anvers Island, SE of the center of the island, and 6 miles north of Börgen Bay. Discovered by de Gerlache in 1898, and named by Charcot in 1903–5 for his ship, the *Français*.

**Français Bight** see **Français Cove**

**Français Cove.** 65°04'S, 64°02'W. Also called Français Bight. At the west side of Port Charcot, it indents the north end of Booth Island, in the Wilhelm Archipelago. Discovered by Charcot in 1903–5, and named by him for his ship, the *Français*, which moored here during the 1904 winter.

**Français Glacier.** 66°30'S, 138°10'E. 12 miles long. 4 miles wide. At the very SW of Commonwealth Bay, on the coast of Adélie Land. It flows to the coast just west of Ravin Bay. In 1840 Dumont d'Urville named a feature in this spot as Baie des Ravins (Bay of Ravines), but saw no glacier. The AAE 1911–14 saw no glacier here, and they would have had it been here. It was here during Operation Highjump, 1946–47, so had to have been formed between 1914 and 1946, surely. It was named Glacier Endurance by the French in 1949–51, but, in order to avoid confusion with the other Endurance Glacier, it was renamed for the *Français*.

**Français Glacier Tongue.** 66°31'S, 138°15'E. 3 miles long. The seaward extension of the Français Glacier. Charted in 1951 by the French, and named by them in association with the glacier.

**France.** Pierre Bouvet was an early explorer who sailed as far south as 54°S, and discovered Bouvet Island in an attempt to prove or disprove the existence of the "Great Southern Continent." Capt. Yves Kerguélen-Trémarec followed him in 1771–72, and discovered Kerguélen Island (50°S), which he named New France. France's earliest actual Antarctic explorers were Dumont d'Urville and Charcot, and on April 1, 1938, France claimed Adélie Land, between 136°E and 142°E. This was France's only Antarctic claim, and was administered as part of Terres Australes et Antarctiques Françaises, and controlled by the governor of Madagascar until the signing of the Antarctic Treaty in 1959, of which France was one of the 12 original signatories. The USA and the USSR do not recognize, and never did, France's claim to Adélie Land, and the two superpowers call this territory the Adélie Coast. In 1948–49 France tried an expedition to Antarctica, but they could not get to land because of the ice. French polar exploration is under the direction of the Expéditions Polaires Françaises, which, in 1947, became an organ of the National Center for Scientific Research. The French Polar Expedition (q.v.) took place in 1949–53. In 1950 Port-Martin was established, but that was consumed by fire in 1952, and replaced by Dumont d'Urville station in 1956, set up by Robert Guillard's 1955–56 expedition. Dumont d'Urville Station and Charcot Station were France's only two IGY stations. Bertrand Imbert led the 1956–57 program, and Gaston Rouillon led the program through IGY itself, 1957–59. Robert Faure was leader of the 1959–61 expedition.

**Cape Frances.** 67°30′S, 164°45′E. On the east side of Sturge Island, in the Balleny Islands. In 1841, Ross, from a distance, thought that Sturge Island was 3 individual islands, and named the center one Frances Island. Scott, in 1904, rectified this situation and redefined everything, naming this cape in order to preserve Ross' naming in the area.

**Frances Island** *see* **Cape Frances**

**Francey Hill.** 70°43′S, 67°02′E. Snow-covered. 3 miles south of Mount McKenzie, in the Aramis Range of the Prince Charles Mountains. Named by the Australians for R.J. Francey, cosmic ray physicist at Mawson Station in 1964.

**Mount Francis.** 72°14′S, 168°45′E. 2,610 m. Overlooks Tucker Glacier from the north. Between the Tyler and Staircase Glaciers, in the Admiralty Mountains. Named for Henry S. Francis, Jr., National Science Foundation Director of International Cooperation and Information. He was at Little America in 1958 and in certain subsequent years.

**The** *Francis Allyn.* US sealer from New London, in the South Shetlands in 1873–

75, 1875–77, and 1877–79, under the command of Capt. R.H. Glass. In 1877–78 it picked up Mr. King, the sole survivor of the wintering sealers left on Rugged Island by the *Florence* the season before. In 1887–89 the *Francis Allyn* was at the Crozet Islands, the Kerguélen Islands, and South Georgia (none of which are in Antarctica), under Capt. Joseph J. Fuller. In 1893–94 Fuller brought it to the Kerguélens and Bouvetøya (neither of which is in the Antarctic).

**Francis Island.** 67°37′S, 64°45′W. Also called Robinson Island. 7 miles long. 5 miles wide. 12 miles ENE of Cape Choyce, 15 miles off the east coast of Graham Land, in the Larsen Ice Shelf. Discovered aerially by the USAS in 1940. Charted by the FIDS in 1947, and named by them for S.J. Francis, FIDS surveyor.

**Francis Peaks.** 67°39′S, 50°25′E. A group of peaks and ridges, 1 mile SE of Mount Gordon, in the Scott Mountains of Enderby Land. Named by the Australians for R.J. Francis, physicist at Mawson Station in 1961.

**Francisco de Gurruchaga Refugio.** Argentine refuge hut built at Harmony Cove, Nelson Island, in 1954.

**Franck Nunataks.** 71°26′S, 72°20′W. 3 miles in extent. At the base of Beethoven Peninsula, in the SW part of Alexander Island. Named by the UK for the composer.

**Mount Frank Houlder** *see* **Mount Houlder**

**Frank Newnes Glacier.** 71°28′S, 169°19′E. Flows into the head of Pressure Bay, on the north coast of Victoria Land. Charted by Borchgrevink in 1898–1900, and named by him for Frank Newnes, son of the expedition's sponsor, Sir George Newnes.

**Mount Franke.** 84°37′S, 177°04′W. 1,600 m. Between Mount Wasko and Mount Cole, on the west side of the Shackleton Glacier. Discovered by the USAS 1939–41. Surveyed by Crary in 1957–58, and named by him for Lt. Cdr.

Willard J. Franke, USN, VX-6 member at Little America in 1958.

**Frankenfield Glacier.** 71°46'S, 98°18' W. In the NE part of the Noville Peninsula, on Thurston Island. Flows into the Bellingshausen Sea between Mount Feury and Mulroy Island. Named for Lt. (jg) Chester Frankenfield, meteorologist on the Bellingshausen Sea Expedition, who established an automatic weather station on Thurston Island in Feb. 1960.

**The *Franklin*.** US sealer from New London. In the South Shetlands in 1871–72, under the command of Capt. James Holmes, and in company with the *Peru*. It was back in the South Shetlands in 1873–74 under Capt. Chester, and in 1874–75 under Capt. Buddington. This is probably the same ship which had been at the Kerguélen Islands (not in Antarctica) in the 1859–62 period under the command of Capt. Church (q.v.).

**Cape Franklin** *see* **Franklin Point**

**Mount Franklin.** 78°05'S, 154°57'W. Between Breckinridge Peak and Washington Ridge, in the southern group of the Rockefeller Mountains, on Edward VII Peninsula, in Marie Byrd Land. Discovered on Jan. 27, 1929, during Byrd's 1928–30 expedition, and named by the USAS from West Base, 1939–41. They established a seismic station camp on the peak.

**Franklin D. Roosevelt Sea** *see* **Amundsen Sea**

**Franklin Island.** 76°05'S, 168°18'E. 7 miles long. A small, rocky, volcanic pile in the Ross Sea, 80 miles east of Cape Hickey, Victoria Land. Discovered and landed on by Ross on Jan. 27, 1841. Named by him for Sir John Franklin, the Arctic explorer.

**Franklin Point.** 63°56'S, 61°29'W. Forms the west end of Intercurrence Island, in the Palmer Archipelago. Charted by Foster in 1829 as Cape Franklin. Later redefined.

**Franklin Shoals.** 76°15'S, 167°E. A submarine feature of the Ross Sea,

around Franklin Island. Named in association with the island.

**Franko Escarpment.** 83°02'S, 49°W. In the Pensacola Mountains.

**Fraser, Capt.** Commander of the *Sprightly* during its first South Shetlands tour, 1820–21.

**Fraser, Francis C.** British zoologist based in South Georgia (54°S) in 1926–27, 1928–29, and 1930. He also worked in Antarctic waters on the *Discovery* in 1927, and on the *Discovery II* in 1929 and 1931.

**Fraser Point.** 60°41'S, 44°31'W. Also spelled (erroneously) as Frazier Point. Between Marr Bay and Mackintosh Cove, on the north coast of Laurie Island, in the South Orkneys. Mapped by Bruce in 1903, and by Petter Sørlle in 1912–13. Remapped in 1933 by the personnel on the *Discovery II*, who named it for Francis C. Fraser.

**Mount Frazier.** 77°53'S, 154°56'W. The most northerly of the Rockefeller Mountains. 1 mile north of Mount Jackling, on the Edward VII Peninsula of Marie Byrd Land. Discovered on Jan. 27, 1929, during Byrd's 1928–30 expedition, and later named Mount Irene Frazier, for the wife of Russell G. Frazier. The name was later shortened.

**Frazier, Capt.** Edmund Fanning (q.v.) claimed that a navigator of this name had sighted the South Shetlands in 1712 and named them South Iceland or New South Iceland.

**Frazier, Paul W.** Cdr., USN. Navigator and projects officer on Operation Windmill, 1947–48. Head of Ship Operations during Operation Deep Freeze I (1955–56), and during Operation Deep Freeze II (1956–57) he was leader of the traverse which left Little America V to set up Byrd Station, 600 miles away.

**Frazier, Dr. Russell G.** Medical officer at West Base during the USAS 1939–41.

[1]**Frazier, William.** Seaman on the Wilkes Expedition 1838–42. Joined in the USA. Run at Sydney.

²**Frazier, William.** Ordinary seaman on the Wilkes Expedition 1838–42. Joined at Rio. Lost in the *Sea Gull* in late April 1839.

**Frazier Glacier.** 77°05'S, 161°25'E. Between the Clare Range and Detour Nunatak, flowing into the Mackay Glacier east of Pegtop Nunatak, in Victoria Land. Named in 1964 for Lt. (jg) W.F. Frazier, officer-in-charge at Byrd Station in 1963.

**Frazier Islands.** 66°14'S, 110°10'E. Four rocky islands, including Nelly Island, Dewart Island, and Charlton Island, in the eastern part of Vincennes Bay, 8 miles WNW of Clark Peninsula. Named for Cdr. Paul W. Frazier.

**Frazier Point** *see* **Fraser Point**

**Frazier Ridge.** 79°09'S, 86°25'W. On the west side of Webster Glacier, extending north from Founders Escarpment to Minnesota Glacier, in the Heritage Range. Named by the University of Minnesota Geological Party of 1963–64 for Sgt. Herbert J. Frazier, radioman with the 62nd Transportation Detachment who helped the party.

**Frazil ice.** Canadian term for ice-spikes formed in water moving fast enough to prevent the formation of a sheet of ice. Tiny crystals, they become pancake ice in the calm sea.

**Frecker Ridge.** 70°49'S, 166°13'E. On the west side of Kirkby Glacier, in the Anare Mountains of Victoria Land. 5 miles long, it terminates at Mount Gale. Named by the ANARE for Sgt. R. Frecker, RAAF, on the ANARE flights from the *Thala Dan* here in 1962.

**Fred Cirque.** 72°34'S, 0°25'E. On the west side of Roots Heights, in the Sverdrup Mountains of Queen Maud Land. Named by the Norwegians as Fredbotnen for Ernest Fredrick "Fred" Roots.

**Fredbotnen** *see* **Fred Cirque**

**The *Frederick*.** American sealing brig of 147 tons, built at Guilford, Conn., in 1815, and registered by William A. Fanning on Sept. 30, 1818 (Fanning had bought it in New Haven). In 1819–20 it made a successful sealing voyage along the west coast of South America, with Ben Pendleton as captain, and a crew of 21. It was reregistered on May 2, 1820, and was flagship on the Fanning-Pendleton Sealing Expeditions of 1820–21 and 1821–22, both times with Pendleton as skipper.

**Frederick H. Rawson Mountains** *see* **Rawson Mountains**

**Frederick Rocks.** 62°32'S, 60°56'W. A group of rocks in water, in Barclay Bay, off the north coast of Livingston Island, in the South Shetlands. Named in 1958 by the UK for the *Frederick*.

**Fredriksen Island.** 60°44'S, 45°W. 2½ miles long. ½ mile wide. ½ mile SE of Powell Island, in the South Orkneys. Discovered by Palmer and Powell in Dec. 1821. Named by Petter Sørlle in 1912–13. It is part of SPA #15.

**The *Free Gift*.** 2-masted, 52-ton schooner, 56 feet, 7 inches long, built at Pawtucket, R.I., in 1807. It was registered on May 15, 1820, and was one of the vessels on the Fanning-Pendleton Sealing Expeditions of 1820–21 and 1821–22, under the command of Capt. Ben Cutler, and with a crew of 11.

**Freeborn Johnston Glacier** *see* **Johnston Glacier**

**Mount Freed.** 71°29'S, 164°20'E. 2,120 m. Between Champness Glacier and McCann Glacier, in the south part of the Bowers Mountains. Named for Cdr. M.G. Freed, legal officer on the staff of the commander, US Naval Support Force, Antarctica, 1966–68.

¹**Cape Freeman.** 67°20'S, 164°35'E. Forms the north end of Sturge Island, in the Balleny Islands. Named for Capt. H. Freeman.

²**Cape Freeman.** 67°59'S, 65°22'W. Also called Cape Engel. Forms the southern fringe of Seligman Inlet, and the northern fringe of Trail Inlet, on the Larsen Ice Shelf coast of the Antarctic Peninsula. Charted by the FIDS in 1947,

and named by them for R.L. Freeman, FIDS surveyor at Base E.

**Mount Freeman.** 72°43'S, 168°21'E. 2,880 m. Surmounts the base of Walker Ridge, 2 miles NW of Mount Lepanto, in the Victory Mountains of Victoria Land. Named for Lt. Elliot R. Freeman, USNR, helicopter commander in Antarctica in 1968.

**Freeman, Capt. H.** Commander of the *Sabrina* in 1838–39, during Balleny's expedition.

**Freeman, J.D.** Sailmaker on the *Peacock* during the Wilkes Expedition 1838–42. Later joined the *Porpoise* at Columbia River, toward the end of the expedition.

**Freeman Glacier.** 66°10'S, 132°24'E. A channel glacier which flows to the west side of Perry Bay, just east of Freeman Point. Named for J.D. Freeman.

**Freeman Point.** 66°09'S, 132°06'E. Ice-covered. Just west of Freeman Glacier, on the Wilkes Coast. Named for J.D. Freeman.

**Freeth Bay.** 67°44'S, 45°39'E. 5 miles wide. On the coast of Enderby Land. 12 miles west of Spooner Bay, in Alasheyev Bight. Visited by D.F. Styles's ANARE party from the *Thala Dan* in Feb. 1961, and named for Gordon Freeth, Australian minister for the interior.

**Freimanis Glacier.** 72°06'S, 168°15'E. Flows for 25 miles, then into Tucker Glacier between Mount Greene and Novasio Ridge, in the Admiralty Mountains. Named for Harry Freimanis, aurora scientist and scientific leader at Hallett Station in 1962–63.

**Fremouw Peak.** 84°17'S, 164°18'E. 2,550 m. In the SW sector of the Queen Alexandra Range. Forms the south side of the mouth of Prebble Glacier. Named for Edward J. Fremouw, aurora scientist at South Pole Station in 1959.

**French, Theodore.** Ship's cook on the Wilkes Expedition 1838–42. Joined in the USA. Discharged on Aug. 5, 1839.

**French Passage.** 65°10'S, 64°20'W. A marine passage through the Wilhelm Archipelago. Petermann Island, the Stray Islands, the Vedel Islands, and the Myriad Islands are on the north of it. The Argentine Islands, the Anagram Islands, the Roca Islands, and the Cruls Islands are on the south of it. Navigated in 1909 by the *Pourquoi Pas?* under Charcot. Named for the French by the BGLE 1934–37.

**French Polar Expedition.** 1949–53. A 1948–49 expedition, led by André-Franck Liotard had been abandoned because of impassable ice, and in 1949 the *Commandant Charcot* set out from France, skippered by Max Douguet, on an expedition led again by Liotard. They took a motor-launch, a 165 hp Stinson aircraft, dogs, sledges, and Weasels (q.v.). They landed on the coast of Adélie Land on Jan. 20, 1950, and set up Port-Martin Station. 11 men wintered-over in 1950 and 12 expeditions were successfully carried out under intensely difficult conditions, inside 6 months, using dogs and Weasels. The fourth ever colony of emperor penguins was found, at Pointe Géologie. On Jan. 9, 1951, the *Commandant Charcot* returned and replaced Liotard's group with Barré's. Some expeditions were carried out by the 17 men on this wintering party of 1951. On Jan. 23, 1952, fire broke out at Port-Martin, and the station was ruined. On Feb. 2, 1952, the *Tottan* arrived to relieve the expedition. René Garcia was to have led the 1952 wintering party but he returned on the *Tottan,* leaving Mario Marret in charge of Adélie Land that year. Marret had been dropped off with 3 other men at Base Marret (as it is now called) on Pétrel Island, where they constructed a wooden building which is now an historic site (q.v.). Soon thereafter, on its way back to France from Port-Martin, the *Tottan* dropped off another 3 men at Pétrel Island, thus bringing to 7 the number of men in Adélie Land that winter (Port-Martin is also now a historic site). In 1953 the *Tottan* returned and took everyone back to France, and Adélie Land remained deserted until 1956. Other personnel associated with this series of expeditions (collectively called the French Polar Expedition) were Raoul Desprez (the chef), Jean Sapin-Jaloustre (biologist in 1950, relieved by Jean Cendron for 1951 and by Jean Prévost for 1952), François Tabuteau (Cendron's assistant), Bertrand Imbert (seismologist in 1951), Jean Rivolier (doctor in 1952), Fritz Loewe (Australian observer in 1951–52).

**Cape Freshfield.** 68°22'S, 151°05'E. Ice-covered. Between Deakin Bay and the Cook Ice Shelf, on the George V Land coast. At one time in the early 20th century this was thought to be the Cape Hudson (q.v.) discovered by Wilkes in 1840. Mapped by the Far Eastern Party of the AAE 1911–14, and named by Mawson for Douglas Freshfield, once president of the Royal Geographical Society.

**Freshfield Nunatak.** 80°28'S, 24°53' W. In the Shackleton Range.

**Isla Fresia** *see* **Mügge Island**

**Freud Passage** *see* **Pampa Passage**

**Mount Freya.** 77°35'S, 160°51'E. East of Mount Thor, in the Asgard Range of Victoria Land. Named by the New Zealanders in 1958–59 for the Norse goddess.

**Freyberg Mountains.** 72°10'S, 163°45' E. In the area of the Rennick Glacier, in Oates Land. Comprises the Alamein Range, Monte Cassino, Mount Baldwin, and Gallipoli Heights. Named by the New Zealanders in 1963–64 for Lord Bernard Freyberg, the most famous of all the NZ generals.

**Peak of Frezeland** *see* **Mount Friesland**

**Friar Island.** 64°55'S, 63°55'W. Just NE of Manciple Island, in the Wauwermans Islands. Named by the UK in 1958 for the *Canterbury Tales* character.

**Fricker Glacier.** 67°03'S, 65°W. 10 miles long. Just north of Monnier Point, it flows into the SW side of Mill Inlet, on the east coast of Graham Land. Named

by the FIDS in 1947 for Karl Fricker, German Antarctic historian.

**Mount Fridovich.** 85°27'S, 148°12'W. 440 m. At the north side of the terminus of the Leverett Glacier, it marks the western limit of the Harold Byrd Mountains. Named for Lt. (jg) Bernard Fridovich, USN, meteorologist at McMurdo Station in 1957.

**The *Fridtjof*** *see* **The *Frithiof***

**Fridtjof Island.** 64°53'S, 63°22'W. 1½ miles NE of Vazquez Island, off the SE side of Wiencke Island. Discovered by de Gerlache in 1897–99, and named by him, presumably for Fridtjof Nansen, the great Arctic explorer.

**Mount Fridtjof Nansen.** 85°21'S, 167°33'W. Also seen as Mount Nansen (there is another Mount Nansen, though). 4,070 m. Between the heads of the Strom and Axel Heiberg Glaciers, in the Queen Maud Mountains. Discovered by Amundsen in 1911, and first named by him as Olavshøi, and later renamed for the famed Arctic explorer.

**Fridtjof Sound.** 63°34'S, 56°43'W. 6 miles long. 2 miles wide. Separates Andersson Island and Jonassen Island from Tabarin Peninsula, at the NE end of the Antarctic Peninsula. Nordenskjöld discovered it in 1901–4, and named it for the *Fridtjof* (also seen as the *Frithiof*— q.v.).

**Friederichsen Glacier.** 66°38'S, 64°09' W. Also called Bailey Glacier. 7 miles long. Flows into Cabinet Inlet, just north of Mount Hulth, on the east coast of Graham Land. Named by the FIDS for Ludwig Friederichsen (*see* **Mapping**).

**Friedmann Nunataks.** 70°55'S, 65°30'W. 6 miles SE of the Braddock Nunataks, on the west edge of the Dyer Plateau, in Palmer Land. Named for Herbert Friedmann of the Smithsonian Institution, author of the article, "Birds of the United States Antarctic Service Expedition 1939–41," in the *Proceedings of the American Philosophical Society,* Vol. 89–1945.

**Friends, Frederick.** Ordinary seaman on the Wilkes Expedition 1838–42. Joined at Oahu. Served the cruise.

**Friends of the Earth.** An environmental group which, in 1984, began their concerned involvement with the future of Antarctica.

**Mount Fries.** 80°57′S, 156°35′E. 1,985 m. Just south of the mouth of the Zeller Glacier. One of the westernmost summits along the south wall of the Byrd Glacier. Named for Robert H. Fries, aurora scientist at Amundsen-Scott South Pole Station in 1963.

**Mount Friesland.** 62°40′S, 60°12′W. Also called Mount Barnard, Barnard Peak, Peak of Frezeland, Friesland Peak, Friezland Peak. 1,790 m. 3 miles ENE of False Bay, on Livingston Island, in the South Shetlands. In the early 1900s it became Barnard Peak, but later its name reverted to Mount Friesland.

**Friesland Island** *see* **Livingston Island**

**Friesland Peak** *see* **Mount Friesland**

**Friesland Point** *see* **Renier Point**

**Frietus, Isaac.** Ordinary seaman on the Wilkes Expedition of 1838–42. Joined at Madeira in 1838. Discharged March 31, 1840.

**Frietus, Vincent.** 2nd class boy on the Wilkes Expedition 1838–42. Joined at Rio. Run at Valparaiso.

**Frigate Range.** 82°48′S, 162°20′E. Extends east for 12 miles from Mount Markham, in the Queen Elizabeth Range. Named by the New Zealanders in 1961–62 for the NZ frigates in Antarctic waters.

**Frigga Peak.** 66°25′S, 64°W. 1,570 m. On the south side of the Anderson Glacier, on the east coast of Graham Land. Named by the FIDS in 1947 for Frigga, the cloud-spinning goddess in Norse mythology. Clouds formed on this peak earlier than on any other in the area.

**Friis Hills.** 77°45′S, 161°25′E. A cluster of ice-free hills, 6 miles in extent, and reaching a height of 1,750 m. At the north side of the bend in Taylor Glacier, in Victoria Land. Named for Herman R. Friis (1906–1989), director of the Center for Polar Archives, in the National Archives. He was US exchange scientist at Showa Station in 1969–70.

**Friis-Baastad, Kåre.** Capt. A member of the Norwegian air unit during the NBSAE 1949–52.

**Friis-Baastad Peak.** 72°53′S, 3°18′W. Ice-free. At the south side of Frostlendet Valley. 1 mile SE of Mana Mountain, in the Borg Massif of Queen Maud Land. Named by the Norwegians for Capt. Kåre Friis-Baastad.

**Friis-Baastadnuten** *see* **Friis-Baastad Peak**

**Fringe Rocks.** 66°04′S, 65°55′W. Rocks in water which form the western limit of the Saffery Islands, off the west coast of Graham Land. Charted by the BGLE 1934–37. Named by the UK in 1959 for their position on the fringe of the ships' passage between the Saffery Islands and the Trump Islands.

**Mount Frishman.** 71°20′S, 166°56′E. 1,880 m. In the east part of Robinson Heights, in the Admiralty Mountains. Named for Steven A. Frishman, biologist at Hallett Station in 1966–67.

**The *Frithiof*.** (Also seen as *Fridtjof*.) Ship sent down by the Swedes to rescue the lost Nordenskjöld expedition of 1901–4. It reached Snow Hill Island in the 1903–4 season, under the command of Capt. Gyldén, only to discover that the *Uruguay* had already rescued the expedition.

**Cape Fritsche** *see* **Mount Fritsche**

**Mount Fritsche.** 66°S, 62°42′W. Snow-capped. On the coast of eastern Graham Land, on the north side of Richthofen Pass. Wilkins named it on Dec. 20, 1928, as Cape Fritsche, for Carl B. Fritsche of Detroit, Michigan. It was later redefined.

**Fritz, James.** Quarterdeck gunner on the Wilkes Expedition 1838–42. Joined at Rio. Served the cruise.

**Fritzson, Mark.** Seaman on the *Eleanor Bolling* during the first half of Byrd's 1928–30 expedition (i.e., 1928–29).

**Frizzell, George J., Jr.** Crewman on the *Bear of Oakland*, 1933–35.

**Froa** *see* **Couling Island**

**Mount Frödin.** 64°50′S, 62°50′W. On the west coast of Graham Land.

**Frogman Cove.** Unofficial name for a little bay near Vincennes Bay.

**Frölich Peak.** 65°32′S, 63°48′W. 1,035 m. Above Holst Point, at the head of Beascochea Bay, on the west coast of Graham Land. Charted by Charcot in 1908–10. Named by the UK in 1959 for Theodor C.B. Frölich, Norwegian biochemist and vitamin pioneer.

**Frolov Ridge.** 70°45′S, 162°09′E. 11 miles long. Just west of Arruiz Glacier, in the Bowers Mountains. Named by the USSR in 1960–61 for V.V. Frolov, director of the Arctic and Antarctic Scientific Research Institute.

**Front Door Bay.** Unofficial name for a small cove on the west side of Cape Royds, Ross Island. Named by Shackleton's 1907–9 expedition (*see also* **Back Door Bay**).

**Frontier Mountain.** 72°59′S, 160°18′E. 2,805 m. Mainly ice-free. 20 miles SSE of Roberts Butte, in the Outback Nunataks. 11 miles WNW of the Sequence Hills. Named by the New Zealanders in 1962–63 for its location near the edge of the interior ice plateau.

**Frontier Nunataks.** 78°19′S, 88°04′W. An isolated group 20 miles west of the Sentinel Range, in the Ellsworth Mountains. Visited by geologist Thomas Bastien (*see* **Bastien Range**), and named because they are the western outlier of the Ellsworths.

**Mount Frontz.** 85°46′S, 131°46′W. 2,010 m. In the western part of the Wisconsin Range, between Mount Vito and Griffith Peak, on the east side of the Reedy Glacier. Named for Lt. Cdr. Leroy Frontz, aircraft commander in Antarctica in 1966 and 1967.

**Mount Frosch.** 72°46′S, 167°55′E. 2,750 m. Mainly snow-covered. 3 miles NE of Mount Riddolls, at the head of the Borchgrevink Glacier, in the Victory Mountains of Victoria Land. Named for Robert A. Frosch, assistant secretary of the navy for research and development, 1971–72, and administator at NASA in 1978.

**Mount Frost.** 81°12′S, 158°19′E. 2,350 m. In the Churchill Mountains. 4 miles south of Mount Zinkovich, at the south side of the head of Silk Glacier. Named for Lt. Col. Foy B. Frost, commander of the 9th Troop Carrier Squadron, which provided Globemaster airlift support between NZ and Antarctica, and from McMurdo to Byrd, Eights and Amundsen-Scott South Pole Stations in 1962.

**Frost, John.** Bosun on the *Porpoise* during the Wilkes Expedition of 1838–42.

**Frost Cliff.** 75°13′S, 135°43′W. Partly ice-covered. 2 miles east of Mount Steinfeld, on the south side of the divide between the upper reaches of the Hull and Kirkpatrick Glaciers, in Marie Byrd Land. Named for Cdr. William L. Frost, USN, officer-in-charge of Antarctic Support Activities at McMurdo Station in 1970.

**Frost Glacier.** 67°05′S, 129°E. A channel glacier which flows to the head of Porpoise Bay, in East Antarctica. Named for John Frost.

**Frost Rocks.** 65°15′S, 64°20′W. A cluster of rocks SW of the southern Argentine Islands. ½ mile SW of the Whiting Rocks, off the west coast of Graham Land. Named by the UK for Richard Frost, survey assistant of the RN Hydrographic Survey Unit on the *Endurance*, in Feb. 1969.

**Frost Spur.** 82°33′S, 51°59′W. On the north side of the Dufek Massif, between

Lewis Spur and Alley Spur. Named for Charles Frost, National Science Foundation logistics specialist.

**Frostbite.** The freezing of living tissue in any part of the body. It does not always act as expected (*see* **Hare**). The first sign is white patches on the face. If this is noted in one's companion (one should never be out in Antarctica on one's own) it should be dealt with immediately as a medical emergency. This was a major plague to the pioneers, and many of them suffered or died because of it. There were only 3 cases during 1967–68 at McMurdo Station, an example of the greater care taken in recent times.

**Frostlendet Valley.** 72°46′S, 3°18′W. 15 miles long. Ice-filled. On the south side of Høgfonna Mountain, in the Borg Massif of Queen Maud Land. Name means "the frost ground" in Norwegian.

**Frostman Glacier.** 75°08′S, 137°57′W. Flows into the south side of Hull Bay, just west of the Konter Cliffs, on the coast of Marie Byrd Land. Named for Thomas O. Frostman, meteorologist at Plateau Station in 1968.

**Frozen Sea Expedition.** 1982–84. Led by David Lewis, in the *Dick Smith Explorer,* with the intention of spending a winter in the Antarctic. Sydney's Channel 7 TV was a principal supporter, as were Dick Smith and the National Geographic. The sponsor was Lewis's own Oceanic Research Foundation. The main aim was scientific research. Out of the 100 people who volunteered to contribute $3,000 toward the cost of the expedition, Lewis took the following: Mimi George, 31, American anthropologist, photographer, and second-in-command; Gill Cracknell, 24, British geographer and third-in-command—she became the biological projects coordinator; Jannik Schou, 29, a Danish gamekeeper; Jamie Miller, 25, Australian zoologist; Norman Linton-Smith, 57, an engineer/radio operator who signed on at the last moment. Lewis himself was then almost 64, had a stainless-steel hip-joint and a

surgically reattached retina. They left Sydney on Nov. 14, 1982, entered the polar ice pack in late Jan. 1983, after 5,750 miles of sailing. Their first port of call was Davis Station, but before that they had problems in the ice, and had to be pulled out first by the *Polar Star* and then by the *Kapitan Markov.* They finally iced-in deliberately in what they called Winterover Bay, in a cove of Filla Island, in the Rauer Group. On March 4, 1983, the sea froze, and Lewis and George went off on a sledging expedition for 8 days over March–April, 1983. Miller and Linton-Smith found life in Antarctica too difficult and, according to the others, spent most of their time in the base. Ice expeditions followed in May and June 1983, and in early July 1983 Lewis and George went to Davis Station by sledge for fuel, and spent 2 days there. In July–August the four active members of the expedition established depots along the Ingrid Christensen Coast, and in Sept.–Oct. did scientific research there. From Nov. 1983 to Jan. 1984 they did lichen study and plateau reconnaissance trips. Miller was dispatched to Davis Station in mid-Dec. 1983 for insubordination, and thence back to Sydney. On Jan. 26, 1984, the ship sailed out of Filla Island, and after a stop at Davis Station arrived back in Sydney on March 11, 1984.

**Frustration Dome.** 68°S, 64°33′E. A large, crevassed ice-dome. 38 miles SE of Mount Henderson, in Mac. Robertson Land. Named by the Australians because of the frustration experienced here by an ANARE survey party in 1967, due to the weather.

**Frustration Ridge.** 82°12′S, 158°38′E. Forms the northern end of the Cobham Range, in the Churchill Mountains. Named by the New Zealanders in 1964–65 who experienced frustration in climbing it, even though it looked easy.

**Mount Frustum.** 73°22′S, 162°57′E. Also seen spelled (erroneously) as Mount Frustrum. 3,100 m. A pyramidal table mountain, between Mount Fazio and

Scarab Peak, in the south part of the Tobin Mesa, in northern Victoria Land. Named by the New Zealanders in 1962–63 for its frustumlike shape.

**Fry Glacier.** 76°38′S, 162°18′E. Flows from the Convoy Range along the south end of the Kirkwood Range, just to the north of the Mackay Glacier, into Tripp Bay, in Victoria Land. Named by Shackleton in 1907–9 for A.M. Fry, a patron.

**Fry Peak.** 71°03′S, 63°40′W. The most southerly peak in the Welch Mountains of Palmer Land. Named for Lt. Frederick M. Fry, USN, flight surgeon and VX-6 pararescue officer in 1969 and 1970.

**Fry Saddle.** 76°34′S, 161°05′E. An ice saddle at the head of the Fry Glacier. 4 miles WSW of Mount Douglas in Victoria Land. Discovered in 1957 by the NZ Northern Survey Party of the BCTAE, and named by them in association with Fry Glacier.

**Fry Strait** *see* **Fyr Channel**

**Lake Fryxell.** 77°35′S, 163°10′E. 3 miles long. Between the Canada and Commonwealth Glaciers, at the lower end of the Taylor Valley, in southern Victoria Land. Mapped during Scott's 1910–13 expedition. Visited by Troy L. Péwé in 1957–58, and named by him for Dr. Fritiof M. Fryxell, glacial geologist of Augustana College, Illinois.

**Fuchs, Sir Vivian.** British geologist, son of a German farmer who had come to Britain. b. Feb. 1908. "Bunny" Fuchs, as he was known, was geologist and base leader at Base E in 1948, as well as being FIDS leader that winter. He was FIDS leader from 1949–53, and during that time he conceived the idea of a transantarctic traverse. In the mid-1950s he got his BCTAE (British Commonwealth Transantarctic Expedition) together, and in 1957–58 became the first man to cross Antarctica by land. On the completion of his traverse, while at McMurdo Station, he was knighted by telegram. He conducted many expeditions worldwide.

**Fuchs Dome.** 80°35′S, 27°50′W. Over 1,525 m. An ice-covered dome between the Stratton and Gordon Glaciers, in the central portion of the Shackleton Range. Mapped in 1957 by the BCTAE and named for Vivian Fuchs.

**Fuchs Ice Piedmont.** 67°10′S, 68°40′W. 70 miles long. Extends along the entire west coast of Adelaide Island. Mapped in 1909 by Charcot. Named by the FIDS for Vivian Fuchs.

**Mount Fučík.** 71°52′S, 14°26′E. 2,305 m. The central peak of Kvaevefjellet Mountain, in the Payer Mountains of Queen Maud Land. Discovered by Ritscher in 1938–39. The USSR named it in 1963 for Julins Fučík (1903–1943), Czech journalist and author.

**Fuente Island** *see* **Fuente Rock**

**Fuente Rock.** 62°30′S, 59°39′W. Almost ½ mile NE of Ferrer Point, in Discovery Bay, Greenwich Island, in the South Shetlands. The Chileans named it Islote de la Fuente in 1951, and this became Fuente Island in later years in English. It was later redefined as a rock.

**Punta Fuenzalida** *see* **Borge Point**

**Fuglefjellet.** 72°17′S, 0°46′E. 7 miles east of Mount Roer, in the Sverdrup Mountains of Queen Maud Land. Name means "the bird mountain" in Norwegian.

**The *Fuji*.** Japanese icebreaker, the first modern icebreaker produced by that country. It replaced the *Soya* as the relieving ship for Showa Station. Commissioned in June 1965, its first Antarctic trip was for the 1965–66 season. 7,760 tons displacement, 27 foot draft, 330 feet long, 73 foot beam. It had diesel electric engines which gave 12,000 hp maximum, 15 knots cruising speed, and a maximum speed of 17 knots. It could break ice up to 19 feet thick. It made its last Antarctic trip in 1983, and was replaced by the *Shirase*.

**Fukuro Cove.** 69°12′S, 39°39′E. Also spelled Hukuro Cove. 1 mile SW of Mount Choto, it indents the Langhovde

Hills, on the coast of Queen Maud Land. Named Fukuro-ura (pouch cove) by the Japanese in 1972.

**Mount Fukushima.** 71°21'S, 35°40'E. 2,470 m. The highest massif in the Queen Fabiola Mountains. Just north of the Yamato Glacier. 1,600 meters above the surrounding ice surface. Has many ragged peaks. Discovered in 1960 by the Belgian Antarctic Expedition led by Guido Derom, and named by him for Shin Fukushima (*see* **Deaths, 1960**), geophysicist on the Japanese Antarctic Research Expedition of 1960–61.

**Fulgham Ridge.** 84°54'S, 177°24'E. Ice-free. 4 miles long. Forms the SE side of Bowin Glacier, in the Queen Maud Mountains. Named for aviation bosun's mate Donald R. Fulgham, USN, Antarctic Support Activity, at McMurdo Station in 1964.

**Fullastern Rock.** 67°37'S, 69°26'W. An isolated, submerged rock in the middle of Johnston Passage, 7 miles WNW of Cape Adriasola, Adelaide Island. A danger to shipping, it compelled the *John Biscoe* to go full astern to avoid it.

**Fuller Dome.** 86°38'S, 156°18'W. 2,850 m. A dome-shaped, ice-covered mountain at the NW end of the Rawson Mountains, in the Queen Maud Mountains. Named for C.E. Fuller, VX-6 storekeeper in 1966 and 1967.

**Fuller Island.** 66°12'S, 101°E. Also called Ostrov Kashalot (by the USSR). 4 miles long. 1½ miles wide. 2 miles south of Thomas Island, in the Highjump Archipelago, on the south side of Cacapon Inlet. Named for H.F. Fuller, who worked on Bunger's plane in Feb. 1947, during Operation Highjump.

**Fuller Rock.** 68°10'S, 68°54'W. In Marguerite Bay, off the west coast of Graham Land.

**Fulmar Bay.** 60°37'S, 46°01'W. 1 mile wide. Between Moreton Point and Return Point, at the west end of Coronation Island, in the South Orkneys. Discovered by Powell and Palmer in Dec. 1821.

Named by the UK in 1954 for the Antarctic fulmars here.

**Fulmar Crags.** 60°38'S, 45°11'W. They surmount East Cape, the NE extremity of Coronation Island, in the South Orkneys. The FIDS surveyed them in 1956–58, and the UK named them for the Antarctic fulmars which breed here.

**Fulmar Island.** 66°33'S, 93°E. Just south of Zykov Island, in the Haswell Islands. Discovered by the Western Base Party of the AAE 1911–14, and they plotted Fulmar Island and Zykov Island as one island, and called it Fulmar Island, for the rookery of southern fulmars here. The USSR redefined this area in 1956.

**Fulmars.** The fulmar is a type of petrel. There are several varieties seen in Antarctica: The silver-gray fulmar *(Fulmarus glacialoides);* the southern giant fulmar *(Macronectes giganteus);* the Northern giant fulmar *(Macronectes halli);* the Antarctic petrel *(Thassaloica antarctica);* the snow petrel *(Pagodroma nivea),* and the pintado petrel, or cape pigeon *(Daption capensis),* all of which, except the northern giant fulmar (which breeds in lower latitudes), breed on the Antarctic continent. Scavengers, fulmars feed mostly on plankton, fish, penguins, and other birds.

**Mount Fulton.** 76°53'S, 144°54'W. 900 m. Between Mount Passell and Mount Gilmour, in the Denfeld Mountains of the Ford Ranges, in Marie Byrd Land. Named by Byrd in 1939–41 for Arthur Fulton, who helped get insurance for the *Jacob Ruppert,* one of the ships used during Byrd's 1933–35 expedition.

**Fumarole Bay** *see* **Primero de Mayo Bay**

**Fumaroles** *see* **Ice fumaroles**

**The *Fumi Maru No. 18.*** Japanese krill-fishing boat of the 1980s, seen in Antarctica.

**Fungi** *see* **Flora, Molds, Yeast, Bacteria**

**Funk Glacier.** 65°34'S, 63°46'W. Flows into Beascochea Bay to the south of

Frölich Peak, on the west coast of Graham Land. Charted by Charcot in 1908–10. Named by the UK in 1959 for Casimir Funk, pioneer in vitamins.

**Fur seals.** *Arctocephalus gazella.* These are the southern fur seals, which are Otariids, not true seals (those are Phocids), and the only Otariids to breed in the Antarctic. They grow to 4–6 feet long, on average. By the 1870s they had been virtually wiped out (*see* **Sealing**), then a few were seen again, and then they were—as far as the world was concerned—exterminated totally, an extinct species. In the 1920s, however, some were seen again, obviously having hidden from human predators. They are now growing in numbers, but regeneration is slow. There are now about 30,000, which is still dangerously few.

**Furdesanden Moraine.** 71°48′S, 9°37′E. Extends 17 miles on the west side of the Conrad Mountains, in the Orvin Mountains of Queen Maud Land. Discovered by Ritscher in 1938–39. Name means "the furrow of sand" in Norwegian.

**Furman, Robert.** Ordinary seaman on the Wilkes Expedition 1838–42. Joined in the USA. Discharged at Oahu on Oct. 31, 1840.

**Furman Bluffs.** 74°06′S, 113°53′W. A line of steep ice bluffs which form the SE side of Philbin Inlet, on Martin Peninsula, on the coast of Marie Byrd Land. Named for Master Chief Quartermaster James L. Furman, USN, staff assistant with Task Force 43 in 1964–67.

**Furneaux, Tobias.** b. 1735, Stoke Damerel, near Plymouth, Devon. d. Sept. 18, 1781, Swiley, Devon. Entered the Royal Navy at 20, and went around the world with Wallis in 1766–68. He was a lieutenant, and commander of the *Adventure,* during Cook's 1772–75 voyage.

**Furness Glacier.** 61°07′S, 54°52′W. Flows between Cape Belsham and Point Wild, to the north coast of Elephant

Island, in the South Shetlands. Charted and named by Shackleton's 1914–17 expedition.

**Islotes Furque** *see* **Wideopen Islands**

**Fusco Nunatak.** 80°02′S, 80°09′W. The most westerly of the Wilson Nunataks, just west of Hercules Inlet, at the SE end of the Heritage Range. Named for aviation electrician Thomas A. Fusco, USN, air crewman on the first flight from McMurdo Station to Plateau Station on Dec. 13, 1965.

**Mount Futago.** 69°12′S, 39°44′E. Also spelled Mount Hutago. Has two peaks, the northern one being 240 m., and the southern one being 245 m. In the northern part of the Langhovde Hills of Queen Maud Land. Named Futago-yama (twin mountain) by the Japanese in 1972.

**Mount Fyfe.** 82°32′S, 155°10′E. 2,260 m. 3 miles north of Quest Cliffs, in the Geologists Range of Victoria Land. Named by the New Zealanders in 1961–62 for H.E. Fyfe, chief geologist of the NZ Geological Survey.

**Fyfe Hills.** 67°22′S, 49°12′E. A group of low coastal hills south of Dingle Dome, and just east of the Hydrographer Islands, at the head of Casey Bay, in Enderby Land. Discovered by Bruce Stinear's ANARE party of Oct. 1957. Named by the Australians for W.V. Fyfe, surveyor-general of Western Australia.

**The** *Fyr.* Steam whaler owned by the Corral Whaling Co., of Bergen, Norway. In 1912–13 it was operating in the South Orkneys with its sister whaler, the *Corral,* both out of their factory ship, the *Tioga.*

**Fyr Channel.** 60°44′S, 45°41′W. Also called Fyr Strait, and also seen spelled (erroneously) as Fry Strait. 350 yards wide. A marine channel between the SW end of Signy Island and Moe Island, in the South Orkneys. Named Fyr Strait in 1912 by Petter Sørlle, and redefined in 1913 by Hans Borge. It is smaller than a strait. Named for the *Fyr.*

**Fyr Strait** *see* **Fyr Channel**

Gabbro Crest. 83°23'S, 50°22'W. At the northern end of the Pensacola Mountains.

Gabbro Hills. 84°42'S, 173°W. They border the Ross Ice Shelf between the Barrett and Gough Glaciers, and extend south to Ropebrake Pass. Named by the New Zealanders in 1963–64 for the gabbro (a dark, plutonic rock) here.

Mount Gaberlein. 75°04'S, 162°04'E. 1,210 m. 3½ miles NNW of Mount Bellingshausen, in the Prince Albert Mountains of Victoria Land. Named for William E. Gaberlein, USN, chief construction electrician at McMurdo Station in 1962 and 1964.

Gablenz Range. 72°S, 4°30'E. 13 miles long. Includes Skigarden Ridge and Mount Grytøyr. Between the north part of the Preuschoff Range and the Luz Range, in the Mühlig-Hofmann Mountains of Queen Maud Land. Discovered by Ritscher in 1938–39, and named by him for the director of the Lufthansa Corporation.

Gabriel González Videla Station  see Presidente Gabriel González Videla Station

Gabriel Peak. 65°36'S, 62°39'W. 1,220 m. At the confluence of the Starbuck and Jeroboam Glaciers, on the east side of Graham Land. Named by the UK for the *Moby Dick* character.

Lake Gadarene. 71°24'S, 67°35'W. A meltwater lake, 1 mile long, in the George VI Ice Shelf in George VI Sound. Below Swine Hill. Surveyed by the FIDS in 1948. When their dogs saw the water they tried to plunge down the steep ice slopes into it (Biblical reference to the Gadarene swine).

Gadarene Ridge. 76°44'S, 159°33'E. Extends southward from Ship Cone in the Allan Hills of Victoria Land. Named by the NZ Allan Hills Expedition of 1964 for the swine-backed profile of the ridge (*see also* Lake Gadarene).

Gadsden Peaks. 71°38'S, 167°24'E. 2,500 m. 5 miles long. 5 miles WSW of

Lange Peak of the Lyttelton Range, in the Admiralty Mountains. Named for Michael Gadsden, radioscience researcher at McMurdo Station in 1965–66 and 1967–68.

Gagarin Mountains. 71°57'S, 9°23'E. Also called Kurzefjella (not to be confused with the Kurze Mountains). 10 miles long. Between the Kurze Mountains and the Conrad Mountains, in the Orvin Mountains of Queen Maud Land. Named by the USSR for the first man in space, Yuriy Gagarin.

Cape Gage. 64°10'S, 57°05'W. Forms the eastern extremity of James Ross Island, and the west side of the north entrance to Admiralty Sound. Discovered by Ross in 1839–43, and named by him for Vice-Adm. William Hall Gage, lord commissioner of the admiralty.

Gage, H.V. Crew member on the *Discovery* during the BANZARE 1929–31.

Gage Ridge. 66°54'S, 51°16'E. 7 miles long. Partly snow-covered. 2½ miles west of Mount Selwood in the Tula Mountains of Enderby Land. Named by the Australians for H.V. Gage.

Gagge Point. 66°20'S, 66°54'W. The southern extremity of Lavoisier Island, in the Biscoe Islands. Named by the UK for Adolph P. Gagge, US physiologist specializing in the cold.

Gaillard, Jean-Edmond. An élève on the *Zélée* during Dumont d'Urville's 1837–40 expedition. Promoted to ensign on March 6, 1839. Left sick at Bourbon (now known as Réunion), in the Indian Ocean, on July 2, 1840. He died there in 1842.

Gain, Louis. Zoologist/botanist of the *Pourquoi Pas?* with Charcot, 1908–10. Later became the director of the French National Meteorological Office.

Gain Glacier. 71°01'S, 61°25'W. On the east coast of Palmer Land. It flows from Cat Ridge into the Weddell Sea, between Imshaug Peninsula and Morency Island. Named for Louis Gain.

Gair Glacier. 73°03'S, 166°32'E. 10 miles long. Flows from just SE of Mount

Supernal, in the Mountaineer Range of Victoria Land, into Mariner Glacier just north of Bunker Bluff. Named by the NZGSAE 1962–63 for H.S. Gair, geologist and leader that year of the NZGSAE Northern Party.

**Gair Mesa.** 73°28'S, 162°52'E. Also called Gair Tableland. The most southerly of the Mesa Range, in Victoria Land. Named by the Northern Party of the NZGSAE 1962–63 for their leader, H.S. Gair (*see* **Gair Glacier**).

**Gair Tableland** *see* **Gair Mesa**

**Galan Ridge.** 73°10'S, 62°W. Forms the NE rampart of the Dana Mountains, in Palmer Land. Named for Michael P. Galan, at McMurdo Station in 1967, and a member of the South Pole–Queen Maud Land Traverse III (1967–68).

**Galatos Peak.** 71°58'S, 163°43'E. 2,045 m. Marks the NW extremity of the Salamander Range, in the Freyberg Mountains. Named by the New Zealanders in 1963–64 for the Greek village associated with New Zealand general Lord Freyberg in World War II.

**Mount Gale.** 70°46'S, 166°11'E. A promontory at the northern end of Frecker Ridge, in the Anare Mountains of Victoria Land. At the south side of the confluence of the Ludvig and Kirkby Glaciers. Named by the Australians for d'A.T. Gale, hydrographic surveyor with the ANARE here in 1962 (*see also* **Gale Escarpment**).

**Gale Escarpment.** 72°55'S, 75°23'E. East of Mount Harding and Wilson Ridge, in the Grove Mountains. Named by the Australians for d'A.T. Gale, officer-in-charge of the Antarctic Mapping Branch, Australian Division of National Mapping (*see also* **Mount Gale**).

**Gale Ridge.** 83°41'S, 56°27'W. 12 miles long. Extends NW from Mount Dover, in the Neptune Range. Named for Phillip E. Gale, Australian meteorologist at Ellsworth Station in 1962.

**Galen Peak.** 64°22'S, 62°26'W. 3 miles west of Buls Bay, at the south side of the Hippocrates Glacier, in the south part of Brabant Island. Mapped by de Gerlache in 1897–99. Named by the UK for the Roman doctor.

**Gales** *see* **Winds**

**Galileo Cliffs.** 70°46'S, 68°45'W. 5 miles long. Between the Grotto and Jupiter Glaciers, 7 miles west of Ablation Point, in the eastern part of Alexander Island. Named by the UK for the Italian astronomer.

**Galíndez, Ismael F.** Argentine Naval commander, leader of the expedition to Laurie Island in the South Orkneys, on the *Uruguay* in 1904–5. This was the expedition which took over Omond House from Bruce when the Scotsman left in that season, and Galíndez set about the reconstruction and expansion of the station into Orcadas Station. Also that season he led a search party on the *Uruguay* to find the lost Charcot (q.v.), when that Frenchman's expedition was feared lost.

**Galíndez Island.** 65°15'S, 64°15'W. ½ mile long. Just east of Winter Island, in the Argentine Islands of the Wilhelm Archipelago, off the west coast of Graham Land. Discovered by Charcot in 1903–5, and named by him for Ismael F. Galíndez. Faraday Sation is here.

**Galkin Nunatak.** 73°27'S, 65°55'W. Isolated. 35 miles NW of Mount Coman, surmounting the interior ice plateau, near the base of Palmer Land. Named for William L. Galkin, meteorologist at Byrd Station in 1965–66.

**Mount Galla.** 75°56'S, 125°52'W. 2,520 m. Snow-capped. 31 miles east of Mount Petras, on the Usas Escarpment of Marie Byrd Land. Named for Lt. Edward J. Galla.

**Galla, Edward J.** Lt., USN. Medical officer and officer-in-charge at Byrd Station for the winter of 1959, taking over from Lt. Peter Ruseski.

**Gallagher, Fergus.** A cooper on the Wilkes Expedition 1838–42. Joined in the USA. Returned on the *Relief* in 1839.

**Gallaher Peak.** 85°27'S, 138°18'W. 1,005 m. In the Berry Peaks. Between the SE edge of the Ross Ice Shelf and the Watson Escarpment. Named for James T. Gallaher, electrician at Byrd Station in 1958.

**Gallen Nunatak.** 75°48'S, 128°36'W. On the south side of Balchunas Pass. 1½ miles NW of Putzke Peak, in the McCuddin Mountains of Marie Byrd Land. Named for Lt. (jg) Kevin P. Gallen, USN, officer-in-charge of Amundsen-Scott South Pole Station in 1971.

**Gallipoli Heights.** 72°26'S, 163°48'E. A group of peaks and ridges, 7 miles SE of Monte Cassino, in the Freyberg Mountains of Oates Land. Named in association with Lord Freyberg, NZ World War I general, by the New Zealanders in 1963–64.

**Gallows Point.** 64°20'S, 62°59'W. The northern of two low, parallel points which mark the NE extremity of Gamma Island, in the Melchior Islands. Named by the personnel on the *Discovery* in 1927.

**Gallup Glacier.** 85°09'S, 177°54'W. 12 miles long. Flows between Mounts Rosenwald and Black into the Shackleton Glacier, just north of Matador Mountain. Named for Cdr. F.S. Gallup, Jr., USN, VX-6 commander in 1964–65.

**Galtefjellet.** 68°16'S, 58°34'E. The SE of two rock outliers on the south side of Purka Mountain, in the Hansen Mountains. Photographed by the LCE 1936–37, and named by the Norwegians (it means "boar mountain").

**Galten Islands.** 66°23'S, 56°25'E. A small group in the east part of Magnet Bay, 10 miles west of Cape Davis. Photographed by the LCE 1936–37, and called Galten (the boar) by the Norwegians. Bruce Stinear led an ANARE party here in 1957.

**Galyshev Nunatak.** 71°36'S, 12°28'E. At the SW foot of Store Svarthorn Peak in the Mittlere Petermann Range of the Wohlthat Mountains, in Queen Maud Land. Discovered by Ritscher in 1938–39.

Named by the USSR in 1966 for pilot V.L. Galyshev.

**Gam Point.** 61°55'S, 58°W. 2 miles SE of False Round Point on the north coast of King George Island, in the South Shetlands. Originally it was part of what David Ferguson called Pyrites Island (q.v.). Named by the UK in 1960. A "gam" is an informal visit between gangs of whalers or sealers.

**Gamage Point.** 66°46'30"S, 64°03'18" W. Marks the north side of the entrance to Hero Inlet, on the SW side of Anvers Island. Palmer Station is on this point. Named for the Harvey F. Gamage Shipyard in South Bristol, Maine, which built the *Hero,* Palmer Station's supply ship.

**Gamaleya Rock.** 71°44'S, 10°43'E. 2 miles SE of Smirnov Peak, in the Orvin Mountains of Queen Maud Land. Named by the USSR in 1966 for navigation scientist P. Yaroslav Gamaleya.

**Gambacorta Peak.** 84°02'S, 56°03'W. 1,840 m. 4 miles east of Mount Kaschak, in the southern part of the Neptune Range. Named for Capt. Francis M. Gambacorta, captain of the *Wyandot,* 1956–57.

**Gambone Peak.** 71°45'S, 164°14'E. 1,620 m. 7 miles SW of Coronet Peak, at the junction of Leap Year Glacier and Black Glacier, in the Bowers Mountains. Named for Lt. (jg) J.C. Gambone, operations administrative assistant on the staff of the commander, US Naval Support Force, Antarctica, 1967 and 1968.

**Gamburtsev Mountains.** 81°S, 76°E. Also called Gamburtsev Subglacial Mountains. Buried mountains, beneath the South Pole area and the American Highland area, extending north-south. Discovered by the USSR in 1958 using seismics, and mapped by them with seismic reflections through the East Antarctic Ice Sheet. Named by the USSR for Grigoriy A. Gamburtsev (1903–1955), geophysicist.

**Gamma Hill.** 63°34'S, 56°47'W. 300 m. Ice-covered. On Tabarin Peninsula. On the west shore of Fridtjof Sound. The

FIDS did much geophysical (G = gamma in Greek alphabet) work here in 1959-60.

**Gamma Island.** 64° 20′ S, 63° W. Also called Isla Observatorio. 1 mile long. Marks the SW extremity of the Melchior Islands. Charcot discovered it in 1903-5, and named it Île Gouts. The personnel on the *Discovery* in 1927 renamed it for the Greek letter. Melchior Station was built here.

**Gand Island.** 64° 24′ S, 62° 51′ W. 3 miles long. 1½ miles wide. Flat and ice-covered. At the north end of the Schollaert Channel, between Anvers Island and Brabant Island. Discovered by de Gerlache in 1897-99, and named by him for Gand (Ghent) in Belgium, where subscription drives were held to help finance the *Belgica* expedition.

**Gandalf Ridge.** 78° 20′ S, 164° 08′ E. An unofficial name for a part of the McMurdo Volcanics, in southern Victoria Land.

**Gándara Bofil, Comodoro Jorge.** Captain of the *Covadonga* during the Chilean Antarctic Expedition of 1947-48. In 1954-55 he was leader of the Chilean Antarctic Expedition of that year, and his ships were: the *Covadonga*, the *Maipo*, the *Leucotón*, and the *Lautaro*.

**Gándara Island.** 63° 19′ S, 57° 56′ W. Just SW of Kopaitic Island, in the Duroch Islands. Named by the Chileans in 1959 for Comodoro Jorge Gándara Bofil (see above).

**Gangbrekka Pass.** 72° 15′ S, 0° 20′ W. Between Jutulrøra Mountain and Brekkerista Ridge, in the Sverdrup Mountains of Queen Maud Land. Name means "the passage slope" in Norwegian.

**Gannon Nunataks.** 70° 43′ S, 69° 28′ W. On the NE coast of Alexander Island.

**Gannutz Glacier.** 70° 24′ S, 162° 11′ E. Flows from the Bowers Mountains into the eastern part of Rennick Bay, between Weeder Rock and the Stuhlinger Ice Piedmont. Named for Theodore P. Gan-

nutz, biologist at Hallett Station in 1966-67, and scientific leader at Palmer Station in 1968.

**GANOVEX IV.** West German geological and geophysical expedition to northern Victoria Land in the summer of 1984-85. Two Dornier aircraft supported this German Antarctic Northern Victoria Land Expedition, and one of them was shot down over Western Sahara while flying back to West Germany.

**GANOVEX 79.** West German Antarctic Northern Victoria Land Expedition. 1979-80. The *Schepelsturm* left NZ for Cape Adare, and studies of the Robertson Bay area began on Dec. 12, 1979. Sedimentology was the main study. Two Hughes 500-D helicopters and a 558 Sikorsky helicopter were used. The last field camp was evacuated on Feb. 20, 1980, and the ship returned to New Zealand.

**GANOVEX III.** West German Antarctic Northern Victoria Land Expedition. 1982-83. Geological expedition to northern Victoria Land, taken down by the *Polar Queen*, with 4 Hughes 500-D helicopters for air support.

**GANOVEX II.** West German Antarctic Northern Victoria Land Expedition. 1981-82. This was the follow up to *Ganovex 79* (see above). When the expedition ship, the *Gotland II* sank in Yule Bay on Dec. 18, 1981, the expedition was called off.

**Gansevoort, Henry.** Passed midshipman on the *Peacock* during the Wilkes Expedition of 1838-42. Detached at Callao, in 1839.

**Ganymede Heights.** 70° 52′ S, 68° 26′ W. 600 m. Between Jupiter Glacier and Ablation Valley, on the east side of Alexander Island. Named by the UK for one of the planet Jupiter's satellites.

[1]**The Gap** *see* **The Gateway**

[2]**The Gap.** 77° 50′ S, 166° 42′ E. The gap separating Cape Armitage, Observation Hill, McMurdo Station, Pram Point, Scott Base, and Hut Point from the rest of

Hut Point Peninsula, on Ross Island. It runs two miles from Hut Point to Scott Base, and one can cross the peninsula at a relatively low level here. Discovered and named by Scott in 1902.

**Gap Nunatak.** 67°54′S, 62°29′E. 1,030 m. In the center of Hordern Gap, in the David Range of the Framnes Mountains of Mac. Robertson Land. Photographed by the LCE 1936–37, and named Metoppen (the middle peak) by the Norwegians. Renamed by the ANARE for its location in Hordern Gap.

**GAP Project.** GAP stood for Glaciology of the Antarctic Peninsula. It was a British effort in the 1980s to derive a 1,000-year climatic record for the peninsula from evidence of impurities in ice-cores.

**Mount Gara** *see* **Mount Cara**

**Mount Garan.** 67°32′S, 98°55′E. Marked by a cluster of small peaks. 9 miles SW of Mount Strathcona, near the head of Denman Glacier. Named for E.M. Garan, aerial photographer on Operation Highjump, 1946–47.

**Cap García** *see* **Loqui Point**

**Cape García.** 65°44′S, 64°40′W. At the north side of the entrance to Barilari Bay, on the west coast of Graham Land. Discovered and named Cap Loqui by Charcot in 1903–5. He named the south side of the entrance to Barilari Bay as Cap García, for Rear-Adm. García, of the Argentine navy. Charcot's 1908–10 maps show Cap García as the northern feature, and that situation remains today. On those 1908–10 maps he did not use the name Cap Loqui at all, but since then the southern feature has been named Loqui Point (q.v.).

**Mont Garcia** *see* **Mount Zdarsky**

**Garcia, René.** French scientific leader who was due to relieve Barré when the *Tottan* landed at Adélie Land on Feb. 2, 1952. However, the fire at Port-Martin prevented this (*see* **French Polar Expedition**). Later, in 1958, Garcia relieved Jacques Dubois as leader of Charcot Station.

**Garcia Point.** 85°14′S, 170°16′W. Forms the south side of the terminus of DeGanahl Glacier, where that glacier enters Liv Glacier, in the Queen Maud Mountains. Named by the USA for Leopoldo Garcia, meteorologist at Amundsen-Scott South Pole Station in 1965.

**Garcie Peaks.** 69°32′S, 66°48′W. Three small peaks, the highest being 960 m. 5 miles SE of Mount Leo, on the south side of the Fleming Glacier, in the west central part of the Antarctic Peninsula. Named by the UK for Pierre Garcie, pioneer French navigator.

**Garczynski Nunatak.** 85°24′S, 124°48′W. Cone-shaped. The highest in a cluster of nunataks just west of Mount Brecher, on the north flank of the Quonset Glacier, in the Wisconsin Range. Named for Carl J. Garczynski, meteorologist at Byrd Station in 1961.

**Garde Islands.** 65°51′S, 66°22′W. A small group, 5 miles WNW of Lively Point, off the SW side of Renaud Island, in the Biscoe Islands. Named by the UK in 1959 for Vilhelm Garde (1859–1926), Danish oceanographer who began sea-ice reporting in the Arctic in 1899.

**Garden Spur.** 84°33′S, 174°45′W. On the west side of the Longhorn Spurs, 3 miles south of Cape Surprise. Named by the New Zealanders in 1963–64 because of the mosses, algae, and lichens here.

**Gardening.** The only place in Antarctica where this activity is usually possible is the Antarctic Peninsula, sometimes referred to as "The Banana Belt" because of its warmer temperatures during the summer (sometimes as high as 59°F). Then it was only likely as a hobby after bases had been built. For example, Base E, on Stonington Island, in 1946, built a greenhouse to grow flowers and vegetables hydroponically. There is quite a flourishing greenhouse at Arctowski Station.

**Mount Gardiner.** 86°19′S, 150°57′W. 2,480 m. A ridgelike, granitic mountain, 3 miles east of Mount Ruth, at the point in the Queen Maud Mountains where Bartlett Glacier runs into Robert Scott Glacier. Discovered in Dec. 1934 by Quin Blackburn's party during Byrd's 1933–35 expedition. Named by Byrd for Joseph T. Gardiner of Wellington, NZ, agent for Byrd's first two Antarctic expeditions.

**Gardiner, Capt.** Commander of the *Alliance*, 1823–24.

**Gardiner Glacier.** 86°01′S, 131°48′W. On the south side of the Quartz Hills, flowing from the Watson Escarpment into Reedy Glacier. Named for Richard D. Gardiner, construction electrician at Byrd Station in 1962.

**Gardiner Ridge.** 75°39′S, 132°26′W. Extends from Mount Kauffman to Mount Kosciusko, in the Ames Range of Marie Byrd Land. Named for James E. Gardiner, USN, construction driver and member of Merle Dawson's Army-Navy Trail Party which established Byrd Station in 1956–57.

**Mount Gardner.** 78°23′S, 86°02′W. 4,685 m. 1½ miles west of Mount Tyree, in the west central part of the Sentinel Range. Discovered by Charles Bentley during the Marie Byrd Land Traverse Party of 1957–58. Named for Lt. Harvey E. Gardner, USN, pilot in Antarctica in 1957–58 and 1958–59 (*see* **Deaths, 1959**). First climbed on Dec. 31, 1966, by Brian Marts and John Evans.

**Gardner, John A.** Ordinary seaman on the Wilkes Expedition 1838–42. Joined at Callao. Run at Oahu.

**Gardner Bay** *see* **Gardner Inlet**

**Gardner Glacier** *see* **Ketchum Glacier**

**Gardner Inlet.** 74°58′S, 62°52′W. Also called Gardner Bay, American Geographical Society Bay. Ice-filled. The extreme northern point of the Ronne Ice Shelf, at the foot of Mount Austin. Discovered by the RARE 1947–48, and named by Ronne for Irvine C. Gardner, physicist at the National Bureau of Standards, and pioneer in aerial photog-

raphy. He helped get the RARE off the ground.

**Gardner Island.** 68°35′S, 77°52′E. ¾ mile long. 2 miles west of Heidemann Bay, off Breidnes Peninsula, in the Vestfold Hills. Photographed by the LCE 1936–37, and named Breidneskollen (the broad point knoll) by the Norwegians. Renamed by the Australians for Lionel G. Gardner, diesel mechanic at nearby Davis Station in 1958.

**Gardner Ridge.** 86°57′S, 148°24′W. Ice-free. 4 miles SE of the Davis Hills, at the south side of the Klein Glacier, in the Queen Maud Mountains. Named for Eric T. Gardner, of VX-6, photographer here in 1966 and 1967.

**Gårekneet Ridge.** 72°04′S, 14°48′E. 3 miles south of Gårenevkalven Nunatak, in the Payer Mountains of Queen Maud Land. Named by the Norwegians as Gårekneet.

**Gårenevkalven Nunatak.** 72°S, 14°47′ E. 2,250 m. 3 miles north of Gårekneet Ridge, in the eastern part of the Payer Mountains of Queen Maud Land. Named by the Norwegians.

**Garfield Glacier.** 74°57′S, 136°35′W. 6 miles long. Flows between the Peden Cliffs and Cox Point to the east side of Hull Bay, on the Marie Byrd Land coast. Named for Donald E. Garfield, deepcore driller at Byrd Station in 1967–68.

**Gargan, Philip.** Crewman on the *Jacob Ruppert*, 1933–35.

**Gargoyle Ridge.** 82°24′S, 159°30′E. Forms the south end of the Cobham Range, in the Churchill Mountains. Named by the New Zealanders in 1964–65 because of the gargoyle-shaped buttresses on top of the ridge.

**Garland Hershey Ridge** *see* **Hershey Ridge**

**Garner, C.J.** Crewman on the *Bear of Oakland*, 1934–35.

**Garnerin Point.** 64°41′S, 62°10′W. Also called Punta Z. Juts out into Wilhelmina Bay, SE of Pelseneer Island, on the west coast of Graham Land. Charted by de Gerlache in 1897–99. Named by the UK in 1960 for André J. Garnerin (1770–1825), French aeronaut, balloonist, and parachutist.

**Cape Garnet** *see* **Garnet Point, Cape Granat**

**Garnet Hill.** 60°44′S, 45°38′W. 230 m. On the east side of McLeod Glacier, in the southern part of Signy Island, in the South Orkneys. Surveyed by the FIDS in 1947, and named by them for the garnets found here.

**Garnet Point.** 66°57′S, 143°46′E. Also called Cape Garnet. Consists of garnet gneiss. At the west side of the entrance to Watt Bay. Discovered by the AAE 1911–14, and named by Frank Stillwell.

**Garnet Rocks.** 68°21′S, 67°04′W. A group of 3 rocks in water, 2 miles east of the Refuge Islands, in the north part of Rymill Bay, off the west coast of Graham Land. Surveyed by the FIDS in 1948–49, and named by them for the garnet in the rocks.

**¹Garrard Glacier.** 84°07′S, 169°40′E. Flows from the névé between Mount Lockwood and Mount Kirkpatrick, into the Beardmore Glacier south of Bell Bluff, in the Queen Alexandra Range. Named by the New Zealanders in 1961–62 for Apsley Cherry-Garrard. The name Garrard Glacier had been applied by Scott's 1910–13 expedition to the glacier which Shackleton had already called Bingley Glacier (q.v.) in 1908.

**²Garrard Glacier** *see* **Bingley Glacier**

**Garrigan, Matthew.** Landsman on the Wilkes Expedition 1838–42. Joined in the USA. Sent home on the *Relief* in 1839.

**Garrison, Francis.** Seaman on the Wilkes Expedition 1838–42. Joined at Rio. Run on April 9, 1840.

**Cape Garry.** 63°21′S, 62°16′W. The most southwesterly of the points on Low Island in the South Shetlands. It is also the most southerly point on the island. Charted and named by Foster in 1829.

**Garwood Glacier.** 78°01′S, 163°57′E. At the head of the Garwood Valley, near the Wright Valley, in southern Victoria Land. Mapped during Scott's 1901–4 expedition, and named in 1911 by Grif Taylor, during Scott's 1910–13 expedition, for Edmund J. Garwood, professor of geology and mineralogy at the University of London.

**Garwood Point.** 74°14′S, 110°36′W. On Bear Peninsula, on the coast of Marie Byrd Land.

**Garwood Valley.** 78°02′S, 164°10′E. A mostly dry valley which opens on the coast of southern Victoria Land just south of Cape Chocolate, in the area of the Wright Valley. It is occupied, near its head, by the Garwood Glacier. Named in association with the glacier by Grif Taylor, during Scott's 1910–13 expedition.

**Gary Peaks.** 70°54′S, 162°35′E. Two peaks. Form a portion of the north wall of the Sheehan Glacier. 4 miles WSW of Mount Hager, in the Explorers Range of the Bowers Mountains. Named for Gary F. Martin, USN, machinery repairman at Amundsen-Scott South Pole Station in 1965.

**Garzón Point.** 64°55′S, 62°53′W. On the west coast of Graham Land.

**Mount Gass.** 80°27′S, 29°30′W. 6 miles SE of Mount Provender, on the east side of the Blaiklock Glacier, in the Shackleton Range. Named by the BCTAE in 1957 for Sir Neville A. Gass, chairman of BP, a supporter.

**Mount Gaston.** 70°25′S, 65°47′E. ½ mile SE of Mount Tarr, in the Porthos Range of the Prince Charles Mountains. Named by the Australians for J. Gaston, aircraft engineer with the ANARE Prince Charles Mountains Survey Party of 1969.

**Mount Gaston de Gerlache.** 71°44′S, 35°49′E. The most southerly massif in the Queen Fabiola Mountains. Discovered on Oct. 7, 1960, by the Belgian Antarctic Expedition of 1960–61 under Guido Derom, who named it for Gaston de Gerlache.

**Gaston Islands.** 64°28'S, 61°50'W. Two islands and off-lying rocks, 1 mile NW of the tip of Reclus Peninsula, off the west coast of the Antarctic Peninsula. Charted by de Gerlache in 1898. He named one of the islands as Gaston Islet, for his brother Gaston de Gerlache. In 1960 the UK extended the name to the entire group.

**Gaston Islet** *see* **Gaston Islands**

**Cape Gates.** 73°35'S, 122°38'W. Ice-covered. The northwesternmost point of Carney Island, in the Getz Ice Shelf. Named for Thomas S. Gates, under-secretary of the US Navy.

**Gates of Hell.** A pass in the Devil's Glacier, at the top of the Axel Heiberg Glacier. Discovered and named descriptively by Amundsen on Nov. 29, 1911.

**The Gateway.** 83°31'S, 170°58'E. Also called The Gap. Snow-filled. Between Cape Allen and Mount Hope at the NE extremity of the Queen Alexandra Range, allowing passage from the Ross Ice Shelf to the mouth of the Beardmore Glacier westward of Mount Hope. Discovered by Shackleton in 1908, and named by him because it was used to enter Beardmore Glacier.

**Gateway Nunatak.** 77°01'S, 160°18'E. Near the head of the Mackay Glacier, 9 miles west of Mount Gran, in Victoria Land. Named by the NZ Northern Survey Party of the BCTAE in 1957 for its position en route up the Mackay Glacier.

**Gateway Pass.** 71°40'S, 68°47'W. 5 miles long. Between Astarte Horn and Offset Ridge, in eastern Alexander Island. Named by the UK because it provides a route to the interior of Alexander Island from the head of Venus Glacier.

**Gateway Ridge.** 64°43'S, 63°33'W. Also called Orejas Negras (black ears). 715 m. SE of Mount Rennie, on Anvers Island. It separates Hooper Glacier from William Glacier where the two glaciers enter Börgen Bay. Surveyed by the personnel of Operation Tabarin in 1944 and 1945. The snow col at the northern end

of the ridge provides the only sledging route between these two glaciers.

**Gatlin Glacier.** 85°11'S, 173°30'W. 7 miles long. Flows from the Cumulus Hills and Red Raider Rampart into the south side of McGregor Glacier. Named for Harold C. Gatlin, meteorologist at Amundsen-Scott South Pole Station in 1964.

**Gatlin Peak.** 70°47'S, 63°18'W. Snow-covered. 4½ miles NE of Steel Peak at the NE end of the Welch Mountains of Palmer Land. Named for Lt. Donald H. Gatlin, USNR, aerial navigator in Antarctica in 1968 and 1969.

**Gaudis Point.** 67°41'S, 45°47'E. On Alasheyev Bight, about 1½ miles west of Molodezhnaya Station.

**Mount Gaudry.** 67°32'S, 68°37'W. Also called Sommet A. Gaudry, and sometimes seen spelled (erroneously) as Mount Goudry. 2,315 m. Just SW of Mount Barré, and 5 miles WNW of Mount Liotard, in the south part of Adelaide Island. Discovered by Charcot in 1903-5, and named by him for Albert Gaudry, French paleontologist.

**Gaul Cove.** 67°49'S, 67°11'W. Indents the NE side of Horseshoe Island, off Graham Land. Named by the UK for Kenneth M. Gaul, first leader of Base Y in 1955.

**Gaunt Rocks.** 65°17'S, 64°20'W. A small group of rocks in water, 2 miles west of Barros Rocks, in the Wilhelm Archipelago. Charted by the BGLE 1934-37. Named descriptively by the UK in 1959. They are desolate and gaunt looking.

**Gauntlet Ridge.** 73°25'S, 167°35'E. Flat-topped. Mainly ice-covered. It is actually a peninsula which separates the mouths of the Nascent and Ridgeway Glaciers where they discharge into Lady Newnes Bay, in Victoria Land. Named by NZ in 1966 because it looks like a gauntlet from the air.

**The *Gauss*.** Von Drygalski's expedition ship of 1901-3, it was built especially for the Antarctic, and was named for Prof. Karl F. Gauss, the German mathematician who predicted the position of the South Magnetic Pole. 164 feet long, 37 feet wide, 650-ton capacity, 1442-ton displacement. It was icebound (no damage) off the Wilhelm II Coast between Feb. 1902 and Feb. 1903, and after the expedition the ship was sold to Canada.

**¹Mount Gauss** *see* **Gaussberg**

**²Mount Gauss.** 76°19′S, 162°02′E. The most northerly peak in the Kirkwood Range of Victoria Land. Discovered by Scott's 1901–4 expedition, and named for Prof. Karl Gauss (*see* **The** *Gauss*).

**Gaussberg.** 66°48′S, 89°12′E. 370 m. An extinct volcano just west of Posadowsky Glacier, on the Wilhelm II Coast, overlooking the Davis Sea. Discovered in Feb. 1902 by von Drygalski, and named by him for his ship, the *Gauss*. Not to be confused with Mount Gauss.

**Gaussberg Abyssal Plain.** 65°S, 80°E. A submarine feature underneath the Davis Sea, off the Leopold and Astrid Coast.

**Gauthier Point.** 64°50′S, 63°36′W. Also called Punta Gautier (by the Argentines). Forms the northern extremity of Doumer Island, in the Palmer Archipelago. Discovered by Charcot in 1903–5, and named by him for M. Gauthier, builder of the *Français* and the *Pourquoi Pas?*

**Mount Gavaghan.** 70°26′S, 65°27′E. In the Porthos Range of the Prince Charles Mountains, between Mount Kirkby and Mount Creighton. Named by the Australians for E.J. Gavaghan, radio operator at Mawson Station in 1963.

**Gavin Ice Piedmont.** 63°44′S, 59°W. 15 miles long. 3–6 miles wide. In Trinity Peninsula, it extends from Charcot Bay to Russell West Glacier. Named by the UK for Christopher B. Gavin-Robinson, pilot for the FIDASE 1955–57.

**Gaviotín Rock.** 63°08′S, 56°01′W. Also called Gull Rock. A rock in the Larsen Channel, ¼ mile north of the coastal ice cliffs of Joinville Island. 2 miles north of Saxum Nunatak. Named by the Argentines in 1957 (Gaviotín means gull).

**Gavlen Ridge.** 72°39′S, 0°27′E. Forms the southern extremity of Roots Heights, in the southern part of the Sverdrup Mountains of Queen Maud Land. Name means "the gable" in Norwegian.

**Gavlpiggen Peak.** 73°58′S, 5°47′W. Isolated. 2 miles sw of Klakknabben Peak, just north of the Kirwan Escarpment in Queen Maud Land. Name means "the gable peak" in Norwegian.

**Gavronski, William.** Seaman on the *City of New York* during the first half of Byrd's 1928–30 expedition. For the second half (i.e., 1929–30) he switched to the *Eleanor Bolling*.

**Mount Gawn.** 71°55′S, 165°11′E. 2,190 m. In the central part of the King Range, in NW Victoria Land. Named by the New Zealanders in 1963–64 for J.E. Gawn.

**Gawn, J.E.** Radio operator at Scott Base, with the NZ party of the BCTAE 1957–58. He stayed in contact with the party. He was also radio operator at Scott Base in 1963–64.

**Gawn Ice Piedmont.** 79°58′S, 160°12′E. An ice piedmont and snow slope occupying the coastal platform between the Darwin and Byrd Glaciers. Named by the Darwin Glacier Party of the BCTAE in 1957–58 for J.E. Gawn.

**Gawne Nunatak.** 76°03′S, 135°24′W. On the east side of Wells Saddle, between Mount Berlin and Mount Moulton, in the Flood Range of Marie Byrd Land. Named for Steven P. Gawne, ice physicist here in 1971–72.

**Gaylard, Lyman.** Carpenter's mate on the Wilkes Expedition 1838–42. Joined in the USA. Discharged at Sydney.

**Gaynor, W.P.** Crewman on the *Jacob Ruppert*, 1933–35.

**Gaze, I.O.** Member of the Ross Sea party during the disastrous British Imperial Transantarctic Expedition of 1914–17. He was one of the 4 at Cape Evans for the 1915 winter, and again one of the 7 for the 1916 winter. Later became a farmer in Western Australia.

**Gazert, Dr. Hans.** Surgeon on the *Gauss* during von Drygalski's 1901–3 expedition.

**Gburek, Leo.** Geophysicist on the German New Schwabenland Expedition of 1938–39, led by Ritscher.

**Gburek Peaks.** 72°11′S, 0°15′W. They form the west end of the Sverdrup Mountains of Queen Maud Land, and include Mount Jutulrøra and Mount Straumsvola. Discovered by Ritscher in 1938–39, and named by him for Leo Gburek. The original Gburek Peaks were more extensive. The current term applies only to the more westerly of this larger group.

**Gealy Spur.** 84°38′S, 165°13′E. Descends from Mount Marshall to Willey Point, on the west side of the Beardmore Glacier. Discovered by Shackleton in Dec. 1908. Named for William J. Gealy, stratigrapher who found tetrapod fossils here in 1969–70.

**The *Gedania*.** Polish ship in the Antarctic Peninsula area during the 1975–76 summer.

**Cape Geddes.** 60°42′S, 44°35′W. Forms the north end of Ferguslie Peninsula, on the north coast of Laurie Island, in the South Orkneys. Charted by Bruce in 1903, and named by him for Prof. Patrick Geddes, Scottish biologist and sociologist (later knighted).

**Gedges Reef** *see* **Gedges Rocks**

**Gedges Rock** *see* **Gedges Rocks**

**Gedges Rocks.** 65°20′S, 64°32′W. A group of rocks 3 miles NNW of Grim Rock, and 10 miles WSW of Cape Tuxen, off the west coast of Graham Land. The BGLE discovered them in 1934–37, and named them Gedges Reef, for The Gedges, a dangerous reef in Cornwall waters in England. This Antarctic feature later became known as Gedges Rock, and in 1971 the UK redefined it as it is today.

**Mount Geier.** 71°34′S, 62°25′W. Mostly snow-covered. In the north part of the Schirmacher Massif, near the east coast of Palmer Land. Named for Frederick J. Geier, topographic engineer here in 1969–70.

**Geikie Inlet.** 75°30′S, 163°E. On the coast of Victoria Land, between the Drygalski Ice Tongue and Lamplugh Island. Discovered by Scott's 1901–4 expedition, and named by them for the Scottish geologist, Sir Archibald Geikie, director-general of the Geological Survey of the United Kingdom, who helped prepare Scott's expedition.

**Geikie Land** *see* **Geikie Ridge**

**Geikie Nunatak.** 80°24′S, 25°52′W. In the Shackleton Range.

**Geikie Point** *see* **Geikie Ridge**

**Geikie Ridge.** 71°44′S, 169°36′E. 20 miles long. 6 miles wide. A ridge which forms the divide between the Dugdale and Murray Glaciers, in the Admiralty Mountains of Victoria Land. In 1898–1900 Borchgrevink charted it and named it Geikie Land for Sir Archibald Geikie (*see* **Geikie Inlet**). This was later redefined as Geikie Point, and then later still as Geikie Ridge.

**Mount Geissel.** 80°25′S, 81°47′W. 1,430 m. 3 miles south of Mount Simmons, in the Independence Hills of the Heritage Range. Named for Robert H. Geissel, geomagnetist at Plateau Station in 1966.

**Gemel Peaks.** 62°12′S, 58°59′W. Also called Twin Peaks. Two peaks, 1⅓ miles NE of Horatio Stump, on Fildes Peninsula, King George Island, in the South Shetlands. In 1935 the personnel on the *Discovery II* named them Twin Peaks, or Twin Peak. Renamed in 1960 by the UK in order to avoid using the same name as another feature in Antarctica. Gemel means "twin."

**Gemini Nunatak.** 66°08′S, 62°30′W. Has two almost ice-free peaks, one 465 m. and the other 490 m. (hence the name given by the FIDS), connected by a narrow rock ridge. 4 miles south of Borchgrevink Nunatak, on Philippi Rise, on the east coast of Graham Land.

**Gemini Nunataks.** 84°42'S, 176°38'W. Two nunataks of similar size and appearance, in a prominent position near the west wall of the Shackleton Glacier, just SE of Mount Cole. Named by Alton Wade in 1962–63 during the Texas Tech Shackleton Glacier Expedition, for the constellation.

**Mount Genecand.** 66°06'S, 64°39'W. At the head of Barilari Bay, between the Lawrie and Weir Glaciers, on the west coast of Graham Land. Named by the UK in 1959 for Félix Genecand (1874–1957), Swiss mountain climber who invented the tricouni nail for climbing boots just before World War I.

**Cabo General Alvorado** see **Cape Shirreff**

**General Belgrano Station.** 77°59'S, 38°44'W. Argentine scientific station built on the Filchner Ice Shelf in 1955. Named for the patriot Manuel Belgrano (1770–1820), it is a year-round station. The *General San Martín* brought in the first personnel, and the leader of the 1955 and 1956 wintering parties was Hernán Pujato. Leal replaced him for the 1957 winter. A new station, General Belgrano Station II was built at 77°46'S, 38°11'W, and a newer one still, General Belgrano Station III, was built at 77°54'S, 45°49'W.

**General Bernardo O'Higgins Station.** 63°19'S, 57°54'W. Year-round Chilean scientific station set up in the 1947–48 season on Schmidt Peninsula, near Cape Legoupil, on the Louis Philippe Peninsula, right at the top of the Antarctic Peninsula. González Videla, the president of Chile, inaugurated the station in Feb. 1948, during the Presidential Antarctic Expedition, and Capt. Hugo Schmidt Prado was the first commander of the base, for the winter of 1948. Subsequent leaders of wintering-over parties included 1949—Aristides Migueles, 1950—Roberto Labra Nuñoz, 1951—Carlos Reyes, 1952—Aquiles López, 1953—Mario Stock, 1954—Luís Arellano, 1955—Luís Valdes, 1956—Guil-

lermo Chacón, 1957—Luís A. Ovando Palet.

**General Erskine Bay** see **Erskine Iceport**

**The General Knox.** US sealing ship, 266 tons, 96 feet long, built in 1810 at Thomaston, Mass. (now part of Maine), and registered in Salem, Mass., on Aug. 15, 1818. Captain William B. Orne. Left for the Falklands in 1818 as part of the Salem Expedition (q.v.). The ship was joined in the Falklands by the *Nancy*, whose captain told Orne of the discovery of the South Shetlands. The Salem Expedition was in the South Shetlands for the 1820–21 season.

**The General San Martín.** Argentine research ship/icebreaker of 4,854 tons, first sent to Antarctic waters in 1954–55, commanded by L.R. Capurro, to set up General Belgrano Station. In 1955–56 it was commanded by Luís M. Iriate. It has had several seasons in Antarctica since then.

**General San Martín Station** see **San Martín Station**

**The General Scott.** US sealer from New London, in the South Shetlands during the 1821–22 season, under the command of Capt. Sayer.

**Generators.** Scott used an acetylene-gas generator during his 1901–4 expedition, as did Shackleton in 1907–9. In his 1908–10 expedition Charcot used a gasoline-driven electric generator. All of these provided light.

**The Geneva.** Schooner, under the command of Capt. A. Padack, which went sealing with the *Sailor's Return* to the South Shetlands in 1836.

**Genghis Hills.** 80°44'S, 28°02'W. In the Shackleton Range.

**Gentile Point.** 81°07'S, 160°48'E. Ice-covered. 7 miles north of Cape Parr. Juts out into the sea from the Darley Hills, on the west side of the Ross Ice Shelf. Named for Peter A. Gentile, captain of the *Alatna* in 1961, and of the *Chattahoochee* in 1963.

**Gentoo penguin.** *Pygoscelis papua.*
Also called johnny penguin, juanito,
pingüín de pico rojo, and often confused
with the rockhopper and the jackass
penguins. The gentoo inhabits the northern shores of the Antarctic Peninsula,
the Balleny Islands, the South Shetlands,
the South Orkneys, and Peter I Island.
They build large nests on low, flat areas.
They are the only penguins with conspicuous white markings on the tops of
their heads. They grow to about 30
inches tall, weigh about 13 pounds, and
can dive to 350 feet or more. Discovered
by John R. Forster.

**Geode Nunataks.** 69°50′S, 70°08′W.
In the northern part of Alexander Island.

**Cape Géodésie.** 66°40′S, 139°51′E.
Ice-covered. 3 miles NW of the mouth of
the Astrolabe Glacier. Charted by the
French in 1951–52, and named by them
for the extensive geodetic program carried out here.

**Geoffrey Bay.** 66°17′S, 110°32′E. A
cove just east of Budnick Hill, on the
north side of Bailey Peninsula in the
Windmill Islands. Named by the Australians for Geoffrey D.P. Smith, senior
technical officer (buildings) with the
Antarctic Division, Melbourne, who
helped plan and supervise the construction of Casey Station. He had also been
carpenter at Mawson Station in 1961.

**Geoffrey Hills.** 67°36′S, 48°36′E. At
the west end of the Raggatt Mountains,
in Enderby Land. Named by the Australians for Geoffrey D.P. Smith (*see*
**Geoffrey Bay**).

**Geographic South Pole** *see* **South Pole**

**Geography** [general] *see* **Antarctica**

**Glacier Géologie** *see* **Astrolabe Glacier**

**Pointe Géologie** *see* **Géologie Archipelago**

**Géologie Archipelago.** 66°39′S, 139°
55′E. A small archipelago of rocky islands
and rocks, just north of Cape Géodésie
and the Astrolabe Glacier Tongue, off

the Adélie Land coast. It extends from
Hélène Island on the west to the Dumou-
lin Islands on the east. Includes the fol-
lowing features: the Dumoulin Islands,
Hélène Island, Marégraphe Island (Île du
Marégraphe in the original French), Ros-
tand Island (Île Jean Rostand), Carrel
Island (Île Alexis Carrel), Lamarck Island
(Île Lamarck), the Gouverneur Islands,
Pétrel Island (Île des Pétrelles), Bernard
Island (Île Claude Bernard), Lion Island
(Île du Lion), Buffon Island (Île Buffon),
Curie Island, the Fram Islands, Cuvier
Island (Île Cuvier), Ifo Island. In Jan.
1840 Dumont d'Urville's expedition
landed on Débarquement Rock (now in
the Dumoulin Islands). Because of the
rock samples collected they named a
nearby coastal point as Pointe Géologie.
This gave its name to the archipelago in
1952 (named by the French).

**Geologists Range.** 82°30′S, 155°30′E.
35 miles long. Between the heads of the
Lucy and Nimrod Glaciers, overlooking
the Ross Ice Shelf. Named by the New
Zealanders in 1961–62 for all geologists in
Antarctica.

**Geology.** Geologically Antarctica is
probably 3 billion years old. When it was
(theoretically) part of the supercontinent
of Pangaea, it was Precambrian. There
are 4 geological provinces of Antarctica:
Andean Province, which is the Antarctic
Peninsula and the coast of Marie Byrd
Land; Ellsworth Province, which is the
Ronne Ice Shelf and through the Ellsworth Mountains and Marie Byrd Land to
the Ross Ice Shelf; Ross Province, which
is a thin corridor running from the Weddell Sea to the Ross Sea, with its major
constituent being the Transantarctic
Mountains; and the East Antarctic
Shield, which is all of East Antarctica.

**Cape Geology.** 77°S, 162°32′E.
Gravel-covered. Marks the western limit
of Botany Bay, on the south shore of
Granite Harbor, in southern Victoria
Land. Charted and named by the Western Geological Party during Scott's 1910–
13 expedition. They established their
base here.

**Geomagnetic South Pole** *see* **South Geomagnetic Pole**

**Georg Foster Base.** 70°46′S, 11°50′E. East Germany's first scientific station in Antarctica, built on the Princess Astrid Coast, extremely close to the USSR base Novolazarevskaya Station, in the summer of 1986–87. Earth and atmospheric studies were conducted here.

**Georg von Neumayer Station.** 70°37′S, 8°22′W. Year-round West German scientific station built at Atka Iceport on the Princess Martha Coast of New Schwabenland, Queen Maud Land, in the summer of 1980–81. It was completed in March 1981, and named for one of the promoters of the First International Polar Year, a hundred years before, in 1882–83. This station, on the Ekström Ice Shelf, was the replacement for the aborted Filchner Station. It is supplied by the *Polarstern*.

¹**The *George*.** British sealer from Liverpool, in the South Shetlands in 1820–21 under the command of Capt. Richards. Operated mainly out of Rugged Island. Driven out to sea by the weather, it was badly damaged in a gale on Jan. 2, 1821. Eight of the crew were left ashore, to be picked up later by the *Indian*.

²**The *George*.** Sealing schooner out of Stonington, Conn. Was in the South Shetlands for the 1821–22 season, and left Antarctic waters on Jan. 20, 1822.

**Mount George.** 67°43′S, 50°E. Just west of Simpson Peak, in the Scott Mountains. Named by Biscoe in 1832 for one of the Enderby Brothers, his employers. At least, a mountain in this general area was so named. Modern geographers can not identify with accuracy Biscoe's Mount George, so they selected this particular mountain to bear the name of Mr. Enderby.

**George Bay.** A term no longer used. It was a bay on Livingston Island, in the South Shetlands, named by Bransfield for George III when the *Williams* anchored here on Jan. 18, 1820.

**George Bryan Coast** *see* **Bryan Coast**

**George V Coast** *see* **George V Land**

**George V Land.** 68°30′S, 147°30′E. To the east of Adélie Land, it runs from Commonwealth Bay to Oates Land, between the Cook Ice Shelf and the Mertz Glacier Tongue, or more specifically, between Point Alden (142°02′E) and Cape Hudson (153°45′E). Discovered by the AAE 1911–14, and named King George V Coast, for King George V of Great Britain. Mawson claimed it for Britain in 1930–31, and the name became George V Coast. Now recognized (although not everywhere) to be a land, rather than a coast.

**The *George IV*.** British sealer in the South Shetlands for the 1821–22 season, under the command of Capt. Alexander. Based out of Clothier Harbor for the season.

**George IV Sea** *see* **Weddell Sea**

**George Getz Shelf Ice** *see* **Getz Ice Shelf**

**George Glacier.** 70°41′S, 164°15′E. A valley glacier in the west part of the Anare Mountains. It rises east of Mount Burge and flows past Mount Kelly into the Lillie Glacier Tongue, on the coast. Named for Robert Y. George, zoologist at McMurdo Station in 1967–68.

**Mount George Murray.** 75°54′S, 161°50′E. Flat-topped. Mainly ice-covered. Between the heads of the Davis and Harbord Glaciers, in the Prince Albert Mountains of Victoria Land. Discovered by Scott's 1901–4 expedition, and named by them for George R.M. Murray of the British Museum, who helped define the scientific aims of the expedition.

**George Nunatak.** 85°35′S, 145°26′W. 1,050 m. Between the Harold Byrd Mountains and the Leverett Glacier. Named for Paul George, helicopter pilot here in 1962–63.

**The *George Porter*.** US sealer from Nantucket. In the South Shetlands in the 1821–22 season, under the command of Capt. Prince B. Moores.

**George Raynor Peak** *see* **Rayner Peak**

**George VI Ice Shelf.** 71°45'S, 68°W. Occupies the George VI Sound between Alexander Island and the Antarctic Peninsula, and extends from the Ronne Entrance to Niznik Island. Named by the UK in association with the sound.

**George VI Sound.** 71°S, 68°W. Also called Canal Seaver. A 300 mile-long fault depression separating Alexander Island from the Antarctic Peninsula's west coast. 20 miles long, on average, it is shaped like a scimitar, and extends from Marguerite Bay to the Ronne Entrance. It is filled with the ice of the George VI Ice Shelf. Discovered aerially by Ellsworth in 1935. It was the realization of the extent of this floating ice shelf which led the BGLE 1934-37 to determine that Alexander I Land was not a land at all, but an island (Alexander Island). Named King George VI Channel by Rymill, for the king of England. It was later redefined.

**Cape Georges** *see* **Georges Point**

**Georges Bay** *see* **King George Bay**

**Georges Island** *see* **Penguin Island**

**Georges Islands** *see* **Patricia Islands**

**Georges Point.** 64°40'S, 62°40'W. Also called Cape Georges. The northern tip of Rongé Island, west of Arctowski Peninsula, off the west coast of Graham Land. Discovered and named by de Gerlache in 1897-99.

**Georgian Cliff.** 71°15'S, 68°15'W. Along the George VI Sound, just north of the terminus of Eros Glacier, on the east side of Alexander Island. Named by the UK in association with George VI Sound.

**Gerard Bluffs.** 83°37'S, 157°18'E. Ice-free. The most southerly part of the Miller Range. Named by the NZ Southern Party of the BCTAE in 1957-58 for V. Gerard, IGY scientist at Scott Base in 1957.

**Gerasimou Glacier.** 84°42'S, 177°03'W. 5 miles long. Enters the west side of the Shackleton Glacier opposite the Gemini Nunataks, in the Queen Maud Mountains. Named by the Texas Tech Shackleton Glacier Expedition of 1964-65 for Helen Gerasimou, National Science Foundation polar personnel specialist.

**Gerber Peak.** 65°07'S, 63°17'W. 2 miles SSW of Rahir Point, just south of Thomson Cove, Flandres Bay, on the west coast of Graham Land. Charted by de Gerlache in 1897-99. Named by the UK in 1960 for Friedrich Gerber (1797-1872), Swiss veterinarian who first suggested the use of photography for book illustrations, in 1839.

**Gerd Island.** 60°40'S, 45°44'W. 1 mile WSW of Stene Point, at the east side of the entrance to Norway Bight, off the south coast of Coronation Island, in the South Orkneys. Charted by Petter Sørlle in 1912-13, and named by him as Gerdholmane. This was later translated into English.

**Mount Gerdel.** 85°59'S, 149°19'W. 2,520 m. 2 miles SE of Mount Andrews, at the south side of Albanus Glacier. Named for Lt. David H. Gerdel, USN, at Byrd Station in 1965.

**Gerdholm** *see* **Gerd Island**

**Gerlache** *see also* **de Gerlache**

**Cape Gerlache.** 66°30'S, 99°02'E. Also called Cape de Gerlache. Forms the NE tip of Davis Peninsula, 4 miles SE of David Island. Discovered in Nov. 1912 by the AAE 1911-14, and named by Mawson for Adrien de Gerlache.

**Mount Gerlache.** 74°58'S, 162°26'E. Also called Mount de Gerlache. 980 m. On the NE side of the Larsen Glacier, between Widowmaker Pass and Backstairs Passage Glacier, behind Terra Nova Bay, Victoria Land. Discovered by Scott's 1901-4 expedition, and named by him for Adrien de Gerlache.

**Gerlache Channel** *see* **Gerlache Strait**

**Gerlache Inlet.** 74°40'S, 164°06'E. 4 miles wide. Just south of Mount Browning, between the Campbell Glacier and the Northern Foothills, at Terra Nova Bay, in Victoria Land. Named by Scott in 1901–4 for Adrien de Gerlache. The Italian scientific station is here.

**Gerlache Island.** 64°35'S, 64°16'W. The largest of the Rosenthal Islands, off the west coast of Anvers Island. Named Pointe de Gerlache in 1903–5 by Charcot, for Adrien de Gerlache. This became de Gerlache Point, and Gerlache Point, until it was redefined by the FIDS in 1956–58.

**Gerlache Point** *see* **Gerlache Island**

**Gerlache Strait.** 64°30'S, 62°20'W. A deep, wide strait separating Brabant Island from the Danco Coast of the Antarctic Peninsula. Discovered by de Gerlache on the *Belgica* on Jan. 23, 1898, and named by him as the Belgica Strait. It was subsequently redefined as a channel, and renamed the Gerlache Channel. It was later still proved to be a strait, and renamed Gerlache Strait (sometimes seen as de Gerlache Strait), the name honoring Adrien de Gerlache.

**German Antarctic Expedition.** 1911–12. Led by Wilhelm Filchner. Filchner planned to prove or disprove the existence of the Ross-Weddell Graben, and raised the money for the expedition by public lottery. On May 4, 1911, the *Deutschland* left Bremerhaven for Buenos Aires, leaving there on Oct. 4, 1911. On Oct. 18, 1911, they reached South Georgia (54°S). They then explored the South Sandwich Islands, and on Dec. 11, 1911, were in Antarctic waters, heading toward the Weddell Sea. Also on board were Richard Vahsel (ship's captain), Alfred Kling, Dr. König, Erich Barkow, Walter Slossarczyk, Johannes Müller. The *Deutschland* sailed into the Weddell Sea to 77°50'S, sighting land at the Luitpold Coast on Jan. 30, 1912. They charted this coast between 29°W and 37°W, and sailed along what is now the Filchner Ice Shelf. Filchner planned to set up a stationhaus (a winter camp), and then strike out across country to the Ross Sea. On Feb. 9, 1912, they began unloading on the

(Filchner) ice shelf, and by Feb. 17, 1912, the hut (55 feet by 30 feet) was almost completed when the ice started to break up on Feb. 18, 1912. The camp was now on a berg floating north. In addition, huge bergs threatened the ship. They dismantled the hut and got all provisions and materials to the ship by Feb. 20, 1912 – all except one dog who wanted to stay on the berg. For several days the ship drifted, and Filchner built two depots on the ice again. He planned to winter in South Georgia, then come back to Antarctica the following summer. However, by March 6, 1912, they were frozen in, slowly drifting north in the Weddell Sea. In June, Filchner, Kling, and König went off looking for the mythical New South Greenland. On Aug. 8, 1912, Vahsel died, and Kling took over as captain of the ship. On Nov. 26, 1912, the ship freed at 63°37'S, 36°34'W. In early Dec. 1912 they got out of the ice, and on Dec. 19, 1912, they were in South Georgia.

**German New Schwabenland Expedition.** 1938–39. Herman Goering chose Nazi captain Alfred Ritscher to lead this propaganda expedition to Antarctica in the *Schwabenland*. The idea was given the go-ahead (presumably by the Führer) in May 1938, and preparation began in Sept. 1938. The *Schwabenland* left Hamburg on Dec. 17, 1938, in a temperature of 1°F. Also on board were A. Kottas (ship's captain), Herbert Ruhnke, Franz Preuschoff, Herbert Regula, Rudolf Mayr, Karl-Heinz Paulsen, Walter Krüger, Erich Barkley, Herbert Bolle, Wilhelm Gockel, Willy Stein, Richardheinrich Schirmacher, Rudolf Wahr, Emil Brandt, Leo Gburek, Ernst Herrmann, Herbert Bruns, Max Bundermann, Dietrich Witte, Erich Bastlen, Karl Hedden. They took 2 hydroplanes, the *Passat* and the *Boreas,* loaned to Ritscher by Lufthansa, as was the expedition ship, the *Schwabenland.* The ship dropped anchor near the edge of the pack ice at 69°14'S, 4°30'W, on Jan. 20, 1939. That day the first photographic reconnaissance flight was made (Wahr and Schirmacher were the two airplane captains). By Jan. 23, 1939, they had finished their photographic flights—7 long-range ones in all (for details of their photography, see **Aerial photography**). The aircraft were launched from the ship by catapult. When they landed again after a flight, they came down in the sea next to the ship, and a huge crane on board lifted the little aircraft back onto the *Schwabenland*. The Norwegians objected to the Nazi land-grabbing expedition, and on Jan. 24, 1939, they claimed all Antarctic land between 20° W and 45° E. Herr Kapitän Ritscher had other ideas. His plane captains dropped 5-foot-long aluminum darts, their tails engraved with the swastika, all over New Schwabenland. From that height these darts penetrated even solid ice, and were used as markers to stake their claim to the vast area surveyed. They, in fact, claimed the area between 11° W and 19° E, and this newly-surveyed area was called Neu Schwabenland (see **New Schwabenland**), a substantial part of the Queen Maud Land claimed by the Norwegians (it is interesting that, for once, the Nazis were out-claimed). Three landings were made on the continent during the 3 weeks that the ship lay off the coast. On Jan. 29, 1939, Wahr flew a party in the *Passat* to a small bay for 5 hours surveying. On Jan. 30, 1939, the *Boreas* touched down briefly at 70°18′S, 4°22′E, and some men made a landing. On Jan. 31, 1939, Erich Bastlen was flown in the *Boreas* to capture some emperor penguins. On Feb. 5, 1939, one man almost drowned in an unsuccessful attempt to land a large party by boat. The *Schwabenland* arrived at Cape Town on March 1, 1939, and at Hamburg on April 10, 1939. A second expedition was planned but World War II got in the way.

**Germany.** The first German expedition into Antarctica was Dallmann's in 1873–75. The *Valdivia* was there briefly in the 1890s, and in 1901–3 von Drygalski led a government-sponsored expedition. Also government-sponsored were the German Antarctic Expedition of 1911–12, led by Filchner, and the German New Schwabenland Expedition of 1938–39, led by Ritscher. In 1936–37 Germany sent a whaling fleet to Antarctica for the first time. After World War II Germany was split into East Germany (q.v.) and West Germany (q.v.).

**Gerof, Demetri.** b. ca. 1888, Sakhalin, eastern Siberia. d. 1932. Name also seen as Gerov, Girev, Gorev. Russian dog driver on Scott's 1910–13 expedition. He was picked for the expedition by Cecil Meares to help with the dogs in Nikolayevsk, and to bring them to Antarctica.

**Gerontius Glacier.** 69°31′S, 70°34′W. In the north of Alexander Island.

**Gerrish Peaks.** 74°41′S, 111°33′W. 4 miles SE of Hunt Bluff, on the west side of Bear Peninsula, Marie Byrd Land. Named for Samuel D. Gerrish, ionosphere physicist at Byrd Station in 1966.

**Gerritsz, Dirck.** Name also seen as Gherritz. Dutch sailor who made one of the first sightings (unconfirmed—see the Expeditions appendix, and also the entry under **South Shetlands**) of the South Shetlands, in Sept. 1599, when he was blown to 64°S in a storm (so he claimed—it may well be true). This was reported in the book *Description des Indes Occidentales* in 1622.

**Gerry Glacier.** 77°24′S, 152°05′W. On Edward VII Peninsula, it flows between Reeves Peninsula and the Howard Heights to the head of Sulzberger Bay. Named by Byrd for Senator Peter G. Gerry of Rhode Island, a contributor to Byrd's 1933–35 expedition.

**Gertrude Rock.** 71°17′S, 170°13′E. Also called Gertrude. The northern of two rocks in water, The Sisters, off the north end of Cape Adare. Named by Murray Levick of Campbell's Northern Party, during Scott's 1910–13 expedition, for one of the sisters in a popular song of the time (see **The Sisters**).

**Gervaize, Charles.** French élève on the *Astrolabe* during Dumont d'Urville's expedition of 1837–40. He was promoted to ensign on Aug. 20, 1840.

**Gervaize Rocks.** 63°21′S, 58°06′W. A group of rocks in water, 3 miles NNE of Cape Ducorps, Trinity Peninsula. Named by the UK for Charles Gervaize.

**Gessner Peak.** 71°46′S, 6°55′E. 3,020 m. Highest peak on Storkvarvet Mountain, 3 miles north of Habermehl Peak, in the NE part of the Mühlig-Hofmann Mountains of Queen Maud Land. Discovered by Ritscher in 1938–39, and named by him for the manager of the Hansa-Luftbild, an aerial photographic corporation.

**Mount Gester.** 75°01′S, 134°48′W. 950 m. Ice-covered. Flat-topped. Between the Johnson and Venzke Glaciers in Marie Byrd Land. Just south of Mount Kohnen and Bowyer Butte. Named for Lt. (jg) Ronald L. Gester, seismologist at Byrd Station in 1971.

**Gestlingen** *see* **Gosling Islands**

**Getman Ice Piedmont.** 68°06′S, 64°57′W. On the east coast of Graham Land.

**Mount Getz.** 76°33′S, 145°13′W. 1,120 m. 5 miles ESE of Mount Ferranto, in the southern part of the Fosdick Mountains, in the Ford Ranges of Marie Byrd Land. Named by Byrd for George F. Getz, Jr., son of George F. Getz (*see* **Getz Ice Shelf**), and a supporter of the USAS 1939–41.

**Getz Ice Shelf.** 75°S, 125°W. Also called George Getz Shelf Ice, Getz Shelf Ice. Over 300 miles long. 20–60 miles wide. Off the Bakutis Coast and the Hobbs Coast of Marie Byrd Land. It contains several islands—Carney, Siple, Dean, Grant, and Wright. Named by the USAS 1939–41 for George F. Getz of Chicago, who furnished a seaplane for the expedition.

**Getz Shelf Ice** *see* **Getz Ice Shelf**

**Mount Gevers.** 85°50′S, 158°29′W. 1,480 m. At the north side of the Cappellari Glacier, in the Hays Mountains of the Queen Maud Mountains. It is ac-

tually at the point where the Cappellari Glacier enters the Amundsen Glacier. Named by the USA for T.W. Gevers, South African geologist at McMurdo Station in 1964–65.

**Geysen Glacier.** 73°32′S, 64°36′E. Just to the south of the Fisher Glacier, into which it feeds after flowing between Mount Bayliss and Mount Ruker, in the Prince Charles Mountains. Named by the Australians for H. Geysen, officer-in-charge of Mawson Station in 1960.

**Gherritz, Dirck** *see* **Gerritsz, Dirck**

**Giaever, John.** b. 1901, Norway. John Schelderup Giaever. In 1948 he became head of the Norsk Polarinstitutt after a varied and exciting career, often in the Arctic. He led the NBSAE 1949–52 to the Antarctic and in 1957–58 was counselor to the Belgian Antarctic Expedition led by Gaston de Gerlache.

**Giaever Glacier.** 72°37′S, 31°08′E. Flows between Mount Kerckhove de Denterghem and Mount Lahaye, in the Belgica Mountains. Discovered by the Belgian Antarctic Expedition of 1957–58, led by Gaston de Gerlache, and named by him for John Giaever (q.v.), counselor for de Gerlache's expedition.

**Giaever Ridge.** 72°S, 5°W. Also called Førstefjellsryggen. Snow-covered. 70 miles long. On the west side of the Schytt Glacier, in Queen Maud Land. Named by the Norwegians for John S. Giaever.

**Giannini Peak.** 71°S, 62°50′W. 13 miles ESE of Mount Nordhill, in the east part of Palmer Land. On the north side of Dana Glacier, where that glacier swings NE toward Lehrke Inlet. Named for Albert P. Giannini, US biologist at Palmer Station in 1973.

**Giant Fulmars** *see* **Fulmars**

**Giard Point.** 64°26′S, 63°49′W. Forms the south side of the entrance to Perrier Bay, on the NW coast of Anvers Island. Charted by Charcot in 1903–5, and named by him for Alfred Giard, French zoologist.

**Gibb Island** *see* **Gibbs Island**

**Gibbney Island.** 67°33'S, 62°19'E. On the west side of Holme Bay, off Mac. Robertson Land. Photographed by the LCE 1936–37, and named Bryggeholmen (the wharf island) by the Norwegians. Renamed by the Australians for L.F. Gibbney, officer-in-charge at Heard Island Station (53°S) in 1952.

**Gibbon, Dr. G.M.** Ship's surgeon on the *Discovery II* in 1933.

**Gibbon Bay.** 60°39'S, 45°11'W. 1 mile long. A Lewthwaite Strait indentation into the eastern end of Coronation Island, in the South Orkneys, between Rayner Point and The Turret. Discovered by Powell and Palmer in Dec. 1821. Named by the personnel on the *Discovery II* in 1933, for Dr. G.M. Gibbon.

**Gibbon Nunatak.** 85°31'S, 127°36'W. Isolated. On the north side of the Wisconsin Range, 8 miles north of the Lentz Buttress, on the west side of the Davisville Glacier. Named for Thomas L. Gibbon, construction driver at Byrd Station in 1959.

**Gibbons, Barney.** Landsman on the Wilkes Expedition 1838–42. Joined at Rio. Run at Valparaiso.

**Gibbous Rocks.** 61°03'S, 54°59'W. A group 4 miles NW of Cape Belsham, on Elephant Island in the South Shetlands. Named by the UK in 1971. The word gibbous means "humped."

**Mount Gibbs.** 73°49'S, 162°56'E. 3,140 m. On the south side of Recoil Glacier, in the Deep Freeze Range of Victoria Land. Named for Lt. Maurice E. Gibbs, USN, meteorological officer at McMurdo Station in 1967.

**Gibbs Glacier.** 68°28'S, 66°W. 15 miles long. Flows into the north part of the Mercator Ice Piedmont, on the east side of the Antarctic Peninsula. Named by the UK for Peter M. Gibbs, FIDS surveyor at Base Y in 1957, and leader at Base E in 1958. He and Peter Forster surveyed this glacier.

**Gibbs Island.** 61°28'S, 55°34'W. Also called Gibb Island, Gibbs Islands, Rain-off's Island, Narrow Isle. One of the easterly group of the South Shetlands, 14 miles SW of Elephant Island. Named by Weddell, probably in 1823.

**Gibbs Islands** *see* **Gibbs Island**

**Gibney Reef.** 66°15'S, 110°30'E. ½ mile west of Clark Peninsula, in the Windmill Islands. Charted in Feb. 1957 by personnel on the *Glacier,* and named by Lt. Robert C. Newcomb of that cruise, for seaman Joseph Gibney, also a member of that survey party.

**Islote Giboso** *see* **Humps Island**

**Gibraltar Peak.** 72°04'S, 164°59'E. 1 mile SE of Lavallee Peak, in the West Quartzite Range. Named by the New Zealanders in 1967–68 for its similarity to the Rock of Gibraltar in Europe.

**Mount Gibson.** 71°20'S, 66°20'E. 2½ miles west of Mount Cameron, and 3 miles south of Schmitter Peak, in the Prince Charles Mountains. Named by the Australians for P.R. Gibson, plumber at Wilkes Station in 1965.

**Gibson, James H.** Coxswain on the Wilkes Expedition 1838–42. Joined in the USA. Served the cruise.

**Gibson Bay.** 63°19'S, 55°53'W. On the south side of Joinville Island, just west of Mount Alexander, at the junction of Active Sound and the Firth of Tay. Discovered and named on Jan. 8, 1893, by Thomas Robertson of the *Active.*

**Gibson Spur.** 77°20'S, 160°39'E. Just west of the mouth of the Webb Glacier, in Victoria Land. Named by the VUWAE 1959–60 for G.W. Gibson, one of the geologists in the party.

**Mount Giddings.** 67°25'S, 50°47'E. 6 miles SE of Debenham Peak, in the Scott Mountains of Enderby Land. Named by the Australians for J.E. Giddings, cook at Mawson Station in 1961.

**Giddings Peak.** 70°12'S, 64°44'E. Just west of Mount Béchervaise, in the Athos Range of the Prince Charles Mountains. Named by the Australians for A. Giddings, cook at Wilkes Station in 1959.

**Gierloff Nunataks.** 85°31'S, 129°W. 8 miles NW of the Lentz Buttress, at the north side of the Wisconsin Range, in the Horlick Mountains. Named for George B. Gierloff, builder at Byrd Station in 1961.

**Giffard Cove.** 64°37'S, 61°42'W. Also seen spelled (erroneously) as Gifford Cove. 1 mile wide. In the west side of Charlotte Bay, on the west coast of Graham Land. Charted by de Gerlache in 1897–99. Named by the UK in 1960 for Henri Giffard (1825–1882), balloonist.

**Gifford Cove** *see* **Giffard Cove**

**Gifford Peaks.** 79°36'S, 84°48'W. A line of sharp peaks and ridges along the escarpment at the west side of the Heritage Range, between the Watlack Hills and the Soholt Peaks. Named by the University of Minnesota Geological Party of 1963–64, for CWO Leonard A. Gifford, pilot of the 62nd Transportation Detachment, who helped the party.

**Giganteus Island.** 67°35'S, 62°30'E. Just north of the Rookery Islands, in the west part of Holme Bay, Mac. Robertson Land. Photographed by the LCE 1936–37. Named by the ANARE in Dec. 1958 for a giant petrel (*Macronectes giganteus*) rookery seen here at the time.

**Mount Gilbert.** 69°16'S, 66°17'W. 1,420 m. Between the Airy and Seller Glaciers, 5 miles NW of Mount Castro, in the west central part of the Antarctic Peninsula. Named by the UK for William Gilbert (1540–1603), magnetism pioneer.

**Gilbert, John.** Master of the *Resolution* during Cook's 1772–75 voyage.

**Gilbert Bluff.** 74°58'S, 136°37'W. On the south side of the Garfield Glacier, in the McDonald Heights of Marie Byrd Land. Named for James R. Gilbert, biologist near here in 1971–72.

**Gilbert Glacier.** 70°S, 71°W. Empties into Wilkins Sound, on the NW part of Alexander Island.

**Gilbert Grosvenor Range** *see* **Grosvenor Mountains**

**Gilbert Strait.** 63°38'S, 60°16'W. Also called Davies Gilbert Strait, Davis Gilbert Strait. Separates Tower Island from Trinity Island, off the west coast of Antarctic Peninsula. Named by Foster in 1829 for Davies Gilbert, president of the Royal Society, 1827–30, and of the *Chanticleer* expedition committee.

**Gilchrist, Edward.** Acting surgeon on the *Vincennes*, during the Wilkes Expedition 1838–42. Detached at Sydney in March 1840.

**Gilchrist Glacier.** 66°05'S, 114°E. A channel glacier which flows to the Budd Coast, 9 miles NW of the Fox Glacier. Named for Dr. Edward Gilchrist.

**Gilderdale, Capt.** Commander of the *Wilmington* in the South Shetlands for the 1853–54 season.

**Gilderdale, George.** Captain of the *Peru* in the South Shetlands, 1871–72. Could be the same Capt. Gilderdale as immediately above.

**Mount Giles.** 75°09'S, 137°36'W. Also called Mount Carrol Kettering. 820 m. 5 miles SSE of Lynch Point, on the coast of Marie Byrd Land. Mainly snow-covered, it is between the Frostman and Hull Glaciers. Discovered aerially by the USAS from West Base in 1940, and named by Byrd for Walter R. Giles.

**Giles, Walter R.** Technical sgt., US Marines. Co-pilot and radio operator on flights out of West Base during the USAS 1939–41.

**Gill Automatic Weather Station.** 80° S, 179°W. An American AWS at an elevation of approximately 180 feet. Began operating on Jan. 24, 1985.

**Gill Bluff.** 76°14'S, 112°33'W. On the NW side of Mount Takahe, in Marie Byrd Land. Named for Allan Gill, aurora researcher at Byrd Station in 1963.

**Gillan, William.** Seaman on the Wilkes Expedition 1838–42. Joined in the USA. Served the cruise.

**Gillespie Glacier.** 85°11'S, 175°12'W. Just SW of Mount Kenyon. Flows from the west slopes of the Cumulus Hills into Shackleton Glacier. Named for Lester F.

Gillespie, meteorologist at Amundsen-Scott South Pole Station in 1962.

**Mount Gillet.** 72°34'S, 31°23'E. 2,460 m. Just north of Mount Van der Essen, in the Belgica Mountains. Discovered by the Belgian Antarctic Expedition of 1957–58, led by Gaston de Gerlache, and named by him for Charles Gillet, a patron.

**Gillett Ice Shelf.** 69°35'S, 159°42'E. Occupies an indentation of the coast off the Wilson Hills, between the Holladay Nunataks and Anderson Peninsula. Named for Capt. Clarence R. Gillett, US Coast Guard, in Antarctica several times between 1965–66 and 1970.

**Gillett Nunataks.** 75°48'S, 114°43'W. Two nunataks. Mostly snow-covered. At the east end of Spitz Ridge and the Toney Mountain massif, in Marie Byrd Land. Named for Richard D. Gillett, USN, radioman at Amundsen-Scott South Pole Station in 1974.

**Gilliamsen Peak.** 71°51'S, 70°20'W. In the central part of Alexander Island.

**Gillick Rock.** 75°36'S, 129°12'W. An isolated nunatak at the NW end of the McCuddin Mountains, 8 miles north of the summit of Mount Flint, in Marie Byrd Land. Named for Lt. Thomas L. Gillick, USNR, helicopter pilot in Antarctica in 1970 and 1971.

**Gillies, F.J.** Chief engineer of the *Aurora* during the AAE 1911–14.

**Gillies, James M.** Chief engineer of the *Jacob Ruppert*, 1934–35.

**Gillies Islands.** 66°32'S, 96°24'E. Also called Gillies Nunataks. Three grounded islands in the Shackleton Ice Shelf, 3 miles north of Cape Moyes. Discovered by the Western Base Party of the AAE 1911–14, and named by Mawson for F.J. Gillies.

**Gillies Nunataks** *see* **Gillies Islands**

**Gillies Rock.** 83°07'S, 54°45'W. An isolated rock on land, 6 miles north of Mount Dasinger, in the northern part of the Neptune Range. Named for Betty

Gillies, San Diego ham radio operator who, throughout the 1960s, patched Antarcticans through to the USA.

**Gillin, John.** Ordinary seaman on the Wilkes Expedition 1838–42. Joined in the USA. Served the cruise.

**Mount Gillmor.** 70°28'S, 159°46'E. 2,185 m. Largely ice-free. At the south side of the head of the Svendsen Glacier, in the Usarp Mountains. Named for C. Stewart Gillmor, US exchange scientist (ionosphere physicist) at Mirnyy Station in 1961.

**Gillock Glacier.** 72°S, 24°08'E. The Norwegians call it Gillockbreen. 5 miles long. Flows from Mount Walnum to the west of Smalegga Ridge, in the Sør Rondane Mountains. Named by the Norwegians for Lt. Robert H. Gillock (*see* **Gillock Island**).

**Gillock Island.** 70°26'S, 71°52'E. 20 miles long. 2–6 miles wide. Ice-covered. In the east part of the Amery Ice Shelf. Named by US cartographer John H. Roscoe in 1952 for Lt. Robert H. Gillock, USN, navigator on Operation Highjump, 1946–47.

**Mount Gilmour.** 76°56'S, 144°40'W. 4 miles SE of Mount Passel, in the Ford Ranges of Marie Byrd Land. Discovered in 1940 by the USAS from West Base. Named by Byrd for Harold P. Gilmour.

**Gilmour, Harold P.** Recorder/historian on the USAS 1939–41. Based at Little America III (West Base) as administrative assistant to the expedition commander.

**Mount Gilruth.** 71°44'S, 168°48'E. 3,160 m. Mostly ice-covered. 4½ miles ENE of Mount Adam, in the Admiralty Mountains of Victoria Land. Named for Robert R. Gilruth of NASA, who visited McMurdo Station in 1966–67.

**Gimber, H.M.S.** Cdr. Captain of the *Brownson* during Operation Highjump, 1946–47.

**Ginger Islands.** 67°45'S, 68°42'W. A group west of Cape Alexandra, off the south end of Adelaide Island. Named by the UK for Kenneth Ginger, civil hydrographic officer responsible for Admiralty charts of the Antarctic for several years beginning in 1958.

**Giovanni Peak.** 69°50'S, 71°24'W. 750 m. Isolated. On Mozart Ice Piedmont, 1 mile south of Debussy Heights, in the north part of Alexander Island. Named by the UK for the Mozart opera, *Don Giovanni.*

**Giovinco Ice Piedmont.** 84°01'S, 176°10'E. 10 miles wide. Between Canyon Glacier and Perez Glacier, descending to the Ross Ice Shelf. Named for F.A. Giovinco, captain of the *Towle* in 1965.

**Mount Giovinetto.** 78°16'S, 86°10'W. 4,090 m. The summit of a buttress-type mountain, 2 miles north of Mount Ostenso, in the main ridge of the Sentinel Range. Discovered by the Marie Byrd Land Traverse Party of 1957–58, and named by the leader of that party, Charles Bentley, for Mario B. Giovinetto, Argentine glaciologist/observer on US bases for several Antarctic seasons.

**Gipps Ice Rise.** 68°46'S, 60°52'W. 10 miles long. Elliptical in shape. Bounded by an ice cliff on all sides. At the edge of the Larsen Ice Shelf, 35 miles NE of Hearst Island, on the east coast of the Antarctic Peninsula. Discovered by William R. MacDonald of the US Geological Survey, on Dec. 18, 1966, on a flight over the area. Named by the UK for Derek R. Gipps, senior executive officer with the BAS, 1961–73.

**Cabo Giralt** *see* **Cape Shirreff**

**Girard Bay.** 65°08'S, 64°W. 2 miles long. 1 mile wide. Indents the west coast of Graham Land, between Cape Cloos and Mount Scott. Discovered by de Gerlache in 1897–99. Named by Charcot in 1903–5 for Jules Girard of the Paris Geographical Society.

**Girdler Island.** 66°S, 65°39'W. A small island at the south side of Mutton Cove, 175 yards SW of Cliff Island. 8 miles west of Prospect Point, off the west coast of Graham Land. Charted and named by the BGLE 1934–37.

**Girev, Demetri** *see* **Gerof, Demetri**

**Giró Nunatak.** 82°13'S, 42°02'W. 4 miles NW of Vaca Nunatak, in the Panzarini Hills of the Argentina Range, in the Pensacola Mountains. Named by the USA for Capt. G.A. Giró, Argentine officer-in-charge of General Belgrano Station in 1965.

**Giroux, F.W.** Crewman on the *Jacob Ruppert,* 1933–35.

**Mount Gist.** 67°20'S, 98°54'E. 8 miles NW of Mount Strathcona, near the head of the Denman Glacier. Named for Lt. Francis J. Gist, USN, co-pilot and navigator on Operation Highjump, 1946–47.

**Mount Gjeita.** 68°12'S, 58°14'E. Also called Mount Banfield. Highest peak in the Hansen Mountains. 3 miles east of Brusen Nunatak. Photographed by the LCE 1936–37, and named by the Norwegians.

**Gjel Glacier.** 71°53'S, 24°55'E. The Norwegians call it Gjelbreen. 17 miles long. Flows between the Luncke Range and Mefjell Mountain in the Sør Rondane Mountains. Name means "the ravine glacier" in Norwegian.

**Mount Gjelsvik.** 72°30'S, 2°E. 12,008 feet. In Queen Maud Land. Named for Tore Gjelsvik (*see* **Gjelsvik Mountains**) by the Norwegians. This seems to be a term no longer in use.

**Gjelsvik Mountains.** 72°08'S, 2°38'E. 25 miles long. Between the Sverdrup Mountains and the Mühlig-Hofmann Mountains of Queen Maud Land. Named by the Norwegians for Tore Gjelsvik, director of the Norsk Polarinstitutt in Oslo (cf. John S. Giaever).

**Gjelsvik Peak.** 85°19'S, 167°59'W. 3,660 m. 2½ miles NW of Mount Fridtjof Nansen, in the Queen Maud Mountains. Named by the New Zealanders in 1961–62 for Tore Gjelsvik (*see* **Gjelsvik Mountains**).

**Gjelsvikfjella** *see* **Gjelsvik Mountains**

**Mount Gjertsen.** 86°40'S, 148°27'W. 2,420 m. 2 miles NE of Mount Grier, in the La Gorce Mountains of the Queen Maud Mountains. In 1911, while speeding toward the Pole, Amundsen named a mountain in this area as Mount F. Gjertsen, for Hjalmar Gjertsen. Modern geographers could not be sure which mountain Amundsen meant, so they named this one, discovered in Dec. 1934 by Quin Blackburn's party during Byrd's 1933–35 expedition (which Gjertsen also took part in).

**Gjertsen, Hjalmar Frederick.** Norwegian naval lieutenant, second mate on the *Fram* during Amundsen's Norwegian Antarctic Expedition of 1910–12. He was loaned to the *Sir James Clark Ross* Expedition of 1923–24 as ice pilot, and he later commanded the *Nilsen-Alonzo*. He was commodore on the *Jacob Ruppert,* during Byrd's 1933–35 expedition.

**Gjertsen Promontory.** 86°38′S, 148°32′W. At the end of the spur trending north from Mount Gjertsen in the La Gorce Mountains, in the Queen Maud Mountains. Named by the New Zealanders in 1969–70 in asscociation with the mountain.

**Gjeslingene**   *see*   **Gosling Islands**

**Glacial Bay**   *see*   **Lednikov Bay**

**Glacial flour.** Fine, powdery icy material found under a glacier. It washes out as glacier milk.

**Glacial milk**   *see*   **Glacier milk**

**Glacial polish.** This is where the substrate or the sides of valleys have been polished by small rocks carried by a glacier as it flows through the valley.

**Glacial striations.** Scratches on the bedrock made by large rocks carried by glaciers.

**Glacial troughs**   *see*   **Hanging valleys**

**Glacial valleys**   *see*   **Hanging valleys**

**The *Glacier.*** US Navy icebreaker / Antarctic research vessel of 8,300 tons and 21,000 hp. It was the largest icebreaker in the Antarctic, and the most powerful

diesel-electric ship (it had 14 diesel-electric engines) ever built in the USA, until the *Polar Star* in 1976. Built in 1954 by the Ingalls Shipping Corporation, it was completed and commissioned in June 1955. It could break through ice 15 feet thick, and was 100 times more powerful than Byrd's ship of 1928. 310 feet long, it had a heliport housing two helicopters. Nicknamed "Big Red," it was the first icebreaker to be designed and built specifically for the US Navy. It first entered McMurdo Sound on Dec. 18, 1955, and on June 30, 1966, it was transferred to the US Coast Guard. In Feb. 1987, after many adventures, it sailed out of Antarctic waters for the last time, and was decommissioned on June 7, 1987.

**Glacier Bay.** Just east of Paradise Bay, on the Danco Coast of the Antarctic Peninsula. This is a term no longer used.

**Glacier Bight.** 71°48′S, 99°45′W. Also called Glacier Roads. 22 miles wide. It is an indentation into the north coast of Thurston Island, between the Hughes and Noville Peninsulas. Named for the *Glacier.*

**Glacier Bluff.** 62°32′S, 59°48′W. 30 m. An ice cliff which forms the north side of the entrance to Yankee Harbor, in Greenwich Island, in the South Shetlands. Charted and named by the personnel on the *Discovery II* in 1935.

**Glacier Dome**   *see*   **McLeod Hill**

**Glacier milk.** Also called glacial milk. This is wet, white liquid formed from glacial flour (q.v.).

**Glacier Roads**   *see*   **Glacier Bight**

**Glacier Strait.** 73°25′S, 169°25′E. Off the coast of Victoria Land, in the Ross Sea. To the east of it is Coulman Island, and to the west of it are Cape Jones, Borchgrevink Glacier Tongue, and Mariner Glacier Tongue. The *Glacier* was the first vessel to navigate it, in Feb. 1965. Named for this icebreaker, and for the nearby glacier tongues, by M.R.J. Ford, NZ surveyor who was aboard the *Glacier* at that time (*see* **Mount Ford**).

**Glacier tongues.** Portions of a glacier which are afloat in the sea, but still attached to the glacier itself.

**Glaciers.** Streams of ice running down a valley. The original glaciers were streams of ice formed on the tops of high mountains about 50 million years ago, and they ran down valleys to the sea where they formed ice shelves. The more glaciers that fed a common area, the larger the ice shelf thus fed. Some glaciers receded during warmer eras in Antarctica's history, and thus dry valleys were formed. Glaciers either move from high ground to low ground, or they float. If they float they spread. Ice sheets, ice shelves, ice piedmonts and mountain glaciers, are all forms of glacier. The early American sealers would often call glaciers "icebergs." The biggest and fastest-moving glacier is Byrd Glacier, flowing at 7½ feet per day into the Ross Ice Shelf. The longest in the world is the Lambert Glacier, its upper section being known as the Mellor Glacier. Transverse glaciers flow east and west from low divides on the spine of the Antarctic Peninsula. Wilkins mistook these for straits of sea ice while he was flying overhead in 1928–30, because from the air they look like channels. It was only later ground checks which disproved his theory that the Antarctic Peninsula was not part of the continent.

**Glaciologist Bay.** 71°14′S, 5°30′W. 25 miles long. Ice-filled. In the SW part of the Jelbart Ice Shelf, on the Queen Maud Land coast. Named Glasiologbukta (glaciologist bay) by the Norwegians, and later translated into English.

**Glaciology.** The study of ice. It used to mean the study of glaciers only. Much is unexplained about the origins and demise of glaciers and ice sheets. 20,000 years ago North America, then under the Laurentide Ice Sheet, probably looked much like Antarctica does today.

**Glade Bay.** 73°58′S, 115°15′W. An Amundsen Sea indentation into the coast of Marie Byrd Land.

**Cape Glandaz** *see* **Glandaz Point**

**Glandaz Point.** 65°05′S, 63°59′W. Forms the south side of the entrance to Deloncle Bay, on the west coast of Graham Land. Charted by Charcot in 1903–5, and named by him as Cap Glandaz, for a man named A. Glandaz. It was later called Glandaz Point in English.

**Glasgal Island.** 66°12′S, 110°23′E. A small island which marks the SW end of the Donovan Islands, in Vincennes Bay. Named by Carl Eklund in 1957 for Ralph Glasgal, aurora scientist at Wilkes Station in 1957.

**Mount Glasgow.** 71°08′S, 162°53′E. 2,490 m. 4 miles NW of Mount Webb, in the Explorers Range of the Bowers Mountains. Named by the NZGSAE 1967–68 for J. Glasgow, field assistant with the expedition.

**Glashaugen Hill.** 72°12′S, 27°24′E. 2 miles north of the Bleiskoltane Rocks, near the head of Byrdbreen, in the Sør Rondane Mountains. Name means "the glass hill" in Norwegian.

**Glasiologbukta** *see* **Glaciologist Bay**

**Glass, R.H.** Captain of the *Francis Allyn* in the South Shetlands during the 1870s (see that vessel for dates and incidents).

**Glass Point.** 61°56′S, 58°12′W. 4½ miles SW of False Round Point, on the north coast of King George Island, in the South Shetlands. Named by the UK in 1960 for R.H. Glass.

**Glaze.** Called glazed frost in Britain. Ice-coating that forms when supercooled rain, drizzle, or fog drops land on surfaces which have temperatures near or below freezing level.

**Glazed frost** *see* **Glaze**

**Mount Gleadell.** 66°57′S, 50°27′E. 560 m. Ice-free. The highest summit on the headland just north of Observation Island, at the east side of Amundsen Bay. Discovered in Oct. 1956 by P.W. Crohn's ANARE party, and named by the Australians for Geoffrey Gleadell, cook at Mawson Station in 1954.

The *Gleaner*. American whaling brig of 166 tons, built at Troy, Mass. (now part of Maine). Registered in New Bedford, Mass., on May 12, 1818. It left New Bedford at the end of Oct. 1820 for the 1820–21 seal rush in the South Shetlands, under the command of Capt. David Leslie, who owned the vessel with John A. Parker. They arrived too late, and were unsuccessful, leaving Antarctica on March 24, 1821. Thomas A. Boyd succeeded Leslie as captain on July 5, 1821.

Gleaner Heights. 62°35′S, 60°15′W. A series of elevations extending SW from Leslie Hill, in the eastern part of Livingston Island. Named by the UK in 1958 for the *Gleaner*.

Mount Gleaton. 72°12′S, 168°27′E. 2,130 m. Overlooks the Tucker Glacier from the north, near the end of the ridge just north of the Helman Glacier, in the Admiralty Mountains. Named for CWO Clarence E. Gleaton, US Army, helicopter pilot here in 1961–62.

Glee Glacier. 78°16′S, 163°E. Enclosed by the two arms of Dismal Ridge, it flows into Roaring Valley. Named by the New Zealanders in 1960–61, who were always happy to see it through the mists of Dismal Ridge.

Mount Gleeson. 71°15′S, 66°09′E. 6 miles west of Mount Woinarski, in the Prince Charles Mountains. It has a rock ridge extending SE from it for 2 miles. Named by the Australians for T.K. Gleeson, weather observer at Wilkes Station in 1965.

Glen Glacier. 80°44′S, 25°16′W. 7 miles long. Joins Recovery Glacier to the west of the Read Mountains, in the Shackleton Range. Named by the BCTAE in 1957 for Alexander R. Glen, member of the Committee of Management of the BCTAE.

Glen Peak. 66°46′S, 67°24′W. On the north end of Liard Island, in Hanusse Bay. Named by the UK for John W. Glen, British physicist specializing in ice.

Glenzer, Hubert, Jr. Lt. (jg). Pilot on Operation Windmill, 1947–48.

Glenzer Glacier. 65°58′S, 103°15′E. 5 miles west of Conger Glacier, it flows from Knox Land into the east part of the Shackleton Ice Shelf. Named for Hubert Glenzer.

Gless Peak. 72°12′S, 165°51′E. 2,630 m. 2 miles WSW of Cirque Peak, in the Millen Range. Named for Elmer E. Gless, biologist at Hallett Station in 1965–66, 1966–67, and 1967–68.

Glidden, C. Seaman on the *Aurora*, 1914–16.

Glimpse Glacier. 78°16′S, 162°46′E. An alpine glacier. Has two parts to it, separated by an icefall. Flows from the area between Mount Kempe and Mount Huggins. Joins Pipecleaner Glacier 2 miles south of the confluence of that glacier with Radian Glacier. Named by the VUWAE 1960–61 because they went up this glacier in order to get their only glimpse of the Polar Plateau in Jan. 1961.

Glinka Islands. 69°23′S, 72°17′W. A small group in Lazarev Bay, just east of Rothschild Island. Named by the UK for the composer.

Gliozzi Peak. 80°01′S, 81°31′W. 1,475 m. 3 miles south of Plummer Glacier, in the Douglas Peaks of the Heritage Range. Named for James Gliozzi, glaciologist on the USARP South Pole-Queen Maud Land Traverse I (1964–65).

Glitrefonna Glacier. 71°57′S, 25°33′E. At the north side of Mount Bergersen, in the Sør Rondane Mountains. Name means "the glitter glacier" in Norwegian.

The *Globe V*. Whale catcher in East Antarctica waters in 1932–33. Rescued some of Riiser-Larsen's party of that season who had tried sledging on the sea ice.

Globemaster  *see*  Airplanes

The *Glomar Challenger*. Deep sea drilling project ship, drilling sediments in the floors of the Antarctic Ocean since 1972. Built in the late 1960s by Global Marine Inc., it is the sister ship of the *Glomar Explorer*. 400 feet long, 65 feet wide, and 10,500 tons, it has a 142-foot derrick amidships, and can house 70 persons. It can drill to 20,000 feet and bring back core samples from 2,500 feet below the sea floor.

**Glomar Challenger Basin.** 77°30'S, 180°. Submarine feature of the Ross Sea. Named for the *Glomar Challenger.*

**Glopeflya Plain.** 72°07'S, 10°25'E. Ice-covered. Between the Orvin Mountains and the interior ice plateau of Queen Maud Land. Name means "the ravine plateau" in Norwegian.

**Glopeneset.** 72°11'S, 10°E. A promontory, mainly ice-covered, at the south side of Glopeflya Plain and the Orvin Mountains of Queen Maud Land. Name means "the ravine promontory" in Norwegian.

**Glopenesranen Nunatak.** 72°08'S, 10°01'E. Surmounts the northern end of Glopeneset, at the south side of Glopeflya Plain, in Queen Maud Land. Name means "the ravine promontory" in Norwegian.

**Glories** *see* **Phenomena**

*Glossopteris.* A genus of fossil plants dating to the late Paleozoic Era (ending 225 million years ago). Discovered in 1824 and considered to be a fern, it was later declared to be a gymnosperm, and later still an angiosperm, or flowering plant. Wilson discovered some in Feb. 1912. *Gangamopteris* is a variety also found in Antarctica.

**Mount Glossopteris.** 84°44'S, 113°43'W. 2,865 m. Mainly ice-covered. Has exposed horizontal bedding on the northern face. At the NE end of Buckeye Table, in the Ohio Range. Named for *Glossopteris* (see above) by William Long (*see* **Long Hills**) who, with Charles Bentley and Fred Darling, climbed to the top in Dec. 1958.

**Glossopteris Gully.** 70°51'S, 68°06'E. On the east side of Bainmedart Cove, Radok Lake, in the Prince Charles Mountains. Named by the Australians for the *Glossopteris* found here.

**Glover, John.** Captain of the topsail during the Wilkes Expedition 1838–42. Joined at Callao. Served the cruise.

**Glover Rocks.** 67°46'S, 68°55'W. Rocks in water, NNW of Avian Island, off the south end of Adelaide Island. Named by the UK for John Glover, 3rd engineer of the *John Biscoe,* 1962–63, whose ship charted these rocks that summer.

**Gloves.** For the tourist they must be warm, woolen, and waterproof, with thin gloves under the mittens. Mittens are better than fingered gloves (*see also* **Clothing**).

**Mount Glowa.** 75°27'S, 73°17'W. 8 miles west of Mount Hirman, in the Behrendt Mountains of Ellsworth Land. Discovered aerially by the RARE in 1948, and named by Ronne for Col. L. William Glowa, who helped get support for the expedition.

**Gløymdehorten Nunatak.** 72°07'S, 12°09'E. On the west side of Horteriset Dome, just west of the Weyprecht Mountains of Queen Maud Land. Named by the Norwegians.

**Lake Glubokoye.** 67°40'S, 45°52'E. Just east of Lake Lagernoye and Molodezhnaya Station, in the Thala Hills of Enderby Land. Named in 1961–62 by the USSR. Name means "deep."

**Gluck Peak.** 71°39'S, 72°35'W. 500 m. Between the heads of the Weber and Boccherini Inlets, on Beethoven Peninsula, in the SW part of Alexander Island. Named by the UK for the composer.

**Gluvreklett Glacier.** 72°14'S, 2°35'E. Flows between Von Essen Mountain and Terningskarvet Mountain, in the Gjelsvik Mountains of Queen Maud Land. Named Gluvreklettbreen by the Norwegians.

**Gluvrekletten Peak.** 72°12'S, 2°32'E. 2,200 m. Between Terningskarvet Mountain and Nupskammen Ridge, in the Gjelsvik Mountains of Queen Maud Land. Named by the Norwegians.

**Gneiskopf Peak.** 71°56'S, 12°07'E. Also called Gneisskolten. 2,930 m. 5

miles SW of Mount Neustruyev, at the south end of the Südliche Petermann Range of the Wohlthat Mountains in Queen Maud Land. Discovered and named by Ritscher in 1938–39. Name means "gneiss peak."

**Gneiss Hills.** 60°44'S, 45°39'W. Two hills, 270 m. and 260 m. At the west side of McLeod Glacier, in the south part of Signy Island, in the South Orkneys. Surveyed by the FIDS in 1947, and named by them because of a band of pink gneiss outcrops near the summits.

**Gneiss Lake.** 60°44'S, 45°39'W. In the Gneiss Hills, at the west side of McLeod Glacier, in the south part of Signy Island, in the South Orkneys. Named by the UK in association with the hills.

**Gneiss Point.** 77°23'S, 163°44'E. 2 miles north of Marble Point, on McMurdo Sound, in Victoria Land, just in front of the Wilson Piedmont Glacier. Mapped by Scott's 1910–13 expedition, and named by them for the gneissic granite here.

**Gneisskolten** *see* **Gneiskopf Peak**

**Gneysovaya Peak.** 71°33'S, 12°10'E. 2,050 m. Between Krakken Mountain and Sandseten Mountain, in the Westliche Petermann Range of the Wohlthat Mountains, in Queen Maud Land. Discovered by Ritscher in 1938–39. Named Gora Gneysovaya (gneiss mountain) by the USSR in 1966.

**Gnezdovoy Point.** 67°39'S, 46°06'E. On Alasheyev Bight, in Enderby Land. 7½ miles east of Molodezhnaya Station.

**Mount Gniewek.** 79°20'S, 158°57'E. 2,060 m. Ice-covered. Flat-topped. At the north side of Carlyon Glacier, 6 miles SW of Mount Keltie. Named for John J. Gniewek, geomagnetician at Little America in 1958.

**Gnome Island.** 67°33'S, 66°50'W. Between the east end of Blaiklock Island and Thomson Head, near the head of Bourgeois Fjord, off the west coast of Graham Land. Surveyed and named by the FIDS in 1949. It looks like a small gnome coming out of the water.

**Gnomon Island.** 61°06'S, 54°52'W. Just north of Point Wild, Elephant Island, in the South Shetlands. Charted by Shackleton's 1914–17 expedition, and named by them because, when seen from the point, it looks like the elevated arm of a sundial.

**Goat Mountain.** 77°55'S, 163°50'E. 1,640 m. West of Hobbs Glacier, between Hobbs Peak and Mount Kowalczyk, in Victoria Land. Charted by the VUWAE 1960–61, and named by them because a balanced mass of gneiss with a goatlike silhouette protrudes 10 meters above the general profile of the southern slope of the mountain.

**Gobamme Rock.** 68°22'S, 41°56'E. Also called Gobanme Rock. Between Kozo Rock and Byobu Rock, on the coast of Queen Maud Land.

**Mount Gobey.** 72°58'S, 165°15'E. 3,125 m. The highest mountain in the Retreat Hills, at the south edge of the Evans Névé. Climbed on Dec. 26, 1966, by the Northern Party of the NZGSAE 1966–67, who named it for the party's field assistant, D.W. Gobey.

**Gockel, Wilhelm.** Meteorological assistant on the German New Schwabenland Expedition of 1938–39, led by Ritscher.

**Gockel Ridge.** 72°42'S, 0°12'E. Extends from Alan Peak to Nupskåpa Peak, at the south end of the Sverdrup Mountains. Ritscher discovered it in 1938–39, and named it Gockel-Kamm, for Wilhelm Gockel. The name was later translated into English.

**Goddard, Samuel H.** First mate on the *Huron*, 1820–21.

**Goddard Hill** *see* **Bynon Hill**

**Godel Bay** *see* **Godel Iceport**

**Godel Iceport.** 70°09'S, 21°45'E. 5 miles wide. 2½ miles deep. Indentation in the ice shelf of the Princess Ragnhild Coast. Discovered on March 26, 1956, by the *Glacier*. Named Godel Bay. It was later redefined.

**Godfrey Upland.** 68°44′S, 66°23′W. A small remnant plateau, with an undulating surface and a mean elevation of 1,500 m. In southern Graham Land. Named by the UK for Thomas Godfrey (1704–49), American inventor of the quadrant in 1730. It is bounded by the Clarke, Meridian, Lammers, and Cole Glaciers.

**Godfroy, René.** French naval sublieutenant and scientist on the *Pourquoi Pas?* with Charcot in 1908–10. His specialties were tides and atmospheric chemistry. He later became an admiral.

**Godfroy Point.** 65°10′S, 64°10′W. Marks the northern extremity of Petermann Island, in the Wilhelm Archipelago. Discovered by Charcot in 1908–10, and named by him for René Godfroy.

**Goepfert Bluff.** 74°39′S, 110°19′W. On Bear Peninsula, on the coast of Marie Byrd Land.

**Goetschy Island.** 64°52′S, 63°31′W. Also called Priest Island, Islote Grillete. Near the middle of Peltier Channel, in the Palmer Archipelago. Charted and named by Charcot in 1903–5.

**Goettel Escarpment.** 70°14′S, 66°55′W. 5 miles north of the Orion Massif, near the head of Chapman Glacier, in Palmer Land. Named for Capt. Frederick A. Goettel, US Coast Guard, commander of the *Westwind* while the new Palmer Station was being built in 1966–67.

**Goff, Robert G.** Lt. (jg), USN. Co-pilot of planes off the *Pine Island* during Operation Highjump, 1946–47. He was in the plane which found the survivors of the crashed Martin Mariner that expedition.

**Gold.** Has been found in Antarctica.

**The *Gold Ranger.*** British Royal Fleet auxiliary vessel at Deception Island, 1949–50, in company with the *Bigbury Bay.* Captain was W.R. Parker.

**Golden Cap.** 84°20′S, 164°26′E. 2,870 m. A peak, the highest point on the ridge running NW from Mount Falla,

between that mountain and Fremouw Peak, in the Queen Alexandra Range. Named by the Ohio State University party to the Queen Alexandra Range in 1966–67, because the peak consists mainly of a buff-weathering massive sandstone.

**Golden Pass.** 69°23′S, 70°47′W. In northern Alexander Island.

**The *Golden West.*** This US sealer/whaler from New London was at the Kerguélens (not in the Antarctic) under Simeon Church in 1865–68, and under another Capt. Church at the same place in 1868–71. In 1873–74 and 1874–75 it came down to the South Shetlands under Capt. Williams. In 1875–76 it was back at the Kerguélens, again under Williams. In 1878, under John Williams (possibly the same Capt. Williams) it was at Bouvet Island (not in Antarctica).

**Goldenberg Ridge.** 66°28′S, 110°35′E. Almost a mile long. Runs along the east side of Browning Peninsula, at the south end of the Windmill Islands. Named for Burton D. Goldenberg, meteorologist at Wilkes Station in 1962.

**Cape Goldie.** 82°38′S, 165°54′E. At the south side of the mouth of Robb Glacier, 50 miles to the west of the foot of the Beardmore Glacier, it juts out into the Ross Ice Shelf from the western end of the Holland Range. Discovered by Scott in 1902, and named by him for Sir George Goldie, a member of the committee which made the final draft of the instructions for the expedition (i.e., the Royal Society Expedition).

**Goldman Glacier.** 77°42′S, 162°51′E. 2 miles east of Marr Glacier, flowing from the Kukri Hills into Taylor Valley in Victoria Land. Named for Charles R. Goldman, biologist in Antarctica in 1962–63.

**Mount Goldring.** 66°57′S, 66°01′W. On the north side of Murphy Glacier, to the east of Lallemand Fjord, in Graham Land. Named by the UK for Denis C. Goldring, FIDS geologist at Base W in 1957 and 1958.

**Cape Goldschmidt.** 80°41′S, 161°12′E. Ice-covered. Forms the eastern tip of Nicholson Peninsula, at the west side of the Ross Ice Shelf. Named by the NZGSAE 1960–61 for Donald R. Goldschmidt, a member of the NZGSAE 1959–60 and 1960–61 here.

**Goldschmidt Cirque.** 80°44′S, 22°48′W. In the Shackleton Range.

**Goldsmith, Rainer.** Medical officer, member of the Advance Party during the early part of Fuchs' crossing of the continent during the BCTAE 1955–58.

**Goldsmith Glacier.** 78°56′S, 27°42′W. Flows through the Theron Mountains, 6 miles south of Tailend Nunatak. Named by the BCTAE 1956–57, for Rainer Goldsmith.

**Goldstream Peak.** 86°41′S, 148°30′W. In the Queen Maud Mountains.

**Goldsworthy Ridge.** 67°41′S, 63°03′E. Runs north from Mount Henderson, in the NE part of the Framnes Mountains of Mac. Robertson Land. Photographed by the LCE 1936–37. Named by the Australians for R.W. Goldsworthy, survey field assistant with the *Thala Dan* ANARE of 1962.

**Mount Goldthwait.** 77°59′S, 86°03′W. 3,815 m. 2½ miles south of Mount Dalrymple, in the Sentinel Range. Discovered by the Marie Byrd Land Traverse Party of 1957–58, and named by the leader of the party, Charles Bentley, for Richard P. Goldthwait, consultant on the Technical Panel on Glaciology, US National IGY Committee.

**Golubaya Bay.** 69°58′S, 9°50′E. In the SE extremity of Kamenev Bight, along the ice shelf fronting Queen Maud Land. Named Bukhta Golubaya (azure bay) by the USSR in 1961.

**Gomez Nunatak.** 73°57′S, 68°38′W. Isolated. 40 miles SW of Mount Vang, surmounting the interior ice plateau near the base of the Antarctic Peninsula. Named for José M. Gomez, mechanic at Eights Station in 1965.

**Gommen Valley.** 73°53′S, 5°17′W. Ice-filled. Between Tunga Spur and Kuven Hill, near the SW end of the Kirwan Escarpment, in Queen Maud Land. Name means "the gum" in Norwegian.

**Gondola Nunakol** *see* **Gondola Ridge**

**Gondola Ridge.** 77°02′S, 161°45′E. Also called Gondola Nunakol. Just south of Mackay Glacier, in southern Victoria Land. It extends 4 miles NE from Mount Suess. Charted by the Western Geological Party of Scott's 1910–13 expedition, and named by them because Mount Suess looks like a gondola.

**Gondwana Province** *see* **East Antarctica**

**Gondwanaland.** In 1858 A. Snider first proposed the idea of continental drift, i.e., the earth's continents having moved in the past. Eduard Suess, an Austrian geologist, invented the name Gondwanaland in the 1890s, and Alfred Wegener proposed the theory in 1912 of an ancient super-continent formed (as was Laurasia, says the theory) out of the primeval continent of Pangaea about 190 million years ago, and Gondwanaland itself breaking up about 120 million years ago into what are now Africa, Arabia, India, South America, Oceania, and Antarctica. Named for the Gondwana region of India, whose coast seems to fit into the Antarctic coastline. The theory led to the science of tectonics, and remained unaccepted until 1967 when Peter Barrett dug up his labyrinthodont. Countries hold Gondwana symposiums.

**Gonville and Caius Range.** 77°05′S, 162°14′E. Between the Mackay and Debenham Glaciers in Victoria Land. Mapped by Scott's 1910–13 expedition, and named for the Cambridge college, alma mater of several members of the expedition.

**Mount González.** 77°11′S, 144°33′W. 1 mile east of Asman Ridge, in the Sarnoff Mountains of the Ford Ranges, in Marie Byrd Land. Named for Oscar González, Chilean geologist on the USARP Marie Byrd Land Survey II, 1967–68.

**González, Capt.** Ernesto González Navarrete, capitán de fragata (frigate). Captain of the *Iquique* on the Chilean Antarctic Expedition of 1946–47, led by Guesalaga. Leader of the Chilean Antarctic Expedition of 1947–48.

**Gonzalez, Domingo.** Seaman on the Wilkes Expedition 1838–42. Joined at Rio. Returned in the *Relief* in 1839.

**González Videla, Gabriel.** President of Chile from 1946 to 1952. Visited Antarctica during the Presidential Antarctic Expedition of 1948.

**González Anchorage.** 63°19′S, 57°56′W. Called Tenedero González by the South Americans. On the west side of Kopaitic Island, in the Duroch Islands. Charted by the Chilean Antarctic Expedition of 1948, which named it for Capt. González (q.v.), commander of the expedition.

**González Island.** 62°29′S, 59°40′W. A small island on the south side of the entrance to Iquique Cove, Discovery Bay, Greenwich Island, in the South Shetlands. On the west side it is linked to a smaller island by a spit covered at high tide. Charted by the Chilean Antarctic Expedition of 1946–47, and named by them for Capt. González (q.v.).

**Good Glacier.** 84°12′S, 177°50′E. Flows from the Hughes Range between Mount Brennan and Mount Waterman, into the Ross Ice Shelf. Discovered by the USAS Flight C of Feb. 29–March 1, 1940. Named by Byrd for Vice-Adm. Roscoe F. Good, USN, who helped Operation Highjump, 1946–47.

**Mount Goodale.** 85°45′S, 157°43′W. Has double summits of 2,420 m. and 2,570 m. 6 miles SE of Mount Thorne, in the Hays Mountains of the Queen Maud Mountains. Discovered by Gould's party in Dec. 1929, during Byrd's 1928–30 expedition. Named by Byrd for Edward E. Goodale (the man who first saw it).

**Goodale, Edward E.** b. April 7, 1903, Boston, Mass. Meteorologist, he was one of the 6-man Southern Geological Party led by Gould, which surveyed the Queen Maud Mountains during Byrd's 1928–30 expedition. He discovered a lichen at 85°21′S, on Mount Fridtjof Nansen—the most southerly yet discovered. He also discovered Mount Goodale. He later spent much time in the Arctic. In 1955–56 he was IGY representative to the US Naval Support Force, Antarctica, at Little America V. He took part in the ice-breaker reconnaissance of the Budd Coast that year, looking for a site for Wilkes Station. In 1956–57 he oversaw the installation of equipment for, and the erection of buildings at Byrd Station. From 1959–68 he was USARP representative at Christchurch, NZ, and was with the National Science Foundation from 1962.

**Goodale Glacier.** 85°35′S, 156°24′W. Flows from Mount Goodale and Mount Armstrong, along the west side of Medina Peaks, in the foothills of the Queen Maud Mountains. Discovered by Byrd's 1928–30 expedition. Named in association with Mount Goodale.

**Goodall Ridge.** 71°02′S, 66°50′E. Partly snow-covered. 6 miles WSW of Taylor Platform, in the Prince Charles Mountains. Named by the Australians for A.W. Goodall, diesel mechanic at Davis Station in 1964.

**Cape Goodenough.** 66°16′S, 126°10′E. Ice-covered. Marks the west side of the entrance to Porpoise Bay, on the Banzare Coast. Forms the most northerly projection of Norths Highland. Discovered aerially by the BANZARE in Jan. 1931, and named by Mawson for Adm. Sir William Goodenough, president of the Council of the Royal Geographical Society, 1930–33, and patron of the BGLE 1934–37.

**Goodenough Glacier.** 72°S, 66°40′W. Also called Margaret Goodenough Glacier. To the south of the Batterbee Mountains, it flows from the west shore of Palmer Land into the George VI Sound. Discovered in 1936 by Stephenson, Fleming, and Bertram of the BGLE while they were exploring the sound.

Named by Rymill for Margaret Goodenough, wife of Sir William Goodenough (*see* **Cape Goodenough**).

**Goodhue, Nathaniel.** Captain of the foretopsail during the Wilkes Expedition 1838–42. Joined in the USA. Served the cruise.

**Mount Goodman.** 75°14′S, 72°14′W. Marks the NE extremity of the Behrendt Mountains, in Ellsworth Land. Named for Alan L. Goodman, aurora scientist at Eights Station in 1963.

**Goodman Hills.** 69°27′S, 158°43′E. A coastal group, 10 miles in extent. Just south of Cape Kinsey, between the Paternoster and Tomilin Glaciers. Named for Cdr. Kelsey B. Goodman, USN, plans officer on the staff of the commander, US Naval Support Force, Antarctica, 1969–72; assistant for polar regions in the office of the secretary of defense, 1972–74; member of the Advisory Committee on Antarctic Names, 1973–76.

**Goodspeed Glacier.** 77°29′S, 162°25′E. A small hanging glacier on the south wall of the Wright Valley, between the Hart and Denton Glaciers, in Victoria Land. Named by Bob Nichols for Bob Goodspeed. They were both here as geologists at nearby Marble Point in 1959–60.

**Goodspeed Nunataks.** 72°59′S, 61°10′E. A group of three rows of nunataks, 10–15 miles long. At the west end of the Fisher Glacier, in the Prince Charles Mountains. 30 miles WNW of Mount McCauley. Discovered by K.B. Mather's ANARE seismic party in Jan. 1958, and named by the Australians for M.J. Goodspeed, geophysicist at Mawson Station in 1957.

**Mount Goodwin.** 81°16′S, 85°33′W. The second most prominent summit in the Pirrit Hills. Positioned by the US Ellsworth-Byrd Traverse Party on Dec. 10, 1958, and named for Robert J. Goodwin, glaciologist with the party.

**Goodwin, Robert.** Ordinary seaman on the Wilkes Expedition 1838–42. Joined at Callao. Served the cruise.

**Goodwin Glacier.** 65°06′S, 62°57′W. Flows into Flandres Bay, south of Pelletan Point, on the west coast of Graham Land. Charted by de Gerlache in 1897–99. Named by the UK in 1960 for Hannibal Goodwin (1822–1900), US photography pioneer.

**Goodwin Nunataks.** 84°38′S, 161°31′E. Isolated. 10 miles west of the Marshall Mountains, at the south side of the Walcott Névé. Named for Michael L. Goodwin, geomagnetist at South Pole Station in 1960.

**Goodwin Peak.** 85°54′S, 129°11′W. 2,770 m. 3 miles NE of Mount Bolton, at the west side of Haworth Mesa, in the Wisconsin Range. Named for Cdr. Edmund E. Goodwin, Public Affairs officer on the staff of the commander, US Naval Support Force, Antarctica, 1965 and 1966.

**Mount Goorhigian.** 75°03′S, 133°46′W. 1,115 m. The highest mountain in the Demas Range, in Marie Byrd Land. Named for Martin Goorhigian, meteorologist at Byrd Station in 1961.

**Goorkha Craters.** 79°46′S, 159°33′E. A line of snow-free coastal hills, 2 miles east of Cooper Nunatak, between the Carlyon and Darwin Glaciers. Discovered by Scott's 1901–4 expedition, and named by them in association with the Kukri Hills (a kukri is a Gurkha knife).

**Mount Goossens.** 71°19′S, 35°43′E. 2,200 m. Mostly ice-free. Just south of Mount Pierre, in the Queen Fabiola Mountains. Discovered on Oct. 7, 1960, by the Belgian Antarctic Expedition of 1960–61, led by Guido Derom, who named it for Leon Goossens, photographer of the Belgian party which made reconnoitering aircraft flights in the area.

**Gopher Glacier.** 73°28′S, 94°W. Flows from Christoffersen Heights, between the Bonnabeau and Anderson Domes, in the Jones Mountains. Named by the University of Minnesota–Jones Mountains Party of 1960–61. Gopher is the nickname of the university and of the state of Minnesota.

**Gorden, John.** Quartermaster on the Wilkes Expedition 1838–42. Joined in the USA. Served the cruise.

**Cape Gordon.** 63°51′S, 57°03′W. 330 m. A headland which forms the east end of Vega Island. Discovered by Ross in 1839–43, and named by him for Capt. William Gordon, RN, lord commissioner of the admiralty.

**Mount Gordon.** 67°36′S, 50°17′E. 6 miles NE of Simpson Peak, in the Scott Mountains of Enderby Land. A mountain near here was named by Biscoe in 1831 for Lt. Gen. Charles Gordon, brother-in-law of the Enderby Brothers, owners of Biscoe's vessel. The Australians, unable to identify with certainty Biscoe's Mount Gordon, applied the name to this feature.

**Île Gordon Bennett** *see* **Mount Edgell**

**Gordon Glacier.** 80°17′S, 26°09′W. 25 miles long. Flows from Crossover Pass, through the Shackleton Range, into Slessor Glacier. Named by the BCTAE in 1957 for George P. Pirie-Gordon, treasurer for the expedition.

**Gordon Nunataks.** 72°53′S, 63°48′W. In Palmer Land.

**Gordon Peak.** 72°26′S, 0°32′E. Marks the NW end of the Robin Heights, in the Sverdrup Mountains of Queen Maud Land. Named Gordonnuten by the Norwegians for Gordon de Q. Robin (*see* **Robin**).

**Gordon Valley.** 84°22′S, 164°E. West of Mount Falla, in the Queen Alexandra Range. Named for Mark A. Gordon, aurora scientist at Hallett Station in 1959.

**Gordonnuten** *see* **Gordon Peak**

**Mount Gorecki.** 83°20′S, 57°35′W. 1,110 m. At the SE extremity of the Schmidt Hills, in the Neptune Range. Discovered aerially on Jan. 13, 1956 (*see* the Chronology appendix). Named for aviation electronics technician Francis Gorecki, radioman on the P2V-2N making that flight.

**Gorev Island.** 66°32′S, 92°59′E. A tiny island, between Tokarev Island and Haswell Island, and between Buromskiy Island and Poryadin Island, in the Haswell Islands. Discovered by the AAE 1911–14. Named by the USSR for Demetri Gerof (q.v.) (sic).

**Gorgon Peak.** Unofficial name for a peak at the top of the Mawson Glacier, in Victoria Land, to the immediate south of Griffin Nunatak.

**Mount Gorham.** 74°03′S, 62°04′W. Just SW of Mount Tricorn in the Hutton Mountains of Palmer Land. Named for Charles E. Gorham, builder at Amundsen-Scott South Pole Station in 1967.

**Gorki Ridge.** 71°37′S, 11°37′E. 8 miles long. Forms the east wall of Schüssel Cirque, in the northern part of the Humboldt Mountains of Queen Maud Land. Discovered by Ritscher in 1938–39. Named by the USSR in 1963, for the writer Gorki.

**Mount Gorman.** 70°29′S, 64°28′E. In the north part of the Bennett Escarpment, just west of Mount Canham. 2 miles south of the west end of the Corry Massif, in the Porthos Range of the Prince Charles Mountains. Named by the Australians for C.A.J. Gorman, supervising technician (radio) at Wilkes Station in 1962.

**Gorman Crags.** 71°01′S, 65°27′E. A ridge with 4 craggy peaks on it. 5 miles east of Husky Dome, in the Prince Charles Mountains. Named for C.A.J. Gorman (*see* **Mount Gorman**).

**Gornyye Inzhenery Rocks.** 71°32′S, 148°05′E. A group just south of Deildegasten Ridge, in the Östliche Petermann Range of the Wohlthat Mountains, in Queen Maud Land. Discovered by Ritscher in 1938–39. Named by the USSR in 1966 as Skaly Gornykh Inzhenerov (mining engineers rocks).

**Cabo Gorrochátegui** *see* **Cape Wiman**

**Mount Gorton.** 70°01′S, 159°15′E. 1,995 m. 6 miles WSW of Mount Pérez, in the southern part of the Wilson Hills. Discovered in 1961 by Phillip Law of ANARE. Named by the Australians for John Gorton, Australian minister for the navy (later prime minister).

**Gosling Islands.** 60°39′S, 45°55′W. Just south and west of Meier Point, off the south coast of Coronation Island, in the South Orkneys. Petter Sørlle charted them in 1912–13, and named them Gestlingen. On a later chart he changed the name to Gjeslingene (the goslings). The UK translated it, first as Gosling Islets, and then as Gosling Islands.

**Gosling Islets** *see* **Gosling Islands**

**Gossard Channel.** 66°05′S, 101°13′E. A marine channel between the Mariner Islands and Booth Peninsula, in the central part of the Highjump Archipelago. Named for G.C. Gossard, Jr., air crewman on Operation Highjump, 1946–47.

**Gossler Islands.** 64°42′S, 64°22′W. 3 miles in extent. 1½ miles west of Cape Monaco, Anvers Island. Discovered and named by Dallmann in 1873–74.

**Gösta Peaks.** 72°06′S, 2°44′W. The NE peaks of the Liljequist Heights, in the southern part of the Ahlmann Ridge, in Queen Maud Land. Named Göstapiggane by the Norwegians, for Gösta H. Liljequist.

**Gothic Mountains.** 86°S, 150°W. A group in the Queen Maud Mountains, in the vicinity of the Robert Scott Glacier.

**Gothic Peak.** 72°01′S, 164°48′E. 2,085 m. 4 miles NW of Lavallee Peak, in the West Quartzite Range. Named by the New Zealanders in 1962–63 for its likeness to a Gothic cathedral.

**The *Gotland II*.** West German expedition ship of 1981–82. 305 feet long. Ice-strengthened. On the afternoon of Dec. 18, 1981, in Yule Bay, off the coast of northern Victoria Land, it got pinched in the ice. Within 24 hours it was crushed and sunk. All scientific equipment and supplies were lost, although passengers and crew were rescued by 5 helicopters on board. The geology program had to be canceled (*see also* **GANOVEX**).

**Cape Gotley.** 66°42′S, 57°19′E. Also called Cape Eustnes. Forms the eastern extremity of Austnes Peninsula, at the north side of the entrance to Edward VIII Bay. Photographed by the LCE 1936–37, and named Austnestangen (the east cape tongue) by the Norwegians, in association with the peninsula. Renamed by the Australians in 1958 for Aubrey V. Gotley, officer-in-charge of the ANARE party on Heard Island (53°S) in 1948.

**Goudier, E.** Chief engineer on the *Français* during Charcot's expedition of 1903–5.

**Goudier Island.** 64°50′S, 63°30′W. Composed of bare polished rock. 100 yards north of Jougla Point, in the harbor of Port Lockroy, Wiencke Island. Discovered by Charcot in 1903–5, and named by him for E. Goudier.

**Mount Goudry** *see* **Mount Gaudry**

**Mount Gough.** 81°38′S, 159°22′E. Forms the eastern portion of the Swithinbank Range, in the Churchill Mountains. Rises over 1,000 meters above the west side of the Starshot Glacier, where that glacier is joined by the Donnally Glacier. Named by the USA in 1967 for R.P. Gough, surveyor-general of New Zealand.

**Gough Glacier.** 84°42′S, 171°35′E. 25 miles long. Flows from the northern slopes of the Prince Olav Mountains and the base of the Lillie Range, into the Ross Ice Shelf, between the Gabbro Hills and the Bravo Hills. Named by the Southern Party of the NZGSAE 1963–64 for A.L. Gough, surveyor of the party.

**¹Mount Gould** *see* **Gould Peak**

**²Mount Gould.** 85°48′S, 148°40′W. 2,385 m. Surmounts the central part of the Tapley Mountains, in the Queen Maud Mountains. Discovered by Laurence Gould in Dec. 1929, and named by Byrd for him.

**Gould, Charles "Chips."** Carpenter on Byrd's 1928–30 expedition.

**Gould, Dr. Laurence M.** Laurence McKinley Gould. Second-in-command of

Byrd's 1928–30 expedition, he led the Southern Geological Party during that expedition, and was one of the three men trapped in the Rockefeller Mountains in 1929 (*see* **Airlifts**). He was one of the sponsors of the RARE 1947–48, and was the director of IGY, 1957–58. In the 1960s he was president of SCAR (from 1962–70), and chairman of the Committee on Polar Research, and periodically went back to Antarctica (*see also* the Bibliography).

**Gould Bay.** 78°S, 45°W. Also called Larry Gould Bay, Bahía Austral. A Weddell Sea indentation into the Filchner Ice Shelf, at the junction of that ice shelf with Berkner Island. Discovered in 1947–48 by the RARE, and named by Ronne for Laurence Gould (q.v.), one of the sponsors of the RARE.

**Gould Coast.** 84°30′S, 150°W. Between the west side of the Robert Scott Glacier (83°30′S) and the south end of the Siple Coast (153°W). The most southeasterly of the Ross Ice Shelf coasts. Named by NZ in 1961 for Laurence Gould (q.v.), who in 1929 mapped 175 miles of this coast.

**Gould Glacier.** 66°47′S, 64°39′W. Also called Shelby Glacier. 12 miles long. Flows into Mill Inlet, to the west of the Aagard Glacier, on the east coast of Graham Land. Surveyed by the FIDS in 1946–47, and named East Gould Glacier by them for Rupert T. Gould (1890–1948), British polar historian and cartographer. It was thought to be the eastern part of a huge glacier (*see also* **Erskine Glacier**), but was redefined in 1957, and given its own name.

**Gould Island.** 77°08′S, 148°05′W. 2 miles long. Ice-covered. In the Marshall Archipelago, within the Sulzberger Ice Shelf, off the Marie Byrd Land coast. Just north of Spencer Island. 2 miles NE of Steventon Island. Named for Lt. Stuart S. Gould, USNR, dental officer at McMurdo Station in 1967.

**Gould Nunatak** *see* **Gould Nunataks**

**Gould Nunataks.** 66°30′S, 51°42′E. 18 miles SE of Mount Biscoe in Enderby Land. Discovered in Jan. 1930 by the BANZARE, and named by Mawson as one nunatak, Gould Nunatak, for Lt. Cdr. R.T. Gould, RN, of the Hydrographic Dept. of the British Admiralty, who worked on the Admiralty South Polar Chart. Redefined more plurally by the ANARE in 1964.

**Gould Peak.** 78°07′S, 155°15′W. Also called Mount Gould. 1 mile north of Tennant Peak, in the southern group of the Rockefeller Mountains. Discovered by Byrd's 1928–30 expedition, and named Charles Gould Peak by Byrd for Chips Gould. The name was later shortened.

**Goulden Cove.** 62°11′S, 58°38′W. The southern of two coves at the head of Ezcurra Inlet, Admiralty Bay, King George Island, in the South Shetlands.

**Cape Goupil** *see* **Cape Legoupil**

**Goupil, Ernest-Auguste.** Painter on the *Astrolabe* during Dumont d'Urville's expedition of 1837–40. Died at Hobart, Tasmania, on Jan. 4, 1840.

**Gourdin, Jean.** Jean-Marie-Émile Gourdin. Ensign on the *Astrolabe* during Dumont d'Urville's 1837–40 expedition. He died on board, on Dec. 8, 1839.

**Gourdin Island.** 63°12′S, 57°18′W. Also called Gourdin Rock. Largest island in a group of islands and rocks 1 mile north of Prime Head, the most northern tip of the Antarctic Peninsula. Discovered by Dumont d'Urville in 1837–40, and named by him for Jean Gourdin. It was reidentified and charted by the FIDS in 1945–47.

**Gourdin Rock** *see* **Gourdin Island**

**Mount Gourdon** *see* **Gourdon Peak**

**Pointe Gourdon** *see* **Gourdon Peninsula**

**Gourdon, Ernest.** French geologist/glaciologist who joined the *Français* at Buenos Aires in Dec. 1903 for Charcot's first expedition. He was also with that explorer on his second expedition, in the *Pourquoi Pas?* in 1908–10.

**Gourdon Glacier.** 64°15'S, 57°22'W. 4 miles long. On the east side of James Ross Island. It flows into Markham Bay, between Saint Rita and Rabot Points. Surveyed by Nordenskjöld in 1901–4, and named by him for Ernest Gourdon.

**Gourdon Peak.** 65°05'S, 64°W. Also called Mount Gourdon. ½ mile north of Wandel Peak, on Booth Island, in the Wilhelm Archipelago. Charted and named by Charcot in 1903–5 for Ernest Gourdon.

**Gourdon Peninsula.** 64°24'S, 63°12' W. 6 miles long. Snow-covered. Forms the SE side of Lapeyrère Bay, on the NE coast of Anvers Island. In 1905 Charcot named a point near here as Pointe Gourdon, for Vice-Adm. Gourdon of the French navy. Almost certainly this is the feature which the UK redefined as a peninsula in 1956.

**Gourlay, R.** Third engineer on the *Discovery II* in 1933.

**Gourlay Peninsula.** 60°44'S, 45°36' W. Ice-free. 200 yards wide at its base, it widens to 800 yards. Forms the SE extremity of Signy Island, in the South Orkneys. The east end of the peninsula divides into 3 arms, Pantomime, Pageant, and Gourlay Points. Surveyed in 1933 by the personnel on the *Discovery II,* and again in 1947 by the FIDS. Named by the UK in association with Gourlay Point.

**Gourlay Point.** 60°44'S, 45°36'W. The southernmost of the three arms of the east end of Gourlay Peninsula, in the SE end of Signy Island, in the South Orkneys. Charted in 1933 by the personnel on the *Discovery II,* and named by them for R. Gourlay.

**Île Gouts** *see* **Gamma Island**

**Gouverneur Island.** 66°40'S, 139°57' E. Almost 1¼ miles WSW of Pétrel Island. Almost 2½ miles east of Cape Géodésie, in the southern part of the Géologie Archipelago. Charted and named by the French under Liotard in

1949–51. Liotard was the first man to camp on the island. As leader of the French Polar Expedition he was also honorary governor of Adélie Land.

**Gouvernøren Harbor.** 64°32'S, 62°W. Also called Puerto Svend Foyn. Indents the east side of Enterprise Island, in Wilhelmina Bay, off the west coast of Graham Land. Named by whalers using the harbor because the *Gouvernøren I* was wrecked here in 1916.

**The *Gouvernøren I*.** Whaling vessel wrecked in Wilhelmina Bay in 1916.

**Government.** Antarctica is neutral. There is no government. No passports. No border control. Since 1959 the Antarctic Treaty has laid down certain rules, and these rules are worked out by the Treaty nations. Generally, but not always by any means, people abide by these rules. At the individual bases however, a certain local government has been desirable. Naturally at naval bases there are specified leaders, both military and scientific, and the system works—always has. At Little America V, however, during the IGY period, a federal and municipal government was set up at the station, based on the US system. The first session of the Little America Senate convened in early April 1957. Nine elected senators met to discuss recreation, education, and other aspects of station life in Antarctica, and to pass on their comments to the station command. There was a president, a supreme court (3 justices), and an appointed cabinet (5 members). The court was made up entirely of command heads. Captain Mills Dickey himself was president. There was also a Public Works system—"P.W."—which saw to things like chores, work details, etc.—and no strikes. In the USSR station of Mirnyy, G.I. Greku was elected mayor in 1956. The Communist party leader was always the man to fear at the Russian camps. He may also have been the leader at the station. The leader of the French Antarctic Expedition was the honorary governor of Adélie Land. The British sent their first resident stipendiary magistrate to Deception Island in 1910–11. He was there every summer during the whaling seasons until 1931 (*see also* **William Moyes**).

**The *Governor Brooks*.** American sealing schooner of 40 tons, built in Freeport, Maine, in 1816, and registered in Salem, Mass., on July 13, 1818. Captain was Nicholas Withen. It arrived at Yankee Harbor in the South Shetlands as part of the Salem Expedition, on Jan. 19, 1821. It returned for the 1821–22 season, finally leaving Antarctica on March 6, 1822.

**Governor Islands.** 60°30′S, 45°56′W. A group of islands and rocks, ½ mile north of Penguin Point, the NW end of Coronation Island, in the South Orkneys. Discovered by Powell and Palmer in Dec. 1821. Named by Petter Sørlle in 1912–13.

**Governor Mountain.** 69°43′S, 158°43′E. 1,550 m. Mainly ice-free. At the west side of the head of Tomilin Glacier, in the Wilson Hills. Named by the New Zealanders in 1963–64 for Sir Bernard Fergusson (*see* **Fergusson Glacier**), governor-general of New Zealand.

**Mount Gow.** 71°20′S, 162°40′E. 1,770 m. On the east side of the Rennick Glacier in the Bowers Mountains. Named for Anthony J. Gow, glaciologist for most of the summers between 1959 and 1969 at Byrd, McMurdo, and Amundsen-Scott South Pole Stations.

**Gowan Glacier.** 79°07′S, 85°39′W. 15 miles long. In the Heritage Range. Flows from the vicinity of Cunningham Peak in the Founders Escarpment, into Minnesota Glacier, just east of Welcome Nunatak. Named for Lt. Jimmy L. Gowan, USN, doctor and officer-in-charge of Plateau Station in 1966.

**Goward Peak.** 69°36′S, 72°26′W. On an island off the NW coast of Alexander Island.

**Gowlett Peaks.** 69°53′S, 64°55′E. Isolated. 8 miles NE of the Anare Nunataks, in Mac. Robertson Land. Discovered in Nov. 1955 by J.M. Bécher-

vaise's ANARE party, and named by the Australians for Alan Gowlett, engineer at Mawson Station in 1955. It consists of twin peaks and 2 close outliers.

**Goy, Dr.** French surgeon, who arrived at Adélie Land in Jan. 1957 with Jacques Dubois, and was one of the 4 men to winter-over at Charcot Station that year. He performed an appendectomy in the course of his activities.

**Monte Goyena** *see* **Mount Kirkwood**

**Mount Gozur.** 78°07′S, 85°30′W. 2,980 m. Just NW of the head of Young Glacier. 9 miles east of Mount Bentley, in the central part of the Sentinel Range. Named for Capt. Alexander Gozur, USAF, who helped build the South Pole Station in 1956–57.

**Holmen Graa** *see* **Grey Island**

**Graben Horn.** 71°48′S, 12°01′E. Also called Sökkhornet. 2,815 m. A horn-shaped peak on the east side of the Humboldt Graben, in the central part of the Pieck Range, in the Petermann Ranges of Queen Maud Land. Discovered by Ritscher in 1938–39, and named by him in association with the Humboldt Graben. A graben is a rift valley.

**The *Grace*.** British sealer from Plymouth, in South Shetlands waters in 1821–22, under the command of Capt. Rowe. It moored at New Plymouth for the season.

**Cape Grace** *see* **Grace Rocks**

**Mount Grace McKinley** *see* **McKinley Peak**

**Grace Rock.** 62°22′S, 59°01′W. A rock in water, almost a mile off the south coast of Nelson Island, in the South Shetlands. Named by the UK for the *Grace*.

**Grace Rocks.** 66°25′S, 100°33′E. Formerly called Cape Grace. On the south side of the mouth of Apfel Glacier, at its junction with Scott Glacier. Named for Lt. Philip J. Grace, USN, pilot on Operation Windmill, 1947–48.

**Isla Graciela** *see* **Lautaro Island**

**Graduation Ridge.** 71°27'S, 161°42'E. North of El Pulgar. It forms the northern extremity of the Morozumi Range. Named by the NZGSAE 1967–68 because J.A.S. Dow (*see* **Dow Peak**) received his exam results here.

**Grady, S.** Fireman on the *Aurora*, 1914–16.

**Graf Lerchenfeld Gletscher** *see* **Lerchenfeld Glacier**

**The *Graham*.** A whale catcher belonging to the Norwegian factory ship the *Svend Foyn*. The commander was Capt. Skidsmo. At the end of Feb. 1921 it visited Bagshawe and Lester at Paradise Bay, promising to pick them up the following season (*see* **British Imperial Expedition**). It did, on Dec. 18, 1921, but the two refused the lift, their mission not yet completed. They accepted an offer on Jan. 13, 1922, however.

**Mount Graham.** 85°25'S, 146°45'W. 460 m. In the north part of the Harold Byrd Mountains. Named for Lt. Cdr. R.G. Graham.

**Graham, James.** Ordinary seaman on the Wilkes Expedition 1838–42. Joined in the USA. Served the cruise.

**Graham, R.G.** Lt. cdr., USN. The first leader of Little America V. He wintered-over in 1956, and was relieved by Howard Orndorff.

**Graham Coast.** 65°45'S, 64°W. Also called Graham Land (not to be confused with the more important Graham Land—see below). Between Cape Renard and Cape Bellue, on the west side of the Antarctic Peninsula, opposite the Biscoe Islands. Named by the UK for Sir James R.G. Graham, first lord of the admiralty at the time of Biscoe's exploration in the early 1830s.

**Graham Land.** Centers on 66°S, 63°30'W. The northern part of the Antarctic Peninsula, north of a line stretching across the peninsula from Cape Jeremy on the west coast to Cape Agassiz on the east coast. South of this imaginary line is Palmer Land. That has been the situation

since 1964 when the USA, UK, Australia, and New Zealand agreed to bring some sort of order to the confused naming of the Antarctic Peninsula (see that entry for further details). Biscoe annexed what is now Graham Land for Britain in 1831–32, and named it for Sir James R.G. Graham, first lord of the admiralty. In 1934–37 the British Graham Land Expedition explored and charted much of it.

**Graham Passage.** 64°24'S, 61°31'W. Also called Paso Yelcho, Paso Correa. A marine channel separating Murray Island from the west coast of Graham Land. Named by Capt. Skidsmo for his whale catcher, the *Graham*, which was the first to pass through it, on March 20, 1922.

**Graham Peak.** 66°46'S, 50°58'E. 7 miles east of Mount Riiser-Larsen, in the NW part of the Tula Mountains, in Enderby Land. Named by the Australians for N. Graham, cook at Wilkes Station in 1960.

**Graham Spur.** 70°06'S, 62°30'W. Mostly ice-covered. On the NW side of the Hughes Ice Piedmont. 6 miles south of James Nunatak, on the east side of Palmer Land. Named for William L. Graham, biologist and scientific leader at Palmer Station in 1972.

**Gråhorna Peaks.** 71°36'S, 12°16'E. A cluster of peaks 5 miles west of Store Svarthorn Peak, in the Westliche Petermann Range of the Wohlthat Mountains, in Queen Maud Land. Discovered by Ritscher in 1938–39, and named by him as Graue Hörner (gray peaks). Later translated directly into Norwegian.

**Grainger Valley.** 70°45'S, 67°52'E. 12 miles long, and up to 1 mile wide. It separates the Manning Massif from the McLeod Massif, in the eastern part of the Aramis Range of the Prince Charles Mountains. Named by the Australians for D. Grainger, a member of the ANARE Prince Charles Mountains survey party which crossed it in Feb. 1969. He took part in a similar survey the following year.

**Gråkammen Ridge.** 71°41'S, 12°20'E. Between Gråhorna Peaks and Aurdalen Valley, in the Westliche Petermann Range of the Wohlthat Mountains, in Queen Maud Land. Tambovskaya Peak and Mount Solov'yev are on it. Discovered by Ritscher in 1938–39. Named Gråkammen (the gray ridge) by the Norwegians.

**Gramophones.** Phonographs, Victrolas, record-players, record-machines. The term "gramophone" is a trademark. Von Drygalski recorded penguins' voices on an Edison phonograph. Charcot had one on the *Français,* but they played it only every Sunday, to avoid over-familiarity with the records. Shackleton took one on his 1907–9 expedition, and Amundsen had one at Framheim. Scott had one on his 1910–13 expedition. The Ross Sea party of the British Imperial Transantarctic Expedition had a 1912 HMV Gramophone.

**Mount Gran.** 76°59'S, 160°58'E. 2,235 m. Flat-topped. Just west of Gran Glacier, at the top of the Mackay Glacier, in Victoria Land. Discovered by Scott's 1910–13 expedition, and named by them as Mount Tryggve Gran, for Tryggve Gran. The name was later shortened.

**Gran, Tryggve.** Sub-lieutenant in the Norwegian Naval Reserve who, in 1910, at the age of 20, planned to lead his own expedition to Antarctica. He was introduced to Scott in Norway, by Arctic explorer Fridtjof Nansen, and was persuaded to join the *Terra Nova* as ski expert. He was the principal builder of Granite House (q.v.), and was one of the relief party to sight Scott's tent in Nov. 1912. He wrote several books, and on July 30, 1914, he became the first man to fly over the North Sea in Europe.

**Gran Glacier.** 76°56'S, 161°15'E. Flows into the Mackay Glacier between Mount Gran and Mount Woolnough. Named by the NZ Northern Survey Party of the BCTAE in Nov. 1957 for Tryggve Gran (q.v.), and also in association with the nearby mountain which also bears his name.

**Cape Granat.** 67°39'S, 45°51'E. On Alasheyev Bight, in Enderby Land, about ½ mile NE of Molodezhnaya Station. 7 miles NE of Campbell Glacier, in the west part of the Thala Hills. Named Mys Granat (Cape Granet) by the USSR in 1961–62, and this was translated into English as Granat Point. Later redefined.

**Granat Point**   *see*   **Cape Granat**

**Grand Chasms.** 78°35'S, 39°30'W. Two or more deep crevasses in the Filchner Ice Shelf, extending west from 37°W, just west of the Touchdown Hills. 60 miles long, and between ¼ mile and 3 miles wide. Discovered by the BCTAE 1955–58. In 1957 Dr. Edward Thiel and a party from Ellsworth Station studied them, and named them descriptively.

**Sommet du Grand Pérez**   *see*   **Pérez Peak**

**Isla Grande**   *see*   **Guyou Islands**

**Grandidier Channel.** 65°35'S, 64°45'W. A navigable channel which separates the northern part of the Biscoe Islands from the Graham Coast, off the west coast of the Antarctic Peninsula. Charted by Charcot in 1903–5, and named by him for Alfred Grandidier, president of the Paris Geographical Society. Charcot's idea of the Grandidier Channel was much bigger than that applied to it today. Originally it was the entire body of water between the Biscoe Islands and the coast.

**Grange, Jules.** Assistant naturalist/ surgeon on the *Zélée* during Dumont d'Urville's 1837–40 expedition.

**Mount Granholm.** 71°34'S, 167°18'E. 2,440 m. 9 miles SE of Mount Pittard, in the NW part of the Admiralty Mountains of Victoria Land. Named for Nels H. Granholm, biologist at Hallett Station in 1967–68.

**Gränicher Island.** 66°53'S, 67°43'W. Also called Isla Guacolda. A small island, the most northerly of the Bennett Islands, in Hanusse Bay. Named by the UK for Walter H.H. Gränicher, Swiss physicist specializing in ice molecules.

**Granite.** Found in Antarctica.

**Granite Harbor.** 76°53′S, 162°44′E. Between Cape Archer and Cape Roberts, at the foot of the Mackay Glacier, on the east coast of southern Victoria Land. It is a part of McMurdo Sound. Discovered and named by Scott in Jan. 1902. There are great granite boulders on its shores.

**Granite House.** 76°53′S, 162°44′E. On Cape Geology, on the south shore of Granite Harbor. Built in Nov. 1911 by Grif Taylor, Frank Debenham, Robert Forde, and Tryggve Gran (he was the main builder), as their kitchen, so they could live more comfortably in their tent, as they mapped the coast of Victoria Land during Scott's 1910–13 expedition. 9 feet by 6 feet, it was 5 feet 2 inches high, and was a natural granite shelter. Boulders were added to it, and a sledge was placed on top. The men planted kale sprouts, which flourished. By Jan. 12, 1912, they knew that the *Terra Nova* couldn't get through the ice to pick them up, so they started walking back to the Ross Island base. The ship picked them up on Feb. 14, 1912. In Nov. 1959 Granite House was found by 5 US scientists working the area—Robert L. Nichols, Bill Meserve, Bob Goodspeed, Bob Rutford, and Roger Hart. They then discovered that someone in Sir Edmund Hillary's party had been there a couple of years before from Scott Base. It is unclear who really found Granite House.

**Granite Knob** *see* **John Nunatak**

**Granite Knolls.** 77°53′S, 163°29′E. Conspicuous rock outcrops on the NW flank of the Blue Glacier, 5 miles west of Hobbs Peak, in Victoria Land. Named descriptively by Scott's 1910–13 expedition.

**Granite Pillars.** 83°36′S, 170°45′E. Ice-free rock pillars on the west side of the Beardmore Glacier, 2 miles east of Mount Ida, in the Queen Alexandra Range. Discovered by Shackleton in 1908, and named Cathedral Peaks by him. The name was later changed in order to avoid confusion with another feature of that name.

**Granite Spur.** 73°30′S, 94°24′W. Along the north front of the Jones Mountains, ½ mile west of Avalanche Ridge. Named by the University of Minnesota–Jones Mountains Party of 1960–61 because the basement granite is well-exposed here.

**Granitnaya Mountain.** 72°08′S, 11°38′E. 2,880 m. Just east of Skeidshovden Mountain, in the Wohlthat Mountains of Queen Maud Land. Discovered by Ritscher in 1938–39. Named Gora Granitnaya (granite mountain) by the USSR in 1966.

**Grant Island.** 74°28′S, 131°35′W. 20 miles long. 10 miles wide. Ice-covered. 5 miles east of Shepard Island, in the Getz Ice Shelf, off the coast of Marie Byrd Land. Discovered and charted on Feb. 4, 1962, by the personnel on the *Glacier*. Named for Cdr. E.G. Grant, commander of the *Glacier* at the time.

**The *Granville*.** Argentine ship which took part in the Argentine Antarctic Expedition of 1947–48.

**Cabo Granville** *see* **Cape Smith**

**Graphite.** Also called plumbago, or black lead. A mineral consisting of native carbon. Has been found in Antarctica.

**Graphite Peak.** 85°03′S, 172°43′E. 3,260 m. At the NE end of a ridge running NE for 3 miles from Mount Clarke, just south of the head of the Falkenhof Glacier. It is between Mount Clarke and Mount Usher, in the Queen Maud Mountains. Named by the New Zealanders in 1961–62 for the graphite here. Here, on Dec. 28, 1967, the first fossilized land animal was found in Antarctica, by Dr. Peter Barrett. It was the fossilized jawbone of a primitive lizard, labyrinthodont.

**Graptolite Island.** 60°44′S, 44°28′W. ½ mile long. In the NE part of Fitchie Bay, off the SE part of Laurie Island, in the South Orkneys. Named by Bruce in 1903 for the graptolite fossils here. In 1825 Weddell's chart showed 2 islands here. There is only one now.

**Grass.** There are two grasses native to Antarctica, both found at the northern tip of the Antarctic Peninsula. *Deschampsia parvula* and *Deschampsia elegantula.*

**Grass Bluff.** 85°35'S, 177°14'W. Wedge-shaped. 4 miles NW of Fluted Peak, in the southern part of the Roberts Massif. Named for Robert D. Grass, meteorologist at Amundsen-Scott South Pole Station in 1964.

**Grasshoppers.** Portable, battery-operated automatic weather stations used by the Americans in Antarctica.

**Gråsteinen Nunatak.** 71°57'S, 2°W. Isolated, 7 miles SW of Litvillingane Rocks, on the east side of the Ahlmann Ridge, in Queen Maud Land. Name means "the gray stone" in Norwegian.

**Gratton Nunatak.** 86°06'S, 127°46'W. Ice-free. On the south side of the mouth of McCarthy Glacier, where that glacier enters Reedy Glacier. Named for John W. Gratton, construction mechanic at Byrd Station in 1962.

**Graue Hörner** *see* **Gråhorna Peaks**

**Grautfatet** *see* **Schüssel Cirque**

**Grautskåla Cirque.** 71°37'S, 11°22'E. Just north of The Altar, in the Humboldt Mountains of Queen Maud Land. Discovered by Ritscher in 1938–39. Name means "the mash bowl" in Norwegian.

**Gravenoire Rock.** 66°21'S, 136°43'E. A nunatak, 1 mile SE of Rock X, on the east side of Victor Bay. Charted by the French in 1952–53, and named by them because of its resemblance to Gravenoire, the hill overlooking the city of Clermont-Ferrand, in France.

**Graves, Ludwig.** Seaman on the Wilkes Expedition 1838–42. Joined at Rio. Served the cruise.

**Graves Nunataks.** 86°43'S, 141°30'W. A small group near the edge of the Polar Plateau, 14 miles ESE of Beard Peak, in the La Gorce Mountains of the Queen Maud Mountains. Named for Gerald V. Graves, VX-6 photographer in 1966–67.

**Graveson Glacier.** 71°S, 163°45'E. Flows into the Lillie Glacier from between the Posey Range and the Explorers Range, in the Bowers Mountains. Named by the Northern Party of the NZGSAE 1963–64 for F. Graveson, mining engineer at Scott Base in 1963, and who was field assistant with the party.

**Mount Gravier** *see* **Gravier Peaks**

**Sommet Gravier** *see* **Gravier Peaks**

**Gravier Massif** *see* **Gravier Peaks**

**Gravier Peaks.** 67°12'S, 67°20'W. Also called Gravier Massif, Mount Gravier, Sommet Gravier. Ice-covered. 2 miles NE of Lewis Peaks, on Arrowsmith Peninsula, on the west coast of Graham Land. Discovered by Charcot in 1903, and named by him for Charles Gravier, French zoologist.

**Cape Gray.** 66°51'S, 143°22'E. Actually a small rocky island, joined to the ice-cap of the mainland by an ice ramp. It forms the east side of the entrance to Commonwealth Bay. Discovered by the AAE 1911–14, and named by Mawson for Percy Gray.

**¹Mount Gray** *see* **Mount Flint**

**²Mount Gray.** 75°S, 136°42'W. Also called Mount Grey, Mount Jane Wade. On the east side of Hull Glacier, 2 miles north of Oehlenschlager Bluff, on the coast of Marie Byrd Land. Discovered in 1940 during a USAS flight from West Base, and named for Orville Gray.

**Gray, David.** Capt. Whaling skipper out of Peterhead, Scotland. He came close to forming an expedition to the Weddell Sea in 1891, but the effort was abandoned due to lack of funds.

**Gray, Orville.** Aviation machinist's mate at West Base during the USAS 1939–41. He piloted several flights over Marie Byrd Land.

**Gray, Percy.** 2nd officer on the *Aurora* during the AAE 1911–14.

**Gray Glacier.** 82°23'S, 159°35'E. 6 miles long. South of Tarakanov Ridge, in the Cobham Range. It flows into Prince

Philip Glacier, where the two join the Nimrod Glacier. Named by the New Zealanders in 1964–65 for M. Gray, postmaster and assistant radio officer at Scott Base in 1965.

**Gray Hill.** 82°56'S, 48°29'W. 1,020 m. Mainly ice-covered. 2½ miles south of Crouse Spur, on the east side of the Forrestal Range, in the Pensacola Mountains. Named for Master Sgt. Kitt Gray, USAF, flight engineer on the United States Air Force Electronics Test Unit, 1957–58.

**Gray Nunatak.** 65°06'S, 60°05'W. ½ mile west of Arctowski Nunatak, in the Seal Nunataks, off the east coast of the Antarctic Peninsula. Charted by Nordenskjöld's expedition in 1902 during a sledge journey, and named by him for Capt. David Gray.

**Gray Peak.** 84°20'S, 173°56'E. 2,570 m. At the west side of Canyon Glacier, in the Queen Maud Mountains. 4 miles NE of Mount Hermanson. Named for Thomas I. Gray, Jr., Weather Central (q.v.) meteorologist at Little America V, in 1958.

**Gray Rock.** 74°41'S, 163°17'E. An isolated rock on land, 4 miles ENE of Rhodes Head, at the SE side of the Eisenhower Range, in Victoria Land. Named for Alvin M. Gray, radioscience researcher at McMurdo Station in 1965–66.

**Gray Spur.** 85°10'S, 90°29'W. Between Aaron Glacier and Counts Icefall, on the east side of the Ford Massif, in the Thiel Mountains. A small peak rises from the end of the spur. Named for James L. Gray (*see* **Deaths, 1961**).

**Grayson Nunatak.** 76°47'S, 143°48'W. 3 miles west of Mount Crummey, it is the most northwesterly of the Gutenko Nunataks, in the Ford Ranges of Marie Byrd Land. Discovered by the USAS 1939–41. Named for Donald E. Grayson, engineer at Byrd Station in 1970.

**Isla Graziella** *see* **Lautaro Island**

**Grease Ice.** Like frazil ice (q.v.), but in a later stage of development of sea ice. It is frazil which agglutinates into a surface like an oil slick.

**Greason, Sydney.** Commissary steward on the *City of New York* during Byrd's 1928–30 expedition.

**Great Antarctic Horst** *see* **Transantarctic Mountains**

**Great Barrier** *see* **Ross Ice Shelf**

**Great Britain.** Britain has as good a claim on Antarctica, or rather their sector of it (*see* **Territorial Claims** and **British Antarctic Territory**) as anyone, having pioneered exploration and navigation with the likes of Cook, Smith, Bransfield, Weddell, Ross, Scott, Shackleton, Bruce, Rymill, and Fuchs. One of the original 12 signatories of the Antarctic Treaty, in 1959, Great Britain has, or has had, the following scientific stations in Antarctica: Port Lockroy, Base B, Base D, Base E, Base F (Faraday Station), Base H (Signy Island Station), Base J, Base K (Fossil Bluff Station), Base N, Base O, Base W, Base Y, Halley Bay, Halley Station, Rothera.

**Great Hånakken** *see* **Stor Hånakken Mountain**

**Great Icy Barrier** *see* **Ross Ice Shelf**

**Great Mackellar Islet** *see* **Greater Mackellar Island**

**Great Piedmont Glacier** *see* **Wilson Piedmont Glacier**

**Great Southern Barrier** *see* **Ross Ice Shelf**

**Great Wall Station.** 62°13'S, 58°58'W. The first Chinese scientific station in Antarctica. Located on Fildes Peninsula, King George Island, in the South Shetlands, just over a mile from Bellingshausen Station and Teniente Rodolfo Marsh Station. The crew arrived on Dec. 30, 1984, and completed it by Feb. 20, 1985. A monolith has been erected to commemorate the "Great Wall Station, First Chinese Antarctic Research Expedition, 20 February, 1985."

**Greater Antarctica** *see* **East Antarctica**

**Greater Mackellar Island.** 66°58'S, 142°39'E. Also called Great Mackellar Islet. The largest of the Mackellar Islands. 2 miles north of Cape Denison, in the center of Commonwealth Bay. Discovered by Mawson during the AAE 1911–14, and named by him in association with the group.

**Greaves, Capt.** Commander of the British sealer *Brusso,* in the South Shetlands, 1821–22.

**Greaves Peak.** 62°28'S, 59°59'W. 240 m. Double-pointed. Near the NW end of Greenwich Island, in the South Shetlands. Charted by the personnel on the *Discovery II* in 1935, and named by them descriptively as Black Peak. Renamed by the UK in 1961, for Capt. Greaves, in order to avoid duplication with another feature of the name Black Peak.

**Greben Island.** 66°31'S, 93°01'E. Just north of the east end of Haswell Island, in the Haswell Islands. Named by the USSR in 1956 for its shape (greben means comb).

**Greece.** Ratified on June 8, 1987, as the 34th signatory of the Antarctic Treaty.

**Greegor Peak.** 76°53'S, 145°14'W. 550 m. 3 miles WSW of Mount Passel, in the Denfeld Mountains of the Ford Ranges, in Marie Byrd Land. Named for David H. Greegor, biologist on the USARP Marie Byrd Land Survey II, 1967–68.

**Cape Green.** 63°39'S, 56°50'W. An ice cliff which forms the SE extremity of Tabarin Peninsula, at the NE end of Graham Land. Charted by the FIDS in 1946, and named by them for Michael C. Green.

**Green, C.J.** Cook on the *Endurance* during the British Imperial Transantarctic Expedition of 1914–17. He also fulfilled that function on the *Quest,* during Shackleton's last expedition, 1921–22.

**Green, Daniel.** Gunner's mate on the Wilkes Expedition 1838–42. Joined in the USA. Served the cruise.

**Green, Ezra.** Yeoman on the Wilkes Expedition 1838–42. Joined in the USA. Served the cruise.

**Green, James.** Captain of the topsail on the Wilkes Expedition 1838–42. Joined in the USA. Served the cruise.

**Green, John.** Bosun's mate on the Wilkes Expedition 1838–42. Joined in the USA. Discharged at Oahu on Oct. 31, 1840.

**Green, Madison.** Ordinary seaman on the Wilkes Expedition 1838–42. Joined at Rio. Served the cruise.

**Green, Michael C.** FIDS geologist, one of the two victims of the fire at Base D in Nov. 1948 (*see* **Deaths, 1948**).

**Green, Thomas.** Quartermaster on the Wilkes Expedition 1838–42. Joined in the USA. Served the cruise.

**¹Green Glacier.** 64°58'S, 61°52'W. 15 miles long. 4 miles wide. Flows from the plateau of Graham Land, into the west side of Hektoria Glacier, on the east side of the Antarctic Peninsula. Surveyed by the FIDS in 1955. Named by the UK for John R. Green, FIDS leader at Base B in 1950 and at Base F in 1951.

**²Green Glacier.** 79°43'S, 156°10'E. On the west side of Haskell Ridge. Flows from the Darwin Mountains into Darwin Glacier. Named by the Darwin Glacier Party of the BCTAE in 1957 because of the color of the surface.

**Green Ice Rises.** 66°22'S, 97°35'E. 5 miles east of Henderson Island. It is a bump in the ice surface where the Shackleton Ice Shelf runs over an obstruction. Named for Duane L. Green, radio operator and recorder on Operation Windmill, 1947–48.

**Green Island.** 65°19'S, 64°10'W. The most northerly of the Berthelot Islands, just outside Collins Bay, off the west coast of Graham Land. Discovered by Charcot in 1903–5. On the northern slopes of the island is a green growth of moss, 4 acres in extent. Due to this rich growth of vegetation, it is an SPA (*see* **Specially Protected Areas**).

**Green Lake.** 77°33′S, 166°09′E. A little lake, ¼ mile north of Cape Royds, between Pony Lake and Coast Lake, on the west coast of Ross Island. Named for its color by Shackleton's 1907–9 expedition.

**Green Point.** 67°19′S, 59°30′E. Also called Rundneset. Forms the eastern extremity of Fold Island, at the west side of the entrance to William Scoresby Bay. Discovered and named by the personnel on the *William Scoresby* in Feb. 1936.

**Green Reef.** 64°44′S, 63°17′W. A group of low rocks in the Neumayer Channel, just east of Green Spur, Anvers Island. Charted by the *Snipe* in Jan. 1948, and named in association with the nearby spur.

**Green Rocks.** 66°14′S, 110°38′E. A small cluster of rocks in water, ¼ mile east of Honkala Island, and ¼ mile offshore, in the east part of the Swain Islands. Named by Carl Eklund, who surveyed them in 1957, for construction driver 2nd class Sydney E. Green, USN, at Wilkes Station in 1957.

**Green Spur.** 64°43′S, 63°20′W. Green-colored (hence the name given before 1927). Extends from Copper Peak, on the SE side of Anvers Island.

**Green Valley.** 85°04′S, 90°30′W. Ice-filled. Indents the east side of the Ford Massif, just north of Janulis Spur, in the Thiel Mountains. Named by Bermel and Ford, leaders of the Thiel Mountains party here in 1960–61, for David H. Green, camp assistant with the party.

**The *Green Wave*.** US supply ship to McMurdo Station in the 1980s.

**Mount Greene.** 72°07′S, 168°14′E. 2,220 m. On the south side of the mouth of Freimanis Glacier, at the point where that glacier joins Tucker Glacier, in the Admiralty Mountains of Victoria Land. Named for 1st Lt. John H. Greene, US Army, commander of a helicopter detachment here in 1961–62.

**Greene Point.** 73°49′S, 166°09′E. Ice-covered. 7 miles NE of Andrus Point, in Lady Newnes Bay, Victoria Land. Named for Stanley W. Greene, biologist at McMurdo Station in 1964–65.

**Greene Ridge.** 83°13′S, 157°10′E. 5 miles long. Partly ice-covered. Extends northward from Martin Dome to the southern edge of Argosy Glacier, in the Miller Range. Named for Charles R. Greene, Jr., ionosphere physicist at South Pole Station in 1958.

**Mount Greenfield.** 80°46′S, 27°36′W. 1,490 m. South of Fuchs Dome, just west of Stephenson Bastion, in the Shackleton Range. Named by the BCTAE in 1957 for George C. Greenfield, literary agent for the expedition.

**Greenfield, Henry.** Bosun's mate on the Wilkes expedition 1838–42. Joined in the USA. Served the cruise.

**Cape Greenland** *see* **Cape Grönland**

**Mount Greenlee.** 84°50′S, 177°W. 2,030 m. Overlooks the west side of the Shackleton Glacier, just east of Mount Butters. Named by Alton Wade in 1962–63 for David W. Greenlee. Both men were on the Texas Tech Shackleton Glacier Expedition of that year.

**Greenpeace.** International environmental group which, in 1984, began to be concerned about Antarctica and what was happening there in the way of pollution and danger to the native flora and fauna due to tourists. In 1986 it failed to get ashore from its ship, the M.V. *Greenpeace,* in order to build a base, but in 1987 it finally succeeded at Cape Evans on Ross Island, and during the 1987 winter the base was occupied by 3 men and a woman. By 1990 Greenpeace had already collected over a million signatures in favor of preserving Antarctica as a World Park. Its address is 1436 U Street, Room 3, Washington, DC, USA. (*See also* the Bibliography under May.)

**The M.V. *Greenpeace*.** A tug with a speed of 7 knots. It is the flagship of Greenpeace (see above). It tried to reach Ross Island in 1986 with materials to build a base for a 4-man wintering-over party, but was prevented from landing by thick ice, getting to within 25 miles of Cape Evans. It got to the Bay of Whales, and members of the 34-man expedition went ashore briefly.

**Greenshields Peak.** 65°40'S, 64°22'W. Between Leroux Bay and Bigo Bay. 1 mile west of Magnier Peaks, on the west coast of Graham Land. Named by the UK for J. Greenshields, FIDASE pilot, 1955–57.

**Greenstone Point.** 73°30'S, 94°18'W. Along the north front of the Jones Mountains, just east of Austin Valley. Named by the University of Minnesota–Jones Mountains Party of 1960–61 for the color of the rock.

**Greenstreet, Lionel.** First officer on the *Endurance* during the British Imperial Transantarctic Expedition of 1914–17.

**Greenville Valley.** 76°45'S, 160°53'E. Mainly ice-free. South of Elkhorn Ridge, in the Convoy Range of Victoria Land. Contains part of the Northwind Glacier. Named by the NZ Northern Survey Party of the BCTAE in 1957 for the *Greenville Victory*.

**The *Greenville Victory*.** US freighter used during Operation Deep Freeze I and II (i.e., through the immediate pre–IGY period). Nicknamed the *Greenville Vic*.

**Greenwell Glacier.** 71°20'S, 165°E. 45 miles long. Flows between the Mirabito Range and the Everett Range into the Lillie Glacier below Mount Works, in northern Victoria Land. Named for Cdr. Martin D. Greenwell, USN, VX-6 Commander, 1961–62.

**Greenwich Island.** 62°31'S, 59°47'W. Also called Beresino Island, Sartorius Island. 15 miles long. Between ½ mile and 6 miles wide. Between Robert Island and Livingston Island, it is one of the principal islands in the South Shetlands. Yankee Harbor is here. It may originally have been called Lloyd's Land, but in any case it was named with the present name before 1821. Chile claimed and occupied it in 1948.

**Greenwood Valley.** 77°21'S, 162°54'E. Ice-filled. On the west side of the Wilson Piedmont Glacier, between Staeffler Ridge and Mount Doorly, in Victoria Land. Named for Russell A. Greenwood, USN, in charge of heavy equipment maintenance at McMurdo Station in 1962.

**Greer Peak.** 76°47'S, 144°25'W. The most northerly of the Wiener Peaks, in the Denfeld Mountains of the Ford Ranges, in Marie Byrd Land. Named by Byrd for Dr. William E.R. Greer, personal physician to Byrd in the 1950s.

**Cape Gregory** *see* ¹**Gregory Point**

**Mount Gregory.** 82°52'S, 159°44'E. 2,940 m. At the south end of Hochstein Ridge, in the Queen Elizabeth Range, rising from the Cotton Plateau. Named by the Holyoake, Cobham, and Queen Elizabeth Ranges Party of the NZGSAE 1964–65, for M. Gregory, a geologist on the party.

**Gregory Bluffs.** 70°43'S, 165°50'E. Granite bluffs which form the east side of Nielsen Fjord on the north coast of Victoria Land. Named by the ANARE for C. Gregory, ANARE geologist on the *Thala Dan* cruise of 1961–62. He, John Stanwix (*see* **Stanwix Ridge**) and Phillip Law (q.v.) landed a helicopter at the foot of these bluffs in order to study them, on Feb. 12, 1962.

**Gregory Glacier.** 64°08'S, 60°48'W. Flows into Cierva Cove north of Breguet Glacier, on the west coast of Graham Land. Named by the UK in 1960 for H. Franklin Gregory, US helicopter pioneer.

**Gregory Island.** 76°48'S, 162°58'E. A little island off the Victoria Land coast, 2½ miles NE of Cape Archer, just to the north of Granite Harbor. Discovered by Scott's 1901–4 expedition, and named by them as Gregory Point, as they thought it to be a coastal point. It was redefined by Scott's 1910–13 expedition. John W. Gregory was director of the civilian staff of the Royal Society Expedition of 1901–4.

¹**Gregory Point.** 62°55'S, 62°33'W. On the west side of Smith Island, in the South Shetlands, 7 miles SW of Cape Smith. Foster called it Cape Gregory in 1829, but it has since been redefined.

²**Gregory Point** *see* **Gregory Island**

**Gregory Ridge.** 86°03'S, 157°46'W. Descends west from the northern part of Fram Mesa, in the Queen Maud Mountains, and terminates at the east side of the Amundsen Glacier. Named for Lt. Cdr. N.B. Gregory, pilot in Antarctica in 1965.

**Gregory Rock.** 77°40'S, 147°46'W. On the western part of Hershey Ridge, 7 miles WSW of Linwood Peak, in the Ford Ranges of Marie Byrd Land. Named for Elmer D. Gregory, aviation maintenance line crew supervisor at Williams Field in 1967.

**Gremlin Island.** 68°16'S, 67°12'W. A small island just NW of the tip of Red Rock Ridge, off the west coast of Graham Land. Surveyed by the BGLE in 1936. In 1948–49 the FIDS used it as a depot, and a box of rations left there by a sledging party disappeared mysteriously.

**Grenlie, Lloyd K.** Radio engineer on Byrd's 1928–30 expedition. He was stationed on the *Eleanor Bolling*. He had fulfilled a similar function on Byrd's North Pole expedition.

**Gressitt Glacier.** 71°30'S, 161°25'E. 45 miles long. Flows from the area between the Daniels Range and the Emlen Peaks, in the Usarp Mountains, into the Rennick Glacier, just north of the Morozumi Range, in Oates Land. Named for J. Linsley Gressitt, biologist in the Ross Sea area for 6 summers between 1959–60 and 1965–66.

**Grew Peak.** 75°18'S, 110°37'W. Over 1,400 m. On the Mount Murphy massif, in Marie Byrd Land, on the NE spur of the massif, between Benedict Peak and the higher summit peaks. Named for Edward Grew, US exchange scientist at Molodezhnaya Station in 1973.

**Mount Grey** *see* **Mount Gray**

**Grey, James.** Pilot on the Wilkes Expedition 1838–42. Joined at Tongataboo. Discharged at Oahu on Oct. 31, 1840.

**Grey, James H.** Ordinary seaman on the Wilkes Expedition 1838–42. Joined in the USA. Run at Oahu.

**Grey Island.** 60°45'S, 45°02'W. A tiny island, barely ¼ mile long by ⅛ mile wide. Just over ½ mile south of Michelsen Island, near Powell Island, in the South Orkneys. Petter Sørlle named it Holmen Graa (the gray island) in 1912–13. Personnel on the *Discovery II* in the early 1930s translated it into English (using the British form of "grey"). It is part of SPA #15.

**Gribb Bank.** 62°S, 88°E. Submarine feature, out to sea beyond the West Ice Shelf.

**Gribben, W.** Seaman on the *City of New York* during Byrd's 1928–30 expedition.

**Mount Grieg.** 71°27'S, 73°22'W. 500 m. Snow-covered. Overlooks the SE part of Brahms Inlet on Beethoven Peninsula, in the SW part of Alexander Island. Named by the UK for the composer.

**Mount Grier.** 86°41'S, 148°57'W. 3,035 m. On the east side of the Robert Scott Glacier. Forms the most westerly summit in the La Gorce Mountains, in the Queen Maud Mountains. Discovered in Dec. 1934 by Quin Blackburn's party during Byrd's 1933–35 expedition, and named by Byrd for Dr. G. Layton Grier, head of the L.D. Caulk Co., of Milford, Delaware, who contributed dental supplies to Byrd's first two Antarctic expeditions.

**Griffen, John P.** Seaman on the Wilkes Expedition 1838–42. Joined in the USA. Served the cruise.

**Mount Griffin.** 71°11'S, 166°16'E. 1,760 m. 13 miles ESE of Mount Bolt. Marks the southern limit of the Anare Mountains of Victoria Land. Named for CWO Joe R. Griffin, US Army, helicopter pilot here in 1962–63.

**Griffin Nunatak.** 75°55'S, 158°20'E. 2 miles long. Flat-topped. Between Ambalada Peak and Terminal Peak, in the Prince Albert Mountains of Victoria Land, at the top of the Mawson Glacier. Named for Lt. William R. Griffin, USN, officer-in-charge and medical officer of Amundsen-Scott South Pole Station in 1966.

**Mount Griffith.** 85°53'S, 155°30'W. 3,095 m. 4 miles NNE of Mount Vaughan, in the Hays Mountains of the Queen Maud Mountains. Discovered by Gould in Dec. 1929, and named by Byrd for Raymond Griffith of 20th Century–Fox Pictures, who helped assemble movie records of Byrd's 1928–30 expedition.

**Griffith, Clyde W.** Machinist's mate 2nd class, USN. Machinist and tractor operator at West Base during the USAS 1939–41. Initially he was one of the 4 men looking after the Snowcruiser (q.v.).

**Griffith, Griffith.** Captain of the topsail on the Wilkes Expedition 1838–42. Joined in the USA. Run at Sydney.

**Griffith Glacier.** 86°11'S, 149°24'W. Flows from the California Plateau and the Watson Escarpment into the Robert Scott Glacier, between Mount McKercher and Mount Meeks. Named for Lt. Cdr. Philip G. Griffith, aircraft commander in Antarctica in 1966 and 1967.

**Griffith Island.** 66°20'S, 110°29'E. A small island at the south entrance to the Robertson Channel, in the Windmill Islands. Named for Chief Fire Patrolman Russell B. Griffith, USN, at Wilkes Station in 1958.

**Griffith Nunataks.** 76°28'S, 143°45'W. On the south side of Balchen Glacier, between the O'Connor Nunataks and Mount Perkins, in the Ford Ranges of Marie Byrd Land. Discovered aerially by the USAS from West Base in 1940, and named for Clyde W. Griffith.

**Griffith Peak.** 85°47'S, 131°31'W. 1,800 m. In the western part of the Wisconsin Range, at the north side of the mouth of Hueneme Glacier at the junction with Reedy Glacier. Named for Raymond E. Griffith, cook at Byrd Station in 1961 and 1963.

**Griffith Ridge.** 71°22'S, 164°23'E. 5 miles long. In the Bowers Mountains, just within the mouth of Champness Glacier, where that glacier joins Lillie Glacier. Named for Lt. Harry G. Griffith, USN, public works officer at McMurdo Station in 1967.

**Mount Griffiths.** 66°29'S, 54°03'E. Has 2 peaks, 1,650 m. and 1,680 m. 5 miles NW of the Wilkinson Peaks, in the Napier Mountains. Photographed by the LCE 1936–37, and named Mefjell (Middle Mountain) by the Norwegians. The Australians, to avoid duplication, renamed it for G.S. Griffiths, a member of the Australian Antarctic Exploration Committee of 1886.

**Griffiths, E.H.** Crewman on the *Jacob Ruppert*, 1933–34.

**Grigg Peak.** 71°26'S, 167°09'E. 2,130 m. 7 miles west of the north tip of the Lyttelton Range, in the Admiralty Mountains of Victoria Land. Named for Gordon C. Grigg, biologist at McMurdo Station in 1966–67.

**Grikurov Ridge.** 71°17'S, 69°W. Extends for 6 miles westward from the south end of the LeMay Range, in Alexander Island. Named by the UK for Garrik Grikurov, USSR exchange geologist with the BAS here in 1963–64.

**Islote Grillete** *see* **Goetschy Island**

**Grim Rock.** 65°23'S, 64°29'W. A rock in water, 3 miles SSE of Gedges Reef, and 10 miles WNW of Cape Pérez, in the Grandidier Channel, off the west coast of Graham Land. Discovered and named by the BGLE 1934–37.

**Grimes Glacier.** 79°12'S, 84°22'W. Flows from the Anderson Massif in the Heritage Range. Named for Master Chief Equipmentman Paul D. Grimes, USN, who supervised the construction crews while Williams Field was being moved in Feb. 1965.

**Grimes Ridge.** 74°37'S, 110°25'W. Mostly ice-covered. At the north side of

Holt Glacier, on Bear Peninsula, Marie Byrd Land. Named for Capt. E.W. Grimes, in Antarctica with the US Army Aviation Detachment in 1966.

**Grimley Glacier.** 69°09'S, 64°40'W. 15 miles long. 3 miles wide. 3 miles north of Sunfix Glacier. Flows into Casey Glacier, in northern Palmer Land. Named by the UK for Peter H. Grimley of the FIDS, geologist at Base Y and Base E in 1960.

**Mount Grimminger.** 73°18'S, 62°18'W. 1,680 m. Cone-shaped. Mostly ice-covered. On the north side of Meinardus Glacier, just east of its junction with Haines Glacier, on the east coast of Palmer Land. Discovered aerially in Dec. 1940 by the USAS from East Base. Named by the FIDS for George Grimminger.

**Grimminger, George.** US meteorologist and co-author of the Met reports of Byrd's 1928–30 expedition, and Byrd's 1933–35 expedition. He was one of the shore party on the latter expedition.

**Mount Grimsley.** 70°36'S, 66°32'E. 1 mile SW of Mount Abbs, in the Aramis Range of the Prince Charles Mountains. Named by the Australians for S.W. Grimsley, technical officer (ionosphere) at Wilkes Station in 1961 and 1963.

**Grimsley Peaks.** 66°34'S, 53°40'E. Five linear peaks, just south of Stor Hånakken Mountain, in the Napier Mountains of Enderby Land. Photographed by the LCE 1936–37. Named by the Australians for S.W. Grimsley (*see* **Mount Grimsley**).

**Grinda Ridge.** 71°56'S, 4°26'E. 1½ miles long. Just north of Mount Grytøyr, in the Mühlig-Hofmann Mountains of Queen Maud Land. Name means "the gate" in Norwegian.

**Grinder Island.** 77°34'S, 149°20'W. Ice-covered. In the Marshall Archipelago, within the Sulzberger Ice Shelf off the coast of Marie Byrd Land. 7 miles long, and 1 mile wide, it is 13 miles SW of Steventon Island. Named for Harry W. Grinder, aviation structural mechanic, USN, at McMurdo Station in 1967.

**Grinder Rock.** 63°58'S, 61°25'W. The most southerly of a group of rocks extending from the SE end of Intercurrence Island, in the Palmer Archipelago. Named by the UK in 1960 for its tooth-like appearance.

**Grindley Plateau.** 84°08'S, 166°05'E. Ice-capped. Just to the west of the Beardmore Glacier, in the central part of the Queen Alexandra Range. Named for George W. Grindley, senior geologist on the Northern Party of the NZGSAE 1961–62. Named by that party.

**Grinnell Island.** 66°11'S, 110°24'E. ½ mile long. South of Chappel Island, in the Donovan Islands. Named by Carl Eklund for Lt. Sheldon W. Grinnell, USNR, medical officer at Wilkes Station in 1957.

**Griswold, Edward A.** Crewman on the *Bear of Oakland*, 1934–35.

**Grizzly Peak.** 85°58'S, 151°25'W. In the Queen Maud Mountains.

**Grob Ridge.** 83°29'S, 51°22'W. 3 miles long. 3 miles south of Dyrdal Peak, at the south end of the Forrestal Range, in the Pensacola Mountains. Named for Richard W. Grob, cook at Ellsworth Station in 1957.

**Gromov Nunataks.** 67°45'S, 50°40'E. 7 miles ESE of Mount Henry, in the Scott Mountains of Enderby Land. Named by the USSR in 1961–62 for pilot M.M. Gromov.

**The *Grönland*.** Dallmann's ship of 1873–75. The first auxiliary steamship to visit Antarctica. It visited the South Shetlands, the South Orkneys, the Bismarck Strait, and the coast of the Antarctic Peninsula.

**Cape Grönland.** 64°15'S, 63°19'W. Also called Cape Greenland. Forms the northern extremity of Anvers Island. Discovered by Dallmann in 1873–74, and named by him for his ship, the *Grönland*.

**Gross, Henry.** Officer's cook on the Wilkes Expedition 1838–42. Joined in the USA. Run at Oahu.

**Gross Hills.** 79°18'S, 83°22'W. East of Schmidt Glacier, in the Heritage Range. Named by the University of Minnesota Geological Party of 1963–64 for Barton Gross, geologist with the party.

**Grosse Brei-Schüssel** *see* **Schüssel Cirque**

**Grosse Eisebeine** *see* **Ross Ice Shelf**

**Grosses Schwarz-Horn** *see* **Store Svarthorn Peak**

**Grosvenor Mountains.** 85°40'S, 175°E. Also called Grosvenor Range, Gilbert Grosvenor Range. East of Mill Glacier, they extend from Mount Pratt in the north to the Mount Raymond area in the south, and from the Otway Massif in the NW to Larkman Nunatak in the SE. Between the Beardmore and Amundsen Glaciers, in the Queen Maud Mountains. Mount Block and Mount Bumstead are in these mountains. Discovered by Byrd on his Polar flight of Nov. 1929, and named by him for Gilbert Grosvenor, president of the National Geographic Society.

**Grotto Glacier.** 70°45'S, 68°35'W. 25 miles long. 7 miles wide at its mouth. On the east coast of Alexander Island, it flows east into the George VI Sound, between Belemnite Point and Ablation Point. Surveyed in 1936 by the BGLE; and again in 1949 by the FIDS, who named it for the crystal-lined crevasse, or grotto, where they rescued one of their sledge dogs.

**Grotto Island.** 65°14'S, 64°15'W. ½ mile long. 175 yards north of Galíndez Island, in the Argentine Islands. Charted and named in 1935 by the BGLE.

**Ground ice** *see* **Anchor ice**

**Groussac Refugio.** Argentine refuge hut built on Petermann Island in 1955.

**Groux Rock.** 76°13'S, 144°47'W. Isolated. In the north part of the Phillips Mountains, 5 miles ENE of Mount June, in the Ford Ranges of Marie Byrd Land. Named for Roger G. Groux, USN, shipfitter at Byrd Station in 1967.

**Grove Mountains.** 72°45'S, 74°58'E. Also called Grove Nunataks, South Eastern Nunataks. 40 miles by 20. 100 miles east of the Mawson Escarpment, just behind the Amery Ice Shelf, in East Antarctica. Named for Squadron Leader I.L. Grove, RAAF pilot with the ANARE who landed here in Nov. 1958.

**Grove Nunataks** *see* **Grove Mountains**

**Groves Island.** 75°30'S, 143°W. 5 miles long. A grounded island at the northern edge of the Nickerson Ice Shelf, off the Ruppert Coast, between Siemiatkowski Glacier and Land Glacier. Named for Benjamin F. Groves, meteorologist at Byrd Station in 1964.

**Growler.** A piece of floating ice smaller than a bergy bit, just showing above water.

**Growler Rock.** 62°07'S, 58°08'W. Also called Roca Gruñón. A rock in water 1 mile NW of Lions Rump, in the west part of King Georges Bay, King George Island, in the South Shetlands. Charted and named by the personnel on the *Discovery II* in 1937 (*see* **Growler**, above).

**Grubb Glacier.** 64°56'S, 62°38'W. Flows into Lester Cove, Andvord Bay, to the west of Bagshawe Glacier, on the west coast of Graham Land. Named by the UK in 1960 for Thomas Grubb (1800–1878), Irish optician who designed the aplanatic camera lens in 1857.

**Gruber-Berge.** Ritscher discovered and named these mountains in the northern part of the Mühlig-Hofmann Mountains. They have not been identified since, and are not the Gruber Mountains.

**Gruber Mountains.** 71°22'S, 13°25'E. Forms the NE portion of the Wohlthat Mountains, in Queen Maud Land. Discovered by Ritscher in 1938–39, and named later by the Norwegians for Otto von Gruber, the German cartographer who compiled maps of New Schwabenland from the Ritscher expedition's aerial photos.

**Gruendler Glacier.** 72°38′S, 167°28′E. Flows from Malta Plateau near Mount Hussey, into Trainer Glacier, in the Victory Mountains of Victoria Land. Named for James D. Gruendler, glaciologist on Roosevelt Island in 1967–68.

**Mount Gruening** *see* **Mount Jackson**

**Gruening Glacier.** 71°52′S, 61°55′W. Feeds the Hilton Inlet, on the Black Coast of eastern Palmer Land. Discovered aerially by the USAS on Dec. 30, 1940. Named for Ernest H. Gruening, director of the Division of Territories and Island Possessions, US Department of the Interior, in 1939 (he was later a senator from Alaska).

**Grunden, Torals.** One of the Nordenskjöld party forced to winter-over at Hope Bay in 1903.

**Grunden Rock.** 63°24′S, 56°58′W. A rock in water, 15 meters high, surrounded by a group of smaller rocks. Just east of Hut Cove, on the south side of the entrance to Hope Bay, on the NE end of the Antarctica Peninsula. Discovered by Nordenskjöld's expedition in 1901–4. In 1945 the FIDS named the entire group of rocks as Grunden Rocks, for Torals Grunden. In 1951 the Argentines established a lighthouse on the big rock, and in 1952 the name of the feature was singularized, as Grunden Rock.

**Grunden Rocks** *see* **Grunden Rock**

**Grunehogna Base.** 18-man South African research summer station built on the Ahlmann Ridge in Queen Maud Land in 1983.

**Grunehogna Peaks.** 72°03′S, 2°47′W. 2 miles north of Liljequist Heights, in the south part of the Ahlmann Ridge of Queen Maud Land. Named by the Norwegians.

**Roca Gruñon** *see* **Growler Rock**

**Gruvleflesa Knolls.** 71°44′S, 8°50′E. Two low rock knolls rising above the glacial moraine just west of Gruvletindane Crags, in the Kurze Mountains of Queen Maud Land. Named by the Norwegians.

**Gruvletindane Crags.** 71°44′S, 8°59′E. 2,255 m. They form the north end of the Kurze Mountains of Queen Maud Land. Named by the Norwegians.

**Mount Grytøyr.** 72°S, 4°31′E. 2,695 m. Ice-topped. Between the Flogeken Glacier and the Stuttflog Glacier, in the Mühlig-Hofmann Mountains of Queen Maud Land. Named by the Norwegians for B. Grytøyr, meteorologist with the Norwegian Antarctic Expedition of 1956–58.

**Isla Guacolda** *see* **Gränicher Island**

**Guano Island.** 66°46′S, 141°36′E. 350 yards long. 350 yards south of Chameau Island, at the SE end of the Curzon Islands. Charted by the French in 1951, and named by them for the penguin droppings here.

**Guarcello Peak.** 79°55′S, 83°10′W. 2,050 m. 3½ miles SSE of Mount Dolence, in the Enterprise Hills of the Heritage Range. Named for Dominic Guarcello, meteorologist at Little America V in 1958.

**Guard Glacier.** 71°01′S, 62°10′W. Flows along the south edge of the Parmelee Massif into the Murrish Glacier, on the east side of Palmer Land. Named for Charles L. Guard, biologist here in 1972–73, 1973–74, and 1974–75, with David E. Murrish (*see* **Murrish Glacier**).

**Bahía Guardia Nacional** *see* **Maxwell Bay**

**Guardian Islands** *see* **Øygarden Group**

**Guardian Nunatak.** 83°49′S, 173°13′E. 210 m. On the ice-covered spur that descends from Mount Robert Scott ENE toward the west edge of Hood Glacier, near the junction with the Ross Ice Shelf. Named by the New Zealanders in 1959–60 for its guardian-type stance at the entrance to Hood Glacier.

**Guardian Rock.** 67°32′S, 67°17′W. An ice-free rock in water, in Bigourdan Fjord. 1½ miles north of Parvenu Point on Pourquoi Pas Island, just off the west coast of the Antarctic Peninsula. Surveyed by the FIDS in 1948–49, and named by them because it guards the NW entrance to The Narrows.

**Mount Gudmundson.** 79°13'S, 157°51'E. 2,040 m. Mainly ice-free. 6 miles NE of Fault Bluff, in the Cook Mountains. Named for Julian P. Gudmundson, USN, explosives expert at Little America in 1957. He blasted the foundation for McMurdo Station's power plant in 1961.

**Guébriant Islands.** 67°48'S, 68°25'W. Also called de Guébriant Islets. 2 small islands in the north part of Marguerite Bay, 5 miles SE of the SE cape of Adelaide Island. Discovered by Charcot in 1908–10, and named by him for Father Guébriant, the French missionary in China.

**Mount Guéguen.** 65°04'S, 64°W. Also called Guéguen Peak. 365 m. ¼ mile NW of Louise Peak, in the northern part of Booth Island, in the Wilhelm Archipelago. Discovered by Charcot in 1903–5, and named by him for F. Guéguen.

**Guéguen, F.** Stoker on the *Français* in 1903–5, and on the *Pourquoi Pas?* in 1908–10, both times with Charcot.

**Guéguen, J.** Crewmember on the *Français* in 1903–5, and on the *Pourquoi Pas?* in 1908–10, both times with Charcot.

**Guéguen Peak** *see* **Mount Guéguen**

**Guéguen Point.** 65°09'S, 64°07'W. Also called Pointe J. Guéguen. Forms the south end of Hovgaard Island, in the Wilhelm Archipelago. Charted by Charcot in 1908–10, and named by him for J. Guéguen.

**Ensenada Güemes** *see* **Rockpepper Bay**

**Güemes Refugio.** Argentine refuge hut built in 1953 on Duse Bay, Trinity Peninsula.

**Guenter Bluff.** 70°40'S, 159°44'E. On the west side of the Pomerantz Tableland, in the Usarp Mountains. Named for Clarence A. Guenter, para-

psychology worker at Amundsen-Scott South Pole Station in 1967–68.

**Guépratte Island.** 64°30'S, 63°W. 1½ miles long. Ice-covered. Between Anvers Island and Brabant Island, at the east side of the entrance to Fournier Bay. Charcot named it in 1903–5 for Capt. Guépratte of the French Navy. In 1927 the personnel on the *Discovery* renamed it as Discovery Island. However, the original naming is now the official one.

**Île Guernsey** *see* **Mount Guernsey**

**Mount Guernsey.** 69°20'S, 68°14'W. 1,250 m. Isolated. Ice-covered. 6 miles north of Mount Edgell, on the west coast of the Antarctic Peninsula. In 1909 Charcot thought it was an island, and named it Île Guernsey, for the Channel island off the French coast. Redefined by the BGLE in 1936.

**Guerrero Glacier.** 78°32'S, 84°15'W. 7 miles long. Flows from Mount Havener to the south side of Taylor Spur, in the SE part of the Sentinel Range. Named for John F. Guerrero, meteorologist at South Pole Station in 1957.

**Bahía Guesalaga** *see* **Curtiss Bay**

**Guesalaga Toro, Federico.** Capitán de Navío (captain of the Chilean Navy), commander of the first Chilean Antarctic Expedition, in 1946–47. His ships were the *Iquique* and the *Angamos*.

**Guesalaga Island.** 64°16'S, 61°59'W. Also called Bell Island. The northern of two islands off the east side of Lecointe Island, in the Palmer Archipelago. Named by the Chilean Antarctic Expedition of 1946–47, for its commander, Federico Guesalaga Toro (*see* **Guesalaga,** above).

**Guesalaga Peninsula.** 62°29'S, 59°40'W. Shingle-covered. On the east side of Discovery Bay, Greenwich Island, in the South Shetlands. Named by Chile for Capt. Federico Guesalaga Toro (*see* **Guesalaga,** above).

**Guest Island** *see* **Guest Peninsula**

**Guest Peninsula.** 76°18'S, 148°W. 45 miles long. Snow-covered. Mitchell Peak is on it. Between the Sulzberger Ice Shelf and Block Bay, at the foot of the Ford Ranges, on the coast of Marie Byrd Land, jutting out into the Ross Sea. The USAS defined it and mapped it as an island in 1940, and named it Amy Guest Island, for Amy Guest, contributor to Byrd's 1933–35 expedition. This name became shortened to Guest Island. In 1966 it was redefined as a peninsula.

**Guettard Range.** 74°21'S, 63°27'W. Also called Guettard Mountains. 40 miles long. 10 miles wide. NW of Bowman Peninsula, between the Johnston and Irvine Glaciers, on the Lassiter Coast of eastern Palmer Land. Named for Jean-Étienne Guettard (1715–1786), French geologist and naturalist.

**Isla Guido Spano** *see* **Guido Island**

**Guido, Manuel.** 2nd class boy on the Wilkes Expedition 1838–42. Joined at Madeira in 1838. Returned to the USA on the *Relief* in 1839.

**Guido Island.** 64°55'S, 63°50'W. Also called Pardoner Island, Isla Ruy. 1 mile NE of Prioress Island, in the Wauwermans Islands, in the Wilhelm Archipelago. Named by the Argentines as Isla Guido Spano, for Argentine poet Carlos Guido Spano (1829–1918). The name was later shortened.

**Guile Island.** 65°44'S, 65°11'W. 1 mile SW of Duchaylard Island, in the Biscoe Islands. Charted by the BGLE 1934–37. Named by the UK in 1959 because of the dangerous underwater rocks near here.

**Guillard, Robert.** French builder of Dumont d'Urville Station, and leader of the 1956 wintering party here.

**Monte Guillermo** *see* **Mount Banck**

**Guillou, Charles F.B.** Assistant surgeon on the Wilkes Expedition 1838–42. Joined the *Peacock* in Sydney. Detached from the *Flying Fish* at Honolulu, in Nov. 1841. Subsequently court-martialed for insubordination and neglect of duty.

**Gulch Island.** 63°59'S, 61°29'W. Also called Isla Aragay. NW of Small Island, in the Christiania Islands, in the Palmer Archipelago. Named by the UK in 1960 for its deep indentations.

**Gulfplatået** *see* **Edward VIII Plateau**

**Gull Channel.** 68°11'S, 67°W. 175 yards wide. A marine channel between Dynamite Island and Stonington Island, on the west coast of Graham Land. Surveyed by the USAS from East Base in 1939–41, and named by them for the gulls here.

**Gull Rock** *see* **Gaviotín Rock**

**The Gullet.** 67°10'S, 67°38'W. Also called Charcot Strait, Loubet Strait. A marine channel between the eastern extremity of Adelaide Island and the west coast of Graham Land. Named descriptively in 1948 by the FIDS.

**Gulliver Nunatak.** 66°12'S, 62°40'W. 575 m. Flat-topped. Has an ice-free summit. At the north side of Adie Inlet, on the east coast of Graham Land. Named by the FIDS for Jonathan Swift's fictional character, because, from the SE it looks like a giant man lying on his back with his head toward the south.

**Gulls.** The principal gull found in Antarctica is *Larus dominicanus*. More commonly this bird is known as the Dominican gull, the kelp gull, or the southern great black-backed gull. It lays 2 to 3 eggs, and breeds on the Antarctic Peninsula and in the South Shetlands and South Orkneys.

**Mount Gunn.** 76°53'S, 160°42'E. 2,465 m. In the Convoy Range of Victoria Land. 7 miles NW of Mount Gran. Named by the NZ Northern Survey Party of the BCTAE in 1957, for Bernie Gunn.

**Gunn, Bernard M.** Known as "Bernie." Geologist with the NZ party during the BCTAE 1957–58.

**Gunn Peaks.** 73°25'S, 66°36'W. Isolated. 9 miles east of Mount Vang, in southern Palmer Land. Named for Robert C. Gunn, glaciologist at Byrd Station in 1965–66.

**Cape Gunnar** *see* **Cape Kater**

**Gunnar Isachsen Mountain** *see* **Isachsen Mountain**

**Gunnel Channel.** 67° 06′ S, 67° 33′ W. A marine channel. ½ mile wide. 7 miles long. In the south part of Hanusse Bay. It separates Hansen Island from the west coast of Graham Land. Discovered aerially by, and charted by, the BGLE in 1936. Surveyed by the FIDS in 1948, and named by them. The channel looks so narrow that a boat would scrape its gunwhales on either side as it passed through.

**Mount Gunner.** 83° 32′ S, 169° 38′ E. 1,430 m. Partly snow-covered. In the south part of Morris Heights, in the Queen Alexandra Range. Named for John D. Gunner, Ohio State University geologist here in 1967–68. He was in other parts of Antarctica in 1968–69 and 1969–70.

**Gunnerus Bank.** 68° S, 33° E. A submarine feature off the Prince Harald Coast.

**Gunnestad, Lt. Alf.** Pilot with the *Thorshavn* expedition of Lars Christensen's, 1933–34.

**Gunnestad Glacier.** 71° 58′ S, 23° 55′ E. 13 miles long. Flows between Mount Widerøe and Mount Walnum, in the Sør Rondane Mountains. Named Gunnestadbreen (Gunnestad Glacier) by the Norwegians, for Lt. Alf Gunnestad.

**Mount Gunter.** 68° 59′ S, 66° 33′ W. 1,970 m. On the south side of Hariot Glacier, 3 miles east of Briggs Peak, on the west side of the Antarctic Peninsula. Surveyed by the BGLE in 1936–37, and again by the FIDS in 1958. Named by the UK for Edmund Gunter (1581–1626), English mathematician who helped revolutionize navigation.

**Gunther, E.R.** Scientific leader on the *William Scoresby*, 1930–32.

**Guozdén, Helvio N.A.** Leader of the 1956–57 Argentine Antarctic Expedition. His ships were the *General San Martín*, the *Bahía Aguirre*, the *Bahía Thetis*, the *Les Éclaireurs*, the *Chiriguano*, the *Sanavirón*, the *Punta Ninfas*, and the *Punta Loyola*.

**Gurling Glacier.** 70° 34′ S, 62° 20′ W. Flows between Krebs Ridge and Leininger Peak, into the SW corner of Smith Inlet, on the east coast of Palmer Land. Named by the UK for P. Gurling, BAS surveyor here.

**Gurney, Norman A.** Member of the BGLE 1934–37.

**Gurney Point.** 71° S, 67° 27′ W. 610 m. A rocky point which overlooks the George VI Sound, and which marks the western extremity of the rock ridge separating the Bertram and Ryder Glaciers, on the west coast of Palmer Land. Discovered aerially by Ellsworth on Nov. 23, 1935. Surveyed by the BGLE in 1936. Named by the UK in 1954 for Norman A. Gurney.

**Gurnon Peninsula.** 74° 23′ S, 110° 30′ W. 10 miles long. Ice-covered. Between the Park and Bunner Glaciers in the NE part of Bear Peninsula, on the coast of Marie Byrd Land. Named for Lt. P.J. Gurnon, USN, aircraft commander on Hercules planes in 1965–67.

**The *Gus W. Darnell*.** US tanker which supplied McMurdo Station at various times throughout the 1980s.

**Mount Gustav Bull** *see* **Gustav Bull Mountains**

**Gustav Bull Mountains.** 67° 50′ S, 66° 12′ E. Also called Mount Gustav Bull, Mount Bull. A group of mountains, 4 miles inland, just south of the Mawson Coast of Mac. Robertson Land, 10 miles SW of Scullin Monolith. Discovered aerially by the BANZARE in Jan. 1930, and named by Norwegian whalers in Jan. and Feb. 1931 (they were exploring here at that time) for Gustav B. Bull.

**Gutenko, Sigmund.** USN. Chief commissary steward. He was cook and steward at West Base during the USAS 1939–41, and, while on furlough, went to Antarctica again with the RARE 1947–48.

**Gutenko Mountains.** 72° S, 64° 45′ W. Also called Vincent Gutenko Mountains. At the south end of the Dyer Plateau, in central Palmer Land. They include the

Elliott Hills, the Rathbone Hills, the Guthridge Nunataks, and the Blanchard Nunataks. Discovered aerially by the RARE on Nov. 21, 1947, and named by Ronne for Sigmund Gutenko.

**Gutenko Nunataks.** 76°53′S, 143°40′W. 1 mile west of Mount Morgan, in the Ford Ranges of Marie Byrd Land. Discovered aerially by the USAS from West Base, in 1940, and named by Byrd for Sigmund Gutenko.

**Guthridge Nunataks.** 71°48′S, 64°33′W. 22 miles long. 6 miles wide. Between the Rathbone Hills and the Blanchard Nunataks, in the Gutenko Mountains of central Palmer Land. Named for Guy G. Guthridge, National Science Foundation official and editor of the *Antarctic Journal of the US* (*see* the Bibliography under *Antarctic Journal*).

**Gutiérrez Reef.** 63°18′S, 57°55′W. Also called Bajo Gutiérrez. Has 2 fathoms of water over it. 350 yards NNE of the north end of Kopaitic Island, in the Duroch Islands, off Trinity Peninsula. Named by the Chilean Antarctic Expedition of 1947–48 for a bosun on that expedition.

**Guvernørens Islands** *see* **Governor Islands**

**Guy, Adam.** British gentleman who chartered the *San Juan Nepomuceno* out of Buenos Aires in 1819, in order to look for seals in the South Shetlands. He was one of the first sealers in these islands.

**Guy Peaks.** 72°04′S, 99°04′W. A cluster of peaks 3 miles NE of Mount Borgeson, overlooking Peale Inlet, on Thurston Island. Named for Arthur W. Guy, electrical engineer at Byrd Station in 1964–65.

**Guyatt Ridge.** 80°38′S, 29°27′W. In the Shackleton Range.

**Guyou Bay.** 64°06′S, 62°35′W. 4 miles wide. An indentation into the NW part of Brabant Island, between Claude Point and Metchnikoff Point. Discovered by Charcot in 1903–5, and named by him for Capt. Émile Guyou (1843–1915),

of the French Navy, a mathematician who prepared the scientific reports for the expedition, and who did the same for de Gerlache in 1897–99.

**Guyou Island** *see* **Ménier Island**

**Guyou Islands.** 65°03′S, 63°24′W. Also called Isla Chico, Isla Grande. A small group, 2 miles NE of Sonia Point, in Flandres Bay, off the west coast of Graham Land. Charted by de Gerlache in 1897–99, and named by him for Émile Guyou (*see* **Guyou Bay**).

**Gwynn Bay.** 67°05′S, 57°57′E. Just west of Hoseason Glacier, on the coast of Enderby Land. Photographed by the LCE 1936–37, and named Breidvika (the broad bay) by the Norwegians. Renamed by the Australians for Dr. A.M. Gwynn, officer in charge at Macquarie Island Station (not in Antarctica) in 1949.

**Gygra Peak.** 71°58′S, 3°16′E. 1,980 m. Just west of Risen Peak, in the Gjelsvik Mountains of Queen Maud Land. Name means "the giantess" in Norwegian.

**Gyldén, O.** Captain of the *Frithiof*, 1903–4.

**Cape H. Hansen** *see* **Cape Hansen**

**Mount H. Kristensen** *see* **Mount Kristensen**

**H.E. Hansenbreen** *see* **Hansenbreen**

**H.J. Sjögren Fjord** *see* **Sjögren Glacier**

**H.U. Sverdrupfjella** *see* **Sverdrup Mountains**

**Mount Haag** *see* **Haag Nunataks**

**Haag Nunataks.** 77°S, 78°18′W. There are three low elevations here, and they were discovered by the RARE 1947–48. One of them, at 77°40′S, 79°W, was called Mount Haag, by Finn Ronne, for Joseph Haag, head of Todd Shipyards in New York, which worked on Ronne's ship (as it had also done on Byrd's ships during his 1928–30 expedition). Redefined by the VX-6 in 1966.

**Haakon Island** *see* **Dufayel Island**

**Haakon VII Sea.** 68°S, 25°E. Off the Princess Ragnhild Coast.

**Haas Glacier.** 85°45'S, 164°55'W. Flows from Rawson Plateau into the south side of Bowman Glacier in the Queen Maud Mountains. Named for Charles G. Haas, meteorologist at South Pole Station, 1960.

**Habermehl Peak.** 71°49'S, 6°55'E. 2,945 m. 3 miles south of Gessner Peak in the Mühlig-Hofmann Mountains of New Schwabenland. Discovered by Ritscher 1938–39 and named by him for the director of the German Weather Service, and originally called Habermehltoppen.

**Habermehltoppen** see **Habermehl Peak**

**Hachinosu Peak.** 69°01'S, 39°35'E. Also spelled Hatinosu Peak. 45 m. A small hill, it is the highest point on East Ongul Island. 350 yards east of Nishinoura Cove. Named Hachinosu-yama (beehive peak) by the Japanese in 1957.

**Hackapike Bay.** 64°31'S, 62°55'W. An anchorage 4 miles NW of Ryswyck Point, on the NE coast of Anvers Island. Charted and named by the BGLE 1934–37.

**Hackerman Ridge.** 72°39'S, 167°46'E. Between the Gruendler and Rudolph Glaciers in the Victory Mountains of Victoria Land. Named for Norman Hackerman, chairman of the National Science Board of the USA from 1974. He visited Antarctica in 1975 and 1977.

**Mount Haddington.** 64°13'S, 57°38'W. Also called Mount Ross. Also spelled (erroneously) Mount Hadington. 1,630 m. Surmounts the central part of James Ross Island. Discovered and named by Ross on Dec. 31, 1842, for the Earl of Haddington, first lord of the admiralty.

**Haddon Bay.** 63°18'S, 55°44'W. Just east of Mount Alexander on the south coast of Joinville Island. Discovered Jan. 1893 by Thomas Robertson in the *Active*. Surveyed by the FIDS in 1953 and named by the UK in 1956 for Prof. Alfred C. Haddon (1855–1940), who helped Bruce

with his scientific preparation before that explorer first went to the Antarctic in 1893 with the Dundee Whaling Expedition.

**Mount Häderich.** 71°57'S, 6°12'E. 2,885. In the eastern part of Håhellerskarvet in the Mühlig-Hofmann Mountains of Queen Maud Land. Named Häderich-Berg in 1939 by Ritscher, who discovered it. Named for the procurator of Lufthansa. This may not be the actual peak which Ritscher saw and named, but it is in the vicinity.

**Hades Terrace.** 73°41'S, 163°30'E. A bluff, mostly ice-covered, on the east side of Campbell Glacier, just west of Vulcan Hills in the Southern Cross Mountains of Victoria Land. Named by the New Zealanders in 1965–66 for the Greek mythological location.

**Mount Hadington** see **Mount Haddington**

**Hadley Peak.** 85°01'S, 90°40'W. 2,660 m. Surmounts the escarpment at the north edge of the Ford Massif in the Thiel Mountains. Named by Bermel and Ford, leaders of the US Geological Survey Thiel Mountains Party 1960–61 for Jarvis B. Hadley of the USGS, and administrator of their geology programs in Antarctica.

**Hadley Point.** 73°55'S, 113°58'W. On the Marie Byrd Land coast.

**Hadley Upland.** 68°29'S, 66°24'W. A triangular plateau in southern Graham Land. Surveyed by the FIDS in 1948–50 and 1958. Named by the UK for John Hadley (1682–1744), inventor of the quadrant in 1730.

**Haefeli Glacier.** 67°18'S, 66°23'W. 2 miles wide and 6 miles long. At the NW side of Finsterwalder Glacier. It flows toward the head of Lallemand Fjord on the west coast of Graham Land. Surveyed in 1946–47 by the FIDS and named by them for the Swiss glaciologist Robert Haefeli.

**Haffner Glacier.** 71°28'S, 169°24'E. Flows into Berg Bay on the north coast of Victoria Land. Charted by Borchgrevink in 1898–1900, and he named it for Colonel Haffner, director of the Government Survey of Norway.

**Hag Pike.** 68°57'S, 66°59'W. 710 m. Rock column on the north side of the Wordie Ice Shelf near the west coast of the Antarctic Peninsula. Forms part of the west side of the mouth of Hariot Glacier. Surveyed by the FIDS in 1948–50 and in 1958. Named descriptively by the UK (a hag is a tree stump).

**Hageman Peak.** 71°43'S, 70°48'W. On Alexander Island.

**Mount Hager.** 70°53'S, 162°48'E. 2,420 m. 6 miles west of Mount Cantello in the Explorers Range of the Bowers Mountains. Named for Clarence L. Hager, geophysicist at Amundsen-Scott South Pole Station, 1967–68.

**Hagerty Peak.** 75°17'S, 68°11'W. At the SE end of the Sweeney Mountains. Named for Cornelius J. Hagerty, photographer at McMurdo Station, 1960.

**Hagey Ridge.** 74°57'S, 134°56'W. Snow-covered. Between Björnert Cliffs and Johnson Glacier. Forms the east end of McDonald Heights on the coast of Marie Byrd Land. Named for Lt. Donald W. Hagey, USN, officer-in-charge at Byrd Station in 1969.

**Hagfish.** Class: Agnatha. Non-bony, primitive, eel-like, scaleless fish found in Antarctic waters (*see* **Fish**).

**Haggerty, James.** Ordinary seaman on the Wilkes Expedition 1838–42. Joined in the USA. Sent home in the *Relief* in 1839.

**Haggits Pillar.** 67°24'S, 179°55'W. 65 m. A column of rock. 175 yards west of Scott Island. 315 miles NNE of Cape Adare in Victoria Land. Discovered in Dec. 1902 by William Colbeck in the *Morning*, and named during his relief expedition.

**Håhellerbotnen Cirque.** 71°54'S, 6°05'E. On the east side of Håhelleregga Ridge in the Mühlig-Hofmann Mountains of Queen Maud Land. Name means "the shark cave cirque" in Norwegian.

**Håhelleregga Ridge.** 71°52'S, 5°58'E. Just north of Håhellerskarvet in the Mühlig-Hofmann Mountains of Queen Maud Land. Name means "the shark cave ridge" in Norwegian.

**Håhelleren Cove.** 71°55'S, 6°04'E. Indents the north side of Håhellerskarvet in the Mühlig-Hofmann Mountains of Queen Maud Land. Name means "the shark cave" in Norwegian.

**Håhellerskarvet.** 71°57'S, 6°08'E. Partly ice-covered mountain. 2,910 m. Between the Austreskorve and Lunde Glaciers in the Mühlig-Hofmann Mountains of Queen Maud Land. Name means "the shark cave mountain" in Norwegian.

**Mount Hahn.** 69°17'S, 70°14'W. In the northern part of Alexander Island.

**Hahn Island.** 78°15'S, 164°58'E. 1 mile long. 7 miles north of Mount Discovery, on the east side of the Koettlitz Glacier. Named in 1963 for Cdr. James Hahn, USN, public information officer on the staff of the Commander, US Naval Support Force, Antarctica, for several years prior to 1963.

**Haigh Nunatak.** 71°15'S, 71°13'E. 12 miles NE of Pickering Nunatak on the east side of the mouth of Lambert Glacier. Named by the Australians for J. Haigh, geophysicist at Mawson Station, 1965, who accompanied the USSR party which first visited this nunatak in Jan. 1966.

**Hailstorm Island.** 66°13'S, 110°37'E. ¼ mile long. Between Cameron Island and Burnett Island in the central part of the Swain Islands. Named by Carl Eklund for Ken Hailstorm (*see* **Wilkes Station**).

**Hainaut Island** *see* **D'Hainaut Island**

**Haines, William C.** Meteorologist with the US Weather Bureau, he was on Byrd's first two expeditions. Third-in-command on the 1933–35 expedition (Byrd's second expedition). He had also been on Byrd's North Pole expedition.

**Haines Glacier.** 73°21'S, 62°33'W. 4 miles wide. Joins Meinardus Glacier just east of Mount Barkow, on the east coast of Palmer Land. Discovered aerially by the USAS in 1940. Named by the FIDS for William C. Haines.

**Haines Mountains.** 77°34′S, 146°20′W. Ice-capped. 25 miles long. They form the SW wall of Hammond Glacier in the Ford Ranges. Discovered in 1934 during Byrd's 1933–35 expedition, and named by Byrd for William C. Haines.

**Haining, David.** Ordinary seaman on the Wilkes Expedition of 1838–42. Joined at Rio. Lost in the *Sea Gull* in late April 1839.

**Håkollen Island.** 67°S, 57°15′E. Also called Shark Island. 1 mile long. 100 meters high. In the SW part of the Øygarden Group. Photographed by the LCE of 1936–37 and named Håkollen (the shark knoll) by the Norwegians.

**Håkon Col.** 71°54′S, 8°52′E. Also called Håkonbandet. At the south side of Saether Crags in the Kurze Mountains of Queen Maud Land. Named by the Norwegians for Håkon Saether, medical officer with the Norwegian Antarctic Expedition of 1956–57.

**Håkonbandet** *see* **Håkon Col**

**The *Hakurei Maru*.** Ice-strengthened Japanese oil exploration ship which was first in Antarctic waters in the early 1980s on a series of surveying explorations. In 1980–81 it was in the Bellingshausen Sea; in 1981–82 it was in the Weddell Sea; and in 1982–83 it was in the Ross Sea.

**Mount Hal Flood** *see* **Mount Berlin**

**Hal Flood Bay** *see* **Okuma Bay**

**Hal Flood Range** *see* **Flood Range**

**Mount Hale.** 78°04′S, 86°19′W. 3,595 m. 1½ miles NW of Mount Davis in the main ridge of the Sentinel Mountains. Discovered by Charles R. Bentley and his 1957–58 Marie Byrd Land Traverse Party, and named by him for Daniel P. Hale, aurora physicist at Byrd Station and a member of the traverse.

**Hale Glacier.** 72°12′S, 100°48′W. 6 miles long. Just east of Mount Simpson

on Thurston Island. It flows into the Abbott Ice Shelf in Peacock Sound. Named for Lt. (jg) Bill J. Hale, USN, helicopter pilot on the *Burton Island* here in the early part of 1960.

**Hales Peak.** 64°08′S, 62°09′W. Rises from the NE shoulder of Mount Cabeza in the NE part of Brabant Island. Named by the UK for Stephen Hales (1677–1761), the first estimator of blood pressure.

**Haley Glacier.** 71°33′S, 61°50′W. 8 miles long. Flows along the north side of Rowley Massif into Odom Inlet, on the east coast of Palmer Land. Named for Philip H. Haley, biologist at Palmer Station, 1973.

**Half Century Nunatak.** 85°22′S, 178°50′W. 4 miles north of Dismal Buttress, on the west side of the upper Shackleton Glacier. Named by the Southern Party of the NZGSAE of 1961–62. Near here they celebrated the 50th anniversary of Amundsen reaching the South Pole.

**Half Dome Nunatak.** 82°27′S, 159°14′E. 2 miles south of the Cobham Range, at the mouth of Lucy Glacier. Named by the New Zealanders in 1961–62 because it is dome-shaped on one side and has sheer rocky cliffs on the other.

**Half Moon Beach.** 62°29′S, 60°47′W. 1 mile SE of Scarborough Castle on the north coast of Livingston Island in the South Shetlands. Named for its shape by the early sealers, possibly Robert Fildes in 1820–21.

**Half Moon Island.** 62°36′S, 59°55′W. Also called Johnsons Island. Crescent-shaped. 1¼ miles long. In the entrance to Moon Bay on the east side of Livingston Island in the South Shetlands. Probably named by the personnel on the *Discovery II* in 1935.

**Half-Ration Névé.** 73°01′S, 163°30′E. At the head of Aviator Glacier in Victoria Land. The Mesa Range forms much of its western side. Named by the Northern Party of the NZGSAE of 1962–63 because while here they were reduced to half rations due to a delay in resupply because of a blizzard.

**Halfmoon Bluff.** 85°13'S, 175°38'W. Overlooks the east side of Shackleton Glacier, just north of the mouth of Brunner Glacier, in the Cumulus Hills. Named descriptively by the Texas Tech Shackleton Glacier Expedition of 1964–65, for its crescent-shaped top.

**Halfthree Point.** 62°14'S, 58°57'W. Forms the SE end of Fildes Peninsula on King George Island in the South Shetlands. Charted and named by the personnel on the *Discovery II* in 1935.

**Halfway Island.** 64°45'S, 64°12'W. 2½ miles NW of Litchfield Island, off the SW coast of Anvers Island. It lies halfway between Arthur Harbor and Cape Monaco.

**Halfway Nunatak.** 78°23'S, 161°06'E. Isolated. On the west side of The Landing, and almost in the center of the Skelton Glacier's upper portion. Surveyed and descriptively named in 1957 by the NZ party of the BCTAE.

**Hålisen Glacier.** 72°02'S, 8°51'E. A cirque glacier between Hålisrimen Peak and Hålisstonga Peak in the Kurze Mountains of Queen Maud Land. Name means "the slippery ice" in Norwegian.

**Hålishalsen Saddle.** 72°07'S, 9°04'E. An ice saddle between the Kurze Mountains and the interior ice plateau to the south, in Queen Maud Land. Name means "the slippery ice neck" in Norwegian.

**Hålisrimen Peak.** 72°01'S, 8°52'E. 2,655 m. 2 miles NW of Hålisstonga Peak in the Kurze Mountains of Queen Maud Land. Name means "the slippery ice frost" in Norwegian.

**Hålisstonga Peak.** 72°02'S, 8°57'E. 2,780 m. Marks the southern end of the Kurze Mountains in Queen Maud Land. Named by the Norwegians.

**Mount Hall.** 84°55'S, 170°22'W. 2,430. 1½ miles SW of Mount Daniel, at the south end of the Lillie Range, in the foothills of the Prince Olav Mountains.

Discovered and named by Albert P. Crary during his Ross Ice Shelf Traverse of 1957–58, for Lt. Cdr. Ray E. Hall, USN, VX-6 pilot during Operation Deep Freeze.

**Hall Cliff.** 71°59'S, 68°37'W. 1 mile long. Made of sandstone. On the south side of Saturn Glacier, and 1 mile west of Citadel Bastion in eastern Alexander Island. Named by the UK for Asaph Hall (1829–1907), the US astronomer.

**Hall Nunatak.** 78°59'S, 87°24'W. 2 miles SE of Thomas Nunatak, on the ice escarpment at the head of Minnesota Glacier, in the Ellsworth Mountains. Named by the University of Minnesota Geological Party here in 1963–64 for George S. Hall, US helicopter crew chief who helped the party.

**Hall Nunataks.** 70°48'S, 66°45'E. Four nunataks, 6 miles ESE of Mount Bunt in the Aramis Range. Named by the Australians for R.G. Hall, assistant diesel mechanic at Wilkes Station in 1964.

**Hall Peak.** 79°29'S, 83°45'W. 2,170 m. Between the upper reaches of Rennell Glacier, Schmidt Glacier, and Larson Valley, in the Heritage Range. Named by the University of Minnesota Geological Party here in 1963–64 for Walter D.M. (Mike) Hall, geologist with the party.

**Hall Peninsula.** 62°46'S, 61°14'W. 2 miles SW of President Head on the east side of Snow Island in the South Shetlands. Named by the UK in 1961 for Capt. Basil Hall, RN (1788–1844). Weddell, in the early 1820s, had given the name Basil Hall's Island to what is now Snow Island, and the British wanted to preserve Weddell's naming with this peninsula.

**Hall Ridge.** 70°42'S, 63°12'W. Snow-covered. 5 miles south of the Eland Mountains in Palmer Land. Named for Capt. Philip L. Hall, US Army, assistant civil engineering officer on the staff of the Commander, US Naval Support Force, Antarctica, during 1968–69 and 1969–70.

**Hall Rock.** 76°51'S, 159°20'E. 2 miles NW of Carapace Nunatak at the edge of the Polar Plateau in Victoria Land. Named for geologist Bradford A. Hall, who did research here in 1961–62.

**Halle Flat.** 76°40'S, 159°50'E. A flat area just south of Coxcomb Peak in the Allan Hills of Victoria Land. Named by the New Zealanders in 1964 for Thore G. Halle, a pioneer in Antarctic fossils.

**Haller Rocks.** 64°04'S, 62°06'W. Small group in the eastern part of Bouquet Bay, 2 miles NW of the SW end of Liège Island. Named by the UK for Albrecht von Haller (1708–1777), Swiss physiologist.

**Cape Hallett.** 72°19'S, 170°16'E. On the Ross Sea, at the foot of Mount Sabine, on the Borchgrevink Coast. Forms the north tip of Hallett Peninsula in Victoria Land. Hallett Station was here. Discovered in 1841 by Ross, who named it for Thomas R. Hallett.

**Hallett, Thomas R.** Purser on the *Erebus* under Ross, 1839–43.

**Hallett Peninsula.** 72°30'S, 170°10'E. Triangular in shape, and domelike. 20 miles long. It has 1,500 meter cliffs on its seaboard side and 300 meter cliffs on its western side. Extends from Cape Hallett to Cape Wheatstone and is joined to the mainland by a narrow ridge between Tucker Glacier and Edisto Inlet. Named by the New Zealanders in 1957–58 because Hallett Station was built at the north end of the peninsula.

**Hallett Station.** 72°18'S, 170°13'E. A US/NZ IGY station built in 1957 on Seabee Hook, at the tip of Cape Hallett, on Edisto Inlet, on the Victoria Land coast. It was the smallest of the IGY bases on the continent. On relatively ice-free ground, and 16 feet above sea-level, at the foot of Mount Sabine, the site was selected on Feb. 12, 1956, when the *Edisto* sailed in this area looking for a suitable place to build Adare Station, as it was called in the planning stage. Landings began on Dec. 29, 1956. Carl Eklund cleared 8,218 penguins off to another part of the colony (great care was always taken with the penguins). On Jan. 9, 1957, construction began and it was finished by Feb. 12, 1957. The 32 Seabees then left on the *Atka* and the wintering crew was brought in from McMurdo Base, 350 miles away, to inhabit the 10 buildings. That crew comprised Lt. Juan F. Tur, USN, the military leader; Dr. James A. Shear, scientific leader; Clayton E. Ingham, aurora and airglow specialist; John G. Humphries, ionosphere physicist; Michael Langevad, radio technician; (these last 3 were the NZ complement). The US Navy personnel were Robert E. Roy, Richard A. Novasio, Bobby G. Northcutt, Ernie Lee Bingaman, Ray H. Camp, James R. Canavan, E. Roger Evans, Jr., Raymond W. Hennessey, and Harry C. King (this last of the USNR). Meteorology was the specialty science and a runway was built here. On Jan. 16, 1958, R.C. Bornmann took over from Tur as military leader, and Kenneth Salmon took over from Shear as scientific leader. Biology was added after IGY, and the station enlarged and improved. A year-round station from 1957 to 1964, and a summer station from 1964, it was closed altogether on Feb. 19, 1973. Other scientific leaders after IGY were 1959 Charles L. Roberts (US), 1960 R.B. Thomson (NZ), 1961 R. Titus (US), 1962 C.B. Taylor (NZ), 1963 H. Freimanis (US), 1964 N.M. Ridgeway (NZ). The winter populations varied between 7 and 12 scientists, and between 7 and 9 support personnel. The summer populations (after 1964) varied between 2 and 9 scientists, and between 12 and 21 support personnel. In 1986 New Zealanders worked here to reclaim the disused station.

**Halley Bay.** 75°29'S, 26°42'W. A Weddell Sea indentation between the Luitpold Coast and the Caird Coast. The old Halley Bay Station was here.

**Halley Bay Station.** 75°31'S, 26°45'W. In Halley Bay, on the Caird Coast of Coats Land. Dr. David Dalgliesh and 10 men built the British Royal Society IGY

Expedition's base here on the Weddell Sea in Jan.–Feb. 1956. In 1983 a new geophysical observatory was built here, and in 1984 a new station, called Halley Station, was established to replace it.

**Halley Station.** On the Brunt Ice Shelf. British scientists occupied this replacement for Halley Bay Station in Feb. 1984.

**Mount Hallgren.** 73°23'S, 3°22'W. Also called Hallgrenskarvet. Mostly ice-covered. 27 miles SW of Neumayer Cliffs in the Kirwan Escarpment of Queen Maud Land. Named by the Norwegians for Stig E. Hallgren.

**Hallgren, Stig E.** Photographer on the NBSAE 1949–52.

**Haloes** *see* **Phenomena**

**Halpern Point.** 63°18'S, 57°50'W. On the northern coast of Trinity Peninsula, just south of the eastern part of the Duroch Islands. Named for Martin Halpern, geologist here in 1961–62, as leader of the field party from the University of Wisconsin, Madison.

**Halsknappane Hills.** 72°04'S, 6°01'E. A group just west of Skorvehalsen Saddle in the east part of the Mühlig-Hofmann Mountains of Queen Maud Land. Name means "the neck buttons" in Norwegian.

**Halverson Peak.** 71°47'S, 164°44'E. 1,710 m. Marks the east side of the terminus of Rawle Glacier in the King Range of the Concord Mountains. Named for Jack E. Halverson, USN, chief electronics technician at McMurdo Station in 1967.

**Halvfarryggen Ridge.** 71°10'S, 6°40'W. Snow-covered. Separates the Ekström and Jelbart Ice Shelves, on the coast of Queen Maud Land. First named Isrygg (ice ridge) by the NBSAE 1949–52, but renamed by the Norwegians themselves in the late 1950s. Name means "the half way ridge."

**Halvorsen, H.** Norwegian whaling captain who, in 1930, discovered the Princess Astrid Coast while in command of the *Sevilla*.

**Hamarglovene Crevasses.** 71°56'S, 5°05'E. A crevasse field in lower Vestreskorve Glacier, just east of Hamarøya Mountain, in the Mühlig-Hofmann Mountains of Queen Maud Land. Name means "the hammer clefts" in Norwegian.

**Hamarøya Mountain.** 71°56'S, 4°57'E. Isolated. Ice-free. In the middle of the mouth of Vestreskorve Glacier in the Mühlig-Hofmann Mountains of Queen Maud Land. Name means "the hammer island" in Norwegian.

**Hamaröygalten** *see* **Sheehan Islands**

**Hamarskaftet Nunataks.** 71°50'S, 4°58'E. A row of nunataks about 5 miles long. 2 miles NW of Svarthamaren Mountain in the Mühlig-Hofmann Mountains of Queen Maud Land. Name means "the hammer handle" in Norwegian.

**Hamarskorvene Bluff.** 72°01'S, 5°14'E. Just east of Kvithamaren Cliff in the Mühlig-Hofmann Mountains of Queen Maud Land. Named by the Norwegians.

**Hamartind Peak.** 72°33'S, 0°39'E. At the eastern end of the Hamrane Heights in the Sverdrup Mountains of Queen Maud Land. Name means "the crag peak" in Norwegian.

**Hambleton, H.A.** Crew member on the *Bear of Oakland*, 1934–35.

**Hamblin Glacier.** 66°24'S, 65°07'W. Flows to the SE side of Widmark Ice Piedmont in Graham Land. Named by the UK in 1959 for Theodore Hamblin (1890–1952), British designer of snow goggles in the 1930s.

**Hamburg Bay.** 64°30'S, 63°57'W. Also spelled Hambourg Bay. Indents the NW coast of Anvers Island, just south of Bonnier Point. Discovered by Dallmann in 1873–74, who named it for the home port of his expedition.

**¹Mount Hamilton.** 80°40'S, 158°17'E. 1,990 m. At the east edge of Kent Plateau, 7 miles south of Mount Tuatara, in the Churchill Mountains. Discovered during Scott's first expedition, of 1901–4, and named by Scott for Adm. Sir Richard Vesey Hamilton, Arctic explorer, and a member of the Ship Committee for Scott's expedition.

²**Mount Hamilton.** 85°44'S, 151°53' W. 1,410 m. Marks the west end of the Tapley Mountains, at the east side of the lower reaches of the Robert Scott Glacier in the Queen Maud Mountains. Discovered by Gould in Dec. 1929, during Byrd's first expedition, and visited by Quin Blackburn in Dec. 1934 during Byrd's second expedition. Byrd named it for G.C. Hamilton, general manager of the McClatchy Newspapers, of Sacramento, California, who was a contributor to Byrd's second expedition of 1933–35.

**Hamilton, James E.** 1893–1957. British colonial naturalist to the Falkland Islands, he visited Antarctica during the Discovery Investigations of 1925–28.

**Hamilton Bluff.** 69°44'S, 73°56'E. 2 miles west of Palmer Point and 10 miles west of Mount Caroline Mikkelsen on the coast of East Antarctica. Photographed by the LCE 1936–37, and named by the Australians for R. Hamilton, helicopter pilot with the ANARE in 1968.

**Hamilton Cliff.** 85°01'S, 90°18'W. Over 600 m. Forms the NE extremity of the Ford Massif in the Thiel Mountains. Named by Bermel and Ford, leaders of the US Geological Survey Thiel Mountains Party here in 1960–61, for Warren B. Hamilton, USGS representative in charge of geologic studies in the McMurdo Sound dry valley area, 1958–59.

**Hamilton Glacier.** 82°40'S, 160°15'E. 12 miles long. Flows from the NW slopes of the Markham Plateau in the Queen Elizabeth Range, into Nimrod Glacier. Named by the New Zealanders in 1960–61 for W.M. Hamilton, secretary of the NZ Department of Scientific and Industrial Research.

**Hamilton Ice Piedmont.** 74°31'S, 110° 18'W. On the Marie Byrd Land coast.

**Hamilton Point.** 64°22'S, 57°18'W. Marks the south side of the entrance to Markham Bay on the SE side of James Ross Island. Discovered by Ross in 1839–43, and he named it Cape Hamilton for Capt. W.A.B. Hamilton, RN, private secretary to the Earl of Haddington. Nordenskjöld's expedition surveyed it in 1901–4, and the FIDS resurveyed it in 1953. It was redefined.

**Hamm Peak.** 69°43'S, 74°08'E. Just south of Strover Peak, and 6 miles WNW of Mount Caroline Mikkelsen, just behind the coast of East Antarctica. Photographed by the LCE 1936–37, and named by the Australians for G.F. Hamm, officer-in-charge of Mawson Station, 1968. He established a survey station here.

**Hammer Hill.** 61°04'S, 55°21'W. The most northerly hill on Elephant Island in the South Shetlands. Just south of Cape Yelcho. Named by the Joint Services Expedition 1970–71. The name is descriptive.

**Hammer Point.** 62°21'S, 59°39'W. On Robert Island in the South Shetlands.

**Cape Hammersly.** 66°28'S, 115°03'E. Ice-covered. Between Williamson and Totten Glaciers on the Budd Coast. Named for George W. Hammersly.

**Hammersly, George W.** Midshipman on the Wilkes Expedition 1838–42. Joined the *Peacock* at Callao, and transferred to the *Vincennes* at Fiji.

**Hammond, Henry.** Quartermaster on the Wilkes Expedition 1838–42. Joined in the USA. Served the cruise.

**Hammond Glacier.** 77°25'S, 146°W. Also called Hammond Inlet, John Hays Hammond Glacier. On the NE side of the Haines Mountains. Flows for about 40 miles to the Sulzberger Ice Shelf in the Ford Ranges of Marie Byrd Land. Discovered in 1934 during Byrd's second expedition, and named by Byrd for John Hays Hammond, US mining engineer and philanthropist.

**Hammond Inlet** *see* **Hammond Glacier**

**Hamna Bay.** 69°16'S, 39°41'E. An indentation into the west side of the

Langhovde Hills, on the east side of Lützow-Holm Bay. Name means "the harbor" in Norwegian.

**Hamna Icefall.** 69°17′S, 39°43′E. Descends to the south end of Hamna Bay, just east of Hamnenabben Head, on the Queen Maud Land coast. Named by the Japanese in 1963 for nearby Hamna Bay.

**Hamnenabben Head.** 69°17′S, 39°41′ E. Ice-free headland. Forms the south shore of Hamna Bay on the east side of Lützow-Holm Bay. Photographed by the LCE 1936–37, and named by the Norwegians in association with the bay. Name means "the harbor crag" in Norwegian.

**Hamner Nunatak.** 78°33′S, 157°56′E. West of the Warren Range, 5 miles WNW of Wise Peak. Named in 1964 for Karl C. Hamner, biologist at McMurdo Station, 1960–61.

**Mount Hampson.** 66°48′S, 51°11′E. 1 mile north of Mount Rhodes, in the north part of the Tula Mountains in Enderby Land. Named by the Australians for R.V. Hampson.

**Hampson, R.V.** Crew member on the *Discovery* during the BANZARE 1929–31.

**Mount Hampton.** 76°29′S, 125°48′W. 3,325 m. A circular, ice-filled crater occupies most of the summit. It is the most northerly of the extinct volcanoes which form the Executive Committee Range in Marie Byrd Land. Discovered aerially on Dec. 15, 1940, by the USAS 1939–41, and named by them for Ruth Hampton, Department of the Interior member of the USAS Executive Committee.

**Hampton, Wilfred E.** Member of the BGLE 1934–37. He had been in Greenland with Rymill a couple of years before.

**Hampton Bluffs.** 64°25′S, 59°18′W. 3 rock bluffs on the east side of Larsen Inlet in Graham Land. Surveyed by the FIDS in 1960–61, and named by the UK for Ian F.G. Hampton, FIDS physiologist at Base D in 1959 and 1960.

**Hampton Glacier.** 69°20′S, 70°05′W. In the NE part of Alexander Island. 25

miles long. 5 miles wide. Flows along the west wall of the Douglas Range to Schokalsky Bay. The BGLE flew up this glacier in 1937 and photographed it. Wilfred E. Hampton was the pilot. The mouth of the glacier was surveyed in 1948 by the FIDS, and later named by the UK for Hampton.

**Hampton Ridge.** 83°52′S, 167°02′E. 10 miles long. Runs north from Pagoda Peak, between Montgomerie and Mackellar Glaciers in the Queen Alexandra Range. Named for Maj. William C. Hampton, commanding officer of the US Army Aviation Detachment which supported the Texas Tech Shackleton Glacier Expedition of 1964–65.

**Hamrane Heights.** 72°32′S, 0°36′E. Ice-free. Between Skarsdalen Valley and Hei Glacier in the Sverdrup Mountains of Queen Maud Land. Name means "the crags" in Norwegian.

**Hamrehovden** *see* **Trethewry Point**

**Hamreneset** *see* **Bertha Island**

**Hanbury, James G.** Hospital steward on the Wilkes Expedition 1838–42. Joined in the USA. Served the cruise.

**Mount Hancox.** 72°38′S, 166°59′E. 3,245 m. 6 miles SE of Mount Burton, on the northern edge of Malta Plateau in the Victory Mountains of Victoria Land. Named by the Mariner Glacier geology party of the NZGSAE of 1966–67, for G.T. Hancox, senior geologist with the party here.

**Hand Glacier.** 72°58′S, 168°05′E. A valley glacier. Flows from the eastern slopes of the Malta Plateau along the south side of Clapp Ridge into Borchgrevink Glacier, in the Victory Mountains of Victoria Land. Named for Cadet H. Hand, biologist at McMurdo Station, 1967–68.

**Handcock.** Steward on the *Nimrod*, 1907–8.

**Handel Ice Piedmont.** 70°20′S, 71°W. North and west of the Colbert Mountains, between Haydn and Schubert Inlets on the west central coast of Alexander Island. Named by the UK for the composer.

**Handler Ridge.** 72°30'S, 167°E. 10 miles long. Divides the Croll Glacier and the upper section of the Trafalgar Glacier, in the Victory Mountains of Victoria Land. Named in 1969 for Dr. Philip Handler, chairman of the National Science Board.

**Mount Handsley.** 77°56'S, 161°33'E. On the Knobhead massif in Victoria Land. 1½ miles SSE of Knobhead, it overlooks the upper section of the Ferrar Glacier from the NW. Named in 1969 by New Zealand for Jesse Handsley.

**Handsley, Jesse.** Able seaman on the Royal Society Expedition of 1901–4. Sledged up the Ferrar and Taylor Glaciers with Scott in 1903.

**Hanessian Foreland.** 74°42'S, 135°15'W. Snow-covered peninsula, over 20 miles long and 10 miles wide, on the coast of Marie Byrd Land. It extends seaward between Siniff Bay and the western end of the Getz Ice Shelf. Named for John Hanessian, Jr. (1925–1974), IGY planner.

**Hanging valleys.** Also called glacial valleys, or glacial troughs. Stream valleys that have been glaciated, or cut off at the base by a large glacier moving past it, thus leaving a valley suspended, as it were, at the level of glaciation.

**Hanging waterfalls.** Waterfalls flowing over hanging valleys.

**The *Hanka*.** Whalecatcher from which David Ferguson did geological reconnaissance in the area of the Antarctic Peninsula in 1913–14.

**Hanka Island.** 64°51'S, 62°49'W. Near the head of Leith Cove, in Paradise Harbor, off the west coast of Graham Land. Named by David Ferguson in 1913–14.

**The *Hannah*.** Liverpool sealer wrecked in the South Shetlands (at what is now called Hannah Point, on the south coast of Livingston Island) on Dec. 25, 1820. Capt. Johnson was almost certainly its captain.

**Hannah Island.** 76°39'S, 148°48'W. Ice-covered. In the Marshall Archipelago. Between Hutchinson Island and Guest Peninsula, within the Sulzberger Ice Shelf. Named for J.P. Hannah, ionosphere physicist at Byrd Station 1968.

**Hannah Peak.** 82°36'S, 53°10'W. At the SW end of the Dufek Massif, 2 miles NNE of Walker Peak, in the Pensacola Mountains. Named for James L. Hannah, construction electrician at Ellsworth Station, 1957, and at McMurdo Station, 1961.

**Hannah Point.** 62°39'S, 60°37'W. Forms the east side of the entrance to Walker Bay on the south coast of Livingston Island in the South Shetlands. Named by the UK in 1958 for the *Hannah*.

**Hannah Ridge.** 83°36'S, 55°10'W. 5 miles long. Arc-shaped and narrow. It extends westward from the Washington Escarpment just north of Brown Ridge in the Neptune Range of the Pensacola Mountains. Named for Edward L. Hannah, aviation structural mechanic at Ellsworth Station in 1958.

**Hannam, Walter H.** Radioman on the AAE 1911–14.

**Hannam Islands.** 66°55'S, 142°58'E. Three small islands in the eastern part of Commonwealth Bay, between Cape Denison and Cape Gray. Discovered by the AAE 1911–14, and named by Mawson for Walter H. Hannam.

**Hannan Glacier** *see* **Molle Glacier**

**Hannan Ice Shelf.** 67°36'S, 47°35'E. 18 miles wide. On the coast of Enderby Land. It is fed by the Molle and Kichenside Glaciers, and borders McKinnon Island on every side except the north side. Named by the Australians for F.T. Hannan, meteorologist at Mawson Station in 1957.

**Hans-Martin Nunatak.** 71°37'S, 8°56'E. Also called Hans-Martinsteinen. Isolated. 3 miles south of Henriksen Nunataks in Queen Maud Land. Named by the Norwegians for Hans-Martin Henriksen, meteorological assistant on the IGY, 1956–58.

**Hans-Martinsteinen** *see* **Hans-Martin Nunatak**

**Cape Hansen.** 60°40′S, 45°35′W. Also called Cape H. Hansen. Separates Marshall and Iceberg Bays on the south side of Coronation Island in the South Orkneys. Possibly named by Petter Sørlle in 1912–13.

**¹Mount Hansen.** 71°28′S, 12°09′E. Also called Hansenhovden. 1,895 m. 1 mile north of Kåre Bench, and just NW of Daykovaya Peak at the northern end of the Westliche Petermann Range of the Wohlthat Mountains. Discovered aerially by Ritscher's expedition of 1938–39, and later named by the Norwegians for Kåre Hansen, meteorologist with the Norwegian Antarctic Expedition of 1958–59.

**²Mount Hansen** *see* **Mount Henson**

**Hansen, Herbert L.** Meteorologist at South Pole Station, 1957, and US representative at Wilkes Station in 1959 after that station had been taken over by the Australians.

**Hansen, Ludvig.** Tinsmith on the *Fram* during the Norwegian Antarctic Expedition of 1910–12, under Amundsen. He was not one of the shore party.

**¹Hansen Glacier.** 78°21′S, 84°33′W. 10 miles long. Flows from Mount Tuck into Dater Glacier in the Sentinel Range. Named for Herbert L. Hansen.

**²Hansen Glacier** *see* **Hansenbreen**

**Hansen Inlet.** 75°15′S, 63°40′W. Ice-filled. Between Capes Schlossbach and Cox, near the eastern base of the Antarctic Peninsula. Named for B. Lyle Hansen, deep-core drilling chief at Byrd Station between 1966 and 1969 (*see also* **Ueda Glacier**).

**Hansen Island.** 67°06′S, 67°37′W. Also called Isla Tegualda. 6 miles long and 3 miles wide. Just north of The Gullet at the head of Hanusse Bay, off the west coast of Graham Land. Surveyed by the BGLE in 1936, and they called it North Island. Resurveyed by the FIDS in 1948, and renamed by the UK in 1954 for Leganger H. Hansen, manager at Salve-

sen's whaling station on South Georgia (54°S) between 1916 and 1937. He helped the BGLE 1934–37.

**Hansen Mountains.** 68°16′S, 58°47′E. A large group of nunataks 55 miles south of Stefansson Bay, in Kemp Land, behind the Mawson Coast. They extend 25 miles in a NW-SE direction. Photographed by the LCE 1936–37, and named by the Norwegians for H.E. Hansen (*see* **Hansenbreen**).

**Hansen Nunatak.** 74°48′S, 162°20′E. Beehive-shaped. 965 m. Near the terminus of Reeves Glacier, about 3 miles NE of Mount Larsen and 3 miles NW of Teall Nunatak, in Victoria Land. Discovered during Scott's first expedition, 1901–4, and named during Shackleton's 1907–9 expedition, possibly for Nikolai Hanson (people were not so meticulous about spelling one another's names in those days).

**Hansen Rocks.** 67°30′S, 62°54′E. Five small islands just north of Holme Bay, about 1 mile NE of Sawert Rocks, off the coast of Mac. Robertson Land. Named by the Australians for Capt. B.T. Hansen, captain of the *Nella Dan* in 1968, 1969, 1970, and 1972.

**Hansen Spur.** 86°13′S, 159°33′W. Also called Mount Ludvig Hansen. 8 miles long. Descends from the NW side of Nilsen Plateau in the Queen Maud Mountains, and ends at the edge of Amundsen Glacier just east of Olsen Crags. Named for Ludvig Hansen. Amundsen named a mountain somewhere near here Mount L. Hansen, and this naming preserves that spirit.

**Hansenbreen.** 72°06′S, 22°45′E. Also called H.E. Hansenbreen, Hansen Glacier. A glacier, 15 miles long, flowing along the west side of Mount Nils Larsen in the Sør Rondane Mountains. Photographed by the LCE 1936–37, and named by the Norwegians for H.E. Hansen, Norwegian Antarctic cartographer.

**Hansenhovden** *see* **Mount Hansen**

**¹Mount Hanson.** 85°28′S, 147°26′W. 800 m. 1 mile SE of Supporting Party

Mountain in the Harold Byrd Mountains. Discovered by Gould in Dec. 1929 during Byrd's 1928–30 expedition. Byrd named it for Malcolm P. Hanson.

**²Mount Hanson**  *see*  **Hanson Peak**

**Hanson, Malcolm P.** Chief radio engineer on Byrd's 1928–30 expedition, and one of the shore party. He had been assigned to the expedition by the Navy Department, and was a pioneer of Polar radio communication. He had been with Byrd in the Arctic.

**Hanson, Nikolai.** Naturalist on Borchgrevink's wintering-over party of 1899. He contracted scurvy in late July 1899, and died on Oct. 14, 1899, "of unknown causes" (probably scurvy). He was the first human being to be buried on the continent itself (at Cape Adare).

**Hanson Hill.** 63°55′S, 58°49′W. 900 m. Snow-covered. Has two lower summits, one to the north of it, and one to the south. 4 miles SE of Cape Roquemaurel on Trinity Peninsula. Charted by Dumont d'Urville in March 1838, and named Thanaron Hill by the UK in 1948. This name came about because the FIDS, in their fruitless search for Dumont d'Urville's Cap Thanaron in 1946, recommended the preservation of the French explorer's naming. Later, however, the British did find the original Cap Thanaron, and renamed it Thanaron Point, and in 1963 they renamed this hill for Thomas A. Hanson, FIDS surveyor at Base D in 1957–59.

**Hanson Peak.** 71°21′S, 170°18′E. Also called Mount Hanson. 1,255 m. 4 miles south of Cape Adare in the northern part of the Adare Peninsula. Named by New Zealand for Nikolai Hanson.

**Hanson Ridge.** 77°17′S, 163°19′E. Ice-free. 3 miles NW of Spike Cape, near the center of Wilson Piedmont Glacier in Victoria Land. Scott's 1910–13 expedition called it Black Ridge, but it was renamed in 1964 by the USA for Kirby J. Hanson, meteorologist at the South Pole Station in 1958.

**Mount Hanssen.** 85°59′S, 164°28′W. Also called Mount Helmer Hanssen. Ice-covered. 3,280 m. At the most southerly point of Rawson Plateau in the Queen Maud Mountains. Discovered in Nov. 1911 by Amundsen and named by him for Helmer Hanssen.

**Hanssen, Helmer.** b. 1870 in the Vesterålen Islands, Norway. d. 1957. Helmer Julius Hanssen. Deputy leader under Amundsen on the Norwegian Antarctic Expedition 1910–12, and one of the first five men to reach the South Pole, on Dec. 14, 1911. A dog expert, he met Amundsen in 1897 and was with him on the *Gjøa* when Amundsen found the Northwest Passage in the Arctic in 1906. Later he was back in the Arctic with Amundsen.

**Hanusse Bay.** 66°57′S, 67°30′W. Also called Hanusse Fjord. 20 miles long, between the northern parts of Adelaide Island, and Arrowsmith Peninsula. Discovered and charted by Charcot in 1908–10, and named by him for the director of the Hydrographic Service of the French Navy.

**Hanusse Fjord**  *see*  **Hanusse Bay**

**Hånuten**  *see*  **Shark Peak**

**Happy Valley.** 75°22′S, 72°40′W. Ice-filled. 3 miles wide. Over 10 miles long. In the Behrendt Mountains of Ellsworth Land. Named by the University of Wisconsin Traverse Party of 1965–66, while they were surveying the area.

**Harald Bay.** 69°12′S, 157°45′E. Also spelled (erroneously) Harold Bay. 4 miles wide. Indents the coast between Archer Point and Williamson Head. Named by the Australians for Capt. Harald Møller Pederson, captain of the *Magga Dan* during the 1958–59 ANARE season.

**Harbord, A.E.** RN. Second officer on the *Nimrod*, 1907–9.

**Harbord Glacier.** 75°55′S, 162°24′E. Flows along the south side of Mount George Murray, into the Ross Sea south of Whitmer Peninsula, where it forms the Harbord Glacier Tongue. Named in association with the tongue.

**Harbord Glacier Tongue.** 75°55′S, 162°50′E. The seaward extension of Harbord Glacier, on the coast of Victoria Land. At the time that Shackleton's expedition charted it in 1907–9 it extended about 5 miles out into the Ross Sea. Shackleton named it for A.E. Harbord.

**Harbord Ice Barrier Tongue** *see* **Harbord Glacier Tongue**

**Harbord Ice Tongue** *see* **Harbord Glacier Tongue**

**Harbour Glacier.** 64°49′S, 63°26′W. A through glacier, 3 miles long and 1½ miles wide, on the NW side of Wiencke Island. It flows from Port Lockroy to the cove 1 mile east of Noble Peak. In 1944 the FIDS charted it and named it for the harbor of Port Lockroy.

**Harbour Heights** *see* **Arrival Heights**

**¹Mount Harcourt** *see* **Mount Vernon Harcourt**

**²Mount Harcourt.** 83°49′S, 172°25′E. 1,535 m. 5 miles east of Mount Kyffin, at the north end of the Commonwealth Range. Discovered and named by Shackleton's 1907–9 expedition.

**Harden, Thomas.** Officer's cook on the Wilkes Expedition 1838–42. Joined in the USA. Served the cruise.

**Hardiman Peak.** 85°01′S, 169°23′W. 1,210 m. Forms the eastern extremity of the ridge along the north side of Zotikov Glacier in the Prince Olav Mountains. Named for Terrance L. Hardiman, geomagnetist at Amundsen-Scott South Pole Station, 1965.

**Mount Harding.** 72°53′S, 75°02′E. The largest of the Grove Mountains, in the south central part of the group. 4 miles west of Gale Escarpment. Named by the Australians for N.E. Harding, topographer who has contributed enormously to Antarctic map-making.

**Península Hardley** *see* **Ardley Island**

**Mount Hardy.** 66°49′S, 50°43′E. Just east of Mount Oldfield in the NW part of the Tula Mountains of Enderby Land. Named by the Australians for K. Hardy, weather observer at Wilkes Station in 1959.

**Point Hardy** *see* **Sartorius Point**

**Punta Hardy** *see* **Fort Point**

**Hardy Cove.** 62°32′S, 59°35′W. On the east side of Greenwich Island in the South Shetlands. Named by the UK in 1961 to preserve the original naming Point Hardy given to what is now Sartorius Point by Robert Fildes in 1821 for Adm. Sir Thomas Hardy (1769–1839).

**Hardy Rocks.** 66°16′S, 67°17′W. 2 miles west of DuBois Island in the Biscoe Islands. Named by the UK for James D. Hardy, US physiologist specializing in the cold.

**Hare, Charles H.** b. 1884. Ward room assistant and captain's steward on the *Discovery* during the Royal Society Expedition 1901–4. Scott picked him to be part of the shore party. On March 11, 1902, his companion George Vince fell over a cliff, and Hare fell asleep and lay under the snow for about 36 hours. He went 40 hours without food, and about 60 hours without warm food, yet when he walked into camp 2 days later, with search parties out looking for him, he was free of frostbite.

**Hare Peak.** 84°59′S, 174°17′E. 2,970 m. Ice-free. At the north end of the ridge forming the east side of Leigh Hunt Glacier in the Queen Maud Mountains. Named by the New Zealanders in 1961–62 for Charles H. Hare.

**Hargrave Hill.** 64°01′S, 60°11′W. At the south side of the Wright Ice Piedmont, 2 miles NE of the mouth of the Henson Glacier, in Graham Land. Named by the UK for Lawrence Hargrave (1850–1915), Australian inventor of the box-kite, and pioneer of rotary aero engines.

**Hargreaves Glacier.** 69°46′S, 74°20′E. 2 miles west of Mount Caroline Mikkelsen on the Ingrid Christensen Coast. It flows into the central part of the head of Sandefjord Ice Bay. Named by US cartographer John H. Roscoe in 1952 for R.B. Hargreaves (*see* **Hargreavesbreen**).

**Hargreavesbreen.** 72°11′S, 23°13′E. Flows between Mount Nils Larsen and Mount Widerøe in the Sør Rondane Mountains. Named by the Norwegians for R.B. Hargreaves, American aerial photographer on Operation Highjump, 1946–47.

**Hariholm** *see* **Mariholm**

**Hariot Glacier.** 69°S, 66°20′W. Flows along the south side of Morgan Upland, and then into the northern part of the Wordie Ice Shelf, on the west coast of the Antarctic Peninsula. Surveyed by the BGLE in 1936–37. Resurveyed by the FIDS in Dec. 1958. Named by the UK for Thomas Hariot (1560–1621), English navigation pioneer.

**Mount Harker.** 77°18′S, 162°05′E. At the east side of Willis Glacier in the Saint Johns Range of Victoria Land. Charted by Scott's 1910–13 expedition and named by them for Dr. Alfred Harker, British petrologist.

**Mount Harkness.** 86°04′S, 150°36′W. Formerly called Mount Bruce Harkness. 1,900 m. 1½ miles south of Organ Pipe Peaks. Forms part of the east wall of Robert Scott Glacier in the Queen Maud Mountains. Discovered by Quin Blackburn in Dec. 1934, during Byrd's 1933–35 expedition, and named by Byrd in 1935 for Bruce Harkness, a friend of Richard S. Russell, Jr. (q.v.).

**Harlin, Hans.** Member of von Drygalski's expedition of 1901–3.

**Harlin Glacier.** 70°53′S, 160°50′E. Flows from the Polar Plateau near Mount Nero, on the NW side of the Daniels Range. It flows between Sample Nunataks and the north end of the Daniels Range, and then eastward into the lower part of Rennick Glacier. Named for Ben W. Harlin, meteorologist-in-charge at Little America in 1957, and scientific leader at South Pole Station, 1961.

**Harman, John.** Private on the Wilkes Expedition 1838–42. Joined in the USA. Served the cruise.

[1]**Harmon, John.** Captain of the fo'c's'le on the Wilkes Expedition 1838–42. Joined in the USA. Served the cruise.

[2]**Harmon, John.** Seaman on the Wilkes Expedition 1838–42. Joined in the USA. Served the cruise.

**Harmon Bay.** 74°15′S, 110°52′W. On the Marie Byrd Land coast.

**The *Harmony*.** American schooner built in Barnstable, Mass., in 1818. 111 tons, 71 feet long, it was owned by Josiah and William Sampson of Barnstable, and temporarily registered in Nantucket on Aug. 17, 1820. It was in the South Shetlands in 1820–21, under the command of Capt. Nathaniel Ray, and in company with the *William and Mary* under Folger. It was based at Harmony Cove, on Nelson Island, and took 4,500 seal skins, arriving home on June 6, 1821, in company with the *Huntress*. Isaac Hodges succeeded Ray as captain for the 1821–22 season in the South Shetlands.

**Harmony Cove.** 62°19′S, 59°12′W. Between Harmony Point and The Toe on the west side of Nelson Island in the South Shetlands. Named by US sealers in 1820 for the *Harmony*.

**Harmony Point.** 62°19′S, 59°15′W. Just west of Harmony Cove, it forms the western extremity of Nelson Island in the South Shetlands. Charted in 1935 by personnel on the *Discovery II*, and named by them in association with the cove. This is SSSI #14.

**Harmony Strait** *see* **Nelson Strait**

**Mount Harmsworth.** 78°41′S, 160°56′E. 2,765 m. Ice-covered. At the NW side of the head of Delta Glacier, in the Worcester Range. Discovered by Scott's 1901–4 expedition, and named by them for Sir Alfred Harmsworth, later Lord Northcliffe, a contributor to the expedition.

**Harold Bay** *see* **Harald Bay**

**Harold Byrd Mountains.** 85°26'S, 146° 30'W. Also called Byrd Mountains. Between the head of the Ross Ice Shelf and the lower part of Leverett Glacier. Discovered in Dec. 1929 by Gould during Byrd's 1928–30 expedition, and named by Byrd for D. Harold Byrd, a cousin and a contributor to the expedition.

**Mount Harold June** *see* **Mount June**

**Harp Island.** 66°S, 65°40'W. Between Beer and Upper Islands, 8 miles west of Prospect Point, off the west coast of Graham Land. Charted and named descriptively by the BGLE 1934–37.

**Mount Harper.** 84°03'S, 57°03'W. 1,405 m. 2 miles west of Mount Kaschak in the southern Neptune Range of the Pensacola Mountains. Named for Ronald B. Harper, electronics technician at Ellsworth Station, 1958.

**Harper Glacier.** 73°52'S, 163°05'E. Flows between Mount Gibbs and Mount Adamson in the Deep Freeze Range, and enters Campbell Glacier in Victoria Land. Named for Wayne M. Harper, satellite geodesist at McMurdo Station in 1964–65.

**Harpun Rocks.** 64°19'S, 62°59'W. Submerged rocks, 175 yards SE of Bills Point on Delta Island, in the Melchior Islands. Harpun means "harpoon" in Norwegian, and the rocks were probably named by whalers in the early part of the 20th century.

**Harriague, Silvano.** Captain of the *Primero de Mayo* in 1943.

**Harrigan Hill.** 66°19'S, 110°29'E. In the NW part of the Mitchell Peninsula, just east of Pidgeon Island, in the Windmill Islands. Named for Edward C. Harrigan, meteorologist at Wilkes Station, 1961.

**Mount Harrington.** 85°34'S, 164°W. 2,550 m. 4 miles east of Mount Ruth Gade in the Quarles Range of the Queen Maud Mountains. Named for John R. Harrington, meteorologist at Amundsen-Scott South Pole Station, 1962.

**Harris, Alvin.** Sailmaker's mate on the Wilkes Expedition 1838–42. Joined in the USA. Served the cruise.

**Harris, John.** Landsman on the Wilkes Expedition 1838–42. Joined at Rio. Run at Sydney.

**Harris, Nathaniel.** Ordinary seaman on the Wilkes Expedition 1838–42. Joined in the USA. Discharged at NZ, March 31, 1840.

**Harris Peak.** 64°36'S, 61°47'W. 1,005 m. Surmounts the base of Reclus Peninsula on the west coast of Graham Land. Named by the UK in 1960 for Leslie Harris, FIDS carpenter and general assistant at Base O during its first winter of operation in 1956.

**Harris Point.** 81°35'S, 161°32'E. On the west side of the Ross Ice Shelf, 6 miles south of Young Head at the south side of Beaumont Bay. Named for Herman D. Harris, USN, a VX-6 chief hospital corpsman, who built a sick bay at South Pole Station in 1961.

**Harris Rock.** 62°57'S, 56°21'W. The largest and most southerly of a group of three rocks north of Montrol Rock and D'Urville Island. Named before 1960 by the Argentines, for Santiago Harris, a naval captain of that country.

**Harris Valley.** 76°38'S, 159°52'E. Just east of Coxcomb Peak in the Allan Hills of Victoria Land. Named by the New Zealanders in 1964 for Prof. T.M. Harris, paleobotanist.

**Cape Harrison** *see* **Cape Harrisson**

**Mount Harrison.** 70°23'S, 159°46'E. 1,955 m. Between Robilliard and Svendsen Glaciers in the Usarp Mountains. Named for Louis J. Harrison, US Army helicopter mechanic in Antarctica, 1961–62 and 1962–63.

**Harrison, George W.** Passed midshipman on the Wilkes Expedition 1838–42. Joined the *Flying Fish* on the voyage south, and transferred to the *Peacock* at Fiji.

**Harrison, Henry T., Jr.** Meteorologist assigned by the US Weather Bureau to

Byrd's 1928–30 expedition. He traveled down on the *City of New York* as a seaman, and was a member of Byrd's shore party.

**Harrison Bluff.** 77°17'S, 166°23'E. A pale-colored trachyte headland forming the seaward end of Trachyte Hill, and marking the southern end of McDonald Beach, on the western side of Mount Bird, Ross Island. Many skuas nest here. A survey station was placed here by E.B. Fitzgerald of the Cape Bird Party of the NZGSAE of 1958–59. Named by New Zealand for J. Harrison, mountain climbing assistant with the expedition.

**Harrison Glacier.** 66°14'S, 131°15'E. A channel glacier flowing to the Wilkes Coast 12 miles east of Cape Carr. Named for George W. Harrison.

**Harrison Nunatak.** 72°29'S, 96°05'W. Snow-covered. 4 miles south of Savage Glacier in the extreme SE part of Thurston Island. Discovered on helicopter flights from the *Burton Island* and *Glacier* in Feb. 1960, during the USN Bellingshausen Sea Expedition. Named for Henry T. Harrison, Jr., US Weather Bureau meteorologist on Byrd's 1928–30 expedition.

**Harrison Passage.** 65°53'S, 65°11'W. Between Larrouy and Tadpole Islands to the west, and Llanquihue Islands and the west coast of Graham Land to the east. Named by the UK in 1959 for John Harrison (1693–1776), English horologist who solved the problem of determining longitude at sea.

**Harrison Peak.** 72°24'S, 166°39'E. 2,830 m. On the north side of Wood Glacier, 5 miles north of Mount McDonald, in the Victory Mountains of Victoria Land. Named for William R. Harrison, biologist at McMurdo Station, 1967–68.

**Harrison Stream.** 77°17'S, 166°24'E. Flows between Trachyte and Cinder Hills to the north end of Romanes Beach on Ross Island. Named by New Zealand for J. Harrison (*see* **Harrison Bluff**).

**Harriss Ridge.** 70°08'S, 65°08'E. 2 miles NE of Mount Dovers in the Athos Range of the Prince Charles Mountains. Named by the Australians for B. Harriss, helicopter pilot here in 1969.

**Cape Harrisson.** 66°43'S, 99°03'E. Also spelled (erroneously) as Cape Harrison. Just north of Possession Rocks at the point where the Northcliffe and Denman Glaciers meet. Discovered by the AAE 1911–14, and named by Mawson for Charles T. Harrisson.

**Harrisson, Charles T.** Biologist and artist at the Western Base of the AAE 1911–14. Several of his paintings appear in Mawson's book, *Home of the Blizzard.*

**Harrisson Ice Rises.** 66°27'S, 96°39'E. 12 miles WSW of Henderson Island, this local swelling of the ice surface is caused by the Shackleton Ice Shelf passing over an underlying obstruction. Discovered by the Eastern Sledge Party of the AAE 1911–14, and named by Mawson for Charles T. Harrisson.

**Harrop Island.** 67°16'S, 46°52'E. 3 miles NW of Felton Head, just off the coast of Enderby Land. Named by the Australians for J.R. Harrop, weather observer at Wilkes Station, 1960.

**Harrow Peaks.** 74°04'S, 164°45'E. In the eastern part of the Random Hills. To the south of Clausnitzer Glacier, and to the west of Tinker Glacier, overlooking the NW extremity of Wood Bay on the Victoria Land coast. Named for Geoffrey N. Harrow, biologist at McMurdo Station, 1965–66.

**Mount Harry.** 74°14'S, 76°32'W. 14 miles SE of FitzGerald Bluffs in Ellsworth Land. Named for Jack L. Harry, US Geological Survey topographic engineer, a member of the Marie Byrd Land Survey Party of 1967–68.

**Punta Harry** *see* **Spallanzani Point**

**Harry Dodson Island** *see* **Dodson Peninsula**

**Harry Island.** 64°08'S, 61°59'W. Also called Enrique Island. Ice-capped. Has a truncated pyramidal peak on it. At the SE entrance to the channel between Brabant and Liège Islands in the Palmer Archipelago. Discovered by de Gerlache 1897–99, and named by him for a supporter of his *Belgica* expedition.

**Mount Hart.** 72°05′S, 169°05′E. Over 3,000 m. 2 miles NW of Mount Chider in the Admiralty Mountains of Victoria Land. Named for Lt. Vernon D. Hart, officer-in-charge of VX-6 at McMurdo Station, 1968.

**Hart, Asa.** Ordinary seaman on the Wilkes Expedition 1838–42. Joined in the USA. Served the cruise.

**Hart, T. John.** Scientific leader of the *William Scoresby* cruise of 1936–37. He was a member of the zoological staff of the Discovery Committee.

**Hart Glacier.** 77°30′S, 162°23′E. A hanging glacier on the south wall of Wright Valley in Victoria Land, between the Meserve and Goodspeed Glaciers. Named by US geologist Robert Nichols for Roger Hart, geological assistant to Nichols at nearby Marble Point in 1959–60.

**Hart Hills.** 83°43′S, 89°05′W. Mainly snow-covered. They extend 4 miles in a line trending east-west. They are isolated and lie 8 miles west of Pagano Nunatak and 77 miles north of the Ford Massif of the Thiel Mountains. Discovered aerially by Edward Thiel and Campbell Craddock on Dec. 13, 1959, and named by them for Pembroke Hart, seismologist on the US National Committee for the IGY.

**Hart Rock.** 60°41′S, 44°22′W. 10 meters high. 1½ miles NW of Herdman Rocks, and 3 miles NNE of the eastern end of Laurie Island, in the South Orkneys. Charted by Dumont d'Urville in 1838, and named in 1933 by the personnel on the *Discovery II* for T. John Hart.

**Harter Nunatak.** 81°14′S, 84°54′W. Isolated. 4 miles NE of Mount Tidd at the NE side of the Pirrit Hills. Named for Gene L. Harter, meteorologist at Little America, 1957.

**Mount Hartigan.** 76°52′S, 126°W. Mostly snow-covered. Has several indi-

vidually named peaks on it which rise to as high as 2,800 m. Just north of Mount Sidley in the Executive Committee Range of Marie Byrd Land. Discovered aerially on Dec. 15, 1940, by the USAS from West Base, and named for Rear Adm. Charles C. Hartigan, USN, Navy Department member of the Antarctic Service Executive Committee.

**Mount Hartkopf.** 75°59′S, 140°45′W. 1,110 m. On the east side of the upper reaches of Land Glacier, 11 miles SE of Mount McCoy, in Marie Byrd Land. Named for Kenneth W. Hartkopf, ionosphere physicist at Byrd Station, 1963.

**Cape Hartree.** 60°48′S, 44°44′W. Also called Cabo Vitie, Cape McVitie. Forms the SW tip of Mossman Peninsula on the south coast of Laurie Island in the South Orkneys. Discovered by Powell and Palmer in Dec. 1821, and named by Powell.

**Hartsene, Henry J.** Name also spelled Hartstein. Naval lieutenant on the Wilkes Expedition 1838–42. Served on the *Porpoise* 1838–39, then transferred to the *Relief* on June 21, 1839.

**Hartshorne Island.** 64°47′S, 64°23′W. Between Dakers Island and Howard Island in the eastern Joubin Islands. Named for Sidney G. Hartshorne, captain of the *Hero* on its first voyage to Palmer Station in 1968.

**Hartvigsen.** Captain of the whale catcher *Star III* during Larsen's 1923–24 expedition in the *Sir James Clark Ross.*

**Mount Harvey.** 66°55′S, 50°48′E. Snow-free. East of Amundsen Bay, in the Tula Mountains. 6 miles ENE of Mount Gleadell. Discovered in 1955 by an ANARE party led by P.W. Crohn. Named by the Australians for William Harvey, carpenter at Mawson Station, 1954.

**Harvey, Samuel.** Australian captain of the *Venus* in 1831.

**Harvey, W.** Seaman on the *Eleanor Bolling* during Byrd's 1928–30 expedition.

**Harvey, William.** Midshipman on the *Resolution* during Cook's second voyage.

**Harvey Heights.** 64°14′S, 62°24′W. Just north of Mount Parry and west of the head of Malpighi Glacier in central Brabant Island. Named by the UK for William Harvey (1578–1657), the English physician who first demonstrated the circulation of the blood.

**Harvey Islands.** 67°43′S, 45°33′E. Two islands in the west part of Freeth Bay, in Enderby Land. Named by the Australians for R. Harvey, radio officer at Wilkes Station, 1959.

**Mount Harvey Johnston** *see* **Johnston Peak**

**Harvey Johnston Peak** *see* **Johnston Peak**

**Harvey Nunataks.** 66°58′S, 52°E. Four nunataks, 4 miles west of Mount Ryder, in the eastern part of the Tula Mountains in Enderby Land. Named by the Australians for D.J. Harvey, electronics engineer at Mawson Station, 1961.

**Harvey Peak.** 79°13′S, 157°01′E. 2,120 m. Ice-free. 2 miles south of the Finger Ridges in the Cook Mountains. Named for Paul Harvey, a member of the US Army aviation support unit here in 1961–62.

**Harvey Ridge.** 70°59′S, 65°18′E. 2 miles east of the Husky Massif in the Aramis Range of the Prince Charles Mountains. Named by the Australians for S.T. Harvey, senior electronics technician at Wilkes Station, 1965.

**Harvey Shoals.** 68°11′S, 67°09′W. Three shoal patches, no shallower than 3 fathoms. Between Millerand and Northstar Islands in Marguerite Bay. Charted by the Hydrographic Survey Unit from the *John Biscoe* in 1966, and named for Petty Officer Brian E. Harvey, surveying recorder who did all the sounding for this survey.

**Harwell Glacier.** 84°57′S, 171°29′W. 3 miles long. Flows from the north slopes of the Prince Olav Mountains, just east of Mount Smithson, and enters the upper part of Gough Glacier. Named for Lt. Thomas W. Harwell, USN, in Antarctica, 1964.

**Mount Harwood.** 70°44′S, 165°49′E. 1,040 m. Surmounts Gregory Bluffs on the north coast of Victoria Land. Named by the ANARE for T.R. Harwood, second-in-charge of the ANARE expedition of 1962 aboard the *Thala Dan*.

**Haselton Icefall.** 77°21′S, 160°46′E. Flows from the Willett Range between Gibson Spur and Apocalypse Peaks toward Webb Lake in the Barwick Valley of Victoria Land. Named by Parker E. Calkin, US geologist, for fellow geologist George M. Haselton, Calkin's assistant in the field here in 1961–62.

**The *Hashedate Maru*.** Japanese whaler in Antarctic waters in 1947–48.

**Haskard Highlands.** 80°30′S, 29°15′W. In the Shackleton Range.

**Mount Haskell.** 66°45′S, 64°16′W. 1,480 m. At the SW side of Cabinet Inlet between Mounts Denucé and Holmes, on the east coast of Graham Land. The FIDS charted it in 1947 and named it for Daniel C. Haskell (*see* the Bibliography).

**Haskell Glacier.** 73°34′S, 94°13′W. Flows from Christoffersen Heights, then between Prism Ridge and Forbidden Rocks, in the Jones Mountains. Named for Lt. Hugh B. Haskell, USN, co-pilot on a flight of Nov. 25, 1961, from Byrd Station to establish Camp Sky-Hi (later Eights Station).

**Haskell Ridge.** 79°44′S, 156°10′E. 2 miles west of Colosseum Ridge in the Darwin Mountains. Named by the VUWAE 1962–63 for T.R. Haskell, a member of the expedition.

**Haskill Nunatak.** 83°24′S, 51°45′W. 1,710 m. Elongated. 2½ miles west of Dyrdal Peak in the southern Forrestal Range of the Pensacola Mountains. Named for Robert E. Haskill, radioman at Ellsworth Station, 1957.

**Haskins, James.** First class boy on the Wilkes Expedition 1838–42. Joined in the USA. Served the cruise.

**Mount Haslop.** 80°36'S, 30°16'W. 760 m. 2 miles south of Mount Lowe at the western end of the Shackleton Range. Named in 1957 by the BCTAE for Gordon M. Haslop.

**Haslop, Gordon M.** 1922–1961. Flight lieutenant of the RNZAF, who was seconded to the RAF for the BCTAE as second pilot in support of Fuchs during his transantarctic crossing.

**Haslum, H.J.** Second mate on the *Antarctic* during Nordenskjöld's expedition of 1901–4.

**Haslum Crag.** 64°22'S, 56°59'W. Close to the north coast of Snow Hill Island. 2 miles NE of Station Nunatak. Nordenskjöld's expedition called it Basaltspitze. The FIDS surveyed it in 1952, and the UK renamed it for H.J. Haslum.

**Mount Hassage.** 75°51'S, 72°29'W. 1,120 m. Isolated. 12 miles SW of Mount Horne in eastern Ellsworth Land. Discovered by the RARE 1947–48 and was the turnabout point of the RARE plane flight of Nov. 21, 1947. Named by Ronne for Charles Hassage.

**Hassage, Charles.** Chief engineer on the *Port of Beaumont, Texas,* during the RARE 1947–48. He was in charge of Main Base during Ronne's absence.

**Mount Hassel.** 86°28'S, 164°28'W. 2,390 m. Also called Mount Sverre Hassel. The most northeasterly summit of the massif at the head of the Amundsen Glacier in the Queen Maud Mountains. Named by the USA for Sverre Hassel. This may or may not be the Mount S. Hassel hastily positioned by Amundsen on his trek to the Pole in Nov. 1911, but it is in this vicinity.

**Hassel, Sverre.** 1876–1928. Helge Sverre Hassel. Norwegian navigator, sailmaker and saddler who, by the time Amundsen took him south in 1910, had been an Arctic explorer and was now a customs man. Prepared to go as far as San Francisco with the dogs, he was persuaded to go further south than any man had ever been, reaching the South Pole on Dec. 14, 1911. He died at Amundsen's feet.

**Mount Hastings.** 85°34'S, 154°10'W. 2 miles SE of Mount Rigby in the Karo Hills, at the west side of the Robert Scott Glacier. Discovered by Byrd's 1928–30 expedition. Named for James V. Hastings, geomagnetist at McMurdo Station, 1964–65.

**Haswell Island.** 66°31'S, 93°E. The largest of the Haswell Islands, off the coast of East Antarctica, 1½ miles north of Mabus Point. Discovered by the Western Base Party of the AAE 1911–14, and named by Mawson for Prof. William A. Haswell, zoologist at Sydney University and a member of the AAE Advisory Committee.

**Haswell Islands.** 66°32'S, 93°E. Also called Haswell Islets. Group of islets off the East Antarctica coast, not far from Mirnyy Station. Haswell Island is the largest, followed in order of size by Tokarev Island, Zykov Island, Fulmar Island, Poryadin Island, Buromskiy Island, Gorev Island, Greben Island, Khmara Island, and Vkhodnoy Island. Also included in the group, but outside the central area, are Stroiteley Islands and Tyulen'i Islands. Charted by the AAE 1911–14. Mawson called them the Rookery Islands because of the large emperor penguin colony on Haswell Island. Renamed by the Australians in 1955, in association with the largest island.

**Haswell Islets** *see* **Haswell Islands**

**Hatch, Lyranus.** Seaman on the Wilkes Expedition 1838–42. Joined in the USA. Discharged at NZ.

**Hatch Islands.** 66°53'S, 109°16'E. 3 miles east of Ivanoff Head at the head of Vincennes Bay. They mark the division between the Knox Coast and the Budd Coast. Named for Ernest B. Hatch, tractor driver on Operation Windmill, 1947–48.

**Hatch Outcrop.** 72°34'S, 93°20'W. An outcropping of rocks just north of Peeler Bluff in the western part of McNamara Island, in the northern part of the Abbott Ice Shelf. Named for Lt.

Ross Hatch, USN, who helped position this outcrop on Feb. 7, 1961.

**Hatch Plain.** 80°44'S, 25°43'W. Just to the east of the Shackleton Range.

**Hatcher Bluffs.** 86°20'S, 125°36'W. 5 miles south of Metavolcanic Mountain, at the east side of Reedy Glacier. Named for Julius O. Hatcher, construction mechanic at Byrd Station, 1962.

**Hatherton Glacier.** 79°55'S, 157°35'E. Flows from the Polar Plateau along the south side of the Darwin Mountains and enters Darwin Glacier at Junction Spur. Named by the Darwin Glacier Party of the BCTAE in 1957 for Trevor Hatherton, scientific officer in charge of Antarctic Activities, Department of Scientific and Industrial Research, NZ. Hatherton was the first scientific leader of Scott Base (*see also* the Bibliography).

**Hatinosu Peak** *see* **Hachinosu Peak**

**Hatley.** Second captain on Shelvocke's voyage of 1719.

**Hatten Peak.** 72°34'S, 4°10'W. Isolated. 6 miles NW of Veten Mountain. At the NW side of Borg Massif in Queen Maud Land. Name means "the hat" in Norwegian.

**Hauberg Mountains.** 75°52'S, 69°15'W. 35 miles in extent. 12 miles north of Cape Zumberge, and 30 miles south of the Sweeney Mountains in eastern Ellsworth Land. Discovered by the RARE 1947–48 and named by Ronne for John Hauberg of Rock Island, Illinois, a contributor to the RARE.

**The *Hauken*.** One of the first two modern whale catchers (cf. the *Ørnen*), it worked for the *Admiralen* in the South Shetlands 1905–6.

**Hauken Rock.** 62°01'S, 57°33'W. 1 mile east of Ørnen Rocks and 2 miles NE of Cape Melville, the eastern end of King George Island in the South Shetlands. Named by the UK in 1960 for the *Hauken*.

**Haulaway Point.** 68°11'S, 67°W. On the NE side of Stonington Island, just off the west coast of Graham Land. Surveyed by the USAS 1939–41. The FIDS resurveyed it in 1947–48, and named it because it is a good place for hauling supplies ashore.

**Haunn Bluff.** 66°23'S, 110°33'E. Surmounts the eastern part of the southern shore of Odbert Island, in the Windmill Islands. Named for Marvin G. Haunn, meteorologist at Wilkes Station, 1962.

**Haupt Nunatak.** 66°35'S, 110°41'E. 5 miles south of Alexander Nunatak, at the east side of the lower reaches of Vanderford Glacier. About 25 miles down the coast from Wilkes Station. Named for Ensign Richard W. Haupt, USN, assistant hydrographic officer on Operation Windmill, 1947–48.

**Hauron Peak.** 64°56'S, 62°59'W. 1,350 m. 3 miles SE of Mount Banck on the west side of Graham Land. Named by the UK in 1960 for Louis-Arthur D. du Hauron (1837–1920), French color photography pioneer.

**Haven Hill.** 82°53'S, 162°36'E. 2 miles west of Mount Tedrow, on the south side of Kent Glacier in the Queen Elizabeth Range. Named for Stoner B. Haven, biologist at McMurdo Station, 1960.

**Haven Mountain.** 80°02'S, 155°12'E. 2,470 m. 2 miles NE of Three Nunataks in the NW part of the Britannia Range. Named in 1957 by the Darwin Glacier Party of the BCTAE, who sheltered for five days here.

**Mount Havener.** 78°27'S, 84°37'W. 2,800 m. At the head of Guerrero Glacier in the Sentinel Range. Named for Melvin C. Havener, mechanic at South Pole Station, 1957.

**Haver Peak.** 75°09'S, 114°18'W. 4 miles south of Morrison Bluff in the Kohler Range of Marie Byrd Land. Named for Lt. D.J. Haver, USN, assistant officer in charge of the Supply Department at McMurdo Station, 1965 and 1966.

**Havilland Point.** 63°55'S, 60°14'W. 2 miles east of Cape Page on the west coast of Graham Land. Named by the UK in

1960 for Sir Geoffrey de Havilland, British pioneer aircraft designer.

**Havola Escarpment.** 84°45′S, 98°40′ W. Isolated. Snow-covered. Arc-shaped. 30 miles long. Faces south. 30 miles NW of the Thiel Mountains. Named for Major Antero Havola (*see* **Byrd–South Pole Overland Trek**).

**Havre Mountains.** 69°08′S, 71°40′W. They form the NW extremity of Alexander Island, and extend 20 miles between Cape Vostok and Russian Gap. Discovered by von Bellingshausen in 1821, and not again until de Gerlache saw them in 1898. Charcot charted them, and named them Massif Le Havre in 1908–10 for Le Havre, the home port of his expedition.

**Havsbotn.** 69°50′S, 38°45′E. A bay marking the head of Lützow-Holm Bay. Photographed by the LCE 1936–37. The name means "sea bottom" in Norwegian.

**Havstein Island.** 67°07′S, 58°45′E. 3 miles long and 2 miles wide. 1½ miles north of Law Promontory, and 1 mile east of Broka Island. Photographed by the LCE 1936–37. Name means "sea stone" in Norwegian.

**The *Hawea.*** NZ frigate which, with the *Pukaki,* escorted the *Endeavour* to 67°30′S, 179°58′E (about 30 miles inside the Ross Sea pack-ice) in the 1956–57 summer when the *Endeavour* was en route to Ross Island. The two frigates then went investigating the ocean north of Scott Island, and failed to land there. Captain W.J. Brown.

**Mount Hawea.** 82°50′S, 161°52′E. 3,080 m. 4 miles east of Mount Markham in the Frigate Range. Named by the New Zealanders in 1961–62 for the *Hawea.*

**Hawker Island.** 68°38′S, 77°51′E. 1 mile long. Between Mule Island and Mule Peninsula in the Vestfold Hills, in the eastern part of Prydz Bay. Photographed by the LCE 1936–37. Named later by the Australians for A.C. Hawker, radio supervisor at Davis Station, 1957.

**¹Mount Hawkes** *see* **Hawkes Heights**

**²Mount Hawkes.** 83°55′S, 56°05′W. 1,975 m. The highest mountain along the Washington Escarpment, at the east side of Jones Valley in the Neptune Range of the Pensacola Mountains. Discovered aerially on Jan. 13, 1956 (*see* the Chronology), and named for the co-pilot on that flight, William M. Hawkes.

**Hawkes, William M. "Trigger."** Capt., USN. One of the truly seminal figures in Antarctic history, he was on the continent during Operation Deep Freeze I and II, and even then was a veteran. He had been commander of the R4D Dakota airplane unit on the *Philippine Sea,* during Operation Highjump, 1946–47, and had flown the first plane from that aircraft carrier to Little America IV, with Byrd aboard. He was commander of one of the two planes which made the historic first flight from Christchurch, NZ, to McMurdo Sound on Dec. 17, 1955, and on Jan. 13, 1956, was co-pilot on another historic flight (*see* the Chronology). He is perhaps best known for being the co-pilot on the *Que Sera Sera* when it became the first plane to land at the South Pole, on Oct. 31, 1956, thus making Hawkes one of the first 15 men ever to set foot at the Pole.

**Hawkes Heights.** 73°32′S, 169°42′E. An ice-filled crater rising to 2,000 m. Dominate the southern part of Coulman Island in the Ross Sea. Named by the New Zealanders in 1958–59 for William M. Hawkes.

**Hawkins, Samuel N.** Sailmaker on the *Vincennes* during the Wilkes Expedition 1838–42.

**Hawkins Glacier.** 66°34′S, 107°31′E. A channel glacier flowing to the coast 4 miles west of Snyder Rocks. Named for Samuel N. Hawkins.

**Hawkins Peak.** 75°24′S, 110°29′W. 7 miles SE of Mount Murphy in Marie Byrd Land. Named for Maj. Billy R. Hawkins, a member of the US Army Aviation Detachment in Antarctica, 1966–67.

**Hawley, J.** Crewman on the *Jacob Ruppert,* 1933–34.

**Haworth Mesa.** 85°54'S, 128°18'W. Ice-capped. Its summit area is 5 miles long and 3 miles wide, and rises to 3,610 m. Between Sisco Mesa and Mount McNaughton in the western Wisconsin Range. Named for Leland J. Haworth, director of the NSF.

**Mount Hawthorne.** 72°10'S, 98°39'W. Also called Mount Mark. In the Walker Mountains, directly south of the base of Noville Peninsula on Thurston Island. Discovered aerially on Feb. 27, 1940, by Byrd on a flight from the *Bear,* and named by Byrd for Roger Hawthorne.

**Hawthorne, Roger.** Field representative for the USAS 1939-41, at West Base.

**Mount Hay.** 71°06'S, 65°39'E. 11 miles SE of Husky Dome in the Prince Charles Mountains. Named by the Australians for Dr. M. Hay, medical officer and officer-in-charge at Davis Station in 1961.

**Hayden Peak.** 74°41'S, 111°41'W. On the coast of Marie Byrd Land.

**Haydn Inlet.** 70°13'S, 70°45'W. Ice-filled. Indents the western coast of Alexander Island between Mozart Ice Piedmont and Handel Ice Piedmont. It is 27 miles long and 12 miles wide at its mouth, and narrows toward the head. Discovered aerially by the USAS 1939-41. Named by the UK for the composer.

**Mount Hayes.** 66°50'S, 64°10'W. 1,140 m. At the base of Cole Peninsula on the east coast of Graham Land. The FIDS charted it in 1947 and named it for James Gordon Hayes (*see* the Bibliography).

**Hayes, James.** Ordinary seaman on the Wilkes Expedition of 1838-42. Joined in the USA. Served the cruise.

**Hayes, William.** Seaman on the Wilkes Expedition 1838-42. Joined in the USA. Served the cruise.

**Hayes Glacier.** 76°16'S, 27°54'W. Enters the SE part of the Weddell Sea 17 miles WSW of Dawson-Lambton Glacier. Discovered aerially on Nov. 5, 1967, during a Hercules flight over the Caird Coast. Named for Lt. Cdr. Winston R. Hayes, USNR, pilot on that flight.

**Hayes Head.** 74°01'S, 165°17'E. 850 m. A headland. Overlooks the northern extremity of Wood Bay. 3 miles north of Kay Island, on the Victoria Land coast. Named for Miles O. Hayes, geologist at McMurdo Station, 1965-66.

¹**Hayes Peak.** 67°28'S, 60°46'E. Also called Veslekulten. 340 m. Conical. 2 miles south of Cape Bruce and Oom Bay. Discovered in Feb. 1931 by the BANZARE, and named by Mawson for James Gordon Hayes (*see* **Mount Hayes**).

²**Hayes Peak.** 85°20'S, 89°18'W. 2,060 m. Isolated. Just south of the Bermel Escarpment in the Thiel Mountains. Named by Bermel and Ford, leaders of the US Geological Survey Thiel Mountains Party here in 1960-61, for Philip T. Hayes, USGS geologist in the McMurdo Sound dry valley area in 1958-59.

**Hayman Nunataks.** 85°40'S, 179°30'E. Isolated. At the east end of the Grosvenor Mountains. 6 miles north of Larkman Nunatak. Named for Noel R. Hayman, aurora scientist at Hallett Station, 1962.

**Mount Hayne.** 70°16'S, 65°02'E. 2 miles NW of Moore Pyramid on the north side of Scylla Glacier, in the Prince Charles Mountains. Named by the Australians for J.R. Hayne, photographic officer here in 1969.

**Haynes Glacier.** 75°25'S, 109°50'W. Flows to the coast along the east side of Mount Murphy in Marie Byrd Land. Named for Maj. John W. Haynes, US Marine pilot in Antarctica in 1967 and 1968.

**Haynes Table.** 84°49'S, 174°35'E. Snow-covered. 8 miles across. Rises to 3,390 m. South of Mount Odishaw in the Hughes Range, between the heads of the Keltie and Bandau Glaciers. Discovered aerially by VX-6 on the flight of Jan. 12-13, 1956, and named for B.C. Haynes, meteorologist of the US Weather Bureau on Operation Highjump, 1946-47.

**Hayrick Island.** 68°42'S, 67°32'W. Over 150 m. Between Lodge Rock and

Twig Rock in the Terra Firma Islands, off the west coast of Graham Land. The FIDS surveyed it in 1948 and named it for its appearance when viewed from the east.

**Hays Glacier.** 67°40′S, 46°18′E. Flows into the head of Spooner Bay, in Enderby Land. Named by the Australians for J. Hays, US observer with the ANARE here in 1961.

**Hays Mountains.** 86°S, 155°W. Formerly called Will Hays Mountains. In the Queen Maud Mountains, between the Amundsen and Robert Scott Glaciers. They extend from the vicinity of Mount Thorne in the NW to Mount Dietz in the SE. Discovered aerially by Byrd on his South Pole flight of Nov. 28–29, 1929, and named by Byrd for Will Hays, the movie censor.

**The Haystack** *see* **Haystack Mountain**

**Haystack Mountain.** 77°03′S, 162°41′E. Formerly called The Haystack. Over 1,000 m. 1½ miles east of Mount England in the NE part of the Gonville and Caius Range in Victoria Land. Charted and named by Scott's 1910–13 expedition. Its rounded summit looks like a haystack.

**Mount Hayter.** 82°02′S, 157°26′E. 2,690 m. 1 mile SE of Laird Plateau on the west side of Olson Névé. Discovered by the NZGSAE 1964–65, and named by them for Adrian Hayter, leader at Scott Base, 1965.

**Mount Hayton.** 72°03′S, 165°12′E. 2,240 m. In the southern part of the East Quartzite Range. Named by the New Zealand Federated Mountain Clubs Antarctic Expedition 1962–63, for J.S. Hayton, field assistant with the party. It was first climbed on Dec. 18, 1962.

**Mount Hayward.** 78°07′S, 167°21′E. A hill 2 miles SW of Mount Heine on White Island in the Ross Archipelago. Named by the New Zealanders in 1958–59 for V.G. Hayward.

**Hayward, V.G.** Canadian dog driver who formed part of the Ross Sea Party of

Shackleton's British Imperial Transantarctic Expedition of 1914–17. On his way back from the depot-laying expedition across the Ross Ice Shelf, he and leader Mackintosh left the Discovery Hut on May 8, 1916, in an impatient effort to get back to Cape Evans over the soft sea-ice. Expecting to reach base in a couple of hours, the couple did not take a tent or sleeping bags, and a blizzard blew up. They were never seen again.

**Hazard Rock.** 64°59′S, 63°44′W. Isolated. 3 feet high. On the east side of Butler Passage, 2½ miles NE of Cape Renard, off the west coast of Graham Land. Named by Lt. Cdr. F.W. Hunt following his survey in 1952. It is a hazard to shipping.

**Mount Hazlett.** 72°06′S, 167°35′E. 2,080 m. At the south side of the mouth of Montecchi Glacier, where that glacier enters Tucker Glacier in the Victory Mountains of Victoria Land. Named for Paul C. Hazlett, VX-6 member at McMurdo Station, 1968.

**Head, John C.** Captain of the topsail on the Wilkes Expedition 1838–42. Joined in the USA. Served the cruise.

**Head Island.** 64°31′S, 62°55′W. Just over half a mile south of Andrews Point, and close to the NE side of Anvers Island. At the SE side of Hackapike Bay, it is not to be confused with Pear Island and False Island, which are just to the NE. Charted by the BGLE 1934–37, and named descriptively about 1952.

**Head Peak.** 72°10′S, 166°11′E. 3½ miles east of Le Couteur Peak in the Millen Range, in the névé area of the Pearl Harbor Glacier. Named by the New Zealanders in 1962–63 for its position at the head of Pearl Harbor Glacier.

**Heald, William L.** Able seaman, RN. On the Royal Society Expedition of 1901–4. Saved Ferrar's life in 1902 when the latter was dying of scurvy out on the trail.

**Heald Island.** 78°15'S, 163°49'E. 3 miles long. 555 meters high. Projects through the ice of the Koettlitz Glacier just east of Walcott Bay in Victoria Land. Discovered by Scott's 1901–4 expedition, and named by them for William L. Heald.

**Heale Peak.** 81°35'S, 160°04'E. 1,340 m. At the east side of Starshot Glacier, 2 miles north of Adams Peak in the Surveyors Range. Named by the New Zealanders in 1960–61 for Theophilus Heale, a New Zealand surveyor.

**Cape Healey** *see* **Cape Healy**

**Cape Healy.** 71°22'S, 60°58'W. Forms the north side of the entrance to Lamplugh Inlet, on the east coast of Palmer Land. Discovered by the USAS in 1940, and named by them for Joseph D. Healy.

**Healy, Joseph D.** Crewman on the *Jacob Ruppert*, 1933–34, and its 3rd officer, 1934–35, during Byrd's 1933–35 expedition, and dog driver and operations man at East Base during the USAS 1939–41.

**Heap Glacier.** 79°03'S, 159°20'E. 10 miles long. Flows into Mulock Glacier, to the east of Henry Mesa. Named for John A. Heap, a member of the University of Michigan–Ross Ice Shelf Studies party of 1962–63.

**Heaphy Spur.** 77°14'S, 161°15'E. 4 miles long. Descends from the southern side of the Clare Range, and divides the head of the Victoria Upper Glacier in Victoria Land. Named by the USA in 1964 for William Heaphy, a New Zealander who worked many years with USARP.

**Heaps Rock.** 76°S, 132°46'W. Above Bursey Icefalls. 2 miles WNW of Hutt Peak, on the Mount Bursey massif in Marie Byrd Land. Named for Kenneth L. Heaps, meteorologist at Amundsen-Scott South Pole Station, 1970.

**Hearfield Glacier.** 72°26'S, 167°42'E. Flows along the south side of the Cartographers Range into Trafalgar Glacier, just east of Aldridge Peak in the Victory Mountains of Victoria Land. Named by the New Zealanders in 1962–63 for B. Hearfield, a NZ alpinist with the NZGSAE of 1957–58.

**Cape Hearst** *see* **Cape Wilkins**

**Hearst Island.** 69°25'S, 62°10'W. Ice-covered. Dome-shaped. It is a grounded island in the Larsen Ice Shelf, about halfway down the east side of the Antarctic Peninsula. 36 miles long and 7 miles wide, and 4 miles east of Cape Rymill. Discovered aerially by Wilkins on Dec. 20, 1928. He thought it was part of the mainland, and called it Hearst Land for his patron, William Randolph Hearst, the newspaper magnate. The BGLE 1934–37 proved it to be an island, and reduced its proportions to a more correct size. They called it Wilkins Island. It was later renamed to preserve Wilkins' naming.

**Hearst Land** *see* **Hearst Island**

**Heart Lake.** 77°34'S, 166°14'E. On Cape Barne, Ross Island, 350 yards NW of Terrace Lake. Named for its shape by Shackleton's 1907–9 expedition.

**Heathcock Peak.** 86°07'S, 130°40'W. 2,310 m. In the eastern part of the Caloplaca Hills, overlooking the west edge of the Reedy Glacier. Named for Joe D. Heathcock, builder at Byrd Station, 1962.

**Heave-Ho Slope.** 72°32'S, 170°10'E. It falls 450 meters from Quarterdeck Ridge to a saddle at the SW end of Hallett Peninsula. Named by the New Zealanders in 1957–58 who had to manhaul sledges over the soft new snow found here that year.

**Heckmann Island.** 67°20'S, 61°03'E. The largest island in the eastern part of the Thorfinn Islands. 7 miles north of Byrd Head in Mac. Robertson Land. Photographed by the LCE 1936–37. Later named by the Australians for B. Heckmann, chief officer on the *Nella Dan* in 1965.

**Mount Hector.** 64°36'S, 63°25'W. Snow-covered. 2,225 m. Between Mount

Français and Mount Priam in the southern part of the Trojan Range on Anvers Island. Surveyed by the FIDS in 1955, and named by the UK for the Homeric hero.

**Mount Hedden.** 72°05′S, 1°25′E. 1,515 m. A nunatak 1 mile north of Brattskarvet Mountain in the Sverdrup Mountains of Queen Maud Land. Discovered aerially by Ritscher's expedition of 1938–39, and named Hedden-Berg by Ritscher for Karl Hedden. This may or may not be exactly Ritscher's Hedden-Berg, but it is in the general area.

**Hedden, Karl.** A sailor on the German New Schwabenland Expedition led by Ritscher in 1938–39.

**Hedgehog Island.** 72°12′S, 170°E. Also called One Day Islet. Ice-free. A stack in Moubray Bay, 1 mile south of Helm Point. First visited in 1957 by a party from Hallett Station. Named for its shape by the New Zealanders in 1957–58.

**Hedgpeth Heights.** 71°07′S, 167°30′E. Mainly snow-covered. 14 miles long. 2 miles SW of Quam Heights in the Anare Mountains of Victoria Land. Named for Joel W. Hedgpeth, biologist at McMurdo Station, 1967–68 and at Palmer Station, 1968–69.

**Hedin Nunatak.** 75°19′S, 111°17′W. Has an ice-capped flat top. 6 miles WNW of Mount Murphy in Marie Byrd Land. Named for Alan E. Hedin, aurora scientist at Byrd Station in 1962.

**Hedley Glacier.** 77°49′S, 162°07′E. Flows from Mount Coates in the Kukri Hills into Ferrar Glacier in Victoria Land. Named during Scott's 1910–13 expedition, for Charles Hedley, of the Australian Museum, an expert on mollusks.

**Heed Rock.** 64°59′S, 63°47′W. 1 mile south of Brown Island in the Wauwermans Islands of the Wilhelm Archipelago. Named by the UK as a warning to navigators, as the rock is practically hidden.

**Mount Heekin.** 85°03′S, 177°16′W. Ice-free. Overlooks the north side of the mouth of Baldwin Glacier, where that glacier enters Shackleton Glacier. Discovered aerially on Feb. 16, 1947, during Operation Highjump, and named for Robert P. Heekin.

**Heekin, Robert P.** Lt. (jg). Navigator on V6, the second flight on Byrd's South Pole flight of Feb. 16, 1947, during Operation Highjump.

**Mount Heer.** 73°18′S, 62°58′W. On the south side of Haines Glacier, 3 miles north of Mount Barkow, in Palmer Land. Named for Ray R. Heer, Jr., program director (atmospheric physics) at the NSF.

**Heezen Glacier.** 72°40′S, 61°10′W. On the east side of the Antarctic Peninsula.

**Hefferman, William P.** Captain of the topsail on the Wilkes Expedition 1838–42. Joined in the USA. Discharged at Oahu, Oct. 31, 1840.

**Heftye Island.** 71°59′S, 171°06′E. The most southerly of the Possession Islands, east of the south end of Adare Peninsula. Named by the *Antarctic* expedition led by Bull, for Heftye and Son of Christiania (now Oslo), shareholders in the expedition ship.

**Mount Heg.** 72°57′S, 166°45′E. Ice-covered. Forms the south end of a promontory on the west side of Malta Plateau in Victoria Land. On the west is the Seafarer Glacier, on the south is the Mariner Glacier, and on the east is the Potts Glacier. Named in 1972 for James E. Heg, chief of Polar Planning at the NSF.

**Hei Glacier.** 72°29′S, 0°35′E. Flows between Hamrane Heights and Robin Heights in the Sverdrup Mountains of Queen Maud Land. Named Heibreen (the upland glacier) by the Norwegians.

**Heiberg Glacier** *see* **Axel Heiberg Glacier**

**Heidemann Bay.** 68°35′S, 77°58′E. 1 mile long. Indents the seaward end of Breidnes Peninsula in the Vestfold Hills, just south of Davis Station. Photographed by the LCE 1936–37 and later named by the Australians for Frank Heidemann, second mate on the *Kista Dan* in 1957 when, on Jan. 11 of that year, this bay was first visited by an ANARE party.

**Heidemann Glacier.** 82°33′S, 162°50′E. 5 miles long. Flows from the area just NW of Mount Damm in the Queen Elizabeth Range, into Lowery Glacier. Named for Richard P. Heidemann, glaciologist at Roosevelt Island, 1962–63.

**Heikampen Peak.** 72°28′S, 0°41′E. At the SE end of Robin Heights in the Sverdrup Mountains of Queen Maud Land. Name means "the upland mountain top" in Norwegian.

**Heil Peak** *see* **Neill Peak**

**Heilman Glacier.** 82°37′S, 160°46′E. In the northern part of the Queen Elizabeth Range, flowing from Mount Sandved into Nimrod Glacier. Named for William L. Heilman, glaciologist at Roosevelt Island, 1961–62.

**Heim Glacier.** 67°28′S, 65°55′W. 8 miles long. In the SE part of Arrowsmith Peninsula. Flows into the ice in Jones Channel, on the west coast of Graham Land. Discovered aerially in 1936 by the BGLE. Surveyed in 1949 by the FIDS, who named it for Albert Heim, Swiss glaciologist.

**Heimdall Glacier.** 77°35′S, 161°50′E. Just east of Siegfried Peak and Siegmund Peak on the south side of the Wright Valley in the Asgard Range of Victoria Land. Named by the New Zealanders for the Norse mythological character.

**Heimefront Range.** 74°35′S, 11°W. Composed of three groups. Runs NE-SW for 65 miles. 50 miles WSW of the Kirwan Escarpment in Queen Maud Land. Discovered aerially by the NBSAE in Jan. 1952, and named Heimefrontfjella (Homefront Range) by the Norwegians. This seems the likely place to designate what Ritscher named Kottas Berge (the Kottas Mountains) in 1938–39.

**Mount Heine.** 78°05′S, 167°27′E. 760 m. A hill in the northern part of White Island in the Ross Archipelago. Named by the NZGSAE 1958–59 for A.J. Heine, leader of their party, who climbed this hill. Heine spent four summers and one winter in the Antarctic, mostly around McMurdo Sound.

**Heintz Peak.** 70°56′S, 63°42′W. The summit at the north end of the west ridge of the Welch Mountains, 2 miles north of Mount Acton, in Palmer Land. Named for Lt. Cdr. Harvey L. Heintz, USN, Hercules aircraft commander, 1969 and 1970.

**Mount Heiser.** 82°40′S, 162°56′E. Just north of Dorrer Glacier in the Queen Elizabeth Range. Named for Paul W. Heiser, Jr., US aurora scientist at Scott Base, 1959.

**Heiser Ridge.** 83°50′S, 57°09′W. 5 miles long. Between West Prongs and Hudson Ridge in the Neptune Range of the Pensacola Mountains. Named for James R. Heiser, topographic engineer here in 1963–64.

**Mount Heito.** 69°16′S, 39°49′E. Flat-topped. 495 m. On the SE end of the Langhovde Hills in Queen Maud Land. Named Heito-zan (flat-top mountain) by the Japanese in 1972.

**Heito Glacier.** 69°16′S, 39°48′E. Flows along the south side of Mount Heito in the southern part of the Langhovde Hills in Queen Maud Land. Named Heito-hyoga (flat-top glacier) by the Japanese in 1973, in association with the mountain.

**Heksegryta Peaks.** 73°31′S, 3°48′W. Between Belgen Valley and Tverregg Glacier, in the Kirwan Escarpment of Queen Maud Land. Name means "the witch's cauldron" in Norwegian.

**Hektor Icefall.** 62°S, 57°48′W. Extends in an arc about 5 miles long at the head of Sherratt Bay, on the south coast of King George Island in the South Shetlands. Named in 1960 by the UK for the Hektor Whaling Company.

**The Hektor Whaling Company.** In 1921 this Norwegian company took a 21-year lease on Deception Island from the British government, which had claimed it as their own, and were then leasing it out. It set up a whaling station which operated until 1931.

**The *Hektoria*.** 15,000 tons. Ship that took Wilkins from Buenos Aires to Deception Island in 1928 during the Wilkins-Hearst expedition 1928–30.

**Hektoria Glacier.** 65°03′S, 61°31′W. Flows from the area around Mount Johnson into the Larsen Ice Shelf just west of Shiver Point, on the east coast of the Antarctic Peninsula. Discovered aerially by Wilkins on Dec. 20, 1928, and he named it Hektoria Fjords, for the *Hektoria*. These fjords could not be identified during a FIDS survey of 1947, but during a 1955 survey the FIDS found that Wilkins' "long, ice-filled fjords" were, in fact, this glacier and two short unnamed ones.

**Held Glacier.** 84°47′S, 177°W. 3 miles long. Flows from Anderson Heights into the Shackleton Glacier just south of Epidote Peak in the Queen Maud Mountains. Named for Lt. George B. Held, USN, public works officer at McMurdo Station 1964.

**Mount Helen.** 64°32′S, 63°38′W. 1,370 m. 2 miles SW of Mount Achilles in the Achaean Range of central Anvers Island. Surveyed by the FIDS in 1955 and named by the UK for the Homeric heroine.

**Helen Glacier.** 66°40′S, 93°55′E. Flows into the sea as Helen Glacier Tongue on the East Antarctica coast. Discovered in Nov. 1912 by the Western Base Party of the AAE 1911–14, and named by Mawson for Lady Helen Tooth, wife of Sir Lucas Tooth, of Sydney, a patron of the expedition.

**Helen Glacier Tongue.** 66°33′S, 94°E. The seaward extension of Helen Glacier on the coast of East Antarctica. Discovered in Nov. 1912 by the Western Base Party of the AAE 1911–14, and named by Mawson in association with the glacier.

**Mount Helen Washington** *see* **Washington Ridge**

**Helen Washington Bay** *see* **Kainan Bay**

**Helena Island** *see* **Bridgeman Island**

**Îles Hélène** *see* **Hélène Island**

**Hélène Island.** 66°37′S, 139°44′E. 350 yards NW of Ifo Island, marking the west end of the Géologie Archipelago. Charted by the French in 1949–51 and named by them for one of their dogs.

**Helfert Nunatak.** 77°53′S, 87°25′W. 15 miles west of Mount Sharp of the Sentinel Range. Discovered by Charles R. Bentley and his Marie Byrd Land Traverse Party of 1957–58, and named by Bentley for Norbert F. Helfert, meteorologist at Byrd Station in 1957.

**Helfferich Glacier.** 70°35′S, 160°12′E. 8 miles long. Flows from the east slopes of the Pomerantz Tableland in the Usarp Mountains. Named for Merritt R. Helfferich, ionosphere physics worker at Amundsen-Scott South Pole Station, 1967–68.

**Helicopters.** Called "helos" in Antarctica, they were the successors to the autogyros (q.v.), and it wasn't until after World War II that the helo came into its own in Antarctica. 7 Sikorskys were used during Operation Highjump 1946–47, the first time that helos flew on the continent. Operation Windmill 1947–48 was named thus for the helos used during that expedition. IGY (1957–58) saw helos all over the continent. The French used mostly their own 2-seater Djinns, the Japanese used S-58s, the USSR used huge M14s, and the Americans used HO4S-3 Sikorskys. The most popular chopper since then seems to be the French Puma, but in the 1960s the Americans at McMurdo Station were using UH-1B turbopowered Iroquois helos which could go as high as 16,000 feet. On Feb. 4, 1964, three of these flew from Mount Weaver to the South Pole, the first helicopters to arrive at the Pole. The longest Antarctic helo flight took place on Nov. 27, 1968 (*see* the Chronology). These Iroquois were an improvement over the original turbine helos first used in Antarctica in

1961–62 when the US Army flew single-engine UH-1Bs. In the late 1960s the UH-1D replaced the UH-1B. They were superior, even though the flight speed was the same—about 120 mph. In 1971–72 the US Navy replaced these with UH-1Ns, a single-rotor, skid-configured helo made by Bell Helicopter Co. These can be loaded into an LC-130 Hercules aircraft. In the 1980s most nations were using the helo as a fieldwork tool.

**Heliozans.** Spherical, mostly freshwater organisms, a form of protozoans. They are some of the microfauna of Antarctica (*see* **Fauna**).

**Helix Pass.** 71°18′S, 163°18′E. 4 miles ENE of Mount Jamroga in the central Bowers Mountains. Named by the NZGSAE 1967–68 for the zigzagging overnight climb they had to make. The helix is a snail.

**Hell Gates.** 62°40′S, 61°11′W. Passage between the rocks off Devils Point, the SW end of Livingston Island in the South Shetlands. Named by sealers about 1821 because of the loss of shipping and life that had already taken place there.

**Mount Helland-Hansen** *see* **Helland-Hansen Shoulder**

**Helland-Hansen Mountains.** 86°07′S, 169°W. Ice features thought by their discoverer Amundsen in 1911 to be mountains.

**Helland-Hansen Shoulder.** 85°26′S, 168°10′W. Ice-covered ridge which extends southward from the west portion of Mount Fridtjof Nansen, and overlooks the northern side of the head of Axel Heiberg Glacier. Discovered in 1911 by Amundsen and named Mount Helland-Hansen by him for Prof. B. Helland-Hansen of the University of Oslo, Norway. Later redefined.

**Helle Slope.** 71°25′S, 5°15′E. A large ice piedmont on the coast of Queen Maud Land, east of Jutulstraumen Glacier and north of the Mühlig-Hofmann Mountains. Named by the Norwegians for Sigurd Helle, leader of the 1957–58

Norwegian Antarctic Expedition to Queen Maud Land.

**Hellender, John.** Seaman on the Wilkes Expedition 1838–42. Joined at Rio. Served the cruise.

**Hellerman Rocks.** 64°48′S, 64°01′W. A group of seven small islets and rocks, almost half a mile east of Hermit Island, off the SW coast of Anvers Island. Named for Lt. (jg) Lance W. Hellerman, USNR, officer-in-charge of Palmer Station in 1969.

**Helliwell Hills.** 71°50′S, 161°25′E. 18 miles long and 9 miles wide. South of Gressitt Glacier and between Emlen Peaks and the Morozumi Range. Named for Robert A. Helliwell of Stanford University, program director for the USARP study of very low frequency radio noise phenomena.

**Hells Gate.** 74°51′S, 163°48′E. A narrows near the eastern edge of the Nansen Ice Sheet, just north of Evans Cove between Inexpressible Island and the Northern Foothills of Victoria Land. First explored by Campbell's Northern Party during Scott's 1910–13 expedition, and they named it with reason.

**Hells Gate Moraine.** 74°52′S, 163°48′E. The glacial moraine at Hells Gate, at the head of Evans Cove, on the coast of Victoria Land. It extends southward to Hells Gate from nearby Vegetation Island and Cape Confusion. Named by Campbell's Northern Party during Scott's 1910–13 expedition, in association with Hells Gate.

**Helm Glacier.** 83°07′S, 162°30′E. 15 miles long. Flows into Lowery Glacier just west of the Fazekas Hills in the Queen Elizabeth Range. Named by the New Zealanders in 1961–62 for Arthur S. Helm, former secretary of the Ross Sea Committee, and secretary of the NZ Antarctic Place Names Committee from 1957–64.

**Helm Peak.** 69°29′S, 67°50′W. On the west side of the Antarctic Peninsula.

**Helm Point.** 72°11′S, 170°E. Marks the SE tip of Honeycomb Ridge on the west side of Moubray Bay. It is formed from brown granodiorite, and there is much life here, lichens, mosses, petrels. Named by the NZGSAE 1957–58 for Arthur S. Helm (see **Helm Glacier**), who had been of great help to the expedition.

**Helman Glacier.** 72°12′S, 168°28′E. Flows between Mount Gleaton and Taylor Peak into Tucker Glacier in the Admiralty Mountains. Named for Terry N. Helman, USN, radioman at McMurdo Station, 1967.

**Mount Helmer Hanssen** see **Mount Hanssen**

**Helmet Peak.** 62°39′S, 60°01′W. Also called Pico Falsa Aguja. 1,040 m. Just south of the mouth of Huron Glacier in the eastern part of Livingston Island in the South Shetlands. Named by the Discovery Investigations personnel about 1930.

**Mount Helms.** 82°04′S, 87°58′W. Partly snow-covered. Between Mount Semprebon and Mount Oldenburg in the central part of the Martin Hills. Named for Ward J. Helms, radioscience researcher at Byrd Station in 1962.

**Helms Bluff.** 78°29′S, 164°25′E. 10 miles east of Mount Morning in Victoria Land. Named in 1963 for Lt. Cdr. Louis L. Helms, USN, officer-in-charge of VX-6 at McMurdo Station, 1961.

**Hemmen, George E.** British figure of note in Antarctic history. In 1952–53 he was a meteorological observer at Base G on Admiralty Bay, with the FIDS. In 1953–54 he was FIDS leader at Base B on Deception Island, and in 1956 took part in the British Royal Society IGY Expedition. In 1972 he became the long-running executive secretary of SCAR.

**Hemmen Ice Rise.** 77°57′S, 49°46′W. 11 miles long. Off the NW corner of Berkner Island on the Ronne Ice Shelf. Named by the UK for George E. Hemmen.

**Hemmestad Nunataks.** 71°40′S, 8°26′E. A group of 20 or so nunataks extending over 7 miles. They form the NE portion of the Drygalski Mountains in Queen Maud Land. Named by the Norwegians for Arne Hemmestad, mechanic with the Norwegian Antarctic Expedition 1955–57.

**Mount Hemmingsen.** 73°25′S, 61°50′W. At the NE end of the Werner Mountains, on the south side of Meinardus Glacier, 5 miles SW of Court Nunatak, in Palmer Land. Named for Edvard A. Hemmingsen, biologist at McMurdo Station, 1966–67, and at Palmer Station, 1967–68.

**Mount Hemphill.** 70°59′S, 165°06′E. Above 1,800 m. Snow-covered. In the southern part of the Anare Mountains. Between the head of McLean Glacier and Ebbe Glacier. Named for Lt. (jg) Harold S. Hemphill, USN, VX-6 photographic officer in Antarctica, 1962–63 and 1963–64.

**Hemphill Island.** 66°23′S, 110°34′E. Mainly ice-covered. Between Robinson Ridge and Odbert Island in the Windmill Islands. Named for George R. Hemphill, meteorologist at Wilkes Station, 1961.

**Hendersin, Wendell K.** US Navy petty officer, radio operator on the PBM-5 Martin Mariner seaplane which flew off the *Pine Island* on Dec. 30, 1946, for photographic reconnaissance. During a whiteout the plane crashed and Hendersin died (see **Deaths, 1946**).

**Hendersin Knob.** 72°08′S, 101°26′W. Also spelled (erroneously) Henderson Knob. Ice-covered. Between the heads of Craft and Rochray Glaciers in the SW part of Thurston Island. Named for Wendell K. Hendersin.

**The *Henderson*.** Destroyer escort ship of the Western Task Group during Operation Highjump 1946–47. The captain was Cdr. Claude E. Bailey.

**Cape Henderson.** 66°11′S, 100°44′E. Ice-free. It is overlain by morainic drift. Marks the NW end of the Bunger Hills. Named for the *Henderson*.

**¹Mount Henderson.** 67°42′S, 63°04′E. 970 m. 5 miles SE of Holme Bay, and 5 miles NE of the north end of the Masson Range. Discovered in Feb. 1931 by the BANZARE, and named by Mawson for Dr. W. Henderson, director of the Australian Department of External Affairs, and a member of the Australian Antarctic Committee of 1929.

²**Mount Henderson.** 78°11′S, 167°20′ E. A hill 2 miles WSW of Isolation Point in the south-central part of White Island, in the Ross Archipelago. Named by the NZGSAE 1958–59 for G.B. Henderson, a member of that expedition.

³**Mount Henderson.** 80°12′S, 156°13′ E. 2,660 m. 5 miles west of Mount Olympus, in the Britannia Range. Discovered and named by Scott's 1901–4 expedition.

**Henderson, James.** Quartermaster on the Wilkes Expedition 1838–42. Joined in the USA. Served the cruise.

**Henderson Bluff.** 83°05′S, 50°35′W. 1,660 m. On the west side of the Lexington Table, 9 miles north of Mount Lechner, in the Forrestal Range of the Pensacola Mountains. Named for John R. Henderson, geophysicist in the Pensacola Mountains, 1965–66.

**Henderson Glacier.** 79°47′S, 82°25′ W. 7 miles long. In the Enterprise Hills, of the Heritage Range. Flows from Schoeck Peak and Hoinkes Peak into Union Glacier, just east of Mount Rossman. Named for Felix E. Henderson, meteorologist at Eights Station, 1965.

**Henderson Island.** 66°22′S, 97°10′E. Ice-covered. 9 miles long. 240 meters high. 9 miles SE of Masson Island, in the Shackleton Ice Shelf. Discovered in Aug. 1912 by the Western Base Party of the AAE 1911–14, and named by Mawson for Prof. G.C. Henderson of Adelaide, a member of the AAE Advisory Committee.

**Henderson Knob** *see* **Hendersin Knob**

**Hendrickson Peak.** 85°56′S, 132°49′ W. Over 2,000 m. At the west side of the Reedy Glacier, 2 miles west of May Peak

in the Quartz Hills. Named for George Hendrickson, glaciologist at Byrd Station, 1962–63 and 1963–64.

**Henfield, Joseph.** Commander of the brig *Catharina* in the South Shetlands in the 1820–21 season.

**Henfield Rock.** 62°19′S, 59°35′W. 2 miles NW of Newell Point, Robert Island, in the South Shetlands. Named by the UK in 1961 for Joseph Henfield.

**Hengist Nunatak.** 69°S, 70°14′W. Isolated. Flat-topped. Over 610 m. On the Roberts Ice Piedmont, 10 miles north of Mount Calais in the NE part of Alexander Island. Surveyed by the FIDS in 1948. Named by the UK for the 5th century Saxon chief.

**Henkes Islands.** 67°48′S, 68°56′W. Group of small islands and rocks 2 miles in extent, 1 mile SW of Avian Island, just off the southern end of Adelaide Island. They include Preston Island. Discovered by Charcot in 1908–10, and named by him for one of the Norwegian directors of the Magellan Whaling Company at Punta Arenas, Chile. Charcot's naming included a far wider area of rocks and islands between Cape Adriasola and Cape Alexandra, and in 1963 the UK restricted the term.

**Henkle Peak.** 74°39′S, 75°50′W. 15 miles north of Mount Rex in Ellsworth Land. Named for Charles R. Henkle of the US Geological Survey, a topographic engineer with the Marie Byrd Land Survey Party of 1967–68.

**Mount Henksen.** 66°46′S, 51°04′E. Between Peacock Ridge and Mount Parviainen in the northern part of the Tula Mountains in Enderby Land. Named by the Australians for H. Henksen.

**Henksen, H.** Crew member on the *Discovery* during the BANZARE 1929–31.

**Point Hennequin.** 62°08′S, 58°24′W. Forms the east side of the entrance to Martel and Mackellar Inlets, on the east side of Admiralty Bay, King George Island, in the South Shetlands. Named by Charcot in 1909.

**Mount Hennessey.** 72°14′S, 164°45′E. 2 miles north of Mount Tukotok in the Salamander Range of the Freyberg Mountains. Named for Raymond W. Hennessey, aerographer at Hallett Station, 1957.

**Hennessy Islands.** 65°53′S, 65°43′W. 2 miles in extent. 4 miles SE of Jurva Point, the SE end of Renaud Island, in the Biscoe Islands. Named by the UK in 1959 for Jack Hennessy (1885–1954), deputy marine superintendent of the Met. Office 1940–54, who collected and published reports on sea ice observations in Antarctic waters for the entire first half of the 20th century.

**The *Henrik Ibsen*.** Norwegian whaler in the South Shetlands in the 1929–30 season. It transported the Wilkins-Hearst expedition part of the way.

**Henriksen Nunataks.** 71°30′S, 9°E. 10 miles north of the Kurze Mountains in Queen Maud Land. Named by the Norwegians for Hans-Martin Henriksen, meteorological assistant with the Norwegian Antarctic Expedition 1956–58.

**[1]The *Henry*.** 3-masted American sealing schooner of 150 tons, built at Saybrook, Conn., in 1817. 83 feet long, it was registered on June 24, 1817. It went down to the South Shetlands, 1820–21, with a crew of 26 officers and men led by Capt. Benjamin J. Brunow, as part of the New York Sealing Expedition. The following season it was again part of the New York Sealing Expedition, again under Brunow, and in 1822–23 it returned alone, this time under Capt. Robert Johnson.

**[2]The *Henry*.** British sealer in the South Shetlands 1821–22, commanded by Capt. Kellick. Not to be confused with its American namesake, also in South Shetlands waters the same season.

**[1]Mount Henry.** 67°43′S, 50°17′E. 1,500 m. 1 mile east of Simpson Peak in the Scott Mountains of Enderby Land. In 1831 John Biscoe named a feature in this area for Henry Enderby, his employer, but later geographers could not find this

feature, and therefore named this mountain thus, in order to preserve Biscoe's naming.

**[2]Mount Henry.** 83°52′S, 172°04′E. 1,675 m. In the Commonwealth Range. 4 miles SE of Mount Kyffin on the east side of the Beardmore Glacier. Discovered and named by Shackleton's 1907–9 expedition.

**Henry, Clifford D.** Capt. USN. A part of Military Sealift Command. He was no fewer than 14 times in the Antarctic, as support to USARP. He died on his ship, the *Private John R. Towle,* on Feb. 16, 1975, while returning from Antarctica.

**Henry, Wilkes.** Nephew of Charles Wilkes, leader of the Wilkes Expedition of 1838–42, a member of which this midshipman became when he joined the *Vincennes* at Callao. He transferred to the *Peacock,* and was killed at Malolo on July 24, 1840.

**Henry Bay.** 66°52′S, 120°45′E. At the eastern end of the Sabrina Coast. The Henry Islands are in the western part of this bay. Named for Wilkes Henry.

**Henry Ice Rise.** 80°35′S, 62°W. Triangular-shaped. 70 miles long. Between the Korff Ice Rise and the southern part of Berkner Island on the Ronne Ice Shelf. Named for Capt. Clifford D. Henry.

**Henry Inlet.** 71°54′S, 100°20′W. Ice-filled. 12 miles long, and narrow. Indents the north coast of Thurston Island, just east of Hughes Peninsula. Named for Robert Henry, photographer's mate on the USN Bellingshausen Sea Expedition 1959–60.

**Henry Islands.** 66°53′S, 120°38′E. A group of 4 small islands in the western part of Henry Bay. Named for Wilkes Henry.

**Mount Henry Lucy.** 85°11′S, 170°26′E. Also called Mount Lucy. 3,020 m. 2½ miles SSE of Mount White at the southern end of the Supporters Range. Discovered by Shackleton's 1907–9 expedition and named by them for Sir Henry Lucy, who had been a great help to the expedition.

**Henry Mesa.** 79°05'S, 159°04'E. Wedge-shaped. 2 miles in extent. 4 miles south of Mulock Glacier on the west side of Heap Glacier. The ice-covered summit is 1,430 meters high and flat except for a cirque which indents the north side. Named for Capt. B.R. Henry, commander of the *Eastwind* in 1964, and commander of the US ship group of Operation Deep Freeze 65.

**Henry Moraine.** 71°57'S, 9°38'E. On the NW side of Mount Bjerke in the Conrad Mountains of Queen Maud Land. Named by the Norwegians for Henry Bjerke, mechanic with the Norwegian Antarctic Expedition of 1957–59.

**Henry Nunataks.** 75°08'S, 72°36'W. 6 miles west of the Merrick Mountains in eastern Ellsworth Land. Named for K.C. Henry, engineman at Eights Station, 1963.

**Henryk Arctowski Station** *see* **Arctowski Station**

**Henrysanden** *see* **Henry Moraine**

**Mount Henson.** 84°50'S, 168°21'W. Also spelled (erroneously) as Mount Hansen. 905 m. Ice-free. At the NE end of the Mayer Crags, it forms the NW portal to Liv Glacier where that glacier enters the Ross Ice Shelf. Discovered in Nov. 1929 during Byrd's 1928–30 expedition, and named for Matthew Henson, a member of Peary's party to the North Pole in 1909.

**Henson Glacier.** 64°06'S, 60°11'W. Flows from the Detroit Plateau of Graham Land into the Wright Ice Piedmont 2 miles SW of Hargrave Hill. Named by the UK for William S. Henson (1805–1888), British aeronautical pioneer.

**Heppinstall, Pat.** On Oct. 15, 1957, this American airline stewardess became one of the first two women ever to visit an American base in Antarctica (*see also* **Ruth Kelley** and **Women in Antarctica**).

**Herald Reef.** 65°11'S, 64°11'W. Also called Arrecife Baeza. 1 mile SW of Petermann Island, on the north side of French Passage, in the Wilhelm Archipelago.

Charted by Charcot in 1908–10. Named by the UK in 1959 because it heralds the approach to French Passage from the east.

**Herbert, Wally.** Walter W. Herbert. NZ explorer who in 1956 and 1957 was an assistant surveyor at Base D, for the FIDS. In 1961–62 he was leader of the Southern Party of the NZGSAE, which went down the Axel Heiberg Glacier, confirming the difficulty of the route pioneered by Amundsen in 1911–12.

**Herbert Mountains.** 80°21'S, 25°30'W. On the east side of Gordon Glacier in the Shackleton Range. Named by the BCTAE for Sir Edwin Herbert, chairman of the Finance Committee and member of the Committee of Management of the BCTAE, 1955–58.

**Herbert Plateau.** 64°32'S, 61°15'W. This is a part of the central plateau of Graham Land, between Blériot and Drygalski Glaciers. Named by the UK in 1960 for Wally Herbert.

**Herbert Range.** 85°22'S, 165°30'W. In the Queen Maud Mountains, extending from the edge of the Polar Plateau to the Ross Ice Shelf, between the Axel Heiberg Glacier and the Strom Glacier. Named by New Zealand for Wally Herbert.

**Herbert Sound.** 63°55'S, 57°40'W. Also called Estrecho Azopardo. Extends from Cape Lachman and Keltie Head on the NW to the narrows between The Naze and False Island Point on the SE. Separates Vega Island from James Ross Island, and connects Prince Gustav Channel with Erebus and Terror Gulf. On Jan. 6, 1843, Ross discovered a broad embayment east of the sound, which he named Sidney Herbert Bay, for Sidney Herbert, first secretary to the admiralty. The actual sound, as we know it today, was discovered and charted by Nordenskjöld's 1901–4 expedition, and he decided that the two stretches of water should be redefined as one feature, and named it Sidney Herbert Sound. Since then, however, it has been redefined again. The embayment discovered by

Ross is now considered to be the western edge of the Erebus and Terror Gulf, and the name Herbert Sound has been restricted to the area west of the narrows between The Naze and False Island Point.

**Herbertson Glacier.** 77°42'S, 163°48' E. Flows from the cliff which forms the south edge of New Harbor, 5 miles WSW of Butter Point, in Victoria Land. Named by Scott's 1910–13 expedition for geographer A.J. Herbertson of Oxford University.

**Herbies.** Weather condition created when fierce winds blow snow or ice crystals through the atmosphere, obscuring vision to less than 100 feet.

**Herbst Glacier.** 75°40'S, 132°07'W. The eastern glacier of the two which flow from the northern slopes of Mount Kosciusko into Brown Valley in the Ames Range of Marie Byrd Land. Named for Emmett L. Herbst of Holmes and Narver, Inc., who was part of the drilling program at Byrd Station in 1968–69. Between 1971 and 1976 he was several times in the Antarctic.

**Mount Hercules.** 77°29'S, 161°27'E. Flat-topped. Between Mount Aeolus and Mount Jason in the Olympus Range of Victoria Land. Named by the New Zealanders in 1958–59 for the Greek mythological hero.

**Hercules, Santo.** Seaman on the Wilkes Expedition 1838–42. Joined in the USA. Discharged in NZ.

**Hercules Inlet.** 80°05'S, 78°30'W. Ice-filled. Forms a part of the SW edge of the Ronne Ice Shelf, to the east of the Heritage Range, and to the south of the Skytrain Ice Rise. Named for the Hercules aircraft.

**Hercules Névé.** 73°04'S, 165°15'E. At the northern edge of the Mountaineer Range in Victoria Land. It is bounded by Astronaut Glacier, Deception Plateau, the Retreat Hills, and various other glaciers such as Meander and Gair Glaciers. Named by the New Zealanders in

1966–67 for the American C-130 Hercules aircraft.

**Cape Herdman.** 72°39'S, 60°37'W. Ice-covered. 12 miles ENE of Mount Reynolds. Forms the south side of the entrance to Violante Inlet, on the east coast of Palmer Land. Discovered aerially by the USAS in 1940. Named by the FIDS for Henry F.P. Herdman.

**Herdman, Henry F.P.** British oceanographer and for many years after 1924 a member of the hydrological staff of the Discovery Committee. Scientific leader on the *Discovery II* expedition of 1937–39 from Jan. 1938 until May 1939, and on the last Antarctic expedition of that vessel in 1950–51.

**Herdman Rocks.** 60°42'S, 44°20'W. Two rocks. 15 meters high. 1½ miles SE of Hart Rock, and 3 miles NE of the eastern end of Laurie Island in the South Orkneys. Charted by Dumont d'Urville in 1838. Re-charted by the personnel on the *Discovery II* in 1933, and named by them for Henry F.P. Herdman.

**Hergert, Richard.** Midshipman on the *Adventure* during Cook's second voyage.

**Heritage Range.** 79°45'S, 83°W. Also called Wexler Mountains. 100 miles long and 30 miles wide. South of Minnesota Glacier, it forms the southern half of the Ellsworth Mountains. This major range was named in continuation of the main theme of feature-names in this range — American heritage.

**Cape Herlacher.** 73°51'S, 113°56'W. Ice-covered. Forms the north end of Martin Peninsula in Marie Byrd Land. Named in 1955 for Carl J. Herlacher, the principal Antarctic cartographer with the US Navy Hydrographic Office from 1937 onward.

**Mount Hermanson.** 84°23'S, 173°32' E. Ice-covered. In the Queen Maud Mountains. 3,140 m. At the head of the Cunningham Glacier, 4 miles SW of Gray Peak. Named for Capt. J.M. Hermanson, USN, air operations officer at McMurdo Station, 1957–58. In 1959 he was chief of staff to the US Antarctic Projects Officer.

**Isla Hermelo**  *see*  **Delta Island**

**Hermelo, Ricardo.** Leader of the Argentine Antarctic Expedition of 1947–48 until March 1948.

**Hermes Glacier.** 68°59′S, 65°15′W. 8 miles long. Flows into Weyerhaeuser Glacier in northern Graham Land. Discovered and named by the FIDS in Jan. 1960. It provided a road out of the mountains, and was named for the Greek god of the roads, Hermes. This began the British practice of naming features in the area for Greek mythological figures.

**Hermes Point.** 73°35′S, 166°13′E. The seaward end of a ridge from the Mountaineer Range, at the confluence of the Icebreaker Glacier and the Fitzgerald Glacier, on the coast of Victoria Land. Named for Agustive A. Hermes, Jr., USN, aviation structural mechanic at Williams Field, 1967 and 1968.

**Hermit Island.** 64°48′S, 64°02′W. Almost 1 mile long. 1½ miles SE of Bonaparte Point, off the SW coast of Anvers Island. Named by the UK in 1958 for the FIDS surveyor who spent time alone on this island in Jan. 1957, making observations.

**Hermitage Peak.** 81°26′S, 160°29′E. 750 m. 4 miles north of Mount Ubique. In the Surveyors Range. Named by the New Zealanders in 1960–61 for the Military School of Surveying in England.

**Hernandez, Antonio.** Officer's steward on the Wilkes Expedition 1838–42. Joined at Callao. Discharged at California.

**¹The Hero.** American sealing sloop of 44 tons built at Groton, Conn., in 1800. 47 feet 3 inches long, it was registered on July 5, 1820, and was at that time part owned by its captain, Nat Palmer, who left from Stonington, Conn., as part of the Fanning-Pendleton Sealing Expedition of 1820–21. There was a crew of 5 that year, including Palmer. It was back in the South Shetlands the following

season, as part of the Fanning-Pendleton Sealing Expedition 1821–22, this time under the command of Harris Pendleton. Phineas Wilcox was the first mate. The vessel was sold at Coquimbo, Chile, on Oct. 11, 1822.

**²The Hero.** Small, wooden-hulled American motor research vessel belonging to the NSF, which served Palmer Station between 1968 and 1984, before being retired due to dry rot in the timbers. 300 tons, it was named for Palmer's old sloop, and was framed with large oak timbers. Ketch-rigged, it had 2 decks and a superstructure. The mast was made of Oregon fir. It had 2 engines, and carried a crew of 12, as well as 8 scientists, and first pulled into its assigned home port of Palmer Station on Dec. 25, 1968, under the command of Capt. Sidney G. Hartshorne. 125 feet long, this floating lab operated in Antarctic waters between November and April every year, and wintered in South America. The best remembered captain was Pieter Lenie, who became skipper in 1972. On April 15, 1984, the *Hero* left Arthur Harbor for the last time, and was retired in October of that year, in favor of the *Polar Duke*.

**Hero Bay.** 62°31′S, 60°27′W. 17 miles wide. Indents for 6 miles on the north side of Livingston Island between Cape Shirreff and Williams Point, in the South Shetlands. In the 1930s this bay was named Blythe Bay, but that name had already been given in 1822 to another, smaller bay on the SE side of Desolation Island. The confusion has since been cleared up, and this bay was renamed for the *Hero,* Palmer's vessel of the 1820s.

**Hero Inlet.** 64°46′S, 64°04′W. At the south side of Palmer Station, between Gamage Point and Bonaparte Point, on the SW side of Anvers Island. Named for the *Hero,* the research vessel of the 1960s and 1970s, which used to use this inlet as a turning basin when docking at Palmer Station season after season.

**The Heroic Era.** A term, nothing more, indicating the first two decades of the 20th century as applied to Antarctic exploration. Author James Gordon Hayes reckons 1895 to be the first year of the Heroic Age of exploration, land traverses, and epic endurance, when great scientific and geographic inroads were made on the southern continent. These were the voyages of Scott, Amundsen, Shackleton and Mawson, Nordenskjöld, Borchgrevink, de Gerlache and von Drygalski, Filchner, Shirase, Bruce and Bull, national heroes most of them, who boldly went where no man had gone before. Rather than the ship versus the elements, it was humans against the unknown and the inhospitable. It was the Edwardian era, when the gentleman was role model, and nobility and purity of spirit were applied to exploration and captured the attention of the civilized world. Author Charles Neider puts Shackleton's death, on Jan. 5, 1922, as the end of the Heroic Era, but that date is too dependent on one man. It was all over by 1916.

**Mount Herr.** 85°45′S, 149°32′W. 1,730 m. 5 miles NW of Mount Gould in the Tapley Mountains. Named for Lt. Arthur L. Heer, Jr., VX-6 aircraft commander at McMurdo Station, 1962–63 and 1963–64.

**Caleta Herradura** see **Lystad Bay**

**Isla Herradura** see **Horseshoe Island**

**Herrin Peak.** 79°16′S, 85°45′W. 1,755 m. Snow-covered. 6 miles south of Landmark Peak on the east side of Gowan Glacier, in the Heritage Range. Named by the University of Minnesota Geological Party of 1963–64, for John M. Herrin, helicopter crew chief with the 62nd Transportation Detachment, who helped the party that year.

**Herring Island.** 66°24′S, 110°38′E. 2 miles long. 1 mile east of Cloyd Island, in the southern part of the Windmill Islands. Named for Lt. Charles C. Herring, USN, photographic officer on Operation Windmill, 1947–48.

**Herring Nunataks.** 83°12′S, 51°22′W. Two nunataks 3 miles NW of Mount Lechner in the western Forrestal Range of the Pensacola Mountains. Named for Earl F. Herring, aviation storekeeper at Ellsworth Station, 1957.

**Herrington Hill.** 66°15′S, 66°42′W. On the east side of Lavoisier Island in the Biscoe Islands, 5 miles south of Benedict Point. Named by the UK for Lovic P. Herrington, US physiologist specializing in the cold.

**Herrmann, Ernst.** Geographer on the German New Schwabenland Expedition of 1938–39.

**Herrmann, John.** Photographer on Byrd's 1933–35 expedition.

**Herrmann Mountains.** 72°33′S, 0°30′E. Between Reece Valley and Kvitsvodene Valley in the Sverdrup Mountains of Queen Maud Land. They include Hamrane Heights and Roots Heights. Discovered by Ritscher's 1938–39 expedition, and named for Ernst Herrmann.

**Herrmann Nunatak.** 76°15′S, 143°47′W. 4 miles NE of the Phillips Mountains, in Marie Byrd Land. Discovered by the USAS 1939–41. Named for John Herrmann.

**Herron, Lewis.** Cooper on the Wilkes Expedition 1838–42. Joined in the USA. Served the cruise.

**Cape Herschel** see **Cape Sterneck**

**Mount Herschel.** 72°12′S, 169°31′E. 3,335 m. Just over 1½ miles NE of Mount Peacock, it overlooks the terminus of Ironside Glacier from the south, in the Admiralty Mountains. Discovered in 1841 by Ross, who named it for the astronomer, Sir John Herschel. First climbed in 1967 by Dr. Michael Gill of Sir Edmund Hillary's party.

**Herschel Heights.** 71°53′S, 69°38′W. A complex of nunataks. Mimas Peak, on the east, is the highest. SW of Enceladus Nunataks, near the head of Saturn Glacier, in SE Alexander Island. Named by the UK for Sir William Herschel, the astronomer who discovered the moons Mimas and Enceladus.

**Hershey Ridge.** 77°40′S, 147°10′W. Also called Garland Hershey Ridge. Ice-covered. Extends for 30 miles between McKinley Peak and the Haines Mountains, in the Ford Ranges of Marie Byrd Land. Discovered in 1934 during Byrd's second expedition, and named for Garland Hershey, noted American geologist.

**The *Hersilia*.** American sealing brig of 131 tons, 68 feet long with a square stern. 22 feet 8 inches wide, with a depth of 10 feet 1 inch, it was built by Christopher Leeds of Stonington and Mystic, Conn., and was registered July 20, 1819, and owned by William A. Fanning. About July 22, 1819, it left Stonington and, after searching unsuccessfully for the mythical Aurora Islands, it arrived at Hersilia Bay, Rugged Island, in the South Shetlands on Jan. 23, 1820, the first American sealer in these parts. Here it met a "black brig from Buenos Aires." This was probably the *San Juan Nepomuceno*, but it might have been the *Espírito Santo* which was also in these waters at that time. Captain James P. Sheffield was in command of a crew of 19, and in 15 days they collected 8,868 seal skins, which, on their return to Stonington on May 21, 1820, they sold for $22,146.49. This was the brig's maiden voyage and the commercial success of it revived the declining sealing industry, opening up a rush to the South Shetlands in the 1820–21 season. Other personnel on the *Hersilia* during its first voyage were Elof Benson, first mate; Nat Palmer, second mate; William A. Fanning. The vessel was reregistered, due to partial change of ownership, on July 28, 1820, and on its second voyage of 1820–21 it formed part of the Fanning-Pendleton Sealing Expedition of that season. Still commanded by Sheffield, this time the first mate was Daniel W. Clark, and the number of crew was 17 on average. That second season in the South Shetlands it pulled in over 18,000 seal skins, and then, still part of the Fanning-Pendleton Sealing Expedition, it sailed into the Pacific. On May 13, 1821, off the coast of Chile, the brig was seized by the Spanish, and turned into a warship. It

was not long after burned in the fire of Arauco. A new ship of the same name was built in Stonington, Conn., in 1822, and registered Dec. 9, 1822, at New London. Capt. James P. Sheffield commanded.

**Hersilia Cove.** 62° 38′ S, 61° 13′ W. Indents the north side of Rugged Island, in the South Shetlands. Discovered Jan. 22, 1820, and named in Feb. 1820 by James P. Sheffield, captain of the *Hersilia*.

**The *Hertha*.** Norwegian sealer under the command of Capt. C.J. Evensen, which sailed to the Antarctic in company with the *Castor*. Mostly in the South Shetlands, it did explore the west side of the Antarctic Peninsula as far south as Alexander Island. It was often in contact with the *Jason*, commanded by Larsen.

**Hertha Nunatak.** 65° 09′ S, 59° 59′ W. 1 mile NW of Castor Nunatak in the Seal Nunataks, off the east coast of the Antarctic Peninsula. Discovered in Dec. 1893 by Carl Anton Larsen and named by him for the *Hertha*. Larsen mapped it as an island, and it was not until 1902 that the Nordenskjöld expedition defined it correctly.

**Hervé.** A member of the *Pourquoi Pas?* during Charcot's 1908–10 expedition.

**Hervé Cove.** 62° 11′ S, 58° 33′ W. 2 miles SW of Point Thomas, on the south side of Ezcurra Inlet, Admiralty Bay, King George Island, South Shetlands. Charted by Charcot in 1908–10, and named by him for a member of the expedition (*see* **Hervé**).

**Hervéou, F.** Seaman on the *Français* during Charcot's 1903–5 expedition.

**Hervéou Point.** 65° 04′ S, 64° 03′ W. Between Port Charcot and Salpêtrière Bay, on the west side of Booth Island in the Wilhelm Archipelago. Charted by Charcot in 1903–5 and named by him for F. Hervéou.

**Herzog Ernst Bucht**   *see*   **Vahsel Bay**

**Hesperus Nunatak.** 71° 31′ S, 69° 21′ W. 2 miles SW of Titania Peak, and 18 miles west of the Venus Glacier in the SE part of Alexander Island. Named by the UK. Hesperus is an alternative name for the planet Venus.

**Hess Glacier.** 67°13′S, 65°05′W. 5 miles long. Its terminus is 10 miles SW of Monnier Point, on the east coast of Graham Land. Charted in 1947 by the FIDS, who named it for Hans Hess, German glaciologist.

**Hess Mesa.** 77°38′S, 160°47′E. Between Koenig Valley and Mudrey Cirque in the Asgard Range of Victoria Land. Named for L.O. Hess, captain of the *Maumee* in 1970 and 1971.

**Hess Mountains.** 72°S, 62°30′W. On the east side of the Antarctic Peninsula.

**Hessler Peak.** 79°37′S, 84°02′W. 1,670 m. At the south end of Dunbar Ridge in the Heritage Range. Named for Victor P. Hessler, ionosphere physicist and exchange scientist at Vostok Station, 1965–66 and 1966–67.

**Hesteskoen Nunatak.** 71°52′S, 27°15′E. 2,350 m. Horseshoe-shaped. 4 miles north of Balchen Mountain in the Sør Rondane Mountains. Photographed by the LCE 1936–37. Name means "the horseshoe" in Norwegian.

**Heth Ridge.** 69°58′S, 159°45′E. 3 miles long. 4 miles south of Hornblende Bluffs. Near the head of Suvorov Glacier, in the Wilson Hills. Named for Samuel R. Heth, biologist at Hallett Station, 1968–69.

**Hette Glacier.** 71°43′S, 26°35′E. 6 miles long. Flows between Hettene Nunataks and Austhamaren Peak in the Sør Rondane Mountains. Name means "the cap glacier" in Norwegian.

**Hettene Nunataks.** 71°45′S, 26°25′E. At the west side of Hette Glacier in the Sør Rondane Mountains. Name means "the caps" in Norwegian.

**The Hetty.** London sealer in the South Shetlands 1820–21. Captain Ralph Bond.

**Hetty Rock.** 62°40′S, 60°44′W. Marks the eastern end of the foul ground which extends eastward from John Beach on the

south side of Livingston Island in the South Shetlands. Named by the UK in 1958 for the *Hetty*.

**Heuser Nunatak.** 72°02′S, 160°38′E. 3 miles south of Mount Phelen, it marks the southern extremity of the Emlen Peaks in the Usarp Mountains. Named for Charles M. Heuser, biolab technician at McMurdo Station, 1966–67.

**Heverley Nunataks.** 75°33′S, 128°34′W. Isolated. 14 miles NE of Mount Flint in the McCuddin Mountains of Marie Byrd Land. Named for Harry W. Heverley, USN, builder at Amundsen-Scott South Pole Station in 1971, and at McMurdo Station in 1962 and 1966.

**Hewitt Glacier.** 83°17′S, 167°50′E. 15 miles long. Flows from the eastern slopes of the Holland Range between Lewis Ridge and Mount Tripp, into Richards Inlet. Named by the New Zealanders in 1959–60 for Leonard R. Hewitt, leader at Scott Base in 1959.

**Mount Hewson.** 73°58′S, 162°38′E. 3,720 m. 6½ miles WSW of Mount Adamson in the Deep Freeze Range of Victoria Land. Named by the Southern Party of the NZGSAE 1962–63 for Ronald W. Hewson, leader and surveyor of the party. He had also been a surveyor for the Northern Party of the NZGSAE 1961–62.

**Hewson Glacier.** 84°12′S, 169°45′E. 15 miles long. In the Queen Alexandra Range. It flows into the Beardmore Glacier, just north of The Cloudmaker. Named by the New Zealanders in 1961–62 for Ronald W. Hewson (*see* **Mount Hewson**).

**Heyer, Henry R.** Quartermaster on the Wilkes Expedition 1838–42. Joined in the USA. Served the cruise.

**Heywood Island.** 62°20′S, 59°41′W. Also called Isla de la Colina. Crescent-shaped. 1½ miles WNW of the northern tip of Robert Island in the South Shetlands. This was one of the group named by Powell in 1822 as Heywood's Isles, for Capt. Peter Heywood, RN. In 1935 the personnel on the *Discovery II* named this specific island as Hummock Island. Later air photos show that, in fact, there is not a real group of islands here, but rather a series of single ones, and so the name Heywood Isles was eliminated, and, in order to avoid duplication (there was already another Hummock Island off the coast of the Antarctic Peninsula), and also in order to preserve Powell's original naming, the name Heywood Island was given.

**Heywood Lake.** 60°41′S, 45°37′W. The most northerly of the lakes in Three Lakes Valley in NE Signy Island in the South Orkneys. Named by the UK for Ronald B. Heywood, BAS limnologist on Signy Island in 1962–63 and 1970–71.

**Hibbert Rock.** 67°47′S, 69°02′W. A drying rock SE of League Rock, off the south end of Adelaide Island. Named by the UK for William Hibbert, second engineer on the *John Biscoe* in 1962–63.

**Cape Hickey.** 76°05′S, 162°38′E. On the coast of Victoria Land, just east of Charcot Cove and Marin Glacier. It forms the outer, north portal of the re-entrant through which Mawson Glacier flows to the Ross Sea. Named in 1964 for Lt. John Hickey, USN, VX-6 pilot in Antarctica in 1962.

**Mount Hicks.** 71°08′S, 64°39′E. Has two peaks. 12 miles SW of Husky Dome in the Prince Charles Mountains. Named by the Australians for Dr. K.E. Hicks, medical officer at Wilkes Station in 1963 and 1965.

**Hicks, Robinson.** Ordinary seaman on the Wilkes Expedition 1838–42. Joined in the USA. Run at Sydney.

**Hicks, William H.** Ordinary seaman on the Wilkes Expedition 1838–42. Joined in the USA. Sent home on the *Relief* in 1839.

**Hicks Ridge.** 71°09′S, 162°40′E. Between Mount Soza and Morley Glacier in the Explorers Range of the Bowers Mountains. Named for Thomas Hicks, USN, cook at McMurdo Station in 1967.

**Hidden, Capt.** Commander of the *Flying Cloud* in the South Shetlands, 1853–54.

**Hidden Bay.** 65°02′S, 63°46′W. 3 miles long. Between Cape Renard and Aguda Point on the west coast of Graham Land. Charted by de Gerlache in 1897–99. Named by the UK in 1958 because, from the north, it is hidden by the Screen Islands.

**Hidden Col.** 85°32′S, 156°W. In the north part of the Medina Peaks, 3½ miles SW of Marks Point, between the lower reaches of the Amundsen Glacier and the Robert Scott Glacier. It provides a good sledging route between these two glaciers. Named by the New Zealanders in 1969–70 because it is hidden behind ridges and spurs of the peaks near it.

**Hidden Lake.** 64°02′S, 58°18′W. 1½ miles long. Between Lagrelius Point and Cape Obelisk in the western part of James Ross Island. Discovered in 1945 by the FIDS, who named it because it is hidden by the highlands around it.

**Hidden Valley.** 78°10′S, 163°52′E. Ice-free. Just south of Miers Valley. An alpine glacier once flowed through here and coalesced with the Koettlitz Glacier. The mouth of the valley is totally blocked by the moraine of the Koettlitz Glacier. Named by the New Zealanders in 1960–61 because it is hidden.

**Hiegel Passage.** 66°23′S, 110°27′E. Marine passage between Ardery Island on the north and Holl and Ford Islands on the south, in the Windmill Islands. Named for Cdr. James A. Hiegel, USN, leader of Mobile Construction Battalion Number One, who supervised the building of Wilkes Station in Feb. 1957.

**Higashi-naga-iwa Glacier.** 68°27′S, 41°38′E. Flows to the sea at the eastern side of Naga-iwa Rock in Queen Maud Land. Named Higashi-naga-iwa-hyoga (eastern long rock glacier) by the Japanese.

**Lake Higashi Yukidori.** Little lake in Yukidori Valley.

**Higgins Canyon.** 84°47′S, 114°41′W. Ice-filled. Just east of Schulthess Buttress, on the north side of Buckeye Table in the Ohio Range of the Horlick Mountains. Named for Merwyn D. Higgins, geologist here in 1961–62.

**Higgins Nunatak.** 79°39'S, 82°27'W. The largest of the Samuel Nunataks, near the south end of the group, in the Heritage Range. Named for utilitiesman John C. Higgins, USN, at McMurdo Station in 1966.

**Mount High.** 73°34'S, 62°05'W. On the south side of Douglas Glacier, in the central portion of the Werner Mountains in Palmer Land. Named for Harvey W. High, cook at Amundsen-Scott South Pole Station, 1967.

**High Nunatak.** 80°03'S, 82°35'W. Isolated. 4 miles east of Liberty Hills in the Heritage Range of the Ellsworth Mountains. Named for Elmer High, helicopter crew chief here in 1963–64.

**High Peak**  *see*  **Mount Camber**

**High Point**  *see*  **Edinburgh Hill**

**High Stile.** 60°35'S, 45°30'W. A pass at the head of the Sunshine Glacier, at a height of 455 m., at the junction of the SW ridge of Mount Nivea and the east end of the Brisbane Heights, in the central part of Coronation Island in the South Orkneys. Surveyed and named by the FIDS in 1948–49 for its appearance and height.

**Highest Points in Antarctica.** The average height of Antarctica is 7,000–8,000 feet. It is the highest continent in the world (Asia is next, at an average of 3,000 feet). Without the ice, though, it would average only 1,500 feet. The massive ice sheets of East Antarctica reach heights of 11,500 feet above sea level, and the highest point on the whole ice cap is 13,450 feet, also in East Antarctica. The highest peaks in Antarctica are Vinson Massif, 5,140 m. (16,864 ft.); Mount Tyree, 4,965 m. (16,290 ft.); Mount Shinn, 4,800 m. (15,750 ft.); Mount Gardner, 4,685 m. (15,375 ft.); Mount Epperly, 4,600 m. (15,100 ft.); Mount Kirkpatrick, 4,528 m. (14,855 ft.); Mount Elizabeth, 4,480 m. (14,698 ft.); Mount Markham, 4,350 m. (14,290 ft.); Mount

Bell, 4,305 m. (14,117 ft.); Mount Mackellar, 4,295 m. (14,098 ft.). Other notable peaks include Anderson, Bentley, Kaplan, Jackson, Sidley, Ostenso, Minto, Miller, Long Gables, Dickerson, Giovinetto, Wade, Fisher, Fridtjof Nansen, Wexler, Lister, Shear, Odishaw, Donaldson, Ray, Sellery, Waterman, Anne, Press, Falla, Rucker, Goldthwait, Morris, Erebus, Campbell, Don Pedro Christopherson, Lysaght, Huggins, Sabine, Astor, Mohl, Frankes, Jones, Gjelsvik, and Coman.

**Highet, W.B.** An M.D. who served as a crewman on the *Bear of Oakland*, 1934–35.

**Highjump Archipelago.** 66°05'S, 101° E. 50 miles long, and between 5 and 15 miles wide. North of the Bunger Hills, it extends from the Taylor Islands, just NW of Cape Hordern, to a group of ice rises which terminate just west of Cape Elliott. Includes Thomas Island, Fuller Island, Foster Island, Dieglman Island, Currituck Island, Chernyy Island, Mariner Islands. Named for Operation Highjump.

**Hikae Rock.** 68°S, 43°58'E. 1 mile east of Rakuda Glacier, along the ice coast of Queen Maud Land. Named Hikae-iwa by the Japanese.

**The *Hilda Knudsen*.** Norwegian whaler in the Antarctic in 1930–31 under the command of Capt. Daehli.

**Cape Hill**  *see*  **Mount Hill**

**Mount Hill.** 70°56'S, 61°42'W. 945 m. 8 miles SW of Cape Sharbonneau at the eastern side of the head of Lehrke Inlet, on the east coast of Palmer Land. Discovered by personnel from East Base in 1940 during the USAS. They named it Cape Hill for Archie C. Hill. It was redefined in 1947.

**Hill, Archie C.** Cook at East Base during the USAS 1939–41.

**Hill, Edward.** Seaman on the Wilkes Expedition 1838–42. Joined in the USA. Discharged at Oahu, Nov. 2, 1840.

**Hill, Joe, Jr.** Mechanic and dog driver in the shore party on Byrd's 1933–35

expedition. He wrote *In Little America with Byrd* in 1937 (q.v. in the Bibliography).

**Hill, Leonard C.** British lieutenant on the *William Scoresby* in Jan.–Feb. 1931, and then on every voyage of the *Discovery II* from 1931–39. From 1937–39 he was its captain.

**Hill Bay.** 64°11'S, 62°08'W. 5 miles long. 2 miles wide. Indents the eastern coast of Anvers Island, between Spallanzani Point and Mitchell Point. Named by the UK for Leonard C. Hill.

**Hill Glacier.** 73°03'S, 75°40'W. Flows from the west central part of Spaatz Island, at the south side of the Ronne Entrance. Named for Lennie J. Hill, topographic engineer here, and a member of the Marie Byrd Land Traverse Party 1967–68.

**Hill Nunatak.** 84°S, 54°45'W. At the SE end of the Neptune Range in the Pensacola Mountains. 8 miles ENE of Gambacorta Peak. Discovered aerially on Jan. 13, 1956 (*see* the Chronology), and named for Jack O. Hill, aerial photographer on this flight.

**Hill Peaks.** 76°54'S, 146°42'W. A small group 2 miles SW of Mount Dane in the western part of Radford Island, in Sulzberger Ice Shelf off the Marie Byrd Land coast.

**Hillary, Sir Edmund.** One of the major names of the 20th century, the first man to climb Mount Everest. A true hero, this NZ explorer and mountain climber was born in Auckland as Edmund Percival Hillary on July 20, 1919. A beekeeper by profession, and a mountain climber by calling, he reached the peak of his career in 1953 when he and Tenzing Norkay reached the top of the world, and he was knighted on July 16 of that year (Tenzing received the George Medal). He wrote *High Adventure*, a book about mountain climbing. In 1957–58 he commanded the NZ party of the BCTAE, and it was his mission to lay depots for his leader Fuchs' return from the Pole during the latter's transantarctic crossing.

Hillary set up Scott Base on Ross Island, was its first commander, and explored the Ross Sea Basin. Then he went via the Skelton Glacier to lay Depot 700 en route to the Pole. This was meant to be his furthest point south, but with a month to wait for Fuchs he decided to go for the Pole, reaching there on Jan. 4, 1958, the third leader to reach 90°S by land. He did it by tractor. As his mission had been to wait for Fuchs at Depot 700 and guide Fuchs back to Scott Base, it was considered by many that the New Zealander had stolen Fuchs' thunder. There was some acrimony, and Hillary's good taste was called into question. In 1967 Hillary was back in Antarctica, leading the first ascent of Mount Herschel, and in 1982 he visited the continent again, this time as a DV (Distinguished Visitor—q.v.), in the company of Prime Minister Robert Muldoon (*see also* the Bibliography).

**Hillary Canyon.** 72°S, 172°W. Submarine feature of the Ross Sea.

**Hillary Coast.** 79°20'S, 161°E. On the western edge of the Ross Ice Shelf, between Minna Bluff and Cape Selborne. Named by New Zealand in 1961 for Sir Edmund Hillary.

**Hillier Moss.** 60°43'S, 45°36'W. A wet, level, low-lying area, which has many small pools and extensive carpets of moss. 350 yards north of Lenton Point in the SE part of Signy Island in the South Orkneys. Named by the UK for Edward R. Hillier, BAS medical officer and leader of Signy Island Station in 1967.

**Hilton, Donald S.** Surveyor at East Base during the USAS 1939–41.

**Hilton Bay** *see* **Hilton Inlet**

**Hilton Inlet.** 71°57'S, 61°20'W. Ice-filled. 12 miles wide. Recedes about 22 miles west from its entrance between Cape Darlington and Cape Knowles, on the east coast of Palmer Land. Discovered by the USAS in 1940, and named for Donald S. Hilton.

**Hinckley Rock.** 83°04′S, 55°14′W. 4 miles NW of Gillies Rock in the northern Neptune Range of the Pensacola Mountains. Named for Neil Hinckley, a member of the US Air Force Electronics Test Unit 1957–58.

**Hind Turret.** 77°38′S, 161°37′E. At the south (hind) side of Obelisk Mountain in the Asgard Range of Victoria Land. Named by the US and NZ for its shape.

**Mount Hindson** *see* **Mount Ancla**

**Cape Hinks.** 69°10′S, 63°10′W. Also called Cape Cross. Headland surmounted by a high, ice-covered dome. Marks the northern end of Finley Heights on the east coast of Palmer Land. Discovered aerially by Wilkins on Dec. 20, 1928. Later named for Arthur R. Hinks, secretary of the Royal Geographical Society, 1915–45.

**Mount Hinks.** 67°53′S, 66°03′E. 595 m. 350 yards south of Mount Marsden in the Gustav Bull Mountains of Mac. Robertson Land. Named by the BANZARE under Mawson on Feb. 13, 1931, for Arthur R. Hinks (*see* **Cape Hinks**).

**Hinks Channel.** 67°16′S, 67°37′W. Arc-shaped. In the northern part of Laubeuf Fjord. 2 miles wide. 11 miles long. Extends from The Gullet, and separates Day Island, on the west, from Arrowsmith Peninsula and Wyatt Island, on the east. Off the west coast of the Antarctic Peninsula. Surveyed in 1936 by the BGLE, and resurveyed in 1948 by the FIDS, who named it for Arthur R. Hinks (*see* **Cape Hinks**).

**Cape Hinode.** 68°07′S, 42°38′E. 3 miles west of Akebono Glacier on the coast of Queen Maud Land. Named Hinode-misaki (sunrise cape) by the Japanese.

**Hinode Peak.** 69°10′S, 42°35′E. 120 m. 3 miles SW of Cape Hinode on the coast of Queen Maud Land. Named Hinode-yama (sunrise mountain) by the Japanese.

**Hinton Glacier.** 80°03′S, 157°10′E. In the Britannia Range. Flows between the Forbes and Dusky Ridges into Hatherton Glacier. Named for Chief Construction Mechanic Clarence C. Hinton, Jr., USN, at McMurdo Station in 1963.

**Hippo Island.** 66°25′S, 98°10′E. Also called Hippo Nunatak. ½ mile long. On the Shackleton Ice Shelf, 1½ miles north of Delay Point. Discovered by the Western Base Party of the AAE 1911–14, and named by Mawson for its shape.

**Hippo Nunatak** *see* **Hippo Island**

**Hippocrates Glacier.** 64°22′S, 62°22′W. 3 miles long. 2 miles wide. Flows into Buls Bay on the east side of Brabant Island. Named by the UK for the ancient Greek doctor.

**Cape Hippolyte** *see* **Hippolyte Point**

**Hippolyte Point.** 64°41′S, 63°07′W. Also called Cape Hippolyte. Marks the NE end of Lion Island, just east of Anvers Island. Charted and named by de Gerlache 1897–99.

**Mount Hiram** *see* **Mount Hirman**

**Mount Hirman.** 75°28′S, 72°46′W. Also spelled (erroneously) as Mount Hiram. Marks the southern end of the Behrendt Mountains in Ellsworth Land. Named for Joseph W. Hirman, scientific leader at Eights Station, 1965.

**Mount Hiroe.** 69°21′S, 39°47′E. 316 m. ½ mile NW of Breidvågnipa Peak, and just over 1¼ miles NE of Hiroe Point, on the Queen Maud Land coast. Photographed by the LCE 1936–37 and later named Hiroe-yama (broad bay mountain) by the Japanese in 1973.

**Hiroe Point.** 69°22′S, 39°44′E. Just over 1¼ miles SW of Mount Hiroe on the Queen Maud Land coast. Marks the southern end of Breidvåg Bight. Photographed by the LCE 1936–37, and later named Hiroe-misaki (broad bay point) by the Japanese in 1973.

**The *Hissem*.** US ship DER-400 in Antarctica in 1963–64.

**Historic sites.** This entry does not give just any sites which any one might conceivably label historic. Certain specific sites were created in Antarctica, and the idea came from a consultative meeting of the Antarctic Treaty system. 43 of these special sites were nominated, and others followed later. Scott's Discovery Hut is the most revered of all. The original 43 were: 1. Flagmast at the Pole erected in Dec. 1965 by the first Argentine Overland Expedition to the South Pole. 2. Rock cairn and plaques at Showa Station in memory of Shin Fukushima (*see* **Deaths, 1960**). Erected Jan. 11, 1961. Some of Shin's ashes are in the cairn. 3. Rock cairn and plaque on Proclamation Island, Enderby Land. Erected by Mawson in Jan. 1930 to commemorate the BANZARE landing here. 4. Plaque at the Pole of Inaccessibility, and a bust of Lenin, marking USSR conquest of this spot in 1958. 5. Rock cairn and plaque at Cape Bruce, Mac. Robertson Land. Erected in Feb. 1931 by Mawson to commemorate his BANZARE landing here. 6. Rock cairn at Walkabout Rocks, Vestfold Hills. Erected by Wilkins in 1939. 7. Stone with inscribed plaque, erected at Mirnyy Observatory, in memory of Ivan F. Khmara (*see* **Deaths, 1956**). 8. Metal monument-sledge at Mirnyy Observatory, in memory of Anatoliy Shcheglov, who died in Antarctica. 9. Cemetery on Buromskiy Island, near Mirnyy Observatory, in which are buried those Communist bloc members who died in the Mirnyy fire (*see* **Deaths, 1960**). 10. Buildings at Dobrowolski Station with plaque erected in 1959 on a concrete pillar commemorating the opening of Oasis Station in 1956. 11. Heavy tractor at Vostok Station, with plaque, in memory of the opening of the station in 1957. 12. Cross and plaque at Cape Denison. Erected in 1913 to commemorate Ninnis and Mertz (*see* **Deaths, 1913**). 13. Hut at Cape Denison, built Jan. 1912 by the AAE 1911–14, as their main base. 14. Remains of rock shelter at Inexpressible Island, Terra Nova Bay, built in March 1912 by Campbell's Northern Party. 15. Shackleton's Cape Royds hut built in Feb. 1908. Restored by the New Zealanders in 1961. 16. Scott's Cape Evans

hut built in Jan. 1911. Restored by the New Zealanders in 1961. 17. Cross on Windvane Hill, Cape Evans, erected by the Ross Sea Party of Shackleton's British Imperial Transantarctic Expedition of 1914–17. In memory of the three who died (*see* **Deaths, 1916**). 18. Scott's Hut Point hut built in Feb. 1902. Partially restored in 1964 by the USA and NZ. 19. Cross at Hut Point erected Feb. 1904 by Scott to commemorate George Vince (q.v.). 20. The Polar Party Cross (q.v.) on Observation Hill. 21. Stone hut built at Cape Crozier by Wilson in July 1911. 22. Borchgrevink's Cape Adare hut built Feb. 1899. There are three huts at Cape Adare, two are Borchgrevink's and one is Campbell's from 1911–13. Only Borchgrevink's southern one is any good now. 23. Nikolai Hanson's grave at Cape Adare. 24. Amundsen's cairn on Mount Betty erected Jan. 6, 1912, by the Norwegian. 25. Hut and plaque on Peter I Island built by Nils Larsen in Feb. 1929 at Framnaesodden. Inscribed "Norvegia-ekspedisjonen 2/2 1929." 26. Abandoned installation of San Martín Station on Barry Island in the Debenham Islands, with cross, flagmast, and monolith built in 1951. 27. Cairn and plaque on Megalestris Hill, Petermann Island, erected by Charcot in 1909. Restored by the FIDS in 1958. 28. Rock cairn at Port Charcot, Booth Island, with wooden pillar and plaque inscribed with the names of Charcot's *Français* crew of 1903–5. 29. Lighthouse named "Primero de Mayo" on Lambda Island, erected 1942. First Argentine lighthouse in the Antarctic. 30. Shelter at Paradise Harbor erected in 1950 near the Presidente Gabriel González Videla Station to honor the first head of state to visit Antarctica (Videla). 31. Memorial plaque marking the position of a cemetery on Deception Island where about 40 Norwegian whalers were buried in the first half of the 20th century. Swept away by a volcanic eruption in Feb. 1969. 32. Concrete monolith erected 1947 near Capitán Arturo Prat Station on Greenwich Island. Point of reference for Chilean hydrographic work. **33.** Shelter and cross with plaque near Capitán Arturo Prat Station on Greenwich Island. Named in memory of Lt. Cdr. González Pacheco (*see* **Deaths, 1960**). **34.** Bust of Arturo Prat erected in 1947 at the Chilean scientific station which bears his name. **35.** Wooden cross and statue of the Virgin of Carmen, erected in 1947 near Capitán Arturo Prat Station on Greenwich Island. **36.** Metal plaque at Potter Cove, King George Island, erected by Dallmann, on March 1, 1874, to commemorate his expedition of that year. **37.** Statue of Bernardo O'Higgins, erected 1948, in front of the Chilean scientific station which bears his name. **38.** Nordenskjöld's Snow Hill hut built in Feb. 1902. **39.** Stone hut at Hope Bay built in Jan. 1903 by J. Gunnar Andersson's party. **40.** Bust of General San Martín, grotto with a statue of the Virgin of Luján, and a flag mast at Esperanza Station, erected by the Argentines in 1955. Together with a cemetery honoring members of Argentine expeditions who died here. **41.** Larsen's Paulet Island hut built in Feb. 1903. **42.** Stone hut built by Bruce on Laurie Island in 1903; the Argentine meteorological and magnetic observatory built in 1905 in the same place; and a graveyard with seven tombs. **43.** Cross erected at Piedrabuena Bay by the Argentines in 1955. Others created since include the Richard E. Byrd Memorial (q.v.); Base Marret (*see* **French Polar Expeditions**); Port-Martin (q.v.); a monolith at 61°03′S, 54°50′W, on the beach at Elephant Island, where the *Yelcho* rescued Shackleton's party in 1916; a cross on Pétrel Island to commemorate the death of André Prudhomme in 1959; a plaque at Metchnikoff Point on Brabant Island, built by Gaston de Gerlache to commemorate his father's stay here Jan. 30–Feb. 6, 1898; a Polish plaque at Fildes Peninsula commemorating the 1975–76 Polish Antarctic Expedition; a monolith on Fildes Peninsula commemorating the establishment of China's Great Wall Station; the site of the first Indian landing on Antarctica, at 70°45′S, 11°38′E—this took place

on the Princess Astrid Coast on Jan. 9, 1982, and was the beginning of Operation Gangotri (q.v.).

**Mount Hitchcock** *see* **Hitchcock Heights**

**Hitchcock Heights.** 68°46′S, 64°51′W. Mostly ice-covered. 1,800 m. Between the Maitland and Apollo Glaciers on the south side of Mobiloil Inlet, on the east coast of the Antarctic Peninsula. Discovered aerially by Wilkins on Dec. 20, 1928. Named in 1952 for Charles B. Hitchcock of the American Geographical Society who made the first reconnaissance map of this area.

**Hiyoko Island.** 69°S, 39°33′E. Just over ½ mile SW of Nesøya in the NE part of Lützow-Holm Bay. It is the most easterly of three small islands ½ mile NW of the strait separating Ongul Island from East Ongul Island. Named Hiyoko-jima (baby chick island) by the Japanese in 1972.

**Mount Hjalmar Johansen** *see* **Johansen Peak**

**Hjart Island.** 69°38′S, 39°16′E. 2 miles west of the Skallen Hills in the eastern part of Lützow-Holm Bay. Photographed by the LCE 1936–37, and later named Hjartøy (heart island) by the Norwegians for its shape.

**Hjelmkalven Point.** 71°40′S, 26°22′E. On the north side of Vesthjelmen Peak, at the east side of the mouth of Byrdbreen in the Sør Rondane Mountains. Photographed by the LCE 1936–37, and later named by the Norwegians.

**Hjörnehorna** *see* **Eckhörner Peaks**

**Hjort Fracture Zone.** Centers on 62°S, 163°E. Submarine feature.

**Hjort Massif.** 72°08′S, 61°24′W. On the east side of the Antarctic Peninsula.

**Hjorth Hill.** 77°31′S, 163°37′E. Ice-free. 760 m. Just north of New Harbor and 2 miles south of Hogback Hill in Victoria Land. Named by Scott's 1910–13 expedition for the makers of the primus stoves used by the expedition.

**Cape Hoadley.** 66°28'S, 99°56'E. Forms the west portal of the valley occupied by the Scott Glacier. Discovered by the Western Base Party of the AAE 1911–14, and named by Mawson in Nov. 1912 for C.A. Hoadley.

**Hoadley, C.A.** Geologist with the Western Base Party during the AAE 1911–14.

**Lake Hoare.** 77°38'S, 162°51'E. 2 miles long. Between Lake Chad and Canada Glacier in the Taylor Valley of Victoria Land. Named by the New Zealanders in 1963–64 for R.A. Hoare, a physicist here.

**Hoarfrost.** The deposit of ice crystals on objects exposed to the free air.

**Hobbie Ridge.** 73°09'S, 165°41'E. Projects from the middle of the head of Meander Glacier, 5 miles south of Mount Supernal, in Victoria Land. Named for John E. Hobbie, biologist at McMurdo Station, 1962–63.

**Cape Hobbs** see **Hobbs Islands**

**Mount Hobbs.** 83°45'S, 58°50'W. 1,135 m. The highest summit in the Williams Hills in the Neptune Range of the Pensacola Mountains. Named for Ensign James W. Hobbs, USN, at Ellsworth Station, 1958.

**Hobbs Coast.** 74°50'S, 132°W. Extends along the coast of Marie Byrd Land from Cape Burks to a point on the coast opposite eastern Dean Island, at 74°42'S, 127°05'W. Discovered by the USAS 1939–41 and named for Prof. William H. Hobbs, US glaciologist (1864–1953).

¹**Hobbs Glacier.** 64°18'S, 57°26'W. Inside a steep, rock-walled cirque at the NW side of Hamilton Point. It flows into the south part of Markham Bay on the east coast of James Ross Island. Discovered and surveyed by Nordenskjöld in 1901–4, and he named it for Prof. William H. Hobbs (see **Hobbs Coast**).

²**Hobbs Glacier.** 77°54'S, 164°24'E. 7 miles long. 2 miles south of the Blue Glacier, on the coast of Victoria Land. Explored during Scott's first two expeditions, and named by Scott on the last

one, for Prof. William H. Hobbs (see **Cape Hobbs**).

**Hobbs Islands.** 67°19'S, 59°58'E. Also called Kringholmane. A group 10 miles NE of William Scoresby Bay. The largest of the group was discovered on Feb. 18, 1931, by the BANZARE, and named Cape Hobbs by Mawson for Prof. William H. Hobbs (see **Hobbs Coast**). Explorations by the *William Scoresby* in 1936 and by the LCE 1936–37 showed it to be part of the island group, and not a cape as Mawson had thought. It was subsequently redefined.

**Hobbs Peak.** 77°53'S, 163°56'E. 1,510 m. Between the Hobbs Glacier and the Blue Glacier in Victoria Land. Named by the New Zealanders in 1960–61 in association with the glacier of the same name.

**Hobbs Point.** 64°37'S, 62°03'W. The NE end of Brooklyn Island in Wilhelmina Bay, off the west coast of Graham Land. Charted by de Gerlache in 1897–99. Named by the UK in 1960 for Graham J. Hobbs, FIDS geologist at Base O in 1957 and 1958.

**Hobbs Stream.** 77°55'S, 164°30'E. Seasonal meltwater stream. Flows from the mouth of Hobbs Glacier into Salmon Bay on the coast of Victoria Land. Named by the New Zealanders in 1958–59 for the glacier.

**Hobby Rocks.** 68°35'S, 77°54'E. Three small islands off the Vestfold Hills. They mark the western side of Davis Anchorage. Photographed by the LCE 1936–37, and later named by the Australians for D. Hobby, diesel mechanic at Davis Station, 1960.

**Hobnail Peak.** 78°32'S, 161°53'E. Triangular rock bluff just south of Mount Tricouni, on the east side of the Skelton Glacier in Victoria Land. Named in 1957 by the NZ party of the BCTAE and named in association with Clinker Bluff and Mount Tricouni (qq.v.).

**Hobsen, Samuel.** Armorer on the Wilkes Expedition 1838–42. Joined in the USA. Returned home in the *Relief* in 1839.

**Hobson Glacier.** 77°06'S, 162°28'E. Between the Mackay and Debenham Glaciers.

**Mount Hochlin.** 72°05'S, 4°03'E. Icetopped. 2,760 m. East of Festninga Mountain in the Mühlig-Hofmann Mountains of Queen Maud Land. Named by the Norwegians for L. Hochlin, radio operator and dog driver on the Norwegian Antarctic Expedition 1956–58.

**Hochstein Ridge.** 82°45'S, 159°47'E. 12 miles long. Extends north from Cotton Plateau between Prince Edward Glacier and Prince of Wales Glacier in the Queen Elizabeth Range. Named for Manfred Hochstein, glaciologist at Roosevelt Island, 1961–62, 1962–63, and 1963–64.

**Hockey Cirque.** 83°17'S, 156°30'E. A glacial cirque ½ mile wide, along the east wall of Ascent Glacier in the Miller Range. Named by the Ohio State University Geological Party of 1967–68 for the game of ice hockey they played here.

**Hodge Escarpment.** 83°03'S, 50°11' W. In the Pensacola Mountains.

**Hodgeman, Alfred J.** Cartographer and assistant meteorologist with the AAE 1911–14.

**Hodgeman Islands.** 67°01'S, 144°14'E. Close to the coast. 4 miles WSW of Cape de la Motte, in the eastern part of the entrance to Watt Bay. Discovered by the AAE 1911–14, and named by Mawson for Alfred J. Hodgeman.

**Hodges, Capt.** Commander of the *Salisbury* in the South Shetlands, 1820–21.

**Hodges, Isaac.** Took over command of the *Harmony* from Nat Ray on Aug. 1, 1821, for that vessel's second Antarctic season, 1821–22.

**Hodges, William.** b. 1744, London. d. March 6, 1797, Brixham, Devon. Painter on the *Resolution* during Cook's second voyage.

**Hodges Point.** 67°21'S, 65°03'W. Terminates in an impressive black cliff. 6 miles ENE of Cape Northrop on the east coast of Graham Land. Twin summits on the point rise to 960 m. and 940 m. Named by the UK for Ben Hodges, general assistant with the BAS Larsen Ice Shelf party of 1963–64.

**Cape Hodgson.** 78°07'S, 166°05'E. The most northerly cape on Black Island, in the Ross Archipelago. Named by the New Zealanders in 1958–59 for Thomas V. Hodgson.

**Hodgson, Thomas V.** 1864–1926. Thomas Vere Hodgson. Marine biologist on the Royal Society Expedition of 1901–4. Later, curator of Plymouth Museum, England.

**Hodgson Nunatak.** 74°17'S, 100°04' W. 5 miles south of Teeters Nunatak and 20 miles NW of Mount Moses in the Hudson Mountains. Named for Ronald A. Hodgson, USN, builder at Byrd Station in 1966.

**Hodson, Arnold.** Governor of the Falkland Islands who, in Feb. and March 1928, made an official visit to the South Orkneys, Palmer Archipelago, and the South Shetlands, on the *Fleurus*. Possibly the first ever Distinguished Visitor (q.v.) to Antarctica.

**Mount Hoegh.** 64°50'S, 62°48'W. 890 m. 1½ miles SSE of Duthiers Point, on the west coast of Graham Land. Charted by de Gerlache 1897–99. Named by the UK in 1960 for Emil von Hoegh (1865–1915), German designer of the first double anastigmatic camera lens in 1893.

**Hoek Glacier.** 66°S, 65°04'W. Flows to the west coast of Graham Land, to the south of Llanquihue Islands. Charted by the BGLE 1934–37. Named by the UK in 1959 for Henry W. Hoek (1878–1951), German-Swiss ski pioneer.

**Hoel Mountains.** 72°S, 14°E. In Queen Maud Land. They include the Payer Mountains and the Weyprecht Mountains. Named by the Norwegians for Adolf Hoel, Norwegian geologist and Arctic explorer.

**Mount Hoffman.** 81°19'S, 85°15'W. 1½ miles SSW of Mount Tidd, in the southern portion of the Pirrit Hills. Named for Daniel Hoffman, mechanic with the US Ellsworth-Byrd Traverse Party of 1958–59, which positioned this peak on Dec. 7, 1958.

**Hoffman Glacier.** 83°22'S, 167°40'E. 10 miles long. Flows from Mount Miller in the Holland Range, into the Lennox-King Glacier south of Rhodes Peak. Named for Lt. Cdr. Robert D. Hoffman, USN, commander of the *Mills* in 1965.

**Hoffman Point.** 79°20'S, 160°30'E. Ice-covered. At the south side of the mouth of Bertoglio Glacier, where that glacier flows into the Ross Ice Shelf. Named for Cdr. G.L. Hoffman, USN, commander of Mobile Construction Battalion Eight at McMurdo Station, 1964.

**Mount Hofmann.** 82°40'S, 160°36'E. 2,000 m. Snow-covered. Between the mouths of the Hamilton and Heilman Glaciers in the northern part of the Queen Elizabeth Range. Named for Walther F. Hofmann, glaciologist on the Ross Ice Shelf, 1962–63.

**Mount Hogan** *see* **Mount Loweth**

**The Hogback** *see* **Hogback Hill**

**Hogback Hill.** 77°29'S, 163°36'E. 735 m. Just north of Hjorth Hill, and 4 miles west of Cape Bernacchi, in Victoria Land. Charted and named by the Scott expedition of 1910–13, because of its rounded shape.

**Mount Hoge.** 72°35'S, 31°25'E. 2,480 m. Between Mount Van der Essen and Mount Brouwer in the Belgica Mountains. Discovered by the Belgian Antarctic Expedition of 1957–58, under Gaston de Gerlache, who named it for Edmond Hoge, member of the scientific committee of the expedition.

**Høgfonna Mountain.** 72°45'S, 3°33'W. Flat. Snow-topped. 3 miles SE of Høgskavlen Mountain in the Borg Massif of Queen Maud Land. Name means "the high snowfield" in Norwegian.

**Høgfonnaksla Ridge.** 72°44'S, 3°34'W. Forms the north end of Høgfonna Mountain in the Borg Massif of Queen Maud Land. Name means "the high snowfield shoulder" in Norwegian.

**Høgfonnhornet Peak.** 72°46'S, 3°37'W. Surmounts the southern extremity of Høgfonna Mountain in the Borg Massif of Queen Maud Land. Name means "the high snowfield horn" in Norwegian.

**Hogg Islands.** 67°31'S, 61°37'E. ½ mile south of Kamelen Island in the northern part of the Stanton Group. Photographed by the LCE 1936–37. Later named by the Australians for Dr. J. Hogg, medical officer at Mawson Station in 1969.

**Hoggestabben Butte.** 72°S, 3°58'E. 2,410 m. 3 miles north of Mount Hochlin, it is the highest northern outlier of that mountain, in the Mühlig-Hofmann Mountains of Queen Maud Land. Name means "the chopping block" in Norwegian.

**Høghamaren Crag.** 72°34'S, 0°36'E. 1 mile SW of Hamartind Peak in the Sverdrup Mountains of Queen Maud Land. Name means "the high crag" in Norwegian.

**Hogmanay Pass.** 69°15'S, 64°07'W. 1,230 m. Just SW of Scripps Heights. Leads from the head of Casey Glacier to the middle of Lurabee Glacier, in northeastern Palmer Land. Named by the UK because it was used as a good sledge route by a FIDS survey party in Dec. 1960. The pass was approached on the last day of the year, the feast of Hogmanay.

**Høgsaetet Mountain.** 72°35'S, 3°23'W. Just NE of Raudberget in the Borg Massif of Queen Maud Land. Name means "the high seat" in Norwegian.

**Høgsenga Crags.** 71°53'S, 5°23'E. Form the northern extremity of Breplogen Mountain in the Mühlig-Hofmann Mountains of Queen Maud Land. Name means "the high bed" in Norwegian.

**Høgskavlen Mountain.** 72°40'S, 3°43'W. Flat. Snow-topped. Just NE of

Domen Butte in the Borg Massif of Queen Maud Land. Name means "the high snowdrift" in Norwegian.

**Høgskavlnasen Point.** 72°42'S, 3°45' W. Forms the southern extremity of Høgskavlen Mountain in the Borg Massif of Queen Maud Land. Name means "the high snowdrift point" in Norwegian.

**Høgskavlnebbet Spur.** 72°38'S, 3°39' W. Extends north from Høgskavlen Mountain in the Borg Massif of Queen Maud Land. Name means "the high snowdrift spur" in Norwegian.

**Høgskavlpiggen Peak.** 72°39'S, 3°45' W. On the west part of Høgskavlen Mountain, in the Borg Massif of Queen Maud Land. Name means "the high snowdrift peak" in Norwegian.

**Høgskotet Spur.** 72°31'S, 3°30'W. On the north side of Borg Mountain, in the Borg Massif of Queen Maud Land. Name means "the high bulkhead" in Norwegian.

**Hoinkes Peak.** 79°52'S, 82°58'W. 1,840 m. At the head of Henderson Glacier. Forms part of the west wall of that glacier. In the Heritage Range. Named for Herfried C. Hoinkes, meteorologist at Little America, 1957.

**Holane Nunataks.** 71°58'S, 0°29'E. Two isolated nunataks. 20 miles west of the northern extremity of the Sverdrup Mountains in Queen Maud Land. Named by the Norwegians.

**Holcomb Glacier.** 75°35'S, 142°48'W. Flows to the coast of Marie Byrd Land 9 miles SE of Groves Island. Named for Leroy G. Holcomb, ionosphere physicist at Byrd Station, 1971.

**Holden, Benjamin.** Private on the Wilkes Expedition 1838–42. Joined in the USA, along with the other marines, and died of smallpox at Callao on July 8, 1839. He was buried on San Lorenzo Island.

**Holden Nunataks.** 72°42'S, 65°W. In Palmer Land.

**Mount Holder** *see* **Houlder Bluff**

**Holder Peak.** 69°45'S, 74°31'E. Just north of Young Peak, and 2 miles east of Mount Caroline Mikkelsen, near the coast of East Antarctica. Photographed by the LCE 1936–37. Norwegian cartographers, using these photos, mapped it along with Mount Young, as Tvillingfjell (twin mountain). It was later renamed by the Australians for J. Holder, weather observer at Davis Station, 1963, and a member of the ANARE party that surveyed this area.

**Holdfast Point.** 66°48'S, 66°36'W. At the east side of Lallemand Fjord, 12 miles SW of Cape Rey in Graham Land. Named by the UK for the pack-ice which, south of this point, seems to hold fast while the pack to the north breaks out sooner.

**Mount Holdsworth.** 72°08'S, 166°35' E. A granite peak surmounting the small massif which forms the west wall of Midway Glacier, in the Victory Mountains of Victoria Land. Named by the New Zealand Federated Mountain Clubs Antarctic Expedition of 1962–63, for G. Holdsworth, leader of the northern party of this expedition.

**Holdsworth Glacier.** 86°30'S, 154°W. 8 miles long. Flows from Fuller Dome into the SE side of Bartlett Glacier, in the Queen Maud Mountains. Named for Gerald Holdsworth, geologist at McMurdo Station, 1965–66.

**Hole Rock.** 61°53'S, 57°44'W. Also called Roca de la Ventana, Roca Perforada. The largest of several rocks just north of North Foreland, the NE cape of King George Island, in the South Shetlands. Charted in 1937 by personnel on the *Discovery II,* and named by them for the conspicuous hole which runs through it.

**Holgersen, Holger.** Leader of the *Bråtegg* expedition of 1947–48. He was a Norwegian oceanographer.

**Holiday Peak.** 78°06'S, 163°36'E. Over 800 m. Between the lower ends of Miers Glacier and Adams Glacier. Named by the VUWAE of 1960–61, because of its prominent position overlooking the expedition's camp at Christmas of 1960.

**Holl, Richard C. Lt., USNR.** Photogrammetrist with the US Navy Hydrographic Office, who took part in Operation Windmill in 1947–48, as a surveyor.

**Holl Island.** 66°25'S, 110°25'E. Triangular-shaped. Almost 1¾ miles long. Marks the SW end of the Windmill Islands. Named for Lt. Richard C. Holl.

**Holladay Nunataks.** 69°31'S, 159°19' E. A cluster, 3 miles in extent. They occupy the central part of the peninsula between the terminus of Tomilin Glacier and the Gillett Ice Shelf. Named for Billy W. Holladay, chief aviation electronics technician, USN, maintenance control chief at McMurdo Station, 1968.

**Holland Range.** 83°10'S, 166°E. 60 miles long. Just west of the Ross Ice Shelf. It extends from the Robb Glacier to the Lennox-King Glacier. Named by the Ross Sea Committee during the BCTAE, for Sir Sidney Holland, prime minister of New Zealand, and a supporter of New Zealand's participation in that expedition.

**Hollick-Kenyon, Herbert.** British-born Canadian transport pilot with Canadian Airways who had been a pilot in the RAF during World War I. With Ellsworth in the co-pilot's seat, he became the first man to make a transantarctic crossing, in the *Polar Star,* from Nov. 23–Dec. 15, 1935.

**Hollick-Kenyon Peninsula.** 68°35'S, 63°50'W. Also called Kenyon Peninsula. An ice-covered spur jutting out from the main mountain mass of the Antarctic Peninsula. It projects over 40 miles in a NE arc from its base between Mobiloil and Casey Inlets into the Larsen Ice Shelf. Cape Agassiz is at its tip. Discovered aerially by Ellsworth in 1935. Named for Herbert Hollick-Kenyon.

**Hollick-Kenyon Plateau.** 78°S, 105° W. Also called Kenyon Plateau. 1,200 m.–1,800 m. above sea level. Between the northern portion of the Ellsworth Mountains, to the east, and Mount

Takahe and the Crary Mountains, to the west. Discovered aerially by Ellsworth and Herbert Hollick-Kenyon, Nov.–Dec. 1935, and named by Ellsworth for his pilot on that flight.

**Hollin Island.** 66°19'S, 110°24'E. 1 mile long. North of Midgley Island in the Windmill Islands. Named for John T. Hollin, glaciologist at Wilkes Station, 1958.

**Mount Hollingshead.** 70°41'S, 66°10' E. 3 miles east of Mount Dowie in the Aramis Range of the Prince Charles Mountains. Visited in Jan. 1957 by the ANARE southern party led by W.G. Bewsher, and named by the Australians for John A. Hollingshead, radio supervisor at Mawson Station, 1956.

**Mount Hollingsworth.** 67°15'S, 50°21' E. 1 mile south of Priestley Peak, just south of Amundsen Bay, in Enderby Land. Named by the Australians for R.J.T. Hollingsworth, geophysicist at Mawson Station, 1961.

**Hollingsworth Cliffs.** 80°26'S, 25°33' W. In the Shackleton Range.

**Hollingsworth Glacier.** 75°33'S, 159° 57'E. Flows from the vicinity east of the Ricker Hills, into David Glacier just east of Trio Nunataks, in Victoria Land. Named for Jerry L. Hollingsworth, meteorologist at Amundsen-Scott South Pole Station, 1966.

**Mount Holloway.** 84°45'S, 163°36'E. 2,650 m. Between Swinford Glacier and Table Bay, in the Queen Alexandra Range. Named for Harry L. Holloway, biologist at McMurdo Station, 1964–65.

**Holluschickie Bay.** 63°59'S, 58°16'W. On the west coast of James Ross Island. Between Matkah and Kotick Points. Surveyed by the FIDS in 1945. Named by the FIDS in 1952 for the young seals (the holluschickie) in Kipling's *Jungle Book.* There were many young seals here in that year.

**Holman Dome.** 66°27'S, 98°54'E. A dome-shaped nunatak 2 miles SW of Watson Bluff, on the east side of David

Island. Discovered by the AAE 1911–14, and named by Mawson for William A. Holman, premier of New South Wales.

**Mount Holmboe.** 77°20′S, 86°35′W. 1,730 m. 1 mile north of Mount Liavaag and 7 miles NW of Mount Weems near the extreme north end of the Sentinel Range. Discovered aerially by Ellsworth on Nov. 23, 1935, and later named for Dr. Jorgen Holmboe.

**Holmboe, Dr. Jorgen.** Meteorologist on the first three of Ellsworth's expeditions in the 1930s.

**Holme Bay.** 67°35′S, 62°42′E. 22 miles wide. Contains many islands. Indents the coast 5 miles north of the Framnes Mountains. Photographed in Jan.–Feb. 1937 by the LCE 1936–37, and named by the Norwegians for the "holmen" (islands) in the bay.

**Holmen Graa** *see* **Gray Island**

**Mount Holmes.** 66°47′S, 64°16′W. 1,440 m. 3 miles NW of Mount Hayes. On the east coast of Graham Land. Charted in 1947 by the FIDS, and named by them for Maurice Holmes, bibliographer of Captain Cook.

**Holmes, James.** Captain of the *Franklin* in the South Shetlands, 1871–72.

**Holmes, Jeremiah.** A Stonington, Conn., mariner who was a principal owner of the fleet sent out in 1820–21 to the South Shetlands under the command of Alexander Clark. Holmes commanded the *Emeline* on this trip.

**Holmes, Silas.** Assistant surgeon on the Wilkes Expedition 1838–42. Joined the *Porpoise* in Sydney, and transferred to the *Peacock.*

**Holmes & Narver, Inc.** Support contractor out of Orange, California, who began work for the USARP in early 1968. On April 1, 1980, ITT/Antarctic Services, Inc., took over the contract (see entry under ITT for what a support contractor does). (*See also* **Antarctic Services Associates.**)

**Holmes Bluff.** 74°59′S, 133°43′W. Marks the north end of the Demas Range

on the coast of Marie Byrd Land. Algae, lichens, and petrels are found here. Discovered aerially by the USAS 1939–41. Named for Thomas J. Holmes, meteorologist at Byrd Station, 1961.

**Holmes Glacier.** 66°46′S, 126°54′E. Flows into the western part of Porpoise Bay about 10 miles south of Cape Spieden. Named for Silas Holmes.

**Holmes Hills.** 72°08′S, 63°25′W. In Palmer Land.

**Holmes Island.** 65°41′S, 65°15′W. 1½ miles long. South of Vieugué Island in the Biscoe Islands. Charted by the BGLE 1934–37. Named by the UK for Bryan Holmes, FIDS surveyor at Base J in 1957.

**Holmes Rock.** 62°23′S, 59°50′W. 1 mile NW of Emeline Island, in the Aitcho Islands of the South Shetlands. Named by the UK in 1961 for Jeremiah Holmes.

**Holmes Summit.** 80°40′S, 24°39′W. In the Shackleton Range.

**Holness, A.** Fireman on the *Endurance* during Shackleton's 1914–17 expedition. At 11 p.m. on April 9, 1916, while in his sleeping bag on an ice floe, the ice opened up and he fell into the water. Shackleton rescued him.

**Holst Peak.** 71°20′S, 70°06′W. 1,000 m. Pyramidal. Between the south end of the Walton Mountains and the LeMay Range in the central part of Alexander Island. Named by the UK for the composer.

**Holst Point.** 65°32′S, 63°50′W. At the head of Beascochea Bay, on the west coast of Graham Land. It divides the bay into two arms. Charted by the BGLE 1934–37. Named by the UK in 1959 for Axel Holst (1860–1931), Norwegian vitamin pioneer.

**Mount Holt.** 69°25′S, 71°43′W. In the north of Alexander Island.

**Holt, Samuel B.** Captain of the hold on the Wilkes Expedition 1838–42. Joined in the USA. Discharged at Oahu, Oct. 31, 1840.

**Holt Glacier.** 74°41′S, 110°18′W. On Bear Peninsula, it flows to the sea between Grimes Ridge and Jones Bluffs, in Marie Byrd Land. Named for Joseph V. Holt, a member of the US Army Aviation Detachment in Antarctica, 1965–66.

**Holt Nunatak.** 64°17′S, 59°21′W. At the NE corner of Larsen Inlet in Graham Land. Named by the UK for the Holt Manufacturing Co., of Stockton, California, which, in 1906, began making commercial chain-track tractors, and the Holt Caterpillar Tractor Co., of New York, founded in 1908.

**Holt Peak.** 79°45′S, 81°04′W. Icefree. 850 m. Surmounts the NE end of the Meyer Hills in the Heritage Range. Named for William C. Holt, aurora scientist at Ellsworth Station, 1961.

**Holt Point.** 66°17′S, 110°30′E. Marks the western extremity of Bailey Peninsula, at the eastern side of the Windmill Islands. Named for James R. Holt, USN, photographer's mate at Wilkes Station, 1958.

**Holtanna Peak.** 71°55′S, 8°22′E. 2,650 m. Its eastern portion is occupied by a small cirque glacier. 1 mile north of Mundlauga Crags in the eastern part of Fenriskjeften Mountain in Queen Maud Land. Name means "the hollow tooth" in Norwegian.

**Holtedahl, Olaf.** Norwegian geologist who, with Ola Olstad, went down to the Antarctic on the *Norvegia* in 1927–28. While the ship was being repaired in South Georgia, the two scientists went island-hopping in the South Shetlands and the Palmer Archipelago, using local Norwegian whalers as lifts.

**Holtedahl Bay.** 66°07′S, 65°20′W. 10 miles long. Average of 6 miles wide. Between Prospect Point and Black Head, on the west coast of Graham Land. Discovered by the BGLE 1934–37, and named by Rymill for Olaf Holtedahl.

**Holtedahl Mountains** *see* **Kurze Mountains**

**Holtedahl Peaks.** 71°47′S, 8°58′E. North of Steinskaret Gap. They form the northern portion of the Kurze Mountains

in Queen Maud Land. The Norwegians in 1966 inadvertently called the whole range Holtedahlfjella (Holtedahl Mountains) for Olaf Holtedahl, not realizing that they had already been named the Kurze Mountains. Consequently the term has become more restricted.

**Holtedahlfjella** *see* **Kurze Mountains**

**Holth, Baard.** Capt. Commander of the *Wyatt Earp* during Ellsworth's 1933–34 and 1934–35 expeditions. He had already had experience in the Antarctic, as a whaler.

**Holth Peaks.** 77°25′S, 86°43′W. 2 miles NW of Mount Lymburner near the north end of the Sentinel Range. Discovered aerially on Nov. 23, 1935, by Ellsworth. Named for Capt. Baard Holth.

**Holyoake Range.** 82°13′S, 160°E. In the southern part of the Churchill Mountains. It extends for about 25 miles between Prince Philip Glacier and Errant Glacier. Named by New Zealand for Keith Holyoake, prime minister of NZ from 1960–72, and who, as minister of agriculture in the 1950s supported NZ participation in the BCTAE.

**Holzrichter Glacier.** 84°50′S, 172°30′W. Flows from the NE slopes of the Prince Olav Mountains, between Mount Wade and Mount Oliver, into the Gough Glacier just north of Mount Dodge. Named for Capt. Max A. Holzrichter, USN, deputy commander and chief of staff, US Naval Support Force, Antarctica, 1964 and 1965.

**Mount Homard.** 80°40′S, 29°50′W. 1,200 m. Near the head of Blaiklock Glacier, 2 miles south of Trey Peaks, in the western part of the Shackleton Range. Named in 1957 by the BCTAE for Roy Homard.

**Homard, Roy.** Sgt. Major Desmond E.L. "Roy" Homard. Engineer who crossed the continent with Fuchs (he was also a member of the Advance Party) during the BCTAE.

**Hombron, Jacques Bernard.** Naturalist/surgeon on the *Astrolabe* during Dumont d'Urville's 1837–40 expedition.

**Hombron Rocks.** 63°28'S, 58°42'W. 8 miles NE of Cape Roquemaurel and 3 miles off the northern coast of Trinity Peninsula. Discovered by Dumont d'Urville, and named by him for Jacques Hombron. Charted by the FIDS in 1946.

**Home Beach.** ¼ mile long. On North Bay, just north of Cape Evans, Ross Island.

**Home Lake** *see* **Pony Lake**

**Homerun Range.** 71°40'S, 166°35'E. 28 miles long. Between 2 and 7 miles wide. East of Everett Range, at the heads of the Ebbe and Tucker Glaciers in Victoria Land. In 1962–63 the New Zealand Federated Mountain Clubs Expedition used a bluff near here as their turnabout point and called it Homerun Bluff. The name of the range comes from that.

**Homeward Point.** 64°51'S, 63°37'W. Forms the west side of the entrance to Security Bay on Doumer Island in the Palmer Archipelago. Charted by Charcot in 1903–5. Named by the British Naval Hydrographic Survey Unit in 1956–57 because it marked the way home for their surveyors after a day's work in the Bismarck Strait. Port Lockroy was their base.

**Homing Head.** 67°48'S, 67°16'W. Headland at the NE side of Sally Cove on Horseshoe Island, off the coast of Graham Land. Named by the UK in 1958. The headland is black and formed from sheer cliffs 60 meters high. It served as a homing landmark for returning FIDS sledging parties.

**Homresund** *see* **Macfie Sound**

**Honabron Rock** *see* **Hombron Rocks**

**Honeycomb Glacier.** 72°07'S, 169°52'E. Flows from the Mount Whewell massif, between there and Honeycomb Ridge, into Moubray Bay. Named by the New Zealanders in 1957–58 in association with the ridge.

**Honeycomb Ridge.** 72°05'S, 169°58'E. Extends north from the mouth of Ironside Glacier, on the west side of Moubray Bay. Named by the New Zealanders in 1957–58 for its honeycombed appearance.

**Honkala, Rudolf A.** Known as Rudy. Chief meteorologist at Wilkes Station, 1957.

**Honkala Island.** 66°14'S, 110°37'E. ¾ mile long. At the SE side of Burnett Island in the Swain Islands. Surveyed by Carl Eklund in 1957. He named it for Rudolf A. Honkala.

**Honnør Glacier.** 69°23'S, 39°50'E. Flows to the east side of Lützow-Holm Bay, to the north of Byvågåsane Peaks. When the LCE 1936–37 photographed the area, they found a glacier tongue extended seaward from this glacier, and named the tongue Honnørbrygga (the honor wharf). In the late 1950s the Japanese found that the tongue had broken off, and amended the name slightly for the glacier itself, which remained.

**Honnywill Peak.** 80°31'S, 29°08'W. 1,220 m. Just SE of Williams Ridge on the west side of Stratton Glacier in the Shackleton Range. Named in 1957 by the BCTAE for Eleanor Honnywill, assistant secretary to the expedition.

**Honores Rock.** 62°30'S, 59°43'W. ½ mile SW of Ferrer Point in Discovery Bay, Greenwich Island, South Shetlands. Named Islote Cocinero Honores by the Chilean Antarctic Expedition of 1947 for the cook on the *Iquique*. The name was later shortened to Islote Honores, and then translated to Honores Rock.

**Hood Glacier.** 83°55'S, 173°10'E. 25 miles long. Flows from Siege Dome in the Commonwealth Range. It enters the Ross Ice Shelf between the Commonwealth Range and the Separation Range. Discovered by Shackleton on his way to the Pole in 1908, and it was named for Adm. Sir Horace Hood, RN, under whom Lt. Jameson B. Adams had served in the *Berwick*.

**Hoodwink Island.** 67°01'S, 66°52'W. 1 mile east of Arrowsmith Peninsula, in Lallemand Fjord, Graham Land. Named by the UK because this island was mistaken for another by the FIDS during a survey.

**Mount Hook.** 83°20'S, 50°W. In the Pensacola Mountains.

**Hook Island.** 65°38'S, 65°10'W. 1 mile NE of Vieugué Island in the Biscoe Islands. Charted by the BGLE 1934–37. Named by the UK in 1959 for its shape when seen aerially.

**Hooke, Leslie A.** Radio operator on the *Aurora* as part of the Ross Sea Party during Shackleton's 1914–17 expedition. He was on the ship when it floated away from the shore party. Later he was managing director of a business in Sydney.

**Hooke Point.** 67°11'S, 66°42'W. Near the head of Lallemand Fjord, in Graham Land. Named by the UK for Robert Hooke (1635–1703), pioneer in the study of ice crystals.

**¹Cape Hooker.** 63°18'S, 61°59'W. Forms the east end of Low Island, in the South Shetlands.

**²Cape Hooker.** 70°38'S, 166°45'E. On the NE part of the peninsula that includes Davis Ice Piedmont, on the north coast of Victoria Land. With Cape Dayman to the ESE it forms an outer entrance point to Yule Bay. Discovered by Ross in 1841, and named by him for Joseph Dalton Hooker.

**Mount Hooker.** 78°06'S, 162°42'E. Over 3,800 m. Just south of Mount Lister in the Royal Society Range of Victoria Land. Discovered by the Royal Society Expedition of 1901–4, and named by them for Joseph Dalton Hooker.

**Hooker, Joseph Dalton.** b. June 30, 1817, Halesworth, Suffolk. d. Dec. 10, 1911, Sunningdale, Berks. Botanist who, with his father, Sir William Jackson Hooker, founded Kew Gardens in London. He was assistant-surgeon/botanist on the *Erebus* under Ross, from 1839–43, and wrote about it (*see* the Bibliog-

raphy). He fell into the sea at Franklin Island on Jan. 27, 1841, and was almost crushed by the ship. He was later knighted.

**Hooker Glacier.** 78°04'S, 163°06'E. On the east side of the Royal Society Range, it flows into the Blue Glacier from the slopes of Mount Hooker. Named for Mount Hooker by the NZ Blue Glacier Party of the BCTAE in 1957.

**Hooper, Frederick J.** 1891–1955. Petty officer, RN. Joined Scott's 1910–13 expedition as a steward, but transferred to the shore party. Was one of the search party who found Scott's tent in Nov. 1912.

**Hooper, G.** Representative of and nautical adviser to the NZ government, he was administrator of the Ross Dependency, and as such took part in Larsen's whaling expedition of 1923–24 in the *Sir James Clark Ross*.

**Hooper Crags.** 78°25'S, 16°43'E. 3 miles long. At the south side of Foster Glacier in the Royal Society Range. Named in 1963 for Lt. Benjamin F. Hooper, VX-6 helicopter pilot at McMurdo Station in 1960.

**Hooper Glacier.** 64°44'S, 63°37'W. 3 miles long. Flows from the col north of Mount William into the west side of Börgen Bay on Anvers Island. Surveyed by the FIDS in 1955, and named by the UK for Peter R. Hooper of the FIDS, leader and geologist at Base N in 1955 and 1956.

**Hoopers Shoulder.** 77°32'S, 166°53'E. An independent cone at a height of 1,800 m. On the western slopes of Mount Erebus on Ross Island. When seen from McMurdo Sound it looks like a huge, black pyramid. Named by Frank Debenham during the second ascent of Mount Erebus, for Frederick J. Hooper, who was on this ascent party.

**Hop Island.** 68°50'S, 77°43'E. One of the largest of the Rauer Islands. 3 miles long. 1 mile WSW of Filla Island. Photographed by the LCE 1936–37, and named Hopøy by the Norwegians.

**Hopalong Nunatak.** 81°33'S, 28°45' W. The highest and most westerly of the Whichaway Nunataks. Named in 1957 by the BCTAE to honor the Australian geologists who have worked in this area (hopalong signifies kangaroo).

**The *Hope*.** Whaler which, after a tour in South Shetlands waters, discovered the *Jenny* floating in the Drake Passage in Sept. 1840.

**Lake Hope.** 63°25'S, 57°01'W. A small lake ½ mile north of Mount Flora, just east of the head of Hope Bay, Trinity Peninsula. Named by the Argentines for the bay.

**¹Mount Hope** *see* **Mount Bransfield**

**²Mount Hope.** 69°46'S, 64°34'W. 2,860 m. Forms the central and highest peak of the Eternity Range in northern Palmer Land. Discovered aerially by Ellsworth on Nov. 21, 1935, and named by him. In Nov. 1936 Rymill surveyed it and named it Mount Wakefield during the BGLE. It was later found that the two were the same, and the original name was retained.

**³Mount Hope.** 83°31'S, 171°16'E. 835 m. Marks the western side of the terminus of Beardmore Glacier at its confluence with the Ross Ice Shelf. Named by Shackleton in 1908-9. He climbed this mountain, and from its peak saw the Beardmore Glacier, which gave him hope for the ascent to the Polar Plateau. This was the southernmost depot laid by the Ross Sea Party in 1916.

**Hope, Royal.** Landsman on the Wilkes Expedition 1838-42. Joined at Rio. Run at Oahu.

**Hope Bay.** 63°23'S, 57°W. 3 miles long. 2 miles wide. Indents the tip of the Antarctic Peninsula, and opens on Antarctic Sound. Discovered Jan. 15, 1902, by Nordenskjöld, who named it to commemorate the winter spent here by Andersson, Duse, and Grunden. It is the home of the world's largest colony of Adélie penguins.

**Hope Island.** 63°03'S, 56°50'W. Also called Hope Isle, Isla Esperanza. Largest of a group of small islands 6 miles west of D'Urville Island, off the NE tip of the Antarctic Peninsula. Named by Powell before 1822. In 1837-40 Dumont d'Urville charted an island in the same position, and named it Daussy Island. Powell's naming is the official one.

**Hope Isle** *see* **Hope Island**

**Hope Point.** 67°23'S, 59°36'E. Marks the western end of Bertha Island in the William Scoresby Archipelago. Charted and named by the personnel on the *William Scoresby*, in Feb. 1936.

**Mount Hopeful.** 62°02'S, 58°06'W. 1½ miles north of the head of King George Bay, and 1½ miles SE of Rea Peak on King George Island, in the South Shetlands. Named by the UK in 1960 for the *Hopefull;* they amended the spelling somewhat.

**The *Hopefull*.** British schooner, Rea's flagship during his 1833-34 cruise. Owned by Enderby Brothers, it rescued the crew of the *Rose*, its consort ship, when the latter vessel went down.

**Hopkins Glacier.** 66°36'S, 65°42'W. Flows into Darbel Bay south of Erskine Glacier, on the west coast of Graham Land. Named by the UK in 1958 for Sir Frederick Hopkins (1861-1947), vitamin pioneer.

**Hopøy** *see* **Hop Island**

**The *Horatio*.** London sealer in the South Shetlands, 1820-21, under the command of Capt. Weeks.

**Horatio Stump.** 62°13'S, 59°01'W. A flat-topped hill. 165 m. Just east of Flat Top Peninsula at the SW end of King George Island, in the South Shetlands. Named by the UK in 1960 for the *Horatio*.

**Cape Hordern.** 66°15'S, 100°31'E. Also called Hordern Peninsula, Mount Hordern. Ice-free. At the NW end of the Bunger Hills. Named Hordern Island by Mawson for Sir Samuel Hordern of Sydney, a patron of the AAE 1911-14. Later redefined by the USA.

**Mount Hordern.** 67°56'S, 62°29'E. 1,510 m. 4 miles south of Mount Coates in the David Range of the Framnes Mountains. Discovered in Feb. 1931 by the BANZARE, and named by Mawson for Sir Samuel Hordern (*see* **Cape Hordern**).

**Hordern Gap.** 67°53'S, 62°30'E. 3 miles wide. Between Mount Coates and Mount Hordern in the David Range of the Framnes Mountains. Photographed by the LCE 1936–37, and later named by the ANARE in association with the nearby mountain.

**Hordern Island** *see* **Cape Hordern**

**Hordern Peninsula** *see* **Cape Hordern**

**Horgebest Peak.** 72°34'S, 0°27'E. Just east of Fred Cirque in Roots Heights, Sverdrup Mountains in Queen Maud Land. Name means "mountain beast" in Norwegian.

**Horizon.** At the South Pole the horizon is 7 miles away.

**Horlick Ice Stream.** 85°17'S, 132°W. To the north of the main mass of the Horlick Mountains. Flows into the lower part of the Reedy Glacier. Named in association with the Horlick Mountains.

**Horlick Mountains.** 85°23'S, 121°W. East of Reedy Glacier in the Transantarctic Mountains. They include the Wisconsin Range, the Long Hills, and the Ohio Range. Parts of the mountains were discovered aerially by Kennett L. Rawson on Nov. 22, 1934, and other parts were discovered from the ground by Quin Blackburn in Dec. 1934, both times during the 1933–35 expedition of Admiral Byrd. Named by Byrd for William Horlick, of Horlick's Malted Milk Company, a supporter of this expedition.

**The Horn.** 63°39'S, 57°34'W. 220 m. Has a sheer cliff of red rock on its western side. Surmounts the NW cape of Eagle Island, in the Prince Gustav Channel, between Trinity Peninsula and Vega Island. Discovered and named descriptively by the FIDS in 1945.

**Horn Bluff.** 68°21'S, 149°45'E. A prominent rocky headland on the northern side of the coastal island at the western side of Deakin Bay. 325 meters high. It is marked by the columnar structure of the dolerite forming the upper part of it. Discovered and mapped as part of the mainland by the AAE 1911–14, and named by Mawson for W.A. Horn of Adelaide, a patron of the expedition. In 1962 aerial shots taken by the ANARE showed it to be on an island.

**Horn Peak** *see* **Kemp Peak**

**Hornblende Bluffs.** 69°54'S, 159°45'E. 1,050 m. 2 miles SE of Mount Ellery, and near the head of Suvorov Glacier, in the Wilson Hills. Named by the New Zealanders in 1963–64 for the hornblende found here.

**Mount Horne.** 75°46'S, 71°44'W. Also called Mount Bernard Horne. 1,165 m. Highest mountain in the Quilty Nunataks. 12 miles ENE of Mount Hassage in the eastern part of Ellsworth Land. Discovered by the RARE 1947–48, and named by Ronne for Bernard Horne of Pittsburgh, who furnished certain clothing for the expedition.

**Horne Glacier.** 71°17'S, 164°56'E. A valley glacier, 6 miles long. Flows from the Everett Range, between Mounts Works and Calvin, and enters the lower part of Greenwell Glacier. Named for Lt. Robert P. Horne, USNR, Hercules aircraft pilot in 1968 and 1969.

**Horne Nunataks.** 71°42'S, 66°46'W. 6 nunataks. On the north side of Goodenough Glacier. 7 miles inland from the west coast of Palmer Land. Named by the UK for Ralph R. Horne, BAS geologist at Base E and Base T during the 1964–65 season.

**Horner Nunatak.** 74°16'S, 72°45'W. 1 mile east of Staack Nunatak, in eastern Ellsworth Land. Named for Stanley Horner, radioscience researcher at Byrd Station, 1962–63.

**Hornet** *see* **Kemp Peak**

**Hornet Peak.** 72°12'S, 2°59'W. 3 miles west of Snøhetta Dome, near the south end of the Ahlmann Ridge in

Queen Maud Land. Name means "the horn" in Norwegian.

**Horney Bluff.** 80°09'S, 159°40'E. Ice-free. 15 miles long. Extends eastward along the north side of Byrd Glacier from Merrick Glacier toward Cape Kerr. Named for Capt. Harry R. Horney, Byrd's chief of staff during Operation Highjump, 1946–47.

**Horniston, Charles E.** Seaman on the Wilkes Expedition 1838–42. Joined at Rio. Run at Valparaiso.

**Horns.** Sharp, isolated peaks, created by two or more glaciers eating away rock on all sides of a mountain peak.

**Mount Hornsby.** 64°14'S, 59°15'W. Snow-capped. On the south side of the middle reaches of the Sjögren Glacier, Trinity Peninsula. Surveyed by the FIDS in 1960–61, and named by the UK for Richard Hornsby and Sons of Grantham, designers of the first caterpillar tractors.

**Horntind** see **Branson Nunatak**

**Horntvedt, Capt. Harald.** Skipper of the *Norvegia*, 1927–28.

**Horowitz Ridge.** 77°37'S, 162°05'E. Between David and King Valleys in the Asgard Range of Victoria Land. Named by biologist Roy E. Cameron in 1966–68 for Prof. Norman Horowitz, who suggested the Antarctica dry valleys–planet Mars analogy. Cameron was there to carry out these studies.

**Horrall Glacier.** 75°S, 114°28'W. In the Kohler Range of Marie Byrd Land. It flows from Faulkender Ridge into the Kohler Glacier at Klimov Bluff. Named for Thomas R. Horrall, glaciologist with the Marie Byrd Land Survey Party of 1966–67.

**Horrocks Block.** 71°35'S, 68°22'W. A large rectangular outcrop of mainly sandstone, on the north side of Venus Glacier, 2 miles SW of Keystone Cliffs, on the east side of Alexander Island. Named by the UK for Jeremiah Horrocks, the astronomer who first observed a transit of Venus, in 1639.

**Horsa Nunataks.** 68°56'S, 70°18'W. Isolated. 5 partly snow-covered nunataks. Over 610 m. On the Roberts Ice Piedmont, 14 miles north of Mount Calais, in the NE part of Alexander Island. Surveyed by the FIDS in 1948. Named by the UK for the 5th century Saxon chief.

**Horse Bluff.** 71°18'S, 67°34'W. On the west coast of Palmer Land.

**Horses.** Filchner took horses with him on his expedition of 1911–12. Shackleton and Scott were the principal exponents of the pony as a means of getting to the Pole (*see* **Ponies**).

**¹Horseshoe Bay** see **Lystad Bay**

**²Horseshoe Bay.** 77°32'S, 166°12'E. A cove just north of Cape Royds on the west side of Ross Island. Discovered and named descriptively by Scott's 1901–4 expedition.

**Horseshoe Harbor.** 67°36'S, 62°52'E. In Holme Bay, Mac. Robertson Land, it is formed by the horseshoe-shaped rock projections of West Arm and East Arm. Mawson Station is at the head of this harbor. Photographed by the LCE 1936–37. First visited by an ANARE party led by Phillip Law, who selected this as the site for Mawson Station. Named by Law for its shape.

**Horseshoe Island.** 67°51'S, 67°12'W. Also called Isla Herradura. 6½ miles long. 3 miles wide. Occupies most of the entrance to Square Bay, on the west coast of Graham Land. Discovered and named descriptively by the BGLE in 1936–37. Base Y was here.

**Horseshoe Island Cove** see **Lystad Bay**

**Horseshoe Islands** see **Forge Islands**

**Horseshoe Mountain.** 77°34'S, 159°57'E. Just west of Mount Fleming, on the north side of the head of Taylor Glacier, near the edge of the Polar Plateau in Victoria Land. Discovered and named descriptively by Scott's 1901–4 expedition.

**Horseshoe Nunatak.** 81°52'S, 158°25'E. 5 miles west of Mount Hoskins, on the north side of the upper portion of Starshot Glacier, in the Churchill Mountains. Charted and named descriptively by the New Zealanders in 1964–65.

**Horseshoe Valley.** 80°05′S, 82°W. Icefilled. In the southern Heritage Range. It is outlined by the semicircular arrangement of the Independence Hills, Marble Hills, Liberty Hills, and Enterprise Hills, hence the descriptive name.

**Horst.** A fault block belt, the classic example of which is the Great Antarctic Horst, more commonly known as the Transantarctic Mountains.

**Hortebrekka Slope.** 72°07′S, 12°34′E. A crevassed ice slope, which marks the eastern edge of Horteriset Dome, just west of the Weyprecht Mountains, in Queen Maud Land. Named by the Norwegians.

**Horteflaket Névé.** 71°56′S, 12°45′E. A névé at the head of Musketov Glacier, between the Petermann Ranges and the Weyprecht Mountains, in Queen Maud Land. Named by the Norwegians.

**Horten Peak.** 72°04′S, 3°11′E. 2,470 m. South of the summit of Risemedet Mountain in the Gjelsvik Mountains of Queen Maud Land. Named by the Norwegians.

**Horteriset Dome.** 72°05′S, 12°22′E. A broad, ice-covered hill 13 miles west of the south part of the Weyprecht Mountains in Queen Maud Land. Named by the Norwegians.

**Horton, W.A.** Lt. Cdr., RN. Chief engineer on the *Discovery II,* 1929–31.

**Horton Glacier.** 67°33′S, 68°30′W. On the west side of Graham Land.

**Horton Ledge.** 85°41′S, 69°05′W. Caps the SW end of the Pecora Escarpment in the Pensacola Mountains. Named for Edward C. Horton, Jr., electronics technician at Plateau Station, 1966.

**Horvath Island.** 66°19′S, 67°08′W. Just north of Watkins Island, in the Biscoe Islands. Named by the UK for Stephen M. Horvath, US physiologist specializing in the cold.

**Hoseason, James.** First mate on the *Sprightly,* 1824–25. He did a survey of Hughes Bay, Graham Land.

**Hoseason Glacier.** 67°06′S, 58°07′E. 12 miles long. Flows into the sea between West Stack and East Stack, 15 miles east of Edward VIII Bay. Photographed by the LCE 1936–37. Visited in 1954 by an ANARE sledging party and named by the Australians for Richard Hoseason of the ANARE, who died on Heard Island (53°S) in 1952.

**Hoseason Harbor** *see* **Mikkelsen Harbor**

**Hoseason Island.** 63°44′S, 61°41′W. 6 miles long. 3 miles wide. 20 miles west of Trinity Island, in the Palmer Archipelago. Named for James Hoseason.

**Hoshka Glacier** *see* **Hoshko Glacier**

**Hoshko Glacier.** 71°49′S, 163°24′E. Also spelled Hoshka Glacier. A cirque-type glacier in the Lanterman Range of the Bowers Mountains, flowing from between Bowers Peak and Mount Edixon into the lower part of the Canham Glacier. Named for Lt. John Hoshko, Jr., USNR, public affairs officer on the staff of the commander, US Naval Support Force, Antarctica, 1966–68.

**Mount Hoskins.** 81°50′S, 159°03′E. 2,030 m. On the west side of Starshot Glacier, 4 miles south of Mount Lindley. Discovered by Scott's 1901–4 expedition and named by them for Sir Anthony Hoskins, a member of the expedition's Ship Committee.

**Hoskins Peak.** 67°46′S, 67°36′W. 3 miles west of Contact Peak in southern Pourquoi Pas Island, Graham Land. Surveyed by the FIDS from 1956–59. Named by the UK for Arthur K. Hoskins, FIDS geologist at Base E in 1958, and at Base Y in 1959.

**Hospital Cove** *see* **Yankee Harbor**

**Hospital Point.** 62°32′S, 59°47′W. Also called Punta Alfaro. On the north side of Yankee Harbor, just east of Glacier Bluff, on Greenwich Island, in the South Shetlands. Charted and named

Rocky Point by personnel on the *Discovery II* in 1935. In order to avoid duplication, the UK rejected this name in 1961, and renamed it for Hospital Cove (*see* **Yankee Harbor**).

**Host Island.** 64°56′S, 63°55′W. Just SE of Manciple Island in the Wauwermans Islands, in the Wilhelm Archipelago. Named by the UK in 1958 for one of the *Canterbury Tales* characters.

**Hotels** *see* **Tourism**

**Mount Hotine.** 81°43′S, 160°E. 2 miles north of Mount McKerrow in the Surveyors Range. Named by the New Zealanders in 1960–61 for Martin Hotine (*see* **Hotine Glacier**).

**Hotine Glacier.** 65°08′S, 63°52′W. 10 miles long. Divided at its mouth by Mount Cloos. Flows into both Deloncle and Girard Bays, on the west coast of Graham Land. Charted by de Gerlache in 1897–99. Named by the UK in 1959 for Brigadier Martin Hotine, British director of Overseas Surveys.

**Hough Glacier.** 78°32′S, 84°20′W. In the SE part of the Sentinel Range, just south of Mount Tuck. It flows for 10 miles between the Guerrero and Remington Glaciers. Named for Willi S. Hough, ionosphere physicist at South Pole Station, 1957.

**Houk, Vernon N.** Lt. Took over as officer-in-charge of South Pole Station from John Tuck on Nov. 19, 1957. He was also the medical officer.

**Houk Spur.** 85°01′S, 64°45′W. Ice-free. Extends from the SW side of Mackin Table, 1 mile north of Mount Dumais, in the southern Patuxent Range of the Pensacola Mountains. Named for Lt. Vernon N. Houk.

**Mount Houlder** *see* **Houlder Bluff**

**Houlder Bluff.** 61°06′S, 54°51′W. Overlooks Point Wild on the north coast of Elephant Island in the South Shetlands. Named Mount Frank Houlder by Shackleton's 1914–17 expedition for the owner of the Houlder Steamship Line which assisted the expedition. Later

called Mount Houlder, and later still, redefined.

**Houle Island.** 66°42′S, 141°12′E. 1 mile west of Ressac Island, and 3½ miles NNE of Zélée Glacier Tongue. Charted by the French in 1949–51, and named by them because the surf (houle means swell in French) breaks over this low-lying island.

**Houliston Glacier.** 72°S, 164°34′E. Flows between Neall Massif and the West Quartzite Range into Black Glacier. Named by the New Zealanders in 1967–68 for R. Houliston, electrician at Scott Base that season.

**Hourglass Buttress.** 86°40′S, 146°28′W. In the Queen Maud Mountains.

**Hourglass Lake.** 77°21′S, 161°04′E. Small meltwater lake between Webb Lake and Lake Vashka in the Barwick Valley, Victoria Land. Named descriptively in 1964 by US geologist, Parker Calkin.

**Hourihan, John J.** Captain of the *Merrick* during Operation Highjump, 1946–47.

**Lake House.** 77°42′S, 161°24′E. In the extreme west end of the Pearse Valley, north of Friis Hills, in Victoria Land. Named by the VUWAE 1963–64, for D.A. House, chemist and member of this party.

**Houser Peak.** 68°22′S, 65°33′W. On the eastern side of Graham Land.

**Houston Glacier.** 70°34′S, 62°03′W. Flows from Eielson Peninsula into Smith Inlet, on the east coast of Palmer Land. Named for Robert B. Houston, USN, radioman at Palmer Station in 1973.

**Cap Houzeau de Lehaie** *see* **Lehaie Point**

**¹Hovde Bay.** 69°10′S, 39°45′E. On the east shore of Lützow-Holm Bay, just north of Langhovde Hills. Photographed by the LCE 1936–37, and named Hovdebukta (the knoll bay) by the Norwegians, in association with the hills nearby.

**²Hovde Bay** *see* **Hovde Cove**

**Hovde Cove.** 69°15′S, 76°50′E. Also called Hovde Bay, Amanda Bay. A small coastal re-entrant within Prydz Bay, just east of Flatnes Ice Tongue. Photographed by the LCE 1936–37, and named Hovdevika by the Norwegians.

**Hovde Glacier.** 69°15′S, 76°55′E. Just west of Brattstrand Bluffs on the SE shore of Prydz Bay. A short tongue from this glacier extends seaward to nearby Hovde Island. Photographed by the LCE 1936–37. In 1952, using photos taken during Operation Highjump, the US cartographer John H. Roscoe named it Hovde Ice Tongue, for the island. However it has since been redefined as a glacier.

**Hovde Ice Tongue** see **Hovde Glacier**

**Hovde Island.** 69°15′S, 76°52′E. In Prydz Bay, at the extremity of the small glacier tongue formed by Hovde Glacier. Photographed and named Hovden (the knoll), for its shape, by the LCE 1936–37.

**Hovdebrekka Slope.** 72°03′S, 11°48′E. A crevassed ice slope several miles long. It trends northeastward from Skeidshovden Mountain in the Wohlthat Mountains of Queen Maud Land. Name means "the knoll slope" in Norwegian.

**Hovdebukta** see **Hovde Bay**

**Hovdeknattane Rocks.** 72°07′S, 11°39′E. Jut out from the SW part of Hovdebrekka Slope, just north of Skeidshovden Mountain in the Wohlthat Mountains of Queen Maud Land. Name means "the knoll rocks" in Norwegian.

**Hovden** see **Hovde Island**

**Hovdeöyane** see **Stanton Group**

**Hovdeskar Gap.** 71°47′S, 11°39′E. Just east of Mount Skarshovden at the head of Skarsbrotet Glacier in the Humboldt Mountains of Queen Maud Land. Discovered during Ritscher's 1938–39 expedition. Name means "knoll gap" in Norwegian.

**Hovdevika** see **Hovde Cove**

**Hovgaard Island.** 65°08′S, 64°08′W. 3 miles long. 1½ miles SW of Booth Island,

in the Wilhelm Archipelago. Discovered and named Krogmann Insel by Dallmann, in Jan. 1874. De Gerlache independently called it Hovgaard Island in Feb. 1898, and this latter name stuck. This was the scene of Charcot's picnic (see Picnics).

**How, Walter E.** Able seaman on the *Endurance* during Shackleton's 1914–17 expedition. He later lived in London.

**Cape Howard.** 71°25′S, 61°08′W. Also called Cape Rusty. Flat-topped. Snow-covered. At the end of the peninsula separating Lamplugh and Odom Inlets, on the east coast of Palmer Land. Discovered in 1940 by the USAS. Named for August Howard, founder of the American Polar Society, and editor of the *Polar Times*.

**Mount Howard.** 75°40′S, 161°16′E. 1,460 m. 8 miles SE of Mount Joyce in the Prince Albert Mountains of Victoria Land. Discovered by Scott's 1901–4 expedition, who named it for Lord Howard de Walden, who helped Scott experiment with sledges before the expedition.

**Howard, A.** Hydrologist on the BANZARE 1929–31.

**Howard, Emanuel.** Ordinary seaman on the Wilkes Expedition 1838–42. Joined in the USA. Served the cruise.

**Howard, Patrick.** Mechanic on Ellsworth's 1935–36 expedition.

**Howard, W.E.** Crew member on the *Discovery* during the BANZARE 1929–31.

**Howard Bay.** 67°28′S, 61°04′E. Also called Ufsöyvågen. 2 miles wide. Between Byrd Head and Ufs Island. Discovered in Feb. 1931 by the BANZARE, and named by Mawson for A. Howard.

**Howard Glacier.** 77°40′S, 163°05′E. Small alpine glacier just west of Crescent Glacier. It flows from the Kukri Hills into the Taylor Valley, in Victoria Land. Named by Troy L. Péwé, the US glaciologist here in 1957, for Arthur D. Howard, geomorphologist at Stanford University, and glaciologist in Antarctica during Operation Highjump, 1946–47.

**Howard Heights.** 77°27'S, 151°40'W. A snow-covered coastal promontory rising to a height of 515 m. Between Stewart and Gerry Glaciers on the north side of the Edward VII Peninsula. Named by Byrd for Roy W. Howard of the Scripps-Howard Newspapers, patrons of Byrd's second expedition to Antarctica.

**Howard Hills.** 67°06'S, 51°09'E. Just south of Beaver Glacier in the NE part of the Scott Mountains in Enderby Land. They contain low hills and meltwater lakes. Named by the Australians for W.E. Howard.

**Howard Island.** 64°47'S, 64°23'W. Just south of Hartshorne Island in the eastern part of the Joubin Islands. Named for Judson R. Howard, mate on the *Hero* during its first voyage to Palmer Station in 1968.

**Howard Nunataks.** 77°30'S, 87°W. 15 nunataks off the extremity of the mountainous ridge at the NW corner of the Sentinel Range. Discovered aerially by Ellsworth on Nov. 23, 1935. Named for Patrick Howard.

**Howard Peaks.** 74°15'S, 163°42'E. At the south side of Tourmaline Plateau, running across the Deep Freeze Range, in Victoria Land. Named for Hugh C. Howard, cook at McMurdo Station, 1963–64, 1964–65, 1965–66, and 1966–67.

**Howchin Glacier.** 78°12'S, 163°22'E. Between the Ward and Walcott Glaciers, on the east side of the Royal Society Range in Victoria Land. Discovered by Grif Taylor's party during Scott's 1910–13 expedition, and named for Prof. W. Howchin, geologist of Adelaide.

**Mount Howe.** 87°22'S, 149°30'W. Also called Mount Louis McHenry Howe. 2,930 m. An elongated mountain at the east of the Robert Scott Glacier, near the head of that glacier, directly opposite Mount McIntyre. This is the most southerly mountain in the world. Discovered in Dec. 1934 by Quin Blackburn during Byrd's 1933–35 expedition. Named by

Byrd for Louis McHenry Howe, secretary to President Roosevelt.

**Howe Glacier.** 86°14'S, 149°12'W. Flows into the Robert Scott Glacier just north of Mount Russell, in the Queen Maud Mountains. Named for Robert C. Howe, VX-6 photographer in Antarctica, 1966 and 1967.

**Howell, John D.** Lt. cdr., USN. Plane commander and pilot of planes flying off the *Pine Island* during Operation Highjump, 1946–47.

**Howell Peak.** 70°58'S, 160°E. 1,750 m. At the NW end of the Daniels Range in the Usarp Mountains. Named for Kenneth R. Howell, meteorologist at Amundsen-Scott South Pole Station, 1967–68.

**Howison, James R.** Captain's clerk on the Wilkes Expedition 1838–42. Joined the *Vincennes* at Callao, and transferred to the *Relief* in 1839.

**Howkins, G.** Meteorologist at Base B, on Deception Island, during the second phase of Operation Tabarin, 1944–45.

**Howkins Inlet.** 73°40'S, 60°54'W. Ice-filled. Recedes SW 6 miles between Cape Brooks and Lamb Point, on the east coast of Palmer Land. Discovered aerially by the USAS in 1940. Named by the FIDS in 1947 for G. Howkins.

**Hoyt Head.** 74°59'S, 134°36'W. Headland which forms the NE end of Bowyer Butte, at the west side of the Venzke Glacier on the Marie Byrd Land coast. Discovered aerially in Dec. 1940 by the USAS from West Base. Named for Lt. Ronnie A. Hoyt, USNR, officer-in-charge of Byrd Station, 1971.

**The Hub**   *see*   **Hub Nunatak**

**Hub Nunatak.** 68°37'S, 66°05'W. Beehive-shaped. In the lower part of Lammers Glacier on the Antarctic Peninsula. Near the center of the Traffic Circle, and hence the name given by the USAS from East Base who discovered it in 1940.

**Mount Hubbard.** 72°08'S, 99°45'W. In the Walker Mountains. 6 miles east of Mount Noxon, on Thurston Island.

Named for Harold A. Hubbard, geologist on the *Burton Island* during the USN Bellingshausen Sea Expedition 1959–60.

**Hubbard, Edwin.** Seaman on the Wilkes Expedition 1838–42. Joined in the USA. Served the cruise.

**Hübl Peak.** 64°43'S, 62°29'W. West of Stolze Peak on Arctowski Peninsula, on the west coast of Graham Land. Named by the UK in 1960 for Artur von Hübl (1853–1932), Austrian surveyor who designed the first stereocomparator, in 1894.

**Mount Hubley.** 78°05'S, 86°46'W. Snow-covered. An outlying mountain to the west of Mount Hale, in the Sentinel Range. Named for Richard C. Hubley, glaciologist on the US National IGY Committee.

**Hubley Glacier**  *see*  **Joyce Glacier**

**Hubley Island**  *see*  **Berkner Island**

**Mount Huckaby.** 85°54'S, 127°03'W. Ice-free. Wedge-shaped. 2,620 m. Surmounts the eastern wall of the Olentangy Glacier, just east of Haworth Mesa, in the western Wisconsin Range. Named for Cdr. Donnie W. Huckaby, VX-6 maintenance officer at McMurdo Station in 1962–63 and 1963–64.

**Mount Huckle.** 69°38'S, 69°48'W. Mainly ice-covered. 2,500 m. Near the north end of the Douglas Range in eastern Alexander Island. 7 miles SSE of Mount Spivey on the west side of the Toynbee Glacier, and 9 miles inland from the George VI Sound. Surveyed by the FIDS in 1948, and named for Sydney R. Huckle, general assistant at Base E, 1948–49.

**Huddle Rocks.** 65°25'S, 64°59'W. 1½ miles NW of Symington Islands, in the Biscoe Islands. Named by the UK for the way the rocks are grouped.

**Hudman Glacier.** 78°54'S, 84°12'W. Between Marze Peak and Miller Peak at the south end of the Sentinel Range. It flows into Minnesota Glacier. Named for Capt. Rayburn A. Hudman (*see* **Deaths, 1956**).

**¹Cape Hudson.** 68°20'S, 153°45'E. Also called (by the USSR) Mys Voronina. At the northern end of the Mawson Peninsula, in George V Land. Capt. William L. Hudson, of the *Peacock*, sighted land in this area on Jan. 19, 1840, and his commander, Wilkes, first applied the name to a cape in the area. Later studies indicate that this is the cape that Wilkes called Hudson, even though looming (q.v.) caused him to chart it over 100 miles north of where it really is.

**²Cape Hudson**  *see*  **Cape Freshfield**

**Hudson, Henry.** Seaman on the Wilkes Expedition 1838–42. Joined in the USA. Served the cruise.

**Hudson, Hubert T.** b. 1886. Killed in action, 1942. Navigating officer on the *Endurance* during Shackleton's 1914–17 expedition. Later a commodore, RNR.

**Hudson, William H.** Midshipman on the *Peacock* during the Wilkes Expedition 1838–42.

**Hudson, William L.** He accepted the post of second-in-command of the Wilkes Expedition 1838–42, on June 16, 1838, and was also captain of the *Peacock* during the same voyage.

**Hudson Glacier.** 66°35'S, 125°23'E. Term no longer used.

**Hudson Island.** 66°39'S, 108°26'E. The largest of the Davis Islands. In the western part of Vincennes Bay. Named by the Australians for Capt. R. Hudson, leader of the helicopter team with ANARE, which was in the area in 1959–60.

**Hudson Mountains.** 74°25'S, 99°30'W. Also called Noville Mountains. 70 miles in extent. Just east of Cranton Bay and Pine Island Bay, at the eastern extremity of the Amundsen Sea. To the south of the Cosgrove Ice Shelf, and to the north of the Pine Island Glacier. Discovered on a flight from the *Bear* in Feb. 1940, during the USAS. Named for Capt. William L. Hudson.

**Hudson Nunatak.** 70°54'S, 65°17'E. 2½ miles west of Mount Bewsher in the

Aramis Range of the Prince Charles Mountains. Named by the Australians for Dr. J.W. Hudson, medical officer at Mawson Station, 1966.

**Hudson Ridge.** 83°47'S, 56°39'W. 5 miles long. 4 miles north of Heiser Ridge in the Neptune Range of the Pensacola Mountains. Named for Peter M. Hudson, aviation machinist at Ellsworth Station in 1958.

**Huemul Island.** 63°40'S, 60°50'W. Also called Islote Clavo, Megaptera Island. Off the north end of Trinity Island, in the Palmer Archipelago. Charted by Charcot, 1908–10. Named by the Chilean Antarctic Expedition of 1946–47 for the particular type of deer which appears on the Chilean national shield.

**Hueneme Glacier.** 85°49'S, 131°15'W. 8 miles long. Flows from the Wisconsin Range into the Reedy Glacier, between Griffith Peak and Mickler Spur. Named for Port Hueneme, California, home of the US Naval Support Force, Antarctica.

**Mount Huffman.** 75°19'S, 72°16'W. 4 miles NE of Mount Abrams, in the Behrendt Mountains of Ellsworth Land. Named for Jerry W. Huffman, scientific leader at Eights Station, 1963.

**Hufford, Lawrence.** Seaman on the Wilkes Expedition 1838–42. Joined in the USA. Sent home on the *Relief* in 1839.

**Hugershoff Cove.** 64°38'S, 62°23'W. 2 miles NW of Beaupré Cove in Wilhelmina Bay, on the west coast of Graham Land. Charted by de Gerlache in 1897–99. Named by the UK in 1960 for Carl R. Hugershoff (1882–1941), German aerial photography pioneer.

**Mount Huggins.** 78°17'S, 162°29'E. 3,735 m. Conical. Surmounts the heads of Allison, Dale, and Potter Glaciers in the Royal Society Range. Discovered by the Royal Society Expedition 1901–4, who named it for Sir William Huggins, president of the Royal Society 1900–5.

**Huggins, Francis G.** Seaman on the Wilkes Expedition 1838–42. Joined at the Sandwich Islands. Served the cruise.

**Huggler Peak.** 79°07'S, 84°41'W. Snow-covered. 1,580 m. In the northern part of the Anderson Massif, in the Heritage Range. Named for John Q. Huggler, USNR, storekeeper at McMurdo Station, 1966.

**Hugh Mitchell Peak** *see* **Mitchell Peak**

**Mount Hughes.** 79°31'S, 157°23'E. 2,250 m. Between Mount Longhurst and Tentacle Ridge in the Cook Mountains. Discovered by Scott's 1901–4 expedition, and named by them for J.F. Hughes, honorary secretary of the Royal Geographical Society, who helped prepare the expedition.

**Hughes, Arthur.** Private on the Wilkes Expedition 1838–42. Joined in the USA. Served the cruise.

**Hughes, Edward.** British sealer, commander of the *Sprightly,* in 1824–25. He did some charting.

**Hughes, Henry.** Ordinary seaman on the Wilkes Expedition 1838–42. Joined in the USA. Discharged at Oahu, Oct. 31, 1840.

**Hughes, John.** 2nd class boy on the Wilkes Expedition 1838–42. Joined at Callao. Run at Oahu.

**Hughes Bay.** 64°13'S, 61°20'W. Also called Hughes Gulf. Between Cape Sterneck and Cape Murray, on the west coast of the Antarctic Peninsula. Named for Edward Hughes. 20–25 miles wide, this is the site of the first landing on the actual continent, by John Davis, in 1821.

**Hughes Bluff.** 75°24'S, 162°12'E. 310 meters high. On the south side of David Glacier, 6 miles west of Cape Reynolds, in Victoria Land. Named for Garrett A. Hughes, researcher in cosmic radiation at McMurdo Station, 1966.

**Hughes Glacier.** 77°44'S, 162°27'E. Small alpine glacier flowing toward Lake Bonney in the Taylor Valley, from the Kukri Hills on the south, in Victoria

Land. Named by Grif Taylor's Western Geological Party during Scott's 1910–13 expedition for Prof. McKenny Hughes, Cambridge geologist.

**Hughes Gulf**  *see*  **Hughes Bay**

**Hughes Ice Piedmont.** 70°12′S, 62°15′ W. Between Cordini Glacier and Smith Inlet, on the east coast of Palmer Land. Named for Terence J. Hughes, glaciologist at Deception Island and McMurdo Sound in 1970–71, and at Deception Island in 1973–74.

**Hughes Island.** 70°44′S, 167°39′E. Ice-covered. The most easterly of the Lyall Islands. Just outside the eastern part of the entrance to Yule Bay in Victoria Land. Named for Lt. Ronald M. Hughes, USN, medical officer at McMurdo Station, 1966.

**Hughes Peninsula.** 71°52′S, 100°35′ W. Ice-covered. 18 miles long. West of Henry Inlet on the north side of Thurston Island. Named for Jerry Hughes, photographer's mate on the USN Bellingshausen Sea Expedition of 1959–60.

**Hughes Point.** 73°30′S, 94°16′W. On the west side of the terminus of Exum Glacier in the Jones Mountains. Named by the University of Minnesota–Jones Mountains Party of 1960–61 for Wayne B. Hughes, assistant USARP representative at McMurdo Station that season.

**Hughes Range.** 84°30′S, 175°30′E. Surmounted by 6 prominent summits, of which Mount Kaplan is the highest. East of Canyon Glacier in the Queen Maud Mountains. It extends 45 miles from the confluence of the Brandau and Keltie Glaciers in the south, to the Giovinco Ice Piedmont in the north. Discovered aerially by Byrd on Nov. 18, 1929, and named by Byrd for Charles Evans Hughes, secretary of state and chief justice of the USA, and Byrd's advisor and counselor.

**Hugi Glacier.** 66°11′S, 65°07′W. Flows into the head of Holtedahl Bay, on the west coast of Graham Land. Charted by the BGLE 1934–37. Named by the UK in 1959 for Franz J. Hugi (1796–1855), the father of winter mountaineering.

**Hugo Island.** 64°59′S, 65°46′W. Formerly called Victor Hugo Island. Ice-covered. 1 mile long. It has several rocky islands and pinnacles off its eastern side, in the western approach to Bismarck Strait. 40 miles west of Cape Monaco, Anvers Island. Charcot discovered and named it in 1903–5, for the novelist Victor Hugo.

**Isla Huidobro**  *see*  **Alpha Island**

**Huie Cliffs.** 83°19′S, 51°03′W. In the Pensacola Mountains.

**Isla Huinca**  *see*  **Wyatt Island**

**Cape Huinga.** 82°31′S, 165°10′E. Overlooks the Ross Ice Shelf, at the northern side of the mouth of the Robb Glacier. Named by the NZGSAE's Southern Party, 1959–60, who gathered here in Nov. 1959. (Huinga means gathering in Maori).

**Huitfeldt Point.** 65°59′S, 64°44′W. SE of Vorweg Point, on the SW side of Barilari Bay, on the west coast of Graham Land. Charted by the BGLE 1934–37. Named by the UK in 1959 for Fritz Huitfeldt, Norwegian ski pioneer.

**Hukuro Cove**  *see*  **Fukuro Cove**

**Hulcombe Ridge.** 70°24′S, 66°15′E. Extends 1½ miles in a north-south direction. 3 miles west of Wignall Peak in the Porthos Range of the Prince Charles Mountains. Named by the Australians for G.C. Hulcombe, diesel mechanic at Davis Station, 1962.

**Huldreskorvene Peaks.** 72°S, 6°05′E. Just north of Skorvehalsen Saddle and west of Tussenobba Peak in the Mühlig-Hofmann Mountains of Queen Maud Land. Named by the Norwegians.

**Huldreslottet Mountain.** 72°58′S, 3° 48′W. Ice-free. The most southerly summit in the Borg Massif of Queen Maud Land. Name means "the fairy castle" in Norwegian.

**Hull Bay.** 74°55′S, 137°40′W. Also called Cordell Hull Bay. Ice-filled. 25

miles wide. Fed by the Hull Glacier, which descends into the bay between Lynch Point and Cape Burks, on the coast of Marie Byrd Land. Discovered by the USAS 1939–41. Named in association with the glacier.

**Hull Glacier.** 75°05'S, 137°15'W. Also called Cordell Hull Glacier. 35 miles long. Flows between Mount Giles and Mount Gray into Hull Bay, in Marie Byrd Land. Discovered by the USAS 1939–41, and named for Cordell Hull, US secretary of state.

**Hulot Peninsula.** 64°29'S, 62°44'W. Forms the SW end of Brabant Island. Charted in 1903–5 by Charcot, who named it for Baron Hulot, a friend.

**Mount Hulshagen.** 72°31'S, 31°16'E. 2,100 m. 1 mile NW of Mount Bastin on the north side of the Belgica Mountains. Discovered by the Belgian Antarctic Expedition of 1957–58 under Gaston de Gerlache, who named it for Charles Hulshagen, vehicle mechanic with the expedition.

**Mount Hulth.** 66°41'S, 64°11'W. 1,470 m. On the west side of Cabinet Inlet, and south of the mouth of Friederichsen Glacier, on the east coast of Graham Land. It has sheer black cliffs on its east side. Charted by the FIDS in 1947, and named by them for J.M. Hulth, Swedish polar bibliographer.

**Hum Island.** 67°21'S, 59°38'E. Also called Sundholmen. In the William Scoresby Archipelago, between the western ends of Bertha Island and Islay. Discovered and named in Feb. 1936 by personnel on the *Discovery II*.

**Humann Point.** 64°24'S, 62°41'W. Forms the north side of the entrance to Duperré Bay on the west side of Brabant Island. Charted by Charcot 1903–5, and named by him for Vice-Adm. Humann of the French Navy.

**Mount Humble.** 67°40'S, 49°29'E. 1,450 m. Highest mountain in the Raggatt Mountains. Named by the Australians for J. Humble, cosmic ray physicist at Mawson Station in 1960.

**Humble Island.** 64°46'S, 64°06'W. Almost ½ mile SE of Norsel Point in Arthur Harbor, off the SW coast of Anvers Island, in the area of Palmer Station. Surveyed by the FIDS in 1955. Named by the UK in 1956 because of its insignificant position between Litchfield Island and the coast of Anvers Island.

**Humble Point.** 61°11'S, 54°08'W. 5 miles SW of Cape Lloyd on the west coast of Clarence Island in the South Shetlands. Named in the 1950s by the Argentines as Punta Baja (Low Point), but as this was rather a dull name, and repetitive of several others of similar names, the UK changed the name in 1971 to Humble Point.

**The *Humboldt*.** Took the first Peruvian Antarctic Expedition to the required latitude, in Jan.–March 1988, and conducted ecosystem studies in the Bransfield Strait.

**Humboldt Graben.** 71°45'S, 11°55'E. Glacier-filled. 20 miles long. Between the Humboldt Mountains and the Petermann Ranges in Queen Maud Land. Discovered aerially during Ritscher's 1938–39 expedition, and named by him in association with the mountains.

**Humboldt Mountains.** 71°45'S, 11°30' E. Also called Alexander Humboldt Mountains. Just west of the Petermann Ranges. They form the most westerly part of the Wohlthat Mountains in Queen Maud Land. Discovered by Ritscher's 1938–39 expedition, and named by them for Alexander von Humboldt, the founder of ecology.

**Humboldtsökket** *see* **Humboldt Graben**

**Humidity.** The absolute humidity in Antarctica is always very low, whereas the relative humidity can be quite high.

**Mount Hummel.** 74°28'S, 131°19'W. Snow-capped. In the east central part of Grant Island, off the Marie Byrd Land coast. Discovered and charted from the *Glacier* on Feb. 4, 1962. Named for Lt. (jg) William T. Hummel, USNR, helicopter pilot on the *Glacier* at the time.

**Mount Hummer.** 83°17'S, 50°06'W. In the Pensacola Mountains.

**Point Hummer.** 74°22'S, 110°15'W. On the eastern ridge of Bear Peninsula, Marie Byrd Land.

**¹Hummock Island** *see* **Heywood Island**

**²Hummock Island.** 65°53'S, 65°29'W. Also called Isla Mogote. 1 mile long. 4 miles west of Larrouy Island, and 5½ miles NW of Ferin Head, off the west coast of Graham Land. Discovered and named by the BGLE 1934–37.

**Hummocks.** In the Antarctic sense of the word, it means small hills or ridges of ice formed by pressure.

**¹The Hump.** 64°21'S, 63°15'W. Dome-shaped summit on the north shore of Lapeyrère Bay, in northern Anvers Island. Named descriptively.

**²The Hump** *see* **Hump Passage**

**Hump Island.** 67°36'S, 62°53'E. Just east of the East Arm of Horseshoe Harbor in Holme Bay, Mac. Robertson Land. Photographed by the LCE 1936–37. Later named by the ANARE for its appearance.

**Hump Passage.** 85°27'S, 170°12'W. A wide gap just SE of Barnum Peak. Liv Glacier flows off the Polar Plateau and then through this passage. Byrd called it The Hump when he flew over it on his way to the Pole in 1929. Renamed in 1961–62 by the New Zealanders.

**Humpback whale.** *Megaptera novaeangliae*, or *Megaptera nodosa*. Black baleen whale with long, narrow flippers, which frequents Antarctic waters. It is 40–50 feet long, and is an endangered species. In the 20th century a reported 68,294 have been killed.

**Mount Humphrey Lloyd.** 72°19'S, 169°27'E. Also called Mount Lloyd. 2,975 m. Between the heads of Towles Glacier and Manhaul Glacier in the Admiralty Mountains of Victoria Land. Discovered in 1841 by Ross, who named it for the Rev. Dr. Humphrey Lloyd, of Trinity College, Dublin, who had a great interest in the Antarctic.

**Humphreys Hill.** 67°14'S, 66°50'W. Between the mouths of Brückner Glacier and Antevs Glacier on Arrowsmith Peninsula, Graham Land. Named by the UK for William J. Humphreys (1862–1949), US meteorologist.

**Humphries Glacier.** 72°51'S, 168°50' E. Just east of Ingham Glacier, it flows into Borchgrevink Glacier just NW of Mount Prior in the Victory Mountains of Victoria Land. Named for John G. Humphries, NZ ionosphere scientist at Hallett Station, 1957.

**Humphries Heights.** 65°03'S, 63°52' W. Extend SW from False Cape Renard to Deloncle Bay, on the west coast of Graham Land. Charted by de Gerlache in 1897–99. Named by the UK in 1959 for Col. G.J. Humphries, deputy director of Overseas Surveys.

**Humps Island.** 63°59'S, 57°25'W. Also called Islote Giboso. ½ mile long. Has two summits near the west end. 4 miles SSE of the tip of The Naze, on James Ross Island. Discovered by Nordenskjöld's expedition of 1901–4. Surveyed by the FIDS in 1945, and named by the UK in 1948 for its shape.

**Hungary.** Ratified on Jan. 27, 1984, as the 29th signatory of the Antarctic Treaty. It has established no presence on the continent.

**¹Mount Hunt** *see* **Hunt Mountain**

**²Mount Hunt.** 67°07'S, 144°18'E. 520 m. Dome-shaped. Surmounts the promontory which terminates in Cape de la Motte. Discovered by the AAE 1911–14, and named by Mawson for H.A. Hunt (*see* **Hunt Glacier**).

**Hunt, James.** Private on the Wilkes Expedition 1838–42. Joined in the USA. Served the cruise.

**Hunt Bluff.** 74°37'S, 111°46'W. 3 miles long. 2 miles south of Jeffrey Head on the west side of the Bear Peninsula in Marie Byrd Land. Named for Lt. Robert B. Hunt, USNR, medical officer at Byrd Station, 1966.

**Hunt Glacier.** 76°52'S, 162°25'E. On the east coast of Victoria Land, it flows into Granite Harbor north of Dreikanter Head. Named by Scott's 1910–13 expedition for H.A. Hunt, Australian meteorologist who had helped write up the scientific reports of Shackleton's 1907–9 expedition.

**Hunt Island** *see* **Papua Island**

**Hunt Mountain.** 82°05'S, 159°16'E. Also called Mount Hunt. 3,240 m. In the northern part of the Holyoake Range. It is the highest point in that range. Named by the NZGSAE 1960–61 for Capt. P.J. Hunt, Royal Engineers, leader of the southern party of the expedition that year.

**Hunt Nunataks.** 70°11'S, 64°53'E. A 2 mile-long line of nunataks, just east of Mount Béchervaise in the Athos Range of the Prince Charles Mountains. Named by the Australians for P. Hunt, helicopter pilot here in 1969.

**Hunt Peak.** 67°18'S, 68°02'W. 610 m. Marks the northern side of the entrance to Stonehouse Bay on the east coast of Adelaide Island. Discovered and surveyed by Charcot in 1909. In 1948 the FIDS resurveyed it and named the point on which it then stood as Hunt Point, for Sgt. Kenneth D. Hunt, mechanic for the FIDS Norseman airplane in 1950. In 1957–58 the FIDS found no appreciable point in the area, and transferred the name to the peak.

**Hunt Point** *see* **Hunt Peak**

**Hunt Spur.** 85°59'S, 146°50'W. Descends from Mount Warden, along the NW face of the Watson Escarpment. Named for Glenn C. Hunt, aviation electronics technician with VX-6, who was in the Antarctic five summers with Operation Deep Freeze.

**Cape Hunter.** 66°57'S, 142°21'E. On the west shore of Commonwealth Bay, 8 miles west of Cape Denison. Discovered in 1912 by the AAE, and explored in 1913 by Mawson, who named it for John G. Hunter.

**Mount Hunter.** 64°05'S, 62°24'W. 1,410 m. 4 miles WSW of Duclaux Point

on Pasteur Peninsula, Brabant Island. Named by the UK for John Hunter, the Scottish surgeon.

**Hunter, John G.** Chief biologist on the AAE 1911–14.

**Hunter Glacier.** 71°44'S, 163°E. 7 miles long. Flows from the central part of the Lanterman Range in the Bowers Mountains, and enters Rennick Glacier at Mount Lugering. Named for Lt. Cdr. William G. Hunter, executive and operations officer at McMurdo Station, 1964.

**The *Huntress*.** 2-masted American sealing schooner of 80 tons, 68 feet long, built in Barnstable, Mass., in 1817. Left Nantucket on Aug. 4, 1820, bound for the South Shetlands, with Capt. Christopher Burdick commanding, William Coleman first mate, and a total crew of about 15. Burdick was one of four owners. On Nov. 22, 1820, at the Falklands, it teamed up with the *Huron* and the *Cecilia,* and finally left Antarctica on March 10, 1821, arriving back in Nantucket on June 10, 1821.

**Huntress Glacier.** 62°41'S, 60°17'W. Flows into the head of False Bay, Livingston Island, in the South Shetlands. Named by the UK in 1958 for the *Huntress.*

**Huon Bay.** 63°23'S, 58°W. 8 miles wide, between Cape Ducorps and Cape Legoupil, on the north coast of Trinity Peninsula. Dumont d'Urville named a cape in this area Cap Huon, for Félix Huon de Kermadec (*see* **De Kermadec**). In 1946 the FIDS, failing to find the cape, gave the name to this bay.

**Hurd Peninsula.** 62°41'S, 60°23'W. Between South Bay and False Bay on the south coast of Livingston Island in the South Shetlands. Named by the UK in 1961 for Capt. Thomas Hurd, RN, second hydrographer to the admiralty, 1808–23.

**Cape Hurley.** 67°36'S, 145°18'E. Ice-covered. Marks on the east the mouth of the depression occupied by the Mertz Glacier. Discovered by the AAE 1911–14, and named by Mawson for Frank Hurley.

**Mount Hurley.** 66°17'S, 51°21'E. Snow-covered massif with steep, ice-free slopes. 7 miles south of Cape Ann and 3 miles south of Mount Biscoe. Discovered in Jan. 1930 by the BANZARE, and named by Mawson for Frank Hurley.

**Hurley, Frank.** b. 1885, Sydney. d. 1962, Sydney. James Francis Hurley. Captain Frank Hurley, or "Cap," was the dominant Australian documentary filmmaker (of all time, probably). In 1911 he went to the Antarctic with Mawson on the AAE 1911–14. In 1915 he was stranded with Shackleton after the *Endurance* went down on the British Imperial Transantarctic Expedition. On one occasion "Cap" dived into the water to save his negatives. He was south with Mawson again during the BANZARE 1929–31, and wrote the books *Argonauts of the South* in 1925, and *Shackleton's Argonauts* in 1948. Tony Buckley made a documentary about his life in 1973 called *Snow, Sand and Savages.* Hurley's Antarctic documentaries were *Home of the Blizzard/Dr. Mawson in the Antarctic/Life in the Antarctic* (1913 — official year of production); *In the Grip of Polar Ice* (1917); *Southward Ho with Mawson* (1929); *Siege of the South/With Mawson to the Frozen South* (1931); *Endurance* (1933 — a rerelease of *In the Grip of Polar Ice*); *Antarctic Pioneers* (1962 — co-photographed and narrated only).

**Hurley Glacier.** 67°34'S, 68°32'W. On the west side of Graham Land.

**The *Huron*.** Square-rigged American sealing ship of 250 tons, 89⅔ feet long, built at Guilford, Conn., in 1819. Owned by 19 persons, it was registered at New Haven, and sailed from there on March 20, 1820, with a 31-man crew, commanded by John Davis. Samuel H. Goddard, first mate; Charles Philips, second mate. Bound for the South Shetlands it met the *Huntress* at the Falkland Islands on Nov. 11, 1820, and Davis constructed the *Cecilia* as a tender from a kit he had brought with him on the *Huron.* On Nov. 22, 1820, the three vessels sailed together for the sealing grounds of the South Shetlands for the 1820–21 season. The *Huron* and the *Cecilia* left Antarctica for the Falklands on March 30, 1821, and the 2 vessels were back in the South Shetlands for the 1821–22 season. They left finally on Feb. 17, 1822, and, going via the Falklands again, arrived home on June 17, 1822.

**Huron Glacier.** 62°38'S, 60°02'W. Flows into Moon Bay, Livingston Island, in the South Shetlands. Named by the UK in 1958 for the *Huron.*

**Hurst Peak.** 79°34'S, 84°35'W. 1,790 m. At the south end of Webers Peaks in the Heritage Range. Named by the University of Minnesota Geological Party, 1963–64, for aviation machinist James E. Hurst, crew member on the LC-47 which made the first 1963–64 flight to the Ellsworth Mountains.

**Huskies** *see* **Dogs**

**Husky Dome** *see* **Husky Heights, Husky Massif**

**Husky Heights.** 84°53'S, 176°E. Also called Husky Dome. Flat. Ice-covered. 4 miles SE of Haynes Table, overlooking the head of Brandau Glacier in the Queen Maud Mountains. Named by the NZGSAE 1961–62 for their husky dog teams, which they drove to the summit of these heights.

**Husky Massif.** 71°S, 65°09'E. 2,100 m. 2½ miles long. 6½ miles SW of Mount Bewsher in the Aramis Range of the Prince Charles Mountains. First seen from Mount Bewsher by an ANARE field party in Jan. 1957, and named Husky Dome to commemorate the husky dogs used by the party. In 1970 the Australians redefined the feature slightly.

**Husky Pass.** 71°40'S, 163°34'E. Between Lanterman Range and Molar Massif in the Bowers Mountains. At the head of Sledgers Glacier. Named by the New Zealanders in 1963–64 for the husky dog teams, whose bravery and devotion made possible the conquest of much of the continent.

**Mount Hussey.** 72°46'S, 167°31'E. 2,790 m. On the spur at the head of Gruendler Glacier in the Victory Mountains of Victoria Land. Named for Keith M. Hussey, geologist at McMurdo Station, 1966–67.

**Hussey, L.D.A.** Assistant surgeon and meteorologist on Shackleton's last two expeditions. He played his banjo for his 21 mates on Elephant Island in 1916 while they waited for Shackleton. He also informed Lady Shackleton of her husband's death. He was later a doctor in England.

**Husted, George.** Quartermaster on the Wilkes Expedition 1838–42. Joined in the USA. Discharged at Oahu, Nov. 2, 1840.

**Hut Cove.** 63°24'S, 56°59'W. Also called Caleta Choza. In the eastern part of Hope Bay, between Seal Point and Grunden Rock, at the NE end of the Antarctic Peninsula. Discovered by J. Gunnar Andersson's party during the Nordenskjöld expedition of 1901–4. Named in 1945 by the FIDS not only for their own hut here, but also for the Swedes' hut in 1903.

**Hut Point.** 77°51'S, 166°38'E. 1 mile NW of Cape Armitage, at the south end of Hut Point Peninsula. Discovered in 1902 by Scott and named by him for his hut (the Discovery Hut).

**Hut Point Peninsula.** 77°46'S, 166°51'E. Long and narrow. Between 2 and 3 miles wide, and 15 miles long. Projects SW from the slopes of Mount Erebus on Ross Island. The Royal Society Expedition 1901–4 built its hut here, at Hut Point, and the peninsula itself took on various names over the next decade, i.e., Winterquarters Peninsula and Cape Armitage Promontory. It was not until Scott's second expedition, 1910–13, that the peninsula became known by its present name. McMurdo Station and Scott Base are both here.

**Hut Point Road.** Antarctica's most famous road, it leads out of McMurdo

Station for Scott Base and Williams Field. Built by the Americans.

**Mount Hutago** *see* **Mount Futago**

**Hutcheson, Guy.** Radio engineer in Byrd's shore party during the 1933–35 expedition.

**Hutcheson Nunataks.** 76°17'S, 143°27'W. On the north side of Balchen Glacier, between the Phillips Mountains and Abele Nunatak, in Marie Byrd Land. Discovered by the USAS 1939–41. Named for Guy Hutcheson.

**Hutchinson Island.** 76°47'S, 148°53'W. Ice-covered. 15 miles long. 10 miles east of Vollmer Island in the Marshall Archipelago. Named for Lt. (jg) Peter A. Hutchinson, USN, operations officer on the *Glacier* along this coast in 1961–62.

**Hutchison Hill.** 66°56'S, 65°42'W. 1½ miles NE of Lampitt Nunatak on Avery Plateau, Graham Land. Readily visible from Darbel Bay. Named by the UK in 1960 for Sir Robert Hutchison, British nutritionist.

**Hutt Peak.** 76°01'S, 132°39'W. Snow-covered. In the central part of the Mount Bursey massif, in Marie Byrd Land. Named for Charles R. Hutt, seismologist at Amundsen-Scott South Pole Station, 1970.

**Hutto Peak.** 79°17'S, 85°53'W. 1,620 m. Just below the Founders Escarpment, between the upper parts of the Gowan and Splettstoesser Glaciers, in the Heritage Range. Named for Chief Yeoman Grey H. Hutto, USN, in Antarctica in 1964–65 and 1965–66.

**Hutton Cliffs.** 77°44'S, 166°51'E. On the west side of Hut Point Peninsula on Ross Island, about 2 miles north of Ford Rock. Discovered by Scott's 1901–4 expedition, and named by Scott for Captain Hutton of the Canterbury Museum, NZ.

**Hutton Mountains.** 74°12'S, 62°20'W. In SE Palmer Land. Bounded on the SW by Johnston Glacier; on the NW by Squires Glacier; on the north by Swann Glacier; on the east by Keller Inlet.

Named by the USA for James Hutton (1726–1797), Scottish geologist.

**Isla Hyatt** *see* **Laktionov Island**

**Mount Hyatt.** 74°53'S, 64°47'W. In the southern part of the Latady Mountains. 5 miles west of Schmitt Mesa, in Palmer Land. Named for Gerson Hyatt, builder at McMurdo Station, 1967. He helped build Plateau Station that year.

**Hyde, William.** Carpenter's mate on the Wilkes Expedition 1838–42. Joined in the USA. Served the cruise.

**Hyde Glacier.** 79°48'S, 83°42'W. Flows through the Edson Hills into the Union Glacier, in the Heritage Range. Named for William H. Hyde, ionosphere physicist at Little America in 1958.

**Hydrodist Rocks.** 63°44'S, 60°55'W. Four rocks, one dries at low tide and two are submerged. 4 miles west of Trinity Island in the Palmer Archipelago. Their position was fixed in Jan. 1964 by a helicopter-borne hydrodist off the *Protector.*

**Hydrographer Islands.** 67°23'S, 48°50' E. Also called Field Islands. Just south of Sakellari Peninsula, Enderby Land. Named Ostrova Hidrografov (Hydrographer Islands) by the USSR. They include McIntyre Island.

**Hydrozoans** *see* **Sessile Hydrozoans**

**Hydrurga Rocks.** 64°08'S, 61°37'W. East of Two Hummock Island in the Palmer Archipelago. Named by the UK in 1960 for the leopard seal *(Hydrurga leptonyx).*

**Hyperion Nunataks.** 72°04'S, 68°55' W. 10 nunataks south of Saturn Glacier. 8 miles west of Corner Cliffs, in the SE part of Alexander Island. Discovered aerially on Nov. 23, 1935, by Ellsworth, and surveyed in 1949 by the FIDS. Named by the UK for Hyperion, one of the planet Saturn's satellites.

**Ian Peak.** 71°31'S, 164°E. 3 miles NW of Mount Stirling, in the Bowers Mountains. Overlooks the heads of Leap Year Glacier and Champness Glacier. Named by the New Zealanders in 1968 for Ian Smith, NZ scientist in Antarctica that year.

**Iapetus Nunatak.** 71°36'S, 70°15'W. An isolated nunatak at the SW edge of Satellite Snowfield, between the Walton Mountains and the Staccato Peaks, in the southern part of Alexander Island. Named by the UK for the satellite of the planet Saturn.

**Ibar, Mario.** Lt. Chilean army officer who signed the official act of inauguration of Capitán Arturo Prat Station on Greenwich Island in 1947.

**Ibar Rocks.** 62°27'S, 59°43'W. To the immediate east of Canto Point, Greenwich Island, in the South Shetlands. The Chileans named the larger, western one of the group as Islote Ibar, or Islote Teniente Ibar, for Mario Ibar. The name Ibar Rocks was later used to take in not only the two visible rocks, but also a submerged rock nearby to the NE.

**Icarus Point** *see* **Cañón Point**

**Ice.** Frozen water. There are about 7 million cubic miles of ice in Antarctica, which is more than 90 percent of all the world's ice. 97.6 percent of Antarctica is ice and snow, the average thickness of which is 6,500 feet. (*See also* **Glaciers, Icebergs, Ice shelves, Depth of ice,** and related entries.)

**Ice barrier.** The old name for an ice shelf.

**Ice Bay** *see* **Amundsen Bay**

**The *Ice Bird*.** David Lewis's 10 meter steel sloop in which, in 1972–73, he sailed alone to Antarctica. It had a plastic dome which enabled Lewis to look out while sheltered below. On Nov. 29, 1972, at 60°S, he had his first capsize, and on Dec. 13, 1972, at 61°S, his second. The mast and the self-steering mechanism were smashed, and on Jan. 29, 1973, Lewis made it to Palmer Station, and the boat was repaired by Lewis and the Americans there. Lewis left Antarctica, and returned for his boat in Nov.

1973, did a tour in it, and then set sail for Cape Town.

**Ice blink.** A whiteness in the sky caused by the reflection of ice ahead.

**Ice budget.** Net surface ice accumulation + inflow of land ice + increments by bottom freezing, minus calved ice, minus bottom melting, minus surface melting.

**Ice caps.** An ice cap is smaller than an ice sheet, and is a dome-shaped glacier covering a highland area less than 50,000 square kilometers in size. Ice caps were formed millions of years ago, and are drifting 27.3 feet per annum, in the direction of 43°W.

**Ice core** *see* **Core samples**

**Ice crystals.** Minute crystals of ice which fill the air at the South Pole and environs. In the summertime they cause the phenomena (q.v.) of refraction, some of which are seen in Antarctica.

**Ice feet.** Fringes of ice found on the coast. They are usually formed by sea spray, and do not answer to tidal movement. There are notable ones at Cape Evans and at Land's End.

**Ice fish.** *Cryocraco antarcticus.* Coastal fish (*see also* **Fauna, Fish**).

**Ice-free areas.** Between 1 and 5 percent of Antarctica is ice-free, and not all of these areas have yet been discovered. The largest ice-free area is the Ross Desert (q.v.). *See also* **Lakes** (some lakes have unfrozen water), **Oases, Dry valleys.**

**Ice fumaroles.** A fumarole is a secondary vent in the side of a volcano, from which issue gasses and water vapor. Ice fumaroles are the result of condensation and freezing of the water vapor around and above fumaroles located in Antarctic volcanoes.

**Ice islands** *see* **Icebergs**

**Ice needles.** Also called ice prisms. Very small, hexagonal, unbranched ice crystals, in the form of columns, shafts, or plates. They are formed only at very low temperatures. When reflecting sunlight they are called diamond dust (q.v.).

**Ice pack** *see* **Pack-ice**

**Ice piedmont.** A broad area of lowland ice fed by two or more valley glaciers.

**Ice prisms** *see* **Ice needles**

**Ice rind.** A shiny skin of new ice formed from grease ice, or by direct freezing.

**Ice rise.** A dome-shaped feature created by a rock feature beneath it. Usually found on an ice shelf.

**Ice sheets.** Large masses of perennial ice on land. Must be more than 50,000 square kilometers in area, otherwise they are ice caps.

**Ice shelves.** Large, semipermanent, glacier-fed areas of ice attached firmly to the continent, but with no bedrock below. Formerly called ice barriers, because they blocked the way to the South Pole. The biggest is the Ross Ice Shelf.

**Ice streams.** Large glacier-type flows of ice. They differ from glaciers in that glaciers are bounded and their flow is ordered by rock, while the ice streams are so influenced by ice sheets.

**Ice tongues.** Tongues of ice jutting out into the sea from an ice shelf. They differ from glacier tongues, in that they are not the seaward extensions of glaciers.

**Iceberg Alley.** There are two places in Antarctica with this name, or rather, nickname. Both are spectacular showcases for scores of bergs going north. One is just outside Vincennes Bay, and the other is in the Lemaire Channel, off the west coast of the Antarctic Peninsula.

**Iceberg Bay.** 60°39'S, 45°32'W. 3 miles wide. Indentation in the south coast of Coronation Island, in the South Orkneys, between Cape Hansen and Olivine Point. Named by Matthew Brisbane in 1823.

**Iceberg Point.** 64°38'S, 63°06'W. 8 miles WSW of Ryswick Point, on the east side of Anvers Island. First mapped by de Gerlache in 1897–99. Named before 1927.

**Icebergs.** Large chunks of ice split off, or calved, from the ice shelves or ice tongues of Antarctica. 138 cubic miles of iceberg are calved from Antarctica every year (although see B-9). This ice then floats, normally as far north as 40°S, although one was spotted as far north as 26°30′S in the Atlantic in 1894. As icebergs age they disintegrate and turn pale blue. Bottle-green icebergs are rare, but one notable one was seen in Moon Bay on March 10, 1976. Seven-eighths of an iceberg is below water, and partly because of this, bergs are a danger to shipping. Even a small one, with its jagged, rocklike edges, can rip open a ship's hull. The largest ones are the tabular bergs (q.v.), one of which was larger than Belgium. What the early sailors called icebergs were often glaciers, and what we call icebergs they often called ice islands (*see also* **Rotten Bergs**).

The *Icebird.* Australian icebreaker which, in late 1985 tried to assist the trapped *Nella Dan* off Enderby Land, but almost got caught itself in the 13-foot-thick pack-ice. On Jan. 6, 1986, it reached the South Magnetic Pole.

**Icebreaker Glacier.** 73°37′S, 166°10′E. A valley glacier. 10 miles NE of Mount Monteagle. Flows from the Mountaineer Range in Victoria Land, and feeds Lady Newnes Bay. Named by the New Zealanders in 1959 for the icebreaker ships of Antarctica.

**Icebreakers.** Clumsy vessels which lead modern Antarctic convoys. As over 95 percent of the matériel used by USAP is delivered to Antarctica by ship, the main purpose of the icebreakers is to free the way through the pack-ice for the supply ships to get to the bases. Icebreakers have no keels, but barrel-shaped hulls that prevent the ships from being crushed if the ice moves in. As the ice presses in from both sides, the hull pops up and out of the water. They do not have sharp bows, and do not cut the ice, but rather charge it, crushing it with the weight of the vessel. They chop out berths in the ice for other ships. Some used to have an extra propellor in front, to suck the water out of the ice shelf in order to make it easier to crack the ice, but these propellors were subject to damage, so now the standard icebreaker still has the step on the front (formerly to hold the propellor), just like it does in the rear, which enables the ship to give the ice an extra bang, from both ends. The *Glacier* is the world's largest icebreaker, and the USA has been using icebreakers in Antarctica since Operation Highjump, 1946–47. The main one belonging to Argentina is the *General San Martín,* which first went to Antarctica in 1954, and Japan has had three—the *Soya* (during IGY), the *Fuji* (launched in 1965), and the *Shirase* (from 1983). The USSR has its own, as do the British and others.

**Icefall Nunatak.** 78°18′S, 158°38′E. 1,760 m. Ice-free. In the area of the Skelton Icefalls. Named in 1964.

**Icenhower, Joseph,** Cdr., USN. Captain of the *Sennett* during Operation Highjump, 1946–47.

**Iceports.** Term coined by the Americans in 1956. An iceport is an indentation, more or less permanent but subject to change in configuration, in ice shelves. It offers anchorage to a ship and offers access to the shelf itself by one or more natural ice ramps. Atka Iceport is the most well known.

**Ichime Glacier.** 68°23′S, 42°08′E. Also called Itime Glacier. Feeds the coast of Queen Maud Land just west of Kasumi Rock. Named by the Japanese.

**Ickes Mountains.** 75°30′S, 139°35′W. In Marie Byrd Land. Discovered aerially on Dec. 18, 1940, by the USAS. Named for Harold L. Ickes, who served as US secretary of the interior from 1933–46. Although Ickes objected, the name became official in 1966.

**Mount Ida.** 83°34′S, 170°29′E. 1,565 m. A bare rock mountain, 2 miles west of Granite Pillars, in the Queen Alexandra Range, just to the east of the Beardmore Glacier. Discovered by Shackleton's expedition of 1907–9, and named by

Shackleton for Ida Jane Rule of Christchurch, NZ, who later married Edward Saunders, secretary to Shackleton while the explorer worked on his book.

**Idun Peak.** 77°38′S, 161°26′E. Between Mount Thundergut and Veli Peak in the Asgard Range of southern Victoria Land. Named for the Norse goddess.

**Ifo Island.** 66°38′S, 139°44′E. At the west end of the Géologie Archipelago. Charted and named by Liotard in 1951. The name comes from the French expression "il faut," meaning "one must."

**Igloo Hill.** 64°33′S, 61°47′W. 280 m. Completely ice-covered. In the central part of Reclus Peninsula, on the west coast of Graham Land. Named by the UK in 1960.

**Igloo Spur.** 77°33′S, 169°16′E. 160 m. A mile south of Cape Crozier, on Ross Island. Named for Wilson's stone igloo here. He called it Oriana Ridge, and his hut he called Oriana Hut, for his wife, Oriana.

**IGY** *see* **International Geophysical Year**

**Il Polo Glacier.** 69°50′S, 74°45′E. Feeds the Publications Ice Shelf, and flows between the Polar Times Glacier and the Polarforschung Glacier on the Ingrid Christensen Coast. Named in 1952 by US cartographer John H. Roscoe for the Italian polar journal, *Il Polo.*

**Iliad Glacier.** 64°27′S, 63°27′W. Feeds Lapeyrère Bay from the central highlands of Anvers Island. Flows between the Achaean Range and the Trojan Range. Surveyed in 1955 by the FIDS, and named by the UK for Homer's epic poem.

**The M.V.** *Illiria.* Lindblad Travel's ship of 1987–88. Built in Italy in 1962, rebuilt in 1982 and 1985, it was certified by the American Bureau of Shipping in 1986. Registered in Greece, with Piraeus as its home port, its official # is 5588. It is 333 feet long, 48 feet wide, with a maximum draft of 17 feet. It has a displacement tonnage of 3,755, and a deadweight tonnage of 950. It has two 2,900 hp engines, and a cruising speed of 15.5 knots. It has 3 decks—Lido, Promenade

and Main, has 83 officers and crew, and can accommodate 140 guests. It is equipped with Denny-Brown stabilizers and other modern equipment. Lindblad replaced it in 1988–89 with the *Antonina Nezhdanova.* The *Illiri* was then hired by Travel Dynamics.

**Illusion Hills.** 73°28′S, 162°18′E. Small, escarpmentlike hills between the Lichen Hills and the Vantage Hills, at the head of the Rennick Glacier in Victoria Land. Named by the New Zealanders in 1963 because of their illusory distance.

**Mount Imbert.** 72°34′S, 31°28′E. 2,495 m. In the eastern part of the Belgica Mountains. Discovered by the Belgians in 1958, and named by them for Bertrand Imbert.

**Imbert, Bertrand.** French seismologist. Was in Adélie Land in 1951. Led the French Polar Expedition of 1955–56, and was leader of the 1957 wintering party at Dumont d'Urville Station. He was the first French representative to SCAR, in 1958.

**Mount Imhotep.** 64°21′S, 62°24′W. In the southern part of Brabant Island, near the head of Hippocrates Glacier. De Gerlache was the first to map it, in 1897–99, and it was remapped in 1959. Named by the UK for the Egyptian historical personage.

**Imshaug Peninsula.** 70°53′S, 61°35′W. Snow-covered. On the south side of Lehrke Inlet, on the east coast of Palmer Land. Mapped by the Americans in 1974. Named for Henry A. Imshaug, biologist in Antarctica in the 1960s and 1970s.

**In the Footsteps of Scott Expedition.** 1985–86. The expedition which proved that heroes like Scott and Amundsen still exist, most notably in the form of Robert Swan, the leader of this expedition. It took Swan 4 years to get this expedition together, at a cost of $4 million, with over 1,000 sponsors. What Swan wanted to do was duplicate Scott's last expedition as much as possible and to eschew the benefits of the modern world as best he could, in order to get a taste of what it was like for Scott to have gone to the Pole, and also to see whether he, Swan, could do it too. They trained for a year, and then left England in the *Southern Quest,* their supply ship. The ship, with 29 people aboard, followed the *Terra Nova's* 1910 course exactly, to Cape Evans, Ross Island. 5 men disembarked, Swan, Roger Mear, Gareth Wood, Mike Stroud (the doctor), and John Tolson, and set up Jack Hayward Base. On June 28, 1985, Wood, Mear, and Stroud went to Cape Crozier, duplicating the "worst journey in the world" undertaken many years before by Wilson, Bowers, and Cherry-Garrard. They returned to Jack Hayward Base on July 26, 1985. Originally Swan and Mear were the two scheduled to ski to the Pole, but they quarreled all the time, so a third was picked at the last moment, to keep the peace. This was Wood. Stroud and Tolson remained at Base. On Oct. 26, 1985, the Polar party set out, manhauling 42-pound sledges containing 311 pounds of equipment and supplies each. They carried their rubbish, in order not to despoil Antarctica. No radios. No dogs. No air support. Just the way it was done in 1911—with the only difference being in the number of men and the knowledge that the Pole was there (Scott did not have this luxury. He was going into the unknown. There should be a psychological equation which proves how much more difficult this makes such a venture). Averaging 12 to 15 miles a day, they arrived safely at Amundsen-Scott South Pole Station at 11:53 p.m. on Jan. 11, 1986. There they got the news that the *Southern Quest* was sinking in McMurdo Sound. Crushed by the ice, it went down a few minutes after Swan's party arrived at the Pole. The 3 Polarfarers were looked after at Amundsen-Scott, and then flown back to McMurdo Station in an LC-130 Hercules. On Jan. 15, 1986, 26 of the expedition members returned to Christchurch, NZ, on a US flight, while 3 stayed on at Ross Island to winter-over for 1986 and to clean up Jack Hayward Base. USAP billed them only for the flight from Antarctica to Christchurch. (*See also* the Bibliography, under Mear.)

**Inaccessible Cliffs.** 82°33′S, 160°48′E. A line of steep cliffs interrupted by several glaciers. They form the northern escarpment of the Queen Elizabeth Range. Named by the New Zealanders in 1963.

**Inaccessible Island.** 77°40′S, 166°22′E. 95 m. Snow-free. The northernmost and second largest of the Dellbridge Islands, in McMurdo Sound. The world's most southerly emperor penguin colony is here. It is one mile SW of Cape Evans, Ross Island. Discovered and named by Scott in 1902.

**Inaccessible Islands.** 60°35′S, 46°38′ W. They vary in height between 120 and 250 meters. A small group of islands, the most westerly of the South Orkneys, 20 miles west of Coronation Island. Discovered and named by Powell on Dec. 6, 1821.

**Inca Point.** 62°18′S, 59°12′W. On Nelson Island, in the South Shetlands.

**Inclusion Hill.** 77°15′S, 166°25′E. 335 m. Steeply conical. It is a trachyte plug, with much basalt. Between McDonald Beach and the Mount Bird Ice Cap, about 4 miles south of Cape Bird, on Ross Island. Explored by the New Zealanders in 1958–59, and named by them.

**Independence Hills.** 80°25′S, 81°33′ W. 10 miles long. 3 miles SE of the Marble Hills in the Heritage Range. They form the south segment of the west wall of Horseshoe Valley. Named by the USA in continuation of the "heritage" theme dominant in this area.

**Index Peak.** 65°49′S, 64°26′W. Over 1,220 m. 7½ miles SE of Cape García on the west coast of Graham Land. Named by the UK for its likeness to an index finger.

**Index Point.** 73°21′S, 167°55′E. Ice-covered. Forms the east end of the Mountaineer Range in Victoria Land. Lies at the terminus of the Mariner Glacier, 1½ miles west of Emerging Island. Named by the New Zealanders in 1966 for its likeness to an index finger.

**India.** India began Operation Gangotri in Jan. 1982, which was the setting up of Dakshin Gangotri on the Princess Astrid Coast. On Aug. 19, 1983, it was ratified as the 28th signatory of the Antarctic Treaty, and on Sept. 12, 1983, achieved Consultative status within the Treaty system. That year India sent 28 scientists to its permanent weather station.

**The *Indian*.** A Liverpool sealing brig in the South Shetlands for the 1820–21 season, under the command of Capt. Spiller. It brought home some of the crew of the wrecked *Cora,* including Capt. Fildes, as well as 8 of the crew of the damaged *George.*

**Indian-Antarctic Basin** *see* **South Indian Basin**

**Indian Rocks.** 62°29′S, 60°17′W. In Hero Bay, in the South Shetlands. Named by the UK in 1958 for the *Indian.*

**Indicator Island.** 65°15′S, 64°16′W. 175 yards long. A tiny member of the Argentine Islands, just to the NW of Galíndez Island. Charted and named in 1935 by the BGLE who had put a windsock on the island to indicate wind direction for their plane.

**Indrefjord** *see* **Bell Bay**

**Indrehovdeholmen Island.** 69°11′S, 39°33′E. 1½ miles west of Langhovdekita Point in the eastern part of Lützow-Holm Bay. Photographed and mapped by the LCE 1936–37, and named by them for its position among the islands of the Langhovde Hills. Name means "the inner knoll" in Norwegian.

**¹Inexpressible Island.** 74°54′S, 163°39′E. Also called Oscar Island. 7 miles long. In Terra Nova Bay, Victoria Land. First called the Southern Foothills, as opposed to the Northern Foothills just to the north. Campbell's Northern Party wintered here, in 1912, in a snow cave, and changed its name to what it is today.

**²Inexpressible Island** *see* **Oscar Point**

**Inexpressible Island Automatic Weather Station.** 74°54′S, 163°36′E. An American AWS at an elevation of approximately 260 feet. On Inexpressible Island, in Terra Nova Bay, Victoria Land.

**Inferno Peak.** 72°07′S, 165°59′E. 3 miles north of Le Couteur Peak, in the northern end of the Millen Range, in Victoria Land. Named by the New Zealanders in 1963 for the reddish color of the peak.

**Inferno Ridge.** 79°26′S, 84°13′W. 8 miles long. Between the Schneider and Rennell Glaciers, in the Heritage Range. Named by the University of Minnesota Geological Party here in 1963–64, because the area is deeply dissected and composed of black rocks.

**Isla Ingeniero Pereira** *see* **Snodgrass Island**

**Ingham Glacier.** 72°50′S, 168°38′E. 3 miles west of Humphries Glacier, it flows into Borchgrevink Glacier in the Victory Mountains of Victoria Land. Named for Clayton Ingham, who was a member of Hallett Station's first wintering-over party, in 1957.

**Cape Ingrid.** 68°46′S, 90°42′W. Also called Kapp Ingrid Christensen. A promontory which separates Norvegia Bay and Sandefjord Cove, on the west side of Peter I Island. Discovered by Eyvind Tofte in 1927. Named for Lars Christensen's wife.

**Ingrid Christensen Coast.** 69°30′S, 76° E. Also called Ingrid Christensen Land. Lies between Jennings Promontory (72° 33′E) and the western end of the West Ice Shelf (81°24′E), just to the east of the Amery Ice Shelf. Discovered on Feb. 20, 1935, by Klarius Mikkelsen in the *Thorshavn,* and named by him for the wife of his boss, Lars Christensen. On that same day a landing party including Caroline Mikkelsen went ashore.

**Inland Forts.** 77°39′S, 161°03′E. Peaks between Northwest Mountain and Saint Pauls Mountain, in the Asgard Range of Victoria Land. Discovered and named descriptively by members of Scott's 1901–4 expedition.

**Inman Nunatak.** 74°49′S, 98°54′W. 6 miles east of Mount Manthe, in the SE part of the Hudson Mountains. Named for Martin M. Inman, aurora scientist at Byrd Station in 1960–61 and 1961–62.

**Inner Harbor.** 64°19'S, 63°W. Also called Puerto Interior. In the Melchior Islands. Formed by the semi-circular arrangement of Lambda, Delta, Epsilon, and Alpha Islands. Surveyed and named by the personnel on the *Discovery* in 1927. Resurveyed by the Argentines in 1942, 1943, and 1948.

**Innerskjera** see **Rookery Islands**

**Mount Innes-Taylor.** 86°51'S, 154°27'W. 2,730 m. 1 mile north of Mount Saltonstall, on the south side of Poulter Glacier, in the Queen Maud Mountains. Discovered in Dec. 1934 by Quin Blackburn's party during Byrd's 1933–35 expedition. Named by Byrd for Alan Innes-Taylor.

**Innes-Taylor, Alan.** Seaman on the *City of New York* during Byrd's 1928–30 expedition. He was one of the shore party, chief of Trail Operations, during Byrd's 1933–35 expedition.

**Innes-Taylor Inlet** see **Nantucket Inlet**

**Innes Wilson, J.** see **Wilson, J. Innes**

**Innfjorden** see **William Scoresby Bay**

**Innhovde Point.** 69°52'S, 37°10'E. On Fletta Bay, on the SW side of Lützow-Holm Bay. Named by the LCE 1936–37. Name means "inner knoll" in Norwegian.

**Innviksletta** see **Edward VIII Ice Shelf**

**Inott, Robert.** Captain of the *Samuel,* 1820–22.

**Insanity.** Used to be a danger. The cold and the isolation had its effects on the pioneers. Only a few cases of insanity were reported, although one wonders if all the cases were talked about. Probably not. Tollefsen and Knudsen went mad during the *Belgica*'s enforced winter-over in 1898. Whitfield went slightly insane after the winter-over with Scott in 1903, and George P. Abbott went insane in 1912. The danger is nowhere near as great today.

**Insects** see **Fauna**

**Mount Insel.** 77°23'S, 161°32'E. The highest point in the NE part of the Insel Range, in Victoria Valley. Named by the New Zealanders in 1959 because of its position in the Insel Range.

**Insel Range.** 77°24'S, 161°20'E. Also called Island Range. Ice-free, flat-topped peaks resembling islands (in German insel means island), in the Victoria Valley area. Separates McKelvey Valley from Balham Valley. Mount Insel is its most salient feature. Named by the New Zealanders in 1959.

**Insomnia.** Known as "the Big Eye" in Antarctica. Affects many people wintering over, as well as those in the summer season who can not get used to the perpetual light. It can become a bad problem.

**Inspections.** According to Article VII of the Antarctic Treaty, signatory countries have the right to inspect the Antarctic premises (i.e., the bases) of another nation. Advance notice must be given (presumably so that no *real* secrets are discovered). New Zealand was the first to avail itself of this opportunity, when it inspected McMurdo Station in 1963.

**Inspiration Rocks.** 73°26'S, 94°05'W. At the northern edge of the Cache Heights in the Jones Mountains. Named and mapped by the University of Minnesota–Jones Mountains party here in 1960–61. From here you can see practically all of the Jones Mountains.

**Instefjorden** see **Shirase Glacier**

**Instekleppane Hills.** 70°02'S, 38°53'E. On the east side of Shirase Glacier. Mapped by the LCE 1936–37, and named by them. Name means "the innermost lumps" in Norwegian.

**Insteodden Point.** 69°58'S, 38°46'E. On the east side of Havsbotn, at the extreme SE corner of Lützow-Holm Bay. Mapped by the LCE 1936–37, and named by them. Name means "the innermost point" in Norwegian.

**Institut Geologii Arktiki Rocks.** 70°56'S, 11°30'E. Extend for 20 miles. 7 miles south of the Schirmacher Hills in Queen Maud Land. Discovered by Ritscher in 1938–39. Named by the USSR in 1963 for their Institute of Arctic Geology.

**The *Instituto de Pesca I*.** Uruguayan trawler out of Montevideo, under the command of Capt. Ryan, loaned to

Shackleton by the Uruguayan government in June 1916, so that he could make his second (unsuccessful, as it turned out) attempt to rescue his men trapped on Elephant Island.

**Intention Nunataks.** 72°56′S, 163°46′E. Between Solo Nunatak and the Forgotten Hills, at the SW edge of the Evans Névé, in Victoria Land. It was intended to put a weather station here, but it never happened. Named by the New Zealanders in 1963.

**Intercurrence Island.** 63°55′S, 61°24′W. Also called Isla Intersección. 4½ miles long. The largest of the Christiania Islands, off Liège Island. The origin of this name is unknown, but it was named sometime in the 19th century.

**International Antarctic Glaciological Project.** A cooperative venture of the 1970s, begun in 1969, and taken part in by Australia, France, USSR, Great Britain, and the USA. They studied a large part of the East Antarctic ice sheet, between 60°E and 160°E, and between the coast and 80°S.

**International cooperation.** Being the most hostile environment on earth, Antarctica has inspired men of all nations to help each other out, rather than drain their energies fighting, when a lot of the time it is all they can do to stay alive. Some of the sealers used to scrap a bit in the South Shetlands, but it was comparatively rare and nothing serious. When an expedition from one nation met one from another nation, relations were almost always friendly. Even when Dumont d'Urville met Ringgold off the coast of East Antarctica, the lack of pleasantries was due to a misinterpretation of signals on both sides. Scott and von Drygalski worked together scientifically in 1901–3, and in 1929–31 the BANZARE met the Norwegians and worked out an exploration agreement so that they would not be in each other's way. In 1947–48 the RARE teamed up with the FIDS. And so on.

There are many cases of expeditions helping out others, icebreakers from one country freeing another country's ship from the pack-ice (often at risk to their own safety). But nowhere is international cooperation better exemplified than in the International Geophysical Year (IGY), and its successor institution, the Antarctic Treaty. During IGY, observers were invited from different countries to work at the bases of others, and the scientific and military harmony evident in Antarctica over that year produced enormous results, not only scientifically but also in the idea that a cold peace may have some influence on the cold war going on back home. The Antarctic Treaty was inspired by this. Territorial claims made by certain countries have been put on hold (not disallowed), and everyone realizes that cooperation is best if Antarctica is to be preserved. The case of Leonid Kuperov (q.v.) is interesting as a single case of international cooperation. Another is the case of Louis Roode. At 2:45 p.m., on Nov. 3, 1987, a Hercules LC-130, piloted by Lt. Cdr. Bradley Lanzer, USN, took off from McMurdo Station, and after 6 hours, 45 minutes, landed at Sanae Station on the other side of the continent, to pick up 26-year-old Louis Roode, who had a kidney problem. Lanzer (an American) then flew Roode (a South African) back to McMurdo via the South Pole, arriving at Williams Field (McMurdo's airport) at 7:34 a.m., on Nov. 4, 1987. Lanzer had traveled a total distance of 4,291 miles, in 17 hours flight time, the longest nonstop flight (including landing and almost immediate takeoff at Sanae Station ever started and completed in Antarctica. Roode was then flown to New Zealand. Another case was in Oct.–Nov. 1985, when the US ship *Polar Duke* went to Chile and brought back 17 tons of snow-removal equipment and 41,000 gallons of fuel for the Chileans at Teniente Rodolfo Marsh Station, who could not begin their summer program because of a snowed-in runway and failure of equipment. Antarctica abounds with such stories.

**International Geophysical Year.** Better known as the IGY. July 1, 1957–Dec. 31, 1958. The first, and to date, biggest international scientific onslaught on Antarctica, a long "year" in which 67 countries participated in ambitious scientific programs on the continent. 12 major countries built a network of scientific stations (see USA, USSR, Argentina, Australia, Belgium, Chile, France, Great Britain, Japan, New Zealand, Norway, South Africa), studying oceanography, meteorology, glaciology, the sun, geomagnetism, seismology, the ionosphere, cosmic rays, aurora, airglow, rocketry, gravity measurements, and some biology, zoology and geology. The stations were built before the event began, and scientists for the first time were able to concentrate on their studies without having to worry too much about staying alive. Their navies backed them up. IGY had its origins in the First International Polar Year (see **International Polar Years**) of 1882–83, even though the context of that event was almost wholly Arctic, as was the second one, in 1932–33. The International Polar Commission held their meetings every 50 years, and in 1949 Lloyd Berkner proposed a Third International Polar Year. On April 5, 1950, James Van Allen, the US physicist, had a small dinner party at his home in Maryland, and proposed more frequent programs — every 25 years — to take advantage of technological development, the interest in the Poles, and in addition, the maximum sunspot activity that was expected to take place in 1957–58. The idea grew, and the International Council of Scientific Unions (ICSU) adopted a formalized version. In 1952 ICSU appointed a committee that became known as CSAGI (Comité Spéciale de l'Année Géophysique Internationale), which coordinated planning for the IGY. Plans widened to study the whole earth, and simultaneous studies all over the world were scheduled to take place, and satellites were to be launched by the USA and USSR for the exploration of space. World data centers were established to collect all the information and make it freely available to all scientists. The next big ICSU meeting came in Rome in 1954, featuring Outer Space and Antarctica as the main topics. In July 1955 the First Antarctic Conference was held, in Paris, to plan the expeditions, and shortly thereafter the Advance Parties went south. The USA's part in the IGY began in 1954–55 when the *Atka* went around Antarctica looking for suitable base sites. On Dec. 17, 1955, the US Navy arrived in McMurdo Sound in the form of Task Force 43 under the command of George Dufek. Operation Deep Freeze had begun. Albert Crary was the senior US scientist who coordinated all scientific activities for his country, while Admiral Byrd was the planner-in-chief and overall head of the US effort. Coastal bases were established first in the summer of 1955–56, and the US started the first regular aircraft flights. The next summer great tractor traverses were run over the continent (by other countries as well), setting up inland bases, and a massive airdrop created the South Pole Station. IGY was inaugurated by ICSU (to which the USA belongs with its National Academy of Sciences) at one minute past midnight on July 1, 1957, and was presided over by Prof. Sydney Chapman. Perhaps the highlight of the IGY was Fuchs leading the British Commonwealth Transantarctic Expedition of 1957–58, the first party ever to cross the continent by land. Originally 69 scientists had gone down at the beginning of IGY, a number which grew dramatically over the course of the "year," and when IGY closed officially at midnight on Dec. 31, 1958, more than 10 tons of scientific data were brought out of Antarctica. One development of IGY was the Antarctic Treaty.

**International Polar Commission.** In 1879, 11 participating countries met in Hamburg, and agreed to hold an International Polar Year in 1882–83. It was decided to hold one every 50 years, the second one being scheduled for 1932–33. IGY replaced the commission.

**International Polar Years.** Conceived by Lt. Karl Weyprecht, an Austrian naval man and Arctic explorer, the International Polar Commission organized the first International Polar Year in 1882–83. 11 countries took part, with Georg von Neumayer presiding. It was devoted almost wholly to Arctic research, and to ground level at that. Although 4 geomagnetic and meteorological stations were planned for the Southern regions, only the German station at Royal Bay, in South Georgia (54°S), materialized. Antarctica was left out totally from the second International Polar Year, in which 34 nations took part. In the Arctic balloons went up to a height of 33,000 feet. The major result of these International Polar Years was the International Geophysical Year.

**International Square.** Where the foreign flags hang at McMurdo Station.

**International Symposium on Antarctic Geology.** Held in Cape Town in 1963, and in Oslo in 1970.

**International Symposium on Antarctic Glaciology.** A series of meetings, sponsored by SCAR. The third symposium took place at the Institute of Polar Studies, Ohio State University, in Sept. 1981, the first such meeting in 13 years.

**International Weddell Sea Oceanographic Expeditions.** A series of scientific expeditions more commonly known by their initials, IWSOE. The first one was Jan. 20–March 15, 1968. Its mission — to investigate the vast mass of the Weddell Sea, generally below ice, which had had extremely limited study up till that time. The *Glacier,* under Capt. O.L. Dawson, and the *General San Martín,* were the US and Argentine icebreakers involved. They placed 4 Norwegian instrumented buoys on the continental slope of the Weddell Sea to measure, for 12 months,

the temperatures and currents of the bottom water. Also 70 oceanographic stations were placed on the ice all over the Weddell Sea in order to study the biological and physical characteristics of the sea. IWSOE 1969 was Part II of the experiment, a follow-up to the preceding year's effort. It went to pick up the results, and retrieved the 4 buoys submerged in the Weddell Sea, and surveyed and studied more of the Weddell Sea. The third phase of IWSOE began in 1977, and was designed to do what could not be done on the second. Overall the IWSOE gave a better understanding of Antarctic bottom water.

**Intrusive Spur.** 73°30′S, 94°25′W. At the north side of the Jones Mountains, 1 mile east of Avalanche Ridge. Mapped and named by the University of Minnesota–Jones Mountains Party here in 1960–61, because the intrusive complex of the basement rocks of the Jones Mountains is well exposed on this spur.

**Bahía Inútil** *see* **Curtiss Bay**

**Inverkeith Hill** *see* **Mount Inverleith**

**Mount Inverleith.** 64°55′S, 62°45′W. Also called Inverleith Hill, Inverkeith Hill. 1,495 m. On the west coast of Graham Land, near the head of Skontorp Cove. First charted and named Inverleith Hill by David Ferguson, in 1913–14.

**Inverleith Harbor.** 64°32′S, 63°W. A bay between Andrews Point and Briggs Peninsula, on the NE coast of Anvers Island. Also at one time called Leith Harbour, it was discovered by Scottish whalers.

**Inverleith Hill** *see* **Mount Inverleith**

**Invertebrates.** Animals without a backbone. More than 90 percent of all living animals do not have a vertebral column. They range in size from minute protozoans to giant squids. There are many in Antarctica (*see* **Fauna**).

**Ionosphere Bay.** 66°46′S, 141°35′E. On the east side of Cape Découverte, in Adélie Land. Charted and named by the French in 1951.

**Isla Iota** *see* **Peace Island**

**Mount Iphigene.** 76°30'S, 145°54'W. Just west of Ochs Glacier, at the neck of Guest Peninsula, in the Fosdick Mountains of Marie Byrd Land. Discovered in 1929 by Byrd's 1928–30 expedition, and named by Byrd for Mrs. Iphigene Ochs Sulzberger, daughter of Adolph Ochs and wife of Arthur Sulzberger.

**The *Iquique*.** Chilean naval frigate which, with the *Angamos,* formed the Chilean Antarctic Expedition of 1946–47. The ship was commanded that season by Capt. González. It landed the first party at Capitán Arturo Prat Station, and on Feb. 20, 1947, made a visit to Base E on Stonington Island, leaving this British station the following day. The captain on the 1949–50 expedition was Balaresque, and on the 1952–53 expedition was Victor Wilson.

**Surgidero Iquique** *see* **Primero de Mayo Bay**

**Iquique Cove.** 62°29'S, 59°40'W. Also called Caletón Iquique. On the east side of Discovery Bay on Greenwich Island, in the South Shetlands. It is right next to Capitán Arturo Prat Station. Named by the Chileans for the *Iquique*.

**Mount Irene Frazier** *see* **Mount Frazier**

**Cape Irízar.** 75°33'S, 162°57'E. A headland which forms the northern end of Lamplugh Island, off the coast of Victoria Land. Discovered by Scott in 1904, and named by him for Julián Irízar.

**Irízar, Julián.** Argentine Naval attaché in London, he was captain of the *Uruguay* in 1903–4 during the relief of Nordenskjöld's expedition.

**¹Irízar Island** *see* **Jonassen Island**

**²Irízar Island.** 65°13'S, 64°12'W. ½ mile long. In the Argentine Islands. Discovered by Charcot in 1903–5. Named by him for Julián Irízar. Recharted by the BGLE in 1935.

**Iron.** Shackleton found it in Antarctica, as did Mawson. It has since been found several times.

**Ironside Glacier.** 72°08'S, 169°40'E. 30 miles long. Flows from Mount Minto in the Admiralty Mountains, between Mount Whewell and Mount Herschel, into Moubray Bay in Victoria Land. At its mouth it is joined by Honeycomb Glacier. Named by the New Zealanders in 1958 for its spectacularness and power.

**Iroquois Plateau.** 83°48'S, 54°W. Ice-covered. East of the southern part of the Washington Escarpment, in the Pensacola Mountains. Named for the Iroquois helicopter (Bell UH-1).

**Irvine Gardner Glacier** *see* **Ketchum Glacier**

**Irvine Glacier.** 74°42'S, 63°15'W. 40 miles long. Feeds Gardner Inlet, in Palmer Land, from between the Guettard Range and the Rare Range. Discovered by Ronne in 1947–48, who named it for George J. Irvine, engineer who had outlined the RARE photographic program.

**Mount Irving.** 61°17'S, 54°08'W. Also called Mount Bowles. Dominates the southern part of Clarence Island, in the South Shetlands. Named by the UK for Rear-Adm. Sir Edmund George Irving, hydrographer of the navy from 1960–66.

**Irving, J.C.C.** Captain of the *William Scoresby,* 1930–31.

**Irving Island.** 66°25'S, 67°04'W. At the NE end of the Barcroft Islands, in the Biscoe Islands. Named by the UK for Laurence Irving, US polar physiologist.

**Irwin Glacier.** 71°07'S, 163°25'E. A steep glacier in the Bowers Mountains which flows from the Edlin Névé, merging with Montigny Glacier, then both flow into the Graveson Glacier. Named for Carlisle S. Irwin, glaciologist in the Meserve Glacier studies of 1966–67.

**Cape Irwyn.** 84°41'S, 170°05'W. Also called Cape Smith. Forms the northern end of the Lillie Range in the foothills of the Prince Olav Mountains, at the edge of the Ross Ice Shelf. Named by the New Zealanders in 1964 for Irwyn Smith, radio operator at Scott Base in 1963–64.

**Mount Isabelle** *see* **Mount Izabelle**

**Isachsen, Gunnar.** Norwegian major, co-leader, with Riiser-Larsen, of the *Norvegia* expedition of 1930–31.

**Isachsen Mountain.** 72°11′S, 26°15′E. Also called Gunnar Isachsen Mountain. 3,425 m. In the Sør Rondane Mountains. Named by the Norwegians for Major Gunnar Isachsen.

**Isacke Passage.** 66°54′S, 67°15′W. A marine channel in Hanusse Bay, between Liard Island and Arrowsmith Peninsula, on the west coast of Graham Land. Charcot discovered it, and charted it, in 1908–10, and the UK later named it for Capt. Christopher J. Isacke, RN, commander of the *Endurance*, 1972–74.

**Isaiah Bowman Glacier** *see* **Bowman Glacier**

**Isbrynet Hill.** 73°09′S, 4°28′W. SW of Penck Ledge, in the area of the head of Penck Trough, in Queen Maud Land. Name means "the ice-rim" in Norwegian.

**Isdalen Valley.** 71°44′S, 12°30′E. Ice-filled. Between Aurdalsegga Ridge and Isdalsegga Ridge in the Südliche Petermann Range of the Wohlthat Mountains, in Queen Maud Land. Discovered by Ritscher in 1938–39. Name means "the ice valley" in Norwegian.

**Isdalsegga Ridge.** 71°45′S, 12°33′E. Forms the east wall of Isdalen Valley, in the Südliche Petermann Range of the Wohlthat Mountains, in Queen Maud Land. Name means "ice valley ridge" in Norwegian.

**¹Iselin Bank** *see* **Iselin Seamount**

**²Iselin Bank.** 73°S, 179°30′W. A submarine feature of the Ross Sea.

**Iselin Seamount.** 70°45′S, 178°15′W. Also called Iselin Bank (although not to be confused with the other feature with this name, for which, see above). A submarine feature.

**Île Iseult** *see* **Yseult Island**

**Isfjorden** *see* **Amundsen Bay**

**Isfossnipa Peak.** 73°09′S, 1°30′W. 2 miles SE of Austvorren Ridge, in Queen Maud Land. Photographed from the air by Ritscher's 1938–39 expedition. The name means "icefall peak" in Norwegian.

**Mount Isherwood.** 74°59′S, 113°43′W. A flattish, ice-covered mountain with steep rock slopes. 4 miles WSW of Mount Strange, in the Kohler Range of Marie Byrd Land. Lichens are to be found here. First photographed in 1947 from Operation Highjump aircraft. Named in the 1960s for William F. Isherwood, geophysicist in the Antarctic, 1965–66 and 1966–67.

**Ishmael Peak.** 65°53′S, 62°25′W. 4 miles south of Spouter Peak, on the east coast of Graham Land, in the area of the head of Leppard Glacier. Surveyed by the FIDS in 1947 and 1955. Named by the UK for the *Moby Dick* character.

**Ising Glacier.** 72°24′S, 0°57′E. Flows between Isingen Mountain and Kvitkjølen Ridge, in the Sverdrup Mountains of Queen Maud Land. First photographed aerially by Ritscher's expedition of 1938–39. Name means "the icing glacier" in Norwegian.

**Isingbreen** *see* **Ising Glacier**

**Isingen Mountain.** 72°23′S, 1°04′E. Between Ising Glacier and Rogstad Glacier in the Sverdrup Mountains of Queen Maud Land. First photographed aerially by Ritscher's expedition of 1938–39. Name means "the icing" in Norwegian.

**Isingsalen Saddle.** 72°20′S, 1°02′E. An ice saddle between Isingen Mountain and Salknappen Peak, in the Sverdrup Mountains of Queen Maud Land. First photographed aerially by Ritscher's expedition of 1938–39. Name means "the icing saddle" in Norwegian.

**Isingufsa Bluff.** 72°21′S, 1°13′E. A rock bluff forming the NE corner of Isingen Mountain, in the Sverdrup Mountains of Queen Maud Land. First photographed aerially by Ritscher's 1938–39 expedition. Name means "the icing bluff" in Norwegian.

**Isklakken Hill.** 71°56′S, 27°26′E. A rocky hill 2 miles east of Balchen Mountain, at the east end of the Sør Rondane Mountains. Name means "the ice lump" in Norwegian.

**Iskollen Hill.** 72°51'S, 4°09'W. Also called Repke Mountain. Snow-covered with a few rock outcrops at the summit. SW of Raudberg Valley in the SW part of the Borg Massif, in Queen Maud Land. Name means "the ice hill" in Norwegian.

**Bahía Isla Neny** *see* **Neny Bay**

**Island Arena.** 79°49'S, 156°35'E. A valley with a lateral lobe of the Darwin Glacier occupying it. It indents the northern side of the Darwin Mountains between Colosseum Ridge and Kenneth Ridge. Richardson Hill, an islandlike nunatak, rises above the ice of the valley. Named by the New Zealanders in 1963.

**Island Lake.** 77°38'S, 166°26'E. About 500 yards east of Cape Evans, Ross Island. It has two small (unnamed) islands within it. Named by Scott during his 1910–13 expedition.

**Island Range** *see* **Insel Range**

**Islands Point.** 71°28'S, 169°31'E. Separates Berg Bay and Relay Bay on the west shore of Robertson Bay, in northern Victoria Land. Named by members of Scott's 1910–13 expedition because of Sphinx Rock (an island), just to its north.

**The *Islas Orcadas*** *see* **The *Eltanin***

**Islay.** 67°21'S, 59°42'E. Also called Islay Island. An island, 2 miles long. 1½ miles north of Bertha Island, in the William Scoresby Archipelago. Discovered in Feb. 1936 by personnel on the *William Scoresby*, who named it for the Scottish isle.

**Islay Island** *see* **Islay**

**Isocline Hill.** 83°31'S, 157°36'E. In the southern part of the Augen Bluffs, in the Miller Range, overlooking Marsh Glacier. Named by the Ohio State University Geological party of 1967–68 because an isoclinal fold is well-exposed on the side of this hill.

**Isolation Point.** 78°13'S, 167°30'E. A small volcanic peak projecting through the ice sheet covering the SE extremity of White Island, in the Ross Archipelago. Aptly named in 1959 by the New Zealanders.

**Isopods.** Crustaceans which lie on the sea bed near the shore. Crablike, and foraging, some are parasitic (*see also* **Fauna**).

**Isrosene Mountains.** 71°53'S, 26°35'E. Two nunataks, 6 miles WNW of Balchen Mountain, protruding through the west part of Byrdbreen in the Sør Rondane Mountains. Name means "the ice roses" in Norwegian.

**Isrugg** *see* **Halvfarryggen Ridge**

**Istind Peak.** 72°06'S, 2°23'W. Also called Sukkertoppen. Partly ice-covered. 1 mile south of Tindeklypa on the east side of the Ahlmann Ridge in Queen Maud Land. First photographed aerially by Ritscher's 1938–39 expedition. Name means "ice peak" in Norwegian.

**Istindhalsen Saddle.** 72°05'S, 2°34'W. An ice saddle between Istind Peak and Grunehogna Peaks in the Ahlmann Ridge of Queen Maud Land. Name means "the ice peak neck" in Norwegian.

**Isvika** *see* **Allison Bay**

**Italy.** Ratified as the 24th signatory of the Antarctic Treaty on March 18, 1981. The first Italian Antarctic expedition, in 1986–87, built a year-round station, Baia Terra Nova Station, in Gerlache Inlet, and surveyed the nearby Terra Nova Bay in Victoria Land. Antarctic weather stations were installed and meteorology, atmospheric physics, physical oceanography, and earth and biologic sciences were conducted. On Oct. 5, 1987, Italy became the 20th nation to achieve Consultative status within the Antarctic Treaty system.

**Itime Glacier** *see* **Ichime Glacier**

**ITT/Antarctic Services, Inc.** Took over from Holmes & Narver, Inc., as the National Science Foundation's Antarctic support contractor, on April 1, 1980. It supplied services, managed seasonal construction activities, and provided maintenance and operational support at the US stations on the continent. It provided technical and administrative support to the USAP on a year-round basis. In short, its employees managed Amundsen-Scott South Pole Station, Palmer Station, and Siple Station, and also provided certain services at McMurdo Station (the US Navy does the rest there). ITT's headquarters are at 621 Industrial Avenue, Paramus, N.J., USA, 07652. Tel: (201) 967-0123. Replaced as contractor by Antarctic Services Associates (q.v.) in 1990.

**Ivanoff Head.** 66°53'S, 109°07'E. A small rocky headland, in fact probably an island, 4 miles west of the Hatch Islands, at the head of Vincennes Bay. Named Brooks Island by the USA in 1956. In 1960 it was used as a rescue base by the ANARE when a helicopter, piloted by Capt. P. Ivanoff, crashed here. In 1961 the Australians inadvertently renamed it Ivanoff Head. This name was an unofficial alternative to Brooks Island, and eventually won out, being now the official name.

**Mount Iveagh.** 85°04'S, 169°38'E. In the Supporters Range, overlooking the east side of the Mill Glacier, 5 miles NW of Mount White. Discovered by Shackleton in 1907–9, and named by him for Lord Iveagh, a sponsor.

**Iversen.** Captain of the whale catcher *Star II* during the *Sir James Clark Ross* expedition of 1923–24.

**Iversen Peak.** 84°37'S, 111°26'W. 3 miles ENE of Urbanak Peak at the NE end of the Ohio Range, in the Horlick Mountains. Surveyed in Dec. 1958 by the USARP Horlick Mountains Traverse Party. Named for Frede Iversen, ionosphere physicist at Byrd Station in 1960.

**Ives Tongue.** 67°21'S, 59°29'E. A narrow tongue of land projecting from an island between Fold Island and the coast of Enderby Land. Discovered and named in Feb. 1936 by the personnel on the *William Scoresby.*

**Ivory Hills** *see* **Ivory Pinnacles**

**Ivory Pinnacles.** 63°49'S, 59°08'W. Also called Ivory Hills. Two ice-covered peaks reaching 1,120 m. On the west side of Pettus Glacier, 9 miles SE of Cape Kjellman, in northern Graham Land. Charted and named by the FIDS in 1948.

**Ivory Tower.** 85°28'S, 142°24'W. A peak in the Queen Maud Mountains.

**Mount Izabelle.** 72°10'S, 66°30'E. Also spelled (erroneously) as Mount Isabelle. Bare rock. 12 miles SW of the Shaw Massif in the Prince Charles Mountains. Discovered on Nov. 28, 1956, from an ANARE Beaver aircraft. Named for B. Izabelle, weather observer at Mawson Station, 1957.

**J. Carlson Bay** *see* **Carlsson Bay**

**Pointe J. Guéguen** *see* **Guéguen Point**

**The *J.H. Bull.*** Norwegian whaler which replaced the *Norvegia* in Antarctic waters beginning in the 1935–36 season. That year it conducted whaling reconnaissance in the Amundsen Sea.

**Mount J.J. Thompson.** 77°41'S, 162°15'E. In the Taylor Valley, overlooking Lake Bonney, between the Rhone and Matterhorn Glaciers, in Victoria Land. Named by Grif Taylor in 1911, during Scott's 1910–13 expedition.

**Mount J. Stubberud** *see* **Mount Stubberud**

**Jabet, Jacques.** Bosun on the *Français,* 1903–5, during Charcot's first expedition to Antarctica.

**Jabet Peak.** 64°49'S, 63°28'W. Also called The Ridge. 545 m. On Wiencke Island. Charcot first charted it in 1903–5, and named it for Jacques Jabet.

**Lake Jabs.** 68°33'S, 78°15'E. On Breidnes Peninsula, in the Vestfold Hills. Named by the Australians for B.V. Jabs, weather observer at Davis Station in 1961.

**Jaburg Glacier.** 82°45'S, 53°W. Behind the Cordiner Peaks and the Dufek Massif, in the northern Pensacola Mountains. Named for Conrad J. Jaburg, USN, helicopter pilot at Ellsworth Station in 1957.

**Jack, A. Keith.** Australian physicist, one of the Ross Sea party during the British Imperial Transantarctic Expedition of 1914–17.

**Jack Hayward Base.** Established in 1985 on Ross Island, 200 yards from Scott's old base, at Cape Evans, as the base for the In the Footsteps of Scott Expedition. Named for a benefactor. Essentially it was a 16 by 24 foot hut with a generator. Mike Stroud and John Tolson looked after it while Swan, Mear, and Wood were en route to the Pole.

**Jack Paulus Skiway.** Amundsen-Scott South Pole Station's landing field, named in 1981 for Jack Paulus (Lt. Cdr. John F. Paulus), who retired from the US Navy on June 26, 1981, after 20 years service. He was with VXE-6 from 1971–81, and had been in Antarctica for 9 summers, including an earlier stint in 1969–70 when he flew the first 6 women to the South Pole (*see* **Women in Antarctica**).

**Jacka Mountains** *see* **Lazarev Mountains**

**Jackass penguin.** The true jackass penguin is *Aptenodytes demersa,* or *Spheniscus demersus,* and is found only off the coast of South Africa. Another species, the rockhopper penguin, is also called the jumping jackass, but this is not found south of 60°S either. The gentoo penguin is often confused with, and often called, the jackass, and it is this one that writers mean when they say they saw a jackass penguin south of 60°S.

**Mount Jackling.** 77°54′S, 154°58′W. In the Rockefeller Mountains. Discovered on Jan. 27, 1929, during a flight on Byrd's 1928–30 expedition. Named by the USAS in 1940.

**Mount Jacklyn.** 70°15′S, 65°53′E. In the eastern part of the Athos Range, in the Prince Charles Mountains. Named by the Australians for Robert Jacklyn, cosmic ray physicist at Mawson Station in 1956.

**Mount Jackman.** 72°23′S, 163°14′E. 1,920 m. In the Freyberg Mountains.

Named for Warren A. Jackman, photographer here in 1959–60.

**Mount Jackson.** 71°23′S, 63°22′W. Also called Mount Gruening, Mount E. Gruening, Mount Ernest Gruening. 13,750 feet. In Palmer Land, it is the highest point on the Antarctic Peninsula. In 1928 Wilkins turned back north at this point, on his expeditionary flight of that year. Named Mount Andrew Jackson by the USAS 1939–41 for the former president of the USA. The name was later shortened.

**Jackson, Archibald.** 1st class boy on the Wilkes Expedition 1838–42. Joined in the USA. Discharged at Oahu, Oct. 31, 1840.

**Jackson Glacier.** 74°47′S, 135°45′W. About 10 miles long. Flows into Siniff Bay from the McDonald Heights, in Marie Byrd Land. Named for Bernard V. Jackson, scientific leader at Amundsen-Scott South Pole Station in 1971.

**Jackson Peak.** 82°50′S, 53°35′W. 1,255 m. In the Cordiner Peaks. Named for Allen M. Jackson, aviation electronics technician at Ellsworth Station in 1957.

**Jackson Tooth.** 80°25′S, 23°16′W. A peak in the Shackleton Range.

**The *Jacob Ruppert.*** US steel-plated ship used during Byrd's 1928–30 expedition. W.F. Verleger was captain in 1933–34, and S.D. Rose was captain in 1934–35, even though Commodore Hjalmar Gjertsen was in overall command of the ship during the entire expedition.

**Jacob Ruppert Coast** *see* **Ruppert Coast**

**Jacobs Island.** 64°48′S, 64°W. Just over ¼ mile long. Between the Hellerman Rocks and Laggard Island, off Anvers Island, in the vicinity of Palmer Station. Named for Lt. Cdr. Paul F. Jacobs, USN, officer-in-charge of Palmer Station in 1972.

**Jacobs Nunatak.** 84°17′S, 159°38′E. On the west side of the MacAlpine Hills, in the area of Sylwester Glacier. Named for Willis S. Jacobs, scientist at South Pole Station in 1959.

**Jacobs Peak.** 80°05'S, 157°46'E. 2,040 m. In the Britannia Range. Named for John D. Jacobs, US scientist observing at Vostok Station in 1964.

**Jacobsen, Glen.** USN. Commander of the *Atka* during the US Navy Antarctic Expedition of 1954–55.

**Jacobsen Glacier.** 82°58'S, 167°05'E. Flows from Mount Reid in the Holland Range, into the Ross Ice Shelf. Named for H. Jacobsen, master of the *Chattahoochee* in Antarctica, 1964–65.

**Jacobsen Head.** 74°01'S, 113°20'W. An ice-covered headland on the east side of Philbin Inlet, on Martin Peninsula, on the coast of Marie Byrd Land. Named for Cdr. Glen Jacobsen.

**Jacoby Glacier.** 75°48'S, 132°06'W. Between Mount Boennighausen and Mount Andrus in the Ames Range of Marie Byrd Land. Named for William J. Jacoby, driller at Byrd Station in 1968–69.

**Jacques Peaks.** 64°31'S, 61°51'W. 385 m. At the NW end of Reclus Peninsula, in Graham Land. Named by the UK in 1960 for Greville A. Jacques, with the FIDS 1955–57, who landed here to build a survey station.

**Mount Jacquinot.** 63°22'S, 57°53'W. 475 m. On Trinity Peninsula. Probably sighted by Bransfield on Jan. 30, 1820, but named in 1837–40 by Dumont d'Urville for Charles-Hector Jacquinot.

**Jacquinot, A.** Assistant to the scientific corps on the Wilkes Expedition 1838–42. Joined at Rio. Run at Callao.

**Jacquinot, Charles-Hector.** b. March 4, 1796, Nevers, France. d. 1879, Toulon. Commander of the *Zélée* during Dumont d'Urville's 1837–40 expedition, and second-in-command under Dumont d'Urville. By the time the expedition set out he had already had a long naval career, and later was promoted to vice-admiral.

**Jacquinot, Honoré.** Naturalist and assistant surgeon on the *Astrolabe* during Dumont d'Urville's 1837–40 expedition.

**Jacquinot Rocks.** 63°26'S, 58°24'W. 1 mile off the north coast of Trinity Peninsula. Named by the FIDS for Honoré Jacquinot.

**Jade Point.** 63°36'S, 57°34'W. Forms the southern end of Eyrie Bay, Trinity Peninsula. Named by the UK for the green ice covering the lower slopes.

**Jaeger Table.** 82°36'S, 52°30'W. In the Pensacola Mountains.

**Jagar Islands.** 66°35'S, 57°20'E. Also called Jagarane. Off Cape Boothby in Enderby Land. Named by the LCE 1936–37 for jagarane (hunters).

**¹Jagged Island.** 61°54'S, 58°29'W. 2½ miles NNW of Round Point on King George Island, in the South Shetlands. It is jagged, and was named descriptively by personnel on the *Discovery II* in 1935.

**²Jagged Island.** 65°58'S, 65°41'W. Also called Isla Mollada, Isla Velez Sarsfield. 2 miles long. 8 miles west of Ferin Head, off the west coast of Graham Land. Named by the BGLE 1934–37 because it is jagged.

**Jagged Rocks.** 63°24'S, 56°59'W. In Hut Cove, Hope Bay, on Trinity Peninsula. First charted in 1903 by Dr. J. Gunnar Andersson, and named by the FIDS in 1945.

**Jallour Isles** *see*  **Yalour Islands**

**Jalour Islands** *see*  **Yalour Islands**

**Cape James.** 63°06'S, 62°45'W. The southernmost part of Smith Island, in the South Shetlands. Named before 1831, probably by Foster.

**James, David P.** FIDS surveyor at Base D, 1945–46.

**James, Reginald W.** b. 1891. Reginald William James. Physicist on the *Endurance* during Shackleton's British Imperial Transantarctic Expedition of 1914–17. He later lived in Cape Town.

**The *James Caird*.** Shackleton's 22-foot-long open boat which made the trip from Elephant Island to South Georgia in 1916. The largest of the three longboats used by Shackleton on this expedition, it was named by him for his chief backer, Sir James Caird.

**James Duncan Mountains** *see* **Duncan Mountains**

**Mount James E. West** *see* **Mount West**

**James Island** *see* **Smith Island**

**James Lassiter Ice Barrier** *see* **Ronne Ice Shelf**

**The *James Monroe*.** American sealing sloop of 80 tons and a crew of 7, commanded by Nat Palmer as part of the Fanning-Pendleton Sealing Expedition of 1821–22 to the South Shetlands. With the *Dove*, under Powell, it discovered the South Orkneys in Dec. 1821.

**James Nunatak.** 69°59'S, 62°27'W. 410 m. 5½ miles south of Lewis Point, on the east coast of Palmer Land. Named by the FIDS for David P. James.

**Mount James Robertson** *see* **Mount Robertson**

**¹James Ross Island.** 64°15'S, 57°45'W. Off the northern tip of the Antarctic Peninsula, from which it is separated by the Prince Gustav Channel. Maximum height 1,630 m. Length 40 miles. It is rich in fossils. Discovered by Nordenskjöld in Oct. 1903, and named by him for Sir James Clark Ross. It has also been called Ross Island, but this name has been greatly discouraged in favor of the other island of that name in McMurdo Sound.

**²James Ross Island** *see* **Foyn Island**

**James W. Ellsworth Land** *see* **Ellsworth Land**

**Jameson Island** *see* **Low Island**

**Jameson Point.** 63°17'S, 62°17'W. On Low Island. First charted by Charcot in 1908–10. Named for Jameson Island (Weddell's name for Low Island, in the South Shetlands).

**Jamesons Island** *see* **Low Island**

**Jamesway Huts.** 16 by 16 foot frame-type tents built from a kit, and which can be added on to. They are erected by covering semicircular, prefabricated wooden arches with insulated canvas panels called blankets. A Jamesway hut resembles a Quonset hut or a Nissen hut. They are popular in Antarctica because they can be assembled rapidly and can be carried by Hercules LC-130 aircraft.

**Jamieson Ridge.** 80°27'S, 25°53'W. In the Shackleton Range.

**Mount Jamroga.** 71°20'S, 163°06'E. 2,265 m. Between the Carryer and Sledgers Glaciers in the Bowers Mountains. Named for Lt. Cdr. John J. Jamroga, photographer here in 1967–68.

**The *Jane*.** British sealing brig of 160 tons owned by James Strachan, out of Leith, Scotland. It was commanded by Weddell for three successive Antarctic voyages, 1819–21, 1821–22, and 1822–24, with a 22-man crew. After the first voyage Weddell bought a share in the vessel. On Feb. 20, 1823, he reached a southing record of 74°15'S, 34°16'45"W, in the Weddell Sea. The *Jane's* tender was the *Beaufoy of London*, commanded first by Michael McLeod and later by Matthew Brisbane.

**Jane Bank.** 61°45'S, 38°45'W. A submarine feature in the northern Weddell Sea.

**Jane Basin.** 62°15'S, 40°30'W. A back-arc basin in the northern Weddell Sea.

**Jane Col.** 60°42'S, 45°38'W. West of Jane Peak, on Signy Island, in the South Orkneys. Named by the UK for the *Jane*.

**The *Jane Maria*.** American sealing brig of 170 tons, 74 feet long, built in New York in 1796. James Sheffield was its first mate in 1817–18, and its captain in 1818–19. On July 1, 1819, it was registered, and that day left for the Falkland Islands under the command of Robert Johnson. It formed part of the New York Sealing Expedition of 1820–21, and left Antarctica on March 9, 1821, for New York. It was back in the South Shetlands on Oct. 27, 1821, for the 1821–22 season, under the command of Capt. Abraham Blauvelt, and still part of the New York Sealing Expedition.

**Jane Peak.** 60°43'S, 45°38'W. 210 m. A nunatak on Signy Island, in the South Orkneys. Surveyed by the personnel on the *Discovery II* in 1933, and again by the FIDS in 1947. Named by the UK in 1954 for the *Jane.*

**Mount Jane Wade** *see* **Mount Gray**

**Mount Jane Wyatt** *see* **Mount Wyatt**

**Janet Rock.** 66°33'S, 139°10'E. 7½ miles WNW of Liotard Glacier, in the region of the Géologie Archipelago, in East Antarctica. Named by the French in 1953 for philosopher Paul Janet.

**Mount Janetschek.** 74°53'S, 162°15'E. 1,455 m. Between Mount Larsen and Widowmaker Pass, at the mouth of the Reeves Glacier, in Victoria Land. Named for Heinz Janetschek, biologist at McMurdo Station in 1961–62.

**Janke Nunatak.** 75°53'S, 70°27'W. To the immediate north of the Hauberg Mountains, on the Orville Coast. Named for John W. Janke, radioman at Eights Station in 1964.

**Janssen Peak.** 64°53'S, 63°31'W. 1,085 m. On Wiencke Island. Discovered by de Gerlache in 1898. Charted by Charcot in 1903–5, and named by him for astronomer Jules Janssen.

**January Col.** 83°24'S, 162°E. A pass on the north side of Claydon Peak. Named by its first climbers, Hillary's party, in Jan. 1958.

**Janulis Spur.** 85°07'S, 90°27'W. Between Green Valley and Aaron Glacier in the Thiel Mountains. Named by surveying party members Peter Bermel and Arthur Ford in 1961 for their pilot, Lt. George Janulis.

**Janus Island.** 64°47'S, 64°06'W. 350 yards long. It has 3 tiny satellites of its own, to the immediate north. About 1½ miles SW of Palmer Station, Anvers Island. Surveyed by the FIDS in 1955. Named by the UK for the Roman god, because it guards Arthur Harbor.

**Japan.** In 1910–12 the Japanese South Polar expedition took place under the leadership of Shirase. In 1934–35 the first Japanese whaling fleet went to Antarctica, and they have engaged in Antarctic whaling ever since, mostly off the coast of East Antarctica. In 1955 an Antarctic Committee in the Science Council of Japan was formed, and an Antarctic program in the Ministry of Education was also begun. In 1956–57 JARE I (the First Japanese Antarctic Research Expedition) went to Antarctica, for the IGY, and set up Showa Station, the main Japanese base in Antarctica. There has been a JARE every year since. In 1959 Japan was one of the original 12 signatories of the Antarctic Treaty, and later set up another couple of stations, Mizuho Station and Asuka Camp. The National Institute of Polar Research heads the JAREs and maintains the scientific stations. In Dec. 1968 a team of 12 from Showa Station arrived at the South Pole after an 11-week traverse. The round trip was the longest ever to the Pole and back—3,200 miles.

**Japanese Antarctic Research Expeditions.** Known as the JARE, these have occurred every year since 1956–57 (*see* the Expeditions appendix). Some highlights: JARE I. 1956–57. Left Japan on Nov. 8, 1956, on the *Soya,* under the leadership of Dr. Takeshi Nagata. 53 scientists and logistics support personnel, 240 tons of supplies, 18 Sakhalin sledge dogs, and a Cessna 180 light airplane, and two Bell 47-6 helicopters to be used for reconnaissance. On Jan. 7, 1957, the ship arrived at the pack ice. On Feb. 14, 1957, Showa Station was inaugurated, and on Feb. 15, 1957, the *Soya* left the area. On Feb. 16, 1957, it got stuck in the pack ice. On Feb. 28, 1957, the Russian ship *Ob'* helped the Japanese ship out, and it went home to Tokyo. The 11-man wintering party was led by Dr. Eizaburo Nishibori, and it carried out a reconnaissance of the Lützow-Holm Bay area. JARE II. 1957–58. Left Japan on the *Soya* on Oct. 21, 1957, again under Nagata. On Dec. 20, 1957, it arrived at the pack ice, and became stuck here, unable to approach Showa Station. On Feb. 11, 1958, the 11 men from Showa Station were air-lifted to the *Soya,* and on Feb. 14, 1958, Nagata abandoned JARE II because of the ice. They left behind, among other things, the dogs. This caused a scandal in Japan. JARE III. 1958–59. When the *Soya* arrived at Showa Station they found two of the dogs, Taro and Jiro (q.v.) still alive. The 14-man wintering party, led by Masayoshi Murayama, reopened Showa Station and enlarged it. The USSR team visited them. JARE IV. 1959–60. 15 men wintered-over under Tetsuya Torii. JARE V. 1960–61. 16 men wintered-over under Murayama.

**Jaques Nunatak.** 67°53′S, 66°12′E. 3 miles SSW of Mount Kennedy in the Gustav Bull Mountains of Mac. Robertson Land. Named by the Australians for G.A. Jaques, weather observer at Mawson Station in 1967.

**Jardine, D.** A FIDS geologist at Base G, Admiralty Bay, on King George Island, in the South Shetlands, in 1949. He traveled much on the island.

**Jardine Peak.** 62°10′S, 58°31′W. 285 m. On the west side of Admiralty Bay, King George Island, in the South Shetlands. Named by the UK in 1960 for D. Jardine.

**JARE IV Nunataks.** 71°38′S, 35°59′E. Four aligned nunataks in the Queen Fabiola Mountains. Discovered on Oct. 7, 1960, by the Belgian Antarctic Expedition of 1959–61, led by Guido Derom. Named by him for the JARE IV (*see* **Japanese Antarctic Research Expeditions**).

**Jaren Crags.** 71°45′S, 6°44′E. A row of rock peaks forming a bluff just west of Storkvarvet Mountain, in the Mühlig-Hofmann Mountains. Name means "the edge" in Norwegian.

**Jarina Nunatak.** 76°23′S, 160°10′E. In the Mawson Glacier, Victoria Land. Named in 1964 for Lt. Cdr. Michael Jarina, US Navy pilot in Antarctica in 1962.

**Jarl Nunataks.** 71°55′S, 3°18′E. Also called Jarlsaetet. 3 miles north of Risen

Peak, in Queen Maud Land. Named for Jarl Tønnesen, Norwegian meteorologist in Antarctica.

**Jarlsaetet** *see* **Jarl Nunataks**

**Jaron Cliffs.** 76°23′S, 112°10′W. A line of steep, snow-covered cliffs on the south side of Mount Takahe in Marie Byrd Land. Named for Helmut P. Jaron, aurora scientist at Byrd Station in 1963.

**Jarrett, William.** Master-at-arms on the Wilkes Expedition 1838–42. Joined in the USA. Discharged at Oahu on Oct. 31, 1840.

**The *Jason.*** Norwegian whaler in Antarctic waters in 1892–93. Captain was Carl Anton Larsen, and first mate was Søren Andersen. It collected fossils on Seymour Island, discovered the Foyn Coast and much else, visited the South Orkneys, and penetrated the Weddell Sea as far south as 64°40′S, 56°30′W. The ship was back again in 1893–94, and this time penetrated the Weddell Sea to 68°10′S along the eastern coast of the Antarctic Peninsula.

[1]**Mount Jason** *see* **Jason Peninsula**

[2]**Mount Jason.** 77°30′S, 161°35′E. In the Olympus Range of Victoria Land. Named by the New Zealanders in 1959 for the mythological Greek hero.

**Jason Island** *see* **Jason Peninsula**

**Jason Land** *see* **Jason Peninsula**

**Jason Peninsula.** 66°10′S, 61°W. Juts out into the Larsen Ice Shelf from the south of Graham Land's east coast. Its tip is Cape Framnes. Discovered by Larsen in 1893 and named Jason Land by him for the *Jason,* his ship. Renamed by Nordenskjöld in 1902 as Jason Island, and later it was even called Mount Jason. In 1955 the FIDS determined it to be a peninsula.

**Jasper Point.** 62°11′S, 58°55′W. Just to the west of Collins Harbor, on King George Island, in the South Shetlands.

**Jato Nunatak.** 72°21′S, 165°52′E. 8 miles west of Crosscut Peak, in the Millen Range, on the Polar Plateau. Named by the New Zealanders in 1963 for the JATO (jet assisted take-off) planes.

**Jaynes Islands.** 73°59'S, 104°15'W. 20 miles west of Canisteo Peninsula, in the Amundsen Sea. Named for James T. Jaynes, USN, equipment operator at Byrd Station in 1966.

**Île Jean Rostand** *see* **Rostand Island**

**Mount Jeanne** *see* **Jeanne Hill**

**Jeanne Hill.** 65°04'S, 64°01'W. Also called Mount Jeanne. 195 m. On Booth Island, overlooking Port Charcot. Discovered by Charcot in 1904, and named by him for his sister.

**Port Jebsen.** 60°43'S, 45°41'W. On the west side of Signy Island, in the South Orkneys. Charted by Petter Sørlle in 1912–13. Named in association with nearby Jebsen Point.

**Jebsen Point.** 60°43'S, 45°41'W. On the west side of Signy Island, in the South Orkneys. Possibly named in 1912–13 by Petter Sørlle, for one of his men.

**Jebsen Rocks.** 60°43'S, 45°41'W. A chain of rocks extending ½ mile in an east-west direction, ½ mile north of Jebsen Point, on the west side of Signy Island, in the South Orkneys. Charted by Petter Sørlle in 1912–13. Named in association with the point.

**Jefferson, Daniel.** Ordinary seaman on the Wilkes Expedition 1838–42. Joined in the USA. Returned in the *Relief*, in 1839.

**Jefferson, Thomas.** Seaman on the Wilkes Expedition 1838–42. Joined in the USA. Returned in the *Relief*, 1839.

**Jefford, Brian.** FIDS surveyor at Base D in 1948 and at Base G in 1949.

**Jefford Point.** 64°24'S, 57°41'W. A rock cliff with ice on top. On the south coast of James Ross Island. First surveyed by Nordenskjöld's expedition of 1901–4. Resurveyed by the FIDS in 1948 and 1952. Named by the UK for Brian Jefford.

**Jeffrey, D.G.** Navigator on the *Quest*, 1921–22.

**Jeffrey Head.** 74°35'S, 111°45'W. A headland on Bear Peninsula, in Marie Byrd Land, overlooking the Dotson Ice Shelf. Algae and lichens are to be found here. Named for Stuart S. Jeffrey, ionosphere physicist at Byrd Station in 1966.

**Jeffries, Peter H.** Meteorologist in the Advance Party of the BCTAE 1955–58.

**Jeffries, William.** Ordinary seaman on the Wilkes Expedition 1838–42. Joined in the USA. Run at Rio.

**Jeffries Bluff.** 73°48'S, 60°14'W. In the southern part of the Kemp Peninsula, on the east coast of the Antarctic Peninsula.

**Jeffries Glacier.** 79°02'S, 28°12'W. Between Lenton Bluff and Marø Cliffs in the Theron Mountains. Named for Peter H. Jeffries.

**Jeffries Peak.** 64°43'S, 62°W. Between the Leonardo and Blanchard Glaciers, on the west coast of Graham Land, south of Wilhelmina Bay. Named by the UK for 18th-century US balloonist John Jeffries.

**Jekselen Peak.** 72°S, 2°33'W. 1,405 m. In the Ahlmann Range of Queen Maud Land. Name means "the molar" in Norwegian.

**Jelbart, John E.** Australian observer on the NBSAE 1949–52. On Feb. 24, 1951, the Weasel driven by Bertil Ekström plunged over the edge of the Quar Ice Shelf near Maudheim Station. Jelbart was one of those killed.

**Jelbart Glacier** *see* **Utstikkar Glacier**

**Jelbart Ice Shelf.** 71°S, 5°W. Also called Jelbartisen. 40 miles wide. To the west of the Fimbul Ice Shelf, on the coast of Queen Maud Land. Named by the Norwegians for John E. Jelbart.

**Jelbartisen** *see* **Jelbart Ice Shelf**

**Jellyfish.** Class: Scyphozoa. Phylum: Cnidaria. Found in Antarctic waters.

**Isla Jenie** *see* **Pampa Island**

**Mount Jenkins.** 75°08'S, 69°10'W. 1,705 m. In the Sweeney Mountains. Discovered by the RARE 1947–48. Named for W.H. Jenkins, medic at Amundsen-Scott South Pole Station in 1963.

**Jenkins Heights.** 74°48'S, 114°20'W. On Martin Peninsula, on the coast of Marie Byrd Land.

**Jenner Glacier.** 64°27'S, 62°35'W. 3 miles long. Feeds Duperré Bay from the Solvay Mountains on Brabant Island. Discovered before 1953, and later named by the UK for Edward Jenner of smallpox fame.

**Jennings Bluff.** 66°42'S, 55°29'E. 100 m. In the Nicholas Range. Discovered by the BANZARE 1929–31. Photographed by the LCE 1936–37, and named Brattstabben (the steep stump) by them. Renamed by the Australians in 1961 for N.D. Jennings, mechanic at Mawson Station in 1960.

**Jennings Glacier.** 71°57'S, 24°22'E. Also called Jenningsbreen. 10 miles long. In the Sør Rondane Mountains, flowing along the west side of the Luncke Range. Named for Lt. James C. Jennings, USN, who flew over this area during Operation Highjump, 1946–47.

**Jennings Lake.** 70°10'S, 72°32'E. A narrow meltwater lake, 3 miles long, at the foot of the Jennings Promontory, on the eastern flange of the Amery Ice Shelf. Named for Lt. James C. Jennings (see **Jennings Glacier**).

**Jennings Peak.** 71°32'S, 168°07'E. 2,320 m. In the Dunedin Range of the Admiralty Mountains. Named for Cedell Jennings, USN, electrician at McMurdo Station in 1968.

**Jennings Promontory.** 70°10'S, 72°31' E. On the eastern flange of the Amery Ice Shelf, between Branstetter Rocks and the Kreitzer Glacier. Mapped in 1952 by US cartographer John H. Roscoe, and named by him for Lt. James C. Jennings (see **Jennings Glacier**).

**Jennings Reef.** 67°46'S, 68°50'W. Mostly submerged. Between Avian Island and Rocca Island, off the south end of Adelaide Island. Named by the UK for A.J. Jennings, RN, coxswain on the *Quest* in 1963.

**The *Jenny*.** British sealer from the Isle of Wight found drifting by the *Hope* under Capt. Brighton in the Drake Passage in Sept. 1840. All the crew were dead, and the log was entered up to Jan. 17, 1823. It had evidently been to the South Shetlands in the 1822–23 season.

**Jenny Buttress.** 61°59'S, 57°43'W. A rock buttress 2½ miles north of Melville Peak, overlooking Destruction Bay, on the east side of King George Island, in the South Shetlands. Named by the UK in 1960 for the *Jenny*.

**Jenny Island.** 67°44'S, 68°25'W. 2 miles long. Highest point is 500 meters. In Marguerite Bay, 3 miles from Adelaide Island, off the west coast of Graham Land. Discovered by Charcot in 1908–10, and named by him for Bongrain's wife.

**Mount Jensen.** 77°09'S, 162°27'E. Over 1,000 m. Between the Gonville and Caius Range and the Debenham Glacier, to the south of Granite Harbor, in Victoria Land. Mapped and named by Scott's 1910–13 expedition.

**Jensen, Bernhard.** Capt. Commander of the *Southern Cross* during Borchgrevink's 1898–1900 expedition.

**Jensen Glacier.** 85°05'S, 170°48'E. 10 miles long. Flows into Snakeskin Glacier, from between Lhasa Nunatak and the Supporters Range, in the Queen Maud Mountains. Named for Kenard H. Jensen, meteorologist at Amundsen-Scott South Pole Station in 1963.

**Jensen Nunataks.** 73°04'S, 66°05'W. A cluster of isolated nunataks in Palmer Land, 28 miles NE of Mount Vang. Named for Curtis M. Jensen, glaciologist at Byrd Station in 1965–66.

**Cape Jeremy.** 69°24'S, 68°51'W. Juts out from Graham Land into Marguerite Bay, between the Wordie Ice Shelf and the northern entrance to the George VI Sound. Discovered by the BGLE 1934–37, and named by Rymill for Jeremy Scott, son of J.M. Scott, home agent for the expedition.

**Jeroboam Glacier.** 65°38'S, 62°40'W. Runs into Starbuck Glacier, in Graham Land. Named by the UK for the ship in *Moby Dick*.

Jessie Bay. 60°44'S, 44°44'W. Also called Bahía Uruguay. 4 miles wide. On the north side of Laurie Island, in the South Orkneys. Named by Bruce in 1903 for his wife.

Mount Jessie O'Keefe see Mount Blackburn

Jester Rock. 67°52'S, 68°42'W. Also called Page Rock. An isolated rocklet in Marguerite Bay. Between Emperor Island and Noble Rocks in the Dion Islands. Charcot discovered it in 1909. Surveyed by the FIDS in 1948 and named by the UK for a court jester, in association with the courtly theme predominant among the features in this area.

Jetty Peninsula. 70°30'S, 68°55'E. Steep-sided. Flat-topped. Extends for 30 miles. Juts out from the Prince Charles Mountains into the Amery Ice Shelf, in Mac. Robertson Land. Discovered aerially by the ANARE in 1956. Named by the Australians because it looks like a jetty.

Mount Jewell. 66°56'S, 53°09'E. 3 miles south of Mount Cordwell, in Enderby Land. Named by the Australians for F. Jewell, geophysicist at Wilkes Station in 1961.

Jewell, William. Seaman on the Wilkes Expedition 1838–42. Joined in the USA. Discharged at Oahu on Nov. 2, 1840.

Jigsaw Islands. 64°54'S, 63°37'W. Also called Jigsaw Island. Two small islands off the SW coast of Wiencke Island. The British Naval Hydrographic Survey Unit was on one island in 1956–57. Named by the UK to illustrate their difficulty, years later, in finding this station.

Jimmy Automatic Weather Station. 77°48'S, 166°42'E. An American AWS at an elevation of approximately 630 feet. Operated from Dec. 5, 1981, to Dec. 31, 1982. It was reactivated on Feb. 1, 1987.

Jingle Island. 65°23'S, 65°18'W. 1½ miles long. 1 mile NE of Weller Island, in the Pitt Islands of the Biscoe Islands. Named by the UK in 1959 for the Dickens character.

Jinks Island. 65°22'S, 65°38'W. Also called Isla Pedro Nelson. 5 miles north of Pickwick Island, in the Pitt Islands of the Biscoe Islands. Discovered before 1957, and named by the UK in 1959 for the Dickens character.

Mount Jiracek. 73°46'S, 163°56'E. 2,430 m. In the Southern Cross Mountains of Victoria Land. Named for George R. Jiracek, geophysicist at McMurdo Station in 1964–65.

Jocelyn Islands. 67°35'S, 62°53'E. Between the Flat Islands and the Rouse Islands in Holme Bay. They include Petersen Island, Teyssier Island, and Verner Island. Photographed and mapped by the LCE 1936–37, and named by them as Meholmane (the middle islands). Renamed in 1960 by the ANARE for Miss Jocelyn Terry, radio broadcaster from Australia to Antarctica.

Cape Joerg see Cape Agassiz

Joerg Peninsula. 68°30'S, 65°W. 20 miles long. Juts out into the Larsen Ice Shelf from the east side of the Antarctic Peninsula, just north of Mobiloil Inlet. Three Slice Nunatak is on it. First charted in 1940 by the USAS. Named by the UK in 1952 for W.L.G. Joerg (see Joerg Plateau).

Joerg Plateau. A snow-covered upland scattered with mountain peaks, near the Orvile Coast, in the area of the Ronne Ice Shelf. Named by Finn Ronne in 1947–48 during the RARE, for W.L.G. Joerg, US cartographer. This term is no longer used.

Mount Joern. 72°35'S, 160°24'E. 2,510 m. 3 miles NW of Mount Bower, in the Outback Nunataks. Named for Albert T. Joern, scientist at Amundsen-Scott South Pole Station in 1968.

Johannes Müller Crests see Müller Crest

Johannessen, Olav. Captain of the Norsel, 1954–55.

Johannessen Harbor. 65°26'S, 65°25'W. On the NE side of Snodgrass Island, in the Pitt Islands of the Biscoe Islands. First entered by the Norsel in 1955. Named later by the UK for Olav Johannessen.

**Johannessen Nunataks.** 72°52'S, 161° 11'E. A series of rocks, 4 miles long. In the southern end of the Outback Nunataks. Named for Karl R. Johannessen, meteorologist at McMurdo Station in 1967–68.

**Mount Johansen.** 70°32'S, 67°11'E. 1,555 m. In the White Massif, in the Aramis Range of the Prince Charles Mountains. First visited in Dec. 1956 by an ANARE party led by W.G. Bewsher. Named by the Australians for Sgt. G. Johansen, RAAF, air frame fitter at Mawson Station in 1956.

**Johansen.** One of Borchgrevink's wintering-over party during the British Antarctic Expedition of 1898–1900.

**Johansen, Bendik.** Norwegian sailing master and ice pilot. He was on the *City of New York* during Byrd's 1928–30 expedition, starting off as second mate, and becoming first mate and ice pilot later in the expedition. He also took part in Byrd's 1933–35 expedition, being sailing master and ice pilot on the *Jacob Ruppert* for the first half of the expedition, and sailing master and first officer on the *Bear of Oakland* during the second half. In 1939–41 he was ice pilot on the *Bear* during the USAS.

**Johansen, Hjalmar.** b. 1867, Norway. d. Jan. 4, 1913. Champion skier, good dog driver, and former army man, he was with Nansen in the Arctic. He was a sailor on the *Belgica* expedition to Antarctica in 1897–99, and years later was forced on Amundsen by Nansen as part of the Norwegian Antarctic Expedition of 1910–12, despite having drinking problems. He caused Amundsen disciplinary problems at Framheim, and on his return to Norway he succumbed to drink again. A tragic figure all around, he shot himself to death.

**Johansen Islands.** 69°03'S, 72°52'W. A group of low, small, partly snow-covered islands, 12 miles WNW of Cape Vostok, off the NW coast of Alexander Island. Discovered by personnel from the *Bear* in 1940, during flights made by USAS airplanes. Named for Bendik Johansen.

**Johansen Peak.** 86°43'S, 148°11'W. Also called Mount Hjalmar Johansen, Mount Thurston. 3,310 m. In the La Gorce Mountains. Discovered by Byrd on Nov. 28–29, 1929, during his flight to the South Pole. Mapped by Quin Blackburn in 1934 during Byrd's 1933–35 expedition. In 1911 Amundsen named a peak in this general area as Mount H. Johansen, for Hjalmar Johansen. Amundsen was speeding toward the Pole at the time and did not have much time to plot geographic features with much accuracy. In order to preserve Johansen's name in this area, this particular peak was thus named.

**The *John*.** London sealing brig in the South Shetlands in the 1820–21 season, under the command of Capt. John Walker.

**John, D. Dilwyn.** Member of the zoological staff of the Discovery Committee in the 1920s and 1930s. He was chief scientist on the *William Scoresby* from Dec. 1927 to April 1929. He was leader of the *Discovery II* expedition of 1931–33, and in 1934 he was back on that ship, but not as leader.

**John Beach.** 62°39'S, 60°46'W. At the west side of the entrance to Walker Bay, on the south coast of Livingston Island, in the South Shetlands. Fildes charted it in 1820–22, and named it Black Point. It was renamed in 1958 by the UK for the *John*.

**¹The *John Biscoe*.** The first of two British ships with the name (named for John Biscoe, the 19th-century British navigator in Antarctica). This one was a FIDS relief vessel from 1947–56. Captain from 1947–48 was A.M. McFie, from 1948–50 it was Henry Kirkwood, and from 1950–55 it was William Johnston, the man most identified with both vessels of this name. Chief engineer most of this time, 1948–55, was Herbert Ward. In 1956 its name was changed to the *Pretext,* and shortly thereafter to the *Endeavour* (q.v.), under which name it continued to sail to Antarctica. It was replaced as a FIDS ship by the new *John Biscoe* (see below).

²**The *John Biscoe*.** British ship of 1,584 tons, launched in June 1956. It was a replacement for the old *John Biscoe* (which became the *Endeavour*—see above). William Johnston was its skipper from 1956–62, and Herbert Ward its chief engineer. It was still active in Antarctica throughout the 1970s and 1980s. In Nov. 1973 it brought David Lewis (q.v.) back to Palmer Station to pick up his boat. In mid–Nov. 1985 it got caught in the pack ice near Adelaide Island, and was abandoned on Nov. 18. The crew was rescued by the *Polarstern* and the *Polar Duke*. On Nov. 20 the *Polarstern* broke the ship free and it was reclaimed by its crew.

**John Bowman Peak** *see* **Bowman Peak**

**John Carlson Bucht** *see* **Carlsson Bay**

**John Hayes Hammond Inlet** *see* **Hammond Glacier**

**John Hays Hammond Glacier** *see* **Hammond Glacier**

**John Nunatak.** 81°12'S, 85°19'W. Also called Granite Knob. An isolated granite nunatak, 4 miles north of the Pirrit Hills. Named for Orlan F. John (*see* **Deaths, 1960**).

**John O'Groats.** The eastern end of Cape Denison, East Antarctica.

**John Peaks.** 60°43'S, 45°04'W. 415 m. Snow-covered. On the extreme SW of Powell Island, in the South Orkneys. Charted in 1933 by personnel on the *Discovery II*, who named them for D.D. John.

**John Quincy Adams Glacier** *see* **Adams Glacier**

**John Shepard Island** *see* **Shepard Island**

**Cape John Wheeler** *see* **Cape Wheeler**

**Johnny penguin** *see* **Gentoo penguin**

**Mount Johns.** 79°37'S, 91°14'W. 90 m. A solitary nunatak, 50 miles west of

the Heritage Range. Discovered on Jan. 27, 1958, by the Marie Byrd Land Traverse Party of 1957–58, and named for Robert H. Johns, meteorologist at Byrd Station in 1957.

**Johns Glacier.** 85°48'S, 136°30'W. 8 miles long. In the Watson Escarpment, it flows into the Kansas Glacier. Named for Antarctic veteran Lt. Ernest H. Johns, USN.

**Johns Hopkins Ridge.** 78°09'S, 162°27'E. Runs northward from Mount Rücker for 6 miles, in the Royal Society Range. Named in 1963 for the American university.

**Johns Knoll.** 71°59'S, 7°59'E. A crevassed ice-knoll in the lower part of the Vinje Glacier, in Queen Maud Land. Named Johnsbåen (John's sunken rock) by the Norwegians, for John Snuggerud, Norwegian radio technician in Antarctica in the late 1950s.

**John's Peak.** On Coronation Island, in the South Orkneys. A term no longer used.

**John's Range** *see* **Saint Johns Range**

**Cape Johnson.** 74°04'S, 165°09'E. Ice-covered. In the northern part of Wood Bay, Victoria Land. Discovered by Ross in 1841, and named by him for Capt. Edward John Johnson, RN.

¹**Johnson, Capt.** British commander of the *Hannah* during the 1820–21 season in the South Shetlands. The ship was wrecked on Dec. 25, 1820. It is unclear who this captain was.

²**Johnson, Capt.** British commander of the *Mellona* during the 1821–22 season in the South Shetlands. His first name was probably Thomas.

**Johnson, Francis.** Ordinary seaman on the Wilkes Expedition 1838–42. Joined in the USA. Sent home on the *Relief* in 1839.

**Johnson, Henry.** Ordinary seaman on the Wilkes Expedition 1838–42. Joined in the USA. Served the cruise.

**Johnson, James.** His tender (or shallop) was found in the South Shetlands on Jan. 31, 1830, by the *Penguin* and the *Annawan,* during the Palmer-Pendleton Expedition. Johnson must have been a sealer of the 1820s.

¹**Johnson, Robert.** American sealing captain in the South Shetlands in 1820–21, on the *Jane Maria* (he also commanded its tender, the *Sarah*), as part of the New York Sealing Expedition. In Jan. 1821, he made an exploratory cruise as far south as 66°S, 70°W. In 1821–22 he was back again in the South Shetlands, this time as commander of the *Wasp,* for the second phase of the New York Sealing Expedition. In 1822–23 he was back on his own, this time as commander of the *Henry.*

²**Johnson, Robert.** Seaman on the Wilkes Expedition 1838–42. Joined in the USA. Lost at sea in the *Sea Gull* about April 29, 1839 (not in Antarctic waters).

**Johnson, Robert E.** US Naval lieutenant who commanded the *Relief* in the early stages of the Wilkes Expedition 1838–42. At Tierra del Fuego, still on the way south, he transferred to command of the *Sea Gull.* He spent Dec. 10–17, 1838, looking for the thermometers Foster had left on Deception Island some years before. He did not find them. He was transferred again, before the disappearance of the *Sea Gull* in April 1839, and was detached at Honolulu in Nov. 1841.

**Johnson, T.** Crewman on the *Bear of Oakland,* 1934–35.

**Johnson, William.** Seaman on the Wilkes Expedition 1838–42. Joined in the USA. Sent home on the *Relief,* 1839.

**Johnson, William Floyd.** US representative at Ellsworth Station after the IGY (1957–58) when that station was taken over by Argentina.

**Johnson Bluff.** 84°49′S, 170°31′E. Overlooks the Keltie Glacier, where that glacier meets the Beardmore Glacier. Named for Dwight L. Johnson, biologist at McMurdo Station in 1963.

**Johnson Col.** 78°22′S, 85°10′W. Situated at 1,800 m. 2 miles WSW of Mount Farrell in the Sentinel Range. Named for Earl F. Johnson, USN, utiliesman at South Pole Station in 1957.

**Johnson Glacier.** 74°55′S, 134°45′W. Flows between the McDonald Heights and Bowyer Butte into the Getz Ice Shelf, on the coast of Marie Byrd Land. Named for Roland L. Johnson, USN, bosun's mate on the *Glacier* in 1961–62.

**Johnson Island.** 72°51′S, 93°55′W. 9 miles long and 5 miles wide. Ice-covered. In the Abbott Ice Shelf. At first it was thought to be an ice rise. Named for Theodore L. Johnson, electrical engineer at Byrd Station in 1964–65.

**Johnson Neck.** 79°27′S, 82°20′W. An isthmus which joins the Dott Ice Rise to the east side of the Pioneer Heights, in the Heritage Range. Named for Douglas J. Johnson, meteorologist at Byrd Station in 1965.

**Johnson Nunatak** *see* **Lyon Nunataks**

**Johnson Nunataks.** 85°02′S, 92°30′W. Two isolated nunataks, 3 miles west of Reed Ridge, in the Thiel Mountains. Named by geologists Peter Bermel and Arthur Ford for American geologist Charles G. Johnson, on the *Glacier* in 1958–59.

**Johnson Peaks.** 71°21′S, 12°26′E. A cluster of detached peaks forming the north end of the Mittlere Petermann Range, in the Wohlthat Mountains of Queen Maud Land. Discovered in 1938–39 by Ritscher and later named Johnsonhorna by the Norwegians, for Rolf Johnson, Norwegian steward on the Norwegian Antarctic Expedition of 1958–59.

**Johnson Spur.** 78°37′S, 84°W. On the east side of the Sentinel Range. Named for William F. Johnson, meteorologist at South Pole Station in 1957.

**Johnsons Dock.** 62°40′S, 60°22′W. A cove in the east side of South Bay, on Hurd Peninsula, Livingston Island, in the South Shetlands. Named about 1821 for Robert Johnson, commander of the *Jane Maria*.

**Johnson's Island** *see* **Half Moon Island**

**Isla Johnston** *see* **Lobel Island**

**¹Mount Johnston.** 64°44'S, 61°48'W. Has two snow-covered summits. Between Wilhelmina Bay and Hektoria Glacier, in Graham Land. Surveyed by the FIDS in 1955. Named by the UK for Capt. William Johnston.

**²Mount Johnston.** 71°31'S, 67°24'E. 1,770 m. The highest and southernmost peak of the Fisher Massif, just west of the Lambert Glacier. First visited in Oct. 1957 by Bruce Stinear and his ANARE party. Named by the Australians for airman D.M. Johnston, at Mawson Station in 1957.

**Johnston, T. Harvey.** Prof. Chief biologist on the BANZARE 1929–31.

**Johnston, William.** Capt. British captain of the FIDS relief ships *John Biscoe* (from 1950–55), *Shackleton* (1955–56), and the new *John Biscoe* (1956–62).

**Johnston Glacier.** 74°25'S, 62°20'W. Also called Freeborn Johnston Glacier. Feeds Nantucket Inlet from Mount Owen, in Palmer Land. Discovered by the RARE 1947–48, and named by Ronne for Freeborn Johnston, a Washington scientist helpful to the expedition.

**Johnston Heights.** 85°29'S, 172°47'E. 3,220 m. Snow-covered. They form the SE corner of the Otway Massif, in the Grosvenor Mountains. Named for David P. Johnston, geologist here in 1967–68.

**Johnston Passage.** 67°37'S, 69°24'W. A north-south channel separating the Amiot Islands from Adelaide Island. Named by the UK for Capt. William Johnston.

**Johnston Peak.** 66°16'S, 52°06'E. Also called Mount Harvey Johnston, Harvey Johnston Peak. 8 miles north of Mount Marr, in Enderby Land. Discovered in Jan. 1930 by the BANZARE, and named by Mawson for T. Harvey Johnston.

**Johnston Spur.** 74°23'S, 63°02'W. In the central part of the Guettard Range. Named for Thomas M. Johnston, equipment operator at Amundsen-Scott South Pole Station in 1965.

**Mount Johnstone.** 85°03'S, 167°45'W. 1,230 m. On the east side of Liv Glacier, in the Queen Maud Mountains. Named for C. Raymond Johnstone, logistics officer at McMurdo Station in 1965.

**Johnstone Glacier.** 71°52'S, 163°53'E. 1 mile east of Zenith Glacier, in the Bowers Mountains. Named by the New Zealanders for Ian Johnstone, chief scientific officer at Scott Base in 1967–68.

**Johnstone Ridge.** 80°08'S, 156°40'E. Ice-free. In the Britannia Range. Extends 7 miles northward from Mount Olympus toward the south side of the Hatherton Glacier, in Victoria Land. Named for Graeme N. Johnstone, scientist in Antarctica, 1962 and 1964.

**Joice Icefall.** 72°23'S, 166°21'E. Flows from the Polar Plateau through the Millen Range, into the Lensen Glacier. Named by the New Zealanders in 1963 for I. Joice, there at the time.

**Joides Basin.** 75°S, 174°E. A submarine feature of the Ross Sea.

**Joines, John.** Sailmaker on the *Porpoise* during the Wilkes Expedition 1838–42. Joined in the USA. Detached at Callao.

**Joint British-American Weddell Coast Sledge Party** *see* **Weddell Coast Sledge Party**

**Joint Services Expedition.** 1970–71. Also called the UK Joint Services Expedition. As its name implies it was a British expedition composed of personnel from the army, navy and air force. The expedition was based on the *Sultan* at Elephant Island, in the South Shetlands, and it was an expedition to explore the island. Capt. John P. Elder was surveyor.

**Joinville Island.** 63°15'S, 55°45'W. Just off the northern tip of the Antarctic Peninsula. Discovered by Dumont d'Urville on Feb. 27, 1838, and named by him for the Prince de Joinville.

**Jökelen** see **Mount Elkins**

**Jøkulfallet.** 71°51'S, 6°42'E. An icefall on the north side of Jøkulkyrkja Mountain, in the Mühlig-Hofmann Mountains. Name means "the glacier fall" in Norwegian.

**Jøkulgavlen Ridge.** 72°42'S, 3°21'W. Flat-topped. It forms the southern part of Jøkulskarvet Ridge, in the Borg Massif of Queen Maud Land. Name means "the glacier gable" in Norwegian.

**Jøkulhest Dome.** 71°52'S, 6°42'E. An ice-capped summit of Jøkulkyrkja Mountain in the Mühlig-Hofmann Mountains. Name means "the glacier horse" in Norwegian.

**Jøkulkyrkja Mountain.** 71°53'S, 6°40' E. The USSR calls it Massiv Yakova Gakkelya. 2,965 m. Ice-topped. In the Mühlig-Hofmann Mountains. Name means "the glacier church" in Norwegian.

**Jøkulskarvet Ridge.** 72°40'S, 3°18'W. Has an ice-capped summit. Just NE of Høgfonna Mountain, in the Borg Massif of Queen Maud Land. Name means "the glacier mountain" in Norwegian.

**Mount Joli.** 66°40'S, 140°01'E. A hill with 3 summits, the highest being 38 m. On the NE side of Pétrel Island, in the Géologie Archipelago. Charted by the French in 1951, and named by them for the summit in the European Alps.

**Joliffe, T.A.** Captain of the *William Scoresby*, 1931–32.

**Jon Islet** see **Låvebrua Island**

**Jona Island.** 66°55'S, 67°42'W. One of the Bennett Islands. Named by the UK for Franco P. Jona, US physicist.

**Jonassen, Ole.** Seaman on Nordenskjöld's 1901–4 expedition. He was one of the main party on Snow Hill Island.

**Jonassen Island.** 63°33'S, 56°40'W. 2½ miles long. In the south entrance to Antarctic Sound. Named Irízar Island in 1904 by Nordenskjöld, for Capt.

Julián Irízar. The name was later changed by the USA for Ole Jonassen.

**¹Cape Jones** see **Jones Ridge**

**²Cape Jones.** 73°17'S, 169°13'E. Also called Cape Constance. Just SE of Mount Lubbock, it forms the southern tip of Daniell Peninsula, in Victoria Land. Discovered in Jan. 1841 by Ross, and named by him for Capt. William Jones, RN.

**Mount Jones.** 77°14'S, 142°11'W. 12,040 feet. The northernmost summit of the Clark Mountains, in the Ford Ranges of Marie Byrd Land. Discovered aerially in 1940 during the USAS, and named for Clarence F. Jones, an American professor (see **Clark Mountains**).

**Jones, Harold D.** FIDS airplane mechanic at Base E, 1947–49. Part of the team which discovered the Jones Channel in 1949.

**Jones, J.** Seaman on the *Eleanor Bolling* during the second half of Byrd's 1928–30 expedition, i.e., 1929–30.

**Jones, John.** Ordinary seaman on the Wilkes Expedition 1838–42. Joined at Sydney. Served the cruise.

**Jones, Dr. Lois M.** In the 1969–70 season, this geochemist from Ohio State University was included in USARP, and led an all-women research team in Antarctica (see **Women in Antarctica**), a geology team dedicated to working in the dry valleys of Victoria Land, notably the Wright and Taylor Valleys. On Nov. 19, 1969, she became one of the first women ever to stand at the South Pole. Before she went she received a letter of commendation from President Nixon.

**Jones, Dr. S.E.** Medical officer at the Western Base during the AAE 1911–14.

**Jones, Thomas.** Seaman on the Wilkes Expedition 1838–42. Joined in the USA. Sent home on the *Relief* in 1839.

**Jones, William.** Seaman on the Wilkes Expedition 1838–42. Joined at Rio. Served the cruise.

**Jones Bluffs.** 74°47'S, 110°20'W. Just south of the Holt Glacier, on Bear Peninsula, on the coast of Marie Byrd Land. Named for Lt. Cdr. S.W. Jones, USN, part of Operation Deep Freeze 66 and 67.

**Jones Channel.** 67°30'S, 67°W. An ice-filled marine channel. 8 miles long. Between 1 and 2 miles wide. Between Blaiklock Island and the southern part of Arrowsmith Peninsula, Graham Land. Discovered by Harold D. Jones in 1949, and named for him by the UK.

**Jones Escarpment.** 70°S, 64°21'E. Extends south from the Riddell Nunataks. 12 miles NNW of Mount Starlight, in Mac. Robertson Land. Named by the Australians for W.K. Jones, geophysicist at Wilkes Station in 1960.

**Jones Glacier.** 66°36'S, 91°30'E. A channel glacier. 5 miles wide. 6 miles long. Flows into the Davis Sea, just to the east of Krause Point. Named for Ensign Teddy E. Jones, USNR, photo interpreter with Operation Windmill, 1947–48.

**Jones Mountains.** 73°32'S, 94°W. An isolated group, extending 27 miles in an east-west direction, on the Eights Coast of Ellsworth Land, overlooking the Bellingshausen Sea. First seen in Nov. 1940 during a flight from the *Bear*. Named by Edward Thiel and J. Campbell Craddock, geologists, for Thomas O. Jones, head of the Office of Antarctic Programs for the National Science Foundation.

**Jones Nunatak.** 69°47'S, 159°04'E. At the head of Noll Glacier, in the Wilson Hills. Named for Frank E. Jones with VX-6 in 1967 and 1968.

**Jones Peak.** 85°05'S, 172°W. 3,670 m. Ice-free. 5 miles WNW of Mount Fisher, at the head of De Ganahl Glacier, in the Prince Olav Mountains. Named for John M. Jones of the National Academy of Sciences.

**Jones Point.** 64°39'S, 62°18'W. Juts out into Wilhelmina Bay, 6 miles SE of Cape Anna, on the west coast of Graham Land. First charted by de Gerlache in 1897–99, and named by the UK in 1960 for Sir Bennett M. Jones, a pioneer aerial surveyor.

**Jones Ridge.** 66°36'S, 99°25'E. Has a sharp peak at its seaward end. Right at the point where the Denman Glacier meets the coast of East Antarctica. Discovered by the Western Base Party of the AAE 1911–14, and named Cape Jones by them, for Dr. S.E. Jones. Redefined in 1955.

**Jones Rocks.** 66°34'S, 97°50'E. 4 miles SW of Avalanche Rocks, on the east shore of the Bay of Winds. Discovered by the AAE 1911–14, and named by Mawson for Dr. S.E. Jones.

**Jones Valley.** 83°55'S, 56°50'W. Snow-covered. Between West Prongs and Elliott Ridge, in the southern part of the Neptune Range, in the Pensacola Mountains. Named for Lt. (jg) James G.L. Jones, USN, at Ellsworth Station in 1958.

**Jorda, Henry P.** Lt. cdr., USN. Pilot with VX-6 during Operation Deep Freeze I (1955–56).

**Jorda Glacier.** 81°18'S, 159°49'E. 15 miles long. Flows from the Churchill Mountains, between Mount Coley and Pyramid Mountain, and merges with the lower Nursery Glacier, and thus helps feed the Ross Ice Shelf. Named for Henry Jorda.

**Jordan Nunatak.** 72°09'S, 101°16'W. Between the heads of the Rochray and Cox Glaciers, in the SW part of Thurston Island. Named for Joe Jordan, US Army helicopter mechanic on the Ellsworth Land Survey of 1968–69.

**Jorff, Charles.** Ordinary seaman on the Wilkes Expedition 1838–42. Joined at Valparaiso. Served the cruise.

**Islote Jorge** *see* **Walsham Rocks**

**Jorge Island.** 62°23'S, 59°46'W. One of the Aitcho Islands, in the South Shetlands. Named by the Chilean Antarctic Expedition of 1949–50 for the son of the *Lautaro's* commander, Capt. José Duarte.

**Mount Jorgen Stubberud** *see* **Mount Stubberud**

**Jorgensen, O.** Norwegian captain of the experimental whaling ship *Thulla* in 1911–12.

**Jorgensen Nunataks.** 83°43'S, 164°12' E. Two rock nunataks in the Queen Elizabeth Range, in the area of Mount Picciotto. Named for Arthur E. Jorgensen, meteorologist at South Pole Station in 1958.

**Islotes Jorquera** *see* **Myriad Islands**

**Jorum Glacier.** 65°14'S, 62°03'W. Flows into Exasperation Inlet, on the east coast of Graham Land, just north of Caution Point. Surveyed by the FIDS in 1947 and 1955. A jorum is a large drinking bowl, and the UK named it because the head of this glacier looks like one.

**Isla José Hernández** *see* **Midas Island**

**Joseph, Francis.** Seaman on the Wilkes Expedition 1838–42. Joined in the USA. Served the cruise.

**Joseph, John.** Captain's steward on the Wilkes Expedition 1838–42. Joined at Valparaiso. Served the cruise.

**Joseph Ames Range** *see* **Ames Range**

**Joseph Cook Bay** *see* **Cook Ice Shelf**

**Mount Joseph Haag** *see* **Haag Nunataks**

**Mount Josephine.** 77°33'S, 152°48'W. 6 miles SE of Bowman Peak, in the Alexandra Mountains of Marie Byrd Land. Discovered on Dec. 5, 1929, by Byrd on a fly-over during his 1928–30 expedition. Named by him during his 1933–35 expedition for Josephine Clay Ford, daughter of Edsel Ford.

**Mount Josephine Petras** *see* **Mount Petras**

**Joss, T.W.** Crewman on the *Bear of Oakland*, 1934–35.

**Joubert Rock.** 68°12'S, 67°41'W. About 35 feet under the water. 5 miles SW of Pod Rocks, in Marguerite Bay, off the west coast of Graham Land. Charted in 1966 by the personnel on the *John Biscoe*, and named for that ship's third

officer, Arthur B.D. Joubert, officer of the watch at point of discovery of the rock.

**Joubin Islands.** 64°47'S, 64°27'W. Also called the Joubin Archipelago. A group of small islands in the lee of the southern part of Anvers Island, 3 miles SW of Cape Monaco. They include Hartshorne Island, Dakers Island, Bielecki Island, McGuire Island, Trundy Island, Howard Island, Ouellette Island, Robbins Island, and Tukey Island. Discovered by Charcot in 1903–5, and named by him for French naturalist Louis Joubin.

**Jougla Point.** 64°50'S, 63°30'W. Forms the west side of the entrance to Alice Creek in Port Lockroy, on the west side of Wiencke Island. Discovered by Charcot in 1904 and named by him as Jougla Peninsula. It was later redefined.

**Joungane Peaks.** 72°04'S, 0°17'W. 4 small peaks in the Sverdrup Mountains of Queen Maud Land.

**Journal Peaks.** 72°41'S, 64°55'W. Two groups of peaks and nunataks 17 miles SE of the Seward Mountains in central Palmer Land. Named for the *Antarctic Journal of the USA* (*see* the Bibliography).

**Lake Joyce.** 77°43'S, 161°37'E. ½ mile long. 140 feet deep. Covered by 22 feet of very clear ice. In Pearse Valley, just south of Taylor Valley, in southern Victoria Land. Named in 1964 by the New Zealanders for Ernest Joyce.

**Mount Joyce.** 75°36'S, 160°51'E. 1,830 m. Dome-shaped. 8 miles NW of Mount Howard, in the Prince Albert Mountains. Between the Mawson and David Glaciers in Victoria Land. Mapped by Shackleton's expedition of 1907–9, and named by them for Ernest Joyce.

**Joyce, Ernest E.M.** 1875–1940. Ernest Edward Mills Joyce. Able Seaman, RN, on the Royal Society Expedition of 1901–4, with Scott. In 1907–9 he was in charge of provisions and dogs on the *Nimrod* during Shackleton's British Antarctic Expedition of that period. Joyce later selected the dogs for the AAE 1911–14. He bought them in Copenhagen and took them to Tasmania. His last Antarctic venture was as part of the Ross Sea depot-laying party during the British Imperial Transantarctic Expedition of 1914–17. He was one of the three depot-layers to survive, and took over from Mackintosh as leader. He wrote *The South Polar Trail* in 1929.

**Joyce Glacier.** 78°02'S, 163°50'E. Also called Hubley Glacier. Immediately north of Péwé Peak, between the Miers and Garwood Glaciers, in southern Victoria Land. Named by the New Zealand Blue Glacier Party of 1957–58 for Ernest Joyce.

**Jubany Base.** 62°14'S, 58°38'W. Argentine scientific station on King George Island, in the South Shetlands. Originally it was a refuge hut built at Potter Cove in 1948, and called Teniente Jubany Refugio. It was still operating into the 1990s.

**Judas Rock.** 63°52'S, 61°07'W. 5 miles west of the SW end of Trinity Island, in the Palmer Archipelago. Discovered before 1950, and named in 1960 by the UK because its isolated danger poses a threat of betrayal.

**Mount Judd.** 85°04'S, 170°26'E. Over 2,400 m. In the Supporters Range of the Queen Maud Mountains. Named for Robert C. Judd, meteorologist at Amundsen-Scott South Pole Station in 1964, and at Hallett Station in 1964–65.

**Judith Glacier.** 80°29'S, 158°49'E. 9 miles long. Flows from Mount Hamilton into Byrd Glacier, in the Queen Maud Mountains. Named for Cdr. J.H. Judith, USN, commander of the *Edisto* in 1964.

**Mount Jukkola.** 71°51'S, 64°38'W. A nunatak in the southern-central portion of the Guthridge Nunataks, in the Gutenko Mountains, of southern Palmer Land. Named for Lt. Lloyd A. Jukkola, USN, officer-in-charge of Palmer Station in 1973.

**Jule Peaks.** 72°S, 5°33'W. A small group of isolated peaks about 35 miles WNW of Borg Mountain, in Queen Maud Land. Named Juletoppane (Christmas peaks) in Norwegian.

**Cape Jules.** 66°44'S, 140°55'E. 3 miles west of the Zélée Glacier Tongue. Discovered by Dumont d'Urville in 1837–40, and named by him for his son Jules (also the admiral's name). Charted in 1912–13 by the AAE 1911–14, and again by the BANZARE in 1931.

**Mount Jumper.** 78°14'S, 85°37'W. 2,890 m. 7 miles east of Mount Viets, in the central part of the Sentinel Range. Named for Maj. Jesse T. Jumper.

**Jumper, Jesse T.** Maj., USAF. One of the men who helped build the South Pole Station in 1956–57.

**Cape Juncal.** 62°58'S, 56°27'W. Forms the NW end of D'Urville Island, in the area of Joinville Island, off the northern tip of the Antarctic Peninsula. Named by the Argentines in 1957 for the Argentine Naval victory of 1827.

**Junction Corner.** 66°30'S, 94°43'E. A point at the west side of the Shackleton Ice Shelf, where that body meets the mainland. Discovered and named by the AAE 1911–14.

**Junction Knob.** 77°36'S, 161°39'E. At the junction of Odin Glacier and Alberich Glacier, in the Asgard Range of Victoria Land. It is a small but distinctive peak.

**Junction Spur.** 79°53'S, 157°29'E. Forms the eastern end of the Darwin Mountains, right where the Darwin Glacier meets the Hatherton Glacier. Mapped and named by the Darwin Glacier Party of the BCTAE 1956–58.

**Mount June.** 76°15'S, 145°07'W. Also called Mount Harold June. 6 miles west of Mount Paige, in the Phillips Mountains of Marie Byrd Land. Discovered in Dec. 1929 during a fly-over on Byrd's 1928–30 expedition, and named for Harold I. June.

**June, Harold I.** Pilot and radioman on Byrd's 1928–30 expedition. He was one of the three men trapped in the Rockefeller Mountains (*see* **Airlifts**) between March 7 and 10, 1929. He was also one of Byrd's companions on his historic flight to the Pole on Nov. 29, 1929, in the *Floyd Bennett*. He came back with Byrd on the 1933–35 expedition, and was co-leader of the party which set up Bolling Advance Weather Station for Byrd to winter-over alone in the winter of 1934.

**June Island.** 68°08′S, 67°07′W. In the Debenham Islands. Charted by the BGLE 1934–37. Named by Rymill for one of Frank Debenham's daughters.

**June Nunatak.** 85°14′S, 169°29′W. In the Liv Glacier. Named by the New Zealanders in 1962 for Harold I. June.

**Juno Peaks.** 71°58′S, 69°47′W. Two steep-sided nunataks with a little rock to the west of them, in southern Alexander Island. Named by the UK for the asteroid.

**Jupiter Amphitheater.** 71°34′S, 161°51′E. A beautiful, steep-sided, glacier-filled valley in the eastern Morozumi Range. One gets into it between Sickle Nunatak and Mount Van Veen. Named in 1968 by the New Zealanders for the airplanes of that name.

**Jupiter Glacier.** 70°57′S, 68°30′W. 10 miles long, and 5 miles wide at its mouth. A little glacier feeding the George VI Sound from Alexander Island. First photographed aerially on Nov. 23, 1935, by Ellsworth. Surveyed many times, and named by the FIDS in 1950 for the planet.

**Jurien Island.** 63°29′S, 59°51′W. Also called Dumoulin Rock. North of Tower Island. Charted and named by Dumont d'Urville on March 4, 1838.

**Jurva Point.** 65°50′S, 65°49′W. Also called Punta Reyes. The southeastern-most point on Renaud Island, in the Biscoe Islands. Named by the UK in 1959 for Risto Jurva, Finnish oceanographer.

**Mount Justman.** 84°34′S, 172°56′W. 740 m. In the northern section of the Gabbro Hills, between Olliver Peak and Mount Roth, on the edge of the Ross Ice

Shelf. Named for Lt. Cdr. L.C. Justman, USN, in Antarctica in 1964.

**Jutland Glacier.** 71°55′S, 166°12′E. 15 miles long. 4 miles wide. Flows into the Greenwell Glacier in the Victory Mountains of Victoria Land. Named by the New Zealanders in 1963 for the World War I naval battle.

**Jutulgryta Crevasses.** 71°16′S, 0°27′E. A crevasse field 12 miles long. To the east of Jutulstraumen Glacier in Queen Maud Land. Name means "the giant's cauldron" in Norwegian.

**Jutulhogget Peak.** 72°02′S, 2°51′E. On Jutulsessen Mountain, in the Gjelsvik Mountains of Queen Maud Land. Named by the Norwegians.

**Jutulpløgsla Crevasses.** 72°28′S, 1°35′W. A crevasse field halfway up Jutulstraumen Glacier, in Queen Maud Land. Name means "the giant's plowed field" in Norwegian.

**Jutulrøra Mountain.** 72°15′S, 0°27′W. In the western part of the Sverdrup Mountains, overlooking Jutulstraumen Glacier, in Queen Maud Land. Name means "the giant's pipe" in Norwegian.

**Jutulsessen Mountain.** 72°02′S, 2°41′E. 2,370 m. 63 miles west of Svarthamaren, in the Gjelsvik Mountains, in the Mühlig-Hofmann Mountains of Queen Maud Land. The Norwegian Antarctic Research Expedition of 1984–85 set up an automatic weather station here. Name means "the giant's seat" in Norwegian.

**Jutulstraumen Glacier.** 71°35′S, 0°30′W. 120 miles long. Flows from the Sverdrup Mountains of Queen Maud Land, into the Fimbul Ice Shelf. Name means "the giant's stream" in Norwegian.

**Mount K. Olsen** *see* **Olsen Crags**

**Mount K. Prestrud** *see* **Mount Prestrud**

**Mount K. Sundbeck** *see* **Mount Sundbeck**

**Kabuto Rock.** 68°03′S, 43°36′E. A large blunt rock sticking out of the coast halfway between Chijire Glacier and

Rakuda Glacier, in Queen Maud Land. Named by the Japanese.

**Kado Point.** 69°39'S, 39°22'E. On the eastern side of Lützow-Holm Bay, it is the western extremity of the Skallen Hills, on the coast of Queen Maud Land. The Japanese named it Kado-misaki (corner point) in 1972.

**Kaggen Hill.** 72°03'S, 26°25'E. A small, ice-covered hill in Byrdbreen, 7 miles east of Mount Bergersen, in the Sør Rondane Mountains. Name means "the keg" in Norwegian.

**Isla Kahn** *see* **Challenger Island**

**Kainan Bay.** 78°07'S, 162°30'W. Also called Helen Washington Bay. An iceport which indents the front of the Ross Ice Shelf 37 miles NE of Roosevelt Island. Discovered by Scott in Jan. 1902. It was here that Shirase landed on Jan. 16, 1912, and he named it for his ship, the *Kainan Maru*. It has an ice shelf, on which Little America was located.

**The *Kainan Maru*.** 100-foot-long Japanese auxiliary schooner which was the expedition vessel for Shirase's Japanese South Polar expedition of 1911-12. Nomura was the skipper. The name means "Southern Pioneer" in Japanese.

**Kaino-Hama Beach.** 69°01'S, 39°34'E. 350 yards south of Kitami Beach, on the south side of East Ongul Island. Name means "beach of shells" in Japanese.

**Cape Kaiser.** 64°14'S, 62°01'W. The north end of Lecointe Island. Discovered by de Gerlache in 1897-99, and named by him for a supporter.

**Isla Kaiser** *see* **Lecointe Island**

**Kaiser Wilhelm Archipelago** *see* **Wilhelm Archipelago**

**Kaiser Wilhelm Land** *see* **Wilhelm II Land**

**Kaiser Wilhelm II Coast** *see* **Wilhelm II Land**

**Kakure Rocks.** 67°57'S, 44°47'E. Two rocky exposures along the east wall of the Shinnan Glacier, at the western end of Enderby Land. Named Kakure-iwa (hidden rocks) by the Japanese.

**Kalafut Nunatak.** 77°46'S, 145°36'W. Marks the SE end of the Haines Mountains, in the Ford Ranges of Marie Byrd Land. Named for John Kalafut, glaciologist at Byrd Station in 1966-67 and 1968-69.

**Kaldager, A.** Capt. Sailing master on the *Sir James Clark Ross* during Larsen's 1923-24 whaling expedition to Antarctica.

**Kallenberg, Paul.** Crewman on the *Bear of Oakland*, 1933-35.

**Kal'vets Rock.** 71°47'S, 11°09'E. 2 miles WSW of the summit of Mount Flånuten, on the west side of the Humboldt Mountains, in Queen Maud Land. Discovered by Ritscher in 1938-39. Named by the USSR for O.A. Kal'vets, one of their pilots.

**Kame Island.** 67°58'S, 44°12'E. 4 miles east of Cape Ryugu, close to the shore of Queen Maud Land. Named Kame-shima (turtle island) by the Japanese because of its shape.

**Kamelen Island.** 67°31'S, 61°37'E. 45 m. 3 miles SW of the Einstoding Islands, in the north part of the Stanton Group. Photographed by the LCE 1936-37. Name means "the camel" in Norwegian.

**Kamenev Bight.** 69°55'S, 9°30'E. 25 miles wide. In the ice shelf fringing the coast of Queen Maud Land. Its western end is Cape Krasinskiy. It is 60 miles NW of the Schirmacher Hills. Named by the USSR for S.S. Kamenev, organizer of Arctic expeditions.

**Kamenev Nunatak.** 71°41'S, 63°W. 7 miles west of Mount Whiting, in Palmer Land, inland from Odom Inlet. Named by the USA for Yevgeniy N. Kamenev, USSR geologist, exchange scientist to McMurdo Station in 1972, and who was in Palmer Land in 1972-73.

**Kamenistaya Platform.** 70°35'S, 68°47'E. On Jetty Peninsula, near the Amery Ice Shelf. Soyuz Station is at its foot.

**Kaminski Nunatak.** 83°36'S, 54°12'W. Cone-shaped. 1½ miles SE of Rivas

Peaks, in the Neptune Range of the Pensacola Mountains. Named for Francis Kaminski, aerographer at Ellsworth Station in 1958.

**Mount Kammuri.** 69°13'S, 39°45'E. 340 m. 1½ miles SSE of Mount Choto, in the central part of the Langhovde Hills, on the coast of Queen Maud Land. Named Kammuri-yama (actually Kanmuri-yama), meaning "crown mountain," by the Japanese in 1973.

**Lake Kamome.** 69°01'S, 39°35'E. In the Langhovde Hills, in Queen Maud Land. Named by the Japanese.

**Kamp Glacier.** 71°45'S, 25°24'E. 8 miles long. In the Sør Rondane Mountains. Name means "the crag" in Norwegian.

**Kampekalven Mountain.** 71°56'S, 7°46'E. 2,200 m. Forms the NE end of the Filchner Mountains in Queen Maud Land. Name means "the crag calf" in Norwegian.

**Kamskaya Peak.** 71°57'S, 13°25'E. 2,690 m. The highest peak of Dekefjellet Mountain, in the Weyprecht Mountains of Queen Maud Land. Discovered by Ritscher in 1938–39. Named by the USSR in 1966, probably for the Kama River in their homeland.

**Kanak Peak.** 79°16'S, 158°30'E. 2,410 m. Ice-free. 6 miles north of Mount Gniewek, and north of the head of Carlyon Glacier, in the Cook Mountains. Named for Lt. Cdr. R.A. Kanak, USN, commander of the *Durant* in 1963.

**Kaname Island.** 69°21'S, 37°36'E. A small, isolated island, 22 miles NW of Padda Island, in Lützow-Holm Bay. Discovered by Japanese helicopter fly-overs in 1969–70, and named by them as Kaname-jima (main island) in 1972.

**Mount Kane.** 73°58'S, 62°59'W. 6 miles WSW of Squires Peak, in the Playfair Mountains of southern Palmer Land. Named for Alan F. Kane, construction mechanic at Amundsen-Scott South Pole Station in 1964.

**Kane, Capt.** Commander of the *Sarah E. Spear* on its second voyage to the South Shetlands, in 1853–54.

**Kane Rocks.** 85°18'S, 166°45'E. 3 miles long. In the Dominion Range, between the Koski and Vandement Glaciers. Named for Henry Scott Kane, scientist at Amundsen-Scott South Pole Station in 1964, and a member of the South Pole–Queen Maud Land Traverses of 1964–65 and 1965–66.

**Kani Rock.** 68°02'S, 43°12'E. Between Umeboshi Rock and Chijire Rocks, on the Queen Maud Land coast. The Japanese named it Kani-iwa (crab rock).

**Mount Kanmuri** *see* **Mount Kammuri**

**Kannheiser Glacier.** 72°10'S, 101°52'W. 4 miles long. 12 miles ESE of Cape Flying Fish, on Thurston Island. It flows into the Abbott Ice Shelf. Named for Lt. Cdr. William Kannheiser, USN, helicopter pilot on the *Glacier* here in 1960.

**Kansas Glacier.** 85°42'S, 134°30'W. 25 miles long. Runs from Stanford Plateau to enter Reedy Glacier just north of Blubaugh Nunatak. Named for the University of Kansas, in Lawrence, Kansas, which has sent several researchers to Antarctica.

**Kapellet Canyon.** 71°53'S, 6°47'E. An indentation into the east side of Jøkulkyrkja Mountain, in the Mühlig-Hofmann Mountains. Name means "the chapel" in Norwegian.

**The *Kapitan Bondarenko*.** USSR ship, sister vessel to the *Mikhail Somov*. In 1985 it was trapped in the ice off Marie Byrd Land for 133 days. In 1986 it broke a rudder off Russkaya Station. It took 6 solid days to effect a temporary repair, and then it made New Zealand for proper repairs.

**The *Kapitan Gotsky*.** A USSR diesel electric cargo ship of the icebreaker class, in Antarctic waters in the 1970s.

**The *Kapitan Markov*.** A USSR ice-strengthened cargo ship of the 1980s.

**Mount Kaplan.** 84°33'S, 175°19'E. The highest mountain in the Hughes Range. 3 miles SE of Mount Wexler. Discovered by Byrd on Nov. 18, 1929. Surveyed by Crary in 1957–58, and named by him for Joseph Kaplan, chairman of the US National Committee for the IGY, 1957–58.

**Kappa Island.** 64°19'S, 63°W. Also called Isla Donati. ½ mile long. South of Beta Island, and east of Theta Island, in the Melchior Islands. Explored by the personnel on the *Discovery* in 1927, and named by them for the Greek letter.

**Kar Plateau.** 76°54'S, 162°40'E. 1,000 feet high. A small, mainly snow-covered plateau, just to the north of the Mackay Glacier Tongue, in Victoria Land, on the coast of Granite Harbor. Named by Scott's 1910–13 expedition. Kar means "snow" in Turkish.

**Karaali Rocks.** 75°23'S, 137°55'W. A small group on the east side of the Coulter Heights, 5 miles east of Matikonis Peak, in Marie Byrd Land. Named for Atok Karaali, ionosphere physicist at Plateau Station in 1968.

**Karamete Point.** 69°09'S, 35°26'E. Just east of Kita-karamete Rock, on the east side of the Riiser-Larsen Peninsula, on the coast of Queen Maud Land. Named Karamete-misaki (back gate point) by the Japanese in 1963.

**Kåre Bench.** 71°29'S, 12°10'E. 1,810 m. A flat-topped mountain, 1 mile south of Mount Hansen, and just SW of Daykovaya Peak, at the north end of the Westliche Petermann Range, in the Wohlthat Mountains of Queen Maud Land. Discovered by Ritscher in 1938–39. Named Kåreseten by the Norwegians, for Kåre Hansen, a meteorologist on the Norwegian Antarctic Expedition of 1958–59.

**Karelin Bay.** 66°30'S, 85°E. An indentation into the West Ice Shelf, immediately NW of Leskov Island. Named by the USSR in 1956 for Dmitri Karelin, professor of oceanography, a meteorologist, and sea ice–forecasting pioneer.

**Karelin Islands.** 65°35'S, 65°35'W. Also called Islas Uribe. 3 miles in extent. 3 miles SE of Tula Point on Renaud Island, in the Biscoe Islands.

**Kåreseten** *see* **Kåre Bench**

**Cape Karl Andreas** *see* **Cape Andreas**

**Karlsen Rock.** 60°21'S, 46°W. Also called Karsten Rock. 10 miles NNW of Penguin Point, on Coronation Island, in the South Orkneys. It is submerged. Sørlle charted and named it in 1912–13.

**Karm Island.** 66°59'S, 57°27'E. 1½ miles long. 1 mile SE of Shaula Island in the south part of the Øygarden Group. Photographed by the LCE 1936–37, and named by them as Karm (the name means "coaming" in Norwegian). First visited in 1954 by an ANARE sledging party led by Robert Dovers.

**Karo Hills.** 85°34'S, 154°10'W. Ice-free foothills extending for 12 miles along the west side of the terminus of the Robert Scott Glacier from Mount Salisbury to the edge of the Ross Ice Shelf. Discovered during Byrd's 1928–30 expedition, and later named for Adm. H. Arnold Karo, director of the US Coast and Geodetic Survey, 1955–65.

**Karpf Point.** 66°54'S, 64°23'W. On the north side of Mill Inlet, 3 miles south of Mount Vartdal, on the east coast of Graham Land. Charted by the FIDS, and named by them for Alois Karpf, polar writer.

**Mount Karpinskiy.** 72°12'S, 18°25'E. Isolated. 9 miles south of Zhelannaya Mountain, in the Russkiye Mountains of Queen Maud Land. Named by the USSR in 1959 for A.P. Karpinskiy, president of the Academy of Sciences of the Russias.

**Karsten Rock** *see* **Karlsen Rock**

**Kartografov Island.** 69°12'S, 157°43'E. A small island in the west part of the mouth of Harald Bay, in Oates Land. Named by the USSR in 1958. The name means Cartographers' Island.

**Mount Kaschak.** 84°02'S, 56°40'W. 1,580 m. 4 miles west of Gambacorta

Peak, in the southern part of the Neptune Range of the Pensacola Mountains. Named for John P. Kaschak, aviation machinist at Ellsworth Station in 1958.

**Kasco Glacier** *see* **Waverly Glacier**

**Ostrov Kashalot** *see* **Fuller Island**

**Kastor Nunatak** *see* **Castor Nunatak**

**Kasumi Glacier.** 68°20'S, 42°21'E. Flows into the sea off Queen Maud Land, just east of Kasumi Rock. Named by the Japanese.

**Kasumi Rock.** 68°22'S, 42°14'E. Also called Mondai Rock. On the coast of Queen Maud Land, between Ichime Glacier and Kasumi Glacier. Named by the Japanese.

**Katedralen Canyon.** 71°52'S, 6°33'E. An ice-filled indentation into the NW side of Jøkulkyrkja Mountain, in the Mühlig-Hofmann Mountains of Queen Maud Land. Name means "the cathedral" in Norwegian.

**Cape Kater.** 63°46'S, 59°54'W. Forms the west side of the entrance to Charcot Bay, on the west coast of Graham Land. Discovered by Foster in 1828–31, and named by him for Capt. Henry Kater, a planner of Foster's *Chanticleer* expedition. Nordenskjöld renamed it Cape Gunnar in 1901–4, but the older name prevails.

**Kater Rocks.** 63°46'S, 59°53'W. 1 mile NW of Cape Kater, in Graham Land. Charted and named by Nordenskjöld's 1901–4 expedition (*see* **Cape Kater** for further details).

**Mount Katherine Paine** *see* **Mount Paine**

**Mount Kathleen.** 83°46'S, 172°48'E. Also seen as Mount Catherine. 900 m. The central and highest summit on Ebony Ridge, and the northernmost of the mountains in the Commonwealth Range. It overlooks the Ross Ice Shelf, at the foot of the Beardmore Glacier. Shackleton discovered it in 1908 and named it for his sister.

**Katie Automatic Weather Station.** 77° 42'S, 167°42'E. American AWS at an elevation of approximately 130 feet. It began operating on Feb. 9, 1983, and ceased operating on Jan. 5, 1986.

**Kats Pillar** *see* **Petes Pillar**

**Mount Katsufrakis.** 82°58'S, 161°38'E. On the east side of the Markham Plateau, in the Queen Elizabeth Range. Named for John P. Katsufrakis.

**Katsufrakis, John P.** American radio scientist, one of Antarctica's most seasoned veterans. At the time he won the National Science Foundation's Distinguished Public Service Award in 1981, he had spent 17 summers in Antarctica. He helped put Siple Station together in the early 1970s.

**Kattaugo Rocks.** 69°46'S, 37°31'E. 5 miles east of Såta Nunatak, at the base of Botnneset Peninsula, on the south side of Lützow-Holm Bay. Photographed by the LCE 1936–37, and later named Kattaugo (the cat's eyes) by the Norwegians.

**Mount Kauffman.** 75°36'S, 132°25' W. 2,365 m. A volcano at the NW end of the Ames Range, in Marie Byrd Land. Algae and lichens are to be found here. Named for Cdr. S.K. Kauffman, USN, who led the building of Plateau Station in 1965–66.

**Kauffman Glacier.** 71°15'S, 61°18'W. 7 miles long. Broad and smooth. Flows into Palmer Inlet, on the east coast of Palmer Land. Named for Thomas A. Kauffman, biologist and station scientific leader at Palmer Station in 1973.

**Kavenagh, W.** Able seaman on the *Aurora*, 1914–16.

**Kavrayskiy Hills.** 70°27'S, 161°05'E. Ice-covered coastal hills south of Rennick Bay, and on the west side of the lower end of the Rennick Glacier. Charted by the USSR in 1958, and named by them for Vasiliy V. Kavrayskiy (1884–1954), geodesist and cartographer.

**Kay, Joseph W.** Lt. Director of the Rossbank Observatory in Tasmania. He was third lieutenant on the *Terror* during Ross' expedition of 1839–43.

**Kay Island.** 74°04'S, 165°19'E. 2 miles east of Cape Johnson, in the north part of Wood Bay, Victoria Land. Discovered by Ross in 1841, and charted by him as a group of 3 islands, the Kay Islands, named for Lt. Joseph W. Kay. Only one island remains here, Kay Island.

**Kay Islands** *see* **Kay Island**

**Kay Nunatak.** 68°41'S, 64°40'W. 500 m. At the south side of Mobiloil Inlet, it forms the northernmost outlier of the Hitchcock Heights, on the east coast of the Antarctic Peninsula. Wilkins photographed it aerially on Dec. 20, 1928, and Ellsworth did the same on Nov. 23, 1935. In 1952 the USA named it for John D. Kay of the American Geographical Society, who first made a map of this area.

**Kay Peak.** 75°14'S, 110°57'W. 760 m. Pyramidal. In the area of Mount Murphy, in Marie Byrd Land. Named for Lt. Cdr. W. Kay, USN, leader of the Construction Unit at Amundsen-Scott South Pole Station in 1973.

**Kaye Crest.** 72°06'S, 4°24'E. A ridge between the Preuschoff Range and the Gablenz Range, in the Mühlig-Hofmann Mountains of Queen Maud Land. This may be what Ritscher called Kaye-Kamm (Kaye crest) in 1938–39. That feature was in this area somewhere, but Ritscher's mapping was not accurate, so the modern geographers have allocated this feature to bear the name.

**Kazanowska, Maria.** Commander, USN. She was on the Antarctic Treaty inspection team aboard the *Polar Star* in 1982–83. She was the first woman at a Japanese station, when the team landed to inspect Showa Station in Feb. 1983.

**Kazanskaya Mountain.** 71°58'S, 13°15'E. 2,690 m. Forms the north end of Snøskalegga Ridge, in the Weyprecht Mountains of Queen Maud Land. Discovered aerially by Ritscher's expedition of 1938–39. Named by the USSR in 1966.

**Mount Kazukaitis.** 72°01'S, 101°09'W. In the Walker Mountains, at the base of Hughes Peninsula, in the west part of Thurston Island. Named for photographer Frank Kazukaitis, USN, here in 1960, and for several years afterward.

**Kealey Ice Rise.** 77°15'S, 83°W. 40 miles long. 15 miles wide. Forms a western lobe of the larger Fowler Ice Rise. Just north of the junction of Talutis Inlet and Carlson Inlet, at the SW side of the Ronne Ice Shelf. Named for Lt. Gerald P. Kealey, USN, medical officer at Amundsen-Scott South Pole Station in 1971.

**Kearns, William H., Jr.** Lt. (jg). Co-pilot of the Martin Mariner which crashed on Dec. 30, 1946, on Thurston Island, during Operation Highjump. He was actually piloting the plane at the time of the crash, and broke his arm.

**Kedd, John.** Seaman on the Wilkes Expedition 1838–42. Joined in the USA. Run at Sydney.

**Keel Hill.** 85°06'S, 174°13'W. Ice-free. On the north side of McGregor Glacier, 1½ miles east of Crilly Hill, in the Queen Maud Mountains. Named by the Texas Tech Shackleton Glacier Expedition of 1964–65, for Elbert E. Keel, a member of the supporting US Army Aviation Detachment.

**Keel Island.** 67°21'S, 59°19'E. 1 mile south of Fold Island, off the coast of Enderby Land. Photographed by the LCE 1936–37, and named Kjölen (the keel). Visited by an ANARE party in 1956.

**Cape Keeler.** 68°51'S, 63°13'W. 520 m. Ice-covered. Forms the south side of the entrance to Revelle Inlet, on the east coast of Palmer Land. It juts out into the Larsen Ice Shelf, just north of Hearst Island. Discovered on Dec. 20, 1928, by Wilkins as he flew over, and named by him for Fred E. Keeler of the Lockheed Corporation. Cape Keeler Advance Base was here in 1947–48 (*see* **RARE**).

**Keenan, Samuel.** Seaman on the Wilkes Expedition 1838–42. Joined in the USA. Discharged at Oahu on Oct. 31, 1840.

**Keep Rock.** 62°48′S, 61°37′W. Almost a mile WSW of Castle Rock, off the west side of Snow Island, in the South Shetlands. Named by the UK in 1952 following a survey by Lt. Cdr. F.W. Hunt, RN. Named in association with nearby Castle Rock.

**Kehle Glacier.** 78°56′S, 160°18′E. Flows from the Worcester Range into Mulock Glacier. Named in 1964 for Ralph Kehle, glaciologist at Little America in 1959–60.

**Keim Peak.** 70°44′S, 159°52′E. 2,045 m. On the southern spur of the Pomerantz Tableland, in the Usarp Mountains. Named for Mike B. Keim, USN, VX-6 aerial photographer in Antarctica in 1962–63 and 1963–64.

**Mount Keinath.** 74°32′S, 163°57′E. 1,090 m. On the east side of the terminus of the Boomerang Glacier, in the Deep Freeze Range of Victoria Land. Named for Gerald E. Keinath, biolab administrator at McMurdo Station in 1965–66.

**Mount Keith.** 70°54′S, 163°19′E. 1,530 m. Between Rastorguev Glacier and Crawford Glacier, in the Bowers Mountains. Named for John D. Keith, USN, builder at Amundsen-Scott South Pole Station in 1965.

**Kellas Islands.** 67°33′S, 62°46′E. Two small islands, ½ mile south of the Parallactic Islands in Holme Bay, Mac. Robertson Land. Named by the Australians for W.R. Kellas, weather observer at Mawson Station in 1960.

**Keller Inlet.** 74°15′S, 61°05′W. On the east coast of Palmer Land.

**Keller Massif** *see* **Keller Peninsula**

**Keller Peninsula.** 62°05′S, 58°26′W. Also called Keller Range, Keller Massif. Separates Mackellar and Martel Inlets, on the south central side of King George Island, in the South Shetlands. Named by Charcot in Dec. 1909. The Brazilian scientific station of Comandante Ferraz is here.

**Keller Range** *see* **Keller Peninsula**

**Kelley, Ruth.** American airline stewardess who, with Pat Heppinstall, was one of the first two women ever to visit an American Antarctic station, when the first ever commercial flight to Antarctica landed at McMurdo Station on Oct. 15, 1957.

**Kelley Massif.** 70°39′S, 63°35′W. 10 miles long. Just west of the Eland Mountains, on the south side of Clifford Glacier, in Palmer Land. Named for Capt. Hugh A. Kelley, USN, commander of Antarctic Support Activities, 1968 and 1969.

**Kelley Nunatak.** 85°39′S, 146°44′W. On the north side of the Leverett Glacier, 12 miles NE of Mount Gould. Named for Herbert O. Kelley, radioman at Byrd Station in 1958.

**Kelley Peak.** 80°10′S, 82°50′W. 1,710 m. Forms the south end of the Liberty Hills, in the Heritage Range. Named for air crewman Charles C. Kelley, USN (*see* Deaths, 1966).

**Kelley Spur.** 82°37′S, 52°08′W. 2 miles east of Spear Spur, on the south side of the Dufek Massif, in the Pensacola Mountains. Named for Samuel Kelley, VX-6 photographer in Antarctica many times between 1964 and 1970.

**Kellick, Capt.** Commander of the *Henry*, 1821–22. He reported about 20 US vessels in the South Shetlands that season.

**Kellick Island.** 61°55′S, 58°26′W. ½ mile long. 1 mile NE of Round Point off the north coast of King George Island, in the South Shetlands. Named by the UK in 1960 for Capt. Kellick.

**Kellogg Glacier.** 71°51′S, 62°41′W. 9 miles long. At the base of Condor Peninsula, on the east side of Palmer Land. Flows along the north side of Boyer Spur, and merges with Gruening Glacier just inland from the NW head of Hilton Inlet. Named for Karl S. Kellogg, geologist on the Lassiter Coast in 1972–73.

**Kellum, John.** Quartermaster on the Wilkes Expedition 1838–42. Joined in the USA. Served the cruise.

**Mount Kelly.** 70°47′S, 164°19′E. 1,110 m. 3 miles NW of Mount Burch, in the western part of the Anare Mountains. Named by the Australians for 2nd Lt. R.M. Kelly, here in 1962 with the ANARE party led by Phillip Law.

**Kelly Glacier.** 72°19′S, 168°55′E. Flows from Mount Peacock in the Admiralty Mountains, and enters Tucker Glacier just south of Mount Titus. Named for Lt. Anthony J. Kelly, USN, medical officer at Hallett Station in 1961.

**Kelly Nunataks.** 77°17′S, 141°44′W. They mark the eastern extremity of the Clark Mountains, in the Ford Ranges of Marie Byrd Land. Named for John David Kelly, ionosphere physicist at Byrd Station in 1958.

**Kelly Plateau.** 81°24′S, 159°30′E. 15 miles long. Ice-covered. Between 2 and 4 miles wide. On the east side of the Churchill Mountains, between the lower parts of the Jorda and Flynn Glaciers. Named for Cdr. George R. Kelly, USN, commander of VX-6 in 1964.

**Kelly Spur.** Unofficial name for a feature in the area of the Dufek Massif, in the Pensacola Mountains.

**Kelp Gulls** *see* **Gulls**

**Mount Kelsey.** 80°27′S, 22°19′W. In the Shackleton Range.

**Kelsey, Lawrence D.** Radio operator on the RARE 1947–48.

**Kelsey Cliff.** 74°30′S, 62°18′W. SE of Mount Owen, at the east end of the Guettard Range, in Palmer Land. Named by Ronne for Lawrence D. Kelsey.

**Cape Keltie.** 66°03′S, 133°26′E. Ice-covered. 11 miles west of Cape Cesney, on the Wilkes Coast. Discovered from

the *Aurora* during the AAE 1911–14, and charted at 66°05′S, 133°E. Named by Mawson for Sir John Scott Keltie, secretary of the Royal Geographical Society, 1892–1915. This feature was later recharted.

**Mount Keltie.** 79°15′S, 159°29′E. 2,640 m. Between Mounts Kosko and Chalmers in the Conway Range. Discovered during Scott's 1901–4 expedition, and named for Sir John Scott Keltie (*see* **Cape Keltie**).

**Keltie Glacier.** 84°53′S, 170°20′E. 30 miles long. Flows from the Pain Névé around the southern end of the Commonwealth Range, to the south of the Hughes Range, in the Queen Maud Mountains. It enters the Beardmore Glacier at Ranfurly Point. Shackleton discovered it in 1908, and named it for Sir John Scott Keltie (*see* **Cape Keltie**).

**Keltie Head.** 63°47′S, 57°41′W. Also called Cape Scott Keltie. A headland which rises to an ice dome 395 meters high. It forms the NW end of Vega Island. Discovered by Nordenskjöld's expedition of 1901–4, and named by Nordenskjöld for Sir John Scott Keltie (*see* **Cape Keltie**).

**Kelvin Crests.** 69°10′S, 66°35′W. 5 miles long. On the north side of the Airy Glacier, they are a line of steep-sided elevations with ice-covered cliffs. In the Antarctic Peninsula. Named by the UK for the physicist, Lord Kelvin.

**Cape Kemp.** 64°52′S, 63°39′W. Forms the SW tip of Doumer Island. Charted by Charcot in 1903–5. Named in 1927 by the personnel on the *Discovery*, for Dr. Stanley Kemp.

**Mount Kemp** *see* **Mount Kempe**

**Kemp, Peter.** British sealing captain who, while working for Bennett and Sons, whalers, as captain of the *Magnet*, discovered Kemp Land (otherwise known as the Kemp Coast) on Dec. 26, 1833. He fell overboard on his way back home and was drowned.

**Kemp, Dr. Stanley W.** Stanley Wells Kemp. British marine biologist, zoologist, and oceanographer. Director of Research with the Discovery Committee, 1924–36. He led the *Discovery* cruise of 1925–26, and the cruise in 1926–27 of the *William Scoresby* and the *Discovery*. He led the 1929–31 cruise of the *Discovery II*.

**Kemp Coast** *see* **Kemp Land**

**Kemp Land.** 67°15′S, 58°E. Also called Kemp Coast. Between the head of Edward VIII Bay (at 56°25′E) and William Scoresby Bay (at 59°34′E), in eastern Enderby Land. Discovered by Peter Kemp on Dec. 26, 1833, and named for him.

**Kemp Peak.** 67°26′S, 59°24′E. Also called Horn Peak, Stanley Kemp Peak. 340 m. Just SE of Stefansson Bay. Discovered on Jan. 30, 1930, by the BANZARE, and named by Mawson for Dr. Stanley Kemp. The Norwegians later applied their own name, Hornet (the horn), but the Australians reinforced the original naming in the 1950s.

**Kemp Peninsula.** 73°08′S, 60°15′W. 305 m. 26 miles long. Between 5 and 12 miles wide. Ice-covered. To the north of the Lassiter Coast, on the east coast of Palmer Land. Discovered aerially in 1940 by the USAS from East Base. Named by the FIDS for Dr. Stanley Kemp.

**Kemp Rock.** 71°58′S, 171°06′E. Between Foyn Island and Bull Island in the Possession Islands. Named for William R. Kemp, USN, VX-6 photographer here in 1958.

**Nunatak Kempbell** *see* **Campbell Nunatak**

**Mount Kempe.** 78°19′S, 162°43′E. 3,005 m. Between Mount Huggins and Mount Dromedary, in the Royal Society Range of Victoria Land. Discovered by Scott's 1901–4 expedition, and named by them for Sir Alfred Bray Kempe, treasurer of the Royal Society.

**Kempe, Arthur.** First lieutenant on the *Adventure* during Cook's second voyage, 1772–75.

**Kempe Glacier.** 78°18′S, 162°54′E. Runs toward Roaring Valley from the Mount Kempe area. Named by the New Zealanders in 1960–61 in association with the mountain.

**Kendall, Edward N.** Lt., RN. 1800–1845. Surveyor who made the first survey of Deception Island in Jan.–March 1829, while part of Foster's *Chanticleer* expedition of 1828–31.

**Kendall Basin.** 80°15′S, 25°39′W. In the Shackleton Range.

**Kendall Group** *see* **Kendall Rocks**

**Kendall Rocks.** 63°28′S, 59°51′W. A group of pillar-shaped rocks, 3 miles north of Tower Island, to the west of the Antarctic Peninsula. First mapped by Bransfield in 1820–21, but not named by him. Charted erroneously by Foster in 1828–31, and named by him as the Kendall Group, for Lt. Edward N. Kendall. Dumont d'Urville recharted them in 1838–42, and redefined them.

**Kendall Terrace.** 62°55′S, 60°42′W. An ice-free, volcanic ash terrace on the NW side of Deception Island, in the South Shetlands. Named for Lt. Edward N. Kendall.

**Mount Kendrick.** 86°22′S, 156°40′W. 3,610 m. Ice-covered. On the east side of the Nilsen Plateau, at the head of the Bartlett Glacier, in the Queen Maud Mountains. Named for Capt. H.E. Kendrick, on Operation Deep Freeze 67.

**Kenfield Nunatak.** 73°46′S, 99°03′W. Isolated. 8 miles SE of the head of the Cosgrove Ice Shelf, and 17 miles ENE of Pryor Cliff, at the extreme north end of the Hudson Mountains. Named for Richard E. Kenfield, topographer at Byrd Station, 1963–64.

**Kennar, Thomas.** Petty officer, RN, on the Royal Society Expedition of 1901–4.

**Kennar Valley.** 77°46′S, 160°20′E. To the immediate west of Turnabout Valley, in southern Victoria Land. Named for Thomas Kennar.

**Cape Kennedy.** 66°30′S, 98°32′E. On the east side of Melba Peninsula, 4 miles SW of David Island. Discovered by the

AAE 1911–14, and named by Mawson for A.L. Kennedy.

**¹Mount Kennedy** *see* **Kennedy Peak**

**²Mount Kennedy.** 67°52′S, 66°13′E. Ice-free. 1 mile south of Mount Rivett, in the Gustav Bull Mountains of Mac. Robertson Land. The BANZARE made a landing near here at Scullin Monolith on Feb. 13, 1931. Mawson named it for A.L. Kennedy.

**Kennedy, A.L.** Cartographer with the Western Base Party during the AAE 1911–14. He did a remarkable job. He was back with Mawson on the BANZARE 1929–31, this time as a physicist.

**Kennedy, L.H.** Crewman on the *Jacob Ruppert*, 1933–34.

**Kennedy Peak.** 67°13′S, 99°11′E. Also called Mount Kennedy. 2 miles south of Mount Barr Smith, on the west side of the Denman Glacier. Named for A.L. Kennedy.

**Kennel Peak.** 75°01′S, 133°44′W. Over 800 m. ½ mile north of Rockney Ridge, in the Demas Range of Marie Byrd Land. Named for A. Alexander Kennel, ionosphere physicist and station scientific leader at Amundsen-Scott South Pole Station in 1969.

**Kenneth Ridge.** 70°57′S, 71°30′E. The northernmost of three rock outcrops in the northern part of the Manning Nunataks. Named by the Australians for Kenneth A. Smith, radio officer at Mawson Station in 1969, who surveyed here that year with the ANARE.

**Mount Kennett.** 67°03′S, 65°10′W. 1,360 m. Between Quartermain Glacier and Fricker Glacier, on the east side of Graham Land. Mapped by the FIDS in 1947–48, and named by the UK for Peter Kennett, general assistant with the BAS Larsen Ice Shelf Party of 1963–64.

**Mount Kennett Rawson** *see* **Rawson Plateau**

**Kennett Ridge.** 79°51′S, 156°45′E. 6 miles long. Descends eastward from the NE end of Midnight Plateau into the Darwin Mountains. Named by the VUWAE

1962–63 for J.P. Kennett, geologist with the expedition.

**Mount Kenney.** 84°44′S, 175°28′W. 2,030 m. In the Cathedral Peaks, 3 miles east of Shackleton Glacier, and 10 miles NW of Mount Wade, in the Prince Olav Mountains. Named for 1st Lt. Leroy S. Kenney, VX-6 pilot.

**Kenney Glacier.** 63°25′S, 57°02′W. 1 mile long. Flows from The Pyramid and The Saddlestone into Depot Glacier, near the head of Hope Bay, at the north end of the Antarctic Peninsula. Named by the FIDS in 1956 for Richard R. Kenney, assistant surveyor at Base D in 1954 and 1955.

**Kent Cooper Glacier** *see* **Cooper Glacier**

**Kent Gap.** 83°17′S, 50°30′W. Ice-filled. It connects the heads of May Valley and Chambers Glacier, and marks the divide between Lexington Table and Saratoga Table, in the Forrestal Range of the Pensacola Mountains. Named for Kenneth R. Kent, electronics technician at Ellsworth Station in 1957.

**Kent Glacier.** 82°50′S, 163°10′E. Flows from the east side of Markham Plateau, in the Queen Elizabeth Range, for about 15 miles, then enters Lowery Glacier. Named by the New Zealanders in 1960–61 for the English county.

**Kent Plateau.** 80°44′S, 157°50′E. 12 miles long. 4 miles wide. Ice-covered. Between the area of Mount Egerton and Kiwi Pass, and that of Mount Hamilton, in the Churchill Mountains. Named for Cdr. Donald F. Kent, USN, logistics officer to Adm. Dufek at the beginning of Operation Deep Freeze.

**Mount Kenyon.** 85°13′S, 174°52′W. 2,260 m. Just to the east of the Shackleton Glacier. 1 mile NW of Schenk Peak, in the northern part of the Cumulus Hills. Named by Alton Wade for his alma mater, Kenyon College, Gambier, Ohio.

**Kenyon Peaks.** 84°33′S, 163°36′E. A small group of basalt peaks 3 miles NW of Storm Peak, in the Marshall Mountains, at the extreme south of the Queen Alexandra Range. Named by the Ohio State University party here in 1966–67, for one of their party, D. Kenyon King.

**Kenyon Peninsula** *see* **Hollick-Kenyon Peninsula**

**Keohane, Patrick.** From Cork, Ireland. Petty officer, RN. One of the support party (with Wright, Atkinson, and Cherry-Garrard) during Scott's push to the Pole in 1911.

**Mount Kerckhove de Denterghem.** 72°37′S, 31°08′E. 2,400 m. Just north of Mount Collard, in the Belgica Mountains. Discovered by the Belgians in 1957–58, and named by them for Count Charles de Kerckhove de Denterghem, a patron of the expedition that year.

**Kerguélen Plateau.** 60°S, 83°E. A subsurface feature beyond the Gribb Bank.

**Mount Kernot** *see* **Øydeholmen**

**Cape Kerr.** 80°03′S, 160°26′E. High. Snow-covered. On the north side of Barne Inlet, on the west side of the Ross Ice Shelf. Discovered and named by Scott on his Royal Society Expedition 1901–4, for Lord Walter Kerr, Admiral of the Fleet, one of the Sea Lords who supported the expedition.

**Mount Kerr.** 70°26′S, 65°38′E. ½ mile south of Mount Creighton, in the Porthos Range of the Prince Charles Mountains. Named by the Australians for A.G. Kerr, physicist at Mawson Station in 1967.

**Kerr.** The bagpipe-player on Bruce's 1902–4 Scottish National Antarctic Expedition.

**Kerr, A.J.** Merchant Navy man. Second engineer on the *Endurance,* during Shackleton's British Imperial Transantarctic Expedition of 1914–17. He was back with Shackleton, as chief engineer on the *Quest,* 1921–22. He retired to England.

**Kerr, G.** Crewman on the *Jacob Ruppert,* 1933–34.

**Kerr Point.** 64°42′S, 62°38′W. 2 miles SE of Georges Point, on the east side of

Rongé Island, off the west coast of Graham Land. Charted by de Gerlache in 1897–99, and named by the UK in 1960 for Adam J. Kerr, second officer of the *Shackleton,* here in 1956–57.

**Kershaw Ice Rumples.** 78°45′S, 75°40′W. A large area of disturbed ice between the Fletcher Ice Rise and the Korff Ice Rise, in the SW part of the Ronne Ice Shelf. Named by the UK for John E.G. (Giles) Kershaw, senior pilot with the BAS, 1974–75. Kershaw died in a plane crash in Antarctica in early March 1990. He was 41.

**Kershaw Peaks.** 64°56′S, 63°08′W. 5 main peaks, the highest being 820 m. West of the mouth of the Miethe Glacier, on the west coast of Graham Land. Named by the UK in 1960 for Dennis Kershaw of the FIDS, assistant surveyor at Base N in 1956 and at Base O in 1957.

**Kessens Peak.** 86°51′S, 146°41′W. 2,660 m. 5 miles SE of Mount Paine, in the La Gorce Mountains of the Queen Maud Mountains. Named for Gerard R. Kessens of VX-6, photographer here in 1966 and 1967.

**Kessler, Charles L.** Seaman on the *Eleanor Bolling* during Byrd's 1928–30 expedition. In later life he was a captain in the US Navy, and director of the Selective Service System for Virginia. He revisited Antarctica in 1962 and 1965.

**Kessler Peak.** 83°37′S, 167°50′E. 2,180 m. Cone-shaped. In the Queen Alexandra Range, at the east side of the Lennox-King Glacier, 4 miles SW of Mount Rotolante. Named for Charles L. Kessler.

**Kester Peaks.** 82°49′S, 48°23′W. Three aligned rock peaks 5 miles south of Mount Malville, on the east side of the Forrestal Range, in the Pensacola Mountains. Named for Larry T. Kester, VX-6 photographer in 1964.

**Ketchum, Gerald L.** USN. The commander of the *Burton Island* during Operation Highjump, 1946–47, and commander of Task Force 39 which conducted Operation Windmill, 1947–48.

Deputy commander of Task Force 43 under Dufek during Operation Deep Freeze.

**Ketchum Canyon.** 64°S, 131°E. A submarine feature off the Wilkes Coast. Named for Gerald Ketchum.

**Ketchum Glacier.** 75°S, 63°45'W. Also called Irvine Gardner Glacier, Gardner Glacier. 50 miles long. At the base of Palmer Land. It flows between the Latady Mountains and the Scaife Mountains into Gardner Inlet. Discovered by the RARE 1947–48, and named by Ronne for Gerald Ketchum.

**Ketley Point.** 64°42'S, 62°46'W. Forms the west end of Rongé Island, off the west coast of Graham Land. Charted by de Gerlache in 1897–99. Named by the UK in 1960 for John Ketley, FIDS assistant surveyor at Base O in 1956 and at Base N in 1957 (cf. Kershaw Peaks).

**Keuken Island** *see* **Keuken Rock**

**Keuken Rock.** 68°35'S, 77°50'E. Off the Vestfold Hills, almost 1½ miles SW of Barratt Island. Photographed by the LCE 1936–37, and later named by the Australians for J. Keuken, weather observer at Davis Station in 1959.

**Kevin Islands.** 63°17'S, 57°44'W. A cluster of small islands and rocks, lying close to the northern coast of Trinity Peninsula, between Halpern Point and Coupvent Point. Named for Kevin M. Scott, geologist here in 1961–62 with the University of Wisconsin.

**The Keyhole.** 78°07'S, 163°41'E. A narrow defile carved by the ice. Between the Adams Glacier and Hidden Valley. You go through it to get to Hidden Valley. Named by the New Zealanders in 1960–61 because it does lead to that valley.

**Lake Keyhole.** 78°08'S, 163°41'E. To the south of The Keyhole (q.v.). A very small lake, it was named by the New Zealanders in 1960–61 in association with The Keyhole.

**Keyhole Island.** 68°47'S, 67°20'W. 5 miles SE of the Terra Firma Islands in the

SW part of Mikkelsen Bay, off the west coast of Graham Land. Surveyed and named by the FIDS in 1948. An ice-arch has been formed here by the island's ice-cap.

**Keys Glacier.** 74°48'S, 114°W. On Martin Peninsula, on the coast of Marie Byrd Land.

**Mount Keyser.** 66°56'S, 52°23'E. Also called Keyser Nunatak. 3 miles east of Mount Ryder, in the eastern part of the Tula Mountains of Enderby Land. Named by the Australians for D.O. Keyser (*see* **Keyser Ridge**).

**¹Keyser Nunatak** *see* **Mount Keyser**

**²Keyser Nunatak.** 77°36'S, 145°55'W. 605 m. At the north of the terminus of Reynolds Glacier, in the Haines Mountains of Marie Byrd Land. Named for Lt. (jg) Teddy H. Keyser, USN, Hercules aircraft navigator in Antarctica in 1968.

**Keyser Ridge.** 73°57'S, 63°28'E. 11 miles long. Snow-covered. 26 miles SSE of Mount Bayliss, in the Prince Charles Mountains. Named by the Australians for D.O. Keyser, radio officer at Mawson Station in 1961, here with the ANARE on an expedition that year.

**Keystone Cliffs.** 71°35'S, 68°13'W. 610 m. They mark the east face of the ridge between Mercury Glacier and Venus Glacier, on the east coast of Alexander Island. Surveyed by the BGLE in 1936. Named by the FIDS in 1948 because the geologic structures in the cliffs provided the key to the general tectonic structure of the area.

**Khamsin Pass.** 69°29'S, 67°45'W. On the west coast of Palmer Land.

**Khmara Bay.** 67°20'S, 49°E. Directly south of Zubchatyy Ice Shelf and Sakellari Peninsula, in Enderby Land. Named by the USSR in 1957 for I.F. Khmara (*see* **Khmara Island**).

**Khmara Island.** 66°33'S, 93°E. Formerly called Khmary Island. 1 mile SW of Haswell Island, in the Haswell Islands. Named for I.F. Khmara (*see* **Deaths, 1956**).

**Khmary Island** *see* **Khmara Island**

**Mount Khmyznikov.** 71°52'S, 11°39'E. 2,800 m. In the northern part of the Skeidsnutane Peaks of the Betekhtin Range, in the Humboldt Mountains of Queen Maud Land. Discovered aerially by Ritscher's expedition in 1938–39, and named by the USSR in 1966 for P.K. Khmyznikov, hydrographer.

**Mount Kibal'chich.** 71°56'S, 14°19'E. 2,500 m. The highest of the Kvaevenutane Peaks, in the Payer Mountains of Queen Maud Land. Discovered aerially by Ritscher's expedition in 1938–39, and named by the USSR in 1963 for N.I. Kibal'chich, Russian revolutionary.

**Kichenside Glacier.** 67°46'S, 47°36'E. Also called Shaw Glacier. 15 miles long. Between 3 and 5 miles wide. Flows into the Hannan Ice Shelf, on the coast of Enderby Land. Named by the Australians for Sq. Ldr. J. Kichenside, RAAF, officer commanding the Antarctic Flight at Mawson Station in 1960.

**Kidd Islands.** 66°27'S, 65°59'W. A small group in Darbel Bay, just south of the Darbel Islands, off the west coast of Graham Land. Named by the UK in 1960 for D.A. Kidd, physicist specializing in ice crystals in the 1880s.

**Cape Kidson.** 73°24'S, 60°45'W. Rises to 300 m. It is an abrupt rock scarp which forms the north side of the entrance to New Bedford Inlet, on the east coast of Palmer Land. Discovered in 1940 by the USAS. Named by the FIDS for Edward Kidson, NZ meteorologist, and author of the meteorological reports of Shackleton's expedition of 1907–9, and also of the AAE 1911–14.

**Kidson Island.** 67°12'S, 61°11'E. Also seen spelled (erroneously) as Kidston Island. ½ mile long. 15 miles NNE of Byrd Head. Discovered in Feb. 1931 by the BANZARE, and named by Mawson for Edward Kidson (*see* **Cape Kidson**).

**Kidston Island** *see* **Kidson Island**

**Kieffer Knoll.** 82°29'S, 162°39'E. Marks the extreme NE corner of the Queen Elizabeth Range. Named for Hugh H. Kieffer, glaciologist at Roosevelt Island in 1961–62.

**Kiel, Max R.** Seabee driver known as "Fat Max." While part of a tractor party, sledging fuel to be cached on the trail to Marie Byrd Land (for the party led by Jack Bursey), he died on March 5, 1956, when the 35-ton D-8 tractor he was driving crashed into a crevasse 110 miles from Little America V. It was the second death during Operation Deep Freeze (*see* **Deaths**).

**Kiel Field.** Also called Max Kiel Airfield. Runway behind Little America V during the IGY. It was 6,000 feet long. Named for Max Kiel.

**Kiel Glacier.** 78°08'S, 154°W. Broad, and heavily crevassed. Flows just east of the Rockefeller Mountains into Prestrud Inlet, in Edward VII Land. Named for Max Kiel.

**Mount Kiffin** *see* **Mount Kyffin**

**Kikko Terrace.** 68°08'S, 42°40'E. 150 m. 1½ miles SSE of Cape Hinode. The Japanese named it Kikko-ga-hara (tortoise shells terrace), and in 1973 they themselves renamed it in English.

**Kilby Island.** 66°16'S, 110°31'E. Barely ¼ mile long. Just NE of McMullin Island, in the entrance to Newcomb Bay, in the Windmill Islands. Named for Arthur L. Kilby, photographer on Operation Highjump, 1946–47, and on Operation Windmill, 1947–48.

**Kilby Reef.** 66°17'S, 110°32'E. Small and isolated. Just over 200 yards SE of Kilby Island, in the Windmill Islands (hence the name). Surveyed in Feb. 1957 by Lt. R.C. Newcomb, USN, of the *Glacier*.

**Kiletangen Ice Tongue.** 69°57'S, 26°25'E. On the east side of Tangekilen Bay, on the coast of Queen Maud Land. First photographed aerially by the LCE 1936–37. Name means "the bay tongue" in Norwegian.

**Kilfoyle Nunataks.** 70°43'S, 65°51'E. Two nunataks. 1½ miles SW of Mount

Dowie, in the Aramis Range of the Prince Charles Mountains. Named by the Australians for B. Kilfoyle, physicist at Mawson Station in 1966.

**Killer Nunatak.** 71°54'S, 160°28'E. 2,080 m. A granite nunatak. Near the center of the Emlen Peaks, 5 miles NW of Mount Phelen, in the Usarp Mountains. Named by the New Zealanders in 1963–64 because of its outline resemblance to the dorsal fin of a killer whale.

**Killer Ridge.** 77°12'S, 162°06'E. Part of the Gonville and Caius Range, between the Debenham and Mackay Glaciers in Victoria Land. It rises to over 1,000 meters between the Crisp and Miller Glaciers. Charted by Scott's 1910–13 expedition. It looks like a killer whale in outline.

**Killer Whale Rocks.** Unofficial name for a group of rocks just over a mile to the SW of Palmer Station, between Janus Island and Litchfield Island.

**Killer whale.** *Orcinus orca.* Also called the grampus. It is actually the largest of the dolphins (sic), and can grow to 31 feet long. It is one of the most intelligent of aquatic animals. Killer whales hunt in packs and feed on penguins and other birds, seals, whales, and other dolphins, but not on humans (as a rule, that is, although there is no question that *Orcinus orca* is easily capable of feeding on a human). Killers cruise right to the edge of the Antarctic pack-ice, appearing even in McMurdo Sound.

**Killermet Cove.** 64°52'S, 63°07'W. The southern of two coves indenting the west side of Bryde Island, off the west coast of Graham Land. Named by the FIDS in 1960 because 3 members of their 1957 circumnavigation of Bryde Island were chased into this cove in their dinghy by six killer whales.

**Killingbeck Island.** 67°34'S, 68°05'W. Just east of Rothera Point, off the SE coast of Adelaide Island. Named by the UK in 1964 for one of their glaciologists, John B. Killingbeck, here over the 1960–63 period.

**Mount Kinet.** 73°14'S, 165°54'E. 2,180 m. On the south side of the upper Meander Glacier, 5 miles SE of Hobbie Ridge, in the Mountaineer Range of Victoria Land. Named for Urbain J. Kinet, biologist at McMurdo Station in 1965–66.

**The *King*.** Argentine ship which took part in the Argentine Antarctic Expeditions of 1946–47 and 1947–48.

**¹Cape King**  *see*  **King Point**

**²Cape King.** 73°35'S, 166°37'E. Forms the seaward end of the west wall of Wylde Glacier, where that glacier enters Lady Newnes Bay, on the coast of Victoria Land. Named for Geoffrey A. King, ionosphere physicist at Hallett Station in 1958.

**¹Mount King.** 67°04'S, 52°52'E. Unofficial name for a mountain in Enderby Land.

**²Mount King.** 69°53'S, 69°26'W. 1,890 m. Flat-topped. Mostly ice-covered. Between the Sedgwick and Tumble Glaciers, on the east coast of Alexander Island. Surveyed by the BGLE in 1936. Named by the FIDS in 1948 for William B.R. King, professor of geology at Cambridge.

**King.** The mate on the *Florence* in the 1876–77 season. He was leader of the crew that was forced to winter-over on King George Island in 1877. They all died except King.

**King, Capt.** Commander of the *Tenedos* in the South Shetlands for the 1856–60 period.

**King, Elijah.** Ordinary seaman on the Wilkes Expedition 1838–42. Joined in the USA. Served the cruise.

**King, Harry R.** 2nd mate on the *Eleanor Bolling* during the first half of Byrd's 1928–30 expedition. He was replaced in 1929 by Harry Adams.

**King, John.** Seaman on the Wilkes Expedition 1838–42. Joined in the USA. Discharged at Oahu on Oct. 31, 1840.

**King, William H.** Corporal of the Marines on the Wilkes Expedition 1838–42. Joined in the USA. Served the cruise.

**King Cliffs.** 72°14′S, 96°10′W. Ice-covered. They form the south side of the larger north arm of Morgan Inlet, on Thurston Island. First investigated in 1960 by the USN Bellingshausen Sea Expedition. Named for Charles E. King, geologist here with the Ellsworth Land Survey in 1968–69.

**King-David Junction.** Unofficial American name given to a dry valley in southern Victoria Land.

**King Edward VIII Gulf** *see* **Edward VIII Bay**

**King Edward Ice Shelf** *see* **Edward VIII Ice Shelf**

**King Edward Plateau** *see* **Polar Plateau, Edward VIII Plateau**

**King Edward VII Land** *see* **Edward VII Land, Edward VII Peninsula**

**King Edward VII Peninsula** *see* **Edward VII Peninsula**

**The *King George.*** Liverpool sealing brig in the South Shetlands in the 1820–21 season under the command of Capt. J. Roberts. It was the first vessel to anchor in Potter Cove. It was back again in 1821–22, again under Roberts. In 1822–23 Capt. Alexander commanded a vessel to the South Shetlands. It was probably the *King George.*

**King George Bay.** 62°06′S, 58°05′W. Also called Georges Bay, Baie Saint Georges, Bahia 25 de Mayo. Indentation into the south coast of King George Island, in the South Shetlands, between Lions Rump and Turret Point. Named by Bransfield on Jan. 24, 1820, for the King.

**King George V Land** *see* **George V Land**

**King George Island.** 62°S, 58°15′W. Also called King George's Island, Isla 25 de Mayo (by the South Americans), Waterloo Island (by the USSR). 43 miles long. 16 miles wide at its broadest. The largest of the South Shetland Islands.

Discovered by Smith on Oct. 16, 1819. He landed on it and named it for George III of Great Britain. There are 7 scientific stations on the island.

**King George VI Channel** *see* **George VI Sound**

**King George Straits** *see* **Nelson Strait**

**King Glacier.** 83°27′S, 170°15′E. NW of Mount Ida, it flows from the Queen Alexandra Range, between the Beaver and Beardmore Glaciers, into the Ross Ice Shelf. Named for Lt. Hugh A. King, officer-in-charge of Hallett Station in 1964.

**King Haakon VII Plateau.** This is the Polar Plateau (q.v.), whereon lies the South Pole. It was named thus on Dec. 14, 1911, by Amundsen, for his king, but the term Polar Plateau is now used instead.

**King Haakon VII Sea** *see* **Haakon VII Sea**

**¹King Island** *see* **King Peninsula**

**²King Island.** 65°30′S, 64°03′W. Close to the south central shore of Beascochea Bay, in Graham Land. Named by the UK for Charles Glen King, US biochemist and Vitamin C pioneer.

**King Leopold and Queen Astrid Coast** *see* **Leopold and Astrid Coast**

**King Oscar Land** *see* **Oscar II Coast**

**King Peak.** 85°21′S, 88°12′W. 2,200 m. A rock peak on the eastern end of the Bermel Escarpment, 1½ miles WNW of Mount Powell in the eastern part of the Thiel Mountains. Named by Bermel and Ford (*see* **Bermel Escarpment** for more details on these two gentlemen) for Clarence King, first director of the US Geological Survey, 1879–81.

**King penguin.** *Aptenodytes patagonicus.* Its Spanish name is "pingüin real." Discovered by Miller. 3 feet tall, it is similar to the emperor penguin (making the king the second largest species of penguin), but the king has brighter yellow coloring than its bigger cousin. It weighs 30–40 pounds, and lays a single egg. Kings are not seen in the Antarctic proper (i.e., south of 60°S) anymore, although in 1833 some were seen in the South Shetlands. It is doubtful whether the species was ever a resident of true Antarctic climes (too cold), but some sources say that they used to live in the South Shetlands and South Orkneys, but were exterminated by the sealers.

**King Peninsula.** 73°12′S, 101°W. 100 miles long. 20 miles wide. Ice-covered. South of Thurston Island, it forms the south side of Peacock Sound. It juts out from the continent between the Abbott Ice Shelf and the Cosgrove Ice Shelf, ending in the Amundsen Sea. First thought to be a long island, King Island (as it was named), it was proved to be a peninsula by 1966 US Navy photos. Named for Fleet Admiral Ernest J. King, USN, who approved the preliminary work for Operation Highjump, 1946–47.

**King Pin.** 77°27′S, 163°10′E. 820 m. A nunatak above the Wilson Piedmont Glacier, between Mount Doorly and Hogback Hill. Named by the VUWAE 1958–59 for the US helicopter, *King Pin,* which flew the party to this area, and performed a similar service for other NZ parties.

**King Point.** 63°09′S, 55°27′W. The western flange of Ambush Bay, on the northern coast of Joinville Island. Discovered on Dec. 30, 1842, by Ross, who named it Cape King for Capt. Philip P. King, RN (1793–1856), naval surveyor.

**King Range.** 71°52′S, 165°03′E. 14 miles long. 5 miles wide. In NW Victoria Land. Named for Cdr. James P. King, USN, staff meteorological officer on Operation Deep Freeze, 1962–64.

**King Ridge.** 84°38′S, 64°05′W. A narrow ridge, 3 miles long. 2 miles SW of Wrigley Bluffs, in the Anderson Hills of the central part of the Patuxent Range of the Pensacola Mountains. Named by Ronne for Col. J. Caldwell King, US Army, who had helped him on the RARE 1947–48.

**King Sejong Station.** 62°13′S, 58°45′W. Established on Feb. 17, 1986, on Barton Peninsula, King George Island, in the South Shetlands. This is Korea's only (as of 1990) Antarctic scientific station, part of the Korean Antarctic Research Program. Named for a king of the Yi dynasty. It consists of 6 major buildings and 2 research observatories.

**King Valley.** 77°37′S, 162°03′E. A small dry valley above the Conrow Glacier, west of Horowitz Ridge, in southern Victoria Land. Named by Roy E. Cameron, leader of a USARP biological party here in 1967–68, for Jonathan A. King, a member of the party.

**King Wilhelm II Land** *see* **Wilhelm II Land**

**Kingsland, Charles.** Ordinary seaman on the Wilkes Expedition 1838–42. Joined at Upolu. Served the cruise.

**Kingyo Rock.** 68°37′S, 41°E. At the south side of Omega Glacier, where that glacier meets the sea, on the coast of Queen Maud Land. The Japanese named it Kingyo-iwa (goldfish rock).

**Kinnear Mountains.** 69°32′S, 67°40′W. A small group, rising to a height of over 875 m. West of Prospect Glacier, at the southern edge of the Wordie Ice Shelf. Discovered by the BGLE in 1936, and named by them for Sir Norman B. Kinnear, British Museum ornithologist who helped the expedition.

**Cape Kinnes.** 63°22′S, 56°33′W. Also spelled Cape Kinness. Forms the western end of Joinville Island. Named by the Dundee Whaling Expedition of 1892–93 for R. Kinnes, a sponsor.

**Kinnes Cove** *see* **Suspiros Bay**

**Kinntanna Peak.** 71°53′S, 8°21′E. 2,725 m. 1 mile north of Holtanna Peak, in the eastern part of Fenriskjeften Mountain, in Queen Maud Land. Name means "the molar" in Norwegian.

**Kinsella Peak.** 83°41′S, 56°53′W. On the south side of Gale Ridge, 5 miles west of Mount Cowart, in the Neptune Range of the Pensacola Mountains. Named for

William R. Kinsella, electronics technician at Ellsworth Station in 1958.

**Cape Kinsey.** 69°20'S, 158°35'E. Ice-covered. On the east side of Davies Bay. Discovered in Feb. 1911 by Harry Pennell on the *Terra Nova,* and named by him for J.J. Kinsey, official representative in Christchurch, NZ, of Scott's 1910–13 expedition.

**Mount Kinsey.** 84°55'S, 169°18'E. 3,110 m. At the eastern edge of the Beardmore Glacier, 5 miles SW of Ranfurly Point, in the Supporters Range. To the south of the Keltie Glacier, in the Queen Maud Mountains. Named by Shackleton in 1909 for J.J. Kinsey, who conducted the affairs of Shackleton's 1907–9 expedition in New Zealand.

**Kinsey Ridge.** 75°20'S, 139°08'W. Flat-topped. Partly ice-covered. In the middle of the Strauss Glacier, near the coast of Marie Byrd Land. Named for James H. Kinsey, aurora scientist at Byrd Station in 1963.

**Kinzl Crests.** 67°05'S, 66°18'W. 2,135 m. Three peaks. 3 miles east of Salmon Cove and Lallemand Fjord, in Graham Land. Named by the UK for Hans Kinzl, Austrian glaciologist.

**Kirby, Allen W.** Captain of the hold on the Wilkes Expedition 1838–42. Joined in the USA. Discharged at Oahu on Nov. 2, 1840.

**Kirby Cone.** 85°54'S, 136°26'W. A sharp peak to the NW of Michigan Plateau. Named for Charles H. Kirby, radioman at Byrd Station in 1961.

**Kirk Glacier.** 72°02'S, 169°09'E. Runs along the south side of Fischer Ridge, into Ironside Glacier, in the Admiralty Mountains of Victoria Land. Named for Edward Kirk, USN, at McMurdo Station in 1967.

**Mount Kirkby.** 70°26'S, 65°15'E. Flat-topped. 3 miles east of the Crohn Massif, in the Porthos Range of the Prince Charles Mountains. First visited in Dec. 1956 by the ANARE party led by W.G. Bewsher. Named by the Australians for

Sydney L. Kirkby, surveyor at Mawson Station in 1956, and later surveyor on the *Thala Dan* cruise of 1962. He was also at Mawson Station in 1960.

**Kirkby Glacier.** 70°43'S, 166°09'E. 20 miles long. Flows from the central Anare Mountains to the sea, just north of Arthurson Bluff, in northern Victoria Land. Named by the ANARE for Sydney L. Kirkby (*see* **Mount Kirkby**).

**Kirkby Head.** 67°17'S, 46°29'E. On the east side of the entrance to Alasheyev Bight, in Enderby Land. First visited in Nov. 1960 by Sydney L. Kirkby (*see* **Mount Kirkby**).

**Kirkby Shoal.** 66°15'S, 110°31'E. A couple of hundred yards NW of Stonehocker Point, on Clark Peninsula. First charted by Cdr. d'A.T. Gale of the ANARE in 1962, and named by the Australians for Sydney L. Kirkby (*see* **Mount Kirkby**).

**Kirkcaldy Spur.** 76°38'S, 159°48'E. On the NW side of Coxcomb Peak, in the NW part of the Shipton Range, in the Allan Hills of Victoria Land. Named by the New Zealanders in 1964 for J.F. Kirkcaldy, professor of geology at Queen Mary College, London.

**Mount Kirkpatrick.** 84°20'S, 166°25'E. 4,528 m. Ice-free. The highest point in the Queen Alexandra Range. 5 miles west of Mount Dickerson, it overlooks the Beardmore Glacier. Discovered by Shackleton in 1907–9, and named by him for a Glasgow businessman sponsor.

**Kirkpatrick Glacier.** 75°09'S, 136°W. 12 miles long. Flows along the south side of McDonald Heights to enter the east side of the Hull Glacier, near the Marie Byrd Land coast. Named for Cdr. Thomas W. Kirkpatrick, US Coast Guard, in Antarctica in 1972 and 1973.

**Mount Kirkwood.** 63°01'S, 60°39'W. Also called Mount David, Monte Goyena. 460 m. 3 miles west of Entrance Point, in the south part of Deception Island, in the South Shetlands. First charted by Foster in 1829. Named by the

UK in 1950 for Cdr. Henry Kirkwood, RN, commander of the *John Biscoe,* 1948–50, and later captain of the *Endeavour,* 1956–58.

**Kirkwood Islands.** 68°22′S, 69°W. A scattered group of reefs and rocks with one larger island. In the center of Marguerite Bay, 15 miles SSW of the Faure Islands. Sighted in 1949 by the crew of the *John Biscoe,* and named by them in 1950 for Capt. Henry Kirkwood, RN (*see* **Mount Kirkwood**).

**Kirkwood Range.** 76°30′S, 162°E. A coastal range of mountains between the Mawson and Mackay Glaciers in southern Victoria Land.

**Kirton Island.** 67°30′S, 63°38′E. In the Robinson Group. 3 miles west of Cape Daly, in Mac. Robertson Land. Photographed by the LCE 1936–37, and later named by the Australians for M. Kirton, geophysicist at Mawson Station in 1959.

**Kirwan Escarpment.** 73°25′S, 3°30′W. Trends NE-SW for about 90 miles, south of the Penck Trough, in Queen Maud Land. The northern end is the Neumayer Cliffs. Named for Laurence P. Kirwan, director of the Royal Geographical Society.

**Kirwan Inlet.** 72°21′S, 68°50′W. Indentation into the SE corner of Alexander Island. It is 12 miles wide at its mouth, and indents the coast for 7 miles. It opens on George VI Sound, and is ice-filled. Named by the FIDS for Laurence P. Kirwan (*see* **Kirwan Escarpment**).

**The *Kista Dan*.** Used by the ANARE as an expedition ship. During the 1954–56 period, when it took the personnel down to create Mawson Station in 1954, its captain was Hans C. Petersen. The captain in 1956–57 was K. Hindberg.

**Kista Nunatak.** 69°47′S, 37°17′E. ½ mile south of Såta Nunatak, on the east side of Fletta Bay, on the SW coast of Lützow-Holm Bay. Photographed by the LCE 1936–37. Name means "the chest" in Norwegian.

**Kista Rock.** 69°44′S, 74°24′E. A small island 1 mile north of Mount Caroline Mikkelsen. It is the southernmost of a chain of small islands off the coast of East Antarctica. Photographed by the LCE 1936–37. Named by the Australians who landed here in 1957 for their ship, the *Kista Dan.*

**Kista Strait.** 67°35′S, 62°51′E. Between the Flat Islands and the Jocelyn Islands, in Holme Bay, Mac. Robertson Land. Photographed by the LCE 1936–37. First navigated by the *Kista Dan* in 1954, en route to what was to become Mawson Station.

**Kita-Karamete Rock.** 69°04′S, 35°23′E. 9 miles north of Minami-karamete Rock, on the east part of the Riiser-Larsen Peninsula of Queen Maud Land. The Japanese named it Kita-karamete-iwa (north back-gate rock) in 1972.

**Kitami Beach.** 69°01′S, 39°34′E. In the south part of Nishino-ura Cove, on East Ongul Island. Named Kitami-hama (north-looking beach) by the Japanese.

**Kitano-Seto Strait.** 69°S, 39°35′E. A narrow strait between Nesøya and East Ongul Island, in the Flatvaer Islands. Photographed by the LCE 1936–37. Surveyed by the Japanese in 1957, and named Kitano-seto (northern strait) by them because of its northern location within the island group.

**Kitano-Ura Cove.** 69°S, 39°36′E. Indentation into the northern side of East Ongul Island. Photographed by the LCE 1936–37. Surveyed by the Japanese in 1957. Name means "northern cove" in Japanese.

**Kitchen, J.** Captain of the *Ann,* in the South Shetlands during the 1821–22 season.

**Kitching Ridge.** 85°12′S, 177°06′W. A rock ridge on the west side of the Shackleton Glacier, between Bennett Platform and Matador Mountain, in the Queen Maud Mountains. Named by the USA for South African vertebrate paleontologist James W. Kitching, who first found fossils here while he was an exchange scientist with the Ohio State University Byrd Institute of Polar Studies 1970–71 geological party here.

**Kite Stream.** 77°23'S, 162°07'E. In the area of the Wright Valley, in southern Victoria Land.

**Kitney Island.** 67°31'S, 63°04'E. 1 mile ENE of Smith Rocks, off the coast of Mac. Robertson Land. Named by the Australians for V.J. Kitney, supervising radio technician at Mawson Station in 1968.

**Kitson, E.W.** Captain of the *Carnarvon Castle,* 1943.

**Kitticarrara Glacier.** 77°43'S, 163°02' E. 1 mile south of Howard Glacier, in the Kukri Hills, flowing into Ferrar Glacier, in southern Victoria Land. Named in 1910–13 by Grif Taylor during Scott's last expedition, for a sheep station in New South Wales, Australia. Frank Debenham suggested the name.

**Kivi Peak.** 86°22'S, 129°39'W. 2,390 m. Marks the south end of Cleveland Mesa, on the east side of the Michigan Plateau. Named for Stephen Kivi, utilitiesman at Byrd Station in 1962.

**Kiwi Pass.** 80°48'S, 158°E. Also called Kiwi Saddle. A high pass in the Churchill Mountains, just NE of Mount Egerton. Named by the New Zealanders in 1960–61 as a nickname for a New Zealander.

**Kiwi Saddle** *see* **Kiwi Pass**

**Kizahashi Beach.** 69°28'S, 39°35'E. At the head of Osen Cove, Skarvsnes Foreland, on the coast of Queen Maud Land. Named Kizahashi-hama (stair beach) by the Japanese in 1972.

**Mount Kizaki.** 70°45'S, 65°46'E. 4 miles SW of Mount Davie, in the Aramis Range of the Prince Charles Mountains. Named by the Australians for K. Kizaki, glaciologist at Mawson Station in 1966.

**Kizer Island.** 77°14'S, 150°50'W. 15 miles long. Ice-covered. The most westerly of the large, grounded islands in the Sulzberger Ice Shelf. 10 miles SW of Cronenwett Island. Named for Lt. T.L. Kizer, USN, helicopter pilot on the *Gla-*

cier who sighted the island aerially on Jan. 26, 1962.

**Kjelbotn, Olav.** In 1933, with Devold and Riiser-Larsen, he attempted sledge explorations of the Princess Ragnhild Coast.

**Kjelbotn Peak.** 72°14'S, 26°34'E. 3,210 m. Between Isachsen Mountain and Devold Peak, in the Sør Rondane Mountains. Named by the Norwegians for Olav Kjelbotn (they actually called the feature Kjelbotnnuten).

**Kjelbotnnuten** *see* **Kjelbotn Peak**

**Kjellberg, Sigvard.** Photographer with the Norwegian air unit of the NBSAE 1949–52.

**Kjellberg Peak.** 72°56'S, 3°45'W. At the head of Frostlendet Valley, about 4 miles west of Ryvingen Peak, in the southern part of the Borg Massif of Queen Maud Land. Named Kjellbergnuten by the Norwegians for Sigvard Kjellberg.

**Kjellbergnuten** *see* **Kjellberg Peak**

**Cape Kjellman.** 63°44'S, 59°24'W. Marks the east side of the entrance to Charcot Bay, on the west side of Trinity Peninsula. Charted by Nordenskjöld's expedition of 1901–4, and named by Nordenskjöld for Prof. Frans Kjellman, Swedish botanist.

**Mount Kjerka.** 68°03'S, 66°04'E. Also called Church Mountain. 865 m. At the south end of the Gustav Bull Mountains. 11 miles south of Mount Marsden, in Mac. Robertson Land. Photographed by the LCE 1936–37. Name means "the church" in Norwegian.

**Mount Kjerringa.** 66°29'S, 55°11'E. 1,220 m. Isolated. 8 miles north of Aker Peaks, and 26 miles west of Magnet Bay. Photographed by the LCE 1936–37. Name means "the old woman" in Norwegian.

**Kjølrabbane Hills.** 72°16'S, 3°22'W. A small group between Lyftingen Peak and Styrbordsknattane Peaks, near the SW end of the Ahlmann Ridge of Queen Maud Land. Name means "the keel hills" in Norwegian.

**Kjuka Headland.** 69°36'S, 39°44'E. 300 m. Just north of Telen Glacier, on the east side of Lützow-Holm Bay. Photographed by the LCE 1936–37. Name means "the lump" in Norwegian.

**Kjukevåg Bay.** 69°36'S, 39°41'E. On the east coast of Lützow-Holm Bay, in the area of Telen Glacier. Photographed by the LCE 1936–37. Name means "lump bay" in Norwegian, and was so named because it is near Kjuka Headland.

**Kjuklingen Nunatak.** 68°13'S, 58°27' E. One of the Dyer Nunataks. 1½ miles east of Mount Gjeita, in the Hansen Mountains. Name means "the chicken" in Norwegian. Photographed by the LCE 1936–37.

**Kjuringen** *see* **Rayner Peak**

**Klakkane Island.** 67°15'S, 59°46'E. A group of small islands 1½ miles east of Farrington Island, in the William Scoresby Archipelago. Photographed in Jan. 1937 by the LCE 1936–37. Name means "the lumps" in Norwegian.

**Klakknabben Peak.** 73°57'S, 5°42'W. Isolated. 2 miles NE of Gavlpiggen Peak, just north of the Kirwan Escarpment, in Queen Maud Land. Name means "the lump peak" in Norwegian.

**Klarius Mikkelsenfjell** *see* **Mikkelsen Peak**

**Klebelsberg Glacier.** 67°23'S, 66°19' W. 7 miles long. 2 miles wide. At the south side of Finsterwalder Glacier, it flows from the central plateau of Graham Land toward the head of Lallemand Fjord. It merges with Sharp Glacier where that glacier enters the fjord. Named by the FIDS in 1948 for Raimund von Klebelsberg, Austrian glaciologist.

**Klein Glacier.** 86°48'S, 150°W. Near the edge of the Polar Plateau, it flows into the Robert Scott Glacier just to the south of the La Gorce Mountains. Named for Lt. Cdr. Verle W. Klein, VX-6 pilot in 1966 and 1967.

**Klenke, William J., Jr.** Airplane mechanic on Ellsworth's 1935–36 expedition.

**Klenova, Marie V.** USSR professor and marine geologist, the first woman to do research in Antarctica. A member of the Council for Antarctic Research of the USSR Academy of Sciences, she had worked for 30 years in the North Polar regions, and then went to the Antarctic in the summer of 1956 with a USSR oceanographic team to map uncharted areas of the coast. She worked on the *Ob'* and the *Lena,* making shipboard observations, and at Mirnyy Station too.

**Klevekampen Mountain.** 71°58'S, 7° 41'E. Ice-free. 3 miles east of Kubus Mountain, in the Filchner Mountains of Queen Maud Land. Name means "the closet crag" in Norwegian.

**Klevekåpa Mountain.** 72°02'S, 7°37' E. 2,910 m. Ice-capped. NW of the mouth of Snuggerud Glacier, in the Filchner Mountains of Queen Maud Land. Name means "the closet cloak" in Norwegian.

**Klevetind Peak.** 71°59'S, 7°37'E. 2,910 m. Immediately south of Klevekampen Mountain, in the Filchner Mountains of Queen Maud Land. Name means "the closet peak" in Norwegian.

**Mount Kleynshmidt** *see* **Enden Point**

**Klimov Bluff.** 74°51'S, 113°52'W. Partly ice-free. Faces east. On the west side of Kohler Glacier, 1 mile SE of Mount Bray, in Marie Byrd Land. Named by the USA for L.V. Klimov, USSR exchange scientist at McMurdo Station in 1966, and again on the USARP Marie Byrd Land Survey Party of 1966–67.

**Klinck Nunatak.** 72°04'S, 63°59'W. On the east side of Palmer Land.

**Kling, Alfred.** Navigator of the *Deutschland,* 1911–12. He, König, and Filchner went out looking for New South Greenland in June 1912. He took over the ship on the death of Vahsel on Aug. 8, 1912.

**Klinger Ridge.** 74°43'S, 114°W. On Martin Peninsula, on the coast of Marie Byrd Land.

**Klo Rock.** 63°55'S, 60°46'W. On the east side of the entrance to Mikkelsen

Harbor, on Trinity Island, in the Palmer Archipelago. Charted and named in 1914–15 by Hans Borge.

**Kloa Point.** 66°38′S, 57°19′E. Juts out into the sea from the Edward VIII Plateau, 3 miles north of Cape Gotley. Photographed by the LCE 1936–37. Name means "the claw" in Norwegian.

**Cape Klövstad.** 71°39′S, 170°06′E. A rock point between Colbeck Bay and Protection Cove, in the southern part of Robertson Bay, in northern Victoria Land. First charted by Borchgrevink in 1898–1900, and named by him for Dr. Herlof Klövstad.

**Klövstad, Dr. Herlof.** Medical officer on Borchgrevink's 1898–1900 expedition.

**Kloyd Island** *see* **Cloyd Island**

**Klumpane Peaks.** 71°57′S, 3°24′W. A group of small rock peaks on the east side of the mouth of Strengen Valley, on the Ahlmann Ridge of Queen Maud Land. Name means "the lumps" in Norwegian.

**Klung Island.** 67°33′S, 62°59′E. Largest of the Klung Islands in Holme Bay, Mac. Robertson Land. Photographed by the LCE 1936–37, and named by the Australians in association with the group.

**Klung Islands.** 67°33′S, 63°E. A group of small islands (Klung Island is the largest), ½ mile east of Welch Island, in the NE sector of Holme Bay. Photographed by the LCE 1936–37, and named by them as Klungholmane (the bramble islands).

**Knack Point.** 85°15′S, 118°50′W. At the extreme north end of the Long Hills, in the Horlick Mountains. Named for Joseph V. Knack, meteorologist at Byrd Station in 1958.

**Knallen Peak.** 72°16′S, 3°56′W. A small rock peak, 2 miles west of Pyramiden Nunatak, at the east side of the head of Schytt Glacier, in Queen Maud Land. Named by the Norwegians.

**Knappane Peaks.** 72°38′S, 4°12′W. A string of separated rock peaks just west of Nålegga Ridge, on the west side of Borg Massif, in Queen Maud Land. Name means "the buttons" in Norwegian.

**Knappen Peak.** 69°27′S, 39°40′E. 220 m. Ice-free. Just east of Osen Cove, on Skarvsnes Foreland, on the east side of Lützow-Holm Bay. Photographed by the LCE 1936–37. Name means "the button" in Norwegian.

**Knattebrauta Nunataks.** 72°27′S, 0°18′E. A line of nunataks trending NE-SW, 4 miles north of Robin Heights, in the Sverdrup Mountains of Queen Maud Land. Name means "the crag slope" in Norwegian.

**Knerten Rock.** 71°33′S, 2°52′W. Isolated. 7 miles north of Vesleskarvet Cliff, in the NW part of the Ahlmann Ridge of Queen Maud Land. Name means "the nipper" in Norwegian.

**Knezevich Rock.** 76°10′S, 112°W. On the lower part of the north slope of Mount Takahe in Marie Byrd Land. At the east side of the mouth of Clausen Glacier. Named for Nick Knezevich, Jr., USN, electronics technician at Amundsen-Scott South Pole Station in 1974.

**Knife Point.** 60°43′S, 45°37′W. On the south side of Borge Bay, just SE of Mooring Point, on the east side of Signy Island, in the South Orkneys. Named earlier than 1927, and probably descriptively.

**Knight, Stephen.** Ship's cook on the Wilkes Expedition 1838–42. Joined in the USA. Discharged at Oahu on Oct. 31, 1840.

**Knight Island.** 64°55′S, 64°01′W. 1½ miles long. 1 mile west of Reeve Island, in the Wauwermans Islands of the Wilhelm Archipelago. Named by the UK in 1958 for the character in the *Canterbury Tales.*

**Knight Nunatak.** 69°23′S, 158°52′E. Isolated. 4 miles SSE of Cape Kinsey and 3 miles NE of Mount Conrad, in the Goodman Hills. Named for Melvin W. Knight, USN, involved in Operation Deep Freeze in 1967, 1968, 1969, and 1970.

**Knight Rocks.** 62°50′S, 61°35′W. A group of small rocks, 4½ miles WNW of the south end of Snow Island, in the South Shetlands. Named by the UK in 1952 after Lt. Cdr. F.W. Hunt's survey of 1951–52, because of their proximity to Castle Rock (a play on chess words).

**Knob Lake.** 60°42′S, 45°37′W. The central lake in Three Lakes Valley, in the NE part of Signy Island, in the South Orkneys. Named by the UK because of the rock knob in the southern part of the lake.

**Knob Point.** 77°48′S, 166°40′E. Juts out from Hut Point Peninsula, Ross Island, into Erebus Bay, just to the north of Danger Slopes. Named by US biologist Gerald L. Kooyman, here in 1963–65, but the name had been used by others before him.

**Knobble Head.** 63°09′S, 56°32′W. Also spelled Nobble Head. Forms the eastern extremity of Bransfield Island, in Antarctic Sound. It is a descriptive name, applied by the FIDS in 1960–61.

**Knobhead.** 77°55′S, 161°32′E. Also called Knobhead Mountain. 2,400 m. A mountain, south of the west end of the Kukri Hills, it overlooks the Ferrar and Taylor Glaciers, in Victoria Land. Discovered by Scott's 1901–4 expedition, and named descriptively by them.

**Knobhead Mountain** *see* **Knobhead**

**The Knoll.** 77°31′S, 169°21′E. 370 m. Snow-free. ½ mile north of Cape Crozier, on Ross Island. Discovered on Scott's 1901–4 expedition, and named aptly by them.

**The *Knorr*.** US academic research ship in Antarctic waters in the 1980s.

**Knotten Nunatak.** 71°37′S, 2°19′W. 5 miles SW of Krylen Hill, in the northern part of the Ahlmann Ridge of Queen Maud Land. Name means "the knob" in Norwegian.

**Cape Knowles.** 71°48′S, 60°50′W. 305 m. Marks the north side of the entrance to Hilton Inlet, it juts out from the east coast of Palmer Land just above Hilton

Inlet. Discovered by the USAS from East Base in 1940. Named for Paul H. Knowles.

**Knowles, Charles.** Ordinary seaman on the Wilkes Expedition 1838–42. Joined in the USA. Served the cruise.

**Knowles, Paul H.** Geologist at East Base during the USAS 1939–41.

**Knowles Passage.** 66°26′S, 110°28′E. A marine passage between Holl Island and Petersen Island, in the Windmill Islands. Named for Lt. Lloyd C. Knowles, USN, engineer officer on the *Burton Island* here during Operation Windmill, 1947–48.

**Knox, Samuel R.** Passed midshipman on the Wilkes Expedition 1838–42. He was commander of the *Flying Fish* on its first, non-Antarctic cruises and in 1840 was acting master on the *Vincennes,* in the Antarctic.

**Knox Basin** *see* **South Indian Basin**

**Knox Coast.** 66°30′S, 105°E. Between Cape Hordern (at 100°31′E) and the Hatch Islands (at 109°16′E), on the coast of Wilkes Land, to the west of Vincennes Bay. Discovered by Wilkes on Feb. 14, 1840, and named by him as Knox's High Land, for Samuel Knox. The name has been variously seen since as Knox Coast and Knox Land.

**Knox Land** *see* **Knox Coast**

**Knox Peak.** 84°49′S, 116°39′W. A nunatak between Vann Peak and Lackey Ridge, at the west end of the Ohio Range. Named for Arthur S. Knox, Antarctic cartographer.

**Knox's High Land** *see* **Knox Coast**

**Knuckey Peaks.** 67°54′S, 53°32′E. A group of isolated peaks, 30 miles SE of the McLeod Nunataks and 15 miles west of the Doggers Nunataks, in Enderby Land. Discovered in Dec. 1958 by an ANARE dog-sledge party and named by the Australians for a member of that party, G.A. Knuckey, surveyor at Mawson Station in 1958.

**Knuckle Reef.** 67°50'S, 67°22'W. Off Beacon Head, Horseshoe Island. Named descriptively by the UK in 1958.

**Knudsen, Engebrecht.** One of the Norwegian seamen who went insane on the *Belgica* during the 1898 wintering-over. He died shortly after the expedition ended.

**Knut Rocks.** 71°24'S, 13°02'E. 5 miles east of Deildegasten Ridge, in the SW portion of the Gruber Mountains of Queen Maud Land. Discovered aerially by Ritscher's expedition of 1938–39, and later named Knutsufsene by the Norwegians, for Knut Ødegaard, radio operator with the Norwegian Antarctic Expedition of 1958–59.

**Mount Knut Sundbeck** *see* **Mount Sundbeck**

**Knutsufsene** *see* **Knut Rocks**

**Ko-iwa Rock.** 68°42'S, 40°33'E. Also called Oden Rock. 3½ miles west of Oku-iwa Glacier, on the coast of Queen Maud Land. Named Ko-iwa (small rock) by the Japanese.

**Koala Island.** 67°34'S, 47°53'E. Just west of Pinn Island, and north of McKinnon Island, off the coast of Enderby Land. Named by the Australians for their native animal.

**Koch Glacier.** 64°27'S, 62°30'W. 3 miles long. Just east of Jenner Glacier, on the south side of Brabant Island. The UK named it for Robert Koch (1843–1910), German bacteriologist.

**Koechlin Island.** 66°42'S, 67°38'W. Off the NE coast of Alexander Island, about 4½ miles south of the Sillard Islands. Named by the UK for René Koechlin, Swiss glaciologist.

**Bahía Koegel** *see* **Suspiros Bay**

**Koehler Nunatak.** 74°52'S, 98°08'W. Isolated. 20 miles ESE of Mount Manthe, at the SE end of the Hudson Mountains. Named for Walter Koehler, helicopter pilot in the area in 1968–69.

**Koenig Valley.** 77°36'S, 160°47'E. Ice-free. Just east of Mount Thor, in the Asgard Range of Victoria Land. Named for Ervan R. Koenig, scientific leader at McMurdo Station in 1972, and station manager there in 1973–74 and 1974–75.

**Koerner Bluff.** 76°S, 133°04'W. A bare rock on the NW edge of Mount Bursey, in the Flood Range of Marie Byrd Land. Named for Roy M. Koerner, glaciologist with the Byrd Station Traverse, 1962–63, who had been a FIDS assistant meteorologist and glaciologist at Base D between 1957 and 1960.

**Koerner Rock.** 63°19'S, 57°05'W. 4 miles SW of Cape Dubouzet, Trinity Peninsula. Named by the UK for Roy M. Koerner (*see* **Koerner Bluff**).

**Koerwitz Glacier.** 85°42'S, 154°24'W. Flows from Mount Griffith in the Hays Mountains, to the Karo Hills. Byrd's 1928–30 expedition was the first to see and map it, and it was later named for Peter H. Koerwitz, biolab manager at McMurdo Station in 1965.

**Koether Inlet.** 71°56'S, 97°20'W. 18 miles long. Ice-filled. An indentation into the northern side of Thurston Island, between Evans Peninsula and Edwards Peninsula. Named for Ensign Bernard Koether, navigator on the *Glacier* during the Bellingshausen Sea Expedition of Feb. 1960.

**Koettlitz, Reginald.** 1861–1916. Surgeon and botanist on the Royal Society Expedition of 1901–4. He invented the pyramid tent while in the Arctic.

**Koettlitz Glacier.** 78°20'S, 164°30'E. West of Mount Morning and Mount Discovery, it flows from the area of Mount Cox, between Brown Peninsula and the mainland of southern Victoria Land, to empty into the Ross Ice Shelf at McMurdo Sound. Discovered by Scott's 1901–4 expedition and named by them for Reginald Koettlitz.

**Koffer** *see* **Coffer Island**

**Kogot Point.** 67°40'S, 45°44'E. On Alasheyev Bight, in Enderby Land, about a mile east of Molodezhnaya Station. Named by the USSR.

**Kohl, Dr.** German surgeon on the *Sir James Clark Ross* expedition of 1923–24.

**Mount Kohler.** 77°17'S, 145°35'W. 480 m. On the south side of the Boyd Glacier, 4 miles east of Mount Woodward, in the Ford Ranges of Marie Byrd Land. Named by Byrd in 1940 for Herbert V. Kohler, Jr., and Ruth DeYoung Kohler II, son and daughter of Herbert V. Kohler, sponsor of Byrd's 1933–35 expedition.

**Kohler Dome.** 76°02'S, 134°17'W. 2,680 m. A rounded, snow-covered elevation. In the eastern part of the Mount Moulton massif in Marie Byrd Land. Named for Robert E. Kohler, geomagnetist at Byrd Station in 1970.

**Kohler Glacier.** 74°55'S, 113°45'W. Flows from the Kohler Range (hence the name) into the Dotson Ice Shelf, in Marie Byrd Land.

**Kohler Head.** 75°48'S, 162°51'E. On the north side of Whitmer Peninsula, on the coast of Victoria Land. Named for John L. Kohler, USN, construction electrician at McMurdo Station in 1966–67.

**Kohler Range.** 75°05'S, 114°15'W. Also called Walter Kohler Range. 40 miles long. Behind the Dotson Ice Shelf, in Marie Byrd Land. Its features include Mount Isherwood, Mount Strange, Mount Bray, Morrison Bluff, Early Bluff. Discovered aerially by Byrd on Feb. 24, 1940, during the USAS, and named for Walter J. Kohler, a supporter of Byrd's 1933–35 expedition.

**Kohmyr Ridge.** 82°47'S, 160°10'E. Just east of Hochstein Ridge, in the NW part of the Queen Elizabeth Range. Named for Walter D. Kohmyr, meteorologist at McMurdo Station in 1963–64.

**Mount Kohnen.** 75°S, 134°47'W. A peak on the SW corner of Bowyer Butte, in Marie Byrd Land. Named for Heinz Kohnen, geophysicist at Byrd Station in 1970–71.

**Koke Strand.** 69°13'S, 39°40'E. A beach just south of Mount Choto, in Fukuro Cove, in the Langhovde Hills on the coast of Queen Maud Land. There is a notable moss deposit here. Named Koke-daira (moss strand) by the Japanese in 1963.

**Kolich Point.** 77°21'S, 163°33'E. Between Spike Cape and Gneiss Point, on the coast of Victoria Land. Named for Thomas M. Kolich, geophysicist on the Ross Ice Shelf Project in 1973–74.

**Koll Rock.** 67°24'S, 60°41'E. Also called Blake Island. ½ mile south of Oom Island, on the west side of Oom Bay, in Mac. Robertson Land. Photographed by the LCE 1936–37, and later named by the Norwegians as Kollskjer (knoll rock).

**Koloc Point.** 74°11'S, 111°24'W. Ice-covered. Marks the northern extremity of Bear Peninsula, in Marie Byrd Land. Named for Lt. Cdr. Bohumil Koloc, Jr., USN, helicopter pilot in Antarctica in 1966 and 1967.

**Mount Kolodkin.** 71°45'S, 12°37'E. 2,525 m. 1½ miles SE of Pinegin Peak, in the Südliche Petermann Range of the Wohlthat Mountains. Discovered by Ritscher in 1938–39, and named by the USSR in 1966 for Kolodkin, designer of the *Vostok* and *Mirnyy*, von Bellingshausen's old ships.

**Cape Kolosov.** 66°29'S, 50°16'E. On the east side of the entrance to Amundsen Bay. Named by the USSR for V. Kolosov, polar aviation navigator who died in the Arctic.

**Mount Kolp.** 81°39'S, 161°42'E. 1,010 m. Ice-free. A coastal mountain 7 miles WNW of Cape Laird, on the west side of the Ross Ice Shelf. Named for Lt. H.R. Kolp, US Marines, VX-6 executive in 1955–56.

**Kolven Island.** 67°33'S, 61°29'E. Also called Alfons Island. A small island ½ mile east of Stedet Island, and just NE of Falla Bluff, in Utstikkar Bay, in Mac. Robertson Land. Photographed aerially by the LCE 1936–37, and later named Kolven (the club) by the Norwegians.

**Komandnaya Nunatak.** 72°12'S, 14°31'E. The eastern and highest of the

Rokhlin Nunataks, in the south part of the Payer Mountains of Queen Maud Land. Discovered by Ritscher in 1938–39, and named by the USSR in 1966 as Gora Komandnaya (command mountain).

**Komatsu Nunatak.** 71°54′S, 161°11′E. 1,840 m. 4 miles west of Mou..it Van der Hoeven, in the western part of the Helliwell Hills. Named for Stanley K. Komatsu, US biologist at McMurdo Station in 1966–67 and 1967–68.

**The *Komet*.** Hilfskreuzer 45 of the German Navy. It cruised along the Antarctic coast between Cape Adare and the Shackleton Ice Shelf, in the summer of 1940–41.

**Koms Glacier.** 72°03′S, 25°18′E. 5 miles long. Flows between Mefjell Mountain and Komsa Mountain, in the Sør Rondane Mountains. Name means "Lapp cradle" in Norwegian. The Norwegians call it Komsbreen.

**Komsa Mountain.** 72°05′S, 25°21′E. 2,960 m. Between Koms Glacier and Salen Mountain, in the Sør Rondane Mountains. The name means "the Lapp cradle" in Norwegian.

**Komsomol′skaya Hill.** 66°33′S, 93°01′E. 35 m. The northernmost point of Mirnyy Station. Immediately south of Mabus Point, on the coast of East Antarctica. Discovered by the AAE 1911–14. Named by the USSR in 1956. Name means "young communist" in Russian.

**Komsomol′skaya Station.** 72°08′S, 96°35′E. USSR IGY station built in 1957 as an operational support station. Later moved to 74°06′S, 97°30′E. Name means "young communist."

**Komsomolskiy Peak.** 75°45′S, 63°25′E. 130 miles SSE of Mount Menzies, in Mac. Robertson Land. Discovered aerially by the USSR on Dec. 7, 1958, and named by them. The name means "communist" in Russian.

**Kon-Tiki Nunatak.** 82°33′S, 159°52′E. 1,300 m. Raftlike (hence the name, given for Thor Heyerdahl's 1947 trans–Pacific raft). On top of the Cooper Ice-

falls, in the center of the Nimrod Glacier. Discovered and named by the New Zealanders in 1961–62.

**König, Dr.** Austrian on the *Deutschland* with Filchner in 1911–12. He, Filchner, and Kling went out looking for New South Greenland in June 1912. He planned a 1913–14 expedition to the Filchner Ice Shelf, but Shackleton beat him to it, and it was aborted. König never went to Antarctica again.

**Kønig Haakon** *see* **King Haakon**

**Konter, Richard W.** Seaman on the *City of New York,* during Byrd's 1928–30 expedition.

**Konter Cliffs.** 75°06′S, 137°48′W. On the east side of the terminus of the Frostman Glacier, on the coast of Marie Byrd Land. Named for Richard W. Konter.

**Mount Koob.** 84°53′S, 169°02′W. 1,600 m. The highest peak in the Mayer Crags, in the Queen Maud Mountains. 4 miles NW of Mount Ferguson. Named for Derry D. Koob, biologist at McMurdo Station in 1964–65 and 1965–66.

**Mount Koons.** 72°43′S, 160°22′E. 1 mile east of Miller Butte, in the Outback Nunataks. Named for Robert W. Koons.

**The *Koonya*.** A steel-hulled steamer chartered by Shackleton's 1907–9 expedition to help the *Nimrod* (Shackleton's expedition ship) to Antarctica in order to save fuel for the *Nimrod*. This service was paid for by the Union Steamship Co., which owned the *Koonya,* and by the New Zealand government. It towed the *Nimrod* out of Lyttelton Harbour, NZ, on Jan. 1, 1908, and 1,500 miles later, on Jan. 15, 1908, in Antarctic waters, it cast off the tow and returned home. F.P. Evans was captain of the *Koonya* which, on this trip, became the first steel vessel to cross the Antarctic Circle.

**The *Kooperatsiya*.** USSR expedition ship used by the Soviet Antarctic Expeditions of 1956–57 and 1957–58. Captain A.S. Yantslevich.

**Kooperatsiya Ice Piedmont.** 70°15′S, 160°25′E. At the SW side of Yermak

Point, on the west shore of Rennick Bay. Named by the USSR in 1958 for their ship, the *Kooperatsiya*. Actually they called the western portion of Rennick Bay Zaliv Kooperatsiya, and the Americans, who still call the whole embayment Rennick Bay, use the Russian term for the ice piedmont here.

**Koopman Peak.** 85°29'S, 125°35'W. Over 2,200 m. 2 miles north of Moran Buttress, on the north side of the Wisconsin Range. Named for Kenneth E. Koopman, Navy yeoman in Antarctica in 1965–66 and 1967.

**Kooyman Peak.** 82°43'S, 162°49'E. 1,630 m. Just south of the Dorrer Glacier, in the Queen Elizabeth Range. Named for Gerald L. Kooyman, biologist at McMurdo Station in 1963–64 and 1964–65.

**Kopaitic Island.** 63°19'S, 57°55'W. Immediately west of Cape Legoupil, in the Duroch Islands. Named by the Chilean Antarctic Expedition of 1946–47 for Lt. Boris Kopaitic O'Neill.

**Mount Kopere.** 82°17'S, 158°51'E. 1½ miles NW of Lyttelton Peak, in the central sector of the Cobham Range. Named descriptively by the New Zealanders in 1964–65 for the appearance of the peak's triangular cross-section which suggests an arrowhead (kopere in Maori means "arrow").

**Korea** *see* **South Korea**

**Koren, Johan.** Norwegian sailor on the *Belgica*, 1897–99.

**Korff Ice Rise.** 79°S, 69°30'W. 80 miles long. 20 miles wide. 50 miles ENE of Skytrain Ice Rise, in the SW part of the Ronne Ice Shelf. Discovered by the US-IGY Ellsworth Traverse Party of 1957–58, and named by them for Prof. Serge A. Korff, member of the National Committee for the IGY.

**Mount Korsch.** Unofficial name for a mountain in the Queen Elizabeth Range.

**Mount Kosciusko.** 75°43'S, 132°13'W. 2,910 m. Forms the central part of the Ames Range, in Marie Byrd Land. Named for Capt. Henry M. Kosciusko, USN, commander of the Antarctic Support Activities group in 1965–67.

**Kosco, George F.** Capt., USN. Chief aerologist and chief scientist on Operation Highjump, 1946–47.

**Kosco Glacier.** 84°27'S, 178°W. 20 miles long. Flows from the area of the Anderson Heights, in the Bush Mountains, and enters the Ross Ice Shelf between Wilson Portal and Mount Speed. Discovered by the USAS 1939–41, and later named for Capt. George F. Kosco.

**Kosistyy Point.** 67°43'S, 45°44'E. On Alasheyev Bight, in Enderby Land, about 3½ miles west of Molodezhnaya Station.

**Koski Glacier.** 85°17'S, 167°15'E. 7 miles long. Flows from the east-central part of the Dominion Range, just north of the Vandament Glacier, ending at the Mill Glacier just SE of Browns Butte. Named for Raymond J. Koski, engineer at Amundsen-Scott South Pole Station in 1962–63, 1963–64, and 1964–65.

**Mount Kosko.** 79°09'S, 159°33'E. 1,795 m. 6 miles north of Mount Keltie, in the Conway Range. Named for Arno Kosko, ionosphere physicist at Byrd Station in 1963.

**Kosky Peak.** 70°57'S, 63°28'W. 1½ miles south of Mount Nordhill, in the Welch Mountains of Palmer Land. Named for Capt. Harry G. Kosky, US Coast Guard, captain of the *Westwind* in 1971.

**Koslov Nunataks** *see* **Kozlov Nunataks**

**The *Kosmos*.** Norwegian factory whaling ship in Antarctic waters in 1929–30 and 1930–31, under the command of Capt. Hans Andresen. The ship supplied coal to the BANZARE ship *Discovery* on Dec. 29, 1930. Also aboard was the whale fishing inspector, Capt. Dingsør.

**Mount Kostka.** 70°42'S, 164°49'E. 1,210 m. On the west side of Zykov Glacier, 3 miles SE of Saddle Peak, in the

Anare Mountains. Named by the USSR in 1961 for Czech aerologist O. Kostka (see **Deaths, 1960**), a member of the Soviet Antarctic Expedition of 1959–61.

**Kotick Point.** 64°S, 58°22'W. The southern entrance point to Holluschickie Bay, on the west coast of James Ross Island. Named by the UK for Kipling's character in *Jungle Book.*

**Kottas, A.** Captain of the *Schwabenland,* 1938–39, during Ritscher's expedition.

**Kottas Mountains** *see* **Heimefront Range**

**Kotterer Peaks.** 70°11'S, 64°26'E. Between the Wignall Nunataks and Mount Starlight, in the Athos Range of the Prince Charles Mountains. Named by the Australians for C. Kotterer, weather observer at Davis Station in 1964.

**Kouperov, Leonid** *see* **Kuperov, Leonid**

**Kouperov Peak.** 75°06'S, 133°48'W. 890 m. At the southern end of the Demas Range, in Marie Byrd Land. Named by the US for Leonid Kuperov (q.v.).

**Kovacs Glacier.** 83°11'S, 49°15'W. In the Pensacola Mountains.

**Mount Kowalczyk.** 77°56'S, 163°47'E. 1,690 m. 1 mile south of Goat Mountain, at the head of Hobbs Glacier, in Victoria Land. Charted by members of Scott's 1910–13 expedition, and named by the USA in 1964 for Chester Kowalczyk, chief of the US Navy Oceanographic Office's Photogrammetry Branch.

**Cape Koyubi.** 69°14'S, 39°38'E. In the Langhovde Hills, jutting out to sea from Queen Maud Land. Named Koyubi-misaki (little finger point) by the Japanese in 1972 (see *also* **Cape Nakayubi**).

**Kozlov Nunataks.** 66°37'S, 51°07'E. 8 miles north of Mount Parviainen, in the Tula Mountains of Enderby Land. Named by visiting USSR geologists in 1961–62 for M.I. Kozlov, USSR polar pilot.

**Kozo Rock.** 68°23'S, 41°54'E. On the coast of Queen Maud Land, between the Narabi Rocks and Gobamme Rock. Named Kozo-iwa (youngster rock) by the Japanese.

**Krakken Hill.** 71°57'S, 26°14'E. In Byrdbreen, 5 miles east of Bautåen Peak, in the Sør Rondane Mountains. Name means "the stool" in Norwegian.

**Krakken Mountain.** 71°32'S, 12°09'E. 1 mile north of Sandseten Mountain in the Westliche Petermann Range. Discovered by Ritscher in 1938–39. Later named Krakken (the stool) by the Norwegians.

**Kramer Island.** 77°14'S, 147°10'W. 2 miles long. Ice-covered. In the Marshall Archipelago, between Nolan Island and Court Ridge, in the Sulzberger Ice Shelf. Named for Michael S. Kramer, meteorologist at Byrd Station in 1968.

**Kramer Rocks.** 65°26'S, 64°02'W. Two rocks in the northern part of Beaschochea Bay, 3 miles SE of Cape Pérez, on the west coast of Graham Land. Named by the UK in 1959 for J.G.H. Kramer, Austrian Army physician who, in 1737, discovered a cure for scurvy.

**Krank Glacier.** 83°08'S, 162°05'E. 5 miles long. It flows into Helm Glacier, just south of Mount Macbain, in the Queen Elizabeth Range. Named for Joseph P. Krank, Weather Central (q.v.) meteorologist at Little America V in 1957.

**Kranz Peak.** 86°31'S, 155°24'W. 2,680 m. 6 miles NW of Mount Przywitowski, between the heads of the Holdsworth and Bartlett Glaciers, in the Queen Maud Mountains. Named for Cdr. Arthur C. Kranz, staff meteorological officer, US Naval Support Force, Antarctica, 1966 and 1967.

**Kråsen Crevasse Field.** 71°48'S, 0°58' W. 15 miles long. In the lower part of the Jutulstraumen Glacier, in Queen Maud Land. Kråsen means "the crop" in Norwegian.

**Krasheninnikov Peak.** 71°41'S, 12°40' E. 2,525 m. On the south side of Svar-

thausane Crags, in the Südliche Petermann Range. Discovered by Ritscher in
1938–39, and named by the USSR in 1966
for geographer S.P. Krasheninnikov.

**Krasin Nunataks.** 68°18′S, 50°05′E. 10
miles SE of Alderdice Peak, in the Nye
Mountains of Enderby Land. Named by
the USSR in 1961–62 for the icebreaker
*Krasin.*

**Cape Krasinskiy.** 69°50′S, 8°30′E.
Separates Dublitskiy Bay from Kamenev
Bight, on the coast of Queen Maud
Land. Named by the USSR in 1961 for
G.D. Krasinskiy, organizer of polar air
expeditions.

**Krasnaya Nunatak.** 68°18′S, 49°42′E.
4 miles south of Alderdice Peak, in the
Nye Mountains of Enderby Land.
Named by the USSR in 1961–62 as Gora
Krasnaya (red mountain).

**Krasnov Rocks.** 71°48′S, 10°20′E. 2
miles SSE of Mount Dallmann, in the Orvin Mountains of Queen Maud Land.
Named by the USSR in 1966 for
geographer A.N. Krasnov.

**Krat Rocks.** 68°34′S, 77°54′E. An area
of submerged rocks off the Vestfold
Hills, at the west side of Davis Anchorage, almost a mile due south of Bluff
Island. The area is 100 yards by 60 yards,
with a depth of at least 4 feet. Named by
the Australians for I. Krat, chief engineer
on the *Thala Dan,* which in 1961 carried
an ANARE party to the area.

**Kraul, Otto.** German Naval captain,
ice pilot on the German New Schwabenland Expedition of 1938–39, led by
Ritscher.

**Kraul Mountains.** 73°30′S, 14°10′W.
The Norwegians call them Vestfjella.
They extend for 70 miles from Veststrau-
men Glacier, going north, in New
Schwabenland. Discovered in 1938–39
by Ritscher's expedition, and named by
Ritscher for Otto Kraul.

**Krause Point.** 66°34′S, 91°04′E. A
low, ice-covered point jutting out into
the Davis Sea between Cape Torson and
Cape Filchner. Named for Glenn R.

Krause, photogrammetrist with the Navy
Hydrographic Office, surveyor with Operation Windmill, 1947–48.

**Kraut Rocks.** 76°04′S, 136°11′W. On
the SW slopes of the Mount Berlin massif,
in Marie Byrd Land. Named for William
F. Kraut, USN, radioman on the Byrd
Station Land Traverse of 1956–57.

**Mount Krebs.** 84°50′S, 170°20′W.
1,630 m. A rock peak in the Lillie Range,
4 miles north of Mount Daniel, in the
foothills of the Prince Olav Mountains.
Discovered by the US Ross Ice Shelf
Traverse Party of 1957–58 under Albert
P. Crary, and named by him for Cdr.
Manson Krebs, VX-6 pilot.

**Krebs Glacier.** 64°38′S, 61°31′W.
Flows into the head of Charlotte Bay, on
the west coast of Graham Land. Charted
by de Gerlache in 1897–99. Named by
the UK in 1960 for Arthur C. Krebs
(1850–1935) who flew the first dirigible,
in 1884.

**Krebs Ridge.** 70°33′S, 62°25′W.
Forms the north wall of Gurling Glacier,
on the east coast of Palmer Land. Named
for William N. Krebs, biologist at Palmer Station in 1972.

**Krech, Capt.** Captain of the *Valdivia,*
1898–99.

**Kreiling Mesa.** 83°12′S, 158°E. Partly
ice-covered. On the south side of the
mouth of Argosy Glacier, in the Miller
Range. Named for Lee W. Kreiling,
traverse engineer at McMurdo Station in
1961, a member of the Ellsworth Land
Traverse of 1961–62, and on Roosevelt
Island in 1962–63.

**Kreitzer, William R.** Lt., USN. Air-
craft commander during Operation
Highjump, 1946–47. He operated off the
*Currituck,* over East Antarctica, with
Bunger and William J. Rogers, Jr.

**Kreitzer Bay** *see* **Vincennes Bay**

**Kreitzer Glacier.** 70°25′S, 72°30′E.
Comes off the Grove Mountains, and
flows between Jennings Promontory and
the Reinbolt Hills, to enter the Amery
Ice Shelf. Named in 1952 by US cartog-

rapher John H. Roscoe, for Lt. William R. Kreitzer. Not to be confused with Kreitzerisen.

**Kreitzerisen.** 72°13′S, 22°10′E. A glacier, 8 miles long, flowing between the Tertene Nunataks and Bamse Mountain, in the Sør Rondane Mountains. Named for Lt. William R. Kreitzer. Not to be confused with Kreitzer Glacier.

**Krichak Bay.** 68°28′S, 151°12′E. An indentation into the Cook Ice Shelf, in East Antarctica.

**Krieger Peak.** 71°46′S, 70°35′W. In the southern part of Alexander Island.

**Krigsvold Nunataks.** 75°38′S, 137°55′W. At the head of the Strauss Glacier, in Marie Byrd Land. Named for Sgt. Alvin I. Krigsvold, member of the Byrd Station Land Traverse of 1956–57.

**Krill.** The most important organism in the higher food chain in the Antarctic, krill is a small, shrimplike (1–2 inches long when mature) marine animal which is cannibalistic and can live to more than 2 years. It has antennae, a tail-fin, gills, thoracic legs, swimmerets, and a carapace. It congregates in vast, dense schools, and thus has great value as food for the large whales and seals who eat tons of it. A blue whale can eat 360 tons a year. Krill concentrate in the top few meters of water when ice is present, but disperse to depths of over 300 feet when the sea is ice-free. In 1981 the US research ship *Melville* discovered a school of 10 million tons of krill near Elephant Island, the largest swarm of sea animals ever seen. 82 species of krill have been described, the largest and best known being *Euphausia superba* (which has 11 pairs of legs). Krill can be marketed, and is to some extent, but the going is tough. Krill are fished by the USSR and Japan, and may one day be part of the human diet, although they're not exciting to eat, unless heavily sauced, spiced, or seasoned.

**Mount Kring.** 74°59′S, 157°54′E. A nunatak on the northern edges of the upper reaches of David Glacier, 13 miles SW of Mount Wood, in Victoria Land.

Named by NZ cartographer D.B. McC. Rainey, for US Marine Sgt. Arthur L. Kring, VX-6 navigator who helped NZ field parties out in this area.

**Kring Island** *see* **Kring Islands**

**Kring Islands.** 67°10′S, 58°30′E. Two islands and many rocks on the east side of Bell Bay, on the Enderby Land coast. Photographed by the LCE 1936–37, and mapped by the Norwegians from these aerial photos as being one island which they called Kringla (the ring). This was translated into English as Kring Island. ANARE photos of 1959 show the feature more accurately.

**Kringholmane** *see* **Hobbs Islands**

**Kringla** *see* **Kring Islands**

**¹Mount Kristensen** *see* **Mount Christensen**

**²Mount Kristensen.** 86°20′S, 159°40′W. 3,460 m. On the west side of the Nilsen Plateau, 2 miles SE of Lindstrøm Peak, in the Queen Maud Mountains. Named by the USA in 1967 for H. Kristensen. Somewhere in this area was Mount H. Kristensen (q.v.), named by Amundsen in 1911.

**Kristensen, H.** An engineer on the *Fram*, 1910–12.

**Kristensen, Leonard.** Norwegian Naval captain, skipper of the *Antarctic* during Henryk Bull's 1894–95 expedition to Antarctica. He found the first vegetation south of the Antarctic Circle, and was leader of the boat which made the first substantiated landing on the continent, on Jan. 24, 1895, at Cape Adare.

**Kristensen Rocks.** 71°55′S, 171°11′E. Twin rocks 1 mile south of Possession Island in the Possession Islands. Named for Leonard Kristensen.

**Kristiania Island** *see* **Christiania Island**

**Proliv Krivoy** *see* **Robertson Channel**

**Krogh Island.** 66°17′S, 67°W. 5 miles long. Just west of Lavoisier Island, in the Biscoe Islands. Named by the UK for

August Krogh (1874–1949), Danish physiologist dealing with the cold.

**Krogmann Island**  *see*  **Hovgaard Island**

**Krogmann Point.** 65°08'S, 64°08'W. The western end of Hovgaard Island, in the Wilhelm Archipelago. Named in order to preserve the original name of the island (*see* **Hovgaard Island**).

**Krok Fjord.** 68°40'S, 78°E. Also called Krok Inlet. A narrow fjord, 11 miles long, between Mule Peninsula and the Sørsdal Glacier Tongue, at the south end of the Vestfold Hills. Photographed by the LCE 1936–37. Named descriptively by the Norwegians (the name means "the crooked fjord"), and translated occasionally into English as Crooked Fjord.

**Krok Inlet**  *see*  **Krok Fjord**

**Krok Island.** 67°02'S, 57°46'E. Also called Crooked Island. 1 mile long. 1 mile south of Abrupt Island, and 6 miles west of Hoseason Glacier. Photographed by the LCE 1936–37, and later named by the Norwegians (the name does mean "crooked island").

**Krok Lake.** 68°37'S, 78°24'E. Also called Krokvatnet, Crooked Lake. 4 miles long. In the SE part of the Vestfold Hills. Aptly named by the Norwegians (the name does mean "crooked lake").

**Krokvatnet**  *see*  **Krok Lake**

**Kroner Lake.** 62°58'S, 60°35'W. Also called Lake Pennilea, Laguna Verde. Circular. 350 yards in diameter. On Deception Island, in the South Shetlands. Immediately to the west of Whaler's Bay. Its name was Tokroningen ("the two-kroner piece") between 1905–31, a name given by whalers, but it was renamed in 1950 by the UK, but still preserving the theme of Norwegian money. It was landlocked, but after the volcanic activity of 1969 it was opened to the sea.

**Mount Kropotkin.** 71°54'S, 6°35'E. On the west side of Jøkulkyrkja Mountain, in the Mühlig-Hofmann Mountains of Queen Maud Land. Named by the USSR in 1961 for the scientist P.A. Kropotkin.

**Kroshka Island.** 70°40'S, 2°05'E. The smaller of two ice-covered islands lying close together in the Fimbul Ice Shelf. Named by the USSR in 1961 as Kupol Kroshka (crumb dome).

**Krout Glacier.** 84°53'S, 172°12'W. 4 miles long. Flows from the Prince Olav Mountains, between Mount Sellery and Mount Smithson, and enters Gough Glacier just east of Mount Dodge. Named for Walter L. Krout, USN, equipment operator 1st class, in Antarctica in 1964.

**Kruber Rock.** 71°45'S, 11°05'E. 3 miles WNW of Mount Flånuten, on the west side of the Humboldt Mountains in Queen Maud Land. Discovered by Ritscher in 1938–39, and named in 1966 by the USSR for geographer A.A. Kruber.

**Krüder, Ernst-Felix.** Captain of the *Pinguin*, 1940–41.

**Mount Krüger.** 72°36'S, 0°57'E. 2,655 m. Also called Kvitskarvet. 8 miles SW of Kvithø Peak, in the Sverdrup Mountains of Queen Maud Land. Discovered by Ritscher in 1938–39, and named for Walter Krüger.

**Krüger, Walter.** Meteorological assistant on the German New Schwabenland Expedition of 1938–39, led by Ritscher.

**Krügerfjellet**  *see*  **Mount Krüger**

**Kupol Kruglyy**  *see*  **Blåskimen Island**

**Krylen Hill.** 71°33'S, 2°10'W. 5 miles SW of Valken Hill, in the northern part of the Ahlmann Ridge of Queen Maud Land. Name means "the hump" in Norwegian.

**Krylov Mountain**  *see*  **Ristelen Spur**

**Krylov Peninsula.** 69°05'S, 156°20'E. Ice-covered. Just west of Lauritzen Bay, between the Usarp Mountains and the Cook Ice Shelf, in Oates Land. Named by the USSR for mathematician Alexiy Krylov.

**Krylvika Bight.** 71°20'S, 2°W. A southern lobe of the Fimbul Ice Shelf, indenting the coast of Queen Maud Land for about 30 miles between Båkeneset Headland and Trollkjelneset Headland. Name means "the hump bay" in Norwegian.

**Kubbestolen Peak.** 71°47′S, 8°54′E. 2,070 m. Ice-free. At the NW end of Vinten-Johansen Ridge, in the Kurze Mountains of Queen Maud Land. Name means "the log chair" in Norwegian.

**Kuberry Rocks.** 75°17′S, 138°31′W. At the north end of Coulter Heights, 6 miles NW of Matikonis Peak, near the coast of Marie Byrd Land. Named for Richard W. Kuberry, geomagnetist at Byrd Station in 1969–70.

**Kubitza Glacier.** 70°24′S, 63°11′W. Flows into Clifford Glacier, just east of Mount Samsel, in Palmer Land. Named for J.T. Kubitza, chief builder in the construction detachment at Palmer Station in 1969–70.

**Kubus Mountain.** 71°59′S, 7°21′E. Also called The Cube. 2,985 m. Shaped like a cube (kubus in Norwegian). 3 miles SE of Trollslottet Mountain in the NW part of the Filchner Mountains of Queen Maud Land. Discovered by Ritscher in 1938–39.

**Kubusdaelda.** 71°59′S, 7°26′E. A steep, ice-filled ravine between Kubus Mountain and Klevekampen Mountain in the Filchner Mountains of Queen Maud Land. Name means "the cube dell" in Norwegian, and was named in association with Kubus Mountain.

**Kubusdalen.** 71°58′S, 7°14′E. An ice-filled valley between Trollslottet Mountain and Kubus Mountain in the Filchner Mountains of Queen Maud Land. Name means "the cube valley" in Norwegian, and was named in association with Kubus Mountain.

**Kuhn Nunatak.** 84°06′S, 66°34′W. One of the Rambo Nunataks, 3 miles SW of Oliver Nunatak, on the west side of the Foundation Ice Stream, in the Pensacola Mountains. Named for Michael H. Kuhn, meteorologist at Plateau Station in 1967.

**Kuiper Scarp.** 71°26′S, 68°27′W. An east-west escarpment along the south side of Uranus Glacier, on the east side of Alexander Island. Seen aerially, and photographed, by Ellsworth on Nov. 23, 1935, and later named by the UK for Gerard P. Kuiper, US astronomer who discovered the Uranus satellite, Miranda.

**Kujira Point.** 69°36′S, 38°16′E. Also spelled Kuzira Point. Forms the northern extremity of Padda Island, in Lützow-Holm Bay. Photographed by the LCE 1936–37. Named by the Japanese in the early 1960s as Kujira-misaki (whale point).

**Kukri Hills.** 77°44′S, 162°42′E. Also seen (erroneously) as Kurki Hills. Between the Taylor Valley and the Ferrar Glacier, just behind New Harbor on McMurdo Sound, in southern Victoria Land. 25 miles long and over 2,000 meters high. Discovered by Scott's 1901–4 expedition, and named for their resemblance to a Gurkha's knife.

**Kulen Mountain.** 72°39′S, 3°18′W. On the NW side of Jøkulskarvet Ridge, in the Borg Massif of Queen Maud Land.

**Kullen Knoll.** 72°04′S, 2°44′W. 2 miles north of Gösta Peaks, in the southern part of the Ahlmann Ridge of Queen Maud Land.

**Kuno Cirque.** 80°41′S, 24°55′W. In the Shackleton Range.

**Kuno Point.** 66°24′S, 67°10′W. The SW end of Watkins Island, in the Biscoe Islands. Named by the UK for Japanese physiologist Yas Kuno, whose specialty was human perspiration.

**Kuperov, Leonid.** Name also spelled Kouperov. USSR ionosphere physicist and exchange scientist at Byrd Station who got sick there, and the Americans went to great trouble and expense to fly him out on April 9, 1961. The plane that did so made the first nocturnal flight and landing in Antarctic history.

**Kuperov Peak** *see* **Kouperov Peak**

**Kupriyanov, Ivan.** Officer on the *Mirnyy*, 1819–21.

**Mount Kurchatov.** 71°39′S, 11°14′E. 2,220 m. Rises from the base of Sponskaftet Spur in the Humboldt Mountains of Queen Maud Land. Discovered aerially by Ritscher's expedition of 1938–39, and named by the USSR in 1963 for scientist I.V. Kurchatov.

**Kurki Hills** *see* **Kukri Hills**

**Mount Kurlak.** 84°05′S, 168°E. Ice-covered. 3 miles SE of Mount Bell, in the Queen Alexandra Range. Named for Lt. Cdr. William B. Kurlak, USN, aircraft commander in Antarctica in 1964.

**Kurtse Mountains** *see* **Kurze Mountains**

**Kurumi Island.** 69°01′S, 39°28′E. Between Ongulkalven Island and Ongul Island, in Lützow-Holm Bay. Photographed by the LCE 1936–37, and later named by the Japanese as Kurumi-shima (walnut island), a descriptive name.

**Kurze Mountains.** 71°53′S, 8°55′E. 20 miles long. 6 miles wide. In the Orvin Mountains of Queen Maud Land. Between the Drygalski Mountains and the Gagarin Mountains and Conrad Mountains. Discovered aerially in 1938–39 by Ritscher, and named by him for the director of the Naval Division of the German Admiralty. This name has also been seen misspelled as Kurtse Mountains. Later the Norwegians renamed them Holtedahlfjella, but the original name is recommended.

**Kurzefjella** *see* **Gagarin Mountains**

**Kusunoki Point.** 65°33′S, 65°59′W. On the NW coast of Renaud Island, in the Biscoe Islands. Named by the UK for Kou Kusunoki, sea ice specialist.

**Kutschin, Alexandr.** Name also spelled Kutchin. Russian oceanographer on the *Fram*, 1910–12, during Amundsen's expedition.

**Kutschin Peak.** 86°25′S, 159°42′W. 2,360 m. On the west slope of the Nilsen Plateau, 6 miles south of Mount Kristensen, at the east side of the Amundsen Glacier, in the Queen Maud Mountains. Named for Alexandr Kutschin.

**Kuven Hill.** 73°52′S, 5°15′W. Between Gommen Valley and Kuvsletta Flat, near the SW end of the Kirwan Escarpment, in Queen Maud Land. Name means "the hump" in Norwegian.

**Kuvsletta Flat.** 73°50′S, 5°14′W. A small, flat, ice-covered area between Utrinden Point and Framranten Point, near the SW end of the Kirwan Escarpment in Queen Maud Land. Name means "the hump plain" in Norwegian.

**Kuvungen Hill.** 73°50′S, 5°09′W. Just SE of Framranten Point, near the SW end of the Kirwan Escarpment, in Queen Maud Land.

**Kuzira Point** *see* **Kujira Point**

**Kuznetsov Canyon.** 64°S, 135°E. A submarine feature off Adélie Land.

**Kvaevefjellet Mountain.** 71°52′S, 14°27′E. 6 miles long. Surrounded by Mount Fucik, at the north end of the Payer Mountains. Discovered by Ritscher in 1938–39. Named by the Norwegians.

**Kvaevenutane Peaks.** 71°57′S, 14°18′E. A small cluster of peaks which include Mounts Kibal'chich and Brounov. 2 miles SW of Kvaevefjellet Mountain (hence the name later given by the Norwegians), in the Payer Mountains of Queen Maud Land.

**Kvalfinnen Ridge.** 72°08′S, 26°24′E. 2,670 m. On the west side of Byrdbreen, and ½ mile north of Isachsen Mountain, in the Sør Rondane Mountains. Name means "the whale fin" in Norwegian. It is a descriptive name.

**Kvamsgavlen Cliff.** 71°46′S, 11°50′E. At the SE corner of Storkvammen Cirque, on the east side of the Humboldt Mountains in Queen Maud Land. Discovered by Ritscher in 1938–39, and later named by the Norwegians.

**Kvars Bay** *see* **Kvarsnes Bay**

**Kvars Promontory** *see* **Kvarsnes Foreland**

**Kvarsnes Bay.** 67°03′S, 56°49′E. Also called Kvars Bay. A small bay at the SW side of Kvarsnes Foreland, on the south part of Edward VIII Bay. Photographed by the LCE 1936-37.

**Kvarsnes Foreland.** 67°02′S, 57°E. Also called Kvars Promontory. It juts out into the south side of Edward VIII Bay, just west of the Øygarden Group. Photographed by the LCE 1936-37.

**Kvassknatten Nunatak.** 72°27′S, 0°20′E. One of the Knattebrauta Nunataks, in the Sverdrup Mountains of Queen Maud Land. Name means "the sharp crag" in Norwegian.

**Kvasstind Peak.** 72°31′S, 3°23′W. In the NE part of Borg Mountain, in Queen Maud Land. Name means "sharp peak" in Norwegian.

**Kvea Valley.** 71°55′S, 4°30′E. Rectangular. Ice-filled. Between Grinda Ridge and Skigarden Ridge, north of Mount Grytøyr, in the Mühlig-Hofmann Mountains. Name means "the sheepcote" in Norwegian.

**Kvervelnatten Peak.** 73°31′S, 3°53′W. 2 miles SW of Svartbandufsa Bluff, in the Kirwan Escarpment of Queen Maud Land.

**Kvinge Peninsula.** 71°10′S, 61°10′W. Snow-covered. On the north side of Palmer Inlet, it ends in Cape Bryant, on the east coast of Palmer Land. Named by the USA for Thor Kvinge, Norwegian oceanographer, a member of the International Weddell Sea Oceanographic Expeditions of 1968, 1969, and 1970.

**Kvithamaren Cliff.** 71°59′S, 5°02′E. Just east of Slokstallen Mountain, in the Mühlig-Hofmann Mountains of Queen Maud Land. Name means "the white hammer" in Norwegian.

**Kvithø Peak.** 72°29′S, 1°13′E. Isolated. 7 miles SE of Kvitkjølen Ridge, in the Sverdrup Mountains of Queen Maud Land. Name means "the white hill" in Norwegian.

**Kvitholten Hill.** 71°49′S, 5°51′E. Snow-covered. At the east side of the Austreskorve Glacier, and just south of Sagbladet Ridge, in the Mühlig-Hofmann Mountains. Name means "the white grove" in Norwegian.

**Kvithovden Peak.** 72°22′S, 0°45′E. At the north end of the Kvitkjølen Ridge, in the Sverdrup Mountains of Queen Maud Land. Name means "the white peak" in Norwegian.

**Kvitkjølen Ridge.** 72°24′S, 0°49′E. Between Kvitsvodene Valley and Ising Glacier, in the Sverdrup Mountains of Queen Maud Land. Name means "the white keel" in Norwegian.

**Kvitkleven Cirque.** 72°S, 7°43′E. Ice-filled. On the south side of Klevekampen Mountain in the Filchner Mountains of Queen Maud Land. Name means "the white closet" in Norwegian.

**Kvitøya** see **White Island**

**Kvitskarvet** see **Mount Krüger**

**Kvitskarvhalsen Saddle.** 72°30′S, 0°51′E. An ice-saddle between Mount Krüger and Robin Heights, in the Sverdrup Mountains of Queen Maud Land. Name means "the white mountain neck" in Norwegian.

**Kvitsvodene Valley.** 72°26′S, 0°45′E. 5 miles long. Ice-filled. Between Kvitkjølen Ridge and Robin Heights, in the Sverdrup Mountains of Queen Maud Land. Named by the Norwegians.

**Mount Kyffin.** 83°47′S, 171°38′E. Also spelled (erroneously) as Mount Kiffin, Mount Kyftin. 1,670 m. A reddish-brown mountain at the extreme north end of the Commonwealth Range, just to the west of the Beardmore Glacier. Discovered during Shackleton's 1907-9 expedition, and named by them for Evan Kyffin-Thomas, a newspaper friend of Shackleton's.

**Mount Kyftin** see **Mount Kyffin**

**Mount Kyle.** 71°57′S, 168°35′E. 2,900 m. On the north side of Denning Glacier, in the Admiralty Mountains of Victoria Land. Named for Ricky L. Kyle, USN, utilitiesman at McMurdo Station in 1967.

**Kyle, J.T.** A crew member of the *Discovery* during the BANZARE 1929-31.

**Kyle Cone.** 77°31′S, 169°16′E. An exposed volcanic cone near Cape Crozier, just over a mile WNW of The Knoll, on Ross Island. Named by the New Zealanders for P.R. Kyle, geologist who examined it in 1969–70.

**Kyle Nunataks.** 66°47′S, 51°20′E. Three nunataks. 2½ miles east of Mount Hampson, in the northern part of the Tula Mountains of Enderby Land. Named by the Australians for J.T. Kyle.

**Kyrkjebakken Slope.** 71°54′S, 6°32′E. An ice-slope on the west side of Jøkulkyrkja Mountain, in the Mühlig-Hofmann Mountains of Queen Maud Land. Name means "the church hill" in Norwegian.

**Kyrkjedalen Valley.** 71°50′S, 6°53′E. Ice-filled. Between Jøkulkyrkja Mountain and Habermehl Peak, in the Mühlig-Hofmann Mountains. Name means "the church valley" in Norwegian.

**Kyrkjedalshalsen Saddle.** 71°47′S, 6°53′E. An ice-saddle between Gessner Peak and Habermehl Peak, in the Mühlig-Hofmann Mountains of Queen Maud Land. Name means "the church valley neck" in Norwegian.

**Kyrkjeskipet Peak.** 71°52′S, 6°48′E. 3,085 m. Just north of Kapellet Canyon, it dominates the NE part of Jøkulkyrkja Mountain, in the Mühlig-Hofmann Mountains. Name means "the church nave" in Norwegian.

**Kyrkjetorget.** 71°54′S, 6°57′E. A flat, ice-filled amphitheater on the east side of Jøkulkyrkja Mountain, in the Mühlig-Hofmann Mountains. Name means "the church marketplace" in Norwegian.

**L.A.S.** *see* **Little America**

**Mount L. Hansen** *see* **Hansen Spur**

**The *L.P. Simmons.*** US sealer from New London in the South Shetlands 1873–75, under Capt. Potts.

**L.V.T.** *see* **Amphibious Vehicles**

**Laager Point.** 62°38′S, 61°09′W. Between Point Smellie and Ocoa Point, on the western coast of Byers Peninsula, Livingston Island, South Shetlands.

**Islote Labbé** *see* **Labbé Rock**

**Islotes Labbe** *see* **Stray Islands**

**Labbé Rock.** 63°17′S, 57°56′W. Also called Islote Labbé. Almost ¾ mile NW of Largo Island in the Duroch Islands. Named by the Chilean Antarctic Expedition of 1947 for First Lt. Custodio Labbé Lippi, navigation officer on the *Angamos.*

**Labyrinth.** 77°33′S, 160°50′E. An extensive flat upland area which has been much eroded, at the west end of the Wright Valley in Victoria Land. Named by the New Zealanders in 1958–59 for the appearance of a labyrinth created by the eroded dolerite of which it is formed.

**Cape Lacaze-Duthiers** *see* **Duthiers Point**

**Mount Lacey.** 70°11′S, 64°43′E. Pyramidal. Has two sharp peaks. 1 mile west of Mount Béchervaise in the Athos Range of the Prince Charles Mountains. Sighted by an ANARE party led by J.M. Béchervaise in Nov. 1955, and named by the Australians for R.H. Lacey, surveyor at Mawson Station in 1955, who plotted it.

**Lachal Bluffs.** 67°30′S, 61°09′E. Just south of Ufs Island on the coast of Mac. Robertson Land. Photographed by the LCE 1936–37. Named by the Australians for R. Lachal, assistant cook at Mawson Station, and geological field assistant in 1965.

**Cape Lachman.** 63°47′S, 57°47′W. Marks the northern tip of James Ross Island. Discovered during Nordenskjöld's 1901–4 expedition. He named it for J. Lachman, a patron.

**Lachman Crags.** 63°52′S, 57°50′W. Escarpment running in a north-south direction for 5 miles, 3 miles SSW of Cape Lachman, on James Ross Island. Its high point is 620 m. Charted by the FIDS in 1945, and they named it in association with the cape.

**Lackey Ridge.** 84°49′S, 116°15′W. 4 miles long, running east-west, it forms the west end of Buckeye Table in the Ohio Range of the Horlick Mountains.

Named for Larry L. Lackey, geologist with the Ohio State University expedition here in 1960–61.

**Laclavère Plateau.** 63°27'S, 57°47'W. 10 miles long. Between 1 and 3 miles wide. Between Misty Pass and Theodolite Hill on Trinity Peninsula. It is just south of General Bernardo O'Higgins Station. Named by the UK in 1963 for Georges R. Laclavère, French cartographer and president of SCAR from 1958.

**La Conchée.** 66°47'S, 141°29'E. A rocky island, ¼ mile long, between Pascal Island and Monge Island, almost ¾ mile NE of Cape Mousse. Charted in 1950 by the French, and named by them for one of the forts guarding the Golfe de Saint-Malo, in France.

**¹Mount Lacroix.** 65°03'S, 63°58'W. 640 m. It has a rounded summit and red vertical cliffs. Surmounts the NE end of Booth Island, in the Wilhelm Archipelago. Charted by Charcot in 1903–5, and named by him for Alfred Lacroix (*see* **Lacroix Glacier**).

**²Mount Lacroix** *see* **Lacroix Nunatak**

**Lacroix Glacier.** 77°40'S, 162°33'E. Between Suess and Matterhorn Glaciers. It flows into the Taylor Valley in Victoria Land. Charted and named by the British Antarctic Expedition of 1910–13, led by Scott, for Alfred Lacroix, French geologist.

**Lacroix Nunatak.** 66°51'S, 141°20'E. Also called Mount Lacroix. A ridge of terminal moraine. 1 mile long. 2 miles SW of Cape Margerie. Discovered by the BANZARE from the *Discovery* in 1931, from a distance, and believed to be a 300-meter-high rock peak. Mawson named it for Alfred Lacroix (*see* **Lacroix Glacier**) as Mount Lacroix. Later redefined.

**Lacuna Island.** 65°31'S, 65°18'W. 8 miles east of Tula Point, the north end of Renaud Island, in the Biscoe Islands. Named by the UK because this island lies in a lacuna (or gap) in the vertical air photos taken by the FIDASE in 1956–57.

**The *Lady Francis*.** British sealer from London, in the South Shetlands during the 1820–21 summer.

**Lady Newnes Bay.** 73°40'S, 167°30'E. 60 miles long. Extends along the coast of Victoria Land from Cape Sibbald to Coulman Island. Discovered by Borchgrevink in 1899, and he named it for the wife of Sir George Newnes, principal backer of the expedition.

**Lady Newnes Glacier** *see* **Aviator Glacier**

**Lady Newnes Ice Shelf** *see* **Lady Newnes Bay**

**The *Lady Trowbridge*.** Liverpool sealing brig which was wrecked off Cape Melville, King George Island, South Shetlands, on Dec. 25, 1820. Captain Richard Sherratt.

**Laënnec Glacier.** 64°12'S, 62°13'W. 3 miles long. Flows into Hill Bay, on the east side of Brabant Island. Named by the UK for René T.H. Laënnec (1781–1826), French inventor of the stethoscope.

**Lafarge Rocks.** 63°13'S, 57°33'W. One large rock and several smaller ones, 2 miles NW of Casy Island, and 7 miles west of Prime Head, the northern tip of the Antarctic Peninsula. Discovered by Dumont d'Urville during his 1837–40 expedition, and named by him for Antoine de la Farge.

**Lafond, Pierre Antoine.** French Naval officer on the *Astrolabe* during Dumont d'Urville's expedition of 1837–40. Joined as an élève. Promoted to ensign, Aug. 20, 1839. Put ashore sick at Semarang on Nov. 25, 1839.

**Lafond Bay.** 63°27'S, 58°10'W. A square bay, 3 miles by 3 miles, just south of Cape Ducorps on Trinity Peninsula. Surveyed by the FIDS in 1960–61. Named by the UK for Pierre Lafond.

**LaForrest Rock.** 85°06'S, 164°32'W. 1½ miles west of the mouth of Strom Glacier, on the northern slopes of the Duncan Mountains. Named for B.A. LaForrest, storekeeper on Operation Deep Freeze 66.

**Mount Lagally.** 67°09'S, 67°06'W. 3 miles south of Vanni Peak, in the Dorsey Mountains, on Arrowsmith Peninsula, in Graham Land. Named by the UK for Max Lagally (1881–1945), German glaciologist.

**Lagarrigue Cove.** 64°39'S, 62°34'W. Also called Selvick Cove, Puerto Marinero Lagarrigue. Just SW of Orne Harbor, on the west coast of Graham Land. Originally called Puerto Lote, it was renamed in 1956 by the Argentines for the navy cook with the Argentine Antarctic Expedition of 1947–48 (*see* **Deaths, 1947–48**).

**Bukhta Lagernaya** *see* **O'Brien Bay**

**Lake Lagernoye.** 67°40'S, 45°51'E. Just south of Molodezhnaya Station, and just west of Lake Glubokoye, in the Thala Hills of Enderby Land. Named Ozero Lagernoye (camp lake) by the USSR in 1961–62.

**Laggard Island.** 64°49'S, 64°02'W. 2 miles SE of Bonaparte Point, off the SW coast of Anvers Island. Surveyed by the FIDS in 1955 and named by the UK for its position on the eastern fringe of the islands in the area of Arthur Harbor.

**Låghamaren Cliff.** 72°30'S, 0°30'E. Forms the NW end of Hamrane Heights, in the Sverdrup Mountains of Queen Maud Land. Name means "the low crag" in Norwegian.

**Lågkollane Hills.** 72°08'S, 22°28'E. 7 miles north of Bamse Mountain, between Kreitzerisen and Hansenbreen in the Sør Rondane Mountains. Name means "the low hills" in Norwegian.

**Lagoon Island.** 67°35'S, 68°16'W. Almost ¾ mile NW of Anchorage Island, in the Léonie Islands. In the entrance to Ryder Bay, on the SE side of Adelaide Island. Discovered by Charcot in 1908–10. Named descriptively by the BGLE in Feb. 1936.

**Mount La Gorce** *see* **La Gorce Peak**

**La Gorce Mountain** *see* **La Gorce Peak**

**La Gorce Mountains.** 86°45'S, 146°W. 20 miles in extent. Between the Robison

and Klein Glaciers at the east side of the upper reaches of the Robert Scott Glacier, in the Queen Maud Mountains. Discovered in Dec. 1934 by Quin Blackburn's party during Byrd's 1933–35 expedition. Named by Byrd for John Oliver La Gorce (1879–1959), vice president of the National Geographic Society.

**La Gorce Peak.** 77°37'S, 153°22'W. 8 miles SW of Mount Josephine. It is at the south end of the Alexandra Mountains in Marie Byrd Land, and marks the highest point in those mountains. Discovered in Feb. 1929 during Byrd's 1928–30 expedition, and named by Byrd for John O. La Gorce (*see* **La Gorce Mountains**).

**Lagotellerie Island.** 67°53'S, 67°24'W. 1 mile long. 2 miles west of Horseshoe Island off the west coast of Graham Land. Discovered and named by Charcot in 1908–10. It is SPA #19. It is the home of the only two flowering plants in Antarctica (*see* **Flora**). There is an Adélie Penguin colony, and a Blue-eyed Cormorant colony, here.

**Cabo Lagrange** *see* **Strath Point**

**Cape Lagrange** *see* **Lagrange Peak**

**Mount Lagrange** *see* **Mount Skidmore**

**La Grange, Johannes.** South Africa's most famous Antarctic explorer, J.J. La Grange was a member of the South African Weather Bureau, invited by Fuchs to go on the BCTAE. He arrived in Antarctica on Jan. 28, 1956, and was a member of the Advance Party for the Transantarctic crossing. He then joined Fuchs on the main trek across the continent. He was back in 1959–61 as leader/meteorologist of SANAE I.

**Lagrange Island.** 66°46'S, 141°28'E. Almost ½ mile NE of Newton Island, and 1½ miles north of Cape Mousse. Charted in 1951 by the French, and named by them for Joseph Lagrange (1736–1813), French geometrist.

**La Grange Nunataks.** 80°18'S, 27°50'W. Also called Beney Nunataks. A scattered group extending west for 22 miles from the mouth of Gordon Glacier, on the north side of the Shackleton Range. Named by the UK for Johannes La Grange.

**Lagrange Peak.** 64°28′S, 62°26′W. 450 m. 5½ miles NE of Strath Point on the SE coast of Brabant Island. In 1897–99 de Gerlache charted a point just to the south of this peak, and named it Cape Lagrange for Joseph Lagrange (*see* **Lagrange Island**). On one of the photos taken by the expedition, the name is applied to the southern tip of the island. To avoid confusion, the name has been removed altogether from these areas, and given to the peak.

**Cape Lagrelius**  *see*  **Lagrelius Point**

**Lagrelius Point.** 63°55′S, 58°17′W. Ice-free. On the NW side of James Ross Island, 1½ miles south of Carlson Island. Discovered and surveyed in 1903 by Nordenskjöld, who named it Cape Lagrelius for Axel Lagrelius of Stockholm, a contributor to the expedition. Resurveyed by the FIDS in 1952 and slightly redefined.

**Lågtangen**  *see*  **Low Tongue**

**Laguna Hill.** 62°56′S, 60°42′W. Also called Cross Hill. 160 m. Ice-free. Rises above the lagoon on the SW side of Telefon Bay in Deception Island. Named descriptively as Monte de la Laguna by the Argentines in 1956.

**Mount Lahaye.** 72°36′S, 31°10′E. 2,475 m. On the north side of Giaever Glacier in the Belgica Mountains. Discovered by the Belgian Antarctic Expedition of 1957–58, under Gaston de Gerlache, who named it for Prof. Edmond Lahaye, president of the Belgian National Committee for the IGY.

**Pointe Lahille**  *see*  **Lahille Island**

**Lahille Island.** 65°33′S, 64°23′W. 3 miles long. 2 miles west of Nuñez Point, off the west coast of Graham Land. Discovered by Charcot in 1903–5, and charted by him as a point, Pointe Lahille, named by Charcot for Fernando Lahille, the Argentine naturalist. On his next expedition, in 1908–10, Charcot redefined it.

**Roca Laine**  *see*  **Lone Rock**

**Laine Hills.** 70°46′S, 64°28′W. A cluster of 4 mainly snow-covered hills on the Dyer Plateau, about 16 miles NW of the Welch Mountains, in Palmer Land. Named for Daren Laine, biologist at Palmer Station, 1965.

**Cape Lainez**  *see*  **Lainez Point**

**Lainez Point.** 67°41′S, 67°48′W. Also called Cape Lainez. Forms the north side of the entrance to Dalgliesh Bay, on the west side of Pourquoi Pas Island, off the west coast of Graham Land. Discovered by Charcot, 1908–10, and named by him for Manuel Lainez, founder of the Argentine newspaper, *El Diario*.

**Lair Point.** 62°37′S, 61°02′W. 5 miles SE of Essex Point on the north side of Byers Peninsula, Livingston Island, South Shetlands. Named by the UK in 1961 for the sealers' lair here, a large cave found by the FIDS in 1957–58, almost 140 years after it was last used.

**Cape Laird.** 81°41′S, 162°27′E. 8 miles NW of Cape May, on the west side of the Ross Ice Shelf. Named by the New Zealanders in 1960–61 for Malcolm G. Laird, NZ geologist here that year.

**Laird Glacier.** 84°55′S, 169°55′E. 3 miles long. Flows from the Supporters Range into Keltie Glacier, 4 miles SE of Ranfurly Point. Named for Robert J. Laird, biologist at McMurdo Station, 1963.

**Laird Plateau.** 82°S, 157°E. Over 2,400 m. 1 mile NW of Mount Hayter on the north side of the head of Lucy Glacier. Discovered by the NZGSAE 1964–65 and named for the leader of the expedition, Malcolm G. Laird (*see also* **Cape Laird**).

**Laizure Glacier.** 69°15′S, 158°07′E. Flows into the sea just west of Drakes Head. Named for Lt. (jg) David H. Laizure, USN, navigator on Hercules aircraft during Operation Deep Freeze 68.

**Lajarte Islands.** 64°14′S, 63°24′W. Also called Dufaure de Lajarte Islands. Around the north coast of Anvers Island, just west of Cape Grönland. Discovered by Dallmann in 1873–74. Charted by Charcot in 1903–5, and named by him for Capt. Dufaure de Lajarte of the French Navy.

**Lake Island.** 68°33′S, 77°59′E. Between Plog Island and Flutter Island, in Prydz Bay, just west of Breidnes Peninsula in the Vestfold Hills. Photographed by the LCE 1936–37. Named later by the Australians, because a lake occupies the northern part of the island.

**Lakes.** There are several unfrozen lakes in Antarctica. A lot of the lakes are deep, the deepest being Radok Lake. They are warmer at the bottom than at the top. There are also several highly saline lakes (*see* **Lake Vanda,** for example), the salt being present probably because of chemical weathering of bedrock and soil. Since 1977, George Simmons has pioneered investigative methods of these lakes.

**Lakeside Hotel.** The summer home for the replacement teams and for the rotating crew teams of the *Shirase* at Showa Station.

**Laktionov Island.** 65°46′S, 65°46′W. Also called Isla Hyatt. 2 miles long. 2 miles NE of Jurva Point, Renaud Island, in the Biscoe Islands. Named by the UK in 1959 for A.F. Laktionov, USSR sea ice specialist.

**Lallemand Bay** *see* **Lallemand Fjord**

**Lallemand Fjord.** 67°05′S, 66°45′W. Also called Lallemand Bay. It is, in fact, a bay, 30 miles long in a north-south direction. 9 miles wide. Between Holdfast Point and Roux Island, or between Arrowsmith Peninsula and the west coast of Graham Land. Discovered by Charcot in 1908–10, and named by him for Charles Lallemand, French scientist.

**Mount Lama.** 78°04′S, 163°42′E. Ice-free. Over 800 m. At the end of the ridge north of Miers Glacier, it forms the south rampart of Shangri-la. Named in association with that valley by the New Zealanders in 1960–61.

**Islotes Lamadrid** *see* **Psi Islands**

**Lamarck Island.** 66°40′S, 140°02′E. 175 yards long. 175 yards NE of Rostand

Island, in the Géologie Archipelago. Charted in 1951 by the French, and named by them for Jean-Baptiste Lamarck (1744–1829), the French naturalist.

**Cape Lamb.** 63°54′S, 57°37′W. Forms the SW tip of Vega Island. Discovered during Nordenskjöld's 1901–4 expedition. Rediscovered by the FIDS in 1945. They named it for I.M. Lamb.

**Lamb, I.M.** FIDS botanist on Operation Tabarin at Port Lockroy in 1944. In 1945 he was at Base D, at Hope Bay.

**Lamb Peak.** 79°34′S, 84°57′W. Ice-free. 2 miles SSE of Maagoe Peak in the Gifford Peaks of the Heritage Range. Named for Lt. Cdr. Arthur D. Lamb, operations and communications officer on Operation Deep Freeze 64, 65, and 66.

**Lamb Point.** 73°41′S, 60°48′W. Ice-covered. Forms the south side of the entrance to Howkins Inlet, on the east coast of Palmer Land. Discovered aerially in Dec. 1940, by the USAS 1939–41. Named by the FIDS in 1947 for H.H. Lamb, British meteorologist on the *Balaena,* 1946–47. Using FIDS weather reports he prepared daily forecasts for the whaling fleet.

**Lambda Island.** 64°18′S, 63°W. Also called Isla Primero de Mayo. 1½ miles long. Just NW of Delta Island in the Melchior Islands. Charted by Charcot in 1903–5, and called Île Sourrieu. Renamed by the Discovery Committee in 1927 for the Greek letter.

**Lambert Glacier.** 71°S, 70°E. The longest glacier in the world, it is up to 250 miles long, including its upper section, the Mellor Glacier (q.v.). It is up to 40 miles wide. With the Fisher Glacier limb it forms a continuous ice passage of about 320 miles, which feeds the Amery Ice Shelf from a large area to the east and south of the Prince Charles Mountains. Photographed during Operation Highjump by personnel on the aircraft known as *Baker 3.* In 1952, US cartographer John H. Roscoe, using these photos, delineated what he called Baker Three Glacier. In 1956 the ANARE remapped the area, and renamed the glacier in 1957 for Bruce P. Lambert, director of National Mapping, in the Australian Department of National Development.

**Lambert Nunatak.** 75°25'S, 137°54' W. In the SE part of the Coulter Heights, near the coast of Marie Byrd Land. Named for Paul A. Lambert, USN, senior quartermaster on the *Glacier,* 1961–62.

**Lamberts Peak.** 72°44'S, 74°51'E. 3 miles NNE of the Mason Peaks in the Grove Mountains. Named by the Australians for G. Lamberts, one of the major Australian Antarctic cartographers.

**Lamboley Peak.** 75°04'S, 64°19'W. In the NW part of the Prehn Peninsula, near the base of the Antarctic Peninsula. Named for Paul E. Lamboley, radioman at Amundsen-Scott South Pole Station, 1964.

**Lambrecht, John.** Midshipman on the *Adventure* during Cook's second voyage.

**Lamina Peak.** 70°32'S, 68°45'W. 1,280 m. Pyramidal. Between Mount Edred and the George VI Sound, on the east coast of Alexander Island, 4½ miles inland from the coast of that island, at the southern end of the Douglas Range. Surveyed by the BGLE in 1936, and again in 1949 by the FIDS, who named it for the marked horizontal stratification of the rocks here.

**Lammers Glacier.** 68°37'S, 66°10'W. Flows along the north side of Godfrey Upland into the Traffic Circle and Mercator Ice Piedmont, on the east coast of Graham Land. Named by Finn Ronne in 1947–48 for Lester Lammers, contributor of 13 huskies to the RARE.

**La Molaire.** 66°40'S, 140°01'E. 24 m. A rocky hill on the west side of Rostand Island in the Géologie Archipelago. Charted and named in 1951 by the French, for its shape (like a molar).

**Lamotte, H. de G.** Captain of the *William Scoresby,* 1927–29.

**Mount Lampert.** 74°33'S, 62°39'W. 6 miles west of Kelsey Cliff in the SE part of

the Guettard Range in Palmer Land. Named for Irwin R. Lampert, storekeeper at Amundsen-Scott South Pole Station, 1964.

**Lamping Peak.** 84°14'S, 164°49'E. Between Prebble and Wyckoff Glaciers, on the western slopes of the Queen Alexandra Range. Named for John T. Lamping, geomagnetist at the South Pole Station, 1961.

**Lampitt Nunatak.** 66°57'S, 65°47'W. Near the head of Murphy Glacier, in Graham Land. Named by the UK in 1958 for Leslie H. Lampitt (1887–1957), British chemist and expert on polar rations.

**Lamplugh, Elmer C.** Communications man at East Base during the USAS 1939–41.

**Lamplugh Bay** *see* **Lamplugh Inlet**

**Lamplugh Inlet.** 71°23'S, 61°10'W. Also called Lamplugh Bay. An inlet, 7 miles long, between Capes Healy and Howard, on the east coast of Palmer Land. Discovered aerially by members of East Base in 1940, during the USAS. Named for Elmer C. Lamplugh.

**Lamplugh Island.** 75°38'S, 162°45'E. Ice-capped. 10 miles long. 4 miles north of Whitmer Peninsula, on the coast of Victoria Land. Discovered during Scott's first expedition, 1901–4, and first charted as an island during Shackleton's 1907–9 expedition. Named by Shackleton for G.W. Lamplugh, a patron.

**Lamykin Dome.** 67°27'S, 46°40'E. 525 m. Forms the ice-covered summit of Tange Promontory, on the coast of Enderby Land. Named by the USSR for hydrographer S.M. Lamykin.

**Lana Point** *see* **Café Point**

**Cape Lancaster.** 64°51'S, 63°44'W. Also called Cape Albert Lancaster. Forms the southern extremity of Anvers Island in the Palmer Archipelago. Discovered by Dallmann in 1873–74, and later rediscovered by de Gerlache, who named it for Albert Lancaster, scientific director of the Meteorological Service of the Royal

Observatory of Belgium, and a supporter of the expedition.

**Lancaster Hill.** 65°21'S, 64°W. At the south side of the mouth of Trooz Glacier, on the west coast of Graham Land. Charted by Charcot in 1908–10. Named by the UK in 1959 for Sir James Lancaster, English navigator who in 1601 was the first captain to use fruit juice as a cure for scurvy.

**Lance Rocks.** 82°52'S, 48°19'W. Two rocks at the NE end of Crouse Spur in the Forrestal Range of the Pensacola Mountains. Named for Capt. Samuel J. Lance, USAF, navigator on the US Air Force Electronics Test Unit, 1957.

**Lanchester Bay.** 63°55'S, 60°06'W. 7 miles wide. East of Havilland Point. On the west coast of Graham Land. Named by the UK in 1960 for Frederick W. Lanchester (1868–1946), aeronautics pioneer.

**The** *Lancing.* Norwegian whaler in the South Orkneys, South Shetlands, the waters of the Palmer Archipelago, and South Georgia (54°S), 1925–26. It was built in 1898 as the *Flackwell,* and it was converted to a whaler in 1923, when its name changed. That year, Capt. H.G. Melsom installed the first hauling-up slipway on this ship, which saw the beginning of pelagic whaling in Antarctic waters. It was back in the South Shetlands, 1926–27.

**Land Bay.** 75°25'S, 141°45'W. Also called Emory Land Bay. Ice-filled. 40 miles wide. Indents the coast of Marie Byrd Land just east of Groves Island. Discovered by the USAS 1939–41. Named in association with Land Glacier, which feeds this bay.

**Land-bridges.** Bridges of land connecting one land mass to another.

**Land Glacier.** 75°40'S, 141°45'W. Heavily crevassed. 35 miles long. Flows into Land Bay in Marie Byrd Land. Discovered by the USAS 1939–41, and named for Rear Adm. Emory S. Land, chairman of the US Maritime Commission.

**Land ice.** Ice formed on land, even when it is found floating on the sea.

**Landauer Point.** 67°04'S, 67°48'W. On the east coast of Adelaide Island. Marks the western side of the northern entrance to Tickle Channel in Graham Land. Named by the UK for Joseph K. Landauer, US physicist specializing in ice and glacial flow.

**Mount Landen** *see* **Landen Ridge**

**Landen Ridge.** 66°50'S, 63°54'W. Also called Mount Landen. At the east end of Cole Peninsula in Graham Land. Charted by the FIDS in Dec. 1947. Named that season by Finn Ronne of the RARE, for David Landen, of the US Geological Survey, who helped Ronne with his photographic program.

**Landers Peak.** 69°26'S, 71°16'W. In the north part of Alexander Island.

**Landfall Peak.** 72°01'S, 102°08'W. Near the extreme west end of Thurston Island, 8 miles ENE of Cape Flying Fish. Discovered during flights from the *Bear* in Feb. 1940, during the USAS, and photographed at that time by Earl B. Perce. Named because it is a landmark for ships.

**The Landing.** 78°22'S, 161°25'E. A large, flat snowfield in the upper part of the Skelton Glacier, between Upper Staircase and Lower Staircase. Named in Feb. 1957 by the NZ party of the BCTAE.

**Landing Cove.** 60°44'S, 45°41'W. North of Conroy Point, on the NW side of Moe Island in the South Orkneys. Named by the UK because it is the only place on the island where boats can land.

**Landings.** Probably the first landing south of 60°S was by William Smith in the *Williams* on Oct. 14, 1819, when he landed on King George Island in the South Shetlands. On Jan. 23, 1820, the crew of the *Hersilia* landed in Hersilia Cove, also in the South Shetlands, but they found there an Argentine ship which had undoubtedly already landed men. This ship was either the *San Juan Nepomuceno* or the *Espírito Santo,* and perhaps both these ships had landed crews. On Feb. 4, 1820, Bransfield, in the *Williams* landed on Clarence Island, in the South Shetlands. On Feb. 7, 1821, a Wednesday, at 10 a.m., John Davis is reputed to have made the first landing on the Antarctic Peninsula, at Cape Sterneck, Hughes Bay, although Davis himself did not go ashore. It is also possible that he was pre-empted by Capt. McFarlane (q.v.). On Dec. 12, 1821, Michael McLeod landed in the South Orkneys. On Feb. 21, 1832, Biscoe landed on Anvers Island, considerably further south, and on Jan. 20, 1840, Du Bouzet led a party onto an islet off the coast of Adélie Land during Dumont d'Urville's voyage. On Jan. 27, 1841, a party from Ross' expedition landed on Franklin Island, and on Jan. 24, 1895, came the first undisputed landing on the continental mass of Antarctica. Leonard Kristensen led a boat party ashore from the *Antarctic,* at Cape Adare. First to jump from the boat was Kristensen, or was it Borchgrevink, or was it von Tunzelman? Peter I Island was not landed on until Feb. 2, 1929, when a crew from the *Norvegia* did so. The first woman to set foot on the continent was Caroline Mikkelsen on Feb. 20, 1935.

**Landmark Peak.** 79°10′S, 85°40′W. 1,840 m. 5 miles south of Minnesota Glacier, on the east side of Gowan Glacier, in the Heritage Range. Named by the University of Minnesota Geological Party here in 1963–64, for its prominence as a landmark to flyers in the area.

**Landmark Point.** 67°31′S, 63°56′E. ½ mile SE of Safety Island, on the coast of Mac. Robertson Land. Named by the Australians because it is almost due south from Auster Rookery and provides a good landmark when approaching the rookery along the coast from Mawson Station.

**Mount Landolt.** 78°46′S, 84°30′W. 2,280 m. At the head of Hudman Glacier, in the southern part of the Sentinel Range. Named for Arlo U. Landolt (*see* **Amundsen-Scott South Pole Station**).

**Landon Promontory.** 69°13′S, 69°20′ E. Ice-covered. Domed. On the west side of the Amery Ice Shelf, 5 miles south of Foley Promontory. First visited by an ANARE party led by D.R. Carstens in Nov. 1962. Named by the Australians for I. Landon-Smith, glaciologist at Mawson Station in 1962, and a member of Carstens' party.

**Landrum Island.** 69°14′S, 68°20′W. On the west side of Palmer Land.

**Landry Bluff.** 85°16′S, 175°37′W. In the Cumulus Hills, just north of the mouth of Logie Glacier, where that glacier joins Shackleton Glacier. Named for Edward J. Landry, meteorologist at Byrd Station in 1963, and at Amundsen-Scott South Pole Station in 1965.

**Landry Peak** *see* **Billey Bluff**

**Lands.** If there were no ice in Antarctica, the lands (i.e., Wilkes Land, Ellsworth Land, etc.) would be beneath the sea. The coasts (q.v.) are also called lands, and the two terms have been somewhat interchangeable over the years. The major lands (aside from those listed above) are Queen Maud Land, Marie Byrd Land, Palmer Land, Graham Land, Victoria Land, Enderby Land, and Mac. Roberston Land.

**Lands End.** The western end of Cape Denison.

**Land's End.** ½ mile east of Cape Evans.

**Lands End Nunataks.** 83°43′S, 172°37′ E. Two rock nunataks 2 miles NNW of Airdrop Peak at the northern end of Ebony Ridge, at the east side of the terminus of Beardmore Glacier. They mark the northern end of the Commonwealth Range at the Ross Ice Shelf. Named descriptively by John Gunner of the Ohio State University Institute of Polar Studies. He and Henry H. Brecher measured a geological section here on Jan. 16, 1970.

**Lang Island.** 66°59′S, 57°41′E. 1 mile long. Almost ½ mile wide. Between Abrupt Island and the Øygarden Group. Photographed by the LCE 1936–37. Named Langøy (long island) by the Norwegians.

**Lang Nunatak.** 74°10′S, 66°29′W. Isolated. In the interior of southern Palmer Land. 30 miles west of the head of Irvine Glacier. Named for James F. Lang, USARP assistant representative at Byrd Station, 1965–66.

**Lang Sound.** 67°09′S, 58°40′E. 1½ miles wide at its narrowest, and 9 miles long. Between Law Promontory and the group of islands which include Broka and Havstein Islands. Photographed in Jan.–Feb. 1937 by the LCE 1936–37, and named Langsundet (the long sound) by the Norwegians.

**Lange, Alexander.** 1860–1922. Norwegian pioneer of modern steam whaling. He was manager of the *Admiralen* in the South Shetlands, 1905–6.

**Lange Glacier.** 62°07′S, 58°30′W. Flows into the western side of Admiralty Bay, just south of Admiralen Peak, King George Island, South Shetlands. Charted by Charcot in 1908–10. Named by the UK in 1960 for Alexander Lange.

**Lange Peak.** 71°34′S, 167°42′E. 2,435 m. In the west-central part of the Lyttelton Range in the Admiralty Mountains. Named for Otto L. Lange, biologist at Hallett Station, 1966–67.

**Langevad Glacier.** 73°08′S, 168°50′E. 2 miles south of Bargh Glacier, and just west of Narrow Neck. Flows from the Daniell Peninsula into the lower part of Borchgrevink Glacier, in Victoria Land. Named for Michael W. Langevad, electronics technician at Hallett Station, 1957.

**Langevatnet** *see* **Ellis Fjord**

**Langflog Glacier.** 72°06′S, 4°14′E. Flows between Mount Hochlin and Langfloget Cliff in the Mühlig-Hofmann Mountains of Queen Maud Land. Named Langflogbreen (the long rock wall glacier) by the Norwegians.

**Langfloget Cliff.** 72°06′S, 4°24′E. 6 miles long. At the west side of Flogeken Glacier, in the Mühlig-Hofmann Mountains of Queen Maud Land. Name means "the long rock wall" in Norwegian.

**Langford Peak.** 85°33′S, 135°23′W. Isolated. 2 miles west of the lower part of Reedy Glacier. 5 miles NW of Abbey Nunatak. Named for Lawrence G. Langford, Jr., builder at Byrd Station, 1958.

**Langhofer Island.** 72°32′S, 93°02′W. Ice-covered. At the north edge of the Abbott Ice Shelf. ½ mile east of McNamara Island. Named for Joel H. Langhofer, US Geological Survey topographic engineer on the *Glacier* which lay just off this island on Feb. 11, 1961, making botanical and geological collections here.

**Langhovde Glacier.** 69°13′S, 39°48′E. At the east side of the Langhovde Hills. Flows north to Hovde Bay on the east shore of Lützow-Holm Bay. Named in association with the nearby hills, by the Japanese.

**Langhovde Hills.** 69°14′S, 39°44′E. An extensive area of bare rock hills on the east shore of Lützow-Holm Bay, just south of Hovde Bay. Photographed by the LCE 1936–37. Name means "the long knoll" in Norwegian.

**Langhovde-kita Point.** 69°10′S, 39°37′E. Marks the northern end of the Langhovde Hills, on the east shore of Lützow-Holm Bay. Photographed by the LCE 1936–37. Named Langhovde-kita-misaki (Langhovde north point) by the Japanese for its location in the Langhovde Hills.

**Langley Peak.** 64°02′S, 60°36′W. 3 miles east of Curtiss Bay, on the west end of the Wright Ice Piedmont in Graham Land. Named by the UK for Samuel P. Langley (1834–1906), US aeronautics pioneer.

**Langmuir Cove.** 66°58′S, 67°10′W. At the north end of Arrowsmith Peninsula in Graham Land. Named by the UK for Irving Langmuir (1881–1957), US physicist specializing in the formation of snow.

**Langnabbane** *see* **Wilkinson Peaks**

**Langnes Channel** *see* **Langnes Fjord**

**Langnes Fjord.** 68°30′S, 78°15′E. Also called Langnes Channel, Langnes Inlet,

Long Fjord. 10 miles long. Narrow. Between Langnes Peninsula and Breidnes Peninsula in the Vestfold Hills. Photographed by the LCE 1936–37. Named by the Norwegians in association with the peninsula. In 1952, US cartographer John H. Roscoe, working off photos taken during Operation Highjump, 1946–47, found that the fjord extended further east than was previously thought, and that it included what the Norwegians had mapped separately as an isolated lake, which they had called Breidvatnet.

**Langnes Inlet**   see   **Langnes Fjord**

**Langnes Peninsula.** 68° 28′ S, 78° 15′ E. Also called Long Peninsula. 9 miles long. It is the most northerly of three main peninsulas which comprise the Vestfold Hills. Photographed by the LCE 1936–37 and named by them as Langneset (the long point).

**Langneset**   see   **Langnes Peninsula**

**Langnuten**   see   **Mount Breckinridge**

**Langpollen Cove.** 69° 26′ S, 39° 35′ E. In the NW part of Skarvsnes Foreland, on the east side of Lützow-Holm Bay. Photographed by the LCE 1936–37, and named Langpollen (the long bay) by the Norwegians.

**Langskavlen Glacier.** 72° 01′ S, 14° 29′ E. Flows from the north side of Skavlhø Mountain in the Payer Mountains of Queen Maud Land. Name means "the long snowdrift" in Norwegian.

**Längstans Udde**   see   **Cape Longing**

**Langsundet**   see   **Lang Sound**

**Mount Langway.** 75° 29′ S, 139° 47′ W. Also called Langway Mountain. 760 m. 2½ miles SW of Mount LeMasurier in the Ickes Mountains on the coast of Marie Byrd Land. Named for Chester C. Langway, glaciologist at Byrd Station, 1968–69.

**Langway Mountain**   see   **Mount Langway**

**Cape Lankester.** 79° 16′ S, 160° 29′ E. Snow-covered. At the south side of the entrance to Mulock Inlet, on the west edge of the Ross Ice Shelf. Discovered during Scott's 1901–4 expedition, and named by them probably for Sir Edwin Ray Lankester, director of the Natural History Department of the British Museum from 1898–1907, and founder of the Marine Biological Association in 1884.

**Lann Glacier.** 71° 15′ S, 167° 54′ E. 3 miles long. In the north end of the Admiralty Mountains. 4 miles east of Rowles Glacier, it flows into Dennistoun Glacier. Named for Roy R. Lann, USN, cook at Hallett Station, 1964.

**Mount Lanning.** 77° 47′ S, 85° 45′ W. 1,820 m. At the south side of Newcomer Glacier. 5 miles SE of Mount Warren, in the northern part of the Sentinel Range. Named for 1st Lt. Delmar L. Lanning, USAF, one of the builders of South Pole Station in the summer of 1956–57.

**Lanterman Range.** 71° 40′ S, 163° 10′ E. 35 miles long. 12 miles wide. Forms the SW part of the Bowers Mountains. It is bounded by the Rennick, Sledgers, Black, and Canham Glaciers. Named for Cdr. William Lanterman, aerological officer for Operation Deep Freeze, 1959–62.

**Lantern Fish.** Two types of these deep sea fishes are found in Antarctic waters (*see also* **Fish**).

**Mount Lanyon.** 71° 15′ S, 67° 10′ E. 11 miles south of Taylor Platform in the Prince Charles Mountains. Named by the Australians for J.H. Lanyon, officer-in-charge at Wilkes Station, 1965.

**Lanyon Peak.** 77° 15′ S, 161° 41′ E. 2½ miles east of Victoria Upper Glacier in the Saint Johns Range of Victoria Land. Named for Margaret C. Lanyon, USARP secretary in Christchurch, NZ, for many years in the 1960s and 1970s.

**Lanz, Walter J.** Radio operator from Brooklyn. He was on Ellsworth's first three Antarctic expeditions in the 1930s.

**Lanz Peak.** 77° 17′ S, 86° 17′ W. 1,570 m. Near the extreme north end of the Sentinel Range. 10 miles NNW of Mount

Weems. It is the middle one of three peaks lying in a NE-SW direction. Discovered aerially by Ellsworth on Nov. 23, 1935. Named for Walter J. Lanz.

**Lapeyrère Bay.** 64°23'S, 63°15'W. 7 miles long and 2 miles wide. North of Gourdon Peninsula. It indents the NE coast of Anvers Island. Charted by Dallmann, 1873–74, and again by Charcot in 1903–5. Charcot named it for Rear Adm. Boué de Lapeyrère of the French Navy.

**Laplace Island.** 66°47'S, 141°28'E. Almost ⅓ mile WNW of La Conchée, and ¾ mile north of Cape Mousse. Charted by the French in 1951 and named by them for Pierre de Laplace (1749–1827), French astronomer.

**La Plata Channel** *see* **Plata Passage**

**La Plaza Point** *see* **Plaza Point**

**LaPrade Valley.** 85°11'S, 174°36'W. In the Cumulus Hills. It has steep rock walls and an ice-covered floor. 3 miles long. Extends north to McGregor Glacier, just west of Rougier Hill. Named by the Texas Tech Shackleton Glacier Expedition of 1964–65 for Kerby E. LaPrade, a member of the college and of the expedition.

**Monte Laprida** *see* **Mount Banck**

**Laputa Nunataks.** 66°08'S, 62°58'W. 6 miles NW of Adie Inlet on the east side of Graham Land. Charted by the FIDS in 1947. Named by the UK for the flying island in *Gulliver's Travels*, and in association with nearby Gulliver Nunatak.

**Lapworth Cirque.** 80°44'S, 23°08'W. In the Shackleton Range.

**Isla Larga** *see* **Long Island**

**Punta Larga** *see* **Aguda Point**

**Large Razorback Island** *see* **Big Razorback Island**

**Largo Island.** 63°18'S, 57°53'W. 1 mile long. The largest of the Duroch Islands. 1 mile west of Halpern Point, Trinity Peninsula. Named by the Chileans before 1961.

**Larkman, A.H.** Chief engineer on the *Aurora*, 1914–16.

**Larkman Nunatak.** 85°46'S, 179°23'E. 2,660 m. Isolated. At the SE end of the Grosvenor Mountains. 12 miles east of Mauger Nunatak. Named by the New Zealanders in 1961–62 for A.H. Larkman.

**Larouy Island** *see* **Larrouy Island**

**Estrecho Larrea** *see* **Boyd Strait**

**Larrouy Island.** 65°52'S, 65°15'W. Also spelled (erroneously) as Larouy Island. 5 miles long. 2 miles wide. Rises to a height of 745 meters. In Grandidier Channel, 4 miles north of Ferin Head. Discovered by Charcot in 1903–5. He named it for a French minister plenipotentiary by that name.

**Larry Gould Bay** *see* **Gould Bay**

**Lars Andersen Island** *see* **Andersen Island**

**Lars Christensen Coast.** 69°S, 69°E. Between Murray Monolith (66°54'E) and the head of Amery Ice Shelf (71°E), on the coast of East Antarctica. Named in 1931 for Lars Christensen by his whalers who sailed along this coast.

**Lars Christensen Land** *see* **Lars Christensen Coast**

**Lars Christensen Peak.** 68°46'S, 90°31'W. Also called Christensen Peak. 1,755 m. A rounded dome. In the NE part of Peter I Island. It is the highest point on the island. Named by Eyvind Tofte in Jan. 1927, for his boss Lars Christensen.

**Lars Nunatak.** 71°52'S, 4°13'E. Also called Larsgaddane. Isolated. 5 miles west of Skigarden Ridge in the Mühlig-Hofmann Mountains of Queen Maud Land. Named by the Norwegians for Lars Hochlin (*see* **Mount Hochlin**).

**Larsemann Hills.** 69°24'S, 76°13'E. Also called Larsen Mountains. On the SE shore of Prydz Bay. They extend for 9 miles west from Dålk Glacier. Discovered in Feb. 1935 by Klarius Mikkelsen on the *Thorshavn*, and named by him.

**Cape Larsen.** Toward the north of Seymour Island.

**Mount Larsen.** 74°51'S, 162°12'E. 1,560 m. Has sheer granite cliffs on the north side. 3 miles SW of Hansen Nunatak, at the south side of the mouth of Reeves Glacier, in Victoria Land. Discovered by Scott during his 1901–4 expedition, and named by him for Carl Anton Larsen.

**Larsen, Carl Anton.** b. 1860, Norway. Norwegian whaling captain, the founder of modern factory ship whaling. A captain at 20, he had his first whaling command in 1885. In 1892–93 he was captain of the *Jason,* and explored the Erebus and Terror Gulf, and discovered 50 mysterious clay beads on Seymour Island (*see* **Mysteries**), as well as some of the first fossils (q.v.) in the Antarctic. He was back again in the same vessel in 1893–94, and discovered the Foyn Coast, Oscar II Coast, Mount Jason, and Robertson Island, as well as the Larsen Ice Shelf. In 1901–4 he was back in the Antarctic as skipper of the *Antarctic,* during Nordenskjöld's expedition. In 1904–5 he established the first whaling station on South Georgia (54°S). In 1923 he founded the first factory whaling system when he took the *Sir James Clark Ross* down to Antarctica for the 1923–24 season. As he was taking that ship down again on a 1924–25 cruise he died at the edge of the pack-ice on Dec. 8, 1924, and was replaced by Oscar Nilsen. C.A. Larsen was embalmed in Norway.

**Larsen, Lars.** Veteran polar explorer who was David Lewis' second-in-command during the *Solo* expedition in 1977–78.

**Larsen, Nils.** Norwegian captain. He skippered the *Norvegia* in 1928–29 and 1929–31, and the *Bråtegg* in 1947–48.

**Larsen Automatic Weather Station.** 66°59'S, 60°32'W. On the Larsen Ice Shelf, at an elevation of approximately 65 feet. It started operating on Jan. 1, 1986.

**Larsen Bank.** 66°16'S, 110°32'E. A shoal no shallower than 52 feet. In the north part of Newcomb Bay. ½ mile north of Kilby Island in the Windmill Islands. Discovered and charted in Feb. 1957 by a party from the *Glacier.* Named

by the Australians for Ludvig Larsen, second mate on the *Thala Dan,* the ship used by ANARE in a 1962 survey of Newcomb Bay.

**Larsen Bay** *see* **Larsen Inlet**

**Larsen Channel.** 63°10'S, 56°12'W. A strait between 1 and 3 miles wide. Separates D'Urville and Joinville Islands, to the NE of the tip of the Antarctic Peninsula. Discovered during Nordenskjöld's expedition, in 1902, and named by them for Carl Anton Larsen.

**Larsen Cliffs.** 71°56'S, 6°53'E. Also called Larsenskarvet. Form part of the east face of Jøkulkyrkja Mountain, in the Mühlig-Hofmann Mountains of Queen Maud Land. Named by the Norwegians for Per Larsen, steward with the Norwegian Antarctic Expedition of 1956–57.

**Larsen Glacier.** 75°06'S, 162°28'E. Flows SE from Reeves Névé, through the Prince Albert Mountains, into the Ross Sea, just south of Mount Crummer in Victoria Land. Discovered by David on his way to the South Magnetic Pole in 1908, as part of Shackleton's 1907–9 expedition. He followed the course of this glacier on his way to the plateau beyond. Named in association with nearby Mount Larsen, which was always in view as they climbed the glacier.

**Larsen Ice Barrier** *see* **Larsen Ice Shelf**

**Larsen Ice Shelf.** 67°30'S, 62°30'W. Also called Larsen Barrier, Larsen Ice Barrier. In the NW part of the Weddell Sea. One of the great ice shelves, this one extends along the east coast of the Antarctic Peninsula from Cape Longing to the area just south of Hearst Island. Named for Carl Anton Larsen, who, in Dec. 1893, sailed along it as far south as 68°10'S in the *Jason.*

**Larsen Inlet.** 64°26'S, 59°26'W. Also called Larsen Bay. Ice-filled. 12 miles long. 7 miles wide. Between Cape Longing and Cape Sobral, on the east coast of Graham Land. Named by Edwin Swift Balch, American writer on Antarctica, in

1902, for Carl Anton Larsen, who had reported a large bay in this area in 1893–94.

**Larsen Island** *see* **Monroe Island**

**Larsen Islands.** 60°36'S, 46°04'W. Small group 1 mile NW of Moreton Point, the western extremity of Coronation Island, in the South Orkneys. Discovered in Dec. 1821 by Palmer and Powell. Monroe Island is the biggest in the group. Named by Petter Sørlle in 1912–13 for Carl Anton Larsen.

**Larsen Mountains** *see* **Larsemann Hills**

**Larsen Nunatak.** 64°58'S, 60°04'W. 2 miles north of Murdoch Nunatak in the Seal Nunataks, just off the east coast of the Antarctic Peninsula. Surveyed and named in 1947 by the FIDS for Carl Anton Larsen.

**Larsenskarvet** *see* **Larsen Cliffs**

**Larsgaddane** *see* **Lars Nunatak**

**Larson Crag.** 76°44'S, 161°08'E. Over 1,600 m. At the north end of Staten Island Heights in the Convoy Range. Named in 1964 for Cdr. Wesley Larson, commander of the *Staten Island*, 1959–60.

**Larson Glacier.** 77°28'S, 154°W. Flows from La Gorce Peak in the Alexandra Mountains, and enters the south side of Butler Glacier, on Edward VII Peninsula. Named for Lt. Cdr. Conrad S. Larson, USN, officer-in-charge of the helicopter detachment aboard the *Eastwind* during Operation Deep Freeze I (1955–56).

**Larson Nunataks.** 82°45'S, 48°W. On the east side of the Forrestal Range. 1½ miles SE of Mount Malville, in the Pensacola Mountains. Named for Larry R. Larson, aviation electronics technician at Ellsworth Station, 1957.

**Larson Valley.** 79°32'S, 83°51'W. Ice-filled. Between the south end of Inferno Ridge and Mhire Spur in the Heritage Range. Named for D.L. Larson, USN, snow removal operator at Williams Field, 1965 and 1966.

**The *Las Palmas*.** Spanish ship in Antarctica in 1988–89.

**Lasala Refugio.** Argentine refuge hut built on Deception Island in Jan. 1953, and dismantled by the British the following month (*see* **Wars**).

**Laseron, Charles F.** Taxidermist on the AAE 1911–14.

**Laseron Islands.** 66°59'S, 142°48'E. Ice-capped. 3 miles east of Cape Denison in Commonwealth Bay. Discovered by the AAE 1911–14, and named by Mawson for Charles F. Laseron.

**Lasher Spur.** 69°06'S, 66°42'W. In the central part of the Antarctic Peninsula.

**Lashley Mountains** *see* **Lashly Mountains**

**Lashly, William.** d. 1940. Chief Stoker, RN. Called Stoker Lashly in the records. A versatile, expert sledger, he served with Scott on both his expeditions.

**Lashly Glacier.** 77°57'S, 159°50'E. Between the Lashly Mountains on the west and Tabular Mountain and Mount Feather on the east. It flows into The Portal, in Victoria Land. Named by the NZ party of the BCTAE in 1957 in association with the nearby mountains.

**Lashly Mountains.** 77°54'S, 159°33'E. South of the head of Taylor Glacier, and west of Lashly Glacier, in Victoria Land. Mount Crean is the highest mountain in this small group. Discovered during Scott's 1901–4 expedition, and named by them for William Lashly.

**Mount Lassell.** 71°45'S, 68°50'W. 1,000 m. Snow-covered. Overlooks the head of Neptune Glacier in the SE part of Alexander Island. Named by the UK for William Lassell (1779–1880), English astronomer who discovered Ariel and Umbriel, satellites of the planet Uranus, and also Triton, the satellite of Neptune.

**Bahía Lasserre** *see* **Admiralty Bay**

**Lassiter, James W.** Captain, USAF. Chief pilot on the RARE, 1947–48. In 1957–58 he headed the US Air Force Electronics Test Unit (q.v.).

**Lassiter Coast.** 73°45'S, 62°W. Between Cape Mackintosh and Cape Adams on the east coast of the Antarctic Peninsula. Discovered aerially by the USAS in 1940. Named for James W. Lassiter, by Finn Ronne.

**Lassiter Ice Barrier** *see* **Ronne Ice Shelf**

**Lassus Mountains.** 69°30'S, 71°37'W. 15 miles long and 3 miles wide. 2,000 m. high. They extend south from Palestrina Glacier in the northern part of Alexander Island. Discovered by von Bellingshausen. Photographed aerially by the BGLE in 1936 and subsequently mapped as part of the Havre Mountains. This was later corrected and the new group was named by the UK for the composer.

**Last Cache Nunatak.** 85°33'S, 174°08' W. The last and most southerly of the nunataks on the ridge forming the eastern wall of the Zaneveld Glacier. It is an important landmark for explorers in the area of the head of the Shackleton Glacier. Named by the Southern Party of the NZGSAE of 1961–62. They made their last depot of fuel and food near this nunatak.

**Last Hill.** 63°28'S, 57°05'W. 350 m. Has a rock ridge at its crest and a cliff at its north side. 4 miles SSW of Hope Bay. 2 miles east of the north shore of Duse Bay on Tabarin Peninsula. Charted by the FIDS in 1946, and named by them because it marks the last climb on the sledging route between Hope Bay and Duse Bay.

**Latady, William R.** Aerial photographer on the RARE, 1947–48.

**Latady Island.** 70°45'S, 74°35'W. Ice-covered. 35 miles long. Over 10 miles wide. 45 miles south of Charcot Island, and west of Alexander Island. Discovered aerially, but not recognized for what it was, by Sir Hubert Wilkins, in 1929. Later named by the UK for William R. Latady.

**Latady Mountains.** 74°45'S, 64°18'W. West of Gardner Inlet. Between the

Wetmore and Ketchum Glaciers, in SE Palmer Land. Discovered aerially by the RARE, 1947–48, and named by Finn Ronne for William R. Latady.

**Laternula Lake.** In the Mule Peninsula of the Vestfold Hills.

**Latham Peak.** 66°21'S, 51°48'E. 16 miles SE of Cape Ann, and 8 miles NW of Mount Marr. Discovered by the BANZARE in Jan. 1930, and named by Mawson for Sir John Latham, Australian minister for external affairs.

**Latino Peak.** 72°09'S, 167°33'E. 2,290 m. 4 miles SSW of Mount Hazlett in the Victory Mountains of Victoria Land. Named for Terry L. Latino, USN, constructionman at McMurdo Station, 1967.

**Pico La Torre** *see* **The Tower**

**La Tour** *see* **The Tower**

**Lattemand Bai** *see* **Lallemand Fjord**

**Latty, John.** First class boy on the Wilkes Expedition 1838–42. Joined at Rio. Served the cruise.

**Laubeuf Fjord.** 67°20'S, 67°50'W. 25 miles long in a north-south direction, this sound averages 10 miles wide. Between the east-central part of Adelaide Island and the southern part of Arrowsmith Peninsula, Graham Land. Discovered by Charcot in 1908–10, and named by him for Maxime Laubeuf, French marine engineer who supervised the building of the *Pourquoi Pas?*'s engine.

**Mount Laudon.** 74°13'S, 64°03'W. 7 miles north of Mount Crowell in the NW part of the Guettard Range, in southern Palmer Land. Named for Thomas S. Laudon, geologist at Byrd Station, 1960–61, and a member of the University of Wisconsin geological party to the Eights Station area in the summer of 1965–66.

**Lauff Island.** 73°03'S, 126°08'W. 2 miles north of Cape Dart, Siple Island, off the Marie Byrd Land coast. Discovered aerially during Operation Highjump, 1946–47. Named for Cdr. Bernard J. Lauff, USN, commanding officer of the *Glacier*, 1956–57.

**Launch Channel.** 66°17′S, 110°30′E. Between Bailey Peninsula and Shirley Island, in the Windmill Islands. Named for the only craft which can safely use this shallow channel.

**Launch Rock.** 67°46′S, 68°56′W. Submerged rock, SW of Glover Rocks, off the south end of Adelaide Island. Named by the UK for the *John Biscoe's* launch used to chart this area in 1963.

**Mount Launoit.** 72°34′S, 31°27′E. 2,470 m. Between Mount Brouwer and Mount Imbert in the Belgica Mountains. Discovered by the Belgian Antarctic Expedition of 1958-59 under Gaston de Gerlache, and named by him for the Count de Launoit, a sponsor of the expedition.

**Laurie, A.H.** Scientist on the *William Scoresby*, 1929-33, and on the *Discovery II*, 1930.

**Laurie Automatic Weather Station.** 77°37′S, 170°06′E. Approximate elevation — 80 feet. About 6 miles east of Cape Crozier on Ross Island. Began operating on Dec. 15, 1981, and ended operations on Jan. 12, 1986.

**Laurie Island.** 60°44′S, 44°37′W. Also called Melville's Island. 12½ miles long in an east-west direction. It is the most easterly of the South Orkneys, and has a permanent ice cap. Discovered in Dec. 1821 by Powell and Palmer. Named for R.H. Laurie, Chartseller to the Admiralty, who published a map of the area in 1822 (*see* **Mapping of Antarctica**). Surveyed by Bruce in 1902-4, it was the site of his camp here, a scientific station actually, called Omond House, which in 1904 became the Argentine base of Orcadas.

**Lauritzen Bay.** 69°07′S, 156°50′E. 12 miles wide. Filled with bay ice and ice shelf, it indents the coast of Oates Land between Cape Yevgenov and Coombes Ridge. The west side of the bay is made up of the Coombes Ridge and the Matusevich Glacier Tongue. Named by the Australians for Knud Lauritzen, owner of the *Magga Dan*.

**Laussedat Heights.** 64°47′S, 62°30′W. They extend eastward for 8 miles in the SW part of the Arctowski Peninsula, on the west coast of Graham Land. Named by the UK in 1960 for Aimé Laussedat (1819-1907), the father of photogrammetry.

**The *Lautaro*.** Chilean ship which took part in various Antarctic expeditions which that country undertook in the late 1940s/early 1950s: 1948-49 (Capt. José Duarte), 1950-51, 1953-54 (Capt. Patricio Carvajal Prado), 1954-55 (Capt. Hernán Prat), 1956-57.

**Canal Lautaro** *see* **Argentino Channel**

**Islote Lautaro** *see* **Låvebrua Island**

**Lautaro Island.** 64°49′S, 63°06′W. Also called Isla Cramer, Isla Graciela, Isla Graziella. 1 mile long. Just west of Lemaire Island in the Gerlache Strait. Named by the Chilean Antarctic Expedition of 1948-49 for the *Lautaro*.

**Lauzanne Cove.** 65°05′S, 63°23′W. 2 miles wide. Just south of the Guyou Islands, on the south side of Flandres Bay, on the west coast of Graham Land. Charted by Charcot in 1903-5, and he named it for Stéphane Lauzanne, chief editor of the French newspaper *Le Matin* from 1900 to 1915.

**Lavallee Peak.** 72°04′S, 164°56′E. 2,175 m. Just NW of Gibraltar Peak in the West Quartzite Range. Named for Lt. David O. Lavallee, USN, biological diver at McMurdo Station, 1963-64, 1964-65, and 1966-67.

**Lavallee Point.** 76°37′S, 159°50′E. The most northerly point on Shipton Ridge in the Allan Hills of Victoria Land. Named by the New Zealanders in 1964 for Lt. David O. Lavallee (*see also* **Lavallee Peak**), who helped in establishing the expedition in the Allan Hills that year.

**Låvebrua Island.** 63°02′S, 60°35′W. Also called Islote Chaco, Jon Islet, Islote Lautaro. 95 meters high. Amost ¾ mile east of South Point on Deception Island. Charted by Foster in 1828-31. Named by

Norwegian whalers operating out of Deception Island in the 1920s. Name means "the threshing-floor bridge" in Norwegian, and is descriptive.

**LaVergne Glacier.** 85°19′S, 170°45′W. 7 miles long. Flows along the southern slopes of Seabee Heights, and enters Liv Glacier just SW of McKinley Nunatak. Named for Lt. Cdr. Cornelius B. de LaVergne, deputy commander of Antarctic Support Activity at McMurdo Station, 1961.

**Lavoisier Island.** 66°12′S, 66°44′W. Also called Nansen Island, Isla Serrano, Isla Mitre. 18 miles long and 5 miles wide. Between Rabot and Watkins Islands in the Biscoe Islands. Charted by Charcot in 1903–5, and named by him as Île Nansen, for Fridtjof Nansen, the Norwegian Arctic explorer. Renamed by the UK in 1960 for Laurent Lavoisier, the French chemist and pioneer in the study of metabolism. This change was effected in order to avoid confusion with Nansen Island.

**Lavris Peak.** 76°49′S, 125°56′W. Snow-capped. 2,745 m. In the NE portion of Mount Hartigan, in the Executive Committee Range of Marie Byrd Land. Named for William C. Lavris, meteorological technician at Byrd Station, 1959.

**Roca Law** *see* **Low Rock**

**Law, Phillip Garth.** b. April 21, 1912, Victoria, Australia. Senior adviser to the ANARE in 1947 and 1948, and from 1949 he was leader of ANARE, as well as being, for the same period, director of the Antarctic Division for the Department of External Affairs. As such he was head of all Australia's Antarctic endeavors from 1949–66, and went south on several occasions. In 1954 he established Mawson Station, and in 1957–58 he led a traverse across Australian Antarctic Territory (*see also* the Bibliography).

**Law Dome.** 66°44′S, 112°50′E. A large ice dome which rises to 1,395 m. Directly south of Cape Poinsett. Forms the bulk of the land behind the Budd Coast.

Named by the Australians for Phillip G. Law.

**Law Dome Station.** Australian scientific base on Cape Folger, in the vicinity of the Budd Coast.

**Law Glacier.** 84°05′S, 161°E. 10 miles wide. Between the south end of the Queen Elizabeth Range and the MacAlpine Hills. It flows from the Polar Plateau to the Bowden Névé. Named by the NZ party of the BCTAE in 1957 for B.R. Law, deputy-chairman of the Ross Sea Committee for that expedition.

**Law Islands.** 67°15′S, 59°02′E. Off the east end of Law Promontory, at the west side of the entrance to Stefansson Bay. Photographed by the LCE 1936–37. First visited by an ANARE party led by P.W. Crohn in 1956. Named by the Australians in association with the nearby promontory.

**Law Plateau.** 73°S, 72°E. Between the Mawson Escarpment and the Grove Mountains, behind the Ingrid Christensen Coast. Named for Phillip Law.

**Law Promontory.** 67°15′S, 58°47′E. 15 miles long. Mainly ice-covered. Extends east from the coast at the NW side of Stefansson Bay. Mapped by personnel on the *William Scoresby* in Feb. 1936. Photographed by the LCE 1936–37, and remapped by Norwegian cartographers from these photos. They called it Breidhovde (Broad Knoll). First visited by an ANARE party in 1956, and renamed by the Australians for Phillip Law (q.v.), who flew over and photographed this promontory in Feb. 1954.

**[1]Mount Lawrence.** 67°51′S, 62°31′E. 1,230 m. Just north of Mount Coates in the David Range in the Framnes Mountains of Mac. Robertson Land. Photographed by the LCE 1936–37. Named later by the Australians for J. Lawrence, diesel mechanic at Mawson Station, 1959.

**[2]Mount Lawrence** *see* **Lawrence Peaks**

**Lawrence Nunatak.** 84°50′S, 67°02′W. 1,540 m. 3 miles west of Snake Ridge, along the ice escarpment which trends SW from that ridge, in the Patuxent Range of the Pensacola Mountains. Named for Lawrence E. Brown, surveyor at Palmer Station, 1966.

**Lawrence Peaks.** 72°50′S, 166°20′E. Also called Mount Lawrence. Separate the Seafarer Glacier from the head of the Mariner Glacier. Named by the Northern Party of the NZGSAE of 1966–67 for the leader of that party, J.E.S. Lawrence.

**Lawrie Glacier.** 66°04′S, 64°36′W. Flows into the head of Barilari Bay between Mount Genecand and Mezzo Buttress, on the west coast of Graham Land. Charted by the BGLE 1934–37. Named by the UK in 1959 for Robert Lawrie, British alpine and polar equipment specialist.

**Laws Glacier.** 60°38′S, 45°38′W. Flows into Marshall Bay on the south coast of Coronation Island in the South Orkneys. Surveyed in 1948–49 by the FIDS. Named by the UK for Richard M. Laws, FIDS leader and biologist at Signy Island Station in 1948 and 1949.

**Lawson, Howard.** Crewman on the *Bear of Oakland,* 1933–34.

**Lawson Aiguilles.** 67°50′S, 66°15′E. A line of sharp peaks in the southern part of Mount Rivett, in the Gustav Bull Mountains of Mac. Robertson Land. Named by the Australians for E.J. Lawson, diesel mechanic at Mawson Station in 1967.

**Lawson Nunatak.** 67°56′S, 62°51′E. 2 miles SE of Branson Nunatak in the Masson Range of the Framnes Mountains. Named by the Australians for E.J. Lawson (*see* **Lawson Aiguilles**).

**Lawson Nunataks.** 70°47′S, 159°45′E. A line of nunataks about 4 miles long. 4 miles SW of Keim Peak in the Usarp Mountains. Named for Gerald J. Lawson, biologist at McMurdo Station, 1967–68.

**Lawson Peak.** 66°11′S, 65°36′W. 3½ miles SE of Cape Evensen on the west coast of Graham Land. Named by the UK in

1960 for Sir Arnold Lawson (1867–1947), British ophthalmic surgeon whose work in tinted glass led to improvements in snow goggles.

**Lay-Brother Rock.** 60°34′S, 46°13′W. Also called Roca Monigote. 2 miles SW of Despair Rocks, and 7 miles NW of Route Point, off the west end of Coronation Island in the South Orkneys. Charted and named by personnel on the *Discovery II* in 1933.

**Layman Peak.** 84°51′S, 179°35′E. 2,560 m. 3 miles east of Mount Bellows and 4 miles north of McIntyre Promontory, in the Queen Maud Mountains. Discovered and photographed by the USAS from West Base on Flight C of Feb. 29–March 1, 1940. Surveyed by Albert P. Crary in 1957–58. He named it for Frank Layman, mechanic of the US Ross Ice Shelf Traverse Party of 1957–58, and of the Victoria Land Traverse Party of 1958–59.

**Lazarev, Mikhail.** b. 1788, near Moscow. d. 1851, Vienna. Mikhail Petrovich Lazarev. Russian second-in-command of the von Bellingshausen expedition of 1819–21. As commander of the *Mirnyy,* he circumnavigated Antarctica with the *Vostok,* and was one of the first to sight the continental ice shelf on Jan. 27, 1820. Between 1803–8 he was in the British Royal Navy, and sailed around the world several times in lower latitudes. In 1833 he became captain of the Black Sea Fleet.

**Lazarev Bay.** 69°20′S, 72°W. Rectangular. 15 miles long and 13 miles wide. Between Alexander Island and Rothschild Island, and bounded on the south by ice shelf joining the two islands. Named by the UK for Mikhail Lazarev.

**Lazarev Ice Shelf.** 69°37′S, 14°45′E. Fringes the Princess Astrid Coast of Queen Maud Land between Leningradskiy Island and Verblyud Island. 50 miles long. Named by the USSR for Mikhail Lazarev.

**Lazarev Mountains.** 69°32′S, 157°20′E. Also called Jacka Mountains. On the west side of Matusevich Glacier, to the south of Eld Peak. 25 miles in extent. Named by the USSR in 1957–58 for Mikhail Lazarev.

**Lazarev Scientific Station.** 69° 56′ S, 12° 58′ E. USSR base established on March 10, 1959, and closed in the 1960–61 season.

**Lazarev Sea.** 67° 30′ S, 4° E. Beyond the Fimbul Ice Shelf, in the Weddell Sea.

**Leach Nunatak.** 77° 36′ S, 146° 25′ W. 4 miles WSW of Mount Ronne in the Haines Mountains, in the Ford Ranges of Marie Byrd Land. Named for Edwin B. Leach, USN, aviation electronics technician, the Williams Field division chief responsible for the maintenance of electronic equipment on all US aircraft in 1966–67.

**Leads.** Cracks in the pack ice through which ships pick their way.

**League Island**  *see*  **League Rock**

**League Rock.** 67° 46′ S, 69° 04′ W. Also called League Island. Rounded rock SW of Box Reef, off the south end of Adelaide Island. Named by the UK because it is one league away from Base T on Adelaide Island.

**Leah Ridge.** 70° 13′ S, 65° E. 1 mile NW of Dawson Nunatak and 5 miles SE of Mount Béchervaise in the Athos Range of the Prince Charles Mountains. Named by the Australians for the code word, "Leah," used at Mawson Station to identify the ANARE party which climbed the ridge in Dec. 1966.

**Cape Leahy.** 73° 43′ S, 119° W. Ice-covered. Marks the northern extremity of Duncan Peninsula, Carney Island, on the coast of Marie Byrd Land. Discovered aerially on Jan. 24, 1947, during Operation Highjump, and named by Byrd for Fleet Adm. William D. Leahy, USN, naval adviser to President Truman at the time, and who helped to get the operation off the ground.

**Leal Bluff.** 63° 53′ S, 57° 35′ W. Over 305 m. 2 miles inland from Cape Lamb, on the SW side of Vega Island. Named by the Argentines for Mayor Jorge Leal, deputy leader at Esperanza Station in 1947.

**Lealand Bluff.** 67° 27′ S, 59° 33′ E. At the SW corner of William Scoresby Bay, in the eastern part of Enderby Land. Named by personnel on the *William Scoresby,* here in Feb. 1936.

**Leander Glacier.** 71° 56′ S, 167° 41′ E. Flows from the area west of Mount Black Prince, and then south between Shadow Bluff and McGregor Range, into the Tucker Glacier, in the Admiralty Mountains. Named by the New Zealanders in 1957–58 for their World War II ship, the *Leander* (which did not visit the Antarctic).

**Leap Year Fault.** 72° S, 166° E. 156-mile-long linear feature, mostly under ice, which separates the Robertson Bay geological group (71° 30′ S, 167° E) on the east from the Bowers geological group (72° S, 165° E) on the west, in the Transantarctic Mountains. It stretches from McKenzie Nunatak in the north to Mounts Burton and McCarthy in the south.

**Leap Year Glacier.** 71° 42′ S, 164° 15′ E. Between Molar Massif and Mount Sterling in the Bowers Mountains. It flows into Black Glacier. Named by the Northern Party of the NZGSAE of 1963–64, which arrived here in the new year of 1964 (a leap year).

**Leavett, James.** Captain of the topsail on the Wilkes Expedition 1838–42. Joined in the USA. Served the cruise.

**Leay Glacier.** 65° 10′ S, 63° 57′ W. Flows into Girard Bay to the west of Hotine Glacier, on the west coast of Graham Land. Charted by Charcot in 1908–10. Named by the UK for Petra Leay Searle of the Directorate of Overseas Surveys, who has contributed to the mapping of the Antarctic Peninsula.

**Le Blanc, Ralph Paul.** Lt. (jg) USNR. Co-pilot of *George-1,* the Martin Mariner which crashed on Thurston Island on Dec. 30, 1946 (*see* **Deaths, 1946**), during Operation Highjump. Lt. Kearns was flying the plane at the time, and he pulled Le Blanc from the burning wreckage. But Le Blanc was badly burned and his feet were frozen. His legs had to be amputated en route home on the *Philippine Sea*.

**Cape Lebland** *see* **Cape Leblond**

**Cape Leblond.** 66°04'S, 66°36'W. Forms the north end of Lavoisier Island, in the Biscoe Islands. Charted by Charcot in 1908–10, and named by him for the president of the Norman Geographical Society at Rouen.

**Le Breton, Louis.** Draftsman/surgeon's aide on the *Astrolabe,* during Dumont d'Urville's expedition of 1837–40.

**Mount Lechner.** 83°14'S, 50°55'W. 2,030 m. Surmounts the SW end of Saratoga Table in the Forrestal Range of the Pensacola Mountains. Named for Major Ralph C. Lechner, US Army, airlift coordinator on the staff of the Commander, US Naval Support Force, Antarctica, 1964–66.

**Mount Leckie.** 70°26'S, 66°E. 3 miles east of Martin Massif in the Porthos Range of the Prince Charles Mountains. Named by the Australians for Squadron Leader D.W. Leckie, RAAF, who commanded the Antarctic Flight at Mawson Station in 1956.

**Leckie Range.** 67°55'S, 56°27'E. 50 miles south of Edward VIII Bay. Named by the Australians for Douglas W. Leckie (*see* **Mount Leckie**).

**Mount Lecointe.** 83°09'S, 161°09'E. 3,620 m. 3 miles NW of Mount Rabot in the Queen Elizabeth Range. Named by Shackleton in 1907–9 for Georges Lecointe.

**Lecointe, Georges.** Belgian navigating officer and astronomer. He was hydrographer and captain of the *Belgica* during de Gerlache's expedition of 1897–99. He was also second-in-command of the expedition.

**Lecointe Island.** 64°16'S, 62°03'W. Also called Isla Alice, Isla Kaiser. 4 miles long. 700 meters high. It is separated from the east coast of Brabant Island by Pampa Passage. Surveyed by de Gerlache, 1897–99. He named the northern

extremity of this island as Cape Kaiser. The whole island was later named by the UK for Georges Lecointe.

**Le Couteur Glacier.** 84°42'S, 170°30'W. 15 miles long. Flows from the NW slopes of Mount Hall and Mount Daniel, then along the west side of the Lillie Range into the Ross Ice Shelf. Named by the Southern Party of the NZGSAE of 1963–64, for P.C. Le Couteur, geologist with the New Zealand Federated Mountain Clubs Antarctic Expedition of 1962–63.

**Le Couteur Peak.** 72°09'S, 165°59'E. Between Cirque and Omega Peaks, in the northern part of the Millen Range. Named by the Southern Party of the New Zealand Federated Mountain Clubs Antarctic Expedition of 1962–63 for P.C. Le Couteur (*see* **Le Couteur Glacier**).

**Mount Lecroix** *see* **Mount Lacroix**

**Lécuyer Point.** 64°50'S, 63°30'W. Forms the southern side of the entrance to the harbor of Port Lockroy, Wiencke Island. Discovered and named by Charcot in 1903–5.

**Ledda Bay.** 74°23'S, 131°20'W. 12 miles long. Indents the north side of Grant Island, off the coast of Marie Byrd Land. Discovered and charted by the *Glacier* on Feb. 4, 1962. Named for R.J. Ledda, USN, quartermaster on the ship at the time.

**Lednikov Bay.** 66°34'S, 92°22'E. Also called Glacial Bay. Just west of McDonald Bay on the coast of East Antarctica. Named Bukhta Lednikovaya (glacier bay) by the USSR in 1956, because of its location at the terminus of a small glacier.

**The *Lee*.** US research vessel doing seismic surveys and sampling in Antarctic waters in 1983–84.

**Mount Lee.** 71°27'S, 74°35'W. Also called Mount Paul Lee. 500 m. Isolated. Snow-covered. On the peninsula between Verdi and Brahms Inlets in the SW part of Alexander Island. Discovered by the RARE, 1947–48, and named by Finn

Ronne for Rear Adm. Paul F. Lee, USN, chief of the Office of Naval Research, who authorized Naval support for the RARE.

**Lee Island.** 67°35'S, 62°52'E. Just west of Teyssier Island in Holme Bay, Mac. Robertson Land. Photographed by the LCE 1936–37. Later named by the Australians for R.T. Lee, diesel mechanic at nearby Mawson Station in 1957.

**Lee Lake.** 77°02'S, 162°08'E. A small lake at the SE corner of Redcliff Nunatak on the south side of Mackay Glacier in Victoria Land. Named by Grif Taylor's Western Journey Party, 1910–13, as it is in the lee of Redcliff Nunatak.

**Lee Nunatak.** 71°01'S, 159°58'E. 1,920 m. 4 miles NW of Penseroso Bluff in the NW part of the Daniels Range of the Usarp Mountains. Named for Chun Chi Lee, biologist at McMurdo Station, 1967–68.

**Lee Peak.** 86°25'S, 151°35'W. On the west side of Robert Scott Glacier, 3 miles north of Mount Denauro, in the Queen Maud Mountains. Named for Frank P. Lee, aerial photographer in Antarctica, 1965, 1966, and 1967.

**Mount Leech.** 72°05'S, 99°59'W. 5 miles NW of Mount Hubbard in the Walker Mountains of Thurston Island. Named for Robert E. Leech, entomologist who took part in a USARP airborne insect program in the Ross, Amundsen, and Bellingshausen Seas areas in 1959–60.

**Mount Leek.** 75°49'S, 68°31'W. West of Spear Glacier in the NE part of the Hauberg Mountains, in Ellsworth Land. Discovered aerially by the RARE, 1947–48. Named for Gouke M. Leek, glaciologist at Byrd Station, 1965–66.

**LeFeuvre Scarp.** 69°21'S, 63°18'W. An irregular clifflike elevation of 750 meters in height. 11 miles west of Cape Reichelderfer on the east side of Palmer Land. It marks the north side of the divide between Bingham Glacier and a smaller, unnamed glacier just to the north. Surveyed by the FIDS in 1947. Named by the UK in 1962 for Charles F. LeFeuvre, radio operator at Halley Bay Station in 1956, at Signy Island Station in 1959, and at Base Y and Base E in 1960.

**Lefèvre Point** *see* **Lefèvre-Utile Point**

**Lefèvre-Utile Point.** 64°50'S, 63°31'W. Also called Lefèvre Point. 1 mile west of Curie Point, on the north side of Doumer Island, in the Palmer Archipelago. Discovered and named by Charcot in 1903–5.

**Cape Legoupil.** 63°19'S, 57°55'W. At the NE side of the entrance to Huon Bay, on the north coast of Trinity Peninsula. Discovered by Dumont d'Urville in 1837–40, and named by him for Ernest Goupil (q.v.). The erroneous form of the name, Legoupil, has been used for so long that it has become correct.

**Legru Bay.** 62°10'S, 58°12'W. 2 miles wide. Indents the south coast of King George Island, just NE of Martins Head, in the South Shetlands. Martins Head was named Cap Legru in 1908–10 by Charcot. This situation was later changed.

**Cape LeGuillou.** 63°30'S, 59°52'W. Forms the northern tip of Tower Island, at the NE end of the Palmer Archipelago. Charted by Dumont d'Urville in 1837–40, and named by him for Élie Le Guillou.

**Le Guillou, Élie.** A surgeon on the *Zélée* during Dumont d'Urville's expedition of 1837–40.

**Cape Lehaie** *see* **Lehaie Point**

**Lehaie Point.** 64°30'S, 62°47'W. Also called Cap Houzeau de Lehaie. Forms the SW extremity of Brabant Island. Discovered by de Gerlache in 1897–99, and he named it for M. Houzeau de Lehaie, a supporter. In 1903–5 Charcot charted it, and changed the name from Cape Lehaie to Lehaie Point.

**Massif Le Havre** *see* **Havre Mountains**

**Lehrke, Lester.** Bosun's mate on the *Bear* during the USAS 1939–41, who went ashore at East Base and became that base's sail maker and communications man.

**Lehrke Bay** *see* **Lehrke Inlet**

**Lehrke Inlet.** 70°49′S, 61°45′W. Also called Lehrke Bay. 8 miles wide. Ice-filled. Recedes SW for 17 miles between Cape Boggs and Cape Sharbonneau, on the east coast of Palmer Land. Discovered in Dec. 1940 by members of the USAS from East Base. Named for Lester Lehrke.

**Leigh Hunt Glacier.** 85°S, 174°10′E. 7 miles long. Flows into Brandau Glacier just west of Hare Peak. Named by the New Zealanders in 1961–62 for Leigh Hunt, founder and first chairman of the NZ Antarctic Society.

**Leininger Peak.** 70°34′S, 62°15′W. 1,135 m. At the north side of the base of Eielson Peninsula, on the east coast of Palmer Land. Charted in 1947 by the Weddell Coast Sledge Party. Named by Ronne for Cdr. Joseph A. Leininger, USNR, who devised the plans for the loading of cargo onto the *Port of Beaumont, Texas,* the RARE ship.

**Leipzig Island** *see* **Nelson Island**

**Leister Peak.** 75°10′S, 113°54′W. 3 miles north of Early Bluff in the Kohler Range of Marie Byrd Land. Lichens and mosses are found here. Named for Geoffrey L. Leister, biologist with the USARP Marie Byrd Land Survey Party of 1966–67.

**Leitch Massif.** 71°55′S, 164°36′E. Forms the northern part of the West Quartzite Range, in the Concord Mountains. Named by the Northern Party of the NZ Federated Mountain Clubs Antarctic Expedition, for E.C. Leitch, geologist with this 1962–63 party.

**Leith Cove.** 64°52′S, 62°50′W. Also called Leith Harbor. In the NE part of Paradise Harbor, on the west coast of Graham Land. Named by whalers here for Salvesen and Co., the Leith, Scotland, whaling company.

**Leith Harbor** *see* **Inverleith Harbor, Leith Cove**

**Lekander Nunatak.** 85°04′S, 64°29′W. 1,815 m. On the SW edge of Mackin Table. 2 miles NE of Bessinger Nunatak, in the southern Patuxent Range of the Pensacola Mountains. Named for Bryant A. Lekander, cook at South Pole Station, 1960.

**Mount Leland.** 77°16′S, 161°18′E. A rock peak 1 mile west of Victoria Upper Glacier in Victoria Land. Named for Capt. Bainbridge B. Leland, captain of the *Burton Island,* 1968 and 1969.

**Lemaire Channel.** 65°04′S, 63°57′W. Also called Lemaire Strait. 7 miles long and an average of 1 mile wide. Extends in a NE-SW direction from Splitwind Island and False Cape Renard to Roulin Point and Cape Cloos. It separates Booth Island from the west coast of Graham Land. Discovered by Dallmann, 1873–74. Crossed by de Gerlache in Dec. 1898, and named by him for Charles Lemaire, Belgian explorer.

**Lemaire Island.** 64°49′S, 62°57′W. 4½ miles long. 1½ miles wide. 1 mile west of Duthiers Point off the west coast of Graham Land. Discovered by de Gerlache, 1897–99, and he named it for Charles Lemaire (*see* **Lemaire Channel**).

**Lemaire Strait** *see* **Lemaire Channel**

**Le Marais.** 66°46′S, 141°34′E. A small area, mainly ice-covered but bounded by several rock exposures, forming part of the peninsula behind Cape Découverte. Charted and named in 1951 by the French. The name means "the marsh" in French. During the summer months, muddy pools of melting water form here.

**Lemasters Bluff.** 73°20′S, 162°12′E. A rock bluff at the eastern end of the Lichen Hills in Victoria Land. Named for Lt. Max E. Lemasters, USN, air operations officer at McMurdo Station, 1967.

**Mount LeMasurier.** 75°27′S, 139°39′W. Over 800 m. Ice-free. Between Mounts Vance and Langway, in the central part of the Ickes Mountains, on the coast of Marie Byrd Land. Discovered aerially by the USAS 1939–41. Named for

Wesley E. LeMasurier, geologist with the Marie Byrd Land Survey II, 1967–68.

**LeMay Range.** 70°55′S, 69°20′W. Also called Army Range, United States Army Range. 40 miles long. It has peaks rising to over 2,000 m. Extends in a NW-SE direction from Snick Pass to Uranus Glacier in central Alexander Island. Discovered aerially by Ellsworth on Nov. 23, 1935. Named by Finn Ronne in 1948 for Gen. Curtis LeMay, deputy chief of Air Staff for Research and Development of the USAAF, which furnished equipment for the RARE.

**The *Lena*.** USSR refrigeration ship/research ship/icebreaker. One of the two ships which took down the First Soviet Antarctic Expedition of 1955–56. Captain A.I. Vetrov. It was back again in 1956–57, same captain.

**Lena Bay** *see* **Casey Bay**

**Lena Passage.** 66°34′S, 92°58′E. ½ mile wide. Between the SW part of the Haswell Islands and Vetrov Hill on the coast of East Antarctica. Named by the USSR in 1956 for the *Lena*.

**Lenfant Bluff.** 70°22′S, 160°03′E. A rock bluff marking the south side of the mouth of Svendsen Glacier in the Usarp Mountains. Named for Claude J.M. Lenfant, biologist at McMurdo Station, 1967–68.

**Punta Lengua** *see* **Spit Point**

**Lenie Passage.** 64°44′S, 64°23′W. 1 mile wide. Between the Gossler Islands and the Joubin Islands in the Palmer Archipelago. It runs NW-SE. Named for Pieter J. Lenie, captain of the *Hero* in 1972–73 and 1973–74. In Jan.–Feb. 1973 Lenie became the first to carry out soundings of this passage.

**Leningrad Bay** *see* **Leningradskiy Bay**

**Leningradskaya Station.** 69°30′S, 159°23′E. USSR base in Oates Land, opened Feb. 25, 1971. An average of 17 men winter-over.

**Leningradskiy Bay.** 70°S, 12°30′E. Also called Leningrad Bay. Indents the ice shelf fringing Queen Maud Land, just west of the Lazarev Ice Shelf. Leningradskiy Island is at the head of the bay. Named by the USSR in 1959 for their city.

**Leningradskiy Island.** 70°08′S, 12°50′E. Ice-covered. At the head of Leningradskiy Bay, at the western edge of the Lazarev Ice Shelf, Queen Maud Land. The surrounding ice shelf encircles the island on all but the northern side, and this island rises nearly 100 meters above the level of it. Discovered by the USSR in 1961, and named by them in association with the bay.

**Leniz Gallejo, Clorindo.** Chief stoker on the *Yelcho* when that ship rescued Wild's party from Elephant Island in 1916.

**Leniz Point.** 64°54′S, 63°05′W. Also called Barbaro Point. The northern extremity of the small peninsula on which stands Mount Banck. 1 mile south of Bryde Island on the west coast of Graham Land. De Gerlache made a landing here on Feb. 10, 1898, and charted it. Named by the Chileans before 1951 for Clorindo Leniz Gallejo (*see* **Leniz**).

**Lennard, John.** Seaman on the Wilkes Expedition 1838–42. Joined at Rio. Sent home to the USA on the *Relief* in 1839.

**Lennox-King Glacier.** 83°25′S, 168°E. A valley glacier. 40 miles long. Flows from the Bowden Névé, between the Holland and Queen Alexandra Ranges into Richards Inlet at the Ross Ice Shelf. Named by the New Zealanders in 1959–60 for Lt. Cdr. James Lennox-King, RNZN, leader at Scott Base in 1960.

**Lens Peak.** 66°08′S, 65°24′W. At the south side of Holtedahl Bay, just east of Conway Island, on the west coast of Graham Land. Named by the UK in 1960. Several features in this area were named for things optical.

**Lensen Glacier.** 72°18′S, 166°48′E. Flows into Pearl Harbor Glacier just east of Mount Pearson in the Victory Mountains of Victoria Land. Named by the

New Zealanders in 1962–63 for G.J. Lensen, a member of the NZGSAE of 1957–58, who worked in the area of the Tucker Glacier.

**Lensink Peak.** 71°04′S, 65°25′E. The most easterly of a group of three peaks 5 miles SE of Husky Massif in the Prince Charles Mountains. Named by the Australians for W.H. Lensink, weather observer at Wilkes Station in 1960.

**Lenton, Ralph A.** A major figure in Antarctic history. FIDS radio operator at Signy Island Station in 1948. He also helped with the survey and biological work. He was at Base G in Admiralty Bay in 1949, and in 1951 was FIDS leader at Base B, on Deception Island. In 1952 he was leader of Port Lockroy Station, and in 1954 was the first leader at the new Faraday Station on Galíndez Island in the Argentine Islands. During the BCTAE he was second-in-command of the Advance Party, 1955–56, and in 1956–58 he crossed the continent with Fuchs, as radio operator/carpenter.

**Lenton Bluff.** 79°S, 28°13′W. On the north side of the mouth of Jeffries Glacier in the Theron Mountains. Named in 1956–57 by the BCTAE for Ralph A. Lenton.

**Lenton Point.** 60°44′S, 45°37′W. The SW extremity of a small, rocky peninsula in Clowes Bay on the south side of Signy Island in the South Orkneys. Surveyed in 1933 by personnel of the Discovery Committee, and again in 1947 by the FIDS. Named in 1954 by the UK for Ralph A. Lenton.

**Lentz Buttress.** 85°40′S, 127°36′W. 5 miles ENE of Faure Peak. 2,800 meters high. Forms a projection along the north side of the Wisconsin Plateau in the Horlick Mountains. Named for Lt. Malcolm W. Lentz, USN, officer-in-charge at Amundsen-Scott South Pole Station, 1962.

**Mount Leo.** 69°29′S, 67°W. 1,270 m. Isolated. At the SE end of the Forster Ice Piedmont on the west side of the Antarctic Peninsula. Surveyed by the BGLE in

1936–37, and again by the FIDS in 1958. Named by the UK because it looks like a lion.

**Isla León** *see* **Lion Island**

**Lake Leon.** Unofficial name of a lake just east of Lake Chad in Taylor Valley.

**Seno León** *see* **Lion Sound**

**Leonard Canyon.** 65°S, 145°E. Submarine feature off George V Land.

**Leonardo Glacier.** 64°42′S, 61°58′W. Flows into Wilhelmina Bay between Sadler and Café Points, on the west coast of Graham Land. Charted by de Gerlache in 1897–99. Named by the UK in 1960 for Leonardo da Vinci (1452–1519).

**Léonie Island.** 67°36′S, 68°21′W. The largest and most westerly of the Léonie Islands. 1 mile long. 455 meters high. In the entrance to Ryder Bay on the SE side of Adelaide Island. Discovered and named by Charcot in 1908–10.

**Léonie Islands.** 67°36′S, 68°17′W. Group of small islands in the entrance to Ryder Bay on the SE side of Adelaide Island. In 1908–10 Charcot named the largest of this group as Léonie Island. The BGLE 1934–37 extended the use of the name to cover the whole group. Others in the group include Anchorage Island, Lagoon Island, Limpet Island.

**Leopard Island.** 65°15′S, 64°18′W. 350 yards long. 350 yards west of the SW end of Skua Island in the Argentine Islands, in the Wilhelm Archipelago. Charted and named by the BGLE in 1935.

**Leopard seals.** *Hydrurga leptonyx.* Also called sea leopards. Earless, carnivorous, aggressive, solitary seals of the family Phocidae, they breed exclusively in Antarctica. They have powerful jaws, huge canines and prey on adult and young penguins, young seals and other warm-blooded beings—the only seals to do this. They have black-spotted, gray coats, can grow to 12 feet long and 840 pounds in weight, and are not commercially important.

**Leopold and Astrid Coast.** 67°20'S, 84°30'E. Between the western extremity of the West Ice Shelf (81°24'E) and Cape Penck (87°43'E). Discovered and explored aerially on Jan. 17, 1934, on a flight from the *Thorshavn* by Lt. Alf Gunnestad and Capt. Nils Larsen. Named by Lars Christensen for the King and Queen of Belgium.

**Leopold Coast** *see* **Luitpold Coast**

**Leopold Land** *see* **Luitpold Coast**

**Mount Lepanto.** 72°44'S, 168°27'E. 2,910 m. 2 miles SE of Mount Freeman in the Victory Mountains of Victoria Land. Named by the New Zealanders in 1957–58 for the Battle of Lepanto in 1571.

**Lepley Nunatak.** 73°07'S, 90°23'W. 2 miles SW of Dendtler Island, near the inner part and east end of the Abbott Ice Shelf. Discovered Feb. 9, 1961, by helicopters from the *Glacier* and the *Staten Island*. Named for Larry K. Lepley, oceanographer who was marooned here with three other men from Feb. 12–15, 1961, by a severe snowstorm.

**Le Poing** *see* **Wegger Peak**

**Cerro Le Poing** *see* **Admiralen Peak**

**Leppard Glacier.** 65°58'S, 62°30'W. A valley glacier. Flows into Scar Inlet, to the north of Ishmael Peak, on the east coast of Graham Land. Discovered aerially on Dec. 20, 1928, by Wilkins. Surveyed by the FIDS in 1955, one of the assistant surveyors being Norman A.G. Leppard, for whom the UK named this glacier. Wilkins had thought it was a channel, and called it Crane Channel. He also photographed what is now Crane Glacier. The confusion among the geographic features in this area stems from the Wilkins flights of that year. Wilkins was confused by what he saw below him, and that confusion was perpetuated for years until ground surveys finally correctly identified these features. The UK renamed his Crane Channel.

**Lepreux.** Seaman on Dumont d'Urville's expedition of 1837–40. Died of scurvy off the coast of Chile on April 1, 1838.

**Mount Lepus.** 70°40'S, 67°10'W. Between Millett and Bertram Glaciers. 10 miles east of Wade Point on the west coast of Palmer Land. Named by the UK for the constellation Lepus.

**Lerchenfeld Glacier.** 77°55'S, 34°15'W. Also called Graf Lerchenfeld Gletscher. Flows between Bertrab Nunatak and Littlewood Nunataks. It joins the southern flank of Schweitzer Glacier, before both of them flow into Vahsel Bay. Discovered by Filchner in 1911–12, and he named it for Graf Hugo von und zu Lerchenfeld-Köfering, a supporter.

**Mount LeResche.** 71°31'S, 166°17'E. 2,040 m. At the extreme north end of Homerun Range in the Admiralty Mountains of Victoria Land. Named for Robert E. LeResche, biologist at McMurdo Station, 1966–67 and 1967–68.

**Leroux Bay.** 65°36'S, 64°16'W. 9 miles long and an average of 5 miles wide. Between Nuñez Point and the Magnier Peaks, on the west coast of Graham Land. Discovered by Charcot, and named by him for Commander Leroux of the Argentine navy.

**Mount LeSchack.** 85°25'S, 124°W. 2,265 m. Flat-topped. On the north side of Perkins Canyon in the Wisconsin Range of the Horlick Mountains. Named for Leonard A. LeSchack, traverse seismologist at Byrd Station, 1958.

**Les Dents.** 68°57'S, 70°58'W. Also called The Needles. 4 sharp needle rocks, all of the same height, between Mount Bayonne and Mount Paris, in the northern part of Alexander Island. Discovered by Charcot in 1908–10, and named by him as Les Dents (the teeth).

**The *Les Éclaireurs*.** Argentine vessel on the 1953–54 expedition and the 1956–57 expedition, the latter under Capt. Enrique I. Paquien.

**Leskov, A.** Third lieutenant on the *Vostok* during von Bellingshausen's expedition of 1819–21.

**Leskov Island.** 66°36'S, 85°10'E. Ice-covered. In the West Ice Shelf. 185 m.

high. 6 miles NW of Mikhaylov Island. Discovered by the USSR in 1956, and named by them for A. Leskov.

**Leslie, David.** American sealing captain from New Bedford, Mass. Co-owner and captain of the *Gleaner* during the 1820–21 season in the South Shetlands. He was succeeded as captain by Thomas Boyd, on July 5, 1821, at Valparaiso.

**Leslie Hill.** 62°34′S, 60°12′W. North of Mount Bowles in the eastern part of Livingston Island in the South Shetlands. Named by the UK in 1958 for David Leslie.

**Leslie Peak.** 68°S, 56°30′E. 5 miles south of Mount Cook in the Leckie Range. Named by the Australians for Leslie Miller, radio officer at Mawson Station in 1964.

**Lesser Antarctica** *see* **West Antarctica**

**Lesser Mackellar Island.** 66°58′S, 142°39′E. Just NE of Greater Mackellar Island in the Mackellar Islands. 2 miles north of Cape Denison in the middle of Commonwealth Bay.

**Lesser rorqual** *see* **Minke**

**Lester, M.C.** b. Sept. 25, 1891. d. 1957. Maxime C. Lester. He had been a second mate on a tramp steamer when he became the "surveyor" on the so-called British Imperial Expedition of 1920–22, during which he and Bagshawe wintered alone on Paradise Bay.

**Lester, William J.** Seaman on the Wilkes Expedition 1838–42. Joined at Rio. Served the cruise.

**Lester Cove.** 64°54′S, 62°36′W. Forms the southernmost part of Andvord Bay on the west coast of Graham Land. Charted by de Gerlache, 1897–99. Named by the UK in 1960 for M.C. Lester.

**Lester Peak.** 79°49′S, 83°42′W. Snow-free. At the south side of Hyde Glacier, in the Edson Hills of the Heritage Range. Named for Lester A. Johnson, meteorologist at Little America V in 1958.

**Letourno, Godfrey.** Seaman on the Wilkes Expedition 1838–42. Joined in the USA. Served the cruise.

**Lettau Automatic Weather Station.** 82°41′S, 174°17′W. American AWS at an elevation of approximately 175 feet. Named for meteorologist Bernard H. Lettau. Began operating on Jan. 29, 1986.

**Mount Letten.** 66°55′S, 51°03′E. 1 mile south of Mount Storer, in the Tula Mountains of Enderby Land. Named by the Australians for W.H. Letten.

**Letten, W.H.** Crew member on the *Discovery* during the BANZARE 1929–31.

**The *Leucotón.*** Chilean vessel on the 1951–52 expedition, the 1952–53 expedition (Capt. Reinaldo Roepke), 1954–55 expedition (Capt. German Valenzuela), and the 1955–56 expedition.

**Leuthner, Walter.** Seaman on the *City of New York,* during Byrd's 1928–30 expedition.

**Mount Levack.** 78°18′S, 85°05′W. 2,670 m. 13 miles east of Mount Ostenso in the central part of the Sentinel Range. Named for Maj. Herbert T. Levack, USAF, one of the builders of South Pole Station in 1956–57.

**Levanevskogo Mountain** *see* **Skeidsberget Hill**

**Levassor Nunatak.** 63°40′S, 58°07′W. Horseshoe-shaped. 1 mile inland, in the middle of Cugnot Ice Piedmont, Trinity Peninsula. Surveyed by the FIDS in 1960–61. Named by the UK for Émile Levassor (1844–1897), automobile pioneer.

**Le Vaux Peak.** 76°40′S, 125°43′W. On the east side of the crater rim of Mount Cumming in the Executive Committee Range of Marie Byrd Land. Named for Howard A. Le Vaux, aurora physicist at Byrd Station, 1959, and a member of the Marie Byrd Land Traverse Party of 1959–60.

**Lever Glacier.** 65°30′S, 63°40′W. 1½ miles wide at the mouth. 6 miles long. Flows into the head of the north arm of Beascochea Bay on the west coast of

Graham Land. Discovered and surveyed by Charcot in 1909. Resurveyed in 1935 by the BGLE, and named in 1954 by the UK for William H. Lever, 2nd Lord Leverhulme, patron of the BGLE 1934–37.

**Leverett Glacier.** 85°38′S, 147°35′W. 50 miles long. 3–4 miles wide. Flows from the Watson Escarpment, between the California and Stanford Plateaus, and then, with a change of direction to the WNW, between the Tapley Mountains and the Harold Byrd Mountains. It terminates at the head of the Ross Ice Shelf, just east of Robert Scott Glacier. Discovered in Dec. 1929 by Gould's party during Byrd's 1928–30 expedition, and named by Gould for Frank Leverett, glacial geologist.

**Levi Peak.** 84°08′S, 165°06′E. 2 miles NW of Mount Stanley, at the western edge of the Grindley Plateau. Named for Gene S. Levi, meteorologist at Hallett Station in 1963 and 1964–65.

**Mount Levick.** 74°08′S, 163°10′E. 2,390 m. At the NW side of Tourmaline Plateau in the Deep Freeze Range of Victoria Land. Charted by Campbell's Northern Party during Scott's 1910–13 expedition, and named by them for G. Murray Levick.

**Levick, G. Murray.** Surgeon, RN. He was on Scott's last expedition, 1910–13. Wrote *Antarctic Penguins* in 1914.

**Levy Island.** 66°20′S, 66°35′W. Isolated. Snow-covered. In Crystal Sound. 7½ miles east of Gagge Point, Lavoisier Island. Surveyed by the FIDS in 1958–59. Named by the UK for Henri H. Levy, US physical chemist specializing in determining the location of hydrogen atoms in ice.

**Lewandowski Point.** 75°36′S, 162°13′E. Partly ice-free. On the coast of Victoria Land. Marks the south side of the mouth of Clarke Glacier. Named for John R. Lewandowski, USN, chief construction electrician at McMurdo Station, 1965–66 and 1966–67.

**Cape Lewis.** 66°30′S, 124°30′E. Ice-covered. At the west side of Maury Bay

on the coast of East Antarctica. Named for Thomas Lewis.

**Mount Lewis**   *see*   **Lewis Chain**

**Lewis, David.** b. 1919, NZ. Mountain climber, parachutist, doctor, international yachtsman, explorer, adventurer, daredevil, navigator extraordinaire, one of the great heroes. On Oct. 19, 1972, he left Sydney alone in the *Ice Bird,* bound for Antarctica. He arrived at Oban, Stewart Island, NZ, on Nov. 1, 1972, and left there the following day. He crossed the 50th Parallel on Nov. 5, 1972, and after a series of wild adventures he arrived at Palmer Station on Jan. 29, 1973. He left his broken boat there and left Antarctica on the *John Biscoe,* returning to Palmer Station in Nov. 1973 to finish repairing the *Ice Bird.* On Dec. 12, 1973, he continued south, and around the coast, and then to Cape Town. In 1977–78 he and a crew of 8 sailed to Antarctica in the yacht *Solo.* In 1981–82 he led the *Dick Smith Explorer* expedition to Cape Denison to compare notes with Mawson's old expedition, the AAE 1911–14. In 1982–84 he was back as leader of the Frozen Sea Expedition. He was then in his mid-60s. (*See* the Bibliography, Chronology, and *Ice Bird.*)

**Lewis, James B.** Passed midshipman on the Wilkes Expedition 1838–42. He joined the *Flying Fish* at Fiji, transferred to the *Peacock,* and left sick from Oahu to return home.

**Lewis, John H.** RAF squadron leader who led the air back-up for Fuchs' Antarctic crossing during the BCTAE 1956–58.

**Lewis, Peter.** Ordinary seaman on the Wilkes Expedition 1838–42. Joined at Rio. Served the cruise.

**Lewis, Thomas.** Gunner on the Wilkes Expedition 1838–42.

**Lewis Bay.** 77°22′S, 167°35′E. Indents the north coast of Ross Island between Mount Bird and Cape Tennyson. It is the island's biggest bay. Charted by Scott's 1901–4 expedition. Named by the US in 1964 for Capt. Price Lewis, USN, captain of the *Staten Island* in 1959. In 1963 and 1964 Lewis was assistant chief of staff and ship group commander, US Naval Support Force, Antarctica.

**Lewis Bluff.** 75°53'S, 140°36'W. At the confluence of Paschal Glacier and White Glacier, 7 miles SE of Mount McCoy, on the coast of Marie Byrd Land. Named for David L. Lewis, ionosphere physicist at Byrd Station, 1963.

**Lewis Chain.** 80°23'S, 26°50'W. Also called Mount Lewis. A chain of 4 rock nunataks on the west side of Gordon Glacier in the Shackleton Range. Named by the UK for John H. Lewis.

**Lewis Cliff.** 84°17'S, 161°05'E. 12 miles long. Extends south from Mount Achernar along the west side of the Walcott Névé. Named for Richard E. Lewis, aviation electronics technician, USN, injured during 1956–57.

**Lewis Glacier.** 67°45'S, 65°40'W. The northerly of two glaciers flowing east into Seligman Inlet, on the east coast of Graham Land. Charted in 1947 by the FIDS, who named it for William Vaughan Lewis, British glaciologist.

**¹Lewis Island.** 66°06'S, 134°22'E. 30 meters high. Marks the east side of the entrance to Davis Bay. Named for James B. Lewis.

**²Lewis Island** *see* **Tonkin Island**

**Lewis Nunatak.** 85°40'S, 88°05'W. Isolated. Mainly snow-covered. 10 miles SE of the Davies Escarpment and 14 miles SW of Nolan Pillar, at the south end of the Thiel Mountains. Named by Bermel & Ford, leaders of the US Geological Survey Thiel Mountains party here in 1960–61, for Charles R. Lewis, USGS geologist in the McMurdo Sound and Balaena Islands areas in 1955–56.

**Lewis Passage** *see* **Lewis Sound**

**Lewis Peaks.** 67°15'S, 67°30'W. Two peaks. 1,065 m. 3 miles east of Day Island. Surmounts the west part of Arrowsmith Peninsula, on the west coast of Graham Land. Surveyed in 1909 by Charcot, and again in 1948 by the FIDS. They

named it for Flight Lt. John Lewis, pilot of the Auster aircraft used from the *John Biscoe* for reconnaissance of ice conditions in Marguerite Bay in Feb. 1950.

**Lewis Point.** 69°54'S, 62°25'W. Surmounted by an ice-covered dome. 510 m. At the south side of the mouth of Anthony Glacier, on the east coast of Palmer Land. Charted by the RARE and the FIDS in 1947–48. Named by Ronne for Colonel Richard L. Lewis of the Army Quartermaster Corps, which gave field equipment and clothing to the RARE for testing.

**Lewis Ridge.** 83°13'S, 167°35'E. 14 miles long. Ice-covered. Extends eastward from the Holland Range, between Morton and Hewitt Glaciers, and terminates at Richards Inlet at the Ross Ice Shelf. Named for Cdr. G.H. Lewis, USN, captain of the *Burton Island* in 1964.

**Lewis Rocks.** 76°18'S, 145°21'W. 3 miles in extent. At the SW foot of Mount June in the Phillips Mountains of Marie Byrd Land. Named for John H. Lewis, geologist with the Fosdick Mountains party here in 1967–68.

**Lewis Snowfield.** 71°25'S, 71°20'W. In southern Alexander Island. It extends westward from the Walton Mountains to Beethoven Peninsula, and northward from Bach Ice Shelf to Wilkins Ice Shelf. Named by the UK for Ernest G. Lewis, governor of the Falklands, 1971–74.

**Lewis Sound.** 66°20'S, 67°W. Formerly called Lewis Passage. In the Biscoe Islands, it separates Lavoisier, Krogh, and DuBois Islands from Watkins Island and the Adolph Islands. Named by the UK for Sir Thomas Lewis (1882–1945), British physiologist specializing in the skin's reaction to temperature.

**Lewis Spur.** 82°34'S, 52°13'W. 1½ miles west of Frost Spur on the north side of Dufek Massif in the Pensacola Mountains. Named for Atles F. Lewis, aviation structural mechanic at Ellsworth Station, 1957.

**Lewisohn, Walter P.** One of the shore party on Byrd's 1933–35 expedition. He was the radio operator.

**Lewisohn Nunatak.** 77°38′S, 142°50′ W. Isolated. 10 miles SE of the Mackay Mountains in the Ford Ranges of Marie Byrd Land. Discovered by the USAS 1939–41. Named for Walter P. Lewisohn.

**Lewiston, William A.** Took over as military leader of McMurdo Base from E.E. Ludeman for the winter of 1959.

**Lewthwaite Strait.** 60°42′S, 45°07′W. Also called Spencers Straits. A marine passage 2½ miles wide, between Coronation Island and Powell Island in the South Orkneys. Discovered by Powell and Palmer on Dec. 9, 1821, and named by Powell for London teacher of navigation, Mr. Lewthwaite, with whom Powell left his chart and journal of the Antarctic waters.

**Lexington Table.** 83°05′S, 49°45′W. A high, flat, snow-covered plateau. 15 miles long and 10 miles wide. Just north of Kent Gap and Saratoga Table in the Forrestal Range of the Pensacola Mountains. Discovered aerially on Jan. 13, 1956 (*see* the Chronology). Named for the early US aircraft carrier, the *Lexington* (never in Antarctica).

**Lhasa Nunatak.** 85°07′S, 171°18′E. 9 miles long. Between Snakeskin Glacier and Jensen Glacier, to the east of the Supporters Range. Named by the New Zealanders in 1961–62 for its resemblance to a Tibetan monastery perched on top of a hill.

**Liard Island.** 66°51′S, 67°25′W. 13 miles long. 6 miles wide. Mountainous. Rises to 1,000 m. In the north-central part of Hanusse Bay, off the west coast of Graham Land. Discovered and named by Charcot in 1908–10.

**Mount Liavaag.** 77°22′S, 86°29′W. 1,820 m. Between Mount Holmboe and the Holth Peaks near the north end of the Sentinel Range. Discovered aerially by Ellsworth on Nov. 23, 1935. Named for Liavaag.

**Liavaag.** Norwegian whaling officer. 2nd mate on the *Wyatt Earp* during Ellsworth's first expedition of 1933–34, and during his second expedition of 1934–35. He was first mate on the same ship during Ellsworth's 1935–36 expedition and during the later 1938–39 expedition to the American Highland. On Jan. 15, 1939, he and two other men were standing on a bergy bit when the ice broke. They had been chipping at the bit for water, and they fell in. Liavaag got his knee crushed between two pieces of ice, and Ellsworth cancelled the expedition immediately and quickly sailed to Hobart Town.

**Islotes Libertad** *see* **Wideopen Islands**

**Libertador Refugio.** Argentine refuge hut built on Persson Island in 1955 by Esperanza Station personnel.

**The *Liberty*.** British sealer from Newcastle which sailed in company with the *Mellona* in the South Shetlands, 1821–22. Anchored at Clothier Harbor for most of the season. Captain Peacock commanding.

**Liberty Hills.** 80°06′S, 82°58′W. 10 miles in extent. 7 miles NW of Marble Hills. They form part of the west wall of Horseshoe Valley in the Heritage Range. Named in association with the Heritage motif.

**Liberty Rocks.** 62°19′S, 59°27′W. SE of Mellona Rocks in Nelson Strait in the South Shetlands. Named by the UK in 1961 for the *Liberty*.

**Libois, F.** Engineer / second mechanic / carpenter on the *Français* during Charcot's first expedition of 1903–5.

**Libois Bay.** 65°04′S, 64°03′W. On the west side of Cholet Island. Between Rozo Point, on the NW end of the island, and Paumelle Point on the NW end of Booth Island, in the Wilhelm Archipelago. Charted by Charcot in 1903–5 and named by him for F. Libois.

**Lice.** There are two types in Antarctica: *Mallophaga*, or biting lice (37 species), and *Anoplura*, or sucking lice. They are parasitic on seals and birds (*see also* **Fauna**).

**Lichen Hills.** 73°18′S, 162°E. 2 miles south of the Caudal Hills on the west edge of the upper part of the Rennick Glacier in Victoria Land. Named by the New Zealanders in 1962–63 for the lichens collected here.

**¹Lichen Island.** 69°20′S, 75°32′E. 5 miles north of the Bølingen Islands, and 2½ miles NW of Cleft Island in the southern part of Prydz Bay. First visited on Feb. 5, 1955, by an ANARE party led by Phillip Law. Named by Law for the abundance of lichens here.

**²Lichen Island** *see* Vegetation Island

**Lichen Peak.** 76°56′S, 145°24′W. Also called Botany Peak. Between Saunders Mountain and the Swanson Mountains in the Ford Ranges of Marie Byrd Land. Discovered in Dec. 1934 by Paul Siple's sledge party during Byrd's 1933–35 expedition, and named by Siple for the lichens found here.

**Lichens.** Symbiotic associations of algae and fungi. There are about 350 species of lichens in the Antarctic (*see also* **Flora, Mosses, Liverworts**). They grow preferentially on dark-colored, heat-absorbing rock (this was proved by Byrd's 1933–35 expedition). They are slow-growing and photosynthesize immediately, being particularly well-suited to survival in the extreme cold. Bright orange lichens growing on cliffs in the South Shetlands are visible for several miles. William Napier brought back several specimens of one he found in the South Shetlands in 1820–21. On Jan. 18, 1895, the crew of the *Antarctic* discovered the first lichens within the Antarctic Circle.

**Lie Cliff.** 76°42′S, 117°37′W. At the eastern foot of Mount Steere in the Crary Mountains. Named for Hans P. Lie, ionosphere physicist at Siple Station in 1970–71 and 1973–74.

**Liebig Peak.** 66°46′S, 66°W. On Protector Heights, Graham Land. Named by the UK for Justus von Liebig (1803–1873), German pioneer of physiological chemistry.

**Liebknecht Range.** 71°48′S, 11°22′E. 10 miles long. Forms the SW arm of the Humboldt Mountains in Queen Maud Land. Discovered aerially by Ritscher in 1938–39. Named by the USSR in 1966 for Karl Liebknecht (1871–1919), a German revolutionary.

**Mount Lied.** 70°30′S, 65°33′E. Pyramidal. 7 miles ENE of Mount Mervyn in the Porthos Range of the Prince Charles Mountains. Discovered in 1956 by an ANARE party led by W.G. Bewsher, and named by the Australians for Nils T. Lied (*see* Lied Bluff).

**Lied Bluff.** 68°31′S, 78°16′E. 125 m. A rocky hill 1½ miles north of Club Lake in the north-central part of Breidnes Peninsula in the Vestfold Hills. 125 m. Its southern face is almost perpendicular. Photographed by the LCE 1936–37. First visited in 1958 by an ANARE sledge party led by Bruce Stinear. Named by the Australians for Nils T. Lied, weather observer at Mawson Station in 1956. In 1962 Lied was back at Mawson Station, and just for fun, made the world's longest ever golf drive—across the ice. The ball traveled for 2,640 yards (1½ miles). Lied was at Davis Station in 1957, and these Antarctic stays were sandwiched in between a long ANARE career in the sub–Antarctic islands, from 1951–63.

**Liège Island.** 64°02′S, 61°55′W. Also called Lüttich Island. 9 miles long. 3 miles wide. Just NE of Brabant Island, in the Palmer Archipelago. It is one of the major islands in that chain. Charted by de Gerlache in 1898, and named by him for the Belgian province.

**The *Lientur*.** Chilean oil tanker which took part in the following expeditions undertaken by that country: 1949–50 (Capt. Victor Wilson); 1950–51; 1951–52; 1952–53 (Capt. Luís Mansilla); 1953–54 (Capt. Mario Mutis); 1955–56; 1956–57 (Capt. Jorge Thornton). During 1961–62 it helped transport the University of Wisconsin field party under Martin Halpern which studied the Duroch Islands. Captain that year was Marcos Ortiz.

Isla Lientur  *see*  Enterprise Island

Lientur Channel. 64°50'S, 63°W. Also called Canal Argentino, Brazo Norte, Bryde Channel. Between Lemaire and Bryde Islands. It connects Paradise Harbor with Gerlache Strait, off the west coast of Graham Land. Charted by de Gerlache in 1897–99. Named by the Chilean Antarctic Expedition of 1949–50 for the *Lientur*.

Lieske Glacier. 85°05'S, 156°50'E. Flows from the northern slopes of Mount Olympus in the Britannia Range, then between Johnstone and Dusky Ridges, into Hatherton Glacier. Named for Bruce J. Lieske, meteorologist at Little America in 1957.

Cape Light  *see*  Cape Fiske

Mount Light. 74°16'S, 61°59'W. On the south side of Barcus Glacier, 6 miles ESE of Mount Nash in the Hutton Mountains of Palmer Land. Named by Finn Ronne in 1948 for Richard Upjohn Light, president of the American Geographical Society.

Light Lake. 60°42'S, 45°39'W. A small lake 350 yards east of Thulla Point in the western part of Signy Island in the South Orkneys. Named by the UK for Jeremy J. Light, BAS limnologist and leader at Signy Island Station in 1970–72.

Lightfoot, Henry. Midshipman on the *Adventure* during Cook's voyage of 1772–75.

Lighthouses. The first Argentine lighthouse in the Antarctic was called Primero de Mayo and was erected on Lambda Island in 1942.

Lilienthal Glacier. 64°21'S, 60°48'W. Flows into Cayley Glacier between Pilcher and Baldwin Peaks, on the west coast of Graham Land. Named by the UK in 1960 for Otto Lilienthal (1848–1896), the German aeronautics pioneer.

Lilienthal Island. 66°12'S, 110°23'E. One of the Donovan Islands. Just north of Glasgal Island, in Vincennes Bay. Named by Carl Eklund in 1957 for Billie R. Lilienthal, USN, aerologist at Wilkes Station that year.

Liljequist, Gösta H. Swedish meteorologist on the NBSAE 1949–52.

Liljequist Heights. 72°06'S, 2°48'W. 2 miles south of Grunehogna Peaks, on the Ahlmann Ridge of Queen Maud Land. Named by the Norwegians for Gösta H. Liljequist.

Lillie, Dennis G. British biologist on Scott's last expedition, 1910–13.

Lillie Glacier. 70°45'S, 163°55'E. 100 miles long. 10 miles wide. Between the Bowers Mountains on the west, and the Concord and Anare Mountains on the east. Flows to the coast at Ob' Bay, and forms the Lillie Glacier Tongue, which was discovered during Scott's 1910–13 expedition and named by them for Dennis G. Lillie. Subsequently the whole glacier took the name in association with the tongue.

Lillie Glacier Tongue. 70°34'S, 163°48'E. Also called Lillie Ice Tongue. The seaward extension of the Lillie Glacier into Ob' Bay. Discovered in Feb. 1911 by Capt. Harry Pennell in the *Terra Nova,* and named by him for Dennis G. Lillie of Scott's expedition in McMurdo Sound.

Lillie Ice Tongue  *see*  Lillie Glacier Tongue

Lillie Range. 84°50'S, 170°25'W. Extends northward from the Prince Olav Mountains to the Ross Ice Shelf. Named by the New Zealanders in 1963–64 for A.R. Lillie, professor of geology at the University of Auckland.

Lilliput Nunataks. 66°08'S, 62°40'W. 3 nunataks. From 600 to 700 m. 3 miles north of Gulliver Nunatak on the east side of Graham Land. Named by the UK for the land in *Gulliver's Travels.*

Mount Limburg Stirum. 72°34'S, 31°19'E. 2,350 m. On the north side of Polarinstitutt Glacier, and 1 mile north of Mount Boë in the Belgica Mountains. Discovered by the Belgian Antarctic Expedition of 1957–58, under Gaston de Gerlache, who named it for Count Charles de Limburg Stirum, a patron.

Limestone Valley. 60°42'S, 45°37'W. Extends north from Cemetery Bay on

Signy Island in the South Orkneys. Leads directly to Jane Col, and serves as a route to the west coast of the island. Named by the UK because of the limestone exposure in the cliff above the valley.

**Limit Rock.** 61°54'S, 57°39'W. 2 miles east of North Foreland, the NE cape of King George Island, in the South Shetlands. Charted by personnel on the *Discovery II* in 1937, and named by them because it marks the eastern limit of the foul ground surrounding North Foreland.

**Limitrophe Island.** 64°48'S, 64°01'W. Oval-shaped. ½ mile long. Directly east of Christine Island and 1 mile south of Anvers Island. Named by personnel at nearby Palmer Station in 1972 because it lies near the limit of the usual operation carried out from that station.

**Limont, Joseph.** Seaman on the Wilkes Expedition 1838–42. Joined in the USA. Served the cruise.

**Limpet Island.** 67°38'S, 68°18'W. The most southerly of the Léonie Islands, in the entrance to Ryder Bay, just off the SE coast of Adelaide Island. Surveyed in 1948 by the FIDS, and named by them for the large number of limpet shells found here.

**Limpets.** *Patinigera polaris.* Marine gastropods, snails with flattened shells, found in the Antarctic.

**Linck Nunataks.** 82°41'S, 104°12'W. Four small, ice-covered nunataks at the SE end of the Whitmore Mountains. 3 of them are aligned and together, and the fourth lies 2½ miles away. Surveyed by the Horlick Mountains Traverse Party on Jan. 2, 1959. Named by the party surveyor, William H. Chapman, for M. Kerwin Linck, chief of the Branch of Special Maps at the US Geological Survey.

**Mount Lincoln Ellsworth** *see* **Mount Ellsworth**

**Lincoln Nunatak.** 67°27'S, 68°43'W. Snow-capped. It has a rocky west face. It is at the end of a ridge running westward from Mount Mangin on Adelaide Island.

Named by the UK for Flight Lt. Warren D. Lincoln, RAF, pilot with the BAS Aviation Unit stationed at Base T in 1962–63.

**Punta Lincoyan** *see* **Cape Rey**

**Lind Glacier.** 65°23'S, 64°01'W. Flows from Alencar Peak into the south part of Collins Bay, on the west coast of Graham Land. Charted by Charcot in 1908–10. Named by the UK in 1959 for James Lind (1716–1794), Scottish founder of modern naval hygiene, and pioneer in the fight against scurvy.

**Lind Ridge.** 75°48'S, 132°33'W. Forms the south wall of Coleman Glacier in the Ames Range of Marie Byrd Land. Named for Larry W. Lind, glaciologist at Byrd Station, 1968–69.

**The *Lindblad Explorer*.** Lindblad Travel's ship for 18 years, from 1969–70 until 1987–88. Launched in 1969, it weighed 2,300 tons. Captain Hasse Nilsson.

**Lindblad Travel, Inc.** 1 Sylvan Road North, Westport, Conn., 06881, USA. Or PO Box 912, Westport, Conn., 06881. Tel: (203) 226-8531, or toll-free (800) 243-5657. The president is Lars Eric Lindblad, an Antarctic veteran who came to the USA from Sweden in the early 1950s, and formed his company in 1965 after his first trip to the great white continent with a group that year. A member of the US Tour Operators Association, Lindblad claims to be 37 percent cheaper than any other Antarctic cruising expeditions. There are two tours to choose from, a 16-day and an 18-day, and the prices range from US $3,750 to $10,500 per person (depending on several things). It is cheaper for Intrepids Club Members, the club being formed by Lindblad to offer repeat company travelers special advantages (there are now over 3,000 intrepids). In 1987–88 Lindblad offered 3 tours, but more expensive, ranging from US $5,100 to 24,450, but these were 27-day, 18-day, or 24-day. Included in the price are accommodations, meals (as specified), hotel service charges, taxes and landing fees, sightseeing, shore excursions and landings, visas, transfers, porterage, and lectures by the experts accompanying the tours. Air fare is extra, as are tips. Schedules are subject to weather, politics, etc., and are dictated by el capitán. Like Society Expeditions Cruises and the others (except Mountain Travel, Adventure Network, and maybe a few more), Lindblad, at this stage, offers only a taste of Antarctica, so one cannot expect to follow in the footsteps of Scott and Amundsen (but in fact will be well looked after in comfort). The actual number of days spent south of 60°S are 4, 5, 6, or 7, and you can expect to visit such places as Hope Bay, Paulet Island, Fildes Peninsula, Cuverville Island, Paradise Bay, Port Lockroy, Lemaire Channel, Peltier Island, Argentine Islands, Palmer Station, Deception Island, Arctowski Station, Bellingshausen Station, Nelson Island, Petermann Island, Halfmoon Island, and Greenwich Island—in other words the South Shetlands and Graham Land. In 1968 Lindblad used the *Navarino* (Peter Scott was tour leader). In 1969 the *Aquiles* was used and then from 1969–87 the *Lindblad Explorer* was Lindblad's ship. In 1987–88 they used the *Illiria*, and then in 1988–89 they acquired the *Antonina Nezhdanova*.

**Lindenberg Island.** 64°55′S, 59°40′W. Also called Lindenberg's Sugar-Loaf. Circular. ½ mile across. 11 miles north of Robertson Island, and 35 miles ENE of Cape Fairweather, off the eastern coast of the Antarctic Peninsula. Discovered in Dec. 1893 by Carl Anton Larsen, and named by him for a member of the company of Woltereck and Robertson of Hamburg, which sent Larsen to the Antarctic.

**Lindenberg's Sugar-Loaf** *see* **Lindenberg Island**

**Linder Glacier.** 71°41′S, 163°03′E. Flows from the southern slopes of Mount Bernstein into Hunter Glacier in the Lanterman Range of the Bowers Mountains. Named for Lt. (jg) Michael A.

Linder, USNR, communications and administrative officer at McMurdo Station, 1967.

**Linder Peak.** 79°52′S, 83°12′W. Just south of Mount Dolence in the Heritage Range. Named for Harold W. Linder, geophysicist with the USARP Ross Ice Shelf party, 1961–62.

**Mount Lindley.** 81°46′S, 159°05′E. 1,760 m. On the west side of Starshot Glacier. 4 miles north of Mount Hoskins. Discovered by Scott's 1901–4 expedition, and named by them for Lord Nathaniel Lindley, a member of the committee which made the final draft of instructions for the expedition.

**Lindley, G.P.** Crewman on the *Jacob Ruppert*, 1933–34.

**Lindqvist Nunatak.** 80°39′S, 20°38′W. In the eastern Shackleton Range.

**Cape Lindsay** *see* **Cape Lindsey**

**Lindsay, Kay L.** Australian entomologist at Ohio State University, wife of Antarctic geologist John Lindsay. She was one of Lois Jones' all-women research team of 1969–70. This party (along with some other women—*see* **Women in Antarctica**) flew to the South Pole on Nov. 11, 1969, and became the first women to set foot at 90°S (*see also* **Lindsay Peak**).

**Lindsay Nunatak** *see* **Syningen Nunatak**

**Lindsay Peak.** 84°37′S, 163°32′E. 3,210 m. Basaltic. 4 miles WNW of Blizzard Peak in the Marshall Mountains. Named by the Ohio State University party to the Queen Alexandra Range in 1966–67, for John Lindsay, geologist with the party (*see also* **Kay L. Lindsay**).

**Cape Lindsey.** 61°06′S, 55°29′W. Also spelled (erroneously) as Cape Lindsay. Forms the western extremity of Elephant Island in the South Shetlands. Named before 1822.

**Lindsey, Alton A.** Biologist on the shore party of Byrd's 1933–35 expedition.

**Lindsey Islands.** 73°37′S, 103°18′W. Just off the NW tip of Canisteo Peninsula in the Amundsen Sea. Named for Alton A. Lindsey.

**Lindstrøm, Adolf Henrik.** Cook on the Norwegian Antarctic Expedition of 1910–12, one of the shore party under Amundsen. He had already been to the Arctic with Amundsen.

**Lindstrøm Peak.** 86°18′S, 160°10′W. 2,640 m. 2 miles NW of Mount Kristensen on the west side of the Nilsen Plateau in the Queen Maud Mountains. Named for Adolf Henrik Lindstrøm. Somewhere near here, Amundsen named a mountain as Mount A. Lindström. That was in 1911, when he was racing for the Pole, and the actual peak he had in mind is now not identifiable.

**Line Glacier.** 72°59′S, 167°50′E. Flows from the southern part of the eastern slopes of Malta Plateau, then between Collins Peak and Mount Alberts into Borchgrevink Glacier, in Victoria Land. Named for Kenneth Line, traverse engineer with the USARP glaciological party at Roosevelt Island, 1967–68.

**Line Islands.** 67°56′S, 67°14′W. Between Horseshoe Island and Camp Point, off the west coast of Graham Land. Named by the UK in 1971 for the fact that the islands lie in a straight line.

**Linehan, Father Daniel J.** A priest / seismologist from Boston College who did scientific work on the *Atka* in 1954–55, and then again in the Ross Sea area during Operation Deep Freeze I (1955–56).

**Linehan Glacier.** 83°15′S, 162°41′E. 11 miles long. Flows from the Prince Andrew Plateau along the north side of Turnabout Ridge to enter Lowery Glacier. Named for Father Daniel Linehan.

**Lines, Peter.** Ordinary seaman on the Wilkes Expedition 1838–42. Joined in the USA. Served the cruise.

**Link Island.** 63°16′S, 57°56′W. At the northern edge of the Duroch Islands, 3 miles NW of Halpern Point in Graham Land. Named for David A. Link, field assistant with the University of Wisconsin (USARP) Geological Party here in 1960–61.

**Link Stack.** 65°36′S, 64°34′W. A rocky pillar at the NW end of Chavez Island, off the west coast of Graham Land. Charted by the BGLE in 1934–37. Named by the UK in 1959 because at this point the FIDS winter surveys from Base J were linked with the 1957–58 summer surveys done by the British Naval Hydrographic Survey Unit.

**Linn Mesa.** 73°32′S, 163°20′E. A small mesa 3 miles south of the Chisholm Hills in the Southern Cross Mountains of Victoria Land. Named for Paul E. Linn, USN, utilitiesman at McMurdo Station, 1963 and 1967.

**Linnaeus Terrace.** 77°36′S, 161°05′E. On the southern slopes of the Wright Valley. A scientific area of concentrated activity. It is SSSI #19.

**Linnormegget Hill.** 72°08′S, 14°27′E. 3 miles south of Linnormen Hills in the Payer Mountains of Queen Maud Land. Name means "the dragon's egg" in Norwegian.

**Linnormen Hills.** 72°04′S, 14°33′E. Just east of Skavlhø Mountain in the Payer Mountains of Queen Maud Land. Name means "the dragon" in Norwegian.

**Linsley Peninsula.** 72°03′S, 98°11′W. Ice-covered. Juts out into the southern part of Murphy Inlet, in northern Thurston Island. It divides the inlet into two arms at the head. Named for Lt. Cdr. Richard G. Linsley, USN, Hercules pilot here in 1968–69.

**Linthicum, Francis.** Coxswain on the Wilkes Expedition 1838–42. Joined in the USA. Discharged at Oahu, Oct. 31, 1840.

**Linton-Smith Nunataks.** 70°17′S, 72°45′E. Between Jennings Promontory and Reinbolt Hills on the east side of the Amery Ice Shelf. Named by the Australians for N. Linton-Smith, senior technical officer with the Antarctic Division in Melbourne. He was a member of the

ANARE Amery Ice Shelf glaciological traverse of 1970.

**Linwood Peak.** 77°36'S, 147°13'W. Isolated. On the Hershey Ridge. 14 miles west of Mount Ronne in the Ford Ranges of Marie Byrd Land. Discovered by the USAS 1939–41. Named for Linwood T. Miller.

**The *Lion*.** US whaler/sealer from Mystic, Conn., which, in 1852–53, in company with the *Aeronaut,* was in the South Shetlands, under Capt. Clark. The following season, 1853–54, it was back, this time with the *Aeronaut* and the *Wilmington,* but this time under Capt. G.H. Buckmaster. It was lost on the English Bank (not in the Antarctic) on March 22, 1854.

**¹Lion Island.** 64°41'S, 63°08'W. 1½ miles long. 1 mile wide. Off the east coast of Anvers Island. 1 mile NE of Cape Astrup on Wiencke Island. Discovered by de Gerlache, 1897–99. Named before 1927, it looks like a reclining lion when seen from the SW.

**²Lion Island.** 66°39'S, 140°01'E. 350 yards NNE of Pétrel Island in the Géologie Archipelago. Surveyed and named by the French in 1949–51 for the rock summit of the island, which looks like a lion's head.

**³Lion Island.** 76°51'S, 162°33'E. East of the mouth of Hunt Glacier in Granite Harbor, Victoria Land. Named by Scott's 1910–13 expedition.

**Lion Sound.** 64°40'S, 63°09'W. Small passage between Lion Island and the SE coast of Anvers Island in the Palmer Archipelago. Discovered by de Gerlache, 1897–99. Named before 1927 in association with Lion Island.

**Lions Rump.** 62°08'S, 58°07'W. Also called Cape Lion's Rump. Headland. It forms the western side of the entrance to King George Bay on King George Island in the South Shetlands. Charted and named descriptively by personnel on the *Discovery* in 1927.

**Cape Lion's Rump** *see* **Lions Rump**

**Mount Liotard.** 67°37'S, 68°34'W. Has an ice-covered peak. 2,225 m. Between Mount Gaudry and Mount Ditte in the southern part of Adelaide Island. Discovered and surveyed by Charcot in 1909. Resurveyed in 1948 by the FIDS, who named it for André Franck Liotard.

**Liotard, André Franck.** French explorer and scientist. He spent 1947–48 as an observer at FIDS bases in Antarctica. In 1948–49 he led the abortive French Polar Expedition of that year, but was back again in 1949–50, on the *Commandant Charcot.* He arrived on the coast of Adélie Land on Jan. 20, 1950, and set up Port-Martin Station. On Jan. 9, 1951, he was relieved by the team under Michel Barré.

**Liotard Glacier.** 66°37'S, 139°30'E. Also called Ebba Glacier. A channel glacier. 3 miles wide. 6 miles long. Flows from the continental ice and terminates in a small tongue about 4 miles west of Hélène Island. Named for André Franck Liotard by the USA.

**Liouville, J.** Assistant medical officer and zoologist on the *Pourquoi Pas?* during Charcot's expedition of 1908–10. Later he became director-in-chief at the Institute of Science.

**Liouville Point.** 65°10'S, 64°09'W. Marks the NE end of Petermann Island in the Wilhelm Archipelago. Discovered in 1908–10 by Charcot who named it for J. Liouville.

**Lippert Peak.** 79°59'S, 81°56'W. At the end of a ridge which extends west from Douglas Peaks into Horseshoe Valley. 5 miles SE of Strong Peak in the Heritage Range. Named for George E. Lippert, biologist at Palmer Station in 1965.

**Lippmann Islands.** 65°30'S, 64°26'W. 2 miles in extent. Just NW of Lahille Island off the west coast of Graham Land. In 1903–5 Charcot mapped it as a single island, and he called it Lippmann Islet, for Gabriel Lippmann, the Nobel Prize-winning French physicist. The name was later extended to include the entire group.

**Lippman Islet** *see* **Lippmann Islands**

**Lipps Island.** 64°46'S, 64°07'W. 350 yards west of Litchfield Island, off the SW coast of Anvers Island. Named for Jere H. Lipps, who studied benthic foraminifera here in 1971–74.

**Mount Liptak.** 78°45'S, 84°54'W. Over 3,000 m. Has twin summits. 7 miles SE of Mount Craddock in the Sentinel Range. Named for L.H. Liptak, aviation machinist's mate, USN, who was plane captain on the first reconnaissance flights to this area in Jan. 1958.

**Mount Lira.** 67°52'S, 48°53'W. 5 miles east of Condon Hills, in Enderby Land. Named Gora Lira (lyre mountain) by the USSR in 1961–62. The name is descriptive of the shape.

**Lisboa Island.** 65°11'S, 64°11'W. The most southwesterly of the small islands off the south end of Petermann Island in the Wilhelm Archipelago. Discovered and named by Charcot in 1908–10.

**Lishness Peak.** 78°53'S, 84°45'W. 2,200 m. Near the south end of the Sentinel Range. At the east side of the Nimitz Glacier. 1 mile SE of Wilson Peak. Named for Alton R. Lishness, radio operator on a flight here on Jan. 28, 1958.

**Mount Lisicky.** 78°27'S, 162°05'E. 2,120 m. 7 miles NW of Mount Cocks in the Royal Society Range. Named in 1963 for Capt. Joseph F. Lisicky, US Marines maintenance officer at McMurdo Station in 1959–60 and several summers thereafter.

**Lisignoli Bluff.** 82°31'S, 42°41'W. 610 m. Forms the north end of Schneider Hills in the Argentina Range of the Pensacola Mountains. Named for Cesar Augusto Lisignoli, Argentine glaciologist and leader of Ellsworth Station in 1961.

**Mount Lister.** 78°04'S, 162°41'E. 4,025 m. The highest point in the Royal Society Range in Victoria Land. Discovered by Scott's 1901–4 expedition, and named by them for Joseph Lister, president of the Royal Society, 1895–1900 (*see also* **Lister Glacier**).

**Lister, Dr. Hal.** Glaciologist, one of the first to cross the Antarctic by land, during the BCTAE 1955–58. He was also in charge of South Ice in 1957.

**Lister Cove.** 62°30'S, 60°05'W. Between Williams Point and Edinburgh Hill on the NE coast of Livingston Island in the South Shetlands. Charted and named by Weddell in 1820–23.

**¹Lister Glacier.** 64°05'S, 62°19'W. 5 miles long. 1 mile wide. Flows into Bouquet Bay just south of Duclaux Point on the NE side of Brabant Island. Discovered before 1953. Named by the UK for Joseph Lister (1827–1912), the surgeon (*see also* **Mount Lister**).

**²Lister Glacier.** 77°59'S, 163°05'E. On the east side of the Royal Society Range. Flows NE from a large cirque just north of Mount Lister. Surveyed in 1957 by the NZ Blue Glacier Party of the BCTAE.

**Lister Heights.** 80°31'S, 28°35'W. On the east side of the Stratton Glacier. 4 miles SW of Flat Top in the western part of the Shackleton Range. Named in 1957 by the BCTAE for Hal Lister.

**Lister Nunataks.** 73°27'S, 160°32'E. Isolated. In the northern portion of the Priestley Névé. 15 miles SSW of Brawn Rocks, in Victoria Land. Named for Larry W. Lister, VX-6 helicopter flight crewman in Antarctica in 1966, 1967, and 1968.

**Liston Nunatak.** 70°54'S, 63°45'W. Just NW of Heintz Peak of the Welch Mountains of Palmer Land. Named for Cdr. John M. Liston, USN, operations officer for Antarctic Support Activities in 1969, and executive officer, 1970.

**Mount Liszt.** 71°27'S, 72°57'W. 250 m. Snow-covered. Between the heads of Brahms and Mendelssohn Inlets in the SW part of Alexander Island. Named by the UK for the composer.

**Mount Litchens.** Near the Cordiner Peaks.

**Litchfield, T.E.** 2nd assistant engineer on the *Bear of Oakland,* 1933–34, and 1st assistant engineer, 1934–35, during Byrd's 1933–35 expedition.

**Litchfield Island.** 64°46'S, 64°06'W. ½ mile long. 50 meters high. ½ mile south of Norsel Point, off the SW coast of Anvers Island. There are many birds here, and it is SPA #17. Surveyed by the FIDS in 1955, it was named by the UK for Douglas B. Litchfield of the FIDS, general assistant and mountain climber at Base N in 1955. He took part in the survey of the island that year.

**Litell Rocks.** 71°24'S, 162°E. Within the lower part of the Rennick Glacier, 5 miles east of the north end of the Morozumi Range. Named for Richard J. Litell, NSF public information officer, who was in the Antarctic for four summers between 1960 and 1964.

**The *Litke*.** USSR icebreaker during IGY (1957–58). Capt. K.A. Dublitskiy.

**Litke Nunatak.** 67°36'S, 51°40'E. 10 miles east of Perov Nunataks, at the eastern edge of the Scott Mountains in Enderby Land. Named by the USSR in 1961–62 for the *Litke.*

**Cape Little.** 74°05'S, 61°04'W. Also called Cape Easson. At the eastern extremity of the peninsula between Wright and Keller Inlets on the east coast of Palmer Land. Named by Finn Ronne in 1948 for Delbert M. Little, assistant chief for Operations, US Weather Bureau, who arranged the program for sending weather reports from the RARE in 1947–48.

**¹Mount Little.** 70°30'S, 65°16'E. Just north of Mount Mervyn in the Porthos Range of the Prince Charles Mountains. Named by the Australians for S.G. Little, electrical fitter–mechanic at Mawson Station in 1967 and technical assistant at Casey Station in 1969.

**²Mount Little.** 77°S, 143°51'E. Mostly ice-free. 3 miles SW of Mount Swan in the Ford Ranges of Marie Byrd Land. Named

by Admiral Byrd for Harold H. Little, captain, USN, who contributed to and assisted in Byrd's first two expeditions.

**Little America.** Or L.A.S. (Little America Station). There have been 5 separate Little Americas. Little Americas I, II, III, and IV were all roughly in the same place, near Kainan Bay, at the Bay of Whales, but in Jan. 1955 they were calved off into the sea by 2 enormous icebergs. Little America V was built further to the west.

**Little America I.** 78°34'S, 163°48'W. This was the first Little America, built by Byrd as base camp for his 1928–30 expedition. It was finished in Jan. 1929, and closed after the expedition came to an end, on Feb. 19, 1930. Naturally, this was called simply Little America. Each man had an individual room, there was a mess hall, a gym, a blacksmith's forge, an administrative room, a garage for the tractor, and a hangar for the planes. It had 60-foot-high antennas. **Little America II.** Built over Little America I, this was the base camp for Byrd's 1933–35 expedition. Finished in Feb. 1934, it was bigger and better than the first one. It had electric light and power, broadcasting and field communications, aviation service, 3 planes, an autogiro, four tractors, machine shops, a meteorological station, a lab and scientific staff for 22 branches of science, a dairy plant with 4 head of cattle, medical facilities, galley, library, a meteor observatory, sound motion picture theater, and almost 150 dogs. The radio towers were still visible above the snow in 1947. **Little America III.** Also called West Base, this was one of the two bases for the United States Antarctic Service Expedition 1939– 41 (known as USAS). This site was selected by Paul Siple under the general directions of Admiral Byrd, and set up 7 miles to the NE of the previous Little Americas, at the Bay of Whales, just south of Eleanor Bolling Bight. By March 6, 1940, construction had finished. There were 3 main buildings under one roof, all the buildings being connected by snow tunnels. **Little America IV.**

2½ miles north of Little America III, this was set up on the shore of the Bay of Whales, as the headquarters for Operation Highjump, 1946–47. The site was selected on Jan. 6, 1947, by Campbell and Siple, 1½ miles from the ships bringing the expedition to the Antarctic. Construction began on Jan. 17, 1947, by the Seabees led by Cdr. Reinhardt, all under the directions of Admiral Byrd. It was a temporary tent city, with 54 main tents, several other smaller ones, and an airstrip. 197 men wintered-over. **Little America V.** 78°11′S, 162°10′W. Set up several miles to the NE of the previous sites, it was built in 1956 by Operation Deep Freeze for the IGY. Admiral Byrd directed the construction. It was the nerve center for all the US IGY bases from 1957–58, as well as being the home base for Byrd Station. The top American scientist of the IGY (Albert P. Crary) was here, as were all the military chiefs. It was the field scientific headquarters for the entire US-IGY program, and the headquarters of IGY Antarctic weather control (*see* **Weather Control**). It was the "Capital of Antarctica," an epithet soon taken over by McMurdo Station. Lt. Cdr. R.G. Graham led the first wintering-over party in 1956, and H.W. Whitney was the scientific leader. Lt. Cdr. James E. Waldron, Jr., relieved Graham for the summer of 1956–57, and he was relieved for the 1957 winter by Lt. Cdr. Howard J. Orndorff. Crary, in overall command of the scientific force for the US effort, was scientific leader that winter. On Nov. 28, 1957, Lt. Cdr. T.N. Thompson relieved Orndorff as military leader. The station was not used during the 1959 winter, the headquarters for the Operation Deep Freeze expeditions in subsequent years being transferred to McMurdo Station.

**Little Jeana Weather Station.** A Ross Ice Shelf weather station operated by the USA. Now defunct.

**Little Razorback Island.** 77°40′S, 166°31′E. Also called Razorback Island, Small Razorback Island. Smallest and most

easterly of the Dellbridge Islands in Erebus Bay, off the west side of Ross Island, in McMurdo Sound. Discovered during the Royal Society Expedition of 1901–4, and named by Scott in association with Big Razorback Island.

**Little Rockford Station.** Also known as NAAF Little Rockford. A US camp, rather than a proper station, in Marie Byrd Land. There were 4 wanigans and a radome protecting its weather radar. Six men wintered-over in 1960–61, led by Joseph Nemeth.

**Little Thumb.** 68°19′S, 66°53′W. Also called Thumb, Neny Fjord Thumb. Small, isolated rock tower. 825 m. On the south side of Neny Fjord. Just south of The Spire at the NW end of the Blackwall Mountains on the west coast of Graham Land. Surveyed in 1936 by the BGLE. Climbed Jan. 22, 1948, by the FIDS and by the RARE. Various names referring to the male member are also commonly used for this geographical feature.

**Littleblack Nunataks.** 81°35′S, 156°20′E. A group of about 12 black nunataks at the SE side of the Byrd Névé. It is a scattered group and lies 4 miles SE of All-Blacks Nunataks and 15 miles SW of Mount Nares of the Churchill Mountains. Charted and named descriptively by the New Zealanders in 1960–61.

**Mount Littlepage.** 77°12′S, 160°03′E. Over 2,000 m. Between Mount DeWitt and Mount Dearborn, just west of the north end of the Willett Range in Victoria Land. Named for Jack L. Littlepage, biologist at McMurdo Station in 1959–60, 1961, and 1961–62.

**Littlespace Island** *see* **Sucia Island**

**Littlewood Nunataks.** 77°53′S, 34°10′W. 4 nunataks. Lichen-covered. Each is 50 yards in width. Between Schweitzer and Lerchenfeld Glaciers. They are brick-red in color. Filchner discovered and charted them in 1911–12. On Jan. 28, 1959, John C. Behrendt of the US Geological Survey visited them and named them for William H. Littlewood, an oceanographer with the US Navy Hydrographic Office, who worked in the Weddell Sea area in 1957 and 1959.

**Littleyear, Lawrence.** Private of marines on the Wilkes Expedition 1838–42. Joined in the US. Sent home on the *Relief* in 1839.

**Litvillingane Rocks.** 71°52′S, 1°44′W. Two isolated nunataks. The eastern one has a small outlier. 3 miles south of Bolten Peak, on the east side of the Ahlmann Ridge in Queen Maud Land. Name means "the mountainside twins" in Norwegian.

**Liv Glacier.** 84°55′S, 168°W. A valley glacier. 40 miles long. Flows from the Polar Plateau, just south of Barnum Peak, through the Queen Maud Mountains, into the Ross Ice Shelf between the Mayer Crags and the Duncan Mountains. Discovered in 1911 by Amundsen on his way to the Pole, and he named it for the daughter of Fridtjof Nansen, the Norwegian Arctic explorer.

**Liv Glacier ANAF.** US Auxiliary Naval Air Facility at the foot of the Beardmore Glacier. This was the former Beardmore Glacier Camp which, in 1957 was moved to the Liv Glacier and renamed. Later it took back its original name.

**Livdebotnen Cirque.** 71°45′S, 11°21′E. In the NE side of Mount Flånuten and the west side of Botnfjellet Mountain, in the Humboldt Mountains of Queen Maud Land. Discovered by Ritscher's expedition of 1938–39. Name means "the shelter cirque" in Norwegian.

**The Lively.** The smaller vessel on Biscoe's voyage of 1830–32. It was a 46-ton cutter commanded on the way south by Capt. Smith. About Nov. 1830, at the Falklands, before the expedition hit Antarctic waters, Capt. Avery took over. It was wrecked in the Falklands on the homeward voyage from the Antarctic, in 1832, with its crew of 10.

**Cape Lively** *see* **Lively Point**

**Lively Point.** 65°52′S, 66°11′W. Also called Cape Lively. Forms the southern extremity of Renaud Island in the Biscoe Islands. Named by the UK in 1954 for the *Lively*.

**Liverpool Bay** *see* **Destruction Bay**

**Liverworts.** Small, creeping, mosslike plants of the class Hepatopsida which, along with mosses (q.v.), make up the Bryophytes (*see also* **Flora**), which total 100 or so of the 800 species of plants in Antarctica. They predominate in maritime areas.

**Living quarters.** Originally men lived on the ships themselves, and that could get tiresome. During the Heroic Era the explorers built crude huts, but by Byrd's time, more luxurious living quarters were the order of the day. Nowadays it is all modern conveniences. Men have lived on beaches, ice floes, ice shelves, islands, under boats, in ice caves, in tents, under the ice, in huts, wanigans, scientific stations, in fact most places.

**Livingston Island.** 62°36′S, 60°30′W. Also called Smiths Island, Smolensk Island. The largest of the South Shetlands, it lies between Greenwich and Snow Islands. 38 miles long and from 2 to 20 miles wide. It has two peaks on it, Mount Friesland and Rotch Dome, and the island itself was called Friesland by the early sealers.

**The Livonia.** British sealer from London, in the South Shetlands, 1820–21.

**Livonia Rock.** 62°02′S, 57°36′W. ½ mile south of Cape Melville, the eastern extremity of King George Island, in the South Shetlands. Named by the UK in 1960 for the *Livonia*.

**Lizard Hill.** 63°31′S, 57°01′W. A narrow, curving rock ridge of 355 meters in height. 2 miles SW of Trepassey Bay, and ½ mile east of Ridge Peak on Tabarin Peninsula. Charted in 1946 by the FIDS, who named it descriptively.

**Lizard Island.** 65°41′S, 64°27′W. 2 miles long. ½ mile wide. In the northern part of Bigo Bay on the west coast of

Graham Land. Discovered by the BGLE 1934–37 and named by Rymill for its shape.

**Lizard Point.** 84°48′S, 163°40′E. A low morainic point on the west side of the upper Beardmore Glacier. It marks the south side of the entrance to Table Bay. Named by Scott's 1910–13 expedition.

**Lizards Foot.** 77°13′S, 162°51′E. 570 m. A rocky spur forming the eastern end of the Saint Johns Range in Victoria Land. Charted and named descriptively by Scott's 1910–13 expedition.

**Mount Llano.** 84°48′S, 173°21′W. 1,930 m. In the foothills of the Prince Olav Mountains. 6 miles NE of Mount Wade. Discovered by the US Ross Ice Shelf Traverse of 1957–58 under Albert P. Crary, and named by him for George A. Llano, biologist often in Antarctica.

**Llanquihue Islands.** 65°53′S, 65°06′W. Also called the Straggle Islands. A group to the east of Larrouy Island. They extend northward for 9 miles from the west coast of Graham Land. Charted by the BGLE 1934–37. Named by the Chileans before 1947 for the Chilean province of the same name. The group includes Cat Island and Dog Island.

**Cape Lloyd.** 61°07′S, 54°01′W. Forms the north end of Clarence Island in the South Shetlands. Known originally as Lloyd's Promontory (between 1821 and 1825), and as Lloyds Cape.

**¹Mount Lloyd.** 83°13′S, 165°44′E. 3,210 m. In the Holland Range. North of the head of Hewitt Glacier. 7 miles north of Mount Miller. Discovered and named by Shackleton's 1907–9 expedition.

**²Mount Lloyd** *see* **Mount Humphrey Lloyd**

**Lloyd, William.** Captain of the topsail on the Wilkes Expedition 1838–42. Joined in the USA. Served the cruise.

**Lloyd Hill.** 62°30′S, 59°54′W. 335 m. SW of Mount Plymouth on Greenwich Island in the South Shetlands. Henry Foster in 1829 recorded the name Lloyd's Land for a feature in the area. This may

be an early alternative name for Greenwich Island, but in any case the UK in 1961 named this feature thus, in order to preserve this original naming.

**Lloyd Icefall.** 72°04′S, 165°27′E. At the head of Lillie Glacier. It flows from the Polar Plateau between the King and Millen Ranges. Named by the Northern Party of the New Zealand Federated Mountain Clubs Antarctic Expedition of 1962–63, for R. Lloyd, field assistant with the southern party of that expedition.

**Lloyds Cape** *see* **Cape Lloyd**

**Lloyds Island** *see* **Rugged Island**

**Lloyd's Land** *see* **Greenwich Island, Lloyd Hill**

**Lloyd's Promontory** *see* **Cape Lloyd**

**Loaf Rock.** 64°48′S, 63°55′W. 3 miles west of Biscoe Point, off the SW coast of Anvers Island. Named by the UK in 1958 for its shape like a flat loaf of bread.

**Lobel Island.** 64°59′S, 63°53′W. Also called Loïcq de Lobel Islands, Isla Johnston. Almost 1 mile long. 2 miles SW of Brown Island in the Wauwermans Islands in the Wilhelm Archipelago. Charted by Charcot in 1903–5 and named by him for Loïcq de Lobel, presumably a French friend.

**Lobell, Milton J.** Member of the USAS during its second phase, 1940–41.

**Lobodon Island.** 64°05′S, 61°35′W. Also called Islote Augusto, Islote Cordovez. 3½ miles east of Wauters Point on Two Hummock Island in the Palmer Archipelago. Named by the UK in 1960 for the crabeater seal *(Lobodon carcinophagus)*.

**Locator Island.** 65°11′S, 64°30′W. The highest of the Roca Islands. 350 yards north of the largest island in that group, in the Wilhelm Archipelago. Named by the UK for its use as a landmark when navigating French Passage.

**Mount Locke.** 71°24′S, 169°06′E. Snow-capped. 1,190 m. At the NE end of the DuBridge Range in the Admiralty Mountains of Victoria Land. Named for

Lt. Cdr. Jerry L. Locke, USN, helicopter pilot with VX-6 in 1968.

**Mount Lockhart.** 76°28'S, 145°06'W. Juts out northward from the main massif of the Fosdick Mountains 4 miles NE of Mount Avers in the Ford Ranges of Marie Byrd Land. Discovered aerially on Dec. 5, 1929, by Byrd's 1928–30 expedition. Later named for Ernest E. Lockhart.

**Lockhart, Dr. Ernest E.** Physiologist and radio operator at West Base during the USAS 1939–41.

**Lockhart Ridge.** 85°02'S, 174°50'W. 4 miles long. It extends west along the south side of the Yeats Glacier, and terminates at the Shackleton Glacier. Named by the Texas Tech Shackleton Glacier Expedition of 1964–65 for CWO James J. Lockhart, pilot with the US Army Aviation Detachment which supported the expedition.

**Lockheed Mountains.** On the Antarctic Peninsula. Discovered Dec. 20, 1928, by Wilkins, who named them for his plane.

**Lockley, G.J.** Leader of the 1945 wintering party at Port Lockroy during the second phase of Operation Tabarin. He was the first FIDS leader of the same station in 1946. He was a biologist and meteorologist and a lieutenant with the RNVR.

**Lockley Point.** 64°47'S, 63°23'W. Ice-covered. 1 mile NE of Noble Peak on the NW side of Wiencke Island. Discovered by de Gerlache in 1898. Rediscovered and charted by the personnel on Operation Tabarin in 1944, and later named by the FIDS for G.J. Lockley.

**Port Lockroy.** 64°49'S, 63°30'W. A harbor ½ mile long and wide. Between Flag Point and Lécuyer Point on the west side of Wiencke Island. Discovered by Charcot on Feb. 19, 1904, and named by him for Édouard Lockroy, French politician who helped get government support for Charcot's expedition. There is a British station here (*see under* P for **Port Lockroy Station**).

**Mount Lockwood.** 84°09'S, 167°24'E. 5 miles south of Mount Bell. It forms a part of the east face of Grindley Plateau in the Queen Alexandra Range. Discovered and named by Shackleton in 1908. Dr. C.B. Lockwood of Barts in London, was an old friend of Shackleton's companion, Marshall.

**Lockwood, F.** Seaman on the *City of New York* during Byrd's 1928–30 expedition.

**Cape Lockyer** *see* **Lockyer Island**

**Lockyer Island.** 64°27'S, 57°36'W. 2½ miles long. Off the south shore of James Ross Island, in the SW entrance to Admiralty Sound. Ross named it Cape Lockyer on Jan. 7, 1843. Crozier suggested the name to Ross. Capt. Nicholas Lockyer, RN, was a friend of Crozier's. In 1902 Nordenskjöld's expedition redefined it.

**Lodge Rock.** 68°41'S, 67°32'W. Snow-capped. Less than 30 meters high. Between Barn Rock and Hayrick Island in the Terra Firma Islands, off the west coast of Graham Land. Surveyed in 1948 by the FIDS, who named it for a ledge on this rock where they could drive their sledges safely.

**Mount Loewe.** 70°32'S, 67°43'E. The most northerly of the Amery Peaks. 1,130 m. 6 miles NE of Mount Seaton in the eastern Aramis Range of the Prince Charles Mountains. Discovered by W.G. Bewsher's ANARE party of 1956. Named by the Australians for Fritz Loewe.

**Loewe, Fritz.** Australian member of the 1947–48 ANARE party to the Antarctic on the *Wyatt Earp* (*see* **Australian National Antarctic Research Expeditions**). In 1951–52 he was at Port-Martin with the French, as an observer.

**Loewe Massif.** 70°34'S, 68°E. In the eastern part of the Aramis Range in the Prince Charles Mountains. The surface of the massif is a plateau, from which Mount Loewe and the Medvecky Peaks rise. The plateau is at an average elevation of 1,000 meters above sea level, and

600 meters above the ice on its northern flank. Discovered by W.G. Bewsher's ANARE party of 1956, and named in association with Mount Loewe.

**Lofgren, Charles E.** Personnel officer and member of the shore party of Byrd's 1928–30 expedition.

**Lofgren Peninsula.** 72°08′S, 96°W. Ice-covered. 22 miles long. Juts out between the Cadwalader and Morgan Inlets on the NE side of Thurston Island. Discovered on helicopter flights from the *Glacier* and *Burton Island* during the Bellingshausen Sea Expedition of Feb. 1960. Named for Charles E. Lofgren.

**Loftus Glacier.** 77°33′S, 162°46′E. A valley glacier between Mounts Weyant and McLennan. It flows into Newall Glacier in Victoria Land. Named in 1964 for Chief Journalist Leo G. Loftus, USN, who was at McMurdo Station every summer from 1959 to 1964.

**Logan, Bernard.** Ordinary seaman on the Wilkes Expedition of 1838–42. Joined in the USA. Returned home in the *Relief* in 1839.

**Logan Sprytes.** The most common medium-tracked vehicles in USARP. Navy-operated vehicles, they have an enclosed cargo area, but they are also used with a crew cab and flat bed. They have wide tracks to lower the vehicle's ground pressure.

**Logie Glacier.** 85°18′S, 175°20′W. 10 miles long. 2 miles wide. Flows through the Cumulus Hills into the Shackleton Glacier just NE of Vickers Nunatak. Named by the New Zealanders in 1961–62 for W.R. Logie, NZ field mechanic and maintenance officer who was deputy-leader of Scott Base, 1962–63.

**Loïcq de Lobel Islands** *see* **Lobel Island**

**Mount Loke.** 77°29′S, 162°33′E. A horn-shaped peak on the south wall of the Wright Valley. Between Goodspeed and Denton Glaciers in the Asgard Range of Victoria Land. Named by the New Zealanders for the Norse god.

**Lokehellene Cliffs.** 71°56′S, 8°47′E. They form the west side of Nupsskarvet Mountain in the Kurze Mountains of Queen Maud Land. Name means "the Loke slopes" in Norwegian, for the Norse god.

**Løken, Olav H.** Norwegian glaciologist at Wilkes Station, 1957.

**Løken Moraines.** 66°17′S, 110°37′E. A line of north-south trending moraines. 7 miles long. About a mile inland from the Windmill Islands, just east of the base of Clark, Bailey, and Mitchell Peninsulas. Named by Carl Eklund for Olav Løken.

**Lokey Peak.** 71°50′S, 64°06′W. A nunatak at the SE extremity of the Guthridge Nunataks, in the Gutenko Mountains of central Palmer Land. Named for William M. Lokey, manager of Palmer Station in 1975. He had previously been at McMurdo Station in 1970 and 1974.

**Cape Lola** *see* **Point Lola**

**Mount Lola.** 60°44′S, 44°43′W. 170 m. Surmounts Point Lola at the east side of the entrance to Uruguay Cove, on the north coast of Laurie Island in the South Orkneys. Named by the Argentines before 1930.

**Point Lola.** 60°44′S, 44°43′W. Also called Cape Lola. Forms the east side of the entrance to Uruguay Cove on the north coast of Laurie Island in the South Orkneys. Named by the Argentines before 1930.

**Mount Lombard.** 64°28′S, 59°38′W. Just north of Cape Sobral in Graham Land. It is the highest peak in the immediate area. Named by the UK for Alvin O. Lombard, US tractor pioneer.

**Lomonosov Mountains.** 71°31′S, 15°20′E. An isolated chain. Extends for 18 miles. 20 miles east of the Wohlthat Mountains in Queen Maud Land. Discovered aerially by Ritscher in 1938–39. Named by the USSR in 1961 for scientist M.V. Lomonosov.

[1]**Lone Rock.** 62°21′S, 58°50′W. Isolated. 1½ miles south of the east end of Nelson Island in the South Shetlands.

Charted and named descriptively by personnel on the *Discovery II* in 1935.

²**Lone Rock**   *see*   **Lonely Rock**

**Lonely One Nunatak.** 71°12'S, 161°18' E. 16 miles NW of the Morozumi Range, at the west side of the confluence of the Gressitt and Rennick Glaciers. Named by the New Zealanders in 1963–64 for its isolation.

**Lonely Rock.** 64°06'S, 57°03'W. Isolated. 50 yards long. 4 miles north of Cape Gage, James Ross Island, on the western edge of the Erebus and Terror Gulf. Charted by the FIDS in 1945, and named Lone Rock by the UK for its small size and completely isolated position. In 1963 its name was changed somewhat in order to avoid confusion with the entry above.

**Lonewolf Nunataks.** 81°20'S, 152°50' E. A group of isolated nunataks. 25 miles NW of Wilhoite Nunataks, at the south side of Byrd Névé. Named by the New Zealanders in 1960–61 for their isolation.

**Long, A.K.** Lt. Commander of the *Relief* during the Wilkes Expedition 1838–42.

**Long Fjord**   *see*   **Langnes Fjord**

**Long Gables.** 78°11'S, 86°14'W. Also called Mount Long Gables. Twin peaks (4,150 m. and 4,110 m.) joined by a col. On the main ridge of the Sentinel Range, between Mounts Anderson and Viets. Discovered by the Marie Byrd Land Traverse Party of 1957–58 under Charles R. Bentley, and named by him for Jack B. Long, a member of the party who came to the Antarctic many times to take part in traverses. First climbed on Jan. 12, 1967.

**Long Glacier.** 72°30'S, 96°47'W. 8 miles long. In the SE part of Thurston Island. It flows into the Abbott Ice Shelf, 14 miles west of Harrison Nunatak. Named for Fred A. Long, Jr., VX-6 aviation machinist at Little America in 1957, and elsewhere in Antarctica in 1960–61 and 1962–63.

**Long Hills.** 85°18'S, 118°45'W. 6 miles in extent. Between the Wisconsin and Ohio Ranges in the Horlick Mountains. Named for William E. Long, geologist with the Horlick Mountains Traverse of 1958–59. He was also a member of the Ohio State University expedition to the Horlick Mountains in 1960–61 and 1961–62.

**Long Island.** 63°46'S, 58°12'W. 3 miles long. ½ mile wide. Opposite the mouth of the Russell East Glacier and 2 miles south of Trinity Peninsula in the Prince Gustav Channel. Discovered and named descriptively by the FIDS in 1945.

**Long Peninsula**   *see*   **Langnes Peninsula**

**Long Rock.** 62°42'S, 61°11'W. In Morton Strait, 2 miles north of the east end of Snow Island, in the South Shetlands. Named descriptively by personnel on the *Discovery II* in 1930–31.

**Long Sound**   *see*   **Lang Sound**

**Long Valley.** 86°13'S, 147°48'W. 6 miles long. Ice-filled. Extends NW from Mount Blackburn as far as Griffith Glacier in the Queen Maud Mountains. Named for Walter H. Long, Jr., VX-6 photographer, 1966 and 1967.

**Punta Longavi**   *see*   **Cape Mascart**

**Longhorn Spurs.** 84°36'S, 174°45'W. A high ridge, 12 miles long, extending north from the Prince Olav Mountains between Massam and Barrett Glaciers to the edge of the Ross Ice Shelf. A series of rock spurs extends from the west side. Named by the Texas Tech Shackleton Glacier Expedition of 1964–65 for their resemblance to the horns of longhorn cattle.

**Mount Longhurst.** 79°26'S, 157°18'E. 2,845 m. West of Mill Mountain. Forms the highest point on Festive Plateau in the Cook Mountains. Discovered during Scott's 1901–4 expedition, and named by Scott for Cyril Longhurst, secretary of the expedition.

**Longhurst Plateau.** 79°23'S, 156°20'E. A narrow, snow-covered extension of the Polar Plateau, just west of Mount Longhurst. 2,200 m. 20 miles long. 10 miles wide. Bounded on the south by the upper Darwin Glacier. Bounded on the east by McCleary Glacier. Traversed by the Darwin Glacier Party of the BCTAE in 1957–58, and they named it for the nearby mountain.

**Cape Longing.** 64°33'S, 58°50'W. On the east coast of Graham Land. It forms the southern end of a large ice-covered promontory which marks the west side of the southern entrance to Prince Gustav Channel. Discovered by Nordenskjöld's expedition in 1902, and named by him because when he looked out of his hut on Snow Hill Island, this feature lay in the direction of his "land of longing," i.e., the land he wanted to explore, and so he called it Längstans Udde (Cape Longing).

**Longing Gap.** 64°25'S, 58°57'W. A low isthmus formed in the promontory north of Cape Longing in Graham Land. 2 miles wide. It is used to avoid the long detour around the cape. Named by the UK in association with the cape.

**Longley, William S.** Seaman on the Wilkes Expedition 1838–42. Joined in the USA. Served the cruise.

**Longridge Head.** 67°28'S, 67°40'W. A headland at the north side of Whistling Bay on Arrowsmith Peninsula. Marks the southern end of a small coastal ridge which extends 3 miles northward along the west coast of Graham Land. Discovered by Charcot in 1909. Surveyed by the FIDS in 1948, and named descriptively by them.

**Longs Nunatak.** 66°28'S, 110°43'E. 1 mile NW of Campbell Nunatak. It faces on Penney Bay at the south end of the Windmill Islands. Named by Carl Eklund for Robert L. Long, Jr., ionosphere physicist at Wilkes Station in 1957.

**Mount Longstaff** *see* **Longstaff Peaks**

**Longstaff Peaks.** 82°54'S, 165°42'E. A series of high peaks just west of Davidson Glacier in the north central part of the

Holland Range. Discovered during Scott's 1901–4 expedition, and named Mount Longstaff by them for Llewellyn Wood Longstaff, the main backer of the expedition. The feature was later redefined by New Zealand.

**Longwire Station** *see* **Byrd VLF Substation**

**Mount Loodts.** 72°32'S, 31°11'E. 2,420 m. Just east of Mount Lorette in the Belgica Mountains. Discovered by the Belgian Antarctic Expedition of 1957–58 under Gaston de Gerlache, who named it for Jacques Loodts, geodesist with the expedition.

**The Lookout.** 68°36'S, 77°57'E. A hill 90 meters high. ½ mile from the coast. The highest summit on the western end of the Breidnes Peninsula, Vestfold Hills. Photographed by the LCE 1936–37. First visited by ANARE parties from Davis Station in 1957. Named by the Australians.

**Cape Lookout.** 61°16'S, 55°12'W. Also called Cabo Vigía, Cabo Fossatti. 240 meters high. It is a steep bluff marking the southern extremity of Elephant Island, in the South Shetlands. Named before 1822, by the sealers, for its good location as a lookout spot.

**Lookout Dome.** 83°03'S, 156°27'E. Ice-covered, dome-shaped mountain. 2,470 m. In the Miller Range. Named by the New Zealanders in 1961–62 for its strategic position.

**Lookout Lake.** 68°36'S, 77°57'E. A small lake ½ mile NNE of The Lookout, in the western part of the Breidnes Peninsula in the Vestfold Hills. First visited by ANARE parties from Davis Station in 1957. Named by the Australians in association with The Lookout.

**Looming** *see* **Mirages**

**Mount Lopatin.** 72°51'S, 168°04'E. 2,670 m. 6 miles ESE of Mount Riddolls in the Victory Mountains of Victoria Land. Named by the USA for Boris Lopatin, USSR exchange scientist at McMurdo Station, 1968.

**Monte López**  *see*  **Doumer Hill**

**Mount Lopez.** 72°01'S, 101°53'W. In the Walker Mountains. 5 miles east of Landfall Peak. In the west part of Thurston Island. Named for Maxwell A. Lopez.

**Picacho López**  *see*  **López Nunatak**

**Lopez, Maxwell A.** Ensign, USN, who was killed on Dec. 30, 1946, in the Martin Mariner crash which also killed 2 others (*see* **Deaths, 1946**).

**López Costa, Alfredo.** Leader of the Chilean Antarctic Expedition of 1953–54. His ships were the *Covadonga, Rancagua, Lientur,* and *Lautaro.*

**López Nunatak.** 62°29'S, 59°39'W. Also called Picachos Teniente López, Picacho López. 275 m. Almost a mile SE of Ash Point on Greenwich Island in the South Shetlands. Named by the First Chilean Antarctic Expedition in 1946–47 for Lt. Sergio López Angulo.

**Cap Loqui**  *see*  **Cape García**

**Loqui Point.** 65°55'S, 64°58'W. Marks the south side of the entrance to Barilari Bay, on the west coast of Graham Land. Discovered in 1903–5 by Charcot, who named it Cap García. The north cape of Barilari Bay he named Cap Loqui, for Capt. Loqui of the Argentine navy. However, the maps of Charcot's next expedition, in 1908–10, show Cap García to be the northern one. The southern one (the one he had originally called Cap García) was left unnamed in the 1908–10 map. In order to continue Charcot's naming, the name for the southern cape has now been given as Loqui Point, because Cap García has been accepted all these years as the name for the northern cape. This is a good example of a phenomenon of name changing which happens not infrequently in the Antarctic.

**Lord Bank.** 67°50'S, 69°15'W. In the northern part of Marguerite Bay, off the west coast of the Antarctic Peninsula.

The *Lord Melville.* British sealer from London which was in the South Shetlands for the 1820–21 summer season. Capt. Clark was in command. The ship was wrecked in the early part of 1821 and the chief officer and 10 of the crew were forced to winter-over in 1821 on King George Island.

**Lord Nunatak.** 80°21'S, 24°01'W. In the Shackleton Range.

**Loren Nunataks.** 83°36'S, 53°52'W. 3 miles east of Rivas Peaks in the Neptune Range of the Pensacola Mountains. Named for Loren Brown, Jr., aviation machinist at Ellsworth Station, 1958.

**Lorentzen, Bjarne.** Cook on the Norwegian-British-Swedish Antarctic Expedition of 1949–52, led by John Giaever.

**Lorentzen Peak.** 71°45'S, 2°50'W. 5 miles south of Vesleskarvet Cliff, on the west side of the Ahlmann Ridge in Queen Maud Land. Named by the Norwegians for Bjarne Lorentzen.

**Mount Lorette.** 72°32'S, 31°09'E. Also called Mont Notre-Dame de Lorette, Mont N.-D. de Lorette. Ice-free. 2,200 m. Just west of Mount Loodts in the Belgica Mountains. Discovered by the Belgian Antarctic Expedition of 1957–58, under Gaston de Gerlache, who named it for the patron saint of aviators, Notre Dame de Lorette, partly because it looks like a cathedral in shape.

**Mount Lorius.** 72°28'S, 162°21'E. 1,690 m. 2½ miles north of Mount Allison, in the Monument Nunataks. Mapped by the USARP Victoria Land Traverse Party of 1959–60. Named for Claude Lorius, French glaciologist, a member of the traverse party.

**Lorn Rocks.** 65°31'S, 64°56'W. 12 miles west of the north end of Lahille Island in the Biscoe Islands. Named by the UK because they are forlorn and deserted.

**Lorten**  *see*  **Cleft Island**

**Los Dientes**  *see*  **Les Dents**

**Lose Platte**  *see*  **Loze Mountain**

**Islotes Los Provincianos** *see* **Yoke Island**

**Puerto Lote** *see* **Lagarrigue Cove**

**Loubat Point.** 65°04′S, 63°56′W. Also called Cape de Loubat. Forms the north side of the entrance to Deloncle Bay, on the west coast of Graham Land. Named by Charcot in 1903–5 for Monsieur Loubat, presumably a French friend.

**Loubet Coast.** 67°S, 66°W. Between Cape Bellue and the head of Bourgeois Fjord on the west coast of the Antarctic Peninsula. Explored in Jan. 1905 by Charcot, who named it Loubet Land for Émile Loubet, the president of France. The feature was later redefined slightly as a coast. The British Base W was here.

**Loubet Land** *see* **Loubet Coast**

**Loubet Strait** *see* **The Gullet**

**Loudwater Cove.** 64°46′S, 64°05′W. ½ mile long. Faces west. The southernmost indentation in Wylie Bay. Just north of Norsel Point, on the SW coast of Anvers Island. Surveyed in 1955 by the FIDS, and named by them for the loud noise the water makes as it comes into this cove from the sea.

**Mount Louis McHenry Howe** *see* **Mount Howe**

**Louis Philippe Coast** *see* **Trinity Peninsula**

**Louis Philippe Land** *see* **Trinity Peninsula**

**Louis Philippe Peninsula** *see* **Trinity Peninsula**

**Louis Philippe Plateau.** 63°37′S, 58°27′W. 11 miles long. 5 miles wide. 1,370 m. Occupies the central part of Trinity Peninsula between Russell West Glacier and Windy Gap. Named by the UK in 1948 in order to preserve Dumont d'Urville's 1838 naming of the Trinity Peninsula as Terre Louis Philippe, a name which did not stick. Louis Philippe of France was the honoree.

**Mount Louise** *see* **Louise Peak**

**Louise Island.** 64°36′S, 62°23′W. Ice-covered. Just over ½ mile long. 1 mile east of Cape Anna in the SW side of the entrance to Wilhelmina Bay, on the west coast of Graham Land. Discovered by de Gerlache in 1897–99, and named by him for his sister.

**Louise Peak.** 65°05′S, 64°W. Also called Mount Louise. 625 m. 1 mile north of Gourdon Peak on Booth Island, in the Wilhelm Archipelago. Charted by Charcot in 1903–5 and named by him for the sister of Ernest Gourdon.

**Lovejoy Glacier.** 70°48′S, 160°10′E. Flows between Anderson Pyramid and Sample Nunataks in the Usarp Mountains. In its lower course, it flows into, and with, the Harlin Glacier. Named for Lt. Owen B. Lovejoy, VX-6 pilot in Antarctica in 1962–63 and 1963–64.

**Lovill Bluff.** 73°22′S, 126°54′W. At the west end of Siple Island, off the Marie Byrd Land coast. 14 miles SW of the summit of Mount Siple. It marks the north side of the entrance to Pankratz Bay. Named for James E. Lovill, meteorologist-in-charge at Byrd Station, 1965.

**Low, F.G.** Captain of the *Esther*, 1820–21.

**Low Head.** 62°09′S, 58°08′W. Also called Cape Low Head, Cabo Promontorio Bajo. A headland 1 mile SSW of Lions Rump, the west side of the entrance to King George Bay, on King George Island in the South Shetlands. Charted and named descriptively by personnel on the *Discovery II* in 1937.

**Cape Low Head** *see* **Low Head**

**Low Island.** 63°17′S, 62°09′W. Also called Jameson Island, Jamesons Island. 9 miles long and 5 miles wide. 14 miles SE of Smith Island, it is the most southerly of the main islands in the South Shetlands. Discovered and named by John Davis on Jan. 31, 1821, for its low elevation.

**Low Nunakol.** 77°07′S, 162°14′E. Between the Mackay Glacier and the Gonville and Caius Range in Victoria Land.

**Low Point** *see* **Monroe Point**

**Low Rock.** 62°17′S, 58°39′W. A low rock surrounded by foul ground. 1 mile

SW of Stranger Point, the southern extremity of King George Island in the South Shetlands. Charted, but not named, by David Ferguson in 1913–14. More accurately charted and descriptively named by personnel on the *Discovery II* in 1935 and 1937.

**Low Tongue.** 67°33′S, 62°E. A tongue of rock 175 yards long. Juts out from the coast of Mac. Robertson Land just west of Holme Bay. Photographed by the LCE 1936–37, and named Lågtangen by the Norwegians. The Australians translated it directly into English.

**Lowd, W.H.** Crewman on the *Jacob Ruppert*, 1933–35.

**Mount Lowe.** 80°33′S, 30°16′W. Has two peaks, the higher 990 m. On the south side of the mouth of Blaiklock Glacier, in the western part of the Shackleton Range. Named in 1957 for W. George Lowe.

**Lowe, Charles.** Seaman on the Wilkes Expedition 1838–42. Joined in the USA. Served the cruise.

**Lowe, W. George.** Wallace George Lowe. New Zealand photographer who crossed the continent with Fuchs in 1957–58 on the BCTAE.

**Lowe Bluff.** 85°58′S, 137°12′W. Ice-covered. Between the head of Kansas Glacier and Alaska Canyon, along the Watson Escarpment. Named for William E. Lowe, radioman at Byrd Station, 1957.

**Lowe Glacier.** 82°58′S, 160°25′E. 7 miles long. In the Queen Elizabeth Range. It flows south from a saddle common with the Prince of Wales Glacier 3 miles east of Mount Gregory, and joins the Princess Anne Glacier. Named by the Holyoake, Cobham, and Queen Elizabeth Ranges Party of the NZGSAE, 1964–65, for D. Lowe, a member of the party.

**Lowell, James.** Captain of the Fo'c's'le on the Wilkes Expedition 1838–42. Joined in the USA. Served the cruise.

**Mount Lowell Thomas** *see* **Thomas Mountains**

**Lowell Thomas Mountains** *see* **Thomas Mountains**

**Lower Ferrar Glacier** *see* **Ferrar Glacier**

**Lower Staircase.** 78°25′S, 161°45′E. The lower, eastern portion of the Skelton Glacier, between The Landing and Clinker Bluff in Victoria Land. Surveyed and named descriptively by the NZ party of the BCTAE, 1957–58.

**Lower Victoria Glacier** *see* **Victoria Lower Glacier**

**Lower Wright Glacier** *see* **Wright Lower Glacier**

**Lowery Glacier.** 82°35′S, 163°15′E. 60 miles long. Flows from the Prince Andrew Plateau along the east side of the Queen Elizabeth Range into the Nimrod Glacier. Named by the New Zealand Geological and Topographical Survey Expedition of 1959–60 for J.H. Lowery. A member of one of the field parties on this expedition, he was injured when a Sno-cat fell through a crevasse off Cape Selborne in Nov. 1959.

**Lowest points in Antarctica.** The Bentley Subglacial Trench is 8,326 feet below sea-level. The deepest lake is Radok Lake at a depth of 1,135 feet.

**Mount Loweth.** 73°26′S, 93°31′W. Also called Mount Hogan. 1,420 m. Snow-topped. 6 miles ENE of Anderson Dome in the eastern end of the Jones Mountains. Named for Hugh F. Loweth, US government officer who for many years helped formulate US Antarctic policy.

**Mount Lowman.** 70°39′S, 160°03′E. 1,610 m. On the east-central slopes of the Pomerantz Tableland. 2 miles SE of Rinehart Peak, in the Usarp Mountains. Named for Henry R. Lowman III, biologist at McMurdo Station, 1967–68.

**Mount Lowry.** 84°33′S, 64°09′W. 1,020 m. 2½ miles NW of Wrigley Bluffs in the Anderson Hills in the northern Patuxent Range of the Pensacola Mountains. Named for James K. Lowry, biologist at Palmer Station, 1967.

**Lowry Bluff.** 74°22'S, 163°19'E. 1,070 m. Forms the eastern extremity of Nash Ridge of the Eisenhower Range in Victoria Land. Named for George Lowry, biologist at Palmer Station, 1965–66.

**Loyd, John.** Ordinary seaman on the Wilkes Expedition 1838–42. Joined in the USA. Run at Sydney.

**Loyd, William.** Landsman on the Wilkes Expedition 1838–42. Joined in the USA. Sent home on the *Relief* in 1839.

**Loze Mountain.** 71°37'S, 11°17'E. 2,130 m. Surmounts the west wall of Grautskåla Cirque in the Humboldt Mountains of Queen Maud Land. Discovered aerially by Ritscher's expedition of 1938–39. Named by the USSR in 1960–61 in order to preserve Ritscher's naming of Lose Platte (loose plateau) for an area near here which nowadays can not be determined.

**Mount Lozen.** 72°07'S, 168°24'E. 2,460 m. At the NW side of the head of Tocci Glacier in the Admiralty Mountains. Named for Michael R. Lozen, USN, radioman at McMurdo Station, 1967.

**Mount Lubbock.** 73°13'S, 169°08'E. 1,630 m. Just north of Cape Jones at the south end of Daniell Peninsula in Victoria Land. Discovered in Jan. 1841 by Ross, who named it for Sir John Lubbock, treasurer of the Royal Society.

**Lubbock Ridge.** 84°50'S, 175°25'W. 5 miles long. Extends west from Mount Wade and terminates in a steep bluff at the east side of Shackleton Glacier. Named by Alton Wade, leader of the Texas Tech Shackleton Glacier Party of 1962–63, for Lubbock, Texas, the home of Texas Tech, to which all three members of the party were affiliated.

**Lucas Island.** 68°30'S, 77°57'E. Just west of the Vestfold Hills. 2 miles NW of Plog Island. Photographed by the LCE 1936–37, and called Plogsteinen (the plow stone) by the Norwegians. Renamed in 1958 by the Australians for

W.C. Lucas, diesel mechanic at Davis Station, 1957.

**Lucas Nunatak.** 67°48'S, 62°11'E. 1 mile south of Woodberry Nunataks in the Casey Range of the Framnes Mountains. Photographed by the LCE 1936–37. Named by the Australians for F.M. Lucas, officer-in-charge at Mawson Station in 1962.

**Luck Nunatak.** 75°19'S, 72°32'W. 2 miles SW of Mount Caywood, in the Behrendt Mountains of Ellsworth Land. Named for George D. Luck, aircraft crew member in Antarctica in 1961.

**Mount Lucy** *see* **Mount Henry Lucy**

**Lucy Glacier.** 82°24'S, 158°25'E. Flows from the Polar Plateau, between Laird Plateau and McKay Cliffs, into the Nimrod Glacier. Named by New Zealand for W.R. Lucy, surveyor at Scott Base in 1963–64 and 1964. He also took part in the NZGSAE of 1964–65, as a surveyor with the Geologists Range field party.

**Ludeman, E.E.** Emmett E. Ludeman. Lt. Cdr., USN. Took over from Scott Marshall as officer-in-charge of McMurdo Base on Nov. 28, 1957. He in turn handed over to William Lewiston.

**Ludeman Glacier.** 84°27'S, 172°40'E. A valley glacier. 13 miles long. Flows through the Commonwealth Range into the east side of the Beardmore Glacier at a point 12 miles north of Mount Donaldson. Named for E.E. Ludeman.

**Ludvig Glacier.** 70°45'S, 166°09'E. Flows between Arthurson Bluff and Mount Gale into Kirkby Glacier near the coast of northern Victoria Land. Named by the ANARE for Ludvig Larsen, chief officer of the *Thala Dan,* the ship which carried the ANARE along this coast in 1962.

**Ludwig Glacier** *see* **Ludvig Glacier**

**Mount Ludwig Hansen** *see* **Hansen Spur**

**Luff Nunatak.** 71°06'S, 71°28'E. 3 miles long. West of Foster Nunatak in the Manning Nunataks, in the eastern part of the Amery Ice Shelf. Named by the Australians for T.S. Luff, senior diesel mechanic at Mawson Station in 1970.

**Mount Lugering.** 71°42'S, 162°57'E. Nearly 2,000 m. On the west side of the Lanterman Range of the Bowers Mountains. It marks the north side of the terminus of Hunter Glacier where it joins Rennick Glacier. Named for utilitiesman Donald R. Lugering, USN, at Amundsen-Scott South Pole Station in 1965.

**Mount Lugg.** 71°13'S, 64°43'E. Partly snow-covered. 5 miles south of Mount Hicks in the Prince Charles Mountains. Named by the Australians for Dr. Desmond Lugg (*see* **Lugg Island**).

**Lugg Island.** 68°32'S, 77°57'E. 1 mile NW of Lake Island, off the west end of the Breidnes Peninsula in the Vestfold Hills. Photographed by the LCE 1936–37. Named by the Australians for Dr. Desmond Lugg, medical officer at Davis Station in 1963. He visited the island for biological studies. Lugg was senior medical officer with the Antarctic Division, Melbourne, and officer-in-charge of the ANARE Prince Charles Mountains surveys in 1970 and 1971.

**Luhrsen Nunatak.** 71°59'S, 161°41'E. 3 miles SSE of Mount Alford at the SE end of the Helliwell Hills. Named for Richard H. Luhrsen, assistant to the USARP representative at McMurdo Station, 1967–68.

**Pic Luigi de Savoie** *see* **Savoia Peak**

**Luigi di Savoia Peak** *see* **Savoia Peak**

**Luigi Peak** *see* **Savoia Peak**

**Pico Luís de Saboya** *see* **Savoia Peak**

**Luitpold Coast.** 77°30'S, 32°W. Also called Luitpold Land, Leopold Land, Leopold Coast, Prince-Regent Luitpold Land, Prinzregent Luitpold Land. Beyond the eastern limit of the Filchner Ice Shelf, it extends along the coast of Coats Land from the vicinity of the Hayes Glacier (27°54'W) to the eastern limit of the Filchner Ice Shelf (36°W). Discovered by Filchner on Jan. 30, 1912, and named Prinzregent Luitpold Land for that Bavarian notable.

**Luitpold Land** *see* **Luitpold Coast**

**Luke Glacier.** 65°42'S, 64°02'W. 15 miles long. Flows into the head of Leroux Bay on the west coast of Graham Land. Discovered and surveyed in 1909 by Charcot. Resurveyed by the BGLE in 1935–36 and later named for Lord Luke, the head of Bovril, a contributor to the expedition.

**Lully Foothills.** 70°44'S, 70°02'W. A large group of peaks and nunataks extending 15 miles in a NE-SW direction between Vivaldi Gap and the LeMay Range in the west central part of Alexander Island. Named by the UK for Jean-Baptiste Lully, the composer.

**Lulow Rock.** 85°36'S, 68°30'W. 1,695 m. The most northerly exposed rock along the face of the Pecora Escarpment in the Pensacola Mountains. Named for William F. Lulow, cook at Plateau Station, 1966.

**Lumière Peak.** 65°18'S, 64°03'W. 1,065 m. 3 miles SE of Cape Tuxen on the west coast of Graham Land. Discovered by Charcot in 1903–5 and named by him for Louis Lumière, the movie pioneer.

**Lumus Reef** *see* **Lumus Rock**

**Lumus Rock.** 65°13'S, 65°18'W. 4 miles WNW of Sooty Rock. Marks the SW extremity of the Wilhelm Archipelago. Discovered by the BGLE 1934–37, and named Lumus Reef by them after one of the expedition's cats, the only one to survive the Antarctic winter. Redefined by the UK in 1971.

**Luna Bay.** An Argentine weather station in the South Shetlands (*see* **Moon Bay**).

**Luna-Devyat' Mountain.** 71°40'S, 11°50'E. 1,880 m. Forms the east end of the Eidshaugane Peaks in the Humboldt Mountains of Queen Maud Land. Discovered aerially by the Ritscher expedition of 1938–39. Named by the USSR in 1966 as Gora Luna-Devyat' (Luna Nine Mountain) honoring USSR space scientists.

**Luncke Range.** 72°02′S, 24°42′E. Rises to 3,020 m. The peaks extend in a north-south direction for 10 miles between Jennings Glacier and Gjel Glacier in the Sør Rondane Mountains. Named by the Norwegians for Bernhard Luncke, Norwegian cartographer who plotted the maps in H.E. Hansen's *Atlas of Parts of the Antarctic Coastal Lands* in 1946.

**Luncke Ridge.** 68°29′S, 78°25′E. On the northern side of the eastern extremity of Langnes Fjord in the Vestfold Hills. Photographed by the LCE 1936–37. Later named for Bernhard Luncke (*see* **Luncke Range**).

**Lund Island** *see* **Petermann Island**

**Mount Lunde.** 66°58′S, 50°28′E. A mountain ridge just south of Mount Gleadell in the western part of the Tula Mountains of Enderby Land. Named by the Australians for J. Lunde, senior diesel mechanic at Wilkes Station, 1960.

**Lunde Glacier.** 71°53′S, 6°15′E. 25 miles long. Flows between Håhellerskarvet and Jøkulkyrkja Mountain in the Mühlig-Hofmann Mountains of Queen Maud Land. Named Lundebreen (Lunde Glacier) by the Norwegians for T. Lunde, glaciologist with the Norwegian Antarctic Expedition, 1956–58.

**Lundström Knoll.** 80°31′S, 20°25′W. In the Shackleton Range.

**Lunik Point.** 70°32′S, 163°06′E. Ice-covered. 3 miles NE of Mount Dergach on the west side of Ob' Bay. Named by the USSR for the first USSR moon module.

**Mount Lupa.** 68°26′S, 66°43′W. Flat-topped. Ice-covered. Over 1,625 m. Between the Romulus and Martin Glaciers just ESE of Black Thumb and 5 miles east of the head of Rymill Bay, on the west coast of Graham Land. Surveyed in 1936 by the BGLE. Resurveyed in 1948 by the FIDS, who named it for the she-wolf who raised Romulus and Remus in Roman mythology.

**Lurabee Channel** *see* **Lurabee Glacier**

**Lurabee Glacier.** 69°15′S, 63°37′W. 27 miles long. Flows between Scripps Heights and Finley Heights to the east coast of Palmer Land. Discovered aerially by Wilkins on Dec. 20, 1928. He thought it was a channel, and named it Lurabee Channel for Lurabee Shreck, a woman in San Francisco who had helped Wilkins over the years. The feature was later redefined.

**Lurker Rock.** 68°03′S, 68°44′W. 10 feet high. 3 miles NE of Dismal Island of the Faure Islands in Marguerite Bay. Named by the UK in 1971. It is covered by ice, and lurks in the water, waiting for unsuspecting shipping.

**Lussich Cove.** 62°06′S, 58°21′W. On the east side of Martel Inlet in Admiralty Bay, King George Island in the South Shetlands. Charted by Charcot in 1909, and named by him for Antonio Lussich of Montevideo, who helped the expedition.

**Luther Peak.** 72°22′S, 169°50′E. 820 m. 11 miles SE of Mount Peacock in the Admiralty Mountains. Overlooks Edisto Inlet in northern Victoria Land. Named for Cdr. Roger W. Luther, captain of the *Edisto* in 1956. The peak was charted from radarscope photographs taken in March of that year from the *Edisto*.

**Lüttich Island** *see* **Liège Island**

**Lützow-Holm, Finn.** Commander in the Norwegian Naval Air Service. In 1929–30 he was a pilot on Riiser-Larsen's expedition on the *Norvegia*.

**Lützow-Holm Bay.** 69°10′S, 37°30′E. 120 miles wide. Indents the eastern coast of Queen Maud Land between the Princess Ragnhild Coast and the Prince Olav Coast. The Queen Fabiola Mountains are behind it. Discovered by Riiser-Larsen in two airplane flights from the *Norvegia* on Feb. 21 and Feb. 23, 1931. Named for Finn Lützow-Holm, by Bjarne Aagard in 1935.

**Luz Range.** 72°03′S, 4°49′E. 14 miles long. Just east of Gablenz Range in the Mühlig-Hofmann Mountains of Queen Maud Land. Includes Petrellfjellet. Discovered aerially by Ritscher's expedition of 1938–39. Ritscher named it for the commercial director of Lufthansa.

**Lyall, David.** Assistant surgeon on the *Terror* during Ross' expedition of 1839–43. He was also responsible for botanical research.

**Lyall Islands.** 70°41'S, 167°20'E. Between Cape Hooker and Cape Dayman off the Oates Land coast, just outside the entrance to Yule Bay. There are four islands in the group: Unger Island, Surgeon Island, Novosad Island, and Hughes Island. Discovered by Ross in 1841, and named by him for David Lyall.

**Lyddan Island.** 74°25'S, 20°45'W. Ice-covered. At the SW extremity of the Riiser-Larsen Ice Shelf. 20 miles off the Princess Martha Coast. 45 miles long. It has three narrow arms in the form of a trefoil. Discovered on Nov. 5, 1967, by W.R. McDonald, during a VX-6 reconnaissance flight over the coast in a Hercules. Named for Robert H. Lyddan, chief topographic engineer of the US Geological Survey, a long-time force in Antarctic mapping.

**Lyftingen Peak.** 72°17'S, 3°15'W. Just SE of Kjølrabbane Hills, near the SW end of the Ahlmann Ridge in Queen Maud Land. Named by the Norwegians.

**Mount Lymburner.** 77°26'S, 86°30' W. 1,940 m. 4 miles WNW of Mount Weems near the northern end of the Sentinel Range. Discovered aerially by Ellsworth on Nov. 23, 1935. Named for J.H. Lymburner.

**Lymburner, J.H.** Canadian Airways pilot out of Montreal who was reserve pilot on Ellsworth's 1935–36 expedition. He was the pilot proper on the 1938–39 expedition over the American Highland.

**Lynch, Thomas B.** American sealing captain in the South Orkneys in 1880 as skipper of the *Express.*

**Lynch Island.** 60°39'S, 45°36'W. In the eastern part of Marshall Bay, just off the south coast of Coronation Island in the South Orkneys. Charted by Petter Sørlle in 1912–13. Surveyed in 1933 by personnel of the Discovery Committee. Resurveyed in 1948–49 by the FIDS, who named it for Capt. Thomas B. Lynch. There is a lot of grass here, and it is SPA #14.

**Lynch Point.** 75°05'S, 137°44'W. Between Frostman Glacier and Hull Glacier on the Marie Byrd Land coast. It is at the end of an unnamed peninsula. Named for Ensign William R. Lynch, Jr., USNR, damage control officer on the *Glacier,* in these waters in 1961–62.

**Lynn Automatic Weather Station.** 74° 14'S, 160°30'E. American AWS at an elevation of approximately 5,777 feet. Began operating on Jan. 19, 1988.

**Lynsky Cove.** 66°19'S, 110°27'E. In the north side of Pidgeon Island in the Windmill Islands. Named for Chief Builder James E. Lynsky, USN, at Wilkes Station, 1958.

**The *Lynx.*** Australian sealer out of Sydney Harbor under the command of Capt. Richard Siddons. It was in the South Shetlands in 1820–21, then wintered-over in the Falklands, and was back in the South Shetlands in 1821–22, in company with the *Huron* and the *Cecilia.*

**Lynx Rocks.** 62°32'S, 60°32'W. In Hero Bay to the west of Siddons Point, Livingston Island, South Shetlands. Named by the UK in 1958 for the *Lynx.*

**Lyon Nunataks.** 74°50'S, 73°50'W. Also called Johnson Nunatak. Isolated. 30 miles NW of the Behrendt Mountains in Ellsworth Land. Named for Owen R. Lyon, USN, hospital corpsman and chief petty officer in charge of Eights Station in 1965.

**Lyon Peak.** 63°47'S, 60°48'W. South of Milburn Bay on the west side of Trinity Island in the Palmer Archipelago. Named by the UK in 1960 for Percy C. Lyon (1862–1952), of the British Department of Scientific and Industrial Research, who was chairman of the interdepartmental committee on research and development of the Antarctic area, 1917–20.

**Mount Lysaght.** 82°49′S, 161°19′E. 3,755 m. 1½ miles north of Mount Markham in the northern part of the Queen Elizabeth Range. Discovered and named by Shackleton in 1908.

**Lystad, Isak.** Captain of the *North Star* during the USAS 1939–41.

**Lystad Bay.** 67°50′S, 67°17′W. Also called Horseshoe Bay, Horseshoe Island Cove, Caleta Herradura. 2½ miles wide. Indents the western side of Horseshoe Island in the NE part of Marguerite Bay. Surveyed in 1936–37 by the BGLE. Visited in 1940 by the *Bear* and the *North Star* during the USAS 1939–41. Named for Capt. Isak Lystad.

**Lystad Island** *see* **Omega Island**

**Cape Lyttelton.** 82°21′S, 164°39′E. Also spelled (erroneously) Cape Lyttleton. Forms the southern entrance point of Shackleton Inlet, along the western edge of the Ross Ice Shelf. Discovered during Scott's 1901–4 expedition, and named by them for the NZ town by that name, a town very friendly not only to Scott's expedition, but to others. It was from Lyttelton that Scott set out on the last leg of his journey south, in 1901.

**Lyttelton Peak.** 82°18′S, 158°56′E. Also spelled (erroneously) Lyttleton Peak. 2,335 m. The highest peak in the Cobham Range. Named by the New Zealanders in 1961–62 for the family name of Lord Cobham, former governor-general of New Zealand.

**Lyttelton Range.** 71°33′S, 167°45′E. South of the Dunedin Range in the Admiralty Mountains. 16 miles long. It forms the western wall of the upper part of Dennistoun Glacier. Named by the USA for the NZ town of Lyttelton.

**Lyttelton Ridge.** 66°22′S, 63°07′W. Also called Antarctic Tetons. 425 m. Extends 4 miles in a NW-SE direction along the west side of the Churchill Peninsula, on the east coast of Graham Land. A dark, jagged ridge, it was charted in 1947 by the FIDS, who named it for Oliver Lyttelton, British minister of production, and a member of the War Cabinet which formed Operation Tabarin.

**Cape Lyttleton** *see* **Cape Lyttelton**

**Mount Lyttleton.** 66°24′S, 65°22′W. Mostly snow-covered. Near the head of Cardell Glacier, on the west coast of Graham Land. Named by the UK in 1960 for Westcote R. Lyttleton (1877–1956), pioneer of laminated safety glass for use in snow goggles.

**Lyttleton Peak** *see* **Lyttelton Peak**